CURRENT
BIOGRAPHY
YEARBOOK
1963

CURRENT BIOGRAPHY YEARBOOK

1963

EDITED BY

CHARLES MORITZ

NEW YORK

THE H. W. WILSON COMPANY

PREFACE

The twenty-fourth volume of CURRENT BIOGRAPHY reflects the continuing world trends of the 1960's: the advance of space technology; the emergence of the Asian-African bloc; huge strides forward in international communications represented by such developments as Telstar; a more and more militant battle for civil rights for all Americans; and accelerated progress in the ecumenical movement.

During 1963 the Vatican became more than ever a center of world attention with the death of Pope John XXIII, the elevation of Pope Paul VI, and the convocation of another session of the Second Ecumenical Conference. Shifts in the Kennedy administration resulted in the inclusion of sketches about such relatively recent appointees to the New Frontier as Anthony J. Celebrezze, Kermit Gordon, Francis Keppel, and W. Willard Wirtz. The annual awarding of Pulitzer and Nobel prizes added articles about their recipients to the volume.

CURRENT BIOGRAPHY YEARBOOK 1963 carries on the policy of including new and updated biographical sketches that supersede earlier, outdated articles. Examples are the sketches of such major figures as William Zorach, Lewis Mumford, Katherine Anne Porter, and John Steinbeck.

Sketches have been made as accurate and objective as possible through careful researching by CURRENT BIOGRAPHY writers in newspapers, magazines, authoritative reference books, and news releases of both government and private agencies. Immediately after their publication in monthly issues, articles are submitted to biographees to give them an opportunity to suggest corrections in time for CURRENT BIOGRAPHY YEARBOOK. To take account of major changes in the careers of biographees, sketches have also been revised before inclusion in the yearbook. With the exception of occasional interviews, the questionnaire remains the main source of direct information.

In the back of the volume under *Organizations* can be found the heads of veterans, industrial, fraternal, and professional organizations. Persons who are not professional authors but who have written books are listed under *Nonfiction* or *Literature* in addition to their primary vocational fields.

The pages immediately following contain: *Explanations, Key to Reference Abbreviations; Key to Pronunciation;* and *Key to Abbreviations.* The indexes at the end of the volume are: *Biographical References; Periodicals and Newspapers Consulted; Necrology* (of persons whose biographies have appeared in previous volumes); *Classification by Profession; Cumulated Index,* 1961-63. The 1940-1950 index can be found in the 1950 yearbook, and the 1951-1960 index, in the 1960 yearbook.

For their help in the preparation of CURRENT BIOGRAPHY YEARBOOK 1963 I should like to thank associate editors Miss Evelyn Lohr and Mr. Henry S. Sloan and former associate editor Mrs. Alice Cheyer.

CHARLES MORITZ

Explanations

Authorities for biographees' full names, with some exceptions, are the bibliographical publications of The Wilson Company. When a biographee prefers a certain name form, that is indicated in the heading of the article: for example, Armstrong-Jones, Antony (Charles Robert) means that he is usually referred to as Antony Armstrong-Jones. When a professional name is used in the heading, as for example, Anne Bancroft, the real name (in this case Annemarie Italiano) appears in the article itself.

The heading of each article includes the pronunciation of the name if it is unusual, date of birth (if obtainable), and occupation. The article is supplemented by a list of references to sources of biographical information, in two alphabets: (1) newspapers and periodicals and (2) books. (See the section *Biographical References,* found in the rear of this volume.)

KEY TO REFERENCE ABBREVIATIONS

References to newspapers and periodicals are listed in abbreviated form; for example, "Sat Eve Post 217:14 S 30 '44 por" means *Saturday Evening Post,* volume 217, page 14, September 30, 1944, with portrait. (For full names, see the section *Periodicals and Newspapers Consulted,* found in the rear of this volume.)

January—Ja	July—Jl	Journal—J
February—F	August—Ag	Magazine—Mag
March—Mr	September—S	Monthly—Mo
April—Ap	October—O	Weekly—W
May—My	November—N	Portrait—por
June—Je	December—D	Review—R

KEY TO PRONUNCIATION

ā	āle	N	Not pronounced, but indicates the nasal tone of the preceding vowel, as in the French *bon* (bôN).	û	ûrn; French eu, as in *jeu* (zhû); German ö, oe, as in *schön* (shûn), *Goethe* (gû'tĕ)		
â	câre						
ă	ădd						
ŭ	ăccount						
ä	ärm						
à	àsk			ŭ	tŭb		
ȧ	sofȧ			ŭ	circŭs		
		ō	ōld	ü	Pronounced approximately as ē, with rounded lips: French u, as in *menu* (mē-nü'); German ü, as in *grün*		
ē	ēve	ô	ôrb				
ĕ	ĕnd	ŏ	ŏdd				
ē	makēr	oi	oil				
		o͞o	o͞oze				
g	go	o͝o	fo͝ot				
		ou	out				
ī	īce			zh	azure		
ĭ	ĭll	*th*	*then*				
		th	thin	′ =	main accent		
ᴋ	German ch as in *ich* (ĭᴋ)	ū	cūbe	″ =	secondary accent		

KEY TO ABBREVIATIONS

AAAA	Amateur Athletic Association of America
A.A.U.	Amateur Athletic Union
ABC	American Broadcasting Company
A.C.L.U.	American Civil Liberties Union
ADA	Americans for Democratic Action
AEC	Atomic Energy Commission
AEF	American Expeditionary Force
AFL	American Federation of Labor
AFL-CIO	American Federation of Labor and Congress of Industrial Organizations
ALA	American Library Association
AMA	American Medical Association
A.P.	Associated Press
ASCAP	American Society of Composers, Authors and Publishers
ASNE	American Society of Newspaper Editors
B.A.	Bachelor of Arts
BBC	British Broadcasting Corporation
B.D.	Bachelor of Divinity
B.L.S.	Bachelor of Library Science
B.S.	Bachelor of Science
CAA	Civil Aeronautics Administration
CAB	Civil Aeronautics Board
C.B.	Companion of the Bath
C.B.E.	Commander of (the Order of) the British Empire
CBS	Columbia Broadcasting System
C.E.	Civil Engineer
CEA	Council of Economic Advisers
C.E.D.	Committee for Economic Development
CENTO	Central Treaty Organization
CIO	Congress of Industrial Organizations
C.M.G.	Companion of (the Order of) St. Michael and St. George
Com.	Commodore
CORE	Congress of Racial Equality
D.A.R.	Daughters of the American Revolution
D.C.L.	Doctor of Civil Law
D.D.	Doctor of Divinity
D.Eng.	Doctor of Engineering
DEW	Distant Early Warning Line
D.F.C.	Distinguished Flying Cross
D.J.	Doctor of Jurisprudence
D.Lit.	Doctor of Literature
D.Mus.	Doctor of Music
DP	Displaced Person
D.Pol.Sc.	Doctor of Political Science
D.Sc.	Doctor of Science
D.S.C.	Distinguished Service Cross
D.S.M.	Distinguished Service Medal
D.S.O.	Distinguished Service Order
ECA	Economic Cooperation Administration
ECOSOC	Economic and Social Council
EDC	European Defense Community
ERP	European Recovery Program
ESA	Economic Stabilization Administration
FAO	Food and Agriculture Organization
FBI	Federal Bureau of Investigation
FCA	Farm Credit Administration
FCC	Federal Communications Commission
FEPC	Fair Employment Practice Committee
FHA	Federal Housing Administration
FOA	Foreign Operations Administration
FPC	Federal Power Commission
FSA	Federal Security Agency
FTC	Federal Trade Commission
GATT	General Agreement on Tariffs and Trade
G.B.E.	Knight or Dame, Grand Cross Order of the British Empire
G.C.B.	Knight Grand Cross of the Bath
G.O.P.	Grand Old Party
H.M.	His Majesty; Her Majesty
ICA	International Cooperation Administration
ICBM	Intercontinental Ballistic Missile
ICC	Interstate Commerce Commission
I.C.F.T.U.	International Confederation of Free Trade Unions
IGY	International Geophysical Year
I.L.A.	International Longshoremen's Association
I.L.G.W.U.	International Ladies' Garment Workers' Union
I.L.O.	International Labor Organization
INS	International News Service
IRO	International Refugee Organization
J.D.	Doctor of Jurisprudence
K.B.E.	Knight of (the Order of) the British Empire
K.C.	King's Counsel
K.C.B.	Knight Commander of the Bath
L.H.D.	Doctor of Humanities
Litt.D.	Doctor of Letters
LL.B.	Bachelor of Laws
LL.D.	Doctor of Laws
M.A.	Master of Arts
M.B.A.	Master of Business Administration
MBS	Mutual Broadcasting System
M.C.E.	Master of Civil Engineering
M.D.	Doctor of Medicine
M.E.	Master of Engineering
METO	Middle East Treaty Organization
MGM	Metro-Goldwyn-Mayer
M.Lit.	Master of Literature
M.P.	Member of Parliament
M.P.P.D.A.	Motion Picture Producers and Distributors of America
MRP	Mouvement Républicain Populaire
MSA	Mutual Security Agency
M.Sc.	Master of Science
Msgr.	Monsignor, Monseigneur
NAACP	National Association for the Advancement of Colored People
NAB	National Association of Broadcasters
NAM	National Association of Manufacturers
NASA	National Aeronautics and Space Administration
NATO	North Atlantic Treaty Organization
NBC	National Broadcasting Company
NEA	National Education Association
NLRB	National Labor Relations Board
N.M.U.	National Maritime Union
NRA	National Recovery Administration
NRPB	National Resources Planning Board
NYA	National Youth Administration
O.A.S.	Organization of American States
O.B.E.	Officer of (the Order of) the British Empire
OCD	Office of Civilian Defense
OEEC	Organization for European Economic Cooperation
OPA	Office of Price Administration
OPM	Office of Production Management
OWI	Office of War Information
P.E.N.	Poets, Playwrights, Editors, Essayists and Novelists (International Association)
Ph.B.	Bachelor of Philosophy
Ph.D.	Doctor of Philosophy
PWA	Public Works Administration
Q.C.	Queen's Counsel
RAF	Royal Air Force
RCA	Radio Corporation of America
REA	Rural Electrification Administration
RFC	Reconstruction Finance Corporation
RKO	Radio-Keith-Orpheum
ROTC	Reserve Officers' Training Corps
SAC	Strategic Air Command
SCAP	Supreme Command for the Allied Powers
SEATO	Southeast Asia Treaty Organization
SEC	Securities and Exchange Commission
SHAEF	Supreme Headquarters, Allied Expeditionary Force
SHAPE	Supreme Headquarters, Allied Powers Europe
S.J.D.	Doctor of Juridical Science
SLA	Special Libraries Association
S.T.B.	Bachelor of Sacred Theology
S.T.D.	Doctor of Sacred Theology
TVA	Tennessee Valley Authority
T.W.U.A.	Textile Workers Union of America
UAR	United Arab Republic
U.A.W.	United Automobile, Aircraft, and Agricultural Implement Workers of America
UMT	Universal Military Training
U.M.W.A.	United Mine Workers of America
U.N.	United Nations
UNESCO	United Nations Educational, Scientific, and Cultural Organization
UNICEF	United Nations Children's Fund
UNRRA	United Nations Relief and Rehabilitation Administration
U.P.I.	United Press and International News Service
USO	United Service Organizations
U.S.S.R.	Union of Soviet Socialist Republics
U.S.W.A.	United Steel Workers of America
VA	Veterans Administration
V.F.W.	Veterans of Foreign Wars
W.E.U.	Western European Union
W.F.T.U.	World Federation of Trade Unions
WHO	World Health Organization
WMC	War Manpower Commission
WPA	Work Projects Administration
WPB	War Production Board
YMCA	Young Men's Christian Association
YWCA	Young Women's Christian Association

CURRENT BIOGRAPHY
YEARBOOK
1963

ALANBROOKE, 1ST VISCOUNT *See* Brooke, Alan (Francis), 1st Viscount Alanbrooke

ALBEE, EDWARD (FRANKLIN) (ôl′bē)
Mar. 12, 1928- Playwright
Address: b. c/o William Morris Agency, 1470 Broadway, New York 36

In a play by Edward Albee, somewhat ordinary people talking in platitudes in a setting as familiar as a city park or a living room can shatter an audience. Geri Trotta described his work in *Horizon* (September 1961) as having "a grotesque, almost macabre effect, rather like finding a live tarantula at the bottom of a box of Cracker Jack." An adventurous writer for New York's avant-garde theater, who became known abroad earlier than at home, Albee believes that a playwright should be not only an entertainer, but a social critic. One of his own major targets is complacency. His obscenity, his grim satire, and his hilarious comedy may be taken therefore as the instruments of a high moral purpose. Beginning with *The Zoo Story*, produced off-Broadway in 1960, he quickly developed the stature to challenge Broadway on his own terms with his lengthy *Who's Afraid of Virginia Woolf?* in the fall of 1962.

Edward Franklin Albee was named after the vaudeville-house owner who had founded a chain of theaters in 1883 (with B. F. Keith) and who by adoption became his grandfather. In a sense he has belonged to the theater since two weeks after his birth, in Washington, D.C. on March 12, 1928, when he was adopted by Reed A. Albee, who worked for his father's Keith-Albee Theatre Circuit. Edward Albee does not know his natural parents. Under the care of the well-to-do Albees, he grew up in Manhattan and Larchmont, New York. During the winters the family used to leave their Westchester County home, where they kept a stable, to vacation in Florida or Arizona. "I could swim or ride almost before I could walk," Albee recalled in an interview for *Horizon* (September 1961). "I was always being yanked out of school, so I never had the chance to learn anything."

For his early education, however intermittent, Albee went to Rye Country Day School, also in Westchester. Then at the age of about eleven when — he now feels — he was probably too young to be away from home, he was sent to boarding school. He has said that he did not write *The Catcher in the Rye* or *End As a Man*;

Wide World

EDWARD ALBEE

he lived them. He was a student at Lawrenceville School in Lawrenceville, New Jersey for a year and a half before being expelled for failure to attend classes. His next school was Valley Forge Military Academy in Wayne, Pennsylvania, but after a year of the routine marching, emphasis on discipline, and what was for him "the aridity" of a military school, he transferred to Choate School in Wallingford, Connecticut.

Happier at Choate, Albee remained long enough to graduate, but later as a student at Trinity College in Hartford, Connecticut, where he cut chapel and classes in mathematics, he lacked the interest to try to qualify for a degree. "It was probably a basic discontent with myself that hadn't taken a specific form yet," he explained to a writer for the *New Yorker* (March 25, 1961). "After a year and a half, the college suggested that I not come back, which was fine with me."

The theater had attracted Albee from childhood. He saw his first stage show, the spectacle *Jumbo*, when he was five years old, and he wrote his first play, a three-act sex farce called *Aliqueen*, short-lived even in manuscript, when he was twelve. If he had learned to play the piano,

ALBEE, EDWARD—Continued

he might have fulfilled his dream of becoming a composer. He turned to writing poetry, and at the age of nineteen he had one of his poems published in *Kaleidoscope,* a Texas magazine.

Although still determined to be a writer, he drifted from one odd job to another after he left college. For more than a year he wrote continuity for the music programs presented over radio station WNYC in New York. The advertising agency Warwick & Legler employed him as an office boy; Bloomingdale's department store, as a record salesman; G. Schirmer, Inc., the music publisher, as a book salesman; and the Manhattan Towers Hotel, as a counterman in its luncheonette. Modestly enriched by a trust fund that his maternal grandmother had set up for him in 1949, he went to Florence, Italy in 1952 and spent several months writing a novel in which, as he once remarked in disgust, all the characters talked alike. His novel, like the poetry that he continued to write, went unpublished.

In 1955 Albee took a job that turned out to be his favorite—as a Western Union messenger. He enjoyed walking all over New York and meeting all types of people, but apparently he had set a deadline for the incubating period of his creative talent. When he was almost thirty, in early 1958, an "explosion," as he puts it, took place in his life. Quitting his job with Western Union, he settled down at the kitchen table of his apartment on West Fourth Street, where he was then living, and in three weeks wrote his one-act play *The Zoo Story.*

When Broadway producers to whom he submitted his play stipulated their preference for a three-acter, Albee started *The Zoo Story* on its circuitous journey to off-Broadway. The American composer David Diamond, to whom Albee's composer friend William Flanagan sent it in Florence, passed it along to the Swiss actor Pinkas Braun in Zurich, who brought it to the attention of Mrs. Stefani Hunzinger, director of the drama department of a large German publishing firm. *The Zoo Story* and Samuel Beckett's one-act *Krapp's Last Tape* were paired in their first performance, in German, in a Boleslaw Barlog production at Berlin's Schiller Theatre Werkstadt on September 28, 1959 and were later jointly produced in twelve other German cities.

Both plays had their New York première in a double bill at the Provincetown Playhouse on January 14, 1960. The freshness of concept and manner and the dramatic tension of *The Zoo Story* won the immediate endorsement of reviewers and audiences sympathetic to the experimental theater, and in May 1960 Albee received the Vernon Rice Award for outstanding achievement in an off-Broadway production. Through a conversation that takes place on a Central Park bench between two male strangers of strongly contrasted personalities, *The Zoo Story* deals with the tragedy of alienation, man's struggle to communicate with his fellow man. Albee denied that his play was nihilistic or pessimistic. "My hero is not a beatnik and he is not insane," he told Arthur Gelb of the New York *Times* (February 15, 1960). "He is over-sane. Though he dies, he passes on an awareness of life to the other character in the play."

Like *The Zoo Story,* Albee's *The Death of Bessie Smith,* a one-act play in several scenes, written in 1959, was first presented in German in Berlin, on April 21, 1960. Bessie Smith, the Negro blues singer who died in an accident in 1937, is not the central figure of this drama of racial conflict and does not appear on the stage. Albee probes instead the character of a nurse who denies Bessie Smith admission to a whites-only hospital in the South: the nurse's relationship with her father, with a Negro orderly, and with a would-be-lover intern—all of whom suffer with her the flaws of a tragically "closed" society.

While *The Zoo Story* was still running in New York, *The Death of Bessie Smith* reached off-Broadway on March 1, 1961, having been chosen to fill out a twin bill at the York Playhouse with Albee's one-act, one-scene *The American Dream.* Earlier in the year, on January 24, *The American Dream* had been premièred with *Bartleby,* a musical adaptation by William Flanagan (who also wrote the blues music for *The Death of Bessie Smith*) of Herman Melville's story *Bartleby, the Scrivener.* Albee collaborated with James Hinton, Jr., on the libretto. Coolly received, *Bartleby* closed in early February, and the following month *The Death of Bessie Smith* took its place. Although the Bessie Smith play matched *The American Dream* more evenly than *Bartleby,* for New York audiences, at least, it did not deliver the blow of *The American Dream.* Both *The Death of Bessie Smith* and *The American Dream* were chosen as the best plays of the 1960-61 season by the Foreign Press Association in New York, and in June 1961, when the two plays were running at the Cherry Lane Theatre, Albee won the Lola D'Annunzio Award for sustained accomplishments in original playwriting.

In point of composition (genesis if not exodus, to use the author's terms) *The American Dream* is Albee's second play. He began to write it in February 1959, but unable to "hear" his play, although he could "see" it, he put it aside until the summer of 1960. Meanwhile, in addition to *The Death of Bessie Smith,* he wrote two fifteen-minute plays, *The Sandbox* (a prelude to *The American Dream*) and *Fam and Yam* (a comic dialogue between playwrights), which were shown off-Broadway in May and October, respectively, during 1960.

Albee calls *The American Dream* a comedy—that is, ostensibly a comedy. It is a gruesome and paradoxical treatment of family relationships. In his preface to its publication in book form by Coward-McCann in 1961, he described it as "an examination of the American scene, an attack on the substitution of artificial for real values in our society, a condemnation of complacency, cruelty, emasculation and vacuity; it is a stand against the fiction that everything in this slipping land of ours is peachy-keen." Audiences found much to laugh at, nevertheless, in the clichéd conversation of tyrannical Mommy and submissive Daddy and the sassy remarks of complaining Grandma, who recognizes that the newly arrived handsome young man whom Mommy and Daddy embrace as the American dream is the twin brother of an adopted child tortured and dismembered by them twenty years ago in an effort to correct his faults and get their money's worth.

Some critics were morally offended by *The American Dream*; others thought it tiresome in technique or repetitious or pretentious or tasteless. One of its most enthusiastic reviewers, Whitney Balliett of the *New Yorker* (February 4, 1961), called particular attention to "its horrible aspects, which reach directly back to the butchery and perversion of the Greek theatre."

Whenever Albee was asked when he was going to write a full-length play, he would reply that all his plays were full-length because every play has its own duration. He disclosed, however, at least as early as February 1960 that he was at work on a long play to be called "The Exorcism" and to be subtitled "Who's Afraid of Virginia Woolf?" A central idea of the play is the exorcism of a nineteen-year-old fantasy child created by a middle-aged couple. Before long Albee decided instead to call his third act "The Exorcism" and to make "Who's Afraid of Virginia Woolf?" the play's title. He had seen the question some years earlier scrawled on the blackboard of a Greenwich Village bar. Recalling it when he began to write the play, he requested permission from Virginia Woolf's husband to use her name.

Ever since the New York première of *The Zoo Story,* Albee had been regarded as a brilliant young playwright who had still to fulfill his promise in a sustained work. Although his plays had been applauded in Europe, Turkey, South America, and in several places in the United States, he had not yet passed "the big test" of production on Broadway. On October 13, 1962 his three-act *Who's Afraid of Virginia Woolf?* opened at the Billy Rose Theatre in an excellent production staged by Alan Schneider and starring Uta Hagen and Arthur Hill. The setting of the three-and-a-half-hour-long play is a cottage on a college campus where two faculty members and their wives indulge in a 2:00 A.M.-till-dawn, self-revealing drinking bout in which everyone is psychologically flayed alive.

For John Chapman of the New York *Sunday News* (October 21, 1962) *Who's Afraid of Virginia Woolf?* was "a calculated exercise in depraved obscenity." He was not entirely alone in his view, but for most critics Albee had passed his test, despite his flaws, and he was promoted to the class of a major New York playwright.

The many reviews that called *Who's Afraid of Virginia Woolf?* unnerving, shocking, stunning, and shattering must have been gratifying to Albee, who has said that it is his intention to offend—as well as to entertain. Years earlier, soon after he had begun work on this first long play, he told Arthur Gelb (New York *Times,* February 15, 1960) that his favorite dramatist was Jean Genêt and that, like Genêt, he tried to dig "so deep under the skin that it becomes practically intolerable." It was not Genêt, however, with whom Broadway critics compared Albee after they had seen *Who's Afraid of Virginia Woolf?*, but rather the Eugene O'Neill of *Long Day's Journey Into Night.* Albee acknowledges that he has been influenced by everyone, including Thornton Wilder, Tennessee Williams, and Samuel Beckett, as well as O'Neill. *Who's Afraid of Virginia Woolf?* was cited several times as the best play of the 1962 season. It won the An-

toinette Perry (Tony) Award, the fifth annual ANTA Award, the Drama Critics Circle Award, the Outer Circle Award, and a special award of $500 sponsored by the *Village Voice* and the Philadelphia chapter of ANTA.

Along with Eugene Ionesco, Jack Richardson, and other experimenters, or re-evaluaters, Albee has been identified with the so-called "The Theatre of the Absurd." Albee, who dislikes labels, wrote an article for the New York *Times Magazine* (February 25, 1962) entitled "Which Theatre Is the Absurd One?" He submitted that "the supposed Realistic" theater of Broadway, "in the sense that it panders to the public need for self-congratulation and reassurance and presents a false picture of ourselves to ourselves is, with an occasional lovely exception, really and truly The Theatre of the Absurd." For some years Albee has been writing a stage adaptation of Carson McCullers' story *The Ballad of the Sad Café,* which is scheduled for production in 1963.

Self-possessed and articulate, although his voice in conversation may become almost inaudibly soft, Edward Albee accepts invitations to lecture at colleges and universities, and he has appeared on television. In the past three years he has given dozens of interviews to newspaper and magazine writers, and in one of them, for the New York *Post* (November 4, 1962), he said, "We must try to claw our way into compassion." His interviewers tend to make a point of contrasting the fury of his plays with his polite, relaxed manner and his quiet humor. He is slim, keeps his dark hair close-cropped, and prefers casual clothes. He lives in an apartment in Greenwich Village with books, modern paintings. and two or three cats.

References

> Esquire 55:45+ Ap '61
> Manchester Guardian p7 Je 19 '62 por
> N Y Post p38 Mr 31 '61 por
> N Y Times p33 O 15 '62 por
> Newsweek 57:90+ Mr 13 '61 por; 60:52 O 29 '62 por
> International Who's Who, 1962-63

ALCOCK, NORMAN Z(INKAN) May 29, 1918- Physicist; organization official

Address: b. Canadian Peace Research Institute, 341 Bloor St. W., Toronto 5, Ontario, Canada; h. 145 Lakewood Dr., Oakville, Ontario, Canada

A pioneering effort to utilize man's rational faculties and scientific know-how to find means of averting war in the midst of the perils of the nuclear age is represented by the work of Norman Z. Alcock, president and director of the Canadian Peace Research Institute. A nuclear physicist and engineer by profession, Alcock participated in the research that led to the perfection of radar during World War II. In 1959 he gave up a promising industrial career when he left his position as director of engineering with Canadian Curtiss-Wright Ltd. in order to arouse public interest in the cause of world peace. In his booklet *The Bridge of Reason* (1961) he pre-

Gilbert A. Milne

NORMAN Z. ALCOCK

sents a plan for the possible elimination of war through the worldwide establishment of fact-finding peace research institutes, staffed with competent, independent scholars and scientists.

The Canadian Peace Research Institute, which was incorporated in 1962, is the first of a projected worldwide network of peace research centers. It is described by David Spurgeon in the *Nation* (May 26, 1962) as not a protest group in the classic sense, nor a movement of the Left, but "an expression of the sense of frustration which thoughtful people feel in the face of threatening nuclear calamity, and of their desire to use their intelligence to avert it."

Norman Zinkan Alcock was born in Edmonton, Alberta, Canada on May 29, 1918, the son of Joseph Benjamin Alcock, a breeder and dealer of horses, and Edith Alma (Zinkan) Alcock. He has one sister, Lois, now Mrs. G. W. Light. Alcock received his secondary education at Magee High School in Vancouver, British Columbia, from which he graduated in 1936. He then attended Queen's University in Kingston, Ontario, where he studied electrical engineering and received a number of prizes and scholarships. During summers he worked with the Hydro-Electric Power Commission of Ontario. After graduating from Queen's University with a B.S. degree in 1940, Alcock took graduate courses in the United States at the California Institute of Technology at Pasadena on a Charles Fortescue Fellowship and received the M.Sc. degree in electrical engineering in 1941.

From 1941 to 1945 Alcock served as a junior research engineer with the National Research Council of Canada in Ottawa and at the Telecommunications Research Establishment in Great Malvern, England. During this period he was one of a small group of men who helped to perfect radar for wartime use. From 1943 until 1945 Alcock also was a member of the Royal Canadian Air Force, with the rank of pilot officer, but he was granted an indefinite leave without pay to enable him to continue with his radar research activities.

Alcock served as an assistant research physicist at McGill University in Montreal during 1945-46, working on cyclotron design. In 1947 he joined Atomic Energy of Canada Ltd. as a research physicist and engaged in research on neutron diffraction. Meanwhile, he continued his graduate studies at McGill University under a National Research Council Fellowship, and in 1949 he received the Ph.D. degree in physics after submitting the dissertation "Neutron Diffraction by Gas Molecules."

In 1950 Alcock, together with three of his colleagues from Atomic Energy of Canada Ltd., founded Isotopes Products Ltd. at Oakville, Ontario. The company aimed at putting to peaceful use the knowledge obtained from wartime nuclear weapons research. Alcock served as vice-president and director from 1951 to 1957. Although the company expanded, it needed greater capital and wider markets for the application of radioactive isotopes to industrial use. Consequently, it was sold in 1957 to Canadian Curtiss-Wright Ltd. In 1958 Alcock became general manager of the isotope products division of Canadian Curtiss-Wright Ltd. at Oakville, and he subsequently served as the company's director of engineering.

Motivated by humanitarian idealism, Alcock had long been concerned with the cause of world peace. His intellectual development had been influenced, in large part, by such individuals as H. G. Wells, Bertrand Russell, P. M. Blackett, Barbara Ward, C. Wright Mills, and Brock Chisholm. When in the fall of 1959 Alcock was asked to transfer with his company to Princeton, New Jersey, he chose to give up his $15,000-a-year position. He felt that he could use his talents for something more worthwhile than raising living standards in North America, where such an effort was least needed.

For the next fifteen months Alcock invested his time and his savings in trying to find a formula for peace grounded on methods of science and reason. He undertook studies in psychology and in the social sciences and consulted a number of scholars in these fields. Having conceived of a concentrated worldwide program of research aimed at averting the present drift toward war, Alcock put forth his proposals in a thirty-eight-page booklet, *The Bridge of Reason*. Published at Alcock's own expense by the John Wilkes Press in Oakville, Ontario in 1961, the booklet has sold many thousands of copies.

Alcock's plan is to set up a worldwide network of peace research institutes, staffed by scholars and scientists of all nations who would be engaged in the full-time study of the physical, psychological, social, and economic causes of war and the possible means to avert it. These institutes would be supported by governments as well as by private funds, but they would be politically independent and would function · as fact-finding and suggestive agencies rather than as pressure groups. They would use no classified data, so that findings could be freely communicated among institutes, national governments, and the United Nations.

Alcock proposes that the plan be undertaken as a "crash program," in a similar manner, and with the same sense of urgency, as the wartime radar research program. "We go on preparing for war with billions of dollars, while we appropriate pennies for peace research," Alcock says, pointing out that the current United States defense budget was $40 billion, whereas a requested appropriation of $400,000 for the study of disarmament problems had been repeatedly refused by the United States Senate. Noting that science and reason are the most powerful tools available to humanity, Alcock calls attention to the tremendous progress that has been achieved in technology and in the conquest of diseases. He believes that man's ability to reason critically in the social sciences will bring about equal advances toward the alleviation of social ills, the greatest of which is war.

Among the proposed projects for the peace research institutes are studies of such problems as the economic effects of transition from a wartime to a peacetime economy; the development of safeguards against accidental war and measures to be taken in the event that such a war should break out; the psychological effects resulting from the exclusion of Communist China from the United Nations; and the relationship between national allegiance and loyalty to humanity as a whole. The compilation of a yearbook on world tensions, to be used to predict international crises in a manner similar to the use of weather maps by meteorologists, has also been proposed.

The nucleus of the peace research institutes would consist of small groups of scientists who are internationally minded, co-operative, competent, and "sufficiently foolhardy, or courageous, to drop present quests and throw energies and reputations into a search for peace." A thousand persons, working together, "might just discover the political and social inventions needed for a warless world," Alcock has said. "Therefore let us at once search for these critical few—in the five or ten years left to us they may be our brightest hope." To pessimistic critics who maintain that some sections of humanity, notably the Communist nations, would not respond to his plan, Alcock points out that the response of these nations cannot be known until the program is tried out. He feels that if enough nations join in, the plan might eventually become universal.

As a first step toward the projected establishment of peace research centers throughout the world, the Canadian Peace Research Institute, with headquarters in Toronto, was incorporated in 1962 as a nonpolitical and nongovernmental organization for objective study. Alcock serves as president and director of the institute. The board of directors includes such noted persons as Brock Chisholm, former director general of the World Health Organization; Franc R. Joubin, who discovered and developed Canada's uranium ore reserves; Professor Kenneth E. Boulding of the University of Michigan; Francis G. Winspear, a former president of the Canadian Chamber of Commerce; Walter C. Koerner, a director of the Toronto Dominion Bank; Hugh L. Keenleyside, chairman of the British Columbia Power Commission; Professor Pierre Elliot-Trudeau of the University of Montreal; Gerard Pelletier, editor in chief of the French-Canadian newspaper La Presse; the Right Reverend James S. Thomson, a moderator of the United Church of Canada; and Mrs. W. D. Tucker, a United Nations Association official.

The Canadian Peace Research Institute has some support from Canada's five major peace groups: the Canadian Committee for the Control of Radiation Hazards, the Combined Universities Campaign for Nuclear Disarmament, the Voice of Women, the Society of Friends, and the World Federalists of Canada. It has received endorsement from conservatives and liberals alike and from persons of all walks of life, including political leaders, trade union officials, newspaper editors, writers, broadcasters, entertainers, social workers, and even military-minded individuals. Alcock has personally conferred with government officials, scientists, and business leaders with regard to his program. In 1961 he delivered about 100 lectures to audiences numbering in the thousands.

During the first four years of its existence the Canadian Peace Research Institute hopes to raise $4,000,000 through private subscriptions and government support. Half of this amount is to be used to set up an International Peace Research Fund to provide grants to scholars and to promote peace research centers in other nations. The directors plan to have twenty-five full-time scholars, in such fields as psychology, biology, anthropology, sociology, economics, history, mathematics, and the physical sciences, working at the Canadian institute in 1963. They hope that by 1965 some 1,000 scientists will be working on peace research in institutes in various parts of the world.

Alcock has written many scientific articles for Physical Review and other periodicals. Organizations of which he has been a member include the Physical Society, the Institute of Radio Engineers, and the Canadian Association of Physicists. He belongs to the Professional Engineers of Ontario and to the science research honor society Sigma Xi. On June 29, 1948 Norman Z. Alcock married Patricia Christian Sinclair Hunter, a secretary. With their four children—Stephen, Christopher, David, and Nancy—they live in a large house in Oakville, on the shore of Lake Ontario. Alcock is five feet nine inches tall, weighs 148 pounds, and has brown hair and blue eyes. His favorite recreation is reading. He refuses to build a fallout shelter for his home. He is a friendly and cheerful man, and although he is occasionally faced by taunts of some of his neighbors, who wonder why he does not get a "real" job, he is undeterred in his dedication to his work. "To our generation has fallen the task of outlawing war," he has said. "Towards that goal we should now be striving with our hearts and sinews and minds, but especially we should be striving with our minds."

References

Macleans Mag 75:14+ F 24 '62 por
Nation 194:470+ My 26 '62
Toronto Globe and Mail p7 Ap 21 '61 por
American Men of Science 10th ed (1960-62)

ALI, MOHAMMED Oct. 19, 1909-Jan. 23, 1963
Foreign Minister of Pakistan (1959-63); Ambassador from Pakistan to the United States (1955-59); Prime Minister of Pakistan (1953-55); staunch anti-Communist and supporter of United States policy. See *Current Biography* (October) 1952.

Obituary

N Y Times p35 Ap 1 '63

ALLEN, FLORENCE E(LLINWOOD) Mar. 23, 1884- Judge
Address: b. 112 Federal Bldg., Cleveland 14, Ohio

NOTE: This biography supersedes the article that appeared in *Current Biography* in 1941.

When Florence E. Allen was admitted to the bar in 1914, no one ventured much optimism about how far a woman could advance in the legal profession. Her career is unique in American history because she passed the tests that tremendously expanded the opportunities for women in the field of law, while making her own contributions to the development of the nation's concept and practice of justice. Early recognized for her ability, resoluteness, and sense of ethical responsibility, she scored many firsts for women in the law courts of Ohio. With her appointment by President Franklin D. Roosevelt to the United States Court of Appeals for the Sixth Circuit in 1934, she had new trails to blaze. She became the first woman ever appointed to a United States court of appeals and to any federal court of general jurisdiction, the first woman to sit in the National Judicial Conference, and the first woman to serve as chief justice of a federal court. Since October 1959, having retired from active service, she has held the title of senior judge of the Court of Appeals for the Sixth Circuit.

Edmondson Studio, Cleveland
JUDGE FLORENCE E. ALLEN

The ancestors of Florence Ellinwood Allen were also pioneers. On her father's side she is a descendant of Ira Allen, who moved from England to New England in the mid-seventeenth century. Ethan Allen was one of her forefathers, and, by maternal lineage, so was the Mayflower passenger Samuel Fuller. Like the Allens, the Ellinwoods and Tuckermans of her mother's family were among the earliest settlers of the Western Reserve, which became the state of Ohio. Florence Allen was born on March 23, 1884 to Clarence Emir and Corinne Marie (Tuckerman) Allen in Salt Lake City, Utah. Her father, a former professor of Greek and Latin at Western Reserve College in Ohio, had gone to Utah for reasons of health and had there studied law. When Utah became a state in 1896, he was elected to the House of Representatives in Washington, D.C., and later he was engaged as a manager of mines in Utah and Nevada. Her mother, one of Smith College's first students, was also a leader in community affairs.

There were five other children in the family: Emir (who died in World War I), John (who died as a result of injuries received in the war), Esther, Helen, and Elizabeth. One of her sisters, Esther (Allen) Gaw, became dean of women of Ohio State University. An accomplished musician, their mother gave them an early love of music and organized a family orchestra in which Florence played the piano. After studying Greek and Latin with her father and attending the Salt Lake Academy, Florence Allen entered the New Lyme Institute in Ohio in 1895. At sixteen she enrolled in the College for Women of Western Reserve University, where she was elected to Phi Beta Kappa and earned the B.A. degree with honors in 1904.

Having decided upon a career in music, Miss Allen went to Berlin, Germany with her parents for further study, and from 1904 to 1906 she was also employed as assistant Berlin correspondent for the New York *Musical Courier*. Because of a nerve injury, she had to abandon her ambition to become a concert pianist, but on her return to Cleveland in 1906 she took a position as music critic for the *Plain Dealer,* which she held for three years, and also lectured on music at the Laurel School.

Her interests turned increasingly to civic affairs. In 1908 she obtained her M.A. degree in political science from Western Reserve. Then after a year's study of law at the University of Chicago, she moved to New York, where she worked as a legal investigator for the New York League for the Protection of Immigrants. From 1910 to 1913 she took courses at the New York University Law School, while lecturing on music for New York City's Board of Education. She was awarded the LL.B. degree *cum laude* from New York University in 1913 and was admitted to the Ohio bar in 1914.

To acquire her training in law, Miss Allen had to overcome formidable discrimination against women. The same prejudice faced her in establishing a law practice in Cleveland, but she was able to acquire basic experience as a volunteer counselor for the Legal Aid Society. She also handled much of the legal work of the Woman's Suffrage party of Cleveland and became a leader in the state's campaigns for woman's suffrage. From 1911 to 1913 she served as assistant secretary of the National Equal Suffrage League and as a member of the executive board of the Ohio Woman Suffrage Association. Compelled by the sense of justice that was to distinguish her dedication to law as a jurist, she traveled through Ohio and neighboring states by horse and buggy, wherever there were public gatherings, to plead for women's right to vote, to hold public office, and to enjoy equal opportunities with men.

In 1919 Florence Allen became, by appointment, the first woman to hold the office of assistant prosecutor of Cuyahoga County, Ohio. The following year, by election on a nonpartisan ticket, she became judge of the court of common pleas in Cuyahoga, having led nine other contestants by the largest vote ever given to a candidate for judge of that court. As the first woman to sit in a court of general jurisdiction, she tried 660 cases, of which seven were for murder.

Judge Allen had been elected for a six-year term, but at the end of two years, in 1922, she was nominated by petition for justice to the Ohio Supreme Court. Her subsequent election made her the first woman in the world to serve as judge of a court of last resort, the highest court of a state. In 1928 she was elected to a second six-year term by a majority of 350,000 votes. Among the important decisions that she wrote were those that upheld the constitutionality of the Cleveland city manager plan and the zoning ordinance of Cincinnati.

Shortly before Judge Allen completed her twelfth year on the Ohio Supreme Court in 1934, President Franklin D. Roosevelt appointed her to the United States Court of Appeals for the Sixth Circuit, which encompasses Ohio, Michigan, Kentucky, and Tennessee. Her work over the next twenty-five years covered cases dealing with taxation, patents, personal injuries, forgeries, contracts, interstate commerce, labor laws, problems of school desegregation, and conflicts between federal and state authority. One important trial over which she presided tested the validity of the Tennessee Valley Authority, and her opinion that the statute was constitutional was affirmed by the Supreme Court.

On October 5, 1959 Florence Allen retired from regular active service and assumed the title and status of senior judge of the Court of Appeals for the Sixth Circuit. In a ceremony honoring Judge Allen at the following session of the court, Mrs. Maurine H. Abernathy, then president of the National Association of Women Lawyers, said of her: "Typical of her opinions are her direct attack upon the heart of issues, her closely reasoned discussion, full documentation of the pertinent law, and a clear style of writing. . . . If one may attempt to state Judge Allen's legal philosophy, it is that in order to have freedom, there must be government of laws—not of men—and that our Constitution, correctly construed, guarantees such freedom."

The scholarly preparation, perception, and philosophical understanding with which Judge Allen approached each case in court are also evident in her book of fourteen essays, *This Constitution of Ours* (Putnam, 1940). In interpreting the Constitution "in terms of vital significance

today," she discussed it as an instrument that each generation must use in creating a liberal society for its own times. Professor Harlan Hatcher of Ohio State University described her book in the Columbus *Citizen* as "a little masterpiece glowingly written." She is also the author of *The Treaty as an Instrument of Legislation* (Macmillan, 1952) in the Kappa Delta Pi lecture series.

Especially since World War I, Florence Allen has been convinced that the survival of humanity depends upon outlawing war and has championed the cause of peace and freedom throughout the world under law. She is a member of the International Bar Association; served as chairman of its section on human rights in 1950 and 1952; and presided at meetings of that section in London in 1950, Madrid in 1952, and Monte Carlo in 1954. She addressed the plenary session of the association at the Hague in 1950 and during the same year spoke before a meeting of the International Federation of Business and Professional Women's Clubs at the Guild Hall in London. In the International Federation of Women Lawyers she served as chairman of the committee on international law in 1954 and of the committee on outer space in 1958. She was a principal speaker at the plenary session of the federation in Finland in 1954.

Also prominent in national legal organizations, Judge Allen is a Fellow of the American Bar Foundation and served the American Bar Association as a member of the house of delegates in 1944 and a member of the resolutions committee from 1951 to 1954. The National Association of Women Lawyers awarded her a citation in 1957 for advancing the status of women in the legal profession.

Among Judge Allen's other awards are some twenty-five honorary degrees from colleges and universities, the National Achievement Award for 1938, the Citation for Distinguished Citizen from Denison University for 1956, and New York University's Albert Gallatin Medal for 1960. Also in 1940 she was made an elector of the Hall of Fame in New York City, where she delivered the Susan B. Anthony Address in 1952. She was received into the Order of the Coif by George Washington University in 1955.

Florence E. Allen has blue eyes and auburn hair, is five feet six inches tall, and weighs 150 pounds. Music continues to be one of the joys of her life, and she prefers Bach, Chopin, Brahms, and Beethoven. All her life she has been a nature lover, a mountain climber, and a vigorous walker who takes a poet's delight in the beauty of the outdoors. Maurine Abernathy has said of her, "It has been her practice, in her walks at dawn with her dogs and pruning shears, to rescue young saplings, such as black walnut and sugar maple, from the stranglehold of the wild grapevine."

Judge Allen's church is the Congregational; in politics she is an independent. Her concern for social justice is marked by a liberal and unbiased outlook, and her friendliness and the sincerity of her convictions have made her an inspiring public speaker. In October 1959 many American lawyers paid tribute to her by presenting her portrait to the Court of Appeals for the Sixth Circuit. On that occasion Ohio's Senator Frank J. Lausche

ALLEN, FLORENCE E.—*Continued*

said, "The dominant force of her life has been love of the law. She has become a legend in it." In her reply Judge Allen spoke of her pride in having been a member of a court that aspired to follow the Lord's requirement of judges to do justly: "And, after all, the attainment of justice is the highest human endeavor."

References

International Who's Who, 1962-63
Roosevelt, Eleanor. Ladies of Courage (1954)
Who's Who in America, 1962-63
Who's Who of American Women (1958-59)
World Biography (1954)

AMMANN, O(THMAR) H(ERMANN) Mar. 26, 1879- Engineer

Address: b. Ammann & Whitney, 111 8th Ave., New York 11; h. Kenilworth Rd., Rye, N.Y.

The master bridge builder and designer of the twentieth century is the Swiss-born engineer O. H. Ammann. As chief engineer and director of engineering of the Port of New York Authority, as chief engineer of the Triborough Bridge and Tunnel Authority, and as a private consultant, Ammann has directed the design and construction of most of the important river crossings in recent decades in the New York metropolitan area. They include the George Washington Bridge, the Triborough Bridge, the Bronx-Whitestone Bridge, the Bayonne Bridge, the Throgs Neck Bridge, the Lincoln Tunnel, and the Verrazano-Narrows Bridge, which will be opened to traffic early in 1965.

Other important bridges in the creation of which Ammann participated prominently include the Hell Gate Bridge in New York, the Golden Gate Bridge in San Francisco, the Mackinac Bridge in Michigan, the Walt Whitman Bridge in Philadelphia, and the Delaware Memorial Bridge at Wilmington. Ammann regards as his greatest achievement to date the George Washington Bridge with a span about twice that of any previously built. Although he is now an octogenarian, Ammann continues to be active as the senior partner in the engineering firm of Ammann & Whitney, Consulting Engineers, in New York.

A native of Schaffhausen on the Rhine River in Switzerland, Othmar Hermann Ammann was born on March 26, 1879 to Emmanuel Christian Ammann, a well-to-do hat manufacturer, and Emilie Rose (Labhardt) Ammann. His maternal grandfather was a noted painter. Determined to become an architect, Ammann excelled in mathematics and art at the cantonal college of Zurich, where he also studied philosophy and languages. By the time he entered the Swiss Federal Institute of Technology in 1898 he had changed his field of interest from architecture to engineering. From the latter institute he graduated in 1902 with a civil engineering degree.

Ammann began his career in 1901 as a structural draftsman with the firm of Wartmann and Valette in Brugg, Switzerland. In that year he also practised topographical surveying for the mountain railway from Montreux to the Bernese Oberland and had occasion to design a thirty-foot stone arch. In 1903 he went to Frankfurt, Germany, where he became an assistant engineer with the firm of Buchheim and Heister, working on reinforced concrete design. Ammann came to the United States in 1904 to gain a few years' experience in American bridge building, but he subsequently decided to remain. While working at his first job in the United States, with Joseph Mayer, a New York consulting engineer, Ammann became acquainted with the problem of spanning the Hudson River with a bridge.

From 1904 to 1906 Ammann was a draftsman for the Pennsylvania Steel Company at Steelton, Pennsylvania, working on bridges and steel buildings. In 1906 he went to Chicago, where he designed steel bridges for Ralph Modjeski, but in the same year returned to Pennsylvania Steel Company as assistant engineer, to work on the design of the Queensboro Bridge of New York City. (The Queensboro Bridge was completed in 1909.) As principal assistant engineer with the firm of C. C. Schneider and F. C. Kunz of Philadelphia, which he joined in 1909, Ammann investigated the collapse of the almost completed Quebec Bridge, crossing the St. Lawrence River near Quebec, Canada. He assisted in making a design study for reconstruction of that bridge and also for an arch bridge at St. John, New Brunswick.

From 1912 to 1923 Ammann was principal assistant engineer with Gustav Lindenthal and as such also assistant chief engineer of the New York Connecting Railroad and the North River Bridge Company. During this period he assisted in executing the design and construction of the Hell Gate Bridge and its approaches (completed 1918) in New York City and of the Ohio River Bridge at Sciotoville, Ohio. He also assisted Lindenthal in studies for a proposed bridge to span the Hudson River at 57th Street in New York City and for a railroad freight terminal as part of the bridge project which was to be privately financed.

When that project had to be abandoned in 1923 Ammann established his own practice as consulting engineer. As such he planned and proposed a bridge across the Hudson River between 179th Street in Manhattan and Fort Lee in New Jersey, which later became the George Washington Bridge. In 1924 the Port of New York Authority was authorized by the two states of New York and New Jersey to finance and build this bridge, and Ammann was appointed chief engineer of bridges to direct its planning and construction. In this position he was also in charge of the planning and construction of two bridges across Arthur Kill: the Goethals Bridge and the Outerbridge Crossing, both of which were completed in 1928. He also designed and constructed the longest bridge of arch design in the world, the 1,652-foot Bayonne Bridge across Kill van Kull, which was completed in 1931.

In 1927 Ammann completed plans for the George Washington Bridge. In its design he deviated from conventional practice by omitting deep stiffening trusses along the bridge deck, being convinced that the great suspended mass would provide adequate stiffness. He thereby effected considerable economies and enhanced the graceful appearance of the suspended structure. The design of the towers, developed with the assistance of the architect, Cass Gilbert, also was unusual. They were at first designed to be of massive concrete construction reinforced with a steel skeleton and faced with stone. This design evoked considerable controversy among engineers and architects and as a result was finally replaced by a plain steel design. To meet the demand for rapid transit connections between Manhattan and New Jersey the original design of the bridge provided for the eventual addition of four tracks on a lower deck. It was also visualized at that time, however, that in the not too distant future this deck might be needed for additional vehicular lanes, and this proved to be the case some twenty-five years after the opening of the upper deck. With a span of 3,500 feet and eight traffic lanes the George Washington Bridge set a new record for length and load capacity of suspension bridges. It has since been exceeded in length of span by the Golden Gate Bridge, the Mackinac Bridge and the Verrazano-Narrows Bridge, but with fourteen traffic lanes it still tops all existing bridges in capacity. After four years of construction work the George Washington Bridge was opened to traffic on the upper deck on October 24, 1931.

Ammann served as chief engineer of the Port of New York Authority from 1930 to 1937, and from 1937 to 1939 he was the Port Authority's director of engineering. He was chief engineer in the planning of the 8,216-foot Lincoln Tunnel, connecting midtown Manhattan and Weehawken, New Jersey, which was opened in December 1937. From 1934 to 1939 Ammann also served as chief engineer of the Triborough Bridge and Tunnel Authority, working closely with its chairman, Robert Moses. He directed the planning and construction of the Triborough Bridge, connecting the boroughs of Manhattan, the Bronx, and Queens, which was completed in 1936, and of the Bronx-Whitestone Bridge, completed in 1939. At the same time he played an important role in the construction of the Golden Gate Bridge at San Francisco, serving as a member of its board of engineers from 1929 until 1937, when the bridge was completed. With a span of 4,200 feet the Golden Gate Bridge is at present the longest suspension bridge in the world.

Returning to private practice as a consulting engineer in 1939, Ammann worked on plans for various bridges in the New York City area and for a suspension bridge across the Yorktown River. He participated in the planning of parkways in the New York metropolitan area and served as consultant of the 2,150-foot Delaware Memorial Bridge near Wilmington, Delaware, which was opened in 1951. As a private consultant Ammann also conducted an investigation of the Brooklyn Bridge for the City of New York and investigated the failure of the Tacoma Narrows Bridge in the state of Washington for the Federal Works Administration. He also served as a member of a committee organized by the United States Bureau of Public Roads to conduct studies of the aerodynamic stability of suspension bridges.

Blackstone Studios

O. H. AMMANN

In partnership with Charles S. Whitney, a Milwaukee engineer, Ammann established the engineering firm of Ammann & Whitney in 1946. The firm has undertaken a variety of engineering projects, including bridges, highways, coliseums, auditoriums, floating dry docks, hangars, airports, blast-resistant structures, and military bases in the United States, Europe, Africa, and Asia. In co-operation with the firm of Modjeski and Masters, Ammann & Whitney undertook the planning and construction supervision of the 2,000-foot Walt Whitman Bridge, crossing the Delaware River at Philadelphia, which was financed by the Delaware River Port Authority and opened in 1957. In 1954 Ammann & Whitney made preliminary studies for the Port of New York Authority and the Triborough Bridge and Tunnel Authority for added arterial facilities in the New York metropolitan area, including a Brooklyn-Staten Island Narrows bridge, a Hudson River 125th Street bridge, a bridge across the East River at Throgs Neck between the Bronx and Queens, and a second deck for the George Washington Bridge.

Ammann was a member of the engineering board that drew up the preliminary plans for the Straits of Mackinac Bridge in Michigan, which was opened in 1958. In 1957 the firm of Ammann & Whitney prepared final plans for, and supervised construction of, the Throgs Neck Bridge, which was opened in 1961. Ammann was appointed design consultant for the lower deck of the George Washington Bridge in August 1957. The lower deck, which added six new traffic lanes to the bridge, thus increasing its capacity by 75 percent, was based on Ammann's original design. It was opened to traffic on August 29, 1962. The construction of the Verrazano-Narrows Bridge, connecting Brooklyn and Staten Island at the entrance of New York Harbor, is also based on Ammann's preliminary plans. With a center span of 4,260 feet and two

AMMANN, O. H.—*Continued*

decks, each accommodating six traffic lanes, the Narrows Bridge will be the longest and heaviest suspension bridge in the world when it is opened to traffic early in 1965.

O. H. Ammann has written many articles and papers for technical journals and professional societies. He holds an honorary membership in the American Society of Civil Engineers, of which he was director from 1934 to 1936, and is a Fellow of the American Academy of Arts and Sciences. He also is an honorary member of the alumni association of the Swiss Federal Institute of Technology; the Swiss Society of Engineers and Architects; the honorary engineering fraternity Tau Beta Pi; and Chi Epsilon, the honor society in civil engineering. Other organizations to which Ammann belongs include the American Institute of Consulting Engineers, the Institute of Civil Engineering of Great Britain, the American Society for Testing Materials, the American Railway Engineering Association, the National Society of Professional Engineers, and the Engineers Club of New York City.

Some sixteen honorary degrees and awards have been conferred upon Ammann by New York University, Yale, Columbia, Pennsylvania Military College, the Polytechnic Institute of Brooklyn, and other institutions. In 1918 he received the Thomas Fitch Rowland Prize of the American Society of Civil Engineers. Several of his bridges, including the Triborough Bridge and the Bayonne Bridge, have received awards from the American Institute of Steel Construction for beauty of design. At the ceremonies marking the opening of the lower deck of the George Washington Bridge Ammann was honored by the unveiling of a bronze commemorative bust of himself.

Since 1924 O. H. Ammann has been a citizen of the United States. He was married on July 24, 1905 to Lilly Selma Wehrli, who died in 1933. On March 2, 1935 he married Klary Vogt Noetzli in California. He has three children: Werner, who is a partner in the firm of Ammann & Whitney; George Andrew, an ornithologist with the Michigan Department of Conservation; and Dr. Margot Durrer, a gynecologist. Soft-spoken and unassuming, Ammann has been described as "the antithesis of the mighty structures he has created," and does not like people to cater to him because of age or position. Ammann is of slight build, with blue eyes that peer over horn-rimmed glasses and brown hair that belies his age. For relaxation he works in the garden of his home, and he still enjoys hiking on summer visits to the mountains of his native Switzerland. He likes all forms of music, especially symphonies and operas, and he formerly played the violin. Although he is not a partygoer he often attends professional meetings and conventions. He is a Protestant.

Ammann still commutes daily from his home in Rye, New York to his Manhattan office, which is decorated with drawings and photographs of bridges. He greets visitors at the office in person, and he knows most of the employees by name. Ammann, who builds his bridges "to last forever," believes that a bridge should satisfy its function with simplicity and truthfulness, but he also feels that he owes it to the public to build beautiful as well as useful bridges. Ammann has advocated closer co-operation between the engineer, the architect, and the layman. Although he takes pride in his achievements, he does not believe that any one man can take exclusive credit for the building of a bridge.

References

Civil Eng 23:622 S '53 por
Eng N 160:136+ My 15 '58 pors
N Y Herald Tribune p25 O 24 '57 por
N Y Post p41 Ag 29 '62 por
N Y Times p59 Ag 29 '62 por
American Men of Science 10th ed (1960-62)
Who's Who in America, 1962-63
Who's Who in Engineering, 1959

ANDERSON, SAMUEL W(AGNER) Feb. 6, 1898-Dec. 14, 1962 United States Assistant Secretary of Commerce (1953-55); investment banker. See *Current Biography* (June) 1954.

Obituary

Washington (D.C.) Post B p4 D 15 '62

ARMSTRONG, DAVID W(ILLIAM) Nov. 19, 1885-Feb. 7, 1963 Former national executive director of Boys' Clubs of America (1941-56), with which he was associated since its founding in 1906. See *Current Biography* (July) 1949.

Obituary

Washington (D.C.) Post C p5 F 8 '63

ASHCROFT, DAME PEGGY Dec. 22, 1907- British actress

Address: Manor Lodge, Frognal Lane, London, N.W. 3, England

The traditional theatrical success story often involves an interminable struggle for recognition. But the leading British actress Dame Peggy Ashcroft has, in the words of her biographer, Eric Keown, "climbed to the heights by a straighter path than most actresses succeed in finding, and has wasted commendably little time on the trivial and ephemeral." She achieved recognition as a major actress at the age of twenty-eight, and since then she has demonstrated her versatility, power, and extraordinary dramatic intuition in classical and modern tragedy, in farce, high comedy, and melodrama, and in every medium open to an actress. Her services to the theater and to literature have earned her designation as a Dame of the Order of the British Empire (1956) and an honorary D.Lit. degree from Oxford University, among many other honors.

Peggy Ashcroft, whose full name is Edith Margaret Emily Ashcroft, was born on December 22, 1907 in Croydon, near London, England to William Worsley Ashcroft and his wife, the former Violet (one source gives Violetta) Maud Bernheim. Eric Keown, in his monograph *Peggy Ashcroft* (Rockliff, 1955), suggests that she was influenced in her choice of a theatrical career by the fact that her mother was an amateur actress and that her grandfather instilled in her a precocious love of poetry.

Miss Ashcroft's early love of language developed into a passion for the theater at the Woodford School, Croydon, where she studied elocution as well as the more traditional subjects and played the lead in school plays. In spite of her own theatrical proclivities Violet Ashcroft was not anxious to put her daughter on the stage. But Peggy Ashcroft could not be talked out of her determination to act. In 1923, when she was sixteen, she entered the Central School of Speech Training and Dramatic Art. She studied under its founder, Eileen (one source gives Elsie) Fogerty, as her mother had done before her, and obtained a diploma in dramatic art.

Peggy Ashcroft made her first professional appearance on May 22, 1926. The actress playing Margaret in a Birmingham Repertory Company production of Barrie's *Dear Brutus* had fallen ill, and Miss Ashcroft, who had played the part at the Central School, was rushed to Birmingham for the last seven performances. The company included Ralph Richardson and Edward Chapman, and Miss Ashcroft came away with a profound sense of how little she knew. A bad year followed, during which her mother died and there was no work. Then her luck changed. In May 1927 she appeared at a tiny London theater called Playroom Six, as Bessie in a stage adaptation of Joseph Conrad's *One Day More*. This led, later the same month, to a part as Mary Dunn in *The Return*, a play by the actor Charles Bennett, who had played opposite her in *One Day More*.

Then a chain reaction began. In July 1927 the director Nigel Playfair, who had heard about her performance in *One Day More*, cast her as Eve in a comedy by George Paston, *When Adam Delved*. And Playfair's introduction to John Drinkwater led, in September 1927, to a part as Joan Greenleaf in Drinkwater's *Bird In Hand* at the Birmingham Repertory Theatre. Miss Ashcroft's debut in the West End followed in November of the same crowded year. She had a small part in Playfair's production of *The Way of the World*, which allowed her plenty of time to stand in the wings and study Edith Evans' brilliant performance as Millamant. The following year brought Miss Ashcroft's first tour, as Hester in Sidney Howard's *The Silver Cord*, and a number of parts, including Anastasia Vulliamy in *The Fascinating Foundling*, Mary Bruin in *The Land of Heart's Desire*, Edith Strange in *Earthbound*, Kristina in *Easter*, and Eulalia in *A Hundred Years Old*.

A writer for *Stage* had commended Peggy Ashcroft's performance in *The Return* and described her as "a promising young actress." A far more important accolade came in April 1929, when she played the lead at the Everyman Theatre, Hampstead, in Molly Kerr's modern tragedy *Requital*. The influential critic W. A. Darlington called her "a young actress whose work bears all over it the stamp of an uncommon charm and ability." Some relatively insignificant parts followed before she was assigned the role that first brought her wide recognition. This came in September

Angus McBean, London

DAME PEGGY ASHCROFT

1929 with the opening of Ashley Dukes's adaptation of the best-selling Feuchtwanger novel *Jew Süss*. Miss Ashcroft's performance as Süss's daughter, Naomi, "had the integrity of exquisite simplicity," Eric Keown wrote, "and it took London by storm. . . . For the first time, most of the major critics unbuttoned their collars in unison to announce that an uncommon actress had arrived."

The public shared the critical enthusiasm, and *Jew Süss* ran for 211 performances, one of which was seen by Paul Robeson, then in London to prepare for his Othello. Miss Ashcroft was recruited to play Desdemona opposite Robeson, although her voice was unequal to the demands of the willow song in the last act. (She cannot carry a tune.) This was her first professional appearance in a Shakespearean play, and she joined a cast that included Sybil Thorndike and Ralph Richardson. Robeson's Othello was a memorable one, and it was generally agreed that Miss Ashcroft was a perfect foil for him. It was during this run, which opened in May 1930, that she caught the eye of Walter Sickert, who was to paint her portrait over and over again.

The next two years brought Miss Ashcroft a variety of roles, classical and modern, many of them in short-lived productions. The high points were Maugham's *The Breadwinner*, in which Miss Ashcroft played Judy Battle, and a production of *Romeo and Juliet* at Oxford, where John Gielgud was the newly appointed director of the Oxford University Dramatic Society (OUDS). Then, in September 1932, when Peggy Ashcroft was only twenty-five, she began her first season as the leading lady at the Old Vic. During its eight-month season she played major roles in seven Shakespearean plays, in *She Stoops to Conquer*, in *The School for Scandal*, and in John Drinkwater's *Mary Stuart*. It was an uneven and exhausting season, of which the director Harcourt Williams subsequently wrote: "For various reasons

ASHCROFT, DAME PEGGY—*Continued*

this last season has not been an entirely happy one, but I owed a great deal to the help and cheer that Peggy Ashcroft gave me. Her insight and clearheadedness, and her own particular technique which demands absolute honesty and freedom from any suspicion of false sentiment, were invaluable."

It is some indication of Miss Ashcroft's devotion to her art that, in the midst of the tremendous strains of the Old Vic season she left the cast for three weeks to star in a totally different kind of production. *Fräulein Elsa,* adapted from a story by Arthur Schnitzler, was performed at a theater club in November 1932—a time when it was considered a daring and shocking experiment. Said to be the longest and most arduous part in stage history, it made heavy use of unusually frank interior monologue and required Miss Ashcroft to undress on stage.

In 1933 Miss Ashcroft appeared in her first motion picture, a British production of *The Wandering Jew.* There followed two busy and generally successful years that established her firmly as a competent and versatile performer. Her leap from that point to recognition as a major actress came in October 1935. At that time John Gielgud, who had left Oxford, resurrected and improved upon his OUDS production of *Romeo and Juliet.* The play was staged at the New Theatre, London, and the production was thought by most critics to be the finest they had ever seen. Peter Fleming wrote: "There is a triumphant beauty in Miss Peggy Ashcroft's Juliet, a passion not to be gainsaid. . . . Technically her performance is perfection. . . . She does more than make Shakespeare's expression of Juliet's thoughts seem natural; she makes it seem inevitable."

Peggy Ashcroft reached the top of her profession at the age of twenty-eight and has been there for nearly thirty years. She made her first New York appearance early in 1937 in the role of Lise in *High Tor,* and on her return to England she joined John Gielgud for his season at the Queen's Theatre from September 1937 to 1938. During the 1940's Miss Ashcroft appeared in several Shakespearean plays—including *The Tempest, Hamlet,* and *A Midsummer Night's Dream*—and played roles in *Rebecca, The Importance of Being Earnest, The Dark River,* and *The Duchess of Malfi.* She appeared at Stratford-on-Avon in 1950 in *Much Ado About Nothing* and *King Lear* and in 1953 in *The Merchant of Venice* and *Antony and Cleopatra.*

Perhaps her most overwhelming triumph to date came in November 1954, when she played the title role of *Hedda Gabler,* in London; the role was repeated in Oslo four months later. The production, directed by Peter Ashmore, was an unorthodox one. It brought out a previously unnoticed vein of sardonic comedy and presented a Hedda who was not a tragic figure but a ludicrous bungler. The production caused a storm in Oslo—not of outrage, but of delight. The critic of the Oslo *Aftenposten* wrote: "It is curious to have to register the fact than an English actress has shown the Norwegian public how Hedda should be played. After only a few minutes we realised that she had that rare combination of

emotional receptivity and intellectual capacity that characterises actresses of the first order. . . . There is the most intimate connection between the Hedda Gabler of Peggy Ashcroft and the intentions of Ibsen himself." The final endorsement came from King Haakon of Norway, who saw the play and presented Peggy Ashcroft with the King's Gold Medal.

Another extraordinary interpretation of an Ibsen play brought Miss Ashcroft further acclaim in 1959, when her performance as Rebecca West in *Rosmersholm* was described by W. A. Darlington as the most impressive "since the play was first translated into English." And her endless versatility prompted Kenneth Tynan to write of the 1960 Stratford production of *The Taming of the Shrew:* "Peggy Ashcroft, in prospect an impossible Kate, confounds prophecy by demonstrating herself ideal for the part; it was her predecessors who were impossible."

Although Miss Ashcroft is usually thought of in relation to the classical repertory—especially at the Old Vic and at Stratford-on-Avon—she believes that a serious actress must also be prepared to deal with the life-size roles of contemporary drama. Her 1940 performance in the title role of Clemence Dane's *Cousin Muriel* wrung from the usually sardonic James Agate high praise for "acting of the highest possible intelligence and delicately graded sentiment." In 1947 Peggy Ashcroft played Evelyn Holt in *Edward, My Son,* winning that year's Ellen Terry Theatre Award, and she later starred in the successful New York production of the same play. Her Miss Madrigal in *The Chalk Garden* won her the 1956 London *Evening Standard* drama award.

Other notable performances in modern plays include her Catherine Sloper in *The Heiress* (1949); Hester Collyer in Rattigan's *The Deep Blue Sea* (1952); Shen Te in Brecht's *The Good Woman of Setzuan* (1956); and Julia Raik in Robert Ardrey's *Shadow of Heroes* (1958). Miss Ashcroft finds herself out of sympathy with the fragmentary technique of the film, but she has nevertheless appeared in several, including *The Thirty-Nine Steps, Rhodes of Africa,* and *The Nun's Story,* in which she played Mother Mathilde. She has often performed on radio but was not seen on television until recently, appearing first in 1959 in *Shadow of Heroes.*

In 1951 Peggy Ashcroft was named an Officer of the Order of the British Empire, and in 1956 a Dame of that order. She was elected to the Council of the English Stage Company in 1957 and has since 1962 been a member of the Arts Council. Dame Peggy is an active adherent of the Labour party, and distinguished herself by canvassing for Labour votes at 10 Downing Street when Sir Winston Churchill was in residence there. Her intense feeling for poetry led her in 1943 to found the Apollo Society, which brought together distinguished actors to give poetry recitals during World War II, and she has continued that work since. That her love of great writing is allied to a highly developed literary intelligence has been demonstrated in her acting and confirmed by the honorary D.Lit. degree that Oxford University awarded her in 1961.

Dame Peggy has been married since 1940 to the distinguished barrister Jeremy Nicolas Hutchinson; they have a son and a daughter. Two earlier marriages—to Rupert Hart-Davis in 1929 and to Theodore Komisarjevsky in 1934—were dissolved. In his biographical monograph about Miss Ashcroft, Eric Keown noted: "In writing about her one is often tempted to use the word 'simplicity,' because it gets nearer than any other to the immediate effect of her acting. It sums up conveniently the clarity, sincerity and directness which in a rare degree she brings to the theatre. It acknowledges her power to become by honest means the character she is playing, and it acquits her of all the sins of stage trickery. . . . By nature she is an explorer, more interested in the difficulties of new territory than in the pleasures of the country she already knows."

References

Keown, Eric. Peggy Ashcroft (1955)
Who's Who, 1963
Who's Who in the Theatre (1961)

AUSTIN, WARREN R(OBINSON) Nov. 12, 1877-Dec. 25, 1962 Republican United States Senator from Vermont (1931-46); member of committees on military affairs and foreign relations; United States representative in the United Nations with the rank of ambassador (1946-53). See *Current Biography* (January) 1944.

Obituary

N Y Times p35 Ap 1 '63

BAEZ, JOAN (bī'ĕz) Jan 9, 1941- Folk singer
Address: b. c/o Folklore Productions, 176 Federal St., Boston, Mass.; h. Carmel, Calif.

With little effort on her part, Joan Baez, the "queen of the folk singers," has experienced a phenomenally rapid and almost spontaneous rise to success. After a modest start as a singer in Boston coffeehouses, she became the object of nationwide attention when, still in her teens, she made an unheralded appearance at the Newport (Rhode Island) Folk Festival in the summer of 1959. Since then, on concert tours throughout the United States and on her Vanguard recordings, she has cast a spell over her listeners with renditions of such ballads as "Wildwood Flower," "Barbara Allen," and "All My Trials." Her style is utterly simple and informal, her soprano voice intense and limpid at the same time.

One of three sisters, Joan Baez was born in Staten Island, New York on January 9, 1941. Her father, Dr. Albert V. Baez, who came to the United States from Mexico at an early age, is a physicist. His teaching and research assignments took him to college communities in New York State, California, Bagdhad, and Boston, and finally to Paris, where he is a consultant to UNESCO. Her mother, Mrs. Joan Baez, the daughter of an Episcopal minister and dramatics professor, is of English, Scottish, and Irish background. Because of her dark complexion Joan Baez occasionally experienced race prejudice during childhood, and this left an indelible impression on her.

As a child, Joan Baez showed considerable talent for memorization and mimicry. Although she was exposed to classical music at home, she rebelled against taking piano lessons, and when she began to learn how to play the guitar at the age of twelve, she specialized in rock 'n' roll. At high school in Palo Alto, California, she did not distinguish herself in academic subjects but excelled in music and sang in the school choir.

In early 1958, shortly after she graduated from high school, Joan Baez moved with her family to Boston, where her father taught at Harvard University and at the Massachusetts Institute of Technology. Her interest in folk music was aroused when her father took her one evening to Tulla's Coffee Grinder, a Boston coffee shop where amateur folk singers could display their talents. At Boston University, where she studied for about a month in the Fine Arts School of Drama, she befriended several semiprofessional folk singers. Among them was Debby Green, who taught her songs and guitar techniques and introduced her to several espresso shops around Harvard Square. Gradually she increased her repertoire from a single folk song ("House of the Rising Sun") to scores of Anglo-American ballads, blues, and spirituals, and songs from all over the world.

While perfecting her technique, Miss Baez began to sing professionally in coffeehouses frequented by folk music fans, such as the Golden Vanity, the Ballad Room, and the Club 47, where she performed regularly twice a week for about two years. Her pure soprano voice and her simplicity of style brought her a large following among Harvard students and hangers-on. Her fame soon spread beyond Harvard Square, and she was praised by such noted folk artists as Theodore Bikel and Harry Belafonte, who offered her a spot with his professional singing group.

While on a visit to Chicago, Miss Baez appeared briefly at the Gate of Horn, a night club specializing in folk entertainment. Folk singer Bob Gibson, who heard her there, extended her an informal invitation to the Newport (Rhode Island) Folk Festival, which was held in the summer of 1959. She arrived in Newport in a Cadillac hearse with her name painted on the side (her first and only theatrical stunt). Singing as an unlisted entertainer, she made a great impact upon the 13,000 people who attended the festival. Her appearance led to friendships with folk singer Odetta, with the Weavers, and with members of the Seeger family. Although she received a number of offers to make recordings and to go on concert tours, she turned them down and returned to Boston to resume her coffee-shop appearances.

After appearing again in Newport in the 1960 folk festival Miss Baez made her first album for Vanguard Records, to the guitar accompaniment of Fred Hellerman of the Weavers. The album, simply labeled *Joan Baez* (she does not care for elaborate titles on record albums), scored an immediate success. A spokesman for Vanguard has called it "the highest selling individual female folk album in the history of long-playing records." Her other albums, released by Vanguard, are *Joan Baez, Volume 2, Joan Baez at Newport,* and *Joan Baez in Concert.*

(Continued next page)

William Claxton

JOAN BAEZ

In early 1961 Miss Baez left the Boston area to go on an extended tour, singing to capacity crowds on college campuses and in concert halls throughout the United States. Wherever she sang, reviewers acclaimed her performances. Folk music critic Robert Shelton, reviewing a concert that she gave in New York's Town Hall, wrote in the New York *Times* (November 13, 1961): "Miss Baez did not disappoint the 1,700 who heard her. That superb soprano voice, as lustrous and rich as old gold, flowed purely . . . with a wondrous ease. Her singing, unwinding like a spool of satin, had an understated passion that resorted to no theatrical tricks or extremes of dynamics to stir her listeners."

Miss Baez makes few concessions to public opinion or to "show business." Within a single year she turned down offers for concert engagements that would have netted her some $100,000. At present she limits herself to performing two months out of the year on concert tours and to recording one album a year for Vanguard. Since her appearance at the Gate of Horn in Chicago she has refused night club engagements. She has rejected offers from Hollywood and an offer for a starring role in a Broadway musical. Although she has sung on television, she will appear on television only on her own terms. "The minute you start thinking about making money, you lose the spirit," she told an interviewer for *Newsweek* (November 27, 1961). "I know I'm getting paid a hell of a lot. But really, I don't care about the money."

Although Miss Baez has acquired a command of her guitar by means of practice, she has made no effort to enhance her natural voice through formal training. Her voice ranges over three octaves, and while she usually sings soprano, she sometimes gives renditions (notably of Spanish songs) in an alto voice. In an article in the *Reporter* (January 4, 1962) Nat Hentoff observed: "Her tone is full and firm, and by the supple use

of a strong but disciplined vibrato, she makes vivid all the multi-colored strands of joy, loss, and tenderness in her material." A writer for *Time* (November 23, 1962) noted that "there is little sex in that clear flow of sound. It is haunted and plaintive, a mother's voice, and it has in it distant reminders of black women wailing in the night, of detached madrigal singers performing calmly at court, and of saddened gypsies trying to charm death into leaving their Spanish caves."

Describing her early coffeehouse appearances, Simon Lazarus 3d wrote of Miss Baez: "A mixture of timidity and arrogance, she stands, rather blankly, waiting for requests. The effect of this mien on the audience, combined with her manner of singing, is to make Joan seem at once innocent yet startlingly sophisticated, somewhat shy yet ready to do just what she damn pleases. To many of her following, all this constitutes a mystery, which they denote as a principal source of her fascination" (*Cambridge 38*, April 1961). A year later, Robert Shelton, reviewing a concert that she gave at Carnegie Hall for the New York *Times* (May 19, 1962), measured her development as a performer. "She is . . . emerging from her youthful shyness and beginning to look at members of her audience, not singing in a detached semi-trance, as she had in the past," he reported.

Miss Baez has sometimes been criticized for her failure to undertake original research on folklore and folk music, and for her reliance on others for material. In her defense, she points out that she is more interested in the quality and spirit of her songs than in their origins. Although in the past she has concentrated on tragic ballads, she now makes room for lighter material in her repertoire, especially the "blue grass" type of Southern country music.

A social conscience, Miss Baez feels, is an essential component in the makeup of a folk artist. "I've never met a reactionary folk singer," she once said. "What could he sing?" Although she sometimes includes topical songs on such issues as human brotherhood and disarmament in her concerts, she does not preach but prefers to let her songs speak for themselves. Her hero and inspiration has been Pete Seeger, and she often pays tribute to him during her concerts. When in the spring of 1963 Seeger was banned from the new weekly ABC-TV folk music show *Hootenanny* because of his controversial political background, Joan Baez, along with several other singers, refused to appear on the program.

Since 1961 Joan Baez has made her home in California. At first she lived in a rustic cabin in the rugged Big Sur area, with cats and dogs as her companions; later she moved to more comfortable quarters in Carmel. Miss Baez is slender, with dark eyes, long black hair flowing down her back, and an oval face that a writer for *Show Business Illustrated* (January 23, 1962) has described as "compelling rather than pretty." She uses little makeup or jewelry, and she has been known to take off her shoes during her concerts. Her wardrobe consists of simple blouses and skirts and burlap dresses. Her only extravagances are her Jaguar sports car and the psychoanalytic sessions that she attends regularly. She is fond of sketching but does little reading.

Although Miss Baez has the reputation of being withdrawn and unsociable (her manager, Manuel A. Greenhill, has called her "one big question-mark"), her friends consider her sincere, honest, sensitive, and kind-hearted. Reviewing one of her concerts for the *Christian Science Monitor* (November 6, 1961), Robert Gustafson described her as "gracious, warm, and witty." From time to time she has volunteered her services to institutions for the blind, Negro schools, and such organizations as UNESCO and the Congress on Racial Equality. She does not share her parents' Quaker faith, but regards "living" as her religion.

References

Newsweek 58:84+ N 27 '61 por
Reporter 26:39+ Ja 4 '62
Show Bsns Illus 2:75 Ja 23 '62 por
Time 79:39+ Je 1 '62 por; 80:54+ N 23 '62 por

Wide World

DR. HASTINGS BANDA

BANDA, HASTINGS (KAMUZU) 1906(?)-
Prime Minister of Nyasaland; physician
Address: Office of the Prime Minister, Zomba, Nyasaland

Regarded as a messiah among his own people, Dr. Hastings Banda is the undisputed spokesman for the 2,890,000 African natives of Nyasaland in their quest for independence from federation with Northern and Southern Rhodesia. Since returning to his native country in July 1958 after an absence of over forty years, the American-educated physician has led his people a long way on the road toward self-government. The first step was taken on February 1, 1963 when Nyasaland became internally self-governing and Dr. Banda became its first Prime Minister. The next steps, yet to be achieved, are full independence and separation from the federation. Although Banda, who has called himself the "extremist of extremists," has spent more than a year in prison for his leadership of the native resistance movement against the federation, he is basically conservative and pro-Western in his outlook. He is head of the Malawi Congress party and has served as Nyasaland's minister of natural resources and local government.

The Federation of Rhodesia and Nyasaland in Central Africa, established in March 1953, joins the British protectorates of Northern Rhodesia and Nyasaland with self-governing Southern Rhodesia. Nyasaland is the smallest and poorest of the three territories. Although in the past it had been almost completely dominated by its white minority of some 8,600, new constitutional provisions, adopted in August 1960 largely as a result of Banda's efforts, gave the native population an elected majority in the legislature and strong representation on the executive council.

A native of the Kasungu district of Nyasaland, Hastings Kamuzu Banda was born about 1906 (some sources give 1902) to a poor peasant family of the Chewa tribe. His pagan parents gave him the name Kamuzu (the little root),

because root herbs, prescribed by a medicine man, were believed to have cured his mother's barrenness. He later adopted as his first name the surname of a missionary friend, John Hastings. Banda received his early education at the Livingstonia mission of the Church of Scotland, where he became proficient in English.

Having exhausted all available educational opportunities in Nyasaland, Banda decided, at the age of twelve or thirteen, to leave home, and he set out on foot for the Union of South Africa, without money, spare clothes, or identification papers. Along the way he stopped at a native African hospital in Southern Rhodesia, where he worked as an orderly. The appalling conditions that he saw there helped form his later ambition to become a doctor.

Aided by an uncle, Banda continued his journey. By the time he reached Johannesburg, his destination, he had been traveling for nearly a year and had walked almost 1,000 miles. At Johannesburg he obtained employment as a clerk and interpreter in the Rand gold fields. He remained there for eight years, while continuing his education at night school. After hearing a lecture by the noted Negro political leader and educator, Dr. J. E. Kwegyir Aggrey of Accra, Banda decided in 1923 to go to the United States with the financial aid of an American Methodist bishop.

In the United States Banda obtained a scholarship to attend the Wilberforce Institute, a Negro secondary school near Xenia, Ohio. He supplemented his income with earnings from odd jobs and teaching Sunday school. After graduating from the institute in 1928 Banda entered Indiana University and majored in history and political science. He subsequently transferred to the University of Chicago, where he w the only Negro student at the time, and received his Ph.B. degree there in 1931. H ing decided on a medical career, he then ent

BANDA, HASTINGS—*Continued*

Meharry Medical College in Nashville, Tennessee and qualified for his M.D. degree in 1937.

In 1938 Banda decided to undertake additional medical training in Scotland before returning to Africa. He studied at the universities of Glasgow and Edinburgh and became an elder of the Church of Scotland. He qualified as a licentiate of the Royal College of Surgeons in Edinburgh in 1941 and later studied tropical medicine in Liverpool. (Banda also holds the degrees of Bachelor of Science, Bachelor of Medicine, and Bachelor of Surgery.) Unable to return to Africa because of the war and because of lack of funds, Banda practised medicine in Liverpool and North Shields through the National Health Service during the early years of World War II. In 1944 he worked at a mission for colored seamen at Tyneside, and from 1945 until 1953 he practised in the Kilburn district of London, serving some 4,000 patients, most of them white.

During his stay in England Banda took a lively interest in African affairs. His home in Kilburn became a meeting place for African intellectuals and African nationalist leaders like Kwame Nkrumah of the Gold Coast and Jomo Kenyatta of Kenya. Banda conducted a voluminous correspondence with native leaders in Nyasaland and wrote handbills and pamphlets for the nationalist movement. His efforts resulted in the establishment, in 1950, of the Nyasaland African Congress, which aimed at carrying on the nationalist struggle by means of passive resistance, and he was generally accepted as its leader.

When in 1949 the white settlers of Central Africa drew up plans for a federation of Rhodesia and Nyasaland, based on white supremacy, Banda led the opposition to these plans from England. After the establishment of the federation in 1953, Banda charged the British government with the betrayal of the people of Nyasaland. Returning to Africa in 1953, he lived first in the Gold Coast (which became the independent nation of Ghana in 1957), and practised medicine among the poverty-stricken Zongo people in Kumasi, as well as among the more prosperous Ashanti cocoa farmers. Although he did not participate in Ghanaian politics, he continued to correspond with nationalist leaders in Nyasaland.

Because of widespread unrest among the Nyasaland natives Banda was invited in 1958 to return to his native country and take over direct leadership of the Nyasaland African Congress. Arriving at Blantyre, Nyasaland on July 5, 1958, Banda was greeted by some 4,000 natives who hailed him as a liberator and messiah. As he stood on his native soil for the first time in more than forty years, he called for friendly negotiations between Africans and Europeans, while insisting on government by elected representatives and ultimate freedom from the federation. Having practically forgotten his native Chinyanja tongue, he addressed his countrymen in English.

The Nyasaland African Congress elected Banda president-general at its annual meeting on August 1, 1958. Subsequently, as a means of consolidating his position, he purged the leadership of the congress of all but his most loyal supporters. He denied that he was anti-British and expressed the desire to keep Nyasaland in the British Commonwealth of Nations, believing that the country would fare better in association with Great Britain than under the domination of the white settlers of Rhodesia.

In December 1958 Banda attended the All-Africa People's Conference at Accra, Ghana. In a press conference at Salisbury, Southern Rhodesia, following the conference, he admitted that he was an extremist in the same sense that Cromwell and Churchill had been extremists. On March 3, 1959 Nyasaland's governor, Sir Robert Armitage, declared a state of emergency. The Nyasaland African Congress was outlawed, and Banda was placed under arrest, without any specific charges against him. Later in the month, he and other congress leaders were charged with implication in a plot on the part of the Nyasaland natives for a massacre of the white population and widespread sabotage.

As disorder and violence increased in Nyasaland, the British Conservative government was forced to defend its African policy against Labour and Liberal opposition in the House of Commons. Banda, who had been given a white man's cell at Gwelo prison in Southern Rhodesia, devoted much of his time to working on his memoirs and reading political, economic, and historical works. Although the authorities made every effort to erase Banda's influence over the people, there were indications that he kept in touch with members of the Nyasaland African Congress and that he was largely responsible for the relative calm that had come to prevail among his countrymen.

On September 30, 1959 followers of Banda, under the leadership of Orton Chirwa, formed the Malawi Congress party (Malawi is the proposed name for a future self-governing Nyasaland) with a program dedicated to democracy, Socialism, nationalism, and pan-Africanism. Meanwhile, the clamor for the release of Banda was rising in Africa and England and was supported in Labour and Liberal circles. On the other hand, federal Prime Minister Sir Roy Welensky and other federation officials strongly opposed Banda's release, maintaining that it might bring with it renewed unrest and violence.

On April 1, 1960 Banda was unconditionally released from imprisonment upon orders of the new Colonial Secretary Iain Macleod. The jubilant crowds that welcomed him remained peaceful as a result of instructions by the Malawi Congress party. Before embarking for London to attend a conference on the future of Nyasaland Banda told his countrymen: "Do not spoil my work. If you listen to me, you will have your own government. I want everybody to keep quiet while I go to London." In June 1960 the state of emergency in Nyasaland was lifted.

The several conferences that Banda attended in London during 1960 failed to win him his demand for immediate secession of Nyasaland from the federation. In August, however, Nyasaland did gain a constitution that gave the vote to some 100,000 Africans who met certain income, property, and literacy qualifications and that guaranteed Africans a solid majority on the Nyasaland legislative council. Banda embarked on a tour of Nyasaland in June 1961, marking the beginning of the campaign for the first elections under the new constitutional provisions. Although federation Prime Minister Sir Roy Welensky demanded a postponement, charging that voters were being intimidated by the Malawi Congress party, the elections took place as scheduled, on August 15, 1961. Banda looked upon the elections as a personal contest between himself and Welensky and as a referendum on whether Nyasaland should remain in the federation.

In the elections, in which some 80,000 of Nyasaland's 2,890,000 Africans participated, the Malawi Congress party took all twenty of the legislative seats on the lower roll with 99 percent of the vote, as well as three of the eight seats on the upper roll. (The remaining five upper roll seats went to Welensky's United Federal party.) The Malawi Congress party received considerable support from Nyasaland's Asian minority in the elections. Following the victory Banda told newsmen that he would continue to insist on secession from the federation and that Nyasaland's minority of Europeans would be welcome to remain in the country following independence, provided they were willing to accept the rule of the African majority.

Shortly after the elections Banda was appointed minister of natural resources and local government. Four of his supporters were also given posts in Nyasaland's ten-member executive council. In February 1962 two additional African ministers were appointed by the new governor, Sir Glyn Jones, upon Banda's recommendation, thus giving the Malawi Congress party control of the executive council as well as of the legislature. In July 1962 Banda announced a three-year development program aimed at modernizing agriculture, improving communications, and building up educational facilities.

Banda has negotiated with Great Britain, the United States, and West Germany for financial assistance. On the other hand, he has rejected the plan of federal Prime Minister Welensky for a hydroelectric project because its acceptance would mean continued dependence on the federation. Although Banda is committed to aid Africans in Portuguese colonies in their struggle for independence, he has been compelled to negotiate with Portuguese authorities because landlocked Nyasaland depends on Mozambique ports for its shipping. Once independence is achieved, Banda hopes to solve his country's economic problems through an East African federation with Tanganyika and other countries. On February 1, 1963 he became the Prime Minister of Nyasaland.

Described as a slight, gnome-like man with lively eyes and thinning hair that is beginning to turn grey, Dr. Hastings Banda has a gift for oratory, a good sense of political organization, and a sharp sense of humor that is marked by occasional cynicism. Although he appears mild and soft-spoken, he has an explosive temperament and occasionally displays outbursts of anger. Banda, who neither drinks nor smokes, dresses like a British gentleman and wears Homburg hats. He drives a Mercedes and

lives in a $28,000 home that had been given to him by the Malawi Congress party. Recently he has added the title Ngwazi (the vindicator or redeemer) to his name.

References

> Christian Sci Mon p7 S 12 '62 por
> N Y Herald Tribune p12 Ag 23 '62 por
> N Y Times p6 F 28 '59 por
> Time 73:21 Mr 30 '59 por
> International Who's Who, 1962-63
> Italiaander, Rolf. The New Leaders of Africa (1961)
> Melady, Thomas Patrick. Profiles of African Leaders (1961)
> Segal, Ronald. Political Africa (1961)

BARBER, MARY I(SABEL) 1887(?)-Mar. 10, 1963 Dietitian; head of home economics department of the Kellogg Company of Battle Creek, Michigan (1923-48); food consultant to Secretary of War (1941-45). See *Current Biography* (July) 1941.

Obituary

> Washington (D.C.) Post B p5 Mr 12 '63

BARBER, SAMUEL Mar. 9, 1910- Composer
Address: b. c/o G. Schirmer, Inc., 609 5th Ave., New York 17; h. "Capricorn," Mt. Kisco, N.Y.

> NOTE: This biography supersedes the article that appeared in *Current Biography* in 1944.

For music in a contemporary and original idiom that nevertheless holds to traditional tonality and lyricism, Samuel Barber has twice received the Pulitzer Prize for music. In 1959 he was honored for his opera *Vanessa* and in 1963, for his First Piano Concerto. Some of his admirers, like Nathan Broder, object to oversimplifying Barber's work with the term "neo-Romanticism," and Louis Biancolli of the New York *World-Telegram and Sun,* who unstintingly hails Barber as a stimulating, independent, and versatile composer, asserts that "the only school he belongs to is music."

The appealing melodies and carefully crafted thematic development of Barber's music have long attracted world-renowned conductors, singers, and instrumentalists. He made an early entrance upon the international musical scene, and in 1937 his First Symphony made him the first American composer to be represented at the Salzburg Festival. Barber's work is published exclusively by G. Schirmer, Inc., and is generously represented in the *Schwann Long-Playing Record Catalog.*

Samuel Barber was born in West Chester, Pennsylvania on March 9, 1910 to Dr. Samuel LeRoy Barber, a physician, and Marguerite McLeod (Beatty) Barber. The nephew of the well-known Metropolitan contralto, Louise Homer, his mother's sister, he grew up in a family atmosphere that encouraged his early signs of musical talent, but by no means excluded other of his boyhood interests. At the age of six he began

Wallowitch

SAMUEL BARBER

piano lessons, and he wrote his first composition when he was seven, "Sadness," consisting of twenty-three bars in the key of C minor. His mother scored this and other of his juvenile compositions, including an attempt at an opera, "The Rose Tree," which he wrote at ten to a libretto by the family's Irish cook. "I wrote the heroine's part for my younger sister [Sara], who can still sing every note of it," he told John Ardoin (Musical America, March 1960). "The hero's part was for me. I was a contralto then! We even got a gypsy chorus into it."

For a short time during his early teens Barber was organist at the Westminster Presbyterian Church in West Chester. Although he had been advised to leave school and spend all his time in the study of music, he continued at the West Chester high school until he graduated in 1926. A few years earlier, at fourteen, he had been accepted as a charter student of the newly established Curtis Institute of Music in Philadelphia, where he majored in three subjects: composition with Rosario Scalero, singing with Emilio de Gogorza, and piano with Isabelle Vengerova. He also studied conducting with Fritz Reiner. At Curtis, Barber composed Serenade for String Quartet (1929); "Dover Beach" (1931), for baritone voice and string quartet; and Sonata for Violoncello and Piano (1932). The composer himself was the soloist in a 1936 RCA Victor recording of "Dover Beach," which has become a collector's item. He left Curtis in 1933 and was awarded the Bachelor of Music degree in 1934.

One of his other compositions written at Curtis, a violin sonata, won him in 1928 the $1,200 Bearns Prize of Columbia University, the first of several awards that enabled him to travel and study in Europe. He won his second Bearns Prize for his Overture to The School for Scandal, first performed in August 1933 by the Philadelphia Orchestra under the baton of Alexander Smallens. His overture was described in Musical

America in 1935 as "an appealing work" in which he invested "a broad melody with shimmering color and tender mood." He also won the Pulitzer Traveling Scholarship—in 1935, and again in 1936.

While studying in Rome as the recipient of the Prix de Rome of the American Academy in 1935, Barber wrote his First Symphony (in one movement) which was given its première by the Augusteo Orchestra in Rome in December 1936. Arthur Rodzinski directed its first American performance, by the Cleveland Symphony Orchestra, in early 1937 and later conducted the symphony at the Salzburg Festival. He also introduced Barber's music in England.

Arturo Toscanini further enhanced Barber's reputation at home and abroad. The maestro not only conducted the NBC Symphony Orchestra in Adagio for Strings (1936) and First Essay for Orchestra (1937) at their première in November 1938 but also included the adagio as the only American work in the repertoire of his South American tour. Some critics questioned Toscanini's choice on the ground that Barber's romanticism and preference for strings over brass were not representative of contemporary American music.

During World War II Barber's work underwent a wider development. After teaching orchestration at the Curtis Institute from 1939 to 1942, Barber was inducted into the United States Army in April 1943 and was transferred to the Army Air Forces soon afterward. While stationed at the Fort Worth Army Airfield in Texas, he began a symphony commissioned by the Air Forces. His Second Symphony, Symphony Dedicated to the Army Air Forces, was first performed by the Boston Symphony Orchestra, under Serge Koussevitsky's direction, in early March 1944.

When Koussevitsky presented the symphony in New York City a week later, local critics found it somewhat closer to the modern idiom—less introverted and romantic (though not necessarily of greater musical merit)—than his previous work. The day before, New York audiences had heard Bruno Walter conduct the Philharmonic Symphony in Barber's revised version of his First Symphony. Virgil Thomson described the revised work in the New York Herald Tribune as "a Hamlet-like meditation about Mr. Barber's private problems, the chief of which seems to be laying the ghost of romanticism without resorting to violence."

Another of Barber's wartime compositions, "Commando March," was first played by the Army Air Forces Band in 1943. During the war, also, seventeen of his songs—nonmilitary—were included in the program of the American Music Festival in Washington, D.C. in the spring of 1944, and Jennie Tourel sang a number of them during her concert tour of Brazil the following summer. His music gained a wider audience, too, in England and the USSR.

At the end of World War II, Barber returned to Europe with a 1945 Guggenheim Fellowship, and in 1948 he became a consultant at the American Academy of Rome. Since the war Barber has written most of his music at "Capricorn," a house near Mt. Kisco, New York, which he had bought in 1943 with Gian-Carlo Menotti, a classmate at the Curtis Institute who became his lifelong friend. Here he composed his Concerto for Violoncello and Orchestra, which Raya Garbousova played at its first performance, with the Boston Symphony Orchestra, in April 1946. The concerto won the New York Music Critics Circle Award in 1947.

Among Barber's other major postwar compositions was the ballet *Medea,* commissioned by the Ditson Fund for Martha Graham, who first presented it in 1946 in New York and later in other parts of the United States and in Europe and the Near East. Another Barber ballet, *Souvenirs,* was performed for the first time in November 1955 by the New York City Center Ballet Company to Todd Bolender's choreography. It is now in the City Center's repertory.

James Agee's long prose poem provided the text for Barber's "Knoxville: Summer of 1915," commissioned by Eleanor Steber, who sang it with the Boston Symphony Orchestra in April 1948. The Koussevitsky Music Foundation commissioned his choral piece "Prayers of Kierkegaard," which also had its première with the Boston orchestra, when Leontyne Price sang the soprano solo part in December 1954. Miss Price had earlier, in 1952, introduced Barber's "Hermit Songs," with the composer himself at the piano.

Off and on for some years Barber had been working on an opera that had been commissioned by the Koussevitsky Music Foundation in 1942, but military service and difficulty in finding the right libretto prolonged his labors. In 1957 he completed his four-act opera *Vanessa,* for which Menotti wrote the text. Its premières, in New York in January 1958 at the Metropolitan Opera, with Eleanor Steber singing the title role, and in Europe at the Salzburg Festival later in 1958, were well received, and *Vanessa* earned Barber the Pulitzer Prize for music in 1959. When it was given its second production at the Metropolitan Opera, in 1959, Howard Taubman praised it with some reservations in the New York *Times* (January 8, 1959): "The composer takes some time to arrive at an individual stylistic fusion. There are reminiscences of this composer and that, and in the orchestra at least they form a theatrical current. But good things begin to appear after the opening act. There are places where the music builds a nostalgic atmosphere with grace and color, and some of the climactic passages have eloquence." Again to Menotti's text, Barber wrote the shorter stage work, "A Hand of Bridge," which was premièred at the Festival of Two Worlds in Spoleto, Italy in June 1959.

In 1963 Barber was awarded his second Pulitzer Prize for music for his First Piano Concerto, which he had been commissioned to write by G. Schirmer, Inc., on the occasion of its centennial in 1961. When it was performed on September 24, 1962 at Lincoln Center's Philharmonic Hall in New York, Paul Henry Lang observed in the New York *Herald Tribune*: "Samuel Barber's new piano concerto displays beneath the elegance of its technique a warm sincerity and exquisite command of form. Everywhere one feels sensibility to the higher forms of esthetic experience.

The concerto is bright, virtuoso in the best sense of the word." In another Philharmonic Hall première, in April 1963, Barber's piece for solo soprano and orchestra, "Andromache's Farewell," from Euripides' *The Trojan Women,* also roused the audience to an ovation.

For theme and mood Barber has drawn upon both classical and contemporary writers and poets like Shelley, Matthew Arnold, A. E. Housman, and the medieval Irish bards. He once said in an interview for *Theatre Arts* (January 1958), "I am one of the few composers—if not the only one—who wrote music for *Finnegans Wake.*" Among his favorite authors are Stendhal, Dante, Goethe, Proust, and Melville.

In discussing the development of Barber's style, Nathan Broder has pointed out that much of his more recent work represents a fusion of his early lyricism with elements of his "transitional" period, such as the irregular rhythms and dissonances of his Second Symphony. In the "Prayers of Kierkegaard," the Piano Sonata, and parts of *Vanessa,* for example, Broder sees that "Barber has employed his new technical gains in an attempt to fuse an essentially lyric spirit with an awakened awareness of the restlessness and discordance of our times" (David Ewen, editor, *The New Book of Modern Composers,* Knopf, 1961).

For several years beginning in 1951 Barber served as vice-president of the International Music Council of UNESCO. He is a member of the American Society of Composers, Authors and Publishers and of the National Academy of Arts and Letters. In 1959 Harvard University awarded him an honorary doctorate in music.

The house that Barber shares with Menotti near Mt. Kisco is Scandinavian in style and has two wings at opposite ends so that each musician can work in his own studio without being heard by the other. Barber, who has brown eyes and brown hair, is a handsome man of medium stature. He has never been a publicity seeker, and Broder describes him as "withdrawn and rather cold, though urbane, when with people he does not know well, but a spring of humor occasionally bubbles to the surface." Walking in the country has been one of his favorite forms of relaxation since boyhood. Barber is facile in German, French, and Italian and wrote the German text for *Vanessa.* He does his own orchestration: "It is a great joy for the composer himself," he said in the *Theatre Arts* interview, "to decide which of the ten thousand possibilities he might choose for the color of one chord."

References

Mus Am p4 Mr 60 por
Theatre Arts 42:68+ Ja '58 por

Broder, Nathan. Samuel Barber (1954)
Ewen, David, ed. American Composers Today (1949); The New Book of Modern Composers (1961)
International Celebrity Register (1959)
International Who's Who, 1962-63
Slonimsky, Nicolas. Baker's Biographical Dictionary of Musicians (1958)
Who's Who in America, 1962-63

BEATTY, JIM (bā'dē) Oct. 28, 1934- Middle-distance runner
Address: b. 600 Sierra Madre Villa, Pasadena, Calif.; h. 4040 Nicolet Ave., Los Angeles 8, Calif.

For about the last decade the United States has lagged far behind England, Australia, Ireland, and New Zealand in producing distance runners of international importance. It was Roger Bannister, an Englishman, for example, who in 1954 established a record in the four-minute outdoor mile. One of the athletes who have helped to restore the prestige of the United States in track competition is Jim Beatty, a native of North Carolina, who runs for the Los Angeles Track Club. In August 1962 Beatty set an American record by running an outdoor mile in 3 minutes 56.3 seconds, only 1.9 seconds more than the world mark held by Peter Snell of New Zealand.

Although Beatty draws the most attention for his accomplishments in the mile (track's "glamour race"), he is a runner of many talents, whose legs and constitution are adapted to various distances. In addition to the mile record he holds the American records for the 1,500-meter, the 3,000-meter, and the 5,000-meter runs and the world records for the indoor and outdoor two-mile and indoor mile distances. He was the first to break the four-minute mark for the indoor mile.

James Tully Beatty was born on October 28, 1934 in New York City, the youngest child of Henry Elder Beatty and Mary Elizabeth (Guccione) Beatty. He has a married brother, Henry F., and a married sister, Mrs Mary E. Booker. Jim Beatty lived in New York City until he was four-and-a-half years old, then moved with his family to Charlotte, North Carolina. "My father was a native North Carolinian," he has explained. "My mother was the New Yorker. But my father was always itching to get back to the South."

Wide World

JIM BEATTY

Beatty began his athletic career as a boxer at Central High School in Charlotte. He also played basketball, baseball, and football, but he did not take up track until his junior year. That year he worked as a newsboy and every morning ran the mile from his house to the point where he picked up his papers to begin his route. "I found that because of my boxing I was in good condition," he recalls, "and actually enjoyed the run. Since the distance was one mile, I figured I was a miler." He persuaded his coach to let him run a mile race. He not only won his first mile but set a track record of 4 minutes 54 seconds. Two weeks later he won the state high school championship mile in 4 minutes and 40 seconds, and the following year he again was state champion with a time of 4 minutes 31 seconds. Beatty became captain of the track team at Central High. He was also vice-president of the junior class and a member of the Key Club and the Hi-Y Club.

After graduating from high school in 1953 Beatty entered the University of North Carolina at Chapel Hill, where he was a competent but comparatively obscure distance runner. He became president of the Carolina Athletic Association and a captain of the track and cross-country teams. He won the Atlantic Coast Conference mile and two-mile indoor titles for three consecutive years, won the outdoor mile twice, and won the two-mile run at the Penn Relays twice. In 1955 he placed second in the National Collegiate Athletic Association (NCAA) two-mile championship, and in 1956 he finished second in the NCAA 5,000-meter run. He qualified for the 1956 American Olympic trials in the 5,000-meter event, but failed to make the Olympic team. In addition to participating in athletics, Beatty was president of the junior class, a member of the student legislature, and a member of the Order of the Old Well and of the Order of the Golden Fleece. He graduated from the university with a B.A. degree in English in June 1957.

Beatty did not set foot on a track again until the fall of 1959. From September 1957 to September 1958 he served in the Army National Guard of the United States, rising from the rank of private E-1 to that of private E-2, and then found a job. In July 1959 he watched the meet between the United States and the Soviet Union in Philadelphia. After watching the 1,500-meter event, a friend of Beatty's said, "You could have won that race." Beatty recalls, "I agreed with him and that gave me the incentive to return to racing." He was also influenced by the fact that 1960 was an Olympic year.

Deciding to race again, Beatty quit his job and moved to California so that he could train under the track coach Mihaly Igloi, a Hungarian who had fled his Communist-dominated land in 1956. Beatty had first met Igloi at the University of North Carolina when the Hungarian coach spent four months at Chapel Hill in late 1956. Beatty has said of his tutor: "Europe has produced three great distance coaches in this generation and Igloi is one of them. I had been in retirement thirty months after graduating from North Carolina University and if I was going to return it was under Igloi's supervision or nothing doing."

Beatty took a job as statistical clerk with the Lockheed Aircraft Corporation's missile and space division in Sunnyvale, California. He trained with Igloi at the Santa Clara Valley Youth Village and re-entered competition during the 1960 indoor season. In a two-mile run at Los Angeles he beat Max Truex in the time of 8 minutes 57 seconds. A few weeks later he achieved the upset of that season by beating the favorite, Dyrol Burleson, in the Baxter Mile at the New York Athletic Club meet at Madison Square Garden with a winning time of 4 minutes 5.4 seconds.

Competing outdoors in May 1960 at the California Relays at Modesto, California, Beatty ran the mile in 3 minutes 58 seconds, a record for American citizens. Showing his versatility, a few days later he set a new American mark for 5,000 meters, 13 minutes 51.7 seconds, and he was also clocked in at the three-mile mark with an American record time of 13 minutes 28 seconds. On the basis of his performance in the 5,000-meter race he appeared to be a good prospect to run that distance in the 1960 Olympics in Rome, but he failed to make the finals after suffering a foot injury.

In 1961 the Los Angeles Track Club was established with the purpose of raising the standards of distance running in the United States, and Igloi was hired as its coach. One of the runners who have brought Igloi and the club into the limelight, Beatty had a successful indoor season in 1961 and an even better one outdoors. He was captain of the United States men's track and field team that toured Europe in the summer of 1961. In London, in July, he ran the mile in 3 minutes 59.7 seconds, and at Warsaw he clicked off the 1,500 meters in 3 minutes 40.9 seconds. He lowered this mark in Oslo in August when he ran the 1,500-meter distance in 3 minutes 40.2 seconds. The A.A.U. named Beatty as the All-America miler of the 1961 season.

In January 1962 Beatty was named the outstanding athlete of an indoor invitational meet held in Los Angeles after he beat the Frenchman Michel Jazy by inches with a mile time of 4 minutes 4.8 seconds. On February 10, 1962 he became the world's first sub-four-minute-miler indoors when he ran the distance in 3 minutes 58.9 seconds at Los Angeles. On February 16 at Madison Square Garden Beatty made his twelfth straight indoor triumph by winning the Baxter Mile in a time of 4 minutes .9 seconds. Early in March at the Chicago Daily News Relays he won the mile again, in the time of 3 minutes 59.7 seconds. In 1962 he won the Charles J. Dieges Award for being the outstanding performer of the national indoor A.A.U. championships, and in the same year he also received the Jesse P. Mortensen Award for his contributions to track and field athletics.

Toward the end of March Beatty sustained some leg injuries. ("I'm always getting hurt," he has said. "I've never been able to stay on schedule for twelve months in a row.") Returning to action early in June at Los Angeles,

Beatty set a world outdoor mark of 8 minutes 29.8 seconds for the two-mile run. About two weeks later he ran a mile in 3 minutes 57.9 seconds at the national A.A.U. meet in Walnut, California, and in July at Palo Alto he set an American record for the 1,500-meter run by breasting the tape in a time of 3 minutes 39.9 seconds.

In August 1962 Beatty stirred the track world with a streak of astonishing performances. While in Europe as captain of the United States men's track and field team, he set four American records in sixteen days. Running in Oslo on August 9, he set a new standard for the 1,500-meter run of 3 minutes 39.4 seconds, and at Avranches, France on August 15 he ran 3,000 meters in 7 minutes 54.2 seconds. On August 21, in Helsinki, Finland, he reeled off the mile in 3 minutes 56.3 seconds, a time just 1.9 seconds below the world mark held by Peter Snell of New Zealand. (He ran this record-breaking mile just three days after he clocked 3 minutes 56.5 seconds for a mile on the White City Stadium track in London.) On August 24, also in Finland, he sped through a 5,000-meter run at 13 minutes 45 seconds.

Returning to the United States from his triumphant European tour, Beatty declared: "We're tired of hearing foreigners call Americans soft. We want to show the world that we can excel in distance races as well as in sprints. As the first step I intend to keep trying to break Peter Snell's [mile] record until I do it. But our ultimate goal is winning the distance events in the 1964 Olympics. As of now I think we're already the equal of the rest of the world in distance events. But we've got to be the best." Another record that Beatty has added to his list is the indoor two-mile, which he ran in 8 minutes 30.7 seconds in March 1963.

Beatty trains about four hours a day and runs about 100 miles a week. When running a race he relies absolutely on his coach's instructions. Barrel-chested, short, and light (five feet six inches tall, 128 pounds), he has a powerful kick that gives him extra speed when he needs it in the last few yards of a race. Beatty has black hair and hazel eyes. He is a Democrat and a Roman Catholic. In January 1963 the A.A.U. gave him the 1962 Sullivan Award, the highest amateur sports award in the United States.

On February 20, 1960 Jim Beatty married Barbara Ann Harmon, a secretary and native of North Carolina. He is currently employed as a claims adjuster by the Allstate Insurance Company. Beatty's off-track hobbies include tennis, water skiing, swimming, and photography. "Running is my hobby and I enjoy it," Beatty explains. "But I'm not going to let it dominate my life. Outside of the training end of it, I have no special rules. I eat normally, sometimes go a little too heavy on the dessert; sleep normally and try to live like anyone else, with a lot of good times and laughs along the way."

References

N Y Journal-American p37 Ag 13 '61 por
Sports Illus 12:18+ Je 6 '60 por
Time 59:80+ F 26 '62

BEECHING, RICHARD Apr. 21, 1913- British government official; business executive; physicist

Address: b. British Railways Board, 222 Marylebone Rd., London, N.W. 1, England; h. Little Manor, Lewes Rd., East Grinstead, Sussex, England

Great Britain's railways, which have been publicly owned since soon after the end of World War II, have defied attempts by both Labour and Conservatives to make them a paying proposition. Between 1948 and 1962, they lost nearly $2.7 billion. In 1961 the present Conservative government borrowed an executive from big business, gave him the highest salary ever paid to a British civil servant, and asked him to restore the railways to economic health. He is Dr. Richard Beeching, now chairman of the British Railways Board, who in the spring of 1963 made known his recommendations for the future of the railways. The Beeching report, proposing merciless cuts in existing services, has provoked a major controversy, but it seems to go a long way toward alleviating the economic plight of the railways.

The imperturbable individual at the heart of the storm has been called "the most significant" man in Britain. Beeching began his career as a physicist and worked for some years during and after World War II in the field of armaments design. He entered the world of big business as a scientist, and it was not until his late thirties that he turned to administration. Beeching was technical director of the massive Imperial Chemical Industries when, in 1961, he took a five-year leave of absence to tackle what might be considered Britain's thorniest management problem.

Richard Beeching was born on April 21, 1913 in Sheerness, Kent, England, one of three sons of Hubert J. Beeching, a journalist, and of Annie Beeching. A quiet and studious child, Beeching attended the Maidstone Grammar School and then went on to the Imperial College of Science and Technology at the University of London. There he read physics, graduating in 1934 with the B.S. degree and first class honors. Beeching stayed on at the Imperial College for two years after graduation, earning his Ph.D. in 1936. His thesis, *Electron Diffraction*, was published on both sides of the Atlantic (Methuen; Chemical Pub. Co. of N.Y., 1936).

In 1936 Beeching worked for a short time at the Fuel Research Station in Greenwich, London, leaving in 1937 to join the Mond Nickel Company. He worked in Mond's Birmingham laboratory for five years. After the outbreak of World War II in 1939, the laboratory became involved in the British war effort, and Beeching had a hand in shaping all kinds of military projectiles. His work attracted attention, and in 1943 he joined the Ministry of Supply and was assigned to the armaments design department at Fort Halstead. After the end of the war Beeching remained with the ministry, becoming deputy chief engineer of the armaments design department in 1946.

In 1948 Beeching followed Sir Ewart Smith, his former chief at the Ministry of Supply, to the giant Imperial Chemical Industries. Smith was then technical director of ICI, and Beeching served on his staff for three years until, in 1951, he was given a place on ICI's Terylene Council. The council, concerned with the development of what is now a widely used polyester filament fiber, later became the board of ICI Fibres Ltd. Beeching's first major administrative assignment followed in 1953, when he was sent to Canada as vice-president of ICI (Canada) Ltd. to start the Terylene organization and to complete the plant at Millhaven on the shore of Lake Ontario.

Beeching succeeded so well in his Canadian assignment that in 1955 he was brought back to take up an even more important post as chairman of ICI's metals division, which at that time employed 18,000 people. Early in 1957 he joined the main board of ICI, succeeding Sir Ewart Smith as technical director and later serving for a time as development director as well. Two more company directorships followed—of British Nylon Spinners Ltd. in 1959 and of ICI (Australia and New Zealand) Ltd. in 1960.

It was not until April 1960 that Beeching had his first taste of British transportation problems from an administrative viewpoint. At that time the Minister of Transport asked him to serve on the so-called Stedeford Committee, an advisory group set up to study the operations of the British Transport Commission. The latter body was then responsible for all of the nation's publicly owned transportation facilities, which included the railways, a road haulage company, provincial and Scottish buses, London's subway and bus system, a small amount of shipping, inland waterways and docks, and several hotels.

The railways were at that time in a critical condition. Built up over a period of a century and a quarter by unco-ordinated and competing private interests, they had become increasingly inefficient and expensive. A Labour government had nationalized the railways in 1948 and the Conservatives had inherited them in 1951. Neither administration had been able to achieve either efficiency or economic viability for the railroads. In 1960 the railways were operating on a deficit of £112,000,000.

The Stedeford Committee recommended that the British Transport Commission be broken down into a number of more specialized agencies, of which the most important would be a British Railways Board. The recommendation was accepted, and in March 1961 Beeching was named chairman-designate of the proposed board. He agreed to take up the post on a five-year leave of absence from ICI only on the condition that it meant no loss of salary. It is a measure of the esteem in which Beeching was held, that the government was willing to match his ICI salary of £24,000 (about $67,000) a year. This is the highest salary ever paid to a British civil servant and is more than double that of the Prime Minister.

Although it was two years before the necessary legislative action brought the British Railways Board into formal existence, Beeching actually took charge of Britain's railways in June 1961, when he succeeded Sir Brian Robertson as chairman of the British Transport Commission. The commission ceased operations at the end of 1962 but meanwhile, in April 1962, Beeching had taken over as chairman of an interim body, the British Railways Committee, which on January 1, 1963 became the British Railways Board.

Beeching arrived at the London headquarters of the British Transport Commission in May 1961, a month before his appointment as chairman became formally effective. His assignment was to make the railways pay, and from the beginning he applied the methods of big business. Management structure was simplified, the number and membership of committees were cut, and senior executives were recruited from industry. Throughout the summer of 1961 Beeching accumulated information—from railwaymen about the existing pattern of services and from businessmen about their transportation needs.

In his first annual report, issued in June 1962, Beeching noted that local passenger transportation accounted for nearly half of the railways' total losses, while producing less than 10 percent of the revenue, and he advocated the discontinuance of these services. What the railways could profitably handle, Beeching suggested, was long-distance passenger traffic, coal traffic, mineral traffic, and commuter services around London and a few other large cities. John Cole, writing in the Manchester *Guardian* (June 22, 1962), described the report as being "patently the work of a man who indulges in no train-worship at all, and who regards the present railway network as an uneconomic product of a horse-drawn century."

In his final recommendations, published in March 1963, Beeching proposed to withdraw passenger services from 5,000 route miles out of a total of 17,800 and to close 2,363 out of a total of 4,709 passenger stations. Closing the small stations would cut out the small-scale freight traffic that passed through them, and the railways would concentrate instead on bulk consignments of heavy freight. The argument in favor of these moves was that one-third of railway route mileage in Britain carried only 0.8 percent of passenger traffic and 1.5 percent of total freight tonnage. It was this third that Beeching proposed to eliminate.

There was at first heavy public criticism from those areas that would be most affected by the proposed cuts, and the threat of strikes from railway unions, who had been told that the proposals would throw 70,000 men out of work. But the initial shock was followed by widespread recognition that Beeching's argument was economically unanswerable—that he had been told to make the railways pay and had delivered a plan that could accomplish this. Harold Wilson, the leader of the Labour party, has acknowledged the validity of the Beeching report but deplores the fact that it was not made as part of an overall study of British transportation needs. Beeching believes that his plan, if implemented, would eliminate "much, though not necessarily all," of the railways' deficit by 1970.

In February 1962 Beeching took another assignment for the government as a member of the National Economic Development Council, set

British Railways Board, London

RICHARD BEECHING

up by the Chancellor of the Exchequer "to examine the economic performance of the nation with particular concern for plans for the future." Beeching is a fellow of the Institute of Physics, a companion of the Institution of Mechanical Engineers, an associate of the Institute of Metallurgists, an associate of the Royal College of Science, and a member of the Institute of Transport. He has published a number of papers in journals of scientific and learned societies.

In 1938 Richard Beeching was married to Ella Margaret Tiley. The Beechings, who have no children, live in a large, half-timbered house in East Grinstead, Sussex, where Dr. Beeching pursues his spare-time interests in gardening and painting. The Railways Board chairman is six feet one inch tall and has been described as "bulky and bearlike of figure." He has blue eyes and thinning dark brown hair. According to a profile in the London *Observer* (February 11, 1962), Beeching possesses "a look of extreme common sense and an elusive air of distinction." He is "wholly without personal flamboyance," and he "dresses quietly and without boardroom polish." "What seems to shape Beeching's attitudes," the *Observer* article continues, "is strict loyalty to a code of scientific objectivity. . . . As one of his colleagues puts it, he is 'the sort of battle commander who can make a careful assessment of the casualties needed to win—and then go off to a peaceful lunch.'" At the same time, "he comes as close as one may hope to get in this country to the pure commercial intellectual, the business thinker, the Aristotle of the boardroom."

References

London Observer p21 F 11 '62 por
International Who's Who, 1962-63
Who's Who, 1963

BELLMON, HENRY (LOUIS) Sept. 3, 1921-
Governor of Oklahoma; farmer
Address: b. State Capitol, Oklahoma City, Okla.;
h. Executive Mansion, Oklahoma City, Okla.

For the first time since its admission to the Union in 1907 Oklahoma has a Republican Governor. He is Henry Bellmon, a farmer with little previous experience in public office, who was elected on November 6, 1962 to a four-year term. Before his election Bellmon's only public service was as a member of the Oklahoma House of Representatives from 1946 to 1948; he gained political prominence, however, as chairman of the Republican state committee from 1960 to 1962, at which time he built up a vigorous party organization throughout the state. The Oklahoma legislature is still predominantly Democratic, but the Governor expects to secure its co-operation to put through his programs. "Basically, I am a conservative," Bellmon was quoted as saying in the *Daily Oklahoman* (September 2, 1962), "but I am sure as hell not a John Bircher nor an isolationist."

The oldest of four sons of George D. Bellmon, a pioneer farmer on the Cherokee Strip, and his second wife, Edith (Caskey) Bellmon, Henry Louis Bellmon was born on September 3, 1921 in Tonkawa, Kay County, Oklahoma. (George Bellmon had nine children by his first wife, who died in 1918.) He was brought up on his father's farm near Billings, in Noble County, and attended elementary school at Glenrose, where he completed eight grades in seven years. He next studied at the Marland High School for three years, then at the Billings High School for one year. Although he played on the high school football team, he was more of a student than an athlete. In his senior year at Billings High School he took part in the program of the Future Farmers of America.

Ramon Griffin

HENRY BELLMON

After graduating from high school in 1938 Bellmon enrolled at Oklahoma A & M (now Oklahoma State University) in Stillwater to study agronomy. "I was probably the greenest freshman who ever enrolled there," he has said. He had arrived in Stillwater with only $20 in his pocket and soon found it necessary to get part-time work. At first he picked pears, washed windows, and painted; later he worked in the soils laboratory, served as a student instructor, and wrote a farm column for the *Daily O'Collegian*. An excellent student, he was on the dean's list each semester and finished college in three and a half years. He graduated in 1942 with the B.S. degree and was elected to the scholastic honoraries Phi Eta Sigma and Phi Kappa Phi and the agriculture honorary Alpha Zeta.

Soon after finishing college Bellmon joined the United States Marines for service in World War II. Enlisting as a private, he underwent officer training at Quantico, Virginia and then, as a first lieutenant, served as executive officer and platoon leader of a tank unit of the Fourth Marines in the Marshall Islands, Saipan, Tinian, and Iwo Jima. He was awarded the Legion of Merit for his service in Saipan and the Silver Star for bravery in action on Iwo Jima. Released from active duty in 1946 after forty-two months of service, Bellmon held the rank of major in the Marine Corps Reserve until 1954, when he resigned his commission.

Returning to civilian life, Bellmon acquired control of the family farm with his brother Sheldon and bought three surplus bulldozers with which to do construction and conservation work. They built dams, ponds, and terraces and also did oil trucking. When Sheldon Bellmon was called into the service during the Korean War, the construction business was abandoned and Henry Bellmon bought his brother's interest in the farm. For a semester in 1950 he took graduate work at Colorado A & M, and in 1953 he organized in Noble County a Farm Bureau chapter of which he became charter president. During the Eisenhower administration he proposed a number of changes in the farm program; he suggested, for example, that wheat allotments be based on bushels instead of acres. By 1962 Bellmon was farming 400 acres of his own and 1,000 acres on lease. He held a 505-acre wheat allotment and, in addition, grew maize and raised livestock.

Meanwhile, after his release from military service Bellmon had begun to take part in Republican party work. Although Oklahoma voted Republican in the Presidential elections of 1952, 1956, and 1960 it remains predominantly Democratic on the local levels. Registered Democrats outnumber registered Republicans by about four to one, and what Republican feeling exists can be found largely in the northern counties like Noble. In 1946 Bellmon was elected to a two-year term in the Oklahoma House of Representatives from Noble County. He lost his seat in the national Democratic tide of 1948, and, although his wife represented Noble County on the Republican state committee from 1954 to 1958, Bellmon himself did not again hold political office for ten years.

In 1958 Bellmon became chairman of the Noble County Republican committee, and over the next two years his name became well known in state politics. When in 1960 the party's state chairmanship became vacant, he was chosen to fill it, to the dismay of old-line Republicans. "Of the 300 state committee people I replaced 208 with new, younger people," Bellmon has recalled (*Time,* October 5, 1962). "Overnight, the average age of the party's top workers dropped by about 30 years. . . . Before that, I could always remember being the youngest man in any large crowd of party people. I can still see those meetings: grey-beards and guys on crutches, all saying 'That won't work because we know better.' " After successfully bringing out a large vote for Richard M. Nixon in the Presidential election of 1960 Bellmon set about preparing for the 1962 state elections. He scheduled a calendar of activities, organized "commando" groups of workers for fund raising, advertising, and house-to-house campaigning, and in general rejuvenated the Republican party organization throughout the state. His success in the gubernatorial race in 1962 can thus be attributed in large part to an organization that he himself helped to build up.

In the May 1962 primary elections Bellmon easily won the Republican nomination for the Governorship. In the Democratic primaries Raymond Gary, a former Governor, beat W. P. Bill Atkinson and several other candidates, but since he did not have the necessary majority of votes, a runoff election was held. Atkinson, a wealthy builder who had the support of Senator Robert S. Kerr, won the runoff election by a very narrow margin. The bitterness engendered by this outcome split the Democratic ranks, and in the gubernatorial campaign there were indications that Gary supporters might bolt party lines and vote for Bellmon.

In an energetic campaign Bellmon adopted a slogan of "clean up state government or cough up more taxes" in opposing Atkinson's proposal for a one-cent sales tax increase. He not only benefited from the defection of Gary Democrats, but also from general disaffection with the administration of the incumbent Democratic Governor, J. Howard Edmondson, which had frequently been at odds with the "Old Guard" legislature. "After fifty-five years of Democrats," Bellmon said, "it's up to us to head up an honest hardworking, and harmonious Governor's office."

Elected on November 6, 1962 by a margin of about 77,000 votes and inaugurated on January 14, 1963, Bellmon became Oklahoma's first Republican Governor. He called his election "not a personal victory nor a party victory, but a popular victory based upon a deep-seated feeling that Oklahoma's one-party system of government had been weighed in the balance and found wanting." Bellmon technically succeeded George Nigh, the Lieutenant Governor under J. Howard Edmondson, who took over the Governorship when Edmondson resigned about a week before his term ended so that Nigh could appoint him to the Senate vacancy left by the death of Senator Robert Kerr. Early in February 1963

Bellmon announced his plan to keep in touch with the people through a series of monthly "Main Street meetings" that would carry him to each of the state's seventy-seven counties. He also came out in support of an initiative petition calling for the submission of a "right-to-work" measure to voters at a special election.

Henry Bellmon and the former Shirley Osborn, whom he married in January 1947, have three daughters, Patricia, Ann, and Gail. Bellmon is six feet two inches tall, weighs about 230 pounds, and has an easy smile and an affable manner. He neither smokes nor drinks and has taught an adult Sunday school class at his Presbyterian church. He has also been clerk of the Billings school board and pushed through several new courses and a curb against excessive competitive sports in the lower grades. One of his favorite recreations is fishing.

References

N Y Times p50 N 18 '62 por
Oklahoma City Daily Oklahoman A p9 S 2 '62 pors
Time 80:20+ O 5 '62 por
Who's Who in United States Politics (1950)

BEN BELLA, AHMED Dec. 1919- Premier and President of the Republic of Algeria
Address: Office of the Premier, Algiers, Republic of Algeria

After the establishment of the Republic of Algeria on July 3, 1962 ended more than seven years of bloody warfare, the new nation continued to be torn by bitter political rivalries among its leaders. The man who emerged triumphantly from the power struggle as Premier and President of the new republic is Ahmed Ben Bella, who for years had been in the top ranks of the revolution against French rule. After serving with distinction in the French army during World War II Ben Bella became active in the Algerian nationalist movement and he helped to organize and direct its secret military organization. He was one of the nine "fathers of the Algerian revolution," which was launched on November 1, 1954. During his imprisonment by French authorities from October 1956 until March 1962 he was regarded as a hero and martyr by his people, and after his release he succeeded in wresting power from provisional Premier Benyoussef Ben Khedda, to be designated the first Premier of the Republic of Algeria on September 26, 1962. A year later, on September 15, he was elected President of Algeria almost unanimously, and immediately afterward he appointed himself Premier. A militant Socialist and an associate of Egyptian President Gamal Abdel Nasser, Ben Bella is faced with the arduous task of rebuilding his strife-torn homeland.

Ahmed Ben Bella (some sources refer to him as Mohammed Ben Bella) was born in December 1919 in Marnia, a small mountain town in western Algeria, in the Oranie near the Moroccan border. His father was a merchant of Moroccan origin who had small land holdings. Ben Bella received his education at a small

Wide World

AHMED BEN BELLA

French government school at Marnia. As a boy he excelled at soccer, serving as captain of the local team, and at one time he considered becoming a professional soccer player. While still in his teens he became interested in the Algerian nationalist movement.

During World War II Ben Bella served in France and Italy as a sergeant-major with the Sixth Algerian Tirailleurs of the French Army. At Monte Cassino he carried his company commander to safety under fire, and for a time he assumed command of his battalion. He received five decorations for bravery, including the Médaille Militaire, which General Charles de Gaulle bestowed upon him personally. Although he had strong feelings about discrimination against Moslems in the French army, Ben Bella applied for a commission as a regular army officer at the end of the war. He was turned down as "intelligent and dangerous" by a French general, who did not believe that Algerians should serve as officers. In May 1945, while awaiting demobilization from the army, Ben Bella heard of the brutal suppression of a nationalist revolt in eastern Algeria. He became convinced that armed rebellion was the only solution for Algeria.

Discharged as a warrant officer, first class, Ben Bella returned to his home town, where he became active in the outlawed Algerian People's party (PPA) and in its successor organization, the Movement for the Triumph of Democratic Liberties (MTLD), led by Messali Hadj. As a candidate of the MTLD he was elected to the Marnia municipal council, and he subsequently became deputy mayor, a position rarely attained by a Moslem. Having become disillusioned with the moderate and opportunist policies of Messali Hadj, Ben Bella, together with five other young nationalists, in 1947 founded the Secret Organization (OS), which aimed at armed insurrection while maintaining links with the MTLD. Ben

Bella became commander of the OS in the Oran district, and he subsequently was recognized as its national chief.

In April 1949 Ben Bella, with two companions, staged an armed robbery of the Oran post office, which netted the nationalist movement some 3,170,000 francs. He was arrested in May of the following year, and in March 1952 he was tried with fifty-five other defendants and sentenced to seven years imprisonment at Blida. Five days later he escaped by sawing the bars of his cell with a blade smuggled to him in a bowl of food. After his escape he went into hiding, first in Algeria, then in France, and later in Cairo. His efforts to avoid publicity during this period earned him the nickname Aminedi (the invisible one). In Cairo Ben Bella delivered anti-French speeches over the Voice of the Arabs program, and he formed a friendship with Egyptian President Gamal Abdel Nasser, who chose him as the sole intermediary for Egyptian arms aid to the Algerian rebels.

In July 1954 Ben Bella became one of the original nine members of the Revolutionary Committee for Unity and Action (CRUA), which organized the launching of the revolution, and which subsequently became the Algerian Front of National Liberation (FLN). On November 1, 1954 the FLN and its military arm, the Army of National Liberation (ALN) began the revolutionary struggle for independence from France. Ben Bella commanded the revolutionary forces from the Aurès mountains and traveled widely—to Egypt, Libya, Tunisia, Morocco, Italy, Spain, and Switzerland—to negotiate for the acquisition of arms. On one occasion he narrowly escaped assassination by French agents in Tripoli. To eliminate those of doubtful loyalty, he issued an order in 1955 for the execution of politicians who sought a negotiated settlement with France. In April 1955 he sent a delegation to the African-Asian conference at Bandung, Indonesia, and he subsequently also sent a delegate to the United Nations.

Speaking at FLN headquarters in Cairo in February 1956 Ben Bella said that "every Algerian is a potential guerilla if he could get a gun." He said that the aim of the revolution was to set up a social democratic republic, and added: "We will get . . . arms where we can. And while we are strongly opposed to Communism we will accept arms from . . . anyone . . . who will offer them—even the Devil himself." In August 1956 a congress of FLN leaders adopted the Platform of Soummam, a document opposing dictatorial rule and imposing "collegiate responsibility" among the Algerian nationalist leaders. The document was believed to have been directed largely against Ben Bella, who registered his opposition to it.

On October 22, 1956 a Moroccan plane, carrying Ben Bella and four other Algerian leaders from Rabat to Tunis was intercepted by French authorities and forced to land at Algiers, where the five men were arrested by French police. Taken to Paris, the five FLN leaders were imprisoned without trial at Fresnes prison, an institution for common law prisoners. While in prison Ben Bella educated himself in revolutionary theory. To obtain better conditions for the prisoners, he engaged in hunger strikes and on one occasion came close to collapse. Meanwhile, Ben Bella continued to be regarded as a hero and leader by his countrymen. Keeping in touch through his Moroccan attorney, the FLN leaders consulted him on every major move they made. In September 1957 Ben Bella and his four fellow prisoners were made honorary members of the FLN's new executive committee of co-ordination and execution. With the establishment of a provisional government of Algeria under the Premiership of Ferhat Abbas on September 19, 1958 Ben Bella was named Vice-Premier.

In an amnesty move in March 1959 French President Charles de Gaulle permitted the transfer of Ben Bella and the other four FLN leaders to more dignified quarters on the Ile d'Aix in the Bay of Biscay, where they were treated as political prisoners rather than as ordinary criminals. In September 1959 de Gaulle for the first time recognized the right of Algeria to self-determination. Two months later the Algerian provisional regime proposed to the French government that Ben Bella and his four fellow prisoners open negotiations for Algerian self-determination, but the proposal was rejected by French officials, who regarded it as a calculated insult. The first official direct contact between the French government and Algerian rebel leaders took place at Melun, France in June 1960, but failed to result in an agreement. Further negotiations at Evian-les-Bains, France also resulted in a deadlock because the Algerians made the liberation of Ben Bella and his associates one of the conditions of a cease-fire and the French insisted on a cease-fire before any of the conditions would be met.

In November 1961 Ben Bella and his associates led some 4,000 Algerian prisoners in France in a twenty-day hunger strike, which resulted in the attainment of political status by all Algerian prisoners. Although the five men failed to obtain complete liberation, the conditions of their imprisonment were greatly improved, and they were moved to a new residence, the Château d'Aunoy, near Melun. During final negotiations at Evian-les-Bains in March 1962 Ben Bella kept informed of developments through a private telephone line, and he was given a special military guard against possible attempts by French terrorists to assassinate him. On March 18, 1962 a cease-fire agreement was signed by French and Algerian leaders, and Ben Bella and his four associates were released.

Traveling on an American plane supplied by President John F. Kennedy, Ben Bella visited Morocco and consulted with President Nasser in Cairo before joining the other Algerian leaders at provisional government headquarters in Tunisia. In June 1962 he headed a committee that drew up a platform defining the future policies of an independent Algeria. On the eve of independence there was increasing evidence of a rift between the moderate Premier Benyoussef Ben Khedda (who had succeeded Ferhat Abbas in the Premiership of the provisional government on August 27, 1961) and the more militant Vice-Premier Ben Bella. At a secret FLN meeting in Tripoli in June 1962 Ben Bella reportedly sought to have Ben Khedda removed from office.

The struggle for power intensified after the establishment of the Republic of Algeria on July 3, 1962, following a referendum of the Algerian population. Ben Bella denounced Ben Khedda's dissolution of the ALN's three-man general staff, declaring that the union of the army and the people "constitutes the best guarantee for the achievement of the revolution." He also criticized the government's failure to consult the National Council of the Algerian Revolution (the former rebel parliament), in which he claimed majority support. Furthermore, whereas Ben Khedda believed that the future of Algeria depended on continued co-operation with France, Ben Bella took a more militantly anti-European attitude, maintaining that the Evian agreements, concluded while he was in prison, were incompatible with Algeria's Socialist goals.

While Ben Khedda sought to spread his influence from Algiers to the southeast, Ben Bella entered western Algeria on July 11, 1962, setting foot on his native soil for the first time since his imprisonment. Speaking to enthusiastic crowds on the way to Oran, Ben Bella denied ambitions for personal power and accused the Ben Khedda government of obstructing the revolution. At Oran he called for one-party government and for a strong role for the army, and invited the Europeans of Algeria to help build up the country. Setting up temporary headquarters near Tlemcen, he restored order to western Algeria. His prestige was enhanced when Ferhat Abbas, one of the most respected men in Algerian politics, joined his forces in opposition to Ben Khedda's regime.

On July 22, 1962 Ben Bella and his supporters formed a seven-man political bureau to assume the government of the country. Algeria's leadership crisis appeared to be headed for a solution when, following negotiations, the Ben Khedda government agreed to accept the rule of Ben Bella's political bureau in return for certain concessions. On August 2 the political bureau supplanted the provisional government as the *de facto* government of Algeria, taking over control of the country and of the FLN party pending national elections. On the following day Ben Bella triumphantly entered the city of Algiers, where he was welcomed by an enthusiastic crowd.

Soon after the political bureau assumed control a new conflict arose, when the guerilla military forces of the fourth wilaya (one of Algeria's six military districts), which controlled Algiers and its surrounding territory, resisted Ben Bella's demand for conversion into a peacetime national army. In the ensuing struggle the political bureau was temporarily forced out of power by a junta of guerilla colonels, and Ben Bella and his associates were reported to be in flight to Oran. On September 5, 1962 Ben Bella was back in Algiers, where he announced a cease-fire providing for the demilitarization of Algiers. The political bureau again assumed control, and military forces loyal to Ben Bella were reconstituted as a national popular army under the leadership of Ben Bella's close ally, Colonel Houari Boumedienne.

In Algeria's first national elections, on September 20, 1962, some 90 percent of Algeria's 6,500,000 voters came out to vote for Ben Bella's hand-picked slate of candidates for the new Na-

BEN BELLA, AHMED—*Continued*

tional Assembly. Since there was no opposition party, the election was virtually a ratification of Ben Bella's choices. On September 26 Ben Bella was chosen by the National Assembly as Premier of the first regular government of independent Algeria by a vote of 141 to 13, with 31 blank ballots cast. (The lack of unanimity in the voting surprised some observers.) Presenting his cabinet of eighteen ministers to the National Assembly, Ben Bella declared that Algeria would follow a Socialist domestic policy, and he outlined plans for agrarian reform, industrialization, and education. Regarding foreign policy he said that Algeria would adhere to a neutralist course, and he stressed Algeria's relationship with the Arab world and the African nations. He emphasized that relations between France and Algeria must be based on equality between the two countries. Ben Bella was elected to a five-year term as President in September 1963. He continued to serve as Premier.

In a speech before the United Nations General Assembly on October 9, 1962, following Algeria's admission as the 109th U.N. member, Ben Bella avoided cold war issues and declared that Algeria's foremost aim was to fight colonialism. A few days later he paid a visit to Washington, D.C., where he was greeted by President Kennedy and received the traditional twenty-one gun salute. On the following day he visited Cuba, where he voiced strong support for the government of Premier Fidel Castro.

On the domestic scene Ben Bella faces immense economic problems, largely induced by the mass exodus of Europeans from Algeria. (Some 800,000 out of 1,000,000 Europeans are said to have left the country.) About 70 percent of the Moslem workers are unemployed, and there is much discontent among the hungry peasants. Although the Algerian government has practically no revenue other than a subsidy from France, provided for under the Evian agreement, Ben Bella intends to obtain a revision of the agreement, aimed in particular at eliminating or reducing French military bases and nuclear test sites on Algerian soil.

In dealing with his country's problems Ben Bella takes a pragmatic approach. Although he has clashed with the Algerian Communists, who have refused to become integrated with his FLN party, he is not averse to appropriating Communist techniques from other countries. "I have been compared to Russian Communists, to Chinese Communists, to Nasser, to Castro," he was quoted by a correspondent for *Newsweek* (August 13, 1962) as saying. "I am none of them, but I will borrow ideas from all."

A tall, youthful, well-groomed man of athletic build and stylish appearance, Ahmed Ben Bella is self-assured and arrogant in his manner and usually wears a solemn or sullen expression. He is not considered an intellectual. Maintaining physical fitness through daily exercise, he prefers an austere life and neither drinks nor smokes. Although Ben Bella is said to attract women, he has never married, and he lives in solitude in a simply furnished apartment in Algiers. He is a devout Moslem, but he favors a secular state.

Imbued with the conviction of his own mission, Ben Bella once said: "I was born a revolutionary and will die a revolutionary."

References

    Life 53:89+ N 2 '62 pors
    N Y Post p25 Jl 17 '62 por
    N Y Times p2 N 21 '59 por; p5 Jl 5 '62 por
    Toronto Globe and Mail p7 Mr 19 '62 por
    Clark, Michael K. Algeria in Turmoil (1959)
    International Who's Who, 1962-63
    Segal, Ronald. Political Africa (1961)

BENNY, JACK Feb. 14, 1894- Comedian; actor; violinist

Address: b. c/o CBS Television Network, 485 Madison Ave., New York 22; h. 1002 N. Roxbury Dr., Beverly Hills, Calif.

NOTE: This biography supersedes the article that appeared in *Current Biography* in 1941.

After more than fifty years in show business, the comedian Jack Benny remains an American institution. A star of screen, stage, radio, and television, Benny began his career as a violinist on the vaudeville stage and later switched to comedy monologues. He gained nationwide celebrity as a result of his weekly radio program, which began in 1932 and lasted for twenty-three years. In the role of a self-loving tightwad noted for his look of pained indignation, his off-key violin playing, and his penchant for satirizing the weaknesses of his fellow man, Benny still is a favorite of the multitudes who view him weekly on the *Jack Benny Show* over CBS-TV.

Jack Benny was born Benjamin Kubelsky in Chicago, Illinois on February 14, 1894 to Meyer and Emma (Sachs) Kubelsky, Orthodox Jewish immigrants from Europe. He grew up in Waukegan, Illinois, where his father owned a saloon and later a dry-goods store. A timid boy, Benny was left to shift for himself much of the time because his parents were preoccupied with business. Like many children of Jewish immigrant families, he began to take violin lessons as a child, and he showed so much talent that for a time he wanted to become a concert artist.

When he was fifteen Benny got a job as a violinist in the orchestra of Waukegan's Barrison Theater at a salary of eight dollars a week. By the time he was seventeen he had been expelled from school because he had played in the orchestra pit during matinees instead of attending afternoon classes, and he left home to form a touring vaudeville act with the orchestra leader of the Barrison Theater—Cora Salisbury. The act was billed as "Salisbury and Benny—From Grand Opera to Ragtime" with Benny as a straight violinist. In 1913 he and pianist Lyman Woods established their own vaudeville act, known as "Benny and Woods," performing current popular tunes on the old Orpheum circuit, and making as much as $200 a week.

Benny's first brush with comedy occurred at the Great Lakes Naval Training Station in 1918, following his enlistment in the United States

Navy. Cast in a sailor revue called *Maritime Frolics,* Benny was chosen as the juvenile lead more for his funny way with a line than for his skill with the violin. Convinced that his future in show business lay in comedy monologues rather than in music, he developed a line of patter and returned to vaudeville after his discharge from the Navy. His first stage name was Ben K. Benny, but because he was often confused with Ben Bernie, another comedian who brandished a violin, the boy from Waukegan became Jack Benny.

Benny's comedy won him considerable popularity during the 1920's. He played the famous Palace Theater in New York and toured with other headliners such as the Marx Brothers, Nora Bayes, and Frank Fay. On January 25, 1927 Benny married Sadye Marks, then a salesgirl in the hosiery department of the May Company department store in Los Angeles. Under the name of Mary Livingstone, Mrs. Benny became a part of the vaudeville act, as a foil for her husband's jokes. After appearing in a few Hollywood films, Benny returned to Broadway in 1931 to star as the leading comedian and master of ceremonies in Earl Carroll's *Vanities.*

On March 29, 1932 Benny made his radio debut when newspaper columnist Ed Sullivan invited him to appear on his program. He opened with the announcement, "Ladies and gentlemen, this is Jack Benny talking. There will be a slight pause while you say, 'Who cares?' " Many listeners apparently did care, for within a few weeks he had his own program, which became a weekly fixture on radio—Sunday nights at 7 P.M.—for twenty-three years. In 1950 Benny cautiously entered the new medium of television, appearing at first only infrequently, and gradually increasing his appearances. In August 1955 he dropped his radio program to devote full time to his television show, which appeared on CBS-TV on alternate weeks. Since 1960 the *Jack Benny Show* has been a weekly feature. In 1963 he announced that he would move to NBC-TV in the fall of 1964.

Since his first movie role, in the Metro-Goldwyn-Mayer production *Hollywood Revue of 1929,* Benny has played in about a score of motion pictures. Some were acclaimed as hits, but Benny himself admits that a few were somewhat less than classics. His films include *Transatlantic Merry-Go-Round* (United Artists, 1934), *Broadway Melody of 1936* (MGM, 1935), *College Holiday* (Paramount, 1936), *Artists and Models* (Paramount, 1937), *Artists and Models Abroad* (Paramount, 1937), *Man About Town* (Paramount, 1939), *Love Thy Neighbor* (Paramount, 1940), *Buck Benny Rides Again* (Paramount, 1940), *Charley's Aunt* (Twentieth Century-Fox, 1941), *To Be or Not to Be* (United Artists, 1942), *George Washington Slept Here* (Warner Brothers, 1942), *Meanest Man in the World* (Twentieth Century-Fox, 1943), *Hollywood Canteen* (Warner Brothers, 1944), *It's in the Bag* (United Artists, 1945), *The Horn Blows at Midnight* (Warner Brothers, 1945), and *Somebody Loves Me* (Paramount, 1952). In 1962 he made a brief appearance in the Warner Brothers film *Gypsy,* based on the Broadway musical.

Over the years Benny has created a character and perfected a style that has made him a

JACK BENNY

favorite funnyman among American audiences. In his characterizations he is, for example, not only miserly but so abjectly the slave of wealth that he cannot resist putting on a jeweler's glass to appraise the diamond ring of the girl he is embracing. Not merely vain, he is so concerned with maintaining a youthful appearance that he long ago adopted the age of thirty-nine, at which he has since remained. Not just an execrable fiddler, scratching out his long familiar "Love in Bloom," he is the self-styled Van Gogh of the violin, who quotes a listener's comment, "My God, he's lost his ear!" No ordinary cheapskate, he tells the story about the holdup man who demands, "Your money or your life." There is a long pause and the holdup man asks, "Well?" To which Benny replies, "I'm thinking it over."

An innovator as well as an exploiter of familiar material, Benny was the first comedian willing to let his stooges share some of the laughs; his valet, Eddie (Rochester) Anderson, his singer, Dennis Day, his announcer, Don Wilson, and other familiar members of his radio and television family are almost as famous as he. "The show itself is the important thing," Benny has said. "As long as people think the show is funny it doesn't matter to me who gets the punch lines." He also pioneered in poking fun at commercials. Cleverly inserted into the continuity, they have provided some of the funniest moments in his show.

In 1956 Benny took on a new title—that of concert artist—when he accepted an invitation to join his friend Isaac Stern, the noted concert violinist, in a fund-raising concert with the New York Philharmonic Symphony Orchestra to help save Carnegie Hall. The evening was a success from every point of view and launched Benny on a new (and unpaid) concert career, which he sandwiches between his television and nightclub appearances. Benny's first performances set the tone for his concert career. In the words of Bill Davidson in the *Saturday Evening Post* (March

BENNY, JACK—*Continued*

2, 1963), the comedian "played Beethoven outrageously, argued with the conductor, [and] demanded that the concert master be banished for playing better than he." By early 1963, Benny had played with thirty of the country's important symphony orchestras and had raised more than $3,300,000 for musical and other charities.

In March 1963 Benny returned to the Broadway stage for the first time since 1931. Starring in his own variety show in New York's Ziegfeld Theatre, he played to capacity audiences during the limited engagement, despite the city's newspaper blackout. *Variety* editor Abel Green, reviewing the performance, described the show as a "skillful blend of sight and sound," and summed up: "As something of an American institution . . . Benny in the flesh is a kingsize spectacular" (March 6, 1963).

Noted in real life for his financial acumen, Benny has transacted some of the biggest business deals in the history of show business. (Reportedly he is the most highly paid comedian in the world.) In 1948 he switched his show from the National Broadcasting Company to the Columbia Broadcasting System. In this transaction CBS paid some $2,260,000 for Amusements, Inc., in which Benny had owned a controlling interest, and in 1961 the Music Corporation of America bought Benny's production company, J. & M. Productions, Inc., for some $2,750,000 in MCA stock.

For his volunteer performances Benny received the 1959 Laurel Leaf Award of the American Composers Alliance, citing his distinguished service to music. In 1961 the Carnegie Hall Society honored Benny with a concert entitled "Carnegie Hall Salutes Jack Benny," for helping to save the hall. Van Cliburn, Benny Goodman, Roberta Peters, and the Philadelphia Orchestra under Eugene Ormandy were among those participating in the program. Benny in addition has had a gold violin bow presented to him by the American Federation of Musicians. He has been honored by the March of Dimes, which gave him its Humanitarian Award of the Year in February 1960. The annual poll taken by *Motion Picture Daily* voted Benny best radio comedian in 1951, 1952, 1953, and 1954 and "Champion of Champions" in 1950 and 1952.

Benny's reputation for winning awards was unaffected by his move to television. In 1957 he won a special award from the Academy of Television Arts and Sciences for the best continuing performance by a male entertainer. The *Jack Benny Show* won the academy's Emmy award as the best comedy series in 1959, and the show's writers and production staff have received a number of awards. Benny has also been cited for his extensive touring of military installations and entertaining of troops at home and abroad during World War II and the Korean conflict. Among his friends Jack Benny counts President John F. Kennedy, ex-President Harry S. Truman, and former Vice-President Richard M. Nixon.

Of all the honors Jack Benny has received, perhaps the one that pleased him most was the naming of a junior high school for him in his home town of Waukegan in 1961. It was an accolade especially appreciated by a man who, because he himself never went beyond the ninth grade, has long prized academic achievement. Benny did a special telecast from the $1,250,000 school shortly after it was dedicated in the fall of 1961.

Benny's assured manner of delivery has prompted Ed Wynn to call him "the world's finest comedian—comedian meaning a man who says things funny, as opposed to a comic, who says funny things." Describing Benny's cool and polished style, Edward S. Hipp wrote in the Newark *Sunday News* (March 10, 1963): "He is now without peer as an exponent of the slow take, the meaningful pause, the raised eyebrow, aided by such small tricks as a slight scratching of the head, a stare of incredulity and the ability to make the simple word, 'well,' cover a variety of situations." The late Fred Allen, with whom Benny had been carrying on a good-natured feud for many years, once noted: "Practically all comedy shows on radio owe their structure to Benny's conceptions."

On the other hand, Benny has sometimes been criticized for his lack of versatility and originality. A spokesman for George Q. Lewis' Comedy Workshop has observed: "Jack Benny . . . is a one-dimension comic who has parlayed a stare, and a violin, and a thirty-nine-year-old joke, plus lines about stinginess into a legend. He has developed a symbol—and won accolades for his good cheer, lovability, etc.—but he is not a funny man" (New York *Herald Tribune*, December 15, 1960).

Still happily married after more than thirty-six years, Jack Benny lives in a Beverly Hills mansion with his wife, Mary, who retired from show business in 1957. He often visits his grandchildren, Michael and Maria, the children of his adopted daughter, Joan Naomi. Unlike his stage character, Benny is known as a generous tipper and a popular boss. The affection and respect he has won from his professional associates may be gauged by the many years that his musical director and his four writers have remained with him. Benny plays golf, drives a Rolls Royce, and enjoys listening to other comedians. His chief relaxation today is the violin, to which he devotes two or three hours daily. "When I feel troubled and depressed, I play the violin and the bad mood goes away," he told Bill Davidson (*Saturday Evening Post*, March 2, 1963). He owns a $25,000 Stradivarius. His major interest, however, remains his work.

After more than a half century in show business Jack Benny is still stagestruck, and he has no plans to bring his career to a halt. He has said that he intends to work as long as people will laugh at him, and he has shown an interest in doing a Broadway play, something he has never tried. Benny's material, according to a writer for *Time* (March 8, 1963), "is gauged for longevity rather than flash. His patent for permanence is simply that he can do no wrong." One reason for that may be in Benny's philosophy of comedy. "There are enough basic concepts in life to poke fun at," he once told Hollywood correspondent Erskine Johnson. "Funny things happen to us all the time. The comedian or comedy writer must be alert to these, remember them and invent variations on them. If a gag is hurtful, I don't need it."

References

Am W pl+ Je 23 '63 pors
Coronet 49:16 F '61 por
Sat Eve Post 236:27+ Mr 3 '63 pors
TV Guide 11:15+ Mr 23 '63 por
Time 81:60+ Mr 8 '63 por
International Motion Picture Almanac, 1963
International Television Almanac, 1963
Who's Who in America, 1962-63
Who's Who in World Jewry (1955)

BEN-ZVI, ISAAC Nov. 24, 1884-Apr. 23, 1963 President of Israel; succeeded Chaim Weizmann, Israel's first president, in 1952 and was re-elected in 1957 and 1962; leading spokesman for Palestine Jewry for thirty years before the establishment of Israel in 1948; member of Mapai party; scholar of Middle East history and archaeology. See *Current Biography* (April) 1953

Obituary

N Y Times pl+ Ap 23 '63

BERANEK, LEO L(EROY) (bâr-än′ĕk) Sept. 15, 1914- Acoustician; educator; author

Address: b. Bolt Beranek and Newman Inc., 50 Moulton St., Cambridge 38, Mass.; h. 7 Ledgewood Rd., Winchester, Mass.

An internationally recognized authority on acoustical science, Leo L. Beranek has made major contributions to all aspects of acoustics, including physical acoustics, psychoacoustics, architectural acoustics, electroacoustics, systems research, and noise control. He directed the Electro-Acoustics and Systems Research Laboratory at Harvard University during World War II and has been on the faculty of the Massachusetts Institute of Technology since 1947. As a member of the consulting firm of Bolt Beranek and Newman Inc., of which he has been president since 1953, Beranek has been called upon as acoustical consultant for some of the most important architectural projects in the world, including the Philharmonic Hall at the Lincoln Center for the Performing Arts in New York City, which opened in September 1962.

Leo Leroy Beranek was born on September 15, 1914 in Solon, Iowa, one of two sons of Edward Fred Beranek, a realtor, and Beatrice (Stahle) Beranek. He and his brother, Lyle Edward, were reared in Mount Vernon and Cedar Rapids, Iowa. At the Mount Vernon High School Leo Beranek was active in track and dramatics and played in the school band. Following his graduation in 1931 he entered Cornell College in Mount Vernon, Iowa, where he majored in physics and mathematics and continued his musical activities, playing drums in the college dance band and timpani in the symphony orchestra. To help meet his expenses he operated a radio repair business in his spare time.

After receiving his B.A. degree with distinction from Cornell College in 1936, Beranek entered Harvard University, where he undertook graduate work in physics and communications engineering. He obtained the M.Sc. degree in 1937. From 1937 to 1939 he worked as a research assistant at Harvard, and in 1939-40 he held a Parker Traveling Fellowship at the university. He received the D.Sc. degree in 1940 after submitting a thesis on architectural acoustics. Beranek credits his interest in music and the historic leadership of Harvard University in training acoustical scientists with influencing his choice of a career in architectural acoustics.

In 1940 Beranek was appointed instructor of physics and communications engineering at Harvard, and from 1941 to 1943 he served as assistant professor. Simultaneously, from 1940 to 1943 he was secretary of the National Research Council's committee on sound control in combat vehicles. In 1943 he became director of the Electro-Acoustics Laboratory at Harvard, operating with funds supplied by the federal Office of Scientific Research and Development, and in this post until 1946, he supervised a staff of some sixty employees. During this period the laboratory was engaged in projects aimed at reducing noise in long-range bombers, tanks, and motors, at developing special acoustical sound-locating devices, and at improving hearing aids. It also undertook studies of voice communications at high altitudes and on board ships. According to a noted Air Force general, the laboratory's work in improving communications at high altitudes greatly contributed to the success of bombing missions over Germany during the war. As director of the Systems Research Laboratory at Harvard, during 1945-46 Beranek supervised a staff of about 100 persons engaged in the study of psychophysical problems in the combined operation of radio, telephone, radar, and plotting equipment aboard ships during combat.

From February 1946 to January 1947 Beranek did research on acoustic materials and auditorium design, working jointly at Harvard and the Massachusetts Institute of Technology under a John Simon Guggenheim Fellowship. He was associate professor of communications engineering at M.I.T. from February 1947 to March 1958 and technical director of its acoustic laboratory from 1947 to 1953. As a member of the educational policy committee of the electrical engineering department at M.I.T. from 1950 to 1955, he played an important role in helping to bring about major reforms in the teaching of engineering. In 1953, 1955, 1957, and 1960 he conducted special summer programs at M.I.T. on noise reduction for practising engineers.

Since 1958 Beranek has been a regular lecturer at M.I.T., and he has also lectured on acoustics at the Physical Society of London, the Zurich Federal Institute of Technology, the Swiss Society of Architects and Engineers, the Technical University of Prague, the Polish Academy of Sciences in Warsaw, the Acoustical Institute of Moscow, the University of Moscow, and the Engineering Society of Finland. He was visiting professor at the University of Buenos Aires in 1949. He presented the forty-fifth Thomas Hawksley Lecture at the Institution of Mechanical Engineers in London in November 1958 and repeated this lecture at Bristol and Oxford universities.

(Continued next page)

LEO L. BERANEK

For the federal government, Beranek served from 1949 to 1952 as chairman of the panel on acoustics with the Research and Development Board of the Department of Defense. From 1955 to 1958 he was a member of the armed forces joint committee on hearing and bio-acoustics of the National Research Council, and in 1958-59 he served on the subcommittee on aircraft noise with the National Advisory Committee for Aeronautics.

A registered professional engineer in the Commonwealth of Massachusetts, Beranek became a partner in the firm Bolt Beranek and Newman Inc., in Cambridge in 1948, and he has been its president since 1953. The firm is a research, consulting, and development organization, working in the fields of architectural acoustics, psychoacoustics, engineering psychology, man-machine systems, information systems, applied physics and engineering, chemistry, and bio-medical technology. As a member of the firm Beranek has been called upon as a consultant on some of the most important architectural projects throughout the world, including the United Nations permanent headquarters in New York, the Aula Magna at the University of Caracas in Venezuela, the Kresge Auditorium at M.I.T., the Tanglewood Music Shed in Lenox, Massachusetts, the Congress Hall in Jerusalem, Israel, the Montreal Civic Center in Canada, the Benjamin Franklin Congress Hall in Berlin, and the Philharmonic Hall at the new Lincoln Center for the Performing Arts in New York City. Beranek has also served as a consultant for the Port of New York Authority, General Dynamics Corporation, General Radio Company, Outboard Marine Corporation, and other firms. Since 1952 he has been vice-president of the Blen Corporation in Cambridge.

The opening, on September 23, 1962, of Philharmonic Hall—the first major concert hall to be built in New York City since Carnegie Hall was opened in 1891—culminated a study of several years by Beranek and his associates. During this period Beranek measured and tested some sixty concert halls in twenty countries, listening to concerts and interviewing conductors, musicians, and music critics, in an effort to translate the language of the musician into that of the physicist. He concluded in his study that high-quality musical acoustics depend largely upon three basic factors—intimacy, liveness, and warmth of sound.

Beranek maintains that the design of concert halls is not an exact science, but depends to a large extent on trial and error. He explained the reasons for serious differences between reverberation times calculated during design and those measured after completion of concert halls, in reports to the Acoustical Society of America in Washington, D.C. in May 1958 and to the third international congress on acoustics in Stuttgart, Germany in September 1959. In August 1962, at the fourth international congress on acoustics in Copenhagen, Beranek presented a paper, "Criteria for the Design of Concert Halls and Opera Houses."

The acoustical plans that Beranek worked out with the assistance of Hope Bagenal of England account for some $1,500,000 of the $15,400,000 cost of the nine-story Philharmonic Hall. The building was in effect constructed as a huge musical instrument, capable of being tuned like a piano without altering its basic structure. To obtain an optimum acoustic quality Beranek limited the capacity of the hall to 2,612 seats and took into consideration a variety of factors, including the structure of seats and the space taken up by the audience. He had 136 adjustable panels installed at the ceiling to provide a greater intimacy of sound and to give it balance and blend.

Beranek's plans for Philharmonic Hall differed considerably from the original plans of its architect, Max Abramowitz, who has noted that commonly accepted architectural standards do not necessarily correlate with the acoustic qualities of concert halls. Because Beranek insisted upon features of design that the architects did not wish to include he lost the position of consultant on Philip Johnson's New York State Theater and on the new Metropolitan Opera House at Lincoln Center.

Although during "tuning week" in May 1962 Beranek adjusted Philharmonic Hall to what then seemed to be optimum acoustics, critics detected some shortcomings in acoustic quality at the hall's first concert, on September 23, 1962, featuring the New York Philharmonic Orchestra. Beranek, who also was not entirely satisfied, immediately made a number of adjustments that markedly improved subsequent concerts. Beranek believes that it might take a year before the hall can be brought to its optimum condition. Noting that Philharmonic Hall is "a hall of today and tomorrow, not a hall of the past," Beranek has said, "There is a changing concept of sound. A modern concert hall needn't sound like a hall of 1850. In my personal opinion Philharmonic Hall is brighter and more reverberant than Carnegie."

In April 1963, because the acoustics of Philharmonic Hall were still considered unsatisfactory, it was decided to make several modifications to increase reverberation, among them an incorporation of the adjustable ceiling panels into a smooth continuous canopy. Acoustics is not yet an exact science, and Lincoln Center officials absolved Bolt Beranek & Newman of any blame for the acoustical difficulties.

One of Beranek's major interests is the field of noise abatement. In 1951 he published a method, now widely used, for calculating loudness in sones rather than decibels, thus taking into account pitch as well as intensity. Speaking at a meeting of the American Acoustical Society in New York City in May 1952, he suggested the possibility of countering noises of jet engines by redesign. Beranek's firm has undertaken projects for the reduction of noise in fans, airconditioners, outboard motors, and other appliances. In an article by Ruth and Edward Brecher in the *Saturday Evening Post* (February 6, 1960) Beranek is quoted as saying: "Except for the sonic boom from planes and missiles traveling faster than sound, there's no noise scientific ingenuity can generate that scientific ingenuity can't suppress— if you give us money enough, room enough, and weight tolerance enough."

Beranek has published over seventy-five technical papers on acoustical science. He was a co-author of *Principles of Sound Control in Airplanes*, published in 1944 by the Cruft Laboratory at Harvard University under the auspices of the Office of Scientific Research and Development and the National Defense Research Committee. With Arnold P. G. Peterson he wrote the *Handbook of Noise Measurement*, published by the General Radio Company in 1953. He is the author of *Acoustic Measurements* (Wiley, 1949) and of *Acoustics* (McGraw, 1954), a general textbook for senior and graduate students in the field; and he was editor of *Noise Reduction* (McGraw, 1960). His book *Music, Acoustics and Architecture* (Wiley, 1962), based on his worldwide study of concert halls and opera houses, is regarded as an important contribution to the field. From 1946 to 1960 Beranek was associate editor of the *Journal of the Acoustical Society of America,* and from 1955 to 1959 he was a member of the editorial board of *Noise Control* magazine. In 1962 he became associate editor of *Sound, Its Uses and Control.*

In 1944 the Acoustical Society of America conferred upon Beranek its biennial award for outstanding contributions to acoustics. He received an honorary D.Sc. degree from Cornell College in Iowa in June 1946, and for his contributions to the war effort he was awarded a Presidential Citation of Merit in 1948. In 1961 Beranek received the Wallace Clement Sabine Award of the Acoustical Society of America for internationally recognized achievements in all phases of architectural acoustics. At the time that the award was conferred the president of the International Commission on Acoustics, Professor Willi Furrer of Switzerland, noted that auditorium acoustics was perhaps the "last field of architectural acoustics where fundamental problems are still awaiting their solution." He added that no one knows more in this field than Beranek and "no one seems more likely to find the solutions to the remaining tasks and mysteries."

A member of the Acoustical Society of America since 1939, and a Fellow since 1940, Beranek has served as chairman of a number of its committees. He was vice-president of the society in 1949-50 and president in 1954-55. He has been active on several of the committees and subcommittees of the American Standards Association, particularly as chairman of its acoustical standards board since 1955. Beranek is a Fellow of the American Physical Society, the American Association for the Advancement of Science, the American Academy of Arts and Sciences, and the Institute of Radio Engineers. He is an honorary member of the Audio Engineering Society and a member of Phi Beta Kappa and of the honorary fraternities Eta Kappa Nu and Sigma Xi. Other organizations to which he belongs include the Human Factors Society of America, the Groupement des Acousticiens de Langue Française (Paris), the M.I.T. Faculty Club, and the Winchester (Massachusetts) Country Club.

On September 6, 1941 Leo L. Beranek married Phyllis Knight, who was employed as a dental hygienist during World War II. They have two sons, James Knight and Thomas Haynes. Beranek is five feet six inches tall, weighs 170 pounds, and has brown hair and brown eyes. His religious affiliation is with the Episcopal Church, and he is independent in politics. His favorite recreations are skiing, stamp and coin collecting, photography, and music.

References

J of the Acoustical Society of America 34:246+ F '62 por

American Men of Science 10th ed (1960-62)

Who's Who in America, 1962-63

Who's Who in American Education, 1960-61

Who's Who in Engineering, 1959

BERLIN, IRVING May 11, 1888- Songwriter; music publisher

Address: b. c/o Irving Berlin Music Co., 1650 Broadway, New York 19; h. 17 Beekman Place, New York 22; Livingston Manor, N.Y.

NOTE: This biography supersedes the article that appeared in *Current Biography* in 1942.

After twelve years of restive retirement from show business the perennially youthful Irving Berlin returned to Broadway with his score for the musical comedy *Mr. President* in October 1962. The embodiment of Tin Pan Alley and the most productive songwriter in the United States, Berlin has written over 900 songs and the scores for nineteen Broadway musicals and eighteen films since he wrote the lyrics for "Marie from Sunny Italy" in 1907.

His sentimental and red-white-and-blue melodies and lyrics have brought Berlin millions of dollars, and his morale-building contributions to American patriotism have earned him a gold medal from the Congress of the United States. One of his songs, "God Bless America," threatens to dislodge the national anthem in

IRVING BERLIN

the affections of the populace, while his "Easter Parade" and "White Christmas" have become fixtures of the holidays they celebrate. Jerome Kern once called Berlin "the nearest thing to a native folk singer since Stephen Foster."

Irving Berlin was born Israel Baline on May 11, 1888 in the village of Temun in eastern Russia, one of the eight children of Moses and Leah (Lipkin) Baline. His father was a cantor in a synagogue and a *shochet*—a person who certifies that meat and poultry are slaughtered in accordance with Jewish ritual requirements. Fleeing from pogroms, the family came to the United States in 1893 and settled in a tenement at 300 Cherry Street in the heart of New York's Lower East Side. Two older children were left behind. With other members of the Cherry Street gang Irving Berlin made the swarming streets his playground, swam in the East River, and watched the scows and tugs go by.

When Berlin was eight years old his father died and the boy took to the streets to help support his mother and brothers and sisters. He had had a total of two years of formal education. One of his first jobs was that of guide for Blind Sol, a singing beggar or "busker," with whom he earned an occasional tip on the Bowery for singing. At fourteen he appeared briefly in Edward E. Rice's *The Show Girl* on the road, but although the show eventually reached Broadway, Berlin was left stranded in Binghampton, New York. He also sang at Callahan's, the Chatham, and other popular hangouts near the Bowery, and for a time he plugged songs for Harry von Tilzer, the song composer and publisher, at Tony Pastor's Music Hall in Union Square, reprising songs from a balcony seat for $5 a week.

From 1905 to 1907 Berlin was a singing waiter at the Pelham Café at 12 Pell Street in New York's Chinatown, where he sang, waited on tables, and learned how to pick out tunes on a battered upright piano. Unable to read har-

mony to this day, Berlin picks out the melody with one finger and a pianist-arranger takes down the notes that he plays by ear. Although F sharp is the only key in which he can compose, he has a piano furnished with a clutch that enables him to switch to any key.

It was at the Pelham Café that Berlin wrote the lyrics for his first published song, "Marie from Sunny Italy," released by Joseph W. Stern & Company on May 8, 1907, with music by "Nick" Nicholson, a pianist at the café. With the publication of "Marie from Sunny Italy" Israel Baline was formally recognized as "I. Berlin," the name that appeared on the cover. From his first published lyrics Berlin realized the total of 37 cents.

Impressed by Berlin's flair for versifying in Italian dialect, a vaudeville performer commissioned Berlin to write a few verses for him about Dorando, a popular Italian marathon runner of the day. Although the vaudevillian never returned, Berlin brought his verses to the attention of Ted Snyder, a music publisher. When Berlin improvised a tune to go with the verses, "Dorando" became a popular topical song of 1909, and it introduced its composer to Tin Pan Alley. Snyder hired Berlin as a lyricist for $25 a week, plus royalties, and later took him on as a partner. In the meantime Berlin was continuing to compose his own melodies, and in 1909 his "That Mesmerizing Mendelssohn Tune," setting the famous "Spring Song" to ragtime, made a hit on a small scale. With "Sadie Salome, Go Home," a parody of the dance of the seven veils in Richard Strauss's *Salome*, with lyrics by Edgar Leslie, he achieved his first genuine hit.

"Alexander's Ragtime Band" in 1911 made Berlin an international celebrity. Ragtime, of American Negro origin, consists of a strongly syncopated melody with a regularly accented accompaniment. By making ragtime and its accompanying dance craze popular, Berlin pioneered in making jazz widely acceptable; eventually he became identified in the public mind with all ragtime. Berlin had written his first sensational hit as a piano rag called "Alexander and His Clarinet," which he transformed into a song for the first annual *Frolics* of the exclusive theatrical Friars Club in New York, of which he had become a member. During an engagement in Chicago, Emma Carus, the vaudeville star, made its syncopated march rhythms and simulated bugle calls famous and within a short time "Alexander's Ragtime Band" sold over 1,000,000 copies of sheet music. In 1911 Berlin wrote three more hits in the ragtime idiom: "The Mysterious Rag" (with Ted Snyder), "The Ragtime Violin," and "Everybody's Doin' It Now."

Although Berlin is described today as inordinately shy and reluctant to perform in public, he was an outstanding performer in vaudeville before World War I. He first appeared on Broadway in *Up and Down Broadway* in 1910, with Ted Snyder, at $50 a week. Billed as "the ragtime king," he appeared at the Hippodrome Theatre in London in 1917, where he introduced his "International Rag."

But Berlin was more interested in writing songs than in performing them. He contributed songs to the *Ziegfeld Follies* of 1911, 1919, and 1920 and an entire score to the *Ziegfeld Follies* of 1927. "A Pretty Girl is Like a Melody," written for the *Follies* of 1919, became the unofficial theme song of all the Ziegfeld extravaganzas. With Victor Herbert he collaborated on the music for *The Century Girl* in 1916 and, conscious of his technical limitations, asked Herbert whether he should take time off to study composition. "You have a natural gift for words and music," Herbert told him. "Learning theory might help you a little, but it could cramp your style." Berlin has never forgotten this advice.

His first complete Broadway score was *Watch Your Step,* starring Irene and Vernon Castle, which opened at the New Amsterdam Theatre on December 8, 1914 and popularized "Play a Simple Melody." Following this "syncopated musical" he contributed the entire score to *Stop! Look! Listen!,* which opened on December 25, 1915, and furnished music for *Dance and Grow Thin,* one of the midnight revues popular during the immediate prewar period.

Drafted into the United States Army as an infantry private in 1917, Berlin served at Camp Upton, Long Island, an embarkation point for troops leaving for Europe. He was commissioned to write the songs for *Yip, Yip, Yaphank,* "A Musical 'Mess' Cooked Up by the Boys of Camp Upton," which opened at the Century Theatre in New York in 1918 and ran for 32 performances. In it Berlin sang "Oh, How I Hate to Get Up in the Morning," a hit that was inspired by his fondness for sleeping until noon. (He is an inveterate insomniac.) *Yip, Yip, Yaphank* grossed $150,000 for the building of a service center at Camp Upton. After his discharge with the rank of sergeant, Berlin formed his own music publishing firm in 1919 —the Irving Berlin Music Company.

With Sam H. Harris, the theatrical producer, and Joseph Schenck, the movie magnate, in 1921 Berlin built the Music Box Theatre on 45th Street off Broadway—the first intimate theater designed as a showcase for the revues of one composer. Opening with the first *Music Box Revue* on September 22, 1921, the theater continued to house Music Box revues in 1922, 1923, and 1924. Berlin composed "Say It With Music" as the theme song for his theater. Other haunting Berlin ballads during the 1920's, some inspired by events in his private life, were "All Alone," "Remember," "What'll I Do?" "Always," "Marie," and "Russian Lullaby." More buoyant Berlin products of the period were "Blue Skies" and his score for *The Cocoanuts,* which opened with the Marx Brothers at the Lyric Theatre in New York on December 8, 1925.

After a fallow period during the early years of the Depression, Berlin again became productive in 1932 with "How Deep Is the Ocean?" and "Say It Isn't So." Devoid of the frivolity of his earlier musical scores, his next two musicals were sobered by the social awareness of the early 1930's. *Face the Music,* which opened on February 17, 1932, dealt with political corruption, and *As Thousands Cheer,* as topical as newspaper headlines, introduced "Suppertime," a

dirge about a lynching, along with the now classic "Easter Parade" when it opened on September 30, 1933.

Recruited by the motion picture industry in 1935, Berlin wrote the score for his first film musical, *Top Hat,* in which Ginger Rogers and Fred Astaire introduced "Isn't This a Lovely Day?" and "Cheek to Cheek." It was succeeded by *Follow the Fleet* (1936); *On the Avenue* (1937); *Carefree* (1938); and *Second Fiddle* (1939). *Holiday Inn* (1942) gave another Berlin classic to popular music with "White Christmas." Other films for which Berlin did original songs included *Blue Skies* (1946); *Easter Parade* (1948); *There's No Business Like Show Business* (1954); and *White Christmas* (1954). *Annie Get Your Gun* (1950) and *Call Me Madam* (1953) are film versions of his stage musicals.

"A patriotic song is an emotion, and you must not embarrass an audience with it, or they'll hate your guts," Berlin told Joseph Roddy in an interview for *Look* (October 23, 1962). "It has to be right, and the time for it has to be right." On Armistice Day, 1939 Kate Smith introduced "God Bless America," which Berlin had written in an earlier version for his World War I Army show. Earmarked for the Boy Scouts and Girl Scouts of America, the royalties from this quasi-anthem have totaled hundreds of thousands of dollars. His patriotic motivations have also led Berlin to write "Any Bonds Today?" to promote the sale of World War II defense bonds, "Arms for the Love of America" to boost production in defense plants, and "Angels of Mercy" for the American Red Cross.

Patriotic sentiments also lured Berlin back to the Camp Upton barracks early in World War II to gather material for another all-soldier show, *This Is the Army.* Composed, produced, and staged by Berlin, it opened at the Broadway Theatre on July 4, 1942, played most of the major cities in the United States, and then toured American military bases in Europe, Africa, Australia, and the South Pacific. Singing his old "Oh, How I Hate to Get Up in the Morning" in his high-pitched tremolo and dressed in his World War I uniform, Berlin stayed with the show during its three and one-half year run and appeared in the 1943 film version. The most durable hits in *This Is the Army* (which earned $10,000,000 for Army Emergency Relief) were "This Is the Army, Mr. Jones" and "I Left My Heart at the Stage Door Canteen."

Berlin's last prewar show had been *Louisiana Purchase,* a satire of political bossism, which opened on May 28, 1940 at the Imperial Theatre. After the end of World War II Berlin returned to Broadway with *Annie Get Your Gun,* starring Ethel Merman. Based on the exploits of the sharpshooting Annie Oakley, this greatest of Berlin's stage successes opened at the Imperial Theatre on May 16, 1946 and ran for 1,147 performances. The same theater was the scene of the opening of Berlin's mildly successful *Miss Liberty* on July 15, 1949 and of the highly prosperous *Call Me Madam* on October 12, 1950,

35

BERLIN, IRVING—*Continued*

in which Ethel Merman spoofed Mrs. Perle Mesta, then American Ambassador to Luxembourg.

After composing for two films in 1954, Berlin tried to retire completely, and he fidgeted around with golfing, fishing, and painting before he concluded that he was not the type to retire gracefully. When he returned to Broadway with *Mr. President* in the fall of 1962, he became one of the oldest composers to write the score for a musical comedy. Excited by the prospect of a score by Berlin, a book by Russel Crouse and Howard Lindsay, and direction by Joshua Logan, the public bought $2,500,000 in tickets before the show opened at New York's St. James Theatre on October 20, 1962, with Nanette Fabray and Robert Ryan as its stars. Although *Mr. President* was dismissed by some critics as old-fashioned, tame, flagwaving, and uninspired, audiences appeared to like it and the show seemed assured of a long run. Answering the charge that his score was "corny," Berlin told Abel Green in a telephone interview for *Variety* (September 19, 1962): "If some of Berlin's songs are corny, then it's because they're simple, and all I know is that some of the corniest and simplest songs have lasted, be they 'White Christmas' and 'Easter Parade' or 'My Old Kentucky Home'."

Irving Berlin was married in February 1913 to Dorothy Goetz, who died on July 17 in the same year of typhoid fever contracted in Cuba during their honeymoon. On January 4, 1926 Berlin married Ellin Mackay, the daughter of Clarence H. Mackay, a leading Catholic layman and president of the Postal Telegraph Company, who at first opposed the marriage on social and religious grounds. The marriage was one of the most widely publicized news events of the 1920's. Mr. and Mrs. Berlin have three daughters: Mary Ellin (now Mrs. Marvin Barrett); Linda (now Mrs. Edouard Emmet) and Elizabeth. Their four grandchildren are the offspring of Mary Ellin Barrett. Small, slender, and wiry, Berlin weighs between 140 and 145 pounds. His black hair remains uninvaded by gray, and his brown eyes are still vigilant behind horn-rimmed glasses. He leads the 6,500 members of ASCAP in fees received per year.

President Dwight D. Eisenhower presented Irving Berlin with a gold medal on February 18, 1955 "in national recognition of his services in composing many patriotic songs including 'God Bless America.'" For his work with *This Is the Army* Berlin was awarded a medal of merit by the United States Army, and in April 1963 he won a special Antoinette Perry (Tony) Award for his "distinguished contribution to the musical theater for many years." He belongs to the French Legion of Honor, the Masons, the Elks, and the Lambs and Friars clubs. Bucknell University and Temple University have presented him with honorary degrees.

References

> Ewen, David. The Story of Irving Berlin (1950); Popular American Composers (1962)

Green, Stanley. The World of Musical Comedy (1960)
Who's Who in America, 1962-63
Who's Who in World Jewry (1955)
Woollcott, Alexander. The Story of Irving Berlin (1925)

BEVERIDGE, SIR WILLIAM (HENRY) Mar. 5, 1879-Mar. 16, 1963 Leading architect of the British "welfare state"; author of Beveridge Plan in the 1940's, which laid foundation for national health program and other welfare measures; member of Liberal party. See *Current Biography* (January) 1943.

Obituary

> N Y Times p35 Ap 1 '63

BLANCHARD, HAZEL A(NN) July 29, 1920- School principal; organization official *Address:* b. Rowell Elementary School, Fresno, Calif.; h. 820 McKinley St., Fresno, Calif.

At the annual convention of the National Education Association in July 1962 Mrs. Hazel A. Blanchard, an elementary school principal from California, was elected president of the NEA for 1962-63 to succeed Ewald Turner. She became the head of the world's largest professional organization for teachers after serving for one year as its vice-president and president-elect. She has also held office in the Fresno (California) Teachers Association and the California Teachers Association. Mrs. Blanchard has been principal since 1958 of the Rowell Elementary School in Fresno, from which she took a year's leave to discharge her NEA duties. Before moving to Rowell, she had been principal of the Lane Elementary School in Fresno for six years and a teacher in Fresno elementary schools for seven years. She chose as the 1962-63 NEA theme, "A Great Profession—Ours By Choice."

Hazel Ann Gonser, one of the five children of Nobel Parker Gonser, a merchant, and Hazel Mae (Hemmer) Gonser, was born on July 29, 1920 in Fresno, California. She has two brothers, Lester N., an attorney, and Harold C., a businessman, and a sister, Mrs. Evelyn E. Lehr, a secretary. Her other sister, Mrs. Florence Carpenter, is no longer living. At Laton Joint Union High School in Laton, California, from which she graduated in 1938, Hazel Gonser took part in oratory, debate, journalism, and dramatics.

Speech and dramatics were Miss Gonser's major interests at Fresno State College, and she decided to teach these subjects in high school. As an undergraduate she was president of Tokalon and of Phrateres, vice-president of the student teachers association, and a member of the Triple S Society and the Associated Women Students. She also did backstage work with sets and props for little theater groups. Miss Gonser graduated from Fresno State College with the B.A. degree in June 1942. Her plans for a fifth year of study to obtain teaching certification were dropped because of her marriage on September 2, 1942 to Stewart Edward Blanchard. Her husband was killed in World War II on February 14, 1944, and Mrs. Blanchard resumed her preparation for teaching.

In the summer of 1944 Mrs. Blanchard acquired enough units for an elementary teaching credential, and that fall she began working as a third grade teacher at the Laton Elementary School. Assigned a year later to the elementary schools of the Fresno City Unified School District, she taught the second, fourth, and fifth grades at the Winchell Elementary School from 1945 to 1952. In 1952 she became the principal of another Fresno school, the Lane Elementary School, and in 1958 she was made principal of the Rowell Elementary School, also in Fresno. She holds an administrative credential from Fresno State College.

Although her responsibilities as principal have taken her away from the classroom, Mrs. Blanchard tries to talk with students and personally help them as much as possible. She also works closely with teachers, and at her school, parents are kept directly informed of school programs through "parent clubs," small groups that correspond to children's grade levels. "This kind of direct parent-teacher communication builds a better understanding of the school's activities," Mrs. Blanchard has said. She would like to see more such plans, by which "all of the services available to children are relayed to parents in small group situations."

Active in professional organizations on the local, state, and national levels, Mrs. Blanchard has long been a member of the Fresno Teachers Association (FTA), the California Teachers Association (CTA), and the National Education Association. She was president of the FTA from 1949 to 1951 and of the central section of CTA in 1951-52. In 1957-58 she was president and chairman of the conference committee of the Fresno City Elementary Administrators Association, and she has served as second vice-president (1959-60) and first vice-president (1960-61) of the central section of the California Elementary School Administrators Association.

Since 1954 Mrs. Blanchard has been on the NEA relations commission of the CTA, serving as its chairman from 1958 to 1960, and has attended the annual NEA conventions as a member of the California delegation. She has been a director of the NEA since 1955. In July 1961, at the NEA convention in Atlantic City, New Jersey, Mrs. Blanchard was elected first vice-president and president-elect of the NEA for 1961-62. She succeeded Ewald Turner as president of the association for a one-year term at the NEA's 100th annual convention in Denver, Colorado in July 1962, becoming the first NEA president from California since 1923.

Founded in 1857, the NEA is an organization of elementary and secondary school teachers, principals and administrators, college and university professors, counselors, and others interested in American education. It has 813,000 members. Every facet of educational activity is encompassed by its many departments and committees, and it is affiliated with other groups in the field. The NEA lobbies in Washington, D.C. on education legislation, and it publishes many reports and books in education as well as the *NEA Journal,* the *Research Bulletin,* and the annual *Proceedings.*

Bradford Bachrach

HAZEL A. BLANCHARD

Among the issues discussed at the 1962 convention were how teachers should organize to obtain better employment conditions. NEA members favored "sanctions" and "professional negotiations" as opposed to strikes and collective bargaining, which are advocated by the 80,000-member American Federation of Teachers, an AFL-CIO affiliated teachers' union and an NEA rival. Already tested in California, the practice of applying sanctions to school districts with substandard employment conditions involves making criticism of the district public and, if necessary, advising teachers not to take jobs there. Most NEA members strongly oppose unionization, which they feel is not appropriate to teachers' professional status. In October 1962 Mrs. Blanchard, speaking at a reception given in her honor by the D.C. Council of Administrative Women in Education, declared that teachers should not become part of the labor movement. Labor leaders cannot speak for teachers, she said, "because our commitment is to the total society. To remain independent we must work with all aspects of the whole community."

As the NEA theme for 1962-63 Mrs. Blanchard chose "A Great Profession—Ours by Choice." In an article in the *NEA Journal* (September 1962), she wrote, "Our professional history records constant advance in the teacher's concepts, aspirations, achievements, competence, and status. We have become professionals. In fact, I believe we have chosen a great profession—a profession which is well on its way to achieving its proper place of pre-eminence among all professions." Mrs. Blanchard took a leave of absence for 1962-63 from Rowell Elementary School in order to carry out her official duties. During this year, "booked for more one-night stands than Bob Hope," she traveled about 125,000 miles, visited hundreds of schools, and addressed about 140 audiences in different cities.

(Continued next page)

BLANCHARD, HAZEL A.—*Continued*

Mrs. Blanchard is an honorary life member of the National Congress of Parents and Teachers. She also belongs to the Soroptimists, the Order of the Eastern Star, Alpha Alpha Iota, and Delta Kappa Gamma. The fall 1962 issue of the *Delta Kappa Gamma Bulletin* carried her report on the World Confederation of the Teaching Profession (WCOTP), which she attended in Stockholm, Sweden in August 1962.

Hazel A. Blanchard has blond hair and brown eyes, stands five feet eight inches tall, and weighs 145 pounds. She is a Republican and a Protestant. Her favorite recreations are playing tennis and going to light opera productions. She and her daughter, Pamela Ann Blanchard, live with her mother, Mrs. Hazel Gonser, in Fresno. They are all kept so busy with various activities that they "almost need to make appointments to see each other."

References

California Teachers Association J 57:12+ F '61 pors
Washington (D.C.) Post B p4 Jl 9 '62
Who's Who of American Women (1961-62)

BOHR, NIELS (HENRIK DAVID) Oct. 7, 1885-Nov. 18, 1962 Danish physicist; developed in 1913 the theory of atomic structure that laid the groundwork for modern nuclear physics and the atom bomb; was awarded the Nobel Prize in Physics in 1922. See *Current Biography* (September) 1945.

Obituary

N Y Times p1+ N 19 '62

BOLT, ROBERT (OXTON) Aug. 15, 1924- British writer
Address: Home Farm House, Pylewell, Lymington, Hampshire, England

Less experimental than many of his contemporaries in the so-called "New Wave" of British dramatists, Robert Bolt has been called an "old-style professional," and a master of the "well-made" play. His first success, *Flowering Cherry*, won a London *Evening Standard* award in 1957 as the most promising play of the season, and a later play, *A Man for All Seasons*, won awards from the New York Drama Critics Circle and the American Theatre Wing in 1962. A former teacher, Bolt is one of several young English playwrights who came to the legitimate theater from an apprenticeship in radio and television. Recently he turned to another medium, motion pictures, and his first screenplay, *Lawrence of Arabia*, won a British Film Academy award and a nomination for a 1963 Oscar award of the Academy of Motion Picture Arts and Sciences.

Robert Oxton Bolt was born on August 15, 1924 in Sale, near Manchester, England to Leah (Binnion) Bolt and Ralph Bolt, a shopkeeper who dealt in furniture, glass, and china. He has an older brother, Sydney, who is a lecturer at a technical school in Cambridge. Reared in what

he recently described as an atmosphere of "Northern Nonconformity," Bolt had a "typical petit-bourgeois childhood." Small businessmen like his father had rough going during the Depression, and there was "never any question of foreign holidays or domestic servants." But there was, Bolt recalls, "much emphasis on education, social responsibility, progressive politics; a good deal of Chapel and Sunday School in early years . . . the "Manchester Guardian" and no alcohol . . . all much better fun than it sounds because of the vigour and seriousness."

In 1940 Bolt graduated from the Manchester Grammar School. Never very gregarious, he limited his extracurricular activities to joining the Boy Scouts. In 1941 he became an office boy for the Sun Assurance Company in Manchester, where he ran errands, stoked the boiler, and filed letters. He "hated it as death" and escaped in 1942 when he "scraped" into Manchester University. A year later he was inducted into the Royal Air Force, but, having failed the course in pilot training, he was transferred to the army. Bolt served for a time on the Gold Coast (now Ghana) with the West African Frontier Force. Released in 1946 with the rank of lieutenant, he resumed his studies at Manchester University and became chairman of its Socialist Society. After graduating in 1949 with an honors degree in history he went on to Exeter University College for his teaching diploma, which he received in 1950.

For the next eight years Bolt was a teacher, first at a village school in Devon and then, from 1952 to 1958, at the progressive Millfield School in Street, Somerset, where he taught English. Meanwhile, he began to write plays for the radio, a valuable outlet and training ground for young playwrights in England, where the British Broadcasting Corporation produces some 500 new plays each year. Bolt said recently that he turned to writing because he couldn't "do anything else well enough to earn a living by it." "Always had the gift of the gab," he added, "and a weakness for telling tall stories plus moral preoccupations beyond my moral reach; hence, a writer. But all this is hindsight; it just happened."

Between 1953 and 1958 the BBC broadcast eight of his plays for adults and seven for children. Most of the latter were concerned with the activities of Sir Oblong Fitz-Oblong, an unwilling and not very bright knight who struggles against dragons and wicked barons. Bolt's first radio play, broadcast on February 15, 1953, was *The Master*, about the wandering scholars of the Middle Ages. It was followed in the same year by *Fifty Pigs* and then, in July 1954, by *A Man for All Seasons*, an early version of Bolt's successful stage play about Sir Thomas More. The radio version of *A Man for All Seasons*, which resembled the stage script only in story line, contained few of the dramatic devices that critics who later reviewed the stage production assumed to have been derived from the radio play. The much-praised "common man," who in the final version acts as narrator, chorus, and scene-shifter, does not appear at all in the radio script. The early version of *A Man for All Seasons* was adapted by Bolt for BBC television in January 1957.

Another of Bolt's dramas, *Ladies and Gentlemen*, was also broadcast in 1954, and two more of his radio plays followed in 1955: *The Last of the Wine* and *Mr. Sampson's Sundays*. In 1956 he wrote *The Window* and in 1958, *The Drunken Sailor*, which the author has described as "an attempt to bring together the lyricism and brutality in the life of an eighteenth-century seaman in the British navy." In 1957 he had concentrated on the writing of children's plays.

By 1958 Bolt had already made his mark in the legitimate theater. His first stage play, which was given the equivalent of an Off Broadway production in London by the Theatre in the Round, was an adaptation of the 1955 radio play *The Last of the Wine*, a stylized examination of society's helplessness in the face of the atomic threat. It was followed in 1957 by *The Critic and the Heart*, a more naturalistic play dealing with the sacrifices imposed by the dedicated artist on himself and on others.

Bolt's *Flowering Cherry* opened in London's West End on November 21, 1957 and became one of the critical and popular successes of the year. It concerned Jim Cherry, an insurance salesman possessed by a dream that he will one day return to the rural life of his childhood and plant an orchard, a fantasy that conceals his inability to cope with reality. When he is given a chance to realize the dream he rejects it. Hailed by London critics as a provocative, honest, and mature drama, it ran for 435 performances and won a London *Evening Standard* prize as the most promising play of the year. In New York, however, where it had a brief run in 1959, critics found that it lacked vitality and creativity. Bolt's next play was a hit on both sides of the Atlantic. This was *A Man for All Seasons*, which began a nine-month engagement in London in July 1960 and ran for a year and a half in New York beginning in November 1961.

The "man for all seasons" is Sir Thomas More, who was awarded that epithet by his contemporary Robert Whittinton. Under Henry VIII More was Lord Chancellor of England, but when Henry broke with Rome and placed himself at the head of an autonomous Church of England, More's loyalty to his king conflicted with his loyalty to his church. Because he refused his allegiance to the monarch, he was executed. Bolt's Sir Thomas is witty, moderate, and wise, but uncompromising in his convictions. A man of this world with no relish for martyrdom, he values life but is asked to pay too high a price for it.

In 1962 *A Man for All Seasons* won awards from the American Theatre Wing and the New York Drama Critics Circle. Typical of its critical reception was a review in the New York *Herald Tribune* (November 23, 1961) by Walter Kerr, who found the play "as remarkable in its restraint as in its ultimate fire. . . . What is colloquial falls on the ear with a humorous grace . . . and what is formal is so precisely, trenchantly phrased as to build a reservoir of suppressed power toward an eventual explosion of intelligence and emotion. . . . What Mr. Bolt has done is to make the human mind shine. The glare is dazzling; the experience exhilarating."

ROBERT BOLT

The next play of Bolt's to be produced (although it was written before *A Man for All Seasons*) was *The Tiger and the Horse*, which opened in London on August 24, 1960. Like Bolt's other work, it offered "substantial acting parts for substantial actors." Its title was taken from William Blake's "The tygers of wrath are wiser than the horses of instruction." Set in a great English university, it deals with the dilemma of Jack Dean, once a precociously brilliant astronomer, now a successful "horse of instruction"—Master of his college and Vice-Chancellor-elect. His daughter's fiancé, a student with passionate integrity, asks him to sign a "ban-the-bomb" petition. If he makes so rash a gesture, Dean will lose the Vice-Chancellorship; if he does not, he will lose himself. He signs the petition. In general the critics were cool toward the play, feeling that Dean's renunciation was out of character and that the play did not "hold water" emotionally.

In 1962 Bolt scored a notable success in another medium with his scenario for the motion picture *Lawrence of Arabia*. In the United States he was nominated for an Oscar award in the category of "best screenplay based on material from another medium," and the film won an Oscar as the best picture of 1962. The British Film Academy awarded Bolt a trophy for having written the best British screenplay, and the picture was voted "best film" and "best British film" of 1962. Bolt's scenario has been called "a sophisticated interpretation" of T. E. Lawrence's enigmatic personality. A *Christian Science Monitor* reviewer (December 20, 1962) wrote: "As Robert Bolt sees Lawrence . . . the desert was the instrument both for his fulfillment and his destruction. In the desert, the only deity Lawrence found was himself, and when, in all that emptiness, he discovered his mistake, he loathed himself with an intensity to match his self-adoration."

(Continued next page)

BOLT, ROBERT—*Continued*

In an article written for the London *Observer*, A. W. Lawrence, T. E. Lawrence's brother and literary executor, objected to the script on the grounds of inaccuracy and fictitiousness. Most commentators felt, however, that Bolt had been faithful to the spirit, if not to the letter, of Lawrence's career in Arabia, as recounted in his autobiographical *Seven Pillars of Wisdom*. Hollis Alpert, for example, wrote in the *Saturday Review* (December 29, 1962): "Dramatic necessity would seem to have required a good deal of coalescence, otherwise the film might have become a pageant-like documentary account, instead of the dramatic whole that it is."

Bolt has completed another play, *Gentle Jack*, as well as a screen adaptation of Boris Pasternak's *Doctor Zhivago*. He often contributes articles on political and theatrical subjects to magazines like *Esquire, Saturday Review*, the New York *Times Magazine*, and *Theatre Arts*. Three of his plays have been published in England by William Heinemann, Ltd.: *Flowering Cherry* (1958), *A Man for All Seasons* (1960), and *The Tiger and the Horse* (1961). *A Man for All Seasons* was published by Random House in the United States in 1962.

Although he came to prominence at a time of ferment and experiment in the British theater, Bolt has not so far been an innovator. In *The Angry Theatre* (1962), published in England as *Anger and After*, John Russell Taylor characterized him as "a good, traditional playwright." Bolt himself, speaking in March 1963 at Keele University in North Staffordshire, has expressed reservations about the Theater of the Absurd, which he said has "demolished the meaning of the question we try to ask." But, he added, the realistic drama was "played out." He would like to see the fictional element in drama increased—even to a point where characters wear masks. "As regards the 'renaissance in English theatre,'" he said recently, "I think almost everything remains to be done."

On November 6, 1948 Robert Bolt married Celia Anne Roberts, a painter. They have three children, Sally, Benedict, and Joanna. Bolt has blue eyes and brown hair, is five feet ten inches tall, and weighs 161 pounds. He enjoys talking, eating, walking, and sailing, but does not count reading or writing among his recreations, for he finds them both hard work. He is an honorary life member of the Spares Club, "a cricket and beer" fraternity in Somerset.

By political inclination Bolt is left-wing Labour, but he is not a member of the Labour party nor of any church. He is "passionately attached" to the British tradition of moderation and thinks that "the burning question is how to continue this, not react out of our present torpor into some form of extremism and violence." For this "torpor" he holds both Conservatives and Labour responsible, but considers Labour the more blameworthy "because Tories should be torpid, Labour shouldn't."

Bolt himself can hardly be characterized as torpid. A devoted member of the Campaign for Nuclear Disarmament, he has written articles and plays on the theme and in 1961 went to prison for his beliefs. Jailed during a demonstration, he could have secured his release at any time by promising to "keep the peace" thereafter. He remained in prison for two weeks, however, until Sam Spiegel, producer of *Lawrence of Arabia*, pointed out that by delaying work on the film he was causing hardship to others. *Time* magazine quoted Bolt as saying (January 25, 1963): "Much ink, perhaps some blood, will flow before we arrive at a genuinely modern and credible version of what a human person is. But I think any artist not in some way engaged upon that task might as well pack up and go home."

References

Who's Who, 1963
Who's Who in the Theatre (1961)

BOSCH, JUAN (bôsh hwän) June 30, 1909-
Former President of the Dominican Republic; writer

Address: Puerto Rico

When on December 20, 1962 the citizens of the Dominican Republic voted in the country's first free elections in thirty-eight years, they attempted to restore democracy to the Caribbean island republic by electing Juan Bosch to the Presidency. On September 25, 1963, however, Bosch's government was overthrown by a rightist military coup. A scholar and a writer who has published some fifteen books, Bosch spent twenty-four years in exile in Cuba and other Latin American countries during the dictatorship of the late Rafael Leónidas Trujillo. As a representative of the anti-Communist democratic left, Bosch was determined to raise the living standards of his poverty-stricken countrymen through extensive economic and social reforms. On the international scene Bosch as President maintained a policy of independence and of friendship with the United States.

A native of La Vega, a medium-sized town in the interior of the Dominican Republic, Juan Bosch was born on June 30, 1909 to lower middle-class parents. His father, José Bosch, was Spanish, and his mother, Angela (Gavioñ) Bosch, was Puerto Rican. The poverty that he saw around him made a deep impression on the boy, and he has recalled that at the age of six he was already thinking of ways in which he might help the poor peasants of his homeland. The desire to alleviate poverty remained with him as he matured. At college in Santo Domingo, the capital of the republic, Bosch studied literature. Before he went into exile, he had written three books: *Camino Real* (1933), a collection of short stories; *Indios* (1935), an anthology of Indian legends; and *La Mañosa* (1936), a novel dealing with a revolutionary theme.

Appalled by the massacre of some 15,000 Haitian squatters by Trujillo's order, Bosch left the Dominican Republic in 1937, and in the years that followed he traveled widely throughout Latin America while making Cuba his headquarters. In 1939 he helped to found the Partido Revolucionario Dominicano (PRD), a political party in exile, with a non-Communist leftist orientation. Eight years later he was one of the organizers of the abortive landing from the

Cuban Cayo Confites, one of several unsuccessful attempts to overthrow the Trujillo dictatorship.

During his twenty-four years in exile Bosch became associated with such democratic leaders as Governor Luis Muñoz Marín of Puerto Rico, President Rómulo Betancourt of Venezuela, former President José Figueres Ferrer of Costa Rica, and Victor Raúl Haya de la Torre of Peru. For a time he taught at the Institute of Political Science in Costa Rica, which was sponsored by José Figueres and which counts among its alumni a number of democratic trade union leaders. He also worked as a journalist and wrote several books, some of which were highly acclaimed by critics.

Bosch's writings during the period of his exile include *Mujeres en la vida de Hostos* (San Juan, 1938) and *Hostos, el sembrador* (Havana, 1939), which deal with the noted Dominican man of letters, Eugenio Maria de Hostos y Bonilla. *Dos pesos de agua* (Havana, 1941), *Ocho cuentos* (Havana, 1947), and *La muchacha de la Guaira* (Santiago, Chile, 1955) are collections of short stories. Bosch also wrote *Cuba, la isla fascinante* (Santiago, Chile, 1955); *Cuento de Navidad* (Santiago, Chile, 1956), a story about Christ; *Trujillo; causas de una tiranía sin ejemplo* (Caracas, 1959), an exposé of the Dominican dictatorship; and *Simón Bolívar* (Caracas, 1960), a scholarly biography of the liberator of Spanish America. Some of his books have been translated into English, French, Italian, and German.

For a time Bosch served as political adviser to Cuban President Carlos Prío Socarrás, who was overthrown by Fulgencio Batista in 1952. After a twelve-year stay in Cuba, Bosch fled when dictator Batista ordered his arrest for extradition to the Dominican Republic. He returned to Cuba in 1959, after Fidel Castro came into power, but he left again a year later because it appeared to him that Castro was betraying the original ideals of the revolution and was turning more and more toward international Communism.

On May 30, 1961 the Dominican dictator Trujillo, who had ruled the country for over thirty years, was assassinated. During the Presidency of his successor, Joaquín Balaguer, opposition parties began to come out into the open. On January 1, 1962 a seven-man provisional government, which aimed at effecting the transition from dictatorial rule to democracy, took control of the country. A few days later the Organization of American States lifted the economic sanctions on the Dominican Republic that were imposed in August 1960, and the United States resumed diplomatic relations, which had been suspended for seventeen months. Balaguer was subsequently compelled to resign, and, following a short-lived military coup, the presidency of the seven-member council was taken over by Rafael Bonnelly, who began preparing the country for democratic elections.

Meanwhile, in October 1961, Bosch returned to the Dominican Republic and started to build the PRD into a strong workers' and peasants' movement. Although he had been practically unknown in Dominican politics, he soon became a leading contender for the Presidency of the republic, in the first free elections that the country had experienced since 1924. With the slogan "land and dignity," Bosch campaigned in a "backslapping, handshaking" tour of the country,

Wide World

JUAN BOSCH

appealing to the peasants in the hinterlands, the city workers, and the intellectuals.

During the campaign Bosch promised jobs to the country's 300,000 unemployed and pledged to divide the lands formerly owned by the Trujillo family into sixteen-acre plots, to be distributed among the country's landless *campesinos*. He promised to build new schools, hospitals, and homes for the aged; to provide for improved housing, better transportation, and increased minimum wage levels; and to make such luxuries as television sets and electric refrigerators available to all. Bosch also declared his intention to transfer some private businesses to worker ownership; to work toward economic diversification, making the country less dependent upon its sugar crop; and to co-operate with the Organization of American States.

Although twenty-eight political parties had appeared in the Dominican Republic following the demise of the Trujillo dictatorship, their number was narrowed down to seven by the time of the elections. During the campaign four leftist factions quit the contest and threw their support behind Bosch's PRD. Among the five Presidential candidates Bosch's only serious rival was Dr. Viriato Fiallo, a longtime opponent of Trujillo, representing the moderately rightist Unión Civica Nacional (UCN). The United States government maintained an official neutrality between the two leading factions.

During the last week of the campaign Father Lautico Garcia, a Spanish Jesuit priest, charged in a newspaper article that some of Bosch's earlier writings indicated that he was a Marxist-Leninist. After failing in his efforts to obtain a thirty-day postponement of the elections to enable him to refute the charges, Bosch withdrew from the campaign and accused the UCN and the Catholic Church of using smear tactics against him. In a subsequent nationwide four-hour television debate Bosch compelled Garcia

BOSCH, JUAN—_Continued_

to retract the charges, and, two days before the elections, he dramatically announced that he would remain in the contest.

The elections, which took place on December 20, 1962, were witnessed by the Secretary-General of the Organization of American States, Dr. José A. Mora, and by a group of distinguished scholars and jurists from fifteen American countries, who had been invited by the Dominican government to participate in a Symposium on Representative Democracy. Although election eve was marked by disturbances on the part of supporters of Cuban Premier Fidel Castro, and there were rumors of a right-wing plot to assassinate Bosch, the elections proceeded in a relatively orderly manner.

Bosch received about 648,000 votes out of a total of over 1,000,000, winning a two-to-one victory over Fiallo. The PRD won twenty-two out of twenty-seven seats in the Senate and forty-eight seats in the seventy-four member Chamber of Deputies. (Fiallo's UCN received four seats in the Senate and twenty-one in the lower house.) Following the elections, President Bonnelly of the outgoing interim government declared that the result of the elections would provide "a firm base for democracy." A congratulatory telegram, sent by Fiallo to Bosch, was seen as an indication that democratic rule in the Dominican Republic would be permitted to proceed unhampered.

Shortly after the elections Bosch visited the United States, where he was received by President John F. Kennedy, Secretary of State Dean Rusk, and other officials, and obtained pledges for increased economic and technical aid under the Alliance for Progress program. "He is just the kind of man to make the Alliance for Progress a success in his country," one American official said of Bosch at the time of his visit. Later Bosch went on a one-month trip to Europe to negotiate economic agreements with West Germany and other countries.

On February 27, 1963 Bosch was formally inaugurated as President of the Dominican Republic. Vice-President Lyndon B. Johnson, representing the United States government at the ceremonies, promised American aid in the republic's "struggle for economic progress and social justice." In his inaugural speech Bosch declared his intention to defend the nation's newly won freedom and to promote the economic and social advancement of his people. While pledging to adhere to the inter-American system, he indicated that his government might follow an independent foreign policy similar to that of Brazil and Mexico.

The principal objective of Bosch's administration was to raise social and economic standards of the Dominican people through vigorous reforms. After the Trujillo landholdings had been divided, Bosch planned to expropriate additional property, but he said that this would be done in accordance with due process. He is a Roman Catholic who believes in the separation of church and state, and he maintained that the state must control the educational curriculum. Although he saw little immediate danger to his country from Castro's Cuba, he warned his people of the danger of a resurgence of dictatorship. "There is

which we have been suffering," he said in a speech on March 13, 1963. "There is only one clear dilemma: Communism or democracy. And Communism means death, war, destruction, and the loss of what we own."

The military chiefs of the Dominican Republic, however, describing the government as "corrupt and pro-Communist," ousted Bosch and his cabinet on September 25, 1963. Later exiled, the President went to Puerto Rico. Meanwhile, the leaders of the bloodless coup called together the heads of the rightist political parties to help form a provisional government.

Juan Bosch is a tall, strong-faced man, with white hair and blue eyes, and he is noted for his patience, determination, and oratorical skill. During the course of his fourteen-hour working day he usually sees at least forty persons. He speaks English with difficulty. Bosch met his wife, the former Carmen Quidiello, in Havana in 1941. She is a member of a prominent family of Santiago, Cuba and a playwright. They have a son, Patricio, who is a student at St. Joseph's Academy in South Bend, Indiana; and a daughter, Barbara.

References

Americas 15:14+ Mr '63 por
N Y Times p3 My 4 '63 por
Newsday p50 D 26 '62 por
Philadelphia Inquirer p2 D 24 '62 por
Toronto Globe and Mail p3 Ap 2 '63 por
Who's Who in Latin America Pt 7 (1951)

BRAQUE, GEORGES May 13, 1882-Aug. 31, 1963 French painter and decorator; associated with Fauvism and cubism (which he founded with Picasso) in the early twentieth century; credited with inventing the technique of collage. See _Current Biography_ (November) 1949.

Obituary

N Y Times p1+ S 1 '63

BREZHNEV, LEONID I(LYICH) (brĕzh'nĕf) Dec. 19, 1906- Chairman of the Presidium of the Supreme Soviet of the U.S.S.R.

Address: b. Verkhovny Sovet S.S.S.R., Barsenevskaya 2-20, Moscow, U.S.S.R.

The titular chief of state of the Soviet Union is Leonid I. Brezhnev, who replaced Marshal Kliment Y. Voroshilov as Chairman of the Presidium of the Supreme Soviet of the Union of Soviet Socialist Republics on May 7, 1960. A metallurgical engineer by profession and a member of the Communist party since 1931, Brezhnev has served in various party positions in the Ukraine, Moldavia, and Kazakhstan. He was a political commissar with the Red Army during World War II. He became an alternate member of the Presidium of the Central Committee of the Communist party in 1956 and a full member in 1957. Brezhnev is the fifth· Soviet chief of state since the Bolshevik Revolution of 1917.

Although the real power in the Soviet Union resides with the Premier and Chairman of the Communist party, Nikita S. Khrushchev, Brezh- no longer room for personal dictatorships from nev, as head of the thirty-two-member executive, formally represents the nation. Known abroad as the "President" of the Soviet Union, Brezhnev proclaims all laws and decrees, receives diplomats from foreign countries, and travels widely on official missions. A protégé and close political ally of Khrushchev, Brezhnev is regarded as a possible future successor to the Premiership of the Soviet Union.

Representing the generation that grew to maturity after the Revolution, Leonid Ilyich Brezhnev was born in Dneprodzerzhinsk in the Ukraine on December 19, 1906 into a steel worker's family. He began to work in 1921, at the age of fifteen, studying after working hours at a surveying and land-reclamation high school in Kursk, where he specialized in farm irrigation. He became a member of Komsomol (the Communist Youth League) in 1923.

After graduating from high school in 1927 Brezhnev worked for three years in the Urals, first as a surveyor, then as head of the district land department, as deputy chairman of the Bissert district soviet executive committee, and as assistant chief of the Ural Regional Land Administration. In 1931 he entered the Dneprodzerzhinsk Metallurgical Institute, and following his graduation in 1935 he went to work as an engineer at the Dzerzhinski iron and steel works.

At the time of Premier Joseph Stalin's great purge (1936-38) Brezhnev rose rapidly through the ranks of the Communist party of the Ukraine, and it was during this period that he first became associated with Nikita S. Khrushchev. In May 1937 Brezhnev was elected deputy chairman of the Dneprodzerzhinsk city soviet executive committee, and he subsequently became head of a department of the Dnepropetrovsk regional committee of the Ukrainian Communist party. In 1939 he was elected secretary of the regional committee, remaining in this position until the outbreak of World War II. During the war Brezhnev held various high political posts with the Soviet Army. In September 1943 he was appointed to serve as a colonel with the Eighteenth Army, which defended Novorossiysk. He was subsequently promoted to the rank of major general. In July 1944 he became chief of political administration of the Eighteenth Army, which formed part of the fourth Ukrainian front.

Returning to party work in the Ukraine after the war, Brezhnev was elected first secretary of the Zaporozhye regional committee in 1946. In the following year he was elected a deputy in the Ukrainian supreme soviet and was chosen a member of the central committee of the Ukrainian Communist party. He became first secretary of the Dnepropetrovsk regional committee in November 1947. From 1947 to 1949 he served under the direction of Khrushchev. Transferred to Moldavia in July 1950, Brezhnev became first secretary of the Moldavian Communist party central committee, and in the same year he was elected a deputy in the Supreme Soviet of the U.S.S.R. (the national legislative body). At the nineteenth congress of the Communist party of the Soviet Union, in October 1952, Brezhnev was a member of the credentials commission and was elected to the party's Central Committee.

LEONID I. BREZHNEV

Although the plenum of the Central Committee after the nineteenth congress elected him a secretary and an alternate member of its Presidium, Brezhnev suffered a temporary setback in prestige when he was dropped from the Presidium during the reorganization that followed Stalin's death in March 1953. For the next eleven months he served in the rank of lieutenant general as first deputy head of the central political administration of the Soviet armed forces, with special responsibility for supervising the navy. In February 1954 Brezhnev resumed his upward movement through the party ranks when he was appointed second secretary of the central committee in the Kazakhstan Communist party. He subsequently became a member of its bureau. He was again elected as a deputy of the U.S.S.R. Supreme Soviet in March 1954, and in the following month he became a member of its legislative proposals commission.

In March 1955 Brezhnev was elected a member of the Kazakhstan supreme soviet, and at its first session he was chosen a member of its presidium. From August 1955 to February 1956 he served as first secretary of the central committee of the Kazakhstan Communist party. In Kazakhstan Brezhnev took a leading part in putting into effect the virgin land campaign, instituted by Khrushchev in 1953 to cultivate new lands and reclaim wastelands for the purpose of obtaining an adequate grain supply. At the twentieth congress of the Communist party of the Soviet Union in February 1956 Brezhnev was a member of the commission for drafting resolutions, and he gave a speech on the economic situation in Kazakhstan. The congress elected him an alternate member of the Presidium of the party's Central Committee and one of its secretaries.

In April 1956 Brezhnev headed a party delegation to a congress of the North Korean workers' party, and in July 1956 he attended meetings with government delegations from North Korea and the German Democratic Republic in Mos-

BREZHNEV, LEONID I.—*Continued*

cow. In January 1957 he was present at negotiations between Communist party delegates of Czechoslovakia and the Soviet Union. With the reorganization of the party ranks after the defeat of an "anti-party" group (which had opposed the concentration of power in Khrushchev's hands and his policy of partial de-Stalinization), a plenum of the party's Central Committee elected Brezhnev a full member of its Presidium in July 1957.

Chosen as the keynote speaker at a celebration on April 22, 1959, marking the eighty-ninth anniversary of Lenin's birth, Brezhnev said that the Soviet example had helped to inspire the revolutions in Iraq and Cuba, and he predicted "new great victories of Communism." As a member of the Presidium Brezhnev organized a number of shakeups in lower party ranks, and in January 1960 he presided over the removal of Nicolai Belyaev from his post as first secretary in Kazakhstan. In March 1960 Brezhnev made his first trip beyond the Iron Curtain when he headed the Soviet delegation to the Finnish Communist party congress.

A new shakeup in the Communist party Secretariat early in May 1960 resulted in the reduction of the number of party secretaries from ten to six. Observers viewed the retention of Brezhnev in the Secretariat as an indication of an active role for him. On May 7, 1960 Marshal Kliment Y. Voroshilov, who in the past had been one of Stalin's strongest supporters, resigned as Chairman of the Presidium of the Supreme Soviet of the U.S.S.R. on the basis of ill health, and Brezhnev was appointed in his place. In his acceptance speech Brezhnev expressed thanks to the Supreme Soviet "for this great honor which shows great confidence in me," and said, "I think this honor and confidence is attributed to our glorious Communist party and Central Committee which, directed by the great successor to Lenin, Nikita S. Khrushchev, is leading our people to the victory of Communism."

In July 1960 Brezhnev voluntarily gave up his position as a secretary in the party's Central Committee, because the burden of his chairmanship of the Presidium of the Supreme Soviet made it impossible to carry out both jobs. He was host to Communist representatives from eighty-one nations meeting in Moscow on the forty-third anniversary of the Bolshevik Revolution in November 1960. The meeting resulted in the adoption of a new Communist party manifesto, representing a compromise between the policies of Communist China and the Soviet Union. In February 1961 Brezhnev visited Morocco, where he conferred with King Mohammed V and offered him extensive aid for economic and industrial development. (While Brezhnev was on his way to Rabat, Morocco, the plane carrying him strayed off course and was fired upon by French fighter planes. The incident led to considerable friction between France and the Soviet Union.) Subsequently Brezhnev also visited Ghana, Hungary, and Guinea. (The Order of the Guinean Republic has designated him "Fighter for Independence.")

Speaking at a friendship rally at the Kremlin on June 10, 1961, Brezhnev referred to the just completed talks between Khrushchev and the United States President John F. Kennedy as "encouraging," and expressed support for Indonesian claims on Dutch New Guinea. At a reception held later that day he was presented with the Indonesian Silver Star (first class) by visiting President Achmed Sukarno. In the following month, at a Soviet-Ghanaian friendship meeting in Moscow, Brezhnev supported a proposal by the Ghanaian President, Kwame Nkrumah, to make Africa a zone free of nuclear arms and foreign military bases. At that time he told the Ghanaian delegation that he sympathized with Tunisia in its efforts to oust the French military base at Bizerte. In September 1961 Brezhnev made a nine-day state visit to Finland.

At the twenty-second Communist party congress in Moscow in October 1961 Brezhnev supported Khrushchev against the Chinese Communists by voicing "anxiety and alarm" over the militant policies of Albania's Communist leadership. In November 1961 Brezhnev made a state visit to Sudan and pledged financial and technical aid to that country. Visiting India a month later, he was greeted by Prime Minister Jawaharlal Nehru and a crowd of some 2,000 at the New Delhi airport. The visit coincided with India's invasion of Portuguese Goa, which Brezhnev described as "a great victory of the Indian people over colonialism." On April 24, 1962 the Supreme Soviet re-elected Brezhnev as Chairman of the Presidium by acclamation.

Brezhnev's ten-day state visit to Yugoslavia, beginning on September 24, 1962, was viewed in Moscow and Belgrade as a major step in strengthening fraternal ties between the two nations. At that time the Chinese Communists and their Albanian allies launched vigorous attacks on Tito for what they termed revisionist policies. On his visit Brezhnev praised the Yugoslav government for what he described as its sound foreign policy and its progress toward Socialism and pledged Soviet aid to Yugoslavia in her efforts to "consolidate her Socialist position." On the other hand, he startled Yugoslavs by launching a vigorous attack against what he termed American "militarism" and West German "fascism," and by criticizing the European Common Market as an economic base for predatory imperialism. He presented the Berlin affair as a major crisis and described United States policy toward Cuba as a possible cause of war. His statements were interpreted as efforts to align Yugoslavia more closely with Soviet foreign policy.

A "stocky, bush-browed bureaucrat," Leonid I. Brezhnev is a dynamic speaker and an able politician with a forceful and commanding personality, although one American reporter described him as representing "the new Soviet breed of colorless Communist party managers and industrial technocrats" (New York *Herald Tribune*, May 8, 1960). His portrait is widely displayed in Russian homes, and he is a highly esteemed and personable figure in party circles. The fact that he and other Ukrainians have risen to high rank in the party and the government is seen as an indication of the growing importance of the Ukraine in Soviet affairs. He is married and has a daughter, Galina, who accompanied him on his Yugoslavian trip. Brezhnev has received a number of decorations, including two Orders of Lenin, two Orders of the Red Banner, the Order of the Red Star, the Order of Bogdan Khmelnitsky (second class), and the Order of the Patriotic War (first class).

References

N Y Times p1+ My 8 '60 por
Washington (D.C.) Post A p6 My 8 '60 por
Biographic Directory of the USSR (1958)
Everyman's Concise Encyclopedia of Russia (1961)
International Who's Who, 1962-63
McGraw-Hill Encyclopedia of Russia and the Soviet Union (1961)
Who's Who, 1962
Who's Who in Soviet Social Sciences, Humanities, Art, and Government (1961)
Who's Who in the USSR, 1961-62

BRIGHAM, CLARENCE S(AUNDERS) Aug. 5, 1877-Aug. 13, 1963 Director (1930-63) and president (1955-63) of the American Antiquarian Society; compiler of more than thirty bibliographies, including *History and Bibliography of American Newspapers, 1690-1820* (1947). See *Current Biography* (July) 1959.

Obituary

N Y Times p33 Ag 14 '63

BRODE, MILDRED H(OOKER) (brōd) Apr. 14, 1900- Librarian; organization official
Address: David Taylor Model Basin, Washington 7, D.C.; h. 4607 Connecticut Ave., N.W., Washington 8, D.C.

The president of the Special Libraries Association for 1963-64, succeeding Ethel S. Klahre, is Mildred H. Brode, who has been chief librarian of the David Taylor Model Basin in Washington, D.C. since 1944. Mrs. Brode, who took office on June 11, 1963, at the fifty-third annual convention of the SLA, in Denver, has been interested in the theory and bibliography of science since her college days, and she brings an impressive background in mathematics and physics to her career in librarianship. As president of SLA, she heads an association of about 5,900 special librarians in business, industry, scientific societies, educational and technical institutions, communications media, and other organizations concerned with specialized research and information.

Mildred Hooker Brode was born in Greensboro, Vermont on April 14, 1900 to Alfred Curtis Hooker, the town's postmaster, and Mary Agnes (Lupien) Hooker. Her father was also a building contractor and her mother was a piano teacher. At Hardwick Academy in Hardwick, Vermont, from which she graduated in 1917, Mrs. Brode played on the girls' basketball team and acted in the school dramatic society. During World War I she served for two summers, from May through September, in the Women's Land Army

MILDRED H. BRODE

of America. Her unit was stationed at Scott Farm in Brattleboro, Vermont, which was owned by a Mr. Henderson, and which comprised ten farms that surrounded "Naulauka," the estate on which Rudyard Kipling lived when he was in the United States.

A high school scholarship enabled her to go on to the University of Vermont for the academic year of 1917-18, and senatorial scholarships helped to support her there from 1918 through 1920. At the university she was again active on the women's basketball team and in the dramatic club, and she belonged to Alpha Xi Delta, a social sorority, the literary club, and the YWCA. In 1921 she graduated from the University of Vermont with the Ph.B. degree, having majored in mathematics.

For her postgraduate work Mrs. Brode attended George Washington University in the nation's capital, from 1921 to 1926, where she studied mathematics, physics, and German. During these years she served as an assistant in the university's physics laboratory and worked as an assistant physicist at the National Bureau of Standards. There, in the bureau's radium section, her research was concerned with problems of radioactivity, atomic structure, and X-rays.

For further postgraduate work Mrs. Brode enrolled at the Ohio State University and received her M.Sc. degree in physics in 1931 after submitting a thesis called "Spectra of the Alkali Earth Sub-halides with Special Attention to the Incidence of Isotopes." In 1933 she obtained a B.S. degree in education from Ohio State. During her years of postgraduate study at George Washington University and Ohio State, Mrs. Brode had become interested in the theory and bibliography of science. This led her to attend the Columbia University School of Library Service, which granted her a B.S. in L.S. in 1938. Two years earlier, in 1936, she had been a member of the Harvard-Massachusetts Institute of Tech-

BRODE, MILDRED H.—*Continued*

nology solar eclipse expedition that went to the Soviet Union.

In 1938-39 Mrs. Brode was supervisor of a spectroscopy project at the Massachusetts Institute of Technology. The project resulted in the publication of *Wavelength Tables* (Wiley, 1939), edited by Dr. George R. Harrison, which has become a standard reference work in spectroscopy. In September 1939 Mrs. Brode became a cataloger of scientific and technical books for the Baker Library of Dartmouth College. In this, her first library position, she also cataloged materials in anthropology for the library's important special collection devoted to the American Indian. (Dartmouth College had originally been founded as a school for the Indians.)

After one year as a cataloger, Mrs. Brode became the first woman member of the Baker Library's reference department, and in 1942 she became its head. From 1942 to November 1944 she was concurrently a full-time instructor in physics in the V-12 Navy Officer Training Program, the largest V-12 unit in the United States, and part-time director of the reference department. She was the second woman to teach on the faculty of Dartmouth College; the first had taught Russian during World War I. Recently Mrs. Brode remarked, "It takes a war to permit a woman to invade this stronghold of masculinity!"

In November 1944 Mrs. Brode became chief librarian of the David Taylor Model Basin in Washington, D.C., where she has remained. On MacArthur Boulevard at Carderock, Maryland, on the north side of the Potomac River, the David Taylor Model Basin is located about twelve miles northwest of the Capitol. Authorized by Congress in 1936 and dedicated in 1939, the David Taylor Model Basin provides a facility for the United States Navy and other government and private shipbuilders to test their new ship designs by the use of scale models. The largest research laboratory of its kind, the David Taylor Model Basin includes among its research facilities towing basins, maneuvering and seakeeping basins, circulating-water channels, high-pressure tanks for testing, wind tunnels, and machine, woodworking, and wax-molding shops where models are made and prepared for testing. Research programs are carried out in four laboratories: hydromechanics, structural mechanics, aerodynamics, and applied mathematics.

As the first professional librarian at the David Taylor Model Basin, Mrs. Brode started by bringing together the various collections of books scattered in offices around the Model Basin. From this nucleus she developed a working library to meet research needs. The collection now integrates test data and ship and model plans with reports of government agencies and industrial and university contractors throughout the United States. Mrs. Brode has paid tribute to the late Captain Harold E. Saunders, the designer and director of the Model Basin and author, who inspired her to "build the best possible library and bibliographical services for a research and development laboratory."

The library has reputedly the most complete collection of material dealing with the hydro-

dynamics of ship design, aerodynamics of aircraft design, model testing, and all supporting and related projects. Its present collection numbers over 300,000 plans, 20,000 test folders, 15,000 books, and 125,000 reports and documents, in addition to bound periodicals. It subscribes to 400 journals. The main, classified, and aerodynamics laboratory facilities have a total staff of fifteen persons.

The applied mathematics laboratory at the David Taylor Model Basin has digital and analog computers of an advanced design. These machines serve the research requirements of the Bureau of Ships, and also solve logistic and operational problems for the entire Department of Defense. In co-operation with the staff of the applied mathematics laboratory, Mrs. Brode is establishing a system of automatic information retrieval, working in conjunction with the Bureau of Ships library.

In 1938 Mrs. Brode joined the Special Libraries Association and became active in its Washington, D.C. chapter, the second largest in the United States. She served as chairman of the Washington science-technology group in 1951-52, as treasurer from 1952 to 1955, and as first vice-president and program chairman in 1955. From 1955 to 1957 she was president of the group. She is also a member of the metals division and served on the convention liaison committee in 1961-62. For six years she has been a member of the chapters executive board. Mrs. Brode also belongs to the documentation and military librarians division of the Special Libraries Association. On the national level she was second vice-president and chairman of the convention advisory committee in 1956-57. Elected first vice-president and president-elect in 1962, Mrs. Brode was installed as president of the SLA on June 11, 1963, during its fifty-third annual convention, in Denver.

Mrs. Brode firmly believes in the advantages of having a subject specialist in charge of a special library or information center, with the background knowledge to understand the problems of the research worker and with the ability to index and catalog technical materials accurately. She is also of the opinion that "the special librarian has a unique opportunity and also responsibility in helping the research man to solve his problems of communication and information needs."

As for the function of the Special Libraries Association that she now heads, she feels that it should co-operate with government agencies, scientific and technical societies, and all other organizations interested in the solution of information problems. According to Mrs. Brode, each of the many new tools of mechanized information retrieval available today should be investigated so that it can be correctly applied to meet the needs of a given situation. The Special Libraries Association, she believes, should provide standard criteria for special libraries and should establish educational requirements for special library staffs. She also points out that continuing education should be provided for information workers so that they can become better equipped to meet the needs of library users.

Mrs. Brode helped to organize a council of chief librarians of the East Coast Navy laboratories, established under the sponsorship of the council of chief scientists of these laboratories. This organization exchanges information on research and information procedures and co-operates in solving mutual problems during its two-day meetings, held each year in the spring and fall. Mrs. Brode wrote the charter for the organization and has served as its chairman and host.

Among the papers that Mrs. Brode has prepared for professional meetings were two that she delivered at workshops for military librarians. One dealt with standards for military libraries; the other discussed regulations and procedures for taking inventory in military libraries. She compiles an annotated bibliography on photography for the *British Journal of Photography,* and she has been a joint translator of Russian technical articles.

In addition to belonging to the Special Libraries Association, Mrs. Brode is a member of the American Library Association, the District of Columbia Library Association, the American Documentation Institute, the American Association for the Advancement of Science, and the Business and Professional Women's Club. Her recreations are foreign travel and a "spectator interest" in the performing and visual arts. She occasionally does watercolor painting.

Mildred Hooker Brode is five feet eight inches in height, has hazel eyes and gray hair, and weighs 160 pounds. On October 1, 1926 she was married to Dr. Wallace R. Brode; the marriage ended in divorce in 1937. Her religious affiliation is with the Congregational Church; her political affiliation is with the Republican party.

References

> Special Lib 53:313 Jl-Ag '62 por; 54:321 Jl-Ag '63 por
> Who's Who in Library Service (1955)
> Who's Who of American Women, 1963-64

BROOKE, ALAN (FRANCIS), 1ST VISCOUNT ALANBROOKE July 23, 1883-June 17, 1963 British army officer; chief of the Imperial General Staff (1941-46); during World War II was Winston Churchill's principal strategic adviser; created a viscount in 1946. See *Current Biography* (January) 1941.

Obituary

> N Y Times p37 Je 18 '63

BROOKS, VAN WYCK Feb. 16, 1886-May 2, 1963 Critic and writer of literary history and biography; best known for his five-volume series, "Makers and Finders: A History of the Writer in America, 1800-1915," of which the first book, *The Flowering of New England, 1815-1865* won the Pulitzer Prize for history in 1937. See *Current Biography* (September) 1960.

Obituary

> N Y Times p31 My 3 '63

BROWN, GEORGE (ALFRED) Sept. 2, 1914-
British politician
Address: b. House of Commons, London, S.W. 1, England; h. 77 Court Lane, London, S.E. 22, England

Since November 1960, when he succeeded the late Aneurin Bevan, George Brown has been deputy leader and vice-chairman of the British Labour party. A former trade union official, he is a prominent, if sometimes controversial, member of his party's powerful union element and of Labour's right wing. Brown held office in both postwar Labour governments, as joint parliamentary secretary to the Ministry of Agriculture and Fisheries and then as Minister of Works. Since Labour went out of office in 1951, he has been Opposition spokesman on agriculture, home affairs, and defense, on which he is regarded as one of Parliament's experts. Until recently he served as chairman of the Labour party's organization subcommittee and did much to increase the efficiency and power of the party machine. Some political observers believe that Brown may become Foreign Secretary or Chancellor of the Exchequer if the Labour party should win the next election.

George Alfred Brown was born on September 2, 1914 at 22 Peabody Buildings, Duke Street, Southwark, London. His father, also George Brown, was a truck driver and union man who rose to a position on the executive council of the Transport and General Workers' Union. The younger Brown had his political baptism at the age of eight when, during the 1922 Parliamentary elections, he distributed handbills for George Isaacs, Labour candidate for Gravesend, Kent. Years later he served as Isaacs' Parliamentary private secretary when the latter was Minister of Labour.

At the age of fifteen, without having finished his secondary education, George Alfred Brown left school and went to work as a junior clerk in London's financial district. He continued his education at evening classes organized by such groups as the Workers' Educational Association. In April 1931 he joined the John Lewis Partnership Ltd., a department store chain, for which he worked as a fur salesman until May 1936. Meanwhile, his interest in politics continued unabated. At the age of eighteen he became vice-chairman of the Streatham (London) Labour party and a national committee member of the Labour League of Youth.

Leaving the John Lewis Partnership in 1936, Brown took a job as full-time organizer for the Transport and General Workers' Union, a position he held for eight years. As a trade union official he was automatically exempted from service with the armed forces during World War II. He made his contribution to the war effort as a member of the Hertfordshire war agricultural executive committee and of the Hertfordshire agricultural wages board.

In the general election of 1945 Brown was sponsored by his union as a Labour candidate for the Derbyshire constituency of Belper. He was successful and has been Member of Parliament for Belper ever since. From 1945 to 1947 he served as a Parliamentary private secretary,

GEORGE BROWN

first to George Isaacs, Minister of Labour and National Service, and then, briefly, to Hugh Dalton, Chancellor of the Exchequer. In October 1947 he achieved junior ministerial rank, when he was appointed joint Parliamentary secretary to the Ministry of Agriculture and Fisheries.

When Brown entered the House of Commons in 1945 he was already a fervent admirer of Ernest Bevin, and during his early years in Parliament he tried to organize a backbench movement that would make Bevin Prime Minister, replacing Clement Attlee. The attempt, resisted by Bevin himself, was unsuccessful. Attlee apparently bore Brown no grudge, however, for in April 1951 he took him into his cabinet as Minister of Works. At the same time Brown was made a member of the Privy Council. His tenure as Minister of Works was brief, for the Labour government fell in October 1951. Brown continued to live up to his reputation as a fearless and outspoken member of that large group of Labour M.P.'s who had the backing of trade unions, and he became chairman of the group in 1954.

In June 1955 Brown was elected to the Parliamentary Committee of the Labour party, the "shadow cabinet" whose members are principal spokesmen for the Opposition in their own fields and normally make up the cabinet when their party returns to power. Brown's first role was as Labour spokesman on agriculture. In 1956 he was appointed Opposition spokesman on defense and in 1961, on home affairs. Meanwhile, George Brown's reputation was growing. In May 1956 he created a furore by arguing fiercely with Nikita S. Khrushchev at a private dinner arranged by Labour leaders. In a long and provocative attack on British policy, Khrushchev claimed that Britain had sought in 1941 to "throw the Nazis at Russia's throat." Brown interjected: "God forgive you!" The argument followed, creating a storm

of controversy within the Labour party and the country at large.

Two years later, Brown's stubborn refusal to go against his principles brought him once more into disfavor with some elements in his party. In July 1958 the Conservative government sent British troops into Jordan to support the threatened regime of King Hussein. The Labour Opposition voted condemnation of this action, but Brown abstained because he did not want it to be thought that a future Labour government might fail to honor Britain's obligations to an ally. Brown offered to resign from the Parliamentary Committee, but was persuaded to remain, and since then he has been re-elected annually except in 1958-59.

Brown again incurred some disapproval within his party in 1961-62, when Labour's reservations about British entry into the European Common Market hardened into opposition. Brown himself had favored entry and he never firmly adopted that party line. (In 1963 he announced that if Labour came to power it would seek Britain's entry into the Common Market.) Despite these differences of opinion Brown has in general promoted unity within his party. Throughout the 1950's, when it seemed hopelessly divided, he worked tirelessly to bring various factions together. He was one of the staunchest supporters of Hugh Gaitskell, who became party leader in 1955 and stood with him against massive opposition when Gaitskell fought those who would have committed Labour to unilateral disarmament and widespread nationalization. In November 1960 George Brown was elected deputy leader of the Parliamentary Labour party, succeeding the late Aneurin Bevan.

George Brown has been Labour's deputy leader ever since. Harold Wilson's attempt to wrest the post from him in November 1962 was unsuccessful, and Brown carried the election, 133 votes to 103. With his help, Hugh Gaitskell won his struggle to restore unity to the party. At the same time, as chairman of Labour's organization subcommittee, Brown steadily built up the power and efficiency of the central party machine. In May 1962 Richard C. Wald described him in the New York *Herald Tribune* (May 29, 1962) as "the real power behind the office staff at Transport House, where the machinery of the Labor party is kept oiled," and as "the guiding hand at the recent elections which added more than 500 local government seats to the Labor total."

Hugh Gaitskell died in January 1963, and Brown ran against Harold Wilson and James Callaghan for leadership of the party. Callaghan was eliminated at the first ballot and Wilson won at the second ballot, 144 votes to Brown's 103. Brown continues as deputy leader but, at his own request, has been relieved of his organization subcommittee chairmanship. In March 1963 he accepted the important but less demanding post of chairman of the home policy subcommittee.

Although he now has no specific departmental responsibility in the "shadow cabinet," as deputy leader Brown is in a position to speak for his party on any subject, and he recently did so on economic matters and the need for reform in the House of Lords. He will no doubt continue to be interested in defense, on which he is regarded as one of Parliament's foremost authorities. As early as 1960 he warned that the Conservative government's commitment to the American Skybolt missile was a mistake, and he was vindicated in 1962, when President John F. Kennedy told Prime Minister Harold Macmillan at Nassau that the Skybolt was to be scrapped. In 1963, stating his party's position on several issues, Brown declared that if Labour gained power all efforts to maintain an independent nuclear force would be abandoned. The current advance in technology, he said, would make it impossible for Great Britain to keep up. He added, however, that Great Britain and other NATO nations should strengthen their contribution to conventional forces.

George Brown's Parliamentary interests include education, mining, and overseas affairs as well as agriculture and defense. He has served on the Loveday higher education committee, on the National Youth Advisory Council, and as a governor of Repton School. He represents a constituency in which mining plays an important part, and he made his maiden speech in the House of Commons during a debate on the Coal Bill. He then served on the standing committee that considered the bill. He has also been a member of Labour committees on agriculture and foreign affairs.

In 1952 Brown visited nearly all of the Middle East, and he returned to the region in the Parliamentary winter recess of 1958-59 and in January 1961. During the 1950's he toured Kenya, made a private visit to Spain, and was a member of Parliamentary delegations to Poland, the Netherlands, and Germany. In 1957, at the invitation of the State Department, he visited the United States, where he met politicians and trade union leaders and made an 8,000-mile tour. He visited the United States again in 1963. From 1951 to 1953 and again in 1960, he was a British representative to the Council of Europe's consultative assembly at Strasbourg. Since 1960, as vice-chairman of the defence committee and a member of the executive committee of the Western European Union, he has attended meetings of the union in Washington.

A frequent contributor to magazines and newspapers on political subjects, Brown has been since 1953 industrial adviser to the London *Daily Mirror*. Because of the newspaper's ambivalent editorial policy toward the Labour party and Hugh Gaitskell, this fact caused Brown some political embarrassment when it became known in 1962. But, characteristically, he refused to relinquish the post. As an orator, Brown has been described as "unassuming," but he by no means lacks humor, as he demonstrated on February 12, 1963 with a much-quoted summary of the Conservative government's recent record in foreign affairs. Great Britain had received, he said, a "slap in the face in Paris, the order of the boot in Brussels, and a kick in the Bahamas."

George Brown is married to the former Sophie Levine, whom he met when they were both members of the Labour League of Youth. They have two daughters. The many profiles of Brown that appeared in February 1963, when he was a candidate for leadership of his party, all used the same kind of terms in describing him. He is "a blunt, rough, straightforward, emotional Englishman," said one. He has "a tough, warm-hearted, and certainly likeable personality [and] a foghorn voice," said another. The *Toronto Globe and Mail* (February 7, 1963) carried this assessment: "His patriotism and hatred of injustice, privilege and snobbery are instinctive and formidable. He can be hot-tempered—though his rages seldom last—and erratic in his preliminary judgements, though his instincts and decisions often derive from the rocklike common sense that made [Ernest] Bevin one of Britain's strongest and most successful Foreign Secretaries. Above all, perhaps, he has the courage of his—sometimes erroneous—convictions."

References

New Statesman 64:395 S 28 '62 por
Toronto Globe and Mail p7 F 7 '63 por
International Who's Who, 1962-63
Who's Who, 1963

BRUMEL, VALERI Apr. 14, 1942- High jumper
Address: b. c/o Physical Culture Institute, Moscow, U.S.S.R.

Few athletes within recent years have so dominated one aspect of track and field as has Valeri Brumel, the Russian high jumper. Brumel first appeared on the international scene in August 1960 when he placed second in the high jump in the summer Olympics at Rome. Since then he has been toppling records to the point where his world high jump record stands at an almost incredible 7 feet 5¾ inches.

Until Brumel came along to challenge him, John Thomas, the American high jumper, had held the world high jump record of 7 feet 3¾ inches, but he suffered successive defeats in competition with Brumel when the Russian journeyed to the United States in the winter of 1961 for the American indoor season. Not until February 9, 1963 at the Los Angeles Indoor Games did Thomas finally defeat Brumel. Although both men cleared 7 feet ¼ inch in the high jump, Thomas was declared the winner because he made fewer misses. Nevertheless Brumel still looms as a probable winner of the high jump at the 1964 summer Olympics in Tokyo.

Valeri Brumel was born on April 14, 1942 in the Siberian village of Tolbuzino in the forested and swampy Chita region near Lake Baikal to Nikolai Brumel, a coal mining engineer, and Ludmilla Brumel, a mine technician. He has an older sister who is an electrical engineer and two younger brothers, one of whom is studying to become a builder. Because the battles of World War II raged 3,000 miles to the west of the village the boy and his family were spared the horrors and deprivations of war, and he and his brothers and sisters grew up to be healthy adolescents. In the years after his birth his family resettled first in Yuzhno-Sakhalinsk on Sakhalin Island, then in Lugansk, a city in the coal and iron region of the Ukraine,

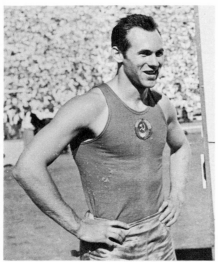

Wide World

VALERI BRUMEL

and finally in Voroshilovgrad, an industrial city in the Ukraine, where they still live.

Attracted by what seemed to him the most graceful of all track and field events, Brumel began to high jump in the fourth grade of Lugansk's Public School 17, where sports were popular. During the summer of 1956 he persuaded his parents to let him remain in town instead of going to a Young Pioneer camp in the country because the biggest track meets of the year took place in that season. It was also the year in which he met his first coach, Pyotr Shein, who having seen the boy jump, invited him to practise at the Vanguard Junior Sports Training School. Shein had Brumel work out with gymnastics, weight lifting, and cross-country running before he let him try his prowess at the high jump bar. By the time he was sixteen Valeri Brumel, while weight lifting, could press thirty-five pounds more than his body weight.

His progress in the high jump was less spectacular. At the age of fifteen he only cleared 5 feet 8⅞ inches, a mark that has been surpassed by many an American schoolboy. On his seventeenth birthday, however, Brumel leaped 6 feet 6¾ inches, and on August 13, 1960 he cleared 7 feet 1½ inches, setting a new European high jump record. The leap won Brumel a place on the Russian track and field team that went to Rome for the 1960 summer Olympics.

The American high jumper John Thomas at that time held the world outdoor record at 7 feet 3¾ inches. He was looked upon as invincible, and few observers gave the three Russians even an outside chance of finishing first in the competition. Under the guidance of Viktor Dyachkov, the coach of the Soviet Olympic high jump team, the three Russians embarked on a strenuous training routine that emphasized mental condition as much as physical well-being.

Dyachkov later wrote in the Soviet magazine *Lehkaia Atletika*: "The essential was to conserve spiritual tranquility and to convince our jumpers that they could manage not only to match the performances of the Americans but even to beat them during the games. . . . Physical training included jumping with weights . . . free jumps, races, and finally movements with weights designed to develop and enforce pure relaxation." Paradoxically it was Thomas' widely touted superiority that gave the Russians grounds for confidence. They felt that the very ease of his victories would prevent Thomas from training himself as arduously as he should for the Olympics at Rome, and they devoted themselves to the psychological preparation of their jumpers.

The Russian strategy worked. Thomas, who could do no better than 7 feet ¼ inch, placed third in the Olympics high jump competition behind Robert Shavlakadze and Brumel, both of whom leaped 7 feet 1 inch. Shavlakadze ranked first because he required fewer jumps than Brumel in clearing the various heights, but after the Olympics ended in Rome he retired from competition.

To the embarrassment of those observers who had dismissed Brumel's feat in Rome as a stroke of luck, in January 1961 the Soviet press announced that Brumel had leaped 7 feet 4½ inches during an indoor meet in Leningrad. (Indoor jumps are not officially recognized as world records, but unofficial records are kept of marks set indoors. Brumel's Leningrad leap was not even given unofficial recognition because he made the jump from a dirt surface.)

When, in the same month, John Thomas cleared 7 feet 3 inches, adding half an inch to his indoor record, the stage was set for the first of the Brumel-Thomas duels in New York's Madison Square Garden, in February 1961. The outcome proved a decisive victory for the Russian visitor. Thomas was unable to clear 7 feet 2 inches, but Brumel propelled himself over that height on his first attempt and then leaped 7 feet 3 inches to tie Thomas' indoor record. A week later the two met again. Thomas cleared only 7 feet 1 inch while Brumel leaped 7 feet 2 inches, and a week after that Thomas cleared 6 feet 10 inches while Brumel soared to 7 feet 3½ inches. Brumel then headed for home, expressing the regret that he had not jumped 7 feet 5 inches.

"I felt sorry for John," Brumel wrote in an article for *Sports Illustrated* (February 4, 1963). "The American press had shifted its tone and unleashed a torrent of abuse against their erstwhile idol. I am most grateful for this rivalry with Thomas, because it helped me so. Keen rivalry gives birth to top results. John is a great friend of mine and an outstanding athlete who has not said his last word in the high jump."

In July 1961 the Soviet Union and the United States competed against each other in a track and field meet in Moscow. While a torrential rain drenched the athletes and the 70,000 spectators in Lenin Stadium, Brumel leaped 7 feet 4 inches to break John Thomas' record of 7 feet 3¾ inches. A few days later Brumel was awarded the highest honor that the Soviet Union can confer upon an athlete—"merited master of sport of the U.S.S.R." Then, on August 31, Brumel boosted his world mark a half inch higher when he soared 7 feet 4½ inches at a meet in Sofia, Bulgaria.

Almost a year passed before Valeri Brumel again broke into the headlines. He was once again in the public eye in July 1962, when he and his teammates flew to Stanford University in Palo Alto, California for another meet between the Russian and American teams. There, under perfect conditions, Brumel improved his world record by jumping 7 feet 5 inches. As he scrambled out of the sawdust pit the first man to reach him and offer congratulations was John Thomas, who had cleared 6 feet 10 inches that day.

After his return to Moscow Brumel leaped 7 feet 5¼ inches on September 29, 1962. He later told reporters that he had jumped in a pair of patched shoes that he had repaired at the last minute. He had found a hole in one of his spiked shoes on arriving at Lenin Stadium. Taking them to a nearby shop, he was told that the cobblers did not repair special footwear. "I wrangled a piece of twine from them," Brumel said, "and somehow sewed up the hole myself. It seems I did a good job."

Brumel returned to the United States in January 1963 to compete in several indoor meets, the first of which was the Millrose Games at Madison Square Garden. Encountering Thomas for the seventh time, Brumel jumped 7 feet 2 inches and Thomas trailed behind with a leap of 7 feet 1 inch. A week later, on February 9, 1963, at the Los Angeles Indoor Games Brumel was defeated by John Thomas for the first time. Both men cleared 7 feet ¼ inch, but Thomas was judged first on the basis of fewer misses. That Brumel's performance was below par may be attributed to a break in his training routine caused by extensive traveling. At the National AAU track and field meet in Madison Square Garden on February 23, 1963 Brumel defeated Thomas by clearing 7 feet 3½ inches to Thomas' 7 feet even. On July 21, 1963, at a track meet between the United States and the Soviet Union in Moscow, Brumel pushed the world high jump record to 7 feet 5¾ inches.

His training methods hold the key to Brumel's success. He is not tall for a high jumper (six feet one inch), and he is deceptively lean in appearance (175 pounds), but he concentrates on speed and on building muscles by lifting weights. He runs 100 meters in 10.7, puts the shot 49 feet, and throws the discus 147 feet. His best broad jump was 23 feet 1¼ inches. "Weight lifting develops practically the same muscles which send a jumper up," Brumel explained in his article for *Sports Illustrated*. "Jumpers, like weight lifters, must be able to concentrate their utmost strength in one quick effort." Charles Coker, the coach of the Los Angeles Striders and a foremost authority on the high jump, attributes Brumel's success to his great speed and his physical strength, while Brumel gives the credit to his own hard work and perseverance.

Valeri Brumel married Marina Larionova, a gymnast whom he met at the Physical Culture Institute in Moscow, in January 1963. He intends to teach physical education when his days of competition are over. His recreations include reading and going to the theater and ballet. He

is studying English at the Physical Culture Institute. At the beginning of 1963 his New Year's resolutions were: to finish his third year at the Institute with excellent marks; to see some new plays in Moscow theaters; to read more well-written books on various subjects; and to improve his chess playing. He would also like to help young athletes as much as possible.

References

N Y Herald Tribune p42 Jl 23 '62 por
N Y Times V p1 S 30 '62 por
Sports Illus 14:20+ F 27 '61 por; 18:38+ F 4 '63 por

BURDICK, QUENTIN N(ORTHROP) June 19, 1908- United States Senator from North Dakota; lawyer

Address: b. Senate Office Bldg., Washington 25, D.C.; h. 1110 S. 9th Ave., Fargo, N.D.

The junior Senator from North Dakota, Quentin N. Burdick, who took office on August 8, 1960 to complete the unexpired term of the late Senator William Langer, is a liberal Democrat and a champion of the interests of the small farmer. As a practising lawyer he was closely associated with the Farmers Union in his home state, and he played an important role in bringing about the affiliation of the Nonpartisan League, representing the liberal farm vote, with the Democratic party in 1956. After making several unsuccessful bids for public office Burdick was elected to the House of Representatives in 1958, to become the first Democratic Congressman in the history of North Dakota. In contrast to the traditional Midwestern isolationism represented by his father, the late Representative Usher L. Burdick, Senator Quentin N. Burdick's views on foreign affairs are frankly those of an internationalist.

Descended from pioneers on both sides of his family, Quentin Northrop Burdick was born on June 19, 1908 in the small farming community of Munich, Cavalier County, North Dakota, to Usher Lloyd and Emma (Robertson) Burdick. He has a brother, the Honorable Eugene A. Burdick, who is district judge in Williston, North Dakota; and a sister, Mrs. Robert Levering, of Frederickstown, Ohio. His maternal grandfather, Hans Robertson, was the first white settler in the area of North Dakota that lies west of Park River. His paternal ancestors had settled in the Devil's Lake area. His father, a lawyer and farmer, served in the House of Representatives for twenty years before his retirement in 1958. He was a Republican who considered himself an independent and was closely associated with Senator William Langer.

At the age of two Quentin Burdick moved with his family to Williston, in the western part of North Dakota, where his father engaged in farming and practised law. He attended public schools in Williston, belonged to the Boy Scouts, and was on one occasion elected honorary mayor by his fellow scouts. At Williston High School he took part in dramatics, debate, and in sports, especially football. He served as captain of the undefeated football team in 1926 and was

QUENTIN N. BURDICK

elected president of his class for three consecutive years. Following his graduation Burdick entered the University of Minnesota in the fall of 1926. There he earned his letter playing football, as his father had done twenty-five years earlier, and he served as commander of his fraternity. A knee injury, which he received on the football field, later disqualified him for World War II military service. After graduating with a B.A. degree in 1931 he entered the University of Minnesota law school, which awarded him the LL.B. degree in the following year.

The country was in the midst of the Depression when Burdick entered his father's law practice in Fargo in 1932 after he had been admitted to the North Dakota bar. Since his clients, mainly farmers and laborers, were generally poor, he derived only a modest income from his law practice. As counsel for the Farmers Union he traveled all over the state, and for several years his principal activity was the handling of foreclosure actions for farmers. "I guess I acquired a social conscience during those bad days, and ever since I've had the desire to work toward bettering the living conditions of the people," Burdick later recalled.

Because of economic conditions Burdick joined the Nonpartisan League (NPL), which had been founded in 1915 for the purpose of improving the conditions of farmers through governmental reforms and co-operative activities. The NPL, which had been dormant for a number of years, was revived in 1932 when William Langer was elected Governor. With the support of the NPL, Burdick ran twice for the office of state attorney and was a candidate for the state senate from the strongly Republican Cass County, but he was defeated in each instance. In 1942 he ran unsuccessfully for Lieutenant Governor with NPL support. During this period the NPL, though politically independent, filed its candidates in the Republican column, and Burdick himself was a registered Republican for ten years.

In 1946, in an effort to unify the Democratic and NPL vote, Burdick ran for Governor as a Democratic candidate, but he was again unsuccessful. In the next few years he continued to try to bring the liberal vote of North Dakota under one banner by aligning the NPL with the Democratic forces of the state. Finally, in 1956, the NPL decided to file its candidates in the Democratic column, thus breaking a political tradition of forty years and paving the way for a two-party system in North Dakota. In the same year Burdick was unanimously endorsed by both the Democratic party and the NPL to run for the United States Senate against Republican candidate Milton R. Young. Although Burdick was defeated by a vote of 155,305 to 87,919, the NPL-Democratic amalgamation made considerable headway in the campaign.

Quentin Burdick's 1956 Senatorial bid had been opposed by his father, who remained in the Republican camp. Although both men were considered liberals and championed the cause of the small farmer, Usher Burdick represented a tradition of isolationism, whereas Quentin Burdick openly endorsed the United Nations, foreign aid, and reciprocal trade agreements. In the spring of 1958, the elder Burdick, fearing defeat in the Republican primary, offered to withdraw his own candidacy if the NPL agreed to back his son as the Democratic candidate for the House of Representatives. Quentin Burdick received the NPL endorsement for the Congressional race on April 1, 1958, and Usher Burdick later retired.

Elected Congressman-at-large in November 1958, Quentin Burdick became the first Democratic member of the House of Representatives from North Dakota since it became a state in 1889. (Four Democratic Senators had previously been elected in the state.) Burdick's election marked the first major victory of the NPL on behalf of a Democratic candidate, and his campaign strengthened the Democratic party. Congratulating the voters of his state upon his son's victory, Usher Burdick noted that his son was "thoroughly honest, and, while he entertains progressive views, he is at the same time a defender of the Constitution" (U.S. News & World Report, November 14, 1958).

As a member of the Eighty-sixth Congress, Burdick requested and obtained membership in the House Interior and Insular Affairs Committee. He became an authority on water resource development and worked on behalf of the Garrison Diversion Project on the Missouri River in his home state. In early 1959 he was one of five Congressmen who helped a Negro boy to enter the Congressional page school. In the voting on key issues during 1959 Burdick supported Hawaiian statehood, TVA bonds, the mutual security act, and the federal highway act. He voted to override the Presidential veto on the public works appropriation bill and opposed the labor-management reporting and disclosure act.

In 1960 Burdick voted for the civil rights act, the school construction assistance act, and the farm surplus act, and he opposed limiting amendments on minimum wage legislation. He was a co-sponsor of the defeated Poage-McGovern-Burdick bill, popularly known as the family-farm-income bill, which was vigorously supported by the North Dakota Farmers Union. This bill, which aimed at closing the gap between large and small farmers, would have assigned to individual farmers a given quota of grain production in bushels, according to the national need. Farmers were to have been paid on the basis of the market price and would have received government support in the event that the price fell below what was termed a "just parity price."

After the death of Senator Langer in November 1959, Governor John E. Davis temporarily appointed C. Norman Brunsdale to the Senate seat. In a special election, called for June 28, 1960 to fill the remaining four and a half years of Langer's term, Burdick was put up as the candidate of the Democratic party and the NPL to run against Governor Davis, the Republican candidate. The campaign was seen by some observers as a referendum on the farm policies of the Eisenhower administration and as a possible indication of trends for the coming national election. Leading spokesmen of both parties, including Presidential candidates John F. Kennedy and Richard M. Nixon, visited North Dakota to deliver major policy speeches and to campaign on behalf of the candidates of their respective parties. During the campaign, in which he received strong support from the Farmers Union, Burdick was charged in an anonymous brochure with having been associated with Henry Wallace in the left-wing Progressive party in 1948, and Republican national committeeman Mark Andrews referred to Burdick as a "left-wing ADA Democrat."

Campaigning mainly on the issue of administration farm policies, Burdick emphasized the need for high price supports and for strict production controls on grains with high surpluses. The campaign slogan "Beat Benson with Burdick" referred to Secretary of Agriculture Ezra Taft Benson, whose soil bank program and efforts to reduce grain price supports were frowned upon by many North Dakota wheat farmers.

Burdick's strength in the rural areas won him the election by a vote of 104,593 to 103,475. Immediately after the election he flew back to Washington to cast his vote in the House for overriding a Presidential veto of a bill increasing the salaries of postal employees. Because of the closeness of the election Davis refused to concede defeat until July 18, when a state canvassing board confirmed Burdick's victory.

On August 8, 1960 Burdick was sworn in as a member of the United States Senate, thus increasing the Democratic majority in the Senate to sixty-six. On the following day he voted to table the Republican civil rights bill, a measure that was opposed by Kennedy as a political move. In the same month he supported efforts to raise minimum wage levels; voted for the bill for medical care for the aged that was co-sponsored by Kennedy; and joined several other leading Democrats in issuing a statement, backed by Kennedy, that attacked the farm policies of Vice-President Nixon. In the Senate, Burdick was assigned to the Interior and Insular Affairs Committee and the Labor and Public Welfare Committee.

Key measures that Burdick supported in 1961 included the school assistance act, the extended Mexican farm labor program, the Peace Corps act, the area redevelopment act, and temporary extended unemployment compensation. He opposed the confirmation of Charles M. Meriwether as director of the Export-Import Bank and voted against amendments to the fair labor standards act that would reduce the number of persons covered by its provisions. As a member of the Labor and Public Welfare Committee he voted against the amended national defense education act because it included a provision for construction loans to private schools. His amendment to the Agricultural Act of 1961, which would have exempted some wheat farmers in disaster areas from the mandatory 10 percent wheat acreage cut, was defeated in the Senate.

In 1962 Burdick supported the administration's civil rights bill, the proposed urban affairs department, the food and agriculture act, the public works bill, and foreign military and economic aid. He opposed the confirmation of John A. McCone as director of the Central Intelligence Agency; the communications satellites act; and tabling the administration's medical care for the aged bill. Burdick's record of support of the Kennedy administration in 1962 was 66 percent on domestic issues, 74 percent on foreign issues, and 69 percent on all issues.

Quentin N. Burdick was married on March 18, 1933 to Marietta Janecky, whom he had met while attending the University of Minnesota. She died on March 14, 1958. Four children were born to this marriage: Jonathan, Jan Mary, Jennifer, and Jessica. On July 7, 1960 Burdick married Mrs. Jocelyn (Birch) Peterson, and they have a son, Gage, born in 1961. (Mrs. Burdick also has two children, Leslie and Birch Peterson, by her previous marriage.) Burdick is an energetic man with a "frontier manner," a rugged and athletic appearance, and a love for all sports. He is five feet eleven and one-half inches tall, weighs 190 pounds, and has hazel eyes and light-brown hair. According to a biographical sketch in the New York *Times* (August 9, 1960), he is "a friendly lawyer-politician whose hair never looks as though it had been combed and whose clothes usually look as if he had worn them to bed the night before." Burdick is a member of the Masonic lodge, the Elks, the Eagles, and Sigma Nu fraternity. His religious affiliation is with the Congregational church. He is said, in the *New Republic* (October 13, 1958), to have a "stern but winning sincerity about his Democratic convictions."

References

N Y Times p12 Ag 9 '60 por
New Repub 139:15 O 13 '58 por
U S News 45:21 N 14 '58 por
Biographic Directory of the American Congress, 1774-1961 (1961)
Congressional Directory (1962)
Who's Who in America, 1962-63

CALDER, (PETER) RITCHIE July 1, 1906-
Journalist; author; educator
Address: b. University of Edinburgh, Edinburgh,
Scotland; h. "The Gables," 74 The Crescent,
Belmont, Surrey, England

Narrowing the gulf between the specialist and
the layman, particularly through scientific journalism, is perhaps the most important overall
achievement of the British author Ritchie Calder,
who has been called "Wellsian in his gift for
expounding facts and theories with lucidity and
liveliness." He has written some twenty books
and has published innumerable articles in over
a thousand newspapers and magazines. Calder,
who has traveled all over the world on special
missions for the United Nations, is now professor
of international relations at the University of
Edinburgh.

Peter Ritchie Calder was born on July 1, 1906
in Forfar, Scotland to David Lindsay Calder, a
jute worker who became a factory manager, and
his wife, the former Georgina Ritchie. There were
four children in the family, a girl and three
boys. Both of Ritchie Calder's brothers entered
the aircraft industry as engineers, but he was
intended for the university, in accordance with
the Scottish tradition that at least one son should,
when possible, follow an academic career.

It was to be a long time before that tradition
was fulfilled. When he was twelve years old, soon
after he began his secondary education at Forfar
Academy, Ritchie Calder had an essay published
in the Forfar *Dispatch*. At fifteen, equipped with
a self-taught proficiency in shorthand, he left
school and joined the Dundee *Courier* as a police
court reporter. Four years later, in 1926, he was
in London, a by-line reporter on a national
newspaper, the *Daily News*. Calder wrote for the
News until 1930, when he worked briefly for the
Daily Chronicle and then moved on to the
Daily Herald, remaining there until 1941.

RITCHIE CALDER

Working in the 1920's as a crime and general
reporter, Calder found himself increasingly fascinated by the science stories to which he was
occasionally assigned. Science journalism was
then in its infancy, and scientists, wrapped in
their own specialties, had little time for their
colleagues in other fields and less for prying
newspapermen. Once, when Calder was interviewing Lord Rutherford, as the incident is
related in the *New Scientist* (January 5, 1961),
the great man threw down a paper crammed
with abstruse mathematics, arguing that no non-
scientist could understand it. The young reporter
produced his own notebook. "If you will transcribe my shorthand," he said, "I will translate
yours."

Calder persevered. As he had once spent his
time with detectives in search of crime news, he
now cultivated scientists to learn about their
work, haunting their laboratories, reading their
books, making many of them his friends. His
conviction that science has an obligation to make
itself understood, and his talent for accurate and
responsible popularization, won him increasing
respect and co-operation. Soon he was writing
regularly on science in the *Daily Herald*. In 1934
his first book appeared, an account of scientific
progress entitled, with characteristic optimism,
Birth of the Future (Barker, Ryerson). It was
followed in quick succession by *The Conquest of
Suffering* (Methuen, 1934) and *Roving Commission* (Methuen, 1935). In his introduction to
Birth of the Future Sir Frederick Gowland Hopkins, then president of the Royal Society, spoke
for many scientists when he said of Calder, "If
this be a journalist, it is a journalist with a
difference."

But Calder's specialization had not limited his
versatility as a journalist. He covered the horrors
and heroism of the Battle of Britain and the
1940-41 blitz in the *Daily Herald* and in two
books, *The Lesson of London* (Secker & Warburg,
1941) and *Carry on, London* (English Universities Press; Musson, 1941). His exposure of
inadequacies in the country's civil defense was
not welcomed by the authorities but Calder, who
was at one point threatened with imprisonment,
was subsequently rewarded by the adoption of
many of the reforms he had advocated. A third
book published during the dark days of 1941 was
Start Planning Britain Now (Routledge). In it,
as forward-looking as ever, Calder was already
offering a policy for postwar reconstruction.

At this point a long gap occurs in Ritchie
Calder's crowded publications list, for in 1941 he
left the *Daily Herald* to become director of plans
in the Foreign Office's political warfare executive.
From headquarters in England, according to a
profile of Calder in the *New Scientist* (January 5,
1961), he was "engaged with a brilliant team of
experts and amateurs in spreading alarm and
despondency in enemy territories, and hope
among the resistance movements." In 1944 both
his home and his offices were wrecked by bombs,
and that summer, already strained and exhausted
by his work at the Foreign Office, Calder collapsed in the street with a brain hemorrhage.
He was for a time in danger of losing his life
but by 1945 recovered sufficiently to join the
staff at General Eisenhower's Supreme Headquarters as special adviser. With the end of the

war he returned to Fleet Street as science editor of the *News Chronicle,* a position he retained until 1956.

It was at this time that Calder embarked on what has become, in effect, a second career— his work for the United Nations and its specialized agencies. In 1946 he served as special adviser at the Famine Conference organized in Washington by the Food and Agriculture Organization. He was a member of the British delegation to UNESCO's first general conference at Paris in 1946 and to its second, in Mexico City, the following year. Three years later, when UNESCO was planning to establish its advisory committee on research in the arid zones, Calder was asked to undertake the first of the wide-ranging missions that have since required him to travel to every part of the world.

Calder's mission to the arid zones of North Africa and the Middle East—from the western Sahara to the salt deserts of Persia—was completed in 1950. His purpose, on this as on later journeys, was to make a synoptic survey—a "reconnaissance," to use his own term, not only of the terrain but of all of the region's problems and possibilities, geological, medical, educational, industrial, and agricultural. Out of this long and arduous journey came a series of articles and broadcasts and a book that discussed, always in human terms, the accomplishments of the U.N.'s technical assistance program, the terrible problems that still face the peoples of the arid zones, and some possible solutions.

Men Against the Desert, as Calder titled his book, was followed by *Profile of Science,* which dealt with such developments as radar and penicillin and new knowledge about vitamins and atomic science. Both books were published in England by George Allen & Unwin in 1951 and in the United States by the Macmillan Company in 1952. Also in 1951 came *The Lamp is Lit,* an informal history of the World Health Organization published by WHO's division of public information. Two years later when *Men Against Ignorance* (UNESCO, 1953), Calder's book about UNESCO, appeared, he was off on a second journey, this time as head of a special information mission to South-East Asia for the U.N. and a half dozen of the specialized agencies. His impressions of the needs and potentialities of Thailand, Indonesia, Burma, India, Pakistan, and Afghanistan were recorded in *Men Against the Jungle* (Allen, G.; Macmillan, 1954).

In 1955 Calder spent four and a half months in the Arctic, at the invitation of the Canadian government and on behalf of the U.N., to investigate the possibilities of development there and to assess the likely consequences of such development in human and technical terms. In 1960 he toured the trouble spots of the Congo as United Nations and WHO consultant. Two books resulted: *Men Against the Frozen North* (Allen, G.; Macmillan, 1957) and *Agony of the Congo* (Gollancz; Doubleday, 1960). Another book is in progress, describing Calder's recent 25,000-mile return trip to South-East Asia—the latest but not necessarily the last of his full-scale missions. "After each long trip I swear I shall

not do another, and then get itchy feet," he wrote in *Men Against the Frozen North.*

During the short intervals between these last three journeys, Calder produced a spate of books. The relation of science to society was discussed in *Science In Our Lives* (Michigan State College, 1954). Then came *Science Makes Sense* (Allen, G., 1955) and three historical books about medicine: one for children, *From Magic to Medicine* (Rathbone, 1957); one for adults, *Medicine and Man* (Allen, G., 1958); and the picture book, *Wonderful World of Medicine* (Garden City, 1958). *Ten Steps Forward* (WHO, 1958) is Calder's second book about the World Health Organization; *The Hand of Life* (Weidenfeld, 1959) is an account of the Weizmann Institute and its work.

Calder's most ambitious work to date is *After the Seventh Day* (Simon & Schuster, 1961), published in England as *The Inheritors* (Heinemann, 1961). It traces the history of man's struggle to master his environment from the earliest use of tools to the present, when he is threatened by nuclear destruction and a population growing faster than its food supply. Calder believes that global co-operation in the application of scientific knowledge provides man's sole hope of survival; that science could create a kind of utopia in which starvation was eradicated, deserts bloomed, and underground cities thrived in Antarctica. The distillation of all that Calder has learned in his work and travels, charged with his unshakable optimism, *After the Seventh Day* might well have been called "Man Against the Earth." Critics found it "brilliant," "exciting," "challenging," and "humane."

Three more of Calder's books appeared in 1962: *The Life Savers* (Hutchinson), *Common Sense About a Starving World* (Gollancz; Macmillan), and *Living With the Atom* (Univ. of Chicago Press). The last book, a review of the development of nuclear energy and its implications for public health, was based on a colloquium held under Calder's chairmanship at the University of Chicago in 1960. Ritchie Calder's books have been translated into nineteen languages. His articles have appeared in over a thousand newspapers and magazines throughout the world, and he has been a frequent broadcaster on radio and television.

His parents' first ambitions for him (and Scottish tradition) were at last fulfilled in October 1961, when Ritchie Calder was appointed to the Sir Montague Burton Chair of International Relations at Edinburgh University. The appointment caused "complications," since no Edinburgh professor may appear ungowned before his students and Calder had neither a degree nor the gown to go with it. This problem was overcome when the university, invoking a centuries-old statute, dubbed Calder an authentic (as distinct from honorary) Master of Arts.

Calder's travels for the U.N., his careers in journalism, writing, and teaching would overwhelm most men. For Calder they are apparently not enough, and he has found time for a large number of additional activities. He was from 1945 to 1958 on the editorial board of the *New*

CALDER, RITCHIE—*Continued*

Statesman. In 1955 and 1958 he served on the U.N. Secretariat during the International Conferences on the Peaceful Uses of Atomic Energy. He works for the U.N. Association in Britain and is a member of its national executive. He is deeply involved in the Workers' Educational Association, of which he is vice-president, and no less busy in the affairs of the British Association for the Advancement of Science. Calder is a founder-member of the Association of British Science Writers (and was for several years its chairman), a Fellow of the Royal Society of Arts, a member of the council of the British Association, and a Fellow of the American Association for the Advancement of Science. In 1957 he was the Charles Beard Lecturer at Ruskin College, Oxford. His clubs include the Savile in England, the Cosmos in Washington, and the Scottish Arts Club.

For his wartime work with the Foreign Office, Calder was created a C.B.E. in 1945. In 1960 he was awarded the Kalinga Prize, given through UNESCO for outstanding achievement in the dissemination of understanding about science. He received the New York Public Library's Jubilee Medal in 1961.

On October 11, 1927 Calder married Mabel Jane Forbes McKail. They have three sons, Nigel, Angus and Allan, and two daughters, Fiona and Isla. Calder is five feet nine inches tall, weighs 182 pounds, and has blue eyes and brown hair. The *New Scientist* profile described him as a "strongly-built dynamic man . . . with a strong voice, a quick wit and a versatile platform approach." He has indeed had much experience on public platforms, political and otherwise, since he joined the Labour party in Dundee in 1924. Since then he has given a great deal of time to Labour meetings. He is a former member of the Fabian Society executive and vice-chairman of the Campaign for Nuclear Disarmament. Among his recreations he lists travel and carpentry, and he says he is "a golfer manqué."

Calder, as the *New Scientist* reported, has been described as a "common law scientist who has lived with science so long that he is married to it by habit and repute." The *New Scientist* commented, "The union has been good for science as well as perpetually fascinating to Calder, for he has made an immense contribution to demolishing the ivory towers, and to giving contemporary science a sense of direction and social purpose."

References

Book Find News Summer '61
New Scientist 9:30+ Ja 5 '61 por
Author's & Writer's Who's Who (1960)
Who's Who, 1963

CAMPBELL, GRACE (MACLENNAN GRANT) Mar. 18, 1895-May 31, 1963 Canadian novelist; author of *Thorn-Apple Tree* and other best sellers. See *Current Biography,* 1948.

Obituary

N Y Times p84 Je 2 '63

CARTER, DON(ALD JAMES) July 29, 1926-
Professional bowler
Address: b. c/o Brunswick Corp., 623 S. Wabash Ave., Chicago, Ill.

With an estimated 30,000,000 Americans participating, bowling has become the nation's top indoor nonspectator sport. Pre-eminent among these Americans is Don Carter of St. Louis, whose proficiency as a professional bowler has won him the title of Mr. Bowling. In late November 1962 Carter confirmed his status as the world's best bowler by winning a fifth World Invitational championship in Chicago—a record for bowling.

For his over-all performance in 1962 Carter was named Bowler of the Year by the Bowling Writers Association of America, the sixth time that the honor was bestowed on him. Carter was the first president of the Professional Bowlers Association and won the first PBA National Open. He is the first professional bowler to reach a six-figure annual income, the first to run six strikes on the *Jackpot* television show, and the first to convert the cash "Sweepstakes" shot on *Make That Spare,* another television bowling show.

Donald James Carter, the younger of two sons, was born on July 29, 1926 in St. Louis, Missouri. (His brother died in 1948.) An all-round athlete at Wellston High School in St. Louis, he won letters for four years of playing baseball and three years of playing football. After his graduation in 1944 he enlisted in the United States Navy and spent two years as a radarman aboard an LST in the South Pacific. He narrowly missed combat action, and was discharged with the rank of a third class petty officer radarman in June 1946.

In the fall of 1946 Bill Beckman of the former Philadelphia Athletics (now the Kansas City Athletics) in the American League signed Carter to a contract as an infielder at a salary of $150 a month. The following spring he was assigned to the Red Springs, North Carolina team in the Class D Tobacco State League, playing the infield and pitching. As a batter, Carter was moderately successful, hitting .302, but as a pitcher he was mediocre, compiling a three won, seven lost record, with an earned run average of 4.19. At the end of the season Carter asked to be released from his contract. "I didn't think I was major league material," he has explained.

Encouraged by his mother, Mrs. Gladys Carter, Don Carter had begun to bowl at the age of thirteen, but not until he joined a St. Louis bowling club in 1942, while in high school, did he really become interested in the sport. Turning his back on professional baseball, Carter returned to St. Louis in 1947 and bowled as often as his pinched budget would allow. During the winter season of 1947-48 he bowled in six leagues. "I bowled because I loved it," he recalls. "You couldn't make any money at it."

In the meantime Carter had worked as an operator of a punch machine, as a pipe fitter's helper, and as a packer of pistons. His mother demanded little board from him so that he could have more money for bowling. In 1948 he became general manager of the Golden Eagle Lanes in St. Louis, but the long hours he spent as alley man, bartender, and janitor left him only a limited amount of time for tournament bowling. He became an instructor, first at Silver Shield Lanes, then at Floriss Lanes, where he was able both to earn money and refine his skill at the game. In September 1951 he was invited to join the Pfeiffer team in Detroit. He received no salary, but he was able to find a job in the recreation department of Detroit at $60 a week.

It was also in 1951 that the *Bowlers Journal* chose Don Carter for its All-American team, and in the years that followed the publication named Carter to eight more All-American squads. In 1952 he won the first of four All-Star bowling championships. He repeated as All-Star winner in 1953, captured the titles of the American Bowling Congress' Team and Team All-Events as a member of the spectacular Pfeiffer bowling crew, and was picked as Bowler of the Year by the Bowling Writers Association of America. In the wake of these achievements Carter was invited to join the Budweiser team of St. Louis, then being formed by Whitey Harris who captained the team for three seasons. "The team was molded around Carter," Harris has explained. "He was the key. Without him there probably wouldn't have been a Budweiser team." As a member of the Budweiser team, Carter played in many places, but his most unusual setting was a St. Louis auditorium in 1955, where he rolled a bowling ball across the stage as part of the sound effects of the *Hudson River Suite*, performed by the St. Louis Symphony under André Kostelanetz. Carter was supposed to simulate the sound of Rip Van Winkle bowling in the Catskills.

Eminently successful, the Budweiser team won the National Team Match Game title against the top competitors of professional bowling for four consecutive years (1956-59). During that period Carter himself was equally successful. He was World's Invitational titlist in 1957 and 1959 and Southern Match Game winner in 1957. Teaming with Tom Hennessey, he won the National Men's Doubles championship in 1958 and 1959. He was named Bowler of the Year in 1954, 1957, and 1958, almost monopolizing the coveted award. In 1960 he won honors in two of the Professional Bowlers Association's leading tournaments by placing first at the PBA National Open Championship in Memphis, Tennessee and first in the PBA Eastern Open at Paramus, New Jersey. That year he captured the World's Invitational title for a third time and again was named Bowler of the Year.

Budweiser having in the meantime withdrawn its sponsorship of the team, Carter reunited its members under the name of Carter Glove. In 1961 Carter Glove won the National Team Match Game title and Carter won the ABC's Masters tournament, the Labor Day Classic, and the World Invitational title. In 1962 he won the PBA Open at Seattle, Houston, and Tucson, and again captured the World Invitational title. His Carter Glove team won the ABC's Classic Division team crown, and Carter was predictably again named Bowler of the Year.

The editor of the *National Bowlers Journal*, Dick Denny, has said of Don Carter that he is as near to being a sports deity as any athlete in

DON CARTER

the United States today. For the last decade he has dominated bowling as Babe Ruth once dominated baseball and as Jack Dempsey once dominated boxing. Yet oddly enough, Carter's bowling style would make a bowling purist cringe. He sights the pins, runs forward, crouching more deeply with each stride, and at the fourth step he releases the ball with his right arm grotesquely bent at the elbow. (Most of the other top bowlers crouch only slightly and keep their arms extended.) Of his style Carter says with a smile: "I guess I just learned to bowl wrong." Much of Carter's success in competition stems from his icy, steel-nerved, and almost calculating approach to the sport. He never speaks to his opponent, for example.

Of Carter's temperament the sports announcer Wynn Elliot has said: "The most obvious quality about him is his competitive control. Great actors, great performers, great athletes, they all have it. The nervous makeup that enables them to maintain their poise while performing under great pressure." Carter is the first to agree that the pressures of professional bowling are tremendous. "The thing about this business is pressure," he once explained. "It's always there. If you press, you pull the ball or maybe push it. I concentrate on trying not to press. That way, I don't get butterflies." His emotional and physical exertions cause Carter to lose eight pounds occasionally while bowling at a major tournament. "But I enjoy it," he has remarked. "When I bowl real well it gives me a big kick."

For the last three years Carter's annual income has exceeded $100,000. Tournaments account for a large part of his earnings and television matches, endorsements of products, and his investments account for the rest. Television has recently become a lucrative outlet for bowlers. Carter, for example, once collected $18,000 for his appearance on television's *Make That Spare*. His name has become profitably associated with such

CARTER, DON—*Continued*

commodities as the Don Carter Glove, the Don Carter Shirt, and the Don Carter Slacks. With a partner he owns Don Carter Lanes, a 28-lane bowling establishment in Rockford, Illinois. He has written a popular paperback called *Ten Secrets of Bowling* for the Cornerstone Library. As a member of the Brunswick Corporation's advisory staff of champions in the bowling division, he is one of a number of big league stars who promote bowling with exhibitions, instruction, and appearances throughout the United States.

In August 1953 Don Carter married the former LaVerne Haverly, who has become one of the nation's leading professional bowlers in her own right. Their two children, Cathy and Jimmy, have already learned to bowl. Carter has said: "Family bowling should be fun. Too often, with parents as teachers, it becomes like so much homework. The children do not enjoy the lessons and the parents become annoyed at slow advancement, and no one enjoys the fun of learning to bowl correctly."

Six feet in height, 193 pounds in weight, Carter is powerfully built, yet round-shouldered. Although he is quiet and somewhat ·shy, he has mastered much of his introversion and handles himself today with dignity and self-assurance. He has confessed to weaknesses for Cadillacs and golfing. A few scares in airplanes have produced his aversion to flying, and he takes a plane only when it is absolutely necessary.

Don Carter is not only the most successful bowler competing today, but also the most popular. At the World Invitational championships in Chicago's McCormick Place in 1962 the crowd cheered his every strike and moaned whenever he happened to throw a "bad ball." Success and money have not blunted his desire for competition. "It's true that money isn't as important as before," he once said, "but I think the desire may be even greater today because I'm at the top and I'd like to stay there."

References

Bowlers J 49:53+ Ja '62 por
Newsweek 51:84+ F 3 '58

CARTON DE WIART, ADRIAN 1880-June 5, 1963 Lieutenant General in the British army; knighted in 1945; commander of British forces in Norway during World War II. See *Current Biography* (May) 1940.

Obituary

N Y Times p35 Je 6 '63

CARVEL, ELBERT N(OSTRAND) Feb. 9, 1910- Governor of Delaware; businessman
Address: b. State of Delaware Executive Department, Dover, Del.; h. Box 111, Laurel, Del.

In the election of 1960 the voters of Delaware, reflecting the general preference of the nation for Democratic candidates, chose Elbert N. Carvel as their Governor for the second time. His earlier four-year term as Governor had begun in

1949 after he had served as Lieutenant Governor. Carvel is president of a prosperous manufacturing concern, the Valliant Fertilizer Company in Laurel, Delaware, and he operates three farms in Delaware and eastern Maryland. Delaware, the second smallest state in area in the United States, is traditionally called a diamond— "diminutive, but having within it inherent value." In 1960 it was also the fifth smallest in population, but its population has since been growing rapidly, particularly in the area around Wilmington, the home of the du Pont chemical enterprises.

Although he has been a resident of Delaware for the greater part of his adult life, Elbert Nostrand Carvel is not a native of that state. He was born to Arnold Wrightson and Elizabeth (Nostrand) Carvel on February 9, 1910 in Shelter Island Heights, New York, near the northeastern tip of Long Island. When he was six years old, however, his father, a businessman, moved his family to Baltimore, Maryland, and it was in the public grade schools of that city that the boy acquired his early education. For four years beginning in 1934 Carvel studied engineering at the Baltimore Polytechnic Institute, and for three years following his graduation in 1928 he attended night classes at the University of Baltimore Law School, where he was awarded his LL.B. degree in 1931. He also studied accounting, at Johns Hopkins University, Baltimore, in the autumn of 1931.

Also in 1931 Carvel was engaged as a sales engineer with the Consolidated Gas and Electric Power and Light Company of Baltimore. He gave up this position in 1936 when he moved to Laurel, Sussex County, Delaware to become general manager, treasurer, and director of the Valliant Fertilizer Company, which had been founded in 1920 and later grew into the state's largest manufacturer of commercial fertilizers. He was elected president of the company in 1945.

Soon after Carvel moved to Delaware in 1936, he also helped to incorporate the Milford Fertilizer Company of Milford, Delaware, of which he was to serve as a director from 1937 to 1941, vice-president and director from 1941 to 1959, and chairman of the board beginning in 1959. He was also a director from 1941 to 1949 of the Sussex Trust Company, and since 1957 he has been a director of the Peoples Bank and Trust Company in Wilmington.

While serving on the 1941-42 Federal Grand Jury, which investigated election practices in Delaware of the 1940 national election, Carvel was so disturbed by the jury's revelations of corruption that he decided to become active in politics and fight for election reforms in his state. A Democrat, he was his party's successful candidate for Lieutenant Governor in 1944, and during his four-year term he served ex officio as president of both the State Senate and the Board of Pardons. He was chairman of the state Democratic party in 1946-47 and a delegate to the Democratic National Convention in 1948.

The Democratic candidate for Governor in 1948, Carvel defeated his Republican opponent in November by 75,339 votes to 64,966. A Democrat was also elected Lieutenant Governor, but the Republicans controlled the State Senate and the House of Representatives, in both cases by a one-seat margin. At the regular 1949 session of the General Assembly (legislature), laws were enacted for financing new school buildings through a $19,000,000 bond issue, and minimum teacher salaries were guaranteed by the state. The legislature also provided for a highway construction program, a payroll withholding system in connection with the state income tax, and an increase in workmen's and unemployment compensation. A public service commission and a state development department were also created. At a special session of the General Assembly an $8,000,000 bond issue was authorized to subsidize a veterans' bonus.

Although the Democrats gained a one-seat majority in the Delaware Senate through the 1950 biennial election, they lost ground in the House of Representatives. At the November 1952 election, when Governor Carvel sought a second term, he was a casualty of the Eisenhower landslide and lost to Republican J. Caleb Boggs. The election reform measures for which he campaigned were not enacted, therefore, until the Democrats gained control of the General Assembly in 1955.

Carvel was again a delegate to the Democratic National Convention in 1952 and 1956 and was again the chairman of the state Democratic committee from 1954 to 1957, but he temporarily split with his party in 1957 when, according to the New York *Times* (November 10, 1960), the "Democratic-controlled legislature passed legislation in [what] he considered [an] unethical manner to take over the Highway Department." In August 1958, however, he accepted the Democratic nomination for the United States Senate seat held since January 1953 by Republican John J. Williams, but in November lost to Senator Williams, who was elected to a second term by 82,280 votes to 75,152.

Re-elected in 1956, Governor J. Caleb Boggs was ineligible under the Delaware constitution for a third term. In 1960 he sought and won the Republican nomination for a United States Senate seat. For the Governorship the Republicans nominated John W. Rollins, who had served as Lieutenant Governor during Governor Boggs's first term. The Democrats nominated Carvel for Governor by acclamation, and at the November election he defeated Rollins by 100,777 to 94,041. Carvel, however, was not to be officially the next Governor of Delaware. Gubernatorial terms in his state do not expire until the third week in January. Thus when on December 30, 1960 Governor Boggs resigned in order to take his United States Senate seat at the opening of the Eighty-seventh Congress, Lieutenant Governor David P. Buckson was sworn in as Governor for what an Associated Press dispatch characterized as "the shortest term a Delaware Governor has ever served—eighteen days."

Since 1960 the Delaware legislature, which formerly met every two years, has held regular sessions annually. Governor Carvel, inaugurated on January 17, 1961, made his recommendations to a General Assembly organized by his own party: the seventeen-member Senate consisted of eleven Democrats and six Republicans, and the thirty-five-member House of Representatives of twenty Democrats and fifteen Republicans. But in neither body was the Democratic majority

The Waller Studio
ELBERT N. CARVEL

decisive or in solid agreement. Thus while the Governor's budget for fiscal 1961 was $72,000,000 (an increase of $5,500,000 over the previous year), the assembly, through additional appropriations, raised expenditures to $82,000,000 without authorizing any new taxes. Regular revenues failed to meet expenditures, and in October the state was forced to borrow over $8,000,000 to meet current obligations. (Subsequently the corporation tax and the taxes on wines and gasoline were increased.)

In September 1961, furthermore, the General Assembly had created a state planning commission without voting an appropriation sufficient to enable it to function and also created a commission on human relations and a department of labor and industrial relations. At the same time, cutbacks in appropriations for welfare led to curtailment of state aid to the needy. On the other hand, the 1961 legislature ratified an interstate compact with New Jersey that created a Delaware River and Bridge Authority making possible new bridges, tunnels, or ferry services. Although the 1961 assembly did not support the Governor in his advocacy of reapportionment of seats, it did pass a municipal home rule bill. Late in December 1961 the assembly overrode the Governor's veto of a bill re-establishing capital punishment, abolished in Delaware in 1958. "The function of the criminal law," Carvel had said in his veto message, "is to protect the law-abiding and not fulfill a lust for revenge."

In his message to the 1962 General Assembly the Governor recommended replacing the existing budget commission by a full-time fiscal office to be appointed by the Governor with approval of the Senate. A General Appropriation Act of over $116,700,000 was passed, and the legislature gave initial approval to a constitutional amendment redefining and somewhat limiting the Governor's veto powers. The Interstate Compact on Mental Health was ratified, and residents of

CARVEL, ELBERT N.—*Continued*

Delaware receiving old age assistance were enabled to share in the benefits of the federal-state medical care program. Late in July 1962 the assembly finally approved, subject to repassage in 1963, a constitutional amendment reapportioning the House and Senate and raising the number of seats to 45 and 21 respectively.

From 1942 to 1955 Carvel was a director of the National Fertilizer Association, and he is now a director of its successor, the National Plant Food Institute. He is a member of the National Joint Committee on Fertilizer Application and the National Planning Association. He also belongs to the Delaware Historical Society and the Sussex County Laymen's League. At the 1963 Southern Governors Conference he was elected vice-chairman of the conference for the following year.

Governor Carvel, who is a vestryman of St. Philip's Episcopal Church in Laurel, was a delegate to the general conventions of the Episcopal Church in 1946 and 1952. He has served three terms on the executive council for the diocese of Delaware. A former member of the Laurel School Board, he was also for fifteen years (1945-60) a trustee of the University of Delaware. He is a 32d degree Mason (Shrine and Scottish Rite) and a member of the Sigma Delta Kappa legal fraternity, the Royal Order of Jesters, and numerous social and service clubs and organizations, including the Lions and the Grange. He has the decoration of Commander of the Netherlands Order of Orange-Nassau.

Elbert N. Carvel married Ann Hall Valliant of Centreville, Maryland on December 17, 1932. They have a son, Edwin Valliant, and three daughters, Mrs. Elizabeth Palmer, Ann Hall, and Barbara Jean. When not occupied with government, politics, business, or farming, Carvel can turn to many hobbies—bridge, color photography, hunting, fishing, boating, chess, reading, golf, and classical music.

References

International Who's Who, 1962-63
International Year Book and Statesmen's Who's Who, 1962
National Cyclopædia of American Biography current vol H (1952)
Who's Who in America, 1962-63
Who's Who in United States Politics (1952)
World Who's Who in Commerce and Industry (1961)

CARY, WILLIAM L(UCIUS) Nov. 27, 1910-
Chairman of the Securities and Exchange Commission

Address: b. Securities and Exchange Commission, 425 2nd St., N.W., Washington 25, D.C.

Created during the Depression, in 1934, to protect the American public against malpractices in the securities markets, the Securities and Exchange Commission is now generally accepted as a useful and necessary watchdog of the financial community. Its present chairman is William L. Cary, a lawyer who specializes in tax and corporation law and a former professor of law at Northwestern and Columbia universities. A few months after he became chairman of the SEC in March 1961 the commission began a full-scale investigation of the securities markets, the first study of its kind in twenty-five years.

William Lucius Cary was born in Columbus, Ohio on November 27, 1910, the second child and only son of William Lincoln Cary and Ellen K. (Taugher) Cary. His father was a utility company lawyer who at the time of his death in 1935 was president of the Newark (Ohio) Telephone Company. Cary recalls that he had "a reasonably pleasant childhood—nothing abnormal, nothing subnormal, and nothing supernormal."

After graduating from high school, Cary went on to Yale University. Elected to Phi Beta Kappa, he graduated from Yale with a B.A. degree in 1931 and continued his education at Yale Law School, from which he graduated with an LL.B. degree in 1934. That same year he qualified for practice in Ohio, Illinois, Massachusetts, the District of Columbia, and New York. He practised law with the firm of Squire, Sanders & Dempsey in Cleveland from 1934 until 1936. Returning to school in 1936, he studied at the Harvard University Graduate School of Business Administration, from which he graduated with an M.B.A. degree in 1938.

In 1938 Cary went to Washington, D.C., where he served as an attorney in the Securities and Exchange Commission, and in 1940 he became a special assistant to the Attorney General in the tax division of the Department of Justice. He left that position in 1942 to become a counsel in the Office of the Coordinator of Inter-American Affairs in Rio de Janeiro, Brazil. During World War II, from 1944 to 1945, Cary served as a captain in the United States Marines with the Office of Strategic Services in Romania and Yugoslavia.

Returning to academic life after the war, Cary lectured on corporation law at the Harvard School of Business Administration from 1946 to 1947, and in 1947 he became a professor of law at the Northwestern University School of Law in Chicago. While in Chicago he served on the tax and corporation laws committees of the American Bar Association and became friends with Adlai Stevenson, for whom he worked in the "Volunteers for Stevenson" in 1952. (He also worked with the "Citizens for Kennedy" in 1960.) During the Korean conflict Cary took leave from Northwestern to serve as deputy counselor for procurement with the Department of the Army from 1951 to 1952, representing the Army before Congressional investigating committees dealing with financing and procurement.

In 1955 Cary left Northwestern University to join the faculty of Columbia University Law School. At Columbia he carried one of the heaviest teaching schedules on the faculty—three courses and two seminars in the fields of corporation law and taxation. While teaching there, Cary compiled a casebook, *Cases and Materials on Corporations*, published in 1956 by the Columbia University Law School. The third edition of the casebook, which is used by law schools throughout the United States, was compiled by Cary with Ralph J. Baker and published by the Foundation Press in 1958. Cary has also written about the effects of taxation upon corporate mergers.

Cary was a visiting professor of law at the University of California at Berkeley in the summer of 1950, at Stanford University in the summer of 1954, and at Yale University in the summers of 1957 and 1958. He has also taught at the University of Istanbul in Turkey. Before he was asked to assume the post with the Securities and Exchange Commission in 1961, he had planned to spend his sabbatical year, 1962, as a visiting professor of law at the London School of Economics. While teaching at Columbia, Cary spent one day a week working as a consultant to the Wall Street law firm of Patterson, Belknap & Webb.

President John F. Kennedy named Cary the fourteenth chairman of the Securities and Exchange Commission on February 3, 1961. Sworn in on March 27, 1961, Cary succeeded Edward N. Gadsby, who resigned the chairmanship but remained a member of the commission. Until June 5, 1961 Cary served out the term of Daniel J. McCauley, Jr., a member who had resigned; he then began serving his own full five-year term. He receives an annual salary of $20,500.

The Securities and Exchange Commission has grown a great deal since its creation. Established under the Securities Exchange Act of 1934 to protect the public and investors against malpractices in American securities and financial markets, the first commission operated on a budget of $1,535,000 and with a staff of 696. Twenty-eight years later the SEC has a budget of some $12,800,000 and a staff of 1,481.

The commission administers a number of laws that provide, among other things, for full public disclosure of pertinent facts about securities offered to the public and listed on exchanges. Information on both exchange-traded and over-the-counter securities must be registered with the SEC. Investment (mutual) companies and investment counselors are required to register with the commission. Although the accuracy of the registrants' statements is not necessarily guaranteed, the sanctions that the SEC can apply—including suspension from the exchange as well as civil and criminal suits—deter misrepresentation in most cases. The commission investigates complaints and irregularities in the sale and purchase of securities.

In June 1961, shortly after he had become chairman of the SEC, Cary appeared before a subcommittee of the House Interstate and Foreign Commerce Committee to endorse a proposed study of the adequacy of the rules of American securities exchanges and associations for protecting investors. A full-scale study of national securities markets had not been made since the 1930's. Cary said the investigation would focus on the growing number of unqualified persons who are dealing in securities; on mutual funds and complaints of "questionable relationships" between funds, brokers, underwriters, and fund directors; and on the over-the-counter market, where there is often insufficient information on stocks issued by companies.

WILLIAM L. CARY

Cary explained that the volume of business in securities has expanded and that more and more people, particularly small investors, are buying stocks. This has led to the proliferation of "inexperienced, freewheeling" brokers and salesmen who do not maintain professional standards of conduct and to the establishment of exchange branch offices that are sometimes inadequately supervised. (In October 1961 the SEC ordered securities houses to maintain more detailed histories of their officers and employees with an eye to weeding out persons with records of unethical conduct.)

Discussing other problems, Cary said that there had been an increase in the number of "hot issues" appearing on exchanges. These stocks, usually bearing a glamorous scientific name, are listed on the market for the first time at prices that are pegged artificially high by various manipulative practices. Cary also mentioned problems connected with the over-the-counter market, on which many stocks are traded. This is a loosely knit market in which individual brokers bring sellers and buyers together without the benefit of an organized exchange. No information is available, Cary said, on the volume of trading in any stock on the over-the-counter market; the volume is an important factor in assessing the price fluctuations of a stock. Cary mentioned the need for investigating unregulated money-lenders who help clients to purchase stock on a margin as low as 25 percent. Federal Reserve rules, which do not apply to these lenders, require that a person borrowing from a bank or broker to buy stocks must himself supply at least 70 percent of the stock value in cash or other collateral.

On September 5, 1961 President Kennedy signed into law a bill authorizing an appropriation of $750,000 for a special study of securities markets. This was later increased by $200,000. At the beginning of the commission's investi-

CARY, WILLIAM L.—*Continued*

gation Cary assured the investment industry that the study would be thorough but would not be a "flamboyant anti-Wall Street publicity venture." He said that if broad abuses of the law were uncovered, the commission would move immediately to end the wrongful practices or sponsor corrective legislation as soon as possible. He subsequently remarked, however, that the regulation of stock trading can best be done by the industry itself.

In November 1961 the SEC issued an important decision, written by Cary, in which it extended the definition of the "insider," whom the law prohibits from using special securities information for private gain. "Insiders" had been defined previously as major stockholders, officers, and directors of a company issuing stock. The new ruling extended the definition to include any person who receives special information through a connection with "insiders."

In August 1962 the SEC made public a controversial report, prepared by the Wharton School of Finance and Commerce, on the $24-billion mutual fund industry. The somewhat critical study contended that the small investor could do as well buying common stocks on his own as he could through a mutual fund. It mentioned complaints of high fees paid to the investment counselors who advise the funds and of high sales commissions that fund subscribers are required to pay. Cary indicated that the SEC special study would expand on the Wharton report. In May 1962 the SEC held public hearings that focused on abuses in selling securities, particularly by employees of mutual companies.

Speaking before the members of the Investment Bankers Association in Hollywood, Florida on November 28, 1962, Cary advised the securities industry to intensify its self-regulation. He warned that if it failed to do so, the government might have to step in "to fill an evident public need," and noted that self-regulation in the over-the-counter market had much room for growth.

The SEC report on the special study, issued in three installments in April, July, and August of 1963, noted that a number of "grave abuses" existed in the securities markets but that the picture was "not one of persuasive and fraudulent activity." Moving with circumspection to avoid upsetting the stock market, the SEC in the main refrained from suggesting correctives imposed from without and adjured the securities industry to set its own house in order.

Cary is a member of the American and New York bar associations, the American Law Institute, and the law fraternity Phi Delta Phi. He belongs to the Century Club in New York and the Metropolitan Club in Washington, D.C. He is a Protestant.

Of medium build with dark, graying hair and blue eyes, he enjoys going for brisk walks, playing tennis, and listening to music. Among his colleagues he has a reputation for "sweetness of temperament combined with a fundamental toughness of fiber." William Lucius Cary married Katherine Lemoine Fenimore Cooper, a great-great-granddaughter of James Fenimore

Cooper, in 1954. They have two daughters, Linn F. C. and Katherine F. C.

References

N Y Post p24 F 6 '61 por
N Y Times p8 F 4 '61 por
Who's Who in America, 1962-63

CASEY, ROBERT J(OSEPH) Mar. 14, 1890-Dec. 4, 1962 Journalist; reporter and foreign correspondent for the Chicago *Daily News* (1920-47); author of thirty-four books, including several on his experiences as a newsman. See *Current Biography* (March) 1943.

Obituary

N Y Times p47 D 5 '62

CELEBREZZE, ANTHONY J(OSEPH) (sĕl"ĕ-brēz'ĭ) Sept. 4, 1910- United States Secretary of Health, Education, and Welfare; lawyer *Address:* b. Department of Health, Education, and Welfare, 330 Independence Ave., S.W., Washington 25, D.C.; h. 7207 Pomander Lane, Chevy Chase, Md.; 9918 Lake Ave., Cleveland, Ohio

With its hundreds of responsibilities and services carried out through an unwieldy complex of numerous divisions, bureaus, and offices, the Department of Health, Education, and Welfare intimately touches many phases of American life. Its Secretary since July 1962, Anthony J. Celebrezze, is a self-made lawyer of Italian descent who for five terms as Mayor of Cleveland had worked closely with people and human issues, as well as complex administrative problems. Among the Kennedy administration's politically explosive programs of which Celebrezze became the champion when he succeeded Abraham A. Ribicoff at HEW were medical care for the aged and federal aid to education.

The ninth of thirteen children, Anthony Joseph Celebrezze was born to Rocco and Dorothy (Marcoguiseppe) Celebrezze in Anzi, a village in southern Italy, on September 4, 1910. (The family name was originally spelled Cilibrizzi.) All of Celebrezze's brothers and sisters were born in the United States; and his father, a railroad track walker, and his mother were both naturalized citizens of the United States. They had visited their native area in the hope of finding better employment. Shortly before Anthony's birth, Rocco Celebrezze went back to America, but he could not afford to send for his wife so that their ninth child could be born in the United States.

Two years later the Celebrezzes were reunited in Cleveland, where the children grew up in a slum area like those that Anthony Celebrezze, as Mayor of Cleveland, later succeeded in having razed. He started working at the age of six, selling newspapers with his brothers at a downtown stand that became known as "Celebrezze Corner." At Central High School in Cleveland he played halfback on the football team in his senior year, and about that time he began to increase his income by boxing on local sports programs. He graduated from high school in 1929, studied for one year at John Carroll University in Cleveland, and then transferred to Ohio Northern University in Ada. To meet his expenses he worked as a gandy dancer for the New York Central Railroad, loading freight and laboring on section gangs. In 1936 he received the LL.B. degree from Ohio Northern and his admission to the Ohio bar.

Celebrezze acquired his early experience in law on the legal staff of the Ohio Bureau of Unemployment Compensation. After three years there, in 1939 he opened his own law office in Cleveland, where he engaged in general practice for the next thirteen years, except for a period of World War II service as a seaman in the United States Navy. Entering politics in 1950, he was elected on the Democratic ticket to the Ohio Senate and was re-elected in 1952. He served on the Senate's judiciary, taxation, veterans affairs and civil defense, elections, and federal relations committees, as well as the committee on television education and bureau of code revision and the Senate highway study commission. In the Senate, according to *Time* (July 20, 1962), he "became Governor Frank Lausche's representative . . . when the Governor passed over the regular minority leader."

When Thomas B. Burke, who served a record span of nine years as Mayor of Cleveland, decided in 1953 not to seek a fifth elected term, the Democratic state machine nominated Albert S. Porter for the office. Celebrezze entered the mayoral race as an independent Democrat and easily defeated Porter in the October primary. Some Democratic leaders ignored Celebrezze's campaign, but Governor Lausche and Mayor Burke campaigned in his behalf, and the Cleveland Federation of Labor and the Congress of Industrial Organizations also endorsed him. In the election on November 3, 1953 Celebrezze won over the Republican candidate, former Juvenile Court Judge William J. McDermott, by a comfortable majority.

Although Celebrezze's relations with several of Cleveland's political leaders and city councilmen remained cool, his popularity with the voters increased. In October 1955 he moved into state prominence by winning a majority of all votes in a three-man contest for the mayoral nomination in the primary, thus becoming, under a two-year-old amendment to the city charter, the only mayoral candidate listed on the November ballot. In the primary two years later he polled 57 percent of all votes and in 1959 was again an easy victor. When he ran for his fifth term, in 1961, he received an unprecedented 73.8 percent of the total vote, carrying every ward in Cleveland.

During his first term as Mayor, in the spring of 1955, Celebrezze formed the Cleveland Seaport Foundation to promote the city as a world trade center, and later in the year he furthered an $8,000,000 seaway bond issue. Among his other accomplishments during almost nine years in office was the inauguration of a $140,000,000 urban renewal undertaking, including the University Circle Cultural, Educational, and Medical Center, a project of special interest to Celebrezze.

Dept. of Health, Education & Welfare
—S. Stanton Singer

ANTHONY J. CELEBREZZE

His program of community progress for Cleveland covered improvements in airports, highways, harbors, recreational facilities, and housing.

A friend of the late Miss Bell Greve, director from 1932 to 1953 of the Cleveland Rehabilitation Center, Mayor Celebrezze was concerned for the welfare of the physically handicapped. His approach to relocation problems was sympathetic and realistic. When twenty-five families of Cuban refugees descended on Cleveland in February 1962, Celebrezze said in a news conference that there were no barriers in Cleveland, and that anyone was welcome. "We have many unemployed here at the present time," he warned, however. "If jobs are available, I should think they'd be given to Clevelanders first." Later in 1962, when twelve Negro "reverse freedom riders" arrived in Cleveland from Centerville, Alabama, Celebrezze severely criticized the Mayor of Centerville, but said that nothing would be done to bar the Negroes from Cleveland because as Americans they had a right to freedom of movement.

As a municipal administrator, Celebrezze was perhaps unique among American mayors in that during his tenure he reduced the number of city employees. In 1958-59 he was president of the American Municipal Association and in 1962, president and director of the United States Conference of Mayors. He was appointed to the Advisory Committee on Intergovernmental Relations by President Eisenhower in 1959 and reappointed by President Kennedy in 1962.

President Kennedy's nomination on July 16, 1962 of Celebrezze to succeed Abraham A. Ribicoff as United States Secretary of Health, Education, and Welfare was unanimously approved by the Senate Finance Committee and on July 20 was approved by voice vote in the full Senate. Since his first news conference, on August 7, Secretary Celebrezze has repeatedly endorsed the

CELEBREZZE, ANTHONY J.—*Continued*

administration's controversial programs of medical care to the aged through Social Security and of federal aid to higher education. Some political observers had speculated that Celebrezze, a Roman Catholic, might modify the administration's stand against aid to parochial schools. In October 1962, however, he said that after a close study of the question he had become convinced that federal aid to private elementary and secondary schools is unconstitutional.

Just before resigning the HEW post to become a candidate for the United States Senate from Connecticut, Ribicoff complained, "The man in my job wears twenty different hats a day, runs 110 different programs and is responsible for seventy-five separate budget items. And the list is growing all the time." He recommended that the department be broken up because its diversity and diffuseness defied successful administration. Celebrezze hopes to reduce his management problems by consolidating some of the department's activities, but he is opposed to splitting the department or transferring any of its offices to other agencies.

The Department of Health, Education, and Welfare was created in April 1953, and at the time of Celebrezze's appointment as Secretary, it was employing around 73,000 persons and spending about $4,605,000,000 a year. The department, which superseded the former Federal Security Agency and certain other agencies, now administers 112 programs allocated to five major divisions—the Public Health Service, the Social Security Administration, the Office of Education, the Office of Vocational Rehabilitation, and the Food and Drug Administration. It also supervises Howard University in Washington and a few other federally aided corporations.

HEW's largest divisions are the Social Security Administration (which includes the Bureau of Old Age and Survivors Insurance, the Bureau of Family Services, the Children's Bureau, and the Bureau of Federal Credit Unions) and the Public Health Service (which covers the Office of the Surgeon General, the Bureau of Medical Services, the Bureau of State Services, the National Institutes of Health, and the National Library of Medicine). The Social Security Administration was budgeted at over $2 billion in the fiscal year which began on July 1, 1961, and the Public Health Service received over $1 billion. Among the functions of the Office of Education is the administration of National Defense Education Act grants-in-aid to states, which in 1961 totaled $436,000,000.

In 1955 Celebrezze received the Brotherhood Award of the National Conference of Christians and Jews, the honorary degree of Doctor of Humanity from Wilberforce University in Ohio, and the decoration of the Order of Merit of the Republic of Italy. He was cited by the United Negro College Fund in 1956. Celebrezze is a stocky, rugged-looking, powerfully built man with black hair and a close-trimmed black mustache. He speaks ordinarily in a low voice, which, however, he does not hesitate to raise for oratorical effect. "Mr. Celebrezze is a driving worker," a *Christian Science Monitor* (July 16, 1962) reporter wrote. "If he has had a weakness it has been that he is reluctant to delegate authority, preferring to have a hand in every action himself."

Anthony J. Celebrezze and his high school sweetheart, Anne Marco, were married on May 7, 1938 and have one son, Anthony, Jr., a midshipman at the United States Naval Academy, and two daughters, Jean Anne and Susan Marie. Mrs. Celebrezze is a graduate of Western Reserve University School of Education and was a teacher in the Cleveland public schools before her marriage. She takes a special interest in the Camp Fire Girls, serving as a member of its national board of directors. Celebrezze's hobby is fishing.

References

N Y Herald Tribune p8 Jl 15 '62; p6 Jl 18 '62
N Y Post Mag p2 Jl 22 '62 por
N Y Times p75 O 9 '55; p35 Jl 15 '62; p46 Jl 29 '62
Newsweek 60:15 Jl 23 '62 por
Time 80:19 Jl 20 '62; 80:14 Jl 27 '62
U S News 53:16 Jl 30 '60 por
Washington (D.C.) Post A p6 Jl 15 '62
Who's Who in America, 1962-63
Who's Who in the Midwest (1960)

CHAMBERLAIN, (GEORGE) RICHARD

Mar. 31, 1935(?)- Actor; singer
Address: b. c/o MGM-TV, 1540 Broadway, New York 36

Since September 28, 1961 one of the most popular of the current television shows has been *Dr. Kildare*, which deals with the problems that challenge a young intern in the course of his hospital training. Richard Chamberlain, who stars in this hour-long weekly melodrama over NBC-TV, plays a dedicated doctor who matures under the guidance of his senior colleague, Dr. Gillespie, acted by Raymond Massey.

Watched by some 80,000,000 fans in thirty-one countries, the show ranks among the top ten in the influential Nielsen ratings. *Dr. Kildare* brought fame to Chamberlain, who earlier had held only minor assignments in motion pictures and television. Ambitious to make a name for himself also as a singer and dancer, he hopes to perform eventually in musical comedies, films, and night clubs. In 1963 Richard Chamberlain was voted the favorite male performer in the *TV Guide* poll.

George Richard Chamberlain, the second son of Elsa and Charles Chamberlain, was born on March 31, 1935 (one source suggests 1936) in Angelus Hospital in Los Angeles, California. His mother is a former singer, and his father owns a plant that manufactures store fixtures. Dick Chamberlain grew up in a comfortable home in Beverly Hills. "My early childhood was so placid and uneventful that I can scarcely remember it," he said in an interview for *McCall's* magazine (August 1962). "I never hated my parents, I played with other nice kids in the neighborhood, and I worshiped my older brother, Bill."

After attending Beverly Vista Grammar School, Chamberlain entered Beverly Hills High School, where he ran on the track team and was elected to Knights and Squires, an honorary society whose members are chosen on the basis of good grades, good conduct, and participation in extracurricular activities. The *Watchtower*, his school yearbook, voted him the "most reserved, most sophisticated, most courteous, and [the student with] the best physique."

Intending to become a designer, Chamberlain continued his studies at Pomona College in Claremont, California, but he switched to painting when he came to view designing as "too commercial." He found his few science courses difficult. As a member of the university track team, he earned his letter by running the 220-yard dash, the quarter mile, and the relay. In his senior year he became interested in dramatics and appeared in *King Lear*, *Arms and the Man*, and *The Lady's Not For Burning*, although he considered himself a "simply terrible actor."

Recalling his college days in an interview in *TV Guide* (March 16, 1963) he said, "I was extremely shy. In college I was a hermit. I sat in my little room and I painted pictures. I was in some sort of a cocoon. . . . Then I discovered acting. The stage seemed like a place where you could escape from the cocoon. It seemed like a place where you could be free. Free to express your emotions . . . free to move . . . free to shout. It seemed like a way to have fun without getting involved in real life." During his last semester he took vocal lessons to improve his speaking voice.

Chamberlain graduated from Pomona College in 1956 with a B.A. degree in art; soon afterwards he was drafted into the United States Army as a private for a two-year tour of duty. He spent sixteen months in Korea as a company clerk and was discharged with the rank of sergeant in 1958. Uncertain about his career plans, he returned to painting but disliked the solitude it entailed. He began to study voice at the Los Angeles Conservatory of Music under Carolyn Trojanowski and took drama lessons with Jeff Corey.

An actor's agent and friend of the family, Lilly Messenger, arranged for Chamberlain to read scripts for television producers. Although still dissatisfied with his acting skills, he secured small parts in *Gunsmoke*, *Rescue 8*, *Bourbon Street Beat*, *Mr. Lucky*, *Thriller*, *The Deputy*, and *Alfred Hitchcock Presents*. He also had parts in two movies, *The Secret of the Purple Reef* (1960), a mystery melodrama, and *A Thunder of Drums* (1961), a Western.

In mid-1960 George Le Maire, a high school classmate of Chamberlain's who had become executive assistant to the head of MGM studios, saw Chamberlain's picture in the Academy Players Directory when he was searching for an actor to play a rich cowboy in a series called *The Paradise Kid*. Chamberlain was screen tested and given the part. Although this pilot film was scrapped, MGM put Chamberlain under a regular term contract in 1960. After his successful appearances in *Dr. Kildare*, a new contract was signed, under which he reportedly makes $1,500 **a week.**

RICHARD CHAMBERLAIN

When MGM executives first considered filming a *Dr. Kildare* television series based on the old movies starring Lew Ayres and Lionel Barrymore, they had planned a half-hour show with Lew Ayres as a mature Dr. Kildare. Later, however, they decided to extend the episodes to sixty minutes and to keep the original format of a young intern and his senior colleague. Raymond Massey was chosen to play the older physician, Dr. Gillespie, and a "good-looking, clean-cut type of youngster" was sought to play Dr. Kildare. Norman Felton, executive producer of the show has described his reaction to Chamberlain's audition for the part. "During Dick's first reading, he was totally unable to bring any variety into his acting, but I saw a great warmth and personal charm. . . . We called him back for a second reading, and again he read badly. But we could find no one really better for the role, so we finally decided to go with Dick." From the day of his debut as Dr. Kildare on September 28, 1961, Chamberlain was an unqualified success.

The *Dr. Kildare* programs center on the emotive aspects of medical practice and tend to pass over its clinical side. Kildare, a dedicated and gentle intern, sympathizes with his patients. According to an article in *TV Guide* (March 16, 1963), Chamberlain projects in his part "neither mysterious nor heroic qualities, but rather the somewhat blank innocence of inexperience. . . . He appears to lack even a nodding acquaintance with passion . . . and is liable to inspire women with an ardent desire to mend his socks." Chamberlain himself considers Kildare "an irreclaimable bore." "If I were to mold Kildare," he says, "I would make him more subject to faults and weaknesses—like the rest of us." For the 1963-64 season the intern Kildare graduated to the status of resident physician. Although he spends his working days in a hospital setting, Chamberlain has little desire to learn more about **medicine.**

(Continued next page)

CHAMBERLAIN, RICHARD—*Continued*

Because the public may one day tire of Dr. Kildare, Chamberlain is perfecting his acting, dancing, and singing to prepare himself for other work. In addition to continuing dancing and singing lessons he works with a rehearsal club of which he is president. A bass-baritone, he made his television singing debut in March 1962 with the number "How About You," on Arthur Freed's *Hollywood Melody*. His first record, "The Theme Music From Dr. Kildare," backed by "A Kiss to Build a Dream On," was released in June 1962, and he is preparing another recording. In April 1963 he performed a duet with his friend Clara Ray at her nightclub debut at the Beverly Hilton Hotel in Los Angeles. After completing the shooting of the last *Dr. Kildare* episode of the 1962-63 season Chamberlain began work on the motion picture *Twilight of Honor,* in which he plays a lawyer. He hopes to undertake musical comedy and nightclub work as well as more films and recordings in the future.

Chamberlain has been affectionately described by the comedienne Carol Burnett as "squeaky clean." He is six feet one inch tall, weighs 175 pounds, and has blond hair and blue eyes. A close friend has called Chamberlain "smart" and "thoughtful," and has said that he is "always evaluating himself." Chamberlain's worst fault, according to his voice teacher, is "a tendency toward self-depreciation." He is said to be well-organized, punctual, thrifty, and considerate of his fellow workers. When he can snatch free time from his long working day, he swims, motors, and runs, or listens to classical, popular, or folk music.

References

Look 26:137+ N 20 '62 pors
McCall's 89:66+ Ag '62 por
Sat Eve Post 236:14+ Mr 30 '63 por
TV Guide 11:9+ Mr 16 '63 por

CHAVAN, Y(ESHWANTRAO) B(ALWAN-TRAO) (chǎ-vän') Mar. 12, 1914- Defense Minister of India

Address: Ministry of Defense, Government of India, New Delhi, India

The appointment of Y. B. Chavan as Defense Minister of India on November 14, 1962 was seen by many observers as signaling a new and closer co-operation between the West and India. Chavan, who has been mentioned as a possible successor to Premier Jawaharlal Nehru, replaced V. K. Krishna Menon in the defense post. Although both Chavan and Menon are longtime disciples of Nehru, they are virtually complete opposites in every other regard. Menon, who was blamed for India's lack of military preparedness in the face of the invasion of India's northern borders, is known for his quick temper and tendency to alienate people. Chavan, who at forty-nine is the youngest member of Nehru's cabinet, is noted for his sense of humor, calm, and ability to make friends. The new Defense Minister has not held a previous post in the national government, but he impressed Indians with his efficiency as chief minister of the state of Maharashtra (formerly

Bombay) from 1956 to 1962, and his appointment as Defense Minister was widely approved throughout India.

Yeshwantrao Balwantrao Chavan was born on March 12, 1914 in Devrashtre, a small village of the Satara district in what is now the western state of Maharashtra. He belongs to the Kshatriya, or warrior, caste and is one of the Mahrattas, a Marathi-speaking people who during the eighteenth century were the leading power group in India. Chavan's father, a poor farmer, died when the boy was three years old, and his mother raised him with the help of one of his two older brothers, who worked at the civil court. Y. B. Chavan also has an older sister.

At Tilak High School in Karad, about ten miles from his village, Chavan obtained his primary and secondary education. At school he organized a student movement against the British government in 1930 and took part in civil disobedience demonstrations in 1932. Because of his political activities he was imprisoned by the British for eighteen months. After his release from jail he enrolled in 1934 at Rajaram College in Kolhapur, then known as the "poor man's college." By the time he graduated with the B.A. degree in 1938 his nationalistic activities had made him a student hero, and his talents as a speaker had enabled him to win several oratory contests. From the Law College at Poona, where he organized study circles, Chavan received the LL.B. degree in 1941.

Returning to Karad, he set up a flourishing law practice and became a member of the Marxist movement started by M. N. Roy. He broke with the Royist group in 1939, however, when Roy advocated Indian support of the British during World War II. Chavan then joined the Indian National Congress party of Mohandas Gandhi and Jawaharlal Nehru, which placed Indian independence before wartime assistance to the British. Taking part in local Congress party politics, he was elected president of the Satara district committee and made a member of the Maharashtra provincial committee in 1940. (He served as secretary of the latter body from 1948 to 1950.) During 1942 and 1943 he directed the Satara district underground activities for Indian independence and opposition to the British war effort, and in 1944 he was arrested by the British after a reward had been offered for his capture.

Released after a year in prison, Chavan returned to his law practice in Karad. In 1946 he was elected to the Bombay state legislative assembly and appointed a parliamentary secretary. As parliamentary secretary he helped organize the Home Guard. He also took a large part in reviving the Tamasha movement, a network of village dramatic societies, which is particularly popular in Chavan's home state of Maharashtra. In 1948, with the help of friends, he founded a Marathi-language daily newspaper, *Prakash*, at Satara. He had earlier established the Marathi weekly, *Lok Kranti*. After the general elections of 1952 had resulted in a victory for the Congress party, Chavan was given the portfolio of civil supplies in the Bombay state ministers' council. When his department was closed down he took over the state ministry for local self-government and forests.

In this twin ministry Chavan improved the administration of the village panchayats. The panchayats, elected by the entire adult population of a village, are responsible for sanitation, provision of medical facilities, civic amenities, and the management of community assets. He also liberalized forest regulations, making many concessions to the people of the Kanara district (now part of Mysore state) and removed many grievances with regard to forest administration in all districts of Bombay state.

Chavan became chief minister of Bombay state on November 1, 1956, after his predecessor, Morarji Desai, had been appointed to the national cabinet in New Delhi. He was returned to the Bombay legislative assembly from the Karad north constituency of Satara district in the general elections of 1957. A reorganization of states in 1956 relieved Bombay of four Kannada-speaking districts and added to its jurisdiction eight Marathi-speaking districts. Bombay remained a bilingual state, however, and friction between its Gujarati-language and Marathi-language populations continued, until it was divided into the states of Gujarat and Maharashtra in May 1960.

Under the ministership of Chavan, who was acceptable to most factions within the state, the rioting and bloodshed connected with the language conflict were reduced. Under his guidance Bombay state also developed into one of the most prosperous areas of the nation, and his encouragement of private industry helped to bring about the present boom in light industry there. After the formation in May 1960 of Maharashtra, which is comprised of twenty-six districts and whose capital is the city of Bombay, Chavan became chief minister of the new state, holding the portfolios of general administration, home, planning, and industry.

During the period of Chavan's incumbency, the legislature passed such important legislation as a "land ceiling" law, a "decentralization of powers" measure, and a law providing for distribution of surplus land to the landless. Chavan was popular with urban industrial workers and with the peasantry and had a reputation within his own party for having a practical, common-sense outlook. He has been described as an efficient administrator, as a political strategist who takes a middle-of-the-road position, and as an undogmatic man who makes few enemies. A reporter for the Manchester *Guardian* (November 15, 1962) wrote, "He is a brilliant coordinator, excelling at getting the best out of everybody without throwing his weight around." In the elections of 1962 Chavan demonstrated his popularity with voters by swinging a landslide victory for the Congress party in Bombay, which returned V. K. Krishna Menon to parliament. Chavan himself was elected to the Maharashtra legislative assembly from the Karad north constituency of Satara district with a large majority.

On November 14, 1962 Chavan was appointed Minister of Defense in the national government, succeeding V. K. Krishna Menon, who had been heavily criticized for leaving India unprepared to resist the Communist Chinese invasion that began on India's northern borders in the

Government of India, New Delhi
Y. B. CHAVAN

fall of 1962. A Manchester *Guardian* writer noted in an editorial on November 15, 1962, "Happily the reports circulating . . . that Y. B. Chavan was to be the new Indian Defence Minister have turned out to be true. . . . Efficient administration is what is above all needed in the Ministry of Defence at present."

Unlike Krishna Menon, Chavan does not believe that India can count upon the Russians to restrain the Chinese Communists from aggression. On his first day in office he set the tone for his new ministry when he said, "No one need have any illusion. A Communist country never gives up violence nor abjures the use of force." He subsequently remarked, "Communist blood is thicker than coexistence water."

Soon after becoming Defense Minister, Chavan toured the battlefront with Premier Nehru. In January 1963 he stated that India planned to increase the size of its military forces, but that expansion would depend largely upon the amount of modern equipment that would be supplied from abroad. (America, Great Britain, and other Western countries have already given some military aid to India and have sent military advisers to determine needs for additional aid.) Ultimately, Chavan said, it would be more economical to produce military equipment in India than to rely on foreign arms shipments, and factories for the manufacture of automatic rifles and ammunition are being given top priority on the Indian agenda.

In February 1963 it was announced that India would double its defense budget to meet the threat of Chinese Communist invasion. Some $1.8 billion were earmarked for the armed forces in the fiscal year beginning April 1, 1963. It is planned to create from six to ten army divisions, improve air force facilities, and generally strengthen defenses. According to diplomatic observers, the replacement of Krishna Menon

CHAVAN, Y. B.—*Continued*

by Chavan has opened the way for smoother co-operation between Indian generals and Western military missions.

Chavan is of medium height, weighs 200 pounds, and prefers native dress. He enjoys sports, music, poetry, and the fine arts. He and his wife, Venutai, have no children. Chavan was a founder of the Satara District Central Co-operative Bank. Interested in social work, he organized the Shivaji Educational Society, which runs a high school and science college at Karad.

References

    Manchester Guardian p20 N 15 '62 por
    N Y Times p8 D 7 '62 por
    Newsday p50 D 6 '62 por
    U S News 53:17 N 26 '62 por
    Asia Who's Who (1960)
    International Who's Who, 1962-63

CHAVEZ, DENNIS Apr. 8, 1888-Nov. 18, 1962 Democratic member of the United States House of Representatives from New Mexico (1931-35); Senator (since 1935); champion of legislation for fair employment practices. See *Current Biography* (March) 1946.

Obituary

    N Y Times p1+ N 19 '62

CHURCHILL, EDWARD D(ELOS) Dec. 25, 1895- Surgeon
Address: b. Massachusetts General Hospital, Boston, Mass.; h. 269 Prospect St., Belmont, Mass.

In his area of specialization—thoracic (chest) surgery—Dr. Edward D. Churchill has helped to advance the frontiers of medical science through applied operative surgery, laboratory research, and teaching. He has been John Homans professor of surgery at the Harvard University Medical School since 1931 and chief of the General Surgical Service at Massachusetts General Hospital since 1948. Churchill was a pioneer in employing surgery in cases of tuberculosis and cancer of the lung. He performed the first successful operation in the United States to relieve constrictive pericarditis, a heart ailment, and he has done valuable work on diseases of the parathyroid glands. During World War II he served as a surgical consultant in the United States Army in the Mediterranean theater, evolving new concepts for management of the wounded in the field.

Born in Chenoa, Illinois on December 25, 1895, Edward Delos Churchill is the son of Ebenezer Delos and Maria A. (Farnsworth) Churchill. He was educated at Northwestern University, from which he received the B.S. degree in 1916 and the M.A. degree in 1917, as well as at the Harvard University Medical School, where he took the M.D. degree *cum laude* in 1920. Churchill completed his student internship at the Faulkner Hospital in Boston during the year 1919-20. He served his surgical internship from 1920 to 1922 and his residency from 1922 through 1924 at Massachusetts Hos-

pital. He was in the medical reserves of the United States Army in 1918.

At the Massachusetts General Hospital Churchill was an assistant in surgery in 1924-25, an assistant surgeon in the out-patient department in 1925-26, an associate in surgery in 1926-27, and an assistant visiting surgeon in 1927-28. From 1928 to 1930 he was an associate surgeon and the director of the surgical research laboratory at Boston City Hospital; he then returned to Massachusetts General Hospital as an associate surgeon. In 1931 Churchill was appointed chief of the West Surgical Service at Massachusetts General Hospital, and in 1948 he became chief of the General Surgical Service, a position he still holds.

Meanwhile, in 1922 Churchill had become a member of the teaching staff, and in 1928 of the faculty, of the Harvard University Medical School. He has encouraged his students to undertake scientific investigations because he believes that new laboratory discoveries are important in the development of improved healing methods. At Harvard University Churchill was an assistant in surgery during 1922-23, an alumni assistant in surgery in 1923-24, and an instructor in surgery from 1924 to 1928. During 1926-27 he studied in Europe as a Moseley Fellow, and on his return became surgical consultant, and later senior physician, at the Rutland (Massachusetts) State Sanatorium for tuberculosis, where he helped introduce the surgical treatment of tuberculosis into New England. From 1928 to 1931 Churchill was an associate professor of surgery at Harvard, and since 1931 he has been the John Homans Professor of Surgery there. This chair is located at Massachusetts General Hospital.

Specializing in thoracic (chest) surgery, Churchill has contributed to this field through laboratory research and applied operative surgery. Early in his career he developed an interest in the functioning and the diseases of the lung. He was the first to use spirometry (measurement of the breathing capacity of the lungs) to determine the reduction of lung ventilation following abdominal operations, and he wrote a paper on this subject with D. McNeil, which appeared in *Surgery, Gynecology, and Obstetrics* in April 1927. In the *Journal of Experimental Medicine*, in April 1929, Churchill and Oliver Cope described a reflex mechanism—rapid shallow breathing resulting from pulmonary congestion—that is now known as the Churchill-Cope reflex.

Churchill has contributed to the early development of surgery for cancer of the lung and pulmonary tuberculosis. At a time when the mortality rates from lobectomy (excision of the lobe of the lung) were about 50 percent because of clumsy techniques and septic complications, Churchill addressed himself to the problem and demonstrated the safety of selectively removing diseased parts of the lung in the treatment of chest diseases. In April 1932, at a meeting of the American Association for Thoracic Surgery, he presented a paper on "The Surgical Treatment of Carcinoma [malignant growth] of the Lung," describing the successful resection (excision of part of an organ) of the diseased lower and middle lobes of the right lung. The case he discussed was the first in which primary healing of the major bronchus was obtained by direct bronchial suture. A year later, in November 1933, Churchill performed the first single stage resection of the right lung for adenocarcinoma.

On July 18, 1928 Churchill performed one of the most notable surgical operations of his career, the decortication of the heart for relief of constrictive pericarditis. This is a condition in which the pericardium, or membranous sac surrounding the heart, tightens and squeezes the heart, causing chronic invalidism. By removing this membrane Churchill completely rehabilitated the patient. This was the first successful operation of its kind in the United States and one of the few in the world at that time. Through a subsequent large series of cases it became established as a dependable and widely used procedure.

During the 1930's Dr. Churchill was one of the medical men at Massachusetts General Hospital who pioneered in the study and treatment of hyperparathyroidism, a condition caused by an increase of its secretion by the parathyroid glands. He was the first to remove a parathyroid adenoma (tumor) from the mediastinum (the area between the two pleural sacs), and he recognized hyperplasia (abnormal multiplication of cells) of the parathyroid and performed a resection on the diseased glands.

The concept of segmental pneumonectomy (removal of lung tissue), to replace the previously advocated total pneumonectomy, was introduced by Churchill in 1939. He suggested also that the bronchopulmonary segment replace the lobe as the surgical unit of the lung, and this idea proved fruitful in the treatment of bronchiectasis (the dilation of the bronchus or bronchial tubes) and in the development of excision surgery for pulmonary tuberculosis.

Before World War II pulmonary tuberculosis was treated by collapse therapy, in which the diseased lung is collapsed and immobilized. Resection was not a recognized form of treating the disease, because it was considered dangerous in the presence of positive sputum due to possibilities of spreading the disease or causing bronchopleural fistula. Ignoring the more orthodox procedures, Churchill performed in 1939 a primary resection by lobectomy on six cases of pulmonary tuberculosis. The publication of the results in a paper in 1943 produced widespread controversy and criticism of its authors, Churchill and Robert Klopstock, but after World War II the use of resection instead of collapsotherapy, in pulmonary tuberculosis cases, with the aid of effective antibiotics became an accepted practice.

During World War II Churchill was commissioned a colonel in the medical corps of the United States Army, and he served in the North African-Mediterranean theater of operations as a surgical consultant from February 1943 to October 1945. He is credited with introducing many new procedures for management of the wounded, and he has written a number of articles about surgery during wartime. Churchill was awarded the Legion of Merit, the Distinguished Service Medal, and the European Theater Service Medal.

Churchill is a consultant to the Surgeon General of the Army, at whose request he made a tour of medical installations of the Far East

DR. EDWARD D. CHURCHILL

Command in January 1953, stopping in Hawaii, Japan, Korea, the Philippines, India, Thailand, Greece, and Italy. He is a charter member of the scientific advisory board of the Walter Reed Army Institute of Research, and he was formerly chairman of the medical advisory committee to the Secretary of War (1946-48), a member of the armed forces medical advisory committee to the Secretary of Defense (1948-51), a member of the committee on veterans' medical problems of the National Research Council, and a senior civilian consultant in thoracic surgery to the Surgeon General of the Army.

The recipient of a Rockefeller Foundation grant in 1958, Churchill visited medical centers in India and took part in the internship-residency program at King George's Medical College at Lucknow University. He has been visiting professor of surgery at the American University of Beirut and acting director of the department of surgery at the American University Hospital. Churchill has served on the editorial board of *Annals of Surgery*.

At present Churchill is special consultant to the chief of the division of general medical sciences of the National Institutes of Health. He serves on the advisory board of the American Hospital in Paris and is a consultant to the medical advisory council of the Shiraz Medical Center, Nemazee Hospital, Iran. Churchill is on the consulting staff of Faulkner Hospital, and he is chairman of the general executive committee of Massachusetts General Hospital. He is also a consultant to the New England Center and a trustee of Boston Medical Library.

Churchill has also been chairman, from 1946 to 1949, of the committee on surgery of the National Research Council; vice-chairman, in 1948-49 and 1953-55, of the task force on federal medical services of the Commission on Organization of the Executive Branch of the Government; a member of the Red Cross advisory

CHURCHILL, EDWARD D.—*Continued*

board on health service; a member of the graduate training committee of the American College of Surgeons; and a trustee of the Boylston Medical Society.

An honorary member of some fifteen foreign medical societies, Churchill is a fellow of the American Academy of Arts and Sciences and an honorary fellow of the Royal College of Surgeons. He holds honorary doctoral degrees from the University of Algiers (1944), Princeton University (1947), Queen's University, in Kingston, Ontario, Canada (1954), and the University of Alabama (1959). Churchill belongs to the American Association for Thoracic Surgery, of which he was president in 1948-49; the American Surgical Association, of which he was president in 1946-47; the Society of Clinical Surgery, of which he was president in 1949-50; and many other American scientific and professional societies. He is a Knight of the French Legion of Honor, an honorary officer of the military division of the Order of the British Empire, a Commander in the Order of the Crown of Italy, and an officer of the Lebanese National Order of the Cedar. He was awarded the Roswell Park Medal of the Buffalo Surgical Society in 1952, the James Ewing Society Annual Award in 1953, and the Henry Jacob Bigelow Medal of the Boston Surgical Society in 1955.

Edward D. Churchill married Mary Lowell Barton on July 7, 1927. They have four children, Mary Lowell, Frederick Barton, Edward Delos, and A. Coolidge. Churchill is a Presbyterian. He belongs to the Aesculapian Club, the Century Association, the Harvard Club of Boston, the Tavern Club, and the Thursday Evening Club. He is a member of Sigma Xi, the honorary science research fraternity, and Delta Tau Delta, a social fraternity.

References

American Medical Directory, 1961
American Men of Science 10th ed (1960-62)
Directory of Medical Specialists, 1959-60
Who's Who in America, 1952-53; 1962-63

CLAPP, GORDON R(UFUS) Oct. 28, 1905-Apr. 28, 1963 President of the Development and Resources Corporation (1955-63), one of whose major projects is a water power system in Iran; former chairman of the board of the Tennessee Valley Authority (1946-54); former deputy city administrator of New York City (1954-55). See *Current Biography* (February) 1947.

Obituary

N Y Times p31 Ap 29 '63

CLARK, SIR KENNETH (MACKENZIE)
July 13, 1903- British art authority; author
Address: h. Saltwood Castle, Hythe, Kent, England

A scholar of international reputation in the art of the Italian Renaissance and something of a Renaissance man himself, Sir Kenneth Clark is a leading representative of a group of British art experts whose influence derives from the new role of government as a patron of the arts. Clark, who was a student of the noted art critic Bernard Berenson, became the youngest man in history to hold the post of director of the British National Gallery. He has also served as Surveyor of the King's Pictures, as a member of the Ministry of Information during World War II, as Slade Professor of Fine Art at Oxford University, as chairman of Great Britain's Arts Council, and as chairman of the Independent Television Authority. His career, his writings, and his work with organizations devoted to the arts have won him several honorary degrees and other distinctions, as well as honorary membership in many learned societies. He received his knightage in 1938 and was named a fellow of the British Academy in 1949 and a Companion of Honour in 1959.

Kenneth Mackenzie Clark was born in London on July 13, 1903, the only child of Kenneth Mackenzie Clark, a prosperous thread manufacturer of Scottish background, and Margaret Alice (McArthur) Clark. The family fortune had been made in the early nineteenth century by Kenneth Clark's great-grandfather, who invented a cotton spool that proved of great value at a time when imports from the Continent to the British Isles were cut off by the Napoleonic blockade. The family traveled widely, and Kenneth Clark spent much of his youth in Scotland, Suffolk, and southern France. His parents had no special academic or artistic background, but in their travels they exposed their son to those influences that made him, at the age of nine, a passionate admirer of great art.

This precocious enthusiasm Clark carried with him to Winchester—one of the greatest of English public schools—and then to Trinity College, Oxford University, where he began his book on the revival of Gothic architecture. He attracted the attention of Bernard Berenson, the great authority on Italian art, and in 1926, after his graduation, he joined Berenson in Florence. Clark worked with Berenson for two years on the revision of the latter's *Drawings of the Florentine Painters.* Clark's own book, *The Gothic Revival: An Essay in the History of Taste* (Scribner, 1929) was welcomed by critics as a concise and informative survey of the Gothic movement.

In 1930 Clark was a member of the committee that arranged in that year a major exhibition of Italian art at Burlington House, in London. He was editor and one of the authors of the exhibition's commemorative catalog and might well have gone on from there to make his mark as a wealthy and knowledgeable dilettante. Instead, in 1931, he chose to accept an invitation to become Keeper of the Department of Fine Arts at Oxford's Ashmolean Museum, the first in a succession of more or less demanding public appointments. The second of these followed in 1934 when he succeeded Sir Augustus Daniel as director of the National Gallery, becoming, at the age of thirty-one, the youngest man ever to hold this post. In 1938 he was created a Knight Commander of the Bath.

Sir Kenneth's years as director of one of England's greatest museums were interrupted by the outbreak of World War II in 1939. He joined the Ministry of Information, serving successively as director of the film division, controller of home publicity, and controller of planning. In 1941 he returned to his post at the National Gallery. His wartime achievements included the organization, with Dame Myra Hess, of a distinguished series of lunchtime concerts at the National Gallery, some of which he conducted himself, and the launching of the War Artists scheme. He served throughout the war as chairman of the War Artists Advisory Committee, which commissioned artists to record various aspects of the British war effort, and marked one of the country's first ventures into state art patronage.

From March 1942 onward Clark also arranged for the return of famous paintings from places of safety to which they had been consigned at the outbreak of the war. The paintings were displayed at the gallery, one at a time, for periods of three weeks, until the end of the war. During the war period he continued to acquire notable paintings for the National Gallery. From 1934 to 1944, as Surveyor of the King's Pictures, he was responsible for what has been described as the world's largest private collection, housed at Hampton Court, Buckingham Palace, Windsor Castle, and elsewhere. Clark's two-volume *Catalogue of the Drawings of Leonardo da Vinci in the Collection of His Majesty the King at Windsor Castle* (Cambridge; Macmillan, 1935), placed the drawings for the first time in chronological order, and established the author as a da Vinci scholar of the first rank.

Clark's next book, *Leonardo da Vinci: An Account of his Development as an Artist* (Cambridge; Macmillan, 1939), was based on Clark's 1936 Ryerson Lectures at Yale University. A reviewer of the 1952 edition of the book wrote in the London *Times Literary Supplement* (July 11, 1952) that it was "the best single book on Leonardo," and praised its "vividness and fluency." Other publications of this period include Clark's edition of the *Last Lectures* of his friend, the critic Roger Fry (Cambridge; Macmillan, 1939); his British Academy lecture *Leon Battista Alberti on Painting* (Oxford, 1944); and his contribution to the Faber Gallery series, *Florentine Paintings, Fifteenth Century* (Faber, 1945; Pitman, 1948).

A writer for the *New Statesman* (December 18, 1954), noting the "extreme restlessness" of Clark's nature, says, "He has never wished to be fashioned in one mould; he has preferred to shift at the bidding . . . of his own temperament." In 1945 Sir Kenneth resigned from his directorship of the National Gallery, and in the following year went to Oxford University where he was Slade Professor of Fine Art until 1950. Here, according to a profile in the London *Observer* (March 30, 1958), "he was at his best. Lecturing to enthusiastic undergraduates, he gave a series of relaxed and witty performances which attained a popularity unmatched by anything similar since the days of Ruskin." A new edition of John Ruskin's *Praeterita* (Hart-Davis; Clarke, Irwin, 1949) contains an introduction by Clark.

Clark's *Landscape Into Art* (J. Murray, 1949), a book published in the United States as *Land-

British Inf. Services

SIR KENNETH CLARK

scape Painting* (Scribner, 1950), is based on his Oxford lectures. It discusses the development of landscape painting as a distinct art form and examines certain of its schools. Clive Bell, reviewing the book in the *New Statesman* (November 26, 1949), noted that Clark has "a turn for historical generalization based on knowledge, the scholar's gift of drawing inferences from apparently disconnected facts and slight indications, expository power and, above all, a love of painting." Even greater enthusiasm greeted the book *Piero della Francesca* (Phaidon, 1951). Stuart Preston in the New York *Times* (August 12, 1951) called it "one of the most important and beautiful art books to have appeared in many years."

According to the London *Observer* profile of Sir Kenneth, it is as a "cultural advocate" that he is happiest. "With quite exceptional gifts of speaking and writing, wide cultural erudition, a combination of traditional social tastes and advanced aesthetic ones, an easy manner and the entrée to all the right people, he is unrivalled as a propagandist for British contemporary art." Clark has proved the truth of this statement by his patronage and effective championing of such artists as Henry Moore and Graham Sutherland. With his wealth and great influence, he has done much to enhance the prestige of British art, in England and abroad. After May 1953, when he was named chairman of the Arts Council of Great Britain, he was able to continue this work on behalf of the government. The council, which Sir Kenneth had helped to found, is a government agency that gives financial support to artists in all fields.

Sir Kenneth remained chairman of the Arts Council until 1960. In August 1954 he accepted an additional heavy responsibility as the first chairman of Britain's Independent Television Authority (ITA). British television had previously been a one-network affair, monopolized by

CLARK, SIR KENNETH—*Continued*

the noncommercial British Broadcasting Corporation. The second network, authorized by the Television Act adopted by Parliament in 1954, was to carry programs created by professional contractors, who would rely for their profits on the sale of advertising time. The function of the ITA was to insure that high standards of taste were maintained in program content and advertising, and it was given absolute authority to enforce its rulings.

Although the introduction of commercial television aroused massive opposition in Parliament and elsewhere, the appointment of Sir Kenneth and his distinguished colleagues on the ITA disarmed criticism. Beverly Nichols commented in an article in *Saturday Night* (October 29, 1955): "I do not think we need greatly fear the impact of the new TV when its direction is in such wise, such sensitive, such searching hands." Examining Sir Kenneth's motives in accepting the post, a writer for the *New Statesman* (December 18, 1954) suggested: "By undertaking an ungrateful and a hard task, he has proved to himself that the man of taste, the virtuoso, can face the dust of the arena."

Meanwhile, Sir Kenneth continued his output of books, articles, and lectures. His book *The Nude; A Study in Ideal Form* (J. Murray; Pantheon, 1956) is an expansion of his A. W. Mellon Lectures in the Fine Arts, which he delivered at the National Gallery of Art in Washington, D.C., in 1953. It formed the basis of a much-praised exhibition at New York's Wildenstein Gallery in 1956. Commending *The Nude* in the *New Yorker* (April 20, 1957), a reviewer wrote: "Probably no one else alive today writes about art with Sir Kenneth's precise combination of intelligence, urbanity and erudition, and certainly his talent has never been better applied than in this volume." Clark's most recent book, *Looking at Pictures* (Holt, 1960), analyzed sixteen more or less familiar masterpieces, showing how they can be approached as a whole, in parts, in relation to the artist's life, and in other ways. "The meaning of a great work of art," he wrote, "must be related to our life in such a way as to increase our energy of spirit."

When Clark left the Independent Television Authority in 1957, independent television was firmly established in Britain. In 1961-62 he returned to Oxford for a year as Slade Professor of Fine Art. He is on the advisory council of the Victoria and Albert Museum, and he is a member of the National Art Collections Fund, the National Theatre Board, the Conseil Artistique des Musées Nationaux, and the Swedish, Spanish, and British Academies. He is much in demand as a lecturer and, as a world authority on Leonardo da Vinci and Piero della Francesca, he is frequently consulted on the authenticity of works attributed to these and other artists.

Sir Kenneth was named a fellow of the British Academy in 1949 and a Companion of Honour in 1959. He holds the Serena Medal of the British Academy (for Italian studies, 1955) and the Banister Fletcher Prize (1958). He has received honorary LL.D. degrees from the universities of Glasgow and Liverpool and honorary D.Lit. degrees from Columbia, Oxford, and London universities. Clark is also an honorary member of the Royal Scottish Academy, an honorary fellow of the Royal Institute of British Architects, and an honorary fellow of the Royal College of Art. His foreign honors include the rank of Commander of the Legion of Honor (France), Commander of the Order of the Crown of Italy, Grand Cross of Merit (Austria), and Commander, Lion of Finland.

On January 10, 1927 Sir Kenneth Clark married Elizabeth Martin, who once was described in the *New Statesman* (December 18, 1954) as "volatile, beautiful, and superbly stylish." They have two sons and a daughter. Sir Kenneth is five feet eleven inches tall, weighs 162 pounds, and has graying dark hair. According to the profile in the London *Observer* (March 30, 1958), he is "suave, aloof, fastidious," widely informed about music, films, literature, and the theater, as well as about his own subjects. In politics, he is "mildly progressive." He is "passionately interested in the welfare of the artist and the diffusion of his work for the benefit of the Common Man. . . . He is, in fact, the nearest thing we have got to the Continental conception of a Minister of the Fine Arts, influencing all our tastes." Sir Kenneth has lived since 1953 at Saltwood Castle, Kent, whose ancient walls are hung with paintings by Sutherland, Degas, and Renoir, as well as with the masterpieces of Renaissance Italy and ancient Greece. His clubs include the Athenaeum, St. James, Beefsteak, Traveller's, and Roxburghe.

References

Burke's Peerage, Baronetage, and Knightage, 1959
International Who's Who, 1962-63
Kelly's Handbook to the Titled, Landed and Official Classes, 1962-63
Twentieth Century Authors (First Supplement, 1955)
Who's Who, 1963

CLAY, CASSIUS (MARCELLUS, JR.) Jan. 18, 1942- Professional boxer
Address: h. 3302 Grand Ave., Louisville, Ky.

According to the proverb, silence is golden, but talk may be worth even more to a strapping and self-confident fighter named Cassius Clay. Although he has been boxing professionally for only three years, he is already a leading contender for the heavyweight crown. Clay turned professional in 1960 after he had won an Olympic gold medal in the light heavyweight division. His fists have brought him nineteen victories (fifteen knockouts) out of nineteen professional fights, and his loud and continual self-adulation ("I'm the greatest") and talent for predictive poetry ("They all must fall/in the round I call") have made him boxing's top drawing card.

When Clay fought Doug Jones in March 1963, Madison Square Garden was sold out for a professional fight for the first time in a decade, and in June 1963, 55,000 paying customers attended his fight with the British and Empire champion, Henry Cooper, in London. "Loud but likeable

Cassius, handsome, intelligent, and witty, can reel off quotable quotes faster than a printing press can get them out," Dan Parker wrote in the New York *Mirror* (June 23, 1963). "People who come to boo him, remain to cheer or at least break up over his drolleries."

Cassius Marcellus Clay, Jr., was born on January 18, 1942 in Louisville, Kentucky to Cassius Marcellus Clay, a commercial artist specializing in sign painting, and Odessa (Grady) Clay. The Clays trace their name back to the times of slavery: the great-great-grandfather of Cassius Clay, Jr., was owned by Cassius Marcellus Clay, American Ambassador to Russia in the 1860's and a relative of Henry Clay. The boxer has a younger brother, Rudolph Valentino Clay, who also plans to become a professional fighter.

Unlike many other present-day fighters, Clay did not know grinding poverty in his youth. "Eating and sleeping, that's the hardest work that boy ever did," his father recalls, and Cassius was well fed—with vegetable soup and steak from the time he was a baby—although his father sometimes had to make sacrifices to pay the food bill. Clay attended DuValle Junior High School and Central High School in Louisville, from which he graduated 376th in a class of 391. He was the neighborhood marble champion and an expert rock fighter, and he owned a bicycle.

It was the theft of Clay's bicycle when he was twelve that might be said to have started the boy on his boxing career. He reported the loss to Joe Martin, a Louisville policeman who also gave boxing lessons in a community gymnasium operated by the city's recreation department. Martin did not recover the bike, but he did persuade Clay to take up boxing. "In the past twenty years I guess I've taught 10,000 boys to box, or at least tried to teach them," Martin has said (*Sports Illustrated*, September 25, 1961). "Cassius Clay, when he first came around here, looked no better or worse than the majority. About a year later, though, you could see that the little smart aleck—I mean, he's *always* been sassy—had a lot of potential. He stood out because, I guess, he had more determination than most boys, and he had the speed to get him some place."

After six weeks of boxing lessons with Martin, Cassius Clay, weighing in at eighty-nine pounds, made his amateur debut in a featured bout on a Louisville television program called *Champions of Tomorrow* and won a split decision. He worked hard at learning to be a fighter, skipping rope for hours to strengthen his legs, flailing away at a heavy punching bag to put power into his blows, and sparring with his own mirror image to perfect his timing. He had one scare: at the age of fifteen he flunked a pre-fight physical because of a heart murmur. But after a four-month rest the murmur disappeared, and Clay resumed fighting.

In his six years as an amateur Clay won 100 out of 108 fights, losing only once during his last two years—to Amos Johnson in the 1959 Pan-American Games trials on a split decision. He won six Golden Gloves titles in Kentucky. In 1959 he took the national Golden Gloves and the A.A.U. light heavyweight championships and in 1960, the national Golden Gloves heavyweight and the A.A.U. light heavyweight titles. By 1960

Wide World

CASSIUS CLAY

Clay wanted to turn professional. Martin, however, advised him to wait. "In boxing," he told Clay, "the Olympic champion is already as good as the No. 10 ranked pro."

Clay tried out and was accepted for the American Olympic team in 1960. In Rome he made an instant hit with the populace by waving, shaking hands, and calling "hello" to everyone as he strolled along the Via Veneto. He met Floyd Patterson, then the heavyweight champion, and told him: "So long, Floyd, be seeing you—in about two years." When a Russian reporter prodded him on the plight of Negroes in the United States, Clay retorted: "Tell your readers we've got qualified people working on that problem, and I'm not worried about the outcome. To me, the U.S.A. is still the best country in the world, counting yours. It may be hard to get something to eat sometimes, but anyhow I ain't fighting alligators and living in a mud hut." Fighting as a light heavyweight at 178 pounds, he disposed of three opponents without difficulty and won the gold medal. "I didn't take the gold medal off for forty-eight hours," he recalls. "I even wore it to bed. I didn't sleep too good because I had to sleep on my back so the medal wouldn't cut me. But I didn't care. I was the Olympic champ."

On his way back to Louisville, Clay stopped off in New York, stayed at the Waldorf Towers suite of an acquaintance, visited Greenwich Village and Times Square, and startled at least a small portion of the citizenry by introducing himself to total strangers as "Cassius Clay, the great fighter." Louisville welcomed him with a giant parade. Clay bought a pink Cadillac, and then, having decided to turn professional, he got down to the serious business of finding a manager. Three days before his first professional fight Clay signed a contract with a syndicate of eleven white businessmen, seven of them millionaires, most of them from Louisville. The Louis-

CLAY, CASSIUS—*Continued*

ville Sponsoring Group, as it is called, is headed by William Faversham, Jr., son of the matinee idol and vice-president of the Brown-Forman Distillers Corporation. The contract gave Clay a $10,000 bonus; a salary of $4,000 for the first two years and $6,000 for the next four; all expenses paid; and a fifty-fifty split on everything Clay earns. Part of Clay's 50 percent is put into a trust or pension fund, upon which he may not draw until he is thirty-five. One of the group's avowed purposes is to guard Clay against bankruptcy when he is too old to fight.

Clay trained first for a short while with Archie Moore, but then Angelo Dundee, a veteran trainer, was hired to get him into shape. "I smoothed Cassius out and put some snap in his punches," says Dundee. "I got him down off his dancing toes so he could hit with power." Clay characteristically remarked: "Dundee gave me the jab. But the rest is me. What changed the most was my own natural ability."

On October 29, 1960 Clay won his first professional fight, against Tunney Hunsaker, by a decision. Victories over LaMar Clark, Tony Esperti, Alonzo Johnson, Alex Miteff, Alejandro Lavorante, Willi Besmanoff, Sonny Banks, and Don Warner, among others, followed. Clay began attracting nationwide attention, most of which he drummed up himself. He would roll into various cities, grant interviews, extoll his own greatness, appear on television, spout poetry, and, in general, grab headlines. Sportswriters dubbed him the "Louisville Lip" and "Cassius the Brashest." The talk paid off: to his fight in October 1961 with Alex Miteff, Clay drew 3,500 fans, paying $12,000. In Los Angeles, 12,000 fans watched him knock out Alejandro Lavorante in five rounds. Clay began composing rhymes naming the round in which he would down his opponent. "They all must fall/In the round I call," he said.

In November 1962 Clay took on Archie Moore, the somewhat aged former light heavyweight champion. In Moore, Clay was confronting a veteran not only of the pugilistic wars, but of the conversational wars as well. Both talked up a magnificent fight, drawing 16,400 patrons who paid a record $182,600 for an indoor fight in California. Clay had said: "When you come to the fight, don't block the aisle and don't block the door/You will all go home after round four." And they did. Clay knocked out Moore at 1 minute, 35 seconds of the fourth round. Clay's next opponent was Charlie Powell. They fought in Pittsburgh on a bitterly cold night in January 1963. A sellout crowd of 11,238 was on hand, and Clay, true to his pre-fight prediction, won by a knockout in the third round. It was his seventeenth professional fight, his seventeenth victory, and his fourteenth knockout. A few cynics suggested that the finish might have been rehearsed. "So what," said Clay. "They can say anything they want as long as they pay their way in."

Clay's self-advertising tactics filled up Madison Square Garden for a professional boxing event for the first time in a decade: his fight with Doug Jones in March 1963 drew over 18,000 customers, paying some $105,000, to cheer him or to watch him get his comeuppance. "If Jones wants to mix/I'll end it in six," Clay rhymed before the fight, "If he gives me some jive/I'll end it in five/ And if he wants more/It'll only go four . . . If he don't want to fight/He can stay home that night." Clay carried the crusade onto television, appearing on the *Tonight* show, and into a Greenwich Village coffeehouse, the Bitter End, where, attired in a tuxedo at noon, he entered a beatnik poetry contest (which, by his own acclamation, he won). Entitled "Ode to a Champion, Cassius Marcellus Clay," his poem said in part: "Marcellus vanquished Carthage/Cassius laid Julius Caesar low/And Cassius will flatten Douglas Jones/With a mighty measured blow." The fighting in this case proved more difficult than the versifying, however. Clever, experienced, and unimpressed by Clay's pre-fight oratory, Jones went the full ten rounds. The decision went to Clay, but some spectators and boxing writers thought the decision a bad one.

In June 1963 Clay went to London to fight the British and Empire heavyweight champion, Henry Cooper. Sporting a bowler, boutonnière, waistcoat, striped pants, and spats, and carrying a furled umbrella, he paraded up and down the streets and blazoned his name throughout London town. He raised the blood pressure of the British by issuing such pronouncements as: "After five rounds, Henry Cooper will think his name is Gordon Cooper: he'll be in orbit." "Gaseous Cassius," as the British press called him, nettled many Londoners who took him seriously. But, as usual, Clay's needling paid off: some 55,000 outraged Englishmen packed Wembley Stadium to see Cooper beat Clay.

On the evening of the fight Clay approached the ring wearing a golden crown of brass with a red velvet interior and a red bathrobe with "Cassius the Greatest" displayed on it. The fight got off to a fast start with Cooper spearing Clay with left jabs and giving him a nosebleed. Clay retaliated in the second round by cutting Cooper on the left eye, and from then on, except for a punch that sent Clay down in the fourth, Cooper, blinded by blood from his eye, was clearly getting the worst of it. In the fifth round the referee stopped the fight. A New York *Times* commentator (June 19, 1963) wrote: "Clay knocked out Henry Cooper . . . in the fifth round tonight, just as he predicted he would. Clay knocked the stuffing out of Cooper and might have dropped him at any time from the third round on. But Cassius wanted it to end in the fifth, and he nearly threw away the fight to get it" (this refers to Clay's fall in the fourth).

Opinion is divided as to whether Clay's bravado is truly a part of his character or just a pose to bolster box-office receipts, but it is generally agreed that Clay's relaxed sense of humor and spontaneity prevents it from becoming obnoxious. "A wise man can act the fool," Clay once said about his role, "but a fool can't act like a wise man." On another occasion he said, "All the time I gotta talk, y'know. People expect it. . . . My mouth is tired." Tired or not, his mouth continues to make him the most colorful boxer in years, one who is revivifying the sport and bringing the fans back to the ring. For some time now Clay has predicted loudly and frequently that he will lay out that "big ugly bear," Sonny

Liston, the present heavyweight champion, in eight rounds. This boast found its way also into a record album, *I Am the Greatest,* which Clay made in August 1963 for Columbia records.

Clay is six feet three inches tall and weighs over 200 pounds. He has a big head; small, well-shaped ears; and a round, rather fleshy face. "His physique, like that of most good heavy-weights, is devoid of the dramatic definition and flashy ripples of the body-builders," a Toronto *Globe and Mail* writer (June 15, 1963) commented. "The muscles are mostly sunk deep under the brown skin . . . and show strikingly only in the slabs curving from the neck along the shoulders." Clay has fast hands, and he has never adopted the American crouch when fighting. He neither drinks nor smokes, and he sticks to a disciplined life with an ease fostered by his ambition to reach the top of his sport. Often asked for his stand on anti-segregation demonstrations, he has replied: "Twice a day people ask me to take part in this. I can't. I'm no leader. . . . Integration's gotta come, but somebody's gotta die first."

References

    N Y Post Mag p2 Mr 17 '63 por
    N Y Times p39 Je 13 '63 por
    Newsday C p24 Ja 29 '63 pors
    Sat Eve Post 234:36+ Mr 25 '61 pors
    Sports Illus 14:39+ S 25 '61 por; 18:18+
      Je 10 '63 pors
    Time 81:78+ Mr 22 '63 pors

CLAY, LUCIUS D(UBIGNON) Apr. 23, 1897- United States Army officer; government consultant; business executive

Address: h. 1040 5th Ave., New York 28

>   NOTE: This biography supersedes the article that appeared in *Current Biography* in 1945.

American determination to stand fast in the face of pressure found a symbol in General Lucius D. Clay when twice since World War II he helped to safeguard the independence of West Berlin against the threat of Soviet domination. Beginning his career as a military instructor, Clay worked on several important engineering projects before World War II. During the war he facilitated the movement of supplies to the battlefronts. As United States deputy military governor and later as military governor in postwar Germany, he supervised the reconstruction of that country, and in 1948 and 1949 he played a major role in organizing the airlift that broke the Soviet blockade of Berlin. His book *Decision in Germany* (1950) is considered the authoritative work on postwar German problems.

Clay revisited Berlin in 1961 as President Kennedy's personal representative, to raise the morale of Berliners in the midst of continuing crisis. In the world of business Clay distinguished himself as chief executive officer of the Continental Can Company, following his retirement from the Army in 1949. In 1963 he headed a committee that made important proposals for improving the foreign aid program of the Kennedy administration.

Wide World

LUCIUS D. CLAY

Lucius DuBignon Clay was born in Marietta, Georgia on April 23, 1897 to Alexander Stephen Clay, a noted lawyer and a United States Senator, and to Sarah (Francis) Clay. He is a descendant of William Clay, who came from England and settled in Virginia in the early eighteenth century. The noted American statesman, Henry Clay, was his great-granduncle. As a boy, Lucius Clay served as a page in the Senate, during his father's term of office.

On the day of his graduation from the United States Military Academy at West Point, June 12, 1918, as a second lieutenant, Clay was promoted to first lieutenant and to captain (temporary). His first assignment was as an instructor at the officers training camp at Camp Humphrey, Virginia. In December 1918 he was assigned to the engineer school at Camp Humphrey, and after completing the civil engineering course there in June 1920, he became assistant professor of military science and tactics at the Alabama Polytechnic Institute at Auburn. He returned to Camp Humphrey in August 1921, serving as engineering officer and instructor at the engineer school for a year and helping to prepare training regulations for the camp in the following year. In 1924 he became an instructor in the engineering department at West Point.

After Clay had completed the company officers course at the Camp Humphrey engineer school in July 1930, he was sent to Corazol in the Panama Canal Zone as a company commander with the 11th Engineers. In September 1931 he was transferred to the office of the district engineer at Pittsburgh, and as assistant district engineer he took charge of the construction of lock and dam number 2 on the Allegheny River. Promoted to the permanent rank of captain on June 19, 1933, Clay went to Washington, D.C. for duty with the river and harbor section of the office of the chief of engineers, during the first

CLAY, LUCIUS D.—*Continued*

two years as an assistant and during the next two years as an officer in charge.

Another appointment that Clay filled in 1934 was United States delegate to the permanent International Congress on Navigation, meeting at Brussels. Assigned to the staff of General Douglas MacArthur at Manila in October 1937, Clay served as adviser to the Philippine government on engineering projects and hydroelectric development. The Army recalled him to the United States in August 1938 to become district engineer at Denison, Texas, in charge of the design and construction of Red River Dam.

In October 1940 Clay was appointed secretary of the airport approval board and assistant to the administrator of civil aeronautics. He organized and directed the establishment of a national system of airports. His work included the improvement and enlargement of 277 airports and the construction of 197 new ones in the United States, Alaska, and the Pacific islands. He had advanced gradually through the ranks and was promoted to brigadier general (temporary) on March 12, 1942. Shortly after the entry of the United States into World War II he went on a special mission to Brazil to establish defense airports.

When he returned to the United States in March 1942, Clay was assigned to the headquarters of the Services of Supply in Washington as deputy chief of staff for requirements and resources. From July 1942 to October 1944 he was assistant chief of staff for matériel (the title was later redesignated director of matériel) at the headquarters of the Army Service Forces, supervising the production and procurement of army supplies. In November 1944 he took command of the Normandy base section of the European Theater of Operations, and he succeeded in greatly expediting the movement of supplies to Allied invading forces through the port of Cherbourg. A month later he joined the staff of the Office of War Mobilization and Reconversion, under the directorship of James F. Byrnes. Released temporarily from active military service, Clay retained his rank and uniform while serving as deputy director for war programs and general administration. The stern military attitude shown in his efforts to bring greater efficiency to the delivery of supplies to the front lines is said to have been resented by some of his civilian colleagues.

At the recommendation of General Dwight D. Eisenhower, Clay was designated in April 1945 as deputy military governor in charge of civilian affairs in the American zone of occupied Germany. In this office he also was United States representative on the Coordinating Committee for Germany. On March 5, 1946 he attained the permanent rank of brigadier general. As deputy military governor Clay helped to establish the four occupation zones of Germany and to set up the four-power Allied Control Council. He undertook the material reconstruction of Germany, the establishment of health, welfare, and educational services, and the elimination of Nazi influences from public life. Although he maintained a tough policy toward Germany, he strongly encouraged the development of democratic institutions in that country. On January 6, 1947 Clay succeeded General Joseph T. McNarney as military governor of the American zone of Germany and as commanding general of the United States forces of occupation in Germany and of United States forces in Europe. (The latter title was redesignated commander-in-chief, European Command, on March 15, 1947.) Clay was promoted to full general (temporary) on March 28, 1947 and major general (permanent) on January 24, 1948.

Meanwhile, friction between the Soviet Union and the Western Allies was mounting. In an effort to drive the Western Allies out of Berlin, the Soviet Union on June 24, 1948 imposed a blockade upon all land traffic between Berlin and Western Germany. The Allies replied to the blockade with an airlift, which for more than a year supplied the isolated city with food, fuel, and military reinforcements. Clay was largely responsible for the effectiveness of the airlift and for the safeguarding of the Western position in Berlin. He also played an important role in the currency reform of 1948, giving West Germany one of the most stable currencies in the world, and he helped to draft the constitution of the Federal Republic of Germany, which was approved in May 1949.

Relinquishing his command in Germany on May 15, 1949, Clay retired from military service effective May 26, 1949. In view of his distinguished record, President Harry S. Truman conferred the rank of full general upon him at the time of his retirement. In his book *Decision in Germany* (Doubleday, 1950) Clay describes in detail the various problems that confronted him during his four years in Germany. A second book by Clay, *Germany and the Fight for Freedom* (Harvard Univ. Press, 1950), based on three Godkin Lectures delivered at Harvard in the spring of 1950, covers much of the same ground.

Free to begin a career in business after he had left the Army, Clay accepted the position of chairman of the board and chief executive officer of the Continental Can Company in 1950. During his chairmanship the Continental Can Company tripled its sales and became the largest manufacturer of containers in the United States. In 1952 Clay helped to persuade General Eisenhower to seek the Republican nomination for the Presidency, and he helped organize the election campaign. He frequently advised the Eisenhower administration on questions concerning Berlin and also offered similar services to the Kennedy administration.

In August 1961 Clay accompanied Vice-President Lyndon B. Johnson to Berlin as a member of a special mission sent by President John F. Kennedy to reassure the German people of the stand of the United States in the face of increased Soviet pressure on the city. Kennedy announced a few days later that Clay would return to Berlin as his personal representative with the rank of Ambassador, to symbolize American determination to resist Soviet attempts to push the Western Allies out of Berlin. Taking a leave of absence from the Continental Can Company for the duration of his mission, Clay arrived in Berlin on September 19, 1961.

When in October 1961 East German authorities prevented Western officials from entering East Berlin, Clay ordered armed convoys to accompany American officials into the Eastern zone. In the ensuing crisis, Soviet and American tanks faced each other across the border, marking the first direct confrontation between United States and Soviet forces in the cold war. Clay noted at the time that the presence of Soviet tanks at the border proved that the East German regime was fully dependent upon the Soviet Union. During a visit to the United States in January 1962, Clay reportedly expressed dissatisfaction over what he regarded as an excessively cautious policy on the part of the State Department. However, both Clay and Secretary of State Dean Rusk subsequently denied rumors of a rift between them.

In May 1962 Clay returned to the United States, having attained the objectives of restoring the morale of the West Berliners and of proving to the Soviet Union that the United States intended to stand firmly on its rights in Berlin. He resumed his position as chairman of the board of the Continental Can Company and continued to serve as a special consultant on Berlin to the Kennedy administration. He feels that some form of settlement might ultimately be reached with the Soviet Union and maintains that it must be achieved through determined and united action on the part of the Western Allies. Emphasizing the importance of building up conventional weapons, Clay has said, "I do not believe that the full implementation of foreign policy can be carried out by waving atom bombs."

President Kennedy appointed Clay in January 1963 to head a permanent advisory committee on foreign aid to study the nation's foreign aid program. In its report of March 1963 the committee maintained that the United States was diluting its efforts by attempting to do "too much for too many." Despite some criticism the report was generally favorably received by supporters as well as by opponents of foreign aid. Its influence was seen in President Kennedy's foreign aid message of April 2, 1963, in which he substantially reduced his earlier budget estimate. Kennedy has also asked the committee to undertake studies of the Export-Import Bank and of the administrative procedures involved in foreign aid.

Although Clay retired in 1962 from the board chairmanship of the Continental Can Company at the mandatory retirement age of sixty-five, he continues to be active in business. In January 1963 he became a senior partner in the banking house of Lehman Brothers. He has served as a director of a number of firms, including General Motors Corporation, United States Lines, Chase Manhattan Bank, Marine Midland Trust Corporation, Newmount Mining Corporation, Metropolitan Life Insurance Company, American Express Company, and the Lehman Corporation. Clay has been vice-president of Columbia-Presbyterian Hospital and a trustee of the Central Savings Bank, the National Fund for Medical Education, the Eisenhower Exchange Fellowships, and the Alfred P. Sloan Foundation. For two years after World War II he served as national chairman of the Crusade for Freedom. He has held membership in the American Society of Civil Engineers and the Society of American Military Engineers. In December 1962 he raised $1,900,000 as ransom for prisoners captured by the Castro regime in Cuba during the abortive Bay of Pigs invasion of April 1961.

In April 1945 Clay received the Distinguished Service Medal for his role as director of matériel during the war and the Legion of Merit for his work on the civil airport program. For his service in Normandy he received a Bronze Star in 1945. He has two Oak Leaf Clusters to the Distinguished Service Medal. Clay also is a Knight Commander (honorary) of the Order of the British Empire and holds the Order of Kutuzov, First Class, from the Soviet Union. Berliners have named a street, the Clay Allee, after him. In May 1962 Mayor Willy Brandt of West Berlin conferred the city's honorary citizenship upon Clay. In June 1962 he received a National Brotherhood Award from the National Conference of Christians and Jews, and in November 1962 the National Institute of Social Sciences awarded him a gold medal for distinguished service to humanity.

On September 21, 1918 Lucius D. Clay married Marjorie McKeown of East Orange, New Jersey. They have two sons, Lucius DuBignon and Frank Butner, both graduates of West Point in the class of 1942. Clay is a wiry man, with the appearance of a noble Roman; he has graying black hair, bushy eyebrows, and a pleasant smile. He speaks with a deep baritone voice and a Southern accent and is noted for his tremendous energy, his autocratic temperament, and his photographic memory. He is a Methodist. His favorite recreations are horseback riding and fishing.

References

Gen Army 1:6+ Jl '53 por
N Y Herald Tribune p3 Ag 19 '61; p29 Ap 7 '63 por
N Y Times p2 Ag 21 '61 por
New Yorker 38:115+ My 26 '62; 39:34+ Mr 30 '63
International Who's Who, 1962-63
National Cyclopædia of American Biography current vol G (1946)
Who's Who, 1963
Who's Who in America, 1962-63

COCHRAN, JACQUELINE (kŏk'răn) 1910(?)- Aviatrix; business executive
Address: b. 630 5th Ave., New York 20; h. Cochran-Odlum Ranch, Indio, Calif.

NOTE: This biography supersedes the article that appeared in *Current Biography* in 1940.

Among the accomplishments of Jacqueline Cochran's life in its course "from sawdust to stardust," as she has described it, are the many world aviation speed records that she has set for both jet and reciprocating aircraft. In acquiring a greater number of speed, distance, and altitude records than any other living pilot, she has made a major contribution to advancements in avia-

JACQUELINE COCHRAN

tion. Her awards include the Clifford Burke Harmon Trophy of the International League of Aviators, which she has won several times, and the Distinguished Service Medal for her work during World War II in organizing the Women's Airforce Service Pilots, the WASPs of the United States Army. In 1958 she became the first woman president of Fédération Aéronautique Internationale. Also a successful businesswoman, she developed a nationally known line of cosmetics; and with her husband, Floyd B. Odlum, she helps operate a 600-acre ranch in California.

Jacqueline Cochran was born in Pensacola, Florida around 1910. (She does not know her real age.) Orphaned in infancy, she lived with a poor family in sawmill camp towns of northern Florida and southern Georgia. "Until I was eight years old, I had no shoes," she wrote in her autobiography, *The Stars at Noon* (Little, 1954). "My bed was usually a pallet on the floor and sometimes just the floor. . . . My dresses in the first seven years of my life were usually made from cast-off flour sacks." A resourceful child, she caught crabs and fish and discovered other ways of getting food for herself, but she was nearly always hungry.

On learning, at the age of six, that her mother and father were foster parents, Jacqueline Cochran grew more independent, determined not to follow their shiftless ways. She remembers the good influence of a Catholic priest and of a teacher, a Miss Bostwick, who taught her cleanliness and gave her a dress. She earned pennies taking care of children, and once, when she was about eight, she was midwife to an eighteen-year-old mother. After winning a longed-for doll, she was deprived of it by her foster mother, who gave it to her own little daughter. "It broke my heart," Miss Cochran recalled in her autobiography. "Years later, when Willie Mae [the daughter] was grown up and had a child of her own, I brought them both to New York to give them a new and better start in life." She made

it a condition that they bring the doll, which she had repaired and dressed in new clothes.

At the age of eight Jacqueline Cochran went to work in the cotton mills of Columbus, Georgia at six cents an hour on a twelve-hour night shift. Despite the poor working conditions, she was happy because she became self-supporting and was able to buy her first pair of shoes. In her spare time she read. Toward the end of a three-month strike at the mill, she found work in a beauty shop where she learned how to give permanent waves. Then moving to Montgomery, Alabama, she was employed in the beauty shop of a department store. She bought a Model T Ford and personally ground the engine valves. Always adept with her hands, she learned to make clothes and do crocheting and needlework.

One of her customers at the beauty shop, a woman judge in the juvenile court, encouraged her to study and arranged for her to go into training as a nurse in a local hospital. Although her grades were low in academic subjects, she excelled in nursing. At the end of three years in training, she worked as a nurse in the impoverished sawmill districts of northern Florida. Before long, however, she moved to Pensacola to return to work in a beauty shop. She was invited to dances at the Pensacola Naval Flying School, where she met many officers who later made their names as captains and admirals.

Then, after she had worked in the cosmetic field for about nine months in Philadelphia, Miss Cochran struck out for New York and was immediately hired by Antoine at his Saks-Fifth Avenue beauty salon. During the winters she worked at Antoine's shop in Miami Beach. In both New York and Florida she met many prominent people, including Floyd Bostwick Odlum, a banker and industrialist, whom she married some years later, on May 11, 1936. It was from her first conversation with Odlum that she got the idea of becoming an airplane pilot. One summer day in 1932 she went out to Roosevelt Field on Long Island, determined to spend her three weeks' vacation learning how to fly.

Exceptionally quick to learn how to handle a plane, Miss Cochran after three days of instruction went off on her first solo flight. She was well aware of her ignorance, but soon after she had obtained her license, in less than three weeks, she insisted on renting a Fairchild plane to fly to Montreal to an air meet of sportsmen pilots. "Flying was now in my blood," she recalled. One of her early friends in aviation, Captain Kenneth P. Behr, who managed Floyd Bennett and later La Guardia airports, has said, "We couldn't help rooting for Jackie. Here she was, a pretty blonde who hadn't even finished grammar school, but she buckled down over the heavy textbooks and mastered celestial navigation and Morse code" (*Reader's Digest*, August 1955).

Miss Cochran resigned her job at Antoine's, headed in her car for San Diego, California, and took courses at a flying school there. But foggy skies and too many students irked her. When she complained to a friend of hers, an air officer attached to the battleship *West Virginia*, about her lack of training and air time, he agreed to give her flight instructions. She bought an old Travelair plane with a Gypsy motor for $1,200, received her training the Navy way, and finally earned a commercial pilot's license.

In 1934 Miss Cochran was the only American woman entrant in the McRobertson London-Melbourne air race. Despite careful preparation for the Australian race, both a Northrop Gamma plane and a "Gee Bee" racing plane, which Miss Cochran and her co-pilots, Wesley Smith and Royal Leonard, planned to fly, had crash landings. Nevertheless, the next year she entered the Bendix transcontinental air race in her Northrop Gamma plane, making an instrument take-off in a fog from Los Angeles on September 2, 1935. On her next try, in the 1937 Bendix race, she won third place. Entering the 1938 race in a Seversky pursuit plane (which she had never flown previously), with a heavy overload of gas, she won first place and much acclaim from the public and her male competitors.

Convinced that woman pilots would be needed in the war effort and encouraged by General Henry H. ("Hap") Arnold and Lord Beaverbrook, Jacqueline Cochran flew a bomber to England in June 1941. For service with the British Air Transport Auxiliary, in which she held the rank of flight captain, she took a group of American women pilots to England for training in 1942. She then headed a woman pilot training program for the United States Army Air Forces, and in July 1943 she was appointed director of the Women's Airforce Service Pilots. More than 25,000 women applied for training in the WASPs; 1,830 were accepted and 1,074 graduated; they flew about 60,000,000 miles for the Army Air Forces. Jacqueline Cochran was commissioned a lieutenant colonel in the Air Force Reserves in 1948. She also holds a commission as lieutenant colonel in the Civil Air Patrol.

When her work organizing the WASPs was completed, Miss Cochran asked the editor of *Liberty* magazine to send her as a correspondent to the Pacific Theater. She interviewed Madame Chiang Kai-shek, reported the Japanese surrender, met Mao Tse-tung and recognized his hard-core Communistic outlook. Later she covered the Nuremberg trials of Nazi officials, talked with the Shah of Iran and Franco of Spain, and visited Russia.

During the war years Miss Cochran was unable to give much of her time to her cosmetics business, which she had started in 1934 with a beauty salon in Chicago and a laboratory in New Jersey. Jacqueline Cochran Cosmetics prospered, however, and each year millions of dollars worth of her products are sold through thousands of outlets. In March 1961 she sold a major interest in her cosmetics firm (but not the controlling interest) to Andrew A. Lynn, who became president and chief executive. Among the best-known products manufactured by her firm are Jacqueline Cochran Flowing Velvet and Shining Hour creams.

Jacqueline Cochran was one of the early supporters of General Dwight D. Eisenhower for the Presidency. While he was still on duty in Europe in 1952, she made a special flight to Paris to show him newsreel films of an "Ike" rally in New York. She believes that the enthusiasm displayed at the rally finally persuaded him to become a Presidential candidate. She, herself, took part in a very colorful political contest in California in 1956 when she contended for the Twenty-ninth District Congressional seat against Dalip S. Saund, a Democrat. Saund won the election by about 3,000 votes.

Flying continued to be the principal interest of Jacqueline Cochran, who was determined to play a role also in the jet phase of aviation. In 1953 she became the first woman in the world to fly faster than sound (to break the sonic barrier). The world jet speed records for both men and women that she set in a Sabrejet in 1953 were: 100 kilometers, 652.552 miles per hour; 500 kilometers, 590.321 miles per hour; and 15 kilometers, 675.471 miles per hour. In 1961, in a Northrop T-38, she broke the 100-kilometer and 500-kilometer speed records that she had established in 1953, and set an altitude record of 55,253 feet.

On June 6, 1960, piloting an A3J plane, she was the first woman to fly at Mach 2 (twice the speed of sound). She achieved another "first" for women on June 15, 1960 when she made an arrested landing in a jet on an aircraft carrier, the USS *Independence*, and was also catapulted from the carrier. A 5,120-mile flight from New Orleans to Hanover on April 27, 1962 made her the first woman to pilot a jet aircraft across the Atlantic Ocean. Flying a Lockheed F-104G Starfighter jet, Miss Cochran set two new records in April and May 1963: She flew ten miles in a 15-25 kilometer straightaway course at 1,273.10 miles an hour; and she covered a 100-kilometer closed course at 1,203.94 miles an hour.

One of the earliest and most significant of her awards in aviation is the Billy Mitchell Trophy (1938). Her other many honors include doctorates from Russell Sage College and Elmira College, Zonta International Achievement Award (1957), Woman of the Year in Business citation (1953 and 1954), and Woman of the Year medal (1954). She has also received the honorary wings of the French, Chinese, Turkish, Spanish and Royal Thailand air forces. Miss Cochran is a director of Northeast Airlines, the African Research Foundation, and the Air Force Academy Foundation. She served for two terms, from 1958 to 1960, as president of the Fédération Aéronautique Internationale, of which she was elected vice-president in 1960. She is chairman of the board of the National Aeronautic Association, the United States affiliate of FAI.

For nine years Jacqueline Cochran was on the national board of directors of the Camp Fire Girls, and she is now an honorary member of the board. Knowing the handicap of inadequate schooling, she has helped a large number of needy children to get an education. She is an excellent cook and has won prizes in needlepoint and tatting. The brown-eyed, blond-haired "glamour girl" of aviation also enjoys golf and dancing. Her husband, Floyd B. Odlum, wrote of her in his preface to *The Stars at Noon*: "Such a person must have many sides to her character and personality, some of which seem to contradict the others. I have said many times that Jackie is fearless, and yet she runs wildly from a snake, and I have seen her almost hysterical from listening to a good old-fashioned ghost story. However, I have never seen her back away from real

COCHRAN, JACQUELINE—*Continued*

danger. . . . Certain it is that she is fearless of death and equally certain it is that she considers a barrier only something to surmount."

References

Clymer, Eleanor and Erlich, Lillian. Modern American Career Women (1959)
Cochran, Jacqueline. The Stars at Noon (1954)
International Celebrity Register (1959)
International Who's Who, 1962-63
Who's Who in America, 1962-63
Who's Who of American Women (1958-59)

COGGESHALL, L(OWELL) T(HELWELL)
(kŏg'ĕ-shôl) May 7, 1901- Medical scientist; physician; university administrator; educator
Address: b. 5801 Ellis Ave., Chicago 37, Ill.; h. 5801 Dorchester Ave., Chicago 37, Ill.

An internationally recognized authority on tropical diseases, Dr. L. T. Coggeshall pursues a dual role as scientific investigator and university administrator. He is the vice-president of the University of Chicago and a member of its board of trustees, and he also holds the Frederick H. Rawson Professorship of Medicine at the university. To his colleagues Dr. Coggeshall is known as one of the most persuasive leaders and successful fund-raisers in medicine, and since World War II he has extended his interests to a wide range of public, private, and professional activities. A realistic but imaginative man, he views the future in terms of increased government involvement in medicine, rapid social change, and unprecedented scientific progress.

Lowell Thelwell Coggeshall was born on May 7, 1901 on a farm in eastern Indiana to William Evart and Flossie Ann (Warren) Cogge-

University of Chicago
DR. L. T. COGGESHALL

shall. He has two brothers, Howard C. and Warren C. Coggeshall, and a sister, Mrs. Lillian Esther Stokes. Coggeshall attended Saratoga High School, where his senior class consisted of only one other student besides himself, and graduated in 1919. He then entered Indiana University at Bloomington, where he waited on tables to help pay for his tuition, and received the B.A. degree in 1922. As a graduate student he taught zoology at Indiana University and, after obtaining the M.A. degree there in 1923, he worked as a research assistant at the University of Wisconsin. In 1924 he taught anatomy at Indiana University, and in the following year he was an instructor in biology at Winona Normal College in Minnesota. During the summers of 1924, 1925, and 1927 Coggeshall was a special staff member of the Rockefeller Foundation International Health Board, and in the summer of 1928 he served as a malariologist for the Georgia state board of health.

After qualifying as an M.D. at Indiana University in 1928 Coggeshall interned at the University of Chicago clinics. He became instructor and secretary in the department of medicine of the University of Chicago in 1931, and assistant professor three years later. In 1935 he left Chicago to join the staff at the International Health Board of the Rockefeller Foundation in New York. There he served as a medical investigator for research in tropical diseases until 1941, when he resigned to become professor of epidemiology and chairman of the department of tropical diseases at the School of Public Health of the University of Michigan.

Coggeshall's specialization in malaria and other tropical diseases proved valuable to the government during World War II. In 1942 he took leave from his post at the University of Michigan to work with Pan-American-Africa Airways in helping to establish medical facilities along air routes that were being plotted by the United States Air Forces through Africa, the Middle East, China, and India. After serving as a special consultant to the Secretary of War, Coggeshall was commissioned a captain in the United States Naval Reserve Medical Corps in January 1944. One of his major assignments was serving as director of a 5,000-bed hospital in Klamath Falls, Oregon, for Navy and Marine personnel suffering from tropical diseases. In 1945 Coggeshall was cited by the Navy and received the Gorgas Medal from the Association of Military Surgeons for his outstanding work in preventive medicine and the treatment of tropical diseases for the armed forces.

In 1946 Coggeshall returned to the University of Chicago as professor and chairman of the department of medicine. In 1947 he became dean of the Division of Biological Sciences, one of the four graduate divisions, which includes the School of Medicine, the university hospitals and clinics, and graduate teaching and research in the nonclinical life sciences. In 1949 Coggeshall was named Frederick H. Rawson Professor of Medicine and resigned his chairmanship of the department of medicine in order to devote full attention to the division's rapidly expanding teaching, research, and hospital facilities.

During Dr. Coggeshall's service as dean of the Division of Biological Sciences from 1947 to 1960 the university spent more than $23,000,000 on research and hospital facilities, and the division's endowment funds grew from $24,000,000 to $48,000,000. The Argonne Cancer Research Hospital, which the university operates for the United States Atomic Energy Commission, was built during this period. It is the first building in the United States specifically designed for exploring the medical uses of radioactive isotopes. Other facilities that Coggeshall had a hand in starting include the Gilman Smith and West Wing hospitals, the Nathan Goldblatt Memorial Hospital, the Chronic Disease Hospital, the W. C. Allee Animal Behavior Laboratory, the Philip D. Armour Clinical Research Building, a diagnostic pavilion, a controlled environment laboratory, and new facilities for interns and residents.

Taking a leave of absence from the University of Chicago, Coggeshall was sworn in on January 31, 1956 to succeed Dr. Chester S. Keefer as special assistant for health and medical affairs to the Secretary of Health, Education, and Welfare. Secretary Marion B. Folsom, who called Coggeshall the "best qualified man" for the position, reportedly spent three months trying to induce him to come to Washington. Among the problem areas scrutinized by Coggeshall in this government post were the slow progress being made against chronic illness and disability, the inadequacy of health insurance, the need to professionalize nursing, and the importance of additional national statistical health surveys. He called for an increase in basic medical research and in medical school construction, to be financed by both public and private funds. He warned, however, against the assumption that unlimited funds would solve all research problems, and he emphasized in particular the need for adequately trained and properly paid personnel.

Revolutionary among Dr. Coggeshall's proposals was that relating to the cost of hospital care. He advocated trying to lower costs by reducing or eliminating some of the expensive equipment and services that most hospitals provide for all patients, but that are actually required only by some. He proposed experimentation in developing sections in which patients with limited medical needs did more things for themselves, such as going to a cafeteria or dining room for their meals, or doing light housekeeping in their rooms. An advisory committee on hospital facilities and services was set up in 1956 to work with Coggeshall in establishing new hospital units as pilot plants. Coggeshall's last official act as special assistant to the Department of Health, Education, and Welfare occurred in December 1956, when he was appointed by President Eisenhower to accompany Vice-President Richard M. Nixon to Vienna. There he investigated the physical and psychological health of Hungarian refugees, to determine their fitness for possible resettlement in the United States.

In 1957-58 Coggeshall served as a member of the Department of Health, Education, and Welfare Secretary's consultants committee on medical research and education. The report of this committee has been important in shaping policy of the federal government and of universities in the fields of medical education and research. Dr. Coggeshall acknowledges the long-standing interest of local, state, and federal governments in medicine and public health, and recognizes that governmental participation in medicine is both permanent and on the increase. He believes, however, that federal funds could be best used to stimulate, assist, and exert leadership, and should not abrogate the responsibilities of other agencies. One such area requiring leadership, Coggeshall believes, is that of medical care for the aged.

Dr. Coggeshall served as president of the American Cancer Society in 1957-58. An advocate of expanded basic research, he was instrumental in the decision of the society to channel more of its funds into this area. He believes that scientific breakthroughs are most likely to occur in biology, in the pre-clinical disciplines on which medicine depends, and he raises the hope that basic research in the life process itself may eventually unlock the riddle of cancer. He anticipates the big strides in the fight against cancer as coming not from surgery or radiation, but ultimately through chemotherapy — the use of chemicals, such as hormones and synthesized drugs.

In 1958 Dr. Coggeshall was a member of two special studies project panels on education for the Rockefeller Brothers Fund. The panels prepared two notable reports: *The Challenge to America: Its Economic and Social Aspects* and *The Pursuit of Excellence: Education and the Future of America*. In the same year he was elected to a three-year membership on the executive board of the World Health Organization. In 1959 Dr. Coggeshall served as a member of the State Department's International Development Advisory Board on foreign aid, heading a subcommittee on health. In the following year he was chairman of the committee on medical care, National Advisory Health Council, United States Public Health Service. In 1961 he served on the United States Public Health Service personnel study advisory committee. Coggeshall was named in 1962 as chairman of the new Commission on Drug Safety of the Pharmaceutical Manufacturers Association. The Commission was established by the ethical drug industry to work on the problem of providing maximum assurance of the safety of new drugs.

Dr. Coggeshall was appointed vice-president of the University of Chicago in 1960, and he was elected a trustee two years later. He is one of the few faculty members, other than the president of the university, ever to become a member of its board. As vice-president, Coggeshall has general responsibility for the educational operations of the university. He works closely with the president of the university and the chairman of the board on questions of policy and planning for the growth and development of the university, and for the most effective use of its resources. Over the years Dr. Coggeshall has published a number of papers on infections, tropical diseases, and medical education.

(Continued next page)

COGGESHALL, L. T.—Continued

In addition to his university duties Dr. Cogge-shall devotes much of his time to civic and organizational affairs. He is a member of the boards of the Rockefeller Foundation and the Josiah Macy, Jr., Foundation, and he has served on the boards of medical advisers of MEDICO and of the Multiple Sclerosis Foundation. He is a past president of the Association of Medical Colleges, the Institute of Medicine of Chicago, and the American Foundation for Tropical Medicine, and he has served as a consultant to a number of federal government departments. In Illinois he has been on the boards of a number of city and state institutions, and from 1958 to 1961 he was a member of the Chicago board of health. Organizations to which he belongs include the National Academy of Sciences, the American Philosophical Society, the American Association for the Advancement of Science, the World Medical Association, the American Leprosy Foundation, the American Epidemiological Society, and many others. He is an honorary member of the American Hospital Association and of the International Academy of Cytology, and an honorary life member of the American Cancer Society.

For his various activities Dr. Coggeshall has received a number of honors and awards. In 1957 he received a Jesuit Centennial Citation as one of Chicago's 100 outstanding citizens. In 1960 he received the Honor Award of the American Medical Writers Association and the Annual Award of the Pharmaceutical Manufacturers Association, and he was honored at a centennial dinner of the New York Medical College. In 1961 Coggeshall received the VIP Award of the Year from Catholic Charities in Chicago; the Founders Day Award from Loyola University; a Chicagoan of the Year Award from the Junior Association of Commerce and Industry; and the Award for Distinguished Achievement from *Modern Medicine*. Honorary doctorates have been conferred on him by Indiana University (1948), Jefferson Medical College (1956), Lake Forest College (1961), and Chicago Medical College (1962).

The lanky scientist and administrator from Indiana married Louise Holland, also an Indiana University graduate, on May 15, 1930. They have two daughters, Diane (Mrs. William Pryor) and Carol (Mrs. Douglas Govan), and one son, Richard Edward Coggeshall, a physician. Dr. L. T. Coggeshall is a Republican and a member of Alpha Omega Alpha, Phi Beta Kappa, Sigma Xi, and Delta Omega honorary fraternities. His clubs are the Chicago Club, the Commercial Club, the Tavern Club, and the University Club in Chicago; the X-Club and the Quadrangle Club at the University of Chicago; and the Cosmos Club in Washington, D.C. He also belongs to the Bandar-Log, the Wayfarers, and Acacia fraternity.

References

    Newsweek 47:60 Ap 16 '56
    Time 67:46+ F 20 '56 por
    American Men of Science 10th ed (1960-62)
    Who's Who in America, 1962-63

COLLINS, JAMES (DANIEL) July 12, 1917-
Philosopher; author; educator

Address: b. St. Louis University, 221 N. Grand Blvd., St. Louis 3, Mo.; h. 5508 Norway Dr., Normandy 21, Mo.

James Collins, a professor of philosophy at St. Louis University and specialist in the history of modern philosophy, sees as his task "a search for wholeness in a jagged world of natural events and interpersonal relations." To it he brings the disciplines of the old commitment he has done so much to renew: the tradition of philosophical theism and realism that flows from St. Augustine, St. Thomas Aquinas, and Cardinal Newman. Aware that while God does not change, man's ideas of Him do, Collins traces the shifting concepts of God through the modern philosophical schools and, in so doing, continues to make a positive contribution to the development of a realistic theism.

The distinguished American Jesuit, Father John LaFarge, has praised Collins as "one of the leading philosophical minds of our country." He spoke not only for Roman Catholics but for the entire body of American intellectuals, to whom Collins has demonstrated the reality of "dialogue" with a persuasive charity as uncommon in the discourse of philosophers as it is in the exchanges of ordinary men.

James Daniel Collins was born on July 12, 1917 in Holyoke, Massachusetts, the only son of Michael Joseph and Mary Magdalen (Rooney) Collins. He has one sister, Elinor, who still lives in Holyoke. His grandparents on both sides of the family had come as Irish immigrants to Holyoke in the 1880's, then known as "Ireland Parish," where they contributed to the engineering and building of the new city. His father worked in furniture sales and advertising. Collins, who obtained his elementary and secondary education in local public schools, recently said: "Before the slogan 'excellence in education' was coined, its reality was put into practice in the Holyoke schools. Since we were surrounded by Connecticut Valley colleges, we aimed at college."

In the summer of 1931 a polio epidemic struck Holyoke, and Collins, who had just graduated from Lawrence Junior High School contracted the infantile paralysis that forced him to spend one year in the hospital and two seasons at the rehabilitation center at Warm Springs, Georgia. He arrived at Warm Springs a few weeks before Franklin D. Roosevelt, recently elected to his first term as President of the United States, and established "informal, friendly terms with him."

Returning to Holyoke, Collins became the first student in Massachusetts to receive public school instruction at home. When he graduated from Holyoke High School in 1937, three years behind his age group, his teachers there pronounced him "the brightest student the high school ever had." It was a confidence he later justified at Catholic University of America in Washington, D.C., from which he graduated in 1941 with a B.A. degree *summa cum laude*, membership in Phi Beta Kappa, and the highest four-year scholastic average in the history of the university. The subject in which he majored was philosophy.

"At fifteen I knew that I had to become a philosopher," Collins recently wrote, "and yet this assurance grew upon me gradually rather than came in a sudden light. Basically, I was 'seduced' into philosophy by following two early interests: in biology, which led me to ask more general questions on the nature and aim of life, and in literature, which introduced me slyly to Plato and Schopenhauer and Nietzsche and thus to the great predicaments in philosophy. I never accepted the C. P. Snow thesis of antipathy between the scientific and humanistic cultures, and my search for ways to unify them and to illuminate them led me to philosophy." Before he graduated from high school he contributed "On Peace," an article with philosophic implications, to *Commonweal*. It appeared on March 5, 1937.

Aided by the Knights of Columbus Fellowship he had received on the basis of an examination mark of 98 percent, Collins spent the next three years in graduate study at Catholic University. He obtained his M.A. degree in philosophy in 1942 and his Ph.D. degree in philosophy in 1944. His doctoral dissertation, *The Thomistic Philosophy of the Angels,* was published by the Catholic University of America in 1947. Collins recalls that he had "two lines of interest" in his extracurricular activities: "helping to read to blind students and fathom their world, and helping Negro friends to live a richer community existence in the bleak Washington areas. The latter focused around Martin de Porres House, under the presiding spirit of that gentlest and firmest of men, Llewellyn Scott, who is still working there to overcome the alienations."

On a Penfield Traveling Fellowship he was granted for 1944-45, Collins engaged in postdoctoral research at Harvard University, where he concentrated on both the medieval Boethius and the modern Immanuel Kant. At the end of the academic year he accepted a post as instructor in philosophy at St. Louis University, an institution founded by the Jesuits. There he has remained and is now professor of philosophy.

Recently explaining his educational credo, Collins wrote: "I regard the discussion over research versus teaching as very unrealistic. My aim has been to unite these two activities and to benefit myself and my students by their mutual enrichment. I deliberately spread out my teaching range rather than concentrate narrowly on graduate studies. I see to it that I meet each year with undergraduates eager about philosophy as well as with graduate students who already have the professional life in mind. Through graduate seminars and dissertations, however, I try to advance the frontier of modern philosophy and to show my students the lasting significance of the great moderns from Descartes and Locke to Kant and Hegel." On another occasion he said that "philosophy should be a personally discovered thing. Students must become directly acquainted with the great sources, raise questions and solve their own problems—but the teacher is always the guide."

His first book was *The Existentialists* (Regnery, 1952), a sympathetic study of the most fashionable of the ideologies of anguish and dread, in which his interest had first been aroused by the late Nathan P. Avery. "All these men," he wrote in the preface, "are occupied with the same generic sort of problems, the problems of existing

JAMES COLLINS

men, despite the enormous differences in historical situation and technique." Those included were Nietzsche, Kierkegaard, Husserl, Sartre, Jaspers, Heidegger, and Marcel, whom he saw as reasserting "the venture of human freedom and its pitfalls" in a "philosophical climate . . . nourished upon pragmatism, scientific methodology, and semantics." Among the reviewers who decided that Collins had made a notable contribution to the contemporary colloquy on the estate of man was William Barrett (New York *Times,* June 1, 1952) who admired the Roman Catholic Collins' sympathetic treatment of the atheistic existentialism of Heidegger.

In his next book, *The Mind of Kierkegaard* (Regnery, 1953), Collins continued his examination of the predicaments of modern philosophy, concentrating on the structure of Kierkegaard's thought and relating it to the intellectual currents of his time. Reviewing it in the New York *Times* (February 7, 1954), the Protestant theologian Reinhold Niebuhr predicted that although many more books will be written about the Danish philosopher, none will be more valuable than *The Mind of Kierkegaard.*

Ostensibly a textbook prepared for university students, his *A History of Modern European Philosophy* (Bruce, 1954) gives substance to Collins' conviction that "a common woof runs through the whole history of philosophy." The great philosophers of all periods, he points out, are concerned with "the problems of the one and the many, the nature and possibility of metaphysics, the starting point and structure of knowledge, the world's relation to God, man's freedom and destiny." Collins therefore views the division between the history of philosophy and philosophy itself as essentially a factitious one. "We should enter into association with a thinker of the past," he once quoted the theologian Karl Rahner as saying, "not only to become acquainted

COLLINS, JAMES—*Continued*

with his views but in the last resort to learn something about the nature of reality."

One critic described Collins' *God in Modern Philosophy* (Regnery, 1959) as "the most detailed and complete attempt to survey the modern philosophies of God available." With it and *The Lure of Wisdom* (Marquette Univ. Press, 1962) and *Three Paths in Philosophy* (Regnery, 1962), Collins moved into the mainstream of his concern: the persistence of God, however shifting the conceptions of Him, as a central problem in the ventures of the great modern philosophers from Descartes and Locke to Kant and Hegel. The changing ideas that man may entertain of an unchanging God, Collins sees as an opportunity, not a disaster. In *The Lure of Wisdom* he recommends that "all the paths should be kept well swept and inviting, even when we accept the long-range goal of working toward a critical unification of the several wisdoms of man. In this way, we can contribute our human share toward the justifying of wisdom by all her children."

As his own share towards that justification, Collins has contributed not only his teaching and his books, but active participation in the American Philosophical Association, the American Catholic Philosophical Association (of which he was president in 1953-54), the International Phenomenological Society, and the Metaphysical Society of America, of which he was president in 1962. Since 1957 Collins has contributed an "Annual Review of Philosophy" to the quarterly *Cross Currents*, and he wrote a similar review for *Thought* from 1951 to 1956. He is the area editor of the *New Catholic Encyclopedia* for the history of Renaissance, modern, and contemporary philosophy.

Collins serves on the editorial boards of the *Modern Schoolman*, the *American Philosophical Quarterly*, and the *Journal of the History of Philosophy*. In 1961 the National Council of Catholic Men inaugurated a program of public recognition of eminent laymen by naming him recipient of its honor in philosophy. In 1962 he received both the Catholic University Alumni Award and the Cardinal Newman Award given annually to a Catholic layman who has made a distinguished contribution to the goals and ideals of the Newman apostolate. As Aquinas Lecturer at Marquette University in 1962, he spoke on "The Lure of Wisdom"; for the second Thomas More Lecture at Yale University in February 1963 he chose as his topic "The Emergence of Philosophy of Religion." In the season of 1961-62 he appeared as one of the main lecturers on a weekly series, "Communism and Freedom," which was telecast on KMOX-TV in St. Louis. He stressed that "Communism is not merely a political movement or an economy, but a definite philosophy which we must learn to interpret."

On June 6, 1945 James Collins married Yvonne Marie Stafford of Adrian, Michigan, who before her marriage engaged in economics research in the Latin American section of the tariff department in Washington, D.C. They have a son, Michael Leo. Collins is a slight man (five feet eight inches in height, 140 pounds in weight) who has blue eyes and brown hair. In religion he is a Roman Catholic, in politics, an independent. Among his recreations are traveling in summer, swimming with his family, stamp collecting on a minor scale, and visiting art collections throughout the United States. The rest of his time he devotes to what he considers the philosopher's mission: "closing the gap between intelligence and life."

References

American Catholic Who's Who, 1962 and 1963
Directory of American Scholars (1957)

COLWELL, EILEEN (HILDA) June 16, 1904-
British children's librarian

Address: b. Central Library, Hendon, London, N.W. 4, England; h. 3 Homefield Court, Hendon, London, N.W. 4, England

England's best-known children's librarian is without question Eileen Colwell, who since 1926 has been librarian in charge of work with children at the Hendon Public Library in London. At a time when few British libraries welcomed juvenile readers she planned and organized her library on modern lines and built it into a model of its kind, which has attracted visiting librarians from all over the world. Miss Colwell is a recognized authority on children's literature and a story-teller of international fame. She was co-founder of what is now the Library Association's Youth Libraries Section, and she has written books and articles and lectured widely on children's literature and library work with children.

Eileen Hilda Colwell, one of the four children of Richard Harold and Gertrude Weiss (Mason) Colwell, was born on June 16, 1904 in Robin Hood's Bay, a fishing village in Yorkshire, England. Her father was a Methodist minister who began his career in the United States but later worked in England. Since he was required to move to a new assignment every three years Eileen Colwell spent her childhood in a succession of homes, including Robin Hood's Bay; a mining town in Durham; and the historic Wiltshire town of Bradford-on-Avon. Encouraged by her parents to browse in the large family library, she became an insatiable reader. She also developed an enthusiasm and talent for telling stories —including many that she made up herself—to anyone who would listen.

Miss Colwell was educated privately until she was nine years old, and she then attended Girls High School in Rotherham and Penistone Grammar School, both in Yorkshire. By the time she graduated in 1921, she knew that she wanted to work with books and, if possible, with children. But teaching did not appeal to her, and librarianship, when her father first suggested it, seemed no more attractive. The British library movement was still in its infancy and offered little scope for work with children. "In most libraries," Miss Colwell wrote in *How I Became a Librarian* (Nelson, 1956), "children were not very welcome, and books for boys and girls, if there were any, were kept in some dark corner and bound in black so as not to show finger marks." Nevertheless, encouraged by the thought that she could perhaps do something to improve this situation, she applied for and obtained a Women's County

Major Scholarship to University College of the University of London. The scholarship was the first ever awarded for training in librarianship in the West Riding of Yorkshire, where Miss Colwell then lived.

The School of Librarianship at the University of London offered the only full-time course in librarianship then available in Great Britain. The curriculum lasted two years and embraced French, Latin, paleography, and literature, as well as classification, cataloging, bibliography, and library administration. Disappointed to find only one or two lectures devoted to library work with children, Miss Colwell nevertheless persevered and ultimately passed the examinations in every subject but Latin. This single failure meant another year at University College, and it was not until 1924 that she received her diploma.

During her college years Miss Colwell learned what she most wanted to know by working whenever she could in children's libraries, reading as many juvenile books as her leisure allowed, and telling stories wherever an audience was available. During vacations she did volunteer work at a settlement in Bow, a slum district in London's East End where children, some of them too poor to own shoes, were enthusiastic users of a ragged collection of donated books. In her third year at college she worked for three months in a London public library, spending much of that time in a basement children's room with no ventilation and no natural light.

Looking for a job after graduation, Miss Colwell was dismayed to discover that many employers were uninterested in "college-trained librarians with no practical experience," but she was finally accepted as a senior assistant in the adult fiction department of the public library in Bolton, a Lancashire industrial town. In the eighteen months that followed Miss Colwell learned a great deal, but although in her leisure time she doggedly continued to read and take notes on children's literature, she seemed no closer to her goal—a library "where children would be welcome and there would be unlimited books for those like myself who loved reading." At last, however, she was put in charge of the juvenile department in one of Bolton's branch libraries—the only modern children's room in the system. She had long coveted the assignment and hastened to put some of her favorite projects into effect. More disappointment followed when she was told to remove the posters she had made to brighten the bare walls, refused permission to hold story hours, and denied the right to select her own books. She realized that she must move on.

The position that she next obtained was in Hendon, a pleasant northern suburb of London, where a temporary part-time assistant was needed to organize a service for children. The project was unusual in that Hendon was proposing to start children's services before it had a library building, a staff, or a chief librarian. At that time Miss Colwell took a risk in exchanging a secure position for a temporary and uncertain one against the advice of almost everyone, but she has been at Hendon ever since.

When Miss Colwell took up her new post in October 1926, her instructions were to lay the

EILEEN COLWELL

foundations of a public library service by opening a number of small library centers in schools. She had three months in which to organize this service and to select, buy, and prepare the books for it. Office equipment was secured, and shelving and stationery were ordered. More gratifying still, Miss Colwell found herself with several hundred pounds to spend on new books of her own choosing—justification at last for her years of study and reading.

The service went into operation on schedule in January 1927 with a collection of books in each of seven schools and a staff of volunteers. Miss Colwell was officially recognized as a full-time employee—something she had been in fact for many weeks. The centers were popular from the beginning, but Eileen Colwell was far from satisfied. The collections were small and the centers open only one night a week. Moreover, she found her service hampered by the lack of an adult library to back up her own meager resources. But more and more centers opened and circulation shot upward—from 25,000 during the first year to 65,000 in the second. Soon work began on Hendon's central library building. It opened in December 1929, complete with a large and cheerful children's room, and Miss Colwell became the first children's librarian there. Her jurisdiction has grown over the years to the point where she is now responsible for Hendon's central children's library, children's rooms in six branches, and fifty school libraries that developed out of the original seven centers.

In the years since 1926 Miss Colwell has experimented with many techniques to make her library more attractive and useful. Story hours, class visits, displays, and booklists have been features of the service from the beginning. Another feature has been an illustrations collection now numbering over 20,000 items that is used by artists and film studios as well as by children. Miss Colwell has always believed that her read-

COLWELL, EILEEN—*Continued*

ers should have a share in running the library and has encouraged them to help with routine tasks. A library magazine was for many years a popular feature, and a library club, a zoo club, music, art, and stamp clubs have all flourished from time to time. The Hendon children's library has produced plays (some of them written by Miss Colwell herself) and puppet shows with puppets made by the children. Miss Colwell held her first Book Week in 1928, long before such weeks became a standard feature of British libraries.

In the midst of this activity Eileen Colwell has never lost sight of the fundamental purpose of a library—to bring books and readers together. She has expressed her philosophy in *How I Became a Librarian*: "To pretend that a book is going to be enjoyed because it is a 'good' book is useless," she wrote. "The best way to influence a child's reading is . . . to leave good books—and plenty of them—in his way for him to find himself." Her extraordinary understanding of both books and children is illustrated by a story told by a former reader at the Hendon children's library who once, ill at home, asked a friend to choose books for her. The problem was referred to Miss Colwell, who not only remembered the child but precisely identified her reading tastes.

"All my life has been full of stories," Eileen Colwell wrote in her autobiography, "stories I have read, stories I have heard and stories I have told to other people." When she first went to Hendon, still unsatisfied with her storytelling technique after years of practice, she invested part of her small salary in elocution lessons. Since then she has told stories to every kind of audience—to adult refugees during the war, to social workers and library students learning storytelling technique, and on radio and television. She has broadcast not only to English listeners but also to the United States, Canada, South Africa, and the West Indies. She was the British storyteller at the Festival of Storytelling during the 1956 ALA conference, and in 1961 she was a guest artist at the first John Masefield Storytelling Festival at the Toronto (Canada) Public Library.

Miss Colwell's first book was *How I Became a Librarian* (Nelson, 1956), an autobiography written with a disarming modesty and simplicity as part of a series of career books. It was followed in 1961 by *Eleanor Farjeon: A Monograph* (Bodley Head) and in 1962 by *Tell Me a Story* (Penguin), a collection for children under five. Another collection, *A Storyteller's Choice* (Bodley Head), appeared in 1963.

Miss Colwell has lectured on children's librarianship, books, and storytelling at her alma mater, the University of London; at other library schools; to publishers and booksellers; and to many other groups and organizations. She is often asked by publishers to read and comment on manuscripts, and at least one author, Malcolm Saville, has dedicated books to her.

Since 1929 Miss Colwell has been a Fellow of the Library Association. In 1937, together with Miss E. G. Hayler of the Croydon Public Library, she founded the Association of Children's Librarians, now the Youth Libraries Section of the

Library Association. She has served as the group's secretary and as its chairman, and she is still a member of the committee. She is also a member of the international jury that awards the Hans Christian Andersen Medal and since 1961 has been chairman of a committee on library work with children of the International Federation of Library Associations. Miss Colwell has served on the Carnegie and Greenaway medal committees since the awards' inception in 1936. These awards are the English equivalents of the American Newbery and Caldecott medals.

Eileen Colwell, who recalls without rancor that she was known as "Tot" at library school, is precisely five feet tall. She is a Methodist and has no political affiliation. Among her favorite recreations are reading, telling stories, writing, making marionettes, and traveling. She has visited most European countries, Canada, and the United States. In an introduction to *How I Became a Librarian*, Phyllis Parrott wrote: "The name of Eileen Colwell is one which springs to mind whenever children's libraries are mentioned. Her work at Hendon has been an inspiration to all; her knowledge of children's literature and children's reading are unequalled; her enthusiasm for her work is infectious and has encouraged countless children's librarians."

References

Junior Bookshelf 14:81 Jl '50 por
Colwell, Eileen. How I Became a Librarian (1956)

COOK, BARBARA Oct. 25, 1927- Actress
Address: b. c/o Actors' Equity Association, 226 W. 47th St., New York 36; h. 6 School St., Port Washington, N.Y.

Barbara Cook, who shines among Broadway's brightest singing stars, is blonde, blue-eyed, and possessed of one of the finest sets of critical notices in the American musical theater. She has been described as "lustrous," "fetching," and "winning and winsome," with "a piquancy in her eyes and a warmth in her voice [plus] the magical quality of lighting up a stage." Her best-known role is that of the librarian in *The Music Man*, a long-run musical that opened in late 1957.

The first signs of Barbara Cook's talent for captivating people appeared when she was a child of four in Atlanta, Georgia, where she had been born on October 25, 1927 to Charles Bunyan and Nell (Harwell) Cook. So pleasing was her voice that friends would call the Cook household and ask Barbara to sing over the telephone. By the time she was seven she had talked her parents into letting her study tap dancing. Although the Cooks were not a well-to-do family, the money was found for her lessons. Barbara remains deeply grateful to her mother for her early encouragement and support.

Two years later the stage-struck youngster was dancing at amateur night performances in neighborhood movie theaters. When she was fifteen she wangled herself a job as a chorus girl in Atlanta's Roxy Theatre and, later, sang over a local radio station, WSB. On graduating from

Girl's High School in Atlanta in 1945, Barbara Cook was ready for Broadway.

It was not, however, until 1948 that the Atlanta soprano moved to New York to seek stardom, and another year and a half passed before she got her first singing engagement—in a Boston night club. Before and after that engagement came singing lessons and the usual jobs that young Broadway hopefuls take to tide them over while waiting for the big break. She worked as a typist, as a file clerk for the Navy's materials distribution office after the war, and as an employee at a post office in Flushing, New York. Eventually she found a summer job as a resort entertainer, did another cabaret stand, and, in May 1951, opened in her first Broadway musical, *Flahooley.* The play was panned by the critics and closed after forty performances, but Barbara Cook, as the romantic lead, appealed to Brooks Atkinson of the New York *Times* as "especially winning."

Summer stock followed, and then, in 1953, Miss Cook was cast in the role of Ado Annie in a New York City Center revival of *Oklahoma!* A typical review was that by William Hawkins, who wrote in the New York *World-Telegram and Sun:* "Barbara Cook is pretty and spirited as Ado Annie, with the voice and energy to take fine care of her immortal numbers, 'I Cain't Say No' and 'All er Nothin.'" Miss Cook next took the role of Carrie Pipperidge in the revival of another Rodgers and Hammerstein classic, *Carousel,* which opened on June 2, 1954. John Beaufort in the *Christian Science Monitor* praised her singing and "that intriguing combination of qualities—the comic spirit and genuine charm." He described her as "the darling of the City Center revival . . . ready for the bigger and better things that undoubtedly await her."

Fresh from her *Carousel* triumph, Miss Cook returned to Broadway on January 27, 1955 in *Plain and Fancy,* a musical hit. In the role of the pert little Amish lass seeking a husband without a beard, Miss Cook won the approval of many critics, including Walter Kerr of the New York *Herald Tribune,* who called her "delightful at every turn; saucy . . . winsome . . . and exuberantly hoydenish." The show ran for more than a year.

In late 1956 and early 1957 Miss Cook gave an enchanting performance as Cunegonde, the heroine of the ill-fated musical version of Voltaire's *Candide.* The show, which had a book by Lillian Hellman, lyrics by Richard Wilbur, and music by Leonard Bernstein, was "a spectacular example of an artistic triumph and a commercial flop," according to *Variety,* and it closed after seventy-three performances at the Martin Beck Theatre. Before the end of the year Miss Cook played in another New York City Center revival of *Carousel,* this time as a very touching Julie Jordan.

Barbara Cook then stepped into one of the most successful of all Broadway musicals, *The Music Man,* by Meredith Willson, which had its première at the Majestic Theatre on December 19, 1957. As Marian, the plain librarian who rⁿforms the fast-talking, heart-of-gold con man (played by Robert Preston), Miss Cook added some new rave notices to her collection. Typical

Bender, N. Y.

BARBARA COOK

was the New York *Post* review by Richard Watts, Jr., who found "that Miss Cook is a charming romantic comedienne with a lovely voice and that she is a blissful dream" in her featured role. To this tribute Frank Aston of the New York *World Telegram and Sun* added: "If all our [librarians] looked, sang, danced and acted like Miss Barbara, this nation's book learning would be overwhelming." For her performance in the play, the young singer won the "Tony" award of the American Theatre Wing as the outstanding featured player of the 1957-58 season.

Before the end of the 1,375-performance run of *The Music Man,* Miss Cook withdrew from the cast to play another role. In May 1960 she appeared as Anna, the British schoolmarm who goes to Siam to teach the royal family, in a City Center revival of *The King and I* by Rodgers and Hammerstein. Brooks Atkinson (New York *Times,* May 12, 1960) thought that in her interpretation of the role Miss Cook gave "the best performance of her career." The veteran critic noted that Miss Cook had previously been playing provincial maidens—"playing them especially well." As a cultivated woman of maturity, Atkinson continued, Miss Cook "gives Anna a cool dignity that adds a little more stature to the part than it has had before."

The next vehicle for Barbara Cook, *The Gay Life,* which reached Broadway on November 19, 1961, was a musical version of Arthur Schnitzler's turn-of-the-century Viennese comedy, *Anatol.* Only a middling hit, it closed at the Shubert Theatre after 114 performances. Reviewers, however, were most enthusiastic about Miss Cook's performance, particularly Walter Kerr, who found little else to praise in the production. The critic for *Life* wrote that "in *The Gay Life* she outshines herself, singing and dancing with a wonderful April zing," and the New York *Times's* Howard Taubman commented, "The integrity of

COOK, BARBARA—*Continued*

her acting and her singing voice gives an oft-told sentimental story the credibility of human warmth." On April 23, 1963 Miss Cook opened in another Broadway musical, *She Loves Me*.

Although her career on the New York stage has brought one personal success after the other, Miss Cook has had her share of disappointments. One of them involved the role of the librarian that she created in the stage version of *The Music Man*. She deeply wanted to play the part in the Warner Brothers motion-picture version of the hit. Instead, it went to Shirley Jones, a star with a Hollywood name.

In addition to the Broadway musical stage, Miss Cook has often performed on television and in concerts. In June 1958, for instance, she opened the eleventh season of the New York Public Library summer record concerts, and in August 1961 she sang on the annual Rodgers and Hammerstein program, the closing concert of the season, at New York's Lewisohn Stadium. On TV she appeared in *Babes in Toyland, Bloomer Girl*, and *Hansel and Gretel* and on many highly rated programs like the *Ed Sullivan Show*, the *Chevy Show*, and the *Bell Telephone Hour*.

Barbara Cook was married on March 9, 1952 to the actor David LeGrant, whom she had met in 1951 when both were members of the social staff at Camp Tamiment in the Pocono Mountains. They both played in *Oklahoma!* in 1953 and have toured on the road together. A son, Adam, was born on November 18, 1959. The LeGrants live in Port Washington, Long Island, where Barbara, in suburban housewife fashion, does the gardening, takes photographs of her family, and knits sweaters for her son. She stands just under five feet four inches and weighs 115 pounds. She is a Democrat. For the role of Lisel in *The Gay Life*, Miss Cook was coached by her husband, who conducts his own dramatic classes.

Miss Cook once said of herself in a newspaper interview: "I'm just interested in working in the theatre and in being as happy as I can be. I don't think being a star is the be-all-end-all. This is a way of life. Sometimes when I'm riding in a taxi at night I look out at the sky-line and I think I'm really a part of this city, and I appreciate the fact that people respect me and respect my work. That's what feels good."

References

N Y World-Telegram p8 Ag 17 '63 por
Who's Who in America, 1960-61

COOPER, LEROY GORDON, JR. Mar. 6, 1927- Astronaut

Address: b. National Aeronautics and Space Administration, Washington 25, D.C.

The need for human skill and judgment in exploring the cosmos was demonstrated when on May 16, 1963 Major Leroy Gordon Cooper, Jr., of the United States Air Force brought his space capsule, *Faith 7*, to a safe landing following mechanical failure. Cooper's successful twenty-two-orbit trip was the sixth manned space flight, and the fourth manned orbital flight, sent aloft

by the United States. It may be the last flight of the National Aeronautics and Space Administration's Project Mercury before a more ambitious program is attempted. Cooper's flight came at a time when the value of the space program of the United States was being questioned by some scientists, government officials, and political leaders, and it injected new life into United States efforts to send a manned spaceship to the moon by 1970. Although the flight fell short of the feat of Soviet astronauts Pavel R. Popovich and Andrian G. Nikolayev who, in separate flights on August 11-12, 1962 simultaneously orbited the earth forty-eight and sixty-four times, respectively, it indicated that the United States was ahead of the Soviet Union in some areas of the space race.

Leroy Gordon Cooper, Jr., the youngest of the seven original astronauts, was born on March 6, 1927 in Shawnee, Oklahoma, the only child of Colonel Leroy Gordon Cooper, Sr. (who died in 1960), and Mrs. Hattie Cooper. Both of his grandmothers, Mrs. Cora Cooper and Mrs. Orena Herd, are still living in Oklahoma. His mother operates a small ranch in Carbondale, Colorado. The elder Cooper, a lawyer and county judge, was also an amateur pilot, who counted among his close acquaintances such noted aviators as Wiley Post and Amelia Earhart. He entered the United States Air Force as a legal officer during World War II and remained with the Air Force until he retired in 1957.

An admirer of the science-fiction hero Buck Rogers, Gordon Cooper, Jr., developed an interest in flying at an early age. He often accompanied his father on flights in his old Command-Aire biplane, and by the time he was seven or eight he was occasionally allowed to take over its controls. He was also fond of fishing and was a Boy Scout. Cooper was educated in the primary and secondary schools of Shawnee, and for a time he also attended high school in Murray, Kentucky. His mother has recalled that although he liked school he was not an outstanding student. During his teens Cooper took odd jobs around the Shawnee airport to earn money for flying lessons, and at sixteen he made his first solo flight.

Upon graduating from high school in 1945 Cooper hoped to qualify for flight training with the Army or Navy, but since the service flying schools were not accepting candidates at the time, he enlisted in the Marine Corps. He completed boot training shortly before the end of World War II and then attended Naval Academy Preparatory School for a few months. Later he served with the Presidential honor guard in Washington, D.C. After his discharge in August 1946 Cooper joined his parents at Hickam Air Force Base in Honolulu and attended the University of Hawaii for three years, earning a commission as a lieutenant with ROTC. He transferred this commission to the Air Force and was recalled to extended active duty in 1949.

After completing his flight training Cooper was assigned to the 86th Fighter Bomber Group in Munich, Germany, where he remained for four years, flying F-84's and F-86's. During this period he attended the European extension of the University of Maryland night school for one year. Later he studied for two years at the Air

Force Institute of Technology at Wright-Patterson Air Force Base in Ohio, where he received a B.S. degree in aeronautical engineering in August 1956. After graduating from Air Force Experimental Flight Test School at Edwards Air Force Base, California, in April 1957, Cooper was assigned to the performance engineering division at Edwards, as a test pilot and aeronautical engineer. There he took part in the flight testing of experimental fighter aircraft. He accumulated a total of about 2,600 hours flying time, 1,600 of them in jet fighters.

When the National Aeronautics and Space Administration called for astronaut trainees to participate in its manned space flight program, Project Mercury, Cooper volunteered out of "plain curiosity." As he learned more about the program his enthusiasm grew, and he was determined to be the first man in space. The announcement that Cooper, with six other test pilots, had been chosen from an original group of 110 volunteers, was made by NASA officials at a press conference on April 9, 1959.

The seven astronaut trainees began their exhaustive training program in May 1959. They acquired a vast amount of scientific knowledge about astronautics and underwent the stresses and strains that they would experience in actual space flight. They were also subjected to many physical and psychological examinations. Unperturbed by the possible perils of space flight, Cooper sometimes upset physicians by his habit of going to sleep during the extensive physical checkups. In August 1959 he was chosen to demonstrate to a group of fifty newsmen at the Naval Air Development Center at Johnsville, Pennsylvania, the probable reactions of an astronaut to the immense pressure involved in a rocket-satellite takeoff. His demonstration included spinning in a giant centrifuge that subjected him to nine times the force of gravity.

Despite Cooper's qualifications, however, NASA officials developed some misgivings about his suitability for Project Mercury, because of his reputation as a complainer and his indifference to the "public image" that the government was trying to build around the astronauts. He was disappointed when Alan B. Shepard, rather than he, was chosen to make the first suborbital flight in May 1961, and when he was passed over on succeeding space flights. When another astronaut-trainee, Donald K. Slayton, was grounded because of a heart flutter, Cooper threatened to quit in protest, but was persuaded to remain in the program by his friend and fellow astronaut Walter M. Schirra.

During the space-flights of the other astronauts Cooper was assigned to ground-support duties. He covered the three-orbit flight by John H. Glenn on February 20, 1962 from Muchea tracking station in Australia. When Malcolm Scott Carpenter made a similar flight on May 24, 1962, Cooper received communications from him at the tracking station at Guaymas, Mexico. In the five months of preparations for the six-orbit flight of Walter M. Schirra on October 3, 1962 Cooper worked closely with Schirra and served as back-up pilot during the flight. After Schirra's flight, it appeared that Cooper would be by-passed for the next space flight, because of his

NASA Photo
LEROY GORDON COOPER, JR.

protest on behalf of Slayton, and because it was felt that the flight should be undertaken by someone with previous space experience. NASA officials reportedly had selected Shepard for the flight. Cooper was finally chosen, however, after Schirra had interceded on his behalf and had threatened to take the case before the press. Informed of his selection on November 13, 1962, Cooper said that he was "very delighted" to have been chosen and that he had been working toward this goal for a long time.

On May 15, 1963, at 8:04 A.M. (Eastern Standard Time), Cooper's space capsule, *Faith 7* (of the same design as the capsules used for the five previous space flights), was successfully launched by an Atlas rocket from Cape Canaveral, Florida. The flight had been postponed several times, and it had originally been scheduled to cover eighteen orbits, but this was extended to twenty-two. The capsule reached a velocity of 17,546 miles per hour and altitudes ranging from 100.2 to 165.8 miles above the earth. During his flight Cooper covered a distance of 595,564 ground miles in thirty-four hours, twenty minutes, and thirty seconds, and he spent thirty-three hours and fifty-four minutes in a state of weightlessness. He flew over some 100 countries and made six trips over the Chinese Communist mainland. (He is the first astronaut to fly over Communist territory.)

A major purpose of Cooper's flight was to obtain medical knowledge concerning the ability of an astronaut to operate a space capsule during extended periods of weightlessness. Instruments attached to his body recorded his water balance, kidney functions, temperature, blood pressure, heartbeat, and respiration. With television, motion picture, and still cameras, Cooper photographed weather phenomena, cloud formations, and stars and beamed television pictures of himself back to earth. He also performed about a dozen experiments designed to furnish informa-

COOPER, LEROY GORDON, JR.—*Cont.*

tion for use in the future two-man Gemini space project and the ultimate Apollo moon project. During his third orbit he ejected a sphere, carrying two flashing beacon lights, to gauge the visibility of nearby lights in space. Another experiment, involving the release of a tethered balloon in the sixth orbit, was unsuccessful owing to the failure of an explosive charge. The capsule also contained Geiger counters to measure radiation encountered in space.

During his flight Cooper slept soundly for about seven and a half hours, exercised with a rubber tension-cord, and experienced some slight difficulty in consuming water and dehydrated food. An important factor in the success of Cooper's flight was his ability to conserve as much of his oxygen, electric power, and hydrogen-peroxide fuel as possible. The flight seemed to be proceeding perfectly until the nineteenth orbit, when the .05G light on the control panel of the capsule lit up unexpectedly. (The light was not supposed to flash on until after the capsule re-entered the atmosphere, when it was subjected to .05 of normal gravity.)

Following instructions from the ground, Cooper turned on his automatic controls during his twentieth orbit, but found that the attitude gyros controlling the positioning of the capsule for return to the ground failed to work. He was forced to steer the capsule manually. During the final orbit another failure occurred when the inverters, which were to provide alternating current for the re-entry control system, did not function. Thus Cooper was compelled to pilot his capsule back to earth without any automatic aids whatever. Guided by the instructions of John H. Glenn, he eased his spacecraft back into the atmosphere, and at 6:24.5 P.M. on the day following his takeoff he made a nearly perfect landing only 7,000 yards from the aircraft carrier USS *Kearsarge,* at a point 115 miles southeast of Midway Island. A medical checkup indicated that Cooper was in good physical condition.

President John F. Kennedy called Cooper's flight "one of the great victories for the human spirit," and the United States Senate adopted a resolution lauding his flight. Messages flooded in from all over the world, including "cordial congratulations" from Soviet Premier Nikita S. Khrushchev. Following a brief reunion with his family in Hawaii, Cooper returned to Florida, where he held a press conference at Cape Canaveral on May 19, 1963 and was enthusiastically welcomed by crowds at Cocoa Beach. On May 21 he went to Washington, D.C., where he was given a White House reception and received the NASA Distinguished Service Medal. Addressing a joint session of both houses of Congress, Cooper paid tribute to members of the armed forces who died for their country and to those who contributed to the success of his flight. He was given a standing ovation. Later he visited New York City, where he was honored with the traditional ticker-tape parade. On May 29 he received his pilot-astronaut wings from the Air Force. Visiting his home town of Shawnee, Oklahoma in the following month, Cooper expressed confidence that the United States would beat Russia in the race to the moon.

Although the astronauts appealed to President Kennedy for another, more extended orbital flight in the Mercury capsule, NASA officials said that Cooper's flight had been so successful that another Mercury flight would probably not be needed before the more elaborate Gemini project, involving a two-man spacecraft, is undertaken in 1964. According to NASA administrator James Webb, Cooper could have remained aloft for ninety-two orbits if he had had enough oxygen and other supplies aboard. Cooper's unlikely report that he saw smoke from the chimneys of Tibet during his flight indicated to some scientists the possibility that an individual's capacity for perception and judgment might be impaired during weightlessness. Cooper was the first of the astronauts to be covered during his flight by a $100,000 individual Aetna life insurance policy, which was issued to each of the seven astronauts on May 8, 1963.

Leroy Gordon Cooper, Jr., who is known as "Gordo" to his friends, was married in 1947 to Trudy Olson, a former drum majorette and flying instructor, whom he met while attending the University of Hawaii. They have two teen-age daughters, Camala K. and Janita L. The Coopers live in a $30,000 ranch house near the NASA spacecraft center in Houston, Texas. Cooper is five feet nine inches tall, and he weighed in at 147 pounds before his space flight. (He lost seven pounds during the flight.) He has brown hair, blue eyes, and a long jaw, and he is described by James Reston in the New York *Times* (May 22, 1963) as "handsome and modest, like the nice guy next door."

Although Cooper is known as a quiet man who shuns publicity, he is also noted for his unpredictable humor and daredevil stunts. He feels that he is destined to go higher and faster than anyone else. He has his own airplane, a Beechcraft Bonanza, and he drives his 1963 Chevrolet at high speeds. His favorite recreations include hunting, fishing, boating, water-skiing, auto-racing, woodworking, and playing the piano. Whenever he has the time he goes picnicking, hiking, and swimming with his family. A religious man, Cooper ended his address to Congress on May 21, 1963 with a prayer: "Help guide and direct all of us that we may shape our lives to be much better Christians, trying to help one another. . . . Help us in our future space endeavors that we may show the world that democracy really can compete and still is able to do things in a big way."

References

Life 54:90+ My 17 '63 pors
N Y Post p27 My 14 '63 por
N Y Times p19 My 16 '63 por
N Y World Telegram p21 My 13 '63 pors
Time 81:17+ My 24 '63 pors

COPELAND, LAMMOT DU PONT May 19, 1905- Industrialist

Address: b. E. I. du Pont de Nemours & Co., Du Pont Bldg., Wilmington 98, Del.; h. Greenville, Del.

The need of American business for attracting "interested owners" to take part in the management of corporations rather than delegating all responsibilities to hired professional managers is a firm conviction of Lammot du Pont Copeland, president, chief executive, and one of the major stockholders of E. I. du Pont de Nemours & Company, the largest chemical firm in the world. Copeland, the eleventh president of the 161-year-old company, was elected on August 20, 1962 to succeed C. H. Greenewalt, who became chairman of the board and finance committee.

For almost thirty-five years, ever since he completed his training as an industrial chemist, Copeland had been advancing in managerial power in the company. Originally a producer of explosives, du Pont now manufactures more than 1,200 diversified chemical products. Through an expanded program of research, modernization, and investment in related companies, Copeland believes, du Pont may soon achieve the long-cherished goal of $3 billion in annual sales.

A great-great-grandson of Éleuthère Irénée du Pont, founder of the company in 1802, and a nephew of three successive presidents, Lammot du Pont Copeland was born on May 19, 1905 to Charles and Louisa d'Andelot (du Pont) Copeland in Christiana Hundred, New Castle County, Delaware. His mother was the sister of Pierre, Irénée, and Lammot du Pont, presidents of the company from 1919 to 1940. His father was associated with the du Pont company as assistant treasurer from 1903 to 1921 and secretary from 1921 to 1935. After resigning as a director in 1942, he was curator of the company's museum until his death in 1944. Lammot Copeland attended the Wilmington Friends School and then Harvard University, from which he obtained the B.S. degree in industrial chemistry in 1928. Although only a few of the more than 1,600 members of the family attempt a career with the du Pont Company, Lammot Copeland cannot remember a time when he did not plan to work in the business.

In September 1929 Copeland joined E. I. du Pont de Nemours & Company as an expediter of small orders at the Fairfield, Connecticut plant, which made fabrics and finishes. After the stock market crash he was laid off during an economy drive when his job was eliminated. Four months later he was rehired as a laboratory technician in the Fairfield plant.

Transferred to the company's headquarters in Wilmington in 1935, Copeland gained wider experience by working in the control section of the finishes division for two years, in the market analysis section for one year, and in general sales as assistant to the manager for three years before he moved to the development department in 1941. He was elected a director of the company in 1942 and the following year a member of the finance committee, which must approve all major appropriations. In 1947 he was named secretary of the company, a position his father once held, and as secretary he began a stockholder relations program. He became director of the secretary department after an organizational change in 1952. His next major promotions, in October 1954, were to a vice-presidency and to the chairmanship of the finance committee. He resigned from the finance committee in 1959 when he was named to the nine-member executive committee,

Karsh, Ottawa

LAMMOT DU PONT COPELAND

which has the important responsibility of deciding what products and research will be developed.

In late 1944 Copeland had been elected a director to the board of General Motors Corporation to represent du Pont's 23 percent stock interest in that company. He served as a member of the audit committee from 1946 to 1949, of the finance committee from 1949 to 1959, and of the bonus and salary committee from 1954 to 1959. Thus Copeland was one of the principal defendants in du Pont's thirteen-year antitrust battle with the government over du Pont's $3.5 billion stock interest in General Motors. He resigned from the General Motors board on December 7, 1959 in compliance with Federal Judge Walter J. LaBuy's decision in Chicago forbidding the interlocking of du Pont and General Motors directors. Copeland did not consider du Pont's interest in General Motors improper, because, he pointed out, du Pont never had received all of the General Motors lacquer and paint business. He was quoted in the New York Times (September 23, 1962) as saying, "Our boys always used to weep and wail that it was harder to sell to G.M."

With the settlement of the antitrust suit, Walter S. Carpenter, chairman of the du Pont board of directors for fifteen years, felt free to retire. At the board of directors meeting on August 20, 1962 C. H. Greenewalt, who had been president, was chosen to be the new chairman of the board and Copeland was elected president. When asked in a press interview about his plans for the future, Copeland explained that he planned no sudden changes, for, he said, "Mr. Greenewalt and I look at life from a similar point of view," and he added that he expected a "continuing and steady growth," with emphasis on research to counteract the low profit margins on chemical staples.

(Continued next page)

COPELAND, LAMMOT DU PONT—Cont.

Under Copeland's direction, du Pont is striving to reach its goal of $3 billion earned from sales. To help achieve this figure du Pont is investing in other companies, such as Block Engineering, Inc., of Cambridge, Massachusetts, which handles technical defense projects, and Cyrogenic Engineering Company, which is engaged in the science of supercold temperatures. Copeland announced in late 1962 a $350,000,000 capital investment program for the improvement of plants, laboratories, and other facilities in 1963. About 15 percent of this expenditure was designated for seventeen du Pont subsidiaries overseas.

One reason for du Pont's pre-eminence in the highly competitive chemical industry has been its development through research of new products such as nylon, orlon, and dacron fibers, Duco finishes, and Mylar plastic film. Delrin, recently perfected, has been called "du Pont's challenge to metal." To carry on its research program du Pont spends more than $90,000,000 a year and employs more than 2,200 scientists and engineers, 450 of them in basic research. The effectiveness of this spending is reflected in the steady increase in du Pont's profits. In October 1962, despite less revenue from the General Motors investments, nine-month earnings per share were reported to be $6.81 in contrast to $6.11 a share in 1961.

When discussing the state of American business in a speech at the annual convention of the Investment Bankers Association on November 27, 1962, Copeland emphasized that industry must spend heavily for research to ensure the growth of American economy. He expressed concern over the public's "misunderstanding" of the profit motive, which he considers the sole incentive for a company "to expand its business, provide more jobs and better opportunities, pay higher wages to employees and engage in research to develop new and better products." Aware of the criticisms of big business, he argued that there is a need for large, growing corporations as well as small and medium companies. Although du Pont is the largest chemical firm in the world, he noted, it receives less than 8 percent of the chemical industry's sales.

Apprehensive that widespread ownership of corporations may lead to lax management, Copeland has suggested that business needs more "truly interested owners" rather than just a greater number of owners. He is convinced that a company manager should receive a major part of his income from company dividends. One of the main stockholders, he owns 190,941 common shares and 338,348 shares of Christiana Securities Company, a holding company with 29.2 percent of the outstanding du Pont shares.

At the age of twenty-five, Copeland had obtained his first experience in helping to determine corporation policies. In 1930 he was elected to the board of the Union National Bank. When this bank merged with the Wilmington Trust Company in 1943, he became a director of the latter and a member of its trust committee. He served as director of the Pennsylvania Railroad Company from December 23, 1953 to October 28, 1959; is at present a director, treasurer, and vice-president of the Christiana Securities Company;

and is a member of the boards of du Pont of Canada Limited in Montreal, Terminal Warehouses Ltd. in Toronto, and the Chemical Bank New York Trust Company. He is also president and a director of the Delaware Realty & Investment Company.

Away from business, Copeland has contributed his time and talents to several educational institutions. He was elected a trustee of the University of Pennsylvania in October 1951 and is a member of the development committee of the Friends School in Wilmington. For his alma mater he served on the committee to reorganize the Harvard Divinity School, on the visiting committee to the Graduate School of Education, on the executive committee of the financial program for Harvard, and as director of the Harvard Alumni Association. Under his leadership, in January 1963 du Pont announced that the company will grant more than $1,780,000 to 168 universities and colleges for the improvement of the education of scientists and engineers.

Another of Copeland's interests is American history. He is president and a director of the Winterthur Corporation, which sponsors a museum of Americana. He is also treasurer and trustee of the Eleutherian Mills-Hagley Foundation, which is concerned with the history of Brandywine Creek, where the first du Pont plants were built. A collector of early American antiques, he is a member of the exclusive Walpole Society, a group of thirty connoisseurs. He belongs to the Huguenot Society of America and the Society of Mayflower Descendants and is lieutenant governor of the Society of Colonial Wars in Delaware.

In October 1962 Copeland was elected vice-chairman of the executive committee of the Planned Parenthood Federation. In local philanthropic and civic organizations, he served in 1948 as campaign chairman for the United Community Fund of Northern Delaware, as director from 1938 to 1959 of the Family Service of Northern Delaware, and he is vice-chairman of the Delaware Safety Council. He is on the board of managers of the Wilmington Institute Free Library and is past president and honorary director of the Wilmington Society of the Fine Arts. He retains his membership in the American Chemical Society and is an honorary member of the American Society of Corporate Secretaries. In 1958 he was made an Officer of the French Legion of Honor and in 1960, an Officer of the Belgian Order of Leopold.

Lammot du Pont Copeland married Pamela Cunningham on February 1, 1930. They have three children: Lammot du Pont Copeland, Jr., Gerret van Sweringen Copeland, and Louisa d'Andelot (Mrs. James Biddle). Copeland was described in the New York Times as "a man who listens attentively and answers forthrightly, often with a humorous aside." He is known as the financial wizard of the family. Active in politics, he has been a delegate to several Republican National Conventions. He is an Episcopalian.

Copeland, whose nickname is "Mots," enjoys hunting and trout and salmon fishing. He has a pistol range in the basement of his home and is a life member of the National Rifle Association.

His clubs include the Vicmead Hunt and the Wilmington Country; the Burlingame (California) Country; and the Harvard, Links, and University in New York City. He lives in a Georgian mansion in New Castle County, Delaware and runs, so far without profit, a 3,000-acre farm.

References

Fortune 66:49 O '62
N Y Herald Tribune p29 Ag 21 '62 por;
p35 N 28 '62 por
N Y Times p3 S 23 '62 por
Newsweek 60:61 S 3 '62 por
Who's Who in America, 1962-63
World Who's Who in Commerce and Industry (1961)

COTY, RENÉ (JULES GUSTAVE) Mar. 20, 1882-Nov. 22, 1962 French statesman; president of the Fourth Republic (1954-59); was instrumental in recalling Charles de Gaulle to power in 1959. See *Current Biography* (April) 1954.

Obituary

N Y Times p29 N 23 '62

CREASEY, JOHN (krē'sĭ) Sept. 17, 1908-
British crime writer
Address: New Hall, Bodenham, Salisbury, Wiltshire, England

One of the best and most productive of crime novelists is the British writer John Creasey. For those of his readers with catholic tastes, there need never be famine: Creasey turns out ten to twelve books a year and has in his time written more than 400. They range from police detective novels to action-adventure and suspense stories, and they generally are "action thrillers . . . without the bedroom scenes." Creasey has worked under twelve pseudonyms and has written several series under his own name. His major hard-cover publishers are Hodder & Stoughton and John Long Ltd. in England and Doubleday & Company, Inc., Charles Scribner's Sons, and Harper & Row in the United States.

Although he does not expect to produce masterpieces at the pace he keeps, Creasey never lets his work fall below a certain level of competence. Critics have found all his series exciting, and *Gideon's Fire* (1961), which he wrote as J. J. Marric, won an Edgar award of the Mystery Writers of America in 1962. Creasey's output can be achieved only through organization and discipline. "You can't wait for the spirit to move you," he says. He is impatient with "Freudian and Jungian poking about in writers' minds to see what makes them tick," and he denies the validity of writing blocks. "Nothing but laziness!" he insists. "And perhaps more than a touch of vanity. It has occurred to me that if writers weren't so desperately eager to write very good books, they wouldn't write such very bad ones" (*New Yorker*, July 16, 1960).

The seventh of nine children of Joseph Creasey, a poor coachmaker, and Ruth (Creasey)

Mark Gerson

JOHN CREASEY

Creasey, John Creasey was born on September 17, 1908 in Southfields, Surrey, England. At two he was stricken with polio and had to learn to walk again four years later. Between 1914 and 1923, except for a year when illness kept him at home, he attended the Fulham Elementary School and the Sloane School in Chelsea, where he held a scholarship. Encouraged by his headmaster, John Creasey began to send his poems and articles to editors from the age of ten. His first story was published in 1925. Creasey has said that he became a writer to make a good living. "I used to be paid five shillings a thousand words," he recalls, "so I got into the habit of writing very fast indeed."

For twelve years after he left school at the age of fourteen and a half Creasey supported himself with factory, clerical, and sales jobs. During this period he did his writing at night, and he was often fired for coming late to work in the mornings. From 1923 through 1925 he worked for a firm of wholesale grocers, and from 1932 to 1935 he held a job with a tire company. During the six years in between he worked for twenty-five different companies in and around London.

Until his first book was published in January 1932 Creasey had received more than 700 rejections for his manuscripts. His first published book was a spy novel, *Seven Times Seven*, which began Creasey's Department Z series (available in England but not in the United States). Through 1942 Creasey turned out about two Department Z books a year. Thereafter, their frequency abated somewhat, probably because around that time he began three new series, including the Dr. Palfrey books. These are "science fiction" mysteries, now numbering over twenty; they also are not published in the United States.

(Continued next page)

CREASEY, JOHN—*Continued*

By 1935 Creasey was making enough money at writing to enable him to give it his full time. In the next five years he began eight different series, producing from seven to fourteen novels a year. Between 1936 and 1939 some fifteen Creasey adventure mysteries dealing with airplanes were published in England. "When I began writing," Creasey has explained (*Newsweek,* February 2, 1959), "I discovered that the only way to make a living at the craft was to publish more than two books a year. Since, at that time, no publisher wanted to print more than two books a year from one author, I just changed names. Then, too, different pen names permit me to write in different tones." Among his earliest pseudonyms are Peter Manton, under which he composed thirteen crime novels between 1937 and 1954, and Norman Deane, under which he wrote twenty-one suspense tales from the late 1930's to 1954. Neither of these series was published in the United States. In 1938, ten years before he first visited the United States, Creasey began to produce Westerns. Inspired by Zane Grey and by the movies, he wrote under the names of William K. Reilly, Tex Riley, and Ken Ranger twenty-nine novels of the American West, which were published in England through 1953. Creasey is the only British member of the Western Writers of America.

Creasey's first American publication, under the name of Anthony Morton, was *The Man in the Blue Mask* (1937), which won the Harrup-Lippincott Cracksman competition. Its English edition, *Meet the Baron,* began an action thriller series that now comprises about forty books. The Baron was originally a gentleman burglar and private sleuth, but the hero of the present Morton books is the reformed Baron, John Mannering, an art dealer who solves cases as an unofficial investigator, often competing with the police.

Lippincott published eight Blue Mask books from 1937 to 1940, but they did not succeed in the United States, although the Baron books remain popular in England. Creasey believes that this is owing to the fact that Americans like to identify with the heroes of thrillers, while the English like their heroes presented at a distance. Another (only partially successful) attempt at bringing the Baron books to the United States was made by Duell, Sloan & Pearce, Inc., between 1949 and 1952, after Creasey had made a book promotion trip to the United States in 1948. Finally, beginning in 1960, Doubleday again brought the Morton books to American readers. Reviewing Morton's *The Double Frame* (1961) in the San Francisco *Chronicle,* L. G. Offord wrote: "The Morton villains are extremely villainous, and Mannering extremely agile in outwitting them." Anthony Boucher, the New York *Times* crime critic, said of *The Double Frame,* however, that it is "competent enough . . . but lacks the imagination and invention and tongue-in-cheek outrage that make the Saint . . . immortal."

Two other action series featuring solo investigators are Creasey's Toff books and the Patrick Dawlish books written under the pseudonym of Gordon Ashe. Amusing accounts of the exploits of the Toff, an aristocratic private eye, the Toff books are enormously popular in England, where about forty-five have been published since 1938. Pat Dawlish, who in recent books has been connected with Scotland Yard, still tangles with criminals primarily on his own as the English member of a semi-official international group called the Crime-Haters. Although about forty Ashe books have been published in England since 1939, Pat Dawlish was not introduced in the United States until 1959. Virginia Kirkus said of Ashe's *The Man Who Laughed at Murder* (1960) that "violence is concentrated and calculated to offer a . . . drastic type of action-entertainment." The New York *Herald Tribune* crime reviewer, James Sandoe, noted: "Flimsy enough to be printed on tissue paper, but Mr. Ashe . . . keeps things moving so fast and so lightly that you'll probably go along quite cheerfully."

Two series that are primarily suspense stories involving ordinary people are the books Creasey has written under the pseudonyms of Jeremy York and Michael Halliday. Forty-two Halliday books since 1937 and over twenty York books since the early 1940's have been published in England; some of each have appeared in the United States since 1957 under the pseudonym Jeremy York. The plots often revolve around an innocent person who falls into the hands of a criminal gang, and the suspense is generated by the race of police or friends to save him before he is killed.

The crime novels of John Creasey have been distributed throughout the world. His first trip around the world in 1950-51, during which he expanded his markets, did more to establish him as a writer of crime fiction than any other single factor. At the end of it Creasey spent five months in New York seeking publishers for his crime books, which, except for a few of the Baron volumes, had not yet been published in the United States. He received sixty-eight rejections at that time because publishers felt that his format would not appeal to American readers. Just before he returned to England, however, Harper & Brothers offered to publish his *Inspector West Cries Wolf* (1950). Under the title *The Creepers,* this book began publication in the United States of the Roger West series, one of Creasey's most popular with American readers. It is his own favorite series.

Creasey began to write the Roger West books in the early 1940's. Suspenseful detective novels starring "Handsome" West of Scotland Yard, they give an excellent picture of police routine and of West's relations with his co-workers and his family. Each book deals with one major crime, and recent volumes have featured hit and run murders, frauds of art masterpieces, racetrack hanky-panky, a strike and murder in a car factory, railroad hijacking, and homicide in a printing plant.

If, as James Sandoe noted in 1961, West sometimes seems "a trifle too good to be true (a sort of grown-up Eagle Scout who would really have to put furrows in his brow with grease-paint)," the same does not hold true of George Gideon, the hero of the books that

Creasey writes as J. J. Marric. Like West, Gideon is a ranking police official at Scotland Yard, but he is a much more rounded character who experiences doubts and failures as well as successes. In each of the nine Marric books that appeared in England and the United States between 1955 and 1963, Gideon tackles several different crimes at once, which heightens the similitude to actual police work. *Gideon's Fire*, which covered rape, embezzlement, murder, and pyromania, won the 1962 Edgar award of the Mystery Writers of America as the best crime book published in the United States in 1961. "J. J. Marric . . . is far and away the best writer of [all the Creasey aliases]," Anthony Boucher wrote in 1961.

Gideon is modeled on Creasey's good friend, Commander George Hatherill of Scotland Yard. Creasey often enlists the help of the Yard and occasionally visits police courts to brush up on his subject. Starting with a theme but no definite plot, he can write a book in six days but now prefers to do it in twelve. Some years ago, after Dorothy Sayers had rebuked him for careless writing, he arranged for two paid readers to scan all his manuscripts for errors, and he bases his revisions on their criticism. Creasey plans his work two years ahead, sticks strictly to schedule, and types his own manuscripts. His books are printed in twenty-three languages and published in hard-cover, original paperback, and reprint editions. A number have been adapted for television, stage, and screen.

Other pseudonyms of John Creasey are Richard Martin and Kyle Hunt. Since 1956 he has published the *Creasey Mystery Magazine* and with Ernest Kay publishes *The New Strand* and *John O'London's Weekly*. He owns a paperback publishing house, Jay Books, and a literary agency, Robert Sommerville Ltd. All in all, his enterprises net him an annual income estimated at $100,000. In 1953 he founded the Crime Writers Association, which numbers over 200 members; he served as its chairman from 1953 to 1957. He is the first Englishman to have been elected a member of the board of the Mystery Writers of America.

Since Creasey was rejected by the armed forces during World War II because of his polio-weakened right leg, he helped to organize local defense groups in Bournemouth and savings groups in the County of Dorset. He was made an M.B.E. in 1946 for his work on behalf of the National Savings Movement. After the war he joined the Rotary and Round-Table service movements in helping the handicapped, the mentally retarded, and war refugees. In 1953 and 1961 he organized special drives for refugee famine relief, and his book *The First Twenty-Five Years of the Round-Table Movement* was published in 1953. Creasey is a member of the Salisbury Preservation Trust and a director of the Salisbury Arts Theatre. As a member of the Salisbury Accident Prevention Committee, he has sponsored a campaign to create a corps of mobile special constables to patrol the roads.

Creasey belonged to the Liberal Party Council from 1948 to 1951, served as president of the Bournemouth Liberal Association from 1945

to 1952, and was a Liberal party candidate in Bournemouth in 1950. He resigned from the party in 1956 over its stand on the Suez crisis but rejoined it in 1962. He hopes to contest another seat for the party in the future. Creasey and his family are now on a second world tour, which began in July 1962 and is scheduled to end late in 1963. On his return he plans to reduce the number of books he writes annually to six or seven. *Round the World in 465 Days* (1953), which he wrote with his wife, and *Let's Look at America* (1956) are based on earlier trips.

A thickset man, Creasey stands five feet ten inches tall and weighs over 200 pounds. He has gray hair and blue eyes and wears glasses. He is a non-drinker and, since 1952, a non-smoker. His recreations are driving and photography. John Creasey married Evelyn Jean Fudge in 1941. They have two sons, Martin John, who paints and writes, and Richard John, who also writes. "I do the best I can," Creasey told a *New Yorker* interviewer in 1960. "I make a great deal of money, and I hope that my sons, who will be much better educated than I was, will come into the business, so to speak. We've a nice little thing here, good for a hundred years, and it would be a pity for it to stop with me."

References

Life 52:21+ Ap 27 '62 por
N Y Herald Tribune Bk R p2 N 23 '58 por
New Yorker 36:25+ Jl 16 '60
Newsweek 53:85+ F 2 '59
Who's Who, 1963

CRESAP, MARK W(INFIELD), JR. Jan. 3, 1910-July 28, 1963 President (1957-63) and vice-president (1951-57) of Westinghouse Electric Corporation; management consultant. See *Current Biography* (October) 1959.

Obituary

N Y Times p19 Jl 29 '63

CROSLAND, (CHARLES) ANTHONY (RAVEN) Aug. 29, 1918- British politician; political theorist; economist
Address: b. House of Commons, London, S.W.1, England; h. Flat 4, 19 The Boltons, London, S.W.10, England

Throughout the 1950's, losing one election after another, the British Labour party was rent by internal struggles between its left-wing and right-wing factions. The left wing preached militant socialism, including nationalization of the means of production, distribution, and exchange, while the right wing sought a less extreme public image that would, it was thought, broaden the party's electoral appeal. A principal draftsman and spokesman of this right-wing "revisionism"—which by and large has triumphed—is the Right Honourable Anthony Crosland.

Now Member of Parliament for Grimsby, in Lincolnshire, Crosland was a friend and adviser of the late Hugh Gaitskell, who became Leader

ANTHONY CROSLAND

of the Labour party in 1955 and who had achieved a large measure of party unity at the time of his death in 1963. Crosland has also modified Labour party thinking through his books, notably the influential *The Future of Socialism* (1956). A former Oxford don, he has been compared to Bernard Shaw, R. H. Tawney, and Sidney and Beatrice Webb as a socialist philosopher and strategist.

Charles Anthony Raven Crosland was born in London on August 29, 1918 to Joseph Beardsell Crosland, a civil servant, and his wife, the former Jessie Raven, a lecturer in medieval languages at the University of London. He has two sisters, one of whom is married to the historian A. J. P. Taylor. At Highgate School in London, Crosland won a scholarship to Trinity College, Oxford. His "excellent middle-class and public school upbringing" was early balanced, according to a *New Statesman* profile (March 19, 1960) by "his rigidly non-conformist background." Already an adherent of the Labour party as an undergraduate, Crosland served in 1939-40 as vice-president of the University Labour Federation.

Interrupting his education in 1940, Crosland enlisted as a private in the Royal Fusiliers for World War II service. He was commissioned in the Royal Welch Fusiliers a year later and in 1942 was transferred to the Parachute Regiment. After serving in North Africa, Italy, and southern France, he finished the war as an intelligence officer in Austria and was discharged in 1945 with the rank of captain. Crosland returned to Trinity College as an undergraduate in 1945, his interest in politics unabated. He became chairman of the Oxford University Democratic Socialist Club and, in 1946, president of the university's famous debating society and political incubator, the Oxford Union. In 1946 he graduated with first class honors in philosophy, politics, and economics.

Crosland stayed on at Trinity as a fellow and lecturer in economics until 1950, serving also as the college's Junior Dean. In 1947 he was elected to the executive committee of the Fabian Society, the influential socialist society that helped to found the Labour party in 1900 and now provides a forum for party intellectuals. Sharing his party's traditional interest in adult education, Crosland became an occasional lecturer for the Workers' Educational Association and for the Oxford Delegacy for Extra-Mural Studies. He also began to publish papers on such subjects as "The Movement of Labour in 1948" (*Bulletin* of the Institute of Statistics) and "Prices and Costs in Nationalised Undertakings" (Oxford Economic Papers, January 1950).

It was not long before Crosland attracted the attention and interest of Hugh Dalton, the Labour economist who had been Chancellor of the Exchequer from 1945 to 1947 and who was still the leader of an influential group of party intellectuals. Crosland was adopted as Parliamentary candidate for South Gloucestershire and won the seat in the 1950 general elections. He also became, according to the *New Statesman* profile, "a member of the happy group who used to meet at the XYZ Club to discuss economics, dine, and drink claret." This group included Dalton and Hugh Gaitskell, who became Crosland's friend and close political associate. Crosland's rapid rise to influence within his party was demonstrated in 1952, when he was one of the contributors to *New Fabian Essays* (Turnstile Press; Praeger), an important symposium edited by R. H. S. Crossman that sought to redefine the Labour party's role in a changing society.

Crosland's South Gloucestershire constituency was much altered in the 1955 re-drawing of political boundaries, and in the general election of that year he campaigned for, but did not win, a different seat, the Test division of Southampton. From 1956 to 1958 he served as secretary of an independent commission of inquiry established under the chairmanship of Hugh Gaitskell to study the co-operative movement in Britain. The movement, which has some twelve million members, operates consumer-owned stores all over Britain through local co-operative societies. In his 1958 report Crosland noted that only 1 percent of the membership attended business meetings and only 2 percent voted in elections. He called for more financial and technical assistance at the national level to raise the sights and increase the efficiency of the local stores. He also argued that the movement had an obligation to assume a wider role—to represent the consumer in all matters of public policy and to combat monopoly and restrictive practices of all kinds.

In the general elections of 1959 Crosland was returned to Parliament for Grimsby, Lincolnshire, which he still represents. He often speaks in the House of Commons on economic and other matters, but has remained a backbencher. Indeed, it is not through his activities in Parliament so much as through his influence on Labour party thinking that Crosland has made his mark on contemporary British politics. This influence has been imposed both through his close association with Hugh Gaitskell and through his writings. Crosland has written many articles for such publications as the *New Statesman, Political Quarterly, Encounter,* the *Listener,* the *Tribune* and the *Banker.* He is also the author of three books: *Britain's Economic Problem* (Cape, 1953); *The Future of Socialism* (Cape, 1956; Macmillan, 1957) and *The Conservative Enemy* (Cape, 1962; Schocken, 1963).

The clearest and most comprehensive statement of Crosland's political philosophy is contained in *The Future of Socialism.* Dr. William Pickles called it "the first thoroughgoing attempt in any language since [1898] to re-examine the whole of the argument for socialism, prune away the irrelevant parts, and re-state what is left in terms of modern facts and needs." Crosland believes that the Labour party has become torpid and complacent, clinging to outworn traditions, doggedly fighting battles no longer relevant to the condition of British society. He outraged party radicals by arguing in *The Future of Socialism* against the socialist doctrine of public ownership, praising some aspects of capitalist economics, and suggesting that the traditionally working-class Labour party should broaden its electoral appeal. Lord Dalton, in his autobiographical *High Tide and After,* called *The Future of Socialism* "a most important book, brilliant, original and brave. It has already had much clarifying influence on current thought, both inside and outside the Labour Party. And its influence will grow."

Crosland's argument was further developed in *The Conservative Enemy,* subtitled "a programme of radical reform for the 1960's." Problems discussed in this collection of essays, some of which had previously appeared as articles, include the place of the public schools, the use of land, the function of public ownership, and the role of the mass media. "A middle-aged Conservatism, parochial and complacent," had settled over the country, Crosland wrote; he suggested that it had affected the Labour party as well as its political opponents. He said that England had become a materialist and Philistine country, with a social structure characterized "by a monstrous degree of élitism, deference, and class differentiation," which had produced a strong spirit of "radical revolt" in the younger generation. He called for a flexible and vigorous Labour party, capable of appealing to the young, the socially mobile, and the previously uncommitted.

Crosland's "revisionism," expressed in his writings and at party councils and conferences, has not been welcomed by members of the Labour party's left wing. He is regarded by them, according to David Marquand (Manchester *Guardian,* November 15, 1962) "as an arch-opportunist, willing to jettison every inconvenient principle for the sake of electoral victory." Mr. Marquand himself believes that Crosland is "a Socialist theorist and a political strategist in one," who recognizes that "the point of political activity is to win power," but who is not interested in power for its own sake. "He wants the Labour Party to win power because he wants it to use power—and he wants it to use power to make effective the Socialist values he holds."

Anthony Crosland was married to Hilary Anne Hathaway Sarson from 1954 to 1958, when the marriage was dissolved. (Some sources give 1952 to 1957.) They had no children. Crosland's interests include jazz and modern art. He has green eyes and brown hair, is six feet one inch tall, and weighs 182 pounds. The *New Statesman* profile describes him as "by instinct, gregarious—a tall, personable figure who engages in the kind of banter which leaves few bruises."

Crosland was chairman of the Fabian Society in 1961-62, and he is still a member of its executive committee. He has served since 1958 as a member of the council of the Consumers' Association and has been active in Civic Trust affairs. Crosland has traveled widely, both for pleasure and on business, visiting Strasbourg, Paris, and Geneva as a member of the Council of Europe subcommittee on full employment, and Germany as a lecturer for the Foreign Office.

Reviewing *The Conservative Enemy* in the Manchester *Guardian* (November 15, 1962), David Marquand wrote: "Page after page of Mr. Crosland's book bears witness to his detestation of class privilege, and his passionate concern for equality. . . . For Mr. Crosland, it is clear, the old slogan really is true: socialism is about equality." "By any reckoning," Marquand believes, Anthony Crosland is "the most impressive Socialist thinker produced by the British Labour movement since the days of Tawney and the Webbs."

References

New Statesman 59:393+ Mr 19 '60 por
Kelly's Handbook to the Titled, Landed and Official Classes, 1963
Who's Who, 1963

CUNNINGHAM, ANDREW BROWNE, 1ST VISCOUNT CUNNINGHAM 1883-June 12, 1963 Chief of Naval Staff of the Royal Navy (1943-46); commander in chief of the Mediterranean fleet (1939-42); created a viscount in 1946. See *Current Biography* (May) 1941.

Obituary

N Y Times p33 Je 13 '63

CURTICE, HARLOW H(ERBERT) Aug. 15, 1893-Nov. 3, 1962 Was associated with General Motors Corporation for forty-four years, as president from 1953 to 1958. See *Current Biography* (March) 1953.

Obituary

N Y Times p88 N 4 '62

DALE, CHESTER May 3, 1883-Dec. 16, 1962 Art collector; from 1955 president of the National Gallery of Art; investment broker. See *Current Biography* (September) 1958.

Obituary

N Y Times p35 Ap 1 '63

DARIN, BOBBY May 14, 1936- Singer; actor
Address: b. c/o Universal-International Pictures,
Universal City, Calif.

Often called the "angry young man" of show
business, Bobby Darin in a few years has reached
the top as a songwriter, singer, and television
and nightclub entertainer. Moreover, he has
fulfilled his childhood ambition to become an
actor; since 1960 he has appeared in six motion
pictures, including *Come September, State Fair,*
and *Pressure Point,* and is under seven-year contracts at both Paramount and Universal-International. Darin broke into the recording field with
an original rock 'n' roll number, "Splish Splash,"
and survived the fate of many teen-age idols
with his jazzed-up version of an old Kurt Weill
tune, "Mack the Knife," from *The Threepenny
Opera.* The record sold over 2,000,000 copies and
won him two "Grammy" awards from the National Academy of Recording Arts and Sciences
in 1959. More important, it gained Darin the
adult audience he wanted without diminishing
his popularity with the juke box set.

His showmanship, versatility, and vitality have
enabled Darin to maintain solid bookings in
nightclubs from New York to Hollywood, and
from Miami to Las Vegas. Although his voice is
generally considered ordinary but pleasant, his
delivery—complete with finger-snapping and
fancy footwork—and his sense of rhythm and
self-assurance generate an excitement that few
audiences can resist. Darin's habit of saying
what he thinks while shunning mention of his
private life has not endeared him to the column-
ists. Described as "bold, brash, and cocky," he
once threatened to quit if he was not a tradition
in show business by the age of twenty-five; he
recently remarked that he was only about four
years behind schedule.

Bobby Darin was born Walden Robert Cassotto on May 14, 1936 in the Italian section of

East Harlem, New York City, to Saverio and
Vivian Ferne (Walden) Cassotto. His father, a
cabinetmaker, died shortly before Bobby was
born. His mother was a descendant of one of the
original English settlers of the Rhode Island
town of Pascoag. She had left college to follow
a career in vaudeville before her marriage. Mrs.
Cassotto along with Bobby's older sister, Vanina,
and her husband, Charles Maffia, raised the boy
from a sickly baby who could tolerate only goats'
milk through a series of painful rheumatic fever
attacks that began when he was eight years old
and recurred each year until he was thirteen.
For most of this time the family, which lived in
the Bronx tenement area, was on home relief, or
or Charles Maffia was working at two jobs to
pay the high medical bills.

Illness kept Bobby from attending school during much of his earlier life, but his mother
taught him at home and he did a great deal of
reading while he was bedridden. His scholastic
record in junior high school was excellent, and
the principal recommended him for admission to
the Bronx High School of Science. Bobby had
chosen this school because of its academic reputation, but once enrolled he found himself out of
his element. The curriculum was difficult, and
his drum playing and flashy attire were ridiculed
by his classmates. "All the arrogance you read
about," he confided in an interview for a *Saturday Evening Post* article (May 6, 1961), "stems
from those days in high school. It all stems from
a desire to be nobody's fool again."

After graduating from high school in 1953,
Darin attended classes in speech and drama at
Hunter College with the intention of becoming
an actor. When a drama teacher told him that
he was good but that the other boys should have
a chance at the leading roles too, Bobby decided
to leave school and go out and succeed his own
way. By this time he could play the piano and
guitar, as well as the drums, and had spent several summers playing with a band in the Catskill
resort areas. He often filled in as a singer, imi-
tator, master of ceremonies, and even busboy. He
also cleaned guns for the Navy and swept up
scraps in a metal factory. "I would work for a
month or two, then quit and make the rounds,
trying to get something in the theater," he
recalls (*Seventeen,* July 1961). "But nothing happened."

Hired by a dancer to play the drums for her
while on tour, Bobby Darin found himself several months later disillusioned, broken-hearted,
and unemployed. He resolved then to get to the
top of the show business world as fast as possible,
and for luck he picked a new name, Darin, from
the telephone directory. He joined another young
hopeful, Don Kirshner, in a cold-water flat, writing and singing radio commercials. With the
proceeds from these, the two cut demonstration
records of their own compositions.

Darin was auditioned by Decca Records in
March 1956 and was given a year's contract. A
few days later he was billed as "the nineteen-
year-old singing sensation" on the Tommy Dorsey
television show, but failed to click. He made
several records for Decca, all unsuccessful, before
his contract expired. In 1957 Atco Records, a
subsidiary of Atlantic Records, signed him for a
year and in 1958, released a recording of his own

BOBBY DARIN

rock 'n' roll number, "Splish Splash." The record hit the market at the peak of the teen-age rock 'n' roll craze and sold more than 100,000 copies in three weeks. But Darin had set his sights beyond the juke box crowd. "There hasn't been an organized teen-age movement for a singer since Eddie Fisher caught on," he observed then. "It's tough these days—the kids are fickle. They do more flipping over the songs than they do over any one singer."

To reach a wider audience, Darin used his earnings from "Splish Splash" to finance an LP album of old favorites, *That's All*. One of the tunes was a new arrangement of Kurt Weill's "Mack the Knife," a song about Macheath, the rogue of Bertolt Brecht and Weill's *Threepenny Opera*, based on the eighteenth-century *The Beggar's Opera* by John Gay. *That's All* sold over 450,000 copies; the single record of "Mack the Knife," issued later in 1959, sold over 2,000,000 copies. The National Academy of Recording Arts and Sciences awarded it a "Grammy" as the best single record of the year and also voted Bobby Darin a "Grammy" award as the best new performer of 1959. The following year he tied with Johnny Mathis for the honor of top male singer of the year in a poll of teenagers taken by the Gilbert Youth Research Company.

Among Darin's other popular records, released by Atco Records, are "Dream Lover," "Queen of the Hop," "Clementine," "Artificial Flowers," and "Beyond the Sea." His album releases are *Bobby Darin; That's All; Darin at the Copa; This is Darin; For Teenagers Only; Love Swings; The Bobby Darin Story; The 25th Day of December with Bobby Darin; Two of a Kind*, with Johnny Mercer; *Twist with Bobby Darin; Bobby Darin Sings Ray Charles;* and *Bobby Darin—Things and More Things*.

Steve Blauner became Darin's manager in 1959 and has been with him ever since. He has been responsible for the extensive publicity campaign and many television and nightclub appearances that have helped Darin's career; it was he who persuaded Darin and Atco to issue "Mack the Knife" as a single record. As a result of Blauner's high-powered publicity campaign, Darin began to make guest appearances on major television programs. He has since been seen on dozens of shows, including the *Ed Sullivan Show, This Is Your Life, What's My Line?* and his own hour-long NBC-TV special, "Bobby Darin and Friends," with Bob Hope and Joanie Summers as his guests, presented in January 1961.

In the nightclub circuit, meanwhile, Darin had given his first solo show at the Cloister in Hollywood and soon afterward, in the summer of 1959, enjoyed a successful engagement with George Burns at the Sahara in Las Vegas. A father-son relationship developed between the two, and Burns once publicly rebuked Darin for losing $1,600 at the gambling tables. The closeness persisted and Darin reportedly refused a chance to play opposite Glenn Ford in *Cry for Happy* to fulfill his promise to appear with Burns at the Sahara in 1960. Darin performed before capacity audiences at many other large nightclubs like the Deauville in Miami, the Sands in Las Vegas, and the Casino Royal in Washington, D.C. before making his triumphant debut at the Copacabana in New York on June 2, 1960.

The critics generally found Darin's singing only fair, but they were almost unanimous in praising his superior showmanship and ability to adapt to a variety of singing styles. At first he was compared to other contemporary singers like Frank Sinatra, Sammy Davis, Jr., and Elvis Presley, but he quickly acquired a stage personality that is Darin's alone. After his first performance at the Copacabana, Barclay Hudson wrote in the New York *World-Telegram and Sun*, "He has a driving, pulsating style, which, combined with an impish, small boy smile, made him irresistible to his fans." His act resembles a cross between the routines of the old song-and-dance man and the hip-grinding pop singer of the rock 'n' roll era. It depends largely on the vitality of his delivery—he kicks, snaps his fingers, bends over backwards, and prances vigorously about the stage. Darin makes his own arrangements mentally, for he neither reads nor writes music. This has not stopped him from learning to play the piano, vibraphones, guitar, bass, and drums. He has made personal appearances in England, Scotland, and Australia. He opened the 1962 Forest Hills Music Festival with a performance that included something for all ages and was awarded a plaque from the New York Heart Association "for meritorious service."

Although Bobby Darin signed his first movie contract in 1959, he waited until he felt he had found a proper vehicle for his acting debut. "I don't think I'm mature enough yet to see what one role it is I want to play but I don't want to be billed as 'Bobby Darin in Rock around the Rumble Hall,'" he told *Newsweek's* Tom Martin (April 9, 1962). His first role was that of an American in Italy in *Come September* (Universal-International, 1961), for which he composed the title song and theme. He portrays a young Nazi-minded American of the 1940's in Stanley Kramer's *Pressure Point* (United Artists, 1962). In a straight dramatic role, he clashes violently with a Negro prison psychiatrist, acted by Sidney Poitier, who is trying to help him. Alton Cook of the *World-Telegram and Sun* (October 11, 1962), who refers to Darin as a seasoned, gifted actor, concludes, "Bobby has been on the verge of winning full acting spurs but he certainly has them now—in shiny gold." A reviewer for the Toronto *Globe and Mail* (October 22, 1962) also commented on Darin's "gift of abrasive characterization" in the domestic comedy *If a Man Answers* (Universal-International, 1962). His other motion pictures are *Too Late Blues* (Paramount, 1961), *State Fair* (Twentieth Century-Fox, 1962), and *Hell is for Heroes* (Paramount, 1962).

Bobby Darin makes as much as $20,000 to $25,000 weekly for nightclub or hotel performances and had a gross income of over $1,000,000 in 1961. He owns two music companies, is incorporated as King Kong, Inc., and has movie contracts with Paramount Pictures and Universal-International Pictures worth about $2,000,000. His brother-in-law, Charles Maffia, acts as his road manager and valet. In 1958 Darin bought a home in Lake Hiawatha, New Jersey, where his sister and her family live. Mrs. Cassotto died in

DARIN, BOBBY—*Continued*

1959, shortly before the release of "Mack the Knife" catapulted her son to success in the world of show business she had taught him to love.

While on location in Rome for the filming of *Come September,* Bobby Darin met Sandra Douvan, an American actress whose stage name is Sandra Dee. They were married on December 1, 1960 and have a son, Dodd Mitchell Cassotto, born on December 16, 1961. Their home is in Hollywood. Darin is five feet nine and a half inches tall and weighs 151 pounds. He has brown hair, "a full and drooping lower lip which lends itself easily to a snarl, and dark-brown eyes which can flash with anger, as if somewhere inside him a switch has been thrown," as Edward Linn pictured him in the *Saturday Evening Post.* He enjoys swimming, golf, and chess and is a member of the Friars and the Limelighters. He belongs to the Episcopal Church.

Partly because of his own comments and partly as a result of his manager's campaign to build him up as a tempestuous, unpredictable performer, Bobby Darin's relations with the press have been stormy. Since his marriage he has been more restrained and communicative and is engaged in some "fence-mending" with the newspapers. Speaking of his work, he once said (*Seventeen,* July 1961), "All I can hope is that my personality comes through and that some people find it entertaining. . . . If I can get some of them to find some part of what I do worth watching or listening to, I'm happy."

References

Life 48:49+ Ja 11 '60 por
McCalls 89:110+ O '61
Newsweek 59:109+ Ap 9 '62 por
Sat Eve Post 234:27+ My 6 '61 por
Seventeen 20:80+ Jl '61 por
Time 77:82 Mr 10 '61 por

DAVEY, JOCELYN *See* Raphael, Chaim

DAVIDSON, ROY E(LTON) July 4, 1901-
Labor union official

Address: b. Brotherhood of Locomotive Engineers, 1102 Engineers Bldg., Cleveland 14, Ohio; h. 16211 Van Aken Blvd., Shaker Heights, Ohio.

The Brotherhood of Locomotive Engineers, which is celebrating its centennial in 1963, is the oldest railroad labor organization in North America. It is also one of the most powerful. Its chief executive, Roy E. Davidson, has been the leading spokesman for five operating railroad unions, representing 200,000 workers, in a dispute with management over work rules that in the summer of 1963 threatened to end in a crippling nationwide railroad strike. Davidson became grand chief engineer of the BLE on August 1, 1960, replacing Guy L. Brown, who retired. In 1962 he was elected for an additional four years in the post.

Davidson was an engineer with the New York Central's Illinois Division-Indiana Harbor Belt Railroad from 1921 to 1947 and worked his way up through the union ranks. He served with

the Brotherhood of Locomotive Firemen and Enginemen as a general chairman and as a road foreman and rules examiner, and after joining the BLE in 1937, he was appointed a general chairman in 1941, an assistant grand chief engineer in 1947, and the first assistant grand chief engineer in 1953.

The third of five children of Frank A. and Sarah L. (Foster) Davidson, Roy Elton Davidson was born in Fairmount, Illinois on July 4, 1901. His father, a coal miner and farmer, had always wanted to work on the railroad. Roy Davidson also "had a hankering for a railroad job," and after attending a one-room elementary school and the Oakwood Township High School, he became a fireman on the Chicago to Danville run of the Illinois Division of the New York Central. "I became a fireman on January 6, 1918," he told Ed Townsend of the *Christian Science Monitor* (August 20, 1960). "I began to shovel what amounted to a mountain of coal. It was a little more lucrative than working on a farm, anyway."

While working as a fireman Davidson took courses at the University of Illinois; many years later, in 1948-49, he attended night classes at the University of Chicago. In the summer of 1918 Davidson joined the Brotherhood of Locomotive Firemen and Enginemen. In 1922 he was appointed general chairman—the equivalent of business agent—for the BLF & E on the New York Central's Illinois Division-Indiana Harbor Belt Railroad; he was one of the youngest men to be given so much responsibility in a railroad labor organization.

Davidson's promotion to engineer in 1921 made him eligible for membership in the Brotherhood of Locomotive Engineers, but he did not join the group until 1937. Instead, he continued to be active in the BLF & E, becoming road foreman (engines) and rules examiner in 1933, after twelve years as general chairman. "This could never happen now," Ed Townsend has commented in the *Christian Science Monitor.* "The two brotherhoods are sharply at odds in a competition that involves jobs. An engineer must belong to the BLE. He at the same time may retain a card in the BLF & E . . . but the BLF & E card by itself is not sufficient for an engineer."

Davidson joined Division 682 of the BLE at Hammond, Indiana in January 1937. Four years later he was appointed general chairman for the engineers of the Illinois Division-Indiana Harbor Belt Railroad, a position he held until May 1947 when he became one of sixteen assistant grand chief engineers, with responsibility for the Chicago area. In July 1953, when Guy L. Brown became the grand chief engineer of the BLE, Davidson was elected first assistant grand chief engineer and alternate grand chief engineer. Davidson has served several times as head of BLE national wage and rule negotiating committees, and in 1960 he was one of the union's two representatives on a six-man arbitration board that overruled industry demands for a 15-cent-per-hour wage cut and awarded the engineers a 4 percent wage increase.

While these negotiations were in progress it was announced that Guy L. Brown would retire as grand chief engineer and that he would be succeeded by Roy E. Davidson. When Davidson took over the post on August 1, 1960 he became the tenth grand chief engineer of the BLE. Two years later, at the BLE convention held in July and August of 1962, he was elected to a regular four-year term. Founded in 1863 in Michigan, the BLE is the oldest railway labor organization in North America. It has 65,000 members in 890 divisions in the United States and Canada and is both a labor and a fraternal organization. It owns office buildings in Cleveland, Ohio and runs the Locomotive Engineers Mutual Life and Accident Insurance Association, of which Davidson, as grand chief engineer, is president.

The tumultuous period of Davidson's leadership of the BLE has been marked by conflict between the railroad companies and the unions over work rules. The controversy began in November 1959 when management demanded that the unions revise work rules to get rid of unnecessary labor that was costing the railroads $600,000,000 a year (principally the 40,000 firemen on diesel engines in freight and yard service.) Representatives of management contended that the railroads were in a poor financial condition as the result of reduced passenger patronage, trucking and airline competition, and rising costs.

The unions have insisted on job security for their members and deny that featherbedding practices exist; they maintain that most of the personnel now employed is necessary for safe and efficient transportation. Writing in a New York *Times* advertising supplement for the BLE (May 5, 1963), Davidson observed: "There is a tendency, in many quarters, to discount the importance of locomotive engineers and railroads and to minimize their future role. In fact, however, the railroads remain the backbone of transportation in both the United States and Canada. . . . The defeatist attitude has been responsible, in large measure, for the drastic reductions in rail passenger service in recent years. It underlies the 'merger mania' which threatens to wipe out competition between railroads. . . . It bred the 'poverty' myth which is advanced as an excuse for poor service and retrogressive wage and rule changes. . . . It is easier to discourage passengers and then ask permission to take a train off . . . than it is to improve the service in the face of competition. . . . It is easier to junk and scrap, to merge and consolidate . . . than to contribute to and participate in the long-run growth of the general economy."

By late 1960 the dispute had reached a crisis stage, accompanied by threats of strikes. James P. Mitchell, then Secretary of Labor, worked out an agreement calling for the creation of a fifteen-man commission to study the question of work rules, which was appointed by President Dwight D. Eisenhower on November 1, 1960. The commission's report, presented to President John F. Kennedy in February 1962, proposed eliminating firemen on freight and yard engines; setting up pay systems to reflect more accurately hours worked; reducing the retirement age for railroad workers gradually; giving workers in local

ROY E. DAVIDSON

and yard service seven paid holidays a year; paying lodging allowances for men away from their home stations; giving the railroads more leeway to reduce train crews; and eliminating extra crews in switching yards by having regular train crews do some switching work.

In the view of the BLE, whose representative on the commission filed a dissent, these recommendations only "enlarged the scope of the dispute." The BLE and four other railroad unions went to court to stop the railroads from putting into effect the job-cutting recommendations or any other unnegotiated changes. In March 1963, however, the United States Supreme Court affirmed, 8 to 0, a United States Court of Appeals opinion that upheld the right of railroads to make extensive work rule changes. To avoid precipitating a strike, the railroad companies did not take immediate advantage of the court rulings. A Presidential emergency board, headed by Judge Samuel I. Rosenman, was appointed to make a further study of the situation. In May 1963 it repeated the proposal that firemen on diesels in yard and freight service be eliminated but added that firemen should be retained where important to safety.

Further negotiations came to nothing, and at the beginning of July 1963 the carriers announced their intention of putting the new court-backed rules into effect. The unions countered with a threat to strike, and as a result of this collapse of collective bargaining, President Kennedy asked Congress to "dispose of the issues in this particular case." Late in August 1963 Congress passed a bill providing for arbitration of the two principal issues in the work rules dispute and barring a strike for 180 days. This action represented the first time in the history of labor during peacetime that Congress imposed arbitration in a labor-management dispute.

(*Continued next page*)

DAVIDSON, ROY E.—*Continued*

Roy E. Davidson married Cecil (or Cecile) May Rinehart on October 31, 1920. They have a married daughter, Mrs. Marilyn Ksir (the New York *Times* gives Mrs. Marilyn Schwandt); three sons, David E., Louis E., and Roy W.; and four grandchildren. Louis and Roy W. Davidson are employed by the Inland Steel Company. Roy E. Davidson is a Mason, a Presbyterian, and a Democrat, and he belongs to the Railway Labor Executives Association. He enjoys photography and occasionally goes fishing. He is a natty dresser and stands five feet seven inches tall. "Mr. Davidson looks every inch an executive," Ed Townsend wrote in the *Christian Science Monitor*. "He would be lost in the midst of any businessman's meeting. His eyes are likely to twinkle when he talks, and when he is serious one cannot escape his deeply penetrating eyes."

References

Christian Sci Mon p9 Ag 20 '60
N Y Times p27 My 18 '60; p12 Jl 11 '63 por
Who's Who in America, 1962-63
Who's Who in Railroading in North America (1959)

DAVIS, TOBÉ COLLER 1893(?)-Dec. 25, 1962 Fashion and merchandising consultant; head (1927-62) of Tobé and Associates, Inc., which advises stores on fashion trends; wrote syndicated newspaper column, "Tobé Says"; founder and head, with Julia Coburn, of Tobé-Coburn School for Fashion Careers. See *Current Biography* (December) 1959.

Obituary

N Y Times p35 Ap 1 '63

DEBYE, PETER J(OSEPH) W(ILLIAM) (dĕ-bī') Mar. 24, 1884- Physicist
Address: h. 104 Highgate Rd., Ithaca, N.Y.

Although Peter J. W. Debye is usually designated a physicist, he might more accurately be called a physical chemist, for much of his pioneering scientific work has advanced the frontiers of chemical knowledge, and the Nobel Prize that he received in 1936 was in chemistry. The prize was awarded for his contributions toward an understanding of molecular structure, and it is with this problem, in many forms, that Debye has been chiefly concerned throughout his career of more than fifty years.

The "Master of the Molecule," as *Time* magazine has called him, is a naturalized American citizen, born in the Netherlands, who was from 1940 to 1952 a professor of chemistry at Cornell University. Since his retirement in 1952 he has held the rank of professor emeritus. From 1935 to 1940, before immigrating to the United States, Debye was the director of the Kaiser Wilhelm Institute (now the Max Planck Institute) for Physics and a professor of physics at the University of Berlin. He has also taught and done research in Zurich, Göttingen, and Leipzig. Among his many contributions to fundamental chemistry are his development of a light-scattering technique for measuring the molecules called polymers; the Debye theory of specific heat of solids; the Debye-Hückel theory of the distribution of ions in chemical materials; and the Debye crystallogram—an X-ray pattern that pictures molecular arrangements within a crystal.

Petrus Josephus Wilhelmus Dibje, who is now known as Peter Joseph William Debye, was born in Maastricht, the Netherlands, on March 24, 1884 to Wilhelmus and Maria (Reumkens) Dibje. He obtained his primary and secondary education at Maastricht schools, including the Hoogere Bürger School, where he studied mathematics, sciences, and languages, and from which he graduated in 1901. Debye next attended the Technische Hochschule in Aachen, where he studied electrical engineering. He graduated in 1905 with the degree of Diplom Ingenieur Electrotechnischer Richtung.

While studying at Aachen, Debye had become interested in physics and chemistry. He was permitted by the physicist Max Wien to conduct experiments after hours, in the school's physics laboratory, and, while still an undergraduate, he became an assistant in technical mechanics to Professor Arnold Sommerfeld. It was at Aachen that he did his first original work—a theoretical analysis of Foucault currents in a rectangular conductor, published in *Zeitschrift für Mathematik und Physik* in 1907—and made a study of the diffraction of light by cylindrical and spherical bodies. When Sommerfeld accepted a professorship of theoretical physics at the Ludwig-Maximilian University in Munich in 1906, Debye went with him and continued to act as his assistant. After completing a thesis on the effects of radiation pressure on spheres of arbitrary electrical properties, Debye received the Ph.D. degree in physics in 1908. In 1910-11 he served as a *Privatdozent*, or lecturer, at the university.

In 1911 Debye succeeded Albert Einstein as professor of theoretical physics at the University of Zurich. The interdependence of chemistry and physics became even more apparent to him as a result of his close association with two colleagues, Kleiner, an experimental physicist, and Alfred Werner, a chemist, and during this year at Zurich, Debye developed his theories of polar molecules and of specific heat of solids. From 1912 to 1914 he was a professor of theoretical physics at the University of Utrecht in the Netherlands, but this sojourn in his native country proved unsatisfactory because the university's research facilities were inadequate.

Consequently, Debye accepted a post as professor of theoretical and experimental physics at the University of Göttingen, where he remained until 1920. In addition to lecturing, he directed the theoretical section of the physics institute and later the entire institute. The research facilities available at Göttingen enabled him to test his ideas on permanent dipoles. In 1916, with Paul Scherrer, he published a paper describing a "powder method" of X-ray diffraction that is now called the Debye-Scherrer method. This technique, used for identifying crystalline substances, consists of forming a diffraction pattern by directing a beam of X-rays onto a powder of crystalline material and photographing the pattern.

(*Continued next page*)

Debye returned to Zurich in 1920 to become professor of experimental physics and director of the physics laboratory at the Eidgenössische Technische Hochschule. Scherrer went with him, and they continued to work on their powder method of X-ray diffraction. At this time Debye also developed a concept of magnetic cooling and an interionic attraction theory of electrolytes. In 1923, with E. Hückel, he set forth a theory of the distribution of ions in chemical materials that became known as the Debye-Hückel theory. This states that the deviation of solutions of electrolytes from the laws of ideal solutions is due to electrical forces between ions.

At the University of Leipzig, where he became director of the physical institute in 1927, Debye experimented with the measurement of interatomic distances in molecules by X-ray scattering in gases and continued his work on dipole moments and electrolyte properties. The Leipzig period proved to be a very fruitful one: he wrote several books, some of which were translated from the German for publication in English. His books include: *Quantentheorie und Chemie* (Quantum Theory and Chemistry) (Leipzig, 1928); *Polar Molecules* (Chemical Catalog Co., 1929); *The Dipole Moment and Chemical Structure* (Blackie, 1931); *The Interference of Electrons* (Blackie, 1931); *The Structure of Molecules* (Blackie, 1932); *The Structure of Matter* (Univ. of New Mexico, 1934); *Magnetismus* (Magnetism) (Leipzig, 1933); and *Kernphysik* (Nuclear Physics) (Leipzig, 1935). In 1954 many of his technical writings were published in *Collected Papers* by Interscience Publishers, Inc. Debye has also written articles for professional journals and encyclopedias, and from 1915 to 1940 he served as an editor of *Physikalische Zeitschrift*.

Attracted by the opportunity to do more research, Debye accepted a professorship of physics at the University of Berlin and the directorship of a proposed Kaiser Wilhelm Institute (now the Max Planck Institute) for Physics. As a Dutch citizen, he had had to obtain the permission of the Queen of the Netherlands and the German Minister of Education to accept the directorship, and in the fall of 1935 he moved to Berlin. His new laboratory contained three-million volt equipment, a laboratory of low temperature production (including apparatus for magnetic cooling), and excellent facilities for chemical research. Debye's contributions to an understanding of molecular structure, made through his work on dipole moments and on the diffraction of X-rays and electrons in gases, won him the Nobel Prize in Chemistry in 1936.

R. M. Fuoss, in the introduction to Debye's *Collected Papers*, said that throughout the five years that Debye spent in Berlin, politics frequently interfered with his research. Finally, with the start of World War II in 1939, he was told that he would have to become a German citizen if he wanted to continue as director of the institute. Debye refused. Told to "stay at home and occupy yourself by writing a book," he managed instead to leave Germany by way of Italy and to reach the United States, where he had been invited to deliver the Baker Lectures at Cornell University. Debye arrived in the United States on February 1, 1940. He became an American citizen in 1946.

Cornell University News Bureau
PETER J. W. DEBYE

Shortly after delivering the Baker Lectures, Debye became a professor of chemistry at Cornell University; in 1948 he became the second Todd Professor of Chemistry, succeeding Dr. John G. Kirkwood. From 1940 to 1952 he also served as head of the chemistry department. Largely owing to his influence, Cornell became one of the first universities to establish a division for teaching and research in solid state physics; Cornell's strength in this field enabled it to obtain a federal grant to build a Materials Science Center. As a teacher, Debye gained the gratitude and respect of many of his students by giving them free time from definitely assigned studies so that they could "develop the ability to think."

During the war years Debye was a consultant in the synthetic rubber program. In June 1952 he retired from his teaching post at Cornell and was given the rank of professor emeritus by the university. Since his retirement Debye has worked in the field of high polymers, the common molecular denominator of rubber, plastics, and proteins, and he developed a method for measuring the giant molecules of high polymers by means of optical waves. The light is beamed at the molecules and scattered by them. The degree of light scattering is easily measured and provides an indication of molecule size. In addition, Debye has continued lecturing throughout the United States and Europe: he is known as an entertaining lecturer with the ability to treat highly complicated subjects in a simple, vivid style. In 1960 he spent much time helping the University of Michigan to establish an institute of science and technology.

The abundant originality of Debye's work is demonstrated by the number of scientific concepts and theories named after him. Besides those already mentioned—the Debye theory of specific heat of solids, the Debye-Hückel theory, and the Debye-Scherrer method—there are: the Debye-Falkenhagen effect, an extension of the

DEBYE, PETER J. W.—Continued

Debye-Hückel theory; the Debye-Sears effect, measuring the velocity and attenuation of compressional waves in a transparent liquid; the Debye frequency and the Debye temperature, both connected with his theory of specific heat; the Debye shielding or screening distance, a concept taken over from the theory of electrolytes and applied to a plasma; the Debye theory of wave mechanics; and the Debye unit, or the Debye, a unit of electric moment. The American Chemical Society has also named a chemistry award after him.

In addition to the Nobel Prize, Debye has been awarded the Rumford Medal (1930) of the Royal Society of London; the Lorentz Medal (1935) of the Royal Netherlands Academy of Sciences; the Franklin Medal (1937) of the Franklin Institute (Philadelphia); the Faraday Medal (1949); and the J. Willard Gibbs Medal (1949), presented by the Chicago section of the American Chemical Society. In 1957 he received the Kendall Award from the American Chemical Society for his work in colloid chemistry, and a paper on the range of molecular forces in the critical opalescence of liquids won him the William H. Nichols Medal of the New York section of the American Chemical Society in 1961. In April 1963 he was given the highest honor in American chemistry, the Priestley Medal, which is awarded annually by the American Chemical Society for distinguished service to chemistry.

A statue of Debye was raised in the City Hall at his birthplace, Maastricht, in 1939. In 1956 he was named a Commander of the Order of Leopold II of Belgium. Debye has received honorary degrees from Harvard University, Brooklyn Polytechnic Institute, St. Lawrence University, Colgate University, the Eidgenössische Technische Hochschule at Zurich, Boston College, and the universities of Oxford, Brussels, Liège, and Sofia. The associations to which Debye belongs include the Royal Society of London, the American Physical Society, the American Chemical Society, the American Philosophic Society, the Franklin Institute, the Electrochemical Society, and the Pontificia Academia Scientiarum. He is also a member of the science academies of the Netherlands, Brussels, Berlin, Göttingen, Munich, Leningrad, Boston, and Washington.

Peter J. W. Debye married Mathilde Alberer on April 10, 1913. Their children are Peter Paul Ruprecht Debye, who is also a physicist, and Mathilde Maria Gabriele (Mrs. Gerhard Saxinger). Debye heartily dislikes card games because he was compelled to take part in family card games in his youth. He enjoys fishing and considers cigar smoking a hobby. When he retired in June 1952 a *Time* writer (June 23, 1952) said of his career at Cornell: "There, perpetually wreathed in cigar smoke, he pioneered in high polymer research, taught Cornell men their chemistry, and each year managed to make them like it."

References

Chem and Eng N 27:1210+ Ap 25 '49
American Men of Science 10th ed (1960-62)

Farber, Eduard, ed. Nobel Prize Winners in Chemistry (1963)
International Who's Who, 1962-63
MacCallum, T. W. and Taylor, Stephen. The Nobel Prize-Winners (1938)
Who's Who, 1963
Who's Who in America, 1962-63

DE KRUIF, PAUL (HENRY) (dĕ krīf')
Mar. 2, 1890- Author; journalist; microbiologist
Address: b. c/o Harcourt, Brace & World, Inc., 750 3d Ave., New York 17; h. Holland, Mich.

NOTE: This biography supersedes the article that appeared in *Current Biography* in 1942.

Convinced that the public must be made aware of the need to eliminate disease, hunger, and other forms of human suffering, Paul De Kruif has for many years crusaded to bridge the gap in time between medical discovery and its practical application. A bacteriologist by training, De Kruif engaged in laboratory research before he began to write for the general public. He is the author of thirteen books, including the best sellers *The Microbe Hunters* (1926) and *The Hunger Fighters* (1928), and he has written over 150 articles for *Reader's Digest* and other popular journals. He collaborated with Sinclair Lewis, providing the medical background for the novel *Arrowsmith* (1925), and he is the co-author, with Sidney Howard, of the play *Yellow Jack* (1934). In his autobiography, *The Sweeping Wind* (1962), he reviews his long career as a fearless and controversial popularizer of the accomplishments of medical science.

Of Dutch ancestry on both sides of his family, Paul Henry De Kruif was born in Zeeland, Michigan on March 2, 1890 to Hendrik and Hendrika J. (Kremer) De Kruif. He has a sister, Lois. In *The Sweeping Wind* De Kruif recalls that his mother was a "tremendous reader." His father "a tough, totally self-made man whose formal schooling had ended at the second grade, was a natural mathematician who . . . solved the fiscal angles of profit and loss in his hard-driving farm-implement business at a glance." He wanted his son to become an engineer, a doctor, or a lawyer.

A magazine article about the noted German bacteriologist and Nobel Prize winner Dr. Paul Ehrlich, which he read during his freshman year at the University of Michigan, implanted in De Kruif an interest in medicine. He graduated with the B.S. degree in 1912, and then, having won a Rockefeller research fellowship, he became a researcher in bacteriology under Professor Frederick G. Novy at the University of Michigan. Preferring the security of the university to the uncertainties involved in private medical practice, De Kruif decided to become a microbiologist. He worked sixteen hours a day and earned his Ph.D. degree in 1916 after submitting a study on the toxicity of normal serum. He was then appointed an assistant professor of bacteriology at the University of Michigan.

Interrupting his career in 1917, De Kruif entered the United States Army. He served as a lieutenant, and later as a captain, with the Sanitary Corps in France, doing research on the bacillus of gas gangrene. Upon his return to the University of Michigan after the war he resumed his research on streptolysin at the medical school and taught serology and advanced bacteriology. During this period he met Rhea Elizabeth Barbarin, a young laboratory assistant, with whom he fell in love. Although he was already married and the father of two boys he determined to go through with his plans for divorce and remarriage, but he lacked the money to meet his responsibilities. Encouraged by H. L. Mencken, then editor of *Smart Set*, to whom he had written for advice, De Kruif decided to embark on popular free-lance writing on the side to supplement his income.

In the meantime De Kruif continued with his laboratory work, doing research on the blood-dissolving poison of hemolytic streptococcus. After reading his first scientific paper—on streptococcus—at a meeting of the Society for Experimental Biology in Cincinnati, he was advised by Dr. Donald D. van Slyke to apply for a position as an associate at the Rockefeller Institute for Medical Research in New York City. Hired by the institute's director, Dr. Simon Flexner, in early 1920, he began research in the epidemiology of upper respiratory and pulmonary infections in rabbits. Working at the Rockefeller Institute during the day, De Kruif spent his evenings in New York literary circles, and he soon made friends with the author Clarence Day and with the literary critic Francis Hackett and his wife Signe.

De Kruif's first important piece of writing was his contribution of the chapter on medicine to the book *Civilization in the United States: An Inquiry by Thirty Americans* (Harcourt, 1922), which was edited by Harold Stearns and contained essays by such noted writers as H. L. Mencken, Lewis Mumford, and Van Wyck Brooks. Although De Kruif was generally unknown and did not have an M.D. degree he was chosen for this assignment because of his association with the Rockefeller Institute. His fee of $50 for the assignment was the first money he ever earned from writing.

Having attained a reputation as "an amusing new journalist in medical science," De Kruif was approached by Glenn Frank, the editor of the *Century* magazine, to write a series of articles on the medical profession. The series was later reprinted in a book, *Our Medicine Men* (Century, 1922). De Kruif criticized the prevalence of cults and of commercialism in modern medicine and maintained that present-day physicians had little right to call themselves scientists, but he also offered some constructive proposals.

Because the descriptions of some of the doctors portrayed in the book were thinly disguised sketches of some of his own noted colleagues, De Kruif resigned from the Rockefeller Institute on September 1, 1922 at Dr. Flexner's request. Rejecting the opinion that "science must be made by a collection of contented human cows or a happy herd of trained seals," De Kruif defended the views that he had expressed in

John Henderson

PAUL DE KRUIF

Our Medicine Men. "My belief demanded that in science every man . . . must call them as he sees them," he recalled in *The Sweeping Wind.* "Science to be vital must grow out of competition between individual brains . . . each man mad for his own idea. . . . This was my vernacular for academic freedom."

While gathering material for a series called "Doctors and Drugmongers" for Norman Hapgood, the editor of Hearst's *International Magazine,* De Kruif met Dr. Morris Fishbein of the American Medical Association. Fishbein introduced him to Sinclair Lewis who already had to his credit the best-selling novels *Main Street* and *Babbitt.* De Kruif and Lewis then began a collaboration on a novel about a physician. It took them to the Caribbean, England, and France, and resulted, after two stormy years, in *Arrowsmith* (Harcourt, 1925). De Kruif's contribution was acknowledged by Lewis in the preface to the novel, and he received 25 percent of the royalties. In 1925 De Kruif became a reporter for the Curtis Publishing Company, and over the years he has written many articles for its publications, notably *Country Gentleman* and *Ladies' Home Journal.*

De Kruif's fame as a medical writer became well established with the publication of *The Microbe Hunters* (Harcourt, 1926), which eventually sold more than 1,000,000 copies and was translated into eighteen languages. The prodigious research he did for this book, and his ability to write accurately and entertainingly on science resulted in revealing portraits of such pioneers in microbiology as Leeuwenhoek, Spallanzani, Pasteur, Koch, Walter Reed, and Paul Ehrlich. H. L. Mencken, writing in the *Nation* (March 3, 1926) called it "an exhilarating and valuable contribution to one of the noblest chapters in the history of mankind."

His friendship with Henry A. Wallace, then the editor of the Iowa farm newspaper *Wallace's*

DE KRUIF, PAUL—*Continued*

Farmer, helped to stimulate De Kruif's interest in the problems of food production. In his book *The Hunger Fighters* (Harcourt, 1928) he described the work of those "obscure and honest men" whose researches helped to increase or improve the yield of foods. A reviewer for *Outlook and Independent* (November 7, 1928) described the writing as "violent, explosive and colloquial, a sort of combination of Emil Ludwig and Sinclair Lewis."

In his book *Seven Iron Men* (Harcourt, 1929) De Kruif tells the story of the Merritt family who discovered the rich iron deposits in the Mesabi range in Minnesota. He continued his sketches of fighters against disease in *Men Against Death* (Harcourt, 1932). He also collaborated with Sidney Coe Howard in writing *Yellow Jack* (Harcourt, 1934), a play dealing with the fight against yellow fever. It was produced in New York City in the spring of 1934 and was released as a motion picture by Metro-Goldwyn-Mayer in 1938.

De Kruif's next book, *Why Keep Them Alive?* (Harcourt, 1936), written in collaboration with his second wife, was an impassioned plea in behalf of children doomed, not by disease, but by starvation in the midst of plenty, and a call for a more equitable distribution of wealth. Although R. A. Kocher wrote in the *New Republic* (March 11, 1936) that the book was "in truth, so overwhelming that it would be impossible for anyone to challenge any essential feature of it," it was not well received by all the critics, and it was largely ignored by scientists and medical men. *The Fight For Life* (Harcourt, 1938), which got a somewhat warmer reception, describes the struggle of physicians, public health officers, and research workers against maternal mortality, tuberculosis, infantile paralysis, and syphilis. Pare Lorentz adapted *The Fight For Life* for his documentary motion picture with the same title, which was released by Columbia Pictures in 1940.

In *Health is Wealth* (Harcourt, 1940) De Kruif calls for preventive medicine through extended public health facilities, and in *Kaiser Wakes the Doctors* (Harcourt, 1943) he examines the medical services available to employees of shipbuilder Henry J. Kaiser. The book *Male Hormone* (Harcourt, 1945) tells of the discovery, synthesis, and application of testosterone. De Kruif describes the struggle of medical scientists against prejudice and ignorance in the book *Life Among the Doctors* (Harcourt, 1949). Waldemar Kaempffert, reviewing the book in the New York *Times* (October 9, 1949), wrote: "As a popularizer of medical science De Kruif has few peers. His method is that of the melodramatist. . . . He is verbose, slangy, sometimes ungrammatical, but never dull."

In *Man Against Insanity* De Kruif gives an account of Dr. John T. Ferguson's efforts to combat mental illness with drugs. Although F. G. Slaughter in the New York *Times* (March 17, 1957) called the book "unquestionably major medical history in the making," Louis Barron in *Library Journal* (March 1, 1957) criticized De Kruif for "his depreciation of psychotherapy

. . . his enthusiastic endorsement of lobotomy, and his negative attitude toward psychiatrists who are attempting to get at causes rather than symptoms." De Kruif's *The Sweeping Wind* (Harcourt, 1962) was described by William Hogan in the San Francisco *Chronicle* (March 5, 1962) as a "frank, blustery, rambling experiment in autobiography by a turbulent man."

De Kruif has also written many articles for popular periodicals. During the 1940's and 1950's in the *Reader's Digest* he publicized new methods of treatment of such diseases as malaria, gonorrhea, rheumatoid arthritis, rabies, epilepsy, bursitis, and cancer. For his zeal in publicizing new drugs and medical techniques he has on occasion been criticized by members of the medical fraternity, but Dr. Beatrice Tucker of Chicago's Maternity Center has said: "By creating a public demand for good medicine, Paul De Kruif has done more than any other man to raise the standards of medical care in this country." In 1939 Dr. Thomas Parran, the Surgeon General of the United States, credited De Kruif with helping through his writings to bring about a reduction in the maternal mortality rate. Although De Kruif has sometimes favored governmental supervision over members of the medical profession, he opposes socialized medicine, which he feels, would hamper scientific initiative.

De Kruif has often worked on scientific and educational committees. In 1934 he helped to organize the President's Birthday Ball Commission for Infantile Paralysis Research, and in 1940 he was secretary of the general scientific committee of the National Foundation for Infantile Paralysis. During World War II he wrote, lectured, and testified before Congressional committees on medical problems relating to the war effort. He has served as a consultant to the Chicago Board of Health and the Michigan State Health Department.

By his first wife, Mary, who at one time taught at Wellesley College, Paul De Kruif has two sons, one of whom—Hendrik—is a physician. On December 11, 1922 De Kruif married Rhea Elizabeth Barbarin, who died in 1957. On September 1, 1959 he was married a third time, to Eleanor Lappage. De Kruif is six feet tall and weighs 215 pounds. Frazier Hunt has written of him: "Physically he's a great hulk of a man. He works like a horse . . . plays like a sea-lion . . . and is as hard as a Dutch sea captain. But underneath this blustering exterior is a gentle, sensitive man, who loves music and books and pictures and birds and friends. Broadly and finely educated, he speaks four languages. . . . All in all, he's a strange genius."

References

Read Digest 49:91+ D '46 por; 50:43+ Ja '47
Sat R 45:19 Mr 31 '62
De Kruif, Paul. The Sweeping Wind (1962)
Twentieth Century Authors (1942; First Supplement, 1955)
Who's Who in America, 1962-63

DE QUAY, JAN EDUARD *See* Quay, Jan
Eduard de

DICKINSON, EDWIN (W.) 1891- Painter;
teacher

Address: 420 W. 119th St., New York 27; Wellfleet, Mass.

When the American Academy of Arts and
Letters elected Edwin Dickinson to its exclusive
ranks in December 1961, it described him as "a
master of painting in the Romantic tradition."
It was a classification on which art critics might
generally agree. Dickinson does have Romantic
characteristics, especially in the sense of mystery
and remoteness that he imparts to his subjects
at times, but he also has a wealth of other characteristics. Over the past fifty years he has drawn
widely but sparingly, and with aesthetic impunity, from both the Old Masters and the many
emerging schools of the modern art revolutionists
to develop his own singular, solitary, and elusive
style. His painting cannot easily be placed in
any category of traditional or avant-garde art.

New York State's fossiliferous Finger Lake district, which in part inspired one of his best-
known paintings, *The Fossil Hunters,* is the
birthplace of Edwin W. Dickinson and was his
boyhood home. He was born in Seneca Falls in
1891, one of four children of Edwin H. Dickinson, a Presbyterian clergyman, and Emma (Carter) Dickinson. His brothers are Howard C.
Dickinson, a lawyer, and Burgess Dickinson, a
musician; his sister is Mrs. Antoinette D. Van
Sickle. When Edwin Dickinson was about twelve
years old his mother died, and the family moved
to Buffalo, New York, where he went to public
schools. He changed schools several times and
did not complete his high school course.

One of Dickinson's recreations in his youth,
along with reading and walking, was traveling in
ships. Hoping to become an officer in the Navy,
he applied for admission to the United States
Naval Academy at Annapolis, but failed the examination in mathematics. Since childhood he
had enjoyed drawing and sketching, and what
he calls a "natural inclination" led him toward
a career in art. At nineteen he went to New
York City, where he attended classes at Pratt
Institute for a year and studied from 1910 to
1913 with William M. Chase and Frank V.
Du Mond at the Art Students League.

In 1912 Dickinson began studying as well in
Provincetown, Massachusetts with Charles W.
Hawthorne, who had also been a pupil of Chase.
Among Dickinson's twenty-seven self-portraits is
an early painting of 1914. "It's the one in which
I breached the painter's rule of never painting
against the light," he said in an interview for
Katharine Kuh's *The Artist's Voice* (Harper,
1960). "The face is in shadow but one eye does
emerge. Charles W. Hawthorne liked this one."
In his *New Yorker* (February 18, 1961) review of
Dickinson's 1961 retrospective exhibition in New
York, Robert M. Coates found Expressionist
undertones in the 1914 *Self-Portrait,* suggestions
of the French Fauves in the 1915 *Provincetown
Window,* and "a mingling of Purist and Abstract
tendencies" in the slightly later *Still Life, White*

Michael Tzovaras, Athens
EDWIN DICKINSON

Plate. But he noted that in general Dickinson
remained untouched by the new techniques of
modern art.

After teaching briefly at the Buffalo Academy
of Fine Arts, Dickinson joined the United States
Navy and served in World War I as a radio
operator from 1917 to 1919. He then went to
Europe to study and paint for a year in Paris,
St.-Tropez, and Spain. During 1920, as he had
done during 1914, he made a number of watercolors, but he realized that oil was the "natural
medium" for him, and his work since then has
been in oil.

Cape Cod, Dickinson believes, has been one of
the most salutary influences on his work. In
1921 he returned to Provincetown, where he lived
and painted until 1937. Then after a year in
Europe and another year in upstate New York,
he settled in Wellfleet, Massachusetts. He still
maintains a home there, although since 1944 he
has spent most of his time in New York City.
A great number of his landscapes and large canvases were painted on Cape Cod. *Wellfleet
Harbor* (1946) and *A Cottage Window and Oar*
(1955) are among his many studies of the area.
"His palette," Dore Ashton has pointed out (New
York *Times,* August 30, 1959), "is geared to the
dimmed blues of the sea, the white-to-taupe tones
of the sands, and the delicate greens of seaside
vegetation." In some measure Dickinson's often
observed kinship with Hawthorne rests on the
Cape Cod motif.

Dickinson acknowledges that he owes much to
his teachers, Hawthorne and Chase, and quite
likely this sense of indebtedness and gratitude
has strengthened his own devotion to teaching.
"I've always done it for pleasure and secondly
as a means of earning a livelihood," he has said
(*The Artist's Voice*). The schools where he has
taught include the Provincetown Art Association
(1929-30), the Art Institute of Buffalo (1939),
the Stuart School in Boston (1940-41), Cooper

DICKINSON, EDWIN—*Continued*

Union in New York City (1945-49), Midtown School in New York City (1946-47), Pratt Institute (1950), Cornell University (1957), and Boston University (1961). Since 1944 he has also been an instructor at the Art Students League.

If in teaching Dickinson found both pleasure and a livelihood, in painting on commission he found only a livelihood and resorted to it only on occasions of economic necessity. His dislike of commissions may perhaps be explained by the fact that so much of his work apparently derives from his interests at the time, his hobbies, his observations while traveling, the personal values of his direct experiences—his own involvement in the objects in his pictures. To a question about the possible symbolism in his self-portraits, he once simply replied that his self-portrait in Civil War uniform (1946), for instance, reflected his special interest over a period of nine years in the Civil War.

Much of Dickinson's work may be grouped into two types. His smaller canvases are likely to be *premiers coups*, spontaneous paintings completed at one sitting in two to four hours and almost never touched again. His 1914 *Self-Portrait* was *premier coup,* as were some sixty paintings that he did during a visit to Europe in 1952. When painting landscapes directly from nature in the United States and abroad, Dickinson has therefore long used the *premier coup,* which has given his pictures a certain freshness. He has described the *premier coup* as "a great teacher."

Quite different in method are Dickinson's large landscape and figure compositions, which because of their size had to be painted in his New York or Massachusetts studios. Composed over a period of several years, some of them required as many as 400 or more sittings. From time to time he found that he needed to erase and repaint a section that hindered the development of his design. As he explained his problem further in *Art USA Now* (edited by Lee Nordness, vol. 1, Viking, 1963), "After working on a composition a year or two or more, my own development during that period made keeping the painting up to date, as it were, impossible. After years of work on it, a painting could not be completely reorganized, nor thrown away, so I often felt forced to stop work on it and begin another."

One of Dickinson's unfinished paintings, *The Fossil Hunters* (1926-28), which is owned by the Whitney Museum of American Art, measures about six feet by eight feet. Painted from models, and recollection and imagination, the picture is representational without being realistic. Its eerie and oppressive mood, suggestive of the Surrealist paintings of the time, is heightened by the way Dickinson handles perspective. Some art critics see his tipped-up picture plane as a device adopted from the Mannerists. Dickinson has explained that he frequently tilts objects, especially in his still-life compositions, to gain a point of view based on fresh, rather than customary, observation. It seems to him fraudulent for a painter to draw from expected observation derived from previous experience when he claims to be drawing from direct observation.

Another painting that Dickinson never completed, *Ruin at Daphne* (1943-53), an acquisition of the Metropolitan Museum of Art, stems from the artist's interest in Roman ruins at Arles, where he lived for a time while visiting Europe in the late 1930's. An architectural fantasy, the painting's intricate pattern of layers and levels of ruined columns, arches, stairways, and pediments appears to some art critics to symbolize inner confusion and uncertainty. Dickinson, who does not name his pictures until he has stopped work on them, is reluctant to discuss the symbolism in his paintings. Once when he was asked whether his large paintings were symbolic, he answered, "I wouldn't be able to say" (*The Artist's Voice*).

Part of the difficulty in classifying Dickinson as a painter arises from his wide technical range. His landscapes may recall Corot and Whistler, and his large canvases may suggest El Greco, Leonardo da Vinci, and Tintoretto. Discussing a "tenuous" link with Surrealism, Coates commented in the *New Yorker* (February 18, 1961), "It's Surrealism with a strange Old Masterish cast, and it is related as much to the painters of the late Renaissance (Caravaggio, Veronese and so on), along with the Englishman Turner, as it is to any of the moderns."

Dickinson's paintings have been exhibited in one-man shows at the Albright Art Gallery in Buffalo (1927), the Passedoit Gallery in New York (several during 1936-43), Wood Memorial Gallery in Provincetown (1939), Farnsworth Museum in Wellesley (1942), and elsewhere. He had retrospective exhibitions in 1958 at the Cushman Gallery in Houston and at Boston University. His work was included in the "Fifteen Americans" show of the Museum of Modern Art in 1952, but he had never had a one-man retrospective exhibition in New York until February 1961 when some 150 paintings and drawings were shown at the Graham Gallery.

In December 1961 Dickinson, who had been a member of the National Institute of Arts and Letters since 1956, was elected to the affiliated fifty-member American Academy of Arts and Letters. Among his awards are the first prize for portrait of the National Academy of Design (1949), a grant in art of the National Institute of Arts and Letters (1954), a Ford Foundation grant (1959), and a Brandeis University creative arts award (1959).

Edwin Dickinson married Frances Foley, an art student, in 1928. They have a daughter, Helen D. Baldwin, and a son, Edwin C. Dickinson. As Roland F. Pease, Jr., described the painter in *Art USA Now,* "Edwin Dickinson's face is as anachronistic as his art: one notices first the splendid gray moustache and beard, at once Edwardian and Renaissance, but it is his eyes that hold one: enigmatic, penetrating, both direct and evasive." A man of many outside interests, as his work also reflects, he especially enjoys reading, walking, conversing, sailing, and target shooting. He is still fond of travel: in the summers of 1959 and 1960, as a passenger on freighters, he visited Mediterranean ports from Gibraltar to Turkey, and he returned to the Mediterranean the following year to spend the winter and spring in Greece.

References

Christian Sci Mon p6 My 1 '59 por
Time 77:60+ F 10 '61 por
Kuh, Katharine. The Artist's Voice (1960)
Nordness, Lee, ed. Art USA Now vol 1 (1963)
Who's Who in American Art (1962)

DORTICÓS (TORRADO), OSVALDO (dôr-tē-kôs') 1919- President of Cuba; lawyer

Address: Palacio Presidencial, Havana, Cuba

Wide World

OSVALDO DORTICÓS

The official chief of state of the Republic of Cuba, President Osvaldo Dorticós, is a "bourgeois Communist" who had been a successful lawyer before he joined Fidel Castro's underground movement against the Cuban dictator Fulgencio Batista. As Minister of Laws of the Revolution in the first cabinet of the Castro regime, which was established in January 1959, Dorticós played an important role in shaping Cuban policies. Since his appointment as President on July 18, 1959, after the forced resignation of his predecessor, Manuel Urrutia Lleo, he has become a leading government spokesman. Although the real power in Cuba remains with Premier Castro, Dorticós is believed to wield considerable influence on the Cuban scene.

Osvaldo Dorticós Torrado was born in 1919 (various sources give April 17, April 27, or June 17) in the port city of Cienfuegos in Las Villas province, some 220 miles east of Havana. His mother is Consuelo Torrado de Dorticós. He has a brother, who is a physician. Dorticós received his early education in Roman Catholic schools. He attended the Colegio Champagnat and the Instituto de Segundo Enseñanza in Cienfuegos, and he studied philosophy and law at the University of Havana. He obtained a bachelor's degree in 1937. Dorticós began his revolutionary activities as a student leader in Cienfuegos during a strike in March 1939.

After receiving his doctor of civil laws degree from the University of Havana in 1941 Dorticós began to build up a moderately successful law practice. He represented some of the largest business firms in his home city, and he served as dean of the Cienfuegos bar association. Subsequently he became vice-president of the Cuban national bar association, and he was a member of the Cuban delegation to the fifth inter-American conference of lawyers.

Having become disillusioned with gradualism as he observed it in Latin America and Western Europe, Dorticós joined Fidel Castro's clandestine revolutionary movement against Fulgencio Batista, and he was arrested on several occasions. In 1957-58 he was a leader of the underground in Cienfuegos, and he acted as a liaison officer between various sections of the revolutionary movement. Arrested in December 1958, Dorticós escaped from prison with the aid of friends and fled to Mexico.

Soon after Castro forces had overthrown the Batista regime and established the revolutionary government in January 1959, Dorticós returned to

Cuba and became Minister of Laws of the Revolution in the new cabinet. He drafted the decrees of Castro into law and played a major role in formulating the policies of the revolutionary government. During the early months of the regime he drafted decrees that modified the constitution of 1940, established agrarian reforms, and took harsh measures against counterrevolutionaries.

On July 17, 1959 Cuban President Manuel Urrutia Lleo was forced by Castro to resign, after he had denounced Communist influences in the government. On the next day Dorticós was installed as President by the Council of Ministers, after two leading contenders for the office had been vetoed by Castro and his advisers as being too pro-American. As an austerity move, approved by Dorticós himself, the salary of the President was reduced from $10,000 to $2,500 per month.

In a television address on the day of his appointment Dorticós called upon the Cuban people to "renew their faith in the high destiny of the homeland—guided by the supreme leader of our revolution, Dr. Fidel Castro." A few days later Dorticós said that the government would continue on its revolutionary path and that agrarian reform was the most important immediate task. He declared that Communism did not pose any threat to Cuba and denied that there were Communists in the government. In the next few months Castro consolidated his position. According to Tad Szulc (New York *Times*, December 18, 1959) the real power in Cuba had come to reside in a small group of left-wing extremists around Castro. President Dorticós and the sixteen-member Council of Ministers were merely called upon to approve the decisions of this unofficial cabinet.

As increasing friction developed between Cuba and the United States in early 1960 Dorticós declared that Cuba was willing to negotiate its differences with Washington, but that it must

DORTICÓS, OSVALDO—*Continued*

insist on respect for its national sovereignty. He said that foreign property taken over under the agrarian reform law would be compensated in the manner "which our constitution authorizes and our financial situation permits." Denying United States charges that the Castro regime had betrayed its original ideals, Dorticós charged that there was an international conspiracy to destroy the Cuban revolution. In February 1960 Dorticós was host to Soviet First Deputy Premier Anastas I. Mikoyan, who visited Cuba to promote commercial and political relations. When in April 1960 the democratic regime of Venezuelan President Rómulo Betancourt was threatened by a right-wing revolt, Dorticós offered Cuban aid in defeating the rebels.

Dorticós embarked on a good-will tour of six Latin American countries in late May 1960 to seek support for Cuba in her conflict with the United States. Although not universally well-received in the countries he visited, he maintained that the people of Latin America stood solidly behind Cuba. His public declaration in Montevideo, that United States citizens had been duly reimbursed for property taken over by the Cuban government, was repudiated in a strong note by the United States State Department. As additional American enterprises were taken over by the Cuban government in the summer of 1960, Dorticós declared that "in the profound revolutionary process we have condemned to death North American imperialism."

In an interview with Max Frankel of the New York *Times* (November 25, 1960) Dorticós said that his government would welcome the resumption of friendly relations with the United States, but that he had little hope that John F. Kennedy's election to the Presidency would change Washington's hostile attitude toward the Castro regime. Therefore, he said, Cuba had no choice but to move closer to the Communist nations. Dorticós maintained that United States hostility to Cuba had been aroused by the agrarian reform law of May 1959 (under which foreign lands were seized), which he described as the essential ingredient of the revolution. He cited Cuba's inability to pay for the lands at the time of seizure.

Under a reorganization and purge of the judicial system in December 1960 Dorticós was authorized to appoint judges with the help of Castro and the Council of Ministers. A previous constitutional provision, requiring judges and law professors to take part in selecting judges, was eliminated. On December 28, 1960 Dorticós received Cuba's first envoy from Communist China. Speaking at a rally in January 1961, Dorticós declared that Cuba reserved the right to claim the site of the United States naval base at Guantanamo bay "in the proper time," but that no attack would be made on the base, despite what he termed attempts to provoke such an attack.

When on April 17, 1961 anti-Castro forces staged their ill-fated invasion attempt at the Bay of Pigs, Premier Castro replaced President Dorticós as commander-in-chief of the armed forces. Castro and Dorticós subsequently issued a joint "exhortation to the peoples of the Americas" for solidarity against the "North American imperialists." After the failure of the invasion Dorticós

proposed negotiations between Cuba and the United States, but he was rebuffed by the State Department on the ground that "Communism in this hemisphere is not negotiable."

At the beginning of September 1961 Dorticós attended a conference of twenty-four "uncommitted" nations at Belgrade. In a violently anti-American speech he denounced United States "imperialism, colonialism, and neocolonialism." He generally echoed Soviet foreign policy views and exhorted other participants at the conference to adopt a more militant attitude against imperialism. Later in the month he visited Communist China and the Soviet Union. Addressing a congress of the Cuban labor confederation in Havana on November 27, 1961, Dorticós declared that political power now resided in the hands of the working class, but he pointed out that the material welfare of the Cuban people would require "years of sacrifice, effort, discipline, and revolutionary enthusiasm." A few days later he proclaimed a law that would provide an immediate death penalty for murderers, saboteurs, and invaders.

Dorticós headed the Cuban delegation to the conference of foreign ministers of the Organization of American States at Punta del Este, Uruguay in January 1962. The conference had been called to consider economic and diplomatic sanctions against Cuba's Communist regime, and Dorticós charged that its purpose was to prepare for new aggressions against Cuba. The conference adopted a compromise resolution by a vote of fourteen to one, with six abstentions, excluding Cuba from participation in the inter-American system on the ground that her Marxist-Leninist regime was incompatible with the objectives of the organization. Pointing out the lack of unanimity on the resolution, Dorticós maintained that the meeting actually resulted in a victory for Cuba. "You may expel us but you cannot extract us from America," he declared. "The United States will continue to have a revolutionary and Socialist Cuba ninety miles from its shores."

In February 1962 Dorticós, with Minister of Industry Ernesto Guevara and the head of the National Agrarian Reform Institute, Carlos Rafael Rodriguez, formed a three-man committee to deal with Cuba's growing economic problems. In March Dorticós became one of the leaders of a twenty-five member directorate of a new "integrated revolutionary organization." Officially described as "the revolutionary Marxist-Leninist organization," representing "the expression of revolutionary power of the working classes," the new organization is viewed by foreign observers as a forerunner of a single political party for Cuba, modeled after the Communist party of the Soviet Union. When anti-Communist demonstrations broke out in the port city of Cárdenas in June 1962 Dorticós reviewed a display of Russian-made tanks and weapons at the site of the disturbance.

On October 8, 1962, while on a ceremonial visit to the United Nations, Dorticós addressed the General Assembly and launched a verbal attack on the United States government, accusing it of using threats of reprisal to keep other nations from shipping supplies to Cuba. He charged the United States with aggression and "acts of war in time of peace," and called on the General Assembly to condemn the United States for violation of the U.N. Charter. After President Kennedy had instituted a naval blockade of Cuba on October 22 to bring about the removal of Soviet missile bases from Cuban soil, Dorticós participated in talks between Castro and Soviet First Deputy Premier Mikoyan, aimed at finding a solution to the ensuing crisis. (Tensions were greatly eased when Soviet Premier Khrushchev agreed to remove offensive weapons from Cuba, and a few weeks later Kennedy called an end to the blockade.)

In contrast to some other leaders of the Cuban revolutionary regime, Osvaldo Dorticós conveys the image of middle-class dignity and respectability. He is five feet eleven inches tall, weighs 180 pounds, and wears horn-rimmed glasses and a moustache. Described by friends as one of the most capable and intelligent members of the Cuban government, he is modest and retiring by nature and friendly and courteous in manner. An abstemious man, he does not indulge in gourmet foods or alcoholic beverages. He seldom sleeps more than six hours a day. His favorite hobby is reading law books. He also likes swimming and fencing, and he was formerly president of the Cienfuegos yacht club. During his youth he was an oarsman with the Cienfuegos rowing club. He and his wife, the former Maria Caridad Molina, have no children.

References

N Y Herald Tribune p2 Jl 19 '59
N Y Times p2 Jl 20 '59 por; p15 O 9 '62 por
Washington (D.C.) Post A p6 Jl 19 '59
Peraza Sarausa, Fermin. Personalidades Cubanas vol. VII (1959)
Who's Who in America, 1962-63

DOUGHERTY, DORA (JEAN) (dô′hēr-tǐ)
Nov. 27, 1921- Pilot; aviation psychologist
Address: b. Bell Helicopter Co., Box 482, Fort Worth 1, Tex.; h. 3616 Landy Lane, Richland Hills, Fort Worth, Tex.

In February 1961 Dr. Dora Dougherty, an aviation psychologist and pilot employed by the Bell Helicopter Company, achieved two world records for women helicopter pilots, previously held by Russians. She flew a Bell 47G-3 helicopter to an altitude of 19,406 feet and a distance of 404.36 miles. Dr. Dougherty also claimed a record in the new category of point-to-point speed by flying 91.6 miles per hour. A human factors engineer with Bell since 1958, Dr. Dougherty conducts research on pilot performance and cockpit design. Before joining Bell she worked for the Martin Company on the Dyna-Soar proposal and, from 1950 to 1957, at the aviation psychology laboratory of the University of Illinois. She has more than 3,700 hours as pilot of fixed-wing aircraft, and she was the sixth woman to earn an airline transport pilot's rating in the United States.

Dora Jean Dougherty was born on November 27, 1921 in St. Paul, Minnesota and moved as

Bell Helicopter Company
DORA DOUGHERTY

a child with her family to Long Island, New York. Living near an airport during her childhood, she became fascinated with flying and preferred building model airplanes to playing with dolls. Her first choice of a career was not, however, aviation; she wanted to be an advertising artist like her father and brothers. While attending Cottey College, a junior college in Missouri, Miss Dougherty learned that a civilian pilot training program had been opened to women, and she was one of the first to enroll. Sent to Sweetwater, Texas for a six-month course in 1940, she received the same type of training as that given to men pilots, except for gunnery.

As a member of the Women's Airforce Service Pilots (WASPS) for two years during World War II, Miss Dougherty ferried planes, towed gunnery targets, and instructed student pilots. After the war, from 1946 to 1949, she worked as a flight instructor at Sky Harbor Airport in Chicago and continued her education at University College, the night school of Northwestern University, from which she received the Ph.B. degree in history in 1949. During the winters, when flight instructors were not in demand, she worked as a secretary during the week and amassed her flying time on Sundays.

In 1949 the University of Illinois, which graduated 200 students each semester from its intensive aviation program, hired Miss Dougherty as a flight instructor. While working in this post she became interested in the research being done at the university's aviation psychology laboratory, and in 1950 she became a research assistant there. Meanwhile, Miss Dougherty studied for the M.A. degree in the psychology of education, which she received from the University of Illinois in 1953.

In the aviation psychology laboratory, research was done to determine ways in which cockpits and instruments could be better adapted to the pilots' needs. Miss Dougherty designed flight

DOUGHERTY, DORA—*Continued*

simulators and displays and used synthetic flight trainers. In 1953 she wrote with others a paper entitled "The Effect of Varying Control Forces in the P-1 Trainer Upon Transfer of Training to the T-6 Aircraft," which appeared in a United States Air Force publication.

Realizing her need for further education, Miss Dougherty took a leave of absence from the laboratory to study for the Ph.D. degree in aeronautical education at New York University. Her doctoral dissertation was called "The Use of Primary Contact Flight Trainers: A Comparison of Two Methods of Pre-flight Instructions." In this project Miss Dougherty set out to learn if a particular training technique could reduce the time an instructor spent with each student pilot, if a psychological test of mechanical ability could predict the fast learner in a group of student pilots, and if there was any difference between men and women in the ability to perform certain flight maneuvers. The results of her study showed that the pilots who received solo practice in the flight trainers were able to achieve the necessary level of proficiency sooner than others. She also learned that the mechanical comprehension test score showed no relationship to the pilot's speed in learning flying maneuvers and that there was no difference in the performance of men and women student pilots. After receiving her Ph.D. degree in 1955 she returned to the aviation psychology laboratory as a research associate.

In 1957 the Martin Company in Baltimore hired Dr. Dougherty as a human engineering specialist, and she continued to design and conduct research on the human factors in aviation. She also worked on the company's Dyna-Soar proposal and wrote several technical papers, including "Human Factors' Aspects in the Design of Space Vehicles." In July 1958 she joined the Bell Helicopter Company, a division of Bell Aerospace Corporation, as a human factors co-ordinator in the electronics department.

In connection with her work at Bell, Dora Dougherty learned to fly helicopters. It was her first encounter with rotary-wing craft, although she had had thousands of hours on fixed-wing airplanes. After only thirty-four hours of helicopter flying experience Miss Dougherty, in a Bell 47G-3, established two world records for women helicopter pilots. On February 8, 1961, starting from Bell's Hurst plant between Fort Worth and Dallas, she climbed to an altitude of 19,406 feet, which surpassed the record that had been achieved by Tatiana Roussian of Russia on March 27, 1959. When a reporter for the *Christian Science Monitor* asked her to comment on this achievement, Miss Dougherty replied, "It was easy. I could have gone much higher. The helicopter was soaring like a rocket."

Two days later Dora Dougherty flew from the Hurst plant to the Hawkins Airport in Jackson, Mississippi, a distance of 404.36 miles in four hours and twenty-six minutes. The distance record had been held by Anna Gueppennere of Russia, who had flown 340.346 miles on June 25, 1960. Miss Dougherty also claimed a third world record for the point-to-point speed of her flight, which averaged 91.26 miles per hour. No previous record for this category had been

established. The helicopter she flew was a standard Bell model, not "souped up" for extra power, which was fully equipped with instruments to record her performance.

Dr. Dougherty's flights climaxed an eleven-day program, sponsored by the Bell Helicopter Company, in which several other records were claimed. The flights were observed by officials of the National Aeronautics Association, the United States representative organization of the Fédération Aéronautique Internationale in France, which officially certifies world aircraft records. All recognized world records for women helicopter pilots had previously been made by Russians.

At present a helicopter's flight instruments are the same as those of a fixed-wing plane, but Dr. Dougherty considers them inadequate. She believes that the shape and placing of instruments should be specially adapted to the needs of helicopter flight. Also, to improve the pictorial representation of speed and altitude, she has designed two "ideal" cockpits, in which pilots are trained and their reflexes studied. Thus she hopes to learn more about what information the pilot needs in flight and how it best can be displayed.

Dora Dougherty has more than 3,700 hours as a pilot of fixed-wing aircraft to her credit. She holds flight instructor's and commercial ratings for single and multiengine airplanes and seaplanes. She is a commercial glider pilot, a qualified ground instructor, and the possessor of an airline transport pilot certificate. For her academic work in aviation, she was given the Amelia Earhart Award in 1957. She got her commercial helicopter rating on December 2, 1959 and became the twenty-seventh member of the Whirly-Girls, an organization of women helicopter pilots.

A member of the American Psychological Association, Dr. Dougherty also belongs to the Institute of Aeronautical Sciences, the Human Factors Society of America, and the Soaring Society of America. She is a captain in the United States Air Force Reserve. She is also a member of the P.E.O. Sisterhood, which sponsors Cottey College, her first alma mater.

Dr. Dougherty, who is single, lives with her mother, Mrs. Lucile W. Dougherty, in the Richland Hills suburb of Fort Worth. She has brown hair and blue eyes. For relaxation on weekends she mows the lawn, reads trade magazines, and flies the glider she bought in 1960.

References

Christian Sci Mon p16 Ap 4 '61 por
Dallas Morning News F 11 '61 por
Directory of the American Psychological Association, 1958

DOWLING, WALTER C(ECIL) Aug. 4, 1905-
Former United States Ambassador to the Federal Republic of Germany
Address: h. Sea Island, Georgia

Throughout the gamut of diplomatic assignments that Walter C. Dowling filled before, during, and after World War II, none was so demanding as his post of United States Ambassador to West Germany, which he held from 1959 to April 1963, when he retired from the post and from the foreign service. Dowling, who attained the rank of Career Ambassador in March 1962, had entered the Foreign Service in 1931 and had served in Italy, Brazil, and South Korea, among other countries, before being sent to the American Embassy in Bonn in 1959.

Walter Cecil Dowling, the son of Walter and Alice (Benton) Dowling, was born on August 4, 1905 in Atkinson, Georgia. In 1925 he graduated from Mercer University in Macon, Georgia with a B.A. degree and soon afterward took a job as a bank clerk. He stayed with the bank until 1929 and then worked as a secretary for two years.

In 1931 Dowling was appointed to the United States Foreign Service and enrolled in the Foreign Service School. Upon completion of the course in 1932, he was sent to Oslo, Norway as vice-consul. He remained in Oslo until 1936 when he was appointed vice-consul at the United States mission in Lisbon, Portugal, where he served until 1938. At the outbreak of World War II he was stationed at the American Embassy in Rome in the post of third secretary, and in December 1941, when the United States declared war on Italy, he was serving as second secretary. Transferred immediately to Rio de Janeiro in Brazil, he held the positions of second secretary and vice-consul at the American Embassy there before becoming consul in April 1944. Later in 1944 he returned to Rome to serve with the office of the United States representative to the Advisory Council for Italy and in early 1945 was appointed second secretary and consul in Rome.

The State Department recalled Dowling to Washington in March 1945 and in September assigned him to administrative work in its division of South European affairs, first as assistant chief and then, beginning in 1947, as associate chief. Briefly in 1949 he was acting chief of the division of Southwest European affairs. He returned to the field in May 1949 with an assignment in Austria. His title of counselor of legation in Vienna was changed in 1950 to counselor of mission, and in 1952 he became Deputy United States High Commissioner for Austria and deputy chief of mission with the personal rank of minister.

Representing the Secretary of State, Dowling took part in London in 1953 in the reopening of negotiations for an Austrian peace treaty with other representatives of the Big Four occupying powers—the United States, Great Britain, France, and the U.S.S.R. The talks, resumed after an interval of more than two years, eventually led to the Austrian State Treaty, which restored sovereignty to the Republic of Austria in 1955.

On July 2, 1953 Dowling was named Deputy United States High Commissioner for Germany, succeeding Samuel Reber, Jr., as the top assistant to High Commissioner James B. Conant, and on May 6, 1955 he became minister-counselor of the American Embassy at Bonn. Europe, however, was not to be Dowling's sole field of operation in the 1950's. A year later, on May 15, 1956, President Eisenhower nominated him Ambassador to the Republic of Korea to suc-

Dept. of State—Whit Keith, Jr.
WALTER C. DOWLING

ceed William S. B. Lacy. Dowling, the fourth United States Ambassador to South Korea since it was founded in 1948, presented his credentials to Korean President Syngman Rhee on July 14. In welcoming the new Ambassador, President Rhee said that "the people of Korea look to American leadership and to American assistance."

The United States' amicable relations with the Republic of Korea were reaffirmed on November 28, 1956, when a treaty of friendship, commerce, and navigation was signed by Dowling and Acting Foreign Minister Cho Chung Hwan of South Korea. The pact was designed to provide a framework within which economic relations between the two countries could develop. Dowling was hastily recalled to the United States for consultation on January 14, 1959, after Korean President Syngman Rhee's Liberal party pushed through the South Korean National Security Act. The new security measure, along with another law, which abolished local elections, was held to be undemocratic by critics of Rhee's party. The bills were passed in the Korean Assembly on December 24, 1958 after members of the opposition Democratic party had been ousted from the hall by specially hired guards.

The enactment of the two laws caused much concern to the United States government, which was chief sponsor of the fledgling South Korean democracy, had fought a war to protect it, and had given hundreds of millions of dollars to support it. According to the New York Times (January 15, 1959), the reasons for calling Dowling back from Korea were to underline the seriousness the United States attached to the developments in Korea and to demonstrate to President Rhee the State Department's complete confidence in Ambassador Dowling, since Rhee had been known to bypass United States Ambassadors.

(Continued next page)

DOWLING, WALTER C.—*Continued*

After the Washington meeting, Dowling went on a vacation trip to Europe. While there, in February 1959, he again was hastily summoned by the State Department. This time he was ordered to return to Seoul to investigate the rapidly deteriorating relations between Japan and Korea. South Korea had become incensed by Japan's plan to return thousands of Korean residents in Japan to Communist North Korea. It was reported that South Korea threatened to use military force to prevent the repatriation move. Dowling was instrumental in getting the two nations to negotiate their differences, and because of his intervention the condition of the Korean residents in Japan was greatly improved, as were relations between the two nations. William J. Jorden of the New York *Times* (July 31, 1959) said of Ambassador Dowling: "In his dealings with the government of President Syngman Rhee he has established a reputation for patience, tact and skill in one of the more difficult and challenging assignments in the foreign service."

With his broad experience in European matters, Dowling seemed an ideal successor to Livingston T. Merchant in the Washington post of Assistant Secretary of State for European Affairs. President Eisenhower made such a nomination in August 1959, and the Senate quickly confirmed his selection. In November 1959, however, less than two weeks after Dowling had returned to the United States from Korea to take up his new assignment, Eisenhower announced his appointment as United States Ambassador to the Federal Republic of Germany, replacing David K. E. Bruce. The appointment of a career diplomat was enthusiastically welcomed by West German Chancellor Konrad Adenauer, who knew Dowling and who sent a message to Washington expressing his delight.

On December 7, 1959, four days after he had presented his credentials in Bonn, Ambassador Dowling visited West Berlin. Reassuring the people of the city of continued American support, he said that he was certain that the freedom of the 2,200,000 people of West Berlin could and would be preserved. He re-emphasized the firmness of the United States position on September 22, 1960 when he made East German border guards back down in their attempt to bar him from the Soviet sector of Berlin. The Communists told Dowling that diplomats not accredited to the East German government, which the United States does not recognize, could not enter East Berlin. It was the first known case of interference by the Communists with an American envoy exercising the United States' hitherto unchallenged right of free circulation throughout Berlin. Ambassador Dowling, who also headed the American military mission in Berlin, informed the guards that he did not recognize their right to control movement across the border. After a few minutes the American envoy was allowed to pass.

As further East German restrictions in and out of the city threatened a major crisis, Dowling told a special session of the West Berlin city government in October 1960 that the United States would continue to discharge its responsibility "until the Berlin question is finally solved within the framework of a reunified Germany." He stressed that the United States would never acknowledge the right of the Soviet Union to transfer its responsibilities in Berlin unilaterally to Communist East Germany. He repeated America's position the following year after John F. Kennedy took office as President of the United States and again after the East Germans had walled off East Berlin. On one occasion he said, "We are in Berlin, together with the other Western powers, because our presence on this part of the free world's soil is needed to protect the right of all free men to govern their lives for themselves." On April 16, 1963 Dowling stepped down from his post as Ambassador to West Germany. He also announced his resignation from the Foreign Service for reasons of ill health.

Walter C. Dowling married Alice Jernigan on December 17, 1930. They have a son, Michael, and a daughter, Patricia (Mrs. Philip Winterer). Dowling is five feet eight inches tall and has brown eyes and red hair. He holds honorary LL.D. degrees from Seoul National University (1959) and Mercer University (1961). His church is the Episcopal. He lists golf and sailing as his favorite recreations and is a member of the Pi Kappa Alpha Club and the Metropolitan Club in Washington.

References

> Department of State Biographic Register, 1962
> International Who's Who, 1962-63
> International Year Book and Statesmen's Who's Who, 1963
> Who's Who in America, 1962-63

DRAKE, FRANK D(ONALD) May 28, 1930-
Astronomer
Address: b. National Radio Astronomy Observatory, Green Bank, W.Va.; h. Arboval, W.Va.

The more that astronomers and biochemists learn about the evolution of the stars and of living beings the more convinced they are becoming that millions of stars, such as our sun, have planets that can support life. In 1960 Dr. Frank D. Drake, who since 1959 has been associate astronomer of the National Radio Astronomy Observatory at Green Bank, West Virginia, took part in Project Ozma, the first important attempt to intercept radio signals from living beings in other planetary systems. He was also the first to make a high resolution study of the Milky Way, the nucleus of our galaxy, and the first to recognize the existence of a high radiation belt surrounding the planet Jupiter.

Drake was among the first half-dozen Americans to get a Ph.D. (from Harvard, in 1958) in the new science of radio astronomy, which studies the heavens by means of the radio waves emitted by a wide variety of celestial objects. Using radio waves 10,000 times longer than the light waves of optical astronomy, he has been able to "see" through cosmic dust to the center of our galaxy and through the perpetual blanket of clouds obscuring the hard surface of the planet Venus.

Frank Donald Drake was born on May 28, 1930 in Chicago, Illinois, the son of Richard C. Drake, a chemical enginer, and Winifred Pearl (Thompson) Drake. He has a brother, Robert H. Drake, and a sister, Alma W. Drake, who is a biochemist with E. I. du Pont de Nemours & Company in Wilmington, Delaware. Brought up in Chicago, Drake graduated in 1947 from South Shore High School, where his extracurricular activities included track, swimming, and chess. At Cornell University, where he held the McMullen scholarship, he majored in engineering physics and received the Bachelor of Engineering Physics degree with honors in 1952. He was named the outstanding graduate of the Naval ROTC program in the same year. Although he had to give much of his free time to waiting on tables in a fraternity, he graduated first in his class.

While he was an undergraduate at Cornell, Drake took a course in astronomy with Dr. R. William Shaw that sharpened his interest in the nature of the universe. Other men whom he credits with having influenced him in the choice of his lifework include Carl W. Gartlein of the Department of Physics, Cornell University; H. I. Ewen of Harvard University; Bart J. Bok of the Harvard University Observatory; and Otto Struve, the director of the National Radio Astronomy Observatory.

The outbreak of the Korean conflict interrupted Drake's academic training, but he continued to broaden his background in physics while serving on the USS *Albany*, of the United States Atlantic fleet, as electronics officer and electronics countermeasures officer, from 1953 to 1955. He had enlisted in the United States Navy as midshipman in 1952 and was discharged with the rank of lieutenant, junior grade, in 1955.

Returning to civilian life, Drake enrolled for graduate work in astronomy at Harvard University, which granted him an M.A. degree in 1956. In 1958 his doctoral thesis on "Neutral Hydrogen in Galactic Clusters" earned him one of the first half dozen American Ph.D. degrees in radio astronomy, from Harvard. While at Harvard Drake held a National Science Foundation Fellowship (1955-56) and the Edwin G. Rice Fellowship of the General Electric Company (1956-57). He also found time, in 1957, to act as director of an astronomical research group at Ewen Knight Corporation, Natick, Massachusetts, where he was responsible for the development of radio sextants for marine navigation.

Radio astronomy emerged as a science in 1932, when Karl G. Jansky, a communications engineer with Bell Telephone Laboratories, in studying the interference of thunderstorms, observed that the level of interference increased regularly each day. He concluded that the Milky Way passing overhead was responsible for the increase of noise or radio interference. Radio astronomy is true astronomy, except that observations are made at radio wave lengths with electronic equipment rather than at optical wave lengths with the eye or analogous equipment. With its ability to span galactic distances and to receive unbelievably weak signals, it has already brought us much information about

FRANK D. DRAKE

the solar system, the Milky Way, and external galaxies.

Since the cost of much scientific equipment for research in radio astronomy and other disciplines is prohibitive for private institutions, Associated Universities, Inc., a nonprofit corporation, was organized in 1946 to establish and maintain, through government contracts and other forms of support, large-scale research devices on behalf of the whole academic community. It is sponsored by nine northeastern universities, and one of its chief projects has been the construction and operation of the National Radio Astronomy Observatory, with the support of the National Science Foundation. The site at Green Bank, West Virginia was chosen because the surrounding Allegheny mountains shield it from the interference of man-made radio signals.

By the time that Drake came to the National Radio Astronomy Observatory in 1958 as assistant astronomer the eighty-five-foot Howard E. Tatel radio telescope was ready to peer into the cosmos in search of new knowledge about the universe. Although, as Drake says, "it clanked like Marley's ghost," the giant dish's reflector surface was accurate to within one-quarter of an inch and could be used at wave lengths as short as 3.5 centimeters.

One of Drake's first projects was the observation of the temperature of the planet Jupiter. Using a radio wave length of 22 centimeters, he calculated from his data an apparent temperature of between 3,000° and 5,000° Fahrenheit. This made little sense, since Jupiter's temperature had already been measured by the Naval Research Laboratory in Washington at minus 189° Fahrenheit and this value had been confirmed by infrared measurements.

Assembling related data from other sources, it soon became clear to Drake that the apparent temperature of Jupiter showed regular dependence upon the lengths of the radio waves

DRAKE, FRANK D.—*Continued*

used in the observations. This led him to the now accepted conclusion that Jupiter has its own radiation belt, similar to the Van Allen radiation belt surrounding the earth. This ocean of deadly atomic particles is 1,000,000 times bigger than the sea of radiation that engulfs our earth and 100 to 1,000 times more lethal. "Any future manned rocket in the vicinity of Jupiter," Drake has said, "would have to take that radiation belt into account."

Another question that intrigued Drake and his colleagues was the nature of our own galaxy, the Milky Way. Astronomers had long known that the Milky Way is shaped like a grindstone, and that its great arms spiral out from the nucleus, but they had never been able to see into the galactic center, hidden from optical view by clouds of cosmic dust. Possessing the means to "see" through that cosmic dust, Drake made the first high resolution map of our galaxy late in 1959 by making measurements at 8,000 megacycles. He found four sources of radiation lying close to the center relatively cool and the inner two so hot that line of the Milky Way, the outer two being he visualizes them as masses of stars equivalent to a billion suns. His observations indicate that each cluster is about forty light years from the center.

Another of Drake's contributions to radio astronomy was his discovery that the planet Venus, with an estimated temperature of 585° Fahrenheit, is too hot to sustain life. He based his temperature estimate on observations that he made during the occultation of Venus between July and October 1959 and on observations made by the Naval Research Laboratory in Washington, D.C. in previous years. Since Venus is perpetually covered with an unbroken layer of clouds, its surface had never been seen, and the radio observations afforded man his first glimpse at the hard surface of the planet. Although Drake and his associates failed in their attempt to discover which way Venus rotates, they were able to estimate the inclination of its axis: similar to that of the earth, inclined about 30° to the plane of the ecliptic.

Project Ozma, the search for radio signals from intelligent beings elsewhere in the universe, has been the most publicized research endeavor at Green Bank. It was named after the queen of L. Frank Baum's imaginary land of Oz—a place "very far away, difficult to reach, and populated by strange and exotic beings." Before they could decide where they should point their saucer-shaped eighty-five-foot antenna, Drake and T. K. Menon, another young astronomer, had to consider a number of pertinent questions. These included the rate at which stars like our sun are born; the number of stars that have planets; the number that have living beings; the number that have an advanced technology; and the length of time that such a technology has existed. Drake and Menon concluded that they would have to look 1,000 light years in all directions to have a reasonable chance of success.

The stars that they chose were Tau Ceti in the Constellation Cetus and Epsilon Eridani in the Constellation Eridanus, some eleven light years (66 trillion miles) away. Both are about the same age as our sun and similar in other respects. From April to July 1960, for six hours a day, the radio telescope was tuned to 21-centimeter waves (1,420 megacycles) coming from cold hydrogen gas in interstellar space, the sharpest, most universal of all radio waves coming from space. The astronomers scanned the tapes for repeated series of uniformly patterned pulses that would indicate an intelligent message or a series of prime numbers, such as 1,2,3,5, or 7, but the only sound that came through the loudspeaker was static and no meaningful bumps superimposed themselves on the formless wiggles on the recording paper. Undiscouraged, Drake plans to try again when more advanced instrumentation becomes available. "In a way, we're like Dorothy making a trip to Oz," he has said. "After we get there and back, we'll never be the same."

During his service in the Navy, Frank D. Drake married Elizabeth Buckner Bell, a professional composer, on March 7, 1953. They have two sons, Stephen David Drake, and Richard Procter Drake. Drake is five feet eleven inches tall, weighs 165 pounds, and has gray eyes and gray hair. His hobbies include automobile tinkering, spelunking, skin diving, sailing, hunting, and playing the piano and accordion. He has published many papers in professional journals and in *Sky and Telescope*, an astronomy periodical. He belongs to the Astronomical Society, the Institute of Radio Engineers, and the International Scientific Radio Union.

References

Sat Eve Post 235:28 F 10 '62 por

American Men of Science 10th ed (1960-62)

DRYFOOS, ORVIL E(UGENE) Nov. 8, 1912-May 25, 1963 President (1957-63) and publisher (1961-63) of the New York *Times*. See *Current Biography* (January) 1962.

Obituary

N Y Times p1+ My 26 '63

DU BOIS, W(ILLIAM) E(DWARD) B(URGHARDT) Feb. 23, 1868-Aug. 27, 1963 Negro writer and teacher; helped found the National Association for the Advancement of Colored People; consultant to United Nations; received World Peace Council prize (1952) and Soviet Lenin Peace Prize (1959); joined Communist party in 1961; became a citizen of Ghana, where he was director of *Encyclopedia Africana*. See *Current Biography* (January-June) 1940.

Obituary

N Y Times p33 Ag 28 '63

DUKE, PATTY Dec. 14, 1946- Actress
Address: 340 W. 72nd St., New York 23

By sixteen Patty Duke had reached a pinnacle of show business that many older actresses might envy. Her extraordinarily skillful performance in her first Broadway role—as the young blind and deaf-mute Helen Keller in *The Miracle Worker*—amazed and captivated audiences for nearly two years (1959-61). Her re-creation of the part in the film of the same name won her an Oscar award as the best supporting actress of 1962. And early in 1962 she again won abundant praise for her work in *Isle of Children*, although the play itself was short-lived. Miss Duke began her career at the age of eight as a television actress. She has appeared in over fifty TV shows and a number of motion pictures and starred in her own television series over ABC-TV beginning in September 1963.

Patty Duke was born in Bellevue Hospital in New York City on December 14, 1946 and named Anna Marie. (Patricia is her confirmation name.) She is the youngest child of John P. Duke, a cab driver, and Frances Duke. When she was six years old, her parents were separated and Mrs. Duke worked as a restaurant cashier to support Patty, her sister, Carol, and her brother, Raymond. The family lived on East 31st Street, and Patty attended the Sacred Hearts of Jesus and Mary School nearby.

Raymond Duke, a few years older than Patty, belonged to the Madison Square Boys' Club and did some acting with this group. When he played the lead in *The Ransom of Red Chief* he attracted the attention of John and Ethel Ross, who specialize in managing child actors, and they began to find him parts on television. Shortly after Patty's eighth birthday, she was introduced to the Rosses by her brother, and, seeing possibilities in her, they decided to take her in hand.

Looking back, Patty remembers herself at that time as "a wide-eyed, skinny kid, sporting a painfully short, scraggly, 'do-it-yourself' haircut" with a "king-sized handicap of a 'dese, dem and dose' sidewalk New Yorkese diction." She began to divide her time between her home and the Rosses' apartment in the West 70's, where Ethel Ross fixed up her appearance, letting her hair grow long enough to be braided, while John Ross coached her in speaking and acting. To get rid of Patty's New Yorkese, Ross taught her many different accents like the British, Italian, Irish, Southern United States, and German. Her biggest asset, according to Ross, was her "strong basic instinct for acting." "She was very observant . . . aware of everything around her," he recalls. "If I asked her to walk like an old lady, she could do it. She had studied old ladies walking."

After a series of discouragingly unsuccessful auditions, Patty Duke got her first part late in 1955 as an extra in a film crowd scene, only to receive her first professional disappointment: after a day of waiting, the extras were told they would not be needed and were dismissed. Shortly thereafter, however, she made her first television appearance, doing a short dance sequence on the *Voice of Firestone* show. In her

PATTY DUKE

first speaking part, at the age of nine, she portrayed an Italian waif in the *Armstrong Circle Theatre* dramatization of the sinking of the *Andrea Doria*.

A number of other television engagements followed. In October 1957 Miss Duke portrayed an English child in *The Prince and the Pauper*, and in May 1958 she was the only non-British cast member in David Susskind's production of *Wuthering Heights*, in which she played the heroine, Cathy, as a child. In October 1958 she appeared in *Swiss Family Robinson*, and in April 1959 in *Meet Me in St. Louis* she danced a waltz clog with Ed Wynn for which she had been coached by Ethel Ross, a former dancer. Patty Duke was cast with Helen Hayes in *One Red Rose for Christmas* in December 1959 and with Sir Laurence Olivier in Graham Greene's *The Power and the Glory* in October 1961. She has appeared several times in the series *Kitty Foyle* and *Brighter Day* and has been a guest on the *Phil Silvers Show*, the *Frankie Laine Show*, and the *Paul Winchell Show*. All in all, she performed on television over fifty times before she had her own show.

Early in 1958 John Ross decided that his protegée should try to branch out into stage work. When he heard that William Gibson's play dealing with the early life of Helen Keller was being readied for Broadway, he began to school Patty Duke to audition for the part of the blind and deaf-mute Helen. Through his training she mastered the straight, unfocused stare of the blind and a complete lack of reaction to sudden or loud noises. (This training was so good that during one performance when a light fell onto the stage, scaring audience and cast alike, she showed no visible reaction.) She also learned to find her way blindfolded around the Ross apartment. When she appeared for the audition, probably the best prepared actress present, she was awarded the role. It brought her

DUKE, PATTY—*Continued*

into association with four of the people who had previously triumphed on Broadway with the play *Two for the Seesaw*: the writer William Gibson, the producer Fred Coe, the director Arthur Penn, and the actress Anne Bancroft.

The Miracle Worker, which opened on October 19, 1959, covers the period of Helen Keller's life from 1882 to 1887 (she was born in 1880). It begins when Mrs. Keller discovers that her daughter has been left deaf, mute, and blind by a childhood illness and ends when Helen's teacher, Annie Sullivan (Anne Bancroft), teaches Helen the word for water, thus breaking through to the understanding locked inside the child's body. Miss Duke mastered the manual alphabet of the deaf for the role.

For her performance Patty Duke won unanimous praise from the critics. Brooks Atkinson in the New York *Times* (October 20, 1959) wrote: "As Helen, little Miss Duke is altogether superb —a plain, sullen, explosive, miniature monster whose destructive behavior makes sympathy for her afflictions impossible, but whose independence and vitality are nevertheless admirable.... Although . . . [her performance] is necessarily wordless it is completely articulate." Richard L. Coe described in the Washington *Post* and *Times Herald* (October 28, 1959) how she portrayed a "tortured, infuriated mind." "The busy little face, the violently active body, the sheer, ghastly loneliness and the triumphant, astonishing breakthrough to the inner mind are expressed in unerring mime," Coe said. On March 7, 1960 Miss Duke achieved stardom when her name was raised above the title of the play, joining Anne Bancroft's. At thirteen she was the youngest person to be so honored. On May 12, 1960 the play was voted the best play of the year by the Outer Circle, an association of drama critics.

For one scene in the play, which calls for a literal knock-down and drag-out battle between Helen Keller and her teacher, both actresses had to wear heavily padded costumes and elbow, leg, and arm guards. Patty Duke had cause to envy the fact that Anne Bancroft could wear a bustle. In the course of this scene, in which Annie Sullivan is trying to force her charge to eat her dinner correctly, furniture, cutlery, and water flew in all directions, occasionally into the audience, and at least one chair gave way during each performance. In the first month of production, forty chairs had been used, proving the point of Annie Sullivan's announcement to the Keller family at the end of the scene: "Helen has folded her napkin, but the dining room's a wreck."

The Miracle Worker ran for 700 performances and closed on July 1, 1961. Except for vacations, Patty Duke played in all the shows except those of the last five weeks; in May she left to begin work on the film version of the play. One of Miss Duke's biggest problems at that time, one common to most child actors, was her rate of growth. When she auditioned for the role of Helen, she was fifty-two inches tall, and a clause in her contract stipulated that if she grew taller than fifty-four inches she could be replaced. Fortunately, she survived the run of the play

and was still small enough to play the eight-year-old Helen in the film at the age of fourteen and a half.

When the movie version of *The Miracle Worker* was released by United Artists in May 1962, film critics repeated the praise of the drama reviewers. Archer Winsten commented in the New York *Post* (May 24, 1962) that her performance was "totally extraordinary" and very realistic, partly because she had "grown into the role" after such a long stage run. On April 8, 1963 Miss Duke became the youngest performer to win an Oscar award of the Academy of Motion Picture Arts and Sciences in a regular category when she was named the best supporting actress of 1962. Earlier, in March 1963, she had been given the Golden Globe award in Hollywood as the most promising future star of the year.

Although *The Miracle Worker* is Miss Duke's best known film to date, it is not her first. In 1957 she and her brother helped to make a documentary, *The Deep Well* (Child Welfare League of America), which dealt with foster care. In 1958 she appeared in *The Goddess* (Columbia Pictures), playing the central figure, a lonely movie star, as a child, and in 1959 she portrayed in *Happy Anniversary* (United Artists) a small girl who blurts out an unfortunate story about her parents over a television show.

On March 16, 1962 Miss Duke opened in her second stage play, *Isle of Children*, in the role of Deirdre Striden, a child afflicted with a fatal illness. Although the play had only eleven performances, she herself won critical acclaim. Walter Kerr paid her perhaps the greatest tribute that a young actress can receive when he wrote in the New York *Herald Tribune* (March 17, 1962), "Miss Duke is not an accomplished child actress, she is an accomplished actress who happens to be a child at the moment."

The year 1963 was an important one for Patty Duke not only because she won the Oscar. In September the series the *Patty Duke Show* had its première on ABC-TV. She starred in the dual role of Cathy, a teen-ager from Edinburgh who is visiting the United States, and Patty, her American cousin. She prepared for the series with her usual thoroughness, learning as much as she could about Scotland and even attending a class of the New York branch of the Royal Scottish Country Dance Society.

Patty Duke has served as the national youth chairman of the Muscular Dystrophy Association of America. In March 1962 she starred on a television program entitled *Talking Hands*, which dealt with the sign language used by the deaf. She has visited Helen Keller a number of times and was thrilled when Miss Keller said how much she enjoyed talking to her. Miss Duke's family now lives in Queens, New York, and she has many friends there. She spends most of her time at the Ross apartment and visits her family on weekends. She has attended the Willard Mace School for professional children and the Quintano School for Young Professionals, where she got good marks. Patty Duke's income is being administered by three trust funds. She is five feet tall, weighs eighty-six pounds, and has green eyes and honey blond hair. Her favorite sports are water skiing, swimming, skin diving, and horseback riding.

References

Coronet 48:131+ Jl '60 pors
N Y Herald Tribune IV p7 Je 9 '63 por
N Y Sunday News p36+ N 8 '59 pors; p7
    N 5 '61 por
N Y Times II p13 My 26 '63 por
Theatre Arts 44:28+ Ja '60 por

Ross, Lillian and Ross, Helen. The Player (1962)

DURRELL, LAWRENCE (GEORGE)

(dûr'ĕl) Feb. 27, 1912- Author

Address: b. c/o National and Grindlay's Bank, Parliament St., Whitehall, London, S.W. 1, England

Rosemarie Clausen

LAWRENCE DURRELL

The Alexandria Quartet, a tetralogy that Lawrence Durrell began in 1957 with *Justine*, explores modern love by means of a literary form based upon a twentieth-century Einsteinian space-time structure. It is written, however, in a baroque prose style hardly typical of that century. With its success in Europe and the United States, almost all of Durrell's earlier work—a spate of previously half-neglected novels, poems, sketches of diplomatic life, Mediterranean travel books, and one or two verse plays—were reprinted. They have since been re-evaluated, both for themselves and for the light they could shed on *The Alexandria Quartet* and its theme of love as a means of self-discovery.

Expatriate Lawrence George Durrell belongs to India by place of birth, to Ireland by parentage, to Great Britain by citizenship, and to the Mediterranean by preference. He was born to Lawrence Samuel and Louisa Florence (Dixie) Durrell on February 27, 1912 near the Himalayas, where his father, an Irish-Protestant engineer, had gone to help build India's first railroads. He was one of four children. His younger brother, Gerald, a "zoomaniac," as Lawrence calls him, is famous as an author and naturalist. Lawrence Durrell retains wonderful memories of his early years in India and of going to school at the College of St. Joseph in Darjeeling.

Durrell was eleven or twelve years old when he first saw England and began attending St. Edmund's School, Canterbury. As a young man, in one of his early letters to Henry Miller, he told about the move from India to England: "Then that mean, shabby little island up there wrung my guts out of me and tried to destroy anything singular and unique in me. . . . I have always broken stable when I was unhappy. The list of schools I've been to would be a yard long. I failed every known civil service exam" (*Lawrence Durrell and Henry Miller; A Private Correspondence*, Dutton, 1963). He also repeatedly failed to enter Cambridge University when he applied for admission.

One of the many odd jobs that Durrell held in London was that of a jazz pianist at the Blue Peter Night Club—until it was raided by the police. He also wrote poems, some of which

were published by the Caduceus Press in 1932 and 1934, and an unsuccessful novel about Bohemian life in Bloomsbury, *Pied Piper of Lovers* (Cassell and Company, 1935). Convinced that he could develop as a writer away from England, in 1935 he persuaded his widowed mother to move to Corfu with her three sons and one daughter and also her one daughter-in-law, the former Nancy Myers, whom Durrell married in the spring of 1935. In his autobiographical *My Family and Other Animals* (Viking, 1956), Gerald Durrell wrote amusingly about their life on Corfu. Surrounded by the hubbub that his brother describes, Lawrence Durrell soon completed his second novel, *Panic Spring*, which Faber & Faber published in 1937. At the suggestion of his publisher that he use a pseudonym because of the failure of his first novel, he wrote under the name of Charles Norden.

Shortly after he arrived in Corfu, in the summer of 1935, Durrell had read for the second time Henry Miller's recently published *Tropic of Cancer*. Both the novel and his correspondence with Miller, which Durrell began in that year with a fan letter, had an enormously liberating effect on the twenty-four-year-old writer. For well over a year he struggled "in the interests of self-discovery," as he has said, on a novel called *The Black Book, An Agon*. In dealing in his own way with the story of the making of a writer and in trying to break out of "the cultural swaddling clothes" symbolized in his book as "the English death," he knew that he had resorted to obscenities and savageries that would make publication in England unlikely. He was not mistaken. Faber & Faber would not accept his book, but the encouragement that he received from T. S. Eliot and Cyril Connolly marked the turning point in his life as a writer. Of it Durrell wrote in his preface to the new, 1960 edi-

DURRELL, LAWRENCE—*Continued*

tion: "This novel—after twenty-odd years—still has a special importance for me. . . . I can't help being attached to it because in the writing of it I first heard the sound of my own voice, lame and halting perhaps, but nevertheless my very own. This is an experience no artist ever forgets —the birth cry of a newly born baby of letters, the genuine article."

Largely through the efforts of Henry Miller, whom Durrell met in Paris for the first time in 1937, *The Black Book* found a publisher in 1938 in Paris—the Obelisk Press. By the time that E. P. Dutton & Company published it in the United States in 1960, *The Black Book* interested critics not so much as a shocking book, but as a seed bed of the style, the techniques, the themes, and the characters that matured in *The Alexandria Quartet*.

For some months in early 1939 Durrell visited England, but he returned to Corfu before the outbreak of World War II, and in late 1940, when the Germans moved into Greece, he was teaching at the British Institute in Kalamata. With his wife and six-month-old daughter, Penelope Berengaria, he escaped to Crete in a caïque. An Australian transport took him from Crete to Egypt in April 1941. He served in Cairo from 1941 to 1944 as foreign press service officer in the British Information Office and in Alexandria in 1944-45 as press attaché.

In Egypt, Durrell was preoccupied with recollections of Greece. By the time that he left Alexandria, he had completed *Prospero's Cell; A Guide to the Landscape and Manners of the Island of Corcyra* (Faber, 1945)—a portrait of Corfu and its people, combining history, description, meditation, and personal experience. He was looking forward, also, to the publication of *Cefalu* (London, Editions Poetry, 1947; republished as *The Dark Labyrinth*, Ace Books, 1958), which he described to Henry Miller in 1945 as "a queer cosmological tale about seven modern European tourists who get lost in the labyrinth in Crete where the minotaur has begun to make a comeback." Another volume from his productive period in Egypt was *Cities, Plains, and People* (Faber, 1946), a book of poems.

The end of the war "liberated" Durrell from Egypt to Rhodes, where he remained until March 1947 as director of public relations for the Dodecanese Islands. His delight in the twelve Grecian islands led to another "travel book," *Reflections on a Marine Venus* (Faber, 1953). In early 1947, when he failed to get an appointment that he wanted on Rhodes, he applied for a transfer from the British Foreign Office to the British Council, hoping to be assigned to Italy or France. He was sent instead to Cordoba, Argentina, where he held the position of director of the British Council Institute from November 1947 to November 1948. His lectures here to an audience of graduate teachers of English were published as *A Key to Modern Poetry* (Peter Nevill, 1952). He suggested in his lectures a great many of the ideas that he developed in *The Alexandria Quartet*. In Argentina, also, he wrote the poems of *On Seeming to Presume* (Faber, 1948) and made a translation from the Greek of Emmanuel Royidis' Rabelaisian satire,

Pope Joan, which was published by Derek Verschoyle in 1954 and reissued in a revised edition by Andre Deutsch in 1960 and E. P. Dutton & Company, Inc., in 1961.

For climate-conscious Durrell, even England was "wonderful" after Argentina, where the damp coldness had depressed him. He spent six months in England before returning to southern Europe, this time to Belgrade, Yugoslavia, where from July 1949 to December 1952 he was press attaché at the British Legation. In letters to Henry Miller he often expressed his disgust with life along Marxist-Leninist lines, at one point calling it "sheer death." His stay in Yugoslavia gave him the raw materials for *White Eagles Over Serbia* (Faber, 1957), an espionage thriller, mainly for teen-agers, about an abortive uprising against Tito. From his work in Belgrade, also, he drew for some of the details of his satiric sketches of life among the diplomats, *Esprit de Corps* (Faber, 1957) and *Stiff Upper Lip* (Faber, 1958).

It was also in Yugoslavia that Durrell completed *Sappho* (Faber, 1950), a play that he had begun thinking about in Rhodes in 1946. "I tried to strike a balance between verse and drama —Eliot made the breakthrough for us," he said in an interview for the Manchester *Guardian* (May 6, 1961). *Sappho* was produced in Hamburg, Germany in November 1959 and in Edinburgh in the summer of 1961, when it received mixed reviews. Lander MacClintock, who wrote a critical essay on Durrell for Henry T. Moore's *The World of Lawrence Durrell* (Southern Illinois Univ. Press, 1962), felt that *Sappho* and Durrell's second play, *Acte*, produced in Hamburg in 1962, "will successfully stand comparison with the plays of any living writer of poetic drama." (Durrell's third verse play, *An Irish Faust*, is scheduled for production in Hamburg in the fall of 1963.)

With no prospects and little money, Durrell quit the Foreign Service in December 1952 and moved to Cyprus. He had been divorced from his first wife and on February 26, 1951 had married Eve (Gipsy). A daughter, Sappho-Jane, had been born to them in 1951. His wife's illness left him for some time during his stay on Cyprus with the day-by-day personal care of his young daughter and also added to his financial burdens, which included the support of his first wife and his older daughter. He was forced to take a job teaching school, instead of giving his full time to writing; and when violence broke out on Cyprus in the Cypriot revolt against British rule, he returned to diplomacy as director of public relations for the British government.

Durrell's reminiscences of his experiences on Cyprus, *Bitter Lemons* (Faber, 1957), won the Duff Cooper Memorial Prize in England in 1957. When E. P. Dutton & Company published its American edition the following year, one reviewer, Gordon Merrick in the *New Republic* (May 26, 1958), complained, "He is obscure, to a point where one may legitimately wonder if obscurity isn't simply a device to disguise his own emptiness." But general opinion of Durrell's sharpness of observation, sensitivity to atmosphere, sense of tragedy and comedy, poetic insight, and lyrical prose, buttressed Gerald Sykes's claim that as a so-called "travel book"

Bitter Lemons could stand on the same shelf as the contributions of Norman Douglas and D. H. Lawrence.

Before he left Cyprus in August 1956, Durrell had just finished a novel about Alexandria called *Justine,* which he described to Henry Miller as his "first *serious* book since *The Black Book,* much clearer and better organized." By that time he had met Claude, a writer. He moved with her to Provence, France in February 1957 and, after being divorced from his second wife, married her on March 27, 1961. With his prose poem *Justine,* which both Faber & Faber and E. P. Dutton & Company published in 1957, he launched *The Alexandria Quartet.* Needing money, he wrote quickly: *Justine* in four months, *Balthazar* (1958) in six weeks, *Mountolive* (1958) in two months, and *Clea* (1960) in seven weeks. All four books were published in a single volume, *The Alexandria Quartet,* in 1962.

In one of several descriptions that he has given of his tetralogy, Durrell explained (*Manchester Guardian,* May 6, 1961), "It is really intended to be a four-dimensional dance, a relativity poem, and ideally the four volumes should be read simultaneously as they cover the three sides of space and one of time. You might call it a sort of stereoscopic narrative with stereophonic personality." He therefore regards the three novels that follow *Justine* not as "sequels" but as "siblings": characters and events are seen from different points of view, in shifting mood and color, through intricate patterns of innumerable subtleties in changing relationships.

"The central topic of the book," Durrell wrote in his introductory note to *Balthazar,* "is an investigation of modern love." Sexual activity, without the pornography of *The Black Book,* is an important study of *The Alexandria Quartet* as a means of exploring the truth about the characters and as a means of man's discovering the truth about himself. *The Alexandria Quartet,* especially *Mountolive,* also tells a story of political intrigue and the whole tetralogy depends for its effectiveness upon Durrell's skill in involving his characters in the exotic city of Alexandria.

Critical commentary on *The Alexandria Quartet* in the United States, England, Germany, and France ranges from quick dismissal to insistence that Durrell be awarded a Nobel Prize (for which he has twice been nominated). Even some of Durrell's admirers question the success of his experimentation with "the relativity proposition," but several scholars of twentieth-century literature suggest that in "extending the novel" he can be mentioned with Marcel Proust and James Joyce. Much of the Durrell controversy centers on his style. As George Steiner pointed out in an essay in *The World of Lawrence Durrell,* Durrell's baroque style is currently out of favor. Steiner wrote, "Touch by touch, Durrell builds his array of sensuous, rare expressions into patterns of imagery and idea so subtle and convoluted that the experience of reading becomes one of total sensual apprehension. . . . No one else writing in English today has a comparable command of the light and music of language."

Durrell's proficiency as a poet has been more popularly appreciated in his prose than in his poetry. He once said, before the publication of *The Alexandria Quartet,* "My poems constitute the only honest sketch of myself I have ever made." Just as his novels and travel books became marketable in the wake of *Justine,* his poetry was reprinted in *Selected Poems* (Grove, 1957) and *Collected Poems* (Dutton, 1960). Reviewers were impressed by the wide range of his interests, his wit and lyricism, his ability to transfix an evanescent sensation in a quotable phrase, and his affinity with the Mediterranean.

For many years, ever since he had drawn up the ground plan during his visit to Argentina, Durrell had been working from time to time on an edition of the selected writings of Henry Miller. His book finally appeared as *The Henry Miller Reader* (New Directions) in 1959. Also in 1959 he published with Alfred Perlès: *Art and Outrage: A Correspondence about Henry Miller between Lawrence Durrell and Alfred Perlès* (London, Putnam). A lifelong friend, Perlès had been associated with Durrell and Miller in the venturous publication of a little magazine, *The Booster,* in 1937-38.

Since 1957 Durrell has lived with his third wife, Claude, in a peasant cottage near Nîmes in Provence, where, he says, he has a "rude notice" on the front gate reading *Keep Out.* In the summer he receives visits from his two daughters and the son and daughter of Claude. He keeps in touch with England, for which he has what he describes as a "love-hate complex," and in 1961 he worked in London on the script of *Cleopatra* for Twentieth Century-Fox. Durrell is a blue-eyed, blond-haired, masculine-looking man who acquired his good manners long before he joined the diplomatic service. As pictured in *Writers At Work: The Paris Review Interviews,* 2d series (1963), "Lawrence Durrell is a short man, but in no sense a small one. . . . He is a voluble, volatile personality, who talks fast and with enormous energy." Not surprisingly, to those who know him as a stylist, he is an accomplished watercolorist.

References

Atlan 208:63+ D '61
Manchester Guardian p4 My 6 '61 por
Moore, Harry T., ed. The World of Lawrence Durrell (1962)
Twentieth Century Authors (First Supplement, 1955)
Wickes, George, ed. Lawrence Durrell and Henry Miller. A Private Correspondence (1963)
Who's Who, 1963
Writers at Work: The Paris Review Interviews, 2d series (1963)

DYKSTRA, JOHN (dĭk'strả) Apr. 16, 1898-
Industrial executive
Address: h. 1147 Glengarry Rd., Birmingham, Mich.

The Ford Motor Company, one of the "Big Three" of the country's automobile makers, had as its sixth president a specialist in manufacturing operations, John Dykstra, who calls himself a "nuts and bolts man." He joined the company in 1947 and was elected president on April 12, 1961, succeeding Henry Ford 2d. Through agreement on division of duties, Ford,

JOHN DYKSTRA

who remained the company's chairman and chief executive officer, retained charge of almost all operations except manufacturing, for which Dykstra was directly responsible. At the end of April 1963, when he had passed his sixty-fifth birthday, Dykstra retired from the Ford post.

Born near Stiens in the Netherlands province of Friesland on April 16, 1898, John Dykstra is one of the four sons of Theodore and Nellie (DeVries) Dykstra. Two of his brothers, James and Theodore, are also engaged in the automobile industry; the third, Richard, is in the ventilating-equipment business. Their father, a master coppersmith who brought his family to the United States in 1902 and settled in Detroit, Michigan, became affiliated with the old Hudson Motor Car Company, and at the time of his death fifty years later was "credited with having developed metal stamping techniques that brought such improvements as the one-piece fender and body panel, that led to modern-day styling" (New York *Times*, June 24, 1952). In 1914, at the age of sixteen, John Dykstra went to work as an apprentice diemaker, and from 1915 until 1917, when he joined the United States Army for World War I service, he took night courses in mechanical engineering at the Cass Technical School in Detroit. He was demobilized in 1919, the year in which he became a naturalized United States citizen.

Returning to Detroit upon his discharge from the service, Dykstra resumed work as a diemaker with a division of the Layton and Lambert manufacturing Company, soon to be absorbed by the Hudson Motor Car Company. For five years beginning in 1921 he took LaSalle Extension University correspondence courses in foremanship and related subjects that proved valuable in the development of his administrative and executive abilities. For the Hudson Motor Car Company he helped to organize body plant operations and eventually became plant manager for sheet metal and body fabri-

cation and assembly. In 1934, after fifteen years with the Hudson company, Dykstra left to join the Oldsmobile Division of General Motors Corporation; five years later he was appointed general superintendent and assistant factory manager. He was named manufacturing manager for Oldsmobile in 1941 and held this position until 1947, when he joined the Ford Motor Company as general production assistant to D. S. Harder, the vice-president in charge of manufacturing.

Reconversion to peacetime production after World War II had found the Ford Motor Company faced with grave managerial problems. The new blood and new ideas that were needed were supplied by the so-called "Whiz Kids," a group of former Air Force statistical control experts engaged by Henry Ford 2d in 1946. In the field of planning and financial analysis, the group included Robert S. McNamara, who was to serve briefly as president of the Ford Motor Company before he became United States Secretary of Defense in January 1961.

With a background strictly concerned with production, Dykstra was general manager of Ford plants in the Detroit area and at Canton and Cincinnati in Ohio. He was named general manager of the former general manufacturing division in 1948 and then, in September 1950, was elected a Ford vice-president in charge of the aircraft engine, tractor, and machined products group. For the next eight years he was responsible for the company's aircraft engine division. He directed the production at the Chicago plant of 3,071 Pratt & Whitney R-4360 Wasp engines for Air Force planes in the Korean war and later, from 1952 to 1958, of 6,195 Pratt & Whitney J-57 jet engines for the Air Force.

After being elected a director of the Ford Motor Company in July 1958, John Dykstra became a member of the executive and operating policy committees, and he has also served on the product planning, scheduling, and styling committees. He is, in addition, a director of such subsidiaries as the Ford Motor Credit Company, the American Road Insurance Company, and the Ford Motor Leasing Development Company. From 1958 to 1961 as vice-president in charge of both manufacturing and the defense products group he spent most of his time on the company's intensified program to improve the quality in the design, manufacture, and assembly of its products. "Inspectors cannot 'inspect' quality into products," he maintains. On one occasion he explored parking lots to buy up rusted cars that he subjected to extensive tests leading to changes in protective coatings. Under Dykstra, the quality of Ford passenger cars and trucks was so notably improved that in October 1960 the company increased the warranty to its purchasers from the then standard three months or 4,000 miles to twelve months or 12,000 miles.

On November 9, 1960 Henry Ford 2d, the president, chairman of the board, and chief executive officer of the Ford Motor Company, turned over the presidency to Robert S. McNamara. Only about a month later, however, McNamara accepted the nomination for Secretary of Defense in the incoming Kennedy administration. Ford again took over the duties of the presidency until April 12, 1961, when John Dykstra was elected the sixth president of the company. Some insiders in the automobile industry speculated about reasons for choosing Dykstra, since in two years he would reach Ford's retirement age of sixty-five, which, however, could be extended by mutual consent for three years.

In announcing Dykstra's election, Henry Ford 2d, who continued as chairman and chief executive officer, noted that the company's eight staff vice-presidents—finance, legal, industrial relations, product planning and styling, engineering and research, marketing, purchasing, and public relations—would still report to him. The manufacturing staff would report directly to Dykstra, as would the vice-presidents in charge of the car and truck, Ford International, general products, stamping and power train, and defense products groups. His primary responsibility, therefore, would lie in operations, the area in which he had concentrated throughout his career.

Despite what Ford described as "a pretty disastrous sales period" for the automobile industry in January and February of 1961, the market began to improve in the spring, and Dykstra predicted for Ford shareholders in May "a fairly satisfactory last three quarters of 1961." During that year Ford earned $409,579,689 as compared with $427,885,948 in 1960 and approximately $454,200,000 in 1955, the company's record year. Although a strike at a stamping plant near Cleveland had halted most of Ford's assembly operations for two weeks in June 1962, the company was able to report record sales, and its second-best earnings, in the half year ending with that month.

The Ford Company announced in September 1961 that it was entering the electronics field through the purchase (concluded two months later) of the Philco Corporation. Later in the month Dykstra disclosed in a speech before the National Defense Transportation Association that his company would bid for the manufacture of the first-stage booster for the Saturn rocket. "This is only one sign," he said, "that we are moving into the defense and space business with both feet." Addressing the American Ordnance Association in December 1962, he urged the creation of "an industrial national guard" to insure the conversion of peacetime industry to war production. "Industry's role no longer fits into two separate compartments marked 'war and peace,'" he pointed out. "Today it must meet both demands simultaneously." In April 1963 it was announced that Dykstra would retire in accordance with the Ford Company's policy at the age of sixty-five, and he did so at the end of the month.

John Dykstra married Marion S. Hyde on March 2, 1918. They have a daughter, Betty H. (Mrs. John Steele), a son, John O. Dykstra, and six grandchildren. A distinguished-looking man, Dykstra has silver hair and blue eyes and stands five feet eleven inches tall. He is said to "make a fetish of neatness" and to have a fondness for things Dutch. He grows tulips, daffodils, and roses in his garden in the Bloomfield Village section of Birmingham, Michigan. At his winter home in Fort Lauderdale, Florida, he goes deep-sea fishing in his Cris-Craft cruiser. He belongs to the Society of Automotive Engineers, the Detroit Athletic Club, the Detroit Golf Club, and the Recess Club. Although he has been called "a hard-driving boss" and "a doer rather than a talker," he becomes extremely articulate when his subject is manufacturing operations or quality. "The best guarantee of quality," he once said, "is pride of workmanship—regardless of the advances that have been made in automatic machinery and plant equipment."

References

Bsns W p33 Ap 15 '61
Christian Sci Mon p10 Ap 13 '61 por
N Y Times p47+ Ap 13 '61 por
Newsweek 57:82 Ap 24 '61 por
Time 77:94+ Ap 21 '61 por
International Who's Who, 1962-63
Who's Who, 1963
Who's Who in America, 1962-63
World Who's Who in Commerce and Industry (1961)

EDEL, (JOSEPH) LEON (ā'děl) Sept. 9, 1907-
University professor; writer
Address: b. Washington Square College, New York University, New York 3

By practising what he teaches about the art of biographical writing, a subject on which he is an authority, Leon Edel won both the 1963 National Book Award for nonfiction and the 1963 Pulitzer Prize in biography. His award-winning books, *Henry James: The Conquest of London, 1870-1881* and *Henry James: The Middle Years, 1882-1895*, both published in 1962, are volumes two and three of his projected four-volume life of James. Edel, who is a professor of English at New York University, has also edited much of James's work and has written on various subjects in the field of literature and psychology, especially the modern novel. John K. Hutchens of the New York *Times* once described him as "a scholar in the great tradition of diligence and responsibility, a critic of insights so original as justly to be called creative, and a stylist of singular grace and charm."

Joseph Leon Edel was born in Pittsburgh, Pennsylvania on September 9, 1907, one of two sons of Simon and Fannie (Malamud) Edel. His younger brother, Abraham Edel, is a professor of philosophy at the City College of New York. Simon Edel, a merchant and entrepreneur, moved his family to Saskatchewan when his sons were still young. While growing up on the Canadian frontier, Leon Edel was oriented toward his life-work in teaching and writing by what he has explained as "a fundamental parental *feeling* about culture and in particular literature: a tradition of writing in the family." Another encouragement came, as he has said, from the isolation of his childhood environment on the prairie— "that is, the longing for the things of the mind and spirit in a community busy with pioneering."

For his early education Edel attended Victoria School in Yorkton, Saskatchewan, and in 1923 he graduated from Yorkton Collegiate Institute, where his extracurricular interests had centered on pub-

New York University—
Pasquale Del Riccio

LEON EDEL

lic speaking, playing the violin, and editing the school's newspaper. Then at McGill University in Montreal, with English as his major subject, he became a member of the editorial board of the *McGill Daily* and was also a founder of the *McGill Fortnightly Review*, which is regarded as having launched "modernism" in Canadian literature, particularly in poetry.

Edel's work at McGill earned him the B.A. degree in 1927 and the M.A. degree in 1928. In his graduate research he had been concerned with the stream-of-consciousness writers, and while investigating their forerunners, he had become interested in Henry James. When he was awarded a fellowship of the province of Quebec for study abroad, he went to the University of Paris (the Sorbonne) to develop his ideas about certain aspects of James's writing. For his state doctorate of letters—Docteur-ès-lettres (d'état)—which the University of Paris granted him in 1932, he wrote two dissertations: *Henry James: Les années dramatiques* (in French) and *The Prefaces of Henry James*, both published in Paris in 1932.

The Depression crushed Edel's hopes for an academic career upon his return home after three and a half years in Paris. He kept variously employed from 1932 to 1943 in tutoring, news broadcasting, news agency work, and free-lance assignments. He acquired some experience in journalism as a reporter and then as a copy desk writer for the Montreal *Daily Star*, and he has also written for New York newspapers. In 1943 he entered the United States Army, in which he served until 1947, rising in rank from private to first lieutenant. He saw action in France, fought in the Battle of the Bulge, and was with the Occupation forces in Germany in 1945-46. During his World War II service he was awarded five battle stars and the Bronze Star Medal.

Although Edel had been earning his living in a generally nonacademic atmosphere, without the security of membership on a university faculty, he had been more or less continually occupied over the years in research and writing on literary subjects, even while in the Army. In Zurich, Switzerland in 1945, about five years after the death of James Joyce, he visited Joyce's grave and also talked with his widow, Nora Joyce, and others who were with Joyce during his last days. From their accounts Edel drew up notes for the final chapter in the novelist's life, *James Joyce: The Last Journey* (Gotham Bkmart, 1947).

Ever since his student days at the Sorbonne, when he had questioned the tendency of contemporary criticism to dismiss too quickly the work of Henry James as a dramatist, Edel had been engaged, as he had said, in a "quest to arrive at the singular story of the novelist's obsession with the theatre." The methods and ideas of his doctoral thesis on James's plays so impressed the James family that Edel was granted priority of access to Henry James's papers and was charged by the novelist's literary executor, his nephew Henry James, with the editing of the plays. A Guggenheim Fellowship, granted in 1936 and renewed for a second year, enabled Edel to carry out considerable research in France, England, and the United States. *The Complete Plays of Henry James* (Lippincott), for which Edel wrote an extended essay on James's dramatic years, appeared in 1949. In the same year his edition of *The Ghostly Tales of Henry James* (Rutgers Univ. Press) was also published.

By the time that he began his career in teaching Edel had therefore set his reputation as a writer and scholar upon a solid foundation. From 1950 to 1952 he held the title of visiting professor at New York University; in 1954 he became associate professor of English; and since 1955 he has been professor of English at NYU. Meanwhile, he lectured at Harvard University in the summer of 1952 and at Princeton University in 1953. During the academic year 1954-55 he was visiting professor of criticism at Indiana University and during the summer of 1955, visiting professor at the University of Hawaii.

In the red-letter year of 1953, productive for Edel in both Jamesian and non-Jamesian studies, Alfred A. Knopf published *Willa Cather, A Critical Biography*, in which Edel shared authorship with E. K. Brown. At the time of his death in 1951, Brown had been working on an authorized biography of Willa Cather, which Edel was then asked to complete. "He has done so with unusual care, and with rare tact," Gordon Roper commented in *Canadian Forum* (July 1953). "The finished volume is a fitting commemoration of two artists, Willa Cather and E. K. Brown." Edel further shared his appreciation of one of America's finest woman novelists in his lecture "Willa Cather, The Paradox of Success," which he gave at the Coolidge Auditorium of the Library of Congress in October 1959.

Literary form rather than biography was the concern of Edel's 1955 study of modern fiction, *The Psychological Novel, 1900-1950* (Lippincott; Grove, 1959, under the title of *The Modern Psychological Novel*). Writing "simply and warmly and with a delectable abundance of appropriate quotations," as a *New Yorker* (June 11, 1955) critic observed, he discussed the stream-of-consciousness novel as a characteristically twentieth-century contribution to fiction writing, with particular reference to the works of James Joyce, Marcel Proust, and Dorothy Richardson.

For no other writer, however, had Edel neglected Henry James. He followed the 1949 publication of the complete plays with many editions of James's writings for various publishers, including *The Selected Fiction of Henry James* (Dutton, Everyman Library, 1953); *The Selected Letters of Henry James* (Farrar, Great Letter Series, 1955); *The Future of the Novel; Essays on the Art of Fiction* (Vintage, 1956); *The American Essays of Henry James* (Vintage, 1956); *The Ambassadors* (Houghton, 1960), and *Guy Domville* (Lippincott, 1961). He also prepared with Dan H. Laurence *A Bibliography of Henry James* (Hart-Davis, 1957) and edited with Gordon N. Ray *Henry James and H. G. Wells: A Record of Their Friendship, Their Debate on the Art of Fiction, and Their Quarrel* (Univ. of Illinois Press, 1958). He is working at present on a projected twelve-volume edition, *The Complete Tales of Henry James* (Lippincott), of which the first two volumes appeared in 1962.

Over a period of more than twenty years Leon Edel had also been studying thousands of James's letters, family papers, uncollected essays, old newspaper records, account books, and other documents in preparation for his biography of Henry James. His first volume, *Henry James: The Untried Years, 1843-1870* (Lippincott), published in 1953, greatly impressed critics because of its accuracy and thoroughness of research, the tact and understanding with which Edel handled his material, and the apparent effortlessness of his narrative. "Mr Edel's first volume," Wayne Andrews wrote in *Commonweal* (May 8, 1953), "is nothing less than a masterpiece."

Equally enthusiastic comment greeted the second and third volumes, *Henry James: The Conquest of London, 1870-1881* and *Henry James: The Middle Years, 1882-1895*, which appeared in 1962. Edel hopes to complete the fourth and final volume by 1966. "The three [volumes] now in print already constitute one of the major literary biographies of our era," Perry Miller wrote in the *Christian Science Monitor* (November 8, 1963). "In every proper sense of a much-abused word, they immediately stand as 'classic.' " Several reviewers had some reservations because of what they regarded as Edel's "excessive praise" of his subject, or occasional unconvincing psychological speculations, or overeagerness to find traces of James's own experiences in his fiction. General critical opinion, however, firmly supported Miller's appraisal.

In March 1963 Edel was awarded the $1,000 National Book Award for nonfiction for the second and third volumes of his life of James, which was cited as "a biography written with exemplary control of its material, with fine psychological insight, and with narrative power." The excellence of the 1962 volumes also won for him, in May 1963, the $500 Pulitzer Prize in biography.

The art of biographical writing has for many years been a subject of special interest to Edel. His Alexander Lectures on biography as a literary form, delivered at the University of Toronto in 1955-56, provided the basis for his *Literary Biography* (Univ. of Toronto Press, 1957; Anchor, 1959). In his review for the New York *Times* (September 4, 1959) John K. Hutchens outlined Edel's picture of the ideal literary biographer: "He is . . . a sensitive critic as well as a scrupulous collector of facts, searches a writer's work not only for its own esthetic sake but for what it says about the writer's inner life, uses the psychoanalyst's techniques but is not confined by them, and by-passes the orthodox biographer's subservience to chronology in favor of grouping for dramatic emphasis outside a fixed-time schedule."

Edel has much fault to find with "the dust cart method" of biographical writing. In his acceptance speech at the fourteenth annual National Book Awards ceremony in New York City, he underscored the importance of selection: "Without selection, all we have is clutter." He went on to say, "It is the inexhaustibility of biographical data that presents to modern biography a challenge to find a method, a theory, a technique, a form. And I like to believe that this award is a recognition of this fact—of the ideal I have set for myself of trying to tell a long and complex life and not engulf the reader in my materials."

Again, in an interview for the *Christian Science Monitor* (March 13, 1963), Edel spoke of the necessity of the humanist scholar to sacrifice the greater part of his findings for the sake of communicating to the statesman and scientist the lasting values of the past. To help make the uses of the past more efficient, he pointed out, "historical re-creation must be more than mere words —scholars talking to scholars—but must be rendered with artistic form and understanding of what is relevant and irrelevant."

Among the honors that Edel received in 1963, besides the National Book and Pulitzer awards, were D.Litt. degrees from Union College and McGill University. In 1959 he was awarded a writing grant by the National Institute of Arts and Letters and in the same year was elected to the American Academy of Arts and Sciences. From 1959 to 1962 he was a Fellow of the Bollingen Foundation. He belongs to the Century Club and to several professional organizations, including the American Studies Association; served from 1957 to 1959 as president of the American Center of P.E.N.; and is organizing chairman of the 1963 congress of the International Federation for Modern Literature and Language at New York University. He is a Democrat.

Leon Edel and his wife, the former Roberta Roberts, whom he married on December 1, 1950, live in Manhattan on Central Park West. They also have a summer home at Gay Head on Martha's Vineyard. A trim man of medium build, Edel is five feet six inches tall and weighs 155 pounds; he has gray hair and brown eyes. He is known for his urbanity and affability. Music and book collecting are his hobbies, and for outdoor recreation he prefers beachcombing and occasional skiing. He sometimes wears Henry James's topaz ring, which was given him by the James family. "I wear it when I go hunting for James material," he once explained. "And I

EDEL, LEON—*Continued*

really think it twinkles with extra brightness when it is in places that it visited before on the finger of its first owner."

References

Christian Sci Mon p9 Mr 13 '63 por
N Y Herald Tribune p10 My 7 '63 por
N Y Times p35 My 7 '63 por

Who's Who in America, 1962-63

EGBERT, SHERWOOD H(ARRY) July 24, 1920- Industrial executive

Address: h. R.R. No. 2, Box 75, New Carlisle, Ind.

Although he had had no experience in the automotive field, Sherwood H. Egbert was hired early in 1961 as president of the Studebaker Corporation to try to restore the company to financial health. There was some danger that the South Bend, Indiana, concern, the smallest of the five American car producers, would be forced to go out of business after over 100 years of manufacturing vehicles. Egbert's imagination, determination, and capacity for hard work were qualities that attracted Studebaker's directors. He also had an excellent record as an executive at the McCulloch Corporation, a maker of chainsaw and outboard motors, where he had risen from assistant purchasing agent to executive vice-president in fourteen years. Besides the sale of its cars—the Lark, the Hawk, the Avanti, and the Wagonaire—Egbert concentrated on a diversification program to put his company on a firmer base. He resigned from Studebaker in November 1963.

Sherwood Harry Egbert, the son of Harry C. and Charlotte (Brown) Egbert, was born on July 24, 1920 in Seattle, Washington and reared in

SHERWOOD H. EGBERT

Easton, Washington, a small community about sixty miles from Seattle. He has a brother, Willard E. Egbert. Harry C. Egbert was a barber who tried unsuccessfully to run a dance hall, and the Egberts were so poor that when their house burned down they were forced to move into tents. Sherwood Egbert remembers eating "plenty of stale bread" and stealing coal from railroad cars to keep the family warm. At the age of twelve he worked as a night flagman with a road repair gang; at fourteen he was driving a truck; and at sixteen he was employed as a laborer and chainman for the Washington State Highway Department. While attending high school he also covered three paper routes and worked at the local airport.

At Easton High School, from which he graduated in 1937, Egbert won sixteen athletic letters and was the state discus champion. He had thought of breaking into professional baseball as a pitcher, but an athletic scholarship enabled him to enroll at Washington State College, where he studied mechanical engineering in 1937-38 and 1939-40. To help pay his college expenses he leased a bulldozer and dug basements at night and on weekends.

Egbert married in 1940 and left college to take a job as a laborer with the Austin Company, a Seattle construction firm. Before the year was out his surveying skills had led to his appointment as assistant chief engineer on a construction project that the Austin Company was doing for the Boeing Airplane Company. In 1941 he was named assistant to the superintendent of general construction for Boeing, but after only one year on this job he entered the United States Marine Corps as a second lieutenant.

For the next three years Egbert served as an engineering officer in the Marine Air Transport Service, which operated a 26,000-mile air route through the Pacific war zones. Because his work involved air transport he decided he ought to learn to fly, and he became a licensed pilot, taking all 250 hours of his flight training at night. He was decorated with the Bronze Star and released from service in 1945 in the rank of major.

On his return to civilian life Egbert worked for a year with the Navy Department's Bureau of Aeronautics in Washington, contributing to the development of turbojet and ramjet engines. In 1946 he joined the McCulloch Corporation in Los Angeles, California, which was then beginning to manufacture chain-saw motors. Egbert was promoted from assistant purchasing agent to purchasing agent, and in 1951 he became vice-president of manufacturing and a director of the corporation. In 1956, when McCulloch purchased the Scott-Atwater Manufacturing Company, a leading manufacturer of outboard motors, Egbert was named chairman of the Scott board of directors, executive vice-president of the McCulloch Corporation, and a member of the McCulloch executive committee. He also became a vice-president of McCulloch divisions in Belgium, Australia, and Canada.

"It was his tenure of 15 years [at McCulloch] that spread the young man's powerhouse reputation," Arthur W. Baum noted in the *Saturday Evening Post* (November 3, 1962). "For one thing, McCulloch was a spectacular manufacturing success, revolutionizing the chain-saw field on an international scale. For another, McCulloch was a vividly colorful company, thanks mainly to Egbert. The firm produced, advertised and packaged in gay pastel splashes." Egbert visited hundreds of industrial plants in search of good ideas. He also traveled an estimated distance of twelve times around the world in establishing McCulloch's foreign manufacturing and sales distribution.

Because of his reputation as a dynamic executive Egbert was chosen president of the ailing Studebaker-Packard Corporation (now the Studebaker Corporation) on December 28, 1960. Signing a five-year, $125,000-a-year contract with stock option, he assumed his new post on February 1, 1961. Studebaker is the smallest of the five American auto makers. The two largest are General Motors and Ford, followed by Chrysler, American Motors, and Studebaker.

Founded in 1852 by Henry and Clement Studebaker, the Studebaker Corporation is one of the oldest producers of vehicles in the United States. Pioneers drove westward in its Conestoga wagons, and the Union Army used its wagons and gun carriages in the Civil War. Although the company went into debt in the 1930's, it prospered in World War II and in early postwar years. In the 1950's, despite one good year—1959, when it introduced the Lark, a roomy compact—Studebaker again went into the red and has been in difficulties ever since. Its merger with the Packard Motor Car Company in 1954 did not help matters, and in 1962 Studebaker dropped the Packard name from its corporate title. There has been much speculation as to whether Studebaker could remain in business; hopes that it could were centered in Egbert, who was given the task of putting the old corporation on its feet again.

True to his reputation for having good ideas and getting them carried out, Egbert instituted effective changes in many different areas of Studebaker operation. Soon after taking office he toured the United States, inspecting dealer installations and obtaining dealers' opinions of the Studebaker line. He got rid of many "dual dealers" whose loyalties to Studebaker suffered because they sold other makes of cars. He had the 1962 line of automobiles styled in record time: the Lark lost its stubby look, and a new Gran Turismo Hawk (a European-looking car with bucket seats, a long, sloping hood, and a walnut-paneled dashboard) was readied for showing in eighteen weeks. Among the 1963 models were the Avanti, a powerful prestige car with a fiberglass body and smooth lines, initially designed by Egbert himself, which was meant to glamorize Studebaker's image; and the Wagonaire, a station wagon with a sliding steel roof, which was called "a roomy, all-purpose vehicle . . . of attractive design" by Joseph C. Ingraham in the New York *Times* (September 8, 1962).

In another area of equal importance to Studebaker's continued solvency, Egbert continued a diversification program begun in the late 1950's. The automobile company already owned Gering Products, Inc., a plastics concern (sold in 1961 at a profit); CTL, Inc., a manufacturer of thermal plastics; Gravely Tractors, Inc.; Clarke Floor

Machine Company; and D.W. Onan & Sons, a producer of generating equipment. To these were added in 1961 Chemical Compounds, Inc., an oil additives company; and in 1962 Schaefer, Inc., maker of frozen food cabinets; Trans-International Airlines; and the Franklin Manufacturing Company, a home appliances manufacturer. Studebaker International, S.A., was set up in Switzerland to expand sales in the foreign market. In addition, Egbert made all-out efforts to obtain military contracts from the United States government; he had a five-man office set up in Washington, D.C. and bought an additional plant. By April 1963 government contracts had exceeded his predicted figure of over $100,000,000.

Among the first changes Egbert had made on coming to South Bend was to have the plant and offices painted and to require the foremen to wear white jackets in the factory, both for appearance and for easy identification. In general, he tried to brighten and freshen Studebaker surroundings, and the employees' morale rose accordingly. He also reorganized management lines to do away with ineffective decision making and lack of communication.

The financial situation at Studebaker improved only slowly, and the automotive division continued to lag in sales. Egbert was considered to be perhaps Studebaker's biggest asset at this time. "Only game fish swim upstream," Charles M. Sievert wrote in the *World-Telegram and Sun* (April 15, 1963). "Studebaker Corporation, with its road ahead all uphill, is lucky to have young Sherwood H. Egbert in the president's chair. . . . Happily for Studebaker shareholders, he is a man who can't even spell discouragement." Before the end of the year, however, he resigned because of differences of opinion over how company policy should be carried out.

Sherwood H. Egbert was married on March 1, 1940 to Doris Ruth McKay; they had two children, Sherwood James and Nancy Lee. He was married for the second time on June 4, 1958, to Diana Nell Johnson, who was an airline stewardess before her marriage. They have three sons, David Sherwood, Gregory Martin, and Robert Paul. Egbert is six feet four inches tall, weighs 185 pounds, and has gray eyes and graying brown hair. He has been described as forthright, unassuming, and cordial, and as operating "on a one-gear ratio—full speed ahead." Swimming, diving, playing golf and tennis, horseback riding, and flying are his favorite recreations. He belongs to the Bel-Air Country Club and the Eldorado Country Club.

References

Fortune 64:96+ D '61 por
N Y Times p33 D 29 '60 por
N Y World-Telegram p24+ Ap 15 '63 por
Newsweek 58:89+ S 25 '61 por
Sat Eve Post 235:30+ N 3 '62 por
Time 77:90 Ap 21 '61 por
Washington (D.C.) Post A p17 D 30 '60 por
Who's Who in America, 1962-63
World Who's Who in Commerce and Industry (1961)

EISENSCHIML, OTTO (ī'zĕn-shĭm'l) June 16, 1880- Chemist; businessman; writer
Address: b. 1637 S. Kilbourn Ave., Chicago 23, Ill.; h. 2300 Lincoln Park West, Chicago 14, Ill.

BULLETIN: Otto Eisenschiml died on December 7, 1963. *Obituary*: N Y Times p35 D 9 '63

Years ago, as a part-time journalist in Pittsburgh, fresh from his native Vienna, the young chemist Otto Eisenschiml learned to heed his editor's advice always to get the story behind the story. Mingling vocation with avocation, Eisenschiml has had a long and varied career as a chemist, scientific and industrial consultant, businessman, historian, public speaker, and writer. Eisenschiml is head of Scientific Chemicals, Inc., a Chicago firm that he founded more than fifty years ago as the Scientific Oil Company. Since 1937 he has published more than a dozen books on the Civil War, writing history as if he were writing an exciting detective story and from time to time outraging traditional scholars.

As Otto Eisenschiml suggests in his autobiography, *Without Fame* (Alliance, 1942), he owes much of his respect for the past and his sense of historic significance to having grown up in the old Austria of the closing years of the nineteenth century. He was born in Vienna on June 16, 1880 to Alexander and Leonore (Koretz) Eisenschiml, both of whom were natives of Bohemia (now Czechoslovakia). His father, having sought his fortune in the United States in his youth, was an American citizen and a veteran of the Civil War. By the time of his son's birth Alexander Eisenschiml had become a prosperous manufacturer of photographic apparatus in Vienna. He died when Otto was eight years old, and his children—two older daughters, Bertha and Helene, besides his son—were reared by their mother in an atmosphere of strict discipline.

OTTO EISENSCHIML

After he had completed grade school, therefore, Otto Eisenschiml was sent to the *Realschule,* to prepare for earning his own living, rather than to the Gymnasium. His mother wanted him to take a commercial course when he finished high school at the age of fourteen, but he had made up his mind to become a chemist and won his mother's consent to his plans by agreeing to support himself while studying and also to help meet family expenses. During his years in the higher grades of the *Realschule* and later at the Kaiserlich-Königliche Technische Hochschule he fulfilled his obligations by tutoring other students and working as a reporter for the newspaper *Neues Wiener Journal*.

In boyhood Eisenschiml had been advised by his father to go to America after completing his education in Europe. He graduated from the polytechnical institute with a diploma in chemical engineering in 1901. Before the year was over he had arrived in the United States (of which he had been from birth a citizen) and had found a job as a chemist with the Carnegie Steel Company in a plant near Pittsburgh, Pennsylvania. His assignment was to analyze the river water used in the plant's boilers and to neutralize its acidity to prevent corrosion. During his three years there he polished his conversational English and responded to every opportunity to learn about the technical operations of the plant. Outside the laboratory he took some lessons in glassmaking.

The American iron and steel industry in the early days of the twentieth century offered the analytical chemist little more to do than what Eisenschiml has called "mere check-up-work." Discouraged by the lack of opportunity for creative contribution, he left Pittsburgh in 1904 and set out for Chicago with the hope of starting a new career. For some months he drifted from one unsatisfactory odd job to another in near poverty, while still fulfilling his financial commitments to his family in Austria.

Eventually he heard of a chance for employment with the American Linseed Company, which operated a linseed oil extracting plant in south Chicago, and he hurried to the John Crerar Library to read the meager material then available on linseed oil. His research gave him a superficial knowledge that helped him to get the job, but when he faced his first practical problem, he had to turn not to books but to firsthand investigation. Charged with explaining why the company's linseed oil discolored when heated in varnish kettles, he found the answer through on-the-spot detective work at the refinery, where he discovered that caustic soda was being used to wash filter cloths.

Eisenschiml's contract with the American Linseed Company gave him the right to work as a consultant on his own time. He often served as an expert in court cases involving the adulteration of linseed oil, and on the basis of his experience he published a series of articles on linseed oil. In 1910 he and another chemist, Norman Copthorne, developed a method of determining the presence of fish oils in vegetable oils, and the method was adopted as official by the United States Department of Agriculture in 1925. Also with Copthorne during World War I he worked out a flexible coating for barbed wire entanglements. Earlier, in excursions into somewhat curious subjects of scientific research, he had developed the first one-piece window envelope for the Window Envelope Company and a patented shoe filler for the Florsheim Shoe Company.

It was partly to supply the Window Envelope Company with a special varnish for its envelopes that Eisenschiml established his own firm in Chicago, the Scientific Oil Company, later called the Scientific Oil Compounding Company and now Scientific Chemicals, Inc. He retained for a time his position as chief chemist of the American Linseed Company, but in 1912 he left to manage his own company, which he described in *Without Fame* as "a chemical consulting office with a manufacturing annex, conducted along the lines of professional ethics." Eventually, however, he gave up his work as a chemist to concentrate on distribution of raw materials. One of his principal concerns as a businessman has been to work out new methods of profit sharing among his employees.

Developments in industrial chemistry and the status of the chemist have long been subjects of intense interest to Eisenschiml. Soon after he moved to Chicago he had started to attend regional meetings of the American Chemical Society, and in 1914, when he was chairman of the society's Chicago section, he founded the Chicago *Chemical Bulletin,* the first chemical newspaper in the United States, which he edited until 1917. He was president of the Chicago Chemists Club in 1922 and of the National Soybean Oil Manufacturers Association in 1928. During World War I he was a member of the Chicago Chemists' Round Table to assist war industries without charge, and during World War II he aided the defense effort through work with the Chicago Technical Societies and the Civil Defense Corps.

Since 1903 Eisenschiml had been gaining national prominence as a lecturer, but neither his career in public speaking nor his achievements in chemistry and industry could fully satisfy his zest for meeting challenges. On a business trip in the West in the summer of 1913, he had visited the battlefield of Custer's last stand and had been so deeply moved by the historic Montana site that he resolved to see every important remaining battlefield in the United States. It was, as he has said, "a vast undertaking" because he studied intensively in preparation for each visit.

Much attracted to battlefields of the Civil War, he tried to find the answers to some of the inconsistencies that he saw in orthodox accounts of events of the period. His investigations of the puzzling circumstances surrounding the death of President Abraham Lincoln resulted in 1937 in his first book, *Why Was Lincoln Murdered?* (Little), in which he argued, while admitting the absence of conclusive proof, that John Wilkes Booth was probably aided in the assassination of Lincoln by Secretary of War Edwin Stanton and Northern radicals. His book was dramatized by Paul Horgan as *Yours, A. Lincoln,* which ran for two performances at the Shubert Theatre in New York City in July 1942.

Although some reviewers of *Why Was Lincoln Murdered?* thought it provocative, admired Eisenschiml's brisk narrative style, and praised his thorough documentation, many tended to regard it more as a demonstration of detective work than as a contribution to history. Eisenschiml answered his critics in "Reviewers Reviewed: A Challenge to Historical Critics," a paper that he read at the William L. Clements Library of the University of Michigan in February 1940. He protested his critics' failure to furnish proof when they refuted the accuracy of his statements. Also in 1940 he published his equally speculative *In the Shadow of Lincoln's Death* (W. Funk), which one reviewer called "a long footnote" to his earlier work.

Among Eisenschiml's other books on the Civil War period are *The Case of A.L.—Aged 56; Some Curious Medical Aspects of Lincoln's Death and Other Studies* (privately printed for the Abraham Lincoln Book Shop, Chicago, 1943); *The Story of Shiloh* (Civil War Round Table, 1946); *The American Iliad; The Epic Story of the Civil War as Narrated by Eyewitnesses and Contemporaries* (with Ralph Newman, Bobbs, 1947; reprinted as the first volume of *The Civil War,* Grosset, 1956); *As Luck Would Have It; Chance and Coincidence in the Civil War* (with E. B. Long, Bobbs, 1948), and *The Celebrated Case of Fitz John Porter; An American Dreyfus Affair* (Bobbs, 1950). He also edited a volume of Civil War letters, *Vermont General; The Unusual War Experiences of Edward Hastings Ripley* (Devin, 1959).

Like *Why Was Lincoln Murdered?*, Eisenschiml's *Why the Civil War?* (Bobbs, 1958) and *The Hidden Face of the Civil War* (Bobbs, 1961) were controversial studies that reviewers found invigorating and generally sound in scholarship, although at times irritating. Few agreed with his conclusions, however, and some wondered whether he intended all his assertions to be taken seriously. One reason for Eisenschiml's unorthodoxy is that he does not copy from other history books, but largely relies upon his own field research. In *O. E. Historian Without an Armchair* (Bobbs, 1963) he tells about his unusual experiences during some forty years of research into obscure or puzzling aspects of the Civil War, of his trips to unreconstructed battle sites, his talks with survivors of the war, and his methods of historical detection.

Among Eisenschiml's books not devoted to the Civil War is *The Art of Worldly Wisdom* (Essential Books, 1947), containing 300 precepts for success based on the original work of Baltasar Gracián y Morales. He also contributed to *Chicago Murders* (edited by S. P. Wright, Duell, 1945) and has written reviews and scientific articles for periodicals.

Often honored for his contributions to both science and history, Eisenschiml received an honor scroll of the Chicago chapter of the American Institute of Chemistry (1949), a citation of the Chicago chapter of the American Chemical Society (1960), a doctorate in literature from Lincoln Memorial University (1937), a diploma of merit from Lincoln College (1960), and distinguished service awards from the Civil War Round Table (1960) and the Illinois Historical

EISENSCHIML, OTTO—*Continued*

Society (1960). He is a member of the National Research Council and the New York Academy of Sciences and a past president and past chairman of the board of directors of the West Side Historical Society.

On January 14, 1912 Otto Eisenschiml married his cousin, Bertha Eisenschimel, whom he had met in Chicago. They have a daughter, Rosalie Ruth, and two sons, Gerald Alexander and Ralph Eugene. Eisenschiml is five feet eight inches tall, weighs 165 pounds, and has hazel eyes and white hair. He mentions only one hobby—reading—but his own books reveal a sense of fun in his outlook on life and a curiosity receptive to many enthusiasms, including music, baseball, and stamp collecting. In *Without Fame* he writes about learning to go without an overcoat in cold weather: "I . . . immediately became known as an eccentric. This as I see it now, is the ultimate goal of human freedom. If you are known as odd, peculiar—cracked, when you are out of earshot—you can do anything you like. You can defy conventions, make your own rules, and still remain reasonably popular. Verily, it is great to be known as an eccentric."

References

Eisenschiml, Otto. Without Fame (1942);
O. E. Historian Without an Armchair (1963)
Who's Who in America, 1962-63

ESHKOL, LEVI (ĕsh-kôl' lē'vē) Oct. 25, 1895-
Prime Minister of Israel

Address: b. Prime Minister's Office, Jerusalem, Israel; h. Busteni St., Jerusalem, Israel

Israel's Prime Minister and Minister of Defense, Levi Eshkol, who succeeded David Ben-Gurion on June 26, 1963 is, like his predecessor, one of the pioneer builders of the Jewish homeland. After immigrating to Palestine in 1914 he helped to establish agricultural settlements there, and he later became one of the founders of his adopted country's central labor movement and political labor party. He also helped to build its defensive military force, and he represented the political and economic interests of Palestine Jewry on missions abroad. A member of Israel's government since its establishment as an independent state in 1948, Eshkol served as Minister of Finance from 1952 to 1963, in which post he undertook a number of reforms. He has successfully mediated inter-party conflicts on the Israeli scene. As Prime Minister, Eshkol is committed to a policy of continued economic progress, of maintaining friendly relations with as many nations as possible, and of strengthening Israel's defenses while exploring means of settling sources of conflict with the Arab countries.

Levi Shkolnik, who later hebraicized his family name to Eshkol (meaning "cluster of grapes"), is a native of Oratova, a village in the Kiev province of the Ukraine. He was born on October 25 (some sources give October 10), 1895 to Joseph and Dvora (Krasniansky) Shkolnik.

His father, who came from a long line of rabbis, was a Talmudic scholar. Eshkol's maternal grandmother managed the family's financial affairs, leasing land from absentee noblemen and trading in such commodities as wheat, iron, coal, and lime. Although fairly prosperous, the family lived in constant terror of the anti-Jewish pogroms then prevalent in Russia.

After receiving a traditional education in his home community Eshkol went to Oman and later to Odessa to prepare for the entrance examinations to the Russian Gymnasium. However, because of the quota limitations on the number of Jewish students permitted to attend the Russian higher schools, he went to Vilna, Lithuania, to attend the Gymnasium there. At Vilna, which was a major center of Zionist activity, Eshkol was active in Zionist work for about three years. His acquaintance with the Zionist leader Yosef Sprinzak inspired him, in 1913, to immigrate to Palestine, then still under Turkish rule.

Carrying only a knapsack, Eshkol arrived at Jaffa, Palestine, in 1914. From there he went to the Jewish settlement at Petach Tikvah. He worked as an agricultural laborer and watchman, and he helped to build the pumping station that brought water from the Yarkon River to irrigate the citrus groves of the settlement. In the evenings he worked as cashier and manager of the workers' kitchen in the village, and he soon was elected to the workers' committee of Petach Tikvah. Later he helped to establish the Atarot and Kiryat Anavim settlements near Jerusalem.

After the outbreak of World War I, Eshkol joined a group of young settlers who cultivated land at Rishon Le-Zion and Petach Tikvah, and during this period he became a member of Hapoel Hatzair, the young worker party. In 1918 he joined the Jewish Legion, which aided British forces against Turkey in exchange for a British promise that a Jewish homeland would eventually be established in Palestine. After serving for two years in the 40th Battalion of the Royal Fusiliers, Eshkol was demobilized in 1920 and, with other members of his group, founded Degania Beth, one of the first of the *kibbutzim* (communal farms) in Palestine.

His skills in economics, administration, and diplomacy were soon recognized by Zionist leaders, and during the post-World War I period Eshkol promoted the interests of the Jews of Palestine at home and abroad. He was an elected representative to the first three sessions of the Assembly of Palestine Jewry, and he was a delegate to all Zionist congresses from the twelfth onward, serving as chairman of the settlement committee at several congresses. In 1921 he took part in the founding convention of Histadruth (the General Confederation of Labor) at Haifa, and he became a member of its executive. During the 1920's he went on Histadruth missions to Lithuania and other countries. With the establishment in 1929 of Mapai, the left-of-center workers party of Israel, Eshkol was elected to its central council and, with Ben-Gurion and others, he became a member of its central committee. For a time he also served as the party's secretary.

After Hitler's rise to power in Germany, Eshkol was for three years director of the agricultural settlement section of the Palestine office in Berlin, and he organized the transfer of immigrants and property from Germany to Palestine. With money borrowed from German Jews he bought industrial, agricultural, and irrigation equipment for Palestine; he also helped to establish the Mekorot Water Company Ltd., the housing companies Shikun Ltd. and Amidar Ltd., and the finance company Nir Ltd. During this period Eshkol also was active in Hehalutz, an organization established to train agricultural pioneers for Palestine, and he worked on its behalf in Germany, Poland, and Lithuania.

In 1942 Eshkol became a member of the executive of the Jewish Agency for Palestine, the central Zionist organization. As director of its settlement department he was in charge of bringing Jewish immigrants into Palestine and settling them in the *kibbutzim*. He had his first opportunity to deal with the problems of city workers in 1944, when Ben-Gurion appointed him secretary of the Tel Aviv Labor Council. Long interested in the problems of security, Eshkol helped to build up Haganah, the Jewish military defense organization. He served on its high command and was its treasurer for a number of years. In 1947, during the critical period preceding Israeli national independence, Eshkol was called upon by Ben-Gurion to occupy a central position on the Haganah staff.

Following the establishment of the independent state of Israel on May 14, 1948, Eshkol was appointed director-general of the Ministry of Defense. In 1951 he was designated Minister of Agriculture and Development, and in 1952 he became Minister of Finance. He also served for a time as deputy Prime Minister and as chairman of the cabinet economic committee. When Ben-Gurion temporarily retired from the government in late 1953 Eshkol was favored by many Israelis as his successor, but the Mapai party chose Foreign Minister Moshe Sharett instead.

As Minister of Finance, Eshkol instituted, among other things, a search for oil resources and fostered the development of a petroleum industry. He also announced the completion of a twenty-year "master" plan for development of the nation's mineral resources and the creation of a chemicals industry. He represented Israel at international conferences and meetings of the International Bank and the International Monetary Fund, and he negotiated with American officials for aid in the development of water resources. Over the years Eshkol made a number of trips to the United States to raise funds for Israel through the United Jewish Appeal and the Israel Bond Organization. He inaugurated a plan for the resettlement and rehabilitation of some 20,000 returned Arab refugees, and he helped to institute a program of economic and technical aid to underdeveloped countries of Asia and Africa.

In April 1958 Eshkol announced a nine-point economic plan to consolidate the gains made during Israel's first ten years of independence. The program called for the increase of exports

LEVI ESHKOL

and the encouragement of private industry, and it included provisions for the building of railroads, harbors, and merchant ships, and for increased housing, citrus cultivation, and electric power production. In the summer of 1959 he introduced legislation in the Knesset (Parliament) providing for increased tax exemptions for foreign investors and other measures aimed at attracting more foreign capital to Israel.

Eshkol's flair for compromise was demonstrated in 1961, when at the request of President Isaac Ben-Zvi he conducted negotiations for the formation of a new coalition government to replace the preceding one, which had fallen as a result of a security controversy. Ben-Gurion had failed in his efforts to win over certain splinter parties needed to form a new government, but Eshkol, after several weeks of painstaking negotiations, finally persuaded the leaders of these parties to relax their conditions and to enter a coalition with the dominant Mapai. The new four-party government, headed by Ben-Gurion, was approved by the Knesset on November 2, 1961 by a vote of 63 to 46.

In February 1962 Eshkol announced a new economic policy instituted by the government as a means of increasing exports and obtaining an accommodation with the European Common Market. The central feature of the program was the devaluation of Israeli currency from a previous rate of 1.8 pounds to the dollar to a new rate of three to one. Although the program met with considerable opposition, including a brief walkout by industrial workers, the government survived three motions of no confidence and its economic policy won final approval by a vote of 66 to 43. To implement the new economic measures Eshkol announced in January 1963 that Israel's fiscal policy for the coming year would involve voluntary freezing of prices, wages, and tax rates, and reductions in government expenditures.

On June 16, 1963 Ben-Gurion announced his resignation from the Prime Ministership. Al-

ESHKOL, LEVI—*Continued*

though he had reportedly intended for some time to retire from politics, his decision was undoubtedly motivated by a number of factors. His conciliatory policy toward West Germany had undergone considerable criticism, and the internal situation in Israel was complicated by the disclosure of activities of German rocket scientists in Egypt, the related resignation of Israel's chief security officer, and the controversial visit of former West German Defense Minister Franz Josef Strauss to Israel in May 1963.

Israel's President, Zalman Shazar, formally designated Eshkol Prime Minister on June 19, 1963, after the secretariat of Mapai had voted to draft Eshkol for this office, with the full backing of Ben-Gurion. On June 24, 1963 Eshkol presented his cabinet to the Knesset and designated it "a government of continuity," representing essentially the policies of the Ben-Gurion regime. The cabinet was approved by the Knesset on June 26 by a vote of 64 to 43. Upon taking office as Prime Minister, Eshkol relinquished his portfolio as Minister of Finance and assumed the Ministry of Defense, which had previously also been held by Ben-Gurion.

Israel's principal long-range internal objective, according to Eshkol, is the cultivation of the Negev desert in the south. One major domestic problem facing the country is the continued vast influx of Jewish immigrants from Asia and North Africa, whose cultural backgrounds differ markedly from that of the previously dominant European Jews. On the international scene Eshkol is expected to continue to follow a policy of friendship with Western European nations, cautious rapprochement with West Germany, and the building of cordial relations with African and Asian countries. He has also adopted a less critical attitude than Ben-Gurion toward American Zionists. While he sees the need for continued intensive armament under present conditions, he has offered to meet with Arab leaders "at any time anywhere," to discuss an overall settlement of outstanding sources of conflict.

Although Eshkol's principles are essentially those of Ben-Gurion, the two men differ markedly in personality. Ben-Gurion is primarily a theorist and a visionary, Eshkol a man of action with an eye for detail and a greater capacity for compromise than his predecessor. In addition to occupying his political offices Eshkol also serves on the board of directors of several companies. He is fluent in Hebrew, Yiddish, German, Russian, and English, and he commands some knowledge of French and Latin. Over the years he has written many articles, notably on agricultural colonization; some of them are included in his book *Be-hevle Hitnahlut* (Problems of Settlement), published in Tel-Aviv in 1958.

Levi Eshkol's first marriage, to Rivka Marshak, by whom he has one daughter, Noa, ended in divorce. His second wife, the former Elisheva Kaplan, who had been a leader in Israel's labor movement, is no longer living. He has three daughters from this marriage: Dvora, Tama, and Ofra. Two of his daughters are married, one is a sergeant in the Israeli army, and another is a teacher of the modern dance. A fairly tall, husky

man, Eshkol can be gregarious and jovial, but he has also been known to show anger and impatience on occasion. Although he sometimes works as much as twenty hours a day he is not an ascetic, and he likes to indulge in good food and an occasional cognac. He is fond of Yiddish jokes, Hebrew and Russian poetry, novels, motion pictures, and the theater. Eshkol lives alone in a stone house in Jerusalem, overlooking the hills of Judea.

References

N Y Herald Tribune II p5 Jl 28 '63 por
N Y Post Mag p2 Jl 7 '63 por
N Y Times p19 N 3 '61 por; p2 Je 25 '63 por
International Who's Who, 1962-63
International Year Book and Statesmen's Who's Who, 1963
Who's Who in Israel, 1962
Who's Who in World Jewry (1955)

FERGUSON, GARLAND S(EVIER) May 30, 1873-Apr. 12, 1963 Former chairman of the Federal Trade Commission (1927-49). See *Current Biography* (July) 1949.

Obituary

N Y Times p19 Ap 13 '63

FINNEY, ALBERT May 9, 1936- British actor
Address: c/o London Artists Ltd., 25 Gilbert St., London, W.1, England

The versatile and nonconformist Albert Finney, who has been called "the most brilliant actor of his age in the English-speaking world" and "the next Olivier," chose his stage career almost by chance. An actor of formidable range, Finney learned to take his profession seriously at the Royal Academy of Dramatic Art in London. After a period of apprenticeship at the Birmingham Repertory Theatre and the Shakespeare Memorial Theatre, he reached early stardom in the play *Billy Liar.* Finney's second film, *Saturday Night and Sunday Morning,* brought him world fame at the age of twenty-five. He has since consolidated his reputation by contributing acting of virtuosity, concentration, and depth to a variety of roles, including the title parts in John Osborne's Brechtian play *Luther* and the motion picture version of Fielding's *Tom Jones.*

Of lower middle-class background, Albert Finney was born on May 9, 1936 in Salford, Lancashire, an industrial suburb on the fringes of Manchester. He has two sisters. His father, also named Albert Finney, is a bookie; his mother is the former Alice Hobson. Finney grew up near the local racetrack and lived only a few streets away from the playwright Shelagh Delaney. At Salford Grammar School his principal interests were athletics and acting: he played cricket, football, and tennis and, between the ages of twelve and seventeen, appeared in some fifteen school plays. Even then he showed a precociously professional approach to acting. Once, when assigned to play a Negro in a school production, he spent hours at the Salford docks studying the mannerisms and speech patterns of West Indian workers.

Academic work had much less appeal for Finney, who twice failed examinations for the British equivalent of a high school diploma. After his second failure Finney's headmaster suggested that he try for a place at the Royal Academy of Dramatic Art in London. Finney had never considered acting as a career and had never heard of RADA. But, having no alternative ambitions and attracted by the idea of student life in London, he applied for and received the Gerald Lawrence Scholarship for a two-year course at the academy.

"I went to RADA mainly because I loved the idea of coming to London and being a student," Finney said recently. "To me a student life meant the chance to get away from home, meant parties and clubs and fun. I soon got over that idea. And I found that acting was really right for me." He appeared in a number of academy productions in character parts and attracted much attention for his performance as Troilus in a modern-dress version of Shakespeare's *Troilus and Cressida*. After seeing the production the critic Kenneth Tynan described Finney as "a smouldering young Spencer Tracy." In his last year at RADA he received the Emile Littler prize as the student having the most outstanding character and aptitude for the theater.

Leaving RADA at the end of 1955, Finney turned down some lucrative offers, including one from the Rank motion picture empire, to join the Birmingham Repertory Theatre. His two years at Birmingham provided him with the broad experience that he sought. Finney's first appearance on the professional stage was in April 1956, when he played Decius Brutus in *Julius Caesar*. Notable among his many performances at Birmingham were those in the title roles of *Hamlet* and *Henry V*, as Francis Archer in *The Beaux Stratagem*, as Face in *The Alchemist*, and as Malcolm in *The Lizard on the Rock*.

Finney's *Henry V* was unanimously admired, but critical opinion differed about his performance in the title role of *Macbeth*. The role happens to be Finney's favorite, but Charles Laughton, who saw his performance at Birmingham, is reported to have said that it was "bloody terrible." Nevertheless, Laughton was enough impressed by Finney's potentialities to offer him a part in the play that he was then casting. This was *The Party*, by the actress Jane Arden, which Laughton directed and in which he starred. It concerned an alcoholic who, by returning unexpectedly from a sanitarium, ruins his daughter's seventeenth birthday party. Finney played Soya Marshall, the daughter's boy friend, who brings about a family reconciliation.

The Party, which opened on May 28, 1958 at the New Theatre, brought Finney for the first time to London's West End. He was favorably mentioned for his performance, but the play itself was not well received and expired after a short run. With characteristic singlemindedness Finney rejected financially attractive offers in favor of another apprenticeship season, this time at the Shakespeare Memorial Theatre, Stratford-on-Avon. Joining the Stratford company for its

ALBERT FINNEY

hundredth anniversary season in 1959, he played Edgar in *King Lear*, Cassio in *Othello*, and Lysander in *A Midsummer Night's Dream*. During the same season, while understudying Sir Laurence Olivier for the title part in *Coriolanus*, he went on in the role for some weeks when Olivier hurt a leg. His vigorous and original interpretation made a great impression and was warmly praised by Olivier himself.

The Stratford season was nevertheless an unhappy time for Finney, who has since referred to it as "a long dark tunnel." His marriage broke up, and an attack of peritonitis cost him the lead in Willis Hall's *The Long and the Short and the Tall*, a part which had been written with Finney in mind. This trying period ended when Finney exchanged Shakespearean doublet and hose for quite different roles in two contemporary productions. One, in which he worked again with Sir Laurence Olivier, was Finney's first motion picture. He appeared for about one minute as the soldier son of a third-rate vaudeville performer in the screen version of John Osborne's play *The Entertainer*. The infinitesimal role marked Finney's first contact with Osborne's work and with the young director Tony Richardson.

Soon afterward, in January 1960, Finney opened in a new musical at London's Royal Court Theatre, the headquarters of the current renaissance of realism in the British theater. He appeared as Ted, the gang leader, in *The Lily White Boys*, Harry Cookson's sardonic musical about the "reformation" of a teen-age gang. Discovering that graft pays better than old-fashioned crime, the Lily White Boys cheerfully embrace respectability. Ted becomes a prosperous Member of Parliament, and the gang members take their place on a committee on juvenile delinquency. Most critics found the play chiefly interesting as a showcase for Finney's talents, and it had a short run.

(*Continued next page*)

FINNEY, ALBERT—*Continued*

Nor was Finney altogether fortunate in his next vehicle. This was *Billy Liar,* by Keith Waterhouse and Willis Hall, which began its run at the Cambridge Theatre, London, in September 1960. In the title part, Finney played a twenty-year-old undertaker's clerk living with his parents in a drab industrial town. Finding his own life intolerable, Billy Liar has substituted fantasy for reality, and the play traces the complications brought about by his compulsive lying. Albert Finney kept the show going by the authority and virtuosity of his acting.

Whatever the merits of the play, Albert Finney made it clear during the run of *Billy Liar* that he would not tolerate inattention. Faced one night with a noisy audience, he stopped suddenly and said: "I'm up here working, so if you won't shut up, go home, and if you won't shut up or go home, I'm going home." Reportedly, no one went home, and the audience remained silent for the rest of the performance. During this period Finney demonstrated his independence in another context, when the producer Sam Spiegel offered him a huge salary and the coveted title role in *Lawrence of Arabia.* But the offer was tied to a long-term contract and, unwilling to become a Hollywood property, Finney turned it down.

Meanwhile, during 1960, Finney had made his second film. It was produced by Woodfall Films, the company formed by John Osborne and Tony Richardson, and based on Alan Sillitoe's novel *Saturday Night and Sunday Morning.* Released in 1961, the film immediately established Finney as an international star. Finney played the young Nottingham factory worker Arthur Seaton, a tough and antisocial product of the Welfare State, who nevertheless possesses a kind of virtue in his stubborn self-reliance. Finney's performance, one of the principal reasons for the film's great success, was described by some critics as "alarming" in its realism. In *Albert Finney,* wrote Archer Winsten in the New York *Post* (April 4, 1961), the film presented "an all-male, high-humor anger the exact likes of which has never before been seen on a screen." *Time* magazine (March 31, 1961) called Finney "at the moment the most brilliant actor of his age in the English-speaking world."

Finney's association with Tony Richardson, begun in *The Entertainer* and *Saturday Night and Sunday Morning* (which Richardson produced), continued. Finney's next role, in John Osborne's play *Luther,* directed by Richardson, was unlike anything he had done before. Osborne's controversial and Brechtian play about the German religious reformer, with Finney in the title role, tried out in Nottingham in June 1961 and opened at the Theatre of the Nations Festival in Paris, with the English Stage Company, the following month. It was then exhibited at the Royal Court Theatre and the Edinburgh Festival before it settled down at the Phoenix Theatre in London. Although critics differed violently about the merits of the play itself, which was obviously modeled on Brecht's *Galileo,* Finney's performance won almost universal acclaim for its "brilliance," "depth," "concentration," and "power." In *Plays and Players*

(September 1961), Caryl Brahms wrote: "This was the most convincing performance that I can remember ever to have seen." *Luther* opened on Broadway, with Finney in the title role, on September 25, 1963.

Equally high praise greeted Finney's most recent stage performance, in Pirandello's *Henry IV* at the Citizen's Theatre, Glasgow, Scotland. Elizabeth Meldrum, writing in the *Guardian* (March 13, 1963), said that Finney's acting gave Glasgow theatergoers "a dose of theatrical excitement from which they are not likely to recover in a hurry" with "an extraordinary, a superb performance to which not only his audience but his colleagues in the cast responded."

In the summer of 1963 Finney was working on a Metro-Goldwyn-Mayer remake of Emlyn Williams' *Night Must Fall* and had completed a film called *The Victors,* in which he plays a Russian soldier. John Osborne's adaptation of Fielding's novel *Tom Jones,* directed for the screen by Tony Richardson, with Finney in the title role, has been scheduled for release in the United States in October 1963. In England, where it was released in June 1963, *Tom Jones* has had an excellent reception and Finney has been praised for his engaging and intelligent performance as the hero. His acting in this role brought him the designation "best male actor" at the 1963 Venice Film Festival.

Although Finney has appeared in several television plays, he has no affection for the medium. In 1961 he was named the "most promising newcomer" by the Varsity Club for his performance in *Saturday Night and Sunday Morning,* and the same year he received the Theatre of the Nations award as the best actor of the season for his *Luther.* Finney was greatly impressed by the early films of Marlon Brando, especially by *On the Waterfront,* and some critics have detected an element of "methodizing" in his acting. Most critics agree, however, that Finney's talent is not the product of technique alone. He has an exceptional gift for concentration, a high degree of natural stage intelligence, and a capacity for meticulous preparation. Required to throw an epileptic fit in *Luther,* for example, he indulged in long discussions with a neurologist about the symptoms of epilepsy. To his irritation, Finney has been repeatedly named as the most likely successor to Sir Laurence Olivier as England's greatest actor, but he insists that he prefers to be known as "the next Finney," not "the next Olivier."

In 1957 Albert Finney married the actress Jane Wenham. He has a son, Simon, by that marriage, which ended in divorce in 1961. Finney is about six feet tall and has blue eyes and auburn hair. An article in the *New Statesman* (July 28, 1961) spoke of his "rough, putty face, with the oddly sensitive mouth, that lumbering grace of gesture, like a delicate footballer," and Donald W. LaBadie in *Show* magazine (June 1963) referred to him as "the prototype of the prole next door." Finney, who is said to be prodigally generous, believes in traveling light, unencumbered by possessions or by people. In the past he could put all his private property into a single suitcase, and he often changed his address.

Allergic to being treated as a celebrity, Finney refuses to act like one. His offstage dress is casual, and he relaxes with judo, weightlifting, dancing, golf, and football. Since the age of fifteen he has been smoking cigars. He enjoys listening to music, playing the guitar, following the adventures of Pogo in the comic strips, and reading books for background to the characters he plays. He is a member of the Church of England.

Finney often changes his mind about the comparative merits of acting on the stage or in films. During the shooting of *Tom Jones* on location he told Elinor Klein of the New York *Herald Tribune*: "At the moment I prefer the theater. . . . An actor is very much alone in films. . . . In the theater the actor is being told when he is or is not communicating immediately and that's what acting is about, really—communicating." His favorite roles are Macbeth and Henry V, both of which he has successfully played. For the time being he is staying away from the role of Hamlet, feeling that he does not respond to it as he should, although he reads the play at least once a year. He betrayed at least one clue to the reason for his potential greatness as an actor when he confided to Donald W. LaBadie (*Show*, June 1963): "There's a side of me that's always taking note of the world around me, of how I'm reacting. It's part of the thing that makes me an actor. But do you know what the other part is? I think I'm trying to find something to get lost in. I'm seeking moments of obliviousness. I never seem to find them in real life."

References

Who's Who, 1963
Who's Who in the Theatre (1961)

FISCHER, BOBBY Mar. 9, 1943- Grand master of chess
Address: b. c/o Robert Rosen, NRB Associates, 485 Madison Ave., New York 22; h. 560 Lincoln Place, Brooklyn, N.Y.

Acknowledged to be the "strongest chess player in the United States" and also perhaps the most controversial, Bobby Fischer is convinced that he can defeat all comers and that he will some day win the world championship, which has not been held by an American for more than 100 years. A chess player since the age of six, Fischer has won the United States championship five times. He first won it in January 1958, when he was fourteen. He was admitted to the ranks of the élite of chess players in September 1958, when he became the youngest international grand master of chess in the history of the game. Since then he has more than held his own among champions at the chess capitals of the world.

Robert James Fischer was born in Chicago on March 9 (one source gives March 12), 1943. His father, a biophysicist, is of German family background. His mother, Mrs. Regina Fischer, who is Jewish, was born in Switzerland and is a former schoolteacher and a registered nurse. Bobby Fischer spent his early years in Oregon, California, and Arizona. Because his parents were divorced when he was

Wide World

BOBBY FISCHER

two years old, he was brought up by his mother and his sister, Joan, who is six years older than he. Mrs. Fischer worked to support the family, and for a time she taught elementary school in Los Angeles and in Phoenix, Arizona. The boy began his schooling at Mobile, near Gila Bend in the western Arizona desert. In 1948 he moved with his mother and sister to Brooklyn, New York, where Mrs. Fischer took up the study of nursing.

At an early age Bobby Fischer mastered puzzles and games that challenged the imagination. He first encountered chess at the age of six, when his sister bought an inexpensive chess set and taught him the basic rules. At first he regarded chess as just another game, but his interest was aroused when in the following year he came upon an old book describing chess games. In January 1951 Fischer attended a chess exhibition at the Brooklyn Public Library. Although he was beaten within fifteen minutes by Max Pavey, an international chess master, his playing impressed Carmine Nigro, the president of the Brooklyn Chess Club, who offered to give him lessons in the game.

Fischer became a regular visitor at the Brooklyn Chess Club, where he soon defeated average adult players. When he was ten he played at the Marshall Chess Club in Manhattan; by the time he was twelve he had been invited to join the Manhattan Chess Club, where he held his own among the best chess players in the United States and became known to newsmen by such nicknames as "the Sweatshirt Kid," "the Boy Robot," or "the Corduroy Killer."

When he was in the fourth grade Fischer received a scholarship to the Community-Woodward School in Brooklyn, a moderately progressive school, where his individuality and preoccupation with chess were encouraged. Although his grades were generally good he showed little interest in academic studies. However, he

FISCHER, BOBBY—*Continued*

was determined to win in competitive sports. His main interest remained chess, and he devoured every book and magazine on the game that he could find, including the Russian chess publication *Shakhmaty*. At Erasmus High School in Brooklyn, Fischer excelled in Spanish, mathematics, and the sciences, but regarded his teachers as "all mental cases" and had few friends his own age.

Fischer's early performances in junior chess tournaments were not particularly spectacular. However, his early setbacks made him more determined than ever to win, and at the age of thirteen he became the youngest player ever to win the national junior championship. In August 1957, at Cleveland, Ohio, Fischer won the tournament for the United States open championship in a field of 175 players, finishing in a tie with the United States champion, Arthur B. Bisguier. The victory enabled him to enter the United States Chess Federation's championship meet at the Manhattan Chess Club, and on January 7, 1958 he dethroned Bisguier as United States champion. His victory won him the Lessing J. Rosenwald and Frank J. Marshall trophies and qualified him to enter the interzonal competition, held in Yugoslavia in August and September 1958. Having won his passage to Europe as a result of his appearance on Garry Moore's television program, *I've Got a Secret,* Fischer made a side-trip to Russia upon the invitation of the Soviet government, before going on to Yugoslavia.

Making his international debut at Potoroz, Yugoslavia, Fischer tied for fifth place and was thus among the six winners of the interzonal tournament, one of whom would eventually play the world champion for the international title. As a result, Fischer was named an international grand master of chess, the youngest player ever to earn this distinction. Back in New York, Fischer successfully defended his United States championship in the Rosenwald trophy tournament in January 1959.

Fischer tied for third place at the international chess tournament at Mar del Plata, Argentina, in April 1959 and at another tournament in the following month at Santiago, Chile. The Jubilee tournament at Zurich, Switzerland in June 1959 resulted in another third-place tie for Fischer. Competing in the world championship challengers' tournament at Bled, Zagreb, and Belgrade, Yugoslavia in September and October 1959, Fischer tied for fifth and sixth place with Svetozar Gligoric of Yugoslavia. When the annual national championship tournament opened in New York in December 1959 Fischer at first refused to take part, protesting against the pairing of players in private rather than openly, in the presence of the participants. He changed his mind, however, and went on to defend successfully his United States title for the third time.

Fischer scored another triumph when he tied for first place with Boris Spassky of the Soviet Union at a tournament at Mar del Plata, Argentina, in April 1960. In October and November 1960 he took part in the Chess Olympics at Leipzig, East Germany, as a member of the United States team, which finished second

to the Soviet Union. On January 2, 1961 he won his fourth consecutive United States chess championship.

In July 1961 Fischer began a scheduled sixteen-game match with Samuel Reshevsky. Since Reshevsky, an Orthodox Jew, would not play on the Sabbath, the twelfth game, which had originally been scheduled for Saturday evening, August 13, was postponed to 11 A.M. the following day. Contending that he was not used to playing in the morning, Fischer refused to appear, and the game was considered a forfeit. When he failed to show up on the following day for the thirteenth game on the grounds that the forfeit was illegal, the entire match was called a forfeiture, and Reshevsky was declared the winner by default. (In April 1962 Fischer sued for resumption of the match with Reshevsky, lest his "reputation as the most skillful and proficient chess player in the United States be irreparably damaged and tarnished.")

At the international chess masters' tournament at Bled, Yugoslavia in October 1961 Fischer finished second to Mikhail Tal, although he did not lose a single game. In December 1961 he refused to take part in that year's United States chess championship tournament, reportedly because the prize of $1,000 was not big enough for him. In March 1962 Fischer won the world interzonal tournament in Stockholm. The victory qualified him to play in the candidates' tournament, the longest and most difficult event in chess and the last step before the world championship.

Playing in a field of eight at Willemstad, Curaçao, in May and June 1962, Fischer tied for fifth place in the candidates' tournament, behind the four Russian contenders. He was thus removed from competition for the world title for the immediate future. After the tournament he openly charged the Russians with using collusive tactics and contended that under the rules of the Fédération Internationale de Échecs (FIDE), the governing body of world chess, only a Russian could win the world championship. He declared that in the future he would refuse to play in any tournament sponsored by FIDE. His charges were published in *Sports Illustrated* (August 20, 1962) and reprinted in several languages. In September 1962 FIDE announced the adoption of new rules aimed at preventing draws in international tournaments, thus making collusion more difficult. FIDE spokesmen denied, however, that Fischer's charges had anything to do with the decision to make these changes.

Fischer first encountered Mikhail Botvinnik, then the world champion, in October 1962 at the Chess Olympics finals at Varna, Bulgaria, in a game that ended in a draw. The series was won by the Russians, and the Americans finished in fourth place. (Botvinnik lost the world championship to Tigran Petrosian, another Soviet grand master, on May 20, 1963.) On January 3, 1963 Fischer regained the United States championship, winning this title for the fifth time. In July 1963 Fischer won the Western open championship at Bay City, Michigan, playing in a field of 160 contestants.

Fischer's chess-playing is characterized by a vast book-knowledge of the game, a rapid sight of the board, an ability to map out effective plans, a flair for discovering new moves, a mastery of thousands of possible openings, a brilliant endgame technique, and a fierce determination to win at all costs. He is at times reckless, sacrificing valuable pieces to gain a more favorable position. An avid student of the techniques of past and present masters, Fischer himself contributes to the literature of chess by writing articles for chess publications. His book, *Games of Chess,* was published by Simon and Schuster in 1959. Erasmus Hall High School, which he left during his junior year, at the age of sixteen, presented him a gold medal for his accomplishments in chess, in January 1959.

In making his way in the world of chess Fischer has had considerable moral support from his mother. In letters to the New York *Herald Tribune* (August 6, 1959) and *Sports Illustrated* (August 17, 1959) Mrs. Fischer appealed for financial aid to enable her son to compete in international tournaments. The letters brought some favorable results. In the fall of 1960 Mrs. Fischer picketed the White House and the offices of the American Chess Foundation and went on a six-day hunger strike in an appeal to provide more funds for the United States team in the 1960 Chess Olympics.

Tall and broad-shouldered, Bobby Fischer is six feet two inches in height. He has light-brown, wavy hair, hazel eyes, sharp features, and a pale complexion. One of his few indulgences is a huge wardrobe of custom-made clothes. Although he derives a substantial income from chess, he prefers a simple life. Fischer now lives alone in the four-room walkup apartment in Brooklyn in which he grew up. (His mother is remarried and makes her home in England). Fischer does not smoke, but he occasionally drinks imported beer, and he likes German food. His interests aside from chess include palmistry, Viennese music, Dixieland jazz, skiing, table-tennis, the stage, and movies. Fischer would some day like to enter the real estate business, after winning the world championship.

References

Harper 224:49+ Ja '62 por
Holiday 33:125+ My '63 por
N Y Post Mag p10 Ap 13 '58 por
N Y Times Mag p38+ F 24 '58 pors
Sat R 46:22+ Ap 27 '63 por
Sports Illus 14:54+ Ja 23 '61 pors

FISTER, GEORGE M(ORGAN) May 22, 1892- Urologist; organization official
Address: b. Suite E-3, 950 25th St., Ogden, Utah; h. 3359 Taylor St., Ogden, Utah

During 1962-63 the president of the American Medical Association was Dr. George M. Fister, who has been practising as a urologist in Ogden, Utah since 1928. When he succeeded Dr. Leonard W. Larson in June 1962 for a one-year term he became the first Utahan to hold this post. Fister was president-elect of the AMA in 1961-62, and he is a past president of the Utah State Medical Association. Like his predecessor, Dr. Larson, he is an opponent of programs for medical care for the aged that would be financed by contributions under the Social Security system. A recent summary of his position stated: "Dr. Fister is for voluntary health care for all regardless of age. He is opposed to taxation by compulsion for medical benefits for any group. He is for medical care for everyone regardless of their ability to pay, and need should be the underlying factor in medical care. It should be an individual problem and not a group problem. In the aged group, for instance, those over 65 should be treated individually and not as a group. The individual should be treated with dignity and respect and receive the best medical care in the world on a voluntary basis."

The only son of George and Jennie (Morgan) Fister, George Morgan Fister was born on May 22, 1892 in Logan, Utah. He had three sisters, of whom only one is now living. Their father, who came originally from Hartford, Connecticut, had joined the United States Cavalry in 1876. He was sent to Fort Bridger, Wyoming and liked the West so much that he decided to remain there after his discharge. He became a merchant of harness and saddlery at Logan, Utah.

George Morgan Fister worked with his father as an errand boy and apprentice. He attended the local elementary school and between 1907 and 1913 studied first at the Brigham Young College in Logan and then at the Utah State Agricultural College (now Utah State University). Utah State, where he majored in mathematics and chemistry, awarded him the B.S. degree in 1913. For most of his undergraduate years he was on the honor roll, and for two years he was manager of the football team. In 1912-13, as a senior, he taught two algebra classes.

In 1913-14 Fister taught mathematics as an instructor at Weber College in Ogden, Utah, and it was during this year that, inspired by his interest in physiological chemistry, he decided to take up medicine. He studied at the University of Chicago, from which he obtained a second B.S. degree in 1916, and at Rush Medical College. Fister supported himself while attending school by selling shoes on Saturdays and knit-goods in the summer and by doing laboratory work in the evenings for Dr. Herman L. Kretchmer, a professor of urology at Rush Medical College. As a result of his association with the department of urology and with Dr. Kretchmer, he chose to make the specialty of urology his own. In December 1917, while still a medical student, Fister enlisted in the United States Naval Reserve for World War I service and was designated a pharmacist's mate. He was never called to active service, however, and was able to continue working for the M.D. degree, which he obtained from Rush Medical College in the spring of 1918.

Fister interned at the Henry Ford Hospital in Detroit, Michigan in 1918-19 and then practised general medicine in Brigham City, Utah for four years. While in Brigham City he served as a captain in the medical detachment of the 116th Cavalry, Utah National Guard. His desire to do special work in urology led him to return to the Henry Ford Hospital, where he worked from 1923 to 1926, and to the Rush Medical College and its affiliate, Presbyterian Hospital, where he worked from 1926 to 1928. In the latter two years

Peter Berkeley's Lainson Studio
DR. GEORGE M. FISTER

Fister practised urology in the out-patient department of Rush Medical College and assisted Dr. Kretchmer at his office and at Presbyterian Hospital. In 1928 he returned to Utah to establish at Ogden a practice in urology that has since been interrupted only by special postgraduate work at London and Vienna in 1936-37.

For the past twenty years Fister has lectured in urology at the University of Utah's College of Medicine in Salt Lake City. He has written many articles, more than thirty of which are scientific papers on the diseases of the genitourinary tract. In 1955 he and Dr. George M. Cochran received the first prize for laboratory research from the American Urological Association—a blue ribbon that was awarded for an exhibit accompanying their paper "Electron Microscope Studies of Human Urine," published in the *Journal of Applied Physics* in 1955. Fister has been affiliated in Ogden, Utah with the Thomas D. Dee Memorial Hospital since 1926, the State Tuberculosis Sanitarium since 1938, and St. Benedict's Hospital since 1941.

In accordance with his desire to be of service to the medical profession Fister has been active in many professional organizations on the local, state, and national levels. He is a founder and past secretary and president of the Ogden Surgical Society and a past president of the Weber County (Utah) Medical Society. He was a counselor from Weber County and then president of the Utah State Medical Association. After serving as a Utah delegate to the American Medical Association from 1949 to 1957, he was elected in June 1957 to the AMA board of trustees, on which he served four years.

Fister was for three years, from 1958 to 1961, the chairman of the AMA council on legislative activities, which analyzes all legislation introduced in Congress that pertains to medicine, medical care, or health, and he helped to form the American Medical Political Action Committee. He was a leader in pressing for the adoption of the Keogh-Smathers bill, which would permit professional men and other self-employed to set up pension plans comparable to those offered by commercial and industrial enterprises to their employees. While a trustee, Fister also had an important part in establishing the AMA Guarantee Loan Fund for medical students, interns, and residents.

When in June 1961 the North Dakota pathologist Dr. Leonard W. Larson was installed as president of the AMA, Dr. Fister was chosen as president-elect. He became the 116th president of the doctors' organization on June 26, 1962. Like his predecessor and his successor, Dr. Edward R. Annis, Dr. Fister opposes the Kennedy administration's bill for medical care of the aged through the Social Security system and favors the existing Kerr-Mills Act, which provides for federal matching funds to states for an expansion of their programs for medical aid to the aged. In his address to AMA delegates as incoming president Fister declared: "I want to assure . . . the citizens of this country that during the next year there will be no letup in our campaign to preserve the high standards of our voluntary, free-choice, medical-care system. There can be no compromise on this principle."

From 1957 to 1962 Fister was a director of the National Association of Blue Shield Plans. A member and past president of the Western section of the American Urological Society, he belonged to the association's scientific awards committee from 1952 to 1958. He is an honorary civilian consultant to the Surgeon General of the United States Air Force and from 1958 to 1961 was a member of the health resources advisory committee of the Office of Civil and Defense Mobilization. In addition, he is on the medical advisory staff of the hospital ship SS *Hope* and a director of the Utah division of the American Cancer Society.

Fister belongs to the medical fraternity Phi Beta Pi, the American College of Surgeons, the American Society for the Study of Sterility, the American Medical Writers Association, the American Association of Railroad Surgeons, and the American Ordnance Association. He is a diplomate of the American Board of Urology and a member of the New York Academy of Sciences, the World Medical Association, and the American Geriatrics Society. In addition, Fister serves on the board of regents of the University of Utah and is a past trustee of Utah State University and of the Utah State School for Deaf and Blind. He belongs to the Utah Historical Society. In 1951 he was cited by the University of Chicago alumni association for public service, and in 1962 he received the distinguished service award from the university's medical alumni association. He also holds an award (1961) for outstanding community service by a physician from the Utah State Medical Association.

On September 23, 1914 George M. Fister married Ruby L. Ostler of Salt Lake City. They have two children, Franklin and Mary (Mrs. William K. Martin), and eight grandchildren. Fister has been described as a quiet, warm, friendly man. He is nearly five feet ten inches in height, weighs 175 pounds, and has blue-green eyes and graying brown hair. He is a baseball fan, and he enjoys "fly fishing on the clear, crystal springs of the West, particularly for rainbow trout." Another of his hobbies is writing short articles and stories about subjects that interest him, and he has amassed several loose-leaf folders of such compositions over the years. Fister has been characterized as a "conservative Republican . . . with a belief that all persons, regardless of occupation or profession, should exercise the basic right of citizenship and demonstrate it by a willingness to work." He is a member of the Church of Jesus Christ of Latter Day Saints, and he belongs to the Ogden Chamber of Commerce, the Ogden Rotary Club, the Fort Douglas Country Club, and the Weber Club.

References

N Y Times p21 Je 27 '62 por
Utah State Alumnus 15:1+ F '62 por
American Medical Directory, 1962
Who's Who in America, 1962-63

FLAGSTAD, KIRSTEN July 12, 1895-Dec. 7, 1962 Norwegian operatic soprano; noted for Wagnerian roles; gave many opera and concert performances in Europe, United States, and Australia; made her debut in 1935. See *Current Biography* (May) 1947.

Obituary

N Y Times p35 Ap 1 '63

FOYLE, WILLIAM ALFRED Mar. 4, 1885-June 5, 1963 Co-founder, with his brother Gilbert, of one of the world's largest bookstores, Foyle's in London. See *Current Biography* (June) 1954.

Obituary

N Y Times p35 Je 6 '63

FRANKLIN, JOHN HOPE Jan. 2, 1915- University professor; historian
Address: b. Brooklyn College, Brooklyn 10, N.Y.; h. 1885 New York Ave., Brooklyn 10, N.Y.

The accomplishments of John Hope Franklin as a Negro teacher, historian, and scholar take on added significance when viewed against the background of the American advance in civil rights during the postwar years. In 1964 Franklin is slated to leave Brooklyn College to become professor in American History at the University of Chicago. He owes his international recognition to his books on American history, including *From Slavery to Freedom* (1947) and *The Militant South* (1956). He is also known for his work in the classrooms of Fisk University, Howard University, Brooklyn College, Cambridge University, and other schools, and for his services in professional, civic, and governmental organizations. As he writes his history of American Negroes, he has to take into account his own career.

The son of a prominent Tulsa lawyer who was also one of the first Negroes to practise law in Oklahoma, John Hope Franklin was born on January 2, 1915 in Rentiesville, Okla-

homa to Buck Colbert and Mollie Lee (Parker) Franklin. He has two sisters, Mrs. Waldo E. Jones, a teacher in Tulsa, and Mrs. Paul McEwen, an investigator with the metropolitan police in Washington, D.C.; his brother, Buck Colbert Franklin, Jr., died in 1947.

When Franklin's father set up his law practice in Tulsa in 1921, his office was burned down by race rioters. He later became the first Negro in his state to sit on a United States district court bench, having been appointed a master in chancery to hear a dispute between members of a Negro church and their pastor. He argued cases before the Oklahoma state supreme court, the Oklahoma criminal court of appeals, and the United States Supreme Court. "My father scorned segregation as a mark of indignity," Franklin has said (*Time*, January 11, 1963). "He paid no attention to signs marked 'Negro' and 'White.' He went where he pleased, mingling with people like any other man."

Franklin attended the Booker T. Washington High School in Tulsa, from which he graduated in 1931. His favorite extracurricular activities there, debating and singing, continued to occupy much of his free time after he entered Fisk University in Nashville, Tennessee, where he held a freshman scholarship and an Alpha Phi Alpha scholarship. At Fisk he also served as president of the student government and of his fraternity and was employed as secretary to the librarian and a helper in the university dining hall. An excellent student, held in "complete fascination" by history, his major subject, he was elected to Phi Beta Kappa and graduated with the B.A. degree, *magna cum laude,* in 1935.

With the encouragement of his professor of history at Fisk, Theodore S. Currier, Franklin went on to graduate courses at Harvard University and obtained his M.A. degree in history in 1936. He returned to Fisk to teach as a substitute in the department of history in 1936-37, but then resumed work at Harvard, studying under an Edward Austin Fellowship in 1937-38 and a Julius Rosenwald Fund Fellowship from 1937 to 1939. He was awarded his Ph.D. degree in history in 1941.

Meanwhile, in 1939, Franklin had accepted a position as instructor in history at St. Augustine's College in Raleigh, North Carolina. During his four years there he also carried on research in original sources on the legal status and economic and social position of the Negro in North Carolina before the Civil War. He published his findings in several articles, including "The Free Negro in the Economic Life of North Carolina" (*North Carolina Historical Review,* July and October 1942) and "Slaves Virtually Free in Ante-Bellum North Carolina" (*Journal of Negro History,* July 1943), and in his book *The Free Negro in North Carolina, 1790-1860* (Univ. of North Carolina Press, 1943). George Streator in *Commonweal* (July 26, 1943) praised his study as "an admirable piece of work," noting that Franklin went "deeper into social and economic factors dragging the free Negro down than many older scholars."

(*Continued next page*)

JOHN HOPE FRANKLIN

Moving from Raleigh to Durham in 1943, Franklin became professor of history at North Carolina College, where he taught for another four years. In 1947 he left North Carolina for Washington, D.C. to take up a new post as professor of history at Howard University. While teaching at Howard he also acted as an adviser to the National Association for the Advancement of Colored People and helped draw up the brief that the association submitted to the United States Supreme Court on segregation in public schools, which the court later outlawed in its historic decision of 1954.

The publication in 1947 of *From Slavery to Freedom: A History of American Negroes* (Knopf), which became a leading college textbook, enhanced Franklin's reputation as a scholar. As he explained in his preface, his effort to consider the forces affecting the development of the Negro in America "involved a continuous recognition of the mainstream of American history and the relationship of the Negro to it." In the opinion of Roi Ottley (New York *Times Book Review* (October 12, 1947), except for a discussion of the Negro in Canada, *From Slavery to Freedom* was a "bulky, unwieldy, conventional history with the studied scholarship of a doctoral thesis." Ottley, however, admired Franklin's forthrightness, as did several other critics, who felt moreover that his sound factual grasp of his subject, his insight, his balanced presentation, and lack of prejudice ensured his book a lasting place among American historical writings. In a second, revised and enlarged, edition (1957), Franklin included the developments of nine post-World War II years, especially important for the American Negro.

While still teaching at Howard, Franklin wrote *The Militant South, 1800-1860*, published in 1956 by the Belknap Press of Harvard University Press. The only other manuscript by a Negro scholar to be published in the Harvard

Historical Series had been W. E. B. Du Bois's study on the slave trade. Unlike Franklin's history textbook, which offered little new material, *The Militant South* is substantially **a** pioneer study. Using original sources, he gathered an impressive body of information on various manifestations of the militant spirit of the ante-bellum South and described the conditions in the South that were responsible for its belligerence.

Just before *The Militant South* appeared, Franklin had been appointed, in February 1956, as professor of history and chairman of the department of history at Brooklyn College in New York. The selection, which gave him the distinction of being the first Negro in the state to head a college department, was made solely on the basis of merit. Besides winning respect for his writings, he had become known in academic circles outside Negro universities as visiting professor at Harvard in 1950, the University of Wisconsin in 1952-53, and Cornell University in 1953.

Because he carried a heavy load of administrative duties at Brooklyn, Franklin had less time for teaching and research than he had enjoyed at Howard. He did, however, publish *Reconstruction After the Civil War* (Univ. of Chicago Press, 1961), a re-examination of political, economic, and social aspects of the postwar period in the light of present-day scholarship; and *The Emancipation Proclamation* (Doubleday, 1963), in which he discussed the significance of the proclamation as a war measure, as a moral force during and following the Civil War, and as an American document of freedom as it relates also to the twentieth century.

Professor Franklin has also contributed to a fuller understanding of the Civil War period through his editing of three books: *The Civil War Diary of James T. Ayers* (Illinois State Historical Society, 1947), Albion Tourgée's *A Fool's Errand* (Belknap Press of Harvard Univ. Press, 1961), and Thomas Wentworth Higginson's *Army Life in a Black Regiment* (Collier Books, 1962). In addition to many articles for periodicals, he has written chapters for several books on American history. Among the more recent is "As For Our History" in *The Southerner as American*, edited by Charles G. Sellers, Jr. (Univ. of North Carolina Press, 1960), a book in which he joined eight other Southerners, both Negro and white, in protesting that Southern historical writing has been seriously distorted.

In April 1963 the University of Chicago announced that Franklin had been appointed professor of American history, to join the Chicago faculty in the fall of 1964. Austin C. Wehrwein reported in the New York *Times* (April 14, 1963): "Dr. Franklin's future colleagues stress that he was selected for his high standing in his field. The appointment was also made because the university hopes that it will encourage Negro intellectuals and make Chicago a center for their research."

At the time of his appointment to the University of Chicago, Franklin was on leave of absence from Brooklyn College for the academic year 1962-63, and was serving as William

Pitt Professor of American History and Institutions at St. John's College, Cambridge University, England. During the year he lectured at some twenty universities in Great Britain, Germany, Italy, and France. He had earlier, in 1954, lectured at Cambridge as a Fulbright professor, and in 1960 he had taught at Australian National University as Distinguished American Fulbright Professor. He has made other trips abroad to lecture in 1951 and 1958 at the Salzburg Seminar in American Studies (of which he is a member of the board of directors), to read a paper at the International Conference of Historical Sciences in Rome in 1955, to represent the American Council of Learned Societies at the Centennial Celebration of Indian Universities in 1957, and to represent the United States Department of State at the independence celebrations in Nigeria in 1960.

Since 1947 Franklin has served on the editorial board of the *Journal of Negro History.* He is a member of the board of trustees of Fisk University and belongs to many professional organizations, including the Mississippi Valley Historical Association (executive committee, 1958-61); American Historical Association (council, 1959-62); American Studies Association (executive council, 1963); and Association for the Study of Negro Life and History. In 1962 President Kennedy appointed him to a three-year term on the Board of Foreign Scholarships. He is also a member of the United States Commission for UNESCO and of the board of directors of the American Council on Human Rights.

In recognition and encouragement of his scholarly achievements Franklin was awarded the Social Science Research Council Fellowship (1945), the Guggenheim Fellowship (1950-51), and the President's Fellowship at Brown University (1952-53). He holds honorary LL.D. degrees from Morgan State College (1960), Virginia State College (1961), and Lincoln University (1961). In December 1962 he became the first Negro member of Washington's Cosmos Club, in an election that brought him wide publicity partly because of the furor raised almost a year earlier when the club rejected the Negro State Department official Carl T. Rowan. Franklin attends the Methodist Church. In politics he is an independent.

When he was an undergraduate at Fisk University, John Hope Franklin met Aurelia Elizabeth Whittington, of Goldsboro, North Carolina, whom he married on June 11, 1940. She is a librarian. The Franklins have one son, John Whittington. Professor Franklin is six feet tall and weighs 190 pounds; his hair is beginning to silver. For recreation he goes fishing or listens to music.

"The writing of history," Franklin has said, "reflects the interests, predilections, and even prejudices of a given generation. This means that at the present time there is an urgent need to re-examine our past in terms of our present outlook." He believes that the advancement of the colored man depends upon the growth of the white man's understanding. *Time* (January 11, 1963) quotes him, "There have been Negroes as talented as I before me, but they could not

get where I have because the white man was not advanced enough to let them." The objectivity that assures his integrity as a scholar does not keep him from eloquent and persuasive argument on occasion, as in an article for the Urban League: "Not only does his Americanism compel the Negro to strive to improve his own status by demanding the rights that are his. It also gives him, as it gives to others committed to the ideals set forth in the American dream, a burning desire to make the system work."

References

N Y Times p1+ F 15 '56 por
Time 81:65 Ja 11 '63 por
Washington (D.C.) Post E p10 Mr 8 '59
Thorpe, Earl E. Negro Historians in the United States (1958)
Who's Who in America, 1962-63
Who's Who in Colored America (1950)

FREYBERG, BERNARD CYRIL, 1ST BARON FREYBERG Mar. 21, 1889-July 4, 1963 Commander of New Zealand Expeditionary Force in the Mediterranean in World War II; Governor General of New Zealand (1946-52); elevated to the peerage in 1951. See *Current Biography* (October) 1940.

Obituary

N Y Times p19 Jl 5 '63

FRIEDMAN, HERBERT June 21, 1916- Astrophysicist
Address: b. Naval Research Laboratory, Washington 25, D.C.

A leading authority in the new field of rocket and satellite astronomy, Dr. Herbert Friedman of the United States Naval Research Laboratory in Washington, D.C. has pioneered in the study of solar radiation and has contributed to many other scientific endeavors. His work has dealt with X-ray spectroscopy and diffraction, electron diffraction and microscopy, nucleonics, and upper atmosphere research, as well as with electron tubes and radio astronomy. Dr. Friedman is currently superintendent of the atmosphere and astrophysics division at the Naval Research Laboratory, which he joined in 1940. Much of his work at NRL has been concerned with the development of radiation detection devices and, since 1949, with upper air research involving rockets, especially in the field of solar-terrestrial relationships.

Herbert Friedman was born in New York City on June 21, 1916, the son of an art dealer and picture framer. He attended Brooklyn public schools and then entered Brooklyn College, where he majored in art. In his junior year he was persuaded by Professor B. Kurrelmeyer to change his major to physics. After graduating with a B.A. degree in 1936 he went on for his graduate studies to Johns Hopkins University, where he also spent a year as an instructor in physics.

After receiving his Ph.D. degree from Johns Hopkins in 1940 Friedman became a physicist with the United States Naval Research Labora-

Official U.S. Navy Photograph
HERBERT FRIEDMAN

tory (NRL) in Washington, D.C., which is administered by the Office of Naval Research, under the Department of the Navy. At first a staff member of the metallurgy division of NRL, Friedman was placed in charge of its electron optics branch in 1943. In this post he undertook research in gaseous discharges, X-ray analysis, and measurements of nuclear radiation. During World War II Friedman was engaged in the development of radiation detection devices, and he is credited with the introduction of Geiger and proportional counter techniques into factory production equipment. An X-ray exposure meter for analyzing crystals, which was designed by Friedman, reportedly saved some 50,000,000 man hours in the manufacture of quartz plates for controlling radio circuits. Friedman's innovation is now standard equipment in all crystal plants.

Friedman's wartime work with NRL led him into rocket astronomy, a new and expanding field of astronomy that uses rockets instead of telescopes or radio waves. It has contributed a great deal to man's knowledge of the sun and the rest of the universe by enabling him, by means of detectors fired into the atmosphere, to examine regions of space completely invisible before, and to study forms of stellar radiation that cannot be observed from the ground. It is making advances in counter and diffraction grating techniques, an example of which is the photography of the sun's surface in the Lyman-alpha line. (Lyman-alpha is the dominant light produced by the excitation of hydrogen atoms.) It has also produced the first ultraviolet pictures of the night sky. Although early work in this field often met with failure for mechanical or other reasons, rocket astronomy was accorded early recognition and experienced successful scientific returns. The first extension of the spectrum into the ultraviolet was accomplished in 1946 by Dr. Richard Tousey and other colleagues of Friedman at NRL, who succeeded in lowering it to about 2,400 Angstrom units.

This was followed by an effort to extend the spectrum to shorter wavelengths.

Friedman obtained the first scientific proof that X-rays emanate from the sun in 1949, when he directed the firing of a V-2 rocket, carrying a detecting instrument, from White Sands, New Mexico. Since then, Friedman has been engaged in extensive research and developmental work in rocket astronomy. His achievements in the field include the first ultraviolet map of celestial bodies; measurements of Lyman-alpha that Dr. Harlow Shapley cited as one of the ten outstanding astronomical events of 1952; new discoveries supporting the theory that stars are being continuously formed; and new data on space radiations affecting the earth and on the nature of gases in space. In 1956 Friedman began working on Vanguard satellites carrying scientific instruments for the purpose of studying X-rays and ultraviolet radiation generated by the sun. Two efforts, in the spring of 1958, to place such a satellite into orbit, proved unsuccessful.

Project Sunflare, the opening event of the International Geophysical Year, was begun in July 1957 under the sponsorship of NRL and under the direction of Dr. Friedman. The purpose of the project was to study the nature and effects of solar flares, which are massive eruptions of uncertain origin on the surface of the sun. They send out streams of electrically charged particles, and they were long thought to be responsible for disturbances in radio communications and the weather. Based on San Nicolas Island off the coast of Southern California, Project Sunflare involved the launching of a Nike-Asp rocket combination to a record altitude of 105 miles, and the firing of fourteen Nike-Deacon rocket combinations to altitudes of from seventy-five to eighty miles. The instruments in the rockets sent back data concerning the nature of X-rays and ultraviolet radiation at various altitudes to ground stations. The presence of X-rays during solar flares supported the view that these solar eruptions are electromagnetic in origin.

Speaking at a meeting of the International Astronomical Union in Moscow in the summer of 1958, Friedman described new findings on ultraviolet light that had been obtained by means of rocket astronomy. During the total solar eclipse of October 1958 Friedman headed an expedition to the Danger Islands in the South Pacific to study the sun's activity. Data received from the firing of instrument-payloaded Nike-Asp rockets, which reached altitudes ranging up to 150 miles, represented the first such observations ever made of a solar eclipse. The experiments provided the first proof that X-radiation came from the sun's corona, or outer atmosphere, and that ultraviolet radiation stemmed from its chromosphere, or inner atmosphere. While on this expedition, Friedman was appointed superintendent of the atmosphere and astrophysics division of NRL. According to the British magazine the *New Scientist*, Friedman's studies of ultraviolet radiation ranked as one of the·two major advances in astronomy during 1958.

In a report to a meeting of the American Association for the Advancement of Science in December 1958 Friedman outlined plans for establishing astronomical observatories on satellites orbiting beyond the earth's atmosphere. He also noted that theories of stellar atmospheres might have to be revised as a result of data obtained from rocket exploration flights, and that some stars appeared to be emitting a far greater amount of radiation than could be explained from their temperatures. Perhaps the most remarkable achievement of rocket astronomy, Dr. Friedman noted, has been the charting of the solar spectrum for the entire range of ultraviolet and X-ray wavelengths. In March 1959, under Dr. Friedman's direction, the ultraviolet gas clouds of the sun were photographed for the first time by a special camera loaded into a rocket, which was fired from the White Sands Proving Ground in New Mexico. It brought back sixty photographs of ultraviolet-emitting clouds of hot hydrogen. The project was a United States contribution to the International Geophysical Year.

Friedman took part in a symposium on problems of space exploration, sponsored jointly by the National Academy of Sciences, the National Aeronautics and Space Administration, and the American Physical Society, at Washington, D.C. in April 1959. In his report he said that rocket astronomy presents problems differing greatly from those of classical astronomy, and that it is carried out under adverse conditions. Noting that it is not necessary to enter outer space to conduct experiments in rocket astronomy, Friedman pointed out that at altitudes greater than 300 kilometers the rocket suffers from the intense fluxes of the Van Allen radiation belt, and that it is necessary to protect detectors from damage by high-energy electron and proton bombardment. Friedman predicted that in the future the birth of stars from dense dust and gas clouds could be observed by means of studies of infrared radiation, and that studies of gamma rays, which travel in relatively straight lines through space, might show the direction of the original center of the universe.

In the summer of 1959, as part of the United States contribution to International Geophysical Cooperation (a follow-up to the International Geophysical Year, which ended December 31, 1958), an NRL team, headed by Friedman, undertook project Sunflare II, a high-altitude rocket study with the purpose of measuring X-radiation. The study indicated that the corona of the sun reached a temperature as high as 190,000,000 degrees Fahrenheit during periods of intense solar activity, about ten times greater than had previously been reported. Friedman also took part in experiments involving Explorer VII, a space satellite launched by the National Aeronautics and Space Administration in October 1959 to measure the sun's radiation and to study the formation of weather. Friedman included in the satellite two sensing devices to measure the intensity of X-rays and ultraviolet radiation in the Lyman-alpha band generated by the sun. The purpose of the experiments was to study increases in intensity and energy of X-radiation during solar flares, and to find out whether there is a similar fluctuation in ultraviolet radiation. Another experiment, reported by Friedman in January 1960, indicated that neutral hydrogen, found throughout the solar system, manifested an ultraviolet glow, apparently as a result of

excitation of the atoms by sunlight. The first X-ray photographs of the sun were taken by a team headed by Friedman with a battery of six cameras aboard an Aerobee-Hi rocket, launched at White Sands, New Mexico in April 1960. One of the most unusual of spacecraft launchings was the simultaneous firing into orbit, on June 22, 1960, of two satellites, one to provide navigation data, the other to study solar radiation. Both were launched by a single rocket. The latter satellite, which was developed by an NRL team headed by Friedman, was equipped to make continuing observations of solar radiation from above the atmosphere of the earth.

Man's knowledge of the entire spectrum of solar radiation was virtually doubled as a result of a rocket launching that was supervised by Friedman in August 1961. The study yielded a spectrum of 5,000 lines from ultraviolet solar radiations. This experiment was of special significance, since it brought back enough data for five years of study and provided important insights into the nature of the sun and its activity. At the third International Space Science Symposium, sponsored by the Committee on Space Research in May 1962, Friedman summarized recent progress in the study of the sun's corona. He noted that such studies should be of great help in the development of a solar storm warning system that would protect space travelers from outbursts of intense solar radiation. Speaking at the centennial meeting of the National Academy of Sciences in 1963, Friedman explained the apparent disappearance of the helium belt from the area around the earth as resulting from the sun's inactivity, and predicted that the belt would return when the sun becomes active again.

An exceedingly productive scientific worker, Friedman held some forty patents, with others pending, as of 1960. He has often addressed scientific groups in the United States, Canada, and Europe, and he is the author or co-author of many scientific papers. Friedman was given the Navy Distinguished Civilian Service Award in 1945, for his contributions toward the speeding up of war production in World War II. In 1950 he received an award for his work in the atomic energy program, and in 1957 the Society for Applied Spectroscopy presented him with its annual award for his development of X-ray spectroscopic techniques. He received the Department of Defense Civilian Service Award in May 1959 for the development of radiation detection devices and for research in astronomy and astrophysics. His distinguished achievements in original research won him election to the National Academy of Sciences in 1960.

Dr. Friedman is also a fellow of the American Rocket Society and the American Physical Society. His professional organizations include the Committee on Cosmic Terrestrial Relations, the American Geophysical Union, the American Optical Society, the National Radio Astronomy Observatory, the Washington Academy of Sciences, and the American Academy of Arts and Sciences.

In 1940 Dr. Herbert Friedman married Gertrude Miller, whom he had met while attending Brooklyn College. The Friedmans have two sons, Paul and Jon, and they live in a brick ranch

FRIEDMAN, HERBERT—*Continued*

house in Arlington, Virginia. A modest and self-effacing man, Friedman is of slight stature, and he has dark hair and dark eyes frequently enlivened by a smile. His favorite recreations are tennis, listening to classical music from a large record collection, and art. He likes to do charcoal landscapes and figure drawings, and once, at White Sands, New Mexico, he caused a minor commotion when a security guard came upon him early on a Sunday morning in a restricted area, sketching a landscape of the distant mountains. Friedman's associates credit him with a great deal of patience and forbearance in view of the complexities of his work as well as its occasional fruitlessness. A colleague once said of him: "I have never known him to have harsh words for anybody."

References

N Y Times p10 Je 23 '60 por
American Men of Science 10th ed (1960-62)

FROST, ROBERT (LEE) Mar. 26, 1875-Jan. 29, 1963 Dean of American poets, unofficial American poet laureate, and voice of New England regionalism; famous for his epigrammatic and colloquial lyrics; won Pulitzer Prize in 1923, 1930, 1936, and 1942. See *Current Biography* (September) 1942.

Obituary

N Y Times p35 Ap 1 '63

GAITSKELL, HUGH (TODD NAYLOR) Apr. 9, 1906-Jan. 18, 1963 British statesman and political party official; Minister of Fuel and Power (1947-50); Chancellor of the Exchequer (1950-51); leader of the Labour party (since 1955); an exponent of moderate Socialism. See *Current Biography* (June) 1950.

Obituary

N Y Times p35 Ap 1 '63

GALLOWAY, IRENE O(TILLIA) Sept. 1, 1908-Jan. 6, 1963 United States Army officer; served in the Women's Army Auxiliary Corps during World War II at the Pentagon and in Europe; director of WAC (1953-57). See *Current Biography* (May) 1953.

Obituary

Washington (D.C.) Post B p2 Ja 7 '63

GARDNER, ED(WARD FRANCIS) June 29, 1905-Aug. 17, 1963 Actor; writer; producer; portrayed Archie, the bartender, on the radio show *Duffy's Tavern* (1941-51). See *Current Biography* (September) 1943.

Obituary

N Y Times p80 Ag 18 '63

GASSER, HERBERT S(PENCER) July 5, 1888-May 11, 1963 Physiologist; won 1944 Nobel Prize for Medicine; director, Rockefeller Institute (1935-53). See *Current Biography* (October) 1945.

Obituary

N Y Times p29 My 13 '63

GILRUTH, ROBERT R(OWE) Oct. 8, 1913- Aeronautical engineer; United States government official

Address: b. c/o National Aeronautics and Space Administration, Langley Field, Va.

When the astronaut John H. Glenn, Jr., made America's first manned orbital space flight in February 1962 he said that his achievement represented the joint effort of some 50,000 dedicated persons. The guiding figure among these 50,000 is Robert R. Gilruth, who as project director of the space task group of the National Aeronautics and Space Administration shoulders responsibility for the direction and operation of the vast manned space program of the United States. Gilruth joined the National Advisory Committee for Aeronautics (NACA) as a flight test engineer in 1937 and conducted a number of major pioneering projects in aeronautics. He became chief of NACA's pilotless aircraft research division in 1945 and was named assistant director of its Langley Laboratory in 1952.

Since 1958, when NACA was expanded in scope to become the National Aeronautics and Space Administration, Gilruth has guided one of man's greatest engineering feats, Project Mercury, which by mid-1963 had conducted six successful manned space flights, the latest being the twenty-two orbit flight completed by Leroy Gordon Cooper, Jr., on May 16, 1963. Gilruth has already begun work on NASA's next step, Project Gemini, involving a two-man spacecraft that would stay aloft for periods up to ten days at a time. Gemini is a technical bridge toward Project Apollo, which aims at sending a manned space vehicle to the moon by 1970.

Robert Rowe Gilruth was born on October 8, 1913 in Nashwauk, Minnesota, to Henry Augustus and Frances Marion (Rowe) Gilruth. His father taught high school chemistry and physics and later was assistant superintendent of schools in Duluth, Minnesota. His mother was a teacher of high school mathematics. Other members of his family also had strong scientific interests. An aunt, May McEwen, was a surgeon in Chicago, and his sister, Jean Marion Gilruth, earned her Ph.D. in zoology at the University of Minnesota. In an interview with Shirley Thomas, published in the fourth volume of her *Men of Space* (Chilton Co., 1962), Gilruth said, "For as far back as I can remember, we always talked of various sciences at home. Being a teacher, my father, of course, was anxious to keep up to date. He was a very avid reader and read such publications as *Scientific American*. We always were a close family, so we would discuss all these issues."

As a boy, Robert Gilruth was much interested in model airplanes. Before the days of balsa wood and tiny gasoline engines, the little planes were powered by rubber bands, and the competition lay in seeing who could keep his plane in the air for the longest time. Wing design was very important, and Gilruth soon became dissatisfied with the published patterns. He began designing his own and later wrote to the National Advisory Committee for Aeronautics in Washington for technical data. The information he received from NACA aroused his interest, and it became the nucleus for his ambition to study aeronautical engineering.

The student of the early 1930's had little choice beyond the established fields of mechanical, civil, and electrical engineering. However, the University of Minnesota offered one of the best courses in aeronautical engineering in the United States, with the noted Professor John Akerman as head of the department. Gilruth took advantage of the opportunity to enter this field. As an undergraduate at the University of Minnesota he worked for a time with Dr. Jean Piccard and his wife, Jeannette, in preparing for the balloon ascension they staged at the Century of Progress exposition in Chicago in 1934. He graduated with a B.S. degree in aeronautical engineering in 1935 and obtained his M.Sc. degree the following year.

When Gilruth joined the staff of the National Advisory Committee for Aeronautics at Langley Field, Virginia as a flight research engineer in January 1937, no one really knew what made an airplane safe and easy to fly. Pilots used their own jargon to describe the behavior of planes, but there were no critical engineering specifications from which to judge plane design. Developing these specifications was one of Gilruth's early responsibilities with NACA, and he worked closely with test pilots to establish such quantitative criteria, based on pilots' experiences in testing a large number of planes. His study resulted in a paper, "Requirements for Satisfactory Flying Qualities of Airplanes," which was published as NACA Report No. 755 and which has since become a classic. It formed the first critical basis for military plane specifications, and its principles have been applied internationally.

Among Gilruth's other contributions were studies of airplane stalling characteristics, longitudinal stability, icing characteristics, and landing properties. In the days when engineers were concerned about the effect of the "sound barrier" on airplane flight, Gilruth saw a way to test models at transonic speeds by means of the wing-flow technique. The wing of a plane flying somewhat below the speed of sound deflects the airstream, and in the region just above the wing the air travels faster than the main stream. Gilruth took advantage of this phenomenon by mounting models of various shapes above the wings and instruments for measuring the effects of the tests within the wings of P-51 planes. In this way he gathered important data for the swept-back wing design developed by his colleague Robert T. Jones.

NASA

ROBERT R. GILRUTH

In 1945 Gilruth was chosen to head NACA's new pilotless aircraft research station at Wallops Island, Virginia, where his mission was to build the research center and to plan and guide its program. Here he made a number of important contributions, including studies of the aerodynamics of airplanes and missiles in the Mach 1 to 3 range, and of heat transfer and the effects of laminar flow and turbulence upon heat transfer. He collected vital information on the reentry problems of intercontinental ballistic missiles, particularly with regard to shape, stability, and choice of materials for nose cones, and he did some of the basic pioneering work on the Atlas, Polaris, and other missiles. In 1952 Gilruth was appointed an assistant director of NACA's Langley Laboratory, supervising three of its research divisions that dealt with pilotless aircraft, structures, and dynamic loads. Under his direction the laboratory undertook further development of high-speed research techniques in free flight and the development of techniques and equipment for research in high-temperature structures, materials, and aircraft loads.

After the launching of the first space satellite, Sputnik I, by the Soviet Union on October 4, 1957, American policy makers, who regarded the Soviet achievement as a stunning blow to United States leadership in science and technology, energetically embarked upon a space program. On July 29, 1958 President Dwight D. Eisenhower signed the National Aeronautics and Space Act, which provided that NACA should form the basis of the National Aeronautics and Space Administration (NASA), a new civilian space agency, whose primary objective would be the development of the manned space program. In early October 1958, after months of study, Gilruth presented a detailed plan for a manned space flight. The program, which included con-

GILRUTH, ROBERT R.—*Continued*

siderations for overall design, aerodynamic data on the capsule, parachute and control systems, and water-impact, was given official approval, and Gilruth was given instructions to proceed immediately with Project Mercury, as it was designated.

Unlike a scientist or engineer occupied with a problem of his own choice and favored with the time and facilities to obtain the best possible answer step by step, Gilruth held top responsibility for an assigned mission of great national urgency and had to work within the bounds of available scientific and technological facilities and strict budget limitations. Soon after Project Mercury got under way the selection of the first astronauts began. On April 9, 1959 NASA officials announced that out of 110 original candidates seven had been chosen to take part in Project Mercury. Meanwhile, as the seven astronauts began their intensive training, teams of specialists were perfecting the Mercury space capsule, its booster rocket and parachute systems, and the pressure suit to be worn by the astronauts. Many problems had to be ironed out, and innumerable tests had to be made, before the first manned space flight could be undertaken.

America's first manned suborbital space flight was successfully completed on May 5, 1961 by Alan B. Shepard, Jr. It was followed in July by an almost identical flight by Virgil I. Grissom. The next major step in Project Mercury was the three-orbit flight of John H. Glenn, Jr., in February 1962, which was largely duplicated by Malcolm Scott Carpenter three months later. There followed the six-orbit flight of Walter M. Schirra, Jr., in October 1962 and the twenty-two orbit flight of Leroy Gordon Cooper, Jr., in May 1963. Each mission placed increased demands on men and equipment and widened the expanding frontiers of outer space.

Although the Soviet Union holds the record for the number of orbits completed by a manned spacecraft and sent the first woman astronaut aloft in June 1963, the United States has held its own in the outer space competition and is believed to have surpassed the U.S.S.R. in some areas. As Project Mercury neared completion, preparation for a second program, known as Project Gemini, was already under way. Gemini, which involves an enlarged version of the Mercury capsule, designed to accommodate two men, is scheduled to send its first manned spacecraft aloft sometime in 1964. The project, which is being conducted under Gilruth's supervision at the new Manned Spacecraft Center near Houston, Texas, will be the final step before Project Apollo, which aims at landing a manned spacecraft on the moon by the end of the 1960's, is attempted.

Gilruth has served on a number of government boards and advisory committees, including the NACA committee on aircraft construction and the scientific advisory board of the Air Force Chief of Staff (1952); the ballistic missile defense committee of the Air Force Chief of Staff (1955);

and the *ad hoc* committee on high temperature research and development facilities in the office of the Assistant Secretary of Defense for research and development (1956). He has been chairman of the panel on aerodynamics and structures of the committee on guided missiles, Research and Development Board. Other panels of which he has been a member include the technical capability panel of the science advisory committee, Office of Defense Mobilization; the industrial survey board of the office of the Chief of Naval Operations; and the NACA subcommittee on high-speed aerodynamics. From 1955 to 1958 he was a director of Dynamic Developments, Inc., in Babylon, New York. He is the author of some fifty technical and scientific papers.

The National Rocket Club elected Gilruth a governor in 1961. He became a fellow of the Institute of Aerospace Sciences in 1959 and of the American Rocket Society in 1960. The Institute of the Aeronautical Sciences conferred upon Gilruth the 1950 Sylvanus Albert Reed Award for the "conception and development of new techniques for obtaining transonic and supersonic data using freely flying models." In July 1951 he received the NACA superior accomplishment award, and in October 1954 the University of Minnesota bestowed upon him its outstanding achievement award. In 1962 he was awarded the Robert H. Goddard Memorial Trophy of the National Rocket Club, the Louis W. Hill Space Transportation Award, and the NASA Distinguished Service Medal, which President John F. Kennedy bestowed on him personally. Indiana Technical College conferred upon Gilruth an honorary D.Sc. degree in May 1962.

Robert R. Gilruth and E. Jean Barnhill were married on April 24, 1937 at the National Cathedral in Washington, D.C. She was the only female aeronautical engineering student at the University of Minnesota when Gilruth studied there, and she had one of the few commercial pilots' licenses held by a woman before World War II. They have a daughter, Barbara, who belonged to the flying team at the University of Minnesota. Gilruth is a medium-sized, calm, pipe-smoking, introverted man with a fringe of graying hair and a monotone in his voice. He takes a great interest in mechanical details. Fond of boating, he invented an effective hydrofoil system enabling a small boat to skim along the surface of the water at high speed. Despite his placid exterior, Gilruth works up a great deal of enthusiasm when he speaks of future plans to conquer space, and he has said to Shirley Thomas, "I think we will astound even ourselves at what we can accomplish."

References

N Y Times p6 Jl 9 '59 por; p16 F 24 '62 por
American Men of Science ·10th ed (1960-62)
Thomas, Shirley. Men of Space vol 4 (1962)
Waters, Frank. Engineering Space Age Exploration: Robert Gilruth (1963)
Who's Who in America, 1962-63

GMEINER, HERMANN (g'mīn'ēr) June 23, 1919- Child welfare worker; social administrator

Address: b. SOS Kinderdörfer, Tuchlauben 7, Vienna 1, Austria; h. SOS Kinderdorf, Imst, Austria

A former medical student who never obtained a university degree and never published an academic paper, the Austrian Hermann Gmeiner has revolutionized the field of child welfare with his network of SOS Children's Villages, which he founded and helped to develop into one of the largest voluntary social welfare organizations of our time. Gmeiner's approach to orphans and abandoned children has won worldwide acclaim. He has been awarded the Austrian Silver Order of Merit, and King Frederik IX of Denmark has presented him with the Danish Order of the Chevalier, First Class. He has been praised by Pope John XXIII in a personal message and twice been proposed for the Nobel Peace Prize by Albert Schweitzer, who has called the SOS Children's Villages "a true contribution to the peace of our world."

The seventh of eight children of Hermann and Angelika (Eberle) Gmeiner, Hermann Gmeiner was born in the village of Alberschwende in the province of Vorarlberg, Austria, on June 23, 1919. His family was poor and life on the family farm difficult. When Hermann was four, his mother died—an event that deeply affected him and that may be assumed to have influenced the course of his life's work and his revolutionary approach to child welfare. By a vote of the Gmeiner children, the widower never remarried. Hermann's eldest sister, then eighteen, looked after the younger children and cared for them like a mother.

Hermann Gmeiner decided early to become a doctor. He went to the one-room elementary school in his native village, then attended secondary school in Feldkirch, some twenty-five miles from Alberschwende. Thus, at the age of twelve—except for help in the form of an occasional food parcel from home—he was entirely on his own. With the aid of a scholarship and earnings from serving as an altar boy in the Roman Catholic church and tutoring younger students in mathematics and Latin, Hermann was able to remain at school.

In 1939, shortly before he was to take his final examinations, Gmeiner was drafted into the German army as a private. He served on the Russian front, rose to the rank of second lieutenant and company commander, received several medals, and was wounded five times. When the war ended Gmeiner returned to the family farm for a year, then completed his studies at Feldkirch and matriculated at the University of Innsbruck, where he studied medicine and philosophy.

By this time Gmeiner had decided to specialize in pediatrics, and he looked forward to the day when he might head a large children's clinic. He had been deeply disturbed by the roaming bands of orphaned children made homeless by the war, and the sight of so many hungry and abandoned children distressed him. "The world these children knew was a world without laws and morals," Gmeiner wrote in his book, *Die SOS Kinderdörfer* (SOS-Kinderdorf-Verlag, 1960).

Simonis, Vienna

HERMANN GMEINER

"They had no chance of a normal upbringing in the ruined cities and large refugee camps of Europe." It also became clear to Gmeiner that impersonal orphan asylums were no answer to the problem. "When we place a child who has just lost his mother or parents in such an institution," he has said, "we complete the process of writing the child out of our normal society."

At Innsbruck, Gmeiner joined the Catholic Students Group, whose activities included helping neglected children. He was particularly disturbed by the suicide of one of the abandoned boys he had tried to help in the Catholic youth group, and the idea of a children's village began to take shape in his mind. His basic principle—as profound as it was simple—was to create a real family for children who did not have one. Gmeiner's explanation of his goal was quoted by Joseph Wechsler in the *New Yorker* (December 22, 1962): "Not life in an orphanage or any other kind of institution, no matter how 'advanced,' where the child was only a temporary charge (and knew it), but life in an ordinary house with a hearth, a living room, and a bedroom, where the child would live with a resident 'mother' and with other children, who would become his 'brothers' and 'sisters.' The houses would be solid and would be comfortable, but not luxurious, corresponding to the homes of factory foremen or white collar workers. A dozen or more such houses would form an SOS Children's Village."

The idea took such hold of Gmeiner that in May 1949 he took his entire capital of 600 Austrian schillings (about $42) and incorporated the SOS Kinderdorf Verein—the SOS Children's Village Association. Soon he left the university to concentrate on raising funds for the Kinderdorf Verein. He got little response from the government officials, religious leaders, and wealthy people to whom he turned at first. Gmeiner then

GMEINER, HERMANN—*Continued*

decided to go directly to the people. With the help of a group of Innsbruck housewives and student friends, he began to ring doorbells and recruit members for the Verein—ordinary people who would pay one schilling (then seven cents) a month toward building and maintaining a Children's Village. Before long Gmeiner had signed up 1,000 members and acquired a site for the first village, offered by the town of Imst, near Innsbruck in the Austrian Tyrol.

The founding of the SOS Village at Imst captured the imagination of many in Austria and across Europe, and the idea spread rapidly. A second village was built at Altmünster in 1954 and a third at Hinterbrühl in 1956. By 1963 there were twenty-seven SOS Children's Villages in Europe, providing homes for more than 1,600 children in Austria alone. The budget had grown to $4,000,000 per year, provided by gifts from millions of members and contributors around the world and supplemented by welfare grants to the children from government funds.

An SOS Village consists of a community house and fifteen to twenty one-family houses, each with its own kitchen, living room, three children's bedrooms, mother's room, and bath—and its own family of nine children of different ages. Often the members of an SOS household include natural brothers and sisters. The children, who at the time of admittance are from three days to twelve years old, are accepted on the basis of need only (there are no racial or religious restrictions) and go to the public school in the nearest community. In a typical SOS Village in Austria, girls stay until they are eighteen; then they leave for job or homemaking training. Boys remain in the village until they are fourteen and then go to an SOS student and apprentice center in Egerdach, near Innsbruck, where they live while obtaining vocational training or further education. Each summer children from SOS Villages throughout Europe meet in a summer camp at Lake Caldonazzo in northern Italy, which Gmeiner himself manages.

It is the mothers around whom family life in the Children's Villages revolves and whose devotion has translated Hermann Gmeiner's theory of child care into successful reality. "The secret of motherliness is the secret of the educational success in the children's villages," Gmeiner has written. The mothers of the SOS Children's Villages are carefully selected single or widowed, childless women in their late twenties to early forties. They receive a monthly household allowance, a small salary, two days off per month, and five weeks' annual vacation. A mother enters an SOS Village for her lifetime. Once a child is placed in her care it remains with her until it leaves the village, and often the children carry their love and devotion for their mother over into their adulthood. Each SOS Village also has a handyman, a laundress, a seamstress, a kindergarten teacher, a nurse, several "aunts" to replace mothers who are sick or on vacation, and five or six people who work in the village office and commissary.

Gmeiner recognizes that masculine authority is important for normal family life, but he decided that it would be hard to find husband-and-wife

teams with the necessary idealism and that many problems would develop with couples that would not arise with mothers alone. Therefore, instead of a father in each house there is a village supervisor or *Dorfleiter* who assumes the father role and to whom mothers may turn for help when needed. "I was sure it would be better to have a manager who would act like a father than a father who would act like a manager," Gmeiner has explained.

The success of Hermann Gmeiner's SOS movement has influenced child care programs around the world. It has also had an impact on thousands of adults, who as contributors to the SOS program have become "godparents" to individual children, with whom they often develop close personal ties. As president of the International Federation of SOS Children's Villages, formed in 1960, Gmeiner spends much of his time traveling to other countries to help set up new villages. At the beginning of 1963 forty SOS Villages were being readied in Australia, Finland, Japan, South Korea, Uruguay, and elsewhere. In 1961 Gmeiner visited the United States, where he met with the Federation's American affiliate, the Friends of SOS Children's Villages, Austria, Inc., and discussed plans for setting up a model village in the United States.

Hermann Gmeiner has blue eyes and blond hair, weighs about 150 pounds, and is about five feet seven inches tall. Joseph Wechsberg in the *New Yorker* (December 22, 1962) described him as a man with a soft voice, who laughs easily and who is short, stocky, and inconspicuous—"the sort of man one doesn't notice on the bus." A bachelor, Gmeiner has a modest room in the community house of the first SOS Children's Village at Imst, where he stays between visits to the different villages, to Austrian SOS Kinderdörfer headquarters in Vienna and Innsbruck, or to other countries. His favorite recreation is skiing. He belongs to the Austrian Automobile and Touring Club and the Rotary Club in Innsbruck. In June 1963 Fordham University awarded him an honorary doctorate.

Gmeiner readily acknowledges his debt to the nineteenth century Swiss educational reformer Johann Pestalozzi. "Pestalozzi believed that children should receive from parents and teachers both instruction and discipline—discipline based on love and understanding," Gmeiner has said. "He had the right idea, but his time didn't understand him. I have been luckier, that's all."

Gmeiner hopes to set up at least one model SOS Village in every country in Europe and in a number of lands on other continents to convince local authorities that reforms in standard child-welfare practices are needed. But he has no illusions about the success of his movement. "Even the best Village mother can never replace the child's real mother," he has said. "Our houses can be only a substitute for the child's missing home and family. And even if we grow and grow, we can accept only a very small number of the children who need our help."

References

Christian Sci Mon p9 Jl 12 '60
New Yorker 38:39+ D 22 '62
Who's Who in Austria, 1959-60

GOLLANCZ, VICTOR (gŭl-ănts´) April 9, 1893- British publisher; humanitarian; author

Address: b. Victor Gollancz, Ltd., 14 Henrietta St., London, W.C.2, England; h. 90 Eaton Place, London, S.W.1, England

"Publisher and Author: Capitalist and Socialist: man of the world and latter day saint: Jew and Christian: rationalist and theologian: rebel and traditionalist." The subject of this string of contradictory epithets, assembled by the late John Strachey, is Victor Gollancz, founder, chairman, and governing director of one of Britain's most successful and controversial publishing houses.

Gollancz, who pioneered in political education at Repton School during World War I, entered publishing in 1920, and founded Victor Gollancz, Ltd., in 1928. He launched the Left Book Club in 1937 in an attempt to expose Nazism and avert World War II, later working with equal devotion to ameliorate the suffering of the Germans after the war. He has since been associated with many humanitarian activities and is at present joint chairman of the National Campaign for the Abolition of Capital Punishment. His horror of war and violence and his reverence for life and freedom have been expressed in the books he has published and in those he has written or edited himself. These include polemical works supporting the many causes he has made his own, several anthologies of religious writings, and two extraordinarily frank, moving, and exuberant volumes of autobiography.

Victor Gollancz was born on April 9, 1893, in Maida Vale, London, the youngest and the only boy in a family of three children. His father, Alexander Gollancz, had a small and moderately successful jewelry business. His mother was the former Nellie Michaelson. The Gollancz family, which had come to England from Poland in the nineteenth century, was an orthodox Jewish one with a long rabbinical heritage.

More than most men, Gollancz has been able to identify the childhood incidents and influences that set him on his course through life. In *My Dear Timothy* he described how a book illustration, depicting a bloody detail of a Crimean cavalry charge, awoke in him at the age of six a horror of war. It became a horror "also of violence, and of flogging, and of capital punishment, and of all the other unspeakable outrages" that never failed to produce in him "a feeling of personal contamination."

His equally powerful hatred of poverty and its corrosive effect on the human spirit, emerged a few years later. Gollancz had gone to the Paddington and Maida Vale High School until he was nine, then to a private school and, at eleven or twelve, to St. Paul's School, Hammersmith. His daily journey from his home in Maida Vale to Hammersmith took him through slums that filled him "with loathing and despair."

Gollancz's incipient pacifism and his precocious concern for social justice, fed by his reading of such authors as Ibsen, Shaw, and Whitman, brought him early into conflict with his father's religious and political conservatism. "By the time I was in my early teens," he wrote in *My Dear Timothy*, "I was in a constant mood of

Wide World
VICTOR GOLLANCZ

protest and indignation." Gollancz was especially outraged by the fact that his sisters were denied any career training, being destined willy-nilly for marriage. This expression of his father's antifeminism, unremarkable as it was at the time, became a symbol for him "of all inequalities, all oppressions, all unwarrantable attempts to interfere in any way . . . with a free, spontaneous, self-directing development of the life and spirit in every human person."

In this mood Gollancz went up to New College, Oxford. There he formed a Liberal club, joined the famous Oxford Union debating society, and became a member of so many clubs and associations that he found little time or inclination to attend lectures. Nevertheless, in 1913, he won the Chancellor's Prize for Latin Prose (with "A Dialogue on Socialism") and, a year later, planned a small volume of feminist essays that was later published by Allen & Unwin.

Not a commercial success, the book was called *The Making of Women: Oxford Essays in Feminism* and included contributions from such distinguished suffragettes as Maude Royden and Eleanor Rathbone. During this period of ardent feminism Gollancz also wrote an unperformed play on the subject, called "Daughters," and braved Oxford masculinity at its height by steaming up and down the river during Eights Week shouting "votes for women" through a megaphone. Afterward, he recalled in *My Dear Timothy*, he hid under a very low table in the classical reading room until "the affair had blown over."

Gollancz had read the New Testament at St. Paul's School and had been profoundly moved and attracted by it, above all by the doctrine that one could and should love his enemies. In 1914, just before he left Oxford, he came close to Christian baptism. But, he wrote in *My Dear Timothy*, he retained a number of reservations about Christian dogma and practice

GOLLANCZ, VICTOR—Continued

and is, moreover, "the sort of Jew . . . who in the presence of antisemitism regards formal apostasy as disgusting." He is uncertain now whether or not he would have proceeded with the baptism, arranged for the fall of 1914; in August of that year the decision was taken out of his hands by the outbreak of World War I. Gollancz, whose present total commitment to pacifism came much later, left Oxford without a degree and enrolled in the officer training corps of the London Inns of Court.

For the first two years of World War I, Gollancz served in England with the Northumberland Fusiliers. According to his own account, he was a rather inept and very bored second lieutenant. Judged unfit for foreign service because of poor eyesight, he managed to have himself assigned to Repton, an ancient and famous "public school" where he was to assist in the training of the school's officer training corps.

In fact, Second Lieutenant Gollancz had little to do with the Repton OTC. Instead, he taught English and Latin and, in time, sparked a kind of revolution. Appalled by the social prejudices and ignorance of his pupils, he began to talk politics to them. From these discussions developed a weekly class, organized by Gollancz and a fellow enthusiast called David Somervell, held on a free afternoon, and attended by a growing number of volunteer students. The class proved so successful that the headmaster was persuaded to introduce courses in modern history, economics, and politics into the curriculum of the entire school. A political club was formed and a political magazine established—A Public School Looks at the World, generally known as "The Pubber." The boys' enthusiasm for modern politics spread to modern poetry, music, and the arts. Other public schools began to follow Repton's lead.

Disaster came late in 1917, at a time when the war was going very badly for the Allies. In an attempt to increase its circulation, an issue of "The Pubber" was made available through a London bookshop. The bookshop was politically suspect, and the issue contained material faintly redolent of pacifism. The War Office intervened, and Gollancz, still officially in the army, was removed from Repton. "The Pubber" was suppressed, but Gollancz's work was not wasted. There is still a class at Repton of the kind he began and—so much have things changed—he was invited not long ago to address it.

Second Lieutenant Gollancz left Repton in the spring of 1918, and, after a brief assignment with the Ministry of Food, was posted to Singapore with the Manchester Regiment. In Singapore he contracted a stomach ailment, and by January 1919 he was back in England. He was soon afterward discharged from the army and, in 1920, joined Ernest Benn, who was then establishing his own publishing house as an offshoot of Benn Brothers. Gollancz remained with Ernest Benn for eight years, serving as managing director and as editor of a paperback series called "The World Today" to which he himself contributed a volume on Industrial Ideals. In 1928 he left Benn to establish Victor Gollancz, Ltd.

The first title on Gollancz's list was R. C. Sheriff's indictment of World War I, Journey's End, which he published in the form of a play and as a novel. In a way, it was prophetic of his publishing style, being both a best-seller and a powerful expression of views close to Gollancz's heart. He has not always been able to combine both elements in the same books, but he has never lost sight of either of them. John Strachey, in The Strangled Cry (Bodley Head, 1962), called him a "rogue elephant among publishers." The term is justified by the stark yellow jackets, often crowded with type, that enclose and identify his books, and by his advertisements—brief, provocative, printed in screaming headlines on any page of a newspaper or magazine but the one devoted to books.

In addition to this flair for projecting the "public image" of his company, Gollancz has demonstrated again and again his instinct for the potential best seller. A high proportion of his authors are American, many of them snapped up by Gollancz himself on his frequent trips to the United States. These qualities, and his capacity for hard work, have made Gollancz an extremely successful publisher. And yet he has insisted repeatedly that the business side of publishing has no appeal for him. Indeed, in My Dear Timothy, he wrote: "I have never ceased to detest, almost daily and with the whole of my being, the commercial necessities that life at Henrietta Street imposes on me."

The best known of Gollancz's crusades was the Left Book Club, founded in 1937 in a desperate effort to avert World War II by revealing the true nature of Nazism. The club was associated with the "united front" movement, which sought to bring together a bloc of nations in opposition to Hitler's expansionist aims, a bloc so powerful that it would act as a kind of "massive deterrent." Although the campaign failed, the club had at one time 50,000 members and the support of such men as Stafford Cripps, Harold Laski, Aneurin Bevan, and Lord Boothby. Gollancz himself worked tirelessly for the campaign and in the year before World War II began addressed one or more meetings almost every night, all over the country.

Gollancz is a Socialist, a supporter of the Labour party; the Left Book Club was anti-Fascist and on the whole pro-Marxist and had many Communist adherents. "For about fifteen months," Gollancz wrote in More For Timothy, "I was as close to the communists as one hair to another and . . . for every minute of those months I was billions of light years away from them—as I have been all my life." In 1941, after the Nazi-Soviet pact, Gollancz edited and published Betrayal of the Left: An Examination and Refutation of Communist Policies from October 1939 to January 1941.

Many of Gollancz's most deeply held convictions have been expressed in the books he has published and in those he himself has written. In 1941 he helped to found the National Committee for Rescue from Nazi Terror, but in 1942, when Lord Vansittart wrote a bitter condemnation of the entire German people, Gollancz angrily rejected so comprehensive an indictment in Shall Our Children Live Or Die? (Gollancz;

Ryerson). At the end of the war, believing as he does that only good should be opposed to evil, he organized the "Save Europe Now" campaign, throwing himself for two years into a struggle for starvation relief in Germany and elsewhere. He wrote *In Darkest Germany* (Gollancz; Regnery; Saunders, 1947) following his 1946 visit to the British Zone, and condemned the harshness of the administration.

Our Threatened Values (Gollancz; Regnery; Saunders, 1947) was a product of the same period. In the violence learned in the European resistance movements, in the intensification of racism and the wartime reversion to barbaric justice, Gollancz saw new threats to civilization. *The Devil's Repertoire* (Gollancz, 1958; Doubleday, 1959) attacked the arguments ranged against unilateral nuclear disarmament. *The Case of Adolf Eichmann* (Gollancz, 1961) examined the moral implications of that trial.

But by no means all of Gollancz's books could be classed as pamphleteering. His growing concern with religious, as distinct from political, questions has been expressed in a series of remarkable anthologies. The first of these was *Man and God* (Houghton, 1951), published in England as *A Year of Grace* (Gollancz, 1950). The book was sub-titled "passages chosen and arranged to express a mood about the human and divine," and its contents came from all faiths and all times, from poets and philosophers as well as from saints and priests. It was gratefully received on both sides of the Atlantic and praised for "renewing a sense of the presence of God in human lives." Gollancz's second anthology, described as "a noble and ennobling work," was *From Darkness to Light* (Gollancz; Harper, 1956). It was followed by *The New Year of Grace* (Gollancz; Doubleday, 1961) and, most recently, by an anthology of prayers "of many people and creeds," jointly compiled by Gollancz and Barbara Greene and called *God of a Hundred Names* (Gollancz, 1962; Doubleday, 1963).

Two volumes have so far appeared of Gollancz's long "autobiographical letter" to his young grandson: *My Dear Timothy* (Gollancz; Longmans, 1952; Simon and Schuster, 1953) and *More For Timothy* (Gollancz; Bond Street Publications, 1953). John Strachey has said of them: "His gusto for life and his intense interest in himself and his own soul, his compassion, his horror of violence, his phobias and weaknesses, his boasts, humiliations and his aspirations—these pour out in his autobiography in a torrent which to some people is merely embarrassing but which others are ready to compare with those of St. Augustine."

In 1937, when Japan attacked China, Gollancz became chairman of the China Campaign Committee. More recently, as chairman of the Jewish Society for Human Service, he organized relief work for Arabs during the Arab-Israel war, and later for Arab refugees in the Gaza strip. In 1955-56 he was chairman of the National Campaign for the Abolition of Capital Punishment, and has since 1960 been joint chairman of that body. Gollancz is a governor of the Hebrew University of Jerusalem. Among his many honors and awards are an honorary doctorate of laws from Dublin University; an honorary doctorate

in jurisprudence from the University of Frankfurt; the 1960 Peace Prize of the West German Book Trade; the Glorious Star of China; the Grand Cross of the Order of Merit of the Federal Republic of Germany; and the Goethe Medal.

Victor Gollancz was married in 1919 to Ruth Lowy. They have five daughters. Gollancz's recreations, listed in *Who's Who,* are: "listening to music, arguing, travelling, playing poorish bridge." He has since 1952 been totally and unequivocally committed to pacifism and describes himself as "a liberal, non-practising Judaeo-Christian."

References

Gollancz, Victor. My Dear Timothy (1952); More For Timothy (1953)
Strachey, John. The Strangled Cry (1962)
Who's Who, 1963

GORDON, CYRUS H(ERZL) June 29, 1908- Orientalist; university professor

Address: b. Brandeis University, Waltham 54, Mass.; h. 130 Dean Rd., Brookline 46, Mass.

With his bold announcement in 1962 that he had identified the Minoan language of ancient Crete as Northwest Semitic, or "Phoenician" in the broad sense of the word, Professor Cyrus H. Gordon dramatically challenged Biblical and classical scholars who hold the orthodox view that Greek and Hebrew civilizations derived independently from different origins. His linguistic findings, he asserted, confirm his long-maintained hypothesis that Greek and Hebrew cultures, the two pre-eminent sources of Western civilization, are parallel structures that developed from the same Semitic foundation in the Eastern Mediterranean. He regards his archeological discoveries as "more important to historians than the Dead Sea Scrolls" and suggests that his work on Greco-Hebrew origins will have a major impact on humanistic research for the next decade. Gordon, who has been professor of Near Eastern studies at Brandeis University since 1956, has made a wide variety of contributions to Near Eastern studies in over 250 articles, monographs, and books, including his recent *Before the Bible* (1963).

As the son of a physician who was proficient in Hebrew and made a hobby of the history of medicine, Cyrus Herzl Gordon was early oriented through his home environment toward the world of the past, especially as revealed in the Scriptures and the classics. He was born to Dr. Benjamin Lee and Dorothy (Cohen) Gordon in Philadelphia, Pennsylvania on June 29, 1908. His brothers are Norman E. Gordon and Maurice B. Gordon (a physician), and his sister is Mrs. Judith Baker. He attended West Philadelphia High School from 1921 to 1924 and played in the school's orchestra.

The University of Pennsylvania, which is noted for its work in archeology, introduced Gordon to the world of archeological discoveries. He entered the university in 1924, chose Hebrew as his major subject, and for recreation turned to playing chess, swimming, and wrestling. Awarded his B.A. degree *cum laude* in 1927, he remained at the University of Pennsylvania for graduate work

CYRUS H. GORDON

and studied under a Harrison Scholarship in 1928-29 and a Harrison Fellowship in 1929-30. For both his M.A. degree, conferred in 1928, and his Ph.D. degree, conferred in 1930, he specialized in Semitics, and for his doctoral thesis he submitted *Rabbinic Exegesis in the Vulgate of Proverbs,* which was published by the University of Pennsylvania Press in 1930.

Eager for archeological field work, Gordon responded to the encouragement of the head of his department, Professor James Montgomery, who was also president of the American Schools of Oriental Research in Jerusalem and Baghdad. In 1931, as a field archeologist of the American Schools of Oriental Research, Gordon set out for the Near East, where he spent the next four years, mainly in Palestine and Iraq. For part of that time, in 1932-33, he held a fellowship from the American Council of Learned Societies.

Among the expeditions of archeological exploration and excavation in which Gordon took part were those at the Judean city of Tell Beit Mirsim, the Maccabean fortress of Beth-Zur, Edom and Moab, King Solomon's Mines, and the Assyrian city of Shibaniba near Mosul in Iraq. He was also a member of the expedition of Sir Leonard Woolley that unearthed the royal tombs at Ur, and in Egypt he helped to decipher the Tell el-Amarna tablets excavated in 1933-34. Working and living close to nomadic tribesmen and to Moslem, Christian, and Jewish groups on all social levels, he gained a wealth of firsthand information of historical and linguistic value. In 1941 he wrote a book about archeology for nonspecialists, *The Living Past* (Day), in which he discussed the discovery and excavation of mounds in western Asia and the rewards of archeological exploration.

Returning from the field to the classroom, Gordon taught Semitics and research at Johns Hopkins University in Baltimore from 1935 to 1938. During the next four years he filled alternate appointments at Smith College in Northampton, Massachusetts, in 1938-39 and 1940-41, and at the Institute for Advanced Study in Princeton, New Jersey, where he could give his time exclusively to research, in 1939-40 and 1941-42. With his *Ugaritic Grammar* in 1940, he set the foundation of his reputation as an authority on Ugaritic, one of the members of the Semitic family of languages. He later wrote *Ugaritic Handbook* (1947), *Ugaritic Literature* (1949), and *Ugaritic Manual* (1955), which were published by the Pontifical Biblical Institute in Rome. He also translated and edited *Loves and Wars of Baal and Anat, and other Poems from Ugarit,* published by the Princeton University Press in 1943.

World War II gave Gordon an opportunity to revisit the Near East. From July 1942 to March 1946 he served in the Army Signal Corps, advancing in rank from second lieutenant to captain. During part of that period he was a technical adviser to the commanding general of the Persian Gulf command as orientalist in the office of technical information, with headquarters in Tehran. He made many trips throughout Arab countries and dealt for the most part with people in diplomatic, military, governmental, and intellectual circles. (He has been a colonel in the Air Force Reserve since 1961 and is a flight commander at the Boston Air Reserve Center.)

After his discharge from military service, Gordon taught for ten years, from 1946 to 1956, at Dropsie College in Philadelphia as professor of Assyriology and Egyptology. Since 1956 he has been professor of Near Eastern studies at Brandeis University in Massachusetts, and since 1958, chairman of the university's department of Mediterranean studies. In 1957-58 he also filled the positions of director of the graduate school and associate dean of the faculty at Brandeis.

The books that Gordon wrote after the war, besides his studies in Ugaritic, included *Lands of the Cross and Crescent; Aspects of Middle Eastern and Occidental Affairs* (Ventnor, 1948); *Smith College Tablets* (Smith College, 1952), which dealt with 110 cuneiform tablets selected from the college collection; *Adventures in the Nearest East* (Phoenix House, 1957); and *Hammurapi's Code: Quaint or Forward-Looking?* (Rinehart, 1957). A revised second edition of his *Introduction to Old Testament Times* (Ventnor, 1953) appeared in 1958 as *The World of the Old Testament* (Doubleday).

When he was a college student, Gordon had taken courses in Greek and Hebrew at the same time, and both subjects, he recalls, were taught as though they were completely unrelated. Through his own later research, partly in his investigations of Ugaritic literature, he became convinced that Greek and Hebrew civilizations, far from having developed independently of each other, were based upon a common Semitic heritage that spread throughout the Eastern Mediterranean in the second millennium B.C.

In some of his books and in his monograph *Homer and the Bible* (Hebrew Union College Annual, 1955) Gordon cited many parallels in early Greek and Hebrew writings that pointed to a common denominator in the two cultures. Regarding Homer and the Bible as summations of civilizations, rather than as beginnings, he had for many years been interested in what produced them. He has described himself as a traditionalist, one who believes that the traditions of the ancient Hebrews and Greeks are historical memories of events and one who interprets Biblical and classical texts literally. He accepts, for example, the statement of King Arius of Sparta, reported in I Maccabees, that the Spartans and Jews are of the stock of Abraham as supporting the claim of the Greeks that they are "Danaoi," the descendants of Danaos, or Dan, the great-grandson of Abraham.

To confirm his hypothesis of a common origin of the heroic ages of Greek and Hebrew cultures, Gordon tracked down linguistic evidence, in addition to literary relationships. As early as 1931, when he made his first trip to the Middle East, he had believed, "Solving the inscriptions of Minoan Crete is the most important problem that faces scholars," as he recalled many years later in an interview for the New York *Times* (April 4, 1962). One set of inscriptions, called Linear B, had been made in a puzzling form of row writing used after the 1450 B.C. Greek invasion of Crete. In 1952 the British architect Michael Ventris deciphered and identified the language of the inscriptions as Greek. Employing Ventris' phonetic values for Minoan syllables as working tools, Gordon set about decoding a script of pictographic and syllabic signs, knows as Linear A, which were found on Cretan stone cult objects dating from the seventeenth to the fifteenth centuries B.C.

In the summer of 1957 Gordon announced that the language of Linear A was Semitic, and at that time he suggested that it might be Akkadian. The Linear A inscriptions on which he worked, however, were merely "the laundry lists of antiquity," as he himself described them, and he conceded the argument of his critics that proof would not be conclusive until he could apply his Semitic key to inscriptions with sentence structure. The publication in England in 1961 of W. C. Brice's *Inscriptions in the Minoan Script of Class A* (Society of Antiquaries) provided Gordon with the clearer photographs and ink copies of Linear A inscriptions. He was able both to offer a translation of a sentence to clinch his theory and to pinpoint the language of the early Cretans as Phoenician, a Semitic language similar to the Akkadian tongue that he had accepted in 1957 "as a working hypothesis."

His decipherment of Linear A enabled Gordon to propose a solution to another Cretan linguistic mystery. For some eighty years scholars had been baffled by the inscriptions in Greek letters found on four tombstones in Crete. They had been written about a thousand years after Linear A but were recognized as Eteocretan (pure Cretan), the pre-Greek language of the island. Having discovered in Linear A that the Minoan language was Phoenician, he was soon able to translate whole phrases of Eteocretan. Gordon published his decipherment of both Minoan Linear A and Eteocretan in the July 1962 issue of the *Journal of Near Eastern Studies* and later discussed some of his linguistic findings in his comprehensive study of Greco-Hebrew origins in *Before the Bible; The Common Background of Greek and Hebrew Civilizations* (Harper, 1963).

In identifying the Minoan language as Phoenician, Gordon said he had proved that Phoenicians had given Crete its language before the coming of the Greeks and thus corroborated his theory of the common Semitic parentage of Greek and Hebrew cultures. As he expected, his assertions have caused something of an uproar among classicists who cling to the view that Minoans were of Indo-European stock. Explaining the implications of his findings, Gordon said, as reported in the London *Times* (April 4, 1962), "The effect that these developments will have on prehistoric and biblical studies will in the long run exceed the impact of the Dead Sea Scrolls. It is safe to predict that quite soon the heroic ages of Greece and Israel will no longer be studied in isolation from each other by any scholar whose work is not to be ephemeral."

Gordon conducted his own explorations in Eastern Mediterranean lands—including Israel, Cyprus, Crete, and Cythera—in 1957, 1958, and 1961. He has also traveled in many European countries. He belongs to the American Oriental Society, Society of Biblical Literature, American Philological Association, American Institute of Archaeology, and American Association of University Professors. The Academy for Liberal Judaism in New York City awarded him its Certificate of Tribute in 1956, and Gratz College in Philadelphia presented him with its Alumni Award in 1961. He was granted a Fulbright Fellowship for 1962-63.

On September 22, 1946 Cyrus H. Gordon married Joan Elizabeth Kendall of Baltimore, a psychologist. Their children have Biblical names—Deborah, Sarah, Rachel, Noah, and Dan. Gordon is five feet eleven inches tall, weighs 185 pounds, and has blue eyes and brown hair. His devotion to his scholarship excludes hobbies. "It isn't just work with me," he explained in the New York *Times* interview. "It's an obsession and a pleasure mixed. There must be easier ways of earning a living—but there's a compulsiveness about it."

References

N Y Herald Tribune Ap 4 '62 por
N Y Times Ap 4 '62 por
Who's Who in America, 1962-63

GORDON, KERMIT July 3, 1916- United States government official; economist
Address: b. Bureau of the Budget, Washington 25, D.C.; h. 7310 Broxburn Court, Bethesda 14, Md.

A key man in carrying out the Kennedy administration's policies designed to improve the nation's economic health is Kermit Gordon, who succeeded David E. Bell as director of the United States Bureau of the Budget on December 28, 1962. An authority on government fiscal policies, Gordon has had much experience in dealing with problems of the national economy, as a government official and as an economic consultant. He was a professor of economics at Williams College for a number of years and has served as an executive with the Ford Foundation. In 1961-62

KERMIT GORDON

he was a member of the influential Council of Economic Advisers, which advised the President on the health of the American economy and helped to formulate fiscal plans to stimulate the economic growth of the nation.

Kermit Gordon was born in Philadelphia on July 3, 1916 to H. B. and Ida E. (Robinson) Gordon. He attended Philadelphia public schools and, after graduating from Upper Darby High School he entered Swarthmore College, where he majored in economics and was elected to Phi Beta Kappa. To help finance his college education Gordon worked as a police reporter on the Philadelphia *Evening Bulletin*. He graduated from Swarthmore in 1938 with a B.A. degree, receiving highest honors in economics. A Rhodes Scholarship enabled him to go to England for the academic year 1938-39 to attend University College of Oxford University. During his year at Oxford, Gordon read economics and played lacrosse against Cambridge. After completing his year abroad he returned to Swarthmore, where he worked as a research associate in economics until 1940. In 1940-41 he was an administration Fellow at Harvard University.

Gordon's first experience with government service was his association, in the late 1930's, with the temporary National Economic Committee. In 1941, after his stay at Harvard, Gordon came to Washington, where he worked in the Office of Price Administration until 1943, when he entered the United States Army as a private. After serving as an economist with the Office of Strategic Services he was discharged in 1945 with the rank of second lieutenant. Returning to Washington, he became a special assistant to the Assistant Secretary for economic affairs under the State Department. Although he returned to university teaching in 1946, he retained his association with the State Department as a consultant until 1953. As consultant to the White House Office in 1950,

he helped to prepare the Gray *Report on Foreign Economic Policies*. He was economic consultant to the Office of Price Stabilization in 1951. Gordon has also served as a consultant to the Brookings Institution and to the United States Council of International Chambers of Commerce.

In 1946 Gordon came to the department of economics at Williams College in Williamstown, Massachusetts, as an assistant professor. He reached the rank of full professor in 1956 and was appointed to the William Bough chair. In 1961 he became David A. Wells Professor of Political Economy. Gordon served on the board of editors of the *American Economic Review* from 1958 to 1960 and was associate to the administrator of the Merrill Foundation for Advancement of Financial Knowledge from 1947 to 1956. In 1956 Gordon left Williams College for a year to become executive associate of the Ford Foundation. He was director of its program in economic development and administration in 1960 and 1961. He has also been a visiting lecturer at the National War College, Harvard University, and the Massachusetts Institute of Technology.

Early in 1961 Gordon took a leave of absence from Williams College to accept an appointment by President John F. Kennedy to the three-man Council of Economic Advisers in Washington. On this job he soon became known as one of the chief economic planners of the New Frontier administration. Set up by the Full Employment Act in 1946, the council advises the President on the health of the economy, recommends policies for economic growth and stability, and evaluates the government's economic program. Other members of the council were James Tobin and chairman Walter W. Heller.

In an interview for the New York *Times Magazine* (July 23, 1961) Harry Schwartz discussed the state of the national economy with the members of the council. Gordon stressed national goals of high employment, more rapid growth in production, and reasonable price stability. Of public regulation of the economy he said, "We ought to look at changes in technology and changes in demand and see if areas that needed public regulation in the past still need it today." He agreed with his fellow members that, except in the case of agriculture, increased competition and more vigorous enforcement of anti-trust laws should be favored.

On January 22, 1962 President Kennedy delivered his annual economic report to Congress, accompanied by an associated report signed by the Council of Economic Advisers. The Presidential report indicated that the economy was responding well to administration efforts to foster economic growth, and that the long-term pace of growth might be increased to 4.5 percent a year during the 1960's. To guard against recessions, the President asked for authority to cut taxes, increase spending for public works, and strengthen the unemployment insurance program. Noting the high rate of unemployment, he said that the nation should aim for a modest target of 4 percent unemployment by mid-1963, which should assure an annual rate of total output of $600 billion dollars by that time.

The report of the Council of Economic Advisers, entitled "Guideposts for Noninflationary Wage and Price Behavior," set forth proposals for the restraint of large companies and strong unions. Although the report offered no specific formula, it recommended that gains in wage and fringe benefits be maintained within the postwar average of productivity gains for the entire private economy, and that industries with productivity gains that are above average reduce prices. The report also dealt with the difficult problem of international payments, and expressed the hope that a reasonable balance could be restored within the next two years, to reverse the trend of large deficits of the previous four years. Joseph A. Loftus wrote in the New York *Times* (January 23, 1962): "Not in some years have professional economists, in a state paper, measured the economy in the human terms found today. . . . The report may become a landmark and a guide to future council members who otherwise might hesitate to speak out."

In the fall of 1962 Gordon had made arrangements to return to Williams College as professor of economics and as chairman of its Center for Development Economics, and he had prepared to teach a seminar called "Current Problems in National Economic Policy." A few weeks later, however, President Kennedy offered him the position of director of the Bureau of the Budget. The President had been impressed by Gordon's work and by his unorthodox, pungent, and incisive opinions. In announcing the appointment the President said: "Kermit Gordon, with his knowledge of public finance and of the relationship between the fiscal policies of the government and of our national economy, has been a valuable member of the Council. . . . I am confident that his performance as budget director will be in the fine tradition of his predecessors." Gordon was sworn in as director of the Bureau of the Budget on December 28, 1962.

Created by act of Congress in 1921, the Bureau of the Budget was originally located in the Treasury Department, but in 1939 it was transferred directly to the Executive Office of the President. In addition to helping the President in preparing the budget and in formulating the government's fiscal program, the bureau is responsible, among other things, for improving the management of finance and accounting of the executive branch and of federal agencies, making recommendations with regard to Presidential action on legislative enactments, and keeping the president informed on the progress of work in federal agencies.

Although the Kennedy Administration's 1964 budget, which was sent to Congress on January 17, 1963, was not primarily the work of Gordon, he had had a hand in its formulation, as a close associate of the previous budget director, David E. Bell. It was estimated that the record 98.8 billion dollar budget would result in an 11.9 billion dollar deficit for the fiscal year ending June 30, 1964. For peacetime, this was exceeded only by the 1958 budget of the Eisenhower administration, which carried a deficit of 12.4 billion dollars. Of the funds provided for in the new budget 51 percent was allocated for defense, space, and international programs; 23 percent for social security, health, and welfare;

6 percent for interest; 5 percent for veterans; and 15 percent for other programs. A major feature of President Kennedy's budget message was his proposed three-year 13.5 billion dollar tax cut, which he saw as an effective means of stimulating the nation's economic growth.

Gordon defended the administration's budgetary plans before the Joint Economic Committee of the Senate and House of Representatives, on January 29, 1963, pointing out that under the present sluggish economy, efforts to balance the budget would be self-defeating. Decreased federal expenditures, he declared, would "reduce private production, employment, profits and wages. This, in turn, would lead to lower federal revenue collections, and a deficit would remain." During the Congressional hearings on the President's tax cut program a few weeks later, Gordon testified before the House Ways and Means Committee, and affirmed the administration's policy to keep the rise in future expenditures well below the rate of increase in revenue. Declaring that the Kennedy program offered "the only true prospect for a balanced budget," he repeated earlier predictions that the budget would be balanced in 1967.

Described as a "hard-headed liberal," Gordon does not belong to any one particular school of economics. Although he believes "in the positive use of fiscal policy to help in the stabilization of the economy," he would rather see economic problems solved by "the virtues of the free market system," wherever this is feasible. He is a member of the American Association of University Professors, American Economic Association, American Association of Rhodes Scholars, and American Civil Liberties Union.

Kermit Gordon was married to Mary King Grinnell of Winnetka, Illinois, on December 25, 1941. They have three children, Katherine, Emily, and Andrew. A round-faced man with thinning hair, Gordon is appreciated in the sober atmosphere of the budget bureau for his sense of humor. His reputation among fellow economists is that of a man who "writes clearly, expresses himself articulately, and listens well." Along with other sports-minded New Frontier colleagues, he can often be found in a softball game in the park behind the White House. One of his friends once said that Gordon has "a down-to-earth view of life that is mixed with an unflagging idealism about long-range human nature. He has a magnificent sense of day-to-day detail, never losing sight of the ideal" (New York *Times,* January 18, 1963).

References

N Y Herald Tribune p33 N 29 '62
N Y Times p4 Ja 18 '63 por
Newsday p46 N 29 '62 por
U S News 53:18 D 10 '62
New Frontiersmen (1961)
Who's Who in America, 1962-63

GRAHAM, PHILIP L(ESLIE) July 18, 1915-Aug. 3, 1963 President and publisher of the Washington *Post* (1946-63); lawyer. See *Current Biography* (February) 1948.

Obituary

N Y Times p1+ Ag 4 '63

GREEN, CONSTANCE (WINSOR) Mc-LAUGHLIN Aug. 21, 1897- Historian; writer
Address: 19 Second St., N.E., Washington 2, D.C.

Constance McLaughlin Green, who won the Pulitzer Prize in history in 1963, feels that a better understanding of the problems of American urban life rests at least in part upon an explanation of how these difficulties came about. Mrs. Green, a grandmother, and a daughter of a Pulitzer Prize winner, received the award for *Washington, Village and Capital, 1800-1878,* the first volume of a two-volume history of the nation's capital. The second volume, *Washington, Capital City, 1879-1950,* has been scheduled for publication in December 1963. Mrs. Green has taught at Smith College and Mount Holyoke College, and she served as a military historian at the Pentagon in Washington from 1948 to 1951.

Constance Winsor McLaughlin Green was born in Ann Arbor, Michigan on August 21, 1897 to Andrew Cunningham McLaughlin and Lois Thompson (Angell) McLaughlin. Her family background gave her a deep-rooted interest in history: her father, a historian and professor, taught American history at the University of Michigan. Two of her brothers are no longer living. A surviving brother, James A. Mac-Lachlan, was a professor at the Harvard Law School. She also has two sisters, Mrs. Esther Donahue, and Mrs. Isabella C. Stephens, a teacher at the Country School in Woodstock, Vermont. Constance McLaughlin grew up in Chicago, where her father had moved his family after he joined the faculty of the University of Chicago. In 1914 she graduated from University High School, where she had been active in sports and had served as a board member of the *Correlator,* the senior yearbook. Before she enrolled at the University of Chicago, she spent one term at Fräulein von Heidenaber's Höhere Töchter Schule in Munich, Germany.

CONSTANCE McLAUGHLIN GREEN

After studying for two years at the University of Chicago, where she majored in history, she transferred to Smith College in Northampton, Massachusetts, which granted her a B.A. degree in 1919. While a Smith undergraduate, she was editor of the *Smith College Monthly.* After receiving her degree she returned to the city in which she had grown up, to teach freshman English at the University of Chicago. She later returned to Smith College to teach freshman English. In 1921, after her marriage to Donald Ross Green, a textile manufacturer, she moved to Holyoke, Massachusetts, and enrolled at Mount Holyoke College in nearby South Hadley, so that she could keep in touch with the academic world after settling down in a small industrial community. She obtained her M.A. degree in history in 1925, after submitting a thesis entitled "The New England Confederation of 1643." It was later published in the first volume of *Commonwealth History of Massachusetts,* edited by Albert Bushnell Hart (States Publishing, 1927). For a while she took a part-time position teaching introductory courses in history at Mount Holyoke College.

From 1925 to 1932 Mrs. Green continued to teach part-time as an instructor at Mount Holyoke, in the meanwhile raising a family. She tried her hand at writing detective stories, but gave it up when she discovered that she was "unable to come up with a plot that had any validity." To sustain her contact with the academic world, she studied for her doctorate at Yale University, and in 1937, one year after her father had won the Pulitzer Prize in history for *The Constitutional History of the United States,* she obtained her Ph.D. degree in history from Yale. In the same year she won Yale's Edward Eggleston Prize in History. Her dissertation, *Holyoke, Massachusetts; A Case History of the Industrial Revolution in America,* was published in 1939 by the Yale University Press.

In 1938 Mrs. Green again returned to Smith College, this time as an instructor in the history department. The following year she became head of the Smith College Council of Industrial Relations, a part-time post she held, with some wartime interruptions, until 1946. She was responsible for directing graduate students engaged in research on the industrial history of the Connecticut Valley. In 1942, soon after the United States entered World War II, she left Smith College to become the United States Army Ordnance Department historian at the Springfield Armory in Springfield, Massachusetts, where she remained until 1945. In the next year her husband died, and Mrs. Green moved to Washington, D.C., where she became consulting historian for the American National Red Cross. In 1948, as chief historian for the Army Ordnance Department, she headed a team of researchers in writing a volume on the technical services. Entitled *The Ordnance Department,* it formed a part of the series, *The United States Army in World War II* (Government Printing Office, 1955). Her co-editors were Harry Thomson and Peter Roots. Mrs. Green left her post at the Pentagon in 1951, reportedly because "the brass tried repeatedly to speed up the historians," according to the Washington *Sunday Star* (May

20, 1962). That same year she became a Commonwealth Fund Lecturer at University College, the University of London.

Returning to Washington in 1952, she became a historian at the research and development board, Office of the Secretary of Defense. In 1954, under a six-year grant from the Rockefeller Foundation, administered by the American University, in Washington, D.C., Mrs. Green was named head of the Washington history project. She completed the project independently from 1960 to 1962 with the help of a grant from the Chapelbrook Foundation of Boston, Massachusetts. The undertaking culminated in the publication of *Washington, Village and Capital, 1800-1878* by Princeton University Press in May 1962. Its companion volume, *Washington, Capital City, 1879-1950*, which will be considerably longer than the first, was scheduled for publication by Princeton University Press in December 1963.

Among the critics who acclaimed Mrs. Green's book was Arthur Schlesinger, Jr., special assistant to President John F. Kennedy. In appraising it for the New York Times *Book Review* (June 17, 1962), he pointed out that Mrs. Green had concentrated on the design of Washington, its special structure, and its problems of municipal housekeeping, and called the book "lucid," "authoritative," and "enthralling." John McKelway described the book in the Washington *Sunday Star* (May 20, 1962) as an "entertaining narrative of the life of the city and its people, many of whom came up from slavery. More than anything else, perhaps, it is a tale of Washington trying to live up to its name." Mrs. Green, who used both manuscript and published sources, has called the book an "interpretive rather than a comprehensive, foolproof history."

In May 1963 members of the Pulitzer Prize committee named Constance McLaughlin Green the recipient of the 1963 Pulitzer Prize in history for *Washington, Village and Capital, 1800-1878*. As soon as she heard the news, Mrs. Green decided to go out and buy her grandson, Andy, a new pair of bright red suspenders. In an interview with Dorothy McCardle of the Washington *Post* (May 8, 1963) she explained that suspenders and Pulitzer Prizes go together in her family. "My mother told my father that she certainly hoped he would not invest the money, but would spend it for some fun or something he really wanted," Mrs. Green recalled. "My father thought a minute, and then he said that yes, he would have some fun with it. He'd go out and buy a new pair of suspenders."

Other books by Mrs. Green include: *History of Naugatuck, Connecticut* (Yale, 1949); *Eli Whitney and the Birth of American Technology* (Little, 1956); and *American Cities in the Growth of the Nation* (De Graff, 1957). Her study, *The Role of Women as Production Workers in War Plants of the Connecticut Valley*, appeared as Volume XXVIII of Smith College Studies in History (1946). She contributed chapters to *The Growth of American Economy*, edited by Harold Williamson (Prentice-Hall, 1944) and to *The Cultural Approach to History*, edited by Caroline Ware (Columbia Univ. Press, 1940). Her shorter works include articles for leading American encyclopedias and for such journals as the *Nation*.

Constance Winsor McLaughlin married Donald Ross Green on February 14, 1921. He died in November 1946. Mrs. Green has three children: a son, Donald Ross Green, is an associate professor of educational psychology at Emory University in Atlanta, Georgia; a married daughter, Mrs. Lois Carr, lives in Annapolis, Maryland; and an unmarried daughter, Elizabeth Langford Green, lives in Philadelphia where she works for a publishing firm and attends law school. There are three grandchildren. Mrs. Green was made an honorary member of Phi Beta Kappa at Smith College in 1943 and received an honorary Litt.D. degree from Smith in June 1963. She belongs to the Literary Society of Washington, D.C., the American Historical Association, Economic History Association, Social Welfare History Group, Urban History Group, and the United States Capitol History Society.

A Washington journalist once described Mrs. Green as small and bouncy, with a "tartness in her talk." (She has blue eyes and light brown hair, is five feet four inches in height, and weighs about 110 pounds.) Her house in Washington is located directly behind the Supreme Court building. Mrs. Green, who is a Democrat and a member of the Congregational Church, lists walking, camping, gardening, and reading detective stories as her favorite recreations. In the summer of 1963 she undertook a project she had long entertained as a possibility: reading Edward Gibbon's *The Decline and Fall of the Roman Empire* in its entirety. She hasn't the slightest intention of ever retiring and is already at work upon her next book, a study of American urban development, which has been contracted by a British publisher. Americans, she feels, should learn more about their past and the origins of their long-enduring problems.

References

N Y Times p35 My 7 '63 por
Washington (D.C.) Post D p5 My 8 '63 por
Washington (D.C.) Sunday Star C p3 My 20 '62 por
Directory of American Scholars (1957)

GREENE, HUGH CARLETON Nov. 15, 1910- British broadcasting executive
Address: b. British Broadcasting Corp., Broadcasting House, London, W.1, England; h. 25 Addison Ave., London, W.11, England

The British Broadcasting Corporation, once known with some condescension as "Auntie," is now offering some of the frankest, liveliest, and most controversial programming in the world. This revolution is, by common consent, the work of Hugh Carleton Greene, director-general of the BBC since 1960. After a distinguished career in journalism, Greene joined the staff of the BBC during World War II. He subsequently spent two years in the British zone of Germany, where he rebuilt a peacetime radio service. In 1950 he received an O.B.E. for his

HUGH CARLETON GREENE

services. Thereafter, apart from a year in Malaya as head of the Emergency Informational Services, he remained at the BBC in a series of increasingly important posts. When he succeeded General Sir Ian Jacob as director-general of the BBC, Greene was director of news and current affairs.

The British Broadcasting Corporation, which is chartered but not owned by the government, carries no advertising on its single television channel and several radio frequencies. It is thus free of both political and commercial pressures. The BBC offered the world's first television service in 1936 and for eighteen years enjoyed a monopoly in video programming, as it still does in British radio. These long years of monolithic autonomy had produced a broadcasting service of unchallengeable integrity and decorum, but one which was widely regarded as lacking in vigor and daring. When an Independent Television Authority was authorized in 1954, offering commercially sponsored programs of mass appeal, it was an immediate success, at one point claiming the loyalty of 70 percent of the viewing audience.

Hugh Carleton Greene was born on November 15, 1910 in Berkhamsted, Hertfordshire, England, to Charles Henry Greene and his wife, the former Marion Raymond Greene. Charles Greene was headmaster of Berkhamsted School, a public school founded in the reign of Henry VIII. He had two daughters and four sons; the latter include Dr. Raymond Greene, a noted physician and mountain climber; and Graham Greene, the novelist and playwright.

Like his brothers, Hugh Carleton Greene was educated at Berkhamsted School. He then went up to Merton College at Oxford University, which awarded him second class honors in the classics in 1931 and in English in 1933 and the B.A. degree in 1935. He obtained the M.A. degree from Oxford in 1958. In 1933 Greene went to Munich, Germany, where he worked for a

time as a correspondent of the New Statesman and the London Daily Herald. In 1934 he joined the Berlin staff of the London Daily Telegraph, and four years later he became the Telegraph's chief correspondent in Berlin.

In May 1939 Greene was expelled from Germany in reprisal for the ousting of certain Germans from Britain, and he became the Warsaw correspondent for the Telegraph. After World War II broke out in September 1939 he covered events as a war correspondent in Poland, Rumania, Bulgaria, Turkey, the Netherlands, Belgium, and France. In the summer of 1940 he joined the Royal Air Force as a pilot officer, but he did not stay in the RAF for long. The British Broadcasting Corporation, then gearing itself for its new role as an agency of psychological warfare, was expanding rapidly, and in October 1940 Greene was assigned to the BBC to help with propaganda broadcasts to Germany. He was promoted to the post of assistant news editor and then made head of the German Service, a position he held until the end of the war.

Late in 1946 the Foreign Office borrowed Greene from the BBC for an important new assignment. He became controller of broadcasting in the British Zone of Germany, and he rebuilt a peacetime radio service, "Nordwest Deutscher Rundfunk," writing its charter on the same lines as the BBC's and serving as its first director-general. Early in 1949 Greene returned to London to head the BBC's East European Service. The following year he was off again on another special government assignment, this time for the Colonial Office in Malaya, where Communist guerrillas were creating havoc. Applying what he had learned about psychological warfare during World War II, Greene spent a year in Malaya as head of the Emergency Informational Services there.

This assignment was followed by what an Observer profile (January 10, 1960) called "odd jobs at the BBC—an economy committee, a spell handling the export of television films." But, the profile added, "by this time he had a powerful supporter in Sir Ian Jacob, at that time head of Overseas Services, and soon to be made Director-General." From 1952 to 1955 Greene was assistant controller of the BBC Overseas Services. In 1955 he served as chairman of a commission of inquiry into the organization of broadcasting in what was then the Federation of Rhodesia and Nyasaland. The same year he became controller of Overseas Services, and in 1956, according to the Observer, he "jumped over several heads and found himself Director of Administration with a place on the Board of Management . . . the eight-member 'Cabinet' of the BBC."

The Observer writer noted further: "A new kind of tough-minded broadcasting was needed for the Overseas Services, and Greene, with a combination of news-sense and showmanship, became one of its cleverest practitioners. It was all a far cry from the admirable but often cosyminded attitudes of the pre-war BBC, and gave Greene, who had never been exposed to the old school, an insight into the real power and flexibility of radio."

In August 1958 Greene became the BBC's first director of news and current affairs, and he did much to overhaul these services. By the summer of 1959, with the retirement of Sir Ian Jacob imminent, the BBC's board had settled on Greene as the next director-general. He took over this post on January 2, 1960. "Whether Greene has the breadth of personality to leave a permanent mark on broadcasting remains to be seen," the *Observer* writer noted a week after Greene's appointment. On this point there is no longer room for doubt. "Auntie" BBC has been rejuvenated.

BBC television dramas, according to *Time* magazine (January 25, 1963), are frank in theme and outspoken in language, and the satiric television program *That Was the Week That Was* "pokes fun at men and institutions in a way that is probably unique in world television." Indeed, the pillorying of public men in "TWTWTW" has been so severe that a Member of the House of Commons recently charged the program with breaching Parliamentary privilege. (His more tolerant colleagues rejected the charge, some disclosing that the program was their favorite viewing.) Neither religion nor the once sacrosanct royal family is safe from the often savage wit of "TW3," as some of its millions of fans call it.

News coverage, on both radio and television, reflects Greene's special interest in this field. The BBC is constitutionally denied the right, as an institution, to editorialize. But, as Greene has said, it is "always entitled to ask questions." In fact, in its reporting of the London race riots of 1958 (when Greene was director of news and current affairs) and in its more recent coverage of alleged police brutality in the handling of ban-the-bomb demonstrators, the BBC's outrage was unmistakeable. In the *BBC Handbook* for 1960, Greene wrote: "I should not for a moment admit that a man who wanted to speak in favour of racial intolerance had the same rights as a man who wanted to condemn it. There are some questions on which one should not be impartial." Even more controversial was Greene's decision to permit the broadcast, early in 1963, of an interview with Georges Bidault, a leader of the underground French terrorist group, Organisation de l'Armée secrète (O.A.S.). Questions were asked in Parliament about what was regarded in some quarters as a studied insult to the French government, but both Greene and the British government defended the BBC's right to present the program "as a matter of interest and information."

The Bidault incident provides some backing for Greene's claim, made during a visit to the United States in 1961, that the BBC is "the most truly independent broadcasting organization in the world." The British government has in theory the power to veto any BBC broadcast but, Greene said, it has never made use of this power, even in wartime. The policy appears to be a sound one in terms of audience appeal. In 1960, when Greene became director-general, British viewers preferred the programs of the BBC's commercial competitor, the Independent Television Authority, in a ratio of 58 to 42. The ratio is now 52 to 48 in favor of the BBC.

Thanks in large measure to the 1962 recommendations of the Pilkington Committee, set up two years earlier to consider the future of British broadcasting, the BBC is now entering a period of great expansion and innovation. Not all of the Pilkington Committee's recommendations were adopted by the government, but those that were will give the BBC a second television channel by 1964 and color television a year later. Greene is also seeking to establish a network of local radio stations on the American pattern to supplement national and regional programming, although this proposal has so far been opposed by the government. In July 1963 it was announced that the British Broadcasting Corporation and the Soviet Ministry of Broadcasting and Television had agreed to a television exchange plan that would include documentaries and cultural programs. Greene headed the team that negotiated the plan.

Hugh Carleton Greene and the former Elaine (Gilbert) Shaplen, whom he married on September 24, 1951, have two sons, Christopher Louis and Timothy Charles. Greene also has two sons, Graham and James, by his first wife, Helga Guinness, to whom he was married from 1934 until 1948, when the marriage was dissolved. According to the *Observer* profile, Greene "goes for long walks in empty places," likes roses, and collects first editions of early detective novels. In 1957 he was co-editor, with Graham Greene, of an anthology called *The Spy's Bedside Book* (Hart-Davis).

Greene has blue eyes and brown hair, is six feet six inches tall, and weighs 215 pounds. The *Observer* describes him as "a large, cool, intelligent man . . . with a striking skull, chubby face and heavy spectacles." He is "far from being remote, though one official calls him a 'lonely tower of a man' and others say he is an enigma, a careerist with private dreams, a bit of a cold fish. He is disconcerting—he will ask an interviewer whether he really *is* a cold fish. He reads quickly, misses nothing, often sits silent and just listens, appears to be better briefed than anyone else: but at the same time he is accessible and considerate, and plays endearing games like cricket and darts. . . . As far as the staff is concerned, he gives them a safe feeling." Three years after the *Observer* profile was written, another journalist, Mary Crozier, wrote in the Manchester *Guardian* (April 4, 1963): "The feet are not cold, but the head is very cool."

On March 26, 1962, at the DuPont Awards Foundation dinner in Washington, D.C., Greene expressed something of his professional philosophy in an attack on broadcasters who claim to "give the public what it wants." "You cannot give everyone what they want all the time," he said. "But you can, under what I should call a free broadcasting system, do your best to think sometimes in terms of the few; sometimes in terms of the many; and even if, as must inevitably be the case, there are many interests which you cannot satisfy, you can at least not kid yourself into thinking that the studied neglect of minorities is justified on democratic grounds."

References

London Observer p4 Ja 10 '60 por
International Who's Who, 1962-63
Who's Who, 1963
Who's Who in America, 1962-63

GREENSTEIN, JESSE L(EONARD) Oct. 15,
1909- Astronomer; university professor
Address: b. Mt. Wilson and Palomar Observatories, California Institute of Technology, Pasadena 4, Calif.; h. 2057 San Pasqual St., Pasadena
10, Calif.

A world authority on the evolution and chemical composition of stars, Professor Jesse L. Greenstein continues to make his regular personal
"runs" in the control chair of the giant 200-inch
Hale telescope at California's Palomar Observatory. He concurrently serves as professor and
head of the department of astronomy at the
California Institute of Technology. Over the
years Greenstein has undertaken, among other
things, projects involving the nature of gas and
dust in interstellar space, and its interaction with
stars; absorption and polarization of light in
space; the study of the composition of stars from
their spectra; nuclear processes in stars; the discovery and study of stars of peculiar composition; and the design and construction of high-
altitude spectrographs for use on rockets and
satellites.

With the aid of Palomar's "big-eye" Greenstein has watched processes ranging from the
helium fusion furnaces of giant red stars having
internal temperatures of five billion degrees, to
the approaching death of white dwarf stars having energy levels so low that their central densi-
ties approach 150 tons per cubic inch. No scientific
recluse, Greenstein is convinced of the need for
public understanding of astronomy. He is active
on a number of governmental and international
bodies, where his insight and special skills in
astrophysics and optics have led to important
contributions.

Jesse Leonard Greenstein, the son of Maurice
and Leah (Feingold) Greenstein, was born in
New York City on October 15, 1909 and grew
up in Manhattan, where his family was engaged
in the real estate business. From 1921 to 1925 he

JESSE L. GREENSTEIN

attended the Horace Mann School, a private
preparatory school for boys. Majoring in astronomy at Harvard University, Greenstein earned
his B.A. degree in 1929 and his M.A. in 1930.
Because of the Depression, Greenstein concluded
that further graduate work offered only a dim
prospect for academic employment. Turning to
the selling of real estate, he bought and sold
bonds, and, in spite of poor business conditions,
found himself with a substantial profit in less
than five years. Then he began to wonder
whether what he was doing was really worth
while, and his basic urge toward astronomy
returned. He quit his business and went back to
Harvard, where he earned his Ph.D. in 1937.

Greenstein was a National Research Council
fellow at Yerkes Observatory of the University of
Chicago from 1937 to 1939. He was appointed
instructor in astrophysics at Chicago in 1939,
assistant professor in 1942, and associate professor in 1947. From 1942 to 1945 Greenstein
also did military research in optical design at
Yerkes Observatory, under the Office of Scientific
Research and Development. In addition to his
Chicago duties he served as a research associate
at the McDonald Observatory of the University
of Texas (1947-48). Greenstein accepted an appointment on the staff of Mount Wilson and
Palomar Observatories of the California Institute
of Technology in 1948. In the following year he
was appointed professor and head of the department of astronomy at Caltech, where he organized a new graduate school in astrophysics in
connection with the observatories.

In December 1949 Greenstein and his Caltech
colleague, Leverett Davis, Jr., presented to the
American Astronomical Society an advanced explanation of the reasons for the partial polarization of light from some stars. Astronomers had
previously believed that iron-containing dust
particles, statically oriented in space, caused the
polarization. The trouble with this theory was
that such particles would have to be at unreasonably low temperatures to escape random
spin. By considering that very strong magnetic
fields exist in space, Greenstein and Davis pictured the iron particles as being in a state of
oriented spin, like a football kicked end over end.
This would account for the polarization, while
avoiding the assumption of unreasonably low
temperatures.

"How did the universe begin?" is a question
toward which Greenstein and William Fowler of
Caltech directed fresh thought in 1955. They
began by questioning one of the prevailing
theories, which holds that the genesis of the
universe lay in one huge cosmic explosion. If
such had occurred, they reasoned, then all stars
should have the same composition. But Greenstein's analyses of stellar spectra showed that
this was not so. In fact, his observations revealed
giant red stars containing very heavy elements,
and still producing them. The earth and sun,
far from being born at the same time as the rest
of the universe may, according to the Greenstein-
Fowler interpretation, be as much as a billion
years younger.

In his studies of the life histories of stars,
Greenstein has been particularly interested in
their senescence. Some 3 percent of all the stars

in our galaxy are dying. These stars are known as white dwarfs. Their luminosities are very low, their fuel has almost burned out, and their size has shrunk to a mere 20,000 miles across, or less. From his Palomar data on more than fifty of these ancients, Greenstein predicts that in about seven billion years, our own sun will be a blue-white dwarf shrunk to a mere pinpoint in the sky, giving off so little heat that the earth's temperature will be 300 degrees below zero. Greenstein makes the point that although the sun's hydrogen will last for billions of years yet, the day must eventually come when it is used up, and that it can never be replaced.

At the annual meeting of the National Academy of Sciences in April 1960, Greenstein, along with William Fowler of Caltech, Fred Hoyle of Cambridge, and E. E. Salpeter of Cornell, proposed the following sequence of events in explaining the formation of the various elements in the stars. Starting in an ordinary star like our sun, hydrogen is fused to form helium with vast energy release. After the hydrogen is consumed, helium fusion begins, the star swells to a red giant with internal temperatures up to five billion degrees, and ever heavier elements up to iron are created by nuclear transmutation. As even higher temperatures are reached, neutrons are released; these combine with iron, and elements up to bismuth are produced.

Upon the eventual collapse of a red giant star, neutrons are released in still greater numbers, again combine with iron, and form elements up to uranium and the transuranium elements. The red giant may then simply shrivel to a white dwarf on its way to coldness and death. It may, however, explode into what is known as a supernova, scattering itself throughout space, where all its elements become available to be gathered up by new stars in the process of formation.

In January 1961 a group of Caltech's radio and optical astronomers disclosed that they had determined the exact location of what they believed to be the first radio star ever found. The astronomers had been puzzled by the behavior of a celestial source of radio signals known as 3C-48. Turning to Greenstein for data from the Hale telescope, they learned that the discovery marked the first time that astronomers had been able to listen to and locate what then appeared to be an individual star that emitted radio signals. Previously discovered celestial radio sources had been gas clouds, galaxies, galaxies in collision, or shells of exploding stars. Later in the same year Greenstein and two colleagues made a spectral analysis of another "oddball" star, known as 3 Centauri A. The study showed that the star had no general magnetic field. It was found to contain the rare helium-3 isotope, as well as krypton, and unusual concentrations of gallium, phosphorus, nitrogen, and iron.

In the spring of 1963 Greenstein and his associates were confronted with another mystery. A celestial radio source known as 3C-273, believed to be a star, was emitting an excessive amount of radio noise. Greenstein and his colleague Maarten Schmidt found that the spectrogram of 3C-273 was unlike that of any star yet studied. The spectral lines were shifted far toward the red, in a manner analogous to the lowering pitch of a train whistle receding into the distance. It appeared that 3C-273 was hurrying out of the universe. If so, the degree of red shift showed it to be traveling at one-sixth the speed of light. In view of its brightness and distance from the earth it was determined that 3C-273 was not a single star but a galaxy, caught perhaps in the act of explosion.

To confirm these assumptions, 3C-48, which bears characteristics similar to those of 3C-273, was re-examined by Greenstein and Schmidt. Although it had previously been believed to be a star, 3C-48 was also determined to be an exploding galaxy, moving away from the earth at one-third the speed of light. The data obtained from these studies appeared to confirm the "expanding universe" theory. According to this theory, galaxies, which obtain their speeds from the general expansion of the universe, are moving away from the earth at velocities approaching the speed of light. The more distant the object, the faster it appears to be going away from the earth. In view of the brightness of such distant objects as 3C-273 and 3C-48, Greenstein believes that astronomers may be able to identify with present telescopes objects as much as ten to twelve billion light-years away.

Living daily with such fantastic facts and figures, Greenstein would hardly be blamed if he indulged in a little science-fiction fantasy. On the contrary, he prefers to confine himself to what he can observe and relate to known physical laws. However, he is entirely in sympathy with those who like to speculate. He once told a staff writer for Fortune (May 1960): "Knowing how hard it is to collect a fact, you understand why most people want to have some fun analyzing it."

Greenstein has contributed to the symposia Astrophysics (McGraw, 1951), edited by Joseph A. Hynek; Modern Physics for the Engineer (McGraw, 1954), edited by Louis N. Ridenour; and Vistas in Astronomy (Pergamon, 1956), edited by Arthur Beer. He is the editor of the Symposium on the Hertzsprung-Russell Diagram, published in Paris in 1959, and of Stellar Atmospheres, published by the University of Chicago Press in 1961. From 1953 to 1959 he was corresponding editor of Annales d'Astrophysique (Paris). Greenstein has written a number of scientific papers and government reports, and he holds patents on various optical devices.

From 1949 to 1952 Greenstein was on the committee on astronomy, advisory to the Office of Naval Research. He has also served on an advisory commission to the National Bureau of Standards, and he is a member of the observatory committee of Mount Wilson and Palomar Observatories. He served the National Science Foundation on the committee of consultants on astronomy and radio astronomy from 1953 to 1957, and on the mathematical, physical, and engineering sciences divisional committee from 1957 to 1960. He was councillor of the American Astronomical Society from 1947 to 1950 and its vice-president from 1955 to 1957. From 1952 to 1958 Greenstein served as president of the commission on stellar spectroscopy of the International Astronomical Union. He is a fellow of the Royal Astronomical Society, a director of the

GREENSTEIN, JESSE L.—*Continued*

Astronomical Society of the Pacific, and a member of the American Academy of Arts and Sciences, the National Academy of Sciences, the Athenaeum Club of Pasadena, and Phi Beta Kappa honorary fraternity.

While engaged in his doctoral studies at Harvard, Jesse L. Greenstein met Naomi Kitay, then an English student at Mount Holyoke. They were married on January 7, 1934, and they have two sons, George Samuel and Peter Daniel. Upon returning home from his occasional all-night sessions at Palomar, Greenstein likes to relax with his family and indulge in his pastime of raising orchids. Summarizing his personal philosophy, he once said that he enjoys "sitting up with the universe," and added: "I didn't get much chance to look out when I was a boy in Manhattan."

References

Fortune 61:149 My '60 por

Sci Am 200:46 Ja '59

Who's Who in America, 1962-63

American Men of Science 10th ed (1960-62)

GRIMOND, JO(SEPH) (grǐ'mŭnd) July 29, 1913- British political leader

Address: b. House of Commons, London, S.W.1, England; h. Old Manse of Firth, Kirkwall, Orkney, Scotland; 71 Kew Green, Richmond, Surrey, England

By common consent, the resurgence of the Liberal party in Great Britain is the almost single-handed achievement of one man. He is the Right Honourable Jo Grimond, Member of Parliament for Orkney and Shetland, who succeeded Clement Davies as leader of the Liberal party in 1956. A Scotsman educated at Eton and Oxford, Grimond began his career as a barrister and was an Army officer in World War II. He worked for UNRRA and the Scottish National Trust before entering Parliament in 1950.

Joseph Grimond (the shortened form, "Jo," is his own choice) was born on July 29, 1913 in St. Andrews, Scotland, to Joseph Bowman Grimond, a successful jute manufacturer, and Helen Lydia (Richardson) Grimond. Jo Grimond was sent to Eton, which enjoys maximum prestige among English public schools. There he played cricket and fives for the school and became a senior prefect. No less outstanding academically, he won a Brackenbury scholarship to Balliol College, Oxford, graduating in 1935 with first class honors in politics, philosophy, and economics.

Grimond inherited his Liberalism from his father and, unlike many Liberals of his generation, has never seriously considered switching to a more fashionable party. This unswerving commitment, according to a profile in the London *Observer* (September 13, 1959), "springs from long reflection on politics . . . and from his Scottish background and origins. . . . Though he was sent away to the sophisticated English world of Eton and Oxford [and] like many

young Scots, he enjoyed and excelled in the upper-class English game of life . . . [he] half-resented the subtle process of anglicisation to which he was subjected. He was always aware that, though his father was well-to-do . . . the Grimond family had risen from quite humble origins only two generations before. Inside the gay Whig patrician was a Scottish radical."

Leaving Oxford, Grimond read law as a Harmsworth Scholar of the Middle Temple, one of London's ancient Inns of Court. In 1937 he was called to the bar and was accredited as a lawyer competent to argue cases in court. He practised as a barrister until the outbreak of World War II in 1939. Meanwhile, his interest in politics, lively even at Eton, had been stimulated by the events of the 1930's. During the great Depression he returned to Scotland to help run a fish marketing co-operative in Dundee for the unemployed. He made his political debut in the general election of 1935, speaking in support of the Liberal candidate for Kincardine and West Aberdeenshire. In 1938 Grimond married into England's most prominent Liberal family.

A few days before the outbreak of World War II, Jo Grimond joined the Second Fife and Forfar Yeomanry, a Scottish Infantry regiment. A year later he was invited to stand as Liberal candidate for Orkney and Shetland, two remote archipelagos off the coast of Scotland comprising several hundred small islands. Grimond, who had never visited these islands, accepted. Then, with the war a more immediate concern, he put the invitation out of his mind. In 1943 complications following an appendectomy took Grimond out of the infantry. He was sent to the Army's Staff College and was a divisional staff officer during the Allied invasion of Normandy. Grimond ended the war at Divisional Headquarters in Hamburg, Germany with the rank of major.

When the Army issued an order that all political candidates should be repatriated in time for the 1945 general elections, Grimond hurried home, paid his first visit to the Orkneys, and vigorously campaigned for the constituency. He lost the seat by only 329 votes to the Conservative incumbent who had held it for fifteen years. From 1945 to 1947, while still in the Army, Grimond was on special assignment as director of personnel at the London headquarters of the United Nations Relief and Rehabilitation Administration (UNRRA). In 1947, upon his return to civilian life, he became secretary of the Scottish National Trust. This body, concerned primarily with the preservation of historic buildings, also owned land and operated a tenant-farming community. His three years with the Trust gave Grimond valuable insight into local Scottish problems.

Grimond's 1945 candidacy had given him a taste for politics and for the Orkneys. In the 1950 elections he stood again for Parliament, and this time he was elected for Orkney and Shetland by over 2,000 votes. He has represented that constituency ever since. Grimond entered a House of Commons that had only nine Liberal members including himself, but membership in a small party had its advantages. Grimond sat on several committees, often spoke on a variety of topics, and was soon appointed Liberal whip.

His prestige soared again after the 1951 elections. Although three of the nine Liberals lost their seats, he was returned with an increased majority. His elevation to the leadership of the party was virtually assured and only awaited the retirement of Clement Davies, the aging incumbent.

Davies retired at the end of the 1956 Liberal party conference. At the time Grimond had already left the conference for a visit to the United States. In one hectic week Grimond flew back from America, accepted the leadership of his party, and ranged it firmly against the Conservative government's policy on Suez, where British troops had been sent in an abortive attempt to prevent Egypt's seizure of the canal.

The British Liberal party is the successor to the Whig party of the eighteenth and nineteenth centuries. It was one of the country's two major political parties until it was supplanted by the Labour party at the 1922 general election. When Grimond became leader in 1956, Liberal fortunes were at a low ebb. The party had only six seats in the House of Commons, and in 1955 it had polled only 722,000 votes out of a total ballot of nearly 35,000,000. As a political force the Liberals were negligible, and few observers would have looked to Jo Grimond to change the situation. He was generally regarded as a charming amateur—intelligent, but a political lightweight.

Within three years of Grimond's election to the leadership, the Liberals had won one by-election, had come second in three more and, according to pollsters, had won the support of between 8 and 15 percent of the electorate. The victory of Grimond's brother-in-law, Mark Bonham Carter, in the by-election in Great Torrington, Devon County, in 1958, constituted the first gain that the Liberal party had achieved in forty years.

Grimond had given the party a platform and an identity. The Liberals were the first to commit themselves to British membership in the European Economic Community; they were against imperialism, an independent nuclear deterrent, and Britain's stifling class distinctions. The party promised more schools, more houses, better planning on pay and pensions. It avoided blind commitment to either Conservative free enterprise or Labour's policy of public ownership, arguing that both systems had their roles to play in a modern economy. It advocated "co-partnership in industry," with workers and management sharing profits and working with, rather than against, each other. Above all, perhaps, Grimond succeeded, as the London Sunday *Times* (June 15, 1958) noted, "in projecting a youthful image of Liberalism which appeals to the new generation of voters."

But in the 1959 elections, when the Conservatives won another smashing majority, many of the Liberal party's gains were swept away. Their share of the ballot rose to 1,640,761 votes of the 27,863,738 cast, but the Liberals came out of the election still with only six of the 630 seats in the House of Commons. Although the party's platform remained virtually unchanged after the 1959 election, its organization was drastically

JO GRIMOND

pruned and revised. A new eight-man organization committee set about streamlining headquarters operations and raising funds. The Liberal war chest increased its assets from $64,000 in 1959 to $560,000 in 1962.

In March 1962 the Liberals won their most spectacular victory to date, when a Liberal candidate, Eric Lubbock, won a by-election at Orpington, Kent, by some 7,000 votes. Orpington, a Conservative stronghold, had gone to that party by 14,000 votes in the 1959 election, and Conservative leaders, admitting that they were shocked by the 1962 result, for the first time began to regard the Liberal resurgence as a serious threat. The Liberals, who have placed themselves firmly on the left as a non-Socialist alternative to the Labour party, have gone on to a series of wins and near-wins in by-elections and impressive gains in local government elections.

It has been pointed out that the Parliamentary Liberal party, which now has seven members in the House of Commons, can still be comfortably accommodated in two London taxicabs. Lacking the funds, the massive party organization, the research facilities, and the specialized manpower of the major parties, Grimond has accomplished the task of injecting new life into the Liberal party by sheer hard work. He must keep abreast of events, find something worthwhile to say on almost every public issue, support his local candidates, travel, and confer with political leaders in other countries. He also continues to take very seriously his responsibilities to his own distant constituents.

In his first eighteen months in Parliament Grimond traveled 80,000 miles between London and Orkney alone. During the first three months of 1963 he spoke with President John F. Kennedy in the United States and with political leaders in Canada and Holland. He conferred with offi-

GRIMOND, JO—*Continued*

cials of the European Economic Community in Strasbourg and Brussels, and addressed the Community's Assembly. At home, he led a recruiting campaign in Wales, addressed many party meetings, paid regular visits to his constituents, and spoke in the House of Commons on a great range of topics. Grimond has called for reform of Parliament and of industrial relations; for the improvement of housing, education, and regional development; for the mobilization of Liberal forces against racial intolerance; and for measures to cope with the Scottish unemployment problem.

In 1959 Grimond's book *The Liberal Future* was published by Faber & Faber. Although it contained an appendix on party policy, it was primarily concerned with stating a Liberal philosophy. Liberals, Grimond wrote, "are optimistic because they have faith in human action based on examination of the facts available to them." They want reason, respect for the individual, and responsible conduct to govern public action. He went on to show how these principles can be applied to political and economic life today. Grimond has also written a number of party pamphlets. He often contributes to newspapers and magazines, and he speaks for his party on radio and television. He is working on another book. Grimond was elected rector of Edinburgh University in 1960, and he became a Privy Councillor in 1961. On his visit to the United States in January 1963 he was a Chubb Fellow lecturer at Yale University. Grimond is a founder-member of the Friends of the Atlantic Union.

In 1938 Jo Grimond married Laura Miranda, daughter of Sir Maurice and Lady Violet Bonham-Carter (who has been described as the "perennial high priestess of the Liberal Party") and granddaughter of Lord Asquith, who in 1908 became Prime Minister of the party's last elected government. They have four children, Andrew, Grizelda, John, and Magnus. Grimond's interests, when he has time for them, include golf, gardening, and walking. His favorite authors include Jane Austen, Bernard Shaw, Joseph Conrad, Evelyn Waugh, and Graham Greene. He reads many political books and articles, pursues an interest in universities, and enjoys sentimental biographies, literary criticism, and the Inspector Maigret stories of Georges Simenon.

According to a profile in the New York *Times* (October 13, 1959), Grimond is "tall and handsome, with blue eyes and graying hair that looks as if it had just been mussed. Many women, it is said, feel an urge to comb it back into place. He has a sort of lazy, natural charm and an unaffected modesty that young voters, in particular, find in refreshing contrast with the usual run of professional politicians. But he speaks in public with a commanding voice and an easy dignity, giving a general impression of an earnest man with a clear mind and a deadly serious intent."

References

London Observer p13 S 13 '59 por
Who's Who, 1963

GRISWOLD, A(LFRED) WHITNEY Oct. 27, 1906-Apr. 19, 1963 President of Yale University (1950-63); teacher of history at Yale (1933-63); noted for his defense of academic freedom and his insistence on excellence in education; author of several books on history and on education. See *Current Biography* (April) 1950.

Obituary

N Y Times p1 + Ap 20 '63

GROSS, PAUL MAGNUS Sept. 15, 1895-
Chemist; educator; organization official
Address: b. Department of Chemistry, Duke University, Durham, N.C.; h. 3816 Dover Rd., Durham, N.C.

A specialist in physical inorganic and fluorine chemistry, a university administrator, and a government consultant in education and science, Paul Magnus Gross succeeded Thomas Park as retiring president and chairman of the board of directors of the American Association for the Advancement of Science on January 15, 1963. He had served in 1962 as president of the A.A.A.S., the world's largest group of related scientific organizations.

The William Howell Pegram professor of chemistry at Duke University since 1920, Gross has played a vital role in building Duke into a leading educational institution. He served as chairman of its department of chemistry from 1921 to 1948, as dean of its Graduate School of Arts and Sciences from 1947 to 1952, and as vice-president of its Division of Education from 1949 to 1960. Gross holds the United States government Medal for Merit for his invention during World War II of a frangible plastic bullet for gunnery training.

Although he now considers himself a Southerner, Paul Magnus Gross was born on September 15, 1895 in New York City and reared there. He is the son of Magnus Gross, an educator and secretary to the board of retirement of New York City, and Ellen Veronica (Sullivan) Gross. His grandfather, who was also named Magnus Gross, was a chemist, an editor, and a prominent figure in New York City educational circles. Paul Gross has two sisters, Mrs. Beatrix Disalvo and Mrs. Ethel Reyling.

After graduating from Townsend Harris High School in New York City, Gross attended the College of the City of New York, where he was on the swimming team. He was elected to Phi Beta Kappa and took his B.S. degree in chemistry from C.C.N.Y. in 1916. While doing graduate work at Columbia University he was an instructor in chemistry at C.C.N.Y. from 1916 to 1918 and served as a second lieutenant in the United States Army Chemical Warfare Service in 1918-19. He obtained the M.A. degree in 1917 and the Ph.D. degree in 1919 from Columbia. A member of Sigma Xi, the honorary science research fraternity, he also belongs to Omicron Delta Kappa, honorary society for leadership and activities, and to Phi Lambda Upsilon, a recognition society in chemistry. He wrote his doctoral thesis, "Factors Affecting the Stability of Addition Compounds in Solution and Their Influence Upon Ionization Equilibria," in an area in which he did much of his later work—the chemistry of solutions.

Gross began his postdoctoral teaching career as an assistant professor of chemistry in 1919 at Trinity College in Durham, North Carolina, which five years later became the nucleus of the newly created Duke University. He was promoted to his present academic post as William Howell Pegram professor of chemistry in 1920, and from 1921 to 1948 he was chairman of the department of chemistry. Soon after arriving at Trinity College in 1919 Gross initiated a long-term study of the fluorination of organic molecules. To this beginning the Duke University chemistry department's reputation as a center for the study of organic fluorine compounds can be traced.

In 1929 Gross studied at the University of Leipzig under Peter Debye, an eminent physicist known especially for his studies of molecular structure. Writing about Gross in *Science* (February 17, 1961), Philip Handler said: "Perhaps the most important single influence on his career was a year spent in Leipzig . . . with Peter Debye, an experience which produced an enduring friendship as well as a series of incisive analyses of molecular structure based upon estimation of dipole moments and magnetic susceptibility." These analyses yielded a number of new insights into the structure of the aromatic class of hydrocarbons and the halogen acids. Upon his return to Duke, Gross and his students undertook several studies of chemical compounds in solution, which culminated in the construction of a critical test of the Debye-Hückel theory—a fundamental concept in modern solution chemistry.

Meanwhile, in 1927, Gross had begun to investigate the cultivation and curing of tobacco, an important product in the economy of North Carolina. The studies that he made with Frederick Wolff of the chemical changes that occur as tobacco ripens and is cured changed the buying practices of the major tobacco companies. In addition, the demonstration by Gross and Wolff that certain strains of aromatic tobaccos could be grown closely spaced in a field without much fertilizer led to continuing research that may allow the American manufacturer to dispense with the foreign aromatic tobaccos that he now imports for blending with domestic leaves. Gross and his colleagues also freed American firms from dependence upon French cigarette papers by showing that cigarette paper could be made in the United States from flax and hemp.

Evidence of Paul Gross's ingenuity and perseverance in solving seemingly insoluble problems is to be found in his contributions to the war effort during the 1940's. Early in World War II he learned that the United States Army Air Force urgently needed improved methods of gunnery training. What was required was a bullet that could be fired through a standard machine gun from a bomber in flight and that would leave a record of hits on target planes without inflicting any damage. Gross was at first refused research funds by the National Defense Research Committee on the grounds that this problem was insurmountable, but, undeterred, he began work on

PAUL MAGNUS GROSS

a frangible bullet at Duke University with some support from the Bakelite Corporation and Princeton University.

After major problems had been solved, Gross and his colleagues obtained a government contract, and about a year later a training system using the frangible bullet was instituted in Army Air Force gunnery schools. For this work Gross was given the Medal for Merit, the United States government's highest civilian award, in 1948. The Presidential citation read: "The Medal for Merit has been awarded to Dr. Paul Magnus Gross for . . . outstanding service to the United States from July 1942 to September 1945. . . . Although a chemist he successfully solved serious problems in the fields of ballistics, machine gun modification, characteristics of armour, electrical circuits, plastics and remote control mechanisms. . . . Dr. Gross persisted until what he believed possible became true, and thereby made an invaluable contribution to the war effort of the United States."

As organized scientific activity increased after World War II, Gross received many calls to public service. He was an incorporator of the Oak Ridge Institute of Nuclear Studies in June 1947 and has served as its president and on its board of directors since 1949. He has been a member of the North Carolina Atomic Energy Advisory Committee since 1959. In September and October of 1949 he attended the General UNESCO Conference in Paris as scientific adviser to the American delegation. From 1950 to 1962 he served on the board of the National Science Foundation, the last five years as chairman. Gross has been a member of the national cancer advisory council of the National Institutes of Health since 1959, and he was chairman of the committee on environmental health of the Department of Health, Education, and Welfare in 1961.

Gross has served education with a devotion equal to that he has given to science. As dean

GROSS, PAUL MAGNUS—*Continued*

of the Graduate School of Arts and Sciences from 1947 to 1952, dean of the university from 1952 to 1958, and vice-president of the Division of Education from 1949 to 1960, he put into practice at Duke his belief that the quality of a school depends on the quality of its faculty. He hired outstanding men in all fields. In addition, he helped to develop the Research Triangle Institute, by means of which the research laboratories of major industrial corporations were brought to an industrial research park near Duke University, the University of North Carolina, and North Carolina State College.

A founder of the Council of Southern Universities, Gross was its president in 1952-53 and has been its treasurer since 1949. For his services from 1953 to 1956 as chairman of the Southern Regional Scholarship Committee for selection of Marshall Scholars to study in Great Britain, Gross was named an Honorary Commander of the civil division of the Order of the British Empire in 1958. Other awards he has received are the Herty Medal (1945), given annually by Georgia State College for Women to the most outstanding scientist in the South; the 1951 Southern Association of Science and Industry award for outstanding work in Southern regional development; an honorary award from the Florida section of the American Chemical Society; the Townsend Harris medal of C.C.N.Y. (1953); and the Carnegie "Manship" award (1954).

Paul Magnus Gross married Gladys Cobb Petersen on August 4, 1918. They have a son, Paul Magnus, Jr., now on the faculty of Wake Forest College, and a daughter, Beatrix Cobb (Mrs. Robert L. Ramey), whose husband teaches at the University of Virginia. Gross rejects any characterization of himself as "a scientific 'long hair'" with little interest in the lighter side of life. He recalls that in the 1920's and 1930's his wife helped to develop student dramatics at Trinity College-Duke University and that he designed and constructed stage sets. His only appearance as a performer was at a faculty party shortly after he had become vice-president of the Duke Division of Education, when he appeared in a skit as a member of a five-piece German street band, his scarlet, brass-buttoned uniform stuffed with pillows, and a huge bass drum, surmounted by cymbals, triangles, and bells, suspended from his neck.

White-haired, blue-eyed Paul Magnus Gross is five feet seven and one-half inches in height, weighs 183 pounds, and is described by colleagues as a man not only of knowledge and skill, but of true wisdom. He likes to relax in the summers at a modest beach house on the North Carolina coast, where he can indulge in his favorite recreations: swimming, sailing, and deep-sea fishing. Among the Grosses' boats are a small sailing craft built by Gross and his son and an ocean-going powered vessel for deep-sea fishing.

Gross is a Fellow of the New York Academy of Sciences and of the American Physical Society. He has served as secretary (1944 through 1945), vice-chairman (1945-46), and chairman (1946-47) of the American Chemical Society's division of physical and inorganic chemistry. Gross has been a member of the American Association for the Advancement of Science since 1930. He was a director of A.A.A.S. from 1955 to 1958, president-elect for the year 1961, and president, succeeding Thomas Park, in 1962. Since January 15, 1963 he has served as retiring president and chairman of the board of directors of A.A.A.S. When Gross was named to A.A.A.S. office in 1961, Philip Handler, a Duke University colleague, wrote in *Science* (February 17, 1961): "A lifetime of successful endeavor as teacher, investigator, and administrator extraordinary have prepared him for the diverse challenges of this position of leadership in American science."

References

Science 133:463+ F 17 '61 por
American Men of Science 10th ed (1960-62)
Who's Who in America, 1962-63

GUEVARA (SERNA), ERNESTO (gā-vä'rä ĕr-nās'tō) June 14, 1928- Cuban political leader; government official

Address: b. Ministry of Industry, Havana, Cuba

The economic czar of the Republic of Cuba, Ernesto "Che" Guevara, is regarded by many observers as the leading intellectual force behind the government of Premier Fidel Castro. Guevara is a native of Argentina and a doctor of medicine who was active in leftist movements of several Latin American countries, including Guatemala, before becoming associated with Castro. He played a major role in the military struggle that led to the overthrow of the Cuban dictator Fulgencio Batista and the establishment of Castro's revolutionary regime in January 1959. An avowed Marxist, Guevara is largely responsible for formulating and carrying out plans for the nationalization of Cuban industry and agriculture and for the political and economic alignment of Cuba with the Soviet bloc. He served as president of the National Bank of Cuba from November 1959 until February 1961, when he was appointed to the newly created cabinet post of Minister of Industry.

Of Spanish and Irish descent, Ernesto Guevara Serna was born on June 14, 1928 in Rosario, eastern Argentina. The nickname "Che" (which is pronounced chā) comes from the Argentine equivalent of "Hey, you." He is the eldest of five children of Ernesto Rafael Guevara Lynch, an architect and builder, and Celia de la Serna de Guevara, who is active in Latin American leftist movements. His paternal grandmother was a United States citizen, born in California. In his childhood (as now) Guevara suffered from asthma, and for this reason his family moved to the mountain town of Alta Gracia. He was given a rugged upbringing by his father, who taught him to shoot, and he ran with street gangs, worked in the vineyards of Cordoba, and swam and played Rugby and golf.

At an early age Guevara avidly read leftist history and sociology books in the family library, and he was particularly influenced by the works of the Chilean Communist poet Pablo Neruda. When he was fourteen he joined a youth group of the Partido Unión Democrática and took part in street fights against supporters of the Argentine dictator Juan Perón. The illness of his paternal grandmother, who had cancer, influenced Guevara in his decision to become a doctor. At the age of nineteen, after graduating from high school with distinction, he entered the medical school of the University of Buenos Aires.

Interrupting his studies in 1952, Guevara went with a friend on a motorcycle and hitchhiking tour through South America. He visited Chile, Peru, Ecuador, Colombia, and Venezuela, and worked for a time as a male nurse in a leper colony. He also tried to visit the United States but was turned back by immigration officials at Miami, Florida. Returning to Argentina, he resumed his studies and graduated with the degree of doctor of medicine and surgery in 1953.

To escape military service in Perón's army Guevara again left Argentina. He became associated with leftist movements in Bolivia, Peru, Ecuador, Panama, and Costa Rica, and he studied the political and economic conditions of the countries he visited. During this period Guevara developed strong feelings against the United States and came to consider himself a Marxist, although he did not have a clear-cut political orientation. Arriving in Guatemala in December 1953, Guevara sold encyclopedias for a while and then held a minor post as an inspector with the agrarian reform movement in the government of the leftist President Jacobo Arbenz Guzmán. When in 1954 the Arbenz regime was overthrown by Colonel Carlos Castillo Armas, covertly supported by the United States Central Intelligence Agency, Guevara made a futile effort to organize a resistance force.

After staying at the Argentine Embassy in Guatemala for two months Guevara went to Mexico, where he met Fidel Castro and his brother Raúl. He joined their revolutionary 26th of July movement, acting as a physician when needed, becoming chief of personnel for Castro's expeditionary force, and helping General Alberto Bayo, an exiled Spanish Republican, to train Cuban guerilla forces. Guevara participated in Castro's ill-fated invasion attempt on the south coast of Cuba's Oriente Province in December 1956, and he was one of twelve survivors of an original force of some eighty men.

Castro set up guerilla headquarters in the Sierra Maestra Mountains of Cuba, and Guevara, who eventually attained the rank of major, became his chief adviser. He subjected the men under his command to rigid training in military tactics and the use of weapons. At night he read to them from literary works, studied revolutionary literature, and formulated future plans for social revolution. In the mountains Guevara set up a weapons plant, a bakery, and a shoe shop. He also established a rebel radio station and a network of schools. In 1958 he conducted the military campaigns that led to the defeat of Fulgencio Batista. His forces swept through Camaguey and Las Villas provinces and fought the decisive battle of Santa Clara. In January 1959, as Castro assumed control of the Cuban government, Guevara took command of La Cabaña fortress, overlooking Havana harbor.

During the first few months of the Castro regime Guevara remained more or less in the background and exercised his influence indirectly.

Wide World

DR. ERNESTO GUEVARA

In the summer of 1959 he visited neutralist countries of Europe, Africa, and Asia as a special envoy of the Castro government with the purpose of negotiating commercial treaties. Upon his return he was named head of the industrial department of the National Institute of Agrarian Reform (INRA), an agency set up to carry out Cuba's agrarian reform law of May 1959. Although Guevara had little background in economics, Castro appointed him on November 26, 1959 to the top economic post in the country, that of president of the National Bank of Cuba, to succeed Dr. Felípe Pazos, a highly respected financial conservative. Upon taking office Guevara pledged that there would be no radical change in government economic policy and declared that rigid import controls to preserve dollar balances would be maintained.

Guevara also undertook the task of training Cuba's civilian militia, and he wrote a training manual, *La Guerra de Guerillas*, published by the Cuban government in 1960. The book, which covers virtually every aspect of the revolutionary struggle, was translated into English and published by the Monthly Review Press in 1961 under the title *Guerilla Warfare*. As head of the National Bank, Guevara was largely responsible for concluding a commercial treaty between Cuba and the Soviet Union in February 1960 under which the Soviet Union agreed to exchange oil, machinery, and other essential products for Cuban sugar.

As relations between the United States and Cuba deteriorated in the spring and summer of 1960, Guevara declared that the American subsidy paid for Cuban sugar amounted to "economic enslavement" and was aimed at hampering Cuba's industrial development. In reply to United States protests against expropriation of foreign property without adequate reimbursement, Guevara declared: "The only way to carry out an agrarian revolution is to take the land first and

GUEVARA, ERNESTO—*Continued*

worry about compensation later." He justified the seizure of American and British oil refineries in June 1960 on the ground that their refusal to process Russian oil was a violation of Cuban law. On the other hand, Guevara declared in an interview with the Australian correspondent Zell Rabin (New York *Herald Tribune,* July 14, 1960) that the Cuban people would resist "to the last drop of blood" any efforts on the part of the Soviet Union to make Cuba a satellite. A five-year agreement for the purchase of Cuban sugar by Communist China, which Guevara had negotiated, was signed on July 23, 1960.

In view of the economic boycott placed on Cuban goods by the United States, Guevara visited Communist countries in the fall of 1960 to build up trade relations with the Soviet bloc. Visiting Peiping in November, he declared that revolution can only be achieved "through armed struggle of the people" and in Moscow the following month he asserted that Cuba stood prepared to fulfill her goal as a model for armed revolution in Latin America. Upon his return to Havana, Guevara announced that a multilateral trade agreement for the purchase of Cuban sugar had been signed by Cuba and the Communist nations to ensure the economic survival of Cuba. The agreement included a promise by the Soviet Union to build 100 industrial plants in Cuba.

On February 24, 1961, in a reorganization of the Cuban government, Guevara was appointed to head a new Ministry of Industry, which took control of the Mining Institute, the Petroleum Institute, the sugar mills, and other agencies formerly under the direction of the INRA. Guevara's post as head of the National Bank went to the former Minister of Commerce, Dr. Raúl Cepero Bonilla. At the same time Guevara announced a new four-year industrial plan to bring the industrial development of Cuba in line with the Communist bloc nations. In a violently anti-American speech on March 28, 1961 he declared that Cuba was engaged in a fight to the death with Yankee imperialism and warned of possible aggression from the United States. During the abortive invasion attempt by anti-Castro Cubans on April 17, 1961 Guevara commanded military forces in Pinar del Rio Province and was reportedly wounded by a stray bullet.

In August 1961 Guevara headed the Cuban delegation to the conference at Punta del Este, Uruguay, which was called for the purpose of setting up President John F. Kennedy's Alliance for Progress program of economic aid to Latin America. Although Guevara delivered a strong anti-American speech and abstained from voting on the final declaration, he took a relatively moderate position and offered proposals for peaceful coexistence between the Alliance for Progress and the Cuban revolution. Following the conference he visited Argentina and Brazil, reportedly to gain Latin American support for the possible reopening of trade relations with the United States. The Brazilian President, Jânio da Silva Quadros, presented Guevara with Brazil's highest decoration, the Grand Cross of the Cruzeirodo Sul, in recognition of his efforts on behalf of economic and cultural relations between the two countries.

As economic conditions in Cuba worsened in late 1961, largely because of shortages, poor harvests, and absenteeism in industry, Guevara's power appeared to be declining. His role as Cuba's economic chief was reportedly overshadowed for a time by a planning board composed of old-line Communists, who were more closely in line with Soviet policies than Guevara, who tended to favor Chinese revolutionary methods. Guevara soon recovered his former influence, however.

In a nationwide broadcast in January 1962 Guevara warned Cubans that they were entering an era of hard work and sacrifice. He pointed out that eventually all consumer goods might have to be rationed, and he appealed to the workers to make every effort to increase sugar production. In February, with President Osvaldo Dorticós and the head of the INRA, Carlos Rafael Rodríguez, Guevara formed a three-man board to deal with Cuba's economic problems. The following month he became one of the twenty-five members of a new directorate of the Integrated Revolutionary Organizations (ORI), the pilot body of a projected Marxist-Leninist party for Cuba.

In August 1962 Guevara went on a special mission to the Soviet Union to obtain a firm commitment from the Soviet government for increased armaments and technical specialists to meet "threats of aggressor imperialist elements." The continued Soviet military buildup on Cuba prompted President Kennedy to institute a blockade of Cuban shipping on October 22, 1962. In the ensuing crisis Guevara was believed to have temporarily left his position as Minister of Industry to assume a military post, and he was reported to have said that Cuba would fire nuclear missiles on American cities in the event of aggression by the United States. Speaking at a ceremony on December 7, 1962, he declared that his government was prepared to export the Cuban revolution to any part of the world where it might be needed.

Laura Bergquist, who interviewed Guevara for *Look* (April 9, 1963), noted that he was "still very much the No. 2 power of the regime." During the interview Guevara said that he had envisioned a Marxist revolution from the beginning and that he could not have worked with a less radical government. He observed that the distinguishing feature of the Cuban revolution is that it was perhaps "more spontaneous" than other Socialist revolutions. He added: "We are part of the Socialist world. Our problems will be solved by our friends."

Although Ernesto "Che" Guevara was proclaimed a "native-born Cuban" by Castro on February 10, 1959, he is still regarded as a foreigner by many Cubans. He was first married in May 1955 to Hilda Gadea, a member of the Peruvian revolutionary movement who introduced him to Castro. He has one daughter from this marriage. After his divorce from his first wife, he married Aleida Marsh, a former schoolteacher who serves as his secretary.

Guevara is a slender man who stands five feet ten inches tall and has brown hair and brown eyes that have a slightly Oriental appearance. Although he has trimmed the shoulder-length hair that he wore in the Sierra Maestra Mountains, he retains a beard and mustache. He generally wears his green battle tunic, paratroop boots, and a black beret with a major's gold star. Guevara has a soft, persuasive voice and a pleasant personality and is said to have a cool, calculating mind. His customary workday is from 3 P.M. to 6 A.M. His hobby is mathematics, and he is also interested in literature, philosophy, and music.

References

N Y Times p10 N 27 '59 por; p2 S 3 '62 por
N Y Times Mag p5+ Je 19 '60 pors
Time 76:36+ Ag 8 '60 pors
Toronto Globe and Mail p8 Ag 12 '61 por
International Who's Who, 1962-63
Matthews, Herbert. The Cuban Story (1961)
Peraza Sarausa, Fermin. Personalidades Cubanas vol VII (1959)

GULLANDER, W(ERNER) P(AUL) July 19, 1908- Organization official; business executive

Address: b. National Association of Manufacturers, 2 E. 48th St., New York 17; h. River House, Bronxville, N.Y.

W. P. GULLANDER

In a major constitutional change, effected in the summer of 1962, the National Association of Manufacturers abandoned its former procedure of electing annually from among the executives of its approximately 17,000 member concerns an unsalaried president to serve for a one-year term. The association's first salaried, full-time chief executive since the end of World War I is W. P. Gullander, who took office for an indefinite term on November 1, 1962. Gullander began his career as an accounting trainee with General Electric Company in 1930 and served General Electric for over twenty years in auditing and managerial capacities. He was financial vice-president of the Weyerhaeuser Timber Company in Tacoma, Washington from 1952 to 1960, and executive vice-president of General Dynamics Corporation from 1960 until he took office as president of the NAM.

Werner Paul Gullander, who is of Swedish ancestry, was born on July 19, 1908 in a Lutheran parsonage in Big Rapids, Michigan. His father, the Reverend Paul Gullander, was a pastor and a former missionary in South Africa. His mother, Elvira Esther (Werner) Gullander, was a schoolteacher. Gullander, who spent most of his early years in Minnesota, attended University High School in Minneapolis, where he was active in athletics and graduated in 1926. He completed his formal education at the University of Minnesota, with the ambition of becoming an educational administrator. However, upon obtaining his B.S. degree in 1930, he was offered a position with General Electric Company, which he accepted.

Gullander was an accounting trainee with General Electric from 1930 until 1933, when he became a traveling auditor. He was promoted to chief traveling auditor in 1938, and he has also served as manager of subcontract operations for the Aircraft Gas Turbine Division of General

Electric. From 1945 to 1948 he was secretary-treasurer of the General Electric Supply Company, and from 1948 to 1951 he served as its district manager. In 1952, after twenty-two years with General Electric, Gullander moved to Tacoma, Washington to become financial vice-president of the Weyerhaeuser Company, a leading lumber firm, which manufactures plywood, hardwood, paperboard, folding boxes, milk cartons, and other wood and pulp derivatives.

In March 1960 Gullander left the Weyerhaeuser Company to become executive vice-president of General Dynamics Corporation, and in July of the same year he was made a director. General Dynamics, one of the main defense contractors in the United States, was the primary contractor on the Atlas intercontinental ballistic missile. Shortly before Gullander joined General Dynamics, the corporation's vice-president, Thomas G. Lanphier, Jr., resigned, because he was unable to see eye to eye with the Eisenhower administration on matters of defense. Gullander remained with General Dynamics for two and a half years, until his installation as president of the National Association of Manufacturers. He had previously served the NAM as a member of its taxation committee.

The National Association of Manufacturers, founded in 1895, represents a membership of some 17,000 manufacturing companies or partnerships that account for about three-fourths of the manufacturing output of the United States. Although the NAM is widely regarded as the voice of big business, in actual fact about 80 percent of its member concerns employ fewer than 500 workers and 45 percent employ fewer than 100 workers. Before the new constitutional provisions went into effect the policies of the NAM, which operated with a staff of 376 and a budget of about $7,000,000, were formulated by twenty-one separate committees, composed of some 3,000 members. For final policy decisions a two-thirds vote of a 170-man board was

GULLANDER, W. P.—*Continued*

needed. The president was chosen annually from among the membership to serve without pay as head of the NAM at the same time that he met his responsibilities to his own firm, thus compounding the difficulties of the association.

Early in 1962 the NAM retained Robert Heller and Associates, a Cleveland firm of management consultants, to explore the means of increasing the association's effectiveness on the American scene and among its own membership. A key recommendation of the firm was that a paid president be installed, who would be able to devote his full time to the affairs of the NAM. The task of finding the new president was vested in an eight-man committee, headed by the NAM's 1961 president, John W. McGovern. The committee eventually recommended Gullander, a man with a reputation as an able specialist in corporate finance, who at the time was reportedly looking for a change of scene.

On September 19, 1962 McGovern announced that a revised constitution, with the creation of the office of permanent president as its principal feature, had been ratified by the NAM membership and put into effect by the executive committee and the trustees. Gullander was elected the association's first full-time president, to take office on November 1, 1962 as a corporate officer, responsible for the management and the administration of the affairs of the association, for a term of indefinite length, and at a salary reported to be $100,000 a year. Donald J. Hardenbrook, the NAM president for 1962, became chairman of the board; the former executive vice-president, Charles R. Sligh, Jr., was elected vice-chairman and a full-time corporate officer and serves as public spokesman for the NAM. The association's other officers continue to be subject to the policy of annual rotation.

Gullander made his public debut as chief executive of the National Association of Manufacturers at the NAM's sixty-seventh annual congress of American industry, held in the Waldorf Astoria Hotel in New York City for three days beginning December 5, 1962. At a press conference before the congress opened Gullander expressed the view that 1963 could well be the year in which the American economy entered a new period of expansion, provided that action were taken to solve basic economic problems and to stimulate growth. He outlined three areas of "constructive action" to help bring this about: tax-rate reform aimed at removing barriers to economic growth; a reduction in government spending; and action to curb what he called "labor monopoly power." He added that the government must adopt an austere program during the period of adjustment until lower taxes could stimulate an upturn of business. Speaking of his own duties, Gullander said: "I'm just one of a bunch of guys running the NAM. My job, basically, will be to mind the store."

Speakers who addressed the 2,000 delegates attending the NAM congress included Governor Nelson A. Rockefeller of New York, former President Dwight D. Eisenhower, the Reverend Billy Graham, the journalist Henry Taylor, and the president of the European Economic Community, Walter Hallstein. A writer for *Newsweek* (December 17, 1962) saw "little evidence of mold-breaking" at the conference and noted that "Gullander neither foresees nor favors any liberalizing of the NAM ideology" although he planned "to be more 'progressive' in getting NAM's idea across."

Testifying before the House Ways and Means Committee on March 14, 1963, Gullander predicted that 10,500,000 Americans would be out of work by 1970 unless the growth of the economy were speeded up. He recommended a $20 billion tax cut over a period of five years, as compared with President Kennedy's proposed $10.3 billion cut over three years. A few weeks later the NAM's government economy committee issued a report recommending a $12.4 billion cut in spending authorizations and a reduction by $6.8 billion of expenditures for fiscal 1964.

Gullander has served as a director of the Hooker Chemical Company of New York, Canadair, Ltd. of Montreal, and the Puget Sound National Bank, and as president and director of the Columbia and Coolitz Railway. He is a former president of the Washington State Research Council and a member of the National Export Expansion Council of the Department of Commerce. He is also a member of the Financial Executives Institute, the National Industrial Conference Board, and the New York Society of Association Executives.

On July 12, 1930 W. P. Gullander married Dorothy Mae Becker, a former teacher of Latin and social studies. They have two daughters, Barbara Louise, who is now Mrs. Donald G. Weinberger of Kansas City, Missouri, and Judith Maria, a student at the University of Puget Sound in Tacoma, Washington. Gullander, who is familiarly known as "Gully," is five feet ten and a half inches tall, weighs 187 pounds, and has gray hair and blue eyes. He is a high-fidelity addict, and he is fond of small boating and golf. His clubs include the Washington Athletic Club in Seattle, the Siwanoy Country Club in Bronxville, New York, the University Club of New York City, the Economic Club of New York City, and the Newcomen Society of North America. He is a Presbyterian, a Republican, and a Shriner. His fraternity is Tau Kappa Epsilon.

Although organized labor has been the NAM's most determined opponent, AFL-CIO men who have worked with Gullander regard him as "honest, fair, and understanding—a person with a reputation for keeping his word," according to Lee Dirks of the *National Observer* (December 3, 1962). Gullander is described in a profile in the New York *Times* (December 6, 1962) as "a typical American business man: affable, approachable, articulate, and a firm believer in the long-held article of faith that if an American youngster gets a good education and works hard at his job, success is inevitable."

References

    Fortune 66:57 N '62 por
    N Y Times p29 D 6 '62 por
    Time 80:78 D 14 '62 por

    Who's Who in America, 1962-63
    World Who's Who in Commerce and
       Industry (1961)

GUTHRIE, WOODY July 14, 1912- Folk singer;
composer; writer
Address: c/o Harold Leventhal, Suite 602, 200
W. 57th St., New York 19

"Some day people are going to wake up to
the fact that Woody Guthrie and the ten thousand songs that leap and tumble off the strings
of his music box are a national possession like
Yellowstone and Yosemite, and part of the best
stuff this country has to show the world," Clifton Fadiman once wrote in a book review for
the *New Yorker* in the early 1940's. A citizen of
the open road since his teens, balladeer Woody
Guthrie has sung and played "for his chips" in
waterfront saloons, on skid rows, and in hobo
jungles all over the United States—experiences
that he has related in his popular autobiography,
Bound for Glory (1943). Although he has written about 1,000 songs, and has been heard by
millions on recordings and in concert appearances and on radio programs, Woody Guthrie
has derived little financial benefit from his
achievements. Many of his songs have become
part of the American folk tradition.

Of Scottish and Irish ancestry, Woodrow Wilson Guthrie was born on July 14, 1912 in Okemah, Ofuskee County, Oklahoma, to Charles
Edward and Nora Belle (Tanner) Guthrie. His
maternal grandmother, Mrs. Lee Tanner, was
one of the first log-cabin schoolteachers in
Ofuskee County. His father, a native of Texas,
was a professional guitarist and trained prize-
fighter who bought athletic equipment for his
children and made his living at a number of
trades. He served for several years as clerk of
the county court and later kept a store and dealt
in real estate. From early childhood, the five
Guthrie children—Roy, Clara, Woody, George,
and Mary Jo—were brought up on the old songs
and ballads that their mother sang to them and
on the Indian square dances and Negro blues
chanted by their father. As a boy Woody
Guthrie sold newspapers, sang and performed jigs
for pennies, and brawled in street gang fights.
He attended school to about the tenth grade in
Okemah and in the oil town of Pampa in the
Texas Panhandle.

Although the Guthries lived under moderately
prosperous circumstances during the height of an
oil boom, the family was soon struck by one disaster after another. Charles Guthrie's land trading business went bankrupt, and he lost a farm
a day for thirty days. Two of the family's
houses were destroyed by fire, and another by
a cyclone. Woody's sister Clara was killed in
an oil stove explosion. His mother had a mental
breakdown and later died in a state asylum.

At thirteen Woody Guthrie was living with
a large family in a two-room house, and he
helped to meet his living expenses by collecting
and selling junk, delivering milk, shining shoes,
washing spittoons, and meeting night trains to
solicit customers for a local hotel. A couple of
years later he hit the trail for Houston, Texas
and the Gulf of Mexico, earning his living by
working at odd jobs and by playing the har-
monica in barber shops and pool halls. Returning to Okemah, he briefly worked in a service

WOODY GUTHRIE

station and then joined his father, who had
become a manager of a block of real estate in
Pampa.

In Pampa, Woody Guthrie was taught guitar-
playing by an uncle, who later got him a job
as a sit-in guitarist with a dance band. For the
next few years he played and sang at country
dances, rodeos, and carnivals, and before long he
began to make up his own songs by putting new
words to the old tunes. Because conditions around
Texas and Oklahoma had worsened as a result
of the dust storms and the Depression, Woody
Guthrie headed west by freight train, working
along the way as a sign painter and as a singer
in saloons.

In California, Woody Guthrie teamed up with
his cousin Jack Guthrie in a fifteen-minute radio
program, and later he and a girl known as
"Lefty Lou" Crissman had a regular radio show
over station KFVD in Los Angeles for about
two years. After appearing for a time over station XELO in Tijuana, Mexico, Guthrie returned
to Los Angeles, where he obtained his own program on KFVD, attended "fancy Hollywood
drinking parties," and saved enough money to
send for his wife and children.

The poverty that he witnessed while singing
in migrant camps and "Hoovervilles" during this
period aroused his social consciousness. He wrote
articles for the *People's World* and teamed up
with actor Will Geer, touring "around the sad
canyons," singing for labor unions, and giving
moral support to striking farm workers. When
his funds ran low he headed for New York City
with $35 borrowed from his brother Roy.

In New York, Guthrie stayed at first in the
Fifth Avenue apartment of Will Geer, but after
a while moved to the Bowery. He sang for labor
groups, wrote a column for the *Daily Worker*,
and met Alan Lomax, who took him to Washington, D.C. to record all the songs he could
remember for the Archive of American Folksong

GUTHRIE, WOODY—*Continued*

of the Library of Congress. After seeing the movie version of John Steinbeck's *Grapes of Wrath* several times he recorded two albums of *Dust Bowl Ballads* for Victor Records. In 1940 he and Pete Seeger toured the South and Southwest, singing in migrant camps and at union meetings.

Returning to New York, Guthrie appeared on a number of radio programs, including *Pursuit of Happiness, Cavalcade of America, We the People, Back Where I Come From, Pipe Smoking Time,* and the WNYC music festivals. He sent for his family in Oklahoma and acquired a new 1941 Pontiac. He soon "got disgusted with the whole sissified and nervous rules of censorship," which the radio stations imposed on his songs and ballads, however, and headed for the South and the West. While touring the mountains of northern California, Guthrie was asked by the Bonneville Power Administration to record the achievements of the dam builders in song. He went to Oregon and made up twenty-six ballads about the Bonneville and Grand Coulee dams for the Oregon Department of the Interior, in which he championed public power.

A few months later, Guthrie joined Lee Hays, Pete Seeger, Millard Lampell, and others in the Almanac Singers, a group which sang in union halls and to audiences of farm and factory workers throughout the United States. Later he and Pete Seeger toured Mexico, made up songs supporting the Allied war effort, and sang on overseas broadcasts for the Office of War Information.

Woody Guthrie's *Bound for Glory*, published by E. P. Dutton & Company in 1943, is an odyssey of his experiences, written in his own rustic vernacular and illustrated with his own sketches. The book was generally well received by critics. Edith Roberts in *Book Week* (April 4, 1943) called it "a huge, rich, juicy chunk of life." Orville Prescott in the New York *Times* (May 22, 1943) disapproved of its bad grammar, but added that it had "more triple-distilled essence of pure individual personality in it than any [book] in years."

In May 1943 Guthrie received a fellowship from the Julius Rosenwald Fund, to enable him to "write books, ballads, songs, and novels that will help people to know each other's work better." Later in the same year he became a member of the National Maritime Union and shipped out as a merchant seaman with his friend Cisco Houston. During his eleven months with the merchant marine Guthrie took part in three invasions and was torpedoed twice. Between trips he met Moses Asch, the son of the author Sholem Asch, and recorded several albums of songs for the Asch Recording Company. Drafted into the Army on V-E Day (May 8, 1945), Guthrie spent some time in military camps but after eight months he was given a dependency discharge and returned to New York. He then attended Brooklyn College for a few weeks on the G.I. bill.

During the next few years Guthrie often traveled from coast to coast, made many concert appearances, and wrote articles on folklore and other subjects for newspapers and magazines.

Renewing his association with the Almanac Singers, he made additional recordings for Moses Asch, who published his second book, *American Folksong* (Disc Company of America, 1947), containing some thirty songs, an autobiographical sketch, and a sketch about the late Huddie Ledbetter (Leadbelly). The book was reissued in 1961 by Oak Publications. For a time Guthrie was associated with Pete Seeger, Lee Hays, Alan Lomax, and others in People's Songs, "a new union of progressive songwriters," and he served on its fifteen-member executive board.

About 1955 Woody Guthrie was stricken by a critical nervous affliction, and since that time he has been hospitalized. In 1956 Pete Seeger, Harold Leventhal, and Lou Gordon established the Guthrie Children's Trust Fund, the purpose of which is to provide for the children of Woody Guthrie and to collect, publish, and safeguard the rights and interests of his musical and literary works. Millard Lampell has undertaken the task of editing the unpublished songs and manuscripts of Woody Guthrie. In 1958 and 1960 the fund published *California to the New York Island,* a book of Guthrie's songs, woven into a script by Lampell.

According to Pete Seeger, Woody Guthrie wrote more than 1,000 songs between 1932 and 1952. He has written songs about virtually everything he has seen, heard, or read, from Einstein's theory of relativity to the simple joys of children. His best-known songs include "So Long It's Been Good To Know You," "Union Maid," "Philadelphia Lawyer," "Jesus Christ" (to the tune of "Jesse James"), "Pretty Boy Floyd," and "Tom Joad." He tells of the trials of the migratory workers in "Hard Traveling," "Blowing Down This Old Dusty Road," and "Do Re Mi"; of the fight against fascism in "Round, Round Hitler's Grave," "Reuben James," and "The Biggest Thing That Man Has Ever Done"; and of the wonders of America in "Oklahoma Hills," "Pastures of Plenty," and "This Land Is Your Land."

Woody Guthrie has sung in New York's Town Hall and Madison Square Garden, but he turned down an engagement in the swanky Rainbow Room atop Rockefeller Center when his prospective employers wanted to deck him out in a clown's costume. Guthrie has made more than twenty albums of records for Stinson Records, Folkways Records, and the Asch Recording Company. The album *Cisco Houston Sings the Songs of Woody Guthrie* was released by Vanguard Records shortly before Houston died in 1961.

A self-taught musician who never learned to read a note of music, Guthrie believes in spontaneity and simplicity. Realizing that his voice does not sound "like dew dripping off the petals of the morning violet," he says: "I had rather sound like the ashcans of the early morning, like the cab drivers cursing at one another, like the longshoremen yelling, like the cowhands whooping, and like the lone wolf barking." In an article in the New York *Times* (April 4, 1943) Guthrie wrote: "I ain't out to say that real honest classical music is better or worse than what you'd call folk music. Both are twin brothers and sisters. Both can learn plenty from the other."

Woody Guthrie was first married in the early 1930's, to Mary Esta Jennings, who bore him three children, Gwendolyn Gail, Carolyn Sue, and Bill Rogers. The marriage ended in divorce. On November 13, 1945 Woody Guthrie married Marjorie Mazia Greenblatt, a dancer and teacher with the Martha Graham Company. They had four children, Cathy Ann (who died in a fire), Arlo Davy, Joady Ben, and Nora Lee. A third marriage, which took place shortly before the onset of Guthrie's illness, also ended in divorce.

Guthrie has been described by John Greenway as "a little weather-worn man with incredibly bushy, wiry hair." Hally Wood Stevenson, who first met Guthrie in 1943, has recalled: "He looked like the Midwest. Sometimes he wore a suit jacket, but it never matched anything.... His speech habits are the talking blues without music. . . . He seldom laughed or smiled. When he did smile, it was a sudden glory that you never forgot." Guthrie was fond of playing chess, and of drawing and painting. His sincerity, tenderness, humor, and identification with the working class are evident in his songs. Cisco Houston compared him with the Biblical prophets, Alan Lomax called him "the best folk-ballad composer whose identity was ever known," and to John Steinbeck, Guthrie represented the essence of the "American Spirit." An advertisement in *Variety* (May 1, 1963) congratulating the Weavers on their fifteenth anniversary was sponsored by Guthrie from Brooklyn State Hospital; it ended with the assurance, "Am still alive an' kickin.' "

References

Greenway, John. American Folksongs of Protest (1953)
Guthrie, Woody. Bound for Glory (1943); American Folksong (1961)
Lawless, Ray M. Folksingers and Folk-songs in America (1960)

HAGEN, UTA (hä'gĕn ōō'tà) June 12, 1919-
Actress

Address: b. Herbert Berghof Studio, 120 Bank St., New York 14; h. 27 Washington Sq. N., New York 11

NOTE: This biography supersedes the article that appeared in *Current Biography* in 1944.

Almost twenty-five years after she had made her debut on Broadway in 1938 as the bewildered little "sea gull," Nina, in *The Sea Gull*, Uta Hagen gave perhaps the most stirring performance of her career in Edward Albee's *Who's Afraid of Virginia Woolf?* as Martha, a many-sided woman with some traits suggesting a bewildered shrike. Diligent in her craft, Miss Hagen had acquired the skill to create Martha through experience in comedy, tragedy, and melodrama in many productions off and on Broadway. Her memorable Desdemona, Shaw's Saint Joan, Odets' country girl, and other roles have made her a favorite First Lady of the theater among New York critics, who twice voted her the best actress of the year in *Variety's* poll:

UTA HAGEN

for Georgie in *The Country Girl* (1950-51) and for Martha in *Who's Afraid of Virginia Woolf?* (1962-63)—performances for which she also won Antoinette Perry (Tony) Awards.

Uta Thyra Hagen was born in Göttingen, Germany on June 12, 1919, the daughter of Oskar Frank Leonard and Thyra A. (Leisner) Hagen. She has a brother, Holger Hagen, an actor in Germany. Her father lectured on the history of art at the University of Göttingen. He was also a musicologist, and for five years after World War I he organized and directed Göttingen's Handel festivals, in which his wife often sang. Visiting the United States in 1924 as a Carl Schurz Foundation Professor, he founded the department of art history at the University of Wisconsin in Madison. When he decided to remain there as head of the department, he moved his family permanently to Wisconsin.

The Hagens made trips back to Europe every few years, and Uta Hagen, who acquired an early enthusiasm for the theater from her parents, saw many stage productions there and in the United States. Acting was her favorite extra-curricular interest at the University of Wisconsin High School, from which she graduated in 1936. She studied for a term at the Royal Academy of Dramatic Art in London, and her eagerness to become an actress apparently led her to decide against completing her college education, for she left the University of Wisconsin in June 1937 after only one semester.

Like many aspiring actresses, Uta Hagen sought an audition from Eva Le Gallienne, who had encouraged newcomers to the stage in her Civic Repertory Theatre. In 1937 she won the role of Ophelia and played opposite Miss Le Gallienne herself, who appeared as Hamlet, in a production of Shakespeare's tragedy in Dennis, Massachusetts. Spared the usual apprenticeship of bit parts, Uta Hagen made her Broadway

HAGEN, UTA—*Continued*

debut at nineteen, on March 28, 1938, as Nina in the Theatre Guild's production of *The Sea Gull* at the Shubert Theatre and, in the opinion of one New York critic, stole some scenes from its stars, Alfred Lunt and Lynn Fontanne.

After touring in *The Sea Gull*, Uta Hagen appeared in stock during the summer of 1938 in Ridgefield, Connecticut in *Arms and the Man*, *The Latitude of Love*, and other plays. Her leading man in *The Latitude of Love* was José Ferrer, whom she was required to knock unconscious, a feat of acting that she performed capably. She and Ferrer were married on December 8, 1938, and during the ten years of their marriage they co-starred in several successful plays and also occasionally performed separately.

In April 1939 Uta Hagen returned to Broadway to play Edith in *The Happiest Days* at the Vanderbilt Theatre, and the following December she opened in Maxwell Anderson's *Key Largo* at the Ethel Barrymore Theatre. In the feminine lead, as Alegre d'Alcala, she appeared opposite Paul Muni, while Ferrer performed in the long prologue of the blank verse drama. During the summer of 1942 she played Desdemona in *Othello* at Cambridge, Massachusetts and Princeton, New Jersey; Paul Robeson as Othello and Ferrer as Iago were also in the cast. Again co-featured with her husband, she had the title role in the comedy *Vickie*, which opened at the Plymouth Theatre in September 1942 to generally unenthusiastic notices.

A year later, however, Uta Hagen scored one of the most impressive successes of her career when she rejoined Ferrer and Robeson in the Theatre Guild's *Othello*, directed by Margaret Webster. The production, which had its première at the Shubert Theatre in October 1943, established the American record for a Shakespearean drama with a run of 295 performances. After its 158th presentation the Ferrers were raised to co-stardom with Robeson. Burton Rascoe of the New York *World-Telegram* praised Miss Hagen's "glorious and heart-gripping performance," and other reviewers suggested that future Desdemonas would find it difficult to improve upon her portrayal.

At the close of the Broadway run in 1944, the Ferrers toured in *Othello* with Robeson, staying only in hotels that accepted the Negro actor. Their close association with Robeson, a leftist, raised some question about their own views. "In due course," as reported in *Time* (May 10, 1963), "they were called to Washington to explain their political beliefs. Ferrer . . . denied any leftist leanings and was not blacklisted. Uta was dismissed without being heard at all. She ended up on TV and Hollywood blacklists nonetheless. She has never made a movie." Television viewers have, however, seen her in *Macbeth, Out of Dust, A Month in the Country*, and other plays.

On an excursion from Broadway in 1947 Uta Hagen performed in several German-language productions, including *The Master Builder*, at the Barbizon-Plaza, playing opposite the veteran actor Albert Bassermann, whom she much admired. Also in 1947 she joined Herbert Berghof, an actor and director, in founding a school for

acting, the Herbert Berghof Studio, where she has since taught a number of classes weekly. (Geraldine Page and Fritz Weaver are among the studio's alumni.) Uta Hagen and José Ferrer were divorced in June 1948, and on January 25, 1951 she married Berghof.

Shortly before her divorce from Ferrer, Miss Hagen opened in a revival of *Angel Street* in January 1948 at New York's City Center. As Mrs. Manningham, she co-starred with Ferrer as the villainous husband in Patrick Hamilton's melodrama. Howard Barnes of the New York *Herald Tribune* credited her with bringing "a particularly scintillating quality to the revival," and called her performance "truly brilliant"—an opinion that Brooks Atkinson of the New York *Times* fully shared.

While touring with the National Company during 1948-49 in the role of Blanche DuBois in Tennessee Williams' *A Streetcar Named Desire*, Uta Hagen received such glowing notices that when Jessica Tandy left the original Broadway cast in 1949, Miss Hagen was called to New York to replace her. She once said in a press interview that she has been discovered or rediscovered as an actress ten times. *A Streetcar Named Desire* provided one such occasion, and *The County Girl* followed soon after with another. As the dowdy wife, Georgie, in Clifford Odets' drama, which premièred in November 1950 at the Lyceum Theatre, she won her first American Theatre Wing Tony award as the best actress of the 1950-51 season, the New York Drama Critics Award, the Donaldson Award, and the annual *Variety* poll of New York drama critics as the best actress of the year.

Again in a Theatre Guild production directed by Margaret Webster, Uta Hagen starred in Shaw's *Saint Joan* at the Cort Theatre in the fall of 1951. Critical notices were especially interesting for their observations on her method of approaching her role. Brooks Atkinson commented on the effective blossoming in the play's last half of ideas that she had planted in the first half. William Hawkins wrote admiringly in the New York *World-Telegram and Sun* (October 5, 1951), "Miss Hagen has that rare gift of creating spiritual energy in the theater, then controlling it at will. She has the authority to compel an audience into silent attention like suspended animation. Unquestionably she is among the theater's greatest in her day."

Two comedy roles followed Saint Joan: the Grand Duchess Tatiana Petrovna at the City Center's *Tovarich* in the spring of 1952 and the rowdy American movie actress at work in Italy in *In Any Language* at the Cort Theatre in the fall of 1952. Both plays were well received, largely because of Miss Hagen's deftness as a comedienne. But Julian Funt's *The Magic and the Loss*, in which she portrayed an advertising executive, closed after twenty-seven performances at the Booth Theatre during April 1954, critics and audiences having found little merit in the play, though much in the players. She toured summer theaters in *The Lady's Not for Burning* and *The Deep Blue Sea* in 1954 and in *Cyprienne* in 1955. Agata in the somewhat disappointing *Island of Goats*, which opened at the Fulton

Theatre in October 1955, was to be her last role in a Broadway play for seven years.

Meanwhile, at off-Broadway's Phoenix Theatre during April-May 1956 Miss Hagen aroused the unqualified admiration of New York critics for the beauty, charm, and subtlety of her portrayal of Natalia Petrovna in Turgenev's *A Month in the Country*. In another play at the Phoenix, the experimental presentation in December 1956 of Bertolt Brecht's *The Good Woman of Setzuan*, she had the dual role of a heart-of-gold prostitute and, in disguise, a male cousin. "A bomb," Uta Hagen acknowledged in an interview for the New York *Post* (April 22, 1963), "but I *worked* on it." On a summer tour in 1957 she appeared as all the women in *The Affairs of Anatol*, and at the Bucks County Playhouse in New Hope, Pennsylvania she portrayed Argia in *The Queen and the Rebels* in August 1959.

Uta Hagen's seven-year absence from Broadway was a period of professional growth and accomplishment independent of commercial rewards. "This whole standard of not being anything unless you're on Broadway is rotten," she protested in the 1963 New York *Post* interview. An earlier article in *Theatre Arts* (November 1951) had pointed out, "According to Uta's standards, it is nonsensical for an actress to remain idle while she could be improving in her craft—whether on Broadway or off." Idealistic about acting, she waited for a role in which she could believe wholeheartedly before she would reappear on Broadway.

The role she found was Martha in Edward Albee's first full-length and first Broadway play, the lacerating *Who's Afraid of Virginia Woolf?*, which began a long run at the Billy Rose Theatre on October 13, 1962. In the demanding part of a college professor's wife who cannot forgive her husband's failure to live up to her expectations, she reveals herself during the psychological flagellation of an all-night drinking bout with another faculty couple to be a vulgar and ruthless woman pitifully seeking love.

Some critics had serious reservations about Albee's play, partly because of its exploitation of obscenity, but they had none about Uta Hagen's acting. "It is a revelation," Emory Lewis wrote in *Cue* (October 27, 1962), "to see Miss Hagen take a rather poor line and make it a great moment." For her performance as Martha she won both her second Tony and the citation of the *Variety* poll of critics as the year's best dramatic actress. Her co-star, Arthur Hill, who played her husband in Albee's drama, won the same awards for a male performer.

Among the distinctions of Miss Hagen's acting is her approach in creating her characters: lucid, analytical, deliberate, and intelligent. "I have to fight continually for subjectivity," she once complained in self-criticism. The magnetic, vibrant qualities of her personality, which make the difference between a competent actress and a star, are said to be also apparent when she is offstage. She has blue eyes and ash-blond hair, is five feet seven and a half inches tall, and weighs 130 pounds. In *Time* (May 10, 1963) her face was described as "forbiddingly experienced," qualifying her to play Martha.

Uta Hagen has a daughter, Leticia Ferrer. When she is not acting, or teaching at the Berghof school, Miss Hagen is likely to spend much of her time knitting, cooking, and swimming. She is a Democrat. In Edward R. Murrow's *This I Believe: 2* (Simon, 1954) she affirmed her faith in the theater and her gratitude to great writers, philosophers, artists, and musicians: "They have helped me to drown out the frenetic racket made by the compromisers who try to bend ideals to fit their practical needs and personal appetites, and to deprive us of our spiritual salvation." Of her own effort to do things well, to be true to herself, and fight the good fight, she wrote: "I was proud the day I first learned to make a good loaf of bread, to have learned a simple thing which others could enjoy. Or to plant a bulb in the ground and tend it and help it grow; or to give birth to a child and help her reach her own individual freedom; or to make a character in a play come off the printed page and become a human being with a point of view who can help others to understand a little more."

References

N Y Post p29 Ap 22 '63 por
Theatre Arts 35:32+ N '51 por
Time 81:82 My 10 '63 por
International Celebrity Register (1959)
Murrow, Edward R. This I Believe:2 (1954)
Who's Who in America, 1962-63
Who's Who in the Theatre (1961)
Who's Who of American Women (1958-59)

HAMILTON, EDITH Aug. 12, 1867- Classical scholar; writer
Address: b. c/o W. W. Norton & Co., 55 5th Ave., New York 3; h. 2448 Massachusetts Ave., N.W., Washington 8, D.C.

> BULLETIN: Edith Hamilton died on May 31, 1963. *Obituary:* N Y Times p21 Je 1 '63

As much at home in Athens of the Periclean Age as in Washington, D.C., Edith Hamilton writes without a hint of pedantry about the significance of ancient civilizations for modern man. Her grace, enthusiasm, scholarly brilliance, and sense of nobility have enabled her perhaps more than any other classicist of the twentieth century to arouse among general readers an interest in the literature and ways of life of the Greeks and Romans. She has also used her gift for literary appreciation to illuminate the worlds of the Hebrew prophets and the early Christians. Especially devoted to the Greeks, she wrote her first book, *The Greek Way* (1930), at the age of sixty-three and became an honorary citizen of Athens at the age of ninety. John Mason Brown described her as "a citizen of two worlds, the ancient and the modern," and as a woman "who would be unusual in any period; in ours she is unique."

Two years after the Civil War had ended in the United States, Edith Hamilton was

Harris & Ewing

EDITH HAMILTON

born in Dresden, Germany, on August 12, 1867. Her parents, Montgomery and Gertrude (Pond) Hamilton, were both American citizens, and they reared their children in Fort Wayne, Indiana. One of Edith Hamilton's sisters, Dr. Alice Hamilton, an authority on industrial medicine, became the first woman to be appointed to the faculty of the Harvard Medical School. A younger brother, Arthur Hamilton, distinguished himself in a field of study more closely related to Edith Hamilton's, as professor of Romance languages at the University of Illinois.

The well-to-do Montgomery Hamilton was, in fact, less interested in earning money than in encouraging his children to use their minds. Contrary to the prevailing views of the time, he believed that learning would not make his daughters unladylike. He started seven-year-old Edith on Latin with *Six Weeks' Preparation for Caesar*. She also, she has said, "came to the Greeks early and . . . found answers in them." Afterward, in and out of school, she read Greek and Latin for pleasure—exactly, she had explained, as she would read French and German. In childhood she liked to recite the poetry of Keats and Shelley, whose delight in classical mythology probably stimulated her own.

In her teens Edith Hamilton attended Miss Porter's Finishing School for Young Ladies in Farmington, Connecticut. When she expressed a desire for further education, Miss Porter, who was concerned primarily with the amenities, assured her that she was capable of becoming learned, but questioned with some dismay the propriety of the ambition and the value of the effort. Edith Hamilton nevertheless entered Bryn Mawr College in Pennsylvania, chose Greek and Latin as her major subjects, and was awarded her B.A. and M.A. degrees in 1894. During the following year she was a Fellow in Latin at Bryn Mawr.

Another scholastic award, the Mary E. Garrett European Fellowship, gave her the opportunity to study in 1895-96 at the universities of Leipzig and Munich. The University of Munich begrudged her the distinction of being the first woman ever admitted to its classes. "They wouldn't let me sit with the young men," she recalled in an interview for the *New Yorker* (May 11, 1957). "I had to take notes at a little desk on the platform, beside the teacher. The head of the university used to stare at me, then shake his head and say sadly to a colleague, 'There, now, you see what's happened? We're right in the midst of the woman question.'"

In 1896, upon her return from Europe, Miss Hamilton was persuaded to direct the Bryn Mawr School in Baltimore, Maryland, which prepared girls for Bryn Mawr College. She remained at the school as headmistress until 1922. Still in the midst of the woman question, she once walked in a suffrage parade, risking criticism of unseemly behavior for a headmistress. A chance remark that she had heard in a lecture at a German university had inspired her with the desire to share what she had discovered about the Greeks and Romans through their literature. For twenty-five years she supervised the education of the 400 students annually enrolled in her school and conveyed to them her appreciation of the values of the classical world, but aside from contributing a few articles on education to magazines, she did not think of writing.

Presumably, and perhaps in so far as she was permitted, Edith Hamilton looked to the Greeks in her work as an educator. Many years after she had retired from teaching she said that although mass education was a "magnificent idea," it produced among other results the disaster of "the deadly commonplace." The Greeks, she pointed out, stressed the differences among pupils and allowed each individual to develop his own capabilities independently: the concept of teaching the same thing to large groups of children was alien to the way of Greece, which had produced more geniuses than any other country.

When she was fifty-five, in 1922, Miss Hamilton left Bryn Mawr School. She then began writing about Greek literature, and a few years later several of her articles appeared in *Theatre Arts Monthly*, including "Greek and the English Genius" (May 1928), "Aeschylus, the First Dramatist" (January 1929), "Sophocles, Quintessence of the Greek" (February 1929), and "Euripides, The Modern Mind" (May 1929).

Edith Hamilton's approach to the ancient world—Greek, Roman, Hebrew, and early Christian—has been primarily through literature. She focused on what people were as they showed themselves to be in their own writings. It was from her articles on Greek drama in *Theatre Arts Monthly* that she developed her first and probably her most honored book, *The Greek Way* (Norton, 1930). In her interpretation of the Greek conception of life, she wanted particularly to make clear the relevance of the Greek ideal, by comparison and contrast, to modern civilization.

As if she had tried to convey in her own book the Greek qualities of directness, aliveness, and striving for perfection, she wrote without footnotes and with a freshness and accuracy that stimulated and illuminated, as well as instructed. At least one reviewer, of the *New Statesman* (September 20, 1930), found her enthusiasm "sustained, but deadly" and complained about inadequate documentation. In much of her later work, also, Miss Hamilton faced occasional charges of oversimplification and omission, but few critics doubted the sensitivity and soundness of her perception. Her books seemed to be vehicles from the old world to the new in which she had absorbed all the pains of scholarship and had passed along only its delights and other rewards.

A new edition of *The Greek Way* was published in 1943 under the title of *The Great Age of Greek Literature* (Norton). Its five additional chapters, dealing with Pindar and Xenophon among other Greek writers, rounded out Edith Hamilton's study of the Athenian writers of the Periclean Age. In partial answer to the interest in Greek literature that she had evoked, she offered in *Three Greek Plays* (Norton, 1937) English translations of Euripides' *The Trojan Women*, Aeschylus' *Prometheus Bound*, and Aeschylus' *Agamemnon*, with introductions for each of the three plays and general essays on translation.

Meanwhile, in 1932, Edith Hamilton had completed *The Roman Way* (Norton), which interpreted the thought and manners of the Romans, again with application to the world of today, as they were presented in the work of great Latin authors like Plautus, Virgil, and Juvenal. Drawing upon both Greek and Roman writers, in 1942 she retold in *Mythology* (Little) the classical myths that through the centuries have provided inspiration and theme for world literature. She also considered in a brief chapter the mythology of the Norsemen.

With no knowledge of the Hebrew language, but with the conviction "that for the English-speaking world the Bible is the Bible in English," Edith Hamilton had turned to the literary achievement of another ancient people in which she saw significance for twentieth-century readers. In *The Prophets of Israel* (Norton, 1936), A. J. Nock commented in the *Atlantic Monthly* (July 1936), "Miss Hamilton has taken the most obscure and difficult portion of the Bible and has given an exposition of it that is remarkably clear, sound, interesting, and above all, attractive. . . . The chief merit of her treatment is its freedom from prepossession." A later edition of the book, *Spokesmen for God; The Great Teachers of the Old Testament* (Norton, 1949), supplied additional commentary on the first five books of the Old Testament. "Here is a work of sheer delight," Robert Peel said of the Bible study in the *Christian Science Monitor* (November 17, 1949), and Philip Burnham in the New York *Times* (January 1, 1950) called it "insistently, a work of intuition, about intuition."

A companion to her books about Greek, Roman, and Hebrew thought, *Witness to the Truth; Christ and His Interpreters* (Norton, 1949), explored a fourth source of modern thought in a study of the teachings of Christ and the interpretations that the evangelists, St. Paul, and writers of the early church gave to His teachings. Returning to the Greeks in 1957 with *The Echo of Greece* (Norton), Edith Hamilton discussed the political ideas of such teachers and leaders as Isocrates, Plato, Aristotle, Demosthenes, and Alexander the Great. In 1961 she edited in collaboration with Huntington Cairns *The Collected Dialogues of Plato* (Pantheon).

In an interview with Rochelle Girson for the *Saturday Review* (August 10, 1957) Edith Hamilton discussed a projected book of essays that would include articles on Goethe and Corneille. She also said that she intended to amend somewhat the critical article on William Faulkner that she had written earlier for the *Saturday Review* (July 12, 1952), having since discovered his compassion in his *Two Soldiers*. She clings, however, to her general view that much of modern fiction, modern poetry (Dylan Thomas, for example), and modern art does not make sense, and she thinks that we live in an age of ugliness. "A man who might be able to do beautiful work is conditioned by his age," she pointed out in the *Saturday Review* interview. "You can't jump from a world war into a renaissance."

Shortly before her ninetieth birthday, in August 1957, Edith Hamilton revisited Greece for the first time since 1929, and in a ceremony at the foot of the Acropolis in the Theatre of Herodes Atticus, she was made an honorary citizen of the City and Demos of Athens and was decorated with the Golden Cross of the Order of Benefaction in the name of King Paul. After the presentation she watched a production of her translation of *Prometheus Bound* in which a company of ANTA players participated.

In February 1958 the Women's National Book Association presented its Constance Lindsay Skinner Award to Edith Hamilton for her contribution to American culture through books. George V. Allen, the director of the United States Information Agency, one of the speakers at the award dinner, said that the USIA included seven of her books in its overseas libraries because a specific mission of his agency was to interpret American ideals to peoples of other countries and that "in her interpretation of the democratic spirit of ancient Greece, Miss Hamilton defines the fundamental of the democratic ideal itself." She is also a recipient of the National Achievement Award (1950) and of honorary D.Litt. degrees from Yale University, the University of Pennsylvania, and the University of Rochester. She is a member of P.E.N., the American Academy of Arts and Letters, and the National Institute of Arts and Letters.

Edith Hamilton has a home in Washington, D.C., and a summer house in Bar Harbor, Maine. In the summer of 1958 NBC-TV filmed an interview with her in Maine for its *Wisdom* series—a conversation that allowed thousands of Americans to share the impression of the *New Yorker* interviewer who had written a year earlier, "Miss Hamilton is as beautiful and wise a person as we have ever met, and we feel

HAMILTON, EDITH—*Continued*

sure that her beauty and her intelligence have been heightened, rather than diminished, by the years."

References

Bul Bibliog 23:183+ My '62
Life 45:79+ S 15 '58 pors
New Yorker 33:36+ My 11 '57
Pub W 173:26+ Mr 17 '58
Sat R 40:29 Ag 10 '57 por
Twentieth Century Authors (1942; First Supplement, 1955)
Who's Who of American Women (1958-59)

HARBACH, OTTO A(BELS) Aug. 18, 1873-Jan. 24, 1963 Broadway song lyricist and librettist; remembered for his lyrics for *Rose Marie, The Firefly, No, No, Nanette, The Desert Song,* and *Roberta;* collaborated with Sigmund Romberg, Jerome Kern, and Rudolf Friml. See *Current Biography* (July) 1950.

Obituary

N Y Times p35 Ap 1 '63

HART, MERWIN K(IMBALL) June 25, 1881-Nov. 30, 1962 Lawyer; founder and president of the New York State Economic Council, a conservative propaganda group; head of a New York chapter of the John Birch Society. See *Current Biography* (October) 1941.

Obituary

N Y Times p88 D 2 '62

HASSEL, KAI-UWE VON (häs'ĕl kī-ōō'vĕ) Apr. 21, 1913- Minister of Defense of the Federal Republic of Germany
Address: b. Ministry of Defense, Bonn, West Germany; h. Petersens Allee 7, Glücksburg, Schleswig Holstein, West Germany

One outcome of the West German government crisis engendered by the *Der Spiegel* affair of October 1962 was the appointment of Kai-Uwe von Hassel as Minister of Defense, to succeed Franz-Josef Strauss on January 9, 1963. Von Hassel began his career as a planter and merchant in East Africa in the 1930's and served as an officer in the German army during World War II. After the war he became active in the civil service and in politics in the state of Schleswig-Holstein, of which he was elected Minister-President in 1954. He is a leading spokesman of the north German Protestant wing of the Christian Democratic Union and has served as one of the four deputy chairmen of that party since 1956. A strong supporter of NATO, von Hassel shares more fully than his predecessor the views of the United States on the defense of Europe.

Kai-Uwe von Hassel, whose given name is of Frisian and Danish derivation, was born on April 21, 1913 on a German plantation in Neuköln, German East Africa (now Gare, Tan-

ganyika), the third of five children of Theodor and Emma (Jebsen) von Hassel. He is descended from a family of military officers and Protestant clergymen. His paternal grandfather was a lieutenant-general in the Imperial German army, and his maternal grandfather served as a National Liberal representative in the Imperial Reichstag. His father, a captain of colonial troops in Africa, resigned his commission in 1909 to become a planter and acquired three farms where he raised coffee, rubber, and livestock.

In 1919, following Germany's loss of its colonies as a result of World War I, the von Hassels were dispossessed and expelled from Africa by the British. The family settled in Glücksburg near Flensburg on the Baltic coast, in the north German state of Schleswig-Holstein. Von Hassel obtained his early education at the Grundschule in Glücksburg and then entered the Reform Realgymnasium in Flensburg, where he did not particularly distinguish himself as a scholar. After he had graduated in 1933 he prepared for a career in agriculture and commerce, attending the Höhere Handelsschule in Hamburg and serving his apprenticeship in a machine factory and on an agricultural estate. In 1935 he returned to Tanganyika, where he worked as assistant, and later manager, on a plantation and became director of the mercantile division for plantations with the former German East Africa Company.

In 1939, when World War II broke out, von Hassel was interned by the British in Dar es Salaam. After his repatriation to Germany in February 1940 he volunteered for service in the Wehrmacht and received a commission as lieutenant of the reserves. He served as a radio signalman and later as a signal translator for English and Swahili. In May 1945 he was taken prisoner by the British and sent to a prisoner-of-war camp in northern Italy.

Upon his return to Schleswig-Holstein in September 1945 von Hassel became head of the office of housing affairs for the Flensburg district. In this position he dealt with problems arising from the vast influx of refugees from the east into Schleswig-Holstein, which at that time was the poorest and most crowded West German state. In 1946 von Hassel became a member of the Christian Democratic Union (CDU), and shortly thereafter he was chosen local party chairman in Glücksburg. He was elected mayor of Glücksburg in November 1947 and a member of the Flensburg county council in 1948. In April 1950 he became chairman of the Glücksburg town council, and a few months later he was chosen deputy chairman of the CDU in Schleswig-Holstein.

Von Hassel was elected to the Schleswig-Holstein Landtag (state legislature) in 1950. He served on several committees, including those on finance, internal administration, commerce, and labor, and he occasionally represented the state's minister of the interior in the Landtag. In September 1953 he was elected a member of the Bundestag (the lower house of the federal legislature), in which he served until October of the following year.

A protégé of Schleswig-Holstein's Minister-President Friedrich Wilhelm Lübke, he was chosen as a compromise candidate to succeed

Lübke by a coalition of the CDU, the Free Democratic party (FDP), and the Refugee party (BHE). Inaugurated as Minister-President on October 11, 1954, he became the youngest chief executive of a state in the Federal Republic. The new government ensured federal Chancellor Konrad Adenauer of a continued two-thirds majority in the Bundesrat (upper house), whose members are chosen by the state governments. Von Hassel became a member of the Bundesrat in 1954 and served as president of that body from September 1955 to August 1956. On one occasion he temporarily replaced federal President Theodor Heuss. In 1955 von Hassel helped to bring about the sweeping victory of the CDU in Schleswig-Holstein. At the national congress of the CDU in the spring of 1956 he was chosen as one of the party's four deputy chairmen.

As Minister-President of Schleswig-Holstein, von Hassel worked toward a solution of the continuing problems of unemployment and refugee resettlement, and he helped solve cultural problems involving the relationship between the Danish minority and the German majority in that state. During the eight years of his administration a number of instances were reported in which former Nazis served in high public office and received government pensions in Schleswig-Holstein. Although von Hassel was not directly involved in any of these cases, he exercised great caution not to antagonize the conservative and nationalist elements of his state. Defending his administration against charges that it had become a haven for prominent ex-Nazis, von Hassel declared before the Schleswig-Holstein Landtag in Kiel in January 1961 that state authorities had acted in these cases according to the letter of the law and with respect for constitutional guarantees.

Since the reconstitution of Germany's armed forces in 1955 von Hassel has been increasingly preoccupied with military affairs. He has repeatedly pointed out the difficulties involved in the defense of Schleswig-Holstein, which is located between the Baltic and North seas and which serves as a bridge between the European mainland and the Scandinavian states. In an interview published in the New York *Times* (March 20, 1960) von Hassel appealed to the United States for a division of Marines to bolster NATO defenses in the Baltic. He has also advanced demands for a local defensive militia. In 1959 von Hassel was considered a possible candidate for the Presidency of the Federal Republic. Following the national elections of September 1961, during which he acted as the CDU's campaign manager, von Hassel was reportedly considered as a contender for the office of Minister of Defense.

On the night of October 26, 1962 the Bonn and Hamburg offices of the leading West German news magazine, *Der Spiegel*, were raided by police, and the publisher and several of his staff members were arrested and charged with treason. The charges arose from an article published in *Der Spiegel* on October 10, purporting to show the inadequacy of West German defenses. Top secret documents were alleged to have been used in the preparation of the article. Because the editors of *Der Spiegel* had

German Inf. Center

KAI-UWE VON HASSEL

frequently been critical of Minister of Defense Franz-Josef Strauss, it appeared as though Strauss were using his powers to conduct a personal vendetta against the magazine.

During the next few weeks West Germany underwent what a Social Democratic spokesman termed "a crisis of the rule of law," and the position of Chancellor Adenauer was weakened by attacks from FDP members of his coalition government. Amid popular demonstrations and charges that the government had used Gestapo methods, Adenauer was compelled to make several changes in his cabinet. Although Strauss was cleared by the Bundestag of charges that he had misused his official position, public pressure compelled him to resign.

In early December 1962 an agreement was reached between CDU and FDP leaders, designating von Hassel as the new Minister of Defense. Von Hassel, who was on a state visit to Africa when the news of the appointment reached him, declined the position at first, but later accepted it upon the urging of his party colleagues. After winding up his affairs in Schleswig-Holstein, he was installed as Minister of Defense by President Heinrich Lübke on January 9, 1963. In this post von Hassel serves as the civilian commander in chief of West Germany's 398,000 defensive troops. In addition, he continues to serve as a member of the Schleswig-Holstein Landtag and retains his positions of leadership in the state and federal CDU organizations. Vice-Chancellor Ludwig Erhard, who has been designated to succeed Adenauer as Chancellor in the fall of 1963, has given assurances that he would retain von Hassel as Minister of Defense. Von Hassel has also gained the confidence of leading members of the Free Democratic and Social Democratic parties.

Although von Hassel has denied that he would follow a "new course" in defense policy, his

HASSEL, KAI-UWE VON—*Continued*

views on the defense of Europe are closer to United States policies than those of Strauss. Whereas Strauss had sought the development of a nuclear force for West Germany, von Hassel favors the continued buildup of the Bundeswehr with conventional weapons. A strong supporter of an integrated NATO force, he regards Western defenses as indivisible, and he is opposed to the idea of an "independent European heartland" advanced by French President Charles de Gaulle. Shortly after taking office, von Hassel conferred with United States Under Secretary of State George W. Ball and with Deputy Secretary of Defense Roswell L. Gilpatric at Bonn, and he accompanied Chancellor Adenauer on a visit to Paris. In late February 1963 Hassel visited Washington, D.C. to confer with President Kennedy and other American leaders on the establishment of a multilateral nuclear force for NATO.

Essentially conservative in his outlook, von Hassel is opposed to proposals for a "greater coalition" that would include the Social Democrats, and he has occasionally expressed strongly nationalist sentiments. An article in *Der Spiegel* (January 16, 1963) said that he criticized the Social Democratic Mayor of West Berlin, Willy Brandt, in a speech in 1960 for having gone into exile during the Nazi era. On several occasions von Hassel has spoken out against recognition of the Oder-Neisse line as Germany's eastern frontier (established by the Potsdam Conference in 1945) as binding, and he has proposed a return to pre-1937 boundaries. His nationalist views, as well as his alleged leniency toward former Nazis in Schleswig-Holstein, prompted the Toronto *Globe and Mail* (December 13, 1962) to editorialize that von Hassel "does not appear to be an improvement" over Strauss.

On the other hand, von Hassel has been a consistent advocate of Great Britain's entry into the Common Market, and he refers to himself as an "out-and-out European." He holds a strong affection for the peoples of the continent of his birth and has made several visits to Africa in recent years. Von Hassel has actively supported the economic development of the new African nations. He is the author of a brochure in the Swahili language entitled *Waafrika Wa Leo*.

Kai-Uwe von Hassel was married in 1940 to Elfriede Fröhlich, a former advertising model, who was born in the former German colony of Samoa. They have a son, Joachim, who is training to be a navy flier, and a daughter, Barbara. Their boxer dog is named Gangster. Von Hassel is six feet tall, has a scholarly appearance, and is calm and contemplative. He is considered more tactful and diplomatic than his predecessor, but on occasion he has delivered militant and provocative campaign speeches. An industrious and energetic man, he generally works fourteen hours a day. His office is decorated with native artifacts from Africa. He is proficient in English, French, and Swahili, as well as German. His hobby is color photography and his favorite subjects are flowers and animals. He was awarded the decoration Grosskreuz Verdienstorden in 1956.

Von Hassel is regarded not as a theoretician but as a sober political realist who looks upon politics as the solution of practical, everyday problems. A colleague once said of von Hassel, as reported in *Die Zeit* (December 21, 1962), that if he were faced with a choice between freedom and order, he would choose order.

References

Christian Sci Mon p2 Ja 10 '63
Der Spiegel 17:17+ Ja 16 '63 pors
Manchester Guardian p7 D 12 '62 por
Newsday p30 F 26 '63 por
Philadelphia Inquirer p2 F 25 '62 por
Time 82:26 D 21 '62 por
International Who's Who, 1962-63
Wer ist Wer? (1962)
Who's Who in Germany (1960)

HATCH, CARL A(TWOOD) Nov. 27, 1889-Sept. 15, 1963 Former Democratic Senator from New Mexico (1933-49); sponsored clean-politics legislation; United States district court judge for New Mexico (1949-63). See *Current Biography* (December) 1944.

Obituary

N Y Times p35 S 16 '63

HERSKOVITS, MELVILLE J(EAN) Sept. 10, 1895-Feb. 25, 1963 Anthropologist; taught at Northwestern University since 1927; founded the first university program of African studies in the United States. See *Current Biography* (November) 1948.

Obituary

N Y Times p35 Ap 1 '63

HESS, VICTOR FRANCIS June 24, 1883- Physicist; university professor

Address: b. Fordham University, New York 58; h. 20 William St., Mount Vernon, N.Y.

Victor Francis Hess, whose discovery of cosmic rays made him the co-recipient of the 1936 Nobel Prize in Physics, has in the course of more than fifty years made basic contributions to an understanding of radiation and its effects on the human body. Before emigrating from Austria to the United States in 1938 Hess was associated with the universities of Vienna, Graz, and Innsbruck. From 1938 to 1958 he was a professor of physics at Fordham University, and since his retirement in 1958, with the title professor emeritus, he has continued to carry on research at the university. Hess holds several honorary degrees, and he has served as consultant to civic and military bodies.

Victor Francis Hess was born to Vinzens and Sarafine (Grossbauer) Hess on June 24, 1883 at Waldstein Castle near Deutsch Feistritz, Styria, Austria, where his father was chief forester on the estate of Prince Oettingen-Wallerstein. He attended the Gymnasium in the nearby city of Graz from 1893 to 1901 and the University of

Graz from 1901 to 1905. In June 1906 Hess obtained the Ph.D. degree in physics *summa cum laude*.

Intending to do postdoctoral work in optics, Hess made arrangements to study under Professor Paul Drude in Berlin. But Drude committed suicide a few weeks before Hess was to become his student, and Hess went instead to the University of Vienna on the invitation of Professor Franz Exner. A pioneer in the study of radiation, Exner, with Egon von Schweidler, interested Hess in investigating radioactivity and atmospheric electricity.

Hess was a demonstrator at the mineralogical institute of the University of Vienna in 1907 and 1908. In 1910 he began lecturing as a *Privatdozent* at the university, and in the same year he was appointed assistant at the new Institute for Radium Research of the Austrian Academy of Sciences, a post he held until 1920. From 1908 to 1920 Hess was also a lecturer in medical physics at the Vienna Veterinary Academy.

In 1911 Hess began the work that twenty-five years later made him a Nobel Prize winner. For some time scientists had been puzzled by the fact that the air in electroscopes—instruments for detecting electrical charges—became electrically charged (ionized) no matter how well the containers were insulated. It was thought that radioactivity from ground minerals was responsible, but if such were the case the effect should have diminished greatly at a height of about 300 meters. In 1910 Theodore Wulf measured ionization at the bottom and top of the Eiffel Tower, which is some 300 meters high, and found that considerably more ionization existed at the top than could be expected if it were caused by ground radiation. His results were not given unqualified acceptance, however. Nor were the experiments of the scientists who in 1909, 1910, and 1911 made balloon ascents to record ionization, for their instruments developed defects.

Reading about these earlier experiments, Hess speculated as to whether the source of ionization could be located in the sky rather than the ground. Before making balloon ascents himself, he determined the height at which ground radiation would stop producing ionization (about 500 meters) and designed instruments that would not be damaged by temperature and pressure changes. He then made ten ascents (five at night)—two in 1911, seven in 1912, and one in 1913—and found that ionization soon ceased to fall off with height and began to increase rapidly, so that at a height of several miles it was many times greater than at the earth's surface. He concluded, therefore, that "a radiation of very high penetrating power enters our atmosphere from above."

After making an ascent during an almost total eclipse of the sun on April 12, 1912 Hess further concluded that, since ionization did not decrease during the eclipse, the sun could not itself be the main source of the radiation. Hess's theory about rays from space did not receive general acceptance at the time he proposed it, but increased research after World War I supported it. First named for Hess, the newly discovered radiation was dubbed "cosmic" by Robert A. Millikan in 1925.

Friedrich Iwan, Innsbruck

VICTOR FRANCIS HESS

In 1919-20 Hess served as an assistant professor at the University of Vienna, and in 1920 he became an associate professor of experimental physics at the University of Graz. In February 1921 he took a leave of absence to make his first trip to the United States, where he became chief physicist and director of a research laboratory, built under his supervision, of the United States Radium Corporation in New Jersey. During his two years in the United States, Hess lectured at several American universities and served as a consultant to the United States Bureau of Mines.

Hess returned to the University of Graz in 1923 and was made a full professor in 1925 and dean of the faculty in 1929. He stayed at Graz until 1931, when he accepted a position as professor of experimental physics and head of the institute for radiation research at the University of Innsbruck. With the support of the Rockefeller Institute, the Austrian Academy of Sciences, the Prussian Academy of Sciences, and the Emergency Society for German Sciences (a university association for the support of science after World War I), Hess founded in the autumn of 1931 a station for the observation of cosmic radiation on Hafelekar mountain near Innsbruck at a height of 2,300 meters (about 7,000 feet).

For his discovery of cosmic radiation Hess was named co-recipient of the Nobel Prize in Physics in 1936; he shared the prize with Professor Carl D. Anderson of the California Institute of Technology, who had discovered the positron. Commenting on the award to Hess, a *Scientific Monthly* writer noted: "After a decision had been made that the first significant work in the field of cosmic rays was to be honored by a Nobel Prize, there was certainly no living person who could for a moment be considered for the award except Dr. Hess."

Hess returned to the University of Graz as professor of physics and director of the physics institute in 1937. Two months after the *An-*

HESS, VICTOR FRANCIS—*Continued*

schluss in March 1938, however, he was dismissed from his post, first, because he had a Jewish wife, and secondly, because he had been a representative of the sciences in the independent government of Chancellor Kurt von Schuschnigg. A sympathetic Gestapo officer warned the Hesses that they would be taken to a concentration camp if they stayed in Austria, and they escaped to Switzerland four weeks before the order came for their arrest.

Offered a full professorship at Fordham University in New York, Hess immigrated with his wife to the United States, where a son of Mrs. Hess already lived. He became an American citizen in 1944. In 1946, less than a year after the atomic bomb was dropped on Hiroshima, he and Paul Luger of Seattle University conducted the first tests for radioactive fallout in the United States. Many of these were made from the eighty-seventh floor of the Empire State Building. Also in 1946 Hess and Frank A. Benedetto of Fordham measured cosmic ray bombardment from the Empire State Building. The following year Hess went from the heights to the depths of Manhattan, measuring the radioactivity of granite in the 190th Street subway station at the base of Fort Tryon Park, which was covered by 160 feet of rock.

In a 1947 issue of the *American Journal of Roentgenology and Radium Therapy*, Hess and William T. McNiff reported that they had worked out "an integrating gamma-ray method" by which they could detect minute amounts of radium in the human body. This new procedure made it possible to detect radium poisoning before it reached a critical stage. In 1948 Hess visited Europe and was a guest professor at the University of Innsbruck.

Two years later, at the request of Mayor William O'Dwyer of New York City, Hess joined five other scientists in investigating the possibility of producing rain artificially in New York State, which at that time was suffering a severe drought. Another project with which he became involved in 1950 was a United States Air Force study to determine the effects of atomic bomb tests in terms of radioactive fallout. Completed in 1955, the study reported a distinction between artificial and natural radiation and found that since the tests there had been a trace of artificial radiation in the atmosphere.

Hess retired from his Fordham professorship after twenty years of service in 1958 and became a professor emeritus, but he continues to do research in his laboratory at the school. His was one of four laboratories in the United States that conducted tests on measurement of radioactivity in the breath of people who worked with radium, and he has also sought to establish a more accurate scale of the toleration limits of radioactivity of the human body. Hess has found that there are individual differences in the amount of radiation a person can tolerate without serious injury. Research in this area is difficult, he has said, for the effects of radioactivity are cumulative and may sometimes take as long as fifty years to make themselves fully felt. For this reason he strongly opposes nuclear weapon test-

ing. "We know too little about radioactivity at this time," he notes, "to state definitely that testing underground or above the atmosphere will have no effect on the human body." Hess has avowed that he intends to dedicate the rest of his working life to further study of the effects of radiation on human beings.

A contributor to many scientific journals and compilations in Europe and the United States, Hess has also written several books, some of which have been translated from the original German. His books include *Luftelektrizität* (Atmospheric Electricity) (Braunschweig, 1928), written with H. Benndorf; *The Electrical Conductivity of the Atmosphere and its Causes* (Constable, 1928); *Ionisierungsbilanz der Atmosphäre* (Ionization Balance of the Atmosphere) (Akademie, 1934); and *Die Weltstrahlung und ihre biologische Wirkung* (Fuessli, 1940), written with Jakob Eugster and published in a revised edition as *Cosmic Radiation and its Biological Effects* by the Fordham University Press in 1949.

Hess holds honorary degrees from the University of Vienna, Loyola University in Chicago and in New Orleans, Fordham University, and the University of Innsbruck. In 1958 the University of Graz held a celebration in honor of the fiftieth anniversary of Hess's completion of his graduate work, and Fordham University awarded him its Insignis and Bene Merenti medals. Hess also received the Lieben Prize of the Austrian Academy of Sciences in 1919, the Ernst Abbé Prize of the Carl Zeiss Foundation in 1932, and the Austrian government's Honorary Insignia for Art and Science in 1959. He is a fellow of the American Physical Society and the American Geophysical Union; one of the handful of American members of the Pontifical Academy of Science in Rome; and a member of the Swiss Physical Society, the Physical Society of London, and the American Meteorological Society. He is a Republican and a Roman Catholic.

On September 6, 1920 Victor Francis Hess married Marie Bertha Warner Breisky, who died on April 2, 1955. On December 13, 1955 he married Elizabeth M. Hoencke, who had nursed his first wife through her final illness. Hess is five feet nine inches tall, weighs 190 pounds, and has blue eyes and white hair. He speaks English well with a slight German accent and in a hoarse whisper, the result of a throat operation he underwent in the 1930's. An avid tennis player in his younger years, he now takes an interest in boxing (Archie Moore is a particular favorite). He also enjoys motoring and was very disappointed when New York State suspended his driver's license recently because he failed its eye test.

References

American Men of Science 10th ed (1960-62)
Heathcote, Niels. Nobel Prize Winners in Physics (1953)
International Who's Who, 1962-63
MacCallum, T. W. and Taylor, Stephen. The Nobel Prize-Winners (1938)
Who's Who in America, 1962-63

HINES, JEROME Nov. 8, 1921- Singer
Address: b. Metropolitan Opera Association, Broadway and 39th St., New York 18

The entirely American-trained basso Jerome Hines, whose majesty of presence and beauty of tone have dignified Metropolitan Opera productions since 1946, has to his credit a number of impressive "firsts." The first really outstanding American-born basso since Herbert Witherspoon (1873-1935), he is the first major American basso in forty years to triumph in important European opera houses and festivals. He is the first native-born American to sing the roles of Boris Godounov and Don Giovanni at the Metropolitan Opera House, the first American to sing the title role in Boito's *Mefistofele,* and the first American to undertake the role of Gurnemanz in Wagner's *Parsifal* at the Bayreuth Festival. To a nobility of bearing enhanced by six feet six and one-half inches of height Hines adds the vocal resources of a range from low F to two octaves above, perfect dynamic control, impeccable focus, and an intelligent interpretation of the text.

The son of Russell Ray Heinz, a Hollywood film executive, and Mildred (Link) Heinz, Jerome Hines was born Jerome Heinz in Los Angeles, California on November 8, 1921. Although he was enough interested in music to study piano for the equivalent of two and one-half years between the ages of seven and twelve, Hines was far more interested in chemistry when he attended Bancroft Junior High School and spent much of his time puttering with a chemical set on his back porch. Encouraged by his mathematical aptitude that became apparent when he engaged a tutor in mathematics, he decided to become a chemist. Having graduated from Fairfax High School, Hines enrolled at the University of California at Los Angeles, where he majored in chemistry and mathematics.

After a year in college Hines auditioned for Edwin Lester, executive director of the Los Angeles Civic Light Opera Association, who recommended that he study voice. Hines became a pupil of Gennaro Curci, who until the time that he died in 1955 remained Hines's only voice teacher. Samuel Margolis of New York has been his only other vocal coach, and much of what Hines has learned about the technical aspects of music he has picked up from the reading of books.

At the age of eighteen, in April 1940, Hines made his professional debut with the Los Angeles Civic Light Opera Association, singing the role of Bill Bobstay in a production of *H.M.S. Pinafore* that starred John Charles Thomas. (He took advantage of this occasion to change his name from Heinz to Hines.) By the time that he had graduated from the University of California in 1943 with a B.A. degree, Hines had behind him some imposing musical accomplishments. He had won a local young artists' competition, had sung on the university's concert series, and in October 1941 had made his debut with the San Francisco Opera as Biterolf in *Tannhäuser.* In 1942 he had made his debut as Ramfis in *Aïda* with the San Carlo Opera and had appeared as soloist with the Los Angeles Philhar-

J. Abresch
JEROME HINES

monic and the Hollywood Bowl Orchestra. In 1943 he sang minor roles with the Opera Association of the Golden West.

After his graduation Hines began to take graduate courses in physics at his alma mater at the same time that he began to move forward in his musical career. In the spring of 1944 he sang Mephistopheles in Gounod's *Faust* in New Orleans with the New Orleans Opera. More and more he was forced to relegate his interest in chemistry and mathematics to the sidelines, but continues his enthusiasm for them. He has contributed articles on such subjects as the operational theory of mathematics to publications like the *National Mathematics Magazine,* and he maintains a chemical laboratory in his home in South Orange, New Jersey, where he and a friend have tried to synthesize amino acids.

Since his gigantic height disqualified him from military service during World War II, Hines contributed to the war effort by working as a chemist for the Union Oil Company of Los Angeles from 1944 to 1945. He continued to sing whenever and wherever he could during this period. In 1945 he appeared at the Oakland (California) Spring Opera Festival, and he returned to the New Orleans Opera Company in 1945 and 1946. In the summer of 1945 he traveled to Central City, Colorado to sing the role of Osmin in Mozart's *Abduction from the Seraglio.* By the end of World War II Jerome Hines had more than twenty-four roles in his operatic repertoire.

Hines auditioned for the Metropolitan Opera company on March 16, 1946 and received a contract one day later. He also won the Metropolitan's $1,000 Caruso Award that year. On November 21, 1946 he made his debut at the Metropolitan Opera House as the sergeant who appears briefly in Act Two of *Boris Godounov,* and New York critics were quick to recognize him as the first important American basso in decades. Later

HINES, JEROME—*Continued*

he sang the more significant role of Pimen in the same opera and then finally moved on to the title role of Boris.

In his seventeen seasons at the Metropolitan Opera House Hines has mastered some thirty-odd roles. Among the more important ones have been the title role in *Boris Godounov*; the title role in *Don Giovanni*; King Marke in *Tristan and Isolde*; King Philip and the Grand Inquisitor in *Don Carlo*; Arkel in *Pelléas and Mélisande*; the Landgraf in *Tannhäuser*; Gurnemanz in *Parsifal*; Ramfis in *Aïda*; Mephistopheles in *Faust*; and Sarastro in *The Magic Flute*. Early in 1948 he created the role of Swallow in Benjamin Britten's *Peter Grimes*. Except for the role of Mosè in Rossini's *Mosè in Egitto* and that of Archibaldo in Montemezzi's *Love of Three Kings*, Hines has undertaken all the basso roles in the operatic repertoire.

In 1949 Hines received the first Cornelius N. Bliss Scholarship, established in memory of a prominent member of the Metropolitan Opera Association's board of directors to further the education and training of promising young singers. (The ultimate aim is to enhance the quality of the Metropolitan Opera Company.) In the summer of 1949 Hines performed at the Goethe Festival in Aspen, Colorado that celebrated the bicentenary of Goethe's birth.

By the season of 1952-53 Hines's career was in full swing. In addition to fulfilling his usual engagements with the Metropolitan Opera Company he went on a coast-to-coast concert tour and attended recording sessions with Arturo Toscanini and the NBC Symphony Orchestra for a performance of Beethoven's *Missa Solemnis* on the RCA Victor label. At both the Glyndebourne Festival in England and the Edinburgh Festival in Scotland he performed the role of Shadow in Stravinsky's *The Rake's Progress* and appeared as King Philip in Verdi's *Don Carlo* at the Teatro Colon in Buenos Aires. He sang the title role in *Don Giovanni* at the Munich Opera Festival in 1954 and returned to Buenos Aires in the same year to sing the title role in Boito's *Mefistofele*.

The first American-born basso to attempt the role of Boris Godounov at the Metropolitan Opera House, Jerome Hines made his first appearance as the crazed Tsar in February 1954 and was tendered an ovation by a crowd that yelled itself hoarse and called him back for seven solo curtain calls. His towering height is perhaps more of an asset in this role than in any other. Writing in the New York *Herald Tribune* (February 12, 1954), Jay S. Harrison reported that Hines "did his homeland proud, and was, in addition, a credit to a role that has toppled many an older and wiser trouper." Since Hines had consulted psychiatric authorities wherever he went while preparing for the role, his insight into the mind of Boris was as much a product of long hours of study as it was of intuition. "We took all the available information on Boris, both in the opera and in history, laid him out on the couch, and applied analysis," Hines once wrote in an article for *Musical America*. "Out of all this came three lines of thinking: one, that the Tzar was a schizophrenic, power-mad with a

guilt complex; two, a manic-depressive type; three, a normal man, the product of a superstitious age and culture who was pushed beyond his moral depth."

For several years Hines had been interested in Passion plays and had been impressed by the fact that no operas had been written on the subject. To fill the gap he composed the music, wrote the libretto, and did the orchestration for *I Am the Way*, the first part of a projected trilogy of music dramas based on the life of Jesus Christ, which was performed for the first time in 1954. Working with volunteers and without the benefit of fees, Hines has taken *I Am the Way* to Salvation Army centers in the Bowery and other depressed areas of New York City. After witnessing one performance, Francis D. Perkins observed in the New York *Herald Tribune* (April 30, 1960): "This work, subtitled *Scenes from the Life of Christ*, has had quite a number of performances here and elsewhere. Both the Bible-based text and the music serve this music drama's admirable purpose appropriately."

In the summer of 1958 Hines won acclaim from European critics and audiences for his performance as Gurnemanz in *Parsifal* at Bayreuth, Germany, where he enjoyed the distinction of being the first American to be selected for the role in the history of the famous Wagner festival. In later summers he added King Marke in *Tristan and Isolde* and Wotan in *Die Walküre* to his Bayreuth repertoire. His debut at La Scala in Milan in the winter of 1958 in the title role of Handel's *Hercules* was a highlight in the festivities commemorating the two-hundredth anniversary of the composer's death. When the Metropolitan Opera House staged its new production of Verdi's *Macbeth* in 1960 he appeared as the luckless Banquo. With soprano Roberta Peters, Hines performed in September 1961 at President John F. Kennedy's first state dinner of the year, for Dr. Manuel Prado, the President of Peru, in the East Room of the White House before an audience of Cabinet members, Senators, and foreign diplomats.

Since Hines had always sung the role in English at the Metropolitan, he feverishly studied Russian in preparation for his tour of the Soviet Union as Boris in September 1962, as part of the cultural exchange program between the United States and Russia. He introduced innovations into the stage business of *Boris Godounov*, playing Boris as dying of a cerebral hemorrhage instead of a skull fracture, and making himself up to look like a Tatar with a short, dark beard and a Mongolian mustache rather than with a long gray beard in the Chaliapin tradition. If Hines had feared that Russian sensibilities might be outraged by such unorthodoxies he was in for a surprise. On the evening of October 23 at the Bolshoi Theater in Moscow, during the height of the Cuban crisis, Premier Nikita S. Khrushchev led a standing ovation and, followed by Deputy Premier Anastas I. Mikoyan, congratulated Hines backstage after the performance, to the accompaniment of popping champagne corks and friendly chitchat. Later explaining his astonishment, Hines asked, "After all, how do you think Americans would react if they saw Yuri

Gagarin on the launching pad at Cape Canaveral?" He also performed in Leningrad, Kiev, and Tiflis.

The basso voice of Jerome Hines has become familiar to listeners beyond the confines of the Metropolitan Opera House through his television appearances on *The Voice of Firestone* and *The Ed Sullivan Show*. He has become known to concert audiences through his performances with the New York Philharmonic Symphony, the Philadelphia Orchestra, and other leading symphonic groups. Collectors have become acquainted with his musicianship on such recordings as *Concert Encores* and *Gospel Hymns of the Salvation Army* for London Records and on *The Holy City*, Verdi's *Macbeth*, and other discs for RCA Victor Records.

On July 23, 1952 Jerome Hines married the Italian-born soprano Lucia Evangelista, whom he met when they sang together at the summer opera in Cincinnati, Ohio. She has abandoned her own career to raise their four sons: David Jerome, Andrew Peter, John Matthew, and Russell Ray. Hines keeps his big frame in shape by training regularly in a gymnasium. His favorite outdoor sports are horseback riding, swimming, ice-skating, skin-diving, and spear fishing off the coasts of California's Palos Verdes, Fort Lauderdale, Florida, and Narragansett, Rhode Island. Hines has an ebullient sense of humor. Interested in hypnotism since his student days at the University of California, he entertains fellow singers on the road by giving demonstrations of hypnosis, and he sometimes hypnotizes himself to sleep during the intermissions of operas in which he is performing. Hines is an articulate and enthusiastic conversationalist, frank about flaws or failures in his performances. He is a partisan of opera in English in the United States, provided that suitable translations are available.

References

Ewen, David. Living Musicians; First Supplement (1957)
Who's Who in America, 1962-63

HOFF, PHILIP H(ENDERSON) June 29, 1924- Governor of Vermont; lawyer
Address: b. State House, Montpelier, Vt.; h. 214 Prospect Parkway, Burlington, Vt.

Philip H. Hoff became the first Democratic Governor of Vermont since before the Civil War by defeating the incumbent Republican, F. Ray Keyser, Jr., in November 1962 by only 1,348 votes. He was installed for a two-year term on January 17, 1963, following a recount by the Vermont legislature. Before his election Hoff served in 1961 and 1962 as representative for the city of Burlington in the Vermont General Assembly. A native of Massachusetts, he has practised law in Burlington since 1951.

Philip Henderson Hoff was born on June 29, 1924 in Greenfield, Massachusetts to Olaf Hoff, Jr., an insurance man, and Agnes E. (Henderson) Hoff. His father, who is now retired, served two terms in the Massachusetts General Court. Philip Hoff has a sister, Dagny Hoff Roseboro, who lives in Ohio, and two brothers, Olaf

Kirk Studio, Burlington, Vt.
PHILIP H. HOFF

Hoff 3d, a Connecticut business executive, and Foster H. Hoff, a high school principal in New York.

Reared in Turners Falls, Massachusetts, Hoff attended Turners Falls High School, where he was a star player on the football team. After graduating in 1942 he entered Williams College in Williamstown, Massachusetts on a one-year athletic scholarship, but his studies were interrupted by World War II service. Hoff served in the United States Navy submarine branch from June 1943 to March 1946. He then returned to Williams College, majored in English literature, and obtained his B.A. degree *cum laude* in 1948.

Hoff obtained his legal education at Cornell Law School in Ithaca, New York. He was elected to the law fraternity Phi Delta Phi, and he graduated in 1951 with the LL.B. degree. To meet part of his expenses he did temporary work for Cornell University, and in 1950 he was employed as a law clerk in the New York City office of Davies, Hardy, Schenck & Soons. In the same year Charles Black, the senior partner of the Burlington, Vermont law firm of Black and Wilson, died. The surviving partner, J. Boone Wilson, who had also attended Cornell, persuaded Hoff to join him in practice in Burlington. Hoff moved there in 1951; he was admitted to the Vermont bar in 1952, and he practised law continuously in that state until his installation as Governor in 1963. His firm, once named Black, Wilson, Coffrin & Hoff and now known as Black, Wilson & Hoff, is engaged in the practice of corporate, banking, and insurance law. Hoff belongs to the Chittenden County, the Vermont, and the American bar associations. He has been a member of the insurance and the labor sections of the American Bar Association.

"Interest in people" and "belief in the responsibility of everyone for good government" are cited by Philip Hoff as factors that influenced him to seek public office. He has served as chair-

HOFF, PHILIP H.—*Continued*

man of the Burlington zoning board and as the Burlington representative to the state General Assembly. In the latter post, which he held in 1961 and 1962, he helped to put through state approval of the Kerr-Mills act, under which federal and state funds are matched for medical care for the aged (Governor Keyser had opposed it).

Even though Republican domination of Vermont politics had not been seriously threatened in over a century, Democratic strength, especially in the industrial areas, had steadily increased, and by the time of the 1956 elections the Democrats were making a strenuous bid to "end 100 years of Republican control." In 1958 the Democrats not only came within 719 votes of electing their gubernatorial candidate, Bernard J. Leddy, but sent William H. Meyer to Washington as Vermont's first Democratic Congressman since the 1850's. Two years later, however, when the outgoing Republican Governor, Robert T. Stafford, unseated Congressman Meyer, the Republican gubernatorial candidate, F. Ray Keyser, Jr., won over the Democrat Russell F. Niquette by 92,780 votes to 71,785—a decisive margin. When, at the primaries in September 1962, Hoff sought the Democratic nomination to contest the election for Governor he encountered no opposition.

According to Herbert S. Hadad of the Boston *Globe* (November 11, 1962), the victory of Philip Hoff over F. Ray Keyser, Jr., on November 6, 1962 "astounded the rest of the country, confounded electronic brains, but surprised nary a native." For, as a New York *Times* correspondent put it (November 9, 1962), "the Democratic theme of 'time for a change' finally fell on receptive ears, and . . . it happened while the Republicans were badly divided." There was dissatisfaction with Keyser for his failure to provide a promised reduction in income tax and more state support of local schools and for his handling of legislative reapportionment and of the Rutland Railroad dispute. The Rutland Railroad, one of the state's two principal carriers, was closed down with the approval of the ICC, resulting in loss of employment and higher shipping rates. Hoff had been the lawyer for the union that wanted to prevent the closing. Furthermore, two Republican leaders in Vermont defected from Keyser's cause and formed the Vermont Independents, who supported Hoff and brought him enough votes to make the difference between winning and losing. The final count of votes, made by legislative committee after the General Assembly had convened in January 1963, was 61,383 for Hoff and 60,035 for Keyser. Hoff was installed in the $13,750-a-year post on January 17, 1963.

Hoff was the only Democrat elected to state office in Vermont in 1962, and the Vermont General Assembly continued to be run by a Republican majority. The Governor's first big task after his election was to make up a budget for the fiscal years 1964 and 1965 and to try to balance the $135,300,000 in budgetary requests with the estimated $110,000,000 in revenues. Soon after his installation Hoff proposed to the General Assembly that it adjourn until January 1964 to allow time for "massive task-force studies

of major problems facing the state," upon which he would base his recommended program. The assembly did not agree to adjourn, but there was some indication that Hoff would call a special legislative session in 1964 so that he could present his program at that time (the Vermont legislature normally meets only in odd years).

Hoff's short occupancy of the Governorship has already been a troubled one. His request for postponement of the assembly session led some constituents to call him a "do-nothing" Governor. He has also alienated members of his own party by appointing Republicans to some of the available jobs, although he has noted that he must have bipartisan support for his appointees. And he has met some resistance to his intention to consolidate in state and regional groupings many of the educational, welfare, health, highway, and other services now performed separately by 246 towns and cities. Late in April 1963 Governor Hoff endorsed a resolution calling for the study of a bill for a state-operated lottery in Vermont; he had previously opposed legalizing pari-mutuel betting in his state.

Philip H. Hoff and the former Joan Brower, whom he married on August 28, 1948, have four daughters: Susan Brower, Dagny Elizabeth, Andrea Clark, and Gretchen Henderson. Hoff has blond hair and blue eyes, stands six feet one inch tall, and weighs 190 pounds. He belongs to the Burlington Rotary Club and is a trustee of the Vermont Rehabilitation Center and a director of the Vermont Children's Aid Society, the Lake Champlain Chamber of Commerce, and the Greater Burlington Industrial Corporation. He and his wife are Episcopalians.

References

Boston Globe p6 N 8 '62; A pl N 11 '62 por

American Bar, 1963
Martindale-Hubbell Law Directory, 1963
Vermont Legislative Directory and State Manual, 1961

HOGGART, (HERBERT) RICHARD (hŏg′ ērt) Sept. 24, 1918- British educator; author

Address: b. Department of English Language and Literature, The University, Birmingham 15, England

Richard Hoggart, a professor of English at the University of Birmingham, first came to public attention in 1957 with the publication of his book *The Uses of Literacy,* a study of working-class attitudes and traditions. In it he drew on his own childhood experiences in the slums of Leeds to show how the media of mass communication are debasing a culture of stability and richness. Hoggart scored another personal triumph in 1960 with his testimony on behalf of the defense in the obscenity trial of D. H. Lawrence's *Lady Chatterley's Lover.* He has served on a number of important committees concerned with education and mass media, and he is a popular lecturer. Hoggart is also the author of the first full-length critical study of the poet W. H. Auden. Since 1957 he has been a fellow of the Royal Society of Literature.

A native of Hunslet, a district of the Yorkshire industrial city of Leeds, Herbert Richard Hoggart was born on September 24, 1918 to Tom Longfellow and Adeline Emma (Long) Hoggart. He has a sister, Molly, and a brother, Tom Longfellow, who is now a headmaster. When his father, a housepainter, died in 1920 his mother, although in poor health, did her best to bring up the children on a charity income equivalent to three dollars a week. Recalling this period of his life in *The Uses of Literacy*, Hoggart records that he and his brother and sister shared pocket money totaling a penny a week. When Mrs. Hoggart died in 1926 the boy went to live with his grandmother. She had been born in a village near Leeds and was superficially educated in a country dame school before she and her husband were drawn to the city and its steel works. "She retained in the vitality of her spirit, in the vigour of her language, and in the occasional peasant quality of her humour, a strength which her children had not," Hoggart has recalled. "She read, without spectacles, many of the books I brought home. I remember especially her reaction to D. H. Lawrence; much of it she admired, and she was not shocked. But of his descriptions of physical sex she said, ''E makes a lot of fuss and lah-de-dah about it.' "

Hoggart attended public elementary schools in Leeds until he was twelve. He then took the examination that was to decide his academic future. If he failed, he would receive low-pressure schooling until he was old enough to work; if he passed, he would attend the vastly superior grammar school. Although he failed, his career was saved by an elementary school headmaster who insisted that the education authorities re-read his scholarship essay. Upon re-reading it the authorities were enough impressed to send him to the Cockburn High School in Leeds. In 1936 a scholarship took Hoggart on to the University of Leeds. Three years later he obtained his B.A. degree with first class honors in English. He also won a Parkinson Graduate Scholarship, spent another year at Leeds, and received his M.A. degree after submitting a thesis on "Literature and Politics in the Reign of Queen Anne."

In 1940 Hoggart enlisted in the Royal Artillery as a private. Commissioned in the educational branch, he served in North Africa, in Pantelleria, and on the Italian mainland. In Italy he founded the Three Arts Club for Allied Forces, edited four anthologies of writings by servicemen, and was a part-time lecturer at the University of Naples. He ended his army service in 1946 as a staff captain.

Hoggart's first civilian teaching post was at the University of Hull, where he went in 1946 as staff tutor in literature in the department of adult education. His first book, *Auden: An Introductory Essay*, was published by Chatto & Windus Ltd. and Yale University Press in 1951. Dismissing the book's subtitle as overly modest, a reviewer in the London *Times Literary Supplement* (August 10, 1951) welcomed it as the first full-length critical study of the literary works of the poet W. H. Auden and praised Hoggart as an admirably direct critic. "He sees

RICHARD HOGGART

Pix

Mr. Auden in the round; like a piece of sculpture he puts him on show, drawing attention here, explaining a typical piece of technique there, and going back again and again to the method of composition itself. This he elucidates with great sensitivity, and as an analysis of modern poetic technique his remarks are worth the attention of any practising poet."

While Hoggart regards his role as a teacher, which he enjoys, as having first call on his time and energy, he fills in his spare time with writing whenever possible. "I am not a natural writer," he told Joseph Minogue in an interview for the Manchester *Guardian* (December 2, 1960), "yet I feel like a man without a job if I go a fortnight without writing anything." *The Uses of Literacy* occupied his evenings and weekends for five years. It was published in 1957 by Chatto & Windus Ltd. in London with the subtitle *Aspects of Working-Class Life, With Special Reference to Publications and Entertainments*. An American edition, published in the same year by Essential Books, Inc., is subtitled *Changing Patterns in English Mass Culture*. The work was recognized at once as an important book by critics on both sides of the Atlantic, and it has scored great popular success, especially with young people.

The Uses of Literacy is a detailed study of English working-class culture and of the changes in it that have been brought about over the past thirty years by the growing influence of the mass media. The book is illustrated with mercilessly exact parodies of the tone and methods of popular journalism, pulp fiction, advertising, and mass-produced entertainment. It is illuminated by the author's own warm but unsentimental recollections of the limited but tight-knit and solidly based society that he knew as a child. According to Joseph Minogue in the Manchester *Guardian* (December 2, 1960), Hoggart seeks to

HOGGART, RICHARD—*Continued*

resist "the building up of a great, near-moronic mass, spooned with opinions, embracing a baseless popular culture, without either old habitual wisdoms or new and intelligently directed energies."

Hoggart spent the academic year 1956-57 as visiting professor of English at the University of Rochester in New York. Returning to Hull, he became senior staff tutor, keeping that position from 1957 until 1959, when he went as senior lecturer in English to the University of Leicester. In October 1962 he took his present post as professor of English at the University of Birmingham.

Meanwhile, the great success of *The Uses of Literacy* has continued to affect his life in a variety of ways. Hoggart, who has been described as "a fluent and exciting speaker," receives some 300 invitations a year to expound his views before various societies. He feels obliged to accept as many of these invitations as possible, often speaking on the European continent and in the United States, as well as in England. He is also much in demand as a speaker on radio and television, and as a book reviewer. In 1958 Hoggart accepted the first of several important public appointments, when he became a member of the Albemarle Committee on Youth Services. The committee's 1960 report led to increased government expenditure on many kinds of youth services and to the establishment of a permanent Youth Service Development Council. Hoggart is a member of this council.

As an authority on the mass media Hoggart was a natural choice for membership of the so-called Pilkington Committee, set up in 1960 to consider the future of British broadcasting and television. The committee's report, issued in June 1962, was a controversial one, regarded in some quarters as biased in favor of the British Broadcasting Corporation and unduly harsh towards Britain's independent television companies. Defining the committee's criteria for democratic broadcasting in the public service, Hoggart has said: "Such broadcasting requires the broadcasters to put on in prime time a fair range or variety of programs, varied in both subjects and moods, rather than to cater for people almost wholly conceived as a relaxed mass."

Hoggart added greatly to his increasing stature as a public figure in October 1960, when he gave evidence as an expert witness in the hotly debated trial of D. H. Lawrence's *Lady Chatterley's Lover.* The novel, then receiving its first British publication in unexpurgated form, was the subject of a Crown case testing a new anti-obscenity law. According to an article written for the British Council by Philip Collins, Hoggart's evidence in favor of the book "marked a turning-point in the trial. Counsel for the Prosecution was clearly worsted in his attempt to upset Hoggart, whose imperturbability owed nothing to dogmatism or to the ivory-tower arrogance often imputed to academics. . . . His triumph was as much a matter of character as of intellectual brilliance." The book was judged not to be obscene. Hoggart's testimony is contained in *The Trial of Lady Chatterley* (Penguin, 1961).

In 1959-60 Richard Hoggart served on the BBC's General Advisory Council. He is also a member of the Books Overseas Committee of the British Council. In the midst of all these activities, he still finds time for writing. His third and most recent book is *W. H. Auden: A Selection* (Hutchinson, 1961), a well-received collection intended primarily for senior grammar school students. Hoggart often writes for magazines on literary and educational topics. He has also contributed to several symposia, including *Conviction* (MacGibbon, 1958), a symposium on the future of the left in Great Britain, edited by Norman Ian Mackenzie; and he wrote the essay on mass communications in *The Modern Age* (Penguin, 1961), the final volume in the *Pelican Guide to English Literature,* edited by Boris Ford.

On July 18, 1942 Richard Hoggart married Mary Holt France, a former schoolteacher. They have three children, Simon David, Frances Nicola, and Paul Richard. Hoggart spends as much time as he can with his family and enjoys "pottering about" in his house and garden. He is five feet seven and a half inches tall, weighs 140 pounds, and has brown eyes and dark-brown hair. He gives his political affiliation as "left" and indicates no church affiliation. Hoggart is essentially an optimist. He is quoted in *Time* (January 25, 1963) as saying: "Old habit patterns are breaking down. Many people are trying to find a new identity. From it all might come one day a fusion of the upper-class sense of service with the working-class sense of clan solidarity and friendship. Then you'd really have something fine."

In trying to answer the question "Who is Hoggart?" Joseph Minogue suggests that "perhaps his own, half-ironic answer is the best—a 'basic provincial Honest Joe.' He is a clever Joe . . . an intellectual without affectation; a sound Yorkshireman with a sharp eye for the shoddy and with an inspiring capacity for hard work built into him. He is also a game 'un, who is not likely to be shouted down by the powerful forces in a struggle which concerns everybody who rejects mass thinking, mass attitudes, and mass behaviour" (Manchester *Guardian,* December 2, 1960).

References

Manchester Guardian p11 D 2 '60 por
Hoggart, Richard. The Uses of Literacy (1957)
Who's Who, 1963

HOLENSTEIN, THOMAS (EMIL LEO) Feb. 7, 1896-Oct. 31, 1962 Swiss statesman; member of the Federal Council and head of the Department of Public Economy (1954-59); president of the Swiss Confederation (1958). See *Current Biography* (May) 1958.

Obituary

N Y Times p31 N 1 '62

HOLLOWAY, STANLEY Oct. 1, 1890- Entertainer; actor

Address: "Nightingales," Penn, Buckinghamshire, England

An all-round entertainer of veteran proficiency in the techniques and traditions of his art, Stanley Holloway has performed in every type of entertainment except the ballet and grand opera. Early in a career that has spanned more than half a century, he became well known to British audiences as a song-and-dance man and then as a monologist especially skillful in using folk humor. Many stage plays and over thirty movies, including *This Happy Breed* and *The Lavender Hill Mob,* have brought him distinction as an actor, particularly as a comedian. In the United States he is identified with Alfred P. Doolittle of Lerner and Loewe's *My Fair Lady,* which opened on Broadway in 1956, and with the English butler of the American television series *Our Man Higgins,* in which he starred in 1962-63.

Stanley Holloway was born in London on October 1, 1890, the son of a law clerk. He received what he describes as a "typically Victorian schooling," attending a free elementary school and then a high school, which charged tuition. The school closed down when he was twelve, much to his satisfaction, and he became an office boy in London's Billingsgate fish market. Here he was surrounded by the Cockney accents that he was to use fifty years later in *My Fair Lady.* One of the minor achievements of his job was learning the fishmongers' code of backward numbers, "eno, owt, eerht," which enabled them to discuss prices with impunity in front of customers.

In addition to a typically Victorian schooling, Holloway had a typically Victorian home life. On Sunday evenings, like every other well-regulated Victorian family, the Holloways would gather round the piano for a family singsong. The talent he showed here resulted in his becoming a choirboy, and by the time he was fourteen he was singing solos with the choir. He also became a soloist in the concert parties that were an annual feature of the entertainment offered at the seaside resorts in Britain, such as Bournemouth, Margate, and Clacton. His next step after the concert parties was to the music hall or vaudeville stage. Since the early 1900's, when Charlie Chaplin was also making his name "on the halls," Holloway has continued to be popular in vaudeville.

By 1913 Holloway had saved enough money to visit Milan to study opera. He stayed in Italy for six months, until the outbreak of World War I in 1914 made it necessary for him to return home. He joined what he calls the "P.B.I. —the poor, bloody infantry" and came out at the end of the war with the rank of lieutenant. In 1919 he made his debut on London's West End, at the Winter Garden Theatre as Captain Wentworth in *Kissing Time.* The following year he appeared at the same theater as René in *A Night Out.*

The early 1920's was a bleak time for England and for the acting profession. Holloway and nine other young actors banded together to do a show based on the concert party idea, essential ingredients being the minimum of props and the

STANLEY HOLLOWAY

maximum of originality. Combining the political key words of the time—"optimism" and "cooperation," the ten performers named themselves The Co-optimists. They opened in London at the Royalty Theatre, which Holloway later called "one of the hottest little theaters in Dean Street," on June 27, 1921. With everything seemingly against it, the show ran through a trade depression, a heat wave, and a coal strike before closing six years later—a run phenomenal for that time. One of Holloway's co-optimists was Bert Coote, the father of Robert Coote, who played Pickering in *My Fair Lady.*

Following the success of *The Co-optimists,* Holloway was engaged for several West End shows during the late 1920's and early 1930's, including *Song of the Sea, Cooee,* a revived *Co-optimists* in 1929, *The Co-optimists of 1930, Savoy Follies, Here We Are Again,* and *Three Sisters.* In 1934 he made his first appearance in the peculiarly British form of entertainment, the Christmas pantomime, when he played Abanazar in *Aladdin* at Birmingham. He repeated this role yearly at Leeds, Golders Green, Edinburgh, and Manchester.

While securing his place on the stage in the 1920's, Holloway also explored opportunities to test his talents in newer fields of entertainment. Movie fans saw him for the first time in *The Rotters* in 1921, and since his first broadcast in 1923 he has been a favorite with radio audiences. He recalls that after the war he was heard on a BBC program with a ten-year-old singer named Julie Andrews, who later starred as Eliza Doolittle in the original cast of *My Fair Lady.*

On the music hall stage, meanwhile, Holloway invented a character for himself, Sam Small, a North countryman who nearly upsets the Battle of Waterloo. When this monologue proved successful, Holloway developed Sam's adventures further. Marriott Edgar wrote a series of twelve monologues for him that tell the story of a

HOLLOWAY, STANLEY—Continued

North country family, the Ramsbottoms. The best-known monologue is *Albert and the Lion,* which in 1957 Milner Productions made into an animated film with Holloway as the narrator.

His work in motion pictures made Stanley Holloway's name known to a wide audience beyond his own country. In the film version of Shaw's *Major Barbara* (United Artists, 1941) one of his fellow actors was Rex Harrison, who also became a member of the original cast of *My Fair Lady.* Featured in two movies about British servicemen in World War II, Holloway played the role of Palmer in *The Way to the Stars* (United Artists, 1945) and of Brewer in *The Way Ahead* (Twentieth Century-Fox), which was released in Great Britain on D Day (June 6, 1944) and had its première in New York in June of the following year. He also appeared in two films that placed Celia Johnson and Noel Coward firmly on the moviegoers' map: in *Brief Encounter* (Universal, 1946) as Albert Godby, the railway station guard, and in *This Happy Breed* (Universal, 1947) as the next-door neighbor. His main screen triumphs have been in comedies such as *Passport to Pimlico* (Eagle-Lion, 1949), *The Lavender Hill Mob* (Universal, 1951), and *The Titfield Thunderbolt* (Universal, 1953).

As Arthur Pemberton in *Passport to Pimlico,* Holloway played one of the British bulldogs determined to stick up for their right to be Burgundian, after a bomb explosion uncovered an old deed making Pimlico, in London, a part of Burgundy. Although not so popular in the United States, it achieved great success in England, where, even in the early 1950's, rationing was still in existence. The movie's airlift (shades of the Berlin airlift) and the bonfire of ration books were extremely funny to a people still sorely restricted.

Along with Alec Guinness as Holland, the master criminal, Holloway shared much of the critics' applause for *The Lavender Hill Mob,* in which he played Pendlebury, the maker of the miniature Eiffel towers used to ship out stolen gold. He gave another notable performance as Lockit, the jailer, in Sir Laurence Olivier's *The Beggar's Opera* (Warner Brothers, 1953); he and Olivier were the only actors in the film whose singing voices were not dubbed. Among Holloway's recent pictures is *No Love for Johnnie* (Rank, 1961).

During the war Holloway had continued with his stage work, and at the time of the London blitz, he recalls, he used to phone "the theatre each morning to see if it was still there." His credits in the early 1940's included *Up and Doing* (1940 and 1941) and *Fine and Dandy* (1942), both at the Saville Theatre. In 1946 he entertained in a pantomime again, this time as Squire Skinflint in *Mother Goose.* His portrayal in May 1951 of the First Gravedigger in *Hamlet* at New Theatre followed his playing the Gravedigger in the Olivier film of *Hamlet* (1948). In 1954, he appeared with the Old Vic Company at the Edinburgh Festival as Bottom in *A Midsummer Night's Dream.* It was in this role and with this company that he first performed in New York, at the Metropolitan Opera House in September 1954.

Holloway's next appearance on the American stage was as that representative of the "undeserving poor," the father of Eliza Doolittle, in Lerner and Loewe's musical adaptation of Shaw's *Pygmalion, My Fair Lady,* which opened at the Mark Hellinger Theatre on March 15, 1956. Playing the part with the "manners and mien of a brewery horse kicking up its heels in the springtime," as Wayne Robinson wrote in *Theatre Arts* (June 1956), Holloway stopped the show almost nightly with his song-and-dance numbers "With a Little Bit of Luck" and "Get Me to the Church on Time."

My Fair Lady ran on Broadway until mid-1962, but Holloway left the American production on December 14, 1957, to open with the other principals in the London production at Drury Lane Theatre Royal on April 30, 1958. Drew Middleton, in describing Holloway's London performance, said that he "seemed a bigger, more impressive, figure" than in New York. Perhaps the greatest praise came from seasoned critic R. E. P. Sensenfelder of Philadelphia, who, after seeing many productions of *Pygmalion,* wrote that Holloway's was the best Alfred Doolittle that he had ever seen. Holloway was chosen in 1963 to play Alfred Doolittle in Warner Brothers film version of *My Fair Lady.*

In October 1960, about a year after he had left the London cast of *My Fair Lady,* Holloway returned to Broadway to bring to the Ethel Barrymore Theatre a one-man show called *Laughs and Other Events.* He tried to epitomize the art of the vaudeville performer with songs and monologues, but the show closed after seven performances. He was perhaps more successful in reaching a similar goal in a record album, *'Ere's 'Olloway* (Columbia Records), which is a collection of the songs and monologues that Alf Doolittle might have heard in the music hall of his day—such classics as "Sweeney Todd the Barber," "Evings's Dorg 'Ospital," and "My Old Dutch." The Sam Small and Albert stories, some of which Holloway used in *Laughter and Other Events,* were also naturals for a record album. These recordings had been brought out by English Columbia in the 1930's and were reissued by Angel in 1955. He made a children's record in the Wonderland series called *The Elephant Alphabet* for Riverside, and in 1962 he recorded the musical *Oliver!* together with Alma Cogen and Violet Carson (Capitol).

Looking back on his career, Holloway remembers how each new entertainment medium was regarded as the potential death of the legitimate theater, down to the very latest so-called assassin —television. He feels that television "will eventually be relegated to the status of a household utility, like the vacuum cleaner and deep freeze." Even if it becomes a household utility, it will be one that has benefited from Holloway's talents.

During the 1930's when television was in its experimental stages in England, he was one of its earliest performers. He has made several appearances in original television productions in the United States, notably as Pooh-Bah in *The Mikado,* which also starred Groucho Marx, on NBC-TV on April 29, 1960. On February 11, 1962 he appeared on NBC-TV's special show *The Broadway of Lerner and Loewe,* with Robert

Goulet, Julie Andrews, Richard Burton, and Maurice Chevalier. Holloway's half-hour weekly television series, *Our Man Higgins*, premièred on ABC-TV on October 3, 1962. Playing an English butler coping imperturbably with the rigors of life in American suburbia, Holloway uses the timing and sly twinkle of a music hall veteran. Although most of the critics condemned the inadequacies of the script, they agreed that Holloway's personality might ensure the series a steady audience.

Stanley Holloway was married first in 1913. In 1939 he married Violet Marion Lane ("Laney"), and they have a son, Julian, who attended Harrow and plans to study acting at London's Royal Academy of Dramatic Art (RADA). On the 1960 New Year's Honours List, Queen Elizabeth II conferred on Holloway the Order of the British Empire for his services to the theater. He is a member of the Garrick and the Green Room clubs. The Holloways attend the Anglican Church in Penn.

Exceptionally vigorous at seventy-two, Holloway plays golf for recreation. He is five feet ten inches tall, weighs 169 pounds, and has brown eyes and brown hair. In *High Fidelity; The Magazine for Music Listeners* (April 1957) Charles Burr described the "real Holloway" as "a dignified, carefully groomed, slightly conscience-stricken Englishman . . . looking very much like the bank president, the well-to-do importer, the special emissary of Her Majesty's government. He seems to be listening for something not quite audible". The latter part of this description is particularly apt, for Holloway lives by some advice given him when he was a very young music hall performer: to listen to every form of entertainment. After the tremendous success of his characterization of Doolittle in *My Fair Lady* one critic seemed to sum up the whole of his talent when he described him as "a gem of an entertainer, sly and effortless with all the gusto of a music hall genius."

References

Hi Fi 7:52+ Ap '57 por
N Y Times II p3 O 2 '60
Who's Who, 1962
Who's Who in the Theatre (1961)

HOLMES, D(YER) BRAINERD May 24, 1921-   Business executive; former United States government official; engineer

Address: b. Raytheon Company, 141 Spring St., Lexington, Mass.

On May 25, 1961 President John F. Kennedy set as a goal for the present decade the landing of Americans on the moon. Directing Project Apollo, the $20 billion American man-to-the-moon program, was one of the responsibilities of D. Brainerd Holmes, who was director of manned space flight programs with the National Aeronautics and Space Administration from November 1961 to September 15, 1963. He brought to the post a rare combination of technical and administrative proficiency and a desire to advance the boundaries of knowledge. An electrical engineer with a record of getting big jobs done on sched-

ule, he worked for the Radio Corporation of America from 1953 to 1961. One of the projects he supervised for RCA was the design and installation of the Ballistic Missile Early Warning System, with stations in Alaska and Greenland. On October 1, 1963 Holmes became a senior vice-president at the Raytheon Company in Lexington, Massachusetts.

Dyer Brainerd Holmes, the son of Theodora P. Holmes and Marcellus B. Holmes, a newspaper advertising executive, was born in Brooklyn, New York City, on May 24, 1921. He grew up in East Orange, New Jersey and attended Newark Academy and Carteret School. In secondary school he distinguished himself in scholarship, student government, and athletics. He was on the varsity football and track teams for two years.

Several first-class schools were interested in enrolling Holmes, but for years he had been determined to go to Cornell University. When he applied for admission to Cornell in 1939 an alumnus who interviewed him wrote: "I do not know of another boy of whom I could so confidently predict a successful career." Awarded a McMullen Scholarship, Holmes studied electrical engineering. He was on the Dean's List throughout his college career. A member of the Sphinx Head and Red Key societies and the honorary engineering societies Tau Beta Pi and Eta Kappa Nu, he was president of his fraternity, Chi Psi, and chairman of the Cornell for Victory Council, a wartime organization. He also played freshman and junior varsity football. He received the B.S. degree from Cornell in 1943. In May 1943, shortly before graduating from Cornell, Holmes joined the United States Naval Reserve as an ensign. He was sent to radar school at Bowdoin College in 1943 and at the Massachusetts Institute of Technology in 1944, and for the remainder of the war he served in a radar maintenance school at Pearl Harbor.

Returning to civilian life, Holmes became a systems engineer with the Western Electric Company, a unit of the Bell System, in Kearney, New Jersey in 1945. For the next eight years he was engaged in development engineering work, at Western Electric from 1945 to 1948 and 1950 to 1951 and at the Bell Telephone Laboratories from 1949 to 1950 and from 1951 to 1953. In 1953 he joined the Radio Corporation of America as a project manager.

Holmes's abilities were thoroughly challenged at RCA, where he was assigned to a series of progressively more difficult projects. His success in handling them accounts for his present reputation. Co-workers regard him as cool and hard-driving, outspoken, yet tactful when the situation requires. The president of RCA, Dr. Elmer Engstrom, who supervised Holmes early in his career with the company, remembers him as an ideal systems man. "The problem with systems engineering," Engstrom has said, "is to find people with a special knack for marrying men, machines, tactics and everything else into one large system. We could see right away that Holmes had the knack."

During his eight years with RCA, from 1953 to 1961, Holmes was responsible for co-ordinating three essential projects: the Navy's ground-to-air antiaircraft missile, Talos; the greatly improved

Wide World

D. BRAINERD HOLMES

electronics system of the Atlas ICBM, which reduced the Atlas countdown from hours to minutes; and the Ballistic Missile Early Warning System (BMEWS), which will give the United States at least fifteen minutes' warning in the event of missile attack.

Holmes directed the design and installation of the giant radar reflectors, as big as up-ended football fields, which can detect missiles coming from all possible directions, including any the Soviet Union might send over the Arctic Ocean. Two tracking stations are in operation: at Thule, Greenland, since 1960, and at Clear, Alaska, since 1961. A third station is scheduled to be built at Fylandsdale, Yorkshire, England. The $1 billion contract for BMEWS that the United States Air Force awarded RCA in 1958 was the biggest in the company's history, and RCA subcontracted parts of the project to about 2,900 other private companies.

Many logistics problems were encountered in setting up the stations. Huge quantities of equipment had to be transported, much of it delicate electronic apparatus that required protection against shock and changes in temperature. Construction of the warning stations at Alaska and Greenland posed special problems because of the terrain and weather. The land on which the radar reflectors were built had to be artificially thawed and then refrozen so that the reflectors would not settle out of line. In spite of the formidable difficulties encountered the first two of the three BMEWS stations were completed on schedule, and costs were kept within the budget. On June 1, 1961 Holmes was made general manager of RCA's major defense systems division in Moorestown, New Jersey.

On September 20, 1961 the National Aeronautics and Space Administration selected D. Brainerd Holmes to direct all United States manned space flights, including the lunar program proposed by President Kennedy. For Holmes, who assumed

the new post in November 1961, accepting the position meant taking a cut in salary to less than half of what he was earning at RCA. However, as his friend Eugene F. O'Neill, head of the Bell Laboratories Telstar program, said, "He has a streak of romanticism, religion, patriotism. In the end it was his desire to push back the boundaries that prevailed."

Project Apollo, the American program to send three men to the moon by 1970, will be preceded by years of other space flights, both manned and unmanned. Many of these are already part of history, and they have brought scientists a great deal of data. The space-flight experience of astronauts who orbited the earth has shown man's ability to function effectively under the condition of weightlessness. An important intermediate step between the present single-astronaut Mercury project and the Apollo program is the so-called Gemini project, under which it is planned that two men will orbit the earth in a capsule for as long as two weeks. During this phase of the space flight program it is hoped that the rendezvous technique will be perfected. The joining together of two vehicles in orbit will be an essential part of the moon trip.

Holmes took part in the important NASA decision, made early in 1962, as to which of three methods should be used in reaching the moon. The direct method of sending a spaceship straight to the moon with everything needed for the round trip requires more rocket power than is technologically available at present. A second method under consideration was the earth orbit rendezvous, in which two ships would link up in earth orbit after having been launched in a precisely timed sequence. One craft would refuel from the other before proceeding to the moon.

The plan that was given priority for the time being as the safest, most feasible, and least costly is the lunar orbit rendezvous. A three-man spaceship, a service module, and a small landing craft would be launched moonwards by a single C-5 Saturn booster and go into lunar orbit, from which the small landing craft would descend to the moon. After completing their explorations the astronauts would return to the command craft, abandon the small ship in lunar orbit, and travel back to earth in the command capsule. Project Apollo is expected to cost about $20 billion within this decade.

D. Brainerd Holmes is a senior of the Institute of Radio Engineers. He is an Episcopalian. On May 22, 1943 he married Dorothy Bonnet of Orange, New Jersey. They are the parents of two teenage daughters, named Dorothy Ann and Katherine Bonnet. On Sundays the family often goes sailing in a nineteen-foot racer. "Brain," as he is called by his wife, has graying brown hair, dresses conservatively, and, when working, wears dark horn-rimmed glasses. He is five feet ten inches tall and weighs 170 pounds. Although an average work day of twelve hours leaves him little or no time for athletics, Holmes keeps fit by means of a daily routine of morning exercises.

References

N Y Times p10 Jl 30 '62 por
Time 80:52 Ag 10 '62 pors

American Men of Science 10th ed (1960-62)

HOLYOAKE, KEITH J(ACKA) Feb. 11, 1904-
Prime Minister of New Zealand; farmer

Address: b. Parliament Bldgs., Wellington, New
Zealand; h. 41 Pipitea St., Wellington, New
Zealand

Every three years when they go to the polls
New Zealanders choose between proponents of a
welfare state and supporters of private enterprise.
With the victory in 1960 of the conservative
National party over the socialist Labour party,
Nationalist leader Keith J. Holyoake succeeded
Labourite Walter Nash as Prime Minister. In
November 1963 he was re-elected to office. A
largely self-educated man and a successful farmer,
Holyoake entered politics through agricultural organizations. He was first elected to the New
Zealand Parliament in 1932 and is looked upon
as an authority on legislative rules and procedures and as an able negotiator, particularly of
trade agreements. As Minister of Agriculture in
the cabinet of Sidney G. Holland from 1949 to
1957, he was considered the most successful incumbent in many years of what had been regarded as politically a suicide post.

Among the distinguished ancestors of New
Zealand's Prime Minister were the early seventeenth-century lexicographer, Thomas Holyoake,
and the lexicographer's son Henry, who became
the headmaster of Rugby School. George Jacob
Holyoake, the nineteenth-century social reformer
and historian of the English co-operative movement, was his great-great-grandfather, and his
great-grandfather, Richard Holyoake, was one of
the original New Zealand Company settlers who
landed at Motueka, South Island, in 1842.

The other of New Zealand's two large islands,
North Island, is the birthplace of Keith Jacka
Holyoake. He was born in Pahiatua on February
11, 1904, the third of seven children of Victor
Holyoake, a fruit and tobacco farmer of moderate
means, and Esther (Eves) Holyoake. His mother,
who had been a schoolteacher before her marriage, taught him to read and write. He attended
elementary school until he was twelve years old,
when, on account of his father's illness, he went
to work on the small family farm. He continued,
however, to study at night and through correspondence courses, acquiring his education at
Hastings on North Island, at the Omokoroa
School in Tauranga, and at the Brooklyn School
in Motueka, South Island.

For twenty-four years beginning in 1917, Holyoake engaged in fruit, hops, and tobacco growing
and in dairy farming at Riwaka, just across the
river from Motueka. He was a member of many
agricultural organizations, including the Motueka
Fruit Growers Association, the New Zealand
Tobacco Growers Federation, and the New Zealand Hop Marketing Committee. He became
well known locally as the president of the
Motueka-Riwaka branch of the Farmers' Union
and an executive of the Motueka and Nelson
Province Progressive Leagues. In 1931 he first
sought election to the New Zealand Parliament
as the candidate of the new National party,
formed that year through a coalition of the Liberals and Reformers. Running for the Motueka
seat, he was defeated by the incumbent member,
G. C. Black, in a close contest. At the by-

National Publicity Studios,
Wellington, New Zealand
KEITH J. HOLYOAKE

election that followed Black's death in 1932,
however, Holyoake outpolled two other candidates and became at the age of twenty-eight the
youngest member of New Zealand's House of
Representatives.

General elections in New Zealand are normally
held every three years. Returned to Parliament
by Motueka in 1935, Holyoake was one of only
twenty Nationalists elected to the House of Representatives as against fifty-three Labour party
members. Labour leader Michael Joseph Savage,
who became Prime Minister, then began to enact
New Zealand's now celebrated social security and
welfare legislation.

At the next election, in 1938, Holyoake lost the
Motueka seat to the Labour candidate, C. F.
Skinner. In 1941 he gave up his Riwaka farm
and returned to North Island to engage in hili-
country sheep raising at Waitahora in the Dan-
nevirke district near his native Pahiatua. When
he left South Island he had completed nine years
of service as Nelson Province president of the
Farmers' Union and three years (1938-41) as
president of the New Zealand Hop Marketing
Committee. In 1940 he was named to the dominion executive of the Farmers' Union, in
which he remained for the next ten years.

Because of World War II, the life of the 1938
Parliament was extended to 1943. At the general
election of that year Holyoake was returned to
the House of Representatives as the member for
Pahiatua. The Labour party, which captured
forty-five seats to thirty-four for the Nationalists,
continued in power under Peter Fraser, who had
become Prime Minister after the death of Savage
in 1940.

It was also in 1943 that Holyoake began a
seven-year tenure as dominion vice-president of
the Farmers' Union and a member of the dominion council of the Farmers' Federation (later

HOLYOAKE, KEITH J.—Continued

Federated Farmers of New Zealand). In 1946 he represented New Zealand at the first World Conference of Farmers, held in London, which established the International Federation of Agricultural Producers. During 1946 he also visited Germany, Canada, and the United States and was a delegate to the Joint Conference of Commonwealth and United States Parliamentary Associations in Bermuda.

Retaining the Pahiatua seat in Parliament by a large majority in 1946—as in all subsequent triennial elections—Holyoake was elected deputy leader of the Nationalist Opposition in 1947. The Nationalists, campaigning in 1949 on a platform that called for governmental economies and a relaxation of import restrictions, won forty-six of the eighty seats in the House of Representatives in November 1949. Their leader, Sidney G. Holland, replaced Labourite Peter Fraser as Prime Minister, and Holyoake became Deputy Prime Minister.

Another post that Holyoake held in the Holland cabinet was that of Minister of Agriculture. In 1952 he led a special mission to London that negotiated under the bulk-purchase agreement with the United Kingdom government a 12½ percent increase in the price of meat. As head of another delegation of New Zealand farm and government representatives, he helped negotiate in London in 1957 an amendment to the Ottawa Agreement giving his country's dairy products duty-free entry into the United Kingdom. Among the international meetings that he attended in the 1950's were the Food and Agricultural Organization Conference in Rome in 1955 (of which he was chairman) and the Colombo Plan Conference in Wellington in 1956.

On September 20, 1957, about two months before the general election, Holland resigned as Prime Minister and Nationalist leader because of ill health. On the same day Holyoake succeeded him in both positions, and a week later he gave up the agriculture portfolio and took on that of Minister for Maori Affairs. His power at this time, however, was short-lived. The election in November gave the Labour party a two-seat majority in the House of Representatives. Walter Nash, who had become Labour leader after Fraser's death in 1950, took office as Prime Minister in December 1957.

During the next three years a continuing recession in the agricultural economy forced the Labour government to the unpopular action of imposing higher taxes and import controls. Even these measures were not enough to permit fulfillment of some of Labour's election promises. At the election of November 1960 the Nationalists, having promised cheaper housing loans and freer private enterprise and an end to compulsory union membership, gained a ten-seat majority in the House of Representatives. Keith Holyoake was sworn in as Prime Minister for the second time, on December 11, 1960, and in addition took on the portfolio of Minister of External Affairs and of Minister in Charge of the Audit Office and the Legislative Department.

In a press interview in January 1961 Holyoake said that his government planned "very little if any change" in New Zealand's social security system, that immigration would be encouraged to offset a labor shortage, and that he hoped to avoid tightening import controls. On record as opposing recognition of Red China, Prime Minister Holyoake conferred with President John F. Kennedy in Washington in March 1961 and joined him in noting "with deep concern the hostile and aggressive attitude of the Chinese Communist regime" in Laos and elsewhere. Later in the month he attended the South East Asia Treaty Organization meeting in Bangkok, Thailand, which discussed plans for the defense of Laos. In the spring he also signed a three-year trade agreement with the Federation of Malaya.

One accomplishment of Holyoake's government during his first year in office was the establishment of a permanent Economic and Monetary Council, charged with recommending "both short-term and long-term measures . . . to promote economic growth and raise living standards." The council is independent of political control and free to publish its reports. In his 1962 New Year's Day message Holyoake warned that because of the United Kingdom's decision to seek membership in the European Economic Community (Common Market), New Zealand might be confronted with the most serious economic problems it had ever had. At the Commonwealth Prime Ministers Conference in London in September 1962 he found "vagueness and generalization" in a Britain-Common Market understanding that New Zealand, which had been sending 90 percent of her agricultural produce to Great Britain under the Commonwealth preference system, would have to be given special treatment if Britain joined. However, he said, if further negotiations proved that New Zealand would be specially protected, he would support Britain's entry into the common market.

When Holyoake took office for the first time as Prime Minister, in 1957, the Toronto *Globe and Mail* described him at the height of his rise to power: "Today, he is a man of distinguished appearance, with greying hair and a deep, well-modulated voice. He has a commanding manner and might pass for an English diplomat. Well-dressed, eloquent, never hustled or heated in debate, he gives an impression of complete control over a situation." In the New Year Honours list of 1963 Holyoake was named a Companion of Honour.

Keith J. Holyoake and Norma Janet Ingram were married on January 11, 1935. Their sons are Roger Henry Jacka and Peter Garden, and their daughters are Diane Flora, Lynley Norma, and Keitha Jennifer Mary. Holyoake and his wife were both formerly prominent in athletics. As a young man he excelled in football, playing Rugby both before and after entering Parliament. For six years he was the president of the Motueka-Golden Bay Rugby Union, and he has also served as president of the New Zealand

Rugby Union. His favorite sport now is tennis, and for other outdoor recreation he turns to gardening.

References

Manchester Guardian p5 S 21 '57
N Y Times p1 N 27 '60 por
Time 76:28+ D 12 '60 por
Toronto Globe and Mail p3+ S 21 '57; p7 Je 16 '59 por
U S News 49:26 D 12 '60
Who's Who, 1962
Who's Who in America, 1962-63
Who's Who in New Zealand (1961)

HORNSBY, ROGERS Apr. 27, 1896-Jan. 5, 1963 Former baseball player; baseball coach; was for many years on the team of the St. Louis Cardinals; held National League records that established him as one of the greatest right-handed hitters in baseball history. See *Current Biography* (September) 1952.

Obituary

NY Times p35 Ap 1 '63

HORNUNG, PAUL (VERNON) (hôrn'ĭng) Dec. 23, 1935- Professional football player
Address: b. Green Bay Packers, 349 S. Washington St., Green Bay, Wis.

Paul Hornung, halfback with the Green Bay Packers, has established himself as one of the most versatile professional players on the sports scene. He is an outstanding runner, blocker, pass receiver, passer, and field goal and point-after-touchdown kicker—talents that have enabled him to lead the National Football League (N.F.L.) in scoring for three consecutive seasons: 1959, 1960, and 1961.

Besides reaping a harvest of personal glory, Hornung has played a key role in the recent rise of the team from Green Bay, Wisconsin, where football is king the year around. In 1958 the Packers finished last in the Western Conference, winning only one game. By 1960 they were good enough to win the Western Conference title. Hornung scored 176 points during the 1960 season, an N.F.L. record. In 1961 Green Bay again was the Western Conference winner, and Hornung scored 146 points. In the 1961 play-off game against the New York Giants, the Eastern Conference Champions, Hornung tallied an additional 19 points (a play-off record) in leading the Packers to a 37-0 win.

Paul Vernon Hornung, an only child, was born on December 23, 1935 in Louisville, Kentucky. (His German surname was originally spelled with an umlaut over the "u.") His mother, Loretta Hornung, and his father, a retired insurance agent, separated when Paul was two years old. Hornung attended Roman Catholic parochial schools in Louisville: first St. Patrick's elementary school, then Flaget High School. At Flaget High he played basketball, baseball, and football. He thought of going to college at the University of Kentucky, but during the fall of

his senior year, 1952-53, the Flaget football team won the state championship. "It felt good playing with a winner and I didn't want to change it," Hornung recalls. "I figured the best way to get with a winner in college was by going to Notre Dame."

For a time during his freshman year Hornung doubted that he would make the Notre Dame football team, but Frank Leahy, who coached the team that year, encouraged him and allowed him to practise with the varsity team. As a sophomore Hornung was a third-string quarterback behind Ralph Guglielmi and Tom Carey, and he played a great deal as fullback. Developing as an all-round player, he soon led the Irish in passing, rushing, scoring, and kickoff and punt returns. He was an All-American and a U.P.I. choice as an outstanding back in 1955, when Notre Dame won eight out of ten games, and in 1956, when it lost eight out of ten. Hornung recalls that his best day as a collegiate player came in 1955, when he gained 259 yards passing and 95 running in the final game with the University of Southern California, which Notre Dame lost 42-20. In 1956, despite Notre Dame's poor record, Hornung received the John W. Heisman Trophy as the year's top collegiate player.

In January of 1957, the year he graduated from Notre Dame with an average a few points below *cum laude,* Hornung signed a three-season contract with the Green Bay Packers that called for an annual salary of $16,000. He was the Packers' bonus choice that year, but their coach, Lisle Blackbourn, viewing Hornung in preseason practice, decided that he couldn't pass well enough to be quarterback, run hard enough to be a fullback, or run fast enough to be a halfback. So Hornung spent his first year as a professional in being shunted from one position to another.

In 1958, under a new coach, Ray ("Scooter") McLean, Hornung's fortunes improved only a little, and the Packers as a team had a miserable year: they won one game, tied one, and lost ten. Hornung maintains that as a result of his failure on the football field his personal reputation was also tarnished and he was pictured in town gossip as "pro football's version of the Playboy of the Western World." Perhaps his attractive appearance and his Notre Dame nickname—Golden Boy—made him particularly vulnerable to this kind of criticism.

Reviewing this period in an article for *Look* (November 20, 1962), Hornung wrote, "Today, four years and many victories later, I realize we were wrong in blaming the whole town for the [gossip] mongering of a few. I also appreciate that the mongerers may have misinterpreted our socializing and our attitude toward them as proof we didn't care whether we won or what they thought. To a certain extent, they were right. There comes a time when chronic losers with no reason for hope begin playing only for the paycheck and praying for the season to end. Down deep, we were more unhappy about losing than anybody else in the town possibly could have been. But we carried a chip against our critics for making bad times even worse." After the arrival in 1959 of Vince Lombardi, who left his post as an assistant coach with the New York

PAUL HORNUNG

Kansas to serve as a jeep driver with a National Guard unit. He managed to play all but two games of the 1961 season with the Packers, however, with the help of weekend passes and a private plane flown by a Green Bay fan. The Packers took the Western Conference title by winning eleven of fourteen games, and on December 31, 1961 they beat the New York Giants 37-0 in the championship play-off game. Despite his part-time playing schedule and his lack of practice sessions Hornung was the N.F.L.'s leading scorer for the third consecutive year with 146 points, not counting the 19 points he tallied in the championship game, a play-off record.

A flock of awards honored Hornung's playing on the football field in 1961. In addition to winning a Corvette sports car (which he gave to his mother) from *Sport* magazine as the outstanding player of the championship game, he was named best player of the N.F.L. by the A.P and U.P.I.; pro player of the year by the Chicago Football Writers, the Columbus Touchdown Club; Wisconsin athlete of the year; and Kentucky athlete of the year. He received the top performance award for football from *Sport*, the Marlboro Award as the pro player of the year from *Sporting News*, the Kansas City Headline Award from the By-Line Club, the Bert Bell Memorial Award from the Maxwell Club of Philadelphia, and the Hickok Award for the month of December.

In July 1962 Hornung was released from the Army when the National Guard unit with which he served was deactivated. He tallied 28 points in Green Bay's opening game with the Minnesota Vikings on September 16, which the Packers won 34 to 7. He played in the next four games, but in the October 14 contest with the Vikings a twisted right knee put him on the sidelines. He sat out the Packers' next six games, except for making a brief appearance in the November 11 game with the Philadelphia Eagles, but in December he was able to help Green Bay win its last three matches. The Packers lost only one of their fourteen 1962 games, gaining the Western Conference championship for the second year in a row, and in the play-off in New York on December 30 they again beat the New York Giants for the N.F.L. championship, 16 to 7. Because of his forced inactivity for almost half of the season, Hornung ended up with an individual score of only 74 points.

In April 1963 Hornung and Alex Karras of the Detroit Lions were suspended for an indefinite period for having broken N.F.L. rules by betting on league games, although no evidence of other wrongdoing was found. Informed of his suspension, Hornung said: "I made a terrible mistake. I realize that now. I am truly sorry."

Unlike many other football stars, Hornung has developed more than one specialty; he can kick, pass, run, and block with equal skill. He has supplemented his contract salary with earnings from personal appearances, testimonials, and modeling men's clothing. A prodigal spender, he likes to dress well, and he drives an expensive convertible. He is six feet two and one-half inches tall, weighs 220 pounds, and has blond hair and green eyes.

Giants to become head coach at Green Bay, the Packers began winning again. "As our fortunes improved, so did my image," Hornung wrote in the *Look* article. "Much of the world is always quicker to recognize the good side of a winner."

To Lombardi goes much of the credit for developing Hornung into a top player. He placed Hornung permanently in the halfback slot and helped him to build his offense around running and passing in this position. In 1959 the Packers won seven out of twelve games, and Hornung led the N.F.L. in individual scoring with 94 points. In 1960 the Packers took their first Western Conference title in sixteen years by winning eight out of twelve games. The game in which Green Bay clinched the title was played in rain and mud at San Francisco against the Forty Niners. The Packers won 13-0, with Hornung scoring all thirteen points. His flair for the dramatic was never more evident than in that game. According to Al Stump, in *This Week* (October 7, 1962), Hornung broke loose on the San Francisco 30-yard line. "Racing unimpeded to the 10-yard line, he had only to walk across," Stump wrote. "But to the delight of the 50,000 spectators, he launched a magnificent dive, flopping into the end zone in a shower of mud and water. He arose, dripping, and delicately removed a gob of mud from one eye."

Green Bay's "Cinderella" season of 1960 was marred only by the 17-13 loss to the Philadelphia Eagles in the N.F.L. championship play-off game in December. During most of the second half of that game Hornung sat on the sidelines because of the recurrence of an old injury—a pinched nerve in his neck that temporarily causes loss of feeling and control in his right arm. Nevertheless, he broke the all-time N.F.L. individual scoring record for a season in 1960 with a total of 176 points—15 touchdowns, 41 extra points, and 15 field goals.

Hornung was inducted into the United States Army in November 1961 and sent to Fort Riley,

Paul Hornung now lives with his mother in Louisville, Kentucky between seasons, and during the season he rents a house in Green Bay with two teammates. Naturally exuberant, with an easy laugh, he is popular with teammates and fans. He never tries to shirk the hard chores of football in favor of making star plays, although he makes many of these, and he has a great deal of self-confidence. "I believe in myself absolutely," he says. "I never think back to any failure, only to successes."

References

Look 26:125+ N 20 '62 pors
N Y Times p16 Ja 1 '62 por
Newsweek 58:43+ O 30 '61
This Week p23+ O 7 '62 pors

HUDDLESTON, (ERNEST URBAN) TREVOR June 15, 1913- Anglican bishop; missionary
Address: Masasi, Southern Region, Tanganyika

An outspoken champion of social justice and racial equality, the Right Reverend Trevor Huddleston, Bishop of Masasi, Tanganyika, lived for twelve years among the natives of South Africa, who know him as Father Huddleston. After serving as curate of a church in Wiltshire, England for three years, and becoming a member of the Community of the Resurrection, an Anglican religious order, Huddleston came to South Africa in 1943 to take charge of Anglican missions in the Negro slums of Johannesburg. Motivated by the belief that respect for the dignity of the individual is a fundamental principle of Christianity, he preached and acted against the South African government's policies of racial segregation and did much to better the living conditions of the native population. He was recalled to England by his order in 1955 to take charge of the training of novices, and he later served as prior of its London House. In late 1960 he returned to Africa as Bishop of Masasi.

Ernest Urban Trevor Huddleston was born on June 15, 1913 in Bedford, England. He has one sister. His father, Captain Sir Ernest Whiteside Huddleston, had a distinguished career in the Royal Indian Marine, of which he was for a time officiating director. His mother was the former Elsie Barlow-Smith. Trevor Huddleston attended Lancing College in Sussex and then went to Christ Church College, Oxford, where he obtained his B.A. degree in 1934 with second class honors in modern history. His M.A. degree followed in 1937.

Having received additional ministerial training at Wells Theological College, Huddleston in 1936 became a deacon, the lowest rank in the ministry of the Church of England. His first post was at St. Mark's Church, Swindon, in Wiltshire, where he served as curate from 1936 to 1939. He became a priest in 1937. In 1939 he left St. Mark's to join the Community of the Resurrection, one of the Church of England's nine religious orders for men, which has as one of its chief aims the adaptation of religious life to the modern world. Huddleston served as a novice at the community's mother house at Mirfield, York-

shire. In 1941 he took his vows as a full member of the Community, and in November 1943 he was appointed prior and priest-in-charge of the order's missions in Sophiatown and Orlando, Negro suburbs of Johannesburg, South Africa. In 1949 he became provincial of the Community of the Resurrection in South Africa, a position he held until 1955.

When Huddleston arrived in South Africa in 1943 to take up his work in Orlando and Sophiatown, both communities were Negro ghettoes from which Johannesburg drew its labor force. Orlando was and still is a "location," an area specifically set aside and developed to house Negro workers. Sophiatown, about five miles west of Johannesburg's center, had none of the order and tidiness of a "location," but was one of the few places in South Africa where Negroes were allowed to own their homes. By 1949, with a population of some 70,000, it had become a desperately overcrowded mixture of small houses and roughly built shanties, and was officially designated a slum. Huddleston's Church of Christ the King stood in Sophiatown, and it was with Sophiatown that he became most closely associated.

In spite of its squalor, Father Huddleston found Sophiatown essentially "a gay place and, for all the occasional moments of violence and excitement, a kindly one too." He became deeply attached to its people. From the first, however, he was distressed by the social conditions under which they lived: the malnutrition, dirt, and disease that were the concomitants of poverty, and the other hardships that he saw as products of the official South African policy of apartheid, or total racial separation.

Aware of his congregation's desperate poverty, and of the hopeless frustration engendered by the apartheid system, Huddleston found it difficult to perform his duties as a priest. He felt that it was useless to tell people not to steal when their children were starving; to tell them to lead blameless lives when men could be separated from their wives by apartheid laws. Accordingly, during his twelve years in South Africa, he worked ceaselessly to improve the lot of the Negro people and became their champion against injustice. South Africa's pass laws were a major target of Huddleston's fight against apartheid. He believed that these regulations, requiring nonwhites to carry passes at all times and produce them on demand, caused more crime than they prevented, and he devoted much time and money to helping members of his staff and congregation imprisoned for pass law offenses. On one occasion, when a schoolboy was jailed after his pass had been deliberately destroyed by the police, Huddleston intervened and was arrested himself, although he later had the satisfaction of a police apology.

In his efforts to alleviate the conditions of South Africa's Negro population Huddleston met with considerable success in raising funds to build a number of facilities, including nurseries, schools, places of worship, and a fine Olympic-size swimming pool in Orlando. He also bought and begged instruments for what became known as the Huddleston Jazz Band, and he invited visiting artists, such as Yehudi Menuhin, to give

HUDDLESTON, TREVOR—Continued

concerts for the Negro population, which had normally been denied any kind of cultural experience by the apartheid laws.

One of the most notable achievements of Huddleston's years in South Africa was the African Children's Feeding Scheme. Although white children had been receiving free lunches in school, Negro children, among whom malnutrition was rife, did not. Huddleston's campaign, which was launched in 1945 with the help of concerned European women, was successful to the extent that the authorities agreed to provide meals for African schoolchildren at a very small cost. The scheme, which eventually provided meals for some 5,000 children a day, was abolished in 1956, soon after Huddleston left South Africa.

As South Africa's Nationalist government tightened its grip, and the apartheid laws grew more and more stringent, Huddleston's opposition to the government and its policy became increasingly overt. In December 1954, when mission schools were ordered to accept government control or lose their subsidies, Huddleston announced his intention of closing St. Peter's, his order's school in Rosettenville. He said that St. Peter's, which had been called "the black Eton," would not participate in "education for servitude." Soon afterwards, in February 1955, Sophiatown was demolished and its residents moved to a new location eight miles further from Johannesburg. Huddleston vehemently opposed the move and accused the government of stealing the freehold rights of the people of Sophiatown.

Huddleston's outspoken opposition to apartheid and baasskap (the idea of white supremacy) created a mounting storm. When the Archbishop of Canterbury visited South Africa in the spring of 1955 he told Huddleston that he was wrong in using political weapons to fight the state authorities. Huddleston rejects this view, and he is quoted by Peter Abrahams in the New York Times Book Review (May 20, 1956) as saying: "I believe that the Christian is bound to act politically, and if the Church refuses to accept responsibility in the political sphere as well as in the strictly theological sphere, then she is guilty of betraying the very foundation of her faith. God is directly concerned in the way men behave to one another—that is, in politics."

In the black slums of Johannesburg, Huddleston was known as Makhaliphile, "the dauntless one." To the South African government, however, he was a thorn in the side. Prime Minister Johannes G. Strijdom denounced him as a fanatic, and accused him of "concentrating on a campaign of misrepresentation to incite the world against South Africa." Microphones were installed secretly in Huddleston's house. His telephone was tapped and his mail was opened. In October 1955 detectives interrupted him in the middle of a scripture lesson and confiscated forty-four documents, including his correspondence with the novelist Alan Paton. There were indications that the government was preparing to take legal action against him.

In November 1955 Father Huddleston was ordered by his superiors in the Community of

Leon Levson

BISHOP TREVOR HUDDLESTON

the Resurrection to return to England. When the news became public, the Golden City Post, South Africa's biggest Negro newspaper, carried the banner headline: "Don't Leave Us, Father," and groups of Africans petitioned Anglican authorities to rescind the transfer. Anglican Bishop Richard Ambrose Reeves of Johannesburg said that the withdrawal was one of the heaviest blows yet suffered by South Africa's non-whites. Prime Minister Strijdom, however, welcomed the news. "Well, thank God," he is reported to have remarked, "that's the last we'll hear of him." The bitterness that the South African government felt toward Huddleston is typified by the sentiments of a government official who wrote to him: "If ever a man deserved to be drummed out of a country, to be ignominiously deported as an undesirable immigrant or, in the last resort, to be strung up from the nearest lamppost as a renegade, it was you."

Leaving South Africa in February 1956, Huddleston went first to the United States, where he spoke about conditions in South Africa on radio and television, and before many audiences. After his return to England in April 1956 he continued his campaign against apartheid. He argued for the removal of South Africa from the British Commonwealth, organized a partially successful British boycott of South African goods, and urged that British and American artists and athletes refuse to perform in South Africa before segregated audiences.

Huddleston's book, Naught for Your Comfort, was published in early 1956 by William Collins Sons & Company Ltd. in England, and by Doubleday & Company in the United States. It described his experiences during his twelve years in South Africa and carried an impassioned plea for social justice for South Africa's Negro population. The book was received with great interest in Britain and the United States and won the $1,000 Anisfield-Wolf Award as an important contribution to the literature of race relations, but in South Africa the book was branded as seditious and copies were seized by the police. Some incidents from *Naught for Your Comfort* were later dramatized and included in the prize-winning film *Let My People Go,* prepared in 1960 by a team of British documentary film makers headed by John Krish.

From 1956 to 1958 Huddleston served as guardian of novices in the mother house of the Community of the Resurrection at Mirfield, Yorkshire, and from 1958 to 1960 he was prior of the Community's London House. But his heart was still in Africa. "I long to go back," he had said in 1956, "and I hope and pray to go back. All my roots are there. I have no interests elsewhere. England bores me to sobs."

In 1960 Huddleston's wish was fulfilled. On August 4 of that year he was elected Bishop of Masasi, in Tanganyika. His consecration followed on November 30. Huddleston hopes to spend the rest of his life in Tanganyika, where his "palace" is a building fashioned of mud and sticks, with one living room, one bedroom, and a chapel. His cathedral is one of the few stone buildings in the diocese. He spends about two-thirds of his time visiting his scattered flock, and the three hospitals and various schools in his charge. The raising of funds to maintain and extend these facilities is one of his major concerns, and brings him periodically to England.

The Right Reverend Trevor Huddleston has been described as tall, lean, and handsome. In Africa, except when he is in church, he wears a shirt and shorts, with a silver pectoral cross the only mark of his calling. For relaxation he likes to go fishing. In 1956 Huddleston received the honorary degree of Doctor of Divinity from Aberdeen University, Scotland. Lord Altrincham, writing in the Manchester *Guardian* (May 30, 1963), called him "one of the finest Englishmen of his generation . . . a rare man—simple-hearted without being in the least simple, holy, without a trace of sanctimoniousness or priggishness."

References

Manchester Guardian p18 My 30 '63
Read Digest 68:65+ Je '56 por
Huddleston, Trevor. Naught for Your Comfort (1956)
International Who's Who, 1962-63
Who's Who, 1963

HUGHES, HAROLD E(VERETT) Feb. 10, 1922- Governor of Iowa

Address: b. Statehouse, Des Moines, Iowa; h. Governor's Mansion, 2900 Grand Ave., Des Moines, Iowa

Iowa's thirty-fifth Governor, Harold E. Hughes, was relatively new to politics when he was elected to a two-year term on November 6, 1962 to succeed the Republican Norman A. Erbe. He had held only one previous state office—that of commerce commissioner from 1958 to 1962—which he had sought because as a trucking executive

and former truck driver he had been dissatisfied with enforcement of trucking regulations. The new Democratic Governor is a former Republican and a teetotaler who campaigned for a more liberal liquor law. He scored a surprise victory in the November 1962 elections, being the only Democrat to win a state office that year.

The younger of two sons, Harold Everett Hughes was born on a farm near Ida Grove, Iowa on February 10, 1922. His parents, Lewis C. and Etta E. (Kelly) Hughes, had moved to Iowa from Kentucky eleven years earlier. Soon after Harold's birth his father gave up farming and took a job as a bridge construction foreman. Lewis and Etta Hughes still live in Ida Grove, where they run a greenhouse and florist business. Their older son, Jesse, was killed in an automobile accident in June 1942.

As a boy Harold Hughes went hunting and fishing on weekends with his father and brother. At Ida Grove High School he was on the debating team and took part in many musical and sporting events. A bass-baritone, he was a district singing champion, and he played in the school band and was a runner-up in a statewide tuba competition. He was a member of the basketball, football, and track teams. In 1938 he was the state discus-throwing champion, and in 1939 he was chosen as right guard on the all-state football team. Jesse and Harold Hughes, both 200-pounders, were feared players on the football line. "Our opponents said we were as big as elephants, which really made us pachyderms," Hughes recalls. "So Jesse became Big Packy and I became Little Packy." Hughes is still called Pack or Packy by his old friends.

During the summer after he graduated from high school, in 1940, Hughes worked in Iowa City as an assistant steamfitter to save some money for college. He attended the State University of Iowa in 1940-41, but his marriage in the summer of 1941 and his expectation of being called into the service led him to drop out of the university and take a job. He worked with the Des Moines Parks Department until he was called into the United States Army as a private on December 22, 1942.

Trained as a Browning automatic rifleman, Hughes was in combat for fourteen months. He took part in operations in Tunisia in the spring of 1943 and fought in Sicily and southern Italy, including the Anzio beachhead. He contracted malaria in Italy and was sent back to Africa, to an Army hospital, where his condition became critical after he also got jaundice. He was given a medical discharge from the Army on July 10, 1945, still with the rank of private.

Readjustment to civilian life was not easy for Hughes. His war experiences had left him deeply shaken. "I was raised in what people would call a good Christian home with good fundamentalist teachings," Hughes was quoted as saying in the Omaha *Sunday World Herald* (January 13, 1963). "I was taught it was wrong to kill. But in the Army you're given new weapons and taught how to kill in the most efficient manner. It was hard to reconcile this with my religious beliefs." Disturbed by this and by the recurrence of malarial attacks, Hughes tried to find solace in liquor and admittedly did some heavy drinking in the next five or six years.

(Continued next page)

Feiler Studio

HAROLD E. HUGHES

In 1952 Hughes made up his mind to become an abstainer, and he feels that this decision was one of the most important of his life. In 1954 he joined Alcoholics Anonymous, to which he has devoted much of his spare time. "When I stopped drinking," Hughes recalls (Des Moines *Sunday Register,* October 7, 1962), "I again really became active in the Methodist Church I grew up respecting." He helped form total abstinence groups in several churches, joined the choir, taught Sunday school, and served on the finance committee and official board of his church. He even thought about entering the ministry and took two years of correspondence courses at Southern Methodist University. Although he gave up the idea of becoming a minister, he is a lay speaker who is qualified to substitute for ministers who are sick or on vacation.

Meanwhile, following his release from the Army in 1945, Hughes had taken a job in a hardware store. Some months later he began to drive a creamery truck, and then a semi trailer for Hinrich's Truck Line, an Ida Grove firm that operates in the Midwest. He became a livestock buyer for Hinrich's and in 1950, after four years of driving trucks, a manager of the trucking line. In 1953 he was hired as a field representative by the Iowa Motor Truck Association, and for the next two years solicited memberships and explained trucking regulations for the association.

In 1955, feeling that small truckers were not being properly represented by the Iowa Motor Truck Association, he founded his own rate and tariff service, the Iowa Better Trucking Bureau. "My principal objective," Hughes has explained, "was to achieve uniform rates for the small trucker, to increase his income and to protect the shipper from fluctuating, discriminatory rates." Uniform truck rates were achieved in thirty counties. At this time Hughes also published the *Iowa Better Trucking Bureau News* and wrote articles, got photographs, and sold advertising for the paper. His trucking bureau flourished, and he organized, in addition, a general insurance agency and a real estate abstract office.

Hughes entered politics quite by accident in 1957. He had gone to the state commerce commission to complain about laxity in the enforcement of state trucking laws, but had received no satisfaction from the three-man board, which was controlled by Republicans. When the commissioners refused to investigate his complaints, he went to Governor Herschel C. Loveless, a Democrat, who advised him to run for election to the commerce commission himself. "I was angry about conditions that the Republican party wouldn't do anything about," Hughes recalls. He further explains, "I felt that the Republican party had lost sight of its ideals and no longer represented the interests of the common man." Hughes, who had once been a delegate to state G.O.P. conventions, thereupon changed his party affiliation from Republican to Democratic and announced his candidacy for the state commerce commission eighteen months early.

Hughes charged that the commission was permitting flagrant violations of freight-rate regulations, and his campaign got a big boost from a bipartisan legislative committee that was investigating charges of malfeasance by the commissioners. In November 1958 Iowa voters replaced two commissioners with new Democratic members—one of them Harold E. Hughes. Hughes remained on the commission until his election as Governor. "I believe we have restored dignity to the commission and people again have a feeling of confidence and fair play," he said in October 1962. From 1959 to 1962 he was a member of the Interstate Commerce Commission joint boards and of the committee on public safety and education of the National Association of Railroad Utility Commission.

As a result of his experience on the commerce commission Hughes "developed a taste for government and public service." In 1960 he sought the Democratic nomination for Governor, but he was beaten in the June primary by Edward J. McManus, then Lieutenant Governor, who in turn lost the election to the Republican Norman A. Erbe. Hughes again sought the Democratic nomination in 1962 and this time won the primary, defeating the Reverend Lewis Lint, a Methodist clergyman and former secretary of the state tax commission. Hughes's campaign for the Governorship was free of the glad-handing, back-slapping, and baby-kissing that sometimes mark political campaigns. His speeches, according to the Des Moines *Sunday Register,* were longer than most candidates' and were often delivered in an unemotional but convincing manner from prepared texts.

Against the advice of some of his backers, Hughes took a firm stand on several "touchy" issues. He advocated revising state laws to permit the sale of liquor by the drink in bars and restaurants rather than exclusively by the bottle in state-owned stores. The existing laws were unrealistic, he said, and were not being enforced. "We have liquor-by-the-drink now, but illegally," he observed. "What we don't have is proper enforcement and respect for law and order." Hughes was able to take this position despite his personal abstinence because he felt that "drinking itself is not a sin, but the misuse of alcohol is." He also risked repercussions from the old quarrel between rural and urban residents by coming out squarely in favor of "home rule" for municipalities and other urban reform legislation and against a re-apportionment plan supported by rural factions. In addition, he was not afraid to tell voters that tax increases might be necessary to maintain services provided by the state.

On November 6, 1962 Harold E. Hughes was elected Governor of Iowa for a two-year term to end in January 1965, scoring a surprise victory over Erbe with a margin of 40,000 votes. He was the only Democrat to win a state office in traditionally Republican Iowa that year, and he was thus faced with working with a predominant-ly Republican state General Assembly. The New York *Times* (November 8, 1962) ascribed his victory to strong Democratic organizational work, to the growing dissatisfaction among Republicans with Governor Erbe, and to the desire of Iowa voters to see the liquor laws revised. Selling liquor by the drink was made legal in Iowa in July 1963.

In his first address to the state General Assembly on January 17, 1963 and in his budget message two weeks later Hughes recommended, among other things, more state aid to local school districts; a nonpolitical civil service; higher salaries for state officials; funds to enable Iowa to take part in the Kerr-Mills program for medical aid to the aging (more limited than the Kennedy administration proposal); a public defender system in Iowa; the use of public school buses by private school pupils; the abolition of the death penalty in his state; increased unemployment and workmen's compensation benefits; permitting the "union shop"; and a Fair Employment Practices Act. He also suggested certain revisions that would make the tax structure more equitable and recommended some rise in personal and corporate income taxes and an extension of the sales tax. The budget he presented was balanced and totaled about $230,000,000.

Harold E. Hughes married Eva Mae Mercer on August 23, 1941. They have three daughters, Connie (Mrs. Dennis Otto), Carol, and Phyllis. Hughes, who has been described as ruggedly handsome, has brown eyes and black hair, stands six feet three inches tall, and weighs 230 pounds. He is an enthusiastic outdoorsman, and hunting, fishing, and trapping are his favorite recreations. He also likes to read the Bible and commentaries on the Bible and enjoys listening to American folk music, especially hymns by Johnny Cash. He belongs to the American Legion, the Masons, the Royal Arch Masons, the Mizpah Commanders, and the Abu Bekr Shrine. From 1957 to 1961 he was a member of the Iowa state commission on alcoholism.

In his first speech to the legislature in January 1963 Hughes said: "It is sometimes said that the knack of skillful government is to hang back, do as little as possible, and make no mistakes. I hope there is another way—for between you and me, this prospect does not invite my soul. Frankly, I expect to experiment and make some mistakes—whether it be in installing new programs in departments or hiring a band. But I can assure you that this new administration will not

stop moving—towards the goals to which we have pledged ourselves with the people of Iowa. . . . The time has come to set aside old prejudices, face our problems squarely, and work together to fulfill our state's immeasurable potential."

References

Des Moines Sunday Register L p5 O 7 '62 por

Omaha Sunday World-Herald Mag p4+ Ja 13 '63 pors

HUMPHREY, HELEN F. Sept. 20, 1909-Aug. 24, 1963 Labor lawyer; former chairman of Wage Stabilization Board enforcement commission. See *Current Biography* (November) 1952.

Obituary

N Y Times p27 Ag 26 '63

HURLEY, PATRICK J(AY) Jan. 8, 1883-July 30, 1963 United States Army officer; staunch Republican who performed several diplomatic missions for President Franklin D. Roosevelt during World War II; Secretary of War under President Herbert Hoover (1929-33); United States Ambassador to China (1944-45). See *Current Biography* (November) 1944.

Obituary

N Y Times p29 Jl 31 '63

HUXLEY, SIR JULIAN (SORELL) June 22, 1887- Biologist; writer

Address: h. 31 Pond St., Hampstead, N.W. 3, England

NOTE: This biography supersedes the article that appeared in *Current Biography* in 1942.

The eminent British biologist, Sir Julian Huxley, has for many years taken all of nature and all of life as his province. His standing as an international figure was indicated when he was appointed as the first director-general of UNESCO (1946 to 1948). Huxley has written scores of books and articles and has lectured throughout the world in an effort to increase man's knowledge and to help man use that knowledge for his betterment. His mastery of the essay has made him a stimulating popularizer of scientific information. But popular acceptance of some of his revolutionary views regarding man's destiny may have to await further advances in the development of the human species—a development that he envisages with characteristic optimism. In a recent proposal that, as usual, provoked more heat than thought, Huxley advocated the deliberate improvement of humanity through the practice of eugenic insemination by preferred donors.

As the grandson of the scientist Thomas Henry Huxley and the grandnephew of Matthew Arnold, Julian Sorell Huxley inherited a

Douglas Glass

SIR JULIAN HUXLEY

family tradition of intellectual integrity and feeling of moral responsibility. He was born on June 22, 1887 to Leonard and Julia Frances (Arnold) Huxley in London's Bloomsbury. His mother's sister, the novelist Mrs. Humphrey Ward, incorporated some of Julian's boyhood traits in the character Sandy of *David Grieve*. Julian is the older brother of the writer Aldous Huxley, and he has a sister, Margaret Huxley, headmistress of a girls' school. His half-brother, Andrew Fielding Huxley, won the 1963 Nobel Prize in Physiology and Medicine.

Leonard Huxley, an essayist who became editor of the *Cornhill*, was master of the Charterhouse at the time of Julian's birth. His mother later founded the successful girls' school, Prior's Field, near Godalming, Surrey. Growing up in a still-rural area of England, Julian Huxley early acquired an interest in natural history, supplemented his own firsthand knowledge with wide reading, and was particularly attracted to bird watching. At Eton, where he was a King's Scholar, he decided upon a career in biology. He then studied at Oxford as a Brakenbury Scholar of Balliol College, won the Newdigate prize in poetry in 1908, and obtained a first in natural science (zoology) in 1909.

Oxford also awarded Huxley the Naples Biological Scholarship, which enabled him to spend the year 1909-10 in research on sponges at the Zoological Station in Naples. He returned from Italy to Balliol to lecture in zoology for two years and to write his first book, *The Individual in the Animal Kingdom,* published in 1912 in the Cambridge University series of manuals of science and literature. In 1912 he accepted an appointment as research associate at the newly established Rice Institute in Houston, Texas, where he founded and developed the department of biology. He had been promoted to assistant professor in 1913 and had spent four years in the United States when he decided in 1916 to go home and enlist in the British Army. During the last

year of World War I he served as staff lieutenant in the Intelligence Corps in Italy.

At Oxford again, after the war, Huxley held the posts of Fellow of New College and senior demonstrator in zoology from 1919 to 1925. He was an organizer and member of Oxford's expedition to Spitsbergen, a Norwegian island located in the north polar regions, in 1921 and wrote about his observations both in the expedition's official reports and in contributions to the London *Times*. The year before, he had begun to build his reputation as a specialist who knew how to explain scientific findings to the layman when he had to correct distortions in the press regarding his experiments on the metamorphosis of the Mexican axolotl, an amphibian resembling a salamander.

In 1925 Huxley was appointed professor of zoology at King's College, London, but at the end of two years he resigned his professorship and became honorary lecturer, a position that allowed him more time for research and writing. From 1926 to 1929 he served also as president of the National Union of Scientific Workers and as Fullerian Professor of Physiology at the Royal Institution. At the suggestion of the Colonial Office he visited East Africa in 1929 to investigate and advise on native education and later published *Africa View* (Harper, 1931), a record in diary form of his trip, interspersed with chapters on social and scientific subjects.

Much of Huxley's laboratory work meanwhile at King's College (where he remained until 1935) probed an extremely complex field of biological research that he had begun to investigate in the early 1920's. The monograph in which he reported some of his most significant contributions to biology, *Problems of Relative Growth* (Dial Press), was intended for specialists. At the time of its publication in 1932, however, he was internationally known for his skill in making scientific information accessible to the nonspecialist—through his lectures, radio broadcasts, and magazine articles and through such books as *Essays in Popular Science* (Knopf, 1927), *What Darwin Really Said* (Routledge, 1929), *Ants* (Smith, 1930), *Bird-Watching and Bird Behaviour* (Musson, 1930), and *The Science of Life* (Doubleday, 1931), on which he collaborated with H. G. Wells and G. P. Wells.

During the period between the two world wars perhaps Huxley's major objective was to make clear the philosophical implications for man of the growing body of scientific fact and the widening application of the scientific method —to use reason and knowledge to develop evolutionary humanism as a religion. In 1923 six of his articles for British magazines, including discussions on science and religion, were collected in *Essays of a Biologist* (Chatto & Windus). He outlined his basic religious beliefs in his controversial *Religion without Revelation* (Harper), which first appeared in 1927 and was revised in 1957. He pointed to new outlets for man's religious spirit in moral dedication to a vision of human destiny, without reliance on mysticism or any belief whatever in the supernatural.

The year 1932, especially, reveals Huxley's versatility—the balanced interests of his lifework. Besides his technical *Problems of Relative Growth,* he produced the first volume of his popular *Introduction to Science,* with Edward Neville da Costa Andrade (Blackwell). He also published *The Captive Shrew* (Harper), a book of verses that he wrote as a relief from laboratory work. For many reviewers, the verses compensated in self-revelation for what they lacked in poetic excellence. Babette Deutsch commented in the New York *Herald Tribune Books* (February 5, 1933), "Mr. Huxley exhibits the awareness, the hungry curiosity, the tenderness, the candor that belong to the rare few." In another 1932 book, *A Scientist Among the Soviets* (Chatto & Windus), based on his visit to Russia during the preceding year, he expressed both his objection to tyranny and his approval of Soviet concentration on scientific research.

Criticizing what he regarded as the inadequacies of England's scientific research and social planning, Huxley wrote *If I Were Dictator* (Harper, 1934) to suggest how the application of reason and scientific information could improve society. His *Scientific Research and Social Needs* (Watts, 1934), stemming from his series of radio talks on BBC, also discussed how science could more fully be used to benefit mankind. Motion pictures offered Huxley another medium for reaching the public. He was general supervisor of biological films for Great Britain Instructional Ltd. from 1933 to 1936 and for Zoological Film Productions Ltd. in 1937. His Oscar-winning *The Private Life of the Gannets,* which he prepared with R. M. Lockley, appeared in 1934.

For seven years after he had left King's College, from 1935 to 1942, Huxley was secretary of the Zoological Society of London. His aims to make the Zoo at Regent's Park "more than a menagerie" were set forth in *At the Zoo* (Allen, G., 1936), but World War II prevented the fulfillment of many of his plans. Before the outbreak of war, as a scientist concerned with international relations, he had written, with A. C. Haddon, *We Europeans* (Harper, 1936), an exposure of the Nordic myth, which won the John Anisfield Award.

During the early years of the war, besides guarding the animals at the Zoo during bombing raids, Huxley often appeared on the BBC Brains Trust program and lectured in the United States on British war aims. He also wrote *The Uniqueness of Man* (Harper, 1941) and his massive *Evolution, the Modern Synthesis* (Harper, 1942). "Evolutionary Ethics," the Romanes Lecture that he delivered at Oxford in 1943, was included with Thomas Huxley's 1893 Romanes Lecture, "Evolution and Ethics," in *Touchstone for Ethics* (Harper, 1947). Concerned about problems that would have to be solved when peace came, he wrote *Reconstruction and Peace* (Routledge, 1942), one of the wartime booklets for which he used the pseudonym Balbus. He served as a member of the commission to make recommendations on higher education in West Africa and of a planning commission for national parks in Great Britain.

In December 1946 Julian Huxley was chosen for a two-year term as the first director-general of the United Nations Educational and Scientific Organization (UNESCO). The post gave him the opportunity to help apply scientific findings on an international scale to man's struggle for progress. Partly because of his atheism, Huxley's appointment was criticized in the United States and elsewhere, but it was soon generally acknowledged that the new organization had been strengthened by the competence and vigor with which he handled his administrative problems and traveled and lectured on behalf of UNESCO throughout the world. His *UNESCO; Its Purpose and its Philosophy* was published by the American Council on Public Affairs in 1947; later some aspects of his work for UNESCO were presented in *From an Antique Land; Ancient and Modern in the Middle East* (Crown, 1954). He was among the originators of UNESCO's mammoth six-volume history of man's scientific and cultural achievements, published jointly by George Allen & Unwin of London and Harper & Brothers of New York, the first volume of which appeared in 1961. He also served in 1960 as adviser to UNESCO on wild life conservation in eastern Africa.

When Huxley revisited the Soviet Union at the end of World War II, he had again been impressed by the importance given to the scientist in the Communist society, but opposed distortion of scientific fact for political reasons, especially in genetics. He later argued for free intellectual inquiry in *Soviet Genetics and World Science; Lysenko and the Meaning of Heredity* (Chatto & Windus, 1949). Among his other postwar books are *Evolution in Action* (Harper, 1953); *Kingdom of the Beasts* (Vanguard Press, 1956); *The Wonderful World of Life; The Story of Evolution* (Garden City Books, 1958); and *Biological Aspects of Cancer* (Harcourt, 1958), based on his lecture as the first Alfred P. Sloan lecturer on cancer at the Sloan-Kettering Institute in New York. Also, as a popularizer of science, he served with James Fisher and others on the editorial board of *Nature: Earth, Plants, Animals* (Doubleday, 1960).

His controversial and philosophical *New Bottles for New Wine* (Harper, 1958), a collection of essays and lectures, and *The Humanist Frame* (Harper, 1961), a collection of essays that he edited and to which he also contributed, contain further expositions of Huxley's humanist creed. According to Huxley, in the present phase of evolution (human or psychosocial), man can consciously control his material environment and can free himself from self-imposed restrictions, such as belief in the supernatural, that have blocked his progress. In 1962 Huxley, who is president of the Eugenics Society, suggested in his Galton Lecture that man could more completely reach his human potentialities through eugenic improvement and proposed a plan of artificial insemination using donors of superior characteristics.

The storms of protest that Huxley's ideas raise intermittently have not hindered international recognition of his contributions to science and twentieth-century thought. His awards include the UNESCO Kalinga Prize in 1953 for distinguished popular scientific writing; the Darwin Medal in 1957 of the Royal Society, of which he has been a Fellow since 1938; and the Linnean Society's Darwin-Wallace Commemorative Medal

HUXLEY, SIR JULIAN—*Continued*

in 1958. Also in 1958 he was knighted. Many universities in Europe, the United States, and South America have awarded Huxley honorary degrees. He was chosen president in 1952 of the first International Congress on Human and Ethical Culture at Amsterdam and gave a keynote speech at the International Planned Parenthood Federation Conference at Delhi in 1959. He is past president of the Institute of Animal Behaviour and past chairman of the Association for the Study of Systematics. His clubs in London are the Savile and Athenaeum.

Shortly after World War I, Julian Huxley married Marie Juliette Baillot of Neuchâtel, Switzerland; they have two sons, Anthony Julian and Francis John Heathorn. Sir Julian is tall and trim and has always had the agility and the outdoor look of a man who likes playing tennis, swimming, mountain climbing, and bird watching. "The enjoyment of the beauty and varied wonder of the natural world—an experience engendered jointly by nature and the capacities of man's mind—is seen as one of the indispensable modes of human fulfillment," he wrote in *Religion without Revelation,* "not to be neglected without peril, involving something essentially religious or holy even though we may not burden it with any such heavy designation."

References

> Clark, Ronald W. Sir Julian Huxley (1960)
> International Who's Who, 1962-63
> Twentieth Century Authors (1942; First Supplement, 1955)
> Who's Who, 1963
> World Biography (1954)

INFELD, LEOPOLD Aug. 20, 1898- Physicist; university professor; author

Address: b. Institute of Theoretical Physics, Warsaw University, ul. Hoza 69, Warsaw, Poland; h. Al.I Armii Wojska Polskiego 16 m. 46, Warsaw, Poland

> NOTE: This biography supersedes the article that appeared in *Current Biography* in 1941.

A leading theoretical physicist, Dr. Leopold Infeld collaborated with the noted scientists Max Born and Albert Einstein in the pioneering work on the theory of fields and the relativity theory. Infeld is the author of many scientific articles and of several books, including *The World in Modern Science* (1934); *The Evolution of Physics* (1938), which he wrote with Einstein; the autobiographical *Quest* (1941); and *Albert Einstein* (1950). Born and educated in Poland, where he began his career as a teacher of science, Infeld came to England and then to the United States in the 1930's. He was associated with Einstein at the Institute for Advanced Study at Princeton, New Jersey before accepting a teaching post at the University of Toronto, Canada. In 1949 he returned to his homeland to settle permanently. In recent years Infeld has spearheaded a movement among Poland's intellectuals for greater freedom from control by Communist theoreticians.

One of the three children of Salomon and Ernestyna (Kahane) Infeld, Leopold Infeld was born on August 20, 1898 in the ghetto quarter of Kraków, Poland, then a part of the Austro-Hungarian Empire. His two sisters were killed by the Nazis during World War II. His father was a successful merchant, and the family lived comfortably despite its enforced restriction to the dark and narrow ghetto. Here Jewish residents had little freedom, and educational opportunities were severely limited.

Leopold Infeld began his education at the traditional Hebrew *cheder.* When he was six years old he was enrolled in a Polish primary school, in keeping with a new government decree requiring public education for all children. There he learned the Polish language and was first introduced to life outside the ghetto. After elementary school Infeld wanted to attend the Gymnasium, the preparatory school for the university, but his father disapproved of academic education and sent him to a commercial secondary school for business training.

After his thirteenth birthday and Bar Mitzvah Infeld asserted his independence. He rejected his religion despite pressures from his family. With the aid of textbooks he taught himself physics, mathematics, and the classics, so that he would be eligible for the university entrance examination *(matura).* In 1916, on his graduation from secondary school, Infeld took his *matura* orals and passed with first honors, but his plans to start an academic career were forcibly postponed by his induction into the Austrian army. Through bribery, Infeld was enabled to desert after a few months and returned to Kraków. There he remained hidden in fear that his desertion would be discovered, but shortly before the Armistice was signed in 1918 Infeld was reclassified as a civilian and admitted to Jagiellonian University in Kraków.

Impatient with the quality of his professional training at Jagiellonian University and harried by anti-Semitism, Infeld decided to emigrate from Poland. He applied for admission at the University of Berlin but its officials rejected him as a candidate for graduate studies in physics. He attributed their action to a prejudice against all Poles. Infeld was, however, not easily discouraged and he sought and obtained help from Professor Albert Einstein in pressing his application. After considerable difficulty he was permitted to matriculate as a special student, auditing courses but receiving no credit for his work. He returned to Kraków where he completed his requirements. When Jagiellonian University awarded him the Ph.D. degree in 1921 Infeld became the first doctor of theoretical physics in Poland.

For eight years Infeld taught on the Gymnasium level in Jewish schools in the provinces, despite the fact that no Polish university had anyone qualified to teach his specialty. Many years later, in his autobiography, Infeld recalled that during the 1920's he became disgusted with the school trustees and his environment. For a time he lost all interest in continuing his scientific studies.

By the late 1920's Leopold Infeld's personal and professional lethargy was alleviated by his membership in the Polish Physical Society and by his marriage to a young woman scientist. He began to work on several research projects and published his results in French and German scientific periodicals, but his career suffered another setback when his Gymnasium was disqualified as the result of an incident for which Infeld was held responsible. He turned the incident to his advantage by leaving the lower schools and obtaining an appointment at the University of Lwów, where he served as a senior assistant from 1929 until 1931, when he was promoted to docent. After the death of his wife in 1933 he published a book they had planned together, which he dedicated to her memory. Translated into English by Louis Infeld, with an introduction by Albert Einstein, the book was published in 1934 in London by Victor Gollancz Ltd. and in New York by G. P. Putnam's Sons with the title *The World in Modern Science: Matter and Quanta.*

On the strength of the book Infeld was awarded a Rockefeller Fellowship. He took a leave of absence from the University of Lwów and used the grant to do postgraduate work at Cambridge University in England during 1934-35. There he became an assistant to Max Born, a German physicist who achieved fame in the late 1920's for his mathematical calculations of the particle and wave aspects of matter. Infeld established as his subject the theory of fields, especially the relativity theory. Born and Infeld collaborated on the development of a field theory that spanned modern quantum mechanics and the electromagnetic wave experiments conducted in the nineteenth century.

As a result of his work in England, Infeld expected the University of Lwów to offer him a full professorship, but his candidacy for promotion was rejected, presumably on the basis of articles he had written against anti-Semitism and Fascism. In 1936 he came to the United States where he received a fellowship at the Institute of Advanced Study at Princeton, New Jersey. There he renewed his friendship with Albert Einstein and worked with him on several research projects involving gravitational waves.

After Infeld's grant expired in 1937 he persuaded Albert Einstein to join him in writing a popular scientific volume. *The Evolution of Physics: The Growth of Ideas From Early Concepts to Relativity and Quanta* (Simon & Schuster, 1938) became a best seller and created Infeld's reputation. Formerly without any rank or prestige, Infeld achieved some distinction in being a co-author with the great scientist. In 1939 Infeld went to Canada to accept a post as lecturer at the University of Toronto. Although by academic standards it was on the same level as the post he had held at the University of Lwów ten years before, he rapidly adjusted to the educational system in North America and one year later he was named a full professor of applied mathematics.

When World War II broke out in Europe Infeld harbored some feelings of guilt that he was not suffering with his people in Poland but enjoying a peaceful and sheltered life in Canada. To ease his mind he began an introspective study of himself that culminated in his auto-

LEOPOLD INFELD

biography entitled *Quest: The Evolution of a Scientist* (Doubleday, 1941). The book, which won the Anisfield-Wolf Prize, covered Infeld's ghetto origins, his emergence into adolescence, and his discovery of theoretical physics. A recurring theme was Infeld's confusion and conflict over the scientist's role in the world struggle. "How can we by our own efforts," asked Dr. Infeld, "prevent or delay the decline of the world in which we live?" He credited the scientist with providing the technology of our age, but added: "Not until today has he begun to notice that the earth on which he moves is covered with sweat and with blood and that in the world in which he lives the son of man has nowhere to lay his head." Waldemar Kaempffert, reviewing the book for the *Saturday Review of Literature* (April 5, 1941), called it "an enthralling human document, . . . which discloses the flowering of an original mind in the face of hardship, frustration, and temporary defeat."

During the 1940's Infeld continued teaching and advancing his research in fundamental physics and the general relativity theory. For a short time he worked on a small and isolated aspect of Canada's atomic project, but he denies that he is an atomic scientist. He stated his liberal anti-war philosophy in *Atomic Energy and World Government,* published in 1946 by the Canadian Institute of International Affairs in Toronto. Two years later he wrote *Whom the Gods Love: The Story of Évariste Galois* (Whittlesey House, 1948), a biography of a French mathematician.

Infeld's definitive volume on his friend and mentor, *Professor Albert Einstein: His Work and Its Influence on Our World* (Scribner, 1950), is less a biography than a comprehensive analysis of Einstein's ideas and their effect on modern theoretical physics. Ernest Nagel, writing in the New York *Times* (February 26, 1950) praised the book and Infeld's "unusual skill

INFELD, LEOPOLD—*Continued*

and luminous simplicity." Infeld discussed the significance of Einstein's revolutionary theories of special and general relativity and his role in the development of quantum mechanics in terms intelligible to the layman.

In the summer of 1949 Infeld made his first trip to postwar Poland. On returning to Canada he announced his intention of taking a one-year leave to lecture at the University of Warsaw. This provoked a parliamentary debate in which the suggestion was made that "appropriate steps be taken to ascertain the circumstances under which Dr. Infeld plans to return to Poland armed with certain atomic knowledge" (*Newsweek,* October 2, 1950). According to statements made in the United States Congress, Infeld was alleged to have had connections with the Soviet atomic spy ring that operated in Canada during World War II. No official action was taken to prevent Infeld from leaving Canada, however, and in October 1950 he notified the university that he planned to remain permanently in Poland. With Professor Wojciech Rubinowicz, Infeld established a new research center in theoretical physics at the University of Warsaw, which has trained a number of scientists in field theory and theoretical nuclear physics. After the establishment, in 1956, of a State Council for the Peaceful Uses of Nuclear Energy, Infeld was appointed its honorary chairman.

In recent years Infeld has been in the vanguard of a movement of Polish scientists and scholars for greater personal and intellectual freedom, and he has asserted that civil and political liberties are indispensable for the victory of Communism over capitalist society. Writing in *Przeglad Kulturalny,* a major weekly cultural magazine, in late 1961, Infeld related his experiences with Polish Marxist theorists, who in the past had subjected scientists to their dogmas. He noted that Polish scientists had succeeded to a large extent in freeing themselves from the dictation of the dogmatists, although some censorship still prevailed. "I agree to the present situation on one condition —that for our children freedom will be on the increase rather than on the decline," Infeld has said. Some of Infeld's colleagues have criticized his views as being too optimistic.

Infeld is the author or co-author of about 100 articles for scientific journals, some of them written in co-operation with Albert Einstein and with Max Born. The monograph *Motion and Relativity,* which he and Jerzy Plebański wrote for the Polish Academy of Sciences, was published in English by the Pergamon Press in 1960. Organizations of which Infeld has been a member include the Royal Society of Canada and the American Physical Society. Since 1953 he has been a member of the Presidium of the Polish Academy of Sciences, and he has been elected to honorary membership in the scientific academies of Hungary and Berlin. The Polish government bestowed upon him the Commander's Cross of Reconstituted Poland (1952), Order of Work of Poland (1954), and the State Scientific First Prize (1955).

Dr. Leopold Infeld's first wife, Halina, died in 1933. Two of his marriages have ended in divorce. On April 13, 1939 he married Helen Schlauch, a college instructor. They have two children, Eryk and Joan. One child, from an earlier marriage, is no longer living. Infeld is six feet tall, weighs 165 pounds, and has gray hair and gray eyes. Although he has never been a member of the Communist party, he has said that he sympathizes with a number of its aims.

References

N Y Times p6 N 27 '61 por
Infeld, Leopold. Quest: The Evolution of a Scientist (1941)
International Who's Who, 1962-63
Who's Who in America, 1962-63

IRENE Dec. 8, 1907-Nov. 15, 1962 Hollywood fashion designer; became head designer for MGM in 1942; formed own company to design and manufacture clothes in 1947. See *Current Biography* (June) 1946.

Obituary

N Y Times p21 N 16 '62

JACOBSSON, PER Feb. 5, 1894-May 5, 1963 Swedish economist and monetary expert; managing director of the International Monetary Fund (1956-63); head of the monetary and economic department of the Bank of International Settlements, Basel, Switzerland (1931-56). See *Current Biography* (October) 1958.

Obituary

N Y Times p1+ My 6 '63

JAGAN, CHEDDI (BERRET) (jā'găn) Mar. 22, 1918- Premier of British Guiana
Address: High St., Georgetown, British Guiana

One of the most controversial political figures in the Western Hemisphere, Premier Cheddi Jagan of British Guiana is a dentist who acquired his political ideas as well as his professional training in the United States. A militant champion of social and economic reform and national independence, Jagan drew worldwide attention in 1953, when he and his colleagues in the left-wing People's Progressive party were ousted from the government by British authorities who feared a Communist coup. Eight years later Jagan, as Premier, was forced to call on Great Britain for help in quelling disorders that threatened his government. Although he describes himself as a Socialist and a Marxist, Jagan has consistently stated his intention to achieve his Socialist goals by democratic means and to follow a neutralist foreign policy.

The only British colony on the South American mainland, British Guiana was acquired from the Dutch in 1814. Bounded by Venezuela, Surinam, Brazil, and the Atlantic Ocean, British Guiana has an area of some 83,000 square miles. Its leading exports are sugar, rice, and bauxite. Of its predominantly poor population of 575,270 about 48 percent are of East Indian descent and some 34 percent are Negro. Although the colony was granted internal self-government in August 1961, internal instability, caused in part by racial tensions, has delayed complete independence.

Cheddi Berret (one source suggests Bharrat) Jagan, the eldest of eleven children, was born on March 22, 1918 at Port Mourant, a sugar plantation in the eastern Berbice section of British Guiana. His grandparents had come as indentured sugarcane laborers from the famine-stricken Behar section of India. Since his father, Cheddi Jagan, worked as foreman of a plantation work gang, young Cheddi Jagan did not experience the abject poverty of most plantation workers, but he saw it all around him and it influenced his later political outlook. After he had completed his elementary education in the village school, his father at considerable financial sacrifice sent him to Queen's College, a secondary school in Georgetown, where he was not an outstanding scholar but excelled as a cricket batsman.

In 1935, after three years of study, Jagan left school and spent a year looking in vain for work. Although he first considered studying law in London, he was too shy to be a lawyer, and in 1936 he decided to take up dentistry in the United States. He studied at Howard University in Washington, D.C. from 1936 to 1938, the second year on a tuition scholarship. To help meet expenses he worked for two summers as a patent medicine salesman in Harlem, New York City. He later held jobs as a tailor and presser and as a night elevator operator. The racial discrimination and economic inequities that he encountered in the United States impressed him very unfavorably.

Jagan attended Northwestern University Dental School in Chicago, where he held a work-loan scholarship, and the doctor of dental surgery degree was conferred upon him in 1942. At this time he began to develop an interest in politics, and he studied the works of Jefferson, Paine, Lincoln, and Marx. Jawaharlal Nehru's autobiography, *Toward Freedom*, particularly inspired him. He attended evening and summer classes in economics, sociology, philosophy, and political science. In Chicago Jagan met Janet Rosenberg, a student nurse then active in leftist campus groups. They were married, and she became a major influence on his political outlook and career.

In 1943 Jagan bought secondhand dental equipment and returned with his wife to British Guiana, where he set up a dental practice in Georgetown, the capital. In 1945 he joined, and was elected treasurer of, the sugar workers' trade union, Man-Power Citizens Association, and in 1946 the Jagans formed the Political Affairs Committee, which sponsored discussion groups and issued a monthly bulletin. A year later Mrs. Jagan founded the Women's Political and Economic Organization. In the general elections of 1947 Jagan won a seat in the British Guiana legislature as a representative of the rural district of Central Demerara, near Georgetown.

Virtually a one-man opposition in the overwhelmingly conservative legislature, Jagan called for constitutional and local government reform, universal adult suffrage, land tenure reform, agricultural marketing facilities, large-scale land

DR. CHEDDI JAGAN

reclamation, and extension of the road program. In 1950 he attended a conference of the Caribbean Commission, a regional organization of the United Nations. As president of the Saw Mill and Wood-workers Union from 1949 to 1953, he went to a conference of the left-wing World Federation of Trade Unions at Berlin in 1951. Meanwhile, in January 1950, the People's Progressive party (PPP), British Guiana's first modern political party, was established, with Jagan as party leader and his wife as executive secretary.

A new constitution, providing for universal adult suffrage, with increased provisions for home rule, was granted in 1953. In the elections in April of that year the PPP obtained 51 percent of the popular vote and won eighteen of the twenty-four seats in the house of assembly. Jagan received the ministry of agriculture, lands, and mines, and as leader of the majority party he was considered chief minister. He immediately launched a vigorous reform program and demanded far-reaching constitutional changes.

On October 6, 1953, amid demonstrations and strikes encouraged by the PPP, the British Colonial Office under the government of Winston Churchill dispatched troops and warships to British Guiana to forestall a suspected attempt "to set up a Communist state." A few days later the British authorities suspended the constitution, dismissed Jagan and five of his ministers, declared a state of emergency, and issued a white paper charging the PPP leaders with efforts to turn British Guiana into a Communist state by means of violence and conspiracy. The British action was endorsed by the United States government. An interim government, consisting of a council appointed by the Governor, Sir Alfred Savage, was instituted in December 1953.

Meanwhile, Jagan went to London, accompanied by Negro leader L.F.S. Burnham, to plead his case with the British government. Although Labour leaders felt that the government had

JAGAN, CHEDDI—*Continued*

resorted to an unnecessary extreme in suspending the constitution, Jagan failed to obtain Labour support for his position. The government's action was endorsed by the House of Commons by a vote of 294 to 256 on October 22, 1953. Jagan then visited India, where he received sympathy for his position, but failed in his efforts to convince Prime Minister Nehru to take the issue before the United Nations.

Returning to British Guiana in January 1954 Jagan launchéd a civil disobedience campaign against the interim government. He was arrested on April 4, 1954 for violating an order restricting him to the city of Georgetown. His wife was arrested on the following day. After his release from prison in September 1954, he continued to be restricted to Georgetown, and for the next four years he practised dentistry. He presented his political and economic position in his pamphlet *What Happened in British Guiana* (Union of Democratic Control, 1954) and in his book *Forbidden Freedom: The Story of British Guiana* (Lawrence and Wishart, 1954).

Trying to end extreme left domination, the PPP in February 1955 demoted Jagan from chairman to vice-chairman and his wife from general secretary to treasurer. Six months later, however, the Jagans were again reinstated in their earlier positions within the party. Meanwhile, L.F.S Burnham had broken with the PPP to form his own party, the People's National Congress (PNC), largely representing the urban Negro population, and based on a policy of moderate Socialism.

In April 1956 the British authorities drafted a new constitution for British Guiana that was aimed at lessening Jagan's power by encouraging other political parties and abolishing the post of chief minister. The restrictions that had confined Jagan to Georgetown were lifted by the Governor, Sir Patrick Renison, in February 1957, and he was permitted to travel to Africa to attend the independence celebrations of Ghana. In the elections of August 12, 1957, in which rivalry between the Indian and Negro factions played an important role, the PPP received 48 percent of the popular vote and won nine of the fourteen elective seats in the twenty-three-member legislative council. Jagan was appointed minister of trade and industry and his wife was named minister of labor, health, and housing. The nine-member cabinet included five PPP members, and it was presided over by the Governor, who retained emergency powers, to be invoked in the event of crisis.

As minister of trade and industry Jagan worked in co-operation with Governor Renison and launched a social and economic reform program, which included large-scale land reclamation measures, the improvement of agricultural marketing facilities, the building of roads, hospitals, and low-income housing, and the expansion of welfare services and educational facilities. On visits to London in 1958 and 1959 Jagan declared that he might have to seek financial aid from the Soviet Union if adequate assistance could not be obtained elsewhere. On a visit to Cuba in April 1960 Jagan negotiated an agreement for the purchase by Cuba of timber and rice from British Guiana. Although he expressed admira-

tion for Cuban Premier Fidel Castro, he later said that his relationship with Castro was solely on an economic level and did not involve any political agreements.

At a constitutional conference in London in March 1960 a new constitution, to be effective in August 1961, was adopted. Under its provisions, British Guiana was granted internal self-government, while the British government retained control over national defense and foreign relations, as well as a veto power over legislation. Jagan, who had insisted upon immediate independence, expressed himself as totally dissatisfied with the discussions.

The elections of August 21, 1961 were marked by racial tensions and charges of Communism. The PPP emerged from the campaign with 42.7 percent of the vote and received twenty of the thirty-five legislative seats. (Eleven seats were won by the PNC and four by the right-wing United Force.) On September 5, 1961 Jagan was sworn in as Premier and appointed a ten-member cabinet in which he assumed the role of minister of planning and development. While stating as his two main objectives the establishment of a socialist economy and the achievement of national independence, Jagan reaffirmed his adherence to parliamentary democracy and neutralism. He disclaimed any intention to nationalize mines and plants at present, though reserving the right to do so in the future. Visiting the United States in October 1961, Jagan conferred at length with President Kennedy and Secretary of State Dean Rusk. Although he found United States officials sympathetic, he did not receive any definite commitments for large-scale economic aid.

As a means of strengthening the country's economy, Jagan, in February 1962, announced a rigid austerity budget. Shortly after its announcement, merchants and civil servants were joined by workers in a wave of strikes and demonstrations aimed at bringing the downfall of Jagan's government. The conflict developed into a racial struggle when Negroes in Georgetown burned and looted Indian-owned shops. Consequently, Jagan was compelled to call on British forces for help in restoring order to the strife-torn country. A revised and modified budget, introduced by Jagan in April 1962, was defeated in the Legislative Assembly then, but was later passed.

In view of the British government's postponement of independence talks, which had been scheduled for May 1962, Jagan visited the U.N. in July and addressed its special committee on colonialism, charging that Britain sought to perpetuate the colonial status of British Guiana. A conference on independence, begun in London on October 23, 1962, ended in a deadlock two weeks later, because of disagreements between Jagan and leaders of the opposition parties. The party leaders declined a British offer for arbitration of their differences. In 1963 British troops were again brought in to quell disturbances occurring during an eleven-week general strike called by the Trade Unions Council to protest a labor bill sponsored by Jagan.

Although Jagan has negotiated economic arrangements with Communist bloc nations, he has repeatedly stressed his neutralism and has declared his intention to accept aid from anyone who offers it without political strings. He describes his goal of establishing a co-operative and Socialist order as "revolutionary," but he points out that these objectives can be attained by democratic means and that capitalism is not synonymous with democracy.

Dr. Cheddi Jagan and Janet (Rosenberg) Jagan have two children, Cheddi, Jr., and Nadira. Mrs. Jagan lost her American citizenship when she voted in British Guiana's 1947 elections. A wiry man of distinguished appearance, Jagan is five feet seven inches tall, has brown eyes and graying hair, and is usually well dressed. Described by a writer for the *Reporter* (November 9, 1961) as "handsome, amiable, idealistic, a demagogue par excellence," with "a fine instinct for the flashing stroke, the dramatic gesture," Jagan conveys the image of a man in a hurry. He is an easy conversationalist who likes a good argument. As a hobby he reads political literature and for relaxation he likes to attend western movies. A Hindu, he is revered by the rural Indian population of British Guiana.

References

> Look 26:66+ Ag 14 '62 pors
> N Y Herald Tribune II p6 Ag 27 '61 por
> N Y Times p18 Ag 23 '61 por
> Toronto Globe and Mail p7 O 20 '61 por
> International Who's Who, 1962-63

JANNEY, RUSSELL Apr. 14, 1884-July 14, 1963 Theatrical producer; author; produced and wrote, with Brian Hooker and Rudolf Friml, the musical *The Vagabond King* (1925); wrote the best seller *The Miracle of the Bells* (1946). See *Current Biography* (March) 1947.

Obituary

> N Y Times p29 Jl 15 '63

JOHN XXIII, POPE Nov. 25, 1881-June 3, 1963 The 262d Supreme Pontiff of the Roman Catholic Church (1958-63); known as a liberal Pope, a champion of world peace and Christian unity; convened the Second Vatican Council of the Church in 1962; issued the encyclical "Pacem in Terris" (Peace on Earth) in 1963. (See *Current Biography* (February) 1959.

Obituary

> N Y Times p1+ Je 4 '63

JOHNSTON, ERIC A(LLEN) Dec. 21, 1896-Aug. 22, 1963 Businessman; was connected with several large companies; president, Motion Picture Association of America (1945-63); president, United. States Chamber of Commerce (1942-46); served in government assignments in the Roosevelt, Truman, and Eisenhower administrations. See *Current Biography* (October) 1955.

Obituary

> N Y Times p1+ Ag 23 '63

JONES, HOWARD P(ALFREY) Jan. 2, 1899-United States Ambassador to Indonesia
Address: b. United States Embassy, Djakarta, Indonesia; h. 6629 Elgin Lane, Bethesda 14, Md.

A diplomat in the true sense of the term, the United States Ambassador to the Republic of Indonesia, Howard P. Jones, can claim much credit for the atmosphere of mutual trust that prevails between Indonesia and the United States. A former journalist and university professor, Jones joined the United States Foreign Service in 1948, and he played an important role in rehabilitating postwar Germany. Transferred to the Far East in 1952, he served in Formosa and Indonesia, then was recalled to Washington to become Deputy Assistant Secretary of State for Far Eastern economic affairs. His appointment to succeed John M. Allison as Ambassador to Indonesia in early 1958 came at a time when relations between Indonesia and the United States threatened to become strained. In the spring of 1962 Jones helped to bring about a settlement of the Dutch-Indonesian dispute over Western New Guinea. A year later he took part in negotiations involving the eventual nationalization of foreign oil companies by the Indonesian government.

Howard Palfrey Jones was born on January 2, 1899 in Chicago to William Cadwallader and Ida May (Noble) Jones. Early in life he decided upon a career in journalism. After graduating from high school, he attended the University of Wisconsin from 1917 to 1920 and then went on to Columbia University, which granted him the Litt.B. degree in 1921. Jones began his career with the New York bureau of the United Press and soon became known as a "boy wonder" of the newspaper world. At the age of twenty-four he was managing editor of a Scripps-Howard newspaper, the Evansville, Indiana, *Press*, and within a few years he became editor-in-chief and a partner in a chain of nine small newspapers in Michigan.

Although Jones had no intention of leaving newspaper work, his interest in the problems of local government led him to return to school and undertake graduate studies in public finance, public administration, and public law. He attended the University of Michigan from 1925 until 1927 and Columbia University in 1929 and 1930. During this period he also taught journalism at both universities. In 1929 Jones obtained a job as public relations secretary with the National Municipal League, a research and educational organization in New York City concerned with problems of state and local government. From 1933 to 1939 he served as executive director of the league and as editor of its organ, the *National Municipal Review*.

In addition to his work with the National Municipal League, Jones was a consultant to the Virginia Commission on County Government in 1931 and a delegate representing the United States Department of State at the International Union of Cities at Lyons, France in 1934. In the latter year he obtained a fellowship from the Oberlaender Trust of the Carl Schurz Memorial Foundation to study public administration in Germany. From 1933 to 1940 he was a member

Department of State—
Whit Keith, Jr.

HOWARD P. JONES

of the governing board of the United States Public Administration Service, and from 1936 to 1938 he was director of research for the New York State Commission on Revision of Tax Laws, which was engaged in an overhaul of the state's tax structure. He also served as a consultant to the Governor's Commission on the New York State Constitutional Convention of 1938.

Having decided to become active in politics, in 1938 Jones ran for the state assembly seat in Rockland County, New York, on the Republican ticket. Although he lost the election, he won the respect of New York Governor Herbert H. Lehman, who in 1939 appointed him to the Civil Service Commission to help develop an expanded state civil service program. Jones remained a commissioner until 1943, when Governor Thomas E. Dewey appointed him deputy comptroller of the state of New York.

A member of the United States Army from 1943 to 1947, Jones served as a major, and later as a colonel, with the staff of the Supreme Headquarters, Allied Expeditionary Forces, under General Dwight D. Eisenhower. He served with the Ninth Army during its advance into Germany and took part in the mission that helped to re-establish the Belgian government after the German occupation. After the war Jones played a key role in German rehabilitation. He helped to set up the German Ministry of Finance, the Bank for Reconstruction, and other financial agencies. In 1948 he joined the United States Foreign Service, and from 1949 to 1951 he was deputy director of the Berlin office of the United States High Commissioner for Germany and Berlin representative of the Economic Co-operation Administration's special mission to Germany. In July 1951 he became director of the Berlin element of the United States High Commissioner's office. For his important role in helping to revive the economy of West Berlin after the

Russian blockade in 1948-49, Jones received the State Department's Meritorious Service Award in 1952.

In 1952 the State Department reassigned Jones from Germany to the Far East. His first post was in Taipei, Formosa as counselor of embassy and deputy chief of mission. Two years later, in 1954, he became director of the United States Operations Mission to the Republic of Indonesia in Djakarta, with responsibility for implementing the American program of technical co-operation and economic assistance.

Recalled to Washington in 1955, Jones was appointed Deputy Assistant Secretary of State for Far Eastern economic affairs, and in this position he kept up his friendships with President Sukarno and other Indonesian officials. An advocate of the policy of keeping Asia free for Asians, Jones urged more United States technical assistance and the investment of private capital in countries like Indonesia, as an antidote to Communism. In 1955 Jones was a member of the United States delegation to the Colombo Plan conference at Singapore, and in 1956 he was chairman of the United States delegation to the United Nations Economic Commission for Asia and the Far East, at Bangalore, India.

In December 1957 Jones had been named to succeed Karl L. Rankin as United States Ambassador to Nationalist China, but owing to a last-minute change in administration plans, he was appointed in January 1958 as Ambassador to Indonesia, succeeding John M. Allison. Reportedly Allison disagreed with State Department policy toward that country. The change in plans was believed to have resulted from the critical situation in Indonesia following the seizure of a number of Dutch companies, and the challenge of the central government in Djakarta by an anti-Communist rebel group in Central Sumatra. Although United States policy toward Indonesia had been officially neutral, State Department spokesmen had on occasion criticized Sukarno's policy of "guided democracy" and Communist influences in the Indonesian government. These comments, in turn, led Indonesians to charge the United States with interference in Indonesian affairs.

When Jones was sworn in as Ambassador to Indonesia on February 21, 1958, Secretary of State John Foster Dulles warned him that he was taking on a tough assignment and one that required "a great effort of statesmanship." On March 10, 1958 Jones presented his credentials to Sukarno, who asked for a greater understanding of his country's problems by the United States. In his speech Jones declared that the two countries were bound together by "belief in God, love of liberty, and respect for the rights of the individual."

Shortly after Jones arrived in Indonesia, fighting resumed between government forces and the rebels on the island of Sumatra, on which are located the multimillion-dollar oil fields of the California-Texas Oil Company and of other American concerns. The rebels asserted their independence from the central government after their demands for greater local autonomy, economic freedom, and the elimination of Communist influences from the government had been ignored. Jones's statement, after his arrival, that the United States had no intention of interfering in Indonesian internal affairs, was viewed as a clear refutation of charges that the United States was supporting the rebels. When an American flyer in the service of the rebels was captured by government forces a few months later, Jones officially expressed regret "that a private American citizen has been involved as a paid soldier of fortune serving with the rebel forces."

After the victory of the central government over the rebels, military leaders took advantage of their increased power and prestige by ordering an end to anti-American demonstrations. The United States reciprocated by starting a program of military and economic aid to Indonesia as a countermeasure to aid from the Soviet Union. Early in 1959 Jones informed Indonesian Foreign Minister Subandrio that $10,000,000 in military aid had been approved by the Eisenhower administration. The move was hailed as proof of United States confidence in Indonesia and paved the way for increased mutual trust between the two nations.

Meanwhile, friction between Indonesia and the Netherlands was mounting over the disputed territory of West Irian (the Indonesian name for the western half of the island of New Guinea). By late 1961 the prospect of war between the two countries was imminent, for President Sukarno threatened the use of force, if necessary, to win the territory from the Dutch. Using his "soft-sell" diplomacy, Jones played a key role in persuading the countries to negotiate. In the process he aroused the indignation of the Dutch for reportedly having shouted the word "merdeka" (freedom) at an Indonesian rally. (He later explained that the word was used by Indonesians as a greeting, with no political implications.) In May 1962 a peaceful solution was reached through the United Nations, whereby Indonesia would eventually take over the territory after a temporary U.N. administration.

Following the settlement of the West Irian problem, Jones presented the Indonesian government with a plan devised by an economic survey team for the growth and development of Indonesia. The plan, involving aid of between $325,000,000 and $390,000,000, included provisions for education and training, transportation expansion, machinery replacement, replenishment of vital material imports, acceleration of rubber and tin production, improvements in the production and distribution of food, improved electric power distribution, and surveys of natural resources. In May 1963 Jones took part in negotiations leading to an agreement between the Indonesian government and foreign oil companies under which the facilities of the companies are to be nationalized within fifteen years, with due compensation to the owners.

Howard P. Jones was married to Mary Rendall on October 22, 1921. The couple had one daughter, Patricia Ann, who is deceased. Their two granddaughters are living in Indonesia. An informal and friendly man, Jones is easily persuaded to entertain at social functions. He has been called "Smiling Jones" by the Indonesian leftist press. In a crowd he is readily identified by his fringe of white hair and by the white sharkskin suits he wears. He and his wife collect Indonesian art objects and batik. Jones is a member of Sigma Nu and Sigma Delta Chi fraternities. He is a Mason. His clubs are the City, the Columbia University Club, and the Cosmos Club in Washington, D.C.

References

N Y Times p12 Ap 5 '62 por
N Y World-Telegram p5 Je 13 '59 por
Newsday p28 Ap 8 '58 por
International Who's Who, 1962-63
Who's Who in America, 1962-63

JONES, JOE Apr. 7, 1909-Apr. 9, 1963 American landscape and mural painter; known for his paintings of social comment in the 1930's and early 1940's. See *Current Biography* (October) 1940.

Obituary

N Y Times p39 Ap 10 '63

KALMUS, HERBERT T(HOMAS) Nov. 9, 1881-July 11, 1963 Inventor of Technicolor; president of Technicolor, Inc. See *Current Biography* (February) 1949.

Obituary

N Y Times p25 Jl 12 '63

KASSEM, ABDUL KARIM (EL-) Nov. 21, 1914-Feb. 9, 1963 Premier of Iraq (1958-63); established revolutionary regime by overthrowing King Faisal II in 1958; rivaled Gamal Abdel Nasser, Premier of Egypt, for leadership of Arab world; overthrown and killed by military junta. See *Current Biography* (November) 1959.

Obituary

Washington (D.C.) Post A p1+ F 11 '63

KAUFFMANN, HENRIK (LOUIS HANS) Aug. 26, 1888-June 5, 1963 Former Danish Ambassador to the United States (1947-58); director, Danish East Asiatic Company (1958-63). See *Current Biography* (April) 1956.

Obituary

N Y Times p14 Je 6 '63

KAWAKAMI, JOTARO (kä-wä-kä-mē) Jan. 3, 1889- Japanese political leader
Address: h. 2-37 Nishihara, Shibuya-ku, Tokyo, Japan

Humanitarian ideals rather than doctrinaire Marxist principles led Jotaro Kawakami, the chairman of the Socialist party of Japan, into the Socialist movement. A former university professor and lawyer, he is the oldest representative of Japanese Socialism and a veteran of the moderate leadership of farmer and labor movements that ended with World War II. He was among the first proletarian party representatives to be

Consulate General of Japan, N.Y.
JOTARO KAWAKAMI

elected to the lower house of the Japanese legislature in 1928.

As chairman of the Right-wing Socialist party in the postwar period Kawakami played a leading role in reuniting the divided Socialist movement in October 1955. He was elected party chairman in March 1961, succeeding Inejiro Asanuma, who had been the victim of a right-wing assassin. Essentially a theoretician, Kawakami represents a policy aimed toward lessening anti-Americanism within Socialist ranks and toward making the party program more flexible and less doctrinaire to broaden its appeal among the Japanese electorate. On the international scene Kawakami has spoken out in favor of worldwide nuclear disarmament.

Jotaro Kawakami was born in Tokyo on January 3, 1889, the eldest son of Shintaro Kawakami. He studied at the law faculty of the Imperial University of Tokyo, and in 1915 he received his B.A. degree in political science. In 1916, after passing his civil service examinations, Kawakami became a teacher at Rikkyo University in Tokyo, and he later taught at Meiji Gakuin University in the same city. From 1918 to 1927 he was a professor at Kansai Gakuin University near Kobe in southern Japan.

Motivated by humanitarian and Christian ideals, Jotaro Kawakami was active in the labor movement of Japan from 1919 onward. He served as an honorary lecturer at the Kobe school of labor, and in 1927 he joined the Farmer-Labor party. He left the teaching profession in 1928 to enter the private practice of law and to run for a seat in the lower house of Japan's parliament, in the first general elections to be held under the universal suffrage act of 1925. Representing Hyogo district, which encompasses the city of Kobe, Kawakami was one of the eight proletarian party candidates to be elected to the House of Representatives. Japan's four left-wing

parties polled about 500,000 votes in this election. Kawakami has since been returned nine times to his seat in the lower house. In 1929 he served as a delegate to the third Pan-Pacific Conference at Kyoto.

Although he represented neither the farm nor the workbench, Kawakami continued to guide and direct farmer and labor movements, and he became an adviser to the Farmer-Labor party. In 1932 he joined the Social Mass party (Shakai Taishuto), organized in July of that year to bring some degree of unity to the farmer and labor groups of Japan. He soon rose to a leading position within that party, becoming chief lieutenant of its de facto leader. Representing Fabian Socialist and anti-Communist principles, the Social Mass party had thirty-six men in the lower house by 1937. It originally stood in opposition to the Imperial government, but in the late 1930's it came out in support of the government's war policies. It was the first party to dissolve itself in July 1940, when the political parties of Japan were superseded by the totalitarian Imperial Rule Assistance Association. During the World War II period the old-line party leaders maintained informal groupings that formed the basis for the postwar political organizations.

In November 1945, following the Japanese surrender, Kawakami joined with other leaders of the non-Communist left to form the Social Democratic party (Shakaito). He became the chairman of its central executive committee. In the first postwar election, in April 1946, the Social Democratic party polled 17 percent of the vote and received ninety-three out of 467 seats in the House of Representatives. In the following year it increased its strength to 143 seats, becoming the largest single party in the lower house. From May 1947 to October 1948 the government of Japan consisted of a coalition between the Social Democratic and Democratic parties. Although during this period the government was headed by a Socialist Prime Minister, Tetsu Katayama, the Social Democrats failed in their efforts to nationalize some of the basic industries of Japan.

In January 1946 the Japanese government, under the direction of the Supreme Command for the Allied Powers, had begun its purge of a number of Japan's political and military leaders from public office for their activities before and during the war. The purge also affected some of the leaders of the Social Democratic party, and in 1948 Kawakami was among those included in the purge.

The peace treaty between Japan and the United States, signed September 8, 1951, and personal and doctrinal differences, led to the division of the Social Democratic party into a right-wing (Uha Shakaito) and a left-wing (Saha Shakaito) Socialist party. The left wing wanted an over-all treaty that would include the Communist countries. It favored complete neutrality and was opposed to any rearmament efforts, and it viewed the party as a proletarian organization that must maintain its doctrinal purity. The right, on the other hand, favored the signing of the peace treaty even though it excluded the Soviet Union. While it opposed rearmament in principle, it foresaw the possible need for a defensive military posture. It favored an appeal to the middle classes as well as to the workers, and it called for a flexible ideology.

After his release from the purge in 1951, Kawakami, as a leading representative of prewar right-wing Socialism, resumed his role in the reconstruction of the Socialist movement. In August 1952, following the restoration of Japanese sovereignty, he was elected chairman of the central executive committee of the Right-wing Socialist party, succeeding Tetsu Katayama. In the elections of October 1952 the right received fifty-seven and the left, fifty-four seats in the House of Representatives, and in the following year the two Socialist factions captured sixty-six and seventy-two seats, respectively. In a worldwide radio broadcast on April 11, 1954, Kawakami issued an appeal against the use of atomic weapons and called for an end to the armaments race.

In December 1954 the two Socialist parties helped to unseat the regime of Shigeru Yoshida and to elect Ichiro Hatoyama as Premier. (Yoshida and Hatoyama represented rival factions among the conservative forces in the country's politics.) Kawakami subsequently explained his party's support of Hatoyama as a strategic move, to give Japan an interim government pending national elections. In the elections of February 1955 Hatoyama was kept in power, and the left and right Socialist factions received eighty-nine and sixty-seven seats, respectively, in the lower house. Although the Socialist parties had earlier supported Hatoyama, they now co-operated with his rivals to isolate the government party.

Meanwhile, Kawakami worked for the reunification of the Socialist movement. In October 1955, after four years of separation, the two Socialist factions were reunited into the Socialist party of Japan. As a result, the two conservative parties—the Liberals (Jiyuto) and the Democrats (Minshuto)—merged into the Liberal Democratic party (Jiyu-Minshuto), giving Japan what amounted to a formal two-party system. Although Kawakami refused to seek a position of power in the reunited Socialist party, he inevitably became one of the fifteen party advisers. In 1957 he headed a delegation of Japanese Socialists that visited the United States. The Socialists reached their high point in the election of 1958 when they obtained 166 seats in the lower house.

At the annual convention of the Socialist party, in March 1960, Kawakami competed with Inejiro Asanuma, a representative of the far left, for the chairmanship of the party, but he was defeated by nineteen votes. On June 17, 1960 Kawakami was stabbed and wounded by a young right-wing fanatic during the riots over the ratification of the United States-Japanese Mutual Security Treaty and the projected visit of President Dwight D. Eisenhower to Japan. (The riots led to the cancellation of Eisenhower's visit.) Four months later Asanuma was stabbed to death by a right-wing assassin, and the next five months were marked by an intensive power struggle within the Socialist party. At the twentieth Socialist party congress, on March 8, 1961, Kawakami was elected party chairman by unanimous consent.

In accepting the chairmanship Kawakami pledged to work toward the goals of strengthening party solidarity, increasing Socialist parliamentary strength by one-third, waging a determined fight against right-wing violence, and carrying out the policies of the party's action program. Over the opposition of left-wing elements the convention rejected the revolutionary and anti-American program that had been laid down by Asanuma three years earlier. Instead, it adopted a moderate program to bring about "structural reform of capitalism" and the achievement of Socialist aims through peaceful revolution, within the framework of the constitution. At the party convention in January 1962 Kawakami was re-elected party chairman without opposition.

Although the forces of the extreme left continue to exercise a strong influence within the Socialist party of Japan, the party obviously has made some headway toward a more moderate and less virulent anti-American policy under the leadership of Kawakami and of its secretary-general, Saburo Eda. Furthermore, although in recent years the United States government had viewed the Socialist party of Japan with some suspicion, relations between the party and the American Embassy in Tokyo have improved since the advent of Edwin O. Reischauer as United States Ambassador to Japan in April 1961.

In late 1962 the Socialist party held 143 seats in the 467-member House of Representatives and sixty-six out of 250 seats in the upper house. To widen the party's appeal among a larger section of the Japanese electorate and to increase its chances for the eventual attainment of political power, Secretary-General Eda demanded a "new perspective for Socialism" at a party conference at Nikko in July 1962. He cited as four major points that should be incorporated in this "new vision" the high standard of living of the United States, the parliamentary democracy of Great Britain, the social security system of the Soviet Union, and the "peace" constitution of Japan, with its emphasis on neutralism and its renunciation of militarism. Although at the party convention in late November 1962 Eda's proposed program was defeated by left-wing forces by a vote of 232 to 211, the convention unanimously re-elected Kawakami as party chairman.

A scholarly man and a Christian, Jotaro Kawakami is a devoted party worker who lacks the ambition and drive of some of the other political leaders of Japan. His mildness and sincerity, his humility, and his conciliatory nature have made him a symbol of unity within the faction-ridden Socialist party of Japan. He and his wife, Sueko Kawakami, have two married daughters and one son.

References

Cur Hist 34:234 Ap '58
Asia Who's Who (1960)
International Who's Who, 1962-63
Japan Biographical Encyclopedia & Who's Who (1961)

KEFAUVER, (CAREY) ESTES July 26, 1903-Aug. 10, 1963 United States Senator from Tennessee since 1949; influential member of important Senate committees; headed Senate investigation of organized crime (1950-51); Democratic candidate for Vice-President in 1956. See *Current Biography* (January) 1949.

Obituary

N Y Times p1+ Ag 11 '63

KELLOGG, WINTHROP N(ILES) Apr. 13, 1898- Experimental psychologist; university professor

Address: b. Florida State University, Tallahassee, Fla.; h. P.O. Box 551, Sarasota, Fla.

An experimental psychologist who has specialized in research on conditioning and learning, Dr. Winthrop N. Kellogg has in recent years done research on how dolphins perceive objects by means of sound. His investigations could yield information that would be valuable in creating sonar devices for underwater detection. Before he became a professor of experimental psychology at Florida State University in 1950, Kellogg was for fifteen years a professor of psychology at Indiana University and the director of the Indiana Conditioning Laboratory. In 1933 he and his wife wrote *The Ape and the Child* (McGraw), describing how they reared a young chimpanzee with their small son to determine the effect of environment on early behavior.

Winthrop Niles Kellogg was born on April 13, 1898 in Mount Vernon, New York to Florence Adele (Bowns) Kellogg and Henry Niles Kellogg, a newspaper publisher. He has a brother, Forest Browns Kellogg, and a sister, Adele K. Archer. Brought up in Mount Vernon, Chicago, and Indianapolis, Winthrop Kellogg attended Culver Military Academy in Culver,

WINTHROP N. KELLOGG

Indiana. He belonged to the Black Horse Troop and took part in track and football. In 1914 he graduated from the academy.

Kellogg attended Cornell University in 1916-17, but World War I interrupted his studies. He entered the Air Service of the United States Army in 1917 as a private and served with the AEF in England and France. Awarded the French Croix de Guerre in 1918, he was discharged with the rank of first lieutenant in 1919. Returning to civilian life, Kellogg enrolled at Indiana University in Bloomington, where he majored in philosophy and psychology, was editor of the student daily newspaper, and belonged to the swimming team. He was elected to Phi Beta Kappa, and he received his B.A. degree *cum laude* in 1922.

For graduate work Kellogg chose Columbia University, from which he received his M.A. degree in psychology in 1927 and his Ph.D. degree in experimental psychology in 1929. From 1927 to 1929 he was an assistant in psychology at Columbia University and did experimental work under the guidance of Professor Robert S. Woodworth. In a number of publications Kellogg reported on his development of improved apparatus and techniques for measuring minute changes in visual and auditory perception and motor responses. His Ph.D. thesis, *An Experimental Comparison of Psychophysical Methods*, was published in the Archives of Psychology series by Columbia University in 1929, and another analysis, *An Experimental Evaluation of Equality Judgments in Psychophysics*, was published in the same series in 1930.

Returning to Indiana University in 1929 as an assistant professor of experimental psychology, Kellogg was promoted to associate professor in 1930 and full professor in 1937. Fascinated by accounts of children raised by animals, Kellogg in 1927 hit upon a plan to investigate the influence of environment on early behavior: he and his wife decided to bring up a young chimpanzee with their small son for a time so that they could study the development of the animal when reared in a human environment.

On June 26, 1931 Professor Robert M. Yerkes of Yale University got for the Kelloggs a young female chimpanzee, seven and a half months old, from the colony at the Anthropoid Experiment Station of Yale University at Orange Park, Florida. The ape, named Gua, and the Kelloggs' son Donald, born on August 31, 1930, lived together as members of the same family until March 28, 1932. Their surroundings and treatment were made as identical as possible. During the nine months of the experiment, the child's and ape's physical growth, sensory reactions, and mental development were continually tested and compared. The results were published in articles in the *Psychological Bulletin* in 1931, 1932, and 1933, and in the book, *The Ape and the Child* (McGraw, 1933). The project was financed by a fellowship grant from the Social Science Research Council (1931-32).

In 1936 Kellogg became director of the Indiana Conditioning Laboratory, which he described in an article in the *American Journal of Psychology* as "designed principally for work on conditioned response and related problems in the field of learning." Besides reporting in professional journals on his research on conditioning techniques and learning behavior of animals, Kellogg prepared a *Handbook of Laboratory Procedure* (Indiana Univ., 1936); *First Course in Experimental Psychology* (Indiana Univ., 1938); and *Review Questions for Introductory Psychology* (Indiana Univ., 1938; 1940). He also contributed a chapter "Conditioning and Motor Learning," to *Methods of Psychology* (Wiley, 1948), edited by T. G. Andrews, and a chapter, "Techniques of Motor Conditioning," to *Readings in Learning* (Prentice-Hall, 1953), edited by L. M. Stolurow.

During World War II, in 1942, Kellogg was commissioned a captain in the United States Army Air Corps and served in South America and Trinidad before his discharge as a major in 1944. Appointed professor of experimental psychology at Florida State University in 1950, he continued to teach and do research. Kellogg began to study the bottle-nosed dolphin (popularly called porpoise) in 1951. His first published reference to porpoise sonar appeared in *Science* in 1952. Since understanding the porpoises' method of navigation could be important for improving man's sonar system, an extensive research program was developed, sponsored, and financed by the Office of Naval Research and the National Science Foundation.

By observing porpoises in the Gulf of Mexico and in public aquariums and by conducting underwater experiments at the Marine Laboratory of Florida State University at Alligator Harbor, Florida, Kellogg discovered that porpoises are able to perceive and identify objects in the water by emitting sounds and "listening" to the echo. He has reported his findings in such periodicals as *Science* and *Natural History*, in psychological journals, and in his book, *Porpoises and Sonar* (Univ. of Chicago Press, 1961). Kellogg has said that the results of his research with dolphins have often been misinterpreted: unlike such experimenters as John C. Lilly, he has never tried to deal with interspecies communication between dolphins and men. He has also conducted experiments to determine the ability of totally blind people to perceive and avoid obstacles and reported in *Science* (August 10, 1962) that "some blind people can observe amazingly well by means of human sonar."

Much of Kellogg's research has been government sponsored. He worked for the Civil Aeronautics Authority in 1939-40, for the United States Public Health Service from 1947 to 1949, for the Office of Naval Research from 1950 to 1956, and for the National Science Foundation from 1954 to 1957 and from 1961 to the present. In the summers he has been a visiting professor at Columbia University in 1933 and 1934 and at the University of Southern California in 1948, 1959, and 1961.

A member of the Oceanographic Institute of Florida State University from 1950 to 1956, Kellogg is a Fellow of the American Association for the Advancement of Science and the American Psychological Association (APA). He was on the APA committee on precautions in animal experimentation from 1943 to 1946 and served as its chairman in 1946. He is a member of the Southeastern Psychological Association, of which

he was president in 1958-59; of the Florida Psychological Association, of which he was president in 1952-53; and of the National Research Council.

Kellogg was chairman of the psychology section of the Indiana Academy of Science in 1945-46, and he was a member of the National Research Council's division of anthropology and psychology from 1951 to 1954. He was on the board of editors of *Comparative Psychology Monographs* from 1942 to 1948 and of the *Psychological Record* from 1959 to 1962. Kellogg has been president of the Indiana University and Florida State University chapters of the science research fraternity Sigma Xi. He also belongs to Sigma Delta Chi and Kappa Sigma.

Winthrop Niles Kellogg and Luella Dorothy Agger were married on December 24, 1920. They had in addition to Donald Agger two children, Jack Stanley, who is no longer living, and Shirley Mae (Mrs. Peter Ingalls). Kellogg is a Republican and a Methodist. He is five feet nine inches tall, weighs 195 pounds, and has blue eyes and brown hair. His hobbies are sailboating and photography.

References

American Men of Science 10th ed (1960-62)
Ethridge, James M. Contemporary Authors (1962)
Who's Who in America, 1962-63
Who's Who in the South and Southwest (1961)

KENDREW, JOHN C(OWDERY) Mar. 24, 1917- British scientist
Address: b. Medical Research Council Laboratory of Molecular Biology, Hills Rd., Cambridge, England; h. 12 Tennis Court Rd., Cambridge, England

Man's understanding of the life process has been increased appreciably in recent years by a string of discoveries relating to basic elements in that process. One of the most important of these discoveries is the determination of the structure of myoglobin by John C. Kendrew, who shared the 1962 Nobel Prize for Chemistry for this work. Myoglobin is one of the globular proteins that absorb oxygen and release it in the blood. Kendrew's deductions about the structure of the myoglobin molecule represent a long stride toward an understanding of how the proteins do their vital work.

Kendrew is deputy chairman of the Medical Research Council's laboratory of molecular biology at Cambridge University, England, and head of the laboratory's structural studies division. He has been working on the structure of myoglobin since 1946. Previously, during World War II, he served as a scientist with the Ministry of Aircraft Production. He still acts as an adviser to the Ministry of Defense and is also a reader at the Royal Institution, editor in chief of the *Journal of Molecular Biology*, and a fellow of the Royal Society. In 1963 he was named a Commander of the Order of the British Empire.

(Continued next page)

B. Gaye

JOHN C. KENDREW

John Cowdery Kendrew was born on March 24, 1917 in Oxford, England, the only child of Wilfrid George Kendrew, a noted climatologist, and his wife, the former Evelyn May Graham Sandberg, an art historian. He went to the Dragon School in Oxford and, for his secondary education, to Clifton College in Bristol. When he graduated from Clifton in 1936, he had already settled on a scientific career. Accordingly, in spite of his Oxford background, he elected to continue his education at Cambridge, which is pre-eminent among English universities in its science program. At Trinity College, Cambridge, where he was senior scholar, Kendrew read for the natural sciences tripos, a two-part examination in which the second part is open only to students who secure honors in the first. Kendrew earned his B.A. degree in 1939 with first class honors in both parts of the tripos. He obtained his M.A. degree in 1943.

Meanwhile, in 1940—a year after the outbreak of World War II—Kendrew had joined the Ministry of Aircraft Production as a junior scientific officer. His work there—reportedly in the field of operations analysis—led him in 1944 to the post of scientific adviser to the Allied Air Commander in Chief, Southeast Asia. At the end of the war in 1945, Kendrew returned to civilian life with the honorary rank of a wing commander in the Royal Air Force. Back at Cambridge, he went to work with Dr. M. F. Perutz in the university's Cavendish Laboratory. He has been at Cambridge ever since. In 1947 Kendrew was elected a fellow of Peterhouse College, Cambridge. He earned his Ph.D. degree in physics in 1949 and his D.Sc. degree in 1962.

The work on which Kendrew embarked when he joined Perutz in 1946 was in the field of X-ray crystallography. Perutz, who had been working in the field for many years, was at that time an Imperial Chemical Industries research fellow. Recognition of the value of the work came in October 1947, when the Medical Research Council's unit for molecular biology was established at the Cavendish Laboratory. The unit at first consisted solely of Kendrew and Perutz, but in time other scientists joined them in the unused shed that had become their laboratory, and research groups elsewhere became involved in their investigations. In March 1962 the unit became the Medical Research Council laboratory of molecular biology and moved into modern quarters at the Cambridge University Postgraduate Medical School.

X-ray crystallography is a technique used to determine the atomic structure of substances. A crystal of the substance under investigation is revolved in a beam of X-rays. In their passage through the crystal, the rays are scattered or diffracted by the electrons that form the outer part of the crystal's component atoms. The rays then fall upon a photographic plate, forming a pattern that gives a clue to the atomic structure of the crystal. According to the New York Times (November 2, 1962), one scientist has described the technique as similar to "bouncing tennis balls off an intricate building and trying to decide what the building looks like from where the tennis balls finally end up."

Perutz had been trying since 1937 to elucidate, by this method, the structure of a protein called hemoglobin. Kendrew's project was a considerably simpler protein—myoglobin, the substance that holds oxygen in the muscles. It is found in great quantities in the muscles of whales and seals and accounts for their ability to dive for prolonged periods. The myoglobin molecule, it was known, consisted of some 150 amino acid units strung together like beads on a wire. These 150 units are made up of about 2,600 atoms of hydrogen, nitrogen, carbon, oxygen, and sulphur. This "string of beads," moreover, is not straight but intricately coiled, like a length of wire that has been crushed into a rough ball. Kendrew's task was to identify the position of each atom in the myoglobin molecule and to plot the molecule's shape.

Proteins are of fundamental importance in the life process. In an article in Scientific American (December 1961), Kendrew wrote: "In a real sense proteins are the 'works' of living cells. Almost all chemical reactions that take place in cells are catalyzed by enzymes, and all known enzymes are proteins." By establishing the structure and three-dimensional shape of myoglobin and hemoglobin, the Cambridge group would be taking an important step towards understanding how they function. But the technique of X-ray crystallography, originated in 1912, was imperfect, leaving one factor in the complex process unresolved. Good results had been obtained by trial and error with such relatively simple molecules as that of vitamin B_{12}, which is made up of about ninety atoms. But for Kendrew, working with a 2,600-atom molecule, the process was inadequate.

The breakthrough came in 1953. Perutz discovered that atoms of mercury, introduced into his hemoglobin crystals, produced a measurable difference in the resulting X-ray patterns. By comparing these patterns with those produced by ordinary hemoglobin crystals and applying an existing mathematical technique, Perutz found a way to eliminate error and guesswork in the interpretation of crystalline structure.

Differences between hemoglobin and myoglobin made it impossible for Kendrew and his assistants to adopt Perutz's method outright. By experimenting, however, Kendrew found that while mercury atoms could not be attached to the myoglobin molecule, certain other heavy atoms could, and with similar effect. The comparative process began. Kendrew took 400 X-ray pictures of an ordinary myoglobin molecule crystal, then 400 of each of five crystals to which heavy atoms had been attached. Then, using Cambridge's EDSAC Mark I computer, Kendrew worked out the density of the molecule at 4,000 different points, plotting the results on a transparent layered map. They showed the belt of highest density, which represented the molecule's main atomic chain. In 1957, from this map, Kendrew was able to build his first model of the molecule, showing its shape but not the location of its constituent atoms. Continuing his research, Kendrew made 10,000 X-ray photographs of the ordinary crystal and the same number of each of the crystals containing heavy atoms. Just in time, Cambridge brought in its EDSAC Mark II computers, which were far faster than the EDSAC Mark I model. Even so, the resulting computations occupied six people for many months.

Kendrew's model of the myoglobin molecule, showing the position of almost every atom, was completed in 1959. His findings were published in the British scientific magazine Nature on February 13, 1960. In the same issue appeared an account of Perutz's necessarily less detailed study of the more complex hemoglobin molecule. The two proteins, performing different functions in different animals, showed a basic similarity in their structures.

For their achievements, Kendrew and Perutz were awarded the Nobel Prize for Chemistry, amounting to nearly $50,000, on November 1, 1962. Kendrew does not regard his work with myoglobin as complete, and he is working towards an even more detailed and revealing analysis of the protein. But, he wrote in Scientific American (December 1961): "Even in the present incomplete state of our studies on myoglobin we are beginning to think of a protein molecule in terms of its three-dimensional chemical structure and hence to find rational explanations for its chemical behavior and physiological function, to understand its affinities with related proteins and to glimpse the problems involved in explaining the synthesis of proteins in living organisms and the nature of the malfunctions resulting from errors in this process. . . . The prospect of establishing a firm basis for an understanding of the enormous complexities of structure, of biogenesis and of function of living organisms in health and disease is now distinctly in view."

Kendrew has been since 1962 the deputy chairman of the Medical Research Council's laboratory of molecular biology and head of its structural studies division. He has served since 1960 as a part-time scientific adviser to the Ministry of Defence and since 1954 as a reader at the Davy-Faraday Laboratory of the Royal Institution, London, which has made important contributions to research in protein structure. A contributor to many scientific journals, he is the editor in chief of the Journal of Molecular Biology. Kendrew is a fellow of the Royal Society, an honorary member of the American Society of Biological Chemists, honorary secretary of the British Biophysical Society, and a member of the council of the Biophysical Society (United States). On June 8, 1963, in Queen Elizabeth's "birthday honours," he was named a C.B.E.

Kendrew, who is unmarried, lists his recreations as skiing and listening to music. He has a large collection of records, mostly classical. He has gray eyes, weighs 147 pounds, and is five feet ten inches tall. The New York Times (November 2, 1962) describes him as a "mild-mannered scientist, far from the public stereotype. Quiet and sensitive, with some gray hair but still youthful in appearance, he . . . does quite a bit of traveling . . . [and] has been to the United States several times."

References

N Y Times p19 N 2 '62 por
Who's Who, 1963

KENNEDY, EDWARD M(OORE) Feb. 22, 1932- United States Senator from Massachusetts
Address: b. Senate Office Bldg., Washington 25, D.C.; h. 1336 31st St., N.W., Washington, D.C.

The youngest of the children of Joseph P. Kennedy and, according to the President of the United States, the best politician in the family, is Edward M. Kennedy, the junior Senator from Massachusetts. Teddy Kennedy won the Senate seat formerly held by his brother John in November 1962, after an election campaign in which he was criticized as a brashly ambitious youth trading on his brother's name and his father's money. Since assuming his Senate seat, however, Kennedy has made a determined effort to play the modest role of a freshman Senator rather than the brother of President John F. Kennedy.

Edward Moore Kennedy was born in Brookline, Massachusetts, a suburb of Boston, on February 22, 1932, the youngest of nine children of Joseph P. and Rose (Fitzgerald) Kennedy. His maternal grandfather was John F. ("Honey Fitz") Fitzgerald, a former mayor of Boston. His paternal grandfather, Patrick J. Kennedy, had served in both houses of the Massachusetts state legislature. Joseph P. Kennedy was appointed by President Franklin D. Roosevelt as chairman of the Securities and Exchange Commission in 1933 and as Ambassador to Great Britain in 1937. He also founded a family fortune that enabled him to set up trust funds giving each of his children $1,000,000 when they reached maturity.

Ted Kennedy's oldest brother, Joseph P., Jr., was killed as a World War II Navy pilot in Europe. His two surviving older brothers are President John F. Kennedy and United States Attorney General Robert F. Kennedy. There were also five sisters: Kathleen, who married the

Halsman, New York City

EDWARD M. KENNEDY

Marquess of Hartington and died in a plane crash in France in 1948; Rosemary, now living in an institution for the mentally retarded; Eunice, who is married to R. Sargent Shriver, Jr.; Patricia, the wife of the actor Peter Lawford; and Jean, the wife of Stephen Smith. As the youngest of nine children in a highly competitive household, Teddy enjoyed no special privileges. He supplemented his ten cent weekly allowance (later increased to a quarter) by earning extra cash for mowing lawns and delivering newspapers. "Even as a child, Ted had a terrific animal energy," his sister Jean has recalled. "You never had to push Ted—you always had to hold him back."

The Kennedys are prominent Roman Catholics, and Teddy received his first communion from Pope Pius XII. Like his brothers, however, he received a secular rather than a parochial education. He also absorbed politics by listening to the rough-and-ready arguments at the family dinner table on domestic and international affairs. Ted Kennedy attended school in England while his father was Ambassador there and, after brief periods in several other schools, including the Milton Academy, a co-educational private school near Boston, he entered Harvard University.

As a freshman at Harvard in the spring of 1951, Kennedy asked a classmate to take an examination for him in Spanish, one of his weaker subjects. The friend was caught, and both boys were suspended. Kennedy then served a two-year hitch in the Army in France and Germany. Readmitted to Harvard after his discharge as a private first class in 1953, Kennedy excelled in public speaking and earned honor grades in history and government during his senior year. As the first-string end on the football team, Kennedy caught a touchdown pass for Harvard's only score in its 21-7 loss to Yale in 1955. He graduated with a B.A. degree in 1956.

Later, during his primary campaign for the Democratic Senatorial nomination in 1962, Kennedy openly admitted the incident that had led to his suspension, and it never became an election issue.

Unable to gain admission to the Harvard Law School, Kennedy spent a year at the International Law Institute at The Hague, in the Netherlands. In 1956 he also spent some time in North Africa as a reporter for the International News Service. Upon his return to the United States he entered the University of Virginia Law School, which granted him his LL.B. degree in 1959. In applying for admission to the Massachusetts bar, Kennedy already indicated the direction his career was to take. "Service in public life," he wrote, "can best be accomplished by an understanding of the legal process, its procedures, functions and limitations. My ambition lies in the public service of this state."

Edward M. Kennedy's first professional exposure to politics came in 1958, while he was still in law school, when he served as campaign manager for his brother John, who was then seeking a second term as Senator from Massachusetts. Ted Kennedy's enthusiasm and performance in this campaign, which culminated in a landslide victory for John F. Kennedy, established his reputation as an adroit politician. In 1960 Ted Kennedy was chosen for the job of co-ordinating the Western states in John F. Kennedy's drive for votes to win the Democratic Presidential nomination, and later, the November election. During the course of the campaign, Ted Kennedy barnstormed through the West in a plane that he piloted himself; rode a bucking bronco in a Montana rodeo; and landed on his feet after making the first ski jump in his life.

In December 1960, traveling at his own expense, Ted Kennedy accompanied members of the Senate Foreign Relations Committee on a fact-finding tour of Africa. He took his first position as a lawyer when he became an assistant to District Attorney Garrett H. Byrne of Suffolk County, Massachusetts, waiving the state salary of $5,000 to serve as a dollar-a-year man. In the summer of 1961 he toured Latin American countries and spoke with students, government officials, and labor leaders. Early in 1962 he visited France, West Germany, Ireland, Belgium, Greece, Poland, and Israel, studying the possible effects of the European Common Market upon industry and employment in Massachusetts.

Originally Edward M. Kennedy had intended to make his first bid for elective office as a candidate for a seat in the House of Representatives. In March 1962, however, he formally announced his candidacy for the seat in the United States Senate previously occupied by his brother and resigned his position as assistant district attorney at the same time. (After John F. Kennedy had been elected President in 1960 Benjamin A. Smith 2d was appointed to occupy the seat on an interim basis until the 1962 election, when the voters would decide who was to occupy it for the remaining two years of the unexpired term.) Ted Kennedy was then just thirty years old, the minimum age for a United States Senator, and his announcement aroused opposition from Republicans and many liberals alike. James Reston, the Washington correspondent of the New York *Times*, wrote: "Teddy's bid for the Senate, at 30 years of age, with the careful connivance of the President, is widely regarded as an affront and a presumption. . . . In the end it is likely to cost the President more votes in the Senate than Teddy will ever give him" (September 21, 1962).

According to *Time* (September 28, 1962), it was Joseph P. Kennedy, Sr., who insisted that his youngest son be given the opportunity to run. Another explanation was forthcoming from Stewart Alsop, who wrote in the *Saturday Evening Post* (October 27, 1962) that the decision was largely determined by a private poll of Massachusetts voters, indicating that the other Democratic aspirant for the Senate seat—Edward J. McCormack, Jr., the Massachusetts attorney-general and nephew of the speaker of the House, John W. McCormack—would probably be defeated by the leading Republican hopeful, George Cabot Lodge, son of the Ambassador and former Senator Henry Cabot Lodge, Jr. The poll also indicated that Ted Kennedy, whose extensive speech-making and campaigning across the state had already made him a well-known figure, could win both the nomination and the election.

Ted Kennedy won the endorsement of the Massachusetts state Democratic convention, at Springfield in June 1962, on the first ballot, and immediately found himself entered in a state-wide primary against McCormack. In the first of two televised "Teddy-Eddie debates" McCormack attacked his opponent with what Robert J. Donovan described in the New York *Herald Tribune* (August 31, 1962) as "a ferocity seldom seen in televised politics." At the start of the debate, McCormack turned to Kennedy and told him: "You never worked for a living. You never held elective office . . . . You lack the qualifications, the maturity of judgment." Then, turning to the audience, McCormack said that if his opponent's name were anything but Kennedy, "his candidacy would be a joke." To indicate his support of the President despite his opposition to the younger Kennedy, McCormack campaigned with the slogan "I back Jack, but Teddy isn't ready."

The attack boomeranged. "Kennedy played it cool under fire," Donovan wrote. "He took the blast with composure and dignity. And to complete the irony of the whole affair, the young man whose qualifications are justly in question looked more like a Senator than he had ever looked before." The vote itself turned out to be no contest. On September 18, 1962 Kennedy won the primary election with a stunning 69 percent of the votes. After the primary a writer for *Time* (September 28, 1962) commented: "Buoyed up by his father's unwavering support, backed by the Kennedy wealth, Teddy also made the best of the Kennedy name, the Kennedy looks, the Kennedy manner . . . . But these qualities alone were not enough . . . . In the end, Teddy won because he staged a campaign unmatched and unmatchable in its energy, enterprise and sheer intensity of purpose."

Aided by the defeated McCormack forces, Kennedy campaigned with equal vigor against his Republican opponent, George Cabot Lodge, for the November elections, in a so-called "battle of dynasties." (In 1916 Kennedy's grandfather, John F. Fitzgerald, had been defeated in a contest for the same Senate seat by Lodge's great-grandfather, Senator Henry Cabot Lodge.) Although Kennedy's campaign slogan—"I can do more for Massachusetts"—was criticized by Lodge as carrying the implication of political patronage, Kennedy easily won the election of November 6, 1962. He received 1,143,021 votes against 863,460 for Lodge and 49,102 for the Harvard professor H. Stuart Hughes, who ran on an independent ticket emphasizing disarmament.

Sworn into office at the opening of the Eighty-eighth Congress on January 9, 1963, Kennedy became a member of the Senate Committee on Labor and Public Welfare. In the Senate he has been particularly concerned with improving economic conditions in his state through defense contract awards and other projects. On this score he has been charged by Republican Senator Kenneth B. Keating of New York with using "a strong and subtle form of pressure" in an effort to lure defense contracts away from New York to Massachusetts. Kennedy's votes during the first few months of 1963 have generally squared with administration policy. In February he voted to invoke cloture on a pending motion to take up a resolution that would change Senate Rule 22, governing the limits of debate. He also voted for the mass transit bill (April), the wilderness preservation bill (April), the upholding of the constitutional authority of the Senate to confirm the incorporators of the Communications Satellite Corporation (April), the feed-grain bill (May), and aid to distressed areas (June).

Active in civic causes, Kennedy is a trustee of Boston University and a member of the advisory board of Emmanuel College. He also serves as president of the Joseph P. Kennedy, Jr., Memorial Foundation, which supports medical causes. In 1961 he became chairman of the American Cancer Crusade in Massachusetts and chairman of the United Fund Health and Fitness Fair, and he is on the executive board of the Massachusetts chapter of the Arthritis and Rheumatism Foundation. In April 1963 he was chosen as chairman of a fund-raising campaign for a Catholic center at the University of Virginia. Kennedy also is judge advocate of the Polish-American Veterans post in Boston, and he is a member of the Pulaski Memorial Committee of Massachusetts. He belongs to the Knights of Columbus.

Edward M. Kennedy and Joan Bennett of Bronxville, New York, were married on November 29, 1959 by Francis Cardinal Spellman. Not only the youngest wife of the youngest Senator in American history, Mrs. Kennedy is also one of the most beautiful newcomers to Washington. The Kennedys have two children, a daughter, Kara, and a son, Edward M., Jr. They live in the fashionable Georgetown section of Washington and also maintain a town house in Boston and a summer home on Squaw Island, near Hyannis Port, Massachusetts. Described by Stewart Alsop in the *Saturday Evening Post* (October 27, 1962) as "a *very* handsome man . . . decidedly better-looking than his brothers, with the precisely balanced features of the old Arrow-collar ads," Teddy Kennedy is six feet two inches

KENNEDY, EDWARD M.—*Continued*

tall and weighs 210 pounds. He enjoys swimming, sailing, golf, reading, and listening to records.

Despite one incident in February 1963, in which he snatched the camera of a newspaper photographer who had snapped an unauthorized picture of him at a skiing resort in Stowe, Vermont (an incident for which Kennedy later apologized), and an earlier incident, when he reportedly jumped fully clothed into a swimming pool at the home of his brother Robert F. Kennedy, the junior Senator from Massachusetts has generally avoided the limelight. He is fully aware of the handicaps as well as the advantages of being the first United States Senator in American history with a brother in the White House. As Richard Starnes wrote in the New York *World-Telegram* (April 13, 1962), after an interview: "Teddy Kennedy is rigidly determined to emerge from the thicket of legend that has been created by others of the clan, and to commence cultivation on his own."

References

Cong Q 20:2008 O 19 '62 por
N Y Herald Tribune II pl+ Ag 4 '63 pors
N Y Post p50 Mr 16 '62 por
N Y Times p27 Mr 15 '62 por
Sat Eve Post 236:55+ Ja 19 '63 pors
Time 80:14+ S 28 '62 pors
Congressional Directory (1963)
International Who's Who, 1962-63

KENNEDY, THOMAS Nov. 2, 1887-Jan. 19, 1963 Labor leader; was active in the Democratic party and served as Lieutenant Governor of Pennsylvania (1935-39); a lifelong officer of the United Mine Workers of America, of which he became president in 1960. See *Current Biography* (June) 1960.

Obituary

N Y Times p35 Ap 1 '63

KEPPEL, FRANCIS Apr. 16, 1916- United States Commissioner of Education; educator

Address: b. Office of Education, Department of Health, Education, and Welfare, Washington 25, D.C.

To answer the urgent need for effective leadership in national education, President John F. Kennedy appointed Francis Keppel in November 1962 as United States Commissioner of Education. In succeeding Sterling M. McMurrin in the difficult post of head of the Office of Education, which has often been a center of controversies and administrative frustrations, Keppel has the qualifications of fourteen years' experience as dean of Harvard University's Graduate School of Education. He earned his present stature among educators by making the school a pacesetter of teacher training for the nation.

Francis Keppel was born in New York City on April 16, 1916, the oldest of five sons of Frederick P. and Helen Tracy (Brown) Keppel. His father

was at that time dean of Columbia College and later, in 1923, became president of the Carnegie Corporation of New York, a foundation for the advancement of higher education. A forward-looking educator and administrator, he encouraged the study of fine arts, organized the American Association for Adult Education, and had some part in initiating Gunnar Myrdal's study of the Negro, *The American Dilemma* (1944).

The intellectual atmosphere in which Keppel grew up was marked by stimulating concern for educational reform. He was reared in New York City and in Montrose, Westchester County, where the family had a home, "Bally Vale." He attended Groton School in Groton, Massachusetts and in 1934 entered Harvard College, from which he graduated four years later with the B.A. degree, his only earned degree. As an undergraduate he had made frequent trips to New York for sculpture lessons. Still interested in sculpturing, after obtaining his degree from Harvard he went to Italy, where he studied at the American Academy in Rome. Becoming aware of his limitations as a sculptor, he returned home after one year.

At Harvard, again, Keppel was employed as assistant dean of freshmen from 1939 until 1941. During part of World War II, from 1941 to 1944, he was secretary of the Joint Army-Navy Committee on Welfare and Recreation in Washington. In 1944 he entered the United States Army's Information and Education Division as a private. He was discharged two years later, in 1946, with the rank of first lieutenant. Returning once more to Harvard after his discharge, he held the position of assistant to the provost of the university during the years from 1946 to 1948.

When Francis Keppel was appointed dean of the Graduate School of Education at Harvard University in June 1948, he was just thirty-two years old. Dr. James Bryant Conant, then Harvard's president, had been seeking a topflight educational administrator to head the Graduate School of Education, but had met with no success. Keppel, whom Conant assigned to the problem, met with the same lack of interest on the part of those educators most sought after. The imagination and enthusiasm shown by his young administrative assistant so impressed Conant, however, that he stopped looking elsewhere and named Keppel himself to the deanship. His task was to equip the school with a revitalized curriculum, increase its endowments, and raise its prestige.

To a marked degree, the development and expansion of the Graduate School of Education expresses graphically the last fourteen years of Francis Keppel's career at Harvard. In the years between 1948 and 1962, full-time enrollment more than quadrupled and admissions applications increased tenfold. During the same period, the faculty, too, quadrupled in size and endowment more than doubled. In 1962 the school enrolled 670 students, more than three-quarters of them on a full-time basis, compared with 39 percent in 1948. More than half of the eighty-three faculty members represented the learned disciplines. Endowment was increased to almost $6,000,000. Also under Keppel, plans were made for the school to occupy in 1963-64 a new campus, the cost of which was estimated at nearly $3,000,000.

As dean, Keppel guided research programs and directed the training of school teachers, administrators, and other educational specialists. In its renascence under his direction, the Graduate School of Education, which had been established in 1920, became a leading institution both for young students acquiring the knowledge and skills needed to begin educational careers, and for experienced teachers and administrators engaged in advanced study and research. Among the more notable alumni, Keppel can include the state commissioners of education of New York and Massachusetts, six city school superintendents —including New York City—and several college presidents.

In his article in *School and Society* (March 9, 1963) Professor Franklin Parker has told in some detail how Keppel changed the character of the Graduate School of Education. Building on the foundation laid by Conant in 1936, Keppel redesigned the Master of Arts in Teaching Program (MAT) to meet the demands and developments taking place in the second half of the century. Conant had tried to attract promising liberal arts graduates into teaching and to bring scholars into touch with public school educators. Keppel realized, however, that not enough liberal arts graduates entered teaching. Many who entered, left the field because of lack of status, inadequate salary, and absence of a recognizable sequence of professional advancement. Keppel saw that in industry, career patterns were based on salary and status rewards for talented people who were willing and able to advance in responsibility. To change the public image of the teaching profession he advocated a direct linking of salary increments to levels of responsibility.

As the first step, Keppel improved recruiting techniques. He linked MAT to twenty-nine (by 1962 the number had increased to forty-five) co-operating liberal arts colleges through the Twenty-Nine College Cooperative Plan. Next, he encouraged participating graduate students to plan their integrated programs early. They prepare for secondary school teaching by study— subject matter and education courses—and by professional salaried internships, carrying progressively increasing responsibility in classroom teaching. Keppel generated interest in the public school curriculum among liberal arts faculty both in co-operating institutions and at Harvard. The MAT program, itself, is administered by the faculty of education and the faculty of arts and sciences. A similar program, Master of Education for Elementary Teaching, was inaugurated in 1951.

In 1957 Keppel created the School and University Program for Research and Development (SUPRAD) to serve as a permanent institutional mechanism for experimenting and improving the areas of teacher training, the learning process, curriculum, and administration. Its members include teachers from the Graduate School of Education and local and regional public school officials and representatives. Since its inception SUPRAD has engaged in some two dozen pilot

Dept. of Health, Education, and Welfare—S. Stanton Singer

FRANCIS KEPPEL

projects, ranging from team teaching and programmed learning to high school mathematics taught by teaching machines.

Keppel regards "the public high school as the educational taproot of American democracy," as Professor Parker has noted. He is a dedicated participant in the struggle to teach Johnny to read. In May 1956 he served as chairman of the Princeton Conference, which brought together just those feuding factions within the world of education—the educationists and representatives of the liberal arts—who had been accusing each other of responsibility for Johnny's inability to read. Keppel deliberately avoided joining battle with either the critics or the supporters of American education. Rather, he focused attention on areas of mutual understanding, conciliation, and the need for scholars and schools to work together. An academic civil war, he warned, would serve only to weaken education, one of the most important instruments of democracy.

The ultimate purpose of programs such as MAT and SUPRAD is to turn out pupils of rising quality. Research-minded as he is, Kepel is quick to warn against miraculous panaceas. Recognizing the need for constant experimentation to solve problems, he cautions against shaky research and premature conclusions in the guise of educational utopias. In 1961 he found that the American public's stultifying complacency of a few years before had turned to mass concern for rebuilding of quality in the schools. At the same time he noted a concomitant tendency for new ideas to become fads before they became facts. Keppel urges the exercise of suspended judgment with respect to unproved promises of quick, inexpensive educational solutions, whether in the form of teaching machines, language laboratories, or team teaching. The alternative to naïve enthusiasm, he fears, may be public and profes-

KEPPEL, FRANCIS—*Continued*

sional disillusionment opposing any further change.

With the appointment in November 1962 of Francis Keppel as United States Commissioner of Education, observers in Washington looked for innovation, although not radical or dramatic, at the Office of Education. Created in 1867, the agency was attached at first to the Department of Interior and from 1939 to 1953 to the Federal Security Agency. In 1953 it became a unit within the Department of Health, Education, and Welfare. An internal reappraisal of the office in 1961 acknowledged its general ineffectiveness and inability to render leadership in the process of shaping national educational goals and policies. Kennedy's first appointee, Sterling M. McMurrin resigned in July 1962 after he had held the commissioner's post a little more than one year, complaining of bureaucracy, insufficient appropriations, and lack of co-operation from government officials and educational associations. Keppel accepted the appointment on November 24, amid rumors of increased status and authoritative powers for both the commissioner and the Office of Education.

Keppel favors federal aid to education as a means of equalizing educational opportunities. He is keenly aware that regional and local financial differences, especially in urban slum areas, give rise to problems that are beyond the scope and resources of these areas to handle. He believes federal funds are necessary to help raise the national quality of education. Increased federal influence, while a concomitant of increased federal spending, need not, according to Keppel, prove inimical to local control.

Like McGeorge Bundy, another Harvard dean, who went to Washington in 1961, Keppel has entered upon his successive posts without the usual advanced degrees. His lack of a doctorate has apparently not adversely affected his career. Keppel relies upon the practical experience gained from his work at Harvard and from the numerous advisory and consultant positions he has also held, both on the national and international scenes. In 1950 President Truman appointed him to the Committee on Religion and Welfare in the Armed Forces. He was named to the executive committee of the National Council of Administrative Leadership in 1956 and the following year attended the Twentieth International Conference on Public Education held in Geneva, Switzerland. During the years from 1957 to 1959 he was chairman of the Council of Cooperation in Teacher Education. In 1960 he served on an educational commission for the Nigerian government and on President Kennedy's task force on education.

In the spring of 1962 Keppel was appointed chairman of the Committee of Consultants for Selection of a Superintendent of the Schools for New York City. The committee chose Dr. Calvin E. Gross, an alumnus of the Harvard Graduate School of Education. Keppel has been a member of the panel on educational research and development of the President's Science Advisory Committee. He has been a trustee of Sarah Lawrence College and Simmons College. In 1957 he received the honorary LL.D. degree from Hamline

University. He is a member of Phi Beta Kappa and Phi Delta Kappa and a Fellow of the American Academy of Arts and Sciences. He has contributed articles to educational journals, and his Horace Mann Lecture of 1961 was published as *Personnel Policies for Public Education* (Univ. of Pittsburgh Press, 1962).

On July 19, 1941 Francis Keppel married Edith Moulton Sawin. They have two daughters, Edith Tracy Drury (Mrs. Samuel S. Drury, Jr.) and Susan Moulton Keppel. He is a Democrat. Possessed of a somewhat dry sense of humor, he confirmed the rumors that he was leaving Harvard for Washington by announcing his small contribution to easing the campus parking problem. His club is the Century Association in New York. He is a dapper, vigorous, and imaginative man, a chain smoker, and a prodigious worker.

References

Nat Observer p1+ D 3 '62
Pub W 182:25 D 3 '62
Sch & Soc 91:126+ Mr 9 '63
Time 88:66 N 30 '62 por
Who's Who in America, 1962-63
Who's Who in American Education, 1959-60

KERR, ROBERT S(AMUEL) Sept. 11, 1896-Jan. 1, 1963 Oil industrialist; Democratic Governor of Oklahoma (1943-47); United States Senator (since 1949); chairman of the Committee on Aeronautical and Space Sciences. See *Current Biography* (May) 1950.

Obituary

N Y Times p35+ Ap 1 '63

KESSING, O(LIVER) O(WEN) Dec. 6, 1890-Jan. 31, 1963 Commissioner and president of the now defunct All-America Football Conference in 1949 and 1950; retired as Admiral of the United States Navy in 1947 after a career of thirty-seven years. See *Current Biography* (June) 1949.

Obituary

Washington (D.C.) Post C p4 F 2 '63

KIMBREL, M(ARVIN) MONROE Aug. 4, 1916- Banker; organization official
Address: b. First National Bank, Thomson, Ga.

M. Monroe Kimbrel, who was head of the American Bankers Association in 1962-63, was one of the youngest presidents to serve in the association's history. A self-styled "country banker," he comes from probably the smallest bank to have produced an A.B.A. president: the First National Bank of Thomson, Georgia, of which he is board chairman, has deposits of less than $5,000,000. Kimbrel served as vice-president of the A.B.A. in 1961-62, and he succeeded Sam M. Fleming as president in September 1962.

The only child of Charlie Clarence and Effie (Folds) Kimbrel, Marvin Monroe Kimbrel was born on August 4, 1916 on his father's farm near

Colquitt, Miller County, Georgia. He attended Miller County High School in Colquitt, where he played baseball and took part in debates, and by the time he was ready for college in 1933 he had already decided to become a country banker. Kimbrel drove a tractor and did other farm chores to raise enough money for a round-trip ticket to the University of Georgia at Athens and a small reserve. When he succumbed to temptation and bought a new bicycle with some of the money, he showed an early ability to handle investments by selling the bike at a profit. He had $95 when he went off to college.

At the University of Georgia he waited on tables and held other jobs to pay his way through school. He obtained his B.S. degree in agricultural economics in three years and was graduated in 1936 in the top 5 percent of his class. His first job was with the Farm Credit Administration in Columbia, South Carolina, where he started as an $80-a-month credit examiner. The pay was low, but he regards the nine years he spent with the farm loan agency as "wonderful experience."

While traveling for the FCA, Kimbrel was assigned temporarily to Thomson, Georgia, where he met his future wife, who was then a cashier with the Georgia Power Company. About 1946 the Kimbrels settled in Thomson, and Kimbrel, having resigned from the FCA, accepted a position as cashier with the First National Bank of Thomson. After successive promotions to vice-president and cashier, and executive vice-president he became in January 1961 chairman of the board and chief executive officer. "I like working in a small bank," Kimbrel explained to an interviewer (Atlanta *Journal and Constitution Magazine*, February 3, 1963). "I feel I can make a real contribution to the economic life of our country here. Most of the banks in our country are small—about ten thousand of them have deposits of only $10,000,000 or less. As a country banker I am familiar with their problems."

In 1947, 1948, and 1949 Kimbrel took courses in commercial banking at the Stonier Graduate School of Banking, which the American Bankers Association conducts at Rutgers University in New Brunswick, New Jersey for bankers on the officer level. He graduated with a certificate in 1949, and his thesis, "Financing the Dairy Industry in Georgia," was selected for library distribution. The thesis is indicative of Kimbrel's concern for the role of banks in supporting agricultural development. The bank of which he is chairman was in 1955 the winner of the Robert Strickland Agricultural Memorial Award, given each year to a Georgia bank for outstanding contributions to farm financing. The winners of the award have formed a scholarship committee, of which Kimbrel is chairman, to aid students at the University of Georgia's College of Agriculture. Kimbrel has also been honored by the Future Farmers of America and by the Georgia Association of Future Homemakers of America. He is a member of the Georgia state advisory committee for Agricultural Extension Service.

Even before Kimbrel was elected to the presidency of the American Bankers Association in September 1962, a writer for *Southern Banker* (February 1961) observed that "his record of

M. MONROE KIMBREL

service already rendered to his profession and to his community might appear to be the accomplishments of a lifetime." In the A.B.A. he had been a member of several committees of the agricultural commission from 1950 to 1952, of the state legislative committee from 1957 to 1961, and of the federal deposit insurance committee; vice-president for Georgia from 1951 to 1953; and regional vice-president from 1953 to 1955. As a member of the A.B.A.'s federal legislative committee since 1955 and as its chairman from 1957 to 1961, he was a leader in helping commercial banks work for the passage of a tax equality bill in Congress. He had also served in 1955-56 as vice-president and in 1956-57 as president of the Georgia Bankers Association.

Monroe Kimbrel was the vice-president of the American Bankers Association in 1961-62, and in September 1962 he was elected president for the following year to succeed Sam M. Fleming. In his new post he expected to exceed the distance of 82,000 miles he had traveled, mostly by air, as vice-president in order to speak on many subjects of interest to bankers. On November 13, 1962, at a dinner honoring him, Kimbrel declared himself in favor of tax reduction as the best method of promoting long-range economic growth in the United States.

Several months later, in March 1963, he observed that President John F. Kennedy's tax reduction proposals "should be acceptable to most segments of the economy," but that the President's suggestions for tax reform "would, if passed, make the entire tax package weighted too heavily on the side of consumption." While disagreeing with those "who think government expenditures should be reduced by the amount of the tax cut," Kimbrel charged that the administration had "failed to tighten the purse strings on expenditures which—although they might be desirable—are not absolutely necessary."

(Continued next page)

KIMBREL, M. MONROE—*Continued*

Addressing a conference sponsored by the A.B.A.'s agricultural committee on November 12, 1962, Kimbrel urged bankers to ensure that their institutions would be able to continue operations in the event of a nuclear attack. He also stressed the importance for small banks of meeting increasing competition by securing "a sound and capable bank management." These banks, he said, should be prepared to pay well to attract good men and, having hired them, should "give them as much training as possible." Kimbrel discussed the educational facilities open to bankers in the A.B.A.'s American Institute of Banking, which he called "the largest adult education program in the world sponsored by an industry." He noted, "In a small bank like mine, it is difficult to free a man for educational activities. . . . However, we found the cost and inconvenience to the bank are more than worthwhile." In subsequent speeches to A.B.A. groups, Kimbrel discussed the United States balance-of-payment problem and deplored the action of the President of France, Charles de Gaulle, in vetoing the entry of Great Britain into the Common Market.

As president of the American Bankers Association, Monroe Kimbrel headed an organization whose membership on August 31, 1962—the end of its fiscal year—numbered 17,582 banks and branches, including 108 members in foreign countries, and comprised over 95 percent of the banks in the United States. Fundamentally an organization "to promote the usefulness of banks," the A.B.A., through twenty-three standing committees, issues studies and reports covering the whole gamut of the banking industry, including federal and state legislation, agricultural financing, bank management, credit policy, economic policy, installment credit, insurance, mortgage financing, and personnel administration. In 1961-62 the A.B.A.'s American Institute of Banking gave courses for bank personnel through chapters and study groups in 570 American cities and towns and through correspondence study. In addition to the institute and the Stonier Graduate School of Banking, the A.B.A. sponsors the National Trust School, conducted at Northwestern University in Evanston, Illinois. It publishes the monthly magazine *Banking*.

Monroe Kimbrel believes that bankers should take part in the affairs of their communities, and he himself has done so. He has served for five years on the McDuffie County Board of Education and has been president of the Rotary Club of Thomson and district governor of Rotary International (1951-52). He has taught a men's Bible class at the Methodist Church in Thomson, of which he is a steward and district lay leader; served as vice-president of the Georgia-Carolina Council of Boy Scouts of America; and acted as a director of the Georgia State YMCA. He is also a member of the board of the Federal Reserve Bank of Atlanta and a trustee of the School of Banking of the South. He is a Democrat. Kimbrel has lectured at banking schools in Georgia, the Carolinas, Pennsylvania, Virginia, and West Virginia, and at the Stonier Graduate School of Banking.

M. Monroe Kimbrel and the former Nita Matlock, whom he married on April 17, 1941, have two children, Jenny Wood and Charles Daniel. Kimbrel has blue eyes and brown hair, stands five feet eleven inches tall, and weighs 145 pounds. He has been described as a "friendly, chatty, personable man who is equally at ease with Wall Street tycoons and overall-clad farmers" (Atlanta *Journal and Constitution Magazine*, February 3, 1963). He is known to most of Thomson's 5,000 inhabitants by his nickname, "Bones." He enjoys fishing, boating, and an occasional game of golf.

Often asked about the factors that led to his success in his profession, Kimbrel has replied, "Hard work, I guess. I still don't know any substitute for that." He is usually in his office from 7:30 A.M. to 6:30 P.M., and he reads five newspapers regularly. "As far back as I can remember, I never had any other career in mind," he told an interviewer for the Augusta *Chronicle Herald* (October 7, 1962), "and I've always been anxious to come to work each morning."

References

Atlanta Journal and Constitution Mag p9+ F 3 '63 por
Augusta Chronicle Herald, E p8 O 7 '62 por
Banking 4:38+ O '62 pors

KIRK, ALAN GOODRICH Oct. 30, 1888-Oct. 15, 1963 United States naval officer; Chief of Staff of American naval forces in Europe during World War II; retired from the navy with the rank of admiral in 1946; United States Ambassador to the U.S.S.R. (1949-52). See *Current Biography* (July) 1944.

Obituary

N Y Times p45 O 16 '63

KRUIF, PAUL (HENRY) DE *See* De Kruif, Paul (Henry)

KUBRICK, STANLEY July 26, 1928- Motion-picture director
Address: b. c/o Harris-Kubrick Pictures Corp., 120 E. 56th St., New York 22

By using natural lighting, paying attention to the accuracy of details, and establishing an unusual rapport with actors, the director Stanley Kubrick has achieved a documentary quality rare in Hollywood films. Kubrick has been obsessively interested in photography since his high school days, and his years of experience as a still photographer for *Look* magazine gave him a knowledge of technique that helped to make him a virtuoso film director.

The youngest of the current crop of independent Hollywood film makers, Kubrick has stirred up more controversy than any director since the Orson Welles of *Citizen Kane*. He launched himself as a director at the age of twenty-two with a documentary film, *The Day of the Fight*. Since then he has directed several low-budget films such as *Fear and Desire* and *The Killing*, the harshly antiwar film *Paths of Glory*, the multimillion dollar epic *Spartacus,* and the highly controversial film version of Vladimir Nabokov's novel *Lolita.* He is especially noted for his films about soldiers and criminals, whom he finds interesting because they are "doomed from the start."

Stanley Kubrick was born on July 26, 1928 in the Bronx, New York to Jacques L. Kubrick, a doctor, and Gertrude (Perveler) Kubrick. He has a sister Barbara (Mrs. Robert Kroner). A lonely child, he spent much of his time watching movies in such local film palaces as Loew's Paradise in the Bronx. He was unhappy at William Howard Taft High School, attending classes irregularly and getting low grades, until he became the official photographer of the school newspaper. He had begun to take candid camera pictures with his father's Graflex early in adolescence; one of his first successes was a series of photographs of his English teacher reading aloud from *Hamlet.* When he was a high school junior, at sixteen, he sold his first picture to *Look* magazine for $25. It showed a grieving newsstand dealer surrounded by newspapers headlining the death of President Franklin D. Roosevelt. Before he accepted *Look's* first offer he found out if the New York *Daily News* would pay more. "They only offered ten," he told Helen O'Brian, *Look's* picture editor, "so you can have it."

After graduating from high school in 1946, Kubrick enrolled briefly at City College of the City of New York, but he left during his freshman year to join *Look's* staff at the age of seventeen. (He had been encouraged by the sale of more pictures to Helen O'Brian.) At *Look* magazine he is remembered for his haphazard modes of dress, his brash precocity, and his habit of carrying his camera in a brown paper bag so that passersby would not mistake him for a camera hobbyist with a fancy leather bag. He photographed theatrical and political celebrities, toured Portugal in quest of pictures, and covered the circus in Sarasota, Florida and Senator Robert A. Taft's pre-election barnstorming in Ohio.

By the age of twenty-one Kubrick had come to the decision that taking still pictures was "too passive" a process. After religiously studying the old movies at the Museum of Modern Art in New York City, he bought a 35-mm. newsreel camera. Aided by Alex Singer, a close friend, he made *The Day of the Fight,* a fifteen-minute documentary film about the last hours before entering the ring of Walter Cartier, a middleweight fighter. It cost Kubrick $800 to make the film, which was based on one of his own picture stories for *Look*; adding an original musical score cost him an additional $3,000. RKO Pathé bought the documentary for $4,000, and when Kubrick saw it screened at New York's Paramount Theatre he decided to spend the rest of his life making movies. He had become a director without having to go through the laborious stages that usually lead up to the profession. The executives of RKO Pathé News then agreed to back Kubrick in making a one-reel documentary called *Flying Padre,* about the Reverend Fred Stadtmueller of Mosquero, New Mexico, who flies in his Piper Cub plane to minister to his widely scattered flock. Kubrick also directed a

Universal Pictures Co., Inc.

STANLEY KUBRICK

short subject on the World Assembly of Youth for the State Department.

With youthful self-confidence Kubrick felt ready to tackle a full-length film. He persuaded a Greenwich Village poet friend, Howard O. Sackler (also a Taft High alumnus) to write a script about four soldiers trapped behind enemy lines and their search for life's meaning and the individual's responsibility to the group. To finance the project Kubrick borrowed money from his father and his uncle and, hiring relatively obscure actors and crew, shot the film on location in the San Gabriel Mountains of California. Finally entitled *Fear and Desire,* the heavily symbolical film was made for $50,000 and was rejected for distribution by every major company until Joseph Burstyn, a distributor of art films, agreed to release it. *Fear and Desire* was visually powerful but murky in meaning, and the public proved apathetic to its merits. Critical reaction was perhaps best summed up by Otis L. Guernsey, Jr., of the New York *Herald Tribune* (April 1, 1953), who wrote: "For all its faults, *Fear and Desire* is twice as constructive, twice as imaginative as most standard movies . . . a searching and original piece of work." "Pain is a good teacher," Kubrick has said of his own experience in making the film.

His second independent feature-length film was *Killer's Kiss,* a story of jealousy and revenge involving a boxer, a taxi dancer, and a racketeer. It was shot on location in the Laurel Gardens boxing arena in New Jersey, a taxi dance hall in Brooklyn, and a mannequin factory on Greene Street in Manhattan. Its production cost of $40,000 was met by Moe Bousel, an owner of two drugstores in the Bronx. *Killer's Kiss* included not only such violent action scenes as a boxing match, a rooftop chase, and a fatal fight in a mannequin factory, but also a symbolic ballet sequence and a dream sequence. Execu-

KUBRICK, STANLEY—*Continued*

tives at United Artists bought the film for $75,000 and offered to finance Kubrick in making "quickies" at $100,000 apiece.

At this point, when Kubrick had realized that visual impact was not enough and that a good story line was also necessary, he met the moneyed James B. Harris, owner with his father of Flamingo Films, a television distribution firm. The two young men established Harris-Kubrick Films Corporation with the aim of making good movies on limited budgets, and in 1955 Harris bought the screen rights of Lionel White's *Clean Break*, a novel about horse racing. Sterling Hayden agreed to play the lead, United Artists invested $200,000 in the project, and Harris contributed $120,000. *The Killing*, as the film was finally entitled, told the story of a race track robbery and multiple murder with a documentary-like realism, a freshness of vision, a precision of detail and of timing that was quickly appreciated by the critics. With Alton Cook of the New York *World-Telegram and Sun* (May 21, 1956) they noted that Kubrick had broadened his technical skill and his narrative ability, and they felt that with *The Killing* Kubrick had fulfilled the promise of his earlier films. Despite the applause from critics the film was shunned by many exhibitors, who hungered for stars. Kubrick earned only his expenses, while Harris lost part of his investment.

One of the admirers of *The Killing* was Dore Schary, head of production for Metro-Goldwyn-Mayer, who offered Kubrick and Harris a forty-week contract to find a project that they would write, direct, and produce. Kubrick selected Humphrey Cobb's bitter antiwar novel *Paths of Glory*, which every major Hollywood studio, including MGM, had rejected. After twenty weeks Kubrick and Harris left MGM and sent their script of *Paths of Glory* to Kirk Douglas who, after some rewriting of the script by Calder Willingham, agreed to star in it. Filmed in Germany on a budget of $850,000, *Paths of Glory* managed to break even after its release by United Artists and was shown in many parts of the world. It was awarded the Grand Prix de la Critique in Brussels, Belgium in January 1959. The story concerns some French generals who during World War I order a needless and futile attack for their aggrandizement and then execute three soldiers for cowardice. William K. Zinsser of the New York *Herald Tribune* (December 26, 1957) admired Kubrick's mastery of the art of cutting and the vividness and skillful composition of his scenes. Bosley Crowther of the New York *Times* (December 26, 1957) thought the "shattering candor" of Kubrick's camera made the execution scene "one of the most craftily directed and emotionally lacerating" that he had ever seen.

Another admirer of Kubrick's directing was Marlon Brando, who in May 1958 hired Kubrick to direct him in *One-Eyed Jacks*. As the months wore on it became increasingly obvious that Brando and Kubrick disagreed over the basic concept of the story. They discussed the conflict amicably, and Kubrick withdrew from *One-Eyed Jacks* on November 19, 1958. Eventually Brando himself directed the film. Unembittered by the

experience, he once said of Kubrick: "Stanley is unusually perceptive and delicately attuned to people. He has an adroit intellect, and is a creative thinker, not a repeater, not a fact-gatherer. He digests what he learns and brings to a new project an original point of view and a reserved passion."

Reluctant to repeat himself, Kubrick next turned to an epic film for Bryna Productions that was released by Universal-International. *Spartacus*, starring Kirk Douglas, Laurence Olivier, Jean Simmons, Tony Curtis, Charles Laughton, Peter Ustinov, and John Gavin, was a $12,000,000 super-spectacle about the gladiator and slave who organized an army that almost overthrew the Roman empire. Kubrick tried to direct *Spartacus* as if he were filming a *Marty*, approaching it in terms of what each scene was about and the plausible behavior of the characters. As a result, *Spartacus* remained dramatic in spite of its thousands of milling extras and huge sets. Brendan Gill of the *New Yorker* (October 15, 1960) was not the only film critic who had expected *Spartacus* to be "a big and tasteless bore," but discovered, to his astonishment that it was not. A reviewer for *Time* (October 24, 1960) deplored the film's recklessness with historical facts, but commended Kubrick's mastery of cast, camera, and cutting.

Kubrick's next production, *Lolita*, released by Metro-Goldwyn-Mayer in 1962, was curiously awaited by readers who wondered how Kubrick would transfer Vladimir Nabokov's controversial novel about a middle-aged professor's obsessive love for a "nymphet" to film. By changing the age of the girl from twelve to about seventeen, Kubrick lessened the novel's shock value and transformed the story to that of an aging man's poignant and doomed love for a teen-aged girl. His astuteness won him a seal of approval from the Production Code Administration and an approval (for adults only) from the Roman Catholic Legion of Decency. Some critics endorsed the result, but others felt that the basic theme of the novel had been destroyed. *Lolita* starred James Mason, Shelley Winters, Sue Lyon, and Peter Sellers.

The protean Peter Sellers, who played Clare Quilty in *Lolita*, will star in the next Kubrick film. Tentatively entitled *Dr. Strangelove, or How I Learned to Stop Worrying and Love the Bomb*, the film satirizes an American college professor, a "nuclear Wise Man," who rises to power in sex and politics. Kubrick has said that the theme of *Dr. Strangelove* is that there is no technical solution to the problem of the nuclear bomb.

In April 1958 Stanley Kubrick married Suzanne Christiane Harlan, a German-born actress. They have three daughters: Anya, Vivian, and Katherine (by a former marriage of the present Mrs. Kubrick). Kubrick has been married twice before. His first marriage, to Toba Metz, a Taft High School classmate, ended in divorce in 1952. His second marriage was to Ruth Sobotka, a dancer with the New York City Ballet. Weighing 155 pounds, Kubrick is five feet eight inches tall and has brown eyes and a shock of brown hair. Once noted for his unkempt appearance and mismatched clothing, he now favors neater, black suits. A solitary, he does without an entourage or a home in Beverly Hills complete with swimming pool, and he has made only one concession to material success by owning a black Mercedes. Kubrick is passionately interested in literature and music and public affairs; when he lived in furnished rooms he kept a stack of books as his only movable property. A friend once observed that Kubrick in Hollywood looks as if he should have "Made in New York" stamped on his forehead. He sets his technical standards so high that he insists on cutting his films, a task that most directors relegate to editors. Someday he would like to try his hand at a film about the American Civil War, based on the Matthew Brady photographs, or a film about World War II.

References

> International Motion Picture Almanac, 1963
> Who's Who in America, 1962-63

KÜNG, HANS (küng) Mar. 19, 1928- Roman Catholic theologian; university professor; author
Address: b. University of Tübingen, Tübingen, West Germany; h. Gartenstrasse 103, Tübingen, West Germany

One of the most promising young theologians of the post-World War II era is the Swiss-born Roman Catholic priest, Dr. Hans Küng, who has been professor of fundamental theology at the University of Tübingen, West Germany, since 1960. A leading spokesman for church reform and for the reunification of Christianity, Küng was appointed by Pope John XXIII as official theologian at the Second Vatican Council, which was convoked in October 1962. For his writings, which include a monumental study of the noted Protestant theologian Karl Barth, and the book *The Council, Reform, and Reunion* (1962), Küng has received wide acclaim from Protestants and Catholics alike. He believes that both Catholicism and Protestantism must undergo extensive reform from within before unification into a universal Christian church can be effected.

Hans Küng was born on March 19, 1928 in Sursee, Switzerland, the son of Hans Küng, a merchant, and of Emma (Gut) Küng. He has five sisters: Marlis, Rita, Margrit, Hildegard, and Irene, all living in Switzerland. Küng obtained his secondary education at the state Gymnasium in Lucerne, where he undertook humanistic studies. After completing his *Abitur* in 1948 he entered the Pontifical German College in Rome, and he then attended the Pontifical Gregorian University in the same city, taking six semesters in philosophy and eight semesters in theology. He also studied in London, Amsterdam, Berlin, Madrid, and Paris. The Gregorian University conferred on him the degree of licentiate in philosophy in 1951 and licentiate in theology in 1955. He received ordination as a priest of the Roman Catholic Church in 1954.

For his postgraduate studies Küng attended the Institut Catholique at the Sorbonne in Paris, where he obtained his doctorate in theology in 1957 after submitting the thesis *Rechtfertigung:*

REV. DR. HANS KÜNG

Die Lehre Karl Barths und eine katholische Besinnung. Published by the Johannes Verlag in 1957, the thesis is an extensive commentary on the work of the noted Protestant theologian, in which Küng concludes that there is an agreement in basic principle between the views of Karl Barth and those of the Roman Catholic Church with regard to the Christian doctrine of justification. This pioneering theological work won high praise from leading Catholic and Protestant theologians, including Barth himself, who viewed it as an important indication of growing reconciliation within the ranks of Christianity. Translated into English by David Granskou, the book is scheduled for publication in New York in 1963 by Thomas Nelson and Sons with the title *Justification: The Doctrine of Karl Barth with a Catholic Reflection*. Karl Barth wrote the introduction.

From 1957 to 1959 Küng served as chaplain at St. Leodegar, the main parish in Lucerne. In 1959 he became an assistant in dogmatic theology at the University of Münster in Westphalia, Germany. Since 1960 he has served as *Ordinarius*, or full professor, of fundamental theology in the Catholic theological faculty of the University of Tübingen, Germany. He is co-editor of the *Tübinger Theologische Quartalschrift*, the oldest Catholic theological journal in the world.

In view of the ecumenical council that was scheduled to be held at the Vatican in the fall of 1962, Küng wrote the book *Konzil und Wiedervereinigung. Erneuerung als Ruf in die Einheit* (Vienna, Freiburg, and Basel, 1960; 5th edition, 1962), which has been translated into French, Dutch, Spanish, and English. Translated into English by Cecily Hastings, it was published in New York by Sheed and Ward with the title *The Council, Reform and Reunion* (1962) and in London as *The Council and Reunion* (1962). In this book Küng concedes that the Roman Catholic Church is not infallible but had in fact erred

KÜNG, HANS—*Continued*

on a number of occasions in the past. He criticizes the "self-righteous 'splendid isolation'" of the church from the leading intellectual currents of the age and notes that there can be no reunion between the Roman Catholic Church and her "separated brethren" without a thorough reform and renewal of Catholicism.

Replying to Protestants who maintain that the Roman Catholic Church is not capable of internal reform, Küng calls attention to successful reforms within the church dating back to the tenth century, as well as the reforms accomplished since the Protestant Reformation by the Jesuits, the Council of Trent, and the Popes Leo XIII, Pius XII, and John XXIII. Among the concrete proposals Küng sets forth in his book are suggestions for granting broader powers to bishops and limiting the authority of the conservative, Italian-dominated Roman Curia; liturgical reform that would allow bishops and diocesan councils the freedom to create rites suited to local needs, including the use of the vernacular in the Mass; the restoration to the laity of the use of the chalice on certain occasions; and the possible reform or abolition of the Index of Prohibited Books. He also proposed a re-examination of such questions as papal infallibility, clerical celibacy, and laws of marriage; and he suggested a Papal declaration of repentance, recognizing the guilt of all for the present unhappy state of the world.

Although Küng does not expect the immediate reunification of all Christianity to result from the decisions of the council, he maintains that "if Catholics carry out Catholic reform and Protestants carry out Protestant reform, both according to the Gospel image, then, because the Gospel of Christ is but one, reunion need not remain a utopian dream. Reunion will then be neither a Protestant return nor a Catholic capitulation, but a brotherly approach from both sides."

The Council, Reform and Reunion became one of the most widely discussed and highly acclaimed theological books of recent years. Episcopal Bishop James A. Pike of San Francisco ordered copies for all the priests in his diocese, and the president of Union Theological Seminary, Henry Pitney Van Dusen, wrote of the book in the *Saturday Review* (June 9, 1962): "It combines in an amazing degree fully informed and authoritative scholarship, fearless and utter fidelity to truth, grace of presentation which can proceed only from uncommon beauty of spirit, and a devoutness so intrinsic, so authentic, that it dares to expose all that outrages and negates that genuine piety." On the other hand, the Right Reverend Monsignor Joseph Clifford Fenton, reviewing the book in the *American Ecclesiastical Review* (September 1962), criticized some of the views expressed in it as "naive," "eccentric," and "utterly unscientific."

Küng is also the author of *Damit die Welt glaube; Briefe an junge Menschen* (Munich, 1962), which was published in English translation as *That the World May Believe* by Sheed and Ward in 1963. Dutch and French editions are in preparation. His book *Strukturen der Kirche* (Vienna, Freiburg, and Basel, 1962) is scheduled for publication in English translation by Thomas Nelson and Sons in 1963 with the title *Structures of the Church*. A Dutch edition was published at Hilversum in 1962 and a French edition is also in preparation. Other books by Küng that are being prepared for publication are *Kirche im Konzil*, which was published as *The Council in Action* by Sheed & Ward in 1963; *Christ in der Welt* (about Thomas More); and *Menschwerdung. Die Christologie Hegels.*

Küng has contributed to encyclopedias and to collections of essays. His article "Justification and Sanctification According to the New Testament" appears in the symposium *Christianity Divided: Protestant and Catholic Theological Issues*, edited by D. J. Callahan and others, and published by Sheed and Ward in 1961. His many articles on theological topics have appeared in newspapers and periodicals in Switzerland, Germany, Holland, and other countries.

When Pope John XXIII convoked the Second Vatican Council in October 1962, to "let some fresh air into the church," he named Küng as the council's official theologian (*peritus*). Speaking at a news conference on December 5, 1962, shortly before the council ended its first session, Küng said that the council had "changed the atmosphere of the whole church." He observed that the new "theology of union" had attained widespread acceptance, and that its development was far more important than the mere promulgation of formal decrees. He also pointed out that a number of major reforms were well under way within the church and that the influence of the conservative Roman Curia had greatly diminished. Küng noted that the council had demonstrated that the Roman Catholic Church is ready to share with Protestants the guilt for a divided Christianity.

In the spring of 1963 Küng visited the United States for a two-month lecture tour. He and three other liberal Catholic theologians were barred from taking part in a lecture series at Catholic University in Washington, D.C. because the university administration did not wish to appear to be taking sides on issues facing the Vatican Council. But he spoke to overflow audiences in cities and at universities from coast to coast, and he received standing ovations. In his lectures he advocated abolition of the Index and of the use of star-chamber techniques in dealing with questions of heresy. He called for a greater role of individual conscience and responsibility in making decisions, and he proposed a public declaration on the part of the church that all men have the right to worship as they choose. "It is urgently necessary for the Church to repudiate all of the methods of totalitarian states, to abandon forever any attempt at coercing conscience or compelling belief," Küng has said.

Dr. Hans Küng is a member of the International Catholic Conference for Ecumenical Questions and of the Arbeitsgemeinschaft Deutscher Dogmatiker. In addition to his native German and classical Latin, Greek, and Hebrew, he knows French, English, Spanish, Italian, and Dutch. Küng is five feet eleven inches tall, weighs 165 pounds, and has blue eyes and wavy blond hair. His favorite recreations are skiing, swimming, and listening to music, and he does much of his writing to the strains of Mozart. He is especially interested in politics, and while visiting the United States he expressed his admiration of President John F. Kennedy. He credits Pope John XXIII with having brought about a new spirit of reform within Catholicism, and says that this spirit is now "living in the whole church."

References

N Y Herald Tribune p7 Ap 21 '63
N Y Post Mag p7 My 5 '63
N Y World-Telegram p6 My 4 '63
Time 79:71+ Je 8 '62 por
Wer ist Wer? (1962)

LA FARGE, OLIVER (HAZARD PERRY)
Dec. 19, 1901-Aug. 2, 1963 Author; anthropologist; champion of the welfare of the American Indian; won 1929 Pulitzer Prize for his *Laughing Boy,* a novel about Navajo life. See *Current Biography* (January) 1953.

Obituary

N Y Times p1+ Ag 3 '63

Studios Jerome

ALBERT LAMORISSE

LAMORISSE, ALBERT (EMMANUEL)
(là-mô-rēs') Jan. 13, 1922- Motion picture writer; producer; director
Address: b. 25 avenue Reille, Paris 14ᵉ, France; h. 44 rue de Verneuil, Paris 7ᵉ, France

Admirers of the individuality of Albert Lamorisse's work have called him at various times "the most original moviemaker in France," one of France's "most gifted creators," and one of "the world's greatest cinematographers." This enthusiasm has been inspired solely by three films that he wrote, directed, and produced—*Crin Blanc (White Mane), Le Ballon Rouge (The Red Balloon),* and *Le Voyage en Ballon (Stowaway in the Sky),* each one praised as an example of movie making at its best. *Crin Blanc* took the 1953 Grand Prix for short films at the Cannes Film Festival, and *Le Ballon Rouge,* a modern film classic, won more than a dozen awards, including an Academy of Motion Picture Arts and Sciences Award for the best original screenplay of 1956 and a Cannes Film Festival Grand Prix for the best short film of 1956. For *Le Voyage en Ballon,* released in Paris in 1960, Lamorisse invented Helevision, a process that enables movies to be filmed from a helicopter.

Albert Emmanuel Lamorisse was born in Paris, France on January 13, 1922, the son of Albert Gusman and Elise (Decaux) Lamorisse. His father was a businessman, and the family, of Flemish descent, was well-to-do. Lamorisse grew up in Paris, attending the Lycée Stanislas, and also in the country, where he went to the École des Roches in Verneuil, Eure District. He did rather poorly in school, but after he had completed his secondary education, he audited classes at the Institut des Hautes Études Cinématographiques. It is said that he took a serious interest in work only when he began his film career in 1945 as a script writer and photographer. In 1946 he went to Tunisia as a tech-

nical assistant on a short feature film *Kairouan.* He developed an enthusiasm for that country and made his own documentary film *Djerba,* about the island of the same name off the coast of Tunisia.

In 1949 Lamorisse returned to Tunisia, where this time he made a film about children, using as his subject the Arab children of the region and their goats. *Bim,* the story of a little goat named Bim, took a year of preparation and four months of shooting. Lamorisse's problems during the shooting included seeing to the hand-feeding of fifty-five bottles of milk a day to the twelve baby goats used in the picture. When the filming was completed, Jacques Prévert saw the results and enthusiastically wrote the commentary.

Lamorisse's next film, which he wrote as well as produced, again told the story of the friendship of a child and an animal. With *Crin Blanc,* released in 1952, Lamorisse moved toward the forefront of French moviemakers. Filmed in the Camargue region in the south of France, which is noted for its desolate terrain and its beautiful wild horses, the movie concerned a small boy who tamed one of the wild horses. It met with international critical acclaim. In addition to the Grand Prix for short films at the Cannes Festival, the awards that it won included the Prix Jean Vigo, the International Prize for Youth, and the Épi d'Or of Rome. *Crin Blanc* was presented before the Queen of England and the King of Greece and has been shown in almost every country of the world.

After the completion of *Crin Blanc,* Lamorisse went to the Gap region of France, in 1952, to work on a film about a boy and two bears. While shooting the outdoor scenes, Lamorisse was caught in an avalanche. The accident cost him five months in the hospital and a year of immobility. When he had recovered, he worked first on an adaptation of *Katrina* in Finland and

LAMORISSE, ALBERT—Continued

then, in 1955, went to Guatemala as a cameraman to help make an experimental color documentary about the country. During this time he dreamed about producing his own film in color.

Later in 1955, feeling that he had acquired the necessary experience and technique, Lamorisse began work on *Le Ballon Rouge*. As a writer, producer, and director of the film, he again penetrated the inner world of a child to tell the story of a little Parisian boy and his red balloon, which follows him wherever he goes. To play the part of the boy, Lamorisse chose his own son Pascal, then five and a half. His daughter, Sabine, also had a role. Lamorisse and his crew, equipped with a technicolor camera, filmed his son and the red balloon as they moved within the daily life of the Paris suburb of Menilmontant. The scenes included a bus stop, a bakery, a market, and a grade school.

When *The Red Balloon* was released in the United States in March 1957, a reviewer for the New York *Times* called it "a little gem" and was particularly delighted with its "remarkable evocation of the city's unique atmosphere." Richard L. Coe wrote in the Washington *Post and Times Herald* (May 31, 1957) of "the ingenuity with which Albert Lamorisse has created a film that can be all things to all people." Coe went on to say, "He has made it, in lovely, soft color, with such perfection of detail that purely as film making it is a triumph." Besides a 1956 Cannes Grand Prix and a 1956 Oscar, the thirty-four minute film won the Grand Prix of the French Cinema, the West German film critics prize for the best foreign film at Hamburg, and similar awards in Tokyo, Mexico, and London. It also received film critics awards in New York and Switzerland in 1957.

Le Voyage en Ballon, Lamorisse's first full-length picture, is a travelogue of France that took two years to film. Once again, Pascal Lamorisse appeared in a film of his father's, this time as a boy who goes on a balloon tour of France with his grandfather. Only three principals appear in the film: the boy; the grandfather, played by André Gille, a balloonist of the old school who is very resentful of the modern craze for speed; and a comic mechanic named Tou-Tou, played by Maurice Baquet.

During the filming of *Le Voyage,* Lamorisse took his cast and a seventy-foot orange-colored balloon to all parts of France. Photographed by movie cameras from an accompanying helicopter, the boy and his grandfather float over such Paris landmarks as Notre Dame and the Eiffel Tower; they witness a stag hunt, a bullfight in the Camargue, and a windjammer race to the Canary Islands, and other spectacular events. Lamorisse ran into several difficulties in filming the picture. Because helium is almost impossible to obtain in France for anything other than military purposes, the balloon had to be filled with hydrogen. Once a ground spark touched off an explosion in which Lamorisse's son and Gille narrowly escaped injury, but the incident was incorporated into the story, as was a forest fire they later witnessed.

In order to photograph his motion picture without the vibration that normally shakes a camera mounted on a helicopter, Lamorisse and his technicians developed Helevision, a "gantry-like camera mount" that cushions vibrations. They also employed a large number of special lenses, including a motor-driven Zoomar to take close-ups of subjects that would be ruffled by the draft from the rotor blades if the helicopter moved too near. According to Joseph Morgenstern in the New York *Herald Tribune* (June 17, 1962), the result was more than successful— "as if the camera were mounted on a perfectly solid track in the sky." Lamorisse, whose Helevision equipment cost him $180,000, discussed the possibility of Helevision in a New York *Post* interview (June 18, 1962): "Doors are opened to subjects that have never been treated before, we can photograph an angel. Now the camera can fly." He believes that when photographed from the air, man and nature are finally seen in their proper perspective. Helevision was also employed successfully in a Swedish children's film *The Wonderful Adventures of Nils* (1962).

Le Voyage, which in final form runs eighty-two minutes, was well-received in both Europe in 1960 and the United States, where it was released as *Stowaway in the Sky* in 1962. André Maurois called it "a film for poets and philosophers," and Jean de Baroncelli of *Le Monde* wrote that it is "a tale of a dream realized. Pure cinema. Above all, a ravishing spectacle." English narration for the film was written by S. N. Behrman and read by Jack Lemmon. United States film rights were acquired by Lemmon's independent company, Jalem Productions, and distributed by Lopert Pictures. Like Lamorisse's other films, *Le Voyage* has won its share of awards, including the Blue Ribbon of the French Movie and Television Critics Association in 1960; prizes from Prague (Concours Technique International du Film), Venice (Prix de l'Office Catholique), and La Plata (Festival International de l'Enfance); and the San Grégorio Prize from the International Festival of Religious Films.

All of Lamorisse's films have received high praise for the excellence of their photography, especially his two color films, *Le Ballon Rouge* and *Le Voyage en Ballon.* His technique of photographing in Eastman color and printing on technicolor stock results, as *Time* (October 24, 1960) described it, in "a Utrillo-like, ethereal aura." Paul V. Beckley in a New York *Herald Tribune* article called Lamorisse "one of the not very large community of filmmakers who can use color convincingly as though it were imperative to the matter at hand and not a mere convention." Beckley continued, "Whether he is moving you to awe with a series of landscapes or with the magnificent dash of a running stag, you cannot miss the exactness of the harmonies he extracts in line, form and color from the world around him. . . . His is the whole world, and a love of nature does not cancel out an enthusiasm for man."

Lamorisse is noted for his deliberately slow and painstaking method of work (which led him, in *Le Ballon Rouge* to go through forty-two different scenarios before he was satisfied). Of his work he says, "I make films in my own way. I am not a professional, I am an amateur." He views the cinema as a "living art," and the only one with so many varied forms of expression. He is very much against the cinema clinging to old ways, believing that it can survive "only by constantly renewing itself."

In speaking of the inspiration for his own films, Lamorisse told Howard Thompson of the New York *Times* (June 17, 1962), "'White Mane' and 'Red Balloon' were meant to convey the dreams of children. And now, in 'Stowaway,' I hope to project the feeling of wonderment." He says that he makes films to bring to life his childhood dreams, and in predicting future films, he sees no lack of material: "I'm still dreaming. I'm a little bit *en retard*. When I'm 80 I'll be making pictures about the things I'm dreaming now." All three of Lamorisse's major films have appeared in book form in the United States. *White Mane* was published in 1954 by E. P. Dutton & Company, and *The Red Balloon* and *Stowaway in the Sky* were published by Doubleday & Company in 1957 and 1962 respectively.

Albert Lamorisse married Claude Jeanne Marie Duparc, a dancer, on November 24, 1947; their children are Pascal (the oldest), Sabine, and Fanny. The family has an apartment on Paris's Left Bank and a country home on the Riviera, in the mountains behind Saint-Tropez. There Lamorisse and his family make wine (red, white, and rosé), which they sell. They also create ceramics, making their own plates and saucers, and they print their own fabrics. Lamorisse is an ardent sportsman and occasionally likes to put all work aside in favor of skiing. He also enjoys fencing, riding, and swimming, and while shooting *Le Voyage*, he became a licensed helicopter pilot as well as a balloonist. His son, who attends school in England, plays the cello and is an expert photographer.

Lamorisse's friends call him Bertie. Trim and wiry-looking, he is five feet ten inches tall and weighs 140 pounds; his eyes are blue and his hair is blond. He has a quiet humor and a self-effacing and genial manner. His church is the Roman Catholic. His honors include Chevalier of the Order of Arts and Letters. In addition to Helevision, he has invented a parlor game called "Risk," which has been selling at the rate of 100,000 a year in the United States and Europe.

References

N Y Herald Tribune IV p4 Je 17 '62
N Y Post p21 Je 18 '62
N Y Times II p9 Je 17 '62
Time 76:65+ O 24 '60

Dictionnaire Biographique Français Contemporain (1954)

LANDAU, LEV (DAVIDOVICH) Jan. 22, 1908- Physicist; author

Address: AN SSSR, Leninsky prosp. 14, Moscow, U.S.S.R.

The recipient of the 1962 Nobel Prize for Physics, Lev Davidovich Landau is recognized as one of the most brilliant and versatile theoretical physicists in the U.S.S.R. Landau developed the abstruse mathematical physical theories needed to explain the behavior of superfluid helium at temperatures near the absolute zero. He is co-author of a series of monographs, virtually constituting an encyclopedia of modern theoretical physics, that have been translated into several languages. An inspiring teacher, Lev Landau is regarded as a major influence in the development of modern Soviet science. He made notable contributions to the development of the first Russian atomic bomb and artificial earth satellites and to studies of quantum theory and cosmic rays. Because he was still hospitalized in November 1962 as the result of an automobile accident, his wife and son went to Stockholm to accept the $50,000 Nobel Prize for him.

Lev Davidovich Landau was born of Jewish parentage on January 22, 1908 in Baku, now the capital of the Republic of Azerbaidzhan on the Caspian Sea. His father was an engineer and his mother was a physician. Lev Landau showed an early interest in science and especially in mathematics; biographical articles in the Soviet press in 1958 said that he could hardly remember not being able to solve problems in differential and integral calculus.

After attending Baku University from 1922 to 1924 Landau transferred to Leningrad University, where he completed his studies in 1927. He published four scientific papers during his last two school years. Having become interested in the new science of quantum mechanics, he introduced at the age of nineteen the concept of the density matrix for energy, now widely used in quantum mechanics. From 1927 to 1929 Landau was at the Leningrad Physical and Technical Institute, working on the theory of the magnetic electron and on quantum electrodynamics. In 1929 he began a year and a half of further study at scientific centers in Denmark, Switzerland, Germany, the Netherlands, and Great Britain. An important influence on his development was his association with the great Danish physicist Niels Bohr in Copenhagen, where the two men began an exchange of ideas and a personal friendship that was to continue for many years. In 1962 Landau told a *Life* reporter who was interviewing him as a Nobel Prize winner: "Please assure me that the pages of your journal will carry my particular thanks to Niels Bohr. I have been a follower of his for many years and he deserves a great part of the credit for my award. He shares my honor. I am very proud."

During the time he spent abroad Landau began investigations that eventually led him to the study of low-temperature physics. In 1930 he calculated the diamagnetism of free electrons quantum-mechanically and put forward a theory of diamagnetism of metals showing that a degenerate ideal electron gas possessed a diamagnetic susceptibility equal to one-third the paramagnetic susceptibility. In 1937-38 this resulted in the explanation of the de Haas-van Alphen effect. At this time Landau obtained a thorough knowledge of and practice in manipulating complicated theoretical Fermi systems, which later helped him to evolve new theories in low-temperature physics.

Landau returned for a short time to Leningrad, but in 1932 he was called to Kharkov to head the theoretical division of its Physical and Technical Institute. Papers he wrote during his

Wide World

LEV LANDAU

mechanics, the theory of field, quantum mechanics, statistical physics, mechanics of continuous media, and electrodynamics of continuous media, Landau and Lifshitz won the Lenin Prize in 1962. The books were published in the Soviet Union beginning in 1938 and have been translated into several languages. Some of the sections are based on the authors' original work.

When Landau arrived at the institute in Moscow, Peter Kapitsa was already working on superfluidity. Landau also turned to this area of low-temperature physics and in 1940 and 1941 made the contributions that twenty years later won him the Nobel Prize. Helium, a very light gas under ordinary conditions, can be condensed to a liquid when chilled to temperatures approaching absolute zero (about -460° F). The helium I form of liquid helium-4 (the common helium isotope) has properties similar to those of other liquefied gases. However, as helium I is cooled below a temperature of about -458° F, it is changed into helium II, the only known superfluid, which since it does not behave like a solid, liquid, or gas, has been called a fourth state of matter.

The viscosity of helium II is so low that it will flow through a microscopic orifice 1,000 times faster than hydrogen gas. It conducts heat 800 times better than copper at ordinary temperatures. It won't boil; if heated slightly, it simply peels off in layers from the top. If an empty glass vessel is partly lowered into a pool of helium II, a thin layer runs up the sides of the vessel, over the rim, and down inside, until the liquid levels inside and out are the same. If the glass vessel is now lifted completely above the surface of the pool, the process is reversed: droplets move from the bottom of the vessel back into the pool until the vessel is empty.

The task of explaining these already known phenomena in rigorous (and complex) mathematical terms was a challenge that Lev Landau successfully solved. He also predicted the possibility that sound waves would travel in helium II at two different speeds. Ordinary sound traveling in liquids is a pressure wave, while Landau's "second sound" is a temperature wave. Although "second sound" had first been predicted in 1938 by L. Tisza, Landau predicted it independently in 1941. V. Peshkov's experimental observations of 1944 proved Landau's views to be correct. As Professor Erik Rudberg of the Royal Academy of Science has pointed out, there is no known practical application for Landau's theory of superfluidity, but the theory does provide insights into the formation under low temperatures of superconductors, which are used in electronic computers and earth satellite equipment.

In 1945 Landau published papers dealing with shock waves at large distances from their place of origin, based on work carried out under the auspices of the engineering committee of the Red Army. The following year he contributed papers describing investigations into the oscillations of plasmas. Having solved the problem of liquid helium II, Landau turned his attention to the properties of the rare helium isotope, helium-3, and predicted that this too would acquire special properties and undergo a phase change if brought close enough to absolute zero. Among the pos-

five years at Kharkov testify to his versatility of outlook and achievement. In 1932 his publications ranged from "On the Theory of Stars" to "On the Theory of Energy Transfers in Collisions." The latter demonstrated one of his specialties: the solution of difficult theoretical problems by ingenious mathematical analysis. In his last two years at the institute he was author or co-author of papers on subjects that included monomolecular reactions, sound dispersion, the kinetic equation of the Coulomb effect, scattering of light by light, properties of metals at very low temperatures, phase transitions, absorption of sound in solids, superconductivity, and the origin of stellar energy. Applying thermodynamics to electronic systems at low temperatures, he introduced the concept of antiferromagnetic ordering as a new thermodynamic phase; developed the thermodynamic theory of magnetic domains (with E. M. Lifshitz); studied phase transitions and determined the relation between transitions of the second order and variation of symmetry of the system; and studied the intermediate state of superconductors and proposed a theory of laminar structure of superconductors.

Meanwhile, at Kharkov, Landau began to attract a number of disciples among the students, one of the first of whom was Evgeny M. Lifshitz, then only seventeen, who became Landau's good friend and collaborator. Convinced that independent creative work in any area of theoretical physics must stem from a good grasp of all its branches, Landau instituted a special program for his students, which they called the "theoretical minimum."

Beginning in Kharkov and continuing in Moscow, where Landau had been summoned by Peter L. Kapitsa to join the Institute for Physical Problems in 1937, Landau and Lifshitz collaborated on an encyclopedic series of monographs on modern theoretical physics that has become a classic. For their books, which deal with sible new properties would be a unique type of wave propagation called "zero sound" and spontaneous occurrence of rotational domains in the substance, capable of causing a suspended containing vessel to begin spinning suddenly. Armed with modern techniques by which they can come within a millionth of a degree of absolute zero, physicists are busy checking Landau's predictions.

At its height, Lev Landau's remarkable career was nearly ended in an automobile accident on January 7, 1962. He was riding as a rear passenger in a light car about seventy-five miles from Moscow. A child darted into the street, and when the driver braked suddenly on the icy road the car spun around and crashed into an oncoming truck. Lev Landau was gravely injured, suffering a skull fracture, broken ribs, brain hemorrhage, ruptured lungs, and severe damage of the nervous system. Within five hours of the time of the accident, a team of top U.S.S.R. medical specialists had gathered at Moscow Hospital #50, where Landau had been taken. Emergency surgery removed immediate pressure on the brain, and famed neurologists from France, Czechoslovakia, and Canada were flown to Moscow for consultation. Conservative views against further surgery prevailed.

Meanwhile, physicists rushed a respirator from the Polio Institute, and doctors and engineers designed a bed with special adjustments. On the fourth day after the accident, Lev Landau's blood pressure fell to zero, and he stopped breathing. He was considered near clinical death, but drug injections and arterial blood transfusions restored the spark of life. On the seventh, ninth, and eleventh days the ordeal was repeated, but the teams of experts who maintained a twenty-four-hour watch would not yield to death.

At last, nearly three months after the accident, Landau was able to recognize his wife and son. Although not yet out of bed in November of 1962 when his Nobel Prize was announced, Landau was able to talk briefly with a Swedish reporter. He seemed delighted that he could remember enough English for the occasion. Finally, some months later, in the spring of 1963, he was able to walk with assistance in the garden near his hospital.

Landau's wife, Konkordia, a former chemist, and his son, Igor, who is studying physics, went to Stockholm to accept the Nobel Prize in his behalf. In addition to the Nobel Prize, Lev Landau has won three Stalin Prizes and a Fritz London Award, given at the Seventh International Conference on Low Temperature Physics in Toronto, Canada in 1960. He was elected a full member of the Academy of Sciences of the U.S.S.R. in 1946. A list of Landau's scientific publications would run to over 100 technical papers and ten books. He is a member of the Danish and Netherlands academies of sciences, an honorary fellow of the Physical Society, a foreign member of the Royal Society (London), and an honorary foreign member of the National Academy of Sciences.

Lev Davidovich Landau, or "Dau," as he is known to his students and colleagues, has a whimsical and light-hearted personality. When John R. Pellam, an American physicist, met him a few months before the automobile accident he

found him to be "a charming and extraordinary person" and "a distinct extrovert." "He likes children," Pellam wrote in Science (November 9, 1962), "and insisted upon making a series of weird and unbelievable faces before our movie camera to entertain ours (they were impressed and delighted)." According to Edward Teller, who met Landau in Europe in the early 1930's, the young Landau argued with some passion about religion with the scientist James Franck, whose religious beliefs he considered "incredibly outmoded for a scientist." Teller says further that Landau at that time "enjoyed making statements calculated to shock members of the bourgeois society." As John Pellam has pointed out, however, Landau "may have mellowed some since." According to the New York Times (November 2, 1962), his Communism is idealistic rather than practical, and he has been called "a salon Communist."

References

Life 53:55+ D 7 '62 por
N Y Times p19 D 2 '62 por
Physics Today 14:42+ '61 por
Science 138:667+ N 9 '62 por
International Who's Who, 1962-63
Who's Who in the USSR, 1961-62

LANGER, SUSANNE K(ATHERINA KNAUTH) Dec. 20, 1895- Philosopher; writer; former college professor
Address: b. c/o Connecticut College, New London, Conn.; h. Neck Rd., Old Lyme, Conn.

In searching for "a firm and free philosophical foundation" for psychology and the social sciences, Susanne K. Langer is dedicated to a systematic study of meanings. Again and again in her writings she insists upon the need "to subject the rough-and-ready notions of ordinary discourse to more and more rigorous definition until we know exactly what our words mean and all the necessary concepts have become clear." Her new key in philosophy depends upon the recognition that man is a symbol-making animal in all forms of intellectual activity, in art and myth as well as science.

The comprehensive and rational theory of art that Mrs. Langer brought to the hitherto inexact realm of aesthetics, in *Philosophy in a New Key, Feeling and Form,* and other books, may profoundly affect twentieth-century thinking in the social sciences. She is one of the few women in the world to win recognition in a field traditionally pre-empted by men. Mrs. Langer, the former wife of the historian William Leonard Langer, has also had a distinguished career in teaching.

Manhattan's German colony, highly cultivated in its traditional music, literature, and philosophy, provided the first of the many sources of the wide learning that underlies Mrs. Langer's own contributions in philosophy. Susanne Katherina Knauth was born on New York's upper West Side on December 20, 1895, one of five children of Antonio and Else M. (Uhlich) Knauth. Her father, a well-to-do lawyer from Leipzig, liked to play the piano and cello. His

Connecticut College

SUSANNE K. LANGER

daughter also studied both instruments and became proficient in the cello. From her mother, whose home in Germany had been Chemnitz, Susanne acquired other appreciations, including a love of poetry, which she learned to read, recite, and write at an early age. Her sisters are Ilse and Ursula, and her brothers are Berthold, an inventor, and Peter, an industrial designer.

The Knauths' preference for speaking German among themselves put Susanne at some disadvantage when she began to attend the Veltin School, a private school not far from her home on the West Side. Her self-education more than compensated. "In my early teens," she recalled in an interview with Winthrop Sargeant for the *New Yorker* (December 3, 1960), "I read 'Little Women' and Kant's 'Critique of Pure Reason' simultaneously." During the family's summer visits to Lake George in upstate New York, she developed an abiding interest in nature study.

Antonio Knauth, according to the *New Yorker* profile, so much disliked "masculine" inclinations in women that he objected to a college education for his daughters. After his death Susanne Knauth entered Radcliffe College in Cambridge, Massachusetts, where she made philosophy her major subject, was elected to Phi Beta Kappa, and in 1920 obtained the B.A. degree. In Cambridge she met William Leonard Langer, then a graduate student at Harvard, whom she married on September 3, 1921. She and her husband studied together at the University of Vienna during the following year.

To complete her graduate work Mrs. Langer returned to Radcliffe, which awarded her the M.A. degree in 1924 and the Ph.D. degree in 1926. In 1924 she also published her first book, *The Cruise of the Little Dipper, and Other Fairy Tales* (Norcross), illustrated by Helen Sewell, to whom many years later Mrs. Langer dedicated *Problems in Art* as her "lifelong So-cratic teacher in the arts." As Winthrop Sargeant has suggested, there was nothing incongruous about her concern as a philosophy student with fairy tales in the *Märchen* tradition when she was to consider myth a central topic in her study of symbols.

For fifteen years, from 1927 to 1942, Mrs. Langer remained at Radcliffe as tutor in philosophy, and during that time she taught occasionally also at Wellesley and Smith colleges. Her own teachers at Radcliffe, Alfred North Whitehead, Henry M. Sheffer, and others, were among the scholars who gave her the starting point for her published work in philosophy. Whitehead wrote the prefatory note to *The Practice of Philosophy* (Holt, 1930), in which she explained the purposes, methods, and achievements of philosophy, with particular attention to the role of symbolic logic in contemporary thinking.

In *The Practice of Philosophy* Mrs. Langer had discussed "the liberation of the mind that comes from training in logic." Her next book, *An Introduction to Symbolic Logic* (Houghton, 1937; Dover, 1953), employed the method of Sheffer, with which she had become familiar at Radcliffe. It was, as she explained, "built around the two great classic feasts of symbolic logic: the Boole-Schroeder algebra, and the logistic masterpiece of Messrs. Whitehead and Russell, Principia Mathematica." She described it as "both a textbook of symbolic logic and an essay on that logic."

When writing *Philosophy in a New Key; A Study in the Symbolism of Reason, Rite, and Art* (Harvard Univ. Press, 1942; Penguin, 1948), the book that made her prominent in aesthetics, Mrs. Langer was substantially influenced by Ernst Cassirer, the German pioneer in the philosophy of symbolism, whose *Language and Myth* (Harper, 1946) she later translated. She maintained that symbolic transformation, or the making of symbols, is a function of the human brain and a basic need of man. Discursive language cannot express all human experience; but the conception of the ineffable also has its forms of logic, its semantics, and its "symbolistic schema."

In further development of her rational system of aesthetics in *Feeling and Form; A Theory of Art* (Scribner, 1953) Mrs. Langer applied to each of the arts her ideas about abstract presentation of emotional experience, or the nature of emotion, through individual systems of symbols. Like *Philosophy in a New Key*, which did, however, attain a fairly wide circulation in its paperback edition, *Feeling and Form* does not appeal to the general reader. Book reviewers disagreed on its merits: although George Boas in *Saturday Review* (June 6, 1953) found it "obscure, dull, and . . . authoritative in tone," Robert Fitzgerald in *Commonweal* (June 5, 1953) admired "the light and warmth and depth of her writing" and R. H. Fogle described it in *Yale Review* (summer 1953) as a "singularly luminous book."

Among Susanne Langer's ideas that differ from generally held views in aesthetics is the tenet that the artist seeks not to arouse or convey feeling, but to portray the nature of feeling. In her ten philosophical lectures printed in

Problems of Art (Scribner, 1957) she discussed symbolism, poetic creativity, abstraction, emotion in art, interrelation among the arts, and similar matters. She explained in a lecture on expressiveness that what the artist expresses is "not his own actual feeling, but what he knows about human feeling. Once he is in possession of a rich symbolism, that knowledge may actually exceed his entire personal experience." She went on to say, "A work of art possesses a conception of life, emotion, inward reality. But it is neither a confessional nor a frozen tantrum; it is a developed metaphor, a non-discursive symbol that articulates what is verbally ineffable—the logic of consciousness itself."

Mrs. Langer contributed articles to *Structure, Method and Meaning: Essays in Honor of Henry M. Sheffer* (Liberal Arts, 1951) and to *Aesthetic Form and Education* (Syracuse Univ. Press, 1958). She edited *Reflections on Art: A Source Book of Writings by Artists, Critics, and Philosophers* (Johns Hopkins Press, 1958). "This is a stimulating volume," Paul Ziff remarked in *Journal of Philosophy* (September 15, 1960). "But it is not for simple souls unwilling to drown themselves in the well of knowledge."

After Mrs. Langer had left Radcliffe in 1942, she taught for a year as assistant professor of philosophy at the University of Delaware in Newark. From 1945 to 1950 she lectured in philosophy at Columbia University, and it was during this period that she wrote *Feeling and Form,* working from 1946 to 1949 under a grant from the Rockefeller Foundation through Columbia. She has also conducted seminars or lectured as visiting professor at New York University, the New School of Social Research, Northwestern University, Ohio University, the University of Washington, and the University of Michigan.

In 1954 Mrs. Langer returned to New England to become professor and chairman of the department of philosophy at Connecticut College in New London, of which she is now professor emeritus and a research scholar in philosophy. Since 1956, as a recipient of a research grant from the Edgar Kaufmann Charitable Trust of Pittsburgh, she has been solely occupied with the writing of a book to be entitled *Mind: An Essay on Human Feeling.* The nine essays—including "The Process of Feeling," "Emotion and Abstraction," and "The Cultural Importance of Art"—published in *Philosophical Sketches* (John Hopkins Press, 1962) are preliminary studies for this work.

"A strong contemplative bent has kept me from entering directly into practical affairs, political, economic or social," Mrs. Langer has said (*Saturday Evening Post,* May 13, 1961). "New theories capable of far-reaching developments seem to me the most immediate challenge." She has misgivings about a society of technical progress that jeopardizes the freedom of man's mind because it does not understand symbolic formulation. "We cannot analyze the contents of those vast symbols—Race, Unity, Manifest Destiny, Humanity—over which we fight so ruthlessly," she wrote in *Philosophy in a New Key;* "if we could, it would mean that they were already furnishing discursive terms,

clear issues, and we would all be busy philosophizing instead of waging holy wars."

As *Problems of Art* shows, Susanne Langer is accustomed to lecturing before different kinds of audiences. Fairly recently, in 1961, she addressed the International Conference on Education at Vassar College and the conference of the Japan Society for the Philosophy of Science held in Nikko. She was the recipient in 1950 of the Radcliffe Alumnae Achievement Medal, and in 1960 she was elected to the American Academy of Arts and Sciences. She holds honorary Litt.D. degrees from Wilson College (1954), Wheaton College (1962), and Western College for Women (1962).

Susanne K. Langer, who was divorced from William Leonard Langer in 1942, has two sons, Leonard C. R. and Bertrand W. Langer, and several grandchildren. She lives and works in a Colonial house in Old Lyme, Connecticut, and for the enjoyment of greater solitude and nearness to nature she has a woodland cabin in New York's Ulster County. Winthrop Sargeant described her in the *New Yorker* as a small, sun-tanned "woman of iron will, impatient of laziness and self-indulgence. She smokes cigarettes in great moderation, and indulges in alcohol only to the extent of an occasional glass of sherry. She does all her own cooking and is rather good at it."

"Despite her professed lack of religion," Sargeant remarked, "Mrs. Langer, like many lovers of art, seems to have a strong streak of instinctive pantheism, which expresses itself not only in a love of nature but also in the cherishing of various objects and pets." She dislikes canned music, whether it emanates from a radio or a phonograph, and finds much pleasure as a cellist in contributing to an evening of live music in the company of a few similarly talented friends.

References

New Yorker 36:67+ D 3 '60 por
Sat Eve Post 234:34+ My 13 '61 por
Twentieth Century Authors (First Supplement, 1955)
Who's Who in the East, 1962-63

LANGNER, LAWRENCE May 30, 1890-Dec. 26, 1962 Founder (1918) and co-administrator, Theatre Guild; founder (1950) and first president, American Shakespeare Festival Theatre and Academy at Stratford, Connecticut; chartered patent agent, associated with Langner, Parry, Card & Langner, New York. See *Current Biography* (September) 1944.

Obituary

N Y Times p36 Ap 1 '63

LAUGHTON, CHARLES July 1, 1899-Dec. 15, 1962 Actor; noted for his motion-picture portrayals of Captain Bligh, Emperor Nero, Rembrandt, and other characters; won an Oscar in 1933 for his performance in *The Private Life of Henry VIII.* See *Current Biography* (November) 1948.

Obituary

N Y Times p35 Ap 1 '63

LAVER, ROD(NEY GEORGE) (lā'vẽr) Aug. 9, 1938- Tennis player
Address: h. 26 Side St., Gladstone, Queensland, Australia

In September 1962 Australia's Rod (Rocket) Laver stepped out onto the hallowed courts of the West Side Tennis Club in Forest Hills, New York to win his fourth major amateur title of the year. Victory in the United States Lawn Tennis Singles Championship gave him the first grand slam in amateur tennis since 1938, when America's Don Budge captured in a single year the Australian, British, and French lawn tennis titles in addition to winning at Forest Hills. Regarded as a worthy successor to such Australian amateur tennis stars of the 1950's as Frank Sedgman, Lew Hoad, and Ashley Cooper, Laver had been a member of the Australian Davis Cup team since 1959 and had been instrumental in seeing that the symbol of international tennis supremacy had not passed out of Australian hands. In his last amateur tennis match, in December 1962, he helped Australia retain the Davis Cup. A few days later he turned professional.

Born on August 9, 1938 in Rockhampton, Queensland, Australia, Rodney George Laver is the third of four children of Roy Stanley Laver and Melba (Roffey) Laver. Rod has two older brothers, Trevor and Robert, and a younger sister, Lois. Their father raised cattle at one time, but is now retired. Rod Laver, who attended primary and secondary schools in Rockhampton, began playing tennis at the age of twelve. His parents were tennis enthusiasts and during the early 1950's they and their three sons took part in tennis tournaments near Rockhampton, picking up many titles and trophies.

At the age of fourteen Laver won his first trophy. The following year he left school to give more time to tennis under the guidance of

Wide World
ROD LAVER

Australia's tennis genius, Harry Hopman. Three years later, in 1956, he captured the United States junior championship. He served during 1957 in the Australian Army. In June 1958, according to an Associated Press dispatch, he "shook American lawn tennis to its roots," by upsetting Barry MacKay of the United States, 6-3, 6-3, in the second round of the Queen's Club Tournament in London. MacKay, at the time, was looked upon as America's best tennis player. Laver was then ranked eighth in his native land, a rating that attested to the wealth of court talent in Australia.

Laver waited in the wings, so to speak, until 1959. Then, when Davis Cuppers Ashley Cooper and Mal Anderson became professionals, Laver was chosen for the Davis Cup team, along with Roy Emerson and Neale Fraser. The Australians turned back the United States team that year three matches to two. Laver lost twice, the second time to Alex Olmedo, in a marathon sixty-six games. Arthur Daley wrote in the New York *Times* (August 31, 1959): "Laver's performance in defeat made the victory of The Chief [Olmedo] all the more noteworthy. The twenty-one year old left-hander [Laver] made chalk shots that would have discouraged anyone less hardy." Olmedo, a Peruvian by birth but a resident of the United States at the time, had led the American Davis Cup team to an upset victory over the Australians in 1958. In September 1959, at Forest Hills, Laver lost to Olmedo in the finals of the men's singles championship.

Again, in early 1960, Laver served notice that he was a tennis player to be reckoned with. Playing the heavily favored Fraser in the finals of the Australian National tennis championship, Laver rallied from a two-set deficit to defeat his countryman, 5-7, 3-6, 6-3, 8-6, 8-6. Before the year was over Fraser beat Laver in the finals of the English championship at Wimbledon and of the United States championship at Forest Hills. Laver did gain some measure of satisfaction at Wimbledon by teaming with America's Darlene Hard to win the mixed doubles title. In December 1960 Fraser and Laver led the Aussies to victory over the challenging Italian teams in the Davis Cup finals.

With Fraser handicapped by a leg injury during much of 1961, Laver was referred to constantly as the world's number one amateur tennis player. He failed, however, to measure up. Only at Wimbledon was he consistently brilliant. In the finals there he defeated America's Chuck McKinley, 6-3, 6-1, 6-4, in only fifty-five minutes. Later, at Forest Hills, Laver lost in the finals to Emerson by a 7-5, 6-3, 6-2 score.

After the 1961 championship matches at Forest Hills, professional tennis czar Jack Kramer offered Laver and Emerson $33,600 each if they would leave the amateur ranks for his pro tour. Both men rejected the offer. In December 1961 they led the Australian team to a one-sided win over the challenging Italians in the Davis Cup finals. The failure of the Italians to win a set in the first three matches enabled the Australians to clinch the best-of-five cup series without loss of a set, marking the first time that a team had done so since 1909.

Reaching top form in the Davis Cup competition, Laver continued his run of championship tennis into 1962. He disposed of Emerson in the finals of the Australian championship, then in rapid order took his measure in the finals of title tourneys in Paris and Rome. Moving on to London, Laver repeated his victory over Emerson with a 6-4, 7-5 triumph in the finals of the Queen's Club Tournament. Emerson failed to reach the championship round at Wimbledon, but that made little difference to Laver. Facing countryman Martin Mulligan in the final round, Laver needed only 51 minutes, 35 seconds to win by a decisive 6-2, 6-2, 6-1. "Rod has never played so well," Mulligan remarked in defeat. "He never let me in the match." The Manchester *Guardian* noted in reporting the match (July 7, 1962): "Mulligan would certainly have found him [Laver] easier to play last year. The difference between Laver then and Laver now is that he has acquired a far greater discipline, both of stroke and of concentration. . . . As well as being the most exciting player at Wimbledon this year, he also has been the most accurate."

The improvement in Laver's playing was also evident at Forest Hills on September 10, 1962 when he again faced Emerson, who had defeated him in the previous year for the United States championship. This time Laver won over Emerson by a score of 6-2, 6-4, 5-7, 6-4, to capture the last of the world's four major titles that make up the grand slam in tennis. In December 1962, in the final Davis Cup match, Laver and Emerson teamed against Mexico's Rafael Osuna and Antonio Palafox. The Australians' doubles victory, 7-5, 6-2, 6-4, completed their 5-0 sweep of the Mexican team and gave Australia the Davis Cup for the eleventh time in the last thirteen years.

For well over a year there had been considerable speculation about whether and when Laver would turn professional. He stirred up some criticism in late December 1962 when he made it obvious during the Davis Cup challenge that he was ready to withdraw from the amateur ranks. In late December he announced that he had accepted a contract with the International Professional Tennis Players Association that would guarantee him $110,000 over a three-year period. In his first professional match, on January 5, 1963, he lost to Lew Hoad, 6-8, 6-4, 6-3, 8-6. By the middle of January Laver had lost his fourth straight match as a professional, when he was defeated by Ken Rosewall, 3-6, 10-8, 6-2, 6-3.

Laver has never talked at length about his expectations in professional tennis, but it is doubtful that he is particularly worried. He is confident in his own ability and is, furthermore, a relaxed sort of person. In late August 1962, for example, while competing in the United States Lawn Tennis Association Doubles Championship at Chestnut Hill, Massachusetts, Laver and his partner, Fred Stolle, were beaten in the quarterfinal round, but only after Laver had spent much of his free time on a nearby golf course. As for his demeanor on the tennis court during the doubles play, the *Christian Science Monitor* reported (August 25, 1962): "He never betrayed the slightest grain of intensity. Boredom would almost be a better description."

Some tennis experts have, in fact, said that Laver's only flaw, or worst weakness, is a tendency to lose interest in a match. Rex Lardner discussed his merits in *Sports Illustrated* (September 17, 1962), "Laver uses his wrists more than any other player in history except Frank Kovacs and he is the first player to combine a whipping wrist action with near-perfect control. Laver can hit a ball flat, with topspin or with underspin, equally well from both sides. . . . Few players have his repertory of strokes, and no player has been able to mask his shots better. . . . But perhaps his greatest ability is to make forcing shots of returns that most players would be happy to get back at all."

Rod Laver's slender figure belies his power on the court: he is five feet nine inches tall and weighs 155 pounds. He has blue eyes, red hair, and a freckled face. Playing golf, dancing, and listening to music, including rock 'n' roll, are his hobbies. He is a member of the Church of England. As an amateur player, he was employed in the sales and public relations division of the Dunlop Rubber Company, where he had worked as a clerk after leaving high school. Laver is known for his court manners. After Laver had won the grand slam, Don Budge said of him: "He has the temperament and every shot in the books. Further, he and Roy Emerson have something else to be proud of—impeccable sportsmanship."

References

N Y Times V p4 Jl 1 '62; p36 S 11 '62 por
Newsweek 58:66 Jl 24 '61 por
Sports Illus 17:51+ S 17 '62 por
Time 80:57 S 21 '62 pors

LEE, PEGGY May 26, 1920- Singer; actress; songwriter

Address: b. c/o Richard St. Johns, 433 S. Spring St., Los Angeles, Calif.

More than two decades have passed since Peggy Lee sang with Benny Goodman's swing band and made her first hit recording. Yet so inexhaustible is her talent and so intense her application to her work that, almost a generation later, she stands at the peak of her career. A product of the big-band era, she derived from that apprenticeship her ability to sing anything from jazz to blues, to sing it with a beat, and with enough volume to be heard above the band. Few vocalists have had her staying power. Peggy Lee is also a successful composer, lyricist, arranger, actress, and businesswoman. To all her careers she brings a perfectionism that leaves the stamp of professionalism on everything she touches.

Of Norwegian and Swedish ancestry, Peggy Lee was born Norma Dolores Engstrom in Jamestown, North Dakota, a farm town on the Great Plains, on May 26, 1920. (One source gives Norma Jean Engstrom.) She was the seventh of eight children born to Marvin Engstrom, a station agent for the Midland Continent Rail Road, and Mrs. Engstrom, who died when the child was four years old. Encouraged by the recognition she had received for her singing with the high school glee club, the church choir, and

Capitol Records, Inc.

PEGGY LEE

semi-professional college bands, Norma headed for Hollywood after she graduated from high school in 1938. With her she took $18 in cash and a railroad pass she had borrowed from her father. Although she got a brief singing engagement at the Jade Room, a supper club on Hollywood Boulevard, she made little impression on the film capital, and she was reduced to working as a waitress and as a carnival spieler at a Balboa midway.

Deciding to try her luck nearer home, she found work as a singer over radio station WDAY in Fargo, North Dakota, whose manager, Ken Kennedy, christened her Peggy Lee. (To supplement her income she worked for a time as a bread slicer in a Fargo bakery.) Her prospects for a career brightened when she moved to Minneapolis, where she sang in the dining room of the Raddison Hotel, appeared on a Standard Oil radio show, and sang with Sev Olsen's band. Miss Lee broke into the big time when she became a vocalist with Will Osborne's band, but three months after she joined the Osborne group it broke up in St. Louis, and she got a ride to California with the manager. It was at the Doll House in Palm Springs, California that Peggy Lee first developed the soft and "cool" style that has become her trademark. Unable to shout above the clamor of the Doll House audience, Miss Lee tried to snare its attention by lowering her voice. The softer she sang the quieter the audience became. She has never forgotten the secret, and it has given her style its distinctive combination of the delicate and the driving, the husky and the purringly seductive. One of the members of the Doll House audience was Frank Bering, the owner of Chicago's Ambassador West Hotel, who invited her to sing in his establishment's Buttery Room.

Benny Goodman discovered Peggy Lee's vocalizing in the Buttery Room at a time when he was looking for a replacement for Helen Forrest.

Miss Lee joined Goodman's band as a vocalist in July 1941, when the band was at the height of its popularity, and for over two years she toured the United States with the most famous swing outfit of the day, playing hotel engagements, college proms, theater dates, and radio programs.

Much of her present success Miss Lee credits to her apprenticeship with the big bands. "I learned more about music from the men I worked with in bands than I've learned anywhere else," she has said. "They taught me discipline and the value of rehearsing and even how to train. . . . Band singing taught us the importance of interplay with musicians. We had to work close to the arrangement." In July 1942 Peggy Lee recorded her first smash hit, *Why Don't You Do Right?* It sold over 1,000,000 copies and made her famous.

In March 1943 Peggy Lee married Dave Barbour, the guitarist in Goodman's band; shortly thereafter she left the band. After her daughter, Nikki, was born in 1944 Peggy Lee and her husband worked successfully on the West Coast. In 1944 she began to record for Capitol Records, for whom she has produced a long string of hits —many of them with lyrics and music by Miss Lee and Dave Barbour. Among them are: *Golden Earrings,* which sold over 1,000,000 copies; *You Was Right, Baby; It's a Good Day; Manana* (which sold over 2,000,000 records); *What More Can a Woman Do?* and *I Don't Know Enough About You.* Today Peggy Lee has a top rating as a songwriter with the American Society of Composers, Authors, and Publishers.

In 1950 Peggy Lee made a first, brief screen appearance in Paramount's *Mr. Music,* starring Bing Crosby. In 1953 she played a featured role opposite Danny Thomas in Warner Brothers' remake of the early Al Jolson talking picture, *The Jazz Singer,* and won praise from a critic of the New York *World-Telegram and Sun* for "a very promising start on a movie career" as "a poised and ingratiating ingenue." Her performance as a despondent and alcoholic blues singer in *Pete Kelly's Blues* (Warner Brothers, 1955) won her a nomination for an award from the Academy of Motion Picture Arts and Sciences. In the 1955 balloting conducted by the Council of Motion Picture Organizations moviegoers voted her the "Audie" statuette.

Peggy Lee has not only appeared in motion pictures but has also written music and lyrics for them. She wrote the theme music for *Johnny Guitar* (Republic, 1954) and for *About Mrs. Leslie* (Paramount, 1954). She contributed the musical score to two George Pal cartoon features, *Tom Thumb* (MGM, 1958), and *The Time Machine* (MGM, 1960), and wrote the lyrics and supplied several voices for the Walt Disney full-length animated cartoon *Lady and the Tramp* (Buena Vista, 1955). For *Anatomy of a Murder* (Columbia, 1959) she wrote the lyrics for "I'm Gonna Go Fishing" to music by Duke Ellington.

In the respect she commands from the critics both as a popular vocalist and as a jazz artist, Peggy Lee is a rarity among singers. Critic George Hoefer of *Downbeat* magazine has called her "the greatest white female jazz singer since Mildred Bailey," and Leonard Feather in *The Encyclopedia of Jazz* (Horizon, 1960) has described her as "one of the most sensitive and jazz-oriented singers in the pop field." Miss Lee won the 1946 polls as best female vocalist of both *Metronome* and *Downbeat* magazines, widely read by jazz buffs, and the 1950 citation as "the nation's most popular female vocalist" from *Billboard,* a trade magazine of show business. A frequent performer on television, she sang on the Thursday night *Revlon Revues* over CBS-TV in 1960, and has appeared on televised musical variety shows starring Perry Como, George Gobel, Steve Allen, and Bing Crosby. In March 1960 she undertook a straight dramatic role in "So Deadly, So Evil," on the *General Electric Theater* over CBS-TV.

In September 1962 Miss Lee reached what she has called the "high spot" in her career when she was selected to appear in Philharmonic Hall of New York's Lincoln Center for the Performing Arts, an auditorium usually available only to those whom the management considers as serious artists. Miss Lee conducted research for, and wrote a program called *The Jazz Tree,* tracing the origins and development of jazz as a native American art form. Originally scheduled for December 1962, the booking was postponed until March 1963 to give Miss Lee enough time to perfect her presentation.

This perfectionist approach to her programs is typical of Miss Lee. She polishes and perfects every aspect of her performances—her special coiffures, her costly wardrobe, her lighting, her entrances and exits, and her musical arrangements. Her perfectionism may derive from her association with Benny Goodman, who has always demanded the best from his performers. Rejecting the improvisatory approach of most jazz singers, Peggy Lee plans every detail of her delivery in advance, including even the movement of her hands. This perfectionism has taken its toll of her health on several occasions; she was hospitalized with virus pneumonia in July 1958 and in November 1961. As a result, Miss Lee has reduced her schedule, confining her public appearances to six weeks each year in New York and Las Vegas, a few television shows, and one or two charity benefits.

Although Miss Lee continues to collaborate with Dave Barbour on words and music, their marriage ended in divorce in 1951. On January 4, 1955 Miss Lee married Brad Dexter, a movie actor. Ten months later they were divorced. Miss Lee's third marriage, to actor Dewey Martin on April 25, 1956, also ended in divorce in 1959. She is five feet seven inches in height, has hazel eyes, and champagne-blonde hair. With her daughter, Nikki, she lives in a rambling contemporary home in Coldwater Canyon, near Hollywood, California. It contains not only a soundproof studio with tape units, microphones, grand piano, and other equipment for writing and recording music, but also an artist's studio in which she paints and sculpts the hands of musicians and the heads of great men like Albert Schweitzer whom she admires. A book of her verse, *Softly, With Feeling,* was published in 1953. In 1958 Miss Lee consolidated her various activities, which include music publishing firms and a production unit for television and films, into a company called Peggy Lee Enterprises. Noted for her generosity,

she has been active in such philanthropies as CARE and WAIF, and in November 1962 was appointed national chairman of the Tom Dooley Foundation.

In spite of her many commitments Peggy Lee makes a point of finding enough time for reading, especially the essays of Ralph Waldo Emerson who, she feels, has a special significance for Americans today. "I wouldn't still be working today if it weren't for the strength I've derived from some of his essays," she once told Neil Hickey in an interview for the *American Weekly* (July 3, 1960). "He said: 'God will not have his work done by cowards.' To me that means: 'Don't let your personal problems get in the way of your life's work.' I've had to remember that rule several times during my career."

References

> International Motion Picture Almanac, 1963
> International Television Almanac, 1963
> Who's Who in America, 1962-63

LEINSDORF, ERICH Feb. 4, 1912- Conductor

Address: b. Boston Symphony Orchestra, Symphony Hall, Boston, Mass.; h. 153 Dean Rd., Brookline, Mass.

> NOTE: This biography supersedes the article that appeared in *Current Biography* in 1940.

When Erich Leinsdorf became conductor and musical director of the Boston Symphony Orchestra in September 1962 he succeeded Charles Munch in what has been called "the most celestial of all conductorial posts." His appointment represented a change for the Boston orchestra from the more flamboyant French-Russian tradition of his predecessors, for he is noted for his precision, and his forte is the German-Austrian repertoire. Born and trained in Vienna, Leinsdorf first came to the United States in 1937 as a protegé of Arturo Toscanini and made his American debut at the Metropolitan Opera House in 1938. Since then, he has been chief conductor of the Rochester Philharmonic Orchestra (1947 to 1956), the New York City Opera (1956), and the Metropolitan Opera (1957 to 1962). He has recorded extensively and has appeared as guest conductor with major orchestras throughout the world.

Erich Leinsdorf was born in Vienna on February 4, 1912 to Ludwig Julius and Charlotte (Loebl) Leinsdorf. His father, an amateur pianist, died when he was three years old. Leinsdorf's musical training began early; by the time he was seven, he was studying the piano, and when he was thirteen he added the cello, musical theory, and composition. After graduating from the University of Vienna in 1930, Leinsdorf entered the State Academy of Music as a scholarship student. He obtained his diploma in 1933 and that year made his debut as a conductor in Vienna.

As an unknown young musician Leinsdorf was confined to such relatively minor posts as assist-

ERICH LEINSDORF

ant conductor of the Vienna Workers' Chorus. Deciding to gamble on a more important job (and lacking money for carfare), he hiked 155 miles to Salzburg, where Bruno Walter was holding auditions for the 1934 festival. Leinsdorf's audition won him the post of assistant conductor, and during his first session he so impressed Arturo Toscanini that he was held over as assistant to Walter and Toscanini for the festivals of 1935, 1936, and 1937. Between summers at Salzburg, Leinsdorf assisted Walter at a music festival in Florence, toured France and Belgium as a symphonic conductor, and spent two seasons in the "Italian operatic backcountry" in Bologna, San Remo, and Trieste. His ability to speak Italian, which he had learned when he was nineteen, stood him in good stead. In 1937 on Toscanini's recommendation, he was hired by the Metropolitan Opera in New York City as assistant to Artur Bodanzky, who was then chief conductor of the Met's German repertory.

Leinsdorf made his American debut at the Metropolitan Opera House on January 21, 1938, leading a performance of Wagner's *Die Walküre*. Writing in the New York *Herald Tribune*, Lawrence Gilman described the newcomer to the podium as "an astonishingly boyish figure" and went on to say: "Though he wiped his brow occasionally with his handkerchief . . . he soon made it evident that he was entirely at home in the great work before him and that he possesses an exceptional gift for eliciting its substance from the players under his command." Three months later Leinsdorf was asked to conduct an Easter performance of Wagner's *Parsifal* on only twelve hours notice. Gilman called the performance "one of the finest that has ever been heard at the Metropolitan."

Although it had been expected that he would substitute for Bodanzky only occasionally, Leinsdorf conducted ten performances during his first season at the Met and thirty-six performances in 1938-39. Three weeks before the start of the

1939-40 season Bodanzky fell ill, and Leinsdorf was entrusted with the preparation and rehearsal of the entire Wagnerian repertory and other operas. Bodanzky died six days before the opening of the season, and the twenty-eight-year-old Leinsdorf was given his job.

Leinsdorf was chief conductor of German operas from 1939 to 1943, during which time he had to contend not only with the musical challenges of the Met, but also with its backstage intrigue. In January 1940 Lauritz Melchior, the Wagnerian tenor, publicly denounced him as being too young and inexperienced to conduct Wagner, and Kirsten Flagstad, then the Met's leading Wagnerian soprano, seconded Melchior. Leinsdorf, however, had the firm backing of Edward Johnson, the manager of the Met, and despite his youth he retained his position.

During the Met's off-seasons Leinsdorf appeared as guest conductor with the NBC Symphony Orchestra (regularly conducted by Toscanini), the Montreal Orchestra, and the San Francisco Opera. In 1943 he left the Metropolitan Opera to succeed Artur Rodzinski as music director and conductor of the Cleveland Orchestra, becoming, at thirty-one, the youngest man ever to head a major American symphony. Only a month later, however, Leinsdorf (who had become an American citizen in 1942) was drafted as a private into the United States Army. When he was released as a corporal on a medical discharge only eight months later, the Cleveland job had already gone to someone else. Over the next three years he appeared as a guest conductor with the Cleveland, at the Met, and elsewhere but held no permanent post.

In 1947 Leinsdorf became music director and conductor of the Rochester Philharmonic Orchestra. This represented something of a comedown, for the Rochester orchestra, though well-respected, is of less consequence in the symphonic hierarchy than the Cleveland, but he stayed there for nine years. "It turned out to be less minor league than I thought it might be," he has since commented. "Some recordings we made there in 1952 and 1953 bear witness that one could get somewhere with an orchestra like that."

Leaving Rochester in 1956, Leinsdorf became director of the New York City Opera. He led this young, adventurous company through what has been described (*Esquire,* February 1962) as "a disastrously overimaginative season of contemporary works." Among the operas that received their American premières at the City Center during the year of his directorship were Carlisle Floyd's *Susannah,* Carl Orff's *The Moon,* and Frank Martin's *The Tempest.* Reviewing the season in the New York *Times,* Howard Taubman wrote: Leinsdorf "has a progressive orientation and is willing to take risks. The failures may be resounding, but they are preferable to tame routine." Despite the fact that the season was a financial failure, Leinsdorf felt the experience helped to convince private foundations of the need for subsidizing contemporary opera productions.

In 1957 Leinsdorf returned to the more staid Metropolitan, assuming, in addition to the conductorship, the newly created post of music consultant. He remained at the Metropolitan for five years, during which time he was responsible for a number of noteworthy productions. Among these were the American première of Verdi's *Macbeth* in 1958-59 and the first performance since 1945 of Wagner's complete *Ring* cycle in 1961-62.

Despite his heavy schedule at the Metropolitan, Leinsdorf was active both as a guest conductor and in the recording studios. Among the orchestras with which he appeared were the Boston Symphony (which he led nearly fifty times before taking it over permanently), the Philadelphia, the Pittsburgh Symphony, the Los Angeles Philharmonic, the Berlin Philharmonic, the Vienna Philharmonic, the Vienna Opera, the BBC Symphony, the London Symphony, the London Philharmonic, and the Israel Philharmonic. He also was on the advisory committee for the new Opera House at the Lincoln Center.

Leinsdorf has made hundreds of recordings, ranging over the repertory from Haydn to Prokofiev. Most notable of his orchestral recordings is a complete set of Mozart's symphonies. He has recorded over a dozen operas, among them Mozart's *The Marriage of Figaro* and *Don Giovanni*, Rossini's *The Barber of Seville*, Verdi's *Macbeth*, and Puccini's *La Bohème, Madama Butterfly*, and *Turandot*. His recording of *Turandot* was hailed by the National Academy of the Recording Arts and Sciences as the best operatic recording of the 1960-61 season and has since become one of the best-selling opera albums of all time. His recording of *Die Walküre*, made in 1962, won the *Saturday Review* critics' poll as the top operatic recording of the year.

With his appointment as conductor and music director of the Boston Symphony Orchestra in 1962, Leinsdorf finally found an instrument worthy of his talents. Generally considered one of the finest orchestras in the world, the Boston Symphony was founded in 1881 by Major Henry Lee Higginson, a Yankee banker. It was his policy to hire the conductor and leave musical matters to him, and the orchestra's directors have followed that policy ever since. For that reason, among others, the Boston symphony has a tradition of unusual conductorial longevity—it has had only eleven conductors over the past eighty-two years. Speaking of his own experiences with the management, Leinsdorf has said: "Whatever came up, the musical necessity had its way. From having seen musical organizations abroad and in this country, this is rare. . . . I have a suspicion it is unique. "

The Boston orchestra is unique in other ways as well. It has the longest season of any privately supported orchestra in the world, performing about fifty weeks each year. Its home season at Symphony Hall is regularly sold out in advance by subscription. In addition, Boston Symphony musicians regularly give a series of Pops Concerts and a Charles River Esplanade series and in the summers perform at the Berkshire Music Festival at Tanglewood, the orchestra's own estate in Lenox, Massachusetts. (As music director, Leinsdorf also holds the post of director of the Berkshire Music Festival and the Berkshire Music Center.) These activities have made the Boston Symphony the most solvent orchestra in the United States: It earns over 70 percent of its expenses, while the national average is only 57 percent.

The Boston Symphony's financial well-being must be considered secondary to its musical accomplishments, however. A critic once called it "one of the very greatest instruments of artistic utterance ever developed by any civilization on earth." Soon after the announcement of his appointment, Leinsdorf said: "I am particularly happy about coming here not as a bricklayer. I don't have to build. I find a magnificent orchestra and a magnificent organization. This enables one to make music without having to go to collect the materials."

Although Leinsdorf's conducting during his first season with the Boston Symphony created a generally favorable impression, not all reviewers were happy with the precision that he seemed to be substituting for Munch's impassioned, if sometimes undisciplined, leadership. Characterizing Leinsdorf's concerts as "superb but not superlative," Harold Rogers in the *Christian Science Monitor* (December 31, 1962) added: "There is no gainsaying that he has done wonders with the orchestra, that he has refined its tone, adjusted its balance, polished its timbres. Yet in nearly everything he does . . . his intelligence holds a slight edge over his emotions. For the finest and greatest music making, of course, the heart should hold a slight edge over the head." Harold C. Schonberg expressed a similar view in the New York *Times* (June 2, 1963). "Already, in the space of one season," he said, Leinsdorf "has made the Boston Symphony a more precise group. . . . Few musicians would deny that he is a steadier conductor than Munch. There is, however, a touch of pedanticism in his work. Perhaps this is purposeful. . . . Greater freedom and more imagination may come as the years roll along."

Whatever the consensus on the 1962-63 season may have been, much satisfaction was expressed with Leinsdorf's vigorous leadership of the 1963 summer season at Tanglewood. He presented thirty-two works new to the Berkshire Music Festival, including the American première of Benjamin Britten's *War Requiem*; gave the first all-Haydn program at Tanglewood; and scheduled a Mozart series and a Prokofiev cycle. Taking a more active part in the Berkshire Music Center than Munch had done, he inspired better organization and the selection of more qualified students. William Bender wrote in the New York *Herald Tribune* (August 26, 1963), "By almost every standard of judgment, Mr. Leinsdorf has done well by his new orchestra, the festival, and the summer music center."

Leinsdorf is a member of the advisory committee on the arts of the National Cultural Center (Washington, D.C.), the visiting committee of the Harvard University board of overseers to the music department, and the music advisory section of the Dartmouth College council on the creative arts. He is an honorary co-chairman of the Friends of Albert Schweitzer (Brookline, Massachusetts) and a fellow of the American Academy of Arts and Sciences. Leinsdorf was awarded the D.Mus. degree by Rutgers University (1952) for his help in forming the Rutgers University Choir and by Baldwin-Wallace College

LEINSDORF, ERICH—*Continued*

(1945). He has written on music for the *Atlantic Monthly,* the New York *Times,* the *Saturday Review* and *High Fidelity.*

Erich Leinsdorf and Anne Frohnknecht, a teacher, were married on August 3, 1939. They have five children: David Immanuel, Gregor Jonathan, Joshua Franklin, Deborah Hester, and Jennifer Gabrielle. From his children Leinsdorf has gained a liking for jazz—"highly intricate jazz and *not* too loud." He collects stamps, and is a connoisseur of wines and an amateur photographer. He is short and compactly built and is always meticulously dressed. Leinsdorf likes to talk and is reputed to be the musical world's greatest wit since the late Sir Thomas Beecham. As a conductor he has a passion for thoroughness and is known as something of a disciplinarian. "I like to have the right note played in the right place," he says.

References

Atlan 210:111+ S '62
Esquire 57:16 F '62
N Y Times p17 S 22 '62 por
Time 80:40 O 5 '62 pors
Ewen, David, ed. Living Musicians (1940; First Supplement, 1957)
Slonimsky, Nicolas. Baker's Biographical Dictionary of Musicians (1958)
Who's Who in America, 1962-63

LEMONNIER, ANDRÉ (GEORGES) 1896-May 30, 1963 French admiral (ret.); chief of the Free French Navy under Charles de Gaulle during World War II and later, chief of the French naval staff; deputy naval commander of SHAPE under Dwight D. Eisenhower (1951-56). See *Current Biography* (November) 1952.

Obituary

N Y Times p21 Je 1 '63

LEQUERICA Y ERQUIZA, JOSÉ FÉLIX DE Jan. 30, 1891-June 9, 1963 Spanish representative to the United Nations (1955-63), Ambassador to the United States (1950-54), and Ambassador to France (1939-44). See *Current Biography* (June) 1951.

Obituary

N Y Times p31 Je 10 '63

LI, C(HOH) H(AO) Apr. 21, 1913- Biochemist; university professor

Address: b. Life Sciences Bldg., University of California, Berkeley 4, Calif.; h. 901 Arlington Ave., Berkeley 7, Calif.

The recipient of the Albert Lasker Award for basic medical research for 1962 is Dr. C. H. Li, professor of biochemistry and experimental endocrinology, and director of the Hormone Research Laboratory of the University of California at Berkeley. The scientist, born in China, has devoted a quarter of a century of research to an effort to understand the chemistry and

nature of the hormones of the front portion of the pituitary gland, the human body's tiny governing gland, located at the base of the brain. Its hormones are the prime movers of reproduction, growth, maturation, and metabolism. Dr. Li and his co-workers have isolated in pure form six of these hormones, including ACTH, the adrenocorticotropic hormone and adrenal booster, used in the treatment of arthritis, and HGH, the human growth hormone or somatotropin, without which human growth could not take place.

Choh Hao Li was born in Canton, China on April 21, 1913, one of the four sons of Kan-chi Li, an industrialist, and the former Mew-ching tsin. One brother, Dr. Choh-ming Li, is a professor of business administration at the University of California at Berkeley; another brother, Dr. Choh-luh Li, is a neurosurgeon at the National Institutes of Health, Bethesda, Maryland; a third brother, Dr. Choh-hsien Li, is director of metallurgical research at the Minneapolis-Honeywell Corporation. Choh Hao Li attended Pui-Ying Middle School in Canton, where his favorite extracurricular activity was tennis. After he graduated in 1929, he continued his studies at the University of Nanking, which granted him his B.S. degree in chemistry in 1933. For the next two years (1933-35) he served as an instructor in chemistry at Nanking.

In 1935 Li came to the United States as a graduate student in chemistry at the University of California. He was granted the Ph.D. degree in 1938 and immediately accepted an appointment as research associate with Professor Herbert M. Evans at the Institute of Experimental Biology. Dr. Li has remained at the University of California throughout his career. In 1941 he was named a lecturer. In 1944 he was appointed an assistant professor and in 1947 an associate professor of experimental biology. In January 1950 he was made professor of biochemistry and experimental endocrinology and director of the Hormone Research Laboratory, part of the University of California's School of Medicine, in San Francisco. Dr. Li also holds faculty appointments in the departments of medicine and pediatrics of the School of Medicine.

In the fall of 1938 Dr. Li had begun his professional scientific career as a research associate with Professor Herbert M. Evans at the Institute of Experimental Biology. His first major contribution to the study of pituitary hormones came in 1940, when he isolated the highly purified interstitial cell-stimulating hormone (ICSH) from sheep glands and, a short time later, from pig glands. In 1942 Dr. Li reported the isolation of two extremely important hormones, the purified crystalline growth hormone and the adrenocorticotropic hormone (ACTH), from sheep and pig pituitary glands. In all, Dr. Li is credited with the isolation and purification of six pituitary hormones.

Since his appointment in 1950 as head of the Hormone Research Laboratory, Dr. Li has directed its work in several critical avenues of investigation. He has assigned primary importance to the isolation, identification, and possible synthesis of biologically active components in the front portion of the pituitary gland. An attempt has been made to determine the nature of these hormones and their physiological functions. These undertakings, in turn, make easier further investigations of the relationship of hormones to diseases and studies of the mechanisms of normal and abnormal growth.

Isolation of a particular hormone, important as it may be, constitutes but a first step in a long series of increasingly complicated investigations. In 1955, after a five-year research program that cost a quarter of a million dollars, Dr. Li and his colleagues determined the composition and structure of the ACTH molecule. It was found to be made up of fairly simple compounds, called amino acids. Thirty-nine of these amino acid residues were discovered, arranged like a straight line of beads. Analysis and determination of the molecular architecture of ACTH pointed the way toward the possibility of eventual synthesis and precise use of the powerful hormone.

Differences noted in the amino acid sequential pattern led Dr. Li to conclude that the potency of ACTH, and probably of other hormones, is associated with a comparatively small area or core of the amino acid residues. Experiments indicated that not all of the thirty-nine amino acids were necessary for the biological activity of the hormone. Dr. Li's core theory of potency was substantiated in 1960 when, with a team of five other scientists, he synthesized a molecule that corresponded to only nineteen of the thirty-nine amino acids of natural ACTH, but which exercised a number of biological functions of the natural hormone. In 1962 a synthesis of a seventeen amino acid peptide possessing ACTH biological activities was achieved.

Dr. Li's continuing efforts to locate the smallest active core of the ACTH molecule opens the door for possible large-scale preparation of a synthetic ACTH for general clinical use. For more than a decade ACTH has been clinically effective in the remission of collagen diseases, notably rheumatoid arthritis. Full use of the hormone has been limited, however, by the presence of undesirable, deleterious side effects. If it is determined that differing biological effects stem from different portions of the ACTH molecule, it may be possible to synthesize specific active cores, designed to achieve specific results, thus eliminating unwanted side effects.

Much of the early hormonal research was performed on the glands of sheep and pigs. Over the years other animals have been used, including cattle. In 1944, twenty-three years after its discovery by Dr. Evans and an associate, the cattle growth hormone was isolated by Dr. Li, and for thirty-five years it provided the foundation for the study of the growth hormone. In 1956 Dr. Li achieved a major breakthrough with the first isolation of growth hormone from human and monkey pituitary glands.

The isolation of the human growth hormone may prove to be the most important among Dr. Li's many achievements. The therapeutic effectiveness of the hormone—both in pituitary dwarfism, caused by a deficiency of growth hormone in the body, and genetic dwarfism, stemming from the defective transmission of genes at birth—has been clinically demonstrated. Experiments with the hormone have apparently

C. H. LI

solved a long-standing biological mystery concerning prolactin, the milk-stimulating hormones in females. Antibodies produced by the injection of human growth hormone into rabbits may suggest new methods in the treatment of cancer.

Considerable difficulties must be overcome, however, before more success can be achieved in these areas. The chief obstacle lies in the fact that while ACTH and other hormones extracted from lower animal life prove effective in human beings, the growth hormones from lower animals are useless in human subjects. Until the hormone can be synthesized or a means found to employ the animal growth hormone successfully in human beings, the only available source remains the human pituitary gland. This gland has been obtained by pathologists at autopsy, but about 1,000 glands are required to obtain one gram of the hormone.

Before an attempt can be made to synthesize HGH, its molecular structure and composition must be established. Although incomplete, Dr. Li's investigations have shown that the human growth hormone has a different chemical composition and structure than the larger, more complicated growth hormones of animals. However, it is believed that there is a similar active core in the growth hormone from all sources. If a method can be devised for obtaining it, the easily available cattle hormone can be used in human beings.

Although one of the most effective methods of controlling cancer is the removal of the pituitary gland, growth of any tissue, normal or abnormal, is thereby made impossible. Less drastic treatment may lie in the direction opened up by growth hormone research. Tests on persons of normal and abnormal stature have revealed that the pituitary growth hormone is present in the blood of abnormally large persons with overactive pituitary glands. The testing method involves the creation of antibodies in rabbits that are then injected into the

LI, C. H.—_Continued_

human subject to measure the amount of growth hormone in the blood. It is hoped that the use of such antibodies may eventually open up a new line of attack on cancer.

At a special scientific gathering at the New York Academy of Medicine held in conjunction with the 1962 Albert Lasker medical research awards, Dr. Li announced what appears to be a second major function for the human growth hormone—that of stimulating milk secretion in the mammary glands. For years, all attempts to find in man or in monkeys prolactin, the milk-stimulating hormone found in lower mammals, had ended in failure. Evidence collected by Dr. Li and his associates at the University of California's Medical Center in San Francisco strongly suggests that the human growth hormone combines in one molecule the functions performed by two separate hormones in most four-footed mammals.

The profound importance of Dr. Li's research efforts and discoveries is reflected by the honors accorded him over the years. In 1947 he received the Ciba Award in Endocrinology, and in 1948 he was a John Simon Guggenheim Memorial Foundation Fellow. He was the first recipient of the American Chemical Society's California section medal in 1951. In 1955 he was awarded the Francis Emory Septennial Prize of the American Academy of Arts and Sciences. He received a gold medal from the Minister of Education of the Republic of China in 1958 and the biennial award from the Chinese-American Citizen Alliance in 1961. The Catholic University of Chile conferred an honorary Doctor of Medicine degree upon him in 1962, and in the same year the Albert and Mary Lasker Foundation gave him the Albert Lasker Award for basic medical research. The Lasker award, consisting of $10,000 in cash and a gold statuette of the Winged Victory of Samothrace symbolizing victory over death and disease, was presented to him by Mrs. Lyndon B. Johnson on November 14, 1962 in New York City. Li was named faculty research lecturer for 1962 at the University of California's San Francisco Medical Center, one of the highest honors that the university faculty can confer on one of its members.

Dr. Li became a Fellow of the American Association for the Advancement of Science in 1950 and of the New York Academy of Science in 1951. He holds honorary memberships in the Harvey Society (New York), Argentina Society of Endocrinology and Metabolism, Academia Sinica (Republic of China), Biological Society of Chile, and is an affiliate of the Royal Society of Medicine in London. Dr. Li also belongs to the American Chemical Society, American Society of Biological Chemists, American Society of Zoologists, Endocrine Society, Biochemical Society (London), and Society of Experimental Biology and Medicine.

Since 1935 Dr. Li has contributed more than 400 articles to scientific journals and books. He has served on the editorial boards of a number of the more specialized publications. In 1947 Dr. Li was the Claude Bernard visiting professor at the University of Montreal, Canada. He was visiting scientist at the Harvard Medical School in Boston in 1955, and in 1958 he served as the China Foundation visiting professor, National Taiwan University, Formosa.

Dr. Li, who became an American citizen in 1955, genuinely appreciates the opportunities for scientific research that are available in the United States. Citing both public and private support for his research projects, he has said, "The United States is one of the very few places in the world where programs like ours could have been carried out." He reserves his greatest tributes, however, for the Hormone Research Laboratory itself.

Over forty visiting scientists and Fellows from nineteen countries have worked at the laboratory since 1950. Dr. Li believes that many accomplishments in basic hormone research stem from the diverse approach to problems taken by this group of scientists who represent many nationalities and scientific disciplines. In accepting the Lasker award Dr. Li said, "We have found that scientific inquiry, in both spirit and practice, is immensely rewarded by the participation of people from many different homelands."

A slim man who looks younger than his age, Dr. Choh Hao Li stands five feet eleven inches tall and weighs 140 pounds. On October 1, 1938 he married Sheng-hwai Lu, a graduate student. They have three children, Wei-i, Ann-si, and Eva. In his rare moments of leisure time he enjoys reading and working on his coin and stamp collections.

References

American Men of Science 10th ed (1960-62)
Leaders in American Science, 1960-61

LOMBARDI, VINCE June 11, 1913- Professional football coach
Address: b. Green Bay Packers, 349 S. Washington St., Green Bay, Wisc.; h. 677 Sunset Circle, Green Bay, Wisc.

Vince Lombardi, who has been head coach and general manager of the Green Bay Packers since 1959, is recognized as a miracle man of present-day football. When he took command of the Packers they were at the bottom of the professional football ladder, and Green Bay, Wisconsin was known as the Siberia of the National Football League, where coaches from other teams threatened to send errant players. But Lombardi molded his group of "has-beens" into a winning team by imparting confidence, training, and know-how; and the Packers won the Western Conference titles in 1960, 1961, and 1962 and the NFL championship in 1961 and 1962. Before coaching at Green Bay, Lombardi had been offense coach with the New York Giants and an assistant coach of the Army team at West Point.

Vincent Thomas Lombardi was born in the Sheepshead Bay section of Brooklyn, New York City, on June 11, 1913 to Henry Lombardi, a meat wholesaler who had emigrated from Italy, and Matilda (Izzo) Lombardi. He has two sisters, Madeline and Claire, and two brothers, Harold and Joseph. As a boy Vince Lombardi planned to enter the Roman Catholic priesthood. He attended Cathedral High School and St. Francis

Preparatory School, both in Brooklyn. While at St. Francis he was a fullback on the football team and belonged to the basketball, baseball, and track teams.

After graduating from St. Francis in 1933 Lombardi entered Fordham University in the Bronx. From 1934 through 1936 he played guard on what was then the most feared line in college football—the "Seven Blocks of Granite." He won three football letters at Fordham and earned a reputation as a scrapper whose violent charges made him appear twice as big as his 172 pounds. Lombardi, who majored in business, was an excellent student and made the Dean's List. He graduated from Fordham with a B.S. degree in 1937.

Lombardi studied nights at the Fordham University School of Law from 1937 to 1939. To pay for his studies he worked days as an insurance investigator and played football on weekends for a minor league professional team called the Brooklyn Eagles. He took his first coaching job in 1939, becoming an assistant football coach at St. Cecilia High School in Englewood, New Jersey. For an annual salary of $1,700 he also taught physics, chemistry, algebra, and Latin. He had great success with the T formation offense, and his football teams won six New Jersey state championships and once picked up thirty-six wins in a row. In 1942 Lombardi became head football, basketball, and baseball coach at St. Cecilia. In 1945 his basketball team won the New Jersey parochial school championship.

At the end of eight years at St. Cecilia, Lombardi returned to Fordham, in 1947, to serve as freshman coach. He installed the T formation for the freshmen, and the following year he coached the varsity offense under Ed Danowski. In 1949 Lombardi became assistant coach under Colonel Earl ("Red") Blaik at the United States Military Academy at West Point, New York. He credits Blaik, who was then a top football coach, with having a marked effect on his career. *Look* magazine (October 24, 1961) quotes Lombardi as saying: "The most important thing that ever happened to me in football was the opportunity to coach under Colonel Blaik. Whatever success I have had must be attributed to 'the old man.' He molded my methods and my whole approach to the game. The unqualified superlative is precarious, but if there is a No. 1 coach of all time, in my opinion it is Colonel Blaik."

In 1954, after five years of shaping the Army's T attack, Lombardi made the big jump to professional football when he was signed as offense coach for the New York Giants. According to the Giants' halfback Frank Gifford, as quoted in *Time* (December 21, 1962), "Vinnie didn't understand our game when he first came here. . . . At first, we players were showing him how it went. By the end of the year, though, he was showing us." Lombardi was convinced that a team could not win in the strong National Football League without a good defense, and he made trades that bolstered the Giants' defense. "A good defense will help the club's morale," he said. In Lombardi's first season the Giants scored 293 points and won seven of twelve games, compared to scoring only 179 points and losing nine games the season before.

Wide World

VINCE LOMBARDI

Lombardi based his offense on what he called "the close-end attack" instead of the league's more popular slot-T formation. In the Giants' offense the ends were closer, with a wide flanker, instead of halfback being between the tackle and a wide end. In 1956 the Giants won their only NFL championship since 1938. The following year they won the Eastern Conference championship but lost to the Baltimore Colts in the league championship game.

On February 2, 1959 Vince Lombardi signed a five-year contract as head coach and general manager of the Green Bay Packers. "While I was with the Giants, my name was mentioned when jobs opened up at Southern California, Washington, Stanford, the Air Force Academy and Pennsylvania, but nothing ever happened," Lombardi has recalled (*Look*, October 24, 1961). "When the Green Bay chance came, I knew it was time to make a move, if ever I was to make one." He resigned his job with the Federation Bank and Trust Company in New York and moved with his family to Green Bay, Wisconsin, a town of 63,000 inhabitants, most of them highly devoted to football and to the Packers.

Among Lombardi's first impressions of the Green Bay team was that the organization was worse but the material much better than he had expected. The team had been run by forty-five directors from all over the state, but Lombardi demanded absolute authority on the football field and the power to hire, fire, and set salaries for players. One of the first things he did was to study movies of past Packer games hundreds of times in order to decide which players to retain and which to discharge. The study of the movies also helped him determine which men to use in certain positions.

By some shrewd trading Lombardi picked up four of his first-stringers from the Cleveland Browns. But it is noteworthy that the majority of the players who later became NFL champions

LOMBARDI, VINCE—*Continued*

had been Packers before Lombardi took over. He brought out their special skills. A good example of this achievement is the transformation of Paul Hornung from a Notre Dame bonus choice who had failed to live up to his promise into a star halfback for Green Bay. "Before Lombardi arrived, I was a jumping jack," Hornung has explained. "Once I was a quarterback, then a fullback. I never knew where I might end up. When he came, everything changed. He said, 'You're going to be my left halfback, period.' Having a coach's backing was like coming out of the dark."

Lombardi worked first on polishing the defense. He launched the team on a vigorous training schedule and established some stringent rules: all players would be on time for meals, meetings, workouts, and the 11 P.M. training camp curfew; those who were late would be fined. "This is a violent sport," he told his players. "To play in this league, you've got to be tough—physically tough and mentally tough." The minds as well as the bodies of the players were shaped for victory. Words like "Spartanism" and "total dedication" were hurled at the team by their fiery coach. Defeatism was banned. "Winning isn't everything," Lombardi emphasized. "It's the only thing!"

The effectiveness of his program was shown in the 1959 league opener against the Chicago Bears. Green Bay won 9 to 6, and in a spontaneous gesture the players carried him from the field on their shoulders. After winning only one out of twelve games in 1958, Green Bay rolled up a 7 won, 5 lost record the first year under Lombardi. In his rookie season as a head coach Lombardi was named National Football League Coach of the Year.

In 1960 the Packers won the Western Conference championship with an 8-4 record, but lost the NFL play-off to Philadelphia by a score of 17 to 13. Green Bay again took the Western Conference title in 1961, winning eleven out of fourteen games. On December 31, 1961 they won their first NFL championship since 1944 by trouncing the New York Giants in the play-off, 37 to 0.

During the 1962 season the Packers rolled up a record of thirteen wins and one loss. They again met the Giants for the world championship on December 30, 1962 and this time beat them by a score of 16 to 7. Following the victory, the Associated Press named the Packers "Team of the Year." Since Lombardi became coach and general manager in 1959 Green Bay has won a total of sixty-two regular, postseason, and preseason games and lost only sixteen. To build a winning team, according to Lombardi, "you must recognize what has to be done, and then you try to do it. It's a matter of recognition, adjustment, and execution, in that order. To play with confidence, a team must feel that everything possible has been done to prepare it fully for the coming game. Nothing's more important than that" (*New Yorker*, December 8, 1962).

Vince Lombardi and the former Marie Planitz, whom he married in August 1940, have two children, Susan and Vincent. Lombardi is five

feet eleven inches tall, weighs 200 pounds, and has brown eyes and graying black hair. He often wears horn-rimmed glasses. Golf is Lombardi's favorite recreation. Active in community life, he has been chairman of the Heart Fund, the March of Dimes, and Wisconsin Dairy Month. He is a Knight of Columbus (fourth degree) and an Elk. He is also a director of the Peoples Bank and Trust Company in Green Bay and of Fordham University.

Under his contract with Green Bay, Lombardi reportedly earns about $50,000 a year. He admits that until 1954, when the school "unwisely" dropped football, he still had hopes of becoming head coach at Fordham University. "A school without football," he said, "is always in danger of deteriorating into a medieval study hall." He wrote a book on professional football, *Run to Daylight!* with W. C. Heinz, which was published by Prentice-Hall, Inc., in 1963. Lombardi considers himself an emotional person; others have noted that he exhibits in his work a talent for analysis, thoroughness, intelligence, pride, and a strong will. Vince Lombardi is popular in Green Bay. A restaurant there has a "Lombardi Room," and the *Vince Lombardi Show* on Wednesday nights during the football season, in which the coach analyzes key plays in the previous Sunday's game, is one of the most popular television programs in Green Bay.

Although college coaching was once his goal Lombardi is now firmly committed to professional football. "In fact, I think I'd be unhappy if I didn't have the added duties of Green Bay's general manager," he has said (*Look,* October 24, 1961). "Tickets, salaries, TV and radio contracts all pose headaches beyond the migraine of trying to win games, but I thrive on work. I'm restless, worrisome, demanding, sometimes impatient and hot-tempered. For these characteristics, a full schedule is the best antidote."

References

Life 53:49+ D 7 '62 pors
Look 25:103+ O 24 '61 pors
New Yorker 38:213+ D 8 '62
Sports Illus 16:13+ Ja 8 '62
Time 80:56+ D 21 '62 pors

LOUTFI, OMAR 1908-May 17, 1963 Egyptian representative to the United Nations (1948-63); United Nations Under Secretary for Special Political Affairs (1961-63). See *Current Biography* (January) 1957.

Obituary

N Y Times p1+ My 18 '63

LOVE, JOHN A(RTHUR) Nov. 29, 1916-
Governor of Colorado; lawyer
Address: b. 136 Capitol Bldg., Denver, Colo.; h. 400 E. 8th Ave., Denver, Colo.

In his first bid for elective office, John A. Love, a Republican, became the thirty-fifth Governor of Colorado after scoring an impressive plurality of more than 86,000 votes over the incumbent Democratic Governor, Stephen L. R. McNichols in the November 1962 election. A politically unknown lawyer, Love campaigned with a pledge to cut taxes and saw his campaign promise fulfilled when, shortly after he took office, the state General Assembly approved a 15 percent across the board reduction in the personal income tax.

John Arthur Love was born on a farm near Gibson City, Illinois on November 29, 1916 to Arthur C. Love, an accountant, and Mildred (Shaver) Love. John A. Love, his brother, Richard, and his sister (now Mrs. A. Morrell) grew up in modest circumstances. When he was four the family moved to Colorado Springs, Colorado, where his father found a job with the *Gazette Telegraph,* a local newspaper. Love attended local elementary schools and in 1934, after graduating from the Cheyenne Mountain School, he enrolled at the University of Denver. To help meet his college expenses he worked at the Denver General Hospital. He also found time to play freshman football and to join the staff of the school newspaper, the *Clarion.* As editor of the *Clarion* in 1937-38, his senior year, he was responsible for several innovations, one of which was to print some editions in reverse with the most important stories in the back of the issue. He reasoned that since many people read their papers from back to front, the best way of getting the top news to them was by putting it on the back pages.

A classmate of Love's recalled in an interview in the Denver *Post* (October 28, 1962): "He was not monied, but he was smart. He earned his way through school by various reputable pursuits. . . . As far as grades were concerned, he always had to work for them. They were good, but he was always so darned busy at something or other that he had to work to keep them good. . . . He had great personal drive. He always knew what he wanted, and he got it. He was an exceptionally well-dressed fellow on a remarkably small wardrobe. He was one of those guys you always knew would wind up right where he is now." After graduating with a B.A. degree in 1938, Love entered the University of Denver Law School, from which he obtained his LL.B. degree in 1941.

Upon graduation, Love passed the state bar examination. However, before he could set up his law practice, the Japanese attacked Pearl Harbor and Love immediately enlisted in the Navy's aviation cadet program. After earning his pilot's wings and commission at Corpus Christi, Texas in October 1942, he was sent to the Pacific, where he piloted amphibious patrol bombers for more than two years as a member of the "Black Cat Squadron." For heroism in combat he was awarded two Distinguished Flying Crosses and the Air Medal with several clusters. Upon his separation from the Navy in 1945, Love returned to Colorado Springs, where he became a partner in the law firm of Love, Cole and Mullett. He confined most of his practice to civil and corporate law.

Since his student days at the University of Denver, Love had been active in the Republican party. In 1947 and 1948 he was president of the El Paso County Young Republicans, and in 1961 he ran unsuccessfully for the chairmanship of the El Paso County G.O.P. He is at present a member of the Republican state central commit-

Lainson Studio, Denver
JOHN A. LOVE

tee and of the El Paso County Republican executive committee. Although he was at the time practically unknown, Love announced in February 1962 that he was "seriously considering whether to seek the Republican nomination for governor." In the Republican primary that year he scored an upset victory over David A. Hamil, an experienced G.O.P. standard bearer who had served in the state legislature. "There was nothing mysterious, no great tactical or strategic knowledge in my pre-assembly campaign," Love told an interviewer for the Denver *Post* (October 28, 1962). "It wasn't hard to get a list of county chairmen and go see them. And it was made easier by my opponent's failure to do so."

In another interview for the Denver *Post* (October 21, 1962) Love said that there were many factors that prompted him to seek the Governorship on his first try for political office, and that "a desire to serve" was his primary motivation. "It's a job which I think I can do, and in all humbleness, I am going to attempt to secure the highest and most effective place in which I can render service," he declared. He also pointed out that he did not believe that prior experience in the state legislature was essential for a Governor. "I think that both Colorado and American history have shown that men who have held high offices without long legislative experience perform their duties at least as well, and in many cases far above average, as those who have not taken that course," he said.

Commenting on his own political orientation, Love pointed out that such designations as "liberal" and "conservative" had been "so used that they are a little shopworn." He noted that he was "no extremist" and "far from the John Birch right wing." The best way to find out where a candidate stood, he said, was to see what action he took on specific issues. Love's foremost campaign pledge was to cut personal state income

LOVE, JOHN A.—*Continued*

taxes, which had recently been raised considerably. "They have been higher than necessary in the past several years, and I propose to attempt to reduce them," he declared.

Although Love's campaign as a political novice was greeted with considerable skepticism by some political experts, including newspapermen, he was, according to the Denver *Post* (October 28, 1962), "expected by a great many persons not given to electoral hallucinations to become the next tenant of the Colorado governor's mansion." In the election of November 6, 1962 Love defeated the incumbent Democratic Governor, Stephen L. R. McNichols, by a vote of 348,790 to 262,456. As James M. Perry wrote in the *National Observer* (April 29, 1963), "Mr. Love clobbered Mr. McNichols and even swept a Republican legislature into office with him. It was, by any standard, a smashing victory."

Less than three weeks after the 1963 Colorado General Assembly convened, it acceded to Governor Love's wishes for a state income tax cut by passing a bill that reduced the tax by 15 percent, retroactive to 1962. It also decreased 1963 state income taxes by about $7,400,000. The two houses of the General Assembly, which for the first time in eight years had large Republican majorities, furthermore showed their support of the new Governor by complying with his wish to make the previously independent department of natural resources a division within his own office. The economy-minded Governor, who cut his predecessor's proposed budget by almost $9,000,000 when he took office, also saw his plan to consolidate the new parks department with the long-established game and fish department approved by the assembly.

One innovation of Governor Love's administration is the so-called Governor's forum. Under this program, the Governor, traveling with selected cabinet members and department heads, conducts two-day meetings in various parts of the state, at which the people from the area are invited to voice questions, comments, and suggestions on current issues. Love has also appointed a special commission to survey the needs and financial problems of local government in Colorado, and he has announced plans for a re-evaluation of the state's higher education. His action of increasing the size of the state Welfare Board and appointing persons of his own choice to the new posts has been accepted without protest.

In a special supplement on Colorado in the New York *Times* (June 16, 1963), Governor Love wrote: "Colorado's government today is sound and operating on the strictest business practices. We are without bonded indebtedness . . . we are on a pay-as-you-go basis both in day-to-day operations and in our capital construction program; our system of taxation is recognized as an outstanding example of equity . . . but it is, nevertheless, under constant and intensive study." Convinced of the need for a greater role for state and local government on the American scene, Love told an interviewer for *Nation's Business* (September 1963): "If we can work right in the precinct, the county and the state, and certainly

in the national elections, we can reverse the trend toward centralization, or at least halt it. I am firmly convinced that this is one of the most important things that we can do to protect the kind of society and government in which we have prospered and progressed."

In 1954 Love was president of the Colorado Springs Chamber of Commerce. (In that year the area was chosen as the site for the Air Force Academy.) A member of several corporate boards, including the board of National Airlines, Love also has oil and ranching interests, and he is division chief of the United Fund. He is a member of the American Bar Association, the Colorado Bar Association, and the El Paso County Bar Association.

John Arthur Love married Ann Daniels of Colorado Springs on October 23, 1942, the same day he won his pilot's wings in the Naval Air Force. They have three children: Dan, an employee of the United Research Company, who is married and lives in Medford, Massachusetts; Andy, a student at Choate School in Wallingford, Connecticut; and Becky, who attends the Graland Country Day School in Denver. Love has been described as ruggedly handsome, with some resemblance to actors William Holden and John Wayne. He is six feet three inches tall, weighs 195 pounds, and has blue eyes and gray hair. His favorite recreations are fishing, swimming, and pheasant and duck hunting. He is also fond of golf and shoots "around 100." When he speaks he is brief and to the point and, according to James M. Perry of the *National Observer* (April 29, 1963), "disarmingly frank." When asked what he thought of being mentioned as a vice-presidential possibility in 1964 by former Vice-President Richard M. Nixon, Love replied: "My position is this. I have a job to do in Colorado." But, he added with a smile, "my mother likes to hear me mentioned for vice-president."

References

Denver Post O 28 '62 por
Nat Observer p1+ Ap 29 '63

LOW, SIR DAVID (ALEXANDER CECIL)
Apr. 7, 1891-Sept. 19, 1963 British political cartoonist and caricaturist; creator of the comic character Colonel Blimp, a symbol of British Conservatism. See *Current Biography* (January-February) 1940.

Obituary

N Y Times p1+ S 21 '63

McCABE, GIBSON Mar. 11, 1911- Publisher
Address: b. Newsweek, 444 Madison Ave., New York 22; h. 120 E. Hartsdale Ave., Hartsdale, N.Y.

According to Gibson McCabe, the president of Newsweek, Inc., and chairman of the executive committee, the magazine industry can expect a bright future because of the development of a more enlightened reading public. "People in greater numbers are getting a better education than ever before," he said in a *Printer's Ink* (September 21, 1962) interview. "The spread of a higher degree of literacy, naturally, creates more readers. Circulations have been climbing for several years now, and they're going to continue going up along with ad linage." Born in Brooklyn, the son of a newspaperman, McCabe has been associated with Newsweek, Inc., since 1942, when he joined the company as circulation director. In September 1962 McCabe became chairman of the Magazine Publishers Association.

Gibson McCabe was born to Robert Copland McCabe, the night city editor of the New York *American*, and Helen Marguerite (Gibson) McCabe on March 11, 1911 in the Flatbush section of Brooklyn, New York City. He has a brother, Robert, Jr., who is in the real estate business. McCabe credits his father's newspaper career with instilling in him a love of journalism. In 1918, when his father was transferred to the Boston *American*, the family moved to Boston, Massachusetts. Five years later the McCabes moved to Baltimore, Maryland, where the father became the managing editor of the Baltimore *News* (now the *News-Post*).

McCabe attended the Tome School in Port Deposit, Maryland from 1923 to 1927. Besides working on the school's publications, he was a member of its tennis and basketball teams. After graduating from the Tome School in 1927 McCabe entered Princeton University, where he majored in French. During his undergraduate days on the New Jersey campus he was a member of the college's tennis team in 1929, 1930, and 1931. In the summers he worked as a runner for Spencer Trask & Company, a New York City stock brokerage house. In 1931 he graduated from Princeton with a B.A. degree.

McCabe's first job after graduation was that of a renting agent for the real estate company Duff & Conger, Inc., where he remained for two years. One day in 1933, while taking a walk, McCabe met a friend who told him that the New York *Times* needed someone to promote the paper's circulation in schools and colleges. McCabe was eager to work for the famous newspaper, and he immediately applied for the position. As the manager of college promotion, McCabe set up a system whereby student representatives at the various schools sold subscriptions for the *Times*. The paper's circulation increased at a rapid rate wherever McCabe put his system into effect.

In 1935 McCabe heard from another acquaintance that the Eton Publishing Company was looking for a circulation manager for school promotion of a new publication, *Young America*. During the seven years that he held this job he built up the magazine's circulation to more than 300,000. In 1942, while walking along Fifth Avenue in Manhattan, McCabe again strolled into some luck. He met the circulation manager of *Time* magazine, who told him that Newsweek, Inc., needed a circulation director. McCabe was interviewed by the publisher of *Newsweek*, Theodore F. Mueller and got the job.

After working with Newsweek, Inc., for about a year McCabe entered the United States Navy. He served from August 1943 through December 1944, and he was released with the rank of lieutenant, junior grade. Beginning in January 1945

GIBSON McCABE

he handled international operations for *Newsweek*, putting out the magazine's "Battle Baby" edition, a stripped-down version without advertisements that was prepared especially for servicemen. He scored a major scoop with the V-E Day number: before the news of the Allied victory in Europe had been cleared for publication he got permission to prepare an advance printing, giving the story of the German surrender. When V-E Day was proclaimed the "Battle Baby" edition was ready for immediate distribution, enabling *Newsweek* to scoop other publications.

Returning to civilian life, McCabe became manager of *Newsweek's* international editions in 1946, advertising manager in 1947, and advertising director in 1949. In 1951 he was named general manager and in 1954 a vice-president of Newsweek, Inc. In 1958, two years after he had become a director of Newsweek, Inc., he succeeded Theodore F. Mueller as publisher of *Newsweek* magazine, and in March 1959 he became the president of Newsweek, Inc. He relinquished his duties as publisher of the magazine in January 1963 and took on the additional title of chairman of the executive committee.

Since McCabe first joined *Newsweek* in 1942 its circulation has climbed from 500,000 to more than 1,500,000. The magazine's ad revenues have risen from $3,906,270 to $25,539,676—an increase of more than 500 percent in twenty years. In August 1961 *Newsweek* became a division of the Washington Post Company. McCabe was pleased with the new ownership because he considers the Washington Post Company an alert and progressive organization. In August 1962 *Newsweek* itself acquired *Art News*, a magazine for art collectors and gallery owners. "The level of public awareness, public interest, and public taste has heightened steadily over the years," McCabe has said (*Printers Ink*, January 6, 1961). "The eagerness for enlightenment . . . the quest for quality . . . have never been so intense. . . .

McCABE, GIBSON—Continued

Few publishers will fail to realize their responsibility (and their own self interest) to continue producing better products by enriching their editorial content and visual appeal."

McCabe, whose interest in selling and salesmanship, whether in circulation or advertising, has never flagged, is convinced that magazines will prosper in relation to how well they serve their readers' interests and retain their readers' loyalty. He is particularly proud of a series of public service messages that his magazine began running in 1958. The full-page spreads deal with subjects like civic awareness, personal responsibility, and interpersonal relations.

McCabe has always shown concern over the fortunes of the magazine industry. On September 18, 1962 he was named chairman of the Magazine Publishers Association (MPA) after serving as vice-chairman for two years. He also served as chairman of the Magazine-Advertising Bureau before that group merged with the MPA. After McCabe's appointment as head of the MPA, one magazine executive said: "There are probably a couple [of] dozen or more publishing executives whose jobs entitle them to head up the MPA, but this time, of all the possibilities, the best of them was picked."

An easygoing man with a deep, soft voice, McCabe has brown hair and brown eyes, is six feet tall, and weighs 175 pounds. His brevity and directness in memoranda and speeches have earned him the nickname "Short-copy" McCabe at Newsweek. Golf and bowling are his favorite recreations. He is the president of the Metropolitan Advertising Golf Association and a member of the Winged Foot Golf Club in Mamaroneck, New York and the Scarsdale Golf Club in Hartsdale. He plays in the low 80's.

Gibson McCabe married Mary Elizabeth Fife, a teacher, on June 27, 1936. They have two daughters, Margaret Anne (Mrs. Melvin Cruger) and Judith Fife (Mrs. Cyrus H. Loutrel 3d). In addition to their Hartsdale home the McCabes have a house in Candlewood Lake, Connecticut. McCabe is chairman of the Publishers Information Bureau, a director of the Advertising Council, and a member of the University and the Chicago clubs. He is an Episcopalian and an independent in politics. He contributed a chapter to How to Get What You Want Out of Life (Appleton-Century, 1962), edited by J. M. Hickerson.

References

Ptr Ink 263:19+ Ap 18 '58 por; 280:52+ S 21 '62 pors
Who's Who in America, 1962-63

McCRACKEN, JAMES (EUGENE) Dec. 16, 1926- Singer

Address: b. c/o Columbia Artists Management, Inc., 165 W. 57th St., New York 19

When the dramatic tenor James McCracken stepped onto the stage of the Metropolitan Opera House as Otello in Verdi's tragic masterpiece on March 10, 1963, his ringing and trumpet-like aria "Esultate" represented not simply a victory in battle but the triumphant return of a native son. During his previous tour of duty at the Metropolitan (from 1953 to 1957), he had seldom sung a role lasting more than a few bars, and many of these were offstage. After four years of carrying a spear as messengers and heralds, McCracken went to Europe in 1957 to gain experience in leading roles in smaller opera houses, and finally stardom in Vienna and Zurich. His Metropolitan comeback was spectacular: the first American-born tenor to attempt the role of Otello in the Metropolitan's long history, McCracken astonished the critics and evoked cheers from the audience.

Supported by a 270-pound frame and a fifty-two-inch chest, McCracken's voice is a powerful one. It is rich in color, exact in placement, and rises without effort to a ravishing upper register. To the dramatic demands of his roles McCracken brings an intelligence and insight rare in an opera singer. These qualities have made him a leading Heldentenor, the world's outstanding Otello, and one of the most exciting singing actors of recent times. He is also that rarity— a dramatic tenor with an international repertory.

Of Scotch-Irish ancestry, James Eugene McCracken was born to John A. McCracken and Doris (Hafey) McCracken in Gary, Indiana on December 16, 1926. His father had a definite musical bent, but his duties as chief of the Gary fire department kept him too busy to do much more than join in local vocal quartets. His mother played the piano by ear and indulged her acting talents in amateur theatricals.

Known to his classmates as "Moose" because he was the heaviest boy in the class, McCracken attended Horace Mann High School in Gary. He sang a leading role in a class production of The Pirates of Penzance, joined the glee club, and was voted "the boy most likely to succeed in music." He also sang in church choirs. After graduating from high school, he enlisted in the United States Navy, where he put his burgeoning tenor voice to good use in the Blue Jackets Choir of the Great Lakes Naval Training Station. Later, when he was assigned to Staten Island, he further performed in naval musical entertainments, and a superior officer was enough impressed by McCracken's voice to advise him to consider singing as a career.

After he was discharged from the Navy, McCracken entered Columbia University under the G.I. Bill to study music. There he worked with Columbia Theatre Associates, gaining experience in productions of Étienne Méhul's Stratonice, Otto Luening's Evangeline, and Douglas Moore's White Wings. Economic pressures led him to take a job in the chorus of the Roxy Theatre, where he sang four shows a day for 291 days a year—sometimes for eighteen hours a day. After several years of this grueling and underpaid employment McCracken looked around for jobs with Broadway musicals. In 1951 he provided the offstage voice of comedian Bert Lahr in Two on the Aisle; in 1951-52 he appeared in A Tree Grows in Brooklyn; and in 1952 he sang in a short-lived revival of Of Thee I Sing. The schedules of the legitimate theater appealed to McCracken because they permitted ample time for auditions and for study with his teacher, Wellington Ezekiel.

In 1952 McCracken made the transition from Broadway to opera when Tibor Kozma gave him an audition for his Central City (Colorado) Opera Company and presented him with a contract. He made his debut as Rodolfo in an English version of *La Boheme* in 1952 and in the same year sang the role of La Couf in Poulenc's *Les Mamelles de Tirésias* with the Lemonade Opera at Brandeis University in Waltham, Massachusetts.

On the advice of Tibor Kozma and scouts from the Metropolitan who had heard his Rodolfo, McCracken auditioned for the Metropolitan and was offered a contract for the season of 1953-54. Of his debut as the toy vendor in *La Boheme*, in November 1953, Jay S. Harrison wrote in the New York *Herald Tribune*: "Mr. McCracken as Parpignol sings no more than a dozen measures. For this reason comment on his operatic abilities must be delayed until another time." Then twenty-six, McCracken felt it would be only a matter of time until he was singing coveted leading roles, but succeeding assignments seldom offered any more substance for criticism than his debut. In short order he settled into the routine of the typical *comprimario,* singing all the behelmeted messengers and liveried retainers in the repertoire. If these walk-ons offered him no opportunity for artistic growth, they kept McCracken so busy that at the end of his first season he had the dubious distinction of having sung 126 roles—more than any other singer in the company. In four years McCracken became convinced that the Metropolitan could not offer him the experience he needed to develop into a leading tenor.

On November 11, 1954 James McCracken had married Sandra Warfield, a mezzo-soprano whom he met when they shared the title roles in a concert version of *Samson and Delilah* in Norfolk, Virginia. In 1957 Miss Warfield advised her husband to leave the Metropolitan and try his luck in Europe, although the move forced her to give up a promising Metropolitan career of her own. McCracken had visited Europe in 1956 to have auditions and to explore the possibilities of singing there, but it was not until the end of the 1956-57 Metropolitan season that he decided to leave the United States.

The first stop for the couple in Europe was Bonn in West Germany, where the tenor had been offered a contract. He made his debut with the German company as Max in *Der Freischütz* and went on to performances as Canio in *Pagliacci,* Manrico in *Il Trovatore,* and Radames in *Aida.* Although McCracken was singing leading roles at last, the house policy of performing all operas in German conflicted with his ambition to develop an international repertoire of works in their original languages.

With the Bonn season behind him McCracken moved to the Verona Arena in 1958, where Herbert Graf was staging *Aida* and *Turandot* under the baton of Tullio Serafin. Graf, who had been impressed with McCracken when they worked together at the Metropolitan, hired him to understudy the two leading tenors during the festival. But bravura performers like Franco Corelli and Carlo Bergonzi seldom find themselves indisposed, and both singers remained remarkably

JAMES McCRACKEN

hearty throughout the engagement. If McCracken remained unheard, Verona had nevertheless provided him with the opportunity of singing for Serafin, and the conductor, always interested in new voices, was impressed. He suggested to McCracken that he gain more experience in Italian roles.

Several trying years of study in Milan for both McCracken and his wife followed, when the couple studied on credit and never sang in public. McCracken often auditioned for the Italian opera companies, only to encounter courteous rejections. His un-Italian name may have contributed to the resistance. Matters began to improve when McCracken was called to Bielefeld and Zurich in 1959 for guest appearances, and later that year he appeared in Athens as Samson in *Samson and Delilah.* Also in 1959 the couple sang in the same opera company, at Split, Yugoslavia, where McCracken sang Faust and Sandra Warfield appeared as Amneris in *Aida.* These minor successes did not keep McCracken from entertaining misgivings about his future, and at times he wondered whether he had acted wisely in leaving the Metropolitan.

In 1960, a banner year for McCracken, the enterprising Washington (D.C.) Opera Society was planning to produce *Otello* for the current season, and having heard of McCracken's commanding presence and rich, dark tenor, decided he was their man. Although McCracken did not yet have the role firmly in his grasp, he accepted the offer and, working in Milan with his teacher, Marcello Conati, he prepared the part in a short time. McCracken flew to Washington for the three performances, the first of which took place on January 22, 1960. He scored a notable success, especially with the Washington critics. Paul Hume, for example, of the Washington *Post* (January 23, 1960) found McCracken "worth seeing, hearing, and remembering."

(Continued next page)

McCRACKEN, JAMES—Continued

Back in Europe, McCracken found himself much in demand. Herbert Graf, who had been engaged as the director of the Zurich Municipal Theatre, Switzerland's leading opera house, was opening his season with a new *Otello* and wanted McCracken to repeat his Washington success. But others had been listening: Mc-Cracken had sung Bacchus in one performance of *Ariadne auf Naxos* at Vienna for Herbert von Karajan as an audition, and the conductor was enough impressed to offer the young singer a contract. The dilemma in which this placed McCracken was resolved when the Vienna State Opera and the Zurich Municipal Theatre agreed to share his talents. Some observers have suggested that Rudolf Bing was the arbitrator, through his European representative.

McCracken concedes that the role of Otello has done a great deal for him, and he has returned the favor. Easily meeting its vocal demands, he has the weight and the dramatic insight to project a clear-cut image of the tormented Moor. Nobody was surprised when he created a sensation in the role in Zurich in 1960, where he sang it twenty times, and then repeated it nine times in Vienna. That season he also sang Samson in Zurich and Florestan, Canio, and Don Alvaro in Vienna.

At the June festival in Zurich in 1961 Rudolf Bing heard his former *comprimario* for the first time in five years, singing the role of Otello. The next day Bing signed McCracken for the same role in the Metropolitan's new production, scheduled for the spring of 1963. In the meantime, McCracken perfected other roles. He opened Zurich's 1961-62 season with a fiery portrayal of Manrico in *Il Trovatore* in a cast that included a complement of American singers. (Mrs. Mc-Cracken sang Azucena.) Later that season the McCrackens sang together in a revival of Meyerbeer's *Le Prophète*.

Although McCracken's debut with the San Francisco Opera Company on October 2, 1962 proved a major event in its history, McCracken considers his return to the Metropolitan Opera House on March 10, 1963 the genuine high point in his American career. "My growth had been in steady logical stages towards that night," he has said. "There was no other goal for me." Although the prolonged New York newspaper strike blacked out local press reports, the news that McCracken's Otello was the sensation of the season got around through television, radio, magazines, and word of mouth. Confined to the Western edition of the New York *Times* (March 12, 1963), Harold C. Schonberg called McCracken "probably the best Otello around." McCracken justified the contention with eight more performances as Otello during the 1962-63 Metropolitan season and went on to further successes as Canio in *Il Pagliacci*. Touring through the major American cities at the end of the season with the Metropolitan Opera, he duplicated his triumphs as Canio and Otello.

By a former marriage, to a childhood sweetheart, McCracken has a son, John; by his marriage to Sandra Warfield he has a daughter, Anna Maureen Giulietta, who was born in Verona and is bilingual in English and Swiss-German. McCracken is five feet ten inches tall and weighs variously between 250 and 285 pounds. He has a burly frame, cherubic features, and a leonine head on which the curly black hair is turning gray. Wholly American in spite of his long European sojourn, he is given to expletives like "gee" and "gosh." His favorite sports are fishing, and shooting movies of Anna taking advantage of the ski slopes near the McCracken home in Dübendorf, not too far from Zurich. So committed is McCracken to the dramatic tenor repertoire that people often ask him when he will brave Wagnerian roles. He answers: "My feeling at the moment is that Wagnerian roles are more vocal than I like to be. Yes, I want to do Wagner, but I'm going to wait until I'm at least forty."

References

Christian Sci Mon p10 Ap 16 '63 por
N Y Post p33 Ap 9 '63 por
Opera N 27:15 Mr 23 '63 por
Time 81:39 Mr 22 '63 por

McDEVITT, JAMES L(AWRENCE) Nov. 3, 1898-Mar. 19, 1963 Director of AFL-CIO Committee on Political Education (1955-63); director AFL League for Political Education (1951-55). See *Current Biography* (March) 1959.

Obituary

N Y Times p36 Ap 1 '63

McDONALD, DAVID L(AMAR) Sept. 12, 1906- United States Navy officer

Address: b. Department of the Navy, The Pentagon, Washington 25, D.C.; h. Admiral's House, Naval Observatory, Washington 25, D.C.

In May 1963 Admiral David L. McDonald was named by President John F. Kennedy to succeed Admiral George W. Anderson, Jr., as Chief of Naval Operations and as a member of the Joint Chiefs of Staff. In April 1963 McDonald had been installed as Commander in Chief of the United States Naval Forces in Europe and just before that assignment he had served as Commander of the American Sixth Fleet, from July 1961 to April 1963. Admiral McDonald assumed his new duties on August 1, 1963, after the usual ceremonies in Washington, D.C. Generally, the appointment to Chief of Naval Operations is for a two-year period, but Admiral Anderson had remained in the position for only one year. Known as a "carrier man," Admiral McDonald had gained experience as a flight training officer, director of military requirements of the Bureau of Aeronautics, and head of the Air Warfare Division of the office of the Chief of Naval Operations before he became Commander of the Sixth Fleet.

David Lamar McDonald, the son of the Reverend William Benjamin McDonald and Mary (David) McDonald, was born at Maysville, Georgia on September 12, 1906. He attended high school in both Maysville and Commerce, Georgia and then entered Riverside Military Academy at Gainesville, Georgia, from which he was graduated in 1924. Later in the year he entered the United States Naval Academy at Annapolis, Maryland. As a midshipman at the academy, he won the Battalion Commander Medal as outstanding rifleman in the class of 1928, the cup awarded for excellence in practical and theoretical ordnance, and the D.A.R. Sword for excellence in practical and theoretical seamanship. McDonald graduated from the naval academy with a B.S. degree on June 7, 1928.

After his graduation from Annapolis, Ensign McDonald spent about twenty-six months of sea duty as a junior officer aboard the battleships USS *Mississippi* and USS *Colorado*. He received his first promotion, to lieutenant (junior grade), in June 1931 and was designated a naval aviator in September of that year. In June 1934, after thirty-two months as a pilot with Fighter Squadron 46 of the carrier USS *Saratoga*, McDonald was assigned to the aviation unit of the cruiser USS *Detroit*. Then in June 1935 he began a three-year tour of shore duty as a flight instructor at Pensacola. On July 1, 1936, while on the teaching staff of the naval air station, he was advanced to full lieutenant. From July 1938 to October 1941 he served as a pilot with Patrol Squadron 42, based first at Seattle, Washington and later in Alaska and the Aleutian Islands.

At the time of the attack on Pearl Harbor, Lieutenant McDonald was serving as flag secretary of the aircraft command of the Atlantic Fleet. Advanced to lieutenant commander on January 1, 1942, he was reassigned to Jacksonville, Florida. In the following May he was made flight training officer on the staff of the commander of the Naval Air Operational Training Command, and on September 15, 1942 he was promoted to full commander.

In April 1944 Commander McDonald joined the carrier USS *Essex* in the Pacific as air officer and executive officer. The *Essex* was the flagship of the Commander of the Task Group that fought in the battle for Leyte Gulf in October 1944. Commander McDonald, who is entitled to wear the ribbon for the Presidential unit citation awarded the USS *Essex*, was awarded the Bronze Star Medal with Combat "V" and was given two Letters of Commendation with Ribbon and Star. One letter of commendation praised Commander McDonald's outstanding service as the executive officer of a large carrier during the several months that preceded the enemy air attack on it in the vicinity of Luzon, Philippine Islands. The letter also cited the commander's abilities in organizational details, the training of the personnel, and the upkeep of the ship's material before the air attack. Owing to the commander's efforts, the USS *Essex* suspended its operations for only thirty minutes after sustaining damage by enemy attack.

Promoted to captain on March 25, 1945, McDonald was reassigned in June 1945 as operations officer on the staff of the Pacific Air Command. He continued in this post until June 1947, when he was called to the Bureau of Aeronautics of the Navy Department in Washington, D.C. There during the next three years he served successively as director of military requirements, aide to the Assistant Secretary of the Navy for air, and aide to the Under Secretary of the Navy.

Official U.S. Navy

ADM. DAVID L. McDONALD

In August 1950 he was assigned to the National War College in Washington, where military officers are trained for extremely responsible duties in the higher echelons of military commands. In 1950-51 he was placed in command of the carrier USS *Mindoro*. In July 1952 McDonald began a two-year tour of duty as assistant chief of staff for operations on the staff of Commander in Chief, Pacific Fleet. For the next sixteen months, beginning in July 1954, he was in command of the carrier USS *Coral Sea*. In November 1955 he reported to Washington for a two-year assignment as director of the air warfare division in the office of the Chief of Naval Operations, then under the command of Admiral Arleigh A. Burke. On January 1, 1956 he was advanced to rear admiral.

From November 1957 to October 1960 Rear Admiral McDonald was assigned to Supreme Headquarters, Allied Powers, Europe to serve as Deputy Assistant Chief of Staff under Air Force General Lauris Norstad. According to a New York *Times* biographical sketch (May 7, 1963), he built up a "reputation as a master diplomat" during those three years. Although soft-spoken to the point of reserve, the writer of the sketch continued, he is "one of the toughest across-the-table operators in uniform."

For nine months beginning in October 1960 McDonald was the commander of Carrier Division 6 in the Mediterranean. Then on July 8, 1961 President Kennedy named him to succeed Admiral George W. Anderson, Jr., who had been named Chief of Naval Operations. McDonald's new command included the Sixth Fleet and all the naval striking and support forces in southern Europe. The Sixth Fleet in 1961 consisted of about fifty vessels (including two or three large carriers), 2,200 aircraft, and nearly 30,000 men. Admiral McDonald in August 1961 indicated that his command was in full combat readiness and

McDONALD, DAVID L.—*Continued*

that its state of alertness would be increased if the Berlin crisis deepened.

On July 28, 1961 McDonald was promoted to vice-admiral, and on April 1, 1963 following his appointment to succeed Admiral Harold Page Smith he was made a full admiral. His new command in April 1963 gave him authority over United States Naval Forces in Europe as well as United States Naval Forces in the Eastern Atlantic and the Mediterranean. McDonald was twenty-eighth in seniority on the list of vice-admirals when he received the promotion to full admiral, a fact that was "enough to tip some old Navy hands that something big was in the wind," according to the New York *Times* sketch. This surmise was justified when on May 6, 1963 President Kennedy announced the nomination of David McDonald to be Chief of Naval Operations succeeding Admiral Anderson, who had received a diplomatic assignment to Portugal. As the New York *Herald Tribune* (May 8, 1963) reported, "The most widely believed explanation of why Anderson was not reappointed is that he was too loud in his opposition to [Defense Secretary] Robert McNamara on two key issues—the TFX contract and the military pay bill." In testifying before the United States Senate on the touchy question of the controversial TFX all-purpose fighter plane, Admiral Anderson was reported to favor a design proposed by the Boeing Aircraft Corporation over one submitted by the General Dynamics Corporation, to which McNamara had awarded a $28,000,000 contract. In spite of some disgruntlement in the corridors of Washington, Admiral McDonald's appointment was approved by the Senate on June 28, 1963.

Before taking office the new Chief of Naval Operations made a quick orientation tour of Asia and on his return reported that United States Polaris-firing submarines would be operating in the Pacific within the next year or earlier. As a member of the Joint Chiefs of Staff he was called as a witness before a Senate subcommittee conducting hearings on the recently concluded United States-British-Soviet Nuclear Test Ban Treaty. He joined with Army General Earl G. Wheeler and Marine Corps Commandant General David M. Shoup in emphasizing their endorsement of the treaty.

David L. McDonald married Catherine Lois Thompson of Rochester, New York on October 7, 1930. They have two children, a daughter, Mary Louise (Mrs. Richard L. Spears of Covina, California), and a son, Thomas Howerth of Falls Church, Virginia. One interviewer at the time of Admiral McDonald's taking command of the Sixth Fleet was impressed by his "friendly manner tempered by an unmistakable no-nonsense self-assurance and determination" (New York *Herald Tribune*, August 6, 1961). The writer of the New York *Times* biographical sketch observed that like Admiral of the Fleet William F. Halsey, Admiral McDonald "always accentuates the positive" although he has not been known as a "hell-for-leather" fighter. "He is just under six feet tall," the New York *Times* profile continued, "and looks younger than his

fifty-six years despite his graying hair. Those who remember him as a golfer who scored in mid-70's while stationed at Pearl Harbor after World War II suggest that he might have made the professional circuit."

References

N Y Herald Tribune II p3 My 12 '63 por
N Y Times p11 Jl 6 '61 por; p22 My 7 '63 por
Time 81:28 My 17 '63 por
Who's Who in America, 1962-63

McGRANERY, JAMES P(ATRICK) July 8, 1895-Dec. 23, 1962 Lawyer; Democratic member of the United States House of Representatives from Pennsylvania (1937-43); Federal Court Judge of the Eastern District of Pennsylvania (1946-52); United States Attorney General (1952). See *Current Biography* (May) 1952.

Obituary

N Y Times p36 Ap 1 '63

McINTYRE, THOMAS J(AMES) Feb. 20, 1915- United States Senator from New Hampshire

Address: b. 5325 Senate Office Bldg., Washington 25, D.C.; h. 45 Roundbay Rd., Laconia, N.H.; 4917 Rodman St., Washington 16, D.C.

The first Democrat from New Hampshire to be elected to the United States Senate in thirty years, following a split within the ranks of the state's Republican organization, is Thomas J. McIntyre, a lawyer, real estate man, and former Mayor of the town of Laconia. He was chosen by the voters of his home state in November 1962 to fill out the unexpired term of the late Senator Styles Bridges, which ends in January 1967, and he succeeds Maurice J. Murphy, Jr., who had been appointed on an interim basis by the Republican Governor, Wesley Powell. McIntyre, who describes himself as a moderate, supported the Kennedy administration on most issues during his first few months on Capitol Hill, although he has criticized some of the administration's fiscal and foreign aid policies. He is a member of the Banking and Currency, Government Operations, and District of Columbia committees in the Senate.

Thomas James McIntyre was born in Laconia, New Hampshire on February 20, 1915, one of the three sons of Thomas James McIntyre, who was in the retail market business, and of Helen Grey (Trask) McIntyre. His brother Richard died in 1933. His other brother, John, his senior by ten years, is his partner in a real estate and building management firm. Brought up in the Roman Catholic faith, Tom McIntyre received his early education at parochial and public schools in Laconia and then entered the Manlius School, a boys' preparatory school in Manlius, New York, where military training is a part of the curriculum. After graduating from Manlius in 1933 he attended Dartmouth College at Hanover, New Hampshire, where he obtained his B.A. degree in 1937. He then entered the Boston University

Law School, and after graduating with the LL.B. degree in 1940 and gaining admission to the New Hampshire bar, he embarked on a practice of law.

In 1942 McIntyre was commissioned a second lieutenant in the United States Army. He served with the 376th Infantry, 94th Division, Third Army, earning four battle stars, the Combat Infantry Badge, and the Bronze Star for meritorious achievement. (Owing to an oversight, McIntyre did not receive the award of the Bronze Star until August 1963, almost twenty years after he had earned it.) After his discharge in 1946 with the rank of major he returned to the practice of law in Laconia and became active in municipal politics. He later joined his elder brother, John McIntyre, as a partner in McIntyre Properties, a firm that owned and managed rental real estate, including the McIntyre, Cook, and Pemaco buildings in Laconia. He also served as vice-president of the Community TV Corporation, which specialized in television antennae. McIntyre has recalled that his law study, his military service, and his general civic interest were factors that determined the future course of his career.

From 1949 to 1951 McIntyre served as Mayor of Laconia, and in 1953 he was city solicitor. At the state Democratic primary in September 1954 McIntyre was nominated to contest the re-election of the moderately liberal Republican, Chester E. Merrow as United States Representative of the First Congressional District of New Hampshire. Because of friction within Republican ranks the Democrats were quite optimistic about McIntyre's chances. When the ballots were counted after the November 1954 election, Merrow's announced margin over McIntyre was only 468 votes. A recount was demanded, but after it was taken McIntyre still trailed Merrow by 397 votes. After this close race McIntyre announced his intention to retire from politics, because he did not care for the rigors of political campaigns. He did, however, continue his association with the Democratic party organization, serving as chairman of the Laconia Democratic City Committee and the Belknap County Democratic Committee, and in 1956 he was a delegate to the Democratic national convention.

In September 1962 McIntyre, who was still remembered by New Hampshire Democrats as a "white hope" of their party, came out of his announced retirement from active politics. At the state Democratic primary held at that time he was unopposed as the Democratic candidate to fill out the unexpired term of the late Republican Senator Styles Bridges, ending January 1967. McIntyre's chances were enhanced by conflicts within the state Republican party. Upon the death of Bridges in November 1961 Governor Wesley Powell had appointed a former aide, Maurice J. Murphy, Jr., to fill the vacancy until the 1962 election, thus alienating William Loeb, the ultraconservative publisher of the influential Manchester *Union Leader*, who had urged the appointment of the late Senator's widow, Mrs. Doloris Bridges.

There were four Republican candidates for the Bridges seat at the September 1962 primary. Candidacies were filed by Murphy and Mrs.

THOMAS J. McINTYRE

Bridges and by the two incumbent New Hampshire Congressmen, Perkins Bass and Chester E. Merrow. Representative Bass won by a narrow margin over Mrs. Bridges, while Governor Powell, seeking nomination for a third gubernatorial term, was defeated by John Pillsbury, who had the support of Loeb and the *Union Leader*. Because of the inherent strength of the Republican party in New Hampshire and the fact that no Democrat had been elected to the Senate from the state since 1932, McIntyre's prospects of being elected were precarious until about the middle of October. At that time the liberal Republican Representative Merrow was reported to be seriously considering endorsing McIntyre, whom he regarded closer to his views than Bass. Later in the month Governor Powell, declaring that he could not support Pillsbury, urged his followers to vote for the Democratic gubernatorial candidate, John W. King.

McIntyre, who had made the Kennedy administration's proposals for federal aid to education and for medical care to the aged under Social Security the chief issues of his campaign, defeated Bass by a vote of 117,612 to 107,199 in the November election. The Democrats also scored a major victory when King defeated Pillsbury for the governorship by a substantial majority. (On the other hand, New Hampshire's senior Senator, Norris Cotton, a Republican seeking a second six-year term, won easily over the Democratic candidate, Alfred Catalfo, Jr.) McIntyre is expected to be a candidate for a full six-year Senate term in 1966.

As the elected replacement for an interim appointee, McIntyre was officially seated in the Senate as early as November 13, 1962, but he was not sworn in until the Eighty-eighth Congress convened on January 9, 1963. At a news conference held upon his arrival in Washington, McIntyre pointed out that while he greatly admired President Kennedy he had to consider his

McINTYRE, THOMAS J.—*Continued*

Republican constituents as well as the Democrats who elected him, and that he would make up his own mind about legislation. He indicated that the President's plan for stand-by authority to reduce taxes might constitute an encroachment on legislative prerogatives, and he took a critical view of United States aid to some Communist countries. To emphasize his independence of the Kennedy administration he added, jokingly, "I once twisted my ankle playing touch football and since I'm a Dartmouth graduate I may have said I didn't like Harvard" (New York *Times,* November 14, 1962).

In the Eighty-eighth Congress, McIntyre was assigned to the Senate committees on Banking and Currency, Government Operations, and the District of Columbia. During the first few months of his Senate term McIntyre voted against the tabling of a question put by Vice-President Lyndon B. Johnson on whether the Senate might close debate by majority vote when considering a change in rules at the beginning of a session (January); against a reduction in the amount of funds to be made available for the Commerce Committee and for an investigation of housing problems (March); and for the upholding of the Constitutional authority of the Senate to confirm the incorporators of the Communications Satellite Corporation (April). He cast his vote for the Russell amendment to strike funds for the Nike-Zeus antimissile system from the defense procurement bill (April), and he endorsed a motion by Senator Margaret Chase Smith of Maine to add $134,000,000 for two additional nuclear submarines to this bill.

McIntyre supported the Kennedy administration on the national wilderness preservation and youth employment acts (April), and the feed grain bill (May), but opposed the administration's mass transportation act (April). He voted for increased area redevelopment aid (June), appropriations for the arms control and disarmament agency (June), the national service corps act (August), and compulsory arbitration of the railroad dispute (August).

Testifying before the House government operations subcommittee in June 1963, McIntyre suggested that the states be asked to relieve the federal government of the burden of the policing responsibilities in the control of water pollution. With regard to New Hampshire's controversial decision to establish a state lottery McIntyre said in May 1963 that because New Hampshire is "a small but honest state" it would make an ideal test area for such an experiment. "If it works, I imagine other states will follow," he declared.

A member of the New Hampshire Bar Association, McIntyre became president of the Belknap County Bar Association in 1962. From 1954 to 1962 he was chairman of the board of trustees of the Taylor Home (formerly Laconia Home for the Aged). He is a member of the Laconia Chamber of Commerce, and he was named a director of the Laconia Industrial Development Corporation in 1962. Other organizations of which he is a member include the Grange, Kiwanis, Knights of Columbus, American Legion, and Veterans of Foreign Wars.

Thomas J. McIntyre and Myrtle Ann Clement were married on May 3, 1941. Mrs. McIntyre was formerly an assistant buyer for a department store and an account executive with a Concord public relations firm. She became interested in politics when her husband first ran for Mayor of Laconia, and she was a Democratic national committeewoman from New Hampshire in 1952 and 1956. The couple has one daughter, Martha Grey McIntyre. Tom McIntyre, who is six feet one inch tall, weighs 195 pounds, and has blue eyes and brown hair, is interested in all sports, especially swimming and bowling. He is also fond of gardening, and he collects United States postage stamps and antique bottles. Another of his hobbies is oil painting, and his landscapes include many snow scenes. The family lives in a white colonial house of which the basement became McIntyre's campaign headquarters in 1962.

References

Christian Sci Mon p5 Ja 8 '63 por
Newark (N.J.) Evening News p3 Ja 7 '63 por
Washington (D.C.) Post F p21 N 11 '62
Congressional Directory (1963)

McKINLEY, CHUCK Jan. 5, 1941- Amateur tennis player
Address: h. 10639 St. Stephens, St. Ann, Mo.

By winning the men's singles title at Wimbledon, England in July 1963, Chuck McKinley, America's exuberant acrobat of the tennis courts, at last lived up to the bright future often predicted for him. McKinley played such superb tennis throughout the tournament that he did not lose a set in seven matches and became the first American since 1955 to capture the Wimbledon crown, by beating Australia's Fred Stolle 9-7, 6-1, 6-4. Once before—in 1961—McKinley had reached the final round at Wimbledon, only to be soundly beaten in straight sets by the Australian Rod Laver, now a professional. McKinley's triumph boosted the sagging prestige of the United States in tennis internationally and justified the hope that in December 1963 the United States might win back the Davis Cup from Australia.

"This year is our year for the Davis Cup," McKinley recently said. "If we don't go all the way this time, we ought to be drawn and quartered." Such statements are typical of McKinley, whose on-court antics have earned him criticism, reprimands, and suspensions. He chastises himself aloud for what he considers stupid errors and once hurled his tennis racket into the spectator stands during the Davis Cup play. On another occasion he whacked the ball at the spectators. But after his Wimbledon triumph all was forgiven him, and he endeared himself to American buffs of amateur tennis by turning down a $50,000 offer to become professional immediately after his win at Wimbledon. McKinley preferred to finish college and play on the Davis Cup team.

Charles Robert McKinley was born on January 5, 1941 in St. Louis, Missouri. His father was a pipe fitter, and Chuck spent his early years in a working-class section on the north side of St. Louis. Oddly enough, tennis held little attraction for him during his formative years: his first love was baseball and his first hero was Stan Musial of the St. Louis Cardinals. During the sweltering summers in St. Louis, Chuck played baseball on school teams. When the weather turned cold he took refuge at a neighborhood YMCA, where he swam and played tennis. There he met Bill Price, a volunteer instructor who was a professional tennis player. When the boy was ten his family moved to the St. Louis suburb of St. Ann, but Chuck kept returning to his old YMCA, and Price soon introduced him to a tennis court. Chuck quickly realized that he enjoyed the game, although he was forced to defend it with his fists against some schoolmates who held a lower opinion of the sport. Before long, Price was spending four hours daily with Chuck McKinley, polishing his game and preparing him for a long series of boys' and junior tournaments.

By the time he was fifteen McKinley had teamed up with Earl (Butch) Buchholz, who grew up in the same neighborhood with Chuck and who is now a professional. "I used to watch those two kids every chance I got," the former amateur star Bill Talbert once recalled. "In my opinion they were the most gifted young players to come along in tennis since Jack Kramer and Ted Shroeder. The chief fault I found with them was their tendency to either forget or ignore their basic strokes. They often gambled with the spectacular shot when the routine play would have been just as effective and much safer."

McKinley won his first big tournament in August 1959, when he defeated veteran Dick Savitt in the finals of the eastern grass court championships at South Orange, New Jersey. He then teamed with Marty Riessen and advanced as far as the quarter finals at the national doubles championships in Brookline, Massachusetts. In September 1959 he beat the Mexican champion Antonio Palafox in an early round of the United States grass court championships at Forest Hills, New York, before losing in the fourth round to Alex Olmedo, who himself was beaten in the final round.

After losing at Forest Hills in 1959, McKinley went to San Antonio, Texas, where he enrolled as a freshman at Trinity University, a small Presbyterian school with a recruiting program that has attracted a number of potential tennis stars. In November 1959 he returned to St. Louis, where he won his third consecutive junior indoor singles championship. He then teamed with Cliff Buchholz, Earl's younger brother, and nailed down his third straight indoor doubles title. In February 1960 McKinley reached the semifinal round of the national indoor championships in New York City; he then went on to Pittsburgh to win the singles title by defeating Barry MacKay and Vic Seixas. Teamed with Bill Talbert, he also gained the doubles crown. By this time McKinley had gained enough confidence to remark: "I used to be so scared when I'd play a top man. Now maybe they're a little bit scared of me."

Wide World

CHUCK McKINLEY

During 1960 McKinley's tennis improved so much that he was named to the Davis Cup team, but he soon plummeted into disfavor from these heights. While playing at Perth, Australia against an underdog Italian squad in the challenge round for the right to play the Australians, the Americans went down to a stunning defeat. So incensed was McKinley at the loss that he hurled his racket into the stands when the Italians clinched the point that eliminated the Yankee players from the challenge competition.

For this unsportsmanlike conduct on an international level McKinley was given a three-month suspension and placed on probation for a year. "That suspension upset me a lot," he explained later. "It meant missing the United States indoor championships, and I had my heart set on winning. When I was banned from playing it upset my confidence and set back my game. . . . I wouldn't be honest if I pretended I really understood why I was suspended. I threw my racket— right. But it wasn't because I was annoyed with the crowd or with anyone else. I was just angry with myself" (New York *World-Telegram and Sun,* July 6, 1961). McKinley came back from the suspension to win the United States eastern grass court championship and to reach the final round at Wimbledon against Rod Laver. But he proved that he was still erratic when he lost in an early round at Forest Hills to the American Whitney Reed.

In February 1961 McKinley squared accounts with Whitney Reed, then considered the leading player in the United States, by defeating him for the national indoor title, 4-6, 6-3, 4-6, 9-7, 10-8. In the fourth set of the three-hour marathon match McKinley was only two points away from defeat, but he recovered sufficiently to achieve a victory that reinforced his tennis reputation. In April 1962 he advanced to the finals of the Dallas Country Club invitation tournament, only to lose in straight sets to Ham Richardson. In June 1962

McKINLEY, CHUCK—Continued

McKinley went to Wimbledon, hoping to win the crown, but he promptly lost in straight sets to Mike Hann of England, who had not been considered a serious threat. There was, however, a reason for McKinley's poor showing on the courts; a week earlier he had pulled a muscle in his forearm, with the result that he could not grip the racket tightly. Returning to the United States, he won the National Clay Court title at River Forest, Illinois. He gained the semifinal round by beating Marty Riessen, his old doubles partner, but, angered at the crowd because he considered it pro-Riessen, McKinley at one point during the match flipped his racket into the air. Later he smashed a ball into the grandstand, scattering the spectators. His next stop, on August 7, 1962, was the Davis Cup American Zone final against Mexico in Mexico City. The Yanks lost, 3-2, but through no fault of McKinley's. He won both his singles matches and almost single-handedly pulled out two sets of the five-set duel of doubles. "McKinley was easily the best player on either team," United States captain Bob Kelleher remarked in the wake of the defeat. "I predict that he will be a factor in amateur tennis for years to come." Recovering from the Davis Cup disappointment, McKinley won the national doubles title with Ralston and the singles event in the Newport invitation tournament. At Forest Hills he made it to the semifinal round before losing to Australia's Roy Emerson, and by the end of 1962 he was ranked in first place by the United States Lawn Tennis Association.

In preparing for the 1963 Wimbledon competition, McKinley concentrated less on winning a series of pre-Wimbledon tournaments than on practising under competitive conditions and sharpening his game and his mental attitude for the big one ahead. As a result he arrived at Wimbledon relaxed, eager, confident, and with his temper well under control. In the final he needed only 77 minutes to dispose of Fred Stolle. "He knocked it down my throat," the Australian said after the match. "In the end I didn't know where to serve or what he was going to do." McKinley said modestly soon after the victory, "If Fred had been serving well, I'd have been in trouble." After his Wimbledon triumph McKinley came home and successfully defended his National Clay Court title, defeating Dennis Ralston in straight sets. In this match McKinley's constant chatter so unnerved his opponent that twice Ralston smashed the ball out of the court in disgust. McKinley then won the grass court championship at the Merion Country Club in Haverford, Pennsylvania by beating the Brazilian Ronald Barnes in straight sets. In the middle of August, McKinley and Ralston together beat the Mexican Davis Cup team, 4-1, in the semifinal round of the American Zone competition. Ralston played better tennis than McKinley, who dropped the opening match to Rafael Osuna. But Ralston won his two singles matches, McKinley won his second singles match, and the two paired for a doubles victory. Ahead lay the goal—final competition with the Australians for the Davis Cup.

In the spring of 1962 Charles McKinley married a former Trinity University co-ed who teaches in a junior high school. Although McKinley's stature (five feet eight inches) is below that of most tennis stars, he considers it no problem on the courts. "My lack of size isn't too severe a handicap," he has said. "I compensate for it because I'm fairly strong and can move quickly with good instinct for anticipation." Resembling a football player more than a tennis star, McKinley has to be careful of his 160-pound weight and not yield too often to his fondness for milk shakes. After winning at Wimbledon McKinley returned to Trinity University as a junior. Now that he has restored the prestige of American tennis after an eight-year hiatus he appears determined to play an active role in the American competition for the Davis Cup.

References

N Y World-Telegram p22 Ag 7 '62
New Yorker 39:91+ Jl 27 '63
Sports Illus 12:34+ My 16 '60 por; 19:12+ Jl 15 '63 por

MacLEAN, BASIL C(LARENDON) Dec. 24, 1895-Feb. 14, 1963 President of the Blue Cross Association (1957-60); New York City Commissioner of Hospitals (1954-57). See Current Biography (May) 1957.

Obituary

N Y Times p36 Ap 1 '63

MADEIRA, JEAN (BROWNING) Nov. 14, 1924- Singer
Address: b. Metropolitan Opera Association, Broadway and 39th St., New York 18; h. 47 Katherine Court, Warwick Neck, R.I.

A leading American contralto of the Metropolitan Opera and the Vienna State Opera, Jean Madeira is best known for her interpretations of flamboyant sorceresses and gypsies, especially Carmen—a role she has sung hundreds of times throughout the Western world. "Carmen is in my blood," she has said. Miss Madeira, who scored her first major successes as an opera singer in Europe, is also notable for such relatively exotic roles as that of Amneris in Aïda, Azucena in Il Trovatore, Delilah in Samson and Delilah, and Klytemnestra in Elektra. She is the only American ever to sing Carmen at the Aix-en-Provence Festival, and in 1955 she made operatic history with the Vienna State Opera, when she received forty-five curtain calls for her performance in that role. A police escort had to be summoned to escort her through the cheering crowds outside the opera house.

Jean Madeira was born Jean Browning in Centralia, Illinois on November 14, 1924 to Lee Roy Browning and Noma Jane (Eubanks) Browning. Her father was a coal miner with Cherokee Indian blood; her mother was a piano teacher of English and Irish ancestry. Miss Madeira said recently that one of the important factors that helped to influence her was her mother, who gave up her own career so that her daughter would have one of her own.

Another factor, according to Miss Madeira, was her childhood love of music and the theater. The opera never came to town, but movies did, and, from time to time, a small traveling chautauqua, with which she would get a chance "to play the fairy queen or something." She also followed and watched the gypsies who came each year with the carnival. The Browning family soon moved to St. Louis, where Miss Madeira began to study piano at the age of five, first with her mother, then with Leo Miller. When she was twelve she appeared as a piano soloist with the St. Louis Symphony, playing the Beethoven Piano Concerto No. 3 in C Minor under the baton of Vladimir Golschmann.

At East St. Louis High School, from which she graduated in 1937, Miss Madeira was active in debating, dancing, and music. During her high school days she became interested in grand opera when Laszlo Halasz brought Bruna Castagna to St. Louis for a production of *Carmen*. After attending it Miss Madeira began to take vocal lessons with Bernard Ferguson, playing piano accompaniments for him in exchange for one year of free lessons.

After high school Miss Madeira took special courses in languages and English at Washington University in St. Louis, and during her free time was piano accompanist for the glee club, leading lady in the Quad show, and a member of Thyrsus, the dramatic society. With some money she had scraped together she went to New York City in 1941 to go on with her studies at the Juilliard School of Music. Auditioning for a piano scholarship, she performed for Olga Samaroff Stokowski and was accepted. Before she left the audition she happened to mention to Madame Samaroff that she had also been studying voice. Madame Samaroff suggested that she audition for voice too and was so impressed with Miss Madeira's way with a French chanson that she promptly recommended her for Juilliard's voice department.

From 1941 to 1945 Miss Madeira was at Juilliard, studying voice with Florence Page Kimball, deportment with Queena Mario, and staging with Alfredo Valenti. A high point of her student career was her singing of the role of Balkis in a Juilliard production of Randall Thompson's opera *Solomon*, a performance favorably reviewed by the press. Another was her rendition, in 1942, of Tchaikovsky's "Adieu Fôrets" on the Metropolitan Opera Auditions of the Air.

In 1943 Miss Madeira obtained a contract with the Chautauqua, New York, Opera Company, and she gained valuable experience in such roles as Ulrica in *The Masked Ball*, Frédéric in *Mignon*, and Delilah in *Samson and Delilah*. She accepted a contract with the San Carlo Opera Company and, touring for two seasons, sang two or three performances each week in such roles as Amneris, Azucena, Carmen, Maddalena in *Rigoletto*, and Lola in *Cavalleria Rusticana*. Her summers were spent in studying voice with Mrs. William Neidlinger, a noted teacher.

Chosen by Gian-Carlo Menotti in 1948 to sing in his *The Medium* in Paris and London as an

JEAN MADEIRA

alternate for Marie Powers, Jean Madeira found Europe "a wonderful experience" and moved every week she was in Paris to get to know as much of the city as possible. Returning to the United States that fall, she auditioned for the Metropolitan Opera and was accepted. For several years she sang a variety of minor roles to gain polish and experience. She made her first public appearances as Carmen and as Azucena on the Metropolitan stage at student matinees. On February 27, 1953 she appeared in the double roles of Baba the Bearded Lady and Mother Goose in Stravinsky's *The Rake's Progress*, undertaking the extra chore of singing Mother Goose on short notice when Martha Lipton fell ill. A critic for the New York *Times* (February 28, 1953) appreciated her "impressive display of stage versatility" and "some of the evening's most impressive singing." Her performance may have been the first time that one person sang two major roles in the same evening in one opera at the Metropolitan. That year when she returned to her home town to sing Carmen at the St. Louis Municipal Opera, a critic for the *Christian Science Monitor* (August 22, 1953) found her "the very embodiment of the part."

Somewhat impatient with her lack of progress at the Metropolitan, Miss Madeira went to the Royal Opera in Stockholm in the fall of 1954 to sing in Saint-Saëns' *Samson and Delilah*. Returning to Europe on tour in 1955, she made her precedent-shattering appearance as Carmen at the Vienna State Opera on September 18. As a member of the company told Sidney Gruson of the New York *Times* (December 25, 1955): "There was a stunning momentary silence when she finished the Habañera. Then the opera house filled with what seemed a mad noise . . . finally the house was stilled . . . But after the second act the audience was screaming again and she had to take 45 curtain calls. Police had to escort her through the crowd that stood waiting for her

MADEIRA, JEAN—Continued

outside the theatre." The next morning the critic of the *Bild-Telegraf* informed his readers that Vienna had a "new darling" and called her Carmen the finest ever heard there. Signed to a contract by the Vienna State Opera, Jean Madeira sang some thirty performances as Carmen, Amneris, Azucena, Klytemnestra, and Herodias before she returned to New York on December 31, 1955.

After her Vienna triumph Jean Madeira's stature at the Metropolitan rapidly increased. After seeing her Amneris on February 8, 1956 and her Azucena on February 28, Paul Henry Lang of the New York *Herald Tribune* (March 1, 1956) remarked: "As far as singing is concerned she is in the prima donna class. When it comes to acting she has it all over the others." On March 17 she made her real New York debut as Carmen on the Metropolitan Opera Stage, and a reviewer for *Time* rhapsodized (March 26, 1956): "She serpentined onstage in a dress of bare-shouldered abandon and the rose in her hand glowed like the apple of Eden. . . . Her big voice had a dark, anthracite sheen, sometimes with more polish than depth, sometimes with not quite enough polish, but always firm and sometimes thrilling. By the time she reached her ultimate scene of terror and death, handsome U.S. Contralto achieved a long-sought objective—to arrive at the top of the operatic heap in her own country." And Jean Madeira, who once had said, "Carmen is in my blood, and I've sung it in every little place I could, almost everywhere in America," told a reporter after the performance, "I'd be glad to sing Carmen for the rest of my life."

In the years that followed, Miss Madeira broadened her repertoire at the Metropolitan: she was called by critics a "powerful and convincing" Erda in *Das Rheingold* and *Siegfried*; a "thoroughly effective" Prince Orlofsky in *Die Fledermaus*; and a "poignant" blind Madelon in *Andrea Chenier*. After listening to her Klytemnestra on a Deutsche Grammophon Gesellschaft recording of Richard Strauss's *Elektra*, released in 1961, a reviewer for the Washington *Post and Times Herald* (December 31, 1961) advised his readers: "For the great singing on the set you must turn to the American, Jean Madeira, whose Klytemnestra is a marvel of deep-throated fear, murderous and foul, but sung with phenomenal effect and in flawless time." New York critics had much the same to say about her Metropolitan performances in the same role, in 1961 and 1962.

Jean Madeira has appeared on opera and concert stages throughout the world. She has sung at Covent Garden, in London; the Teatro Colon, in Buenos Aires; La Scala, in Milan; the Teatro San Carlo, in Naples; the Chicago Lyric Opera; the Paris Opéra; and the Israel National Opera. Her festival engagements have included Bayreuth, Munich, Salzburg, Seville, and Aix-en-Provence. During the opening festival week of Philharmonic Hall at New York's Lincoln Center of the Performing Arts she appeared in a performance of Manuel de Falla's seldom-heard dramatic cantata, *Atlantida*.

Concert singing Jean Madeira finds "the greatest challenge an artist faces," although it offers "the most exciting rewards." Convinced that a large audience for opera remains untapped in the United States, she champions televised opera in English with young and personable singers. "The people would like opera if they could understand it," Miss Madeira maintains.

Jean Browning married Francis Madeira, whom she met while they were both attending Juilliard, on June 17, 1947. He is now a professor of music at Brown University and conductor of the Rhode Island Philharmonic Orchestra. Miss Madeira is five feet eight and one-half inches in height, weighs about 145 pounds, and has jet-black hair, green eyes, and a strong-featured face. Warm and unpretentious, she once said, "Although you need temperament to be an opera singer, I have no temper in my temperament except when I get mad." The Madeiras live in a contemporary house at Warwick Neck on Narragansett Bay, with bayside walls of glass. They enjoy traveling, swimming, and canoeing together, and she likes cooking, riding, sailing, gardening, bicycling, and making hats. From the countries in which she sings she collects recipes, rugs, china, and jewelry. In 1957 she was given a Woman of Achievement award by the city of St. Louis; in 1959 an honorary Master of Arts degree by Pembroke College of Brown University; and in 1962 an alumni citation by Washington University. She is a member of Job's Daughters and of Mu Phi Epsilon, the national honorary music society. She is a Republican and an Episcopalian.

Occasionally Jean Madeira still sits down at the piano. "I play the piano when I'm too sad to sing," she has said, "but that's not too often. I'm always happy because I'm doing what I want to do." Above all she wants to act. "Acting," she says, "is one of the things I like most about opera and singing."

References

Who's Who in America, 1962-63
Who's Who of American Women (1961-62)

MASTROIANNI, MARCELLO (mäs″ trō-yän′ nē) Sept. 28, 1924- Italian actor

Address: b. c/o Titanus Films, Via Sommacampagna 28, Rome, Italy; h. Via Appia Antica, Rome, Italy

After twelve years as a popular stage and screen actor in his native Italy, Marcello Mastroianni attained international stardom in 1960 with his performance in *La Dolce Vita*. In this much publicized and highly controversial film he portrays a society reporter who is corrupted by the wealthy, decadent people he is assigned to cover —a victim of the "sweet life." In this and later films, *La Notte, Bell' Antonio*, and *Divorce—Italian Style*, he has created a new image, which director Michelangelo Antonioni calls "the imperfect man, the unheroic hero"—very different from the virtuous and stalwart hero of another era. Mastroianni began his career in amateur theatricals, and he had attained a reputation on the stage before he entered the movies. He is now a veteran of more than fifty-five films and earns as much as $160,000 for one picture. He has won several acting awards, including two Silver Ribbons from the Italian film critics in 1958 and 1961. Despite his growing popularity in the United States, Mastroianni, who speaks very little English, has thus far rejected offers from Hollywood.

Marcello Mastroianni was born on September 28, 1924 in Fontana Liri, Italy, the son of Ottone Mastroianni, a carpenter, and Ida (Irolle) Mastroianni. His family moved to Turin when he was five years old; a few years later they settled in Rome. After completing school Marcello Mastroianni went to work in his father's carpentry shop. His study of surveying was interrupted during World War II when he was put to work drawing maps for the Germans. "It was all so stupid," he told a *Time* reporter (October 5, 1962). "We were still doing maps of Sicily when the Americans were in Florence."

In 1943 Mastroianni was seized by the Germans and sent to a forced-labor camp in the Italian Alps. Fearing deportation to Germany when the Allied forces advanced toward northern Italy, he and an artist friend escaped and went to Venice, where they eked out a scanty living painting pictures for tourists. Mastroianni returned to Rome the following year, during the American occupation, and was reunited with his family.

His first contact with the film industry came in 1944 when he took a $40-a-month job as a cashier with Eagle Lion Films, an English company making motion pictures in Rome. He also enrolled for some courses at the University of Rome and joined the university's amateur theatrical group, where he met and acted with Federico Fellini and Giulietta Masina, among others. Mastroianni made his acting debut opposite Miss Masina in the university theater center's production of *Angelica* in 1948, and he received one Italian critic's praise for his "enthusiastic inexperience."

A friend was sufficiently impressed with Mastroianni's acting ability to introduce him, in 1948, to the stage and film director Luchino Visconti, who headed Italy's leading theatrical troupe. Hired by Visconti, Mastroianni began working with outstanding actors like Vittorio Gassman and Rina Morelli, although he had had no previous professional acting experience except for a bit part in the film *I Miserabili* (1947), an Italian version of *Les Miserables*. His first notable stage success was as Pilade in Vittorio Alfieri's *Orestia*, and he subsequently had roles with the Visconti troupe in the Italian versions of *Death of a Salesman*, *A Streetcar Named Desire*, *The Glass Menagerie*, *Uncle Vanya*, *The Three Sisters*, and *L'Avare*.

Meanwhile, Mastroianni had begun to act in radio plays, and in 1949 he got his first substantial screen assignment—the portrayal of a city policeman who seduces a servant girl, in *Una Domenica d'Agosto* (A Sunday in August). During the next six years, from 1950 through 1955, he appeared in twenty-seven films, including *Racconto di Cinque Città* (A Tale of Five Cities) (1951): *Le Ragazze di Piazza di Spagna* (The Girls of the Piazza di Spagna) (1952), in which he played a wholesome boy next door; *Febbre di Vivere* (Fever to Live) (1953), in which he

MARCELLO MASTROIANNI

played his first dramatic role; *Giorni d'Amore* (Days of Love) (1954), in which he starred as a young lover; *Tempi Nostri* (Our Times) (1954); and *Tam Tam Mayumbe* (Mayumbe Tom-Tom) (1955).

By 1956 he had become a well-known film actor in Italy, but he was discouraged about the progress of his career. After playing a cab driver in a 1956 movie that starred Sophia Loren, he told a reporter, "I am resigned. I'll be playing taxi cab drivers until the end of my days." He was fortunate, however, in obtaining a variety of roles in subsequent films. In 1957 he co-starred with Maria Schell and Jean Marais in an adaptation of a Dostoevsky story, *Le Notti Bianche* (presented in America as *White Nights* in 1961), which won the Silver Lion award for the best film at the Venice Film Festival in 1957. Mastroianni's portrayal of a hopeful lover in *Le Notti Bianche* won him the 1958 Italian Film Critics' Silver Ribbon for acting. His ability to play an unusual and serious role with both charm and natural ease caught the attention of Italy's leading film directors, and he was later chosen by one of them, Federico Fellini, for the leading male role in *La Dolce Vita*.

Mastroianni played a comical and bungling photographer in the 1958 Italian farce, *I Soliti Ignoti*, which amiably poked fun at *Rififi* and other great robbery films. It enjoyed a successful run in Europe and in the United States, where it was shown with the English title, *Big Deal on Madonna Street*. Paul V. Beckley (New York *Herald Tribune*, November 23, 1960) called it "one of the most irresistible Italian comedies in years." That year Mastroianni also appeared in the French-Italian film *La Loi*.

The phenomenal success of *La Dolce Vita*, first presented in Rome early in 1960 and in New York a year later, transformed Mastroianni from a top Italian star into an international leading man. The film, directed by its writer, Federico Fellini, won the highest award at the Cannes

MASTROIANNI, MARCELLO—*Continued*

Film Festival in May 1960. Although its more sensational aspects at first overshadowed the actors' performances, it was soon evident that movie critics and enthusiastic audiences had agreed upon one thing—the brilliance of Mastroianni's acting.

Mastroianni attributes his belated success to the fact that he was finally cast in a meaningful role. "In *La Dolce Vita* I found my first real role where it was all me, and all right," Mastroianni told Curtis G. Pepper of *Newsweek* (February 18, 1962). "In this I was an intellectual lost in the mainstream of life, not really an intellectual, not really or wholly anything, without the will to arrest my drift." In his more recent films he has portrayed other variations of the unheroic hero, interpreting his roles with such artistry that these characterizations have a universal appeal.

La Notte (1961), shown in America as *The Night* (1962), is another film whose theme reflects the boredom and decadence prevalent in modern society. It tells of a married couple, played by Mastroianni and Jeanne Moreau, who drift aimlessly through a night filled with unattractive pursuits only to face a continuing futility at dawn. Although the film won an award at Berlin's film festival in 1961, it was coolly received by some New York critics, who believed that Mastroianni was given insufficient scope to display his talents.

Mastroianni was again cast as an "imperfect man" in the 1960 *Bell' Antonio*. As the playboy son of a proud Sicilian father, he is forced into an arranged marriage with an heiress, played by Claudia Cardinale. The discovery that he is impotent has both tragic and comic results. When the film reached New York in 1962, the critics praised the performances but felt that the seriousness of the theme was marred by the farcical ending.

Disappointed with the final scenario of the French production *A Very Private Affair*, Mastroianni tried to break his contract to do the film. He was unsuccessful, however, and co-starred with Brigitte Bardot in this 1961 movie (shown in the United States in 1962), in which he played a magazine publisher and playwright with whom the actress falls in love. New accolades were won by Mastroianni for his performance as the debonair, bored Sicilian baron who plans to rid himself of an unwanted wife in the Italian comedy *Divorzio all' Italiana* (*Divorce—Italian Style*). Filmed in 1961, the picture was awarded a prize as the best comedy of the year at the Cannes Film Festival in 1962, with special praise going to Mastroianni. He also won another Silver Ribbon from the Italian film critics in 1961. When *Divorce—Italian Style* began its long run at the Paris Theater in New York on September 17, 1962, it received rave notices. Bosley Crowther of the New York *Times* (September 18, 1962) called Mastroianni's performance "one of the most ingenious and distinctive comic characterizations that has lately been," and Paul V. Beckley of the New York *Herald Tribune* (September 18, 1962) said Mastroianni added "a new dimension to his reputation" in this part. The role also brought Mastroianni a nomination for an Oscar Award of the Academy of Motion Picture Arts and Sciences as the best supporting actor of 1962.

Marcello Mastroianni visited the United States for the first time in October 1962 as a guest of Embassy Pictures, the American distributor of *Divorce—Italian Style*. He has received several offers from Hollywood producers but has not yet succumbed to the lure of the film capital. One of the reasons he gives for this is that he speaks little English and thinks he would be "too lazy" to learn now. Furthermore, he is perfectly content with his lot. "What is being done here in Italy," he told a *Time* (October 5, 1962) interviewer, "is far better and much more mature and advanced than anything cinematic being done elsewhere." Recent pictures in which he has appeared are *Cronaca Familiare* (A Family Diary), *A Tranquil Life in a Country House*, and Fellini's *Otto e Mezzo* (8½). He is scheduled to play Casanova in a lavish motion picture being filmed in Italy, France, Germany, Spain, England, and Switzerland.

Marcello Mastroianni met the actress Flora Carabella at the University of Rome's theater center, and they were married in 1950. They have one daughter, Barbara. Although Mrs. Mastroianni retired from the theater after her marriage, she has acted in occasional French stage plays as well as in the improvised home movies filmed by her husband and a friend. After residing for several years in a rented apartment, the Mastroiannis now own a spacious $125,000 villa on the Via Appia Antica on the outskirts of Rome. The grounds around the villa include the ruins of a Roman aqueduct and a pre-Christian burial ground.

Mastroianni is five feet ten inches tall, weighs about 150 pounds, and has brown hair and brown eyes. He has a good deal of nervous energy, and he is a chain smoker and an espresso coffee addict. For relaxation he watches a new movie or drives one of his two sports cars. Mastroianni, unlike many celebrities, prefers a quiet life with his family and friends to the night clubs or cafés on the Via Veneto. He does not care for publicity and keeps his family life completely separate from his work.

Mastroianni is happiest when in front of a camera. "In front of a camera, I feel solid, satisfied," he has explained. "Away from it I am empty, confused." He spends hours with the writer and director working out his part before any shooting begins, and he seems to exemplify a new kind of movie actor, one who regards himself primarily as a tool of the director. "I'm content to be myself on the screen, if I can do it well," Mastroianni asserts. "That way I let a director use me any way he sees me, to express his own view of modern life."

References

Life 54:79+ Ja 18 '63 pors
N Y Herald Tribune IV p5 F 18 '62
N Y Times II p7 O 28 '62 por
Newsweek 59:96+ F 19 '62 por
Time 80:71 O 5 '62 pors

Chi è? (1957)
Panorama Biografico Degli Italiani D'Oggi
vol II (1956)

MATTEI, ENRICO Apr. 29, 1906-Oct. 27, 1962
Politically powerful president (1953-62) of the
Italian National Hydrocarbon Authority, which
controls oil and gas resources in Italy. See *Current Biography* (April) 1959.

Obituary

N Y Times p13 O 28 '62

MATTINGLY, GARRETT May 6, 1900-Dec.
18, 1962 Historian; authority on early modern
European diplomatic history; professor of history,
Columbia University, 1948-62; received 1960
Pulitzer special citation for his book *The Armada*. See *Current Biography* (November) 1960.

Obituary

N Y Times p36 Ap 1 '63

MAUGHAM, (WILLIAM) SOMERSET
(môm) Jan 25, 1874- Writer
Address: Villa Mauresque, St. Jean, Cap Ferrat,
Alpes Maritimes, France

Perhaps the most financially successful writer
of the twentieth century, Somerset Maugham is
best known for his novels *Of Human Bondage*
(1915), *The Moon and Sixpence* (1919), *Cakes
and Ale* (1930), and *The Razor's Edge* (1944)
and for his short stories. He has been prized
more by the reading public than by the
literary critics, who place him among the competent craftsmen with high commercial standards rather than in the first rank of creative
geniuses. Maugham, however, has achieved his
avowed purpose as a professional author—to entertain his readers.

Earlier in the twentieth century Maugham
was well known as a dramatist, and he helped
to bring back the comedy of manners to the
stage. Forsaking the theater in the early 1930's,
he produced twenty novels and 100 short stories
before he abandoned fiction in its turn. During
the 1950's he devoted himself to essays and
memoirs, and he has now formally retired.
Most of his books have been published by
Heinemann in England and by Doubleday in
the United States.

William Somerset Maugham was born in
Paris, France on January 25, 1874. His paternal
ancestors had emigrated from Ireland to Westmorland in the Lake District of England, where
they became gentlemen farmers and government
officials. His paternal grandfather was a famous
British barrister, and his father, Robert Armand
Maugham, Jr., was a well-known Paris solicitor.
Robert Maugham loved to travel, and it was
from Morocco that he brought home the talisman that Somerset Maugham later adopted as
the personal insignia that adorns the entrance
to his home and the covers of his books.

Somerset Maugham's mother was one of the
Snell family whose descent has been traced back
to the English king Edward I. Of the six
sons she bore, four—Charles, Frederick, Henry,
and the youngest, William Somerset—survived
childhood. Until the age of eight, when his
mother, weakened by tuberculosis, died in child-

Editta Sherman

SOMERSET MAUGHAM

birth, Somerset Maugham led a happy life and
was in most respects thoroughly Gallicized.
After his mother's death he was taken out of
the French school he attended and given English language lessons. Two years later his father
died of cancer, and he was sent to live with
an uncle, the Reverend Henry Maugham, vicar
of All Saints' Church in Whitstable, Kent,
England.

His life at the vicarage in Kent was joyless
in comparison with his early years in Paris.
Shy, sickly, and afflicted with a stammer (which
persisted into adulthod), he felt out of place
at the annex to the King's School in Canterbury,
where he completed his primary schooling. At
the age of thirteen Maugham entered the King's
School. Because of his health he spent two successive winter terms under an English tutor
at Hyères on the French Riviera. The jolting
transition from a happy childhood in France
to a bleak existence in Whitstable was painfully
remembered by Maugham for a long time. He
used the Whitstable scene in a number of his
writings.

After three years Maugham cut short his
secondary schooling and spent an emancipating
year in Heidelberg, Germany. He attended lectures at the University of Heidelberg, and from
an Englishman whom he met he acquired a
love of literature and an acquaintance with the
works of Newman, Meredith, Pater, and Swinburne and Edward FitzGerald's translation of
the Rubáiyát of Omar Khayyám. From Heidelberg he traveled to other parts of Germany
and the Continent. By the time he returned
to Kent at the age of eighteen, he had shed
his token Christianity and acquired a wanderlust that he would never lose.

After a flirtation with accounting Maugham
became a medical student at St. Thomas' Hospital in London in the autumn of 1892. Although he was an apathetic student of medicine
who spent much of his time reading literature

263

MAUGHAM, SOMERSET—*Continued*

and writing in his notebooks, he qualified as a member of the Royal College of Surgeons and as a licentiate of the Royal College of Physicians in 1897. His work in the out-patient department of the hospital brought him into contact with the sick of Lambeth, then a London slum. Almost a transcript of one of his cases, his first published novel, *Liza of Lambeth* (Unwin, 1897), dispassionately told the story of the last year in the life of a young factory girl. Its modest success encouraged him to choose writing rather than medicine as a career.

After qualifying in medicine he spent some time in Italy and in Seville, Spain. (He often returned to Spain in later years and still holds a special affection for that country.) Spain provided the setting of his first short story, "The Punctiliousness of Don Sebastian," which was included in his *Orientations* (1899). From his Spanish notebooks he quarried the material for two books of sketches, *The Land of the Blessed Virgin* (1905) and *Don Fernando* (1935; revised version, 1950).

Returning to England, Maugham settled into a London flat and continued to write novels. During the decade 1898-1908 seven were published: *The Making of a Saint* (1898); *The Hero* (1901); *Mrs. Craddock* (1902); *The Merry-Go-Round* (1904); *The Bishop's Apron* (1906); *The Explorer* (1907); and *The Magician* (1908). Only *Mrs. Craddock,* which treated marriage in a manner that shocked the Edwardians, enjoyed a fair artistic and commercial success. Maugham's average annual income of 100 pounds from writing during these years was supplemented by a small inheritance. Around the turn of the century he lived for a time in Paris.

Popular acclaim and financial independence came to Maugham through the theater. After several of his plays had been turned down by London producers and his play *A Man of Honour* had been briefly performed by the Stage Society in 1903, Maugham deliberately set out to write plays that would please the producers. *Lady Frederick,* an epigrammatic comedy of manners, scored an immediate hit. First presented in October 1907, it still held the boards in 1908 when three other Maugham plays, *Jack Straw, Mrs. Dot,* and *The Explorer* were being exhibited at London theaters.

Beginning with 1909, Maugham wrote as he pleased, turning out comedies that proved popular in spite of their flouting of conventional mores. In addition to two one-acters and three adaptations he wrote twenty-seven full-length plays in all. His plays that reached production before World War I are *Penelope* (1909); *Smith* (1909), an attack on the English caste system; *The Tenth Man* (1910); *The Trivial Shepherd* (1910); *Landed Gentry* (1910); *Loaves and Fishes* (1911); and *The Land of Promise* (1914).

When World War I broke out in 1914 Maugham requested assignment to a Red Cross ambulance unit in France, and he served with it for a few months. In a billet near Ypres, within the sound of the big guns, he corrected the proofs of his autobiographical novel *Of Human Bondage,* published in 1915. By setting down the experiences of his youth in *Of Human Bondage,* Somerset Maugham tried to exorcise some painful memories. Although some of the incidents in the book are fabricated, many correspond to events in his own life. Philip Carey, the protagonist, like Maugham was orphaned at an early age and handicapped (with a clubfoot, analogous to Maugham's stammer). He too endured a difficult childhood in an English vicarage, attended medical school, and felt liberated in Heidelberg and Paris. *Of Human Bondage,* a *Bildungsroman,* dealt with Philip's subjection to the slattern Mildred and his emancipation with the help of the Athelny family. At the time of its publication Theodore Dreiser was one of the few reviewers to appreciate the merits of what is perhaps Maugham's finest contribution to prose fiction.

Maugham's next wartime assignment took him to Switzerland for a year as a British intelligence agent, where he capitalized upon his knowledge of French, German, and Italian. During this period he wrote the plays *Caroline* (1916) and *Our Betters* (first produced in the United States, in 1917). Touring the South Seas after a brief trip to the United States, Maugham amassed a wealth of material that he used in writing his first short stories in twenty years—brought together in *The Trembling of a Leaf* (1921). One was "Miss Thompson," about an encounter between a missionary and a prostitute, which later became celebrated in stage and screen versions under the title *Rain.* In Tahiti Maugham gathered impressions for a novel about the French painter Paul Gauguin, who exchanged the bourgeois respectability of a banking career for the life of a painter in the South Seas.

In the fall of 1917 Maugham discharged perhaps the most important, though ultimately unsuccessful, mission of his career as a secret agent—he was sent to persuade Russia to stay in the war against Germany. From his experiences in Switzerland and Russia derive the stories in *Ashenden, or the British Agent* (1928). He spent the winter of 1917 in Banchory, Scotland, in a tuberculosis sanatorium, and during the summer of 1918, living near London, he wrote *The Moon and Sixpence* (1919), a novel suggested by the life of Gauguin (represented in the book as Charles Strickland) in which Maugham also uses autobiographical elements and airs his views on art, philosophy, and human conduct. Richard A. Cordell in the biography *Somerset Maugham* (1961) noted: "It is safe to say that Strickland's violent tirades against women are an expression of Maugham's misogyny."

Maugham again stayed at Banchory in the winter of 1918 and returned to London the following spring. Three more of his comedies were produced about this time: *Love in a Cottage* (1918), *Caesar's Wife* (1919), and *Home and Beauty* (1919). In the 1920's Maugham traveled abroad every year. His trip to the Far East inspired a volume of sketches, *On a Chinese Screen* (1922); a travel book, *The Gentleman in the Parlour* (1930); a novel, *The Painted Veil* (1925); and the stories in *The Casuarina Tree* (1926) and in *Ah King* (1933). Maugham revisited the Far East in 1959-60. He has also visited Italy, Switzerland, Austria, Germany, the United States, Guatemala, Mexico, Cuba, the West Indies, Australia, the Near East, North Africa, and India. On his trips to India in 1938 and 1939 he gathered material for his novel *The Razor's Edge* (1944).

Meanwhile, until 1933, he continued to write plays—some of them his best. Produced between 1920 and 1933, they were *The Unknown* (1920); *The Circle* (1921); *East of Suez* (1922); *The Camel's Back* (1924); *The Letter* (1927); *The Constant Wife* (1927); *The Sacred Flame* (1928); *The Breadwinner* (1930); *For Services Rendered* (1932); and *Sheppey* (1933). In the 1960's *The Circle* and *The Constant Wife* seem to be the most likely candidates for survival. "He has been called a cynical playwright," Cordell wrote of Maugham, "for suggesting that sexual love does not last forever, that the infidelity of one's mate is more likely to hurt one's pride than one's heart, that people fall out of love . . . that philosophically evil is unexplainable, that literal Christianity is impracticable . . . that vice is not always punished and virtue rewarded in ways that strict moralists would prefer . . . that the moderately immoral seem to live about as happily as the rigidly conventional."

These observations equally apply to Maugham's short stories. In addition to those already mentioned, he produced the collections *Six Stories Written in the First Person Singular* (1931), *Cosmopolitans* (1936), *The Mixture as Before* (1940), and *Creatures of Circumstance* (1947). Modeling many of his characters upon people he has met, he believes that a well-turned plot is essential and that the primary function of fiction is to entertain. Like O'Henry's, Maugham's stories ambush the reader with an unexpected dénouement, but this hinges in Maugham on the disclosure of unconventional ethical views rather than on a twist of the plot. His *Complete Short Stories* was published in 1951.

Cakes and Ale (1930), Maugham's favorite among his novels, is an affectionate recollection of his long but abortive romance with an actress. The original of Rosie in *Cakes and Ale* is artfully disguised, but her promiscuity and charm are faithfully represented in her fictional counterpart. The novel is also a satire of the English literary scene in the late nineteenth and early twentieth centuries, and many readers protested what they thought was Maugham's ridicule of Thomas Hardy in the character of Edward Driffield, the "Grand Old Man of English Letters." Maugham, however, denies that Driffield was modeled upon Hardy.

A procession of novels followed during the 1930's and the 1940's. *The Narrow Corner* (1932) is a lively tale about an exiled doctor, a rascally sea captain, and a youth who take refuge on a Malay island. Next came *Theatre* (1937), *Christmas Holiday* (1939), *Up at the Villa* (1941), and *The Hour Before Dawn* (1942), a propaganda novel that Maugham reluctantly wrote at the request of the British Ministry of Information. His next novel, *The Razor's Edge* (1944), about a young American who repudiated Western materialistic values for Indian mysticism,

sold some 3,000,000 copies and was made into a successful movie. Maugham's last two novels are *Then and Now* (1946) and *Catalina* (1948).

In 1928 Maugham bought the Villa Mauresque at Cap Ferrat on the French Riviera; it has been his permanent home ever since. In 1940, after the fall of France, he went to England and then to the United States, where he lived out the war on the South Carolina estate of Nelson Doubleday. He returned to France in 1946. After his formal retirement from fiction writing in the late 1940's Maugham turned to autobiography and essays in *A Writer's Notebook* (1949), *The Vagrant Mood* (1952), *Ten Novels and Their Authors* (1954), and *Points of View* (1958), which he has said will be the last book to be published during his lifetime. He had earlier written about himself in *The Summing Up* (1938) and *Strictly Personal* (1942). In a series of three articles, "Looking Back," in *Show* magazine in June, July, and August of 1962 Maugham was much more candid about his marriage and other intimate relationships than he had previously been.

During World War I William Somerset Maugham married Gwendolen Syrie Barnardo (Mrs. Henry Wellcombe). They were divorced in 1929. They had a daughter, Elizabeth Mary, who is Lady John Hope. Maugham still likes to travel and to act as host for his friends at the Villa Mauresque. He enjoys playing bridge and reading. Over the years he collected more than thirty-five paintings by modern masters, but the difficulties of guarding them from theft and fire led him to sell them at auction in April 1962. The sale realized $1,466,864, which Maugham said would go into a fund for struggling and aged writers. (He had earlier set up an annual award of £500 to encourage promising young British writers to travel.) *Purely For My Pleasure* (1962) is a collection of reproductions of these paintings with a running commentary by him.

Maugham is a Commander of the Legion of Honor, a Companion of Honour, a Fellow of the Library of Congress, and a Fellow of the Royal Society of Literature. He holds honorary D.Lit. degrees from Oxford and Toulouse universities. On his eightieth birthday he was tendered a dinner by the historic Garrick Club in London; he was the fourth member to be so honored— the others were Dickens, Trollope, and Thackeray.

Maugham is a nonbeliever who in his search among the world's religions has not found one in which he can believe. In his life as in his art he is a hedonist. One of his favorite quotations comes from Fray Luis de Leon: "The beauty of life is nothing but this, that each should act in conformity with his nature and his business."

References

Show 2:60+ Je '62 pors; 2:41+ Jl '62 pors; 2:70+ Ag '62 pors

Cordell, Richard A. Somerset Maugham (1961)

Pfeiffer, Karl G. W. Somerset Maugham (1959)

Twentieth Century Authors (1942; First Supplement, 1955)

Who's Who, 1962

Who's Who in America, 1962-63

MEAD, GEORGE H(OUK) Nov. 5, 1877-Jan. 1, 1963 Head of the Mead Corporation, one of the largest paper manufacturing companies in the United States, for more than fifty years. See *Current Biography* (October) 1946.

Obituary

Washington (D.C.) Post B p5 Ja 2 '63

MEHAFFEY, JOSEPH C(OWLES) Nov. 20, 1889-Feb. 18, 1963 Former United States Army engineer; helped to build Arlington Memorial Bridge in Washington, D.C. (1925-30); Governor of the Panama Canal Zone (1944-48). See *Current Biography* (January) 1948.

Obituary

Washington (D.C.) Post B p10 F 22 '63

MELCHER, FREDERIC G(ERSHOM) Apr. 12, 1879-Mar. 9, 1963 Publisher; president (1933-59) and chairman (since 1959) of R.R. Bowker & Company; co-editor of the company's *Publishers' Weekly* (1918-58). See *Current Biography* (July) 1945.

Obituary

N Y Times p36 Ap 1 '63

MESSMER, PIERRE (AUGUST JOSEPH) Mar. 20, 1916- French Minister of the Armed Forces

Address: b. 14 rue St. Dominique, Paris 7°, France; h. 1 rue du Général Delanne, Neuilly-sur-Seine, France

The French Army, exhausted and demoralized by an unbroken series of defeats stretching back twenty years, was by 1960 bitter and divided. Many of its senior officers were emotionally committed to the idea of a French Algeria and wholly opposed to the French government's policy of self-determination for that tortured land. The man chosen by President Charles de Gaulle to purge the army of disloyalty and to reanimate its fighting spirit was Pierre Messmer, who on February 5, 1960 was called from the Algerian battlefront to succeed Pierre Guillaumat as Minister of the Armed Forces.

Messmer entered political life after a distinguished career as a soldier and colonial administrator. His World War II service with de Gaulle's Free French forces earned him the rank of Commander of the Legion of Honor, among other decorations. He later served as a lieutenant colonel of the reserve in the Algerian campaign and rose to high office in the colonial service during the 1950's. Messmer has retained the post of Minister of the Armed Forces through two changes of government. He recently announced plans for a complete reshaping of France's defense strategy, which is to be built around the country's independent nuclear striking force.

Pierre August Joseph Messmer was born on March 20, 1916, in Vincennes, a town near Paris in the Seine department of France. He went to school in Paris, at the Lycée Charlemagne and the Lycée Louis-le-Grand, and later read law at the University of Paris. Messmer graduated as a doctor of law but, already determined on a career in the colonial service, went on to study from 1934 to 1937 at the École Coloniale (Colonial School), now the École Nationale de la France d'Outre-Mer (National School of France Overseas). He also holds the diploma of the school of oriental languages at the University of Paris.

In 1938 Messmer entered the colonial service as a student administrator, becoming an assistant administrator in August 1939. World War II began a month later, and Messmer was inducted into the services. In June 1940, when the Vichy government signed its armistice with the German invaders of France, Messmer elected to fight on. He joined de Gaulle's Free French forces, serving as a paratroop officer with the Thirteenth Brigade of the Foreign Legion. Messmer fought with the Foreign Legion in Africa, Italy, France, and Germany until 1944, when he joined the staff of General Joseph Pierre Koenig, who was military governor of Paris from August 1944 to July 1945.

Two special assignments took Messmer to the Far East before the end of the war. On the first he went to Calcutta in 1944 as head of a French mission to Lord Mountbatten, Supreme Allied Commander for South-East Asia. The second was considerably more dangerous. Messmer was parachuted into Japanese-held Indochina in 1945 to lay the groundwork for eventual restoration of French administration there. He was captured not by the Japanese but by the Viet-Minh, the Communist-led guerrilla army that, formed to resist the Japanese invaders of Indochina, was equally antagonistic to its former French rulers. Released after a period of harsh imprisonment, Messmer resumed his colonial career in 1946, serving successively as general secretary of the interministerial committee on Indochina and as director of the administrative staff of E. Bollaert, High Commissioner of Indochina.

Returning to Paris, Messmer in January 1951 became chief administrator of the Ministry of Overseas Departments and Territories. A year later, in April 1952, he was named Secretary General and interim Governor of Mauritania, positions that he filled until his appointment as Governor was confirmed in February 1953. Messmer's next post was that of Governor of the Ivory Coast, where he remained from 1954 until February 1956. There followed a brief interlude in Paris when Messmer served as director of the administrative staff of the Minister of Overseas Departments and Territories, and in April 1956 he was named High Commissioner of the French Cameroons (now the Republic of Cameroun).

Two even more important appointments followed. In January 1958 Messmer became High Commissioner of French Equatorial Africa, a group of four French territories that are now independent states—the Central African Republic, Chad, the Congo Republic, and Gabon. Six months later he was named High Commissioner of French West Africa, a similar but even larger group comprising the now independent states of Dahomey, Guinea, the Ivory Coast, Mali, Mauritania, Niger, Senegal and Upper Volta.

A profile of Messmer in the New York *Times* (February 6, 1960) described him as one of the men who "have noted how the tide of events is moving in Asia and in Africa" and have "helped transform what were French African colonies into newly independent republics that want both to be free and to stay economically close to mother France." French West Africa was dissolved in the spread of independence, and the post of High Commissioner was abolished in December 1959. Messmer was sent to Algeria, not as a colonial official but as a lieutenant colonel of the army reserve. At that time, although President de Gaulle had adopted a policy of self-determination for Algeria, that country was still under French domination and the Moslem population was fighting savagely for its freedom. Messmer joined the Eighth Parachute Regiment, then fighting the rebels in the mountains of eastern Algeria. He was not to stay there long.

The French settlers in Algeria were bitterly opposed to de Gaulle's self-determination policy, which would inevitably place the country's rule in the hands of the Moslem majority. On January 24, 1960 the settlers rose against the Paris government in an insurrection that was known to have the support of many military and civilian officials, both in Algeria and in France itself. President de Gaulle survived the crisis and acted swiftly to rid his government of dissident and ineffective elements. In the cabinet shake-up of February 5, 1960 two ministers were ousted and a number of cabinet posts changed hands. Pierre Guillaumat, Minister of the Armed Forces, who was felt to have lost control of the army, was replaced by Pierre Messmer.

Twenty-four hours later Messmer was back in Algeria, together with two other ministers, investigating the causes of the insurrection and identifying its participants. Civil and military purges were followed by sweeping administrative changes designed to reassert the Paris government's authority in Algeria. This was the first of many hurried trips to Algeria that Messmer was to make as Minister of the Armed Forces. His assignment has almost always been the same— to investigate disaffection in the army and to try to prevent its recurrence.

As Minister of the Armed Forces, a post equivalent to that of the United States Secretary of Defense, Messmer is responsible for France's entire military establishment. The French Navy and the Air Force, firm in their loyalty to de Gaulle, have given Messmer little trouble. It is the army, and particularly the regular army, that has provided his most acute and persistent problem. The French Army has a splendid history, both as a fighting force and as a devoted servant of the state, content to fight the wars and leave the thinking to the politicians. World War II changed this. Crushed by Germany and betrayed by the Vichy government, the French Army lost its confidence and acquired a contempt for politicians. There followed twenty years of failure, in the Levant, in Indochina, and at Suez.

Even in Algeria, where between 1954 and the end of 1960 over 10,000 French soldiers died, victory eluded the army. When Messmer took office the army was bitter, exhausted, disunited,

French Embassy Press & Inf. Division

PIERRE MESSMER

and deeply immersed in politics. For many regular soldiers, victory in Algeria had acquired an almost mystical importance as the army's last hope of redeeming its honor. To these men, de Gaulle's decision to give Algeria its freedom seemed the ultimate betrayal.

The crisis came to a head in 1961. On January 2 Messmer went to Algeria and exhorted the army to get out the Moslem vote in the referendum that was to decide for or against self-determination. A typical response from one high-ranking officer was: "We will do our duty and follow your orders, gritting our teeth." Another said the army was "on the verge of despair, possibly of revolt, certainly of scorn." On March 31 plans were announced for a reorganization of the armed forces to concentrate more authority in Messmer's hands. On April 22 General Maurice Challe and three other mutinous generals seized power in Algeria. Paris prepared against invasion.

The coup, which seemed at first to have succeeded, lasted only four days. Messmer attributed its collapse to swift action by de Gaulle and to the loyalty of the great majority of the army. It was nevertheless followed by the arrest of several hundred officers, the dissolution of the crack First Foreign Legion Parachute Regiment, and investigations and "modifications" in other elite regiments. These measures marked the end of overt army resistance to de Gaulle's Algerian policy, but earned Messmer the hatred of the OAS, the terrorist organization established by the white settlers. In March 1962 he escaped assassination by fifteen minutes, when he avoided an OAS booby trap only because he was late for an appointment. The agreement on Algerian independence was followed by the return of French forces to Europe and plans for a complete reorganization of the army.

(Continued next page)

MESSMER, PIERRE—Continued

Messmer has survived two changes of government since he became Minister of the Armed Forces. The first came in April 1962, when Georges Pompidou succeeded Michel Debré as Premier; the second in December of the same year, when Pompidou formed a new government following the November elections. In both cases Messmer retained his position in a cabinet that was little changed. It has been described as a cabinet of "technicians," as distinct from politicians, and one that is completely loyal to President de Gaulle.

Messmer's tenure has paralleled the development of France's nuclear defense strategy. The country's first atomic bomb was exploded in the Sahara on February 13, 1960, nine days after his appointment. His statement then that the test was only the first of a series was greeted by disapproval at home and abroad, but Messmer said that France would continue to work toward a nuclear striking force, and it has. In the May 1963 issue of the *Revue de la Défense Nationale* (Review of National Defense), Messmer announced that France's "first generation" atomic striking force would be in operation by the end of 1963. It would consist of atomic bombs carried by Mirage 4 aircraft. This, he said, would be succeeded in 1969 by submarines carrying missiles equipped with thermonuclear warheads. Conventional forces will meanwhile be reduced.

Messmer's article was seen as a rebuff to the United States, which has sought reinforcement of conventional forces available to the North Atlantic Treaty Organization and has opposed any increase in the membership of the "nuclear club." A defense by Messmer of the French policy appeared in *U.S. News & World Report* for September 24, 1962. In an interview in Paris with Frederick C. Painton, he said: "American nuclear arms . . . are now and will remain at the sole disposition of the President of the United States. And no matter how strong the links of friendship which bind us to the U.S., and despite the common interests we share, we cannot put our national defense in the hands of the United States indefinitely." Fears that the United States might one day withdraw its troops from Europe took Messmer to Bonn in June 1963 for talks with the West German Defense Minister, Kai-Uwe von Hassel, on joint defense plans.

For his services during World War II, Messmer received the high rank of Commander of the Legion of Honor, the Croix de Guerre, and the Resistance Medal. He is a Companion of the Liberation. Messmer has traveled widely and in November 1961 became the first French Defense Minister to visit the United States since World War II. In 1947 Messmer married Elizabeth Gil Duprez de Fravers. They have no children. At the time of his appointment as Minister of the Armed Forces, the New York *Times* (February 6, 1960) described Messmer as "unswervingly loyal to General de Gaulle." He is, the *Times* said, a big man, physically powerful, of demonstrated courage. Pierre Messmer and his wife spend their holidays in Brittany, sailing and playing tennis. He is an enthusiastic elephant hunter and says

that he likes to test his skill and courage tracking down elephants, though he is reluctant to kill his quarry.

References

N Y Times p2 F 6 '60 por
International Who's Who, 1962-63
International Year Book and Statesmen's Who's Who, 1963
Nouveau Dictionnaire National des Contemporains, 1961-62
Who's Who in France, 1961-62

MILAM, CARL H(ASTINGS) Oct. 22, 1884-Aug. 26, 1963 Librarian; executive secretary, American Library Association (1920-48); director, United Nations library (1948-50). See *Current Biography* (June) 1945.

Obituary

N Y Times p33 Ag 28 '63

MILLS, HAYLEY Apr. 18, 1946- Actress
Address: b. c/o Walt Disney Productions, 477 Madison Ave., New York 22

Since the release of Hayley Mills's first picture, *Tiger Bay*, in 1959, the career of the teen-age British actress has made such spectacular progress that one writer described it as "Hayley's comet." She belongs to one of England's leading theatrical families—John Mills, her father, has had a long and distinguished career in motion pictures and on the stage, and her sister, Juliet Mills, made her Broadway debut in *Five Finger Exercise* in 1959. Hayley herself has been enthusiastically praised by Walt Disney, with whom she has a contract, and among other professional admirers of her acting ability is Maurice Chevalier, who co-starred with her in Disney's *In Search of the Castaways* (1962).

Hayley Catherine Rose Vivian Mills was born in London on April 18, 1946, the second daughter of John Mills and Mary Hayley (Bell) Mills. Her mother, a former actress, is a novelist and playwright. Hayley's first school was a nursery in Chelsea, and she also attended Elmhurst Ballet School at Camberley in Surrey, a boarding school that specializes in drama and ballet instruction. Her mother chose the school not because she thought Hayley was a budding dancer, but because she believed that this training would give her daughter grace and poise. At school Hayley's favorite subject was languages, and she put her knowledge of French to good use during 1961 when she attended a finishing school in Switzerland for six months.

The Millses have tried to maintain a close-knit family group, and during her school years Hayley often accompanied her father when he was filming on location outside England. Since Hayley became a star in her own right at the age of twelve, her film schedules have also had to be worked into the family pattern of togetherness. Her career started one day in 1958 when J. Lee Thompson visited the Millses' Sussex home to discuss with John Mills his forthcoming movie, *Tiger Bay*, which Thompson was to direct. At the time of this visit, the script included a part for a small boy who befriends the murderer in the film, a part that had not yet been cast. When Thompson happened to overhear the younger Mills daughter imitate a television commercial for the amusement of her young brother, Jonathan, he decided to rewrite the part for a girl, and urged John Mills to allow Hayley to try for the role.

As a result, therefore, *Tiger Bay* (Rank, 1959) introduced Hayley Mills to the movie world. Based on the French story *Rodolphe et le Revolver* by Noel Calef, the movie setting was transferred to the slum area (Tiger Bay) of Cardiff. Hayley Mills played Gillie, a sly, wide-eyed product of the slum who sees a murder committed, steals the murder weapon, and befriends the killer. Her father played Superintendent Graham, who is in charge of the murder investigation. One critic described the scenes between father and daughter as "a prolonged, one-sided duel—a duel that will be best appreciated by parents who have conducted similar investigations, albeit on less serious matters."

The acting of Hayley Mills and of Horst Buchholz, in the role of the Polish sailor who kills his lady friend, lent credibility to the seemingly implausible friendship between child and murderer. Praising Hayley's acting in the Washington *Post and Times Herald* (February 19, 1960), Richard L. Coe described her performance as "an intensely believable study of a child's shrewd wisdom, loneliness, distrust and self-effacing charm." In the New York *Herald Tribune* (December 15, 1959) Paul V. Beckley commented that "she has none of that indoctrinated cuteness, the machine packaged, pre-cooked, quick frozen 'lovable child' quality which passes for pre-adolescent behavior in so many movies."

Tiger Bay came to the attention of Walt Disney at a time when he was looking for a child actor to play the part of Pollyanna, the heroine of a 1912 novel by Eleanor H. Porter. The sticky sweetness of the original Pollyanna, who always insisted on seeing the silver lining in every cloud, needed an actress who could introduce some wholesome mischief into the part to prevent it from becoming cloying. After Disney had seen *Tiger Bay,* he decided that Hayley Mills was the right actress to play Pollyanna for a modern audience.

Consequently, Hayley signed a five-year non-exclusive contract with the Disney organization. The contract is an agreement for five films, every other one to be made in England, and stipulates that total filming time should not exceed three months in any one year. The dollar value of the contract is $252,000, reportedly the largest amount paid for a child star since Fox signed up Shirley Temple in 1934. Disney is planning to let Hayley age naturally, and in the films she makes for him she will play increasingly older and more mature roles. Disney himself, usually restrained in his comments about his stars, has referred to Hayley as "the greatest movie find in twenty-five years."

As the "Glad Girl" in *Pollyanna* (1960) she was an immediate and popular success in Great Britain and in the United States. The cast of *Pollyanna* included Jane Wyman, Adolph Men-

Walt Disney Productions

HAYLEY MILLS

jou, and Karl Malden. The latter described Hayley as "the most unspoiled professional child actor" he had ever met. Discussing the success of *Pollyanna* in getting away from the saccharinity of the original story, Frank Morriss in the Toronto *Globe and Mail* (July 15, 1960) characterized Hayley's performance as "friendly, frank and extrovert," and went on to say that "she escapes priggishness by a couple of comfortable miles."

With the gross income from *Pollyanna* exceeding $7,000,000, Disney figured that if one Hayley could make this amount, two Hayleys could double it. His figuring proved accurate when her next film, *The Parent Trap* (1961), which starred Hayley in the dual role of twins separated by divorced parents in early childhood, grossed for Disney over $14,000,000. In fact, it became one of the top twenty money-making movies in film history and to date rates as Disney's leading box office attraction.

The next Disney picture starring Hayley Mills, *In Search of the Castaways* (1962), is based on the Jules Verne story *Captain Grant's Children.* A critic in the *National Observer* (December 24, 1962), who coined the phrase a "Vernacular spectacular," commented that it was a "cliff-hanging adventure that makes Pearl White look like *Rebecca of Sunnybrook Farm,*" for the movie includes earthquakes, landslides, giant condors, and an evil Maori chief. Teamed with such established actors as George Sanders, Wilfrid Hyde White, and Maurice Chevalier, Hayley again gave an outstanding performance, this time as Mary Grant searching for her long-missing father.

Summer Magic (1963) starred Hayley Mills in Walt Disney's version of Kate Douglas Wiggin's *Mother Carey's Chickens.* In line with Disney's policy of letting Hayley grow up naturally, *Summer Magic* shows her as a teen-ager in love for the first time. Her screen romances so far

MILLS, HAYLEY—*Continued*

had been limited to some hand holding and one kiss in *In Search of the Castaways*. She has also been cast as Laurel in *The Chalk Garden,* filmed by Universal-International in 1963.

Meanwhile, in the British picture *Whistle Down the Wind,* produced by Richard Attenborough and based on her mother's book, Hayley Mills had the leading role as one of three Lancashire children who mistake an escaped convict for Christ in His second coming. The movie was described in the Manchester *Guardian* after the British première in 1961 as "a small masterpiece" and this praise was echoed in the New York *Times* and the New York *World-Telegram and Sun* in 1962 after the American première. Bosley Crowther in the New York *Times* thought Hayley's performance was "surely one of the most sturdy and eloquent performances of a sensitive child ever done."

Although Hayley Mills is extremely critical of her own singing ability—"I couldn't sing my way out of a paper bag"—she has made several records that have achieved great popularity. In *The Parent Trap* she sang a song designed to satirize the rock 'n' roll craze called "Let's Get Together." This captured the teen-agers' hearts as genuine rock 'n' roll and was included in two records also made for Disney, *Let's Get Together* and *The Parent Trap.* Among her other records are *Johnny Jingo; Ding Ding Ding,* which reached fourth place on the Japanese hit parade; and *In Search of the Castaways.* She has also made an album with Maurice Chevalier entitled *Teen Street.*

For *Tiger Bay,* Hayley Mills won the Best Actress Award (Silver Bear) at the Berlin Film Festival in 1959 and for *Pollyanna,* the "Oscar" of the Variety Clubs of Great Britain and a special award of the Academy of Motion Picture Arts and Sciences. She has also received a British Film Academy Award, a Hollywood Press Association Golden Globe, and an award as Number One Star of Tomorrow in a poll of United States and Canadian exhibitors. In January 1962 she was named Great Britain's top box office attraction. Her fan mail amounts to 7,500 letters a month, and her income is estimated at over $50,000 a year. Her parents, aware of the fact that child actresses sometimes earn big money for only a small portion of their lives, have established a trust fund for Hayley, Sussex Ltd., which three family friends will direct for her until she is twenty-five.

Like many another teen-ager, Hayley has endured two major passions—horses and Elvis Presley. Her passion for horses has proved its staying power: she owns a pony called Arabelle and a mare called Beauty, both of which are stabled at the family's farm in Sussex. She collects records "like a fiend," dabbles in painting, has tried her hand at writing, and also collects china figures—mainly figures of horses.

Hayley Mills has strong views on such teen-age topics as dating—"I don't really agree with dating in the early teens. I believe everything comes in time although lots of people are impatient to grow up"—and on Great Britain's segregated schools (boys and girls)—"Our segregation makes boys and girls terribly shy in their teens." She has received letters from Great Britain's Committee of 100, and though she has not taken part in any demonstrations she has said that she is "worried" about the atomic bomb problem. She wants to marry after her twenty-first birthday and then "have hundreds of kids." Another wish is for a vintage car as soon as she is old enough to drive. She would like to play "a very glamorous period role" and also "something just a little bit mad and with a wild, shrieking scene or two," but more than anything else she wants to be a serious actress. At the age of seventeen she is five feet three inches tall and weighs 100 pounds.

Writing in the *Saturday Evening Post* (August 4, 1962), Pete Martin described Hayley Mills as having "a snub nose, a high dome of a forehead, a stubborn chin and pale-blue eyes." He continued, "When a director asks her to be happy, she can look as if she had just been given the world on a string. When she weeps, her face breaks into fragments of grief." Maurice Chevalier has said of her, "She is not pretty, she is more than pretty. She has youth, which always has a shine upon it. Moreover, she has vivacity, warmth and feminine wisdom." He predicted in an interview for *Parade* (November 5, 1961), "She will become a great, great star, because already—perhaps it is her instinct or her heritage—she knows how to act, how to appeal to the heart."

References

Cosmop 153:48+ D '62 pors
Ladies Home J 79:44+ D '62 pors
Parade p6+ N 5 '61 pors
Sat Eve Post 235:20+ Jl 28-Ag 4 '62 por

MILLS, JOHN Feb. 22, 1908- Actor; director
Address: b. c/o M.C.A. Ltd., 139 Piccadilly, London, W. 1., England

Both in popularity and in talent the Mills family stands at the top among England's theatrical families. John Mills, the father of actresses Hayley and Juliet Mills and the husband of playwright Mary Hayley Bell Mills, heads his family also by virtue of his performances in many plays on the London stage and about a hundred motion pictures. Although Mills has never made a movie in Hollywood, even his *Swiss Family Robinson* (1960) for Disney having been filmed in the West Indies, such British imports as *Great Expectations* (1947) and *Tunes of Glory* (1960) have made him as well known in the United States as almost any Hollywood star. Broadway audiences saw him for the first time in Terence Rattigan's *Ross* (1961-62), in which the disturbing integrity of his portrayal of Lawrence of Arabia was for some New York critics the play's chief recommendation. He has also appeared on television and has directed several motion pictures.

John Lewis Ernest Watts Mills was born in Felixstowe, Suffolk, England, on February 22, 1908 to Lewis and Edith (Baker) Mills. His father was a mathematics teacher at the Naval Training School in Felixstowe, but shortly after the birth of his son he became headmaster of a village school near Yarmouth, and it was here that John Mills spent his boyhood. He attended a Norwich school where Lord Nelson had been educated. At an early age he developed a taste for the stage, writing what he later described as "terrible little plays" at the age of nine and playing Puck by the time he was twelve.

The females in his family encouraged him to be stage struck, for his mother had once been manager of London's Haymarket Theatre, and his sister, Annette, trained to be a dancer. However, the men of the family tried to sway his choice of career toward a different field. His grandfather was a member of the London Corn Exchange, and when it was decided that John should learn the family business, he became a clerk in a corn merchants' office in Ipswich, London.

By the time Mills was nineteen he had discovered that the world of business was not for him, and he determined to try his luck on London's West End. Subsisting meanwhile on a variety of jobs, he got his first chance in the theater in 1929 when he was cast in the chorus of *The Five O'Clock Girl*, which opened at the Hippodrome Theatre on March 21. Following this production he was invited to join a repertory company called The Quaints, which toured India and the Far East.

This repertory tour proved extremely important to Mills's career in two ways. First, it gave him an opportunity to acquire solid dramatic experience, for in the course of the tour he played in *Journey's End, Young Woodley, Mr. Cinders,* and *Hamlet.* Secondly, he met two people during the tour who were to have a major influence on his work: Noel Coward was impressed by his portrayal of Lieutenant Raleigh in *Journey's End* and became his friend, and in Tientsin he was seen and admired by a sixteen-year-old redheaded British girl named Mary Hayley Bell.

On his return to England, Mills was cast as Lord Fancourt Babberley in *Charley's Aunt.* In this production, which opened at London's New Theatre in December 1930, Mills became the youngest actor ever to play the lead role of the comedy. Coward introduced his young protégé to C. B. Cochran, who gave him the juvenile lead, and an opportunity to sing, in the *1931 Revue,* presented at the Pavilion Theatre beginning in March. Then as Birkinshaw in *London Wall* he opened at the Duke of York's Theatre in May 1931, and in October of the same year Coward offered him the part of Joe Marryot in *Cavalcade* at the Drury Lane Theatre. After *Cavalcade,* he played a series of juvenile leads, with some song and dance work in between. By the middle of 1938, realizing that he was in danger of being typecast, he decided to wait for an offer that would give him a chance to develop.

The offer he wanted came in December 1938 when he was invited to join the Old Vic Company to play Young Marlowe in *She Stoops to Conquer* and Puck in the Tyrone Guthrie revival of *A Midsummer Night's Dream.* In Guthrie's 1937 production of *A Midsummer Night's Dream* he had used a boy as Puck, and as Audrey Williamson noted in her book *Old Vic Drama, 2; 1947-1957* (Macmillan, 1957), "how much more a mature and clever actor may make of" the part was obvious from Mills's performance.

Friedman—Abeles

JOHN MILLS

When the Old Vic season finished in February 1939, Mills played Tommy in *We at the Crossroads* at the Globe Theatre, in March. Then in one of the most important parts he has ever played on the English stage, in April 1939 he opened in *Of Mice and Men* as George at the Gate Theatre. To prepare for the role he had perfected his American accent by sitting through the James Cagney movie *Angels with Dirty Faces* seventeen times.

Mills's performance in *Of Mice and Men* pleased Guthrie McClintic, who went backstage to offer the "young American" the leading role in Maxwell Anderson's *Key Largo,* which he was planning to produce on Broadway. World War II intervened, however, and delayed John Mills's Broadway debut. He joined the Royal Engineers as a recruit and spent a year in the ranks. He was commissioned in the Royal Monmouthshire Rifles and served until a duodenal ulcer caused him to be invalided out in 1942.

Meanwhile, Mills had again met Mary Hayley Bell, and he married her in January 1941. Giving up her acting career, she began to write plays for her husband. In the first of these, *Men in Shadow,* Mills starred as Lew at the Vaudeville Theatre presentation beginning in September 1942. Three years later he appeared as Stephen Cass in his wife's *Duet for Two Hands,* which opened at the Lyric Theatre in June and proved a tremendous personal success for both author and actor.

In *Angel,* which had its première at the Strand Theatre in June 1947, Mills displayed his talent as a director rather than an actor. In October of 1950 and 1951 respectively he played Bertie in *Top of the Ladder* and Freddie in *Figure of Fun.* Another play written by his wife, *The Uninvited Guest,* in which he starred in the part of Candy, opened at St. James's Theatre in May 1953. In February 1954 he revived his charac-

MILLS, JOHN—*Continued*

terization of Lord Fancourt Babberley in *Charley's Aunt* at the New Theatre.

Since 1933, when he appeared in *The Midshipmaid,* John Mills has acted in over 100 motion pictures, while his career on the stage also progressed. According to the *Motion Picture Herald-Fame* polls, he was one of the top ten money-making British stars for about nine years between the mid-1940's and the late 1950's. Among his early films that introduced him to American audiences were Carol Reed's *The Young Mr. Pitt* (1942) and Noel Coward's *In Which We Serve* (1942). Describing the latter as "one of the most eloquent motion pictures of these or any other times," Bosley Crowther wrote in the New York *Times* (December 24, 1942) that Mills's acting as Ordinary Seaman Shorty Blake was "incomparable."

His appealing performances as the humanitarian editor George Boswell in *So Well Remembered* (1947) and, especially, as Pip in *Great Expectations* (1947) further endeared John Mills to American moviegoers, as well as to audiences at home. *Great Expectations* was directed by David Lean, who had also directed Mills in Noel Coward's *This Happy Breed* (1947). In 1954 Lean directed another film starring Mills and won a prize at the Fourth International Film Festival in Berlin. The movie, *Hobson's Choice,* which co-starred Charles Laughton and Brenda de Banzie, tells the story of a Lancashire bootmaker and his clash with his eldest daughter. A critic for the New York *Herald Tribune* (June 20, 1954) described Mills in the role of Willie Mossop as the "key figure" in the comedy and pointed out, "Beginning as a man of awkward ways braced into stiff attitudes by an ill-fitting suit, and ending as a man of promise, Mills has been directed by Lean into a concentrated combination of humor, character and period."

John Mills might well be called a veteran of British war movies, having appeared in *The Colditz Story* (1957), *Dunkirk* (1958), *I Was Monty's Double* (1959), and many similar films. One of his finest portrayals in a military movie was in *Tunes of Glory* (1960), in which he co-starred with Alec Guinness. Stephen Watts commented in the New York *Times* (October 2, 1960) that director Ronald Neame "was in the fortunate position of being able to pit two of Britain's most resourceful actors against one another, and there is no doubt that the strength of each brings out the best in the other." For his performance in this picture, Mills won the male acting prize at the International Film Festival in Venice in 1960.

Another movie which put him in uniform, this time a naval uniform, but gave him a very different type of role, was *The Baby and the Battleship* (1957). As the inept sailor who gets left with a baby when on leave in Naples and has to smuggle the infant boy on board ship, Mills was praised by Alton Cook in the New York *World-Telegram and Sun* (October 1, 1957) for providing the "backbone of laughter." "The situations may get silly," Cook added, "but he never does."

In 1948 Mills signed a contract with the J. Arthur Rank Organization that allowed him to star in Rank pictures and to maintain independence as an actor and direct his own films. Under this agreement he produced *The Rocking Horse Winner* (1950) and *The History of Mr. Polly* (1951), a delightful comedy adapted from H. G. Wells's story, in which he played the title role. Under another contract, with Walt Disney, he appeared as the father in *Swiss Family Robinson* (1960). In one of the Rank releases in which he starred, *The Singer, Not the Song* (1962), he played a dedicated Roman Catholic priest in Mexico. "Mills' performance," New York *Herald Tribune* critic Paul V. Beckley found, "is conspicuously the best thing about the picture." His recent films have also included *The Valiant* (1962) and *Tiara Tahiti* (1962).

The father of one of England's leading theatrical families, he has appeared with both his daughters in different movies. Juliet Mills, the elder daughter, who made her Broadway debut in *Five Finger Exercise* in 1959, first appeared with her father in the movie *In Which We Serve* when she was just a few weeks old. Since then she has performed briefly in nine of her father's films. John Mills also helped to launch the career of Hayley Mills, in whose first motion picture, *Tiger Bay* (1959), he played Superintendent Graham.

By 1961 John Mills had long been a familiar figure on the American screen, but he had never appeared on the stage in the United States. He made his Broadway debut in the leading role of Terence Rattigan's play *Ross,* which opened at the Eugene O'Neill Theatre on December 26, 1961. This was his first stage role in seven years. Rattigan's play deals with T. E. Lawrence at the time when he was seeking anonymity in the Royal Air Force under the assumed name of Ross.

As background for his portrayal of Lawrence, Mills could remember a meeting back in the 1930's when he was appearing in *Cavalcade.* Noel Coward had introduced him to a noticeably reserved man called Shaw, and it was not until later that Mills discovered that he had met Lawrence of Arabia. He came to the part in *Ross* with a vivid memory of "the steady, steely blue eyes of the man." Mills further recalled in an interview for the New York *Post* (April 28, 1962), "He had enormous charm without trying to exude it, but there was something very odd about him, something very withdrawn." New York critics generally agreed that Mills handled the difficult role brilliantly. In his next appearance on the stage he portrayed a timid clerk transformed into a would-be dictator, in *Power of Persuasion,* which opened in London at the Garrick Theatre in September 1963.

Mills made his American television debut in 1956 in the *Producers Showcase* production of Somerset Maugham's *The Letter.* He also played the part of a tough British officer stationed in Cyprus in *The Interrogator* on NBC's *Du Pont's Show of the Week* on September 23, 1962. Watching him rehearse for the latter production, producer Lewis Freedman commented to a writer for *Newsweek* (September 24, 1962), "He's honest, you can see he's honest, can't you?"

His honesty is the hallmark of John Mills's acting. Howard Taubman noted his concentration on the truth of the character he was playing during his performance as Ross; a *Time* reviewer wrote of his "lacerating honesty"; and John Chapman in the *Sunday News* (January 7, 1962) said that his acting was "so intense and ... so true that he must be Col. Lawrence as he really was." Insisting on the principle of truth, Mills has tried to pass on his belief to his children: "If an actor will ask himself how a character really thinks and would say a line and not how interesting and dramatic it would be to do it another way, he will be telling the truth and never overact nor underact" (New York *Post*, April 27, 1962).

On his 450-acre farm, about thirty-eight miles from London, John Mills raises a dairy herd of Guernseys and also some Aberdeen Angus cattle. His other home is in Berkeley Square. He has gray eyes and brown hair, is five feet eight inches tall, and weighs 160 pounds. Before his marriage to Mary Hayley Bell he was married to Aileen (Raymond) Mills. In addition to their two daughters, he and Mary Hayley Bell Mills have a son, Jonathan. In 1960 Mills was named a Commander of the British Empire by Queen Elizabeth II. He is a member of the Garrick and the Green Room clubs, and his recreations are polo, riding, swimming, skiing, golf, and tennis —and his "one vice is fast cars."

References

N Y Post p72 Ap 27 '62 por
N Y Sunday News p80+ F 4 '62 por
Shulman, Milton. How To Be a Celebrity (1950)
Who's Who, 1963
Who's Who in the Theatre (1961)

MONTINI, CARDINAL GIOVANNI BATTISTA *See* Paul VI, Pope

MORATH, MAX (EDWARD) (môr-ăth') Pianist; entertainer Oct. 1, 1926-
Address: b. 1130 E. Kenyon Ave., Englewood, Col.

Max Morath is a pianist and entertainer who has almost single-handedly revived the nearly lost art of ragtime piano and launched a whole new folk-cult centering on the turn of the century. He has described that era as one of "consolidation, tranquility, reform, and harmony in our national life . . . a great period of optimism and happiness." Seated at an old upright piano, with a cigar clenched between his teeth, and dressed in a derby hat, chalk-striped suit and sleeve garters, Morath has aroused a great interest in the ragtime era in millions of Americans. In September 1963 he made his first nightclub appearance in New York, at the Blue Angel, and the response from critics and public indicated that Morath had won many converts to a musical period that ended before he was born.

Max Edward Morath was born on October 1, 1926 in Colorado Springs, Colorado, the son of Frederic Palmer Morath, a real estate broker, and Gladys (Ramsell) Morath, who used to play piano accompaniments for silent movies in Colorado Springs. From his mother, now society editor of the Colorado Springs *Gazette-Telegraph*, Max

learned to play the piano. Although she played ragtime, she never consciously taught it to him, according to Morath, who feels it "soaked" into him as a child.

With an older brother, Frederick Ramsell Morath, Max was raised in Colorado Springs and Long Beach, California. He graduated from Colorado Springs High School in 1944, where he had been active in the choir and theater and had written for the school newspaper. At Colorado College, in his home town, he worked his way through school as an announcer, newscaster, and pianist for the local radio station, KVOR, and received his B.A. degree in 1948.

After he graduated from college Morath was a staff announcer for radio station KGHF in Pueblo, Colorado. In 1949-50 he prepared and sold syndicated radio transcriptions in Dallas, Texas, and worked as actor, assistant producer, and salesman. During the next year he was an actor, pianist, singer, and musical director for several stock companies in Phoenix, Arizona. In late 1951 he attended a radio and television institute at Stanford University, where he studied such television techniques as writing, acting, and directing. Applying what he had learned at Stanford, he became a production manager, announcer, and entertainer at television station KKTV, Channel 11, in the latter part of 1952.

Beginning in 1954 Morath spent six summers as music director, intermission pianist, accompanist, and song writer for the Imperial Players at the Melodrama Theatre in the summer resort town of Cripple Creek, Colorado. Winters he spent working in nightclubs and radio and TV stations. During this period Morath began to specialize in ragtime and turn-of-the-century styles and repertoire. A serious student of the social history of the United States from 1890 to 1920, Morath embarked particularly on research in the musical history of the era. He combed libraries, studied ragtime piano rolls, borrowed old sheet music, consulted historical societies, explored antique shops, rummaged through old magazines, and interviewed survivors of the ragtime era. The result was a brand-new kind of act: the showmanship of an old-time ragtime pianist accompanied by scholarly commentaries on the music, mores, and social etiquette of a vanished age. In his nightclub appearances and his television programs Morath has shown such enthusiasm and nostalgia for the ragtime era that he appears to possess a missionary zeal in winning converts to his favorite period of American music.

"Ragtime is the folk music of the city," Morath tells his audiences. "It represents 25 years of a music that's been overlooked. Classic ragtime isn't the honky-tonk music you hear today. That's just a popular misconception. . . . Nobody has paid the classic ragtime much attention because of the attitude that folk music had to come from the hills. We were looking in the wrong direction."

The pianist's big break came in the winter of 1959-60. At the urging of Jim Case and Marvin Hale of KRMA-TV, Denver's educational TV station, Morath wrote and performed a series of twelve programs for the National Educational Television network, entitled *The Ragtime Era.*

(Continued next page)

MAX MORATH

The series traced the development of blues and ragtime, the beginnings of musical comedy, and the rise of Tin Pan Alley. Morath's vintage piano and long-forgotten tunes—among them Scott Joplin's "Maple Leaf Rag," Tom Turpin's "St. Louis Rag," and "Ragtime Nightingale" by Joseph Francis Lamb—as well as his zest and craftsmanship as a showman were a novelty on educational television. As a result of his success many commercial TV stations bought the show, giving Morath a far greater audience than the forty-eight stations covered by the National Educational Television network.

Jack Gould of the New York *Times* (February 21, 1961) called the series "one of the season's more engaging little sleepers." Reviewing one of the programs, which traced the origins of ragtime, Gould noted that the subject "necessarily involved the institution of the sporting house, where the distinctive syncopation flourished amid an appropriately pulchritudinous framework. With an infectiously gay spirit, hilarious but in good taste, the presentation acknowledged, visually and orally, one of the sociological roots of ragtime."

The success of *The Ragtime Era* resulted in many bookings for Morath at concerts and industrial conventions. It also led to a second National Educational Television network series—fifteen half-hour programs entitled *Turn of the Century,* in which Morath presented the social history of the era as reflected in its music. Taped in the winter of 1961-62, each of the programs dealt with a different aspect of the period—its social customs, commercial inventions, political movements, economic development, among others. Lantern slides, photographs, and other props were used by Morath to illustrate the vintage songs with which he recreated an era. In general critics were favorably impressed with the new series. They praised Morath for his piano and song selections and for his interpretation of Americana. One critic recommended that Mor-

ath's "smooth documentary of humor, morals, art, and recreation should be required reading for the too-academically inclined."

Morath's engagement at the Blue Angel in New York in September 1963 was not his first cabaret date, but the warm reviews he received and the response from the sophisticated local nightclub public indicated that he had been launched on a new career. Previously, Morath had played at colleges across the United States and had entertained at industrial conventions. Both audiences and reviewers have appreciated Morath's refreshing treatment of his material. His use of color slides to accompany melodies of the period places ragtime in its proper historical perspective. Perfectly preserved and clearly projected, the slides come from the collection of John Ripley of Topeka, Kansas.

In the summer of 1963 Morath taped a radio series of music and monologues for the Pacific Northwest Bell Company. He also recorded an album of ragtime for the Epic label and prepared a folio of early ragtime piano and vocal music, adding originals by himself. He completed and edited for publication *100 Ragtime Classics,* containing reprints of the outstanding ragtime favorites of the turn of the century.

In his introduction Morath commented on the current ragtime revival and summed up his enthusiasm for the music and the era in which it flourished: "Every day the number of players, both amateur and professional, increases. The crystal clear and highly exhilarating form of piano music called classic ragtime has begun its return to fashion with players of all persuasions—the disciplined classicist, the jazz traditionalist, the contemporary stylist. At its best ragtime can be both introspective and flamboyant, dynamic and gently lyrical. With its quaint name and clouded past, ragtime's vitality and charm have lain dormant these many years, a music misunderstood and short-changed from the beginning. Ragtime is old now, its proud publishers broke and forgotten, its boisterous milieu of the turn-of-the-century America already an almost mythical haven. Ragtime, it seems, is so old, it's new again."

On October 23, 1953 Max Morath married Norma Loy Tackett, whom he met in 1952 when she auditioned for a television show on which Morath appeared. Like Morath, she attended Colorado College. They appeared together on television and with the Imperial Players at the Melodrama Theatre at Cripple Creek, Colorado. The Moraths live in the Denver suburb of Englewood with their three children—Kathryn Annette, Christine Lee, and Frederic Loyd. Morath is five feet eleven inches tall, has blond hair and blue eyes, and is much more youthful in appearance than the image he projects on the television screen. His religious affiliation is with the Protestant Episcopal Church, and his hobbies include collecting music and objects of the turn of the century, prospecting, mountaineering, swimming, and reading.

References

N Y Herald Tribune IV p26 F 5 '61
Newsweek 59:82 Mr 19 '62 por
St. Louis Post-Dispatch Ja 17 '61

MORGENSTIERNE, WILHELM (THOR-LEIF) MUNTHE DE Nov. 4, 1887-July 15, 1963 Norwegian Ambassador to the United States (1942-58). See *Current Biography* (May) 1949.

Obituary

N Y Times p31 Jl 16 '63

MORGENTHAU, HANS J(OACHIM) Feb. 17, 1904- Political scientist; lawyer; university professor; author
Address: b. Department of Political Science, University of Chicago, Chicago, Ill.; h. 5542 S. Dorchester Ave., Chicago 37, Ill.

The distinguished writing and teaching that have made Hans J. Morgenthau one of America's most respected authorities on political science began in pre-Hitler Germany. He fled from Nazism to the United States in 1937, has taught at the University of Chicago since 1943, and has directed the university's Center for the Study of American Foreign and Military Policy since 1950. A proponent of the "realistic" approach to international relations, Morgenthau believes that the United States should be concerned primarily with its national interest rather than with world opinion, and his views have provoked considerable controversy. His most important books include *Scientific Man vs. Power Politics* (1946), *Politics Among Nations* (1948), *In Defense of the National Interest* (1951), *Dilemmas of Politics* (1958), and *The Purpose of American Politics* (1961).

Hans Joachim Morgenthau was born in Coburg, Germany on February 17, 1904, the son of Dr. Ludwig Morgenthau, a physician, and Frieda (Bachmann) Morgenthau. At the age of six he entered elementary school in Coburg, and after completing his studies there in 1914 he attended the Humanistisches Gymnasium, also in Coburg, from which he graduated with highest honors in 1923. From 1923 to 1927 Hans Morgenthau studied history, law, economics, and philosophy at the universities of Berlin, Frankfurt, and Munich. He passed his first law examination at Munich *magna cum laude* in 1927, and after his admission to the bar he practised law in Munich and Wolfrathshausen.

From 1928 to 1930 Morgenthau served as assistant to Professor Sinzheimer in Frankfurt, while practising law in that city. In 1929 he received the degree of Juris Utriusque Doctor (doctor of both canon and civil law), *summa cum laude*, from the University of Frankfurt, after having written the dissertation *Die internationale Rechtspflege, ihr Wesen und ihre Grenzen* (Leipzig, 1929). He then contributed articles to journals and newspapers, including a series about the reform of German law schools, published by the Frankfurter *Zeitung* in 1929-30. It was described by the president of the Prussian board of law examiners as the best series of articles ever written on the subject. After taking his second law examination in 1931 Morgenthau was appointed assistant to the faculty of law at the University of Frankfurt, where he worked with Professor Baum-

University of Chicago

HANS J. MORGENTHAU

gartner. In the same year he became acting president of the labor law court in Frankfurt. He was a member of the Deutsche Gesellschaft für Völkerrecht and of the Internationale Vereinigung für Rechts- und Wirtschaftsphilosophie.

In 1932 Morgenthau went to Geneva, Switzerland to study at the Graduate Institute for International Studies and to take a position as instructor in German public law at the University of Geneva. Because of Hitler's rise to power in Germany, in 1933, Morgenthau decided to remain at Geneva, and he received a grant from the Swiss Committee for the Aid of Refugee Scholars. From 1933 to 1935 he was instructor of public law and political science at the University of Geneva. His writings during this period include *La notion du "politique" et la théorie des différends internationaux* (Paris, 1933) and *La réalité des normes, en particulier des normes du droit international* (Paris, 1934). During 1935-36 Morgenthau taught in Spain, as professor of international law with the Institute of International and Economic Studies in Madrid and as lecturer at the Union of Spanish Societies for International Studies.

Moving to the United States in 1937, Morgenthau became an instructor in government at Brooklyn College in New York City. In 1939 he obtained a grant from the Rockefeller Foundation, through the Emergency Committee in Aid of Displaced Foreign Scholars, and from 1939 to 1943 he was assistant professor of law, history, and political science at the University of Kansas City. Simultaneously from 1940 to 1943, he did research work on a grant from the Penrose Fund, through the American Philosophical Society. He was admitted to the Missouri bar in 1943.

Morgenthau began to teach at the University of Chicago in 1943 as visiting associate professor of political science. He became associate professor in 1945, professor of political science in 1949, and professor of political science and mod-

MORGENTHAU, HANS J.—Continued

ern history in 1961. On October 1, 1963 he assumed the Albert A. Michelson Distinguished Service Professorship. Since 1950 he has served as director of the Center for the Study of American Foreign and Military Policy at the University of Chicago. He was visiting professor at the University of California in Berkeley in 1949 and 1961; at Harvard in 1951, 1959, 1960, and 1961; at Northwestern in 1954; and at Columbia and Yale in 1956-57. In 1961 he was Faith and Freedom Lecturer at the American University in Washington, D.C. He has also lectured at the Armed Forces Staff College; the NATO Defense College; and the Air, Army, Naval, and National War Colleges. In 1958-59 he was a member of the Institute for Advanced Study at Princeton, New Jersey, and from 1958 to 1960 he was an associate of the Washington Center for Foreign Policy Research. He served the United States Department of State as a consultant from 1949 to 1951.

In his book *Scientific Man vs. Power Politics* (Univ. of Chicago Press, 1946) Morgenthau analyzes the underlying philosophy of contemporary Western civilization and concludes that the "scientific man" must give way to the "more than scientific man—the statesman." J. S. Rouceck in *School and Society* (April 19, 1947) described the book as "one of the most important works published in recent years," one that "should be a required reading for all educators," and C. L. Willard in the *Churchman* (March 15, 1947) called it a "brilliant and penetrating study of the critical inability of modern man to cope with political problems." On the other hand, Alfred Werner in *Christian Century* (January 1, 1947) commented that it "will hardly contribute much to the establishment of a better postwar world, for it offers nothing but abysmal pessimism, disguised as realism."

Morgenthau's *Politics Among Nations: The Struggle for Power and Peace* (Knopf, 1948; 1953; 1960), a survey of international politics that is widely used as a college textbook, has been described as "bringing Machiavelli up to date." Barrington Moore wrote in the *American Sociological Review* (April 1949) that it stands "head and shoulders above the crusading or pontifical writings that constitute the major intellectual fare" in the field of international relations. Dexter Perkins, in the *Annals of the American Academy of Social and Political Science* (July 1949), found that its "general tone is so profoundly critical as almost to give one the impression of hopelessness as to the future of international relations."

The four intellectual errors, as Morgenthau calls them, of postwar diplomacy—Wilsonian utopianism, Dumbartian legalism, Trumanian sentimentalism, and neo-isolationism—are the subject of *In Defense of the National Interest: A Critical Examination of American Foreign Policy* (Knopf, 1951), in which he calls upon statesmen to analyze the national interest unemotionally and pragmatically. Although he thought that the book was in its substance "one of the most useful contributions to the understanding of our problems," Crane Brinton

noted in the New York *Herald Tribune Book Review* (July 1, 1951) that it "may well offend unnecessarily a good many intelligent and well-meaning people who ought to be able to learn a lot from it." The book was published in England under the title *American Foreign Policy*.

In *Dilemmas of Politics* (Univ. of Chicago Press, 1958), a collection of essays that he wrote over a period of twenty years, Morgenthau tries to make a distinction between what is new and what is perennial in contemporary political problems, and between what is valid and what has become obsolete in political ideas and institutions. W. S. Fiser wrote in *Ethics* (April 1959) that this book "clearly establishes the author as one of the very few major figures among contemporary political theorists." Another collection of Morgenthau's essays, the three-volume *Politics in the 20th Century* (Univ. of Chicago Press), appeared in 1962.

Continuing debates over the national purpose prompted Morgenthau to write *The Purpose of American Politics* (Knopf, 1960), based on his Albert Shaw Lectures on Diplomatic History, which he delivered at Johns Hopkins University in April 1959. Critically examining the bases of American civilization, he observes that America is essentially revolutionary in its purpose, with a firm belief in "equality in freedom." He notes, however, that the American people have tended to lose sight of their goals through the degeneration of government to a mere instrument of the majority, the excessive role of public opinion, the pressures of conformism, and what he calls "the feudalism of the concentration of private power." Consequently, he declares, "we must restore to the government the ability to govern and to the people the ability to control." Herman Finer in the *New Republic* (November 28, 1960) criticized Morgenthau for his tendency to accept the theory "that the people have no right to participate in the formulation of policy but only to consent to it," and added that "the sweep of his mind is vast in its scope, taut in logic, ingenious in relating principle to action."

Morgenthau has contributed to the *Encyclopædia Britannica* and to the series of articles published under the title *H-Bomb* (Didier, 1950). He was co-editor with Kenneth W. Thompson of *Principles and Problems of International Politics: Selected Readings* (Knopf, 1950), and he edited *Germany and the Future of Europe* (Univ. of Chicago Press, 1951), a series of Harris Foundation lectures by Reinhold Niebuhr and others. He has written many articles and reviews for scholarly periodicals in the fields of law, philosophy, history, and political science, as well as for popular magazines and newspapers.

A champion of military preparedness, Morgenthau believes that the United States should have a three-fold capability for all-out nuclear war, tactical atomic war, and conventional preatomic war. Speaking on a five-member panel on *Open End* (WNTA-TV) on April 10, 1960, he termed "phony" the recent Soviet proposals for total disarmament and declared that historically disarmament had proved impossible and unpractical, unless it was preceded by a settlement of political issues. On the other hand, he takes a dim view on a foreign policy based on a crusading spirit, and he has said that "the anti-Communist crusade as an instrument of foreign policy is likely to destroy all nations, Communist and anti-Communist alike."

Morgenthau also criticizes what he regards an undue American concern with world opinion. "This world opinion we pay so much attention to is largely a myth," he is quoted in *Time* (September 15, 1961) as saying. "Our position should simply be to think and act in terms of our own self-interest. If so-called world opinion supports our self interest, well, that's fine. But if it doesn't . . . we should ignore it." In an article in the *American Political Science Review* (June 1962) Morgenthau evaluates the United States foreign aid program. Noting that large-scale aid is wasted on so-called "bum and beggar nations" that are incapable of genuine economic development, he declared that foreign aid should be strictly tailored to suit the political purposes of the United States.

In another article, in *Commentary* (November 1962), written shortly before President Kennedy imposed a naval blockade on Cuba, Morgenthau wrote that the United States should counter Soviet activity in the Caribbean, either alone, or in concert with Latin American nations, by means of military demonstrations, a blockade, or even an invasion of Cuba. "If we refuse to take any action at all because we take the Russian threat of nuclear war seriously, as we did in 1956 during the Hungarian revolution and the Suez Canal crisis, we will hasten and not prevent the coming of a nuclear war," he wrote.

Although a realist in international politics, Morgenthau believes that the preservation of moral values is essential for the survival of civilization, and he especially insists on the maintenance of high moral standards by members of the academic profession. In an article in the New York *Times Magazine* (November 22, 1959) he condemned Charles Van Doren, a young instructor, who, along with others, had won large sums of money under false pretenses on a television quiz program.

Hans J. Morgenthau was married on July 3, 1935 to Irma Thormann. They have two children, Matthew and Susanna. Morgenthau has been a citizen of the United States since 1943. He is five feet eight inches tall and has gray hair. Morgenthau is fluent in English, French, German, and Spanish, and he is able to read Dutch, Italian, and Portuguese. He belongs to the Quadrangle Club in Chicago, and his professional associations include the American Political Science Association, the International Institute of Philosophy of Law and Legal Sociology, the International Institute of Ibero-American Studies, the American Society of International Law, the American Academy of Arts and Sciences, the American Academy of Political and Social Science, the American Association of University Professors, and the American Philosophical Association. In April 1962 he was nominated temporary chairman of the University of Chicago

chapter of the Councils of the Gradualist Way to Peace.

References

Newsweek 61:48+ Ja 14 '63 por
American Men of Science 10th ed (1960-62)
Twentieth Century Authors (First Supplement, 1955)
Who's Who in America, 1962-63

MORLEY, ROBERT May 26, 1908- British actor and playwright
Address: h. "Fairmans Cottage," Wargrave, Berkshire, England

As a playwright, television personality, and as what Brooks Atkinson has called "an extraordinary actor of first rank," Robert Morley is known to audiences all over the world. He is the author or co-author of seven plays, including the successful *Edward, My Son*. Morley has appeared in nearly thirty motion pictures and innumerable plays, on the stage and on the home screen. Although comedy is Morley's forte, some of his greatest performances have been in roles that were far from comic, notably as Arnold Holt in *Edward, My Son* and as Oscar Wilde in both the stage and screen versions of the Leslie and Sewell Stokes play. Morley, who has also served as a director and a producer, is above all a professional, of whom it has been said that "there is no record of his ever having given a bad performance." He has won awards for his acting both in England and the United States, and in 1957 he was named a C.B.E. for his services to the theater.

Robert Morley was born on May 26, 1908 in Semley, Wiltshire, England to Major Robert Wilton Morley of the British Army and the former Gertrude Emily Fass. A career in the diplomatic corps was planned for him, and he was accordingly educated first at Wellington College and then at schools in Germany, France, and Italy. But Morley, who had made his theatrical debut in kindergarten, had other plans. His early ambition to "loaf about on the stage" was fortified, he maintains, at the ultraconservative Wellington College, where horror greeted his choice of acting as a career.

Morley's parents received the decision with some hesitation and suggested that, as a compromise, he first try a career in business. A brief and boring stint as a beer salesman followed, ending in the mid-1920's, when Morley enrolled in the Royal Academy of Dramatic Art. Leaving RADA, Morley made his first professional appearance on May 28, 1928 at the Hippodrome, Margate, in a play about smugglers called *Dr. Syn*. His first appearance on the London stage came the following year, on December 26, 1929, when Morley played a minor role as a pirate in a Christmas production of *Treasure Island* at the Strand Theatre. Thereafter, until 1935, he played a variety of roles in a succession of touring companies that took him all over England. At one time during this period he supported himself between engagements by selling vacuum

ROBERT MORLEY

cleaners from door to door. "In those six months," he wrote in the New York *Herald Tribune* (February 1, 1953): "[I] learned more about acting . . . than ever before or since on the stage."

In 1935 Morley decided to try his hand at writing a play. The result was a comedy called *Short Story*, which he sent to the actress Marie Tempest. She promptly accepted it, had it rewritten to suit her own subtle and elegant style, and appeared in it with an all-star cast in November 1935. *Short Story*, which ran in London for six months, established Morley's theatrical reputation and led to further success. With the actor Peter Bull, he launched a summer theater at Perranporth, Cornwall, appearing in a variety of roles. In September 1936 he scored his first major success as an actor, when he played the lead at London's Gate Theatre in *Oscar Wilde*, by Leslie and Sewell Stokes.

The Gate, however, was a theater club with a relatively small audience, and in spite of the critical enthusiasm that greeted his Oscar Wilde, Morley was still a long way from stardom. The equally satisfactory reviews of his next performance, as Alexandre Dumas in *The Great Romancer*, still referred to him as an "unknown actor." *The Great Romancer* was withdrawn after a short run in the summer of 1937, but not before Morley had caught the eye of a Metro-Goldwyn-Mayer executive. Morley opened as Henry Higgins in Shaw's *Pygmalion* at the Old Vic in September 1937, but early in 1938 he was off to Hollywood for his first film part, as Louis XVI in MGM's *Marie Antoinette*. When the shooting was over, Morley went to New York's Fulton Theatre, where he opened on October 10, 1938 in *Oscar Wilde*. He repeated his London success in the role and was cited for the best performance of the year by an actor in *Variety*'s poll of the New York drama critics.

In June 1939, shortly before the outbreak of World War II, Morley returned to England, where he played a summer season at Perranporth. In the fall of 1939 he joined Gabriel Pascal for the eight months it took to make the film version of Shaw's *Major Barbara*. Having completed his memorable portrayal of the millionaire arms manufacturer Andrew Undershaft, Morley himself fell on hard times. At that stage of the war, there was little work for actors in England, and the newly married Morley found nothing except an insignificant out-of-town assignment until late in 1941, when the producer Firth Shepard offered him the lead in his London production of Moss Hart and George S. Kaufman's *The Man Who Came to Dinner*. Although Morley had turned down the role in New York, he promptly accepted.

The London production of *The Man Who Came to Dinner* opened at the Savoy Theatre on December 5, 1941, and on the same night Morley's first child was born. He was named Sheridan, after the irascible Sheridan Whiteside of the play, and acquired Alexander Woollcott, on whom the character was modeled, as his godfather. Morley scored a personal triumph in the part, and the play ran, in London and on tour, until 1943, when another slack period followed. Morley's second play, *Goodness, How Sad,* had been produced in London in 1937 with a modest success. In February 1944 he opened in the provinces in his third play, *Staff Dance*. It closed after ten weeks without venturing into London. Another enforced "rest" followed, which lasted until the end of World War II, when Morley approached the producer Henry Sherek with a sales talk for Norman Ginsbury's play *The First Gentleman*. As a result, the play opened at the New Theatre, London in July 1945, with Morley earning enthusiastic notices as the dissipated and unpopular Prince Regent who became England's George IV.

During the sixteen-month run of *The First Gentleman*, Morley appeared in films and began writing a new play, in collaboration with Noel Langley. The play, which had been simmering in his head for over a year, brought him his greatest success to date, as actor and playwright. *Edward, My Son* opened in the provinces in the early spring of 1947, made its London debut on May 31, 1947, and opened a year later at the Martin Beck Theatre in New York. It was still running there in July 1949, when Morley took the play with another company on tour of Australia and New Zealand.

Edward, My Son traced the career of Arnold Holt, a newspaper tycoon who, for the sake of his worthless son, fights his way by cheating, bullying, and lying to wealth and power. At the end of the play he has lost his son, who is killed in the Battle of Britain, and reduced his wife to drunkenness. Although the play was a popular success, most reviewers regarded it as an "actor's play," superficial in its characterization and unoriginal in its ideas. Nevertheless, they welcomed it for its expertise and "inherent theatrical excitement," and both Morley, who played Holt, and Peggy Ashcroft, who played his wife, received enthusiastic notices on both sides of the Atlantic. "What the play lacks in depth and substance," wrote Brooks Atkinson in the New York *Times* (October 1, 1948), "Mr. Morley supplies out of the magnificence of his acting." For his performance in *Edward, My Son,* Morley received both the British Ellen Terry Award for the season's best performance by an actor and the Delia Austrian Medal, awarded by the Drama League of America for the most distinguished performance of the season.

Returning from the Australian tour of *Edward, My Son,* Morley opened in August 1950 in *The Little Hut,* Nancy Mitford's English adaptation of an André Roussin comedy. The play had a long run in London, thanks largely, many critics felt, to Morley's exuberant performance. Two years of film making followed, during which Morley worked on his free adaptation of another Roussin play, *The Ostrich Eggs.* As *Hippo Dancing,* it brought Morley back to the stage in April 1954 as a blustering fruit wholesaler outraged at the unmanly behavior of his two sons. In 1956 Morley played two roles in Gerald Savory's *A Likely Tale,* and in the same year he appeared in his first musical, as Panisse in the British production of *Fanny.* A second Roussin adaptation by Morley, *Hook, Line and Sinker,* starred Morley in 1958, but was coolly received. He has since appeared on the British stage as Mr. Asano in *A Majority of One* (1960), another much-praised performance, and as a Catholic bishop in Robert J. Crean's *A Time to Laugh* (1962).

Robert Morley has appeared in nearly thirty motion pictures since he entered that medium in 1938. They include *The African Queen* (1951), in which he played a naïve missionary; *Curtain Up,* in which he was the bedeviled director of a small-town stock company; *Gilbert and Sullivan* (1953), which starred Morley as the lyricist W. S. Gilbert; *The Final Test* (1954), in which he impersonated a poet; *Beat The Devil* (1954), a parody of the international intrigue genre in which Morley portrayed a seedy gang leader; and *Oscar Wilde,* in which he repeated his stage triumph in the title role. Other screen credits include *The Old Dark House* (1932); *Young Mr. Pitt* (1942); *Melba* (1953); *Outcast of the Islands* (1953); *Beau Brummel* (1954); *The Final Test* (1954); *The Good Die Young* (1955); *Quentin Durward* (1955); *Around the World in Eighty Days* (1956); *The Young Ones* (1958); *Libel* (1959); *The Doctor's Dilemma* (1959); *The Battle of the Sexes* (1960); *The Road to Hong Kong* (1962); *Joseph and His Brethren* (1962); *Murder at the Gallop* (1963); *Nine Hours to Rama* (1963), and *Take Her, She's Mine.*

On December 7, 1955 Morley made his American television debut in *Edward, My Son* on the *United States Steel Hour.* He scored a major success and has since been seen by United States television audiences in a number of roles, including that of Mr. Brownlow in *Oliver Twist,* Tarleton in Shaw's *Misalliance,* and Mr. Jordan in Harry Segall's *Heaven Can Wait.* Television has also brought to a huge audience Morley's extraordinary gifts as a conversationalist, wit, and raconteur. His appearance on David Susskind's *Open End* (November 29, 1959) was hailed as one of the television treats of the season. In February 1963 he appeared alone for a full hour in Standard Oil's *Festival of the Performing Arts,*

discussing his career and delivering opinions on everything from actors to politicians. "His philosophy," wrote Laurence Laurent in the Washington *Post* (February 20, 1963), "comes in rounded epigrams, sometimes biting, sometimes wickedly malicious and always amusing."

Since he wrote *Edward, My Son* (Random House, 1949) with Noel Langley, Morley has written two other plays in collaboration: *The Full Treatment,* with Ronald Gow (1953); and *Six Months' Grace,* with Dundas Hamilton (French, 1958). He is the author of theatrical sketches, poems, short stories, and many newspaper and magazine articles. Although he has frequently expressed his contempt for directors, he has himself directed two plays: *Tunnel of Love* (1957) and *Once More, With Feeling* (1959). He has also been active as a producer.

In 1940 Robert Morley married Joan Buckmaster, a daughter of the actress Gladys Cooper. The Morleys have two sons and a daughter. According to an article that Morley wrote for the New York *Herald Tribune* (February 1, 1953), he has lived since that marriage "happily ever after, bereft of all serious ambition." The couple live in an old cottage on the Thames, and Morley writes, usually by dictation, in a study in the woods. He considers acting the best exercise in the world, and apart from that, limits his recreations to conversation and horse racing. His clubs are the Garrick and Buck's.

Some years ago Mary Braggiotti reported in the New York *Post* (March 30, 1949) that Morley had "very dark red curly hair and eyebrows, a receding hairline, challenging blue eyes and, offstage, an habitually deadpan expression. He talks trippingly on the tongue—and like lightning." In the New York *Times* (October 10, 1948), Brooks Atkinson said of Morley in *Edward, My Son:* "Since he is tall and massive, his acting is in the grand manner. It becomes him; his acting would probably be silly on any other scale. . . . He speaks with a studied authority that might sound like an affectation in an actor of inferior style. . . . But under his gravity there is a very droll and mischievous sense of humor; and Mr. Morley not only impresses the audience with his size and authority but captivates it with some fugitive ironic inflections. And that, perhaps, is the heart of his acting. Without the humor he would be a ham. With it he is one of the most stimulating actors of the day."

References

N Y Herald Tribune IV p3 F 1 '53
N Y Times II p1 O 24 '48
Who's Who, 1963
Who's Who in the Theatre (1963)

MORRIS, WILLIAM RICHARD, 1ST VISCOUNT NUFFIELD Oct. 10, 1877-Aug. 22, 1963 British automobile manufacturer; philanthropist; honorary president of British Motor Corporation (1951-63); endowed Nuffield College at Oxford University and the Nuffield Trust for the Advancement of Medicine. See *Current Biography* (April) 1941.

Obituary

N Y Times p27 Ag 22 '63

MOSBACHER, EMIL, JR. Apr. 1, 1922-
Yachtsman; businessman
Address: b. 515 Madison Ave., New York 22;
h. 384 Rosedale Ave., White Plains, N.Y.

That the America's Cup, the most famous and
coveted international sailing trophy, remains in
the quarters of the New York Yacht Club after
the America's Cup races in September 1962 is
owing in large measure to Emil ("Bus") Mosbacher, Jr. As skipper of the twelve-meter boat
Weatherly, Mosbacher guided her to a 4-1 victory
over the Australian yacht *Gretel*, which had
offered the eighteenth challenge in the 111-year
history of America's Cup competition for world
yachting supremacy. For Mosbacher the triumph
climaxed about thirty-five years of devotion
to the sport of sailing. In the world of
business Mosbacher works for an investment firm
founded by his father.

Emil Mosbacher, Jr., the son of Emil and Gertrude (Schwartz) Mosbacher, was born on April
1, 1922 in Mount Vernon, New York. His father,
now semiretired, founded an oil, natural gas,
and real estate investment company, with which
Mosbacher and his younger brother, Robert, are
associated. They have a sister, Mrs. Barbara
Smullyan. Mosbacher's nickname, "Bus," which
he dislikes, is a contraction of "Buster" and was
bestowed on him during his infancy. Emil and
Robert Mosbacher were introduced to sailing at
an early age by their father, who belonged to
the Knickerbocker Yacht Club and was instrumental in the founding of the Sound Interclub
class of racing sloops.

"Bus" Mosbacher first sailed in a small flat-
bottomed catboat and gradually moved up from
class to class, winning prizes as he went. He was
a junior champion of Long Island Sound and
later intercollegiate champion for two years in a
row. At the Choate School in Wallingford, Connecticut, from which he graduated *cum laude* in

Wide World
EMIL MOSBACHER, JR.

1939, Mosbacher played baseball, hockey, football, golf, and squash and belonged to the rifle,
history, French, and camera clubs and the debating and dramatic councils. At Dartmouth
College in Hanover, New Hampshire he majored
in economics and sailed with the Corinthian
Yacht Club. Dartmouth granted him the B.A.
degree in 1943. From 1942 to 1945 he served
with the United States Navy in the Pacific, advancing in rank from apprentice seaman to lieutenant. On his return to civilian life he resumed
sailing in Long Island Sound.

Having sailed in the Star and Atlantic classes,
Mosbacher took to the bigger International Class
one-design boats—sometimes called the Cadillacs
of Sound fleet racing. In 1950 he won the first of
eight straight season championships in the International Class. It was not until 1958, however,
that he really caught the attention of the yachting world with his superb handling of the
twenty-year-old twelve-meter boat *Vim* in that
year's America's Cup elimination trials, which
were won by the yacht *Columbia*.

The America's Cup, the trophy that has given
rise to the most famous series of international
sailing matches, was first won for the United
States by the New York Yacht Club schooner
America in 1851 in a race with British boats
around the Isle of Wight. Since that time, between 1870 and 1958, British and Canadian
yachtsmen have tried vainly seventeen times to
wrest the America's Cup from its place at the
New York Yacht Club. Before 1958 the races had
been entered by big Class J boats. That year,
after having the rules changed to permit entry of
smaller twelve-meter craft, the New York Yacht
Club received its first challenge for the America's
Cup in twenty years, from a syndicate of the
British Royal Yacht Squadron. Trials were held
in the summer of 1958 to determine who the
American defender of the America's Cup should
be, and the *Columbia, Vim, Weatherly,* and
Easterner competed for the honor. It was these
trials that Mosbacher, in *Vim*, came close to
winning.

In 1959 the eighteenth challenge for an America's Cup race was issued to the New York Yacht
Club by a syndicate of the Royal Sydney Yacht
Squadron of Australia, and from the beginning
Mosbacher was discussed as the possible skipper
of the American defending boat. The race rules
required that the skipper of the American boat
be a member of the New York Yacht Club, and
Mosbacher was not. In 1961 he was proposed
for membership by Harold S. Vanderbilt, who
had defended the cup in the 1930's, and Mosbacher reportedly received more letters of recommendation from members than any other candidate in the history of the club.

At the beginning of the 1962 yachting season
Henry D. Mercer, head of the syndicate that
owned the twelve-meter yacht *Weatherly*, asked
Mosbacher to take her helm for the America's
Cup trials. Mosbacher had the boat stripped of
every ounce of excess weight and used the weight
allowance thus gained to put extra lead into her
keel, giving her greater stability in strong winds.
The *Weatherly* then competed in a series of
elimination trials against *Columbia, Easterner,*
and *Nefertiti* in the summer of 1962 and, win-

ning them, she was selected to defend the America's Cup.

Mosbacher then whipped the boat and ten-man crew into shape for the America's Cup against *Gretel*, the Australian challenger. His triumphs owe as much to the way he selects and commands a crew as to his attention to detail, his skilled starts, and excellent work to windward. "A good crew should serve as assistant eyes," he has said, "but only to give me information. . . . I give the only orders. It is not a democracy." His crewmen, several of whom had worked with him for four years, were loyal to him and appreciated his restraint and coolness in times of stress or error.

Both the challenger and the defender were twelve-meter craft — single-masted sloops, over sixty-five feet long, with a mainsail and spinnaker, designed to international mathematical formula (including length, girth, freeboard, and sail area dimensions), which must result in a rating of twelve meters. The competition was held in the Atlantic Ocean, nine nautical miles south-southeast of Brenton Reef Lighthouse, each race covering twenty-four nautical miles.

The *Gretel*, captained by Jock Sturrock, was more evenly matched with the American boat than had been the case in 1958 and put up a good fight. But the *Weatherly* had an edge on the challengers and won the first race on September 15, 1962 by 3 minutes and 46 seconds. In the second race, however, the Australians turned the tables on the Americans as the *Gretel* led the *Weatherly* home by 47 seconds. The *Weatherly* won the third race with a lead of 8 minutes and 40 seconds. The fourth developed into one of the most exciting races in America's Cup annals. The *Weatherly* won it by 26 seconds, the smallest margin in America's Cup history. Mosbacher's tactical maneuvers largely accounted for the victory. In the somewhat anticlimactic fifth race the *Weatherly* won by 3 minutes and 40 seconds, thus retaining the America's Cup for the United States. "There is no one on this boat who wouldn't give anything he had to bring this happy climax about," Mosbacher said at his moment of triumph. Then he went back to his wife and children, his business, and his impressive array of civic duties, all of which he had been forced to neglect for sailing in the preceding six months.

Emil Mosbacher, Jr., married Patricia Ann Ryan, a graduate of Bennington College in Vermont, on November 24, 1950. They have three sons, Emil 3d, Richard Bruce, and John David. Mosbacher, who has had two operations for blood cancer of the lips, smears zinc oxide on his lips before sailing and has stopped smoking to cut down mouth irritation. Five feet eleven and one-half inches tall and weighing 185 pounds, blond-haired and blue-eyed Mosbacher has an imposing appearance. He is known for his ever-ready smile and his congeniality.

A member of the Mamaroneck Frostbite Association, Mosbacher sails in the winter as well as in the summer. He is on the executive committee of the Yacht Racing Association of Long Island Sound, and he was commodore of the Beach Point Yacht Club from 1952 to 1958. He belongs to the North American Yacht Racing

Union, the United States International Sailing Association, the Ida Lewis Yacht Club, the Storm Trysail Club, and the Royal Corinthian Yacht Club. When not sailing or engaged in business he finds time for golf, squash, and photography.

Mosbacher is a Republican and a member of Christ's Church (Episcopal) in Rye, New York. He belongs to the Choate Club of New York, the Gamma Delta Chi fraternity, and the Dartmouth College clubs in New York City and Westchester County. In 1959 and 1960 he was co-chairman of the Dartmouth College capital gifts campaign, and he is a member of the alumni council of Dartmouth College. He has been a trustee of Lenox Hill Hospital in New York City and co-chairman of the 1962 American Red Cross drive in New York City. He also belongs to the Real Estate Board of New York, the New York Chamber of Commerce, the Bronx Board of Trade, the Westchester County Association, Inc., the New Rochelle Downtown Association, and the Independent Petroleum Association of America. He is a member of the Quaker Ridge Golf Club and the Boulder Brook Club. Mrs. Mosbacher says of her husband: "He's a do-er."

References

> Christian Sci Mon p11 S 26 '62
> N Y Mirror p72 S 9 '62 por
> N Y Post p29 S 28 '62 por
> N Y Times p45 S 26 '62 por
> Sports Illus 12:27+ S 10 '62 por

MOSCONI, WILLIE June 27, 1913- Professional billiard player
Address: b. Brunswick Corp., 623 S. Wabash Ave., Chicago, Ill.; h. 1804 Prospect Ridge Blvd., Haddon Heights, N.J.

Over the last two decades the name Willie Mosconi has been synonymous with the game of pocket billiards. Meticulous, high-strung, and with a flair for the dramatic, Mosconi has proved to be not only the game's most highly skilled player but its best salesman and goodwill ambassador as well. He has been the world's pocket billiard champion almost every year since 1941. He holds several records, including a high run of 526 balls in exhibition play and a high grand average of 18.34 in tournament play. More important, however, from the standpoint of the game's overall popularity, Mosconi has played a major role in establishing billiards as a reputable pastime in the minds of the general public. He has given hundreds of exhibitions and has been a consultant to the Brunswick Corporation, a large manufacturer of billiard and bowling equipment, for about twenty-five years. During the filming of *The Hustler* (1961), about pool players who seek matches for money, Mosconi served as technical adviser, and he has written *Willie Mosconi on Pocket Billiards* (Crown, 1959).

William Joseph Mosconi was born on June 27, 1913 in Philadelphia, Pennsylvania, the oldest child of Helen (Reilly) Mosconi and Joseph Mosconi, a tavern and billiard parlor owner and a former prize fighter. He has four brothers,

WILLIE MOSCONI

Charles, John, Joseph, and Louis, and a sister, Mrs. Marie Maher. Surprisingly enough, the elder Mosconi forbade his son to have anything to do with billiards. He would not permit Willie to play and made certain that the balls and cues were locked up at night. Instead, he had decided that the boy should go into show business. Willie's uncles, Charles and Louis Mosconi, were successful dancers in vaudeville, and at the age of six Willie became their reluctant (and inept) pupil.

One day his Uncle Charley challenged Willie to a game of pool. The youngster ran off fifteen balls, a feat that led his father to discover that he had been practising billiards late at night, using a broomstick and round potatoes in place of a cue and balls. Reconciled to what he could not prevent, Joseph Mosconi arranged a series of exhibition matches for his six-year-old son. The most memorable of these was the boy's game with ten-year-old Ruth McGinnis in Philadelphia's National Billiard Academy, in which he ran forty balls in his first round. Willie played a few more exhibitions and then retired at the age of seven. "I was sick of the game," Mosconi recalls. "First my dad was trying to stop me from learning the game. Now he was trying to ram it down my throat."

Mosconi attended Barrett Junior High School, from which he graduated in 1931, and enrolled at Banks Business College. He was forced to leave school, however, when both his parents became seriously ill, and he took a job as an upholsterer's apprentice. By doing piecework Mosconi soon earned $40 a week, a large sum during the Depression, but as a result of a disagreement with his foreman, he lost this job. On his way home that day he saw a sign advertising a billiard tournament. He entered it and won the first prize of $75.

In 1932 Mosconi came under the sponsorship of Izzie Goodman, owner of the Fox Billiard Academy, who placed him in the 1933 National

divisional tournament in Philadelphia. Mosconi won it and went on to capture the sectional tournament in New York. From New York he went to Minneapolis for the National championships and there finished fourth. Despite his status as a runner-up, Mosconi's overall performance impressed Clyde Storer, then president of the National Billiard Association, a subsidiary of the Brunswick Corporation, which has been the leading manufacturer of billiard tables in the United States since 1845. Storer signed Mosconi to a $600-a-month contract, and at the age of nineteen Mosconi became the youngest member of Brunswick's twenty-one-man billiard staff. "I suddenly realized how much money was to be made at the game," Mosconi recalls. From that time on he made billiards his career.

His first job for Brunswick was to go on a 112-day tour with Ralph Greenleaf, then the world's billiard champion. "I watched him like a hawk," Mosconi relates (*National Bowlers Journal*, July 1962). "I learned all the little tricks and the tremendous horde of knowledge he had accumulated in his career. I also watched for his mistakes." Greenleaf won fifty-seven matches on the tour to Mosconi's fifty. Significantly, most of Mosconi's wins came near the end of the tour, proving that he had learned his lessons well.

In the years that followed, Mosconi was almost always on tour—a tiring but prosperous way of life. In world tournaments from 1933 to 1938 he played well, but never well enough to win. Then, in 1939, public interest in billiards seemed to slacken. In low spirits, Mosconi severed his connection with Brunswick and went to Hollywood, where he spent a restless year. In late 1940 Bob McGirr, one of New York's biggest billiard operators, agreed to sponsor Mosconi in the six-month tournament for the 1941 world's championship.

Mosconi won the 1941 title. A reporter for the *National Bowlers Journal* (May-June 1941) wrote: "Who ever heard of winning a world crown by 32 games? Mosconi did! Then . . . 125-and-out is a remarkable feat in any class of pocket competition. . . . The youthful expert from Philly [Mosconi] won seven games by doing just that. Mosconi's performance was nothing short of fantastic. He had 50 runs of 100 or more in his total of 224 games." Mosconi lost the title in November 1941 but regained it in November 1942. He held the crown from 1944 through 1948, losing it in 1949 to Jimmy Caras, and from 1950 through 1953. In 1954 there was no sanctioned world tournament, and in 1955, when the last such tournament was played, Irving Crane was the champion. Mosconi regained the title from Crane in a challenge match, and no one has challenged Mosconi since.

Mosconi was drafted as a private into the Special Services of the United States Army late in 1944, and by the time he was discharged with the classification T-5 a year later, he was broke. "I was really sick of life in general and the billiard game in particular," he recalled in the July 1962 *National Bowlers Journal* interview. "I wanted a title match so I could get some money and get out quick." C. P. Binner, then Brunswick's promotion manager, heard of Mosconi's dissatisfactions and his need for secure employment. He offered Mosconi a contract, under which the billiard player has been ever since.

He has held an exhibition contract with Brunswick for about twenty-five years—longer than any active bowler or billiard player with the exception of the late Willie Hoppe.

Perhaps his greatest contribution to the game of billiards has been to popularize it through exhibitions and interviews. Partly on Mosconi's suggestion Brunswick designed billiard tables with covers in "decorator colors" like tangerine, blue, white, gold, or gray-beige instead of the traditional green, thus hoping to erase from the public mind the disreputable associations that the game has long carried. Mosconi's own color preference is for the gold covering. "I'd be happy if they never covered another table with the old green cloth," he says. "It just reminds people of the sordid old rooms which have hurt the game." Mosconi is also in favor of making pockets on billiard tables the maximum allowable size. "Why frustrate the new player?" he asks. "Let him make as many shots as possible and you create a new fan."

Mosconi, who earns perhaps $50,000 a year, still gives many exhibitions. In them he usually includes some trick shooting, as, for example, the "machine-gun shot" in which he uses a force-follow with side "English," which caroms the cue ball off each of fifteen balls before counting on a corner pocket shot. He has no intention, however, of defending his world title when the next championship tournament is held, because after all the years he has devoted to the game he "would like to start taking it easy." Probably the fact that he suffered a stroke in 1957 has influenced his decision. "Billiards is a great tranquilizer for the harried executive and anxious housewife," he has explained, "but for the tournament player it can be real torture."

In addition to serving as technical adviser for *The Hustler* (1961), a film that dealt with men who make a living drifting from one city to another in search of pool matches for money, Mosconi has written a book entitled *Willie Mosconi on Pocket Billiards* (Crown, 1959). In his introduction to the book he traces the game back to the fifteenth century and goes on from there to write a concise, informative book about billiards. Mosconi owns the Superior Billiard Academy in North Philadelphia and points out with pride that his clientele consists mostly of college students.

Willie Mosconi and his second wife, Gloria (Marchini) Mosconi, whom he married in February 1953, have a daughter, Gloria Albina. By his first marriage, which ended in divorce, he has two children, William and Candace. Mosconi is five feet seven inches tall, weighs 165 pounds, and has hazel eyes and white hair. He is a Roman Catholic and a member of the Lambs Club in New York. His favorite recreation is playing golf. He enjoys good food and always dresses well. "I always wear a jacket when I play," he has said. "You just can't project the image of a prestige game in your shirtsleeves."

References

N Y Herald Tribune p14 N 17 '62
N Y Times p52 N 15 '62 por
Nat Bowlers Journal & Billiard Revue 49:
  16+ Jl '62 pors
New Yorker 38:29+ Mr 10 '62
Time 65:35 F 7 '55

MOSCOSO (MORA RODRÍGUEZ), (JOSÉ) TEODORO (mōs-cō′sō tā′ō-dō′rō) Nov. 26, 1910- United States government official
Address: b. Agency for International Development, Department of State, Washington 25, D.C.; h. 3900 Watson Place, N.W., Washington, D.C.

The Alliance for Progress is a ten-year, multi-billion dollar co-operative enterprise for the social and economic development of Latin America, exceeding in scope the post-World War II Marshall Plan for Europe. Soon after President John F. Kennedy conceived of it in 1961 he chose Teodoro Moscoso as its chief administrator. Although Moscoso began his career as a pharmacist, he later worked more than twenty years as an economist and administrator with the government of Puerto Rico. As head of its Economic Development Administration from 1950 to 1961 he helped to turn the island commonwealth into a Caribbean showcase through the agricultural and industrial development program known as Operation Bootstrap. He served as United States Ambassador to Venezuela for a few months before being appointed on November 6, 1961 to the Agency for International Development as assistant administrator for Latin America and United States co-ordinator of the Alliance for Progress. Aware that he is racing against overwhelming odds, Moscoso regards himself as an evangelist for progress, and he is convinced that the goals that the Alliance for Progress has set for itself will someday be fulfilled.

José Teodoro Moscoso Mora Rodríguez was born on November 26, 1910 in Barcelona, Spain to Teodoro Moscoso Rodríguez, a pharmacist, and the former Alejandrina Mora Fajardo, who was active in civic and religious affairs. Both of his parents were American citizens. He has a brother, José Guillermo Moscoso, and a sister, Carmen Leonor Moscoso de Cintrón. At an early age Teodoro Moscoso returned with his family to Ponce, Puerto Rico, where his father had established a drug business in 1898. At the Ponce High School, from which he graduated in 1928, he served as class president and as captain of the debating team. Expecting to follow in his father's footsteps Moscoso entered the Philadelphia College of Pharmacy and Science, where he was editor of *The Scope*. Having obtained the Treshman scholarship, Moscoso then attended the University of Michigan, where he majored in chemistry and was assistant editor of the magazine *Gargoyle*. He graduated with a B.S. degree in 1932.

Returning to Puerto Rico, Moscoso served as general manager of the family's retail drug firm in Ponce—Moscoso Hno. & Co., Inc.—from 1932 until 1939—and from 1936 to 1939 he also was president of the wholesale branch of the firm. Interested in housing for low-income groups, Moscoso became a member of the municipal housing authority in Ponce in 1938 and studied housing problems and techniques at night. He soon became vice-chairman of the Ponce housing authority, and in 1941 he was made its executive director. So successful was his operation of the agency that in 1942 Governor Rexford G. Tugwell appointed him housing administrator for all of Puerto Rico.

(*Continued next page*)

TEODORO MOSCOSO

As executive director of Puerto Rico's housing authority, Moscoso directed the building of five huge housing projects for slum dwellers. During this period he also wrote what later became the legislation that formed the basis of Puerto Rico's development program—Operation Bootstrap, or Fomento. The purpose of the program was to lift the island from impoverishment through greater industrialization. (Its economy had been based largely upon the production of sugar, coffee, and tobacco.) In 1942 Moscoso was named as the first president of the Puerto Rico Industrial Development Company, a government corporation designed to bring industries to the island.

Operation Bootstrap was eminently successful. By offering investors the advantages of a stable government, abundant labor, and substantial tax exemptions Moscoso, in co-operation with Governor Luis Muñoz Marin and others, conveyed the image of Puerto Rico as an industrialists' paradise. During the twenty years from 1942 to 1962 more than 700 new industrial plants opened their doors on the island. Unemployment greatly declined during this period, and per capita income rose steadily from less than $200 to over $600 per year. Average life expectancy has increased from forty-six to seventy years. Annual payrolls of industrial plants now exceed $100,000,000.

To stimulate Puerto Rico's negligible tourist trade, Moscoso encouraged the construction of the island's first resort-class hotel, the Caribe-Hilton, which opened in 1949. Although the hotel was at first referred to as "Moscoso's folly," it paved the way for the tourist boom, which now adds over $50,000,000 each year to Puerto Rico's income. In 1950, when the island's government set up an over-all Economic Development Administration, incorporating the Industrial Development Company, Moscoso was appointed chief administrator of the new organization.

On March 29, 1961 President John F. Kennedy appointed Moscoso United States Ambassador to Venezuela, a post that required considerable diplomatic skill. He is the first Puerto Rican ever to serve in such a position. When Moscoso arrived in Caracas in May 1961, leftist students at the Central University of Venezuela threatened hostile demonstrations, and in the following month, when he visited the university, they burned his automobile. "I was a boy once myself," he later said to a group of friendly students. "I have had the same urges."

On November 6, 1961 President Kennedy appointed Moscoso United States co-ordinator of the Alliance for Progress and assistant administrator for Latin America in the Agency for International Development, a position with rank equal to that of an Assistant Secretary of State. His appointment was confirmed by the Senate on February 5, 1962. The idea of the Alliance for Progress was announced by President Kennedy on March 13, 1961 at a White House reception for Latin American diplomats and Congressional leaders. The program officially became an inter-American undertaking in August 1961, when twenty American countries (not including Cuba) signed the alliance charter at the Inter-American Economic and Social Conference in Punta del Este, Uruguay.

The Alliance for Progress, which is known to Latin Americans as La Alianza Para el Progreso, was established in order to foster technical and financial co-operation among the American republics, to strengthen democratic institutions by means of self-help, and to make available the material means needed to carry out comprehensive national programs for social and economic development. The alliance, which is slated to become the largest continuing program of United States foreign economic assistance, is designed to deal with a wide range of social and economic problems, including housing, agrarian reform, industrialization, education, public health, tax reform, and other matters. The Latin American republics have pledged themselves to mobilize their resources to carry out the necessary reforms and self-help measures. The United States has committed itself to make available over a period of ten years a major part of the minimum of $20 billion, which Latin American nations are estimated to need to supplement their own efforts.

Until Moscoso's appointment the preliminary machinery for operating the Alliance for Progress was in the hands of two loosely organized committees of State and Treasury Department officials. The President's special assistant for Latin American affairs, Richard N. Goodwin, also took part in the initial phases of the program. The alliance operates through the Agency for International Development, the new State Department agency responsible for the United States foreign aid program. It also works closely with such other agencies as the Organization of American States, the Inter-American Bank, the Export-Import Bank, Food for Peace, the United States Information Agency, the Peace Corps, and cultural exchange programs. On June 3, 1963 Moscoso was appointed by President Kennedy United States representative on the Inter-American Economic and Social Council of the Organization of American States, a post vacant since the Eisenhower Administration.

The mechanism of the alliance calls for each of the participating countries to draw up and present its own long-term development plan. The plan is then reviewed by a panel of experts from the Organization of American States—"nine wise men," representing eight American countries and Great Britain. In turn this committee counsels and assists each country in evolving a plan that would best accomplish the objectives under the charter of Punta del Este. Critics have charged that the Alliance is simply a system of bilateral relationships between the United States and other O.A.S. members. On June 15, 1963, in a critical report to the Council of the Organization of American States, two Latin American leaders, former Brazilian President Juscelino Kubitschek and former Colombian President Alberto Lleras Camargo, urged the O.A.S. to form an autonomous multinational mechanism to co-ordinate and direct the granting of alliance aid. Two months later plans were drafted for the establishment of a new Inter-American Development Committee, designed to make the Alliance for Progress a truly co-operative enterprise by giving Latin Americans direct responsibility in the planning and execution of policies.

The entire concept of the Alliance for Progress hinges upon effective co-operation between the United States and Latin America. A necessary condition for the success of the program is the full acceptance of the philosophy underlying it. Moscoso's task of selling a peaceful revolution is all the more urgent in view of the tremendous population growth and desperate poverty experienced by Latin Americans. Extremist groups, both left and right, actively and passively militate against the alliance. Moscoso makes no attempt to conceal the fact that one of the chief obstacles to reform in Latin America has been the powerful economic élite, which looks upon the alliance as an attack on privilege and the status quo.

Although Moscoso is distressed by the lag between the alliance's goals and its results, and by Congressional reductions in the amount of money made available to the program, he has remained optimistic with regard to its worth and its prospects for the future. Combining hardheaded practicality with a fiery idealism, he took especial care to *mark*, rather than to celebrate, the first anniversary of the alliance in August 1962. "There will be time enough to celebrate when we have achieved a working alliance and an extensive progress," he declared. In Moscoso's view, economic development is only a means to an end, and only meaningful when allied with social justice. "If the Alianza is left entirely to the economists, the technicians, and the government officials, it cannot fully succeed," he said in an address before the National Press Club in Washington, D.C. on February 15, 1962. "For we are dealing with human emotions and aspirations, not just economic charts, bricks and machinery."

By March 1963 the Alliance for Progress had some 392 separate projects under way that were being carried out in co-operation with local governments and private groups in twenty-three countries. As a result of Moscoso's efforts the establishment of a thirteen-member Latin American Science Board, which would advise the Alliance for Progress on making more effective use of science and technology in raising living standards, was announced on July 1, 1963. As of August 1963 the achievements of the Alliance for Progress in the first two years of its existence include the buildings of some 140,000 dwelling units, 8,200 classrooms, 900 hospitals and health centers, and 1,500 wells and water systems. In addition, some 4,000,000 textbooks have been produced and distributed, 160,000 farm credit loans have been issued, and 15,000,000 people have received food from United States surplus stocks. Tax reforms have been initiated in eleven countries and land reform programs in a dozen.

Moscoso travels extensively both in the United States and abroad introducing, explaining, and publicizing the Alliance for Progress. He has written a number of articles for popular magazines and newspapers and has contributed to *Collier's Encyclopedia* (1963) and the *Grolier Encyclopedia* (1963). He is a recipient of the Rho Chi Medal, and in 1962 he was awarded honorary LL.D. degrees by Fordham University, the University of Notre Dame, and the University of Michigan. Moscoso is a member of the Society for International Development, the Foreign Service Association, and the University of Michigan Alumni Association. He was president of the Pharmacists Association of Puerto Rico in 1938 and of the Puerto Rico chapter of the American Society for Public Administration in 1952. He has also served as a director of the Puerto Rico Urban Renewal and Housing Corporation, the Government Development Bank of Puerto Rico, and the Land Authority of Puerto Rico. His clubs are the Bankers, the Hermitage, and Casino de Puerto Rico, and his fraternities are Rho Chi and the A.F.D.A. in San Juan.

Teodoro Moscoso and Gloria Sánchez Vilella were married on July 3, 1937. They have a son, José Teodoro, and a daughter, Margarita, who is with the Peace Corps. Moscoso, who is known as Teddy to his friends, is soft-spoken but persuasive, and he speaks English with a slight Spanish accent. He is five feet eleven inches tall, weighs 185 pounds, and has brown eyes and thinning black hair. He is a Roman Catholic and a Democrat, and his political affiliation in Puerto Rico was with the Popular Democratic party. When his sixteen hour-a-day work schedule permits, he likes to paint, listen to operatic music, and read the works of his favorite author, Marcel Proust. To remind himself and others of the urgency of his mission, Moscoso has a sign on the wall behind his desk, which reads: "Please Be Brief—We Are 25 Years Late."

References

N Y Post Mag p2 Mr 18 '62 por
N Y Times p6 Mr 30 '61 por
N Y Times Mag p10+ D 17 '61 por
Newsweek 59:54+ F 19 '62 por
Time 78:33 N 17 '61

Who's Who in America, 1962-63

MOSTEL, ZERO (mŏs-tĕl') Feb. 28, 1915-
Actor; painter
Address: b. c/o Toby Cole, 234 W. 44th St.,
New York 36

NOTE: This biography supersedes
the article that appeared in
Current Biography in 1943.

Zero Mostel, who won *Cue* magazine's 1962
Entertainer-of-the-Year award for his performance in the Broadway musical comedy *A Funny
Thing Happened on the Way to the Forum,* is
a study in paradox. A huge clown weighing
around 250 pounds, he has the grace of a ballet
dancer and the physical control of a Chaplin.
A slapstick comic, he has lectured on the philosophy of humor at Harvard University. As a
straight dramatic actor he has won praise for his
portrayals of roles in plays by Ionesco and
Molière. Mostel got his start as an entertainer
doing satirical sketches in Greenwich Village
nightclubs to support himself as a painter; he
still paints several hours daily and is considered
a gifted artist.

Zero Mostel was born Samuel Joel Mostel on
February 28, 1915 in the Brownsville section of
Brooklyn, the next-to-youngest child of his
father's second set of children. By his first wife,
Zero's father—Israel Mostel—had had four children spaced three years apart; four more children,
including Zero, were born of his second marriage, to the former Celia Druchs. All but two
of the eight children were boys. Shortly after
Zero was born his father was put in charge of a
kosher slaughterhouse in Moodus, Connecticut,
and the family moved there. Ten years later the
family moved to the Bronx, where Israel Mostel
made sacramental wine. The Mostels eventually
settled on New York's Lower East Side. There
Zero—who won his nickname because he seemed
to be a hopeless student—attended Public School

Wide World
ZERO MOSTEL

188 and graduated from Seward Park High
School in 1931. As a boy he was extremely thin,
and he loved to do imitations to amuse his classmates. His family, however, frowned on Zero's
clowning, and his father, who died in 1945, never
saw his son perform on stage.

At school Zero discovered his passion and
talent for drawing and painting. His grades were
good enough to win him admission to the tuition-
free College of the City of New York, where he
majored in art and developed a love for serious
literature and drama. He received the B.A. degree in 1935 and then enrolled in New York
University for postgraduate studies in art at
night, working during the day in a men's clothing
factory operated by a brother-in-law. After a
month, however, Mostel quit and wandered off
to Mexico and Louisiana. In the course of working in factories and on the docks he acquired a
social conscience. He obtained a job with the
WPA art program, teaching life drawing and
painting at the 92d Street Young Men's Hebrew
Association in New York City, and lecturing at
the Museum of Modern Art, the Frick Museum,
and the Museum of Science and Industry in New
York.

To keep himself in paints, Mostel began entertaining at neighborhood parties for $5 and sand-
wiches. At an artists' ball he was discovered by
Barney Josephson, the nightclub impresario, who
booked him into his Café Society Downtown at
a salary of $40 a week. Opening on February 16,
1942, Mostel made an immediate hit with his
"Jitterbug in Roseland" routine and his impression of Charles Boyer ("Let me run through
your hair, Hedy—barefoot"). During the next
year he appeared on radio, performed in nightclubs, and made his Broadway debut in the
vaudeville show *Keep 'Em Laughing.* Then the
Paramount Theatre in New York hired Mostel
for two weeks at $1,250 a week.

Mostel then went to Hollywood in the summer
of 1942 to play the dual role of Paliostro and
Rami in the MGM film *DuBarry Was a Lady.*
The comedian's part in the film was trimmed
considerably, however, when the studio discovered
that he had signed a petition protesting the
release of another MGM picture, *Tennessee Johnson.* His action was prompted by his conviction
that the picture was "less liberal-minded than it
should be." An unabashed progressive, Mostel
was also attacked by the ultraconservative newspaper columnist, George Sokolsky, in August 1942
for his satirical portrayal of an isolationist legislator named Senator Polltax T. Pellagra.

Returning to New York, Mostel was booked
into La Martinique at $3,750 per week, but
shortly afterward the United States Army drafted
him at $21 per month. After spending several
months in the infantry at Camp Croft and Fort
Meade, he was discharged and returned to the
entertainment world. Mostel appeared on both
stage and television shows and in motion pictures, but at this point in his career he was cast
not as a fat comedian, but as a fat villain. He
played comedy roles on stage in *Concert Varieties*
(1945); *Beggar's Holiday* (1946); *Lunatics and
Lovers* (1954); and *Good as Gold* (1957). His
serious vehicles included *Flight into Egypt* (1952);
A Stone for Danny Fisher (1954); and *The Good*

Woman of Setzuan (1956). He also appeared in a number of films, including Elia Kazan's *Panic in the Streets* (1950); *Mr. Belvedere Rings the Bell* (1951); *The Guy Who Came Back* (1951); and *The Model and the Marriage Broker* (1952) —all released by Twentieth Century-Fox—and *The Enforcer* (Warner Brothers, 1951).

Because of his political convictions Mostel ran into difficulty in October 1955. Appearing before the House Un-American Activities Committee for questioning about Communist party membership and associations, Mostel invoked the Fifth Amendment. For several years his career languished; he worked occasionally in the theater, but producers remained cautious. Then, in 1958, his old friend Burgess Meredith, who had sat in the audience when Mostel made his nightclub debut in 1942, helped him to take a giant step toward stardom. Meredith staged an off-Broadway production of *Ulysses in Nighttown*, based on a sequence in James Joyce's novel *Ulysses,* and cast Mostel in the leading role—that of Leopold Bloom, Joyce's Everyman.

In the New York *Times* (June 15, 1958) Brooks Atkinson noted that Mostel played his role flawlessly as "the perfect Leopold Bloom" and added: "His vulgar bourgeois of Dublin—sensual, outwardly respectable, inwardly epicene, secretive, cunning, cheap in self-esteem as well as infamy, haunted by a million vicious specters—is the core of the performance." Mostel won the Obie award for the best acting of the Off-Broadway season and, competing with actors from twenty-six countries, walked off with the honors as outstanding actor at an international dramatic festival at the Théâtre des Nations in Paris. For Mostel, who had admired Joyce since his days at City College, the role was a natural. "I was made to play Bloom," he told Maurice Zolotow of the New York *Times* (June 1, 1958). "When Joyce wrote this character, he wrote it for me. It's typecasting, putting me in it."

In January 1961 Mostel astonished audiences and critics with his performance in Eugène Ionesco's avant-garde play *Rhinoceros,* when he turned himself into a rhinoceros while wearing a beret and a bathrobe. Walter Kerr of the New York *Herald Tribune* (January 10, 1961) described the transition as "fantastic," and Howard Taubman of the New York *Times* (January 22, 1961) called the transformation "a performance of brilliant resourcefulness . . . inevitable, sidesplitting, and terrifying." Taubman noted that Mostel shared with certain other fat men the knack of moving on stage with the grace of a ballet dancer.

For his performance in *Rhinoceros* Mostel won his first Antoinette Perry Award ("Tony") as the outstanding actor of 1960-61. Mostel received his second Tony award in 1962-63 for his starring role in *A Funny Thing Happened on the Way to the Forum,* which opened on Broadway in May 1962 and grossed about $3,500,000 by the end of its first year. Based on a classical comedy by the Roman Plautus, the musical was described by *Newsweek* (May 21, 1962) as "highly hilarious fare for anyone with a taste for old-fashioned lowdown comedy." According to the *Newsweek* critic, as the Roman slave Pseudolos, Mostel "mugs and minces with a fat man's ineffable

delicacy; he is a past master of the double-take, the double-entendre, and the double-jointed knee."

Mostel's triumph in *A Funny Thing* has made him one of the theater's most sought-after personalities. In April 1963 he did a one-man show on television's *Festival of the Performing Arts,* described by the New York *Times* critic Jack Gould as "an hour of humor that enjoys an enticing mixture of subtle observation and low comedy, sensitive acting and outrageous horseplay." Mostel had previously appeared over television in *The World of Sholom Aleichem* and *Waiting for Godot,* both on *The Play of the Week.*

Zero Mostel has been married twice. His first marriage ended in divorce. In 1944 he married Kate Harsin, a former dancer with the Rockettes at New York's Radio City Music Hall. The Mostels have two sons—Joshua and Tobias. The family lives in a huge apartment on the upper West Side of Manhattan, where Mostel collects Peruvian textiles, Coptic art, and pre-Columbian figures. A frequenter of museums, he visited the National Gallery almost daily during the five months that he played *Ulysses in Nighttown* in London, and during the run of *A Funny Thing Happened on the Way to the Forum* he took a short vacation to visit the Prado in Madrid.

For all his slapstick on and off the stage, Mostel is regarded as a subtle clown. In the opinion of Burgess Meredith, the late Charles Laughton, and others, Mostel could easily become the finest actor of classic roles, comic or tragic, in America. Regarded as one of the theater's leading intellectuals, Mostel is a serious student of comedy. He once did his own adaptation of Molière's *Imaginary Invalid* and appeared in it at the Brattle Theatre in Cambridge, Massachusetts. Invited to lecture at the Loeb Drama Center at Harvard under the auspices of the Theodore Spencer Memorial fund in May 1962, Mostel gave his view that comedy was "a commonwealth of experience, a shared background of culture, a unifying force . . . clearly social in its meaning." In what might be described as his personal philosophy as well as his creed as an actor, Mostel declared: "Comedy is rebellion against that kind of piety which we may call False Piety . . . against hypocrisy, against pretense, against falsehood and humbug and bunk and fraud, against false promises and base deceivers . . . against all evils masquerading as true and good and worthy of respect."

Mostel started going to the Actors' Studio in 1950 and still enjoys working there from time to time. He particularly admires Charlie Chaplin, W. C. Fields, and the French actor Raimu. He claims to be impervious to theater critics and would one day like to play King Lear. In 1960 he was run down by a bus and nearly suffered the loss of a leg as a result. He recovered his agility almost fully—as audiences and critics watching him cavort in *A Funny Thing* have attested. Since the accident, however, he carries a cane while walking.

At the height of his acting career Mostel maintains an artist's studio on West 28th Street in Manhattan, where he paints every day, usually working on several canvases at a time. He has

MOSTEL, ZERO—Continued

achieved respectable critical standing as an artist, and it is rumored that he has obtained high prices for his paintings. "Painting is a much more creative field than acting," Mostel explained some time ago. "You take up an empty canvas; you fill it. In acting, you've got something to start with."

References

Cue 31:15 D 29 '62 por
N Y Post Mag p10 N 25 '62 por
N Y Times Mag p40+ Je 3 '62 por
New Yorker 37:22+ O 28 '61
International Motion Picture Almanac, 1963

MUIR, P(ERCIVAL) H(ORACE) See Muir, Percy

MUIR, PERCY Dec. 17, 1894- Antiquarian bookseller; bibliographer

Address: b. Elkin Mathews Ltd., Takeley, Bishop's Stortford, Hertfordshire, England; h. Taylors, Takeley, Bishop's Stortford, Hertfordshire, England

In 1950 Percy Muir was elected life president of honor of the International League of Antiquarian Booksellers, an accolade that indicates his standing in his profession. A force in antiquarian bookselling for over thirty years, Muir knows and cares about the contents of books as much as he does about their market value. He pioneered in such collecting fields as first editions of musical compositions and has been prepared to suffer hardship for his bibliographical principles. Muir enjoys an international reputation as a writer and lecturer on bookselling and book collecting and as the creator of some memorable book exhibitions. He quite recently completed what he regards as one of the most important tasks of his career: the preparation of a display of books that have changed man's thinking over the past five centuries. The display formed part of the 1963 International Printing Machinery and Allied Trades Exhibition, held in London from July 16 to July 27.

Percival Horace Muir was born in London on December 17, 1894, the elder son of Charles Henry and Annie (Hancock) Muir. His brother, Alan, who is no longer living, was a civil servant with the Ministry of Supply. Charles Muir's work as an insurance executive involved the family in frequent moves, and Percy Muir attended a series of elementary and secondary schools in southern England.

Since his parents were financially unable to send him on to a university, Muir left school at the age of sixteen to go to work as a junior clerk in the offices of Docker Brothers Ltd., paint and varnish manufacturers, at a salary of five shillings a week. Already drawn to literature, with his "nose always stuck in a book," Muir found the work dull, and in 1911 he took a job with the Christian Evidence Society, a nondenominational evangelical

organization. With it he gained his first experience before an audience, speaking regularly on behalf of the society at London's famous "speaker's corner" in Hyde Park.

When World War I broke out, Muir volunteered for service with the London Scottish Regiment. In the spring of 1915, shortly after he reached France, a shell burst over Muir's trench, killing the men on both sides of him and seriously wounding him in the shoulder. He was invalided back to England for guard duties at the Tower of London. Charles Muir had meanwhile begun to organize entertainments for soldiers in London hospitals, and Percy Muir now joined him, learning to sing, dance, and handle a comedy routine-from Bert Bex, a former entertainer.

As a result of his wounds, Muir was discharged from the Army in October 1916. He rejoined the Christian Evidence Society, remaining there until 1918, when Bert Bex induced him to embark on quite a different career. For the next two years Muir toured England as one half of the popular vaudeville act billed as "Bex and Bex." When the act broke up in 1920, Muir had £50 to invest in a new project, the *Independent Film Review*. The idea was to provide objective assessments of new motion pictures for the guidance of independent theater managers. The service was much needed and was warmly welcomed, but foundered in 1921 for lack of capitalization.

Meanwhile, Muir had already entered the book trade. As early as 1919, when he was not touring with Bex, he had begun to act as a kind of "runner," scouting secondhand book shops for first editions of modern writers and selling them at a minimum of profit to rare book dealers. It was during that year when Muir was still an amateur, that the bookseller Leslie Chaundy told him of a collector who wanted a first edition of John Masefield's *Salt Water Ballads*. Muir knew where to find a copy and, horrified at his own rashness, invested all of £10 in it. Chaundy calmly paid him £15 for the book and assigned him to round up a whole set of Masefield first editions. "It may not have been much of an assignment," Muir wrote later in the *The Book Collector*, "but when I had finished the job I knew quite definitely that I was committed to becoming a bookseller."

In 1921 Muir opened a bookshop, on Warren Street, London, with Harold Edwards, now a noted antiquarian bookseller, as his partner. The partnership was not a success, and in less than a year Muir and Edwards were out of business. For the next two years Muir continued to sell books to the trade, operating out of a single room in his father's house. During his partnership with Edwards, Muir had visited Germany and struck up an acquaintance with the Berlin bookseller Paul Graupe. In 1923 he received an urgent and totally unexpected message from Graupe who had just concluded a deal in Belgium that netted him some £3,000. Unwilling to take the money into Germany, where inflation was rampant, Graupe offered it as a loan to Muir. That same year Muir opened his bookshop at 76A Davies Street, London.

There followed a period when Muir worked at his shop all day and spent his evenings managing dances and "whist drives" for his father, who had discovered that entertainment paid better than insurance. After two years of this exhausting regimen, the Davies Street business was well enough established for Muir to consider abandoning his "moonlighting." At this point his old friend Leslie Chaundy offered him a place on the board of Dulau & Co. Ltd., the oldest antiquarian bookshop in England. With some hesitation, he gave up his own business and accepted.

Muir's misgivings were well founded; his four years at Dulau's were not happy ones. In 1925, when Muir joined the company, it was already in decline, rigid and unimaginative in its methods, and dependent for its existence on a single specialty, its natural history department. Muir's special interest in, and knowledge of, first editions of modern writers was not particularly welcome there; nor was his wish to experiment with new lines and new methods. The firm did a little publishing however, notably of bibliographical and botanical works, and Muir found some satisfaction in handling this end of the business. In 1928 Muir went with Chaundy on a fascinating if frustrating trip to Russia, trying to buy some of the fabulous pre-Revolutionary libraries then being offered for sale by the Bolsheviks. Hopelessly entangled in Soviet red tape, they bought only one library.

Late in 1929, when Muir was offered a partnership at Elkin Mathews Ltd., he accepted with relief. The bookshop, which dated back to 1885, was then controlled by A. W. Evans, whom Muir greatly admired. Evans had gathered around him on the board of Elkin Mathews an extraordinary group of young amateur bookmen, some of them brilliant, some of them wealthy, and all of them notably eccentric. These men, unhampered by formal bookselling training, had tested Evans' theory that collectors could become interested in first editions of such books as *The Origin of Species* and *The Adventures of Sherlock Holmes*—books that were not "literature" but were for other reasons of great interest or importance. During the boom years between 1923 and 1929, Evans' experiment was an immense success. He opened up collecting fields that are now basic.

But Muir had joined Elkin Mathews Ltd. in the year of the Wall Street crash. As the bottom began to slip out of the antiquarian book market, the spendthrift dilettantism with which the company had been run became more and more inappropriate. Faced with the need for economy and efficiency, Muir's partners began to lose interest, and the responsibility of keeping the company afloat fell increasingly to Muir.

In 1935 Muir himself ran into serious trouble. The editor of an American journal for book collectors had asked him for information about a man then operating on the fringes of the British book trade. Muir found that the man was selling forgeries of a gross and amateurish nature, and said so in a private letter. The letter was published. Faced with a libel action, Muir refused on principle to retract. His charges

PERCY MUIR

Today

were substantiated in court, but Muir nevertheless lost the case. The damages awarded to the plaintiff, though moderate, were enough to bankrupt Muir. His directorship in Elkin Mathews was automatically forfeit. Six months later—the minimum time legally permissible—Muir had paid off his debt, was discharged as a bankrupt, and was back on the Elkin Mathews board.

Then, as throughout that agonizing period in his own affairs, Muir continued to wrestle with the shaky fortunes of his firm. During the 1930's he began to explore what was then almost a virgin field, often traveling to Europe in search of first editions of musical works, such as the manuscript of Mozart's Symphony No. 35 in D, K. 385 ("Haffner"), smuggled out of Nazi Germany and sold for $20,000. This and other methods used by Muir to keep the firm of Elkin Mathews Ltd. afloat are described in his *Minding My Own Business* (Chatto & Windus, 1956). Its anonymous reviewer in the London *Times Literary Supplement* (July 13, 1956) commented: "It is obviously to Mr. Muir's own efforts that the survival of Elkin Mathews . . . is principally due."

Muir became managing director in 1939, when with the outbreak of World War II Elkin Mathews Ltd. was evacuated to the village of Takeley, near Bishop's Stortford in Hertfordshire. There it has remained, adjoining his seventeenth-century home, which is itself stuffed to the low beams with books. Muir is now also the company's principal stockholder, sharing the board with his wife and Laurie Deval. In *Minding My Own Business*, he describes the present-day Elkin Mathews as "a decent, intelligently run antiquarian book business of the second or third rank that makes no fortunes for its partners, but provides them with a living and an enormous amount of more or less clean fun."

(Continued next page)

MUIR, PERCY—Continued

Minding My Own Business purports to be an autobiography. In fact, as its reviewers pointed out, it is a self-effacing, affectionate, and highly entertaining history of Elkin Mathews Ltd., its personnel, and some of its colorful patrons (who have ranged from Thomas J. Wise to Queen Mary). Muir is now dealing in the same way with Dulau's in his "Further Reminiscences," which have been appearing in the British quarterly *Book Collector* since 1956.

Percy Muir first broke into print in 1927 with a bibliography of the first editions of Aldous Huxley and T. F. Powys, which was published by Dulau's. Other first edition bibliographies were followed in 1931 and 1934 by *Points, 1874-1930* and *Points, second series, 1866-1934*, both published by Constable, and both dealing primarily with first edition collecting. Then came *Book-Collecting As a Hobby, In a Series of Letters to Everyman* (Gramol, 1944; Knopf, 1947) and its sequel, *Book-Collecting, More Letters to Everyman* (Cassell, 1949). Muir's *English Children's Books, 1600-1900* (Batsford; Praeger, 1954), more literary than bibliographical, updated Darton's *Children's Books in England*. In an agreeable style that conceals considerable learning, he has often contributed to such magazines as the *Colophon* and the *Bookman's Journal*, has prepared some notable catalogs, and between 1940 and 1945 conducted the "Notes on Sales" department of the London *Times Literary Supplement*. Muir was editor of the *Good Housekeeping Book of Fairy Stories* (Gramol, 1946) and of the Antiquarian Booksellers' Association's *Talks on Book-Collecting* (Cassell, 1952), a collection of talks given at the National Book League in 1948-49. He is a founder and member of the *Book Collector*'s editorial board.

In 1951 Muir prepared for the British Council an exhibition called "The Private Press and its Background" and opened it in Oslo, Norway. It is still on tour. Later the same year he paid his only visit to the United States, on a lecture tour organized by his friend William Johnson of the Harvard University Libraries.

Percy Muir married Barbara Kenrick Gowing, now better known under her pseudonym as the novelist Barbara Kaye, in 1935. They have two children, Helen Lisl and David. Muir stands five feet ten inches tall and carries his 196 pounds comfortably. He was once active in the labor movement, but has switched from being a "right-wing Labourite" to being a "left-wing Conservative." He has no religious affiliation. Muir is a former president (1948-50) of the International League of Antiquarian Booksellers' Association; an honorary life member of the National Book League; and a member of the Bibliographical Society. His special interests, apart from bibliography, include music, photography, and gardening, and he is a Fellow of the Royal Horticultural Society and a member of the Bath Club.

References

Muir, Percy. Minding My Own Business (1956)
Who's Who, 1963

MUMFORD, LEWIS   Oct. 19, 1895-   Social philosopher and critic; historian; writer; educator

Address: h. Amenia, N.Y.

> NOTE: This biography supersedes the article that appeared in *Current Biography* in 1940.

In an age of specialization, Lewis Mumford, the social philosopher, cultural historian, and authority on architecture and city planning, remains a "man of the Renaissance." He is engaged "not in finding or fabricating the pieces but in putting them together into a significant picture." Although not a professional architect or city planner, Mumford has received honors and awards for his contributions to these fields, and he has written extensively about them. Without holding any academic degrees, he has served as a professor or lecturer at institutions of higher learning over the years.

Of the twenty books that Mumford has written the more important ones are *Technics and Civilization* (1934), *The Culture of Cities* (1938), *The Condition of Man* (1944), and *The Conduct of Life* (1951), which form his Renewal of Life series; and *The City in History* (1961), for which he won a National Book Award in 1962. In addition, four books have given him a special place as a pioneer in American studies: *Sticks and Stones* (1924), *Golden Day* (1926), *Herman Melville* (1929), and *The Brown Decades* (1931). A vocal critic of the dehumanizing tendencies of modern technological civilization, Mumford is much concerned with the commitment of present-day governments to weapons of mass destruction, with the resulting danger of nuclear war.

Of English and German ancestry, Lewis Mumford was born on October 19, 1895 in Flushing, Long Island, New York, the only child of Lewis Charles Mumford, a lawyer, and of Elvina Conradina (Baron) Mumford. He grew up on the West Side of New York City in modest circumstances, and he began to attend public school in 1901. "I remained a docile pupil, a model pupil, always an excellent pupil in the futile academic sense, until I entered high school, where my interests widened and my marks worsened," Mumford has recalled.

While attending Stuyvesant High School, which he entered in 1909, Mumford played tennis, took part in dramatics, experimented with radio, and contributed to the journal *Modern Electrics*. Although he had an early ambition to become an electrical engineer, his dislike of mathematics and a youthful love affair stimulated his desire to be a writer, and for a time he hoped to become a newspaper reporter or a playwright. After graduating from high school in 1912 Mumford entered the evening division at the City College of New York. Later, until 1919, he also studied at Columbia University, and at the New School for Social Research under Thorstein Veblen. Although he had enough credits for college graduation, he never obtained a degree. "I got what I wanted out of my studies, and have never felt the need for a degree," he has recalled, "because I did not aim to be a teacher."

A major influence on Mumford's intellectual development was Sir Patrick Geddes (1854-1932), a Scottish biologist and also sociologist who pioneered in civic and regional studies. Mumford first encountered Geddes' writings in 1915, although he did not meet the man until 1923. In keeping with Geddes' ideas, Mumford used New York City as a "storehouse and powerhouse," visiting its libraries, museums, and theaters, and studying the architecture of its buildings. He also engaged in what he has called "vocational participation" by working as an investigator in the dress and waist industry in 1916 and as a laboratory assistant with the United States Bureau of Standards early in 1917. From April 1917 to February 1918 he served as a radio electrician, second class, with the United States Navy.

Although Mumford embarked on his writing career with enthusiasm, and began to contribute articles to *Forum* as early as 1914, he had little published during the first few years. He wrote several plays, but he refused to submit them for production, since they did not meet his own standards. He became an associate editor of the *Dial*, which was the most distinguished American literary magazine of its day, in 1919. At the invitation of Victor Branford, a colleague of Geddes, Mumford spent half of 1920 in London, where he served as acting editor of the *Sociological Review*. He also taught a course in Principles of Reconstruction at the Summer School of Civics at High Wycombe. Returning to New York, he resumed his work as a free-lance writer. He contributed to *Civilization in the United States: An Inquiry by Thirty Americans*, edited by Harold Stearns and published by Harcourt, Brace and Company in 1922.

Mumford's first book, *The Story of Utopias* (Boni and Liveright, 1922), is a critical study of the classic utopias of the past. His second book, *Sticks and Stones: A Study of American Architecture and Civilization* (Boni and Liveright, 1924), interprets American architecture in its social context. Mumford traces American cultural history, particularly that of the romantic period, back to its Old World sources in *Golden Day: A Study in American Experience and Culture* (Boni and Liveright, 1926).

In 1923 Mumford became a charter member of the Regional Planning Association of America, an experimental group that paved the way for several successful projects in regional development, including the Tennessee Valley Authority. In 1924 he served as a special investigator for the New York Housing and Planning Commission. In 1926 with Alfred Kreymborg, Paul Rosenfeld, and Van Wyck Brooks he founded the *American Caravan*, a yearbook of contemporary American writing, of which five volumes, edited by Mumford, Kreymborg, and Rosenfeld, were published between 1927 and 1936. In 1925 he edited the regional planning issue of the liberal journal *Survey Graphic*. Mumford went to Switzerland in 1925 and 1929 to lecture at the Geneva School of International Studies, and in 1929 he also served as Guernsey Centre Moore Foundation lecturer at Dartmouth College.

In 1932 Lewis Mumford began to write a column of architectural criticism, "The Sky Line," for the *New Yorker*. During this period he often contributed to such journals as the *American*

Alison Morss

LEWIS MUMFORD

Mercury, New Republic, Freeman, and *Harper's Magazine,* and architectural periodicals. His book *Herman Melville* (Harcourt, 1929), a critical and psychological study of the life and thought of the noted American writer, is based in part on Melville's then-unpublished letters and notebooks. In *The Brown Decades: A Study of Art in America 1865-1895* (Harcourt, 1931) Mumford examined American city planning, architecture, and painting during the thirty years following the Civil War.

In 1931 Mumford projected a book that would trace the relationships between the various aspects of civilization. During a four-month visit to Europe on a Guggenheim Fellowship in 1932 he elaborated the scheme for a single book into a series that culminated in his four-volume Renewal of Life. The first volume, *Technics and Civilization* (Harcourt, 1934), deals with the development of technological civilization since the tenth century and shows how technology might be brought into harmony with human needs and desires. A second volume, *The Culture of Cities* (Harcourt, 1938), traces the history of cities in the western world since the Middle Ages and sets forth proposals for the improvement of modern cities. The book established Mumford's international reputation. Mumford's emphasis on the human factors in city design influenced European city planning, and during World War II the book was used by underground organizations in several occupied countries to train a new generation of planners.

During the 1930's Mumford took an increased interest in education. After teaching briefly at the New School for Social Research he was a visiting professor of art at Dartmouth College from 1931 until 1935. From 1935 to 1937 he was a member of the board of higher education in New York City, and from 1938 until 1944 he was on the commission on teacher education of the American Council on Education. In 1938 he was consultant

MUMFORD, LEWIS—*Continued*

to the city and county park board in Honolulu, Hawaii, and his booklet *Whither Honolulu?* (1938) reports on a study of parks and playgrounds in that city. In 1939 he wrote the narration for a documentary film, *The City*, which was shown at the city planning exhibit at the New York World's Fair.

As early as 1935 Mumford advocated military resistance to the rising totalitarian powers. His article "A Call to Arms," which appeared in the *New Republic* in May 1938, pleaded for a militantly anti-Fascist policy on the part of the United States. In his book *Men Must Act* (Harcourt, 1939) he forcefully called upon democratic nations to adopt a policy of collective security and nonintercourse with Fascist nations. In *A Faith for Living* (Harcourt, 1940) he presented "a program for survivors of the present mass attack on democracy." In 1940 Mumford became a member of the City of Man group, founded by G. A. Borgese, and he helped to draft its manifesto. In June 1940 he resigned as contributing editor of the *New Republic* after thirteen years, because the liberal journal was reluctant to rally to the cause of aid to the Allies. In the fall of 1939 he had resigned as vice-chairman of the American Artists' Congress in protest against its antidemocratic policy in defending the Hitler-Stalin compact.

The Condition of Man (Harcourt, 1944), the third volume in Mumford's Renewal of Life series, is a comprehensive interpretation of the development of modern man, proposing ways in which he might best use the vast powers at his command. The fourth and final volume in the series is *The Conduct of Life* (Harcourt, 1951), which attempts to counteract the current breakdown of the human personality by means of a new humanistic philosophy. Neil Martin, reviewing the book in the *Christian Science Monitor* (October 11, 1951) noted that Mumford "takes top rank among living philosophers," and Waldo Frank in the *Saturday Review of Literature* (September 22, 1951) described Mumford as "another Moses who leads to and sees the promised land, and cannot reach it."

Other works by Mumford include *The South in Architecture* (Harcourt, 1941); *City Development: Studies in Disintegration and Renewal* (Harcourt, 1945); *Values for Survival* (Harcourt, 1946), which consists of essays, addresses, and letters on politics and education, written between 1938 and 1946; *Art and Technics* (Columbia University Press, 1952), dealing with the relationship between man and machine and between man's artistic impulse and technical urge; *The Human Prospect* (Beacon Press, 1955), a series of essays on a variety of topics, edited by Harry T. Moore and Karl W. Deutsch; *From the Ground Up: Observations on Contemporary Architecture* (Harcourt, 1956); and *The Transformations of Man* (Harper, 1956), an interpretation of history from the view of ideal human progress. Mumford also contributed to the volume *Arts in Renewal* (University of Pennsylvania Press, 1951), and he edited the volume *Roots of Contemporary American Architecture* (Reinhold, 1952).

Since the end of World War II Mumford has been increasingly concerned with the moral and practical problems resulting from the reliance of governments on weapons of mass destruction and their neglect of more vital and human objectives. His book *In the Name of Sanity* (Harcourt, 1954) describes the possible consequences of nuclear war and the steps that might be taken to prevent the nuclear extinction of civilization. Mumford also contributed to *Alternatives to the H-Bomb* (Beacon Press, 1955), a symposium organized by the *New Leader*.

Continuing in his role as an educator, Mumford was professor of humanities at Stanford University from 1942 to 1944 and a visiting professor of architecture at North Carolina State College from 1948 until 1952. He delivered the Earle lectures at the Pacific Institute of Religion in 1947 and the Bampton lectures at Columbia University in 1951. In 1955 he served as co-chairman of the Wenner-Gren conference on man's role in shaping the face of the earth. From 1952 to 1959 Mumford was visiting professor of land and city planning at the University of Pennsylvania, and from 1959 to 1961 he was a Ford research professor there. He was also visiting Bemis professor at the Massachusetts Institute of Technology from 1957 to 1960; Ford rotating professor of political science at the University of California, Berkeley, in 1961-62; and Saposnekow lecturer at the City College of New York in 1962.

For his achievements Mumford has received many honors and awards. He held Guggenheim Fellowships in 1932, 1938, and 1956, and he was awarded the Townsend Harris Medal of the City College of New York in 1939. He received the Ebenezer Howard Medal of the Town and Country Planning Association in 1946; the Fairmount Park Association medal of honor in 1953; and the gold medal of the Town Planning Institute of Great Britain in 1957. In 1961 he was the first American to receive the Royal Gold Medal for architecture, which was conferred on him by Queen Elizabeth II on recommendation of the Royal Institute of British Architects. The American Institute of Architects conferred upon him its Award of Merit in 1962.

In March 1962 Mumford received the National Book Award for nonfiction for his book *The City in History: Its Origins, Its Transformations, Its Prospects* (Harcourt, 1961), a philosophical study of the role of cities throughout recorded history. Although Mumford criticizes what he regards as "the spiritual rootlessness and loneliness of the overgrown city," he concludes that "the final mission of the city is to further man's conscious participation in the cosmic and historic process."

Mumford is a member of the American Philosophical Society, the American Society of Architectural Historians, and the National Institute of Arts and Letters. He holds honorary memberships in the American Institute of Architects, the American Institute of Planners, Phi Beta Kappa, and the Town Planning Institutes of Great Britain and Canada. In 1941 Stanford University made him an honorary Fellow. He is an honorary associate of the Royal Institute of British Architects, and he has served as vice-president of the Société Européene de Culture. In December 1962 the American Academy of Arts and Letters elected Mumford president for 1963.

On September 30, 1921 Lewis Mumford married Sophia Wittenberg, who was assistant editor of the *Dial* from 1920 to 1925. They have one daughter, Alison Jane. Mumford dedicated the book *Green Memories: The Story of Geddes Mumford* (Harcourt, 1947) to his son, Geddes, who was killed in combat in Italy in September 1944 at the age of nineteen. Dignified and scholarly in appearance, Mumford is five feet ten and a half inches tall, weighs 175 pounds, and has brown eyes and thinning gray hair. He is a Democrat with Socialist sympathies, and he has consistently opposed totalitarian ideologies. Although he was reared in the Episcopal faith he regards himself as a religious humanist in the tradition of Emerson and Whitman. His favorite recreations are gardening, walking, sketching. His permanent residence is in the small community of Amenia, New York, but he denies that he is a "rural recluse" or that he opposes urban living, since he has habitually spent half the year in the city.

Mumford believes that man's only hope lies in a return to human feelings and sensitivities and to moral values. "The test of maturity, for nations as well as for individuals, is not the increase of power, but the increase of self-understanding, self-control, self-direction, and self-transcendence," he wrote in the *Saturday Evening Post* (April 18, 1959). "For in a mature society, man himself, not his machines or his organizations, is the chief work of art."

References

    International Who's Who, 1962-63
    Twentieth Century Authors (1942; First Supplement, 1955)
    Who's Who, 1963
    Who's Who in America, 1962-63

MURPHREE, EGER V(AUGHAN) Nov. 3, 1898-Oct. 29, 1962 President (1947-62) of Esso Research and Engineering Company. See *Current Biography* (September) 1956.

Obituary

N Y Times p35 O 30 '62

NABARRO, SIR GERALD (DAVID NUNES) June 29, 1913- British politician; industrialist

Address: b. House of Commons, London, S.W.1, England; 28-30 Great Peter St., London, S.W.1, England; h. "The Orchard House," Broadway, Worcestershire, England

The British House of Commons, which has nurtured some notably exotic personalities in its 600 years of history, has since 1950 provided a setting for the Right Honourable Sir Gerald Nabarro, Conservative Member of Parliament for Kidderminster, Worcestershire. Sir Gerald, who flaunts his huge moustaches as defiantly as his frequently controversial opinions, is however, far more than a mere eccentric. He has been almost uniquely successful in implementing his personal

P. A.—Reuter, London
SIR GERALD NABARRO

legislative program and is recognized as a personality of growing importance within his party. Nabarro is the hero of a rags-to-riches story that began in a London slum, included stints as seaman and professional soldier, and led him to considerable wealth as an industrialist before he turned his attention to politics. He received his knighthood in 1963.

Gerald David Nunes Nabarro was born on June 29, 1913 in London to Solomon Nunes Nabarro, a cigar importer and merchant of Sephardic Jewish ancestry, and to Lena (Drucquer) Nabarro. He has a brother, Cedric, and two sisters, Rita and Betty. Another brother, Jack, was killed in action in World War II. Nabarro, who was orphaned at an early age, is proud of the fact that he is a self-made man. He was educated at a London County Council elementary school where he was average at games and, he recalled in a British Broadcasting Corporation interview on March 13, 1963, was in no way outstanding academically, although he did "get into a lot of trouble." At the age of fourteen he left school and went to sea. A year later, claiming that he was eighteen, he enlisted as a private in the regular army. From 1929 to 1937 Nabarro was a professional soldier, rising to the rank of staff sergeant instructor. At this point in his military career, he applied for a commission in the Royal Artillery. He was selected for Sandhurst, the British military academy, but, realizing that the incidental expenses there would be beyond his means, he left the regular army.

Re-entering civilian life in 1937, Nabarro started again at the bottom, working as a laborer in a West of England sawmill. Soon he asked for and received permission to take charge of the mill's night shift and in rapid succession became foreman, cost clerk, works manager, and managing director. He is now a director of several engineering and sawmilling companies

NABARRO, SIR GERALD—*Continued*

and is considered a wealthy man. Andrew Roth's *The Business Background of Members of Parliament, 1961-62* (Parliamentary Profile Services Ltd., 1961) listed him as managing director of No-Nail Boxes Ltd. of Chester and a director of other unspecified companies.

Nabarro's political career began unpromisingly in 1945, when he stood as Conservative candidate for West Bromwich in Staffordshire and was defeated. A few months later he became a prospective candidate for Kidderminster in Worcestershire, a former Conservative stronghold that had just been won by the Labour party. For the next four and a half years Nabarro "nursed" the constituency, making every effort to create an atmosphere favorable to himself for the next election. Meanwhile, having become active in the Young Conservative movement, he served from 1945 to 1948 as chairman of the West Midlands Young Conservative Organization, covering six counties, and he was its president from 1948 to 1950. During his tenure the number of Young Conservative branches in the West Midlands rose from a mere handful to more than 250. From 1946 to 1948 Nabarro served also as vice-chairman of the Midland Union of Conservative Associations. In the general election of 1950, he won back Kidderminster for the Conservatives. He has represented that constituency in Parliament ever since, increasing his majority at each election.

If Nabarro did not immediately achieve general popularity in the House of Commons, he did attract attention. With his extravagant moustaches, his inevitable carnation, his parade ground voice and uninhibited comments, he seemed "all set at first to join the parliamentary eccentrics," according to a profile in the *New Statesman* (July 25, 1959). "Many a time was the former Tory Chief Whip's pallid face seen to flush as Mr. Nabarro rushed thundering, uninvited, into some sophisticated exchange," the profile went on.

Nabarro rapidly succeeded in impressing his image on his party—an image, according to the *New Statesman* profile, "as vivid as that of a neon-lit factory on the fringe of a village at dusk." He worked hard and was soon vice-chairman of the important Atomic Energy Committee. "And suddenly," the *New Statesman* went on, "both the government and the Opposition heard themselves listening to a well-informed and fluent expounder of fuel policies, not in the least eccentric . . . but enterprising, bright with new ideas, not flashy but sober."

Nabarro's methods have not always been entirely in keeping with parliamentary tradition. In January 1955, for example, he opened one of his most notable campaigns by having his parliamentary letters franked: "Gerald Nabarro's Clean Air (anti-smog) Bill Second Reading—Friday, February 4, 1955." But few would question the fact that Nabarro's parliamentary techniques work. Before long he had become the only man of this century to have brought through his own initiative four private bills onto the statute books: a new Coroner's Act (1953); the

Clean Air legislation of 1955-56; the Thermal Insulation (Industrial Buildings) Act of 1957; and the Oil Burners (Standards) Act of 1960.

The interest in industrial affairs demonstrated by this legislative activity is only one of Nabarro's parliamentary concerns. He also specializes in finance and taxation and has said that the cabinet post he most covets is that of Chancellor of the Exchequer. Believing that taxation in general is too high, he favors tax incentives to stimulate production and increase exports. He has moreover fought for these beliefs, and recent reforms and reductions in Britain's stringent purchase tax regulations are owing in part to Nabarro's famous "400 questions" on what he regards as the law's more irrational provisions. Why, for example, had a 30 percent purchase tax been imposed on false beards and moustaches? During the past few years Nabarro has asked hundreds of such questions in the House of Commons, embarrassing the leaders of his own party, to whom the questions were addressed, but delighting the general public.

It is, however, with fuel and power that Nabarro has been most closely associated. He is reputed to have spoken in every debate concerned with fuel, power, and coal since he entered the House of Commons, and he is now vice-chairman of the Conservative Parliamentary Power Committee. He formerly served the same committee as secretary but, reinforcing his reputation for independence, resigned in a dispute with the Minister of Fuel. Nabarro, a member of the Institute of Fuel, is the author of two publications on the subject of fuel and power. The first, written with C. J. M. Alport, was *Make Coal Work Harder,* a pamphlet published in 1951 by the Conservative Political Centre. The second, a longer publication, was *Ten Steps to Power; A National Fuel and Power Policy* (St. Catherine Press, 1952).

Nabarro is a frequent contributor to newspapers and magazines on a variety of topics and a popular figure on British radio and television. He is much in demand as a public speaker and has become something of an institution at by-elections, where he appears regularly to support local Conservative candidates. He is president of the Merseyside branch of the National Union of Manufacturers and a member of that body's National Executive Committee. He is also a member of the Midlands Committee of the Institute of Directors and of the Dee and Clwyd Rivers Board of Navigation Committee, and a governor of the University of Birmingham.

In the New Year Honours of 1963, Nabarro was knighted Sir Gerald Nabarro. Soon afterward James Margach commented in the London *Sunday Times* (March 17, 1963) that Sir Gerald was emerging "as a powerful new personality . . . the Tory Party's biggest personality performer in the country." Margach predicted that Nabarro would shortly be offered one of the top jobs at the Conservative Central Office, "continuing the classic pattern of the rebel and critic of yesterday becoming the Establishment figure of today."

Nabarro, who cheerfully concedes that he attracts a lot of attention, remains a great deal in the public eye, and not always to his advantage. In April 1963, appearing on the BBC radio discussion program *Any Questions,* he caused something of a furore when he reportedly made an anti-Negro statement to another panelist. The remark was deleted when the program was rebroadcast, although Nabarro explained that he had meant no offense. Sir Gerald has weathered similar storms in the past. Once, in 1956, when he was arrested for speeding, he reportedly insulted the police officer and struck his notebook from his hand. In the flurry of bad publicity that followed, a National Coal Board official described Nabarro as "a carpet-bagger and political hoodlum." Sir Gerald, who could have claimed a breach of Parliamentary privilege, rehabilitated himself in public estimation by turning the other cheek. "MP's ought not to be too tender," he commented, "and I don't like privilege."

In 1943 Gerald Nabarro married Joan Maud Violet im Thurn, daughter of Colonel B. B. von B. im Thurn; at the time she was junior commander in the Auxiliary Territorial Service. They have four children, Rupert, Jeremy, Sarah, and Dinah. Sir Gerald is five feet ten inches tall, weighs 174 pounds, and has brown eyes and black hair. His recreations include rifle shooting, riding, tennis, walking, and travel. He is a member of the Church of England and of the Carlton Club. In his profile of Sir Gerald (July 25, 1959), the *New Statesman* writer commented that while the moustache might have to be trimmed and the carnation discarded, "there are those who believe that, stripped of his wraps, Mr. Nabarro, a courageous, intelligent and responsible man, could emerge as a considerable politician."

References

New Statesman 58:103+ Jl 25 '59 por
Kelly's Handbook to the Titled, Landed and Official Classes, 1963
Who's Who, 1963

NABRIT, S(AMUEL) M(ILTON) Feb. 21, 1905- Biologist; university president

Address: b. 3201 Wheeler St., Houston 4, Tex.; h. 3806 Tierwester St., Houston 4, Tex.

The scientist and educator Dr. S. M. Nabrit was named second president of Texas Southern University, a state school for Negroes, in the summer of 1955, when his predecessor, Dr. Raphael O'Hara Lanier, resigned. Nabrit, who is noted for his work on biological regeneration, was dean of the graduate school of arts and sciences of Atlanta University from 1947 to 1955 and served for three years, 1956 to 1959, on the board of the National Science Foundation. He has contributed scientific papers to professional journals and has written book reviews and articles on education for *Phylon, The Atlanta University Review of Race and Culture,* for the *Negro History Bulletin,* and for *Science Education.*

Samuel Milton Nabrit, the son of James Madison and Augusta Gertrude (West) Nabrit, was born on February 21, 1905 in Macon, Georgia. His father, a Baptist minister and a gradu-

Teal Studio, Houston

S. M. NABRIT

ate of Morehouse College in Atlanta, taught at the Central City College in Macon. Samuel Nabrit's sisters are Ann, Lois, and Cecile. His brothers are Henry and James Madison, Jr., who is the president of Howard University in Washington, D.C. In 1912 the Nabrit family moved to Augusta, Georgia, where the father became pastor of the Springfield Baptist Church and a teacher at the Walker Baptist Institute, which Samuel Nabrit attended. The boy studied Latin, Greek, and physics under his father, and he was valedictorian of his graduating class in 1921. His extracurricular activities at high school included playing football and baseball and managing the student paper.

Continuing his education at Morehouse College, Nabrit majored in biology. He played football, joined the Omega Psi Phi social fraternity, and managed the student paper. Dr. John Hope, then president of Morehouse College (later of Atlanta University), firmly believed that Negroes should seek a liberal arts education instead of the more traditional vocational training. He and George Washington Hill both influenced Nabrit's choice of career. Morehouse College, a Baptist-affiliated private liberal arts college for men, has been connected with Atlanta University since 1929 in the Atlanta University System. Under the system Morehouse and Spelman College (for women) give undergraduate courses, and the university takes the responsibility for developing a graduate program.

Upon Nabrit's graduation with a B.S. degree and honors in 1925, Dr. Hope suggested that he remain at the college as a teacher in the zoology department. After taking summer courses at the University of Chicago, Nabrit took up his post at Morehouse, where he retained a faculty appointment for six years (1925-31). During the year 1927-28 Nabrit was granted a leave of absence from the college so that he could study biology at Brown University in Providence,

NABRIT, S. M.—*Continued*

Rhode Island. He attended Brown on a general education board fellowship and received his M.Sc. degree in biology in 1928.

Every summer from 1927 to 1932 Nabrit left Atlanta to do research at the Marine Biological Laboratory at Woods Hole, Massachusetts. He studied, among other things, the regeneration of the tail fins of fish. The results of this work were published in the *Biological Bulletin* and used as the basis for his doctoral dissertation. After studying at Brown University during the academic year 1931-32, Nabrit became the first Negro to earn a Ph.D. degree from that school, in 1932. He was also the first Morehouse College graduate to win a Ph.D. degree. Nabrit was elected to Sigma Xi, the science research honor society. He did postdoctoral work at Teachers College, Columbia University in 1943 and at the University of Brussels in Belgium in 1950.

Named chairman of the biology department of Atlanta University in 1932, Nabrit continued to do research during summers at Woods Hole, Massachusetts. In 1948 he became a member of the Marine Biological Laboratory Corporation, the second Negro scientist to achieve this honor. (Ernest E. Just, an authority on the embryology of marine fauna, was the first.) Nabrit, who had met Dr. Just at Woods Hole, described his impressions of the embryologist in a 1946 issue of *Phylon*. Although busy with teaching and hampered by inadequate library and laboratory facilities and funds, Nabrit continued to do research on regeneration in fish embryos at Atlanta University. Papers describing his work have been published in the *Journal of Experimental Zoology, Anatomical Record, Biological Bulletin,* and the *Journal of Parasitology.*

In 1947 Nabrit was appointed dean of the graduate school of arts and sciences of Atlanta University. In addition to teaching and making scientific investigations, he has tried to improve educational standards for Negroes. He helped to organize the National Institute of Science in 1943 and served as its third president from 1945 to 1946. The purpose of the National Institute of Science is to explore the teaching and research problems of Negro scientists. It has a membership of about 200 people, mainly science teachers in Negro colleges and universities.

Nabrit has written articles on education, such as "The Negro in Science" (*Negro History Bulletin,* January 1957), in which he points out the need for science and mathematics teachers to study in research centers where they can get the best facilities and contact other scientists in their field. His article "Educational Requirements for Those Planning to Study Medicine" (*Science Education,* March 1951) stresses the importance of education for intelligent living and the need for interpreting, rather than merely accumulating, scientific facts. Nabrit has also reviewed books for *Phylon.*

A member of the National Committee for Research in Science Teaching since 1936, Nabrit has been on the committee on higher education of the Southern Regional Board of Control since 1950. He served on the screening committee for faculty fellowships of the Fund for the Advancement of Education from 1950 to 1954, and he

has been the co-ordinator of the Carnegie Foundation grant-in-aid program since 1948. In 1952 he was named to the committee for the training of college teachers of the American Council on Education. Since 1954 he has served on the administrative committee of the Southern Fellowships Fund. Nabrit taught a science workshop at Columbia University in the summer of 1945, at Prairie View A & M College in Texas in the summer of 1946, and at the Hampton Institute in the Virgin Islands in the summer of 1955. The latter program was sponsored by the Ford Foundation.

After the resignation of Raphael O'Hara Lanier as president of Texas Southern University in the summer of 1955, the board of directors of the school appointed Nabrit second president. He assumed the duties of office on September 1, 1955. When Governor Allan Shivers of Texas spoke at his inaugural ceremonies on March 18, 1956 on the Texas Southern University campus, the program was picketed by members of the NAACP because of Governor Shivers' views on segregation.

Established by the state legislature in 1947 as Texas State University for Negroes, the school was named Texas Southern University in 1951. Situated on fifty-three acres in Houston, Texas, the university has a coeducational enrollment of over 3,000 students in its various schools, which include the College of Arts and Sciences, the Graduate School, and schools of law, pharmacy, business, and vocational and industrial education. Nabrit's influence is reflected in the development of a basic skills workshop that prepares students for successful performance in leading universities and of a high school science teachers institute. The university is reputed to have a particularly strong program in the sciences.

The university library contains the Heartman Negro Collection, which includes books, pamphlets, art and music documents, dating from 1600 to the present, on the background and development of Negro people all over the world. As the president of a university for Negroes Nabrit is in a position to provide responsible leadership as American Negroes campaign for civil rights in the South. On March 4, 1960 about 100 Texas Southern University students participated in a sit-in in Houston.

President Dwight D. Eisenhower appointed Nabrit to the National Science Board of the National Science Foundation on May 10, 1956. The board consists of twenty-four members selected by the President on the basis of established records of distinguished service in scientific fields. However, Nabrit resigned on July 28, 1959, along with Logan Wilson, president of the University of Texas at Austin, in conformity with a state ruling barring them from accepting a federal appointment.

Morehouse College conferred an honorary LL.D. degree on Nabrit in 1960, and Brown University gave him an honorary D.Sc. degree in 1962. He is a member of the American Association for the Advancement of Science, the American Society of Zoologists, the New York Academy of Science, and the Society for the Study of Growth and Development, and he belongs to the Beta Kappa Chi and Sigma Pi Phi fraternities.

Samuel Milton Nabrit married Constance Crocker, the private secretary of Dr. John Hope, on August 8, 1927. They have no children. Nabrit enjoys reading and photography and likes to watch baseball and football games.

References

Negro History Bulletin 20:3+ O '56
American Men of Science 10th ed (1960-62)
Who's Who in America, 1962-63

NEHRU, B(RAJ) K(UMAR) Sept. 4, 1909-
Indian Ambassador to the United States

Address: b. 2107 Massachusetts Ave., N.W., Washington 8, D.C.; h. 2700 Macomb St., Washington, D.C.

Since September 1961, when he became the Ambassador from India to the United States, B. K. Nehru has exhibited considerable diplomatic skill in presenting his country's position on a number of difficult questions. These have included India's forcible occupation of the Portuguese enclaves in India, her continued dispute with Pakistan over Kashmir, and possible modifications of India's adamant neutrality in the light of United States help against Red China's aggression on Indian borders. One of India's ablest career civil servants since 1934, Nehru became known as India's greatest fund-raiser while he was Commissioner General of Economic Affairs from 1958 to 1961. Devoted to abolishing the poverty of his country's 438,000,000 people, he was chiefly responsible for obtaining billions of dollars in foreign government and international loans for the implementation of India's Five-Year Plans for economic progress.

Born on September 4, 1909 in Allahabad, India, Braj Kumar Nehru is the son of Brij Lal Nehru, a retired civil servant, and Rameshwari Nehru, a leading Indian social worker who received a Lenin Peace Prize in 1961. He is a cousin of the Indian Prime Minister, Jawaharlal Nehru. After taking his B.S. degree at the University of Allahabad, B. K. Nehru continued his education in England. He received the B.S. degree from the London School of Economics and Political Science, also studied at Balliol College, Oxford University, and read law at the Inner Temple.

Nehru began his career with the Indian civil service in 1934, as the assistant commissioner of Punjab, a former Indian province that was divided between Pakistan and India by the Indian Independence Act of 1947. In 1939 he was assigned to the Indian government's headquarters as under secretary to the Department of Education, Health, and Lands. Transferred to the Ministry of Finance, he served as an under secretary from 1940 to 1944, deputy secretary from 1944 to 1947, and joint secretary from 1947 to 1949. He represented India at a reparations conference in 1945, and at sterling balances conferences between 1947 and 1949.

Nehru's first assignment in Washington, D.C., from 1949 to 1954, was as executive director of the International Bank for Reconstruction and Development, an autonomous institution affiliated

B. K. NEHRU

with the United Nations, which makes loans to member nations and private investors. During the same period he held a minister's post at the Indian Embassy in Washington. From 1949 to 1952 Nehru represented India at the United Nations General Assembly, and from 1951 to 1953 he was a member of the United Nations advisory committee on administrative and budgetary questions. He also attended conferences of the Food and Agriculture Organization in 1949 and 1950.

In 1954 Nehru returned to India, where he became joint secretary with the Department of Economic Affairs for three years. In 1955 he represented India at the Bandung Conference of Asian and African nations, and he served as an adviser to the Sudanese government. Nehru took part in a number of Commonwealth Finance Ministers' Conferences, in 1949-50, 1955-56, 1958, and 1960, and in a Commonwealth Trade and Economic Conference in 1958.

After serving in 1957-58 as secretary in the Indian Department of Economic Affairs, Nehru was appointed in 1958 to the post of Commissioner General for Economic Affairs (he also held the title Ambassador-at-Large). His principal task during the second half of the 1950's was to solicit aid for India through foreign government and international loans and private business investments to implement India's second Five-Year Plan for economic development.

India's population of some 438,000,000 people increases at the annual rate of about forty per 1,000. Many Indians live on a subsistence level, and the average per capita income is merely $70 a year, as compared to $2,700 in the United States. The Five-Year Plans were instituted to speed economic development and raise the standard of living. The first was started in 1951, a year after India had become a sovereign democratic republic in January 1950. Costing about $7 billion, it concentrated on agricultural reforms

NEHRU, B. K.—*Continued*

and brought about a rise in food production. The second Five-Year Plan (1956-61), costing about $14.2 billion, emphasized the development of basic industries and new employment opportunities. Although these goals were to a certain extent realized, their fulfillment also produced some problems.

A severe drain on India's foreign exchange reserves resulted from the unexpectedly heavy flow of imports needed by the new industries, the rise in the prices of these imports, insufficient amount of exports, and increased food imports to make up for inadequate domestic production because of droughts and the comparative neglect of agriculture under the second plan. By seeking foreign aid and cutting the plan back to basic essentials like transport and port improvement, electric power development, and major industrial enterprises, India tried to meet her balance of payment obligations and prevent her second Five-Year Plan from breaking down.

In June 1956 India received a $75,000,000 loan from the International Bank for Reconstruction and Development for expansion of her steel industry. In 1957 Nehru negotiated with the World Bank for further financial assistance, maintaining that India would need over $1 billion in external finances over the next five years, in addition to funds already obtained from the United States, the Colombo Plan, and the International Monetary Fund.

As head of an Indian delegation visiting Washington, D.C. in March 1958, Nehru obtained credits of $150,000,000 from the Export-Import Bank and $75,000,000 from the Development Loan Fund of the International Cooperation Administration, set up by Congress in 1957 to aid underdeveloped nations. In July 1958 he informed the United States and international institutions that India needed $300,000,000 within the next six to nine months and a total of $1.2 billion to $1.4 billion to tide her over until the end of the second plan. If aid were not forthcoming, he said, India would have to stop paying her bills or "starve the economy." Representatives of India's chief creditors, the World Bank, the United States, West Germany, Canada, and Japan, met in August to explore means of providing the necessary funds.

In the fall of 1960 Nehru obtained another loan of $136,000,000 under the auspices of the International Bank for Reconstruction and Development. Provided by the United States, Britain, West Germany, Canada, Japan, and the Netherlands, the loan was designed to see India through her second Five-Year Plan to the spring of 1961. At the same time he asked the so-called "Aid India Club" to provide assurances that it would find the $1 billion needed to start a third Five-Year Plan. He pointed out that all underdeveloped countries do not need the same kind of help, and that India, with a stable government, know-how, a comprehensive economic plan, and trained technicians, lacks only capital. By August 1961 the "Aid India Club" and the International Bank had promised $2.286 billion in aid for the following two years. In August 1962 the United States announced another loan

to India of $24,000,000 for development of additional thermal-power plants.

The third Five-Year Plan, which began in April 1961, will cost about $22 billion. Its goals are to increase national income by 5 percent each year, to achieve self-sufficiency in food grains, to expand basic industries and heavy machinery production plants, to create enough new jobs for India's exploding population, and to continue to reduce inequalities of wealth.

In a major policy speech before the economic and financial committee of the U.N. General Assembly in October 1960, Nehru suggested that the abolition of want in the world is more vital than disarmament. He endorsed a proposal of the Indian delegation chairman, V. K. Krishna Menon, that the industrialized nations set aside 1 percent of their annual income for aid to underdeveloped nations, and that the money be channeled through the U.N. to keep it free of political overtones. The General Assembly later adopted a resolution recommending this transfer of capital.

Nehru has encouraged the investment of foreign private capital in India, citing its stability, its efficient and honest government, technical competence, growing market, and low labor costs. He has urged other nations to lower trade barriers to permit the importation of products manufactured by the new industries of India.

In September 1961 Nehru presented his credentials to President John F. Kennedy as India's new Ambassador to the United States, succeeding M. A. C. Chagla. In December India used military force to settle its long-standing dispute with Portugal over possession of Goa and two other small enclaves in India. Although the United States representative to the U.N., Adlai E. Stevenson, criticized India's use of violence, Ambassador Nehru quickly rose to his country's defense. He argued that the enclaves should naturally belong to India by reason of their geographical location and their predominantly Indian population. He said India had used the least violent method of settling the dispute by occupying the enclaves. "To those post-Goan converts to the creed of nonviolence for other people," he added, "I would submit . . . that if they studied the doctrine of Ahimsa (a word mistranslated into English as nonviolence), they would discover that it does not consist of nonaction or passivity or being pushed around or being deprived of one's rights without resistance, and it does not exclude the use of physical force. The Government of India retains an Army, an Air Force, and a Navy —and these are not for show."

As Ambassador, Nehru has advocated his country's neutralism. His first statement at his new post in Washington defended the failure of the nonaligned nations to criticize the resumption of nuclear tests by the Soviet Union. "We have been very categorical on the resumption of tests. We are against tests anywhere at any time," he said. "However, we rather hesitate to point a finger at anybody."

At present two major problems preoccupy India: the continuing dispute between India and Pakistan over the possession of Kashmir, a state now a part of northern India; and, more vital to India's very survival, the India-Red China military conflict that began in the fall of 1962 on India's northern borders. Nehru has assiduously negotiated for arms aid from the United States, and in the fall of 1962 some $5,000,000 in small arms and equipment was shipped to India. Observers in the United States speculated that India might modify her neutral stand as a result of prompt Western help in countering Red Chinese aggression. Nehru said that although the circumstances would indeed modify Indian foreign policy, he could not predict how.

In July 1935 B. K. Nehru married Hungarian-born Magdalena Friedman, whom he met while he was studying in England. They have three sons, Ashok, Aditya, and Anil. The Ambassador is six feet in height and has broad shoulders and a slim waist. He is known for being absent-minded about small details. His recreations are playing bridge and reading and he belongs to the Gymkhana Club in New Delhi and to the Metropolitan Club in Washington.

References

N Y Times p5 N 22 '62 por
Washington (D.C.) Post C pl S 13 '61 por
Asia Who's Who (1960)
International Who's Who, 1962-63
Who's Who in America, 1962-63

NIKOLAYEVNA-TERESHKOVA, VALENTINA (VLADIMIROVNA) *See* Tereshkova, Valentina (Vladimirovna)

NUFFIELD, 1ST VISCOUNT *See* Morris, William Richard, 1st Viscount Nuffield

NUREYEV, RUDOLF (HAMETOVICH) (noo-rā'yĕv) Mar. 17, 1938- Ballet dancer
Address: b. The Royal Ballet, Covent Garden, London, England

The most exciting young danseur in the West today is Rudolf Nureyev, now a principal dancer with Britain's Royal Ballet and a frequent and favorite partner of the company's prima ballerina assoluta, Dame Margot Fonteyn. Originally a member of Leningrad's Kirov Ballet, Nureyev broke away from the touring Kirov troupe at Le Bourget airport in Paris in June 1961 and sought asylum in France. Audiences and critics alike have welcomed this extraordinary artist with unstinting, sometimes even hysterical, praise; many have compared him to the legendary Nijinsky. He is noted for his seemingly effortless catlike leaps; his exceptional *ballon;* a quality of romance and mystery that he projects from the stage; and his total absorption while dancing. "When I dance with him," Dame Margot has said, "I see not Nureyev but the character of the ballet. I don't see, as I do with others, a man I know and talk to every day. I see the ballet. He is how I would like to be, and he makes it easier for me to dance as I wish." Nureyev has taken roles in all the major classical ballets. In the spring of 1963 he made a tour of North America with the Royal Ballet.

Richard Avedon

RUDOLF NUREYEV

Rudolf Hametovich **Nureyev** was born on March 17, 1938 on a train that was just passing Irkutsk on Lake Baikal en route to Vladivostok, where his father, a soldier, was then stationed. He has three older sisters, Rosa, Rosida, and Lida. Through both parents he is descended from the Tartars, a people whom he has characterized as volatile, passionate, and sensuous with "a curious mixture of tenderness and brutality." Soon after his birth the family moved to Moscow; when their Moscow home was bombed they settled in Ufa, capital of the Republic of Bashkir. Throughout the war they shared a small room with two other families (which may explain why, to this day, Nureyev hates crowds) and lived on meager rations consisting mostly of potatoes. As a child Nureyev was lonely and unhappy. His one solace was music, to which, from the age of two, he would listen by the hour.

When he was seven Rudolf Nureyev learned some Bashkir folk dances at school and helped to entertain wounded soldiers in hospitals. Later, as a member of the Pioneers (Scouts), he learned folk dances of all the Russian republics and gave "folkloric" performances in villages surrounding Ufa. Meanwhile, at the age of eight Nureyev had seen his first ballet, and from that time on he was possessed with the desire to become a dancer. It was not until he was eleven, however, that he had his first ballet lessons. He studied first with Udeltsova, who had been a member of the corps de ballet of Diaghilev's Ballets Russes, and then with Vaitovich, a former soloist with the Kirov.

Envisioning for his son a more secure and "manly" profession, Hamet Nureyev forbade him to continue dancing. As a result the boy had to deceive his family in order to keep on with folk dancing and with walk-on parts at the Ufa Opera that he first obtained at the age of fourteen. Finally leaving school at fif-

NUREYEV, RUDOLF—*Continued*

teen, he supported himself by his Ufa Opera work and by teaching folk dancing at workers' collectives. The following year the director of the Ufa Opera allowed him to dance in the corps de ballet and to attend the dancers' classes. Nureyev had an excellent memory and could reproduce a dance after it had been demonstrated to him once.

When he was seventeen Nureyev was selected to go to Moscow to dance in a folk festival celebrating Bashkir art. While there, he auditioned for and was accepted by the Bolshoi Ballet School, but because the Bolshoi did not maintain a student residence he could not afford to attend. Instead he auditioned for the Leningrad Ballet School, which trains dancers for the Kirov Ballet, the successor to the great Imperial Maryinsky. He was accepted into an advanced grade and in August 1955 entered that "coveted temple of dancing."

Studying ballet with Alexander Pushkin, who became like a "second father" to him, Nureyev soon outstripped his fellow students. He learned parts in *Swan Lake, The Nutcracker, Giselle, Le Corsaire,* and other classical ballets, and, as the best student in his class, was given the right to dance in public leading roles in nine full-length ballets. At the end of his third year he took part in a national classical ballet contest in Moscow, for which he prepared a pas de deux from *Le Corsaire,* variations from *Gayane,* and a pas de deux from *Esmeralda.* He won the contest, and for the first time in his life an audience demanded an encore—for the *Le Corsaire* pas de deux, which he later performed in a ballet film, *A Leap by the Soul.*

As a result of his winning the contest Nureyev was offered upon graduation the rank of soloist (skipping the usual stage in the corps de ballet) by the Stanislavsky, a provincial ballet; by the Kirov; and by the Bolshoi. He chose the Kirov because he felt that the Bolshoi's policies were more traditional and restrictive and that it turned dancers into "mere athletes, record breakers with marvelous muscles of steel but no heart." His first major performance with the Kirov was in *Laurencia,* and he was also seen in *Le Corsaire, Taras Bulba, Giselle,* and *Don Quixote.* He danced in the provinces, appeared at International Youth Festivals in Vienna and Berlin, and in June 1960 danced before Khrushchev and other government officials in Bulganin's villa some sixty miles from Moscow.

When the Kirov decided to tour England and France in the spring of 1961, it was felt that Konstantin Sergeyev, the company's director and leading dancer, was too old to appeal to Western audiences. Nureyev was chosen to replace him as leading dancer, and within a month he perfected his own roles and added the parts of Florimund and the Blue Bird in *The Sleeping Beauty* and Solor in *La Bayadère* to his repertoire. His success with Western critics was immediate. After his first performance in Paris in *La Bayadère,* a French reviewer hailed him as "the Kirov's cosmonaut."

Despite his artistic success, Nureyev had been in trouble with the Kirov authorities ever since his student days. He never participated in group activities, showing an "abnormal taste for solitude"; he refused to join the Communist Youth League (Komsomol) because he felt himself to be apolitical; he criticized the artistic policies of the company as being too static; and he associated with visiting foreign artists. As a result he was unpopular with many of his fellow dancers and harassed by his superiors. Furthermore, as he recalls in his autobiography, *Nureyev* (Dutton, 1963), he, like other Kirov dancers of his rank, appeared on the stage rather infrequently since the troupe gave only fifteen performances a month and many soloists and first dancers were entitled to leading roles. Thus, a desire to dance more, to advance in status more rapidly than was possible at the rigidly stratified Kirov, and to try all kinds of roles—modern and classical—abroad as well as in Russia contributed in large part to his dissatisfactions at home.

In Paris, Nureyev continued to do as he liked, making friends among foreigners and wandering about the city by himself. On June 17, 1961, as the Kirov dancers assembled at Le Bourget Airport before their departure for London, he learned that he was not to accompany them but was to be sent back to Moscow, presumably to be disciplined for "insubordination, non-assimilation, and dangerous individualism." At that instant he decided to seek asylum in Paris. He eluded the Russian security men, jumped over an airport railing, and received sanctuary from the French police. Nureyev has emphasized that a desire for personal freedom and artistic, rather than political, considerations led him to make the break. Eleven months later, in March 1962, Alexander Bland wrote in *Dance Magazine,* "Although he clearly suffers from his total isolation . . . he seems outwardly quite undismayed. He exudes the courage—both moral and physical—which comes from long years of independence and loneliness, together (as he frankly admits) with a strong dose of obstinate egoism. 'I do not like to be pressed,' he says."

Once in the West, Nureyev faced the problem of finding a job and—what was more important—a dance company that would nurture his talents. Two days after the airport incident, he signed a contract with the International Ballet of the Marquis de Cuevas, and on June 23, 1961 he danced Florimund in *The Sleeping Beauty* in Paris. He toured Israel and Italy with the Cuevas company, but his association with it was not a happy one artistically, and in December he did not renew his contract. Meanwhile in the summer of 1961 he had visited Copenhagen, where he met the dancer Erik Bruhn and spoke by telephone with Margot Fonteyn, who had called to invite him to appear in a gala benefit in London in the fall.

On November 2, 1961 Nureyev made his London debut at the gala benefit for the Royal Academy of Dancing. He danced the *Black Swan* pas de deux with Rosella Hightower and a solo especially choreographed for him by Frederick Ashton to Scriabin's *Poème Tragique.* The audience turned the occasion into a demonstration of political sympathy, greeting his every appearance on stage with an ovation. According to a Manchester *Guardian* reviewer (November 3, 1961), he put on a "wonderful display of pyrotechnics," but it was difficult to disentangle his dancing from its "hysterical reception."

Upon his return to the Continent, Nureyev, with Erik Bruhn, Rosella Hightower, and Sonia Arova, formed an independent group to present ballet programs. The two men each contributed some choreography as well as dancing; Nureyev prepared a new version of the adagio in the pas de deux from *The Nutcracker* and a pas de quatre to music by Glazunov. On the second of two Paris appearances, Bruhn pulled a leg muscle. In an outstanding display of stamina and technique, Nureyev danced his own roles and most of Bruhn's as well. Shortly afterwards, on January 19, 1962, he replaced Bruhn on the *Bell Telephone Hour* on American television, appearing with Maria Tallchief in the pas de deux from *Flower Festival in Genzano*. He again danced on the *Bell Telephone Hour* in September 1962, the pas de deux from *Le Corsaire* with Lupe Serrano.

In February 1962 Nureyev appeared for the first time in a full-length production in England, opposite Margot Fonteyn in the Royal Ballet production of *Giselle*. He made his American stage debut in March 1962 with the Ruth Page Chicago Opera Ballet at the Brooklyn Academy of Music, dancing with Sonia Arova the pas de deux from *Don Quixote,* to which he had contributed some of his own choreography. "Nureyev is unquestionably one of the most compelling dance figures of our era," Walter Terry wrote in the New York *Herald Tribune* (March 12, 1962). "In 'Don Q.' he displayed altitudes in leaps and jumps which recalled the legends of Nijinsky. His leg beats were brilliant . . . and his partnering of Miss Arova was both technically secure and elegant." The following October, Nureyev again appeared with the Ruth Page company, in Chicago, as the leading male dancer in the Polovetsian Dances of the opera *Prince Igor*. He also partnered Sonia Arova in Lehar's *The Merry Widow;* the pas de deux from *Le Corsaire.* to which he added some original choreography; and the *Flower Festival in Genzano.*

At the Royal Opera House in London in May 1962 Nureyev danced with Yvette Chauviré in *The Sleeping Beauty* and *Giselle.* "Nureyev brought the house down with a bravura variation danced with the most extraordinary ease," Arnold Haskell wrote of *The Sleeping Beauty* performance in *The Ballet Annual. 1963.* "This showed his considerable powers as a dancer and his exceptional grace. . . . Nureyev is no instinctive dancer but a highly conscious artist whose every gesture is carefully planned." At the end of June 1962 Nureyev partnered Arova in *Swan Lake.*

It was not until late in 1962 that Nureyev found a congenial permanent company: at that time he joined the Royal Ballet in the specially created position of "permanent guest artist" (only British Commonwealth subjects can become regular members). During the ensuing season he and Margot Fonteyn scored notable

triumphs in *Flower Festival in Genzano, Le Corsaire,* and *Les Sylphides.* In March 1963 they danced the première of *Marguerite and Armand,* a short ballet based on Dumas' *The Lady of the Camellias* that Frederick Ashton had choreographed especially for them to Liszt's Piano Sonata in B minor. On opening night Fonteyn and Nureyev took twenty curtain calls and bowed to ten minutes of applause. The London *Times* called Nureyev "an Armand of wild dreams, fierce authority and depths of feeling the choreographer can plumb but not fully chart."

In the spring of 1963 Nureyev accompanied the Royal Ballet on its North American tour. In New York he danced the leading roles in *Giselle, Swan Lake, Marguerite and Armand,* and *Les Sylphides* and was seen in the Blue Bird pas de deux from *The Sleeping Beauty,* the pas de deux from *Flower Festival in Genzano,* and the *Le Corsaire* pas de deux. "Nureyev is always a magnetic personality, and, at his best, a magnificent artist of the dance," Allen Hughes wrote in the New York *Times* (May 14, 1963). "Some of his technical accomplishments in these past weeks have equaled those of any male ballet dancer performing today, and he has infused them with a poetic radiance that has lifted them far above the level of mere athletic tricks."

Nureyev is small, slender, and well-proportioned. with high cheekbones; blue-gray, slightly slanted eyes; and chestnut-colored hair, which he wears somewhat long. Off-stage, according to Alexander Bland, "he is modest, elegant, courteous. and unpunctual." Nureyev speaks English fairly well. He is enthusiastic about modern ballet and admires the work of Alvin Ailey, Martha Graham, and especially George Balanchine, with whom he would like to work. "One thing is certain," according to Bland. "Nureyev is not just one more dancer of first-class talent. He is something much more rare. He is one of those strange, haunted artists that ballet throws up from time to time, dancers through whom some intense, urgent message seems to be passing. Such individual performers are not always the easiest to fit into organizations, or even into society. But what they have to contribute is unique."

References

Dance Mag 36:42+ Mr '62 pors
Look 27:26+ Jl 16 '63 pors
Nureyev, Rudolf. Nureyev (1963)

NYERERE, JULIUS K(AMBARAGE) (nyă-rā'rē) 1923(?)- President of the Republic of Tanganyika
Address: Dar es Salaam, Republic of Tanganyika

Once described by an American official at the United Nations as a "symbol of African hopes, African dignity, and African successes." President Julius K. Nyerere of the Republic of Tanganyika is among the most respected and influential leaders of the newly emerging nations of Africa. A former schoolteacher, he has guided Tanganyika through the various steps toward complete inde-

JULIUS K. NYERERE

pendence since becoming the head of the Tanganyika African National Union in 1954. Nyerere, who is a Socialist and Pan-Africanist, is a force for moderation and racial harmony and has worked in close co-operation with the British authorities in his homeland. He is considered the possible head of any future federation of East and Central African states.

Tanganyika, a former German colony in eastern Africa, came under a League of Nations mandate administered by Great Britain after World War I and was made a United Nations trusteeship territory in 1946. Of its estimated population of 9,237,000 some 98 percent are African, most of them of Bantu stock, belonging to about 120 tribes. Tanganyika lacks the racial tensions that mark some of the other African countries, and its African majority lives in relative peace and harmony with the European, Indian, and Arab minorities. On May 1, 1961 Tanganyika was accorded internal self-government and Nyerere became Prime Minister. Complete independence was granted on December 9, 1961, and a year later the Republic of Tanganyika was proclaimed, with Nyerere as President. Tanganyika is a member of the United Nations, and it retains its ties with Great Britain in the Commonwealth of Nations.

A native of Butiama, on the eastern shore of Lake Victoria, Julius Kambarage Nyerere was born about 1923 (other sources give the year of his birth variously as 1918, 1921, or 1922), one of the twenty-six children of the aristocratic but illiterate chief of the Zanaki tribe, Nyerere Burito, who had several wives. The present chief of the tribe is Wanzagi Nyerere, a half-brother of Julius Nyerere. As a boy, Nyerere herded sheep and led a typical tribal life. He had practically no contact with the civilization of the white man until the age of twelve, when he

entered a Native Authority school at Musoma, twenty-six miles from his home. After completing his elementary schooling in three years instead of the customary four, he obtained his secondary education at a Roman Catholic mission school at Tabora in the Central Province. He was baptized in the Roman Catholic faith at the age of twenty.

Having been selected for teacher training, Nyerere entered Makerere College (now the University College of East Africa) in Kampala, Uganda in 1943. There he organized the Tanganyika Students' Association and the Makerere branch of the Tanganyika African Association, a nonpolitical organization founded by British civil servants in 1929. After receiving his teaching diploma in 1945, Nyerere returned to Tabora as a teacher at St. Mary's mission school. In 1949 he became the first Tanganyikan to study at a British university when he entered the University of Edinburgh on a government scholarship. Upon obtaining his M.A. degree in history and economics he returned to Tanganyika in October 1952 and became a teacher at the St. Francis school in Pugu near Dar es Salaam.

As his interest in politics grew, Nyerere renewed his ties with the Tanganyika African Association and was elected its president in 1953. Under his guidance the association developed into a political organization. On July 7, 1954 it became the Tanganyika African National Union (TANU) and adopted a new constitution, with the central goal of preparing Tanganyika's natives for self-government and independence. The constitution stressed peace, equality, and racial harmony, while opposing tribalism, isolationism, and discrimination. The Governor of Tanganyika, Sir Edward Twining, appointed Nyerere in 1954 to a temporary seat on the Tanganyika legislative council. As a member of the council Nyerere called attention to the limited educational opportunities of the native population and proposed that council representatives be elected instead of appointed. In February 1955 he presented the program of TANU to the Trusteeship Council of the United Nations in New York.

When the headmaster at St. Francis requested that he give up politics, Nyerere decided to follow his conscience and gave up his teaching position instead, to devote his full time to a political career. (He later resumed teaching on a part-time basis.) Touring the country in a battered Land-Rover, he solicited support for the program of TANU, which attained a membership of some 250,000 within a year. Despite his emphatic disavowal of violence, Nyerere was forbidden to speak in public early in 1957 because some of his speeches were termed inflammatory by police. "I am a troublemaker, because I believe in human rights strongly enough to be one," Nyerere told a correspondent for the New York Times (March 31, 1957). He said that his movement would resort to civil disobedience if necessary to attain its goals.

Nominated again as a representative member of the legislative council in 1957, Nyerere resigned after a brief period when it became apparent that the government was unwilling to consider his demands for self-government. Later, relations between Nyerere and the British authorities improved, and in October 1958 he publicly accepted the new Governor, Sir Richard Turnbull, as the man who would guide Tanganyika to self-government.

Meanwhile, in September 1958, some 28,500 voters who met educational and income qualifications went to the polls in Tanganyika's first quasi-democratic elections. Under a "parity" system of representation, each voted for one candidate of each of the three major racial groups—African, Asian, and European. Although Nyerere was highly critical of the system, his TANU party was victorious over the European-backed United Tanganyika party as well as over the radical African National Congress. "Independence will follow as surely as the tickbirds follow the rhino," Nyerere said upon hearing the result.

After the second stage of the elections was completed in February 1959, twenty-eight of the thirty elected seats in the sixty-four-member legislative council were occupied by candidates supported by TANU. (The remaining thirty-four seats continued to be appointed by the Governor.) Although Nyerere declined to accept a ministry in the new government, he was the unquestioned leader of the multiracial elected members organization, which formed a permanent opposition within the legislative council. Under Nyerere's leadership an "unofficial government" also began to take form, to prepare the country for self-government.

In April 1959 Nyerere went to Zanzibar to attend a meeting of the Pan-African Freedom Movement of Eastern and Central Africa (PAFMECA), of which he had previously been elected president. There he was instrumental in bringing the Arab and African parties closer together. Speaking at a meeting of PAFMECA at Nairobi, Kenya in September 1959, he declared that Europeans and Asians were welcome to remain in Africa as equal citizens after independence was achieved.

Great Britain's new Colonial Secretary, Iain Macleod, announced in December 1959 that Tanganyika would be given virtual home rule in late 1960, under constitutional provisions that would include a legislature with a guaranteed African majority. Although Nyerere criticized the retention of income and literacy qualifications, as well as the reservation of a specific number of seats in the legislative council for the European and Asian minorities, the new plan was seen as a definite triumph for him and his party.

In the elections of August 30, 1960 TANU won seventy of the seventy-one seats in the new legislative assembly. Nyerere was sworn in as chief minister on September 3 and became the effective head of government under the new constitution, while Governor Turnbull continued to hold certain veto powers. At a meeting of Commonwealth Prime Ministers in London in March 1961 Nyerere joined other African leaders in denouncing the racist policies of the Union of South Africa and declared that if South Africa remained in the Commonwealth Tanganyika would never join. South Africa subsequently withdrew its membership.

Following a constitutional conference in March 1961, Colonial Secretary Macleod announced that Tanganyika would become internally self-governing on May 1 and totally independent in the

following December. Upon being sworn in as Prime Minister on May 1, 1961, Nyerere called upon his people to concern themselves with the pressing economic problems of the country and not to waste time in fighting colonialism, which had already been overthrown in Tanganyika. Visiting the United States in July 1961, Nyerere warned the West against giving military aid to African nations and called instead for help in fighting poverty, disease, and ignorance. He said that if adequate Western aid were not forthcoming, Tanganyika might be compelled to apply to the Soviet Union for assistance.

On December 9, 1961 Tanganyika obtained complete national independence within the British Commonwealth. When Tanganyika was unanimously accepted as the 104th U.N. member a few days later, Nyerere expressed some concern that his country's independence might slow efforts to attain an East African federation. On January 22, 1962 he resigned as Prime Minister and bestowed the office on his own nominee, former Minister without Portfolio Rashidi Kawawa. Although it was rumored that he was forced out by the more radical elements of his party, his national popularity and political influence appeared undiminished. He later declared that he had resigned to rebuild the TANU party and to "give the country a new purpose" now that independence had been achieved.

The Tanganyika government announced on May 31, 1962 that in the coming December the country would become a republic within the Commonwealth. Following elections, in which Nyerere was chosen President by 97 percent of the vote, the Republic of Tanganyika was officially proclaimed on December 9, 1962—the first anniversary of national independence. The new constitution, modeled after that of Ghana, established a one-party state, outlawed strikes, and greatly increased Nyerere's personal power. A preventive detention act, aimed at curbing racist and antiforeign activities, had been passed by the legislature with Nyerere's approval a few months earlier.

Although Tanganyika appears to have attained a high degree of political stability, the new nation continues to be faced with many problems, notably with regard to economic development, education, medical services, and the shortage of qualified civil servants. In line with the TANU slogan *Uhuru na Kazi* (freedom and work), Nyerere has instituted a successful self-help program, under which roads, schools, clinics, communal farms, and other projects are being built by teams of volunteer workers. In late 1961 Nyerere inaugurated a three-year program for the improvement of agriculture, the exploration of mineral resources, and the expansion of light industry, aided financially by Great Britain, the United States, and West Germany. Nyerere has also pledged his efforts to preserve Tanganyika's wildlife.

Nyerere's "Bantu Socialism" is of the pragmatic rather than dogmatic variety. His conciliatory views on race relations are contained in his booklet *Barriers to Democracy*. Although he admires Ghana's President Kwame Nkrumah and the late Congolese Premier Patrice Lumumba, his policies are far less radical. He is said to have

NYERERE, JULIUS K.—*Continued*

been influenced in his moderate position by Indian Prime Minister Jawaharlal Nehru and by the late Mohandas Gandhi. "I have learned how to be a moderate through observing the inflexible behavior of the Europeans," Nyerere once told Rolf Italiaander (*The New Leaders of Africa*, Prentice-Hall, 1961).

While he was still a teacher, Julius K. Nyerere married a woman from another tribe in an open ceremony, in order to de-emphasize tribal loyalties. His wife, the former Maria Magige, runs a small shop in the native quarter of Dar es Salaam and is president of the Tanganyika Council of Women. They have five sons and one daughter. A slightly built man with graying hair and a small moustache, Nyerere is five feet six and a half inches tall and weighs 125 pounds. Although he is a practising Catholic, his sawed-off front teeth indicate his pagan tribal background. He has been described as mild-mannered and unassuming, with a ready wit and a good sense of humor.

A forceful speaker, given to fiery phrases, he is fluent in both English and Swahili. In 1963 his translation of Shakespeare's *Julius Caesar* into Swahili was published in Dares Salaam. He is a chain smoker and likes an occasional Scotch and soda or gin and tonic, and he claims that he has "all the vices." Having little use for pomp, he prefers to dress informally, in sports shirts, but on public celebrations he wears his native dress. He is a tireless worker and seldom has time for recreation. In 1963 he became the first chancellor of the University of East Africa, formed by three colleges in Uganda, Kenya, and Tanganyika. In 1959 Duquesne University in Pittsburgh, Pennsylvania conferred upon him an honorary LL.D. degree, as a statesman and scholar whose determination and vision had "given new hope to men long weary of racial strife and unresolved national differences."

References

Manchester Guardian p6 My 1 '61 por
N Y Times p12 F 11 '60 por
N Y Times Mag p29+ D 3 '61 pors
Newsweek 58:39+ D 18 '61 por
Sat Eve Post 234:13+ D 2 '61 por
Toronto Globe and Mail p7 D 8 '61 por
International Who's Who, 1962-63
Italiaander, Rolf. The New Leaders of Africa (1961)
Melady, Thomas P. Profiles of African Leaders (1961)
Segal, Ronald. Political Africa (1961); African Profile (1962)
Who's Who, 1963

O'CONNOR, EDWIN (GREENE) July 29, 1918- Writer

Address: b. c/o Little, Brown & Co., 34 Beacon St., Boston 6, Mass.; h. 48 Beacon St., Boston 6, Mass.

The winner of the 1962 Pulitzer Prize for fiction, Edwin O'Connor, has often been cast in the role of spokesman for the Irish in America as a result of his having written *The Last Hurrah*

(1956) and *The Edge of Sadness* (1961). In these two novels he has recorded his informed observations of middle-class Irish-American Catholics. O'Connor writes with humor, compassion, and understanding of the ambiguities of life and the inadequacies of men in a way that transcends specific scene and time, giving his work a universality that accounts for his popularity as a writer.

Edwin Greene O'Connor, the son of John Vincent O'Connor, a doctor, and Mary (Greene) O'Connor, was born in Providence, Rhode Island on July 29, 1918. He spent his early life in Woonsocket and attended public school there. After graduating from La Salle Academy in Providence he enrolled at the University of Notre Dame. O'Connor had intended to study journalism but changed his major to literature at the persuasion of Professor Frank O'Malley (to whom he later dedicated *The Edge of Sadness*), who informed him: "You can learn all you need to learn about journalism in six months. English literature takes a little longer."

Upon his graduation from Notre Dame in 1939 O'Connor became a radio announcer and worked in Providence, Palm Beach, Buffalo, and Hartford. "He wrote and produced radio shows," Edward Weeks, editor of the *Atlantic Monthly*, once commented, "and in the process learned to write with his ears." This ability, plus his own Irish warmth and wit, is evident in the pages of *The Last Hurrah*, of which Clifton Fadiman has written: "Today I find myself remembering not its political theme . . . nor its story . . . but its talk, its spate of wild, outrageous, *useless* talk cascading down every page, talk indulged for its own sake."

During World War II, O'Connor was stationed in Boston as an information officer with the United States Coast Guard, and he liked it so much that he adopted Boston as his home. Returning to civilian life in 1945, he worked for a year as writer and producer of radio shows for the Yankee Network. Then, relying on his savings and on an offer to write a daily television column for a Boston newspaper, O'Connor decided to take his chances as a free-lance writer. His first published works were articles about radio and television for the *Atlantic Monthly*'s "Accent on Living" department from June 1946 through February 1947, and his first short story, "The Gentle, Perfect Knight," appeared in the *Atlantic* in September 1947. This marked the beginning of a happy association between O'Connor and the *Atlantic Monthly*. Its editor, Edward Weeks, has explained: "We soon learned that he is a fastidious worker who goes over and over his manuscripts before submitting them, with the result that there is very little editing left to do."

In 1951 O'Connor's first novel, *The Oracle*, was published by Harper & Brothers. With sometimes biting satire it deals with a comic crisis in the life of a self-inflated radio broadcaster. The book earned praise but not much money in the United States, but it fared somewhat better in Britain, bringing O'Connor enough funds to finance a visit to Dublin, his favorite town after Boston. Returning from Ireland, he wrote a second novel, which fell so far short of his own standards that he suppressed the manuscript.

On his third try O'Connor produced *The Last Hurrah* (Little, 1956), which won the $5,000 Atlantic Prize, was chosen by the Book-of-the-Month Club, and immediately reached the best-seller lists. *The Last Hurrah* is concerned with the last campaign of Frank Skeffington, an aging Irish-American political boss in a city that, despite the author's denials, might be Boston. The book was widely acclaimed as one of the finest American novels ever written about politics and was described by a writer for *Life* as "both an affectionate farewell to—and an exposé of—the old-time city boss who, in his most flamboyant manifestations, was often an Irish-American."

Not all reviewers reacted favorably to *The Last Hurrah*, however. Anthony West, for example, writing in the *New Yorker* (February 11, 1956), said that O'Connor had sentimentalized Skeffington, a "barbaric figure," into a "fairy godmother of widows and orphans" and had soft-pedaled "mean vices" into seeming virtues. But John V. Kelleher pointed out in the New York *Times Book Review* (February 5, 1956), Mr. O'Connor . . . has no doubts about what Skeffington cost the city or the Irish. . . . He also makes it clear, however, that the tragedy is collective, the failure of the Irish as a whole to have the courage of their own qualities and to make better use of them." Appearing in an election year, *The Last Hurrah* was soon viewed as a *roman à clef*, and O'Connor spent considerable time denying that the character of Skeffington was based on James Michael Curley, four times Mayor of Boston and former Governor of Massachusetts. In 1958 O'Connor's book was adapted into a motion picture with the same title, starring Spencer Tracy as Frank Skeffington.

Presumably as a change of pace O'Connor next wrote *Benjy: A Ferocious Fairy Tale* (Little, 1957), illustrated by Ati Forberg. Regarded by some reviewers as an oblique attack upon Momism, *Benjy* is dedicated to "all readers of all ages who have never, at any time, been good little boys or, for that matter, good little girls." Four years later *The Edge of Sadness* appeared (Little, 1961), in which O'Connor wrote of the Irish who are socially and politically secure. Through the eyes of Father Hugh Kennedy, a reformed alcoholic priest, are seen three generations of Irish-Americans: Charlie Carmody, a bouncy octogenarian who all but dominates the book; the Carmody children, Father Hugh's contemporaries; and Ted, the conformist grandchild, who represents the trend of the future. Although most reviewers praised the novel's craftsmanship, some found it rather slick and thin in substance. *The Edge of Sadness* became a best seller, and in May 1962 it was awarded the Pulitzer Prize for fiction. Lewis Nichols, writing "In and Out of Books" for the New York *Times Book Review* (May 20, 1962), remarked that the Pulitzer Prize had gone to the "right writer—if for the wrong book," since he felt *The Last Hurrah* was better than *The Edge of Sadness*.

In May 1963 O'Connor completed his first play, *I Was Dancing*, a light comedy about a retired vaudeville hoofer. Some months later he announced that instead of having it produced as a play, he would first bring it out as a novel,

Paul Berg

EDWIN O'CONNOR

to be published by Atlantic-Little, Brown & Company in the spring of 1964.

Often compared to Dickens because of the warmth and vitality of his characterizations, O'Connor has an almost perfect ear for the lilt and cadence of Irish-American speech and a gift of mimicry that he often demonstrates in a rich brogue for the delectation of his friends and, occasionally, of a lecture audience. Dedicated to producing fiction of high quality, he re-reads writers with similarly high standards, and in the list of his favorite authors Russian writers predominate: Dostoevski, Tolstoy, Gogol, and Turgenev. His English choices include Charles Dickens and Jane Austen. Among his favorite contemporaries are T. S. Eliot, J. F. Powers, J. D. Salinger, and Evelyn Waugh. O'Connor considers it important for a writer to draw upon his imagination instead of relying upon personal experiences. In an interview with George Ryan (*Information,* December 1961) he said: "I'm not much for autobiographical novels in general. Some of them are powerful. But after a writer has done one, he usually has exhausted his material, and from that point on, he may be in danger of doing the same thing over and over again."

O'Connor's friends include literary critics, Boston newspapermen, and a number of Harvard faculty members. He was very close, as friend and editorial adviser, to the late Fred Allen, and he is at present editing a collection of Allen's letters. In addition to the 1962 Pulitzer Prize for fiction, his honors include the Golden Book Award of the Catholic Writers Guild (1957) for *The Last Hurrah* and the Catholic Press Institute Award (1962). Tall and trim in appearance, with blue eyes and blond hair, O'Connor is described as a man with a genial disposition and a warm smile. He is a Roman Catholic.

(Continued next page)

O'CONNOR, EDWIN—*Continued*

On September 2, 1962 he was married to Mrs. Veniette Caswell Weil in Holy Cross Cathedral, Boston.

References

N Y Herald Tribune p14 My 8 '62 por
N Y Times p32 My 8 '62 por
Newsweek 50:118 O 21 '57 por
Who's Who in America, 1962-63

ODETS, CLIFFORD July 18, 1906-Aug. 14, 1963

Playwright; film writer and director; known for his plays of social consciousness, including *Waiting for Lefty* (1935), *Awake and Sing* (1935), and *Golden Boy* (1937). See *Current Biography* (November) 1941.

Obituary

N Y Times p27 Ag 16 '63

ODLUM, MRS. FLOYD B(OSTWICK) *See* Cochran, Jacqueline

OHLIN, LLOYD E(DGAR) Aug. 27, 1918-

Sociologist; educator

Address: b. Columbia University School of Social Work, 2 E. 91st St., New York 28; h. 6 Sunset Dr., Scarsdale, N.Y.

A sociologist who specializes in criminology and corrections, Lloyd E. Ohlin has in recent years addressed his attention to youthful offenders rather than to adult criminals, as he did formerly. A special consultant on juvenile delinquency to the United States Department of Health, Education, and Welfare from 1961 to 1962, he helped to plan and initiate Mobilization for Youth, a multimillion-dollar experimental project to combat juvenile delinquency, which seeks to remold social patterns of New York City's Lower East Side to create better opportunities for the youth who live in that area. Ohlin has been a professor of sociology at the Columbia University School of Social Work (formerly the New York School of Social Work) since 1956 and the director of the school's research center since 1962. From 1953 to 1956 he was the director of the Center for Education and Research in Corrections at the University of Chicago.

Lloyd Edgar Ohlin, one of the three children of Emil Ohlin, a bakery proprietor, and Elise (Nelson) Ohlin, was born in Belmont, Massachusetts on August 27, 1918. After graduating from Belmont High School in 1936 he enrolled at Brown University, where he specialized in sociology and psychology and ran for the track team. A James Wayland Scholar and a member of Phi Beta Kappa, he graduated from Brown with the B.A. degree in 1940. While studying for his master's degree at Indiana University he worked as a research assistant on a prediction study of marital success and failure from 1940 to 1941 and as an instructor in sociology, teaching two introductory courses, from 1941 to 1942. He received his M.A. degree in sociology from In-

diana University in 1942. Two men whom he credits with influencing the direction of his career are Edwin Sutherland, who was a professor of criminology and head of the sociology department at Indiana University, and Ernest Burgess, whom Ohlin met at the University of Chicago, where Burgess was a professor of sociology.

From December 1942 through November 1945 Ohlin served with the counterintelligence corps of the United States Army in Europe, advancing in rank from private to technical sergeant. Returning to civilian life, he began studying for the doctorate at the University of Chicago, from March 1946 to September 1947. (He received the Ph.D. degree from the university in 1954.) In the fall of 1947 Ohlin became a sociologist-actuary with the Illinois Parole and Pardon Board at Joliet Penitentiary, where he interviewed inmates, prepared case materials for parole board dockets, and did research in parole prediction. In January 1950 he was transferred to the Chicago office of the Illinois Parole and Pardon Board, as a supervising research sociologist, and for the next three years he did research on parole board decisions and on parole statistics and prediction; made follow-up studies of the military careers of paroled felons; and conducted an in-service training program for correctional workers.

In July 1953 Ohlin was named the director of the Center for Education and Research in Corrections at the University of Chicago, but before assuming his duties there he spent three months in Korea investigating problems of prisoner-of-war camps for the Human Resources Research Office of George Washington University. As director of the Center for Education and Research in Corrections from 1953 to 1956, Ohlin supervised research on probation and parole organizations and adult correctional institutions, which were studied to determine organizational structure, organizational change, and administrative and work practices. The study included an analysis of casework in correctional settings.

In 1955 Lloyd E. Ohlin was also employed as a part-time consultant to the sheriff of Cook County (Chicago) on correctional problems of the county jail, making a study of the changing structure and program organization of the jail under reform management. In addition, from 1955 to 1956 he acted as a part-time consultant on field research to the survey of the administration of criminal justice in the United States then being made by the American Bar Foundation. He was appointed a professor of sociology in September 1956 to teach in the doctoral program at the New York School of Social Work, but did not occupy the position until December of that year. During the fall of 1956 he helped to complete the first report of the American Bar Foundation survey; he later met with other members of an advisory committee to discuss fuller development of the survey's findings. (Publication of a detailed analysis of the results of the survey is scheduled for 1963.) Ohlin was also for several years a member of the advisory committee on the model penal code of the American Law Institute.

During his first semester at the New York School of Social Work Ohlin visited classes and read extensively in the literature of social work to prepare for his teaching responsibilities. He took part in a doctoral dissertation seminar and in a workshop on the problems of correctional organization and taught some sessions of a course on community organization. In the summer of 1957 he was one of the leaders of an institute at the school on detached group work programs. He later taught a course in delinquency and advanced courses in group work, community organization, and the analysis of the processes of social change. During the fall semester of 1959-60 he was on leave from teaching.

In the 1950's, as the rate and severity of juvenile crime increased, the need to understand the causes of juvenile delinquency and the means to control it became urgent. Turning from adult corrections to the study of young offenders, Ohlin became a leading researcher in the field. In the fall of 1957, at the school's new research center, he began to direct, with Richard A. Cloward, a comparative study of institutions for juvenile offenders, a three-year project sponsored by the Ford Foundation. Observers placed in boys' institutions talked with both inmates and staff in an effort to understand the social patterns of the inmates and the effect on it of staff organization and type of institution. "As in the adult prison," Ohlin has explained (New York Post, June 9, 1961), "we found that psychiatric and social work treatment was resisted because of a strong anti-administration culture among the inmates. And also as with the adults we found a tremendous fear of the future on the part of the inmate —who would have him now that he carried the stigma of having been away? The training school and prison official can only do so much. Most of it is up to the public. And their attitudes have to change. Communities must be put in the position of solving their own problems."

Some of the knowledge gained from the study was disseminated at New York School of Social Work summer institutes on the analysis of delinquent subcultures and on the problems of correctional organization and treatment, in which Ohlin participated. Out of this and later studies, also, came a newly formulated etiology of juvenile delinquency, developed by Ohlin and Cloward in Delinquency and Opportunity: A Theory of Delinquent Gangs (Free Press, 1960). In the book they study gangs of adolescent boys of lower-class urban areas and theorize about the causes behind delinquent "rules of conduct" and the kinds of delinquency practised, such as theft, violence, and the use of drugs. "It is our view," they observe, "that pressures toward the formation of delinquent subcultures originate in marked discrepancies between culturally induced aspirations among lower-class youth and the possibilities of achieving them by legitimate means."

In other words, it is the view of the authors that while American society officially promises its members an equal opportunity to attain the good life—generally equated with material success—factors like education, social position, money, and talent limit the individual in his quest for advancement. Lower-class youth, lacking education and jobs, experience frustration because they are unable to attain the success that the American culture leads them to desire, and this frustration is often turned against society.

Harold Haliday Costain
LLOYD E. OHLIN

Ohlin believes that the responsibility for providing such boys with alternatives to antisocial behavior and with lawful opportunities to better their lot lies with the community itself and that any approach to the problem must be systematic and comprehensive. In 1959 he was one of those who initiated a pilot study that, after some years of planning, gave rise to a massive $12,600,000 project called Mobilization for Youth. Its aim is to reform the social patterns of an entire community to provide better opportunities and goals for its young people.

Announced by President John F. Kennedy in May 1962, Mobilization for Youth is an experimental project to be financed by federal, city, and private funds. It will first be tried out in the Lower East Side of New York City and, if successful there, will serve as a pattern for other cities. Involved in the project will be an urban youth service corps absorbing about 1,000 unemployed out-of-school youth; a youth jobs center for counseling and job placement; revised curricula tailored to "slum children in slum schools"; homework help and reading clinics; three coffee shops for young people, emphasizing cultural activities; an adventure corps for boys nine to sixteen; a pilot narcotics demonstration program; neighborhood service centers for casework for families; classes for adults; neighborhood councils for area improvement; and a training program in behavioral sciences. Recently asked to comment on a current issue in his field, Ohlin said: "I am greatly concerned that more effective work be done to study the processes by which the deteriorated areas in our cities can be made more habitable places for families, and particularly the youth, and I think the most promising work in that area of youth problems is addressed to programs which serve to redevelop the whole structure of youth services and opportunities in these areas in the center of the city."

(Continued next page)

OHLIN, LLOYD E.—*Continued*

From 1961 to 1962 Ohlin took a leave of absence from the New York School of Social Work to serve in Washington, D.C. as a special consultant on juvenile delinquency to the Department of Health, Education, and Welfare. He had served in 1958-59 as part-time director of the school's research center, and on his return from Washington for the beginning of the 1962-63 academic year he assumed full-time duties as director of the research center in addition to his teaching work.

Ohlin has written many articles for professional journals, and he has been a national adviser to *Children,* the journal of the Children's Bureau. He has counseled the National Institute of Mental Health and the Ford Foundation on the distribution of grants in the area of delinquency, and he was consultant to the Youth Study Center of Syracuse University in 1959. From 1956 to 1958 he was a member of the *ad hoc* committee on corrections of the Council on Social Work Education, and he was chairman of the Social Science Research Council committee on the sociocultural contexts of delinquency in 1959 and 1960. He has represented the American Sociological Society at the American Correctional Association, and in 1960 he was the chairman of a committee to create a section on criminology for the American Sociological Society. He has been a member of the professional council of the National Council on Crime and Delinquency (formerly the National Probation and Parole Association) since 1959.

Lloyd E. Ohlin married Helen Barbara Hunter on January 27, 1946. They have four children, Janet, George, Robert, and Nancy. Ohlin is a well-mannered and mild-tempered man with blue eyes and brown hair. He is a Democrat and has no church affiliation. In addition to reading he enjoys swimming, tennis, and sailing, and he plays a recorder with a recorder group.

References

N Y Post p60 Je 9 '61 por
N Y Times p28 Ag 16 '62 por

American Men of Science 10th ed (1960-62)

OLDS, IRVING S(ANDS) Jan. 22, 1887-Mar. 4, 1963 Corporation executive; lawyer; partner of the Case & White law firm of New York (since 1917); chairman of the board of United States Steel Corporation (1940-52). See *Current Biography* (October) 1948.

Obituary

N Y Times p36 Ap 1 '63

OLSEN, JOHN (SIGVARD) Nov. 6, 1892-Jan. 26, 1963 Comedian; as "Ole" Olsen was partner with Harold ("Chic") Johnson in famous vaudeville team that made biggest hit in *Hellzapoppin.* See *Current Biography* (September) 1940.

Obituary

N Y Times p36 Ap 1 '63

O'MAHONEY, JOSEPH C(HRISTOPHER) Nov. 5, 1884-Dec. 1, 1962 United States Senator from Wyoming (1933-52, 1954-61); liberal Democrat who campaigned for the regulation of "big business." See *Current Biography* (October) 1945.

Obituary

N Y Times p88 D 2 '62

ONASSIS, ARISTOTLE SOCRATES Jan. 15, 1906- Businessman; shipping executive

Address: b. Olympic Maritime, S.A., 17 Ave. de Monte Carlo, Monaco; h. Yacht Christina, Monte Carlo, Monaco

Aristotle Socrates Onassis, the Greek shipping magnate, is one of the world's wealthiest men. A pioneer in the use of oil tankers, he now owns more ships than are in the navies of some countries. Onassis began his legendary career at the age of sixteen with $60 in his pocket. Today he travels more than 100,000 miles a year to oversee his vast holdings and maintains his headquarters in an office overlooking the harbor of Monte Carlo, from which he can see the $3,000,000 yacht that he calls home. He also has residences in New York City, Long Island, Paris, Montevideo, and Buenos Aires, where he often entertains world leaders and the elite of international society.

Aristotle Socrates Onassis was born on January 15, 1906 in Smyrna, Turkey, the son of Homer Socrates and Penelope (Dologlou) Onassis. He has a sister, Artemis, and two half-sisters, Merope and Calliroy. His father was a wealthy and influential Greek tobacco merchant whose family had lived in the thriving port city for generations.

When Aristotle was five his mother died, and although his father remarried two years later, he was mostly reared by his religiously strict grandmother named Gethsemane. The boy attended private schools and in 1922, at the age of sixteen, graduated from the Evangeliki Scholi (Evangelical High School), the famous eighteenth-century Greek school of Smyrna, under British patronage.

That same year Turkish Nationalists under Kemal Ataturk captured Smyrna from the Greek army, which had been given administration of the city after World War I. The Turks sacked and burned the city and killed thousands of its Greek inhabitants. Three of Aristotle's uncles were hanged by the Turks, an aunt and her baby died in a burning church, and another uncle collapsed and died of shock. The boy's stepmother and sisters were allowed to go to Greece, and Aristotle worked for the release of his father from a concentration camp. The elder Onassis was later released through the intervention of the American vice-consul, and he and his son joined the rest of the family in Athens.

Back on the Greek mainland the elder Onassis tried to salvage what was left of his once prosperous business, but his drastically reduced income was not enough to support his own family of a wife and four children, and the widows of his brothers and their families. A family council decided that sixteen-year-old Socrates was the most likely candidate to rebuild the family's fortunes. The family scraped enough money together to buy him steamer passage to South America, and with $100 for cash reserves Aristotle Socrates Onassis sailed for Argentina. In September 1923 he arrived in Buenos Aires with $60— just enough to get himself settled in a bare cubicle in a cheap rooming house.

After a training course in switchboard operation Onassis got his first job, with the United River Plate Telephone Company. Since he handled the company's switchboard from 11 P.M. to 7 A.M., he had his days relatively free for other concerns. Obtaining help from a friend of his father and cutting his sleep to two or three hours a day, Onassis set up a modest tobacco importing business. He used his room in his boarding house as his office and tried to make Argentina (which had been importing most of its tobacco from the United States and Cuba) conscious of the merits of Oriental tobacco. Within two years he increased the amount of Oriental tobacco imported by Argentina from 10 to 35 percent. Soon leaving his post at the switchboard, he sold $2,000,000 in Oriental tobacco and made a 5 percent commission on each sale, or $100,000 in the two years.

In 1927 Onassis branched out into the manufacture of cigarettes. His exploits had not gone unnoticed in Athens, and in 1928 the Greek government commissioned him to negotiate a new trade treaty with Argentina. So pleased was the Greek government with the resulting treaty that it appointed Onassis Greek consul general in Buenos Aires as a reward. Continuing to expand his commercial interests, Onassis by this time traded in grains, wool, hides, and whale oil in addition to Oriental tobacco. By the time he was twenty-five Aristotle Socrates Onassis had made his first $1,000,000.

At the depth of the world depression, in 1932, Onassis went into the shipping business. Traveling to Canada he bought six freighters from a Montreal company for a total cost of $120,000— about one per cent of the price it had cost to build them eleven years earlier. Onassis put two of the ships into service and kept the other four in reserve until the freight market picked up and they could be chartered out profitably.

For the next three years the ships broke even, but gradually as the panic receded and freight and ship values improved Onassis kept adding to his fleet. In 1935 he decided to enter the promising oil tanker business. He went to Sweden and ordered the construction of what was then considered a mammoth oil tanker, the 15,500-ton *Ariston*. The *Ariston* was delivered to Onassis in 1938, the first oil tanker to be ordered and owned by a Greek.

By the time World War II broke out, Onassis had three tankers in operation and many cargo vessels of varying size and age. Part of his fleet was bottled up in the Baltic, but he promptly put the rest of his fleet at the disposal of the Allies and reaped impressive profits from the high wartime freight rates. By the time the war ended, he had added to his considerable fortune and had at his command a sizable fleet. When the United States put up for sale twenty-three surplus war tankers and freighters for about $20,000,000, Onassis helped to form several companies that

ARISTOTLE SOCRATES ONASSIS

bought the ships. In October 1953 the United States government charged Onassis with conspiracy to defraud in connection with the purchase, maintaining that Onassis used the American-owned companies as dummy fronts to get the ships in violation of a United States law that prohibited the sale of surplus ships to non-Americans. Onassis eventually paid a $7,000,000 fine and the charge was dropped.

The shipping executive continued to concentrate on building bigger and better "super-tankers" (tankers with more than 25,000 tons capacity). In 1954 alone he commissioned seventeen new tankers with a total capacity of more than 375,000 tons, and shipyards in the United States and West Germany were kept busy turning out tankers for the Greek shipping magnate. "Mr. Onassis is our biggest individual foreign customer," Ludwig Erhard, the West German Minister of Economics, said in 1954, pointing out that German shipyards had more than $70,000,000 in orders from various Onassis companies. In June 1954 the 47,000-ton *King Saud I* was launched in Hamburg, at that time the largest nonpassenger vessel in the world. Although Onassis owns one of the largest independent fleets in the world, his ships sail under the flags of tiny countries without maritime tradition. The ships are registered in Panama, Honduras, Costa Rica, Liberia, and Saudi Arabia, where ship registration fees and wages are low.

In 1948 Onassis decided to take a fling at the whaling business and reportedly cleared almost $8,500,000 in his first season. In 1954 Onassis' whaling fleet sailed into rough waters, however, when it defied the legality of a claim by the governments of Peru, Ecuador, and Chile that their territorial waters extended 200 miles from their coasts. The Peruvian navy seized the whaling ships, which were flying the Panamanian flag, on the high seas, and Onassis eventually paid Peru a $3,000,000 fine, an amount covered

ONASSIS, ARISTOTLE SOCRATES—*Cont.*

by his insurance. In 1956 he sold his whaling fleet to the Japanese.

Onassis broke into the international headlines again in 1953 when he became known as the Man Who Bought the Bank at Monte Carlo. Actually, far from wanting the bank, he was looking for an office near his chateau at Antibes, on the French Riviera, which was also close to Marseilles and Genoa on the Mediterranean, where many of his ninety-one ships were repaired. Since Monte Carlo's long vacant Winter Sporting Club, owned by the Casino, looked like a good prospect for an office building, Onassis asked the directors to rent him the place. "They wouldn't rent it to me, although it had been closed for twenty years. So I did something else," Onassis once explained. The "something else" was the purchase of controlling interest in the Société des Bains de Mer for $1,000,000. Besides the Sporting Club, the Société owned the Casino, the Hotel de Paris, three other hotels, a theater, the golf course at Montagel, and other choice real estate. Onassis subsequently moved the headquarters of his Société Olympique Maritime from its crowded offices in Paris to the more spacious quarters of the Sporting Club.

The Greek shipping executive, whose fortune has been estimated as high as $500,000,000, added another arm to his worldwide enterprises in 1956, when he was awarded a twenty-year contract to run Greece's state airline, a contract that gave him a concession to operate internal air communications on a monopoly basis. The following year Onassis incorporated the state airline as Olympic Airways.

In December 1946, at the age of forty, Aristotle Socrates Onassis married Athina (Tina) Livanos, the seventeen-year-old daughter of Stravros G. Livanos, a wealthy Greek shipowner in New York. Educated at Rosemary Hall in Connecticut and Miss Hewitt's Classes, she is a naturalized American citizen. By that marriage the couple had two children, a son, Alexander, and a daughter, Christina, who also are naturalized American citizens. The marriage was dissolved by divorce in June 1960. Onassis' former brother-in-law, Stavros Niarchos, who married the former Eugenie Livanos, has one of the largest private fleets in the world. The two men have been bitter business rivals and since World War II have been trying to outdo each other in the size of their tankers.

Onassis spends much of his time on his 1,800-ton yacht, *Christina*, a 325-foot vessel that has been called the most sumptuous privately owned yacht in the world. Originally a destroyer escort, it was converted by Onassis at a cost of $3,000,000. With quarters for twenty-five guests and a crew of forty-four, the *Christina* has teakwood decks, a swimming pool with a mosaic floor that can be raised to form a dance floor at the touch of a button, two El Grecos, marble and gold bathrooms, an amphibious airplane, an automobile, and four launches.

On the *Christina*, whose home port is Monte Carlo, "Ari," as Onassis is known to his intimates, does much of his entertaining. Sir Winston Churchill, an old friend, has gone on several Mediterranean cruises on the yacht *Christina*, as have other leaders in politics and the arts. In recent years Onassis has been linked romantically with the opera star Maria Callas, but both have denied any sentimental involvement.

Today Onassis claims both Greek and Argentine citizenship, but after the fall of Smyrna, he became a stateless person who traveled to Argentina on a Nansen passport. He applied immediately for Argentine citizenship after he arrived in Buenos Aires, and it was granted after two years of residence. A few months after becoming an Argentine national, along with thousands of other refugees from Asia Minor, he was also granted Greek citizenship under a settlement reached at the Treaty of Lausanne.

Onassis is of medium height and weight and often hides his eyes behind tinted glasses. He speaks English, Spanish, French, Italian, Turkish, and Greek. Although he smokes heavily, he eats and drinks sparingly. He lists sea sports, particularly yachting, as his favorite recreation. His religious affiliation is with the Greek Orthodox Church. Newsmen who have interviewed Onassis find him both affable and outspoken. After he had bought controlling interest in the Monte Carlo Casino, he was asked if he intended to visit the gaming tables. "I never gamble, it doesn't amuse me," he answered. "I don't oppose it. I understand it. My whole life has been a terrific gamble."

References

Rees, Goronwy. The Multimillionaires (1961)
Who's Who, 1963
Who's Who in America, 1962-63
Who's Who in Greece, 1958-59

O'NEILL, EUGENE F(RANCIS) July 2, 1918- Communications engineer

Address: b. Bell Telephone Laboratories, Murray Hill, N.J.; h. 130 Culberson Rd., Basking Ridge, N.J.

Eugene F. O'Neill, director of the satellite communications laboratory at Bell Telephone Laboratories and project manager of the Bell System's satellite communications program, Project Telstar, has been associated with Bell Laboratories since the beginning of his career. After joining the technical staff at Bell Laboratories in 1941 as a communications engineer, O'Neill worked on radar transmitters, radio communications, and overland and submarine cable systems, and he has been employed in a supervisory capacity at the laboratories since 1952. In 1956 he was placed in charge of the development of Time Assignment Speech Interpolation (TASI) terminals that doubled the capacity of transoceanic telephone cables.

The launching of Telstar, the Bell System's experimental communications satellite, on July 10, 1962 was the culmination of two years of work by a team of scientists, engineers, and technicians headed by O'Neill, who has been described as "the brain behind Telstar." The first privately owned and financed space satellite, Telstar also marks the first international attempt to transmit communications by means of an active repeater satellite. Telstar has transmitted television broadcasts, telephone calls, pictures, and teletype messages between continents and provided information on radiation in space. Radiation muzzled the satellite's communication unit from November 23, 1962 to January 3, 1963. After resuming transmission for about two months, the satellite again went silent at the end of February 1963. A Telstar 2 was launched in May 1963.

Eugene Francis O'Neill was born in New York City on July 2, 1918 to John J. O'Neill and Agnes M. (Willmeyer) O'Neill. His father, a native of Scotland, worked as a milk delivery route man after immigrating to the United States and later became a milk company superintendent. Eugene F. O'Neill has three brothers: Jerome P., a traffic control engineer with the General Railway Signal Company; William H., a tax accountant with General Foods Corporation, and Lawrence M., associate dean of the Columbia University School of Engineering and Applied Science.

O'Neill has recalled that he liked mathematics and technical subjects as a boy and was greatly influenced in this by his oldest brother. After graduating from Public School 71 in New York City he entered Newtown High School in Queens, where he was further influenced in the direction of his vocational goal by Miss Verona Spicer, a teacher of mathematics. At Newtown, O'Neill belonged to several clubs and to the gymnastics team. After graduating from high school in 1936 he attended Columbia College and the Columbia School of Engineering on a Pulitzer Prize scholarship, which his brothers Jerome and Lawrence had also received. Only ten such scholarships were awarded annually to students in about forty high schools, and O'Neill attributes his success in winning one to the training for the competitive scholarship examinations he received from teachers at Newtown.

After briefly considering the study of civil and chemical engineering, O'Neill decided to become an electrical engineer, since he liked physics more than chemistry. He received his B.S. degree in electrical engineering in 1940 and his M.Sc. degree in the same field in 1941. During 1940-41 he served as president of Tau Beta Pi, an engineering honor society. He is also a member of Sigma Xi, the science research honor society. Correcting an erroneous statement that has been published about him, O'Neill points out that he has never taken the Ph.D. degree.

O'Neill joined the technical staff at Bell Telephone Laboratories in New York City in 1941, and he worked on radio communications, airborne and ground radar transmitters, and coaxial cable operations. The research and development unit of the Bell Telephone System, Bell Laboratories, which is jointly owned by the American Telephone and Telegraph Company and Western Electric Company, is considered one of the largest and most important industrial laboratories in the world. It has its main headquarters in Murray Hill, New Jersey and employs some 13,800 people in twelve states, about one-third of them professional engineers and scientists. In addition to its work for the Bell System, Bell

Bell Telephone Laboratories, Inc.
EUGENE F. O'NEILL

Laboratories handles many military projects. The work at Bell Laboratories falls into three general categories: research and fundamental development, systems engineering, and specific development and design. The pioneering work in communications satellites was done at Bell Laboratories by Dr. J. R. Pierce, whose reflecting balloon satellite, Echo I, was launched in August 1960.

From 1952 to 1955 O'Neill was supervisor at Bell Laboratories in New Jersey, working on radio relay systems and on submarine cables, mainly between the United States and Europe. His work during this period involved extensive traveling. From 1956 to 1960 he headed a department at Bell Laboratories that developed Time Assignment Speech Interpolation (TASI) terminals, which doubled the capacity of transoceanic telephone cables that had been recently installed.

In 1961 O'Neill was appointed director of the satellite communications laboratory of Bell Laboratories and project manager for Project Telstar. Before assuming this position O'Neill laid the groundwork for the development of Telstar as head of a department engaged in the design of active satellite communication repeaters and in satellite system co-ordination and equipment design. The principal purpose of Project Telstar was to test the use and reliability of active satellites for the transmission of broadband microwave radio signals. With the increasing volume of overseas telephone calls, the development of a communications satellite system answers a practical need for the Bell Telephone System, since existing overseas circuits via cables and high-frequency radio may eventually be insufficient.

On July 27, 1961 an agreement was signed between the American Telephone and Telegraph Company and the National Aeronautics and Space Administration, according to which Bell Laboratories would design, build, and test the Telstar satellite at its own expense and NASA

O'NEILL, EUGENE F.—Continued

would launch it. The resulting data would be analyzed by NASA and Bell Laboratories and made available to the world scientific community.

About 400 scientists, engineers, and technicians took part in the experiments that led to the development of Telstar. To ensure precision each of the 15,000 components of the satellite was thoroughly tested and inspected. Constructed of aluminum and magnesium, Telstar weighs 170 pounds and has a diameter of thirty-four and one-half inches. Its energy was supplied by 3,600 solar cells that converted the sun's rays into electrical power. The satellite received signals on a frequency of 6,390 megacycles and transmitted them on a 4,170-megacycle frequency. It was capable of reporting on 115 separate items, and it provided the equivalent of 600 telephone channels or one television channel.

An important part of Project Telstar was the construction of an elaborate 380-ton horn antenna, capable of transmitting microwave signals to Telstar and picking up even the faintest radio signals from outer space while screening out surrounding noises. The antenna is located at Project Telstar's ground station at Andover, Maine, and the data it received were relayed for study to the Murray Hill laboratory. On April 3, 1962 Telstar withstood a major test when a telephone conversation between O'Neill and Robert E. Sageman, A.T. & T. co-ordinating engineer, was transmitted over the completed satellite, perched on its tower at Andover, Maine. Later tests for the transmission of photographs and television signals also proved successful.

Telstar was launched at 4:35 A.M. (Eastern Daylight Time) on July 10, 1962 from Cape Canaveral by a NASA three-stage Thor-Delta booster rocket. While the satellite was in its sixth orbit O'Neill, who had kept close track of its movements, reported that it was near enough to Andover to receive signals from the ground station there. Later that day a telephone conversation between the board chairman of A.T. & T., Frederick R. Kappel, at Andover and Vice-President Lyndon B. Johnson in Washington was beamed over Telstar. Also, television pictures were transmitted via Telstar from Andover to British and French stations, and on the following day television broadcasts from England and France were received in the United States. Although O'Neill noted some minor difficulties in the radio command of the satellite two days after its launching, these difficulties were later resolved.

In addition to its communication functions Telstar has provided valuable information on high-altitude radiation, since it passed through the heart of the Van Allen radiation belt. Measurements taken early in September 1962 indicated that Telstar orbited the earth every 157.78 minutes at distances from the earth varying from 592 to 3,531 statute miles.

Telstar's communication unit failed late in November 1962 because of radiation, after the satellite had been used in more than 250 technical tests and in over 400 demonstrations of voice, telegraph, facsimile, telephoto, and television transmission (including forty-seven trans-atlantic television broadcasts). By January 3,

1963 Bell scientists had restored it to working order, but the satellite again went silent at the end of February 1963. Speaking before the Senate Commerce Committee on February 26, 1963, O'Neill explained that the satellite had encountered radiation 100 percent "hotter" than anticipated, but that Bell scientists would redesign future satellites to meet this problem, and he said that satellites for commercial use might be ready in 1967. A Telstar 2 was launched on May 7, 1963. On January 16, 1963 Telstar won a special citation from the Thomas Alva Edison Foundation.

Eugene F. O'Neill was married on October 24, 1942 to Kathryn Mary Walls, whom he had met in high school. They have four children: Kathryn Anne, Kevin, Jane Agnes, and Andrew Thomas. O'Neill objects to the abbreviation of his middle name, "Francis," to "Frank." He is five feet nine inches tall, weighs 185 pounds, and has brown eyes and thinning black hair. Described as a warm and humorous man, he dresses conservatively and does not smoke. He has written articles for Bell Laboratories technical publications. Although he often spends fifteen to eighteen hours a day on the job, away from the laboratories he tries to avoid discussion of his professional work. For relaxation he works in his garden and reads, particularly historical books. He also likes to hike in the hills near his home. He is a Roman Catholic and a Democrat.

Asked to comment on current issues in his profession, O'Neill has said: "I am appalled at the way polysyllabic nonsense is spreading in the technical professions—particularly in the aerospace field—and at the apparent inability of high administrators to detect it for nonsense. [I am] also dismayed at the failure of many people to learn from experience—both good and bad. But [I] am still optimistic for the future of my profession, because of the large number of highly competent young people I see."

References

N Y Times p16 Jl 11 '62 por; p10 Jl 26 '62 por

OXNAM, G(ARFIELD) BROMLEY

Aug. 14, 1891-Mar. 12, 1963 Methodist Bishop; noted as a leader of the liberal cause during the McCarthy era; president of World Council of Churches for North and South America (1948-54); resident bishop of New York (1944-52) and Washington, D.C. area (1952-60). See *Current Biography* (November) 1944.

Obituary

N Y Times p36 Ap 1 '63

PARK, THOMAS

Nov. 17, 1908- Scientist; educator; organization official

Address: b. University of Chicago, Chicago 37, Ill.; h. 5715 S. Blackstone Ave., Chicago 37, Ill.

An animal ecologist whose work with experimental insect populations may have far-reaching implications for mankind, Dr. Thomas Park served in 1962 as retiring president and chairman of the board of directors of the American Association for the Advancement of Science. Dr. Park, a professor of zoology at the University of Chicago, served a one-year term as president, succeeding Chauncey D. Leake, beginning on January 15, 1961; he ended his term as retiring president and chairman of the board of directors of the world's largest group of related scientific organizations on January 14, 1963.

Thomas Park was born on November 17, 1908 in Danville, Illinois, one of two sons of Samuel Thomas Park, a railroad man, and Sophronia (Stealey) Park. His brother, Orlando, is now a professor of zoology at Northwestern University. Thomas Park grew up in Ocean Springs, Mississippi, not far from Biloxi, and in Chicago, where he graduated from Hyde Park High in 1926. Entering the University of Chicago that year, he majored in biology and received his B.S. degree, with honors, in 1930. As an undergraduate, he held jobs as an animal caretaker and a stockroom man to support himself. His interest in the dynamics of insect populations began while he was an undergraduate and continued while he was a graduate student at the University of Chicago, studying under the late W. C. Allee. Having submitted a thesis on "Factors Regulating Initial Growth of *Tribolium* Populations," Park earned his Ph.D. degree from the University of Chicago in 1932. While a graduate student, he was a University Fellow and an assistant in zoology.

Park has said that the factors that influenced him in choosing his lifework were an interest in nature and natural surroundings, succeeded by a desire to study some of these phenomena with greater rigor, through experimentation and quantification. After receiving his Ph.D., Park went to Johns Hopkins University as a National Research Council Fellow (1933-35). He stayed on as an associate in biology at Johns Hopkins (1935-37), continuing to study the dynamics of populations under the influence of the late Raymond Pearl. In 1937 Park returned to the University of Chicago, and there he has remained, as instructor in zoology (1937-39); assistant professor (1939-42); associate professor (1942-47); and, since 1947, as professor of zoology. From 1943 to 1946 he had an opportunity to demonstrate his administrative ability as dean of the Division of Biological Sciences of the University of Chicago. As a Rockefeller Foundation Fellow, Park spent the year of 1948 at Oxford University and worked with Charles Elton, director of the bureau of animal population and reader in animal ecology.

In addition to teaching and conducting research, Park has occupied advisory posts for the United States government. In 1949 he served a four-month appointment in London as scientific attaché in the United States Embassy. From 1956 to 1958 he was a member of the environmental biology panel of the National Science Foundation and served as its chairman in 1957.

Long active in science publishing, Park was editor of *Ecology* from 1940 to 1950. Since 1938 he has served on the editorial board of the *Quarterly Review of Biology*; since 1950 he has been zoological adviser to the *Encyclopaedia Brittanica,* and he is also a member of its board

THOMAS PARK

of editors. He has been editor of *Physiological Zoology* since 1955. From 1951 to 1959 he was a member of the editorial board of *American Naturalist.*

In looking for a president for the American Association for the Advancement of Science, the members of the A.A.A.S. council seek a man who has earned the respect of the scientific community, who has proved his administrative ability, and who has had experience with the problems of the organization of science. Park's qualifications had been subject to the appraisal of other members of the A.A.A.S. since 1954, when he became a member of its board of directors. From 1956 to 1958 he was a member of the association's Newcomb Cleveland Prize committee and from 1955 to 1961 he was chairman of the publications committee. Park continues to serve as a member of the board of directors. He was also a member of the nominating committee of the A.A.A.S. When he learned that Park had been elected to the presidency, Sewall Wright, one of his former professors, remarked that Park "has first-hand familiarity with the potentials of the association for promoting the development of science for the welfare of this country."

The American Association for the Advancement of Science numbers 63,000 individual members and 294 affiliated scientific organizations in all branches of the social, biological, and physical sciences. Since its founding in 1848 the A.A.A.S. has furthered scientific work, facilitated co-operation among scientists, improved the effectiveness of science in the interest of human welfare, and increased public understanding of the importance of science in human progress. The association publishes the weekly journal *Science* and, in addition to its annual winter meetings, sponsors many regional conferences.

Since 1927 Park has been studying the mutual relations and environment of beetles, analyzing their birth rates, death rates, overcrowding, and competition. To learn more about the nature of

PARK, THOMAS—*Continued*

animal competition he chose two species of flour beetles—*Tribolium confusum* and *Tribolium castaneum*—that closely resemble each other, since the closer the resemblance between competing groups the more intense the competition. He placed the two species in the same vial, filled with a mixture of 95 percent flour and 5 percent yeast, and found that under these conditions one species always lived and the other died off. The food supply was ample and the insects did not directly kill each other off. Overcrowding, Park discovered, led to an increase in the death rate, a lowering of the birth rate, an increase in disease or malformation, and general physical deterioration. He also placed each species separately in the same environmental conditions and found that they could maintain a definite population level by themselves. When he varied the humidity and temperature in the container he found that the changes in environment affected the rate at which the species survived individually, and controlled which one of the species survived in the competitive experiments. Under some conditions one species survived, and under others the second species survived. As by-products of his investigations, Park discovered some Mendelian mutations of *Tribolium*.

Some of his colleagues believe that Park's discoveries may have important implications for human beings persisting (with decreasing death rates and without a compensating decrease in birth rates) on an overpopulated planet. Park, however, maintains that it would not be entirely correct to say that what has been learned from insect population studies applies directly to the human population. He says, "Let specialists, if they wish, cross the bridge over to human kind." Because he believes that the human species can avoid the fate of his flour beetles through advances in technology he describes his outlook as "more pessimistic than optimistic, but not melancholy."

Park has published some fifty articles in scientific journals. He is joint author of the widely used *Principles of Animal Ecology* (Saunders, 1949) with Alfred Emerson, W. C. Allee, Carl Schmidt, and Orlando Park. He believes that the scientist is obliged to keep the general public informed of developments in research and to report them in terms the layman can understand. In an interview in *Science News Letter* (January 7, 1961) he said: "We are moving faster in this area than ever before, but the scientist still has not gone far enough in public communication." Park has also voiced the belief that the scientist should participate in public affairs because it breaks down the barrier that traditionally has set the scientist apart from the community.

On July 31, 1928 Thomas Park married Martha Alden Whitehead of Chicago. They have two married daughters, Sherley (Mrs. William R. Hohmann) and Judith (Mrs. Edgar A. Barnett), and several grandchildren. Park is five feet eleven inches in height, weighs 175 pounds, and has hazel eyes and brown hair. Noted for his attitude of deliberate calm, Park has been described by one of his friends as "charming, a very good biologist, an extremely intellectual in-

dependent, and courageous." He breaks down his problems and organizes his work systematically and meticulously. Ever since his boyhood near the Alabama Gulf coast Park has been an enthusiastic salt-water fisherman, who prefers to go after bonefish. He also likes surf-casting and fishes in the bayous for sea trout, flounder, and red snapper. Although he attended night classes for six years at the Art Institute of Chicago, he modestly calls himself only a "Sunday painter." In politics he is an independent. He belongs to the Ecological Society of America, and served as its president in 1958-59, the American Society of Zoologists, the Biometric Society, the Society for the Study of Evolution, and the American Society of Naturalists. His other memberships include Sigma Xi, Phi Delta Theta, and the Quadrangle Club of Chicago.

References

> N Y Times p22 D 26 '61 por
> Sci N L 79:3 Ja 7 '61
> Science 131:502+ F 19 '60 por
> American Men of Science 10th ed (1960-62)
> Who's Who in America, 1962-63

PARTRIDGE, ERIC (HONEYWOOD) Feb. 6, 1894- Writer; linguist
Address: 15 The Woodlands, Southgate, London N. 14, England

In an essay in memory of the famed British lexicographer H. W. Fowler, Eric Partridge wrote admiringly a few years ago of Fowler's wit, his charm and precision of style, his erudition, and his ability to illuminate every subject that he treated. "There is only one Fowler," he remarked, but the same qualities in Partridge's own work have led linguists, book reviewers, and other writers to compare him to Fowler. Partridge's *Usage and Abusage,* first published in 1942 and kept up to date through four subsequent editions, makes him probably the foremost British authority on good English, and his work on slang and on the origin of words vastly enriches his contributions to philology. In Partridge's thirty or more books, the lexicographer, grammarian, and etymologist becomes also a humanistic scholar, an artist, and a philosopher of language.

A native New Zealander who spent many of his growing years in Australia, Eric Honeywood Partridge once described himself as a Colonist with an admiring and understanding, but detached, attitude toward Australians and the development of Australian English. He was born to John Thomas Partridge, a farmer, and Ethel Annabella (Norris) Partridge on February 6, 1894 and was the first white child who could claim Waimata Valley in Gisborne as his birthplace. In 1907 the family moved to Darlington Downs in Queensland, Australia, where Eric attended Toowoomba Grammar School. His boyhood sports were cricket, Rugby football, and lawn tennis.

At sixteen, when he graduated from secondary school, Partridge began to earn his living as a schoolteacher. About three years later, in March

1914, he enrolled in the University of Queensland with the intention of making the classics his major subject. After the outbreak of World War I, however, he enlisted as a private in the Australian infantry and served from 1915 to 1918 in Gallipoli and on the Western Front. He then returned to the University of Queensland to specialize in French and English and in 1921 took his B.A. degree with first-class honors.

From 1921 to 1923 Partridge studied at Oxford University in England under a Queensland traveling fellowship. He received his B.Litt. degree in Anglo-French interaction in literature from Oxford in 1923, and the following year the Paris firm É. Champion published his *The French Romantics' Knowledge of English Literature (1820-1848)*. Also in 1923 he was awarded the M.A. degree by the University of Queensland for his thesis *Eighteenth Century English Romantic Poetry*, published in 1924.

During the next two years Partridge lectured in English literature at the University of Manchester and the University of London. In 1927 he founded in London a small publishing company, the Scholartis Press, of which he was managing director until late 1931. Among the books that his firm published were *Poetical Sketches by William Blake* (1927), for which he wrote an introduction on Blake's lyrical poetry; *Pirates, Highwaymen and Adventurers* (1927), which he edited with an introduction; and *Songs and Slang of the British Soldier: 1914-1918* (1930), which he edited in collaboration with John Brophy.

Partridge's retirement from the Scholartis Press signaled a new direction in his career. As he wrote in autobiographical notes for *Twentieth Century Authors* (H. W. Wilson Company, First Supplement, 1955), "Finally I did what I should have done long before: became a professional writer, mostly on the subject of English—usage, composition, grammar, slang and cant, clichés, jargon, punctuation, [and etymology]." What he called his "inborn sense of literature and language" rejected a cut-and-dried approach. He delighted in treating words discursively, and some of his best-received books, as he has observed, were written in "consecutive English."

His study of the slang of the British soldier and his *Slang To-day and Yesterday* (Macmillan, 1934), which included vocabularies of English, American, and Australian slang, helped Partridge to prepare *A Dictionary of Slang and Unconventional English; Slang—including the Language of the Underworld; Colloquialisms and Catch-Phrases, Solecisms and Catachreses, Nicknames, Vulgarisms, and Such Americanisms as have been Naturalized* (Macmillan, 1937; enlarged fifth edition, 1961). Partridge has pointed out that it is "a book written in a humane spirit and incorporating a vast amount of research (both 'field' and academic)."

Several book reviewers were especially impressed by the individual effort expended in Partridge's contribution to so difficult an area of linguistics. H. L. Mencken, for example, whom Partridge has saluted for his work on the American language, commented on *A Dictionary of Slang* in the *Saturday Review of Literature*

The Sport & General Press Agency, Ltd.
ERIC PARTRIDGE

(April 10, 1937): "Mr. Partridge undertook the whole enterprise on his own, with no help save what he could get from other dictionaries—and that, in many cases, was precious little. His skill, put to the test, turned out to be equal to his diligence, and the result is an extremely learned and useful volume, long yearned for by fans of language."

Another Partridge dictionary of the pre-World War II years that ran into several editions was *Name This Child* (Oxford, 1936; third edition, Hamilton, 1951), in which he told the story, including the origin and the literary and historical associations, of some 25,000 British and American given names. In the late 1930's he worked on several other books, which were not published until after the outbreak of the war, among them, *A Dictionary of Clichés* (Macmillan, 1940). One of his most important books, *Usage and Abusage, A Guide to Good English*, appeared under the Harper & Brothers imprint in 1942. Hamish Hamilton brought out a fifth edition in 1957, and Philosophical Library published an abridged and simplified volume, *The Concise Usage and Abusage*, in 1954. Partridge, who does not intend to compete with Fowler's *Modern English Usage* (1926), describes his book as "less academic and more practical than 'Fowler.'"

As a student of language, Partridge has found his experience in "the university of life," to use his phrase, more valuable than academic instruction. World War II, like World War I, offered him an opportunity to gain practical knowledge of the actual working of the English language. He enlisted in the British Army in September 1940, and after serving for some months as a private in the King's Royal Rifles, he was transferred to the Army Educational Corps, in which he held the rank of lieutenant and then of captain. In January 1942 he was invalided out, but before the end of the year he had enlisted

PARTRIDGE, ERIC—*Continued*

in the Royal Air Force, where he served for the rest of the war as an aircraftsman, during the last six months in the public relations division of the Air Ministry. Two books based directly on his investigations during the war are *A Dictionary of Abbreviations with Especial Attention to Wartime Abbreviations* (Allen, G., 1942) and *A Dictionary of R.A.F. Slang* (Joseph, 1945).

Turning after the war to a quite different subject, Partridge published *Shakespeare's Bawdy; A Literary & Psychological Essay and A Comprehensive Glossary* (Dutton, 1948). His "discursive dictionary," *Name into Word; Proper Names that Have Become Common Property* (Secker & Warburg, 1949), was highly recommended both as a valuable reference work and as a book of entertaining reading—merits that belong also to his *English: A Course for Human Beings* (Macdonald & Co., 1948) and *You Have a Point There; A Guide to Punctuation and Its Allies* (Hamilton, 1953).

Before the war, from 1936 to 1938, while holding a Leverhulme Research Fellowship, Partridge had done some concentrated research on the language of the British-speaking underworld, from the sixteenth to the twentieth centuries. It was not until 1950, however, that his *A Dictionary of the Underworld* (Macmillan) appeared. As its lengthy subtitle indicates, it covers British and American vocabularies of crooks, criminals, racketeers, beggars and tramps, convicts, the commercial underworld, the drug traffic, the white slave traffic, and spivs. Like his *Dictionary of Slang*, it contains a wealth of information that reveals a great deal about social class and social change.

Since 1947 Partridge had been at work on the writing (not the compiling, he emphasizes) of an etymological dictionary, and for a time he had misgivings about its completion because he saw that foundations ready to give financial help to research in other sciences were not attracted to original work in etymology. His *Origins; A Short Etymological Dictionary of Modern English* was published, however, by Routledge & Paul in 1958, and in 1961 an enlarged and revised third edition appeared. "The 'short' of the title," Partridge explains, "could be described as 'Pickwickian' or 'esoteric', for it is a very large book, arranged on new lines and written in consecutive English." His dictionary runs to almost 1,000 pages, examines the histories and relationships of over 10,000 basic words, and provides in three final sections explanations of a large number of prefixes, suffixes, and free components.

Origins was welcomed for the most part as a long-overdue supplement to Skeat's *Etymological English Dictionary* (1879-1882), although B. H. Smeaton protested in *Library Journal* (May 15, 1959) that "the etymological dictionary which takes into account the findings of 20th-century structural linguistics has yet to be written." A reviewer for the London *Times Literary Supplement* (November 21, 1958) found that Partridge had set "a new fashion in the presentation of an old science," and went on to say, "By rigorous selection and skillful organization he has succeeded in giving word-lovers a compact lexicon that is both abundantly informative and delightfully readable."

Similarly informative and readable are Partridge's several collections of essays on language (which for Partridge means language and life), including *From Sanskrit to Brazil* (Hamilton, 1952), *A Charm of Words* (Macmillan, 1960), and *Adventuring Among Words* (Oxford, 1961). Their sprightliness and enthusiasm attest to a labor of love, and the comment in the London *Times Literary Supplement* (October 14, 1960) on *A Charm of Words* is generally applicable: "Always at the back of his most erudite tracking down of the source, one is conscious of the man and the artist, warm, living, human and humorous." In 1963 the Macmillan Company (New York) published Partridge's *The Gentle Art of Lexicography*, which contains some autobiographical details.

Eric Partridge married Agnes Dora Vye-Parminter in 1925, and their daughter, Rosemary Ethel Honeywood Mann, was born in 1933. Partridge has gray-green eyes and pepper-and-salt hair ("What there is of it," he qualifies). He stands five feet eleven inches tall and still has the lean figure that he may have acquired from playing cricket and lawn tennis in the past. He now enjoys those sports as a spectator and belongs to the Surrey and Middlesex county cricket clubs. He is also a member of the Savile Club and the Whitefriars Club. One of his hobbies, he says, is "a critically generous study of human nature."

References

> International Who's Who, 1962-63
> Partridge, Eric. The Gentle Art of Lexicography (1963)
> Twentieth Century Authors (First Supplement, 1955)
> Who's Who, 1963

PATTERSON, ALICIA Oct. 15, 1906-July 2, 1963 Editor and publisher of *Newsday*, the largest daily newspaper on Long Island (1940-63). See *Current Biography* (November) 1955.

Obituary

> N Y Times p27 Jl 3 '63

PAUL VI, POPE Sept. 26, 1897- Supreme Pontiff of the Roman Catholic Church

Address: Vatican City

> NOTE: This biography supersedes the article that appeared in *Current Biography* in 1956.

With the ease and assurance of centuries-old practice that can bring about a new administration without doing violence to continuity of tradition, on June 20, 1963 the Sacred College of Cardinals elected the Archbishop of Milan, Giovanni Battista Cardinal Montini, as the 262d Supreme Pontiff of the Roman Catholic Church. Montini, who took the name of Pope Paul VI, had occasionally been referred to as the spiritual son of both Pope Pius XII and Pope John XXIII.

A scholar and a linguist, intensely interested in international politics and for many years trained in Vatican administration and diplomacy, Pope Paul VI is expected to assure a continuity of Pope John's recognition of the need of the church to adjust to changing world conditions and to deal directly with problems such as Communism instead of ignoring them. Even before his coronation on June 30, he had set an early date, in September, for the resumption of the Second Vatican (Ecumenical) Council, which Pope John had convened in 1962 to study proposals for reform and modernization of some church practices. It reopened on September 29, 1963 with his declaration that its task is "to build a bridge toward the contemporary world."

Like Pope John XXIII, Pope Paul VI is a Lombard, but his background as a member of a landholding, upper-middle-class family contrasts strikingly with the peasant origins of his predecessor. Montini was born in the hamlet of Concesio near Brescia in northern Italy on September 26, 1897. His parents, Giorgio and Giuditta (Alghisi) Montini, in keeping with the family's traditional devoutness named him Giovanni Battista (John the Baptist). He has an older brother, Lodovico, now a Christian Democratic member of the Italian Senate, and a younger brother, Francesco, a physician.

During the five centuries that the Montinis have lived in the Po region, several members of the family have served the church as prelates or priests. The Pope's father was a lawyer and the editor for twenty-five years of a crusading Catholic newspaper *Il Cittadino* (the Citizen) of Brescia. He championed the progressive political views of the Popular party (a forerunner of the Christian Democratic party) in his paper and also as a deputy for three terms in Italy's pre-Fascist legislature.

Boyhood friends now recall Giovanni Battista Montini as an expert tree climber who attributed his fearlessness to keeping his eyes on heaven. His physical frailty, however, made it impossible for him to complete his schooling at the Jesuits' Arici Institute in Brescia, where he had founded a student paper *La Fionda* (the Catapult). Largely through private tutoring and independent study at home he qualified for a degree in 1916 from the Arnaldo Lyceum in Brescia. Rejected for military service, he then began to study for the priesthood and was ordained four years later, on May 29, 1920, at the Church of St. Mary of the Graces in Brescia.

After a summer's service as a parish curate, Montini went to Rome for graduate work at the Gregorian University. He also took courses in literature at the University of Rome. His intensity and brilliance as a scholar came to the notice of Monsignor Giuseppe Pizzardo, who some forty years later, as an influential conservative cardinal, was to vote in the conclave that elected Montini to the papacy. Pizzardo recruited Montini for the Pontifical Ecclesiastical Academy, a training school for Vatican diplomats and officials of the Secretariat of State.

As an apprentice foreign service officer of the Holy See, with degrees in theology, civil and canon law, and philosophy, Montini was sent to Poland in May 1923 to fill the position of secretary to the apostolic nunciature in Warsaw. His health apparently suffered from the change in climate, and at the end of about six months he returned to Rome. He became a *minutante*

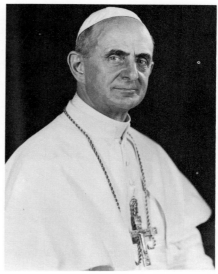

Wide World

POPE PAUL VI

(document writer) in the Secretariat of State at the Vatican and at the same time assumed the far less routine duties of spiritual adviser to the Italian Federation of Catholic University Students. During his ten-year association with that organization, he often saw his students engage in street fighting with Fascist youth groups, and he befriended a number of anti-Fascists, including Alcide de Gasperi and Aldo Moro, who later became leaders of the Christian Democrats.

Eventually, Mussolini's suppression of non-Fascist organizations and the pressure of his own increasing responsibilities at the Vatican forced Montini to give up his work with the student group. As early as 1930 he had caught the attention of Eugenio Cardinal Pacelli, who was then the Secretary of State of Pope Pius XI. Pacelli singled out Montini for special grooming and in 1937 appointed him Substitute Secretary of State for Ordinary (Internal) Affairs and entrusted him with the key to the Vatican's secret code.

When Pacelli became Pope Pius XII in 1939 he relied heavily on Montini as a friend and as a dedicated, tireless steward of the Vatican. Especially after the death in 1944 of Luigi Cardinal Maglione, his Secretary of State, the Pope turned to Montini for advice, because instead of appointing a successor to Maglione, Pius XII chose to cope personally with the duties of the office. Montini dealt with all Papal correspondence, handled many delicate diplomatic problems during World War II, and in the postwar period strengthened the stand of the Catholic Church against Communist aggression by supporting Christian Democratic liberals.

In 1952 Pius XII appointed Monsignor Montini to the post of Pro-Secretary of State for Ordinary Affairs. Monsignor Domenico Tardini, as Pro-Secretary of State for Extraordinary Affairs, had the responsibility of handling concordats. Some

PAUL VI, POPE—*Continued*

observers of events at the Vatican have suggested that Montini, who had been sympathetic toward the worker-priest movement in France and who advocated a more active role for the church in co-operating with organizations for world peace, found himself in conflict with the older, conservative Tardini. Both men declined elevation to a cardinalate in 1953—a refusal that Pope Pius attributed to their modesty. A rumor, however, prevailed that Tardini had rejected the honor to prevent Montini from accepting. "A pasquinade," Xavier Rynne recalled in the *New Yorker* (July 20, 1963), "at once became current: 'When Tardini would not, Montini could not.'"

The Vatican hummed with similar speculation the following year when Pope Pius chose Montini to succeed Ildefonso Cardinal Schuster as Archbishop of Milan. To some observers the appointment meant a banishment of Montini from the center of power of the church and therefore a triumph for the reactionary faction of the Holy See. Others believed that the Pope acted in accordance with a petition from the clergy of Milan that Montini be made Cardinal Schuster's successor. Furthermore, as Archbishop of Milan, traditionally the see of a cardinal, Montini could freely accept the red hat at the next consistory for the election of cardinals.

Giovanni Battista Montini was consecrated Archbishop of Milan on December 12, 1954 at St. Peter's Cathedral in Rome. When he arrived in Milan, in a dramatic gesture of humility he knelt and kissed the frozen ground. Milan, the largest archdiocese in Italy and a stronghold of Communism, challenged Montini to bring the teachings of the Catholic Church to bear on the many social problems that had arisen from the area's enormous postwar industrial expansion. To replace the churches destroyed during World War II he launched a construction program for the building or renovation of about 220 chapels and churches that he felt should be used not only as houses of prayer but as centers of community activity.

Some ninety cases of books had followed Archbishop Montini to Milan, but in becoming "the archbishop of the workers," he found less time for the pleasures of his library. A contemplative, scrutinizing man, whom Pope John XXIII reportedly referred to affectionately as "our Hamlet in Milan," Montini as archbishop expressed another side of his personality. With the zeal of a missionary, he sought a pastoral encounter with the Milanese, and he visited factories, mines, business offices, Communist districts, banks, and chamber of commerce headquarters. He also attended bicycle races. To "the unhappy ones who gather behind Marx," he preached a doctrine of Christian love in an effort to win souls to the church, rather than further alienate them.

Although not yet a cardinal, Montini was among the candidates for the papacy whom the Sacred College of Cardinals considered in the conclave to chose a successor to Pope Pius XII upon his death in October 1958. The election went instead to Angelo Giuseppe Cardinal Roncalli, who as Pope John XXIII called a consistory later in the year, on December 15, and placed

Montini's name at the head of his list of twenty-three new cardinals. Restored to prominence in the diplomatic service of the church, Montini left Milan from time to time to carry out missions for Pope John abroad. In June 1960 he visited the United States to receive an honorary degree from Notre Dame University and also, according to speculations in the press, to explain to American bishops that an editorial in *L'Osservatore Romano* justifying the church's right to influence political thinking did not apply to the United States, where Marxism was not a real threat and where a Catholic, John F. Kennedy, was a candidate for President. Montini later in the year visited South America and in August 1962 made a tour of Africa to report to Pope John on the church's problems in the newly established African states.

The principal act of Pope John's reign was his calling the Second Vatican (Ecumenical) Council to enable the church to consider modifications in its procedures that would allow a more effective handling of present-day problems. Alone of the Princes of the Church, Montini was invited to be a house guest of Pope John at the Apostolic Palace during the first session of the council in late 1962. The Pope, reportedly, listened to the Archbishop in preparing his opening address to the council, and in turn Montini may have been following John XXIII's advice in taking a somewhat nonpartisan stand in council debates.

Pope John XXIII died on June 3, 1963. When the Sacred College of Cardinals met on June 20 to elect a new Pope, Archbishop Montini was the popular favorite and was generally believed to have been also the choice of Pope John, who had, however, avoided influencing the cardinals. On the second day of a relatively brief conclave, in the fifth or sixth ballot (the church prescribes secrecy on details of voting), Montini was elected to rule as the 262d Supreme Pontiff of the Roman Catholic Church. (Pope Pius XII and Pope John XXIII had also been elected as the 262d Pontiff, but their positions were changed during their reigns.) In choosing the name Pope Paul VI, Montini seemed to many Catholics to have announced a program of evangelism and Christian unity such as that undertaken by St. Paul. He was crowned on June 30 in a spectacular open-air ceremony in St. Peter's Square. In his coronation sermon, which he delivered in nine languages—Latin, Italian, French, English, German, Spanish, Portuguese, Polish, and Russian—he declared his intention to encourage "greater mutual comprehension, charity, and peace between peoples."

In a funeral oration in Milan just after the death of Pope John, Archbishop Montini had said, "Pope John has shown us some paths which it will be wise to follow. . . . Can we turn away from paths so masterfully traced? It seems to me we cannot." A few days after his election Pope Paul showed his readiness to follow immediately at least one path of his predecessor when he set September 29, 1963 as the date of the resumption of the Second Vatican Council. He vowed that the continuation of the council would be "the pre-eminent part" of his pontificate.

During the first three months of his rule he gave much attention to streamlining the procedures of the council and to working out plans for the second session, including the decision to permit a number of qualified Catholic laymen to attend. Early in September 1963 in the first direct denunciation of Communism that he made as the Pope, he said that "the council should not be viewed as a subtle but harmful submission to the pragmatism" of the times. He explained that the effort to apply remedies to "a contagious and deadly illness"—errors condemned by the church, such as Marxist atheism—did not signify a change in opinion: "Rather it means trying to fight it not only in theory but in practice."

A slight figure of ascetic appearance, Pope Paul VI is five feet ten inches tall, weighs 154 pounds, and has deep-set blue eyes. When he was Archbishop of Milan, as reported in *Newsweek* (July 1, 1963), he used to watch news programs on television during his dinner hour. Then "for two hours after 9:30 he [dictated] as many as 50 or 60 letters to his secretary as a hi-fi [played] in the background. Montini loves Mozart, but he is also a fan of the French Jesuit guitarist, Father Aimé Duval."

Attempts to evaluate Pope Paul's qualifications as the leader of more than half a billion Roman Catholics throughout the world and to foretell what policies he might adopt, have invited comparison between him and his predecessors. The Most Reverend Egidio Vagnozzi, Apostolic Delegate to the United States, who had once worked with Montini at the Vatican, said of the newly elected Pope, "Pope Paul VI brings to the throne of St. Peter the statesmanship of a Pius XI, the brilliance of mind and deep perception of modern problems of a Pius XII, and the charity, the open-mindedness and universal love of Pope John XXIII." Vagnozzi also spoke of his subtle wit, inspiring enthusiasm, and oratorical talents.

Because of his complexity, Pope Paul VI has often been pictured in the press as a baffling, contradictory, independent man who defies both classification and prediction. There is far less uncertainty about his conception of his role as the Pope: "The papacy," he said in 1960, "seems a solitary, unique phenomenon in the world of today. . . . Upon the Pope must depend the destinies of civilization, not because he disposes of riches, or means, or forces, or power, but because he is in sympathy with every human need, feels repugnance for every human injustice, courage for every ideal principle, and keeps the humility and dignity of the man of God."

References

N Y Post Mag p2 Je 23 '63 por
N Y Times p2 Je 22 '63 por
New Yorker 39:74+ Jl 20 '63
Newsweek 62:42+ Jl 1 '63 pors
Sat Eve Post 263:79+ Jl 27 '63 pors
Time 81:40+ Je 28 '63 por
Washington (D.C.) Post B p5 Je 22 '63 por
Chi è? (1961)
Clancy, John G. Apostle for Our Time; Pope Paul VI (1963)
International Who's Who, 1962-63
Panorama Biografico degli Italiani d'Oggi (1956)
Who's Who in Italy, 1957-58

PEARSON, LESTER BOWLES Apr. 23, 1897- Prime Minister of Canada

Address: b. Parliament Bldgs., Ottawa, Ont., Canada; h. 541 Acacia Ave., Rockliffe Park, Ottawa, Ont., Canada

NOTE: This biography supersedes the article that appeared in *Current Biography* in 1947.

An advocate of harmony among Canada, Great Britain, and the United States, Lester Bowles Pearson became the fourteenth Prime Minister of Canada on April 22, 1963. He succeeds John G. Diefenbaker, whose Progressive Conservative party was defeated by the Liberals in the general elections of April 8, 1963. Canada's leading diplomat, Pearson has served as Ambassador to the United States and delegate to the United Nations and was a major figure in the promotion of the North Atlantic Treaty Organization. He was Secretary of State for External Affairs in the government of Louis St. Laurent from 1948 to 1957, and in January 1958 he became the leader of the Liberal party. For his work in helping to resolve the Suez crisis of 1956 Pearson was awarded the 1957 Nobel Peace Prize.

Lester Bowles Pearson was born in Newtonbrook, Ontario (now part of Greater Toronto) on April 23, 1897. He is the second son of the Reverend Edwin Arthur Pearson, an itinerant Methodist minister, and of Annie Sarah (Bowles) Pearson. After attending the collegiate institutes of Peterborough and Hamilton (Ontario) Pearson entered Victoria College of the University of Toronto at the age of sixteen.

Pearson was about to begin his second year of undergraduate study when World War I broke out. He then joined the university's hospital unit, which later was attached to British forces in Salonika. After serving with this unit as a corporal in 1915-16 Pearson received a commis-

Ashley & Cripps, Toronto

LESTER BOWLES PEARSON

PEARSON, LESTER BOWLES—Continued

sion as a flight lieutenant in the Canadian Army in 1917 and transferred to the Royal Flying Corps. Pearson's flying career was cut short, however, when he crashed on his first solo flight. After a week in the hospital he returned to Toronto, where he resumed his undergraduate training at the university while serving as a training instructor for the remainder of the war.

After obtaining his B.A. degree, with honors in history, from the University of Toronto in 1919, Pearson worked for about two years at the Hamilton, Ontario, branch of Armour and Company. In his free time he kept in shape by playing third base for the Guelph Maple Leafs, a semiprofessional baseball team. With a two-year Massey Foundation Fellowship, Pearson went to England in 1921 and attended St. Johns College, Oxford University. Oxford conferred on him the B.A. degree in 1923 and the M.A. in 1925.

In the meantime, in 1923, Pearson returned to Canada, where he became a lecturer in history at the University of Toronto, while also serving part-time as an ice hockey and football coach. Advanced to an assistant professorship in 1926, he taught at Toronto until 1928, when he was persuaded to take a civil service examination for the position of first secretary with the Department of External Affairs. Having scored the top mark, Pearson was appointed first secretary and remained in the post from 1928 to 1935. He attended the Hague Conference on Codification of International Law and the London Naval Conference in 1930, and in 1931 he served on loan as secretary to Lord Stamp's Royal Commission on Wheat Futures. He was again on loan in 1934-35, this time as secretary of a Royal commission investigating price spreads and mass buying. Pearson also took part in the London and Geneva disarmament conferences in 1933 and 1934, and he attended meetings of the League of Nations.

In 1935 Pearson was sent to London as first secretary in the office of the High Commissioner for Canada. Advanced to secretary with the rank of counselor in 1939, he remained in England through the early part of World War II. In May 1941 he was recalled to Ottawa to become Assistant Under Secretary of State for External Affairs, and in June 1942 he was sent to Washington, D.C. as minister-counselor at the Canadian Legation, which in 1943 was raised to embassy status. Pearson helped to establish the United Nations Relief and Rehabilitation Administration in November 1943 and he represented Canada at UNRRA meetings from 1944 to 1946. Also for a time he served as chairman of its committee on supplies. He also attended the Hot Springs (Virginia) Food Conference in May 1942, was named chairman of the interim commission on food and agriculture in July 1943, and helped to draft the constitution of the United Nations Food and Agricultural Organization (FAO). It was ratified in October 1945.

Promoted to the rank of envoy extraordinary and minister plenipotentiary in the Canadian Embassy in Washington in July 1944, Pearson represented Canada at the Dumbarton Oaks conference, which was held from August to October 1944 to draw up preliminary plans for the establishment of the United Nations. In January 1945 he succeeded Leighton McCarthy as Canadian Ambassador to the United States. As one of the senior advisers to Canada's delegation to the United Nations Conference on International Organization, which met in San Francisco from April to June 1945, Pearson played an important role in helping to formulate the United Nations Charter. He was considered a possible choice for the first Secretary General of the U.N., a position that he would have been glad to accept. However, the Soviet Union insisted on a European, and the appointment went to Trygve Lie of Norway.

Pearson was recalled to Ottawa in 1946 to become Under Secretary of State for External Affairs. In September 1948 he took over the External Affairs portfolio from Secretary Louis S. St. Laurent, who was preparing to succeed the aging Prime Minister Mackenzie King. To provide Pearson with a seat in the House of Commons a vacancy was created in the Algoma East riding of Ontario. In a by-election in October 1948 Pearson, running as a Liberal (although his family background had been Conservative, became its Member of Parliament, and he has retained this seat in succeeding elections.

As Secretary of State for External Affairs, Pearson represented Prime Minister St. Laurent at the London meeting of the Commonwealth Prime Ministers in 1949. He also headed the Canadian delegations to the Commonwealth meeting on foreign affairs at Colombo, Ceylon in January 1950; the Japanese peace treaty conference at San Francisco in September 1951; the Geneva conference on Far Eastern affairs in April 1954; and the nine-power conference on German rearmament held at London in September 1954. For Prime Minister St. Laurent, Pearson drafted the historic speech that first proposed a North Atlantic treaty. He represented Canada at the establishment of the North Atlantic Treaty Organization and the signing of the treaty in Washington, D.C. on April 4, 1949, and he headed the Canadian delegation to NATO meetings until 1957. Pearson also served as chairman of the North Atlantic Treaty Council in 1951-52 and became president of the North Atlantic Treaty Association in 1957.

A member of the Canadian delegation to the United Nations General Assembly from 1946 to 1957, Pearson was chairman of that delegation from 1948 through 1956, and he served as president of the seventh session of the General Assembly in 1952-53. He headed the General Assembly's Political and Security Committee during the special session that paved the way for the establishment of the state of Israel.

On several occasions Pearson acted as an intermediary in resolving differences between the United States and Great Britain. In 1951, however, he delivered one of the most critical speeches of American policy ever made by a Canadian statesman, when he opposed a United States plea that Communist China be declared an aggressor in the Korean war. A milder resolution, suggested by Pearson, was adopted at the following session.

Pearson's skill as a diplomat was demonstrated at the time of the Suez crisis in the fall of 1956, when the United Kingdom, France, and Israel sent troops into Egyptian territory. After much study and negotiation, Pearson drafted and presented a resolution calling for the establishment of an emergency international United Nations force. For his role in the Suez crisis, Pearson was awarded the Nobel Peace Prize on October 14, 1957.

Meanwhile, in Canada's general election of June 10, 1957, the Progressive Conservative party, now under the leadership of John G. Diefenbaker, won 109 seats in the House of Commons and the Liberals received 104. Since it appeared that the Liberals had lost the confidence of the nation after twenty-two years in power, St. Laurent resigned both as Prime Minister and as leader of the Liberal party, and the members of his government, including Pearson, relinquished their cabinet posts.

On January 16, 1958 Pearson was chosen leader of the Liberal party of Canada and of the Opposition in the federal House of Commons. Four days later he delivered a speech calling upon the Conservatives to hand the government over to the Liberals without an election. This gave Prime Minister Diefenbaker a pretext for calling the general election of March 31, 1958, in which the Conservatives obtained an absolute majority by electing 208 representatives, and the Liberals saw their representation reduced to forty-nine seats.

During his first year or so as leader of the Opposition, Pearson appeared to be disillusioned and apathetic, but by early 1960 he began to show increased self-confidence and awareness of the political aspects of his position. In August 1960 he began to rebuild his party by assembling a "Pearson team" of intellectuals, whose purpose it was to develop a dynamic Liberal program. In 1961 he criticized the government for its inability to cope with unemployment and presented a six-point program for recovery. He also proposed that Canada take the lead in establishing a North Atlantic trading community.

In the general election of June 18, 1962 the Liberals increased their representation in the House of Commons to 100, while the Conservatives saw their number of seats reduced to 116. This gave fewer than the 133 needed for a majority. Diefenbaker was, however, able to continue in power after the Social Credit party, with thirty seats, had pledged its support to his government, although his control of Parliament was precarious.

A visit to Ottawa in January 1963 by General Lauris Norstad of the United States, who was retiring as commander of Allied forces in Europe, touched off a sequence of events that culminated in the calling of a new general election. Norstad charged that the Diefenbaker government, by refusing to accept American-controlled nuclear warheads on Canadian bases, was not fulfilling Canada's commitments to NATO. Pearson asserted at the time that he would be ashamed as a Canadian if the government accepted commitments and then refused to live up to them.

In the ensuing political campaign Diefenbaker made nuclear weapons his chief issue. Pearson and the Liberals, on the other hand, emphasized the inadequacies of Conservative fiscal policy, continuing unemployment, and the need to "get Canada moving again, moving forward economically, and back into the councils of the world." In the election of April 8, 1963 the Liberals obtained 128 seats (later increased to 130) to 96 received by the Conservatives, and were thus barely short of a majority. It was not until April 17, after several Social Credit members had pledged support for Pearson, that Diefenbaker conceded defeat and resigned as Prime Minister.

On April 22, 1963 Pearson was sworn in as the fourteenth Prime Minister of Canada. Although he had pledged during the campaign that "more constructive things will be done in the first sixty days of a new Liberal government than in any similar period of Canadian history," his domestic record, at the end of two months, was generally regarded as disappointing. But Pearson's government survived several attempts to defeat it by censure vote during his first few months in office. In foreign relations, Pearson scored some notable successes. His visits to London to confer with Prime Minister Harold Macmillan and to Hyannis Port, Massachusetts to meet President John F. Kennedy did much to restore confidence in Canada abroad. During his visit to the United States in May he confirmed his intention to accept American nuclear warheads for Canadian forces.

Pearson was made an officer of the Order of the British Empire in 1935, and he was admitted to the Privy Council of Canada in 1948. The government of Israel has conferred on him its Medallion of Valor. He holds more than twenty honorary LL.D. degrees, from universities in Canada, the United States, Great Britain, and other countries. Pearson is the author of two books, *Democracy in World Politics* (Princeton Univ. Press, 1955; Oxford, 1956) and *Diplomacy in the Nuclear Age* (Harvard Univ. Press; Oxford, 1959).

On August 22, 1925 Lester Bowles Pearson married Maryon Elspeth Moody of Winnipeg, Manitoba, who was one of his students at the University of Toronto. They have a son, Geoffrey Arthur Holland, a foreign service officer, and a daughter, Patricia Lillian Hannah. About five feet ten inches tall and weighing 168 pounds, Pearson keeps fit through golf and curling. His relaxations are television and reading light novels and detective stories. Described in a profile in the New York *Times* (April 10, 1963) as "boyish, diffident, disarming, a statesman and an unhappy warrior in politics," Pearson still does not care for "the hoopla, the circus part" of political campaigns. His clubs are the Athenæum and the Rideau in Ottawa.

References

Macleans Mag 76:13+ Ap 6 '63 pors
Time 81:33+ Ap 19 '63 pors
Canadian Who's Who, 1958-60
International Year Book and Statesmen's Who's Who, 1963
Who's Who, 1963
Who's Who in America, 1962-63
Who's Who in Canada, 1963

PEASE, LUTE Mar. 27, 1869-Aug. 16, 1963
Political cartoonist; worked for the Newark
Evening News (1914-52); won 1949 Pulitzer
Prize for one of his cartoons. See *Current Biography* (July) 1949.

Obituary

N Y Times p19 Ag 17 '63

PENNEL, JOHN (THOMAS) (pĕn-ĕl') July
25, 1940- Track and field athlete
Address: h. 7300 S.W. 31st St., Miami, Fla.

A wiry young student at Northeast Louisiana
State College, John Pennel, has assured himself a
lasting place in the annals of track and field by
becoming the first athlete in history to pole-vault
higher than 17 feet in official competition. Pennel first attracted national attention on March
16, 1963, when he vaulted 15 feet 9 inches. He
set a new world record a few days later with a
leap of 16 feet 3 inches, and he continued to
improve his standard in succeeding months. His
jump of 17 feet ¾ inch took place on August 24,
1963 at the Gold Coast track and field meet on
the campus of the University of Miami. Pennel's
feat has been hailed as being perhaps of even
greater significance than such classic events as the
first mile run under 4 minutes and the first high
jump of over 7 feet.

John Thomas Pennel was born in Memphis,
Tennessee on July 25, 1940 to William O. Pennel,
a former high school track star who later became
an aviator, farmer, and welding equipment supplier, and to Mrs. Margaret Pennel, a native of
Ireland. He has one brother, William O., Jr., who
is two years older. Unlike many other successful
athletes, John Pennel was not encouraged by his
parents to take part in sports during his boyhood.
His mother, an accordion player, insisted that he
and his brother learn to play musical instru-

ments. William chose the clarinet, while John
selected the sousaphone, a large circular tuba
made famous by the late march king, John Philip
Sousa. At Coral Gables (Florida) High School,
John played the sousaphone in the school band
for three years. His sports were track, football
(he was a halfback), and gymnastics, especially
the rope climb. In his free time he also kept fit
by climbing ropes in his backyard, swinging
around a beanpole, and doing rebound tumbling
exercises.

It was not until his senior year of high school
that Pennel showed any interest in pole vaulting.
One day he happened to see Henry Wadsworth,
the University of Florida pole-vaulting star, in
action. After that, with much encouragement
from Wadsworth, Pennel began to spend less
time on the sousaphone and more at the pole-vaulting pit. He became annoyed when the time
he had to spend practising for a Florida state
band contest cut into his pole-vault training
schedule and contributed to his poor showing at
a track and field meet. Finally he decided to
give up music altogether. His high school athletic
honors included All-City and All-State in track,
the national Junior Olympic championship in
pole vaulting, and a national Athletic-Scholastic
award.

Pennel graduated from high school in 1959 and
was awarded an athletic scholarship to Northeast
Louisiana State College in Monroe, Louisiana.
The scholarship consisted of room, board, tuition,
and $20 a month for laundry. In 1960, his
first year at Northeast Louisiana State College,
Pennel became the first college freshman to clear
15 feet, when he vaulted 15 feet ¼ inch in the
Chattanooga Relays, with an aluminum pole.
He distinguished himself in track events other
than the pole vault by establishing the school
broad jump record of 23 feet 8 inches; achieving 191 feet 9 inches in the javelin throw; and
reaching 6 feet ¼ inch in the high jump. His
accomplishments in track and field earned him
a designation as Athlete of the Year by the Gulf
States Conference in 1962-63. On March 16,
1963, during a wind and rain storm, Pennel
cleared the pole vault bar at 15 feet 9 inches
while competing in the Shreveport Relays. The
following week, during practice, he broke his
favorite fiber-glass pole. On March 23, at the
Memphis Relays, he borrowed the fiber-glass pole
of a rival vaulter, Fred Hansen of Rice University, and set a new world record by leaping
16 feet 3 inches, a half inch above the then
existing mark.

Stepping up his assault on the record books,
Pennel leaped 16 feet 4 inches on April 10, 1963,
during a triangular meet with Northwestern
Louisiana State and McNeese colleges at Natchitoches, Louisiana. He held that mark until April
27, when it was topped by Brian Sternberg, a
sophomore at the University of Washington, who
cleared 16 feet 5 inches at the Penn Relays in
Philadelphia. On April 30 on the campus of
Northeast Louisiana State, Pennel regained the
record with a jump of 16 feet 6¾ inches, but on
May 25 Sternberg cleared the crossbar at 16 feet
7 inches, and on June 7 he improved his mark
to 16 feet 8 inches. On July 2, however, Sternberg sustained a serious injury in a trampoline

Wide World

JOHN PENNEL

accident, which resulted in his paralysis and removed him from further competition.

With Sternberg out of the running, the spotlight focused on Pennel. On July 11, 1963, while traveling in Europe as a member of a United States track and field team, Pennel was chosen to replace Sternberg on the United States team scheduled to compete with a Russian team at a dual meet in Moscow later in the month. On July 13, at the British track and field championship meet at White City Stadium in London, Pennel topped Sternberg's best preaccident record with a vault of 16 feet, 8¾ inches. (The same figure, attained by Pentti Nikula of Finland in February 1963, was not considered a world record at the time, because it was achieved in an indoor arena.)

At the dual meet in Moscow on July 20 and 21 Pennel finished second to his fellow American, John Uelses, who had been the first man in history to vault 16 feet. A few days later Pennel injured his back during practice, and observers doubted that he could take part in a forthcoming competition with a Polish team in Warsaw. But on July 26, while some 20,000 Polish spectators chanted encouragement, and while automobile headlights lit up the vaulting pit, Pennel cleared the bar at a height of 5.10 meters (the equivalent of 16 feet 8¾ inches).

Back in London, on August 5, 1963, competing with the British national team, Pennel set a new world record by jumping 16 feet 10¼ inches before an audience of some 33,000 at the White City Stadium. Reporting on Pennel's performance in London for the New York Times (August 6, 1963), Fred Tupper wrote: "The bar was at a record height now and it was Pennel's third and last try. He got the start he wanted. Pounding down the runway, he slammed his fiber-glass pole into the box and jack-knifed up, up and incredibly over. He just snatched his trailing hand free as he fell into the pit." A few minutes after the jump, Pennel told reporters: "It was the only good run I had. I put everything into that last one." Although he said at the time that he would not compete again outdoors until the 1964 season, he changed his mind after returning to the United States and decided to take part in the Amateur Athletic Union's Gold Coast Track and Field meet, held at the University of Miami later that month.

At the Gold Coast competition, on August 24, 1963, Pennel started with the bar at 15 feet 1 inch. He cleared it easily, but Henry Wadsworth, his only serious competitor, missed on his three attempts. The barrier was then raised to 16 feet 10 ¾ inches, and again Pennel sailed over it with ease. Finally the standard was lifted to 17 feet ¾ inch. On his first attempt Pennel went up and over, seeming to clear the bar by several inches. "I wanted that," he remarked as admirers, including his mother and father, surged around him. "This was a perfect day to wait for. The clouds covered the sun just before the jump and cooled it off. That helped a lot. And there was no wind at all. I felt fine and my form couldn't have been better. I rocked back on the pole farther than I ever did before. I knew one

of these days everything was going to be just right and seventeen feet wasn't going to look too high at all. This was the day. And I could not think of a better place for it than here at home."

Shortly after her son's triumph Mrs. Pennel told reporters: "He came home during practice and told me he had broken seventeen feet. But he said, 'Please, mother, don't let this out until I do it officially.' Today, when he did, I couldn't even get near him to hug him afterward. Everybody smothered him." A half hour after his record-shattering leap Pennel failed in three attempts to clear 17 feet 3⅞ inches. At the Canadian National Exhibition track and field meet on September 2, 1963 he did not equal his previous record, but he became the first to vault 16 feet in a Canadian tournament when he cleared the bar at 16 feet 1 inch.

Pennel has risen to record heights with the aid of the controversial fiber-glass pole, which has revolutionized pole vaulting during the last two years. Before it appeared vaulters used bamboo or metal poles to lift themselves over the crossbar. The glass pole, because of its great flexibility, virtually catapults the vaulter up and over the bar. Don Bragg, the last of the outstanding vaulters to use a metal pole, won the 1960 Olympic gold medal with a leap of 15 feet, 5⅛ inches. At the 1964 Olympic Games, to be held in Tokyo, the champion is likely to top 17 feet. Pennel himself expects to jump at least 17 feet 4 inches before ending his pole-vaulting career. The University of Miami track coach Robert Downes, Pennel's long-time friend and tutor, is convinced that Pennel will eventually reach the 17 feet 6 inch mark.

An all-around athlete, Pennel has run the 100-yard dash in 10.1 seconds and has thrown a softball a distance of 115 feet—an unofficial national record. He is also an excellent swimmer. Pennel's 170 pounds are solidly packed on his five-foot-eleven-inch frame. (One source gives his weight as 165 pounds and his height as five feet ten inches.) According to his coach, Bob Groseclose, Pennel's assets are his strength, good wind, and the finesse of an acrobat. In January 1964 Pennel is scheduled to graduate from Northeast Louisiana State College, where he has maintained a B average. Having majored in physical education, he hopes eventually to become a track and field coach. His more immediate goal is to be chosen for the United States Olympic team and to win the gold medal for pole vaulting at the 1964 Olympics.

The Reverend Michael Hannon, who was chaplain of Northeast Louisiana State's Newman Club for eight years, has said of Pennel, a Roman Catholic: "He's a good kid, unassuming and hard working. He has studied his sport very closely. His fame hasn't gone to his head." For several years John Pennel has served as a volunteer worker in the Miami Boys Club, instructing boys in trampoline, tumbling, and track, and acting as umpire in their softball and baseball games. When a fiber-glass pole manufacturer recently offered to give him four poles, Pennel asked for three 16-foot poles for himself and a 12-foot pole to use in teaching his boys vaulting. He once vaulted in a Seattle exhibition for the

PENNEL, JOHN—*Continued*

benefit of the Brian Sternberg Foundation and donated his winnings on *To Tell the Truth* over television to the same cause.

References

N Y Herald Tribune III p1+ Ag 25 '63 por
N Y Times p34 Ag 6 '63 por
Time 82:52+ Ag 16 '63 por

PERKINS, C(HARLES) H(ARVIE) Aug. 9, 1889-Mar. 6, 1963 Nurseryman; president (since 1928) of Jackson & Perkins Company, Newark, New York, one of the world's largest rose growing firms. See *Current Biography* (June) 1955.

Obituary

N Y Times p36 Ap 1 '63

PERUTZ, M(AX) F(ERDINAND) May 19, 1914- British scientist

Address: b. Medical Research Council Laboratory of Molecular Biology, Hills Rd., Cambridge, England; h. 42 Sedley Taylor Rd., Cambridge, England

One of the most important biological discoveries of recent years was made by a chemist who used the techniques of a physicist. This was the elucidation by Dr. M. F. Perutz of the molecular structure of hemoglobin, one of the largest and most complex of the proteins, the substances described as "the most important constituents of living matter." When Perutz, a co-winner with John C. Kendrew, received the 1962 Nobel Prize in Chemistry, the award recognized not only his discovery of the structure of hemoglobin, but the method he devised to make that discovery possible—one that can be applied in determining the structure of other complex substances.

Perutz is now chairman of the Medical Research Council Laboratory of Molecular Biology at Cambridge University. He was born in Vienna, went to Cambridge in 1936, and began his work on hemoglobin a year later. This research has occupied him ever since, apart from a period during World War II when he helped to investigate the possibility of using ice floes as airports for combined operations headquarters. Perutz is a fellow of the Royal Society and a lecturer at the Royal Institution.

Max Ferdinand Perutz was born in Vienna, Austria, on May 19, 1914 to Hugo and Adele Perutz. Both parents came from families that had made fortunes during the nineteenth century in the textile industry. Max Perutz has a brother, Frank, and a sister, Lotte. He was sent to school at the Vienna Theresianum, a secondary school that had been an army officer's academy in the days of the Empress Maria Theresa.

It was his parents' intention that Perutz would study law and, thus equipped, enter the family textile business. He was, however, influenced by an excellent teacher at the Theresianum and was drawn to chemistry. His parents were soon reconciled to the change of career plans. In 1932 Perutz entered the University of Vienna, where he embarked on a course in inorganic chemistry. His interest in this subject was most limited, for he wrote in his Nobel autobiographical sketch that he "wasted five semesters." He added, "My curiosity was aroused by organic chemistry and especially by a course of organic biochemistry, given by F. von Wessely." It was in von Wessely's class that Perutz heard about work being done in the field of X-ray crystallography at Cambridge University. It was there, he decided, that he would work for his Ph.D. degree.

In 1936 Perutz left Austria and went to England to become a research student at Cambridge's Cavendish Laboratory under Professor J. D. Bernal. X-ray crystallography, the field that Perutz now entered, is a technique for determining the molecular structure of substances. Sometimes called X-ray diffraction, it was introduced in 1912 by Dr. Max von Laue and others. A crystal of the substance under analysis is revolved slowly in a narrow beam of X-rays. As the rays emerge, they strike a photographic plate, producing a series of spots of varying darkness. The position and darkness of the spots, interpreted mathematically, allow the scientist to reconstruct the position of the linked atoms that form the crystal.

A conversation with F. Haurowitz in Prague, in September 1937, turned Perutz's attention to hemoglobin, one of the larger and more complex proteins. Hemoglobin, the substance which carries oxygen in the blood, is of vital importance to the life processes. Perutz's attempt to determine its structure, as a first step towards understanding its physiological functions, was to occupy him for almost twenty-five years.

Perutz learned how to make and interpret X-ray pictures from J. D. Bernal and the physicist Isidor Fankuchen. Early in 1938 Bernal, Fankuchen, and Perutz published a joint paper on X-ray diffraction from crystals of hemoglobin

Wide World

M. F. PERUTZ

and chymotrypsin. They found that chymotrypsin crystals, being twinned, were difficult to work with. Thenceforth, Perutz concentrated on hemoglobin.

While a research student in England, Perutz depended on his parents for his livelihood. After Nazi Germany seized Austria and Czechoslovakia, the family business was expropriated, and Perutz suddenly found himself destitute. Then, when it seemed that he must abandon his work, he was appointed on January 1, 1939 as research assistant to Sir Lawrence Bragg, Cavendish Professor of Physics. His new position as research assistant was a salaried post that had been made possible through a Rockefeller Foundation grant. In 1940 he obtained his Ph.D. degree from Cambridge University.

Since Sir Lawrence Bragg is a Nobel Prize winner in Perutz's own field, the latter had the opportunity to continue his investigations into the structure of hemoglobin—but not, however, without interruption. Perutz has a subsidiary interest in the crystal texture and flow mechanism of glaciers, and his knowledge of glaciers became of prime interest to the military during World War II. When naval officers considered the possibility of using ice floes as aircraft carriers, Perutz was assigned to combined operations headquarters, where he worked under the command of Lord Louis Mountbatten. Although the plans for using the glacial aircraft carriers were never used, Perutz was involved in this work for some time.

Resuming his work with hemoglobin after the war, Perutz secured a research fellowship from the Imperial Chemical Industries in October 1945. It lasted for two years and was followed by further recognition of the importance of his work, which came this time from the Medical Research Council. This is the high-level government agency responsible for allocating public funds voted for the promotion of medical research. In October 1947 the council opened its unit for molecular biology at Cambridge University. Perutz became its first director, and with Dr. John C. Kendrew, who had joined Perutz in 1946, at first represented the unit's entire staff. Working conditions, moreover, were not ideal. According to the New York Times (November 2, 1962), Perutz and Kendrew worked in "a rather tawdry unused hut forty feet long by twelve feet wide" that had been built during the war and had fallen into disuse. But other scientists joined them and out of that hut came the work of four Nobel Prize winners: Perutz and Kendrew in November 1962, Dr. Francis H. C. Crick earlier the same year, and Dr. Frederick Sanger in 1958.

In 1947, however, after ten years' work on the molecular structure of hemoglobin, Perutz was still a long way from his objective. The X-ray diffraction technique, which produces acceptable results with simple substances, had proved a clumsy and an inadequate tool in dealing with hemoglobin. Hemoglobin molecules, though there are about ten million of them to the inch, are relatively very large and immensely complex. The problem, according to an article in the Manchester Guardian (June 25, 1959) is this: "Just as a musical note can be analysed into the several different wave patterns which make it up, so a molecule can be analysed harmonically—though

in three dimensions. But while it is comparatively easy to determine the amplitude of the waves by X-ray techniques, it is impossible to determine directly their phase—that is to say, how they mesh in with one another." In the case of simple molecules, which may contain fewer than 100 atoms, this problem can be overcome by a mixture of intuition and trial and error; with the hemoglobin molecule, made up of thousands of atoms in tangled chains, such an approach proved to be hopelessly inadequate.

Perutz solved this problem in 1953 by developing a technique—the "heavy atom" method—that can now be used to determine the structure of many other substances. John C. Kendrick, who used it in his Nobel Prize-winning work on the structure of myoglobin, described the method in Scientific American (December 1961). Perutz found, Kendrick explained, "that if he made crystals of hemoglobin labeled with mercury, the X-ray pattern differed significantly from that of unlabeled crystals. This made it possible to apply the so-called method of isomorphous replacement in the Fourier synthesis. . . . By comparing in detail the X-ray patterns of crystals with and without heavy atoms it is possible to deduce the phases of all the reflections, and this without any of the guesswork of the trial-and-error method. Thus Perutz's observation for the first time made it possible . . . to solve the complex X-ray pattern of a protein crystal and to produce a model of the structure of the molecule."

Even with the "heavy atom" method and the use of Cambridge University's electronic computers, six years passed before Perutz and his assistants produced their model of the hemoglobin molecule, which shows four chains of amino acids in three dimensions tangled together like a jig-saw puzzle. Perutz published his findings in the British scientific journal Nature for February 13, 1960. Kendrew's more detailed work on the simpler myoglobin molecule appeared in the same issue. On November 1, 1962 the Swedish Royal Academy of Sciences announced that the Nobel Prize for Chemistry had been awarded jointly to M. F. Perutz and John C. Kendrew. They were cited for their determining of the structure of the globular protein molecule, thus adding to the understanding of the basic processes of life. As co-recipients the two scientists shared a prize of $49,656.

If and when it is discovered how the proteins do their work, Perutz will have made a tremendous contribution to that knowledge. In the words of one American scientist, quoted in Newsweek (November 12, 1962): "You can't know how proteins work until you know their three-dimensional structure. They have to be folded up to operate." Perutz has elucidated the three-dimensional structure of one of the most complex of the proteins, and made it possible to do the same for other proteins. In March 1962 Perutz's unit moved into new and more appropriate quarters at the Cambridge Postgraduate Medical Research Council Laboratory of Molecular Biology.

Perutz became a fellow of the Royal Society in 1954, and in 1963 he was named a Commander of the Order of the British Empire. He lectures at the Davy-Faraday Laboratory of the Royal Institution, where his former chief Sir

PERUTZ, M. F.—*Continued*

Lawrence Bragg is scientific director. Perutz is the author of a book on *Proteins and Nucleic Acids* (Elsevier, 1962) and of articles in *Nature,* the *Proceedings of the Royal Society,* and other learned journals. He is an accomplished skier and mountaineer, and in his Nobel autobiographical sketch confessed that his interest in glaciers "was mainly an excuse for working in the mountains." An unexpected by-product of his enthusiasm for skiing and his knowledge of chemistry is a special varnish that he has devised for skis.

On March 28, 1942 Perutz married Gisela Clara Peiser, a medical photographer. They have two children, Vivien and Robin. Perutz is five feet six inches tall, weighs 140 pounds, and has brown eyes. According to an article in the New York *Times* (November 2, 1962), he is "a dark-complexioned man who is now growing bald [and who] still speaks with a trace of a Viennese accent." The New York *Times* continues: "Persons who have interviewed him consider him shy and diffident, a difficult man to draw out. Those who have worked with him describe him as often difficult because of his extreme tenacity."

References

N Y Times p19 N 2 '62 por
Who's Who, 1963

PEW, JOSEPH N(EWTON), JR. Nov. 12, 1886-Apr. 9, 1963 Chairman of the board (1947-63) and vice-president (1912-47) of the Sun Oil Company; prominent and longtime financial supporter of the Republican party. See *Current Biography* (September) 1941.

Obituary

N Y Times p39 Ap 10 '63

PHILLIPS, MORGAN (WALTER) June 18, 1902-Jan. 15, 1963 Former secretary of the British Labour party (1944-61); was an important figure in the Socialist international movement. See *Current Biography* (September) 1949.

Obituary

N Y Times p36 Ap 1 '63

PIAF, EDITH Dec. 19, 1915-Oct. 11, 1963 Parisian *chanteuse*; ballad singer of tragic love affairs; well-known for her original *chansons,* particularly "La Vie en Rose." See *Current Biography* (December) 1950.

Obituary

N Y Times p1+ O 12 '63

PICARD, FRANK A(LBERT) Oct. 19, 1889-Feb. 28, 1963 Judge; appointed to the federal bench for the Eastern District Court of Michigan by President Roosevelt in 1939; was influential in the state Democratic party. See *Current Biography* (March) 1947.

Obituary

N Y Times (Western Edition) p4 Mr 1 '63

PICCARD, JEAN FELIX Jan. 28, 1884-Jan. 28, 1963 Aeronautical engineer; chemist; noted for his stratospheric balloon flights and cosmic ray research; member of the faculty of the University of Minnesota (1937-52). See *Current Biography* (September) 1947.

Obituary

N Y Times p36 Ap 1 '63

PINTER, HAROLD Oct. 10, 1930- British writer; actor
Address: 14 Ambrose Place, Worthing, Sussex, England

The British theater, long the province of middle-class entertainments by middle-class writers, came suddenly to life in 1956 with the production of John Osborne's *Look Back in Anger.* The young writers who followed Osborne, many of them from the working class, swept away the polite tradition of the "well-made" play and filled English theaters with passionate discussion of moral and political issues, and every kind of technical experiment. In the forefront of this revolt is Harold Pinter, a former actor who is still in his early thirties.

Pinter has written two full-length plays, *The Birthday Party* and *The Caretaker;* two film scripts (one of them an adaptation of *The Caretaker*); and eight short plays for radio, television, and the stage. In 1960 he was named the best playwright of the year by the London Drama Critics. He is already a powerful influence on his contemporaries and is being imitated by a whole school of dramatists. His "comedies of menace," which puzzle many critics, have been collectively defined as a new Theatre of Insecurity. Others have associated Pinter's work with the Theatre of the Absurd. But by whatever terms his work is described, most authorities agree that Harold Pinter is technically the most adroit and accomplished of England's New Wave writers, and some critics believe that he is on his way to becoming the greatest living British dramatist.

Harold Pinter was born on October 30, 1930 in the East End of London, an area not unlike New York's Lower East Side. He is the only child of Hyman Pinter, a tailor, and the former Frances Mann. The Pinter family was Jewish and had migrated to Britain by way of eastern Europe from Portugal, where the name had been da Pinta. Harold Pinter was educated at Hackney Downs Grammar School, not far from where he was born, and where his own success in school plays and his admiration for an enthu-siastic drama teacher propelled him toward a stage career.

In 1948 Pinter enrolled at the Royal Academy of Dramatic Art. He did not remain there long, for he found there what he described as "a terrible atmosphere of affectation and unreality, ankle bands and golden hair." In 1949 he joined a repertory company, the first of many, and during the next ten years he toured the provinces of England and Ireland. Under his stage name, David Baron, Pinter was a professional actor until 1959, performing Shakesperian and contemporary roles and, later, taking parts in some of the plays that he had written.

Pinter, who had been writing poetry since he was thirteen, continued to do so during his years on stage. At this time he began to compose short prose pieces, often in monologue or dialogue form. He also set about writing a long autobiographical novel, "The Dwarfs," which has never been completed. In 1956 at a party he witnessed a ludicrous, inexplicable, and somehow disturbing scene that seems to have unlocked his imagination. Pinter came upon two people in a small room. One, a little man with bare feet, was talking brightly and quite intelligently. The other, an enormous truck driver, wearing a cap, barely answered. And all the time, the little man was feeding the other as if he were a child. This incident suggested the theme of Pinter's first play and set the mood of much of his early work. It also provided the setting—the single squalid room—that has enclosed so many of Pinter's plays. Most of Pinter's plays have been published in the United States by the Grove Press: *The Caretaker* and *The Dumbwaiter* in one volume; *The Birthday Party* and *The Room* also in one volume, all in 1961; *A Slight Ache, The Collection,* and *The Dwarfs* under the title *Three Plays* in 1962.

Pinter's first four plays have been called "comedies of menace." They are *The Room* and the *Dumbwaiter* (English title—*The Dumb Waiter*), both written in 1957; *The Birthday Party* (1958), his first full-length play; and *A Slight Ache,* written for radio in 1959. *The Room,* written in four days for an amateur production at the Bristol University department of drama, is about a truck driver and his wife hiding from life in a dingy room. The truck driver leaves reluctantly on a journey and a blind Negro enters. He has been waiting for days to talk to the wife and begs her to come back with him. She refuses, insisting—or pretending—that she does not know him. The husband returns, speaks of his journey, and then turns on the Negro, beating him savagely. As the curtain falls, his wife is struck blind.

Even this very early play had qualities that Pinter has made uniquely his own. John Russell Taylor, the critic, had his own opinion in his book *The Angry Theatre* (Hill & Wang, Inc., 1962), which was published in Britain as *Anger and After* (Methuen, 1962). He speaks of the play's "obsessive dream-like quality," its technique of casting doubt upon clear and unequivocal statements by matching them with equally clear statements to the contrary, and its "almost uncannily accurate reproduction of everyday speech." Like most of Pinter's plays, *The Room* is both comical and frightening—comical in its exact evocation of the stupidities, irrelevancies, and evasions of ordinary speech; frightening in its suggestion that nothing is certain, that some undefined horror is imminent.

In *The Room* violence and horror are brought onto the stage; in Pinter's later "comedies of menace" they remain, as it were, in the wings, never overt, or even precisely defined, but unmistakably present. The *Dumbwaiter,* not performed until 1960, is about two hired killers

HAROLD PINTER

who wait in a squalid basement for their next assignment. Their taut nerves are shattered when a dumbwaiter begins rolling up and down in the empty house, bringing orders for increasingly exotic foods. Eventually it gives a different kind of order; at the end, one killer is waiting for the other, his gun drawn.

Pinter's first full-length play, *The Birthday Party,* takes place in a decrepit seaside boarding house. Stanley, a mild, self-indulgent man who lives there, is visited by two mysterious strangers. They subject him to a merciless cross-examination, throwing at him every kind of accusation, and follow this with a kind of ritual humiliation at his birthday party. Stanley, who insists that it is not his birthday anyway, finally collapses in hysteria. Next morning, numb and silent, Stanley is led by the strangers to a waiting car and some unimaginable punishment.

The Birthday Party was the first of Pinter's plays to be performed professionally. It opened at the Arts Theatre in Cambridge on April 28, 1958 and moved to the Lyric Theatre in London a month later. Derided by the critics, it was, Pinter has said, "a mammoth flop, a flop *d'estime.*" The play closed after a week at the Lyric, and Pinter, then out of work and with a wife and small baby to support, nearly abandoned writing. Help came from two sources: the American producer Roger L. Stevens, who bought an option on Pinter's next three plays, and Donald McWhinnie of the British Broadcasting Corporation's drama department, who commissioned a radio play. *The Birthday Party* was later revived with great success, both on the stage and over television.

The play commissioned by Donald McWhinnie was *A Slight Ache,* broadcast by the BBC on July 29, 1959 and later adapted for the stage. An elderly couple, fascinated by an old match seller who stands by their garden gate and never seems to sell anything, invite him into their house. The old derelict is filthy and re-

PINTER, HAROLD—*Continued*

pulsive, and he never speaks. In the face of this impenetrable silence, the husband becomes increasingly agitated and finally breaks down. The wife sends him out to sell matches, keeping the old man in his place. It was at about this stage in his career that Pinter experimented in another medium, writing a series of seven sketches for the satirical revues *One To Another* and *Pieces of Eight*. These sketches, which have been called "plays in miniature," were enthusiastically received and marked his first popular success.

In April 1960 Pinter's second full-length play, *The Caretaker,* opened in London at the Arts theatre club, subsequently moving to the Duchess Theatre in the West End. Crossing the Atlantic in the next year, the play opened at the Shubert Theatre in New Haven, Connecticut in September 1961 and moved to the Lyceum on Broadway a month later. Acclaimed by both British and American critics, it established Pinter's reputation in the theater world.

Although *The Caretaker* superficially resembles the "comedies of menace," it goes much deeper. The setting is familiar—a squalid attic in an abandoned London house. Even the circumstances are reminiscent of earlier Pinter plays—the two strange brothers who live in the attic and the degraded old vagrant who tries to bluster and wheedle a place in this unattractive ménage. There is menace in *The Caretaker,* but it is not something external, as it was in his first four plays; it resides in the frightening isolation of the three characters, with their total inability to communicate with each other. Each is hopelessly sealed in his own fantasies: the old derelict, with his transparent lies and ludicrous bigotry, the older brother, numbed by electric shock treatment, and the other, malicious in his torment and insanely posing as a man of affairs. When the two brothers reject the despicable old man, they reject their last chance of escaping from themselves; they reject life itself.

Pinter, who has so far completed only two full-length plays, shows no inclination to pause at this point in his career. During the past few years he has adapted *The Caretaker* for the screen, and he has written another screenplay for a film titled *The Servant,* which was shown during the first New York Film Festival in 1963. He has also written five shorter plays for radio and television: *A Night Out, The Dwarfs, Night School, The Collection,* and *The Lovers.* (*A Night Out* and *The Collection* have also been given stage performances.) These plays have for the most part been less obscure and less "menacing" than Pinter's earlier works, with the notable exception of *The Dwarfs.* This exceedingly ambiguous play is derived in part from Pinter's unfinished novel and was first produced in December 1960. The play shows a man struggling desperately to understand himself, and for the first time in his plays, there is an attempt to explain a personality, rather than merely record it.

Martin Esslin, in *The Theatre of the Absurd* (Doubleday, 1962), described Pinter as one of the most promising exponents of that genre

in the English-speaking world, and many critics have pointed out similarities between Pinter's work and that of Ionesco and Beckett. Pinter himself has acknowledged his indebtedness to Beckett, whom he regards as the greatest living writer, as well as to Dostoevski, Joyce, Kafka, and Dos Passos. Moreover, Pinter's plays can be described in the terms Ionesco uses to define the Absurd: "Cut off from his religious, metaphysical, and transcendental roots, man is lost, all his actions become senseless, absurd, useless." Pinter's own comment on attempts to label him is typical: "Sometimes I feel absurd," he told a *Newsday* interviewer (November 26, 1962), "sometimes I don't."

Pinter does not welcome attempts to explain his plays in symbolic terms, although such attempts have been made repeatedly. *The Caretaker,* in particular, has been interpreted as everything from an allegory of the cold war to a modern view of Christ, man, and the devil. "I feel very strongly about the particular," Pinter told Joseph Morgenstern (New York *Herald Tribune,* September 10, 1961), "not about symbolism."

The critic T. C. Worsley defines Pinter's work as the Theatre of Insecurity and attributes the "dazzling clarity and vividness" of his writing to his acute awareness of "the insecurity that lurks behind the lives of most people today," and to his mastery of dialogue. This latter quality is the most praised of all Pinter's abilities. According to Martin Esslin in *The Theatre of the Absurd,* Pinter's "clinically accurate ear for the absurdity of everyday spech enables him to transcribe everyday conversation in all its repetitiveness, incoherence and lack of logic and grammar. . . . He registers the delayed action effect resulting from differences in the speed of thinking between people . . . mishearings; and false anticipation." This dialogue, said John Russell Taylor in *The Angry Theatre,* "'Orchestrated' with overtones and reminiscences, with unexpected resonances for what has gone before" accounts for the "obsessive fascination the most apparently banal exchanges exert in his plays."

It is difficult to overestimate the importance of Pinter's dialogue, since it is the isolation of each individual, his wish to make contact with others and his fear of doing so, which is at the root of much of his work. In an interview with Kenneth Tynan on the BBC (October 28, 1960), Pinter said: "I feel that instead of any inability to communicate there is a deliberate evasion of communication. Communication itself between people is so frightening that rather than do that there is continual crosstalk, a continual talking about other things rather than what is at the root of their relationship."

On September 14, 1956 Harold Pinter married the actress Vivien Merchant (who appeared in the March 1963 production of his television play *The Lovers*). They have a son, Daniel. Pinter, who lists his favorite recreations as drinking and jazz, is a member of the Arts Council Drama Committee and of the Dramatists Club. He has brown eyes and black hair, is five feet eleven inches tall, and weighs about

170 pounds. According to Joseph Morgenstern, he looks in profile like a young Wernher von Braun, while Maurice Zolotow in the New York *Times* (September 17, 1961) has described him as "even-tempered, calm and temperate of speech."

John Russell Taylor in *The Angry Theatre* said of Pinter: "His works are the true poetic drama of our time, for he alone has fully understood that poetry in the theatre is not achieved merely by couching ordinary sentiments in an elaborately artificial poetic diction. . . . Instead he has looked at life so closely that, seeing it through his eyes, we discover the strange sublunary poetry which lies in the most ordinary objects at the other end of a microscope. . . . Because he has achieved this, and he alone among British dramatists of our day . . . he is likely to turn out the greatest of them all."

References

Time 78:76 N 10 '61 por

Esslin, Martin. The Theatre of the Absurd (1962)

Taylor, John Russell. The Angry Theatre (1962)

Department of Defense

STEUART L. PITTMAN

PITTMAN, STEUART L(ANSING) June 6, 1919- United States Assistant Secretary of Defense; lawyer

Address: b. Department of Defense, Washington 25, D.C.; h. 1816 24th St., N.W., Washington, D.C.

During periods of heightened international tension, such as the Cuban crisis of the fall of 1962, the office that Steuart L. Pittman fills as Assistant Secretary of Defense suddenly becomes recognized as crucial because he is responsible for carrying out federal plans for civil defense against nuclear attack. When the world situation is calm, however, he has to cope with public apathy and Congressional irresolution that have blocked the launching of a comprehensive fallout-shelter program. Pittman, a Washington, D.C. lawyer who was appointed to the Pentagon on August 30, 1961, had served the government from 1950 to 1954 on various foreign aid programs and later had been a consultant to a number of governmental departments, agencies, and commissions, including the Second Hoover Commission on Government Reorganization, and the Development Loan Fund.

Steuart Lansing Pittman belongs to a family whose members have lived in Maryland for seven generations. He was born on June 6, 1919 in Albany, New York, where his parents were staying temporarily. His father was a chemical executive. Pittman grew up in New York City and from 1932 to 1937 attended St. Paul's School, Concord, New Hampshire. At Yale University he majored in international relations and received his bachelor's degree *cum laude* in 1941. During his summer vacations he used to hitch-hike and ride freight cars to odd jobs in the West, and he considers this experience to have been as important as any other in his education.

Right after leaving Yale, Pittman joined the African division of Pan American Airways, which had been set up while the United States was neutral to supply the Royal Air Force in Cairo in the early days of World War II. He was stationed on the Gold Coast, and at Khartoum and Cairo, before being sent on to Calcutta, India, where early in 1942 he was appointed assistant operations manager of Pan American's Chinese subsidiary, the China National Aviation Corporation.

As Pittman explained in September 1961 to the Senate Armed Services Committee considering his federal appointment, "The Japanese were coming up through Burma at that time. The operation was largely flying refugees out of Burma and supplying General Chennault's Flying Tiger group with spare parts and gasoline in Burma. Later in 1942 the war in Burma was pretty well lost, and I . . . came home and enlisted in the Marine Corps. I spent part of a year training in the United States and was sent back to China because I had some familiarity with the Chinese." In his three years in the service Pittman rose in rank from private first class to first lieutenant. During the final eighteen months of the war he was the commanding officer of a Chinese-American amphibious guerrilla unit that encouraged and helped active resistance against the Japanese in Wenchow. This adventurous assignment culminated in what has been characterized as "probably the most unusual sea battle of World War II, a fight between sailing junks in the East China Sea." For gallantry in this action Pittman was decorated with the Silver Star.

When he returned to the United States at the end of the war, Pittman decided to become a lawyer because he was advised that legal training would help him get into public service in the field of international economics. He studied at Yale Law School and received his LL.B. degree and admission to the New York bar in February 1948. For the next two years he was

PITTMAN, STEUART L.—*Continued*

associated with the New York City law firm of Cravath, Swaine & Moore.

In 1950 Pittman moved to Washington, D.C. to work as a lawyer on the Marshall Plan. From February of that year until August 1954 he was concerned with the development of successive foreign aid programs and in 1953-54 he served as assistant general counsel of the Foreign Operations Administration. "Almost all my time," he testified during the Senate committee hearing in September 1961, "was devoted to the problem of inducing private investment abroad, and various techniques to bring private enterprise into the foreign aid program. This has been a continuing interest of mine."

Admitted to the District of Columbia bar in 1954, Pittman left government service to help found the Washington law firm later known as Shaw, Pittman, Potts & Trowbridge. As a practising lawyer he specialized in aviation and foreign matters, meanwhile pursuing his primary interest in a series of government consulting assignments. A consultant in 1954 to the Second Hoover Commission on Government Operations, he wrote the staff report on public lending and private capital participation in the government's foreign operations. In 1955 he served as a State Department consultant on the investment guarantee program in South America; then in 1958-59 he spent about half a year as a consultant to the Development Loan Fund, helping first in establishing loan policies and procedures and later in unusual loan negotiations. Also in 1959 he helped in the development of the Straus Report to the Senate Foreign Relations Committee on expanding private investment abroad.

It was in keeping with recommendations of the Second Hoover Commission that Congress on July 1, 1958 established in the executive office of the President an Office of Defense and Civilian Mobilization consolidating the eight-year-old Federal Civil Defense Administration and the Office of Defense Mobilization. A month later Congress passed a law declaring civil defense to be the joint responsibility of federal, state, and local governments, and giving the federal government the right to assist state and local governments and to supply federal financing. The name of the new executive office was changed to Office of Civil and Defense Mobilization, and in October 1958 a master plan for national protection against enemy air and nuclear attack was promulgated by the Eisenhower administration.

In the course of the next three years some progress was made in certain civil defense projects, such as the testing of an alert system (CONALRAD), but efforts to go ahead with a fallout-shelter program were scattered and meager. On July 20, 1961 President Kennedy transferred to the Department of Defense, from the Office of Civil and Defense Mobilization, the responsibility for a greatly expanded civil defense effort that included a nationwide fallout-shelter program. The Department of Defense also became responsible for the existing warning and communication system and for co-operation with state and local governments in post-attack sanitation, law-enforcement, fire fighting, and

other services. The former OCDM was renamed the Office of Emergency Planning and was charged with the duty of handling import restrictions, material stockpiling, and industrial mobilization.

Reportedly on the recommendation of Deputy Secretary of Defense Roswell L. Gilpatric, President Kennedy on August 30, 1961 nominated Steuart L. Pittman for the newly created post of Assistant Secretary of Defense (Civil Defense). By the time of the Senate Armed Services Committee's hearing on his nomination, on September 14, Pittman had "started extricating" himself from his law practice. He promised to sell any securities that the committee felt he should dispose of, including his interest in Electronic Teaching Laboratories, Inc., of Washington, which held contracts to teach foreign languages to government employees. He won bipartisan endorsement from the committee and was confirmed by the full Senate by voice vote on September 15.

One of Pittman's first actions as Assistant Secretary of Defense was to transfer the operating headquarters of the civil defense office from Battle Creek, Michigan to the Pentagon. On December 1, 1961 he announced the start of a nationwide survey of space for community shelters and gave his own endorsement of a family-shelter program. "We think," he said, "that it is possible for people who have back yards and basements and who do not have the resources to buy the kind of shelters that are now on the market to do the job with some work for themselves for as low as $150 or $100 per family." The Defense Department published its much-debated civil defense pamphlet *Fall-out Protection: What to Know and Do About Nuclear Attack* in late 1961, but decided to distribute it on a more modest scale than originally intended.

Regarding the fallout-shelter program in general, Pittman told the military operations subcommittee of the House Government Operations Committee that the administration's program would provide 233,500,000 spaces in the next five years, offering protection for substantially all Americans at an estimated cost of between $5 billion and $6 billion, with the Federal Government paying about $3 billion. For fiscal 1963 the administration proposed a $695,000,000 program to provide community shelters for 20,000,000 persons, but in September 1962 the House and Senate passed a compromise bill adding $38,000,000 to the $75,000,000 already agreed upon and bringing total civil defense appropriations to only $113,000,000. "The actual effect," Pittman commented, "has been to defer until the next Congress the decision as to whether the nation wishes to embark on a comprehensive shelter program such as that proposed by the President." In July 1963, after seven weeks of hearings in which Pittman took part, a House Armed Services subcommittee voted unanimously in favor of a nation-wide fallout-shelter program.

Steuart L. Pittman is described in the New York *Times* as a lean and intense man who "leaves the limelight to others" and who "as a speaker is calm and almost shy." He is married to the former Barbara Milburn White, daughter of Brigadier General Walter White, and he has two children by this marriage and four by a previous marriage. The Pittmans weekend on a family tobacco farm, "Dodon," near Annapolis, Maryland, where they enjoy fishing and swimming in their one-acre pond.

References

N Y Times p19 O 30 '61 por
Newsday p48 N 2 '61 por
Washington (D.C.) Post D p4 S 2 '61 por
Martindale-Hubbell Law Directory, 1961
United States Congress. Senate. Hearing before the Committee on Armed Services, S 14 '61 (1961)

PLISETSKAYA, MAYA (MIKHAILOVNA)
(plĕ-zĕt′ skä-yȧ mä′ yȧ myĭ-kī′ lŭv-nȧ) Nov. 20, 1925- Ballerina
Address: The Bolshoi Theatre, Moscow, U.S.S.R.

Maya Plisetskaya, one of the world's great dancers, has been prima ballerina of the Bolshoi Ballet since the retirement of Galina Ulanova in about 1960. Best known for her portrayal of Odette-Odile in *Swan Lake,* Plisetskaya has also interpreted the leading roles in *Raymonda, The Sleeping Beauty, Don Quixote,* and several modern Soviet ballets. She holds her country's highest artistic title, People's Artist of the U.S.S.R.

Tall, slender, and beautiful, Plisetskaya is famous for a style that combines great technical precision with extraordinary fluidity and, more particularly, for her expressive arms and exceptional elevation. She was first seen by Western audiences in 1959, when the Bolshoi Ballet first toured North America, and she made an indelible impression on them. As John Martin wrote in the New York *Times* (May 24, 1959), "To see a body so responsive to the theatrical moods of the passing moment, so creatively energized, and so completely without technical problems is quite an experience. . . . No wonder audiences scream and yell with delight whenever she appears." Plisetskaya repeated her earlier triumphs in the United States in a tour with the Bolshoi in 1962.

Maya Mikhailovna Plisetskaya was born in Moscow on November 20, 1925 to Mikhail Plisetsky, an engineer, and his wife, the former Raissa Messerer. Of Russian-Jewish background, she comes from a family rich in artistic accomplishments. Her mother is a film actress, and one of her uncles, Azari Azarin, an actor. Another uncle, Asaf Messerer, was a leading dancer of the Bolshoi Ballet and remains with the company as ballet master and choreographer. His sister, Sulamith Messerer, was a prominent Bolshoi ballerina. At the age of four Maya was taken to her first ballet, a performance of *Little Red Riding Hood,* with her Aunt Sulamith dancing the title role. It was then that she decided on her future career. Her brothers, Alexander and Azari, are also dancers with the Bolshoi.

Despite the fact that her arms and legs were too long and that she was tall and gawky, Maya Plisetskaya entered the ballet school of the Bolshoi Theatre in 1934. She studied for six years with Yelizaveta Gerdt, a teacher noted for the "plasticity" and "nobility" she cultivated in pupils, and for one year with the famous teacher Agrippina Vaganova. When she was eleven years old

MAYA PLISETSKAYA

she appeared for the first time on the Bolshoi's great stage, dancing the Breadcrumb Fairy variation from *The Sleeping Beauty.* In 1941 she danced the Grand Pas from *Paquita,* a part considered a milestone for budding ballerinas, and later that year, after her performance at a student recital, she was called "one of the most talented pupils of The School of Choreography." On April 1, 1943, following her graduation from the school, Maya Plisetskaya joined the Bolshoi Ballet company. She entered with the rank of soloist, without having danced in the corps de ballet.

During her first season with the Bolshoi, Plisetskaya was seen in a record number of roles. While this was in part due to a wartime shortage of dancers, a more important factor was the remarkable rapidity with which she learned new parts. In the fall of 1943 she danced a Little Swan and a Possible Bride in *Swan Lake* and, in November, her first important role—the Mazurka in *Les Sylphides.* On April 6, 1944 she had her first leading part in a full-length classical ballet as the Princess in *The Nutcracker.* Among her other early roles were the Lilac Fairy in *The Sleeping Beauty,* the Queen of the Dryads in *Don Quixote,* and a Wili in *Giselle,* all in 1944, and the fairy Autumn in *Cinderella,* in 1945.

Moving on to more complex characters, Plisetskaya first created Myrtha, Queen of the Wilis, in a December 1944 performance of *Giselle.* She danced the imperious ghost-queen with a "cold brilliance" that has made her one of the best contemporary interpreters of the role. On October 13, 1945 she first danced the title role of Alexander Glazounov's *Raymonda,* the first part that placed her in the ballerina class. "I shall work on . . . Raymonda as long as I live," she wrote in her diary at that time. According to one critic, she created "a very expressive image of the beautiful, proud and incorruptible girl."

On April 27, 1947 Plisetskaya made her first appearance as Odette-Odile in Tchaikovsky's *Swan Lake.* This double role—in which the bal-

PLISETSKAYA, MAYA—_Continued_

lerina must be both the lyrical, lovely Queen of the Swans (the White Swan) and the evil daughter of a demonic magician (the Black Swan)— is one of the most demanding in the entire repertoire. A ballerina's being assigned the role is parallel to an actor's obtaining the part of Hamlet.

From the beginning Plisetskaya (who was only twenty-one when she first danced it) showed technical mastery of the role, but critics at first found her wicked Odile more vivid and compelling than the subtler, more elusive Odette. With growing artistic maturity, she has perfected her performance; her Odette is now as profoundly moving as her Odile is dazzling. The role has become one of her finest; in it "she dominates the stage, performs prodigies of technique, but never sacrifices the quality of her characterisation" (_Dictionary of Modern Ballet_, 1959). According to one of her teachers, "You cannot say 'she dances well' or 'she acts well.' Her performance is a complete synthesis of choreography, music and acting."

In March 1948, less than a year after she first created Odile, Plisetskaya again focused on the dark side of human nature with her portrayal of Zarema, the Khan's rejected concubine, in _The Fountain of Bakhchiserai_. Her dancing, Natalia Roslavleva wrote in _Maya Plisetskaya_ (Foreign Languages Publishing Co., 1956), is "technically perfect, expressive and in harmony with the music and action. She convincingly expresses violent human passions in terms of pure choreography."

During the next few years Plisetskaya added a number of minor roles to her repertoire, among them the Street Dancer in _Don Quixote_ (February 1949) and the Queen Maiden in Cesare Pugni's _The Humpbacked Horse_ (October 1949). She also danced in several operas produced at the Bolshoi, appearing as the Beautiful Maiden in Michael Glinka's _Russlan and Ludmilla_ (September 1948), as the Needle-Fish in Rimski-Korsakov's _Sadko_ (May 1949), as the Persian Maiden in Musorgski's _Khovanshchina_ (April 1950), and as the Bacchante in the Walpurgis Night scene from Gounod's _Faust_ (November 1950).

Plisetskaya gave her first performance in the full-length role of Quiteria (or Kitri) in Leon Minkus' _Don Quixote_ on March 10, 1950. Of her performance as the tavern-keeper's daughter whom Don Quixote mistakes for his Princess, Ulanova said: "Plisetskaya's dancing is characterized by breadth, softness, freedom and lightness. She has a forceful, broad leap resembling flight, she has strength and vigor. . . . Her artistic temperament, excellent technique, élan and the all-conquering bubbling optimism of youth reveal themselves in this ballet with full force." On October 3, 1952 Plisetskaya made her debut in another great classical role, that of Aurora in Tchaikovsky's _The Sleeping Beauty_. She danced the part of the Princess with warmth and youthful femininity.

Following her performance in _The Sleeping Beauty_, Plisetskaya took the leading roles in a number of modern Soviet ballets. She danced the Mistress of the Copper Mountain at the première of Prokofiev's _The Stone Flower_ in February 1954. This part of the underground queen who teaches the secrets of stonecraft to the young artisan Danila was created especially for her by the choreographer Leonid Lavrovsky. In January 1955 Plisetskaya danced the Bird-Maiden at the première of _Shuraleh_, a contemporary ballet (with music by F. Yarullin) based on Tartar folk tales. The following February she had the title role in Alexander Krein's _Laurencia_, a ballet based on a play by Lope de Vega. Plisetskaya's interpretation of this Spanish peasant girl who is wronged by the lord of the manor and who incites her fellow villagers to revenge, is one of her most popular parts. She has since added to her repertoire the part of Juliet in Prokofiev's setting of Shakespeare's _Romeo and Juliet_. She first danced the role, originally created by Galina Ulanova, in December 1961.

By 1956 Plisetskaya had become recognized as one of the Bolshoi's leading interpreters of both classic and contemporary roles. John Martin, who saw her dance in Moscow that year, described her in the New York _Times_ (June 5, 1956) as "technically out of this world." Thus, when part of the Bolshoi company visited London in November 1956, British balletomanes were disappointed that Plisetskaya did not make the trip. Officially, it was said that she was too ill to dance, or (in an alternate explanation) that she had remained in Moscow to dance with the part of the company that had been left behind, but unofficially it was rumored that she had not been allowed to tour because she was considered politically unreliable.

Whatever the real reasons for her absence from London, Plisetskaya was permitted to accompany the Bolshoi on its first tour of the United States and Canada in 1959. On her first American tour, Plisetskaya danced in _Swan Lake_, in a new version of _The Stone Flower_ (choreographed by Yuri Grigorovich and first performed by her in March 1959) and in the Walpurgis Night scene from _Faust_. The New York _Herald Tribune_ dance critic, Walter Terry, thought her interpretation of Odette-Odile "vivid . . . and brilliantly danced." He found her "dazzling" as the Mistress of the Copper Mountain, and although he considered the Walpurgis Night scene "corny beyond belief," Plisetskaya, he said, "makes you forget everything but the marvels of her body in motion."

In 1962 Plisetskaya again accompanied the Bolshoi on a North American tour, this time as prima ballerina of the company. She again danced the part of Odette-Odile in _Swan Lake_, impressing several reviewers with the even greater warmth and tenderness that she had developed in her portrayal of Odette. She also performed her most famous recital number, _The Dying Swan_, first on a "Highlights Program" at the Metropolitan Opera House on September 20, 1962 and later on television. Reviewing this brief work, choreographed by Michel Fokine to the music of Saint-Saëns, Walter Terry said in the New York _Herald Tribune_ (September 21, 1962): "What she did was to discard her own identity as a ballerina and even as a human and to assume the characteristics of a magical creature. . . . The audience yelled and cheered, applauded and wept. . . . Indeed, the length of the applause . . . exceeded the length of the solo itself."

Plisetskaya also danced the part of Phrygia in Leonid Yakobson's version of Khachaturian's *Spartacus* (she had appeared as Aegina in this ballet in 1958), but this elaborate and somewhat athletic ballet was a failure with American audiences. "Poor Miss Plisetskaya," wrote Allen Hughes (New York *Times,* September 13, 1962), "never gets to do more than a few rounds of rather ordinary steps." Far more successful was her appearance in *Ballet School,* a novel "choreographic sketch" that her uncle Asaf Messerer prepared at S. Hurok's suggestion for the Bolshoi's 1962 tour. She was also acclaimed for her performance as the Temple Dancer, Nikiya, in Minkus' *Bayaderka,* a role that she had added to her repertoire since her earlier American tour.

Before visiting the United States, Plisetskaya had danced outside the Soviet Union at Communist Youth Festivals in Prague (1947), Budapest (1949), and Berlin (1954) and had toured India in 1954. She has also danced in Poland (1960), Finland (1960), and Egypt (1961). In 1961 she appeared in Paris, where she was acclaimed the world's greatest living ballerina. Plisetskaya has also performed in a number of ballet films, including *Grand Concert* (1951), *Masters of the Russian Ballet* (1954), *Swan Lake* (1957), *Khovanshchina* (1960), *The Way to the Bolshoi Ballet* (1961), and *The Little Humpbacked Horse* (1962). In 1951 Plisetskaya was made an Honored Artist of the Russian Federation, in 1956 a People's Artist of the Russian Federation, and in 1959 a People's Artist of the U.S.S.R.

Maya Plisetskaya has green eyes, auburn hair, and what has been described as an ideal dancer's body. She was married on October 2, 1958 to Rodion Shchedrin, a composer whose work includes a new version of *The Humpbacked Horse* and an opera, *Not Love Alone,* in both of which Plisetskaya has danced. In addition to the dance, Plisetskaya is interested in music and the theater. Her favorite sport is swimming. She has been described as "gay," "dashing," and "irrepressible" and is said to have an excellent sense of humor.

References

Ballet p35 Ap '51 por
Ballet Today Je '60 por
N Y Times II p7 My 24 '59
Bellew, Helene. Ballet in Moscow Today (1956)
Dictionary of Modern Ballet (1959)
Roslavleva, Natalia. Maya Plisetskaya (1956)
Who's Who in the USSR, 1961-62

PLUMLEY, H(AROLD) LADD May 13, 1902- Insurance executive; organization official
Address: b. State Mutual Life Assurance Company of America, 440 Lincoln St., Worcester 5, Mass.; h. 16 Moreland St., Worcester 9, Mass.

As the president for 1962-63 of the Chamber of Commerce of the United States, H. Ladd Plumley served as spokesman for the world's largest organization of businessmen. His own field is insurance, and since the end of World War II he has been associated with State Mutual Life Assurance Company of America in Worcester,

Fabian Bachrach

H. LADD PLUMLEY

Massachusetts, of which he is now chairman of the board and president. At the time of his installation as president of the Chamber of Commerce, he was described in the New York *Times* (May 1, 1962) as a liberal-trade advocate with a global outlook and "a firm believer in the modern theory that today's businessman must also be an activist in public life and politics."

The grandson of a clergyman and the son of an automobile executive, Harold Ladd Plumley was born to Alexander Ralston and Mary Elizabeth (Gearing) Plumley on May 13, 1902 in Waterbury, Connecticut. He spent most of his boyhood in Meriden, not far from the New Britain, Connecticut plant of General Motors Corporation, where his father was employed in the new departure division. In an article in *Nation's Business* (May 1962) Louis Cassels suggested that "as the smallest of four brothers he developed early the fiercely competitive instinct which is still one of his most outstanding traits."

Ladd Plumley entered Hotchkiss School in Lakeville, Connecticut after completing grammar school in Meriden. He took part in football, baseball, and gymnastics and was editor of the literary magazine and a member of the dramatic society. At Williams College in Massachusetts, where Greek was one of his main subjects, he edited the college humor magazine, *Purple Cow.* He received his B.A. degree in 1925.

During one of his summer vacations from college Ladd Plumley had worked as an office boy with the Travelers Insurance Company. After graduation he found full-time employment as an underwriter with the group division at Travelers headquarters in Hartford, Connecticut. He moved up gradually—to group assistant in the agency department in 1932, district group supervisor in 1934, home office group supervisor in Hartford in 1938, and to assistant superintendent of group sales in 1941. In the last of his positions with Travelers he became the principal author in

PLUMLEY, H. LADD—*Continued*

1942 of the War Department's Group Insurance Rating Plan and helped the Maritime Commission and the Navy to establish appropriate standards for insurance with cost-plus contractors.

Later in 1942 Plumley was commissioned a major in the United States Army and assigned to the Office of the Fiscal Director. For much of the remainder of World War II he was in charge of all sales and servicing in the National Service Life Insurance (G.I. Insurance) Program. By the time of his discharge with the rank of lieutenant colonel in 1945, he had become chief of the government life insurance section.

Plumley's return to civilian life came just at a time when the State Mutual Assurance Company of America, in Worcester, was looking for someone to organize a department of group insurance, the branch of the business with which Plumley had been most notably associated. The fifth oldest insurance firm in the United States, State Mutual had been chartered in 1844 and had been a pioneer in the "adoption of cash surrender values, guaranteeing equitable treatment for all policy holders whether or not they were able to fulfill their part of the contract," as Plumley wrote in an article for the *Christian Science Monitor* (March 7, 1960). The values set up by the company were incorporated in the first nonforfeiture law enacted by Massachusetts.

State Mutual described itself in its early reports as "striving to do a safe rather than a large business," and this policy in the main continued until the changes in the insurance field brought about by the New Deal and World War II made a group department inevitable. Plumley, who was well known to Worcester businessmen through his prewar field work for Travelers, was engaged as secretary of the new State Mutual group department late in 1945. The department started with three employees on January 1, 1946 and by February 26 had received its first group premium.

In 1947 Plumley wrote the monograph *Budgeting the Costs of Illness*, published by the National Industrial Conference Board as the first item in its Studies in Individual and Collective Security series. The rapid growth of his group department contributed to State Mutual's attainment in 1948 of its first $1 billion of life insurance in force. By 1951 the group department had grown to $617,292,000 in combined group and casualty coverage.

As his department grew, Plumley himself advanced in the company, becoming a vice-president in 1947 and a director in 1950. On December 18, 1951, after the death of George Avery White, he was elected president of State Mutual, and he retained the presidency when he was elected chairman of the board in 1956. In 1958 he became in addition board chairman of both the Guarantee Mutual Assurance Company of Worcester and the Worcester Mutual Fire Insurance Company. Since it began issuing noncancellable individual and accident policies in 1953, State Mutual has offered complete personal insurance protection. By 1955 the $2 billion mark of insurance in force was reached, and in early 1960 the $3 billion mark was passed. State Mutual, which had over 1,000 home office employees and more than 800 agents, is the twenty-

sixth largest of the country's 1,400 life insurance firms. In other business affiliations, Plumley is a director of Worcester County National Bank and a trustee of the Bank of New York.

A past president of the Worcester Chamber of Commerce, Plumley has been a member of the board of directors of the Chamber of Commerce of the United States since May 1, 1956. He was elected a vice-president on May 3, 1960 and has been chairman of the chamber's policy, Canada-United States, and *Nation's Business* committees, as well as a member of the executive, budget, by-laws, economic security, foreign policy, and Mexico-United States committees. The board of directors elected him on April 19, 1962 to take office on May 2, 1962 as the national Chamber of Commerce's thirty-fifth president, to succeed Richard Wagner, the executive committee chairman of the Champlin Oil & Refining Company.

At a news conference following his election, Plumley spoke of the "disquieting effect" that the recently concluded steel price "tug of war" had produced on businessmen and investors, and he called for increased co-operation among the forces of business, labor, and government. Under his leadership, he pledged, the Chamber of Commerce would "turn its attention to next week's problems and opportunities, rather than to a rehash of last week's events." Later in May he conferred with President John F. Kennedy, and at the President's request the Chamber of Commerce formed a committee to study the problem of reducing the United States deficit in the international balance of payments.

Before the end of 1962 Plumley had made nine trips to Europe on behalf of the Chamber of Commerce, and it was estimated that by the time his term expired on May 1, 1963, he would have traveled some 250,000 miles in the United States and abroad. Besides meeting with Chamber of Commerce groups in other countries, he discussed with high government officials such matters as the implication of the Common Market for American business, the United States balance of payments problem, and the differences between the tax structures of the United States and some of the European countries.

The breadth of the national economy, Plumley believes, has become so great that United States business firms must operate with increasing regard for the world market. He foresees that in competing with other countries America will have an advantage because of its strength in management skill. He is vice-chairman of both the United States management advisory committee and the business and industry advisory committee to the Organization for Economic Cooperation and Development.

Also a leader in Worcester's educational and civic activities, Plumley is a trustee of Becker Junior College, an adviser on business administration to Clark University, and a director of Hahnemann Hospital and Worcester Boys Club. He is also president of the Worcester Oratorio Society, director of the Worcester Orchestral Society, and governor of the Worcester County Musical Association. He belongs to the Newcomen Society, Phi Delta Theta, and several clubs. He is the moderator of the Chestnut Street Congregational Church in Worcester and is a Knight of Justice, Sovereign Order of St. John of Jerusalem, Knights of Malta. His political party is the Republican.

On August 10, 1945 H. Ladd Plumley married Christine A. Larsen of Seattle, Washington, who had been dean of the School of Nursing at the University of California at Los Angeles. He has two daughters, Nancy Phelps (Mrs. David E. Ljungberg) and Susan Winslow (Mrs. A. Paul Arruda, Jr.), and three grandchildren. Plumley is a tall, gray-haired man, a witty conversationalist, and a connoisseur of food and wines. He enjoys fishing and boating and playing golf, billiards, bridge, and poker. Horticulture is one of his favorite hobbies, and he has won awards for raising hybrid irises.

References

Eastern Underwriter 53:3+ Mr 28 '52 por
N Y Herald Tribune p2 Ap 20 '62 por
N Y Times p16 My 1 '62 por
Nations Bsns 50:34+ My '62 pors
Washington (D.C.) Post A p6 Ap 20 '62 por
Who's Who in America, 1962-63
Who's Who in Insurance, 1961
Who's Who in the East, 1962-63
World Who's Who in Commerce and Industry (1961)

POPPER, KARL R(AIMUND) July 28, 1902-
Philosopher; author; educator

Address: b. London School of Economics, Houghton St., London W.C.2, England; h. "Fallowfield," Manor Rd., Penn, Buckinghamshire, England

Karl R. Popper, the Viennese-born professor of logic and scientific method at the University of London, has one foot planted firmly in each of C. P. Snow's "two cultures." Popper, who is also head of the department of philosophy, logic and scientific method at the university's famous London School of Economics, regards himself, with justification, as a humanist. He is a pianist and music lover, and is most popularly known for *The Open Society and Its Enemies,* described by Bertrand Russell as "a vigorous and profound defence of democracy." At the same time, it is generally recognized that Popper's major contributions to contemporary thought have been in the logic of science.

The only boy in a family of three children, Karl Raimund Popper was born on July 28, 1902, near St. Stephan's Cathedral in the heart of Vienna. His father, Dr. Simon Siegmund Carl Popper, was a barrister and solicitor who had taken over the practice from his friend and partner, the last liberal burgomeister of Vienna. The possessor of a 10,000-volume library, Dr. Popper was also a poet, a historian, and an excellent classical scholar, particularly interested in Hellenistic culture. His wife, the former Jenny Schiff, no doubt nurtured her son's abiding passion for music. She had heard Brahms and Liszt perform and she herself, Popper has recalled, "played Mozart and Beethoven very simply and beautifully." Popper's sister, Annie Lothringer, is a writer living in Switzerland; another sister, Dorathea Popper, died in 1934.

Fayer, London

KARL R. POPPER

The attractive world in which Karl Popper grew up was destroyed in the collapse of Austria-Hungary after World War I. The boy was sixteen in 1918 and "hopeful and eager for a better world." Late in that year, too young to matriculate but dissatisfied with the Vienna Gymnasium, his secondary school, he enrolled as a part-time student at the University of Vienna. There, sporadically, he was to study until 1928. He followed no formal course of study and says that during his whole university career he "attended few courses and profited from fewer." Yet he absorbed a great deal, choosing professors who interested him and, since personal contacts between students and faculty were rare, learning more from their books than from themselves. In that period of economic depression and social upheaval, Popper writes, "few of us seriously thought of a career—there was none. We studied for the sake of studying."

It was also a time of intellectual upheaval. Popper became interested in such diverse theories as those of Einstein, Marx, Freud, and Adler. While he was working for a time in one of Adler's clinics for children, an incident took place that had a profound influence on the direction of his thought. It is described in a profile of Popper in the British *New Scientist* (April 2, 1959). One day in 1919 Popper reported to Adler a case that the psychologist diagnosed in terms of his theory of the inferiority complex, even though he had not seen the child. Popper felt that the diagnosis was wrong and asked Adler how he could be certain. "Because of my thousandfold experience," Adler said. "And with this case," Popper retorted, "I suppose your experience is now even thousand-and-one-fold."

Partly as a result of this incident, Popper, at the age of seventeen, formulated the problem (and a solution to it) that he still considers "both the most practical and the deepest problem in the philosophy of science—that of

POPPER, KARL R.—*Continued*

distinguishing between science (such as astronomy) and pseudo-science (such as astrology)." Einstein's theory of gravitation was then becoming known and the hypothesis seemed to Popper "scientific" in a sense that the theories of Adler, Marx, and Freud were not. What was the difference, he asked himself, and how could it be distinguished? Popper's solution to this "problem of demarcation" was to be developed and refined over a period of nineteen years before it was published in 1934 as *Logik der Forschung* (The Logic of Discovery).

Meanwhile, the young student had decided that a man should be able to work with his hands. He apprenticed himself to a cabinet maker but, not surprisingly, found it "extremely difficult to concentrate" on the work. It is perhaps typical of Popper that he conceived some of his most important ideas about the philosophy of science as he worked at the cabinet maker's bench and that these ideas were influenced by his speculations regarding the development of European music. It is equally characteristic of him that, bored as he was, he stayed until he had successfully completed his apprenticeship.

In 1923 Popper sat for his teacher's certificate and found a year's employment as a social worker, caring for delinquent youngsters. At about this time he wrote his first paper, in the philosophy of education. It was called "Über die Stellung des Lehrers zu Schule und Schüler" and was published in 1925 by the magazine *Schulreform*. In that year he became a full-time student, pursuing courses at both the University of Vienna and the Vienna Institute of Education.

Scholarships were unknown then in Vienna, but Popper earned a little by coaching other students for university examinations. In quick succession he wrote a thesis for his secondary school teacher's certificate, another for the certificate of the Institute of Education, yet another for his Ph.D. degree. The doctoral thesis, dealing with dogmatic and critical ways of thinking and their relation to the problem of induction, attracted the attention of one of his professors, Heinrich Gomperz, who introduced him to other philosophers. It was through Gomperz that Popper learned of the work of the Vienna Circle, the group of logical positivists associated in the 1920's and 1930's with the University of Vienna.

The University of Vienna awarded Popper the Ph.D. degree in 1928. Two years later he found a position as a secondary school teacher. He continued his philosophical studies and was attracted by the Vienna Circle's interest in the philosophy of science, "But," as he explained in an autobiographical note for *Twentieth Century Authors* (H. W. Wilson Company, First Supplement, 1955), "I disagreed with their positivist tendencies. . . . I believed that there are genuine problems to be solved, and secrets to be discovered, while they believed that everything is on the surface—that there is no depth." Nevertheless, authorities find in the general orientation of Popper's thought similarities to that associated with the Vienna Circle.

In 1934, feeling that he had in fact solved some of the problems whose existence the Vienna Circle denied, Popper published *Logik der Forschung*, his answer to the "problem of demarcation" between science and pseudo-science. In spite of the book's great impact, it waited twenty-five years for its English translation, by Popper himself, as *The Logic of Scientific Discovery* (Hutchinson in England, Basic Books in America, both in 1959, with a Science Editions paperback in 1961).

In his review of the English translation in the *Spectator* (January 30, 1959), A. J. Ayer called the book "a work of great originality and power." He said: "The method of science, as Popper saw it, was to put up hypotheses and test them by trying to falsify them. So long as they survived these tests, the hypotheses were retained as part of accepted scientific theory; when they failed they were discarded and other hypotheses adopted in their place." Statements that were not susceptible to logical refutation, or that were so limited as to be merely definitions, "were not asserted to be meaningless; but they were to be excluded from the domain of empirical science."

Logik der Forschung caused an immediate stir. Most reviewers praised its boldness and lucidity, and at least one authority found in Popper's thesis a "quality of greatness." Others saw the book as "laborious and complicated" and the thesis as "untenable" or merely a truism. At any rate, it brought its author a flood of lecture invitations and, in 1937, the post of senior lecturer in philosophy at Canterbury University College, Christchurch, New Zealand, where he remained until 1945.

In March 1938 Hitler occupied Austria. Popper, who even as a child had reacted against the nationalistic music of Wagner, determined to write what has become his best-known book, *The Open Society and Its Enemies*, first published in England by Routledge & Kegan Paul in 1945. The enemies of the open society, in Popper's view, are those thinkers—notably Plato, Hegel and Marx—who, believing that history is subject to certain inexorable laws, would impose these laws on humanity at whatever cost to the individual. History cannot progress, Popper says in the book, "only we, the human individuals can do it. . . . Instead of posing as prophets we must become the makers of our fate." Reviewers found it "by far the most important work on contemporary sociology"; "solid, erudite, and challenging"; and even "beyond any doubt a great book."

The Poverty of Historicism, which appeared at almost the same time as *The Open Society*, developed similar arguments. It was originally published serially in the London School of Economics' *Economica* in 1944 and 1945; it made its first appearance as a book in English in 1957 (Routledge in England, Beacon Press in America). It has been widely translated.

The book rejected historical determinism, insisting that man's future is in his own hands and advocating "piecemeal social engineering" rather than "total planning." Some reviewers praised its clarity and cogency, viewing it as a work of great importance; others thought it "ambiguous," "jerky" in exposition, and based on a poor knowledge of sociological literature.

In May 1945 Popper became reader in logic and scientific method at the University of London, exchanging the readership for full professorship in January 1949. Since 1945 he has also been head of what is now the department of philosophy, logic and scientific method at the London School of Economics, which is part of the University of London. The department has become a center of intellectual activity.

Popper's long-awaited *Conjectures and Refutations: The Growth of Scientific Knowledge* (Basic Books; Routledge) was published in 1963. He is at present engaged in writing a sequel to *The Logic of Scientific Discovery* to be called "Postscript: After Twenty Years." Although his book output has so far been relatively small, the number and variety of his articles and published speeches are large. Among the periodicals to which he has contributed are *Mind, Nature,* the *British Journal for the Philosophy of Science,* the *Philosophical Quarterly,* the *Journal of Symbolic Logic, Analysis,* and many others in several countries.

Popper received an M.A. degree *ad eundem* from the University of New Zealand in 1938 and a D.Lit. degree from the University of London in 1948. He is a Fellow of the British Academy and the International Academy for the Philosophy of Science. In 1958-59 he served as president of the Aristotelian Society and in 1959-61 as president of the British Society for the Philosophy of Science. He is a member of the board of the Royal Institute of Philosophy and a member of the editorial board of the *British Journal for the Philosophy of Science.* He is also associated with the periodicals *Ratio,* the *Monist, Erfahrung und Denken,* and *Dialectica.*

He was the Eleanor Rathbone Lecturer at Bristol University in 1956, the Annual Philosophical Lecturer at the British Academy in 1960, the Herbert Spencer Lecturer at Oxford in 1961, and the Shearman Memorial Lecturer at University College, London the same year. Popper has paid a number of visits to the United States, first in 1950 as William James Lecturer at Harvard and then in 1956 as visiting lecturer at Emory University, Atlanta, Georgia. He returned to America as Resident Fellow at the Center for Advanced Studies, Stanford, California in 1956-57 and was back again in the spring of 1962 as visiting professor of philosophy in the University of California at Berkeley.

On April 11, 1930 Karl R. Popper married a school teacher, Josefine Anna Henninger. They live in Penn, Buckinghamshire, a quiet village between London and Oxford. They have no children. Professor Popper, who is now a British subject, lists his favorite recreations as reading and music. Asked if there were any misconceptions about himself that he would like corrected, the author of *The Open Society and Its Enemies* wrote: "Although I abhor Plato's social philosophy, I do not belittle him: I have always acknowledged what I have described as 'Plato's overwhelming intellectual achievement.'"

The *New Scientist* (April 2, 1959) profile of Popper presents him as a man of charm and sensitivity, with a great capacity for friendship, although he is frequently involved in arguments with other scholars. His health is not good, but he works "phenomenally long hours." He is a perfectionist for whom the effort of writing is still considerable, in spite of his grasp of English. "A problem which has engaged my interest during my whole life," Popper has observed, "is that of speaking and writing clearly, simply and unpretentiously. I believe that it is everybody's duty to . . . avoid, like the plague . . . the appearance of possessing wisdom which is too deep to be clearly and simply expressed."

References

New Scientist 5:746+ Ap 2 '59 por
International Who's Who, 1962-63
Koch, Adrienne. Philosophy for a Time of Crisis (1959)
Twentieth Century Authors (First Supplement, 1955)
Urmson, James O., ed. Concise Encyclopedia of Western Philosophy and Philosophers (1960)
Who's Who, 1963

PORTER, KATHERINE ANNE May 15, 1890-
Writer

Address: b. c/o Atlantic Monthly Press, Little, Brown & Co., 34 Beacon St., Boston 6, Mass.

> NOTE: This biography supersedes the article that appeared in *Current Biography* in 1940.

To a master of irony like Katherine Anne Porter it may have seemed only natural that the appearance of her twenty-year endeavor, *Ship of Fools,* was celebrated more as a publishing event of 1962 than as a literary event. The reputation that she had long before established as a short story writer appealing to the connoisseur had made her first full-length novel a best seller before it reached the book stores. Weathering the mixed critical reviews that had never greeted her volumes of short stories, such as *Flowering Judas* (1930) and *Pale Horse, Pale Rider* (1939), *Ship of Fools* brought Miss Porter commercial success for the first time in a long career.

Katherine Anne Maria Veronica Callista Russell Porter was born in Indian Creek, near San Antonio, Texas on May 15, 1890, the fourth of five children of Harrison Boone Porter, a landowning farmer, and Mary Alice (Jones) Porter. Her mother died in early womanhood. She has two sisters, Ann Gay and Mary Alice; her brothers, Paul and John, are no longer living. Her ancestors had come from Warwickshire, England in the mid-seventeenth century. On her father's side of the family she is a lineal descendant of Daniel Boone's brother Jonathan and of Colonel Andrew Porter, a pre-Revolutionary aide to George Washington. The famed short story writer O. Henry (Sidney Porter) was her father's second cousin.

Baptized in the Roman Catholic faith, to which she still adheres, Katherine Anne Porter was educated in convents and private schools for girls in Texas and Louisiana, where the emphasis on deportment perhaps partly accounts for the picture she has of herself as a "precocious, nervous, rebellious, unteachable child." She loved music

Bradford Bachrach

KATHERINE ANNE PORTER

and sang in school and church concerts and choruses. "Badly trained," she recalls, "my singing voice left me early." In girlhood, as in later life, she enjoyed dancing, swimming, and horseback riding.

For Katherine Anne Porter, learning to write, even learning to form letters, had meant learning to write stories. Her literate family background, her early access to good libraries, and her own natural tendency conspired to draw her into a compulsive and persistent absorption in writing. "I did not choose this vocation," she once protested, "and if I had any say in the matter, I would not have chosen it." In an apprenticeship of self-imposed isolation, she began to write and accumulate trunkfuls of manuscripts. Her reading gave her all English literature and all literature in English translation for inspiration, but she had no one to turn to for guidance and encouragement in what she has spoken of as "the single vital issue" of her life. It is not surprising, therefore, since she had been a literary disciple of no one, that critics of her earliest work were struck by the individuality of her talent.

Throughout her life Miss Porter has traveled a good deal and has had many temporary homes in both hemispheres. In 1918-19 she worked as a reporter for the *Rocky Mountain News* in Denver. (She denies a much-quoted report that she once worked on a Dallas newspaper.) After a long bout with influenza, she lived for a considerable time in Mexico, where she became the friend of some of its revolutionary leaders and painters. In 1922 she arranged for the first exhibition of Mexican-Indian folk art in the United States. Wherever she lived, she earned her living through hack writing of all kinds, and later through teaching and lecturing, in order to insure the integrity of her own creative work. She wanted to be personally responsible to the last comma, and she explained on a television pro-

gram in October 1962, "I could not make a living writing because I would not write the kind of books editors wanted me to write because that was mine and I wouldn't tamper with it."

American literature has no sample of Katherine Anne Porter's novice work, since she did not try to publish her stories before she was thirty years old. Her early published stories, which appeared in *Century, transition, Second American Caravan, New Masses,* and *Hound and Horn,* were collected in 1930 in *Flowering Judas* (Harcourt). "'Flowering Judas' is not a promising book," Allen Tate wrote (*Nation,* October 1, 1930); "it promises nothing. It is a fully matured art."

The qualities that reviewers discovered and proclaimed in Miss Porter's first volume became the hallmark of her work as a whole: her mastery in handling her theme with a style both rich and economical, with colorful detail but no decoration, with both subtlety and straightforwardness. Her penetrating and imaginative perception of human motivation allowed her to achieve the inevitable and dramatic climax without resorting to stylistic tricks. Two of the six stories of *Flowering Judas* were set in Mexico; the others had backgrounds in the United States.

In 1931 Miss Porter received a Guggenheim Fellowship, which enabled her to travel, study, and write abroad. She made her first voyage to Europe, and her impressions of that voyage were still vivid in her mind (as she wrote in a foreword to *Ship of Fools*) when in Basel, Switzerland in the summer of 1932 she read Sebastian Brant's fifteenth-century moral allegory, *Das Narrenschiff*. She visited Germany and met some of the Nazi leaders, and for several years she lived in Paris. One of her literary undertakings there was the translation of seventeen French songs, beginning with the twelfth-century "Chanson de Chatelain de Coucy," which were published with music, with words in English and French, and with explanatory notes in *Katherine Anne Porter's French Song-Book* (Harrison of Paris; Minton) in 1933.

Also in Paris, Miss Porter wrote a long short story, *Hacienda; A Story of Mexico* (Harrison of Paris, 1934), based on the visit of the film directors S. M. Eisenstein and G. V. Alexandrov and the cameraman E. K. Tisse to Mexico in 1931. Glenway Wescott in *Images of Truth* (Harper, 1962) thought that this tale about a group of Russian film producers working in Mexico pointed toward *Ship of Fools.* "For some mysterious reason, perhaps nothing but the timing in her life," he suggested, "her recollection of Mexico evidently had lapsed less for her, subsided less, than that of other places she has lived."

Her recollections of Texas did not subside either. In 1937, after she had returned to the United States, Katherine Anne Porter published a short novel, *Noon Wine* (first brought out in book form by Schuman's), whose setting is a dairy farm in southern Texas. A psychological tale about an immigrant Swede from North Dakota who is fleeing pursuit as an escaped homicidal maniac, it seemed to a New York *Times* reviewer "too ironic for ordinary mortals," but its frequent reprintings seem to testify to the validity and appeal of the experience it conveys.

Noon Wine was first reprinted in *Pale Horse, Pale Rider* (Harcourt, 1939), which contained two other short novels, the title story and *Old Mortality*. The two latter stories are related to each other through Miranda, probably in part an autobiographical character, who in *Old Mortality* recounts with another little girl the story of a beautiful Southern belle of fifty years ago. *Pale Horse, Pale Rider* is a bitter, tragic tale of grown-up Miranda's love for a World War I soldier who dies of influenza.

"With these three novelettes, Katherine Anne Porter establishes herself as a prose stylist of first rank," P. T. Hartung wrote in *Commonweal* (May 19, 1939). Christopher Isherwood compared her to Katherine Mansfield, and other reviewers felt that she belonged in the company of Henry James, Hawthorne, and Flaubert. The flawless style that almost all critics acknowledged in the *Pale Horse, Pale Rider* volume owed its very existence to unobtrusiveness. Clifton Fadiman commented in the *New Yorker* (April 1, 1939), "Miss Porter calculates her effects, which is not to say that she gives the effect of calculation."

The nine stories collected in *The Leaning Tower* (Harcourt, 1944) encouraged further comparison with Henry James. In *The Days Before* (Harcourt, 1952), a collection of essays, critical articles, and book reviews that had appeared in periodicals and as book prefaces over a period of some thirty years, Katherine Anne Porter discussed in the title piece the formative years of Henry James. Among the other subjects of her essays were Gertrude Stein and Willa Cather.

The title story of *The Leaning Tower*, a short novel written during World War II, is set in Berlin on the eve of Hitler's rise to power and treats the menace of Nazism with an artistic integrity that resists temptations to propagandize. While writing the story, Miss Porter was also working on her first full-length novel, which she variously called "The Promised Land," "No Safe Harbor," and "Ship of Fools." From time to time since 1940 it had been scheduled for early publication, but it needed many years to grow. Miss Porter has been called a slow writer because of the years of silence between each published volume. Actually, she has said, she wrote *Noon Wine* and *Old Mortality* each in seven days and *Pale Horse, Pale Rider* in nine days—not counting the inestimable amount of time that went into observing, thinking, note taking, and planning for each story.

Although Katherine Anne Porter's literary reputation did not bring large sales of her books, it did help her earn a living. On several occasions she worked as a script writer in Hollywood, on films about Queen Elizabeth I and Madame Sans-Gêne, among others, but she received no screen credits. She was more successful in academic circles. "I did not go to a university," she has said, "until I went there to teach. In the past twenty-four years . . . I have visited as teacher, speaker, or reader of my own work in something near two hundred American and European universities, colleges, and writing conferences." One of the first of these was the Olivet College Writers' Summer Conference in 1937. More recently she was Fulbright lecturer at the

University of Liége, Belgium (1955), writer-in-residence at the University of Virginia (1958-59), and first Glasgow Professor at Washington and Lee University (1959). Other demands on her time included serving as a Fellow of regional American literature in the Library of Congress (1944), representing American literature with five other delegates at the International Festival of Twentieth Century Arts in Paris (1952), and making a summer tour of duty with the Department of State for the United States Information Service (1960).

Meanwhile, Katherine Anne Porter was completing *Ship of Fools*. She had begun actual composition on her novel in August 1941, when she wrote the first fifteen or twenty paragraphs and the last three paragraphs. Because of the organic structure of her story, she has said, she was able to pick up its various strands from time to time as one might do in weaving a tapestry. *Ship of Fools*, which takes its title from Brant's *Das Narrenschiff*, offers a view of life through a moral allegory involving some forty identifiable characters who are passengers aboard the German ship *Vera* on a twenty-seven-day voyage from Veracruz, Mexico to Bremerhaven, Germany. *Ship of Fools* is a novel of theme and character rather than plot. Its main theme—evil and good are in criminal collusion, and one cannot exist without the other—is illustrated by several narrative lines, among them the budding of evil in the German ethos that permitted Hitler's regime.

Presold at the time of its publication by Little, Brown & Company in April 1962, *Ship of Fools* became a Book-of-the-Month Club selection and soon headed the bestselling list. Within a month its screen rights were sold for a guaranteed minimum of $500,000. The majority of critics (about 80 percent) gave it glowing reviews, some of them hailing Miss Porter as a major novelist. Among the dissenting voices was that of the reviewer for the London *Times Literary Supplement* (November 2, 1962), who felt that the book's "moments of great power and compassion" were the accomplishments of a short story writer and who bluntly called the novel "a drastic failure." In *Commentary* (October 1962) Theodore Solotaroff discussed the controversy in a detailed examination openly sympathetic to the unfriendly critics of *Ship of Fools*.

Katherine Anne Porter was living in Washington, D.C. at the time that *Ship of Fools* was published, and in an interview for the Washington *Post and Times Herald* (April 1, 1962) she remarked that none of the reviews had quite hit the point—"that evil is always done with the collusion of good." She explained that the theme of her lifetime had been self-betrayal in all its forms: "Every story I have ever written has that at the center, and you know, I didn't realize it for years." On a television program in October 1962 she said, "Many complain that I have a low view of human nature and that I make things entirely too black. And I think they must have led very sheltered lives."

One of the earliest recognitions of literary merit that Miss Porter received was the gold medal (1940) of the Society for the Libraries of New York University for *Pale Horse, Pale Rider*. She has since been awarded many honorary doc-

PORTER, KATHERINE ANNE—*Continued*

torates and various literary prizes, including the Emerson-Thoreau bronze medal for prose fiction of the American Academy of Arts and Sciences (1962). Although Miss Porter has, as she says, "a deep resistance to joining things," she did serve for two years in the early 1950's as vice-president of the National Institute of Arts and Letters. She belongs to the Democratic party and during President Franklin D. Roosevelt's third campaign trooped about the United States making speeches for him.

In Paris in 1933 Katherine Anne Porter married Eugene Pressly, who was attached to the United States consular service in that city. After her divorce from Pressly, on April 19, 1938 she married Albert Russel Erskine, Jr., a professor of English and one of the editors of the *Southern Review*, from whom she was divorced in 1942. A small, trim woman at seventy-three, she is five feet three inches tall and weighs 116 pounds. Her hair is snow-white and her eyes are blue-gray. "She has in fact a lovely face," Wescott wrote in *Images of Truth*, "of utmost distinction in the Southern way, moonflower-pale, never sunburned." In conversation, as if unleashed from the restraints of the short story, she sparkles with a vivacious, overflowing wit—sometimes formidable and almost always charming.

Asked what she did with her time in recent years when she was not working, Miss Porter replied, "I studied cooking, and music, and grew flowers when I had the chance, and read and listened to music, and enjoyed talk with friends; one does less of these things and more work and meditation as one grows older. All pleasant to have done." For many years she has been promising her readers a biography of Cotton Mather, on which she began work in 1928, and she means to keep the promise.

References

N Y Herald Tribune Bk R p11 Ap 1 '62; p4 N 11 '62
N Y Times Bk R p1+ Ap 1 '62 por
Washington (D.C.) Post F p8 Ap 1 '62 por
Twentieth Century Authors (1942; First Supplement, 1955)
Wescott, Glenway. Images of Truth (1962)
Who's Who in America, 1962-63

POUND, EZRA (LOOMIS) Oct. 30, 1885-
Poet and critic

Address: c/o Messrs. Shakespear and Parkyn, 8 John St., Bedford Row, London, W.C. 1, England

NOTE: This biography supersedes the article that appeared in *Current Biography* in 1942.

T. S. Eliot has said of Ezra Pound that "Mr. Pound is more responsible for the twentieth century revolution in poetry than is any other individual." Many other major English and American poets have acknowledged their indebtedness to Ezra Pound, despite the possible guilt by association with Pound's heresies, which became increasingly economic and political after 1920.

Tagged as a "funny money crank" and a fascist, Pound was incarcerated for twelve years by the United States government, which charged him with treason but never brought him to trial. Meanwhile, he was writing the *Cantos*, which the critic M. L. Rosenthal has called "a gigantic work in progress of a new kind, the boldest experiment in poetry of the twentieth century."

Few expatriates have remained as thoroughly American as Ezra Loomis Pound. Born in Hailey, Idaho on October 30, 1885, he was the only child of Homer Loomis Pound and Isabel (Weston) Pound, both of whom traced ancestry to colonial New England. Henry Wadsworth Longfellow is a distant relative. His grandfather Thaddeus Coleman Pound made a fortune in Wisconsin lumber (and issued his own company scrip until the government stopped him) before entering Republican politics and Congress. Homer Pound, assayer at the government land office in Hailey, became, during the poet's childhood, assistant assayer at the United States Mint in Philadelphia. The family moved to Philadelphia in 1889, after long stopovers at the Weston home in New York City and the Pound farm in Wisconsin. In 1891 they settled in the Philadelphia suburb of Wyncote.

A self-described "lanky whey-faced" boy, Pound studied successively at Cheltenham Military Academy and Cheltenham High School. He traveled to Europe with a great aunt-in-law in 1898 and with his father in 1901. At fifteen he entered the University of Pennsylvania, where he was a fellow student of William Carlos Williams, who weathered all the differences through the years and always remained a friend of Pound. He was also a frequent companion of Hilda Doolittle, the poetess "H.D." Although robust, Pound shunned athletics except for fencing and tennis and wrote daily sonnets, which he periodically destroyed. Transferring to Hamilton College in Clinton, New York at the beginning of his junior year, Pound discovered Provençal poetry under Professor William Pierce Shephard there and took his Ph.B. degree in June 1905.

Returning to the University of Pennsylvania for graduate work in Romanics and English literature, Pound took his M.A. degree in June 1906 and went to Europe on a fellowship granted for the study of Lope de Vega. When the university failed to renew the fellowship he returned to the United States and taught French and Spanish at Wabash College in Crawfordsville, Indiana from September 1907 to mid-winter, when he was dismissed as a "Latin Quarter type." The college paid him for the full year of contract, however, and he was soon on his way back to Europe. Arriving at Gilbraltar in 1908, Pound proceeded (reportedly on foot) to Venice, where, in June 1908, he paid A. Antonini eight dollars—practically all he had left—to print *A Lume Spento*, his first collection of poems. Moving on to London (again reportedly traveling much of the way on foot), he lectured during two winters at the Regent Street Polytechnic Institute.

Overnight fame came to Pound in April 1909 when Elkin published his *Personae*, a collection of poems. The acclaim of London critics crossed the Atlantic, and when Pound visited the United

States in 1910 he found himself well known in his homeland, particularly for "Ballad of the Goodly Fere," about Christ. "All I had to do was to write a ballad about each of the disciples," Pound said later, "and I would have been set for life."

He had already begun to expand his metric virtuosity by his explorations outside the tradition dominated by Shakespeare, Milton, and Tennyson. His translations from Anglo-Saxon, medieval Provençal, medieval Tuscan, and ancient Roman, scattered through *Ripostes* (1912), *Lustra* (1916), and *Umbra* (1920), gave the originals fresh birth in our time without depriving them of the rhythms that gave English verse new possibilities. These translations, with *Cathay* (1915), are collected in *The Translations of Ezra Pound* (New Directions, 1954). *Cathay* was a translation of the Chinese of Rihaku, done for the most part from the notes of Ernest Fenollosa. From Rihaku, Pound learned the ideogram. From Fenollosa's notes he also translated *Certain Noble Plays of Japan* (1916; reissued as *Noh* by New Directions in 1959). The effect of the continual discipline of translation was evident in the economy and freedom from literary incrustation of *Homage to Sextus Propertius* (Elkin Matthews, 1919). Pound later translated Confucius' *Ta Hio* (University of Washington Chapbooks, 1928), *The Unwobbling Pivot and the Great Digest* (New Directions, 1947), and *The Confucian Odes* (Harvard University Press, 1954); and Sophocles' *Women of Trachis* (New Directions, 1957).

Impresario as well as poet, Pound before and during World War I was a colorful figure in London with his red hair and beard, billiard cloth trousers, loose jacket, and cajoling and mocking voice. With T. E. Hulme, Richard Aldington, and H.D., he founded the *Imagiste* movement against overstuffed Georgian verse, and the rules of directness, naturalness, and precision that he formulated still hold true almost half a century later. When Amy Lowell made off with Imagism in 1914, Pound invented Vorticism with Henri Gaudier-Brzeska, the sculptor. *Blast*, the organ of Vorticism, edited by Wyndham Lewis, had two issues, the last in 1915.

Pound's generosity to other writers was particularly notable from 1914 to 1924, when he scoured the little magazines for unknown giants. He brought T. S. Eliot and James Joyce into print and recognition and scrounged money to lure Eliot from his job at Lloyd's Bank and Joyce from destitution. His blue pencil cut Eliot's original *Waste Land* in half and brought William Butler Yeats, older and in mid-career, down from abstraction and artifice to his more natural and enduring later work. (Pound was Yeats's secretary for three successive winters beginning in 1913-14.) Pound's influence can be traced through more than fifty little magazines published between 1912 and 1939. He was London editor of *Poetry* (beginning in 1912), literary editor of *The Egoist* (1914-19), foreign editor of the *Little Review* (1917-19), and art and music critic for guild-socialist Alfred Richard Orage's *New Age*. Orage introduced Pound to

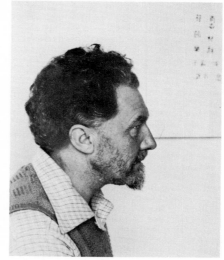

Arnold Genthe

EZRA POUND

Major Clifford Hugh Douglas, the inventor of Social Credit, in 1917.

After World War I Pound was bitter: not only had the lives of men like T. E. Hulme and Gaudier-Brzeska been sacrificed during the war, but the horror of the mass sacrifice had been compounded by the flood of Georgian verse which sentimentalized it and to which the public turned in relief, to the detriment of Pound's poetic cause. His cause would never again be solely poetic. *Hugh Selwyn Mauberly* (Ovid Press, 1920), one of his unquestioned masterpieces, was his poetic farewell to England.

In the Paris of the early 1920's Pound's Montparnasse apartment rivaled the salon of Gertrude Stein as a regular stop in the itinerary of Ernest Hemingway and other expatriate literati. Stein dismissed Pound as a "village explainer," Pound remembered Stein as "that charming old fraud." While in Paris Pound was French correspondent for the American *Dial*. He championed the sculptor Valentin Brancusi and the composer George Antheil and did some sculpturing and composing himself.

Moving to Rapallo, Italy in 1924, Pound continued his prodigious international correspondence and his patronage of other writers. In 1927 he received the *Dial* award of two thousand dollars for his service to letters. During 1927-28 he published *The Exile*, whose platform was Confucian. *The Exile* defined the state "as convenience" and decried "all interference in human affairs by people paid to interfere." In 1928 Pound met Leo Frobenius, Spengler's German source, whose theory of cultures rising with races and perishing with them he had long been imbibing.

Pound's lifetime project, the *Cantos*, which he had begun in London, began to appear in book form in 1925. The *Cantos* are garrulous monologues on the meaning of history, epic and fugue-like in structure. Like conversations, they

POUND, EZRA—*Continued*

are obscure only to the stranger who drops in, and the obscurity, as T. S. Eliot has suggested, disappears after one becomes acquainted with Pound through a study of his other work in chronological order. Faber published the *Cantos* as they appeared during the 1930's and 1940's. All of the *Cantos*—1 through 84—up to and including the *Pisan Cantos* were brought together in the 1949 New Directions edition of *The Cantos of Ezra Pound.*

Pound's concern and involvement with economics increased during the world depression of the 1930's. "Monetary theory is worthy of study because it leads to the contemplation of justice," he wrote in *A Visiting Card,* the fourth in the series of Money Pamphlets that he wrote between 1935 and 1944. Originally published in Italy, the pamphlets, which also included *An Introduction to the Economic Nature of the United States, Gold and Work, What Is Money For?, Social Credit,* and *America, Roosevelt, and the Causes of the Present War,* were published in England by Peter Russell between 1950 and 1952. Pound's *ABC of Economics,* an attempt to interest the lay reader in Social Credit, was published by Faber in 1933. *Jefferson and/or Mussolini* was published by Liveright in 1935. His emphases changed over the years and his identification with American Social Creditors faded as his identification with the Mussolini regime became greater. Pound was never a pure Social Creditor, but his rage against usury remained the same and never lost its basis in Thomas Jefferson and John Adams.

After an absence of twenty-eight years, Pound visited the United States in 1939. The chief purpose of the visit, he said later, was to try to move American governmental policy toward what he considered paths of peace. He tried unsuccessfully, to see President Franklin D. Roosevelt but discussed economics with Secretary of Agriculture Henry A. Wallace and several Congressmen instead. Hamilton College gave him an honorary doctorate in letters during his visit.

After his return to Italy, Pound broadcast on the American hour of Rome Radio two or three times a week beginning in January 1941. Relishing his role as social commentator, he gave free rein to his political and economic ideas in mocking and discursive monologues. After the United States entered World War II in December 1941, Pound went off the air. He tried to board the last diplomatic train taking Americans out of Italy in 1942, but was stopped by American officials.

On January 29, 1942 Pound resumed his broadcasts after he had come to an agreement with the Italian government that "he never be asked to say anything contrary to his conscience...or to his duties as an American citizen." Pound later insisted that he never broke that agreement, but he nevertheless changed his political stance, and the vituperation with which he identified Jews with international finance shocked many who knew his background.

When the victorious American army overran Italy in the spring of 1945, Pound was arrested and taken to the Mediterranean Theater of Operations' Disciplinary Training Center at Pisa. There, confined to a cage, he wrote of his personal tragedy with remarkable lack of self-pity in the *Pisan Cantos:* "Pull down thy vanity/ How mean thy hates..../ But to have done instead of not doing/ This is not vanity. . . ./ To have gathered from the air a live tradition/ Or from a fine old eye the unconquered flame/ This is not vanity" (Canto LXXXI).

Flown to Washington, D.C. in November 1945, Pound was indicted for treason, arraigned, submitted to psychiatric examination, declared to be "mentally unfit" for trial, and remanded to St. Elizabeths Hospital in the Washington suburb of Anacostia. There he remained for twelve years, holed up in a doorless cubicle in the Chestnut Ward except when he was allowed out on the lawn on sunny afternoons. His wife moved nearby and visited him daily. He continued to produce his poetry and conduct his correspondence despite his grim surroundings, and such old friends as T. S. Eliot, E. E. Cummings, and Marianne Moore called on him from time to time. Among the new friends who visited him was the rabid racist John Kasper.

In 1948, while confined at St. Elizabeths, Pound was awarded the Bollingen Prize in Poetry. The event stirred up considerable acrimony, not only in the pages of the *Partisan Review* and the *Saturday Review of Literature,* but also in the popular press. Although he was among those who objected to the award, Peter Viereck wrote in *Commentary* (April 1951): "Much of the moralizing hue and cry against Pound's fascism and Jew-baiting comes not from sincere anti-fascists but from the envy with which the dwarfs of mediocrity forever regard originality and experimentalism in art."

Section: Rock-Drill (Cantos 85 to 95) was published by New Directions in 1956. Archibald MacLeish wrote of it in the New York *Times Book Review* (December 16, 1956): "For forty years the curious structure of the Cantos has been rising, figure by figure, out of the disorder of our time . . . and as the book completes itself, one sees what it is, a true . . . dissent from the dead assumptions . . . for the sake of the ideal of order in men's lives."

The indictment against Pound was dropped on April 18, 1958, and he was released from St. Elizabeths. In July 1958 he returned to Italy, where he has continued working on the *Cantos. Thrones* (New Directions, 1959) carried the number of *Cantos* to 109. By Christmas 1959 he had completed Canto 111 and was hoping "to make it to 120."

Pound's literary criticism, directed mainly to his fellow craftsmen, has been called by T. S. Eliot "the *least dispensable* body of critical writing in our time." Eliot collected *The Literary Essays of Ezra Pound* (New Directions, 1954) from *Pavannes and Divisions* .(Knopf, 1918), *Instigations* (Boni and Liveright, 1920), *Make It New* (Faber; Yale, 1934); *Polite Essays* (Faber, 1937); and *Guide to Kulchur* (Faber, 1938; New Directions, 1952) and various periodicals. Pound has also written *The Spirit of Romance* (Dent; 1910; New Directions, 1952), about the pre-

Renaissance literature of Latin Europe, and *ABC of Reading* (Yale, 1934; New Directions, 1951).

Ezra Pound married Dorothy Shakespear, a native of England, in April 1914. They have a son, Omar Shakespear Pound, and a daughter, Princess Mary de Rachewiltz. In the tower of the Rachewiltz castle near Moreno in the Italian Alps he does his work. The high altitude reportedly aggravates the osteo-arthritic condition of his neck vertebrae that he traces to his confinement at Pisa. On the castle's garden terrace stands the hieratic head of Pound done by Gaudier-Brzeska; in the castle is the clavicord made by his late friend Arnold Dolmetsch. Pound is a big man with green eyes. Although his auburn hair and beard have turned silver, and he sometimes uses a cane, reports suggest that he has as much nervous energy at his command as ever. In September, Ezra Pound was named the 1963 fellow of the American Academy of Poets, receiving with the honor a cash award of $5,000.

References

> International Who's Who, 1962-63
> Kenner, Hugh. The Poetry of Ezra Pound (1951)
> Mullins, Eustace. That Difficult Individual, Ezra Pound (1961)
> Norman, Charles. Ezra Pound (1960)
> Twentieth Century Authors (1942; First Supplement, 1955)
> Who's Who, 1963

POWELL, DICK Nov. 14, 1904-Jan. 2, 1963

Motion-picture actor; first played juvenile singing roles in musical comedies, then tough private detective roles; appeared on radio and television programs, including the *Dick Powell Show*; co-owner of Four Star Television Corporation. See *Current Biography* (February) 1948.

Obituary

N Y Times p36 Ap 1 '63

POWERS, JAMES E(LLIS) July 26, 1910-

Organization official; public official

Address: b. Georgia State Department of Veterans Affairs, Macon, Ga.; h. Colaparchee Dr., Macon, Ga.

Representing some 2,502,546 veterans of the two World Wars and of the Korean conflict, the American Legion is the largest organization of war veterans in the world. Its national commander in 1962-63 was James E. Powers of Macon, Georgia, who was chosen for this office at the Legion's forty-fourth annual convention, held at Las Vegas, Nevada in October 1962. Powers, who was the second Georgian to become national commander, joined Macon's American Legion Post 74 in 1946, following a tour of duty in World War II with the United States Army Transportation Corps in the Pacific, and he became the post's service officer shortly afterward. He was post commander from 1947 to 1950 and department commander for Georgia in 1951-52, and he has been active on several committees of the national organization. Since 1954 he has repre-

Chase

JAMES E. POWERS

sented his state on the Legion's national executive committee. A specialist in the rehabilitation of veterans, Powers has been manager of the Macon office of the Georgia state veterans service department since 1947.

James Ellis Powers was born on July 26, 1910 at Lorane, Bibb County, Georgia, about ten miles from Macon. He is the eleventh of fifteen children of Nathan Abner Powers, a cotton farmer, and Laura Eileen (Ellis) Powers, a schoolteacher. Both of his grandfathers fought in the Confederate army during the Civil War. Three of his brothers served in World War I; his other three brothers, like himself, saw action in World War II. Jimmie Powers was educated in the public schools of Macon and Bibb County. At Lanier High School in Macon he played football and baseball and was a member of the debating team and the literary society. After graduating in 1927 he attended Mercer University in Macon, where he was on the freshman football and baseball teams.

Compelled to give up college after three years because of the Depression, Powers, who had begun his career as a farmer, took a job with the Macon National Bank in 1930. In the following year he was employed by the Buckeye Cotton Oil Company, a subsidiary of Procter and Gamble. Powers became credit manager in the Macon office of the Sherwin Williams Paint Company in 1936, and he held this position at the time he entered the United States Army in 1944. During the prewar years he was active in the Methodist Church, where, among other things, he served as a scoutmaster.

Powers served with the Macon volunteers in the Georgia National Guard before entering the army as a private on April 13, 1944. After completing his basic training in Texas he went to Officers Candidate School in New Orleans, and in 1945 he received his commission as a second lieutenant in the 'Transportation Corps. From

POWERS, JAMES E.—*Continued*

Camp Stoneman, California he was sent to the Pacific for convoy, supply, and amphibious support duties, which took him to Eniwetok, Ulithi, Leyte Gulf, Luzon, Mindanao, Okinawa, and finally to occupation duty in Japan and Korea. When he was placed on reserve status in August 1946 he held the rank of first lieutenant and had four battle stars—two on the Asiatic-Pacific campaign ribbon and two on the Philippine Liberation ribbon.

Upon his return to civilian life Powers resumed his post as credit manager with the Sherwin Williams Company, and he soon joined American Legion Post 74 in Macon. The Legion had been of considerable help to his family in the combat death of one brother and the serious wounding of another. Furthermore, his older brothers, who had served in World War I, were charter members of a local Legion post. Shortly after joining the Legion, Jimmie Powers volunteered to become the post's service officer, and in this capacity he dealt with the problems of disabled veterans and of families of soldiers who were killed. He was so successful in his work on behalf of the disabled that he was offered a full-time position as manager of the Macon office of the Georgia State Department of Veterans Affairs, serving some 25,000 veterans. He was still holding this job at the time of his election as national commander of the American Legion in 1962 despite the fact that he had received a number of other attractive offers for employment in government and private industry.

In 1947 Powers was elected commander of Macon's Post 74 for the first of three successive one-year terms. Largely as a result of his leadership the post's membership more than doubled within a few years, from 620 to 1,260 members, to become the second largest in the state. He has also continued to be service officer of the post. On a state level, Powers became junior vice-commander of the American Legion's Department of Georgia in 1949. He was elected senior vice-commander in 1950 and department commander in 1951. In the years following the end of World War II the state membership had declined considerably, and the organization was operating at a deficit. As commander, Powers saw the need for revising the structure of the state organization and for making the Legion's programs more effective. Under his leadership, revisions were made in the constitution of the state organization, the budget was balanced, and the programs were given new life. Within a few years the membership rose to an all-time high of 58,000.

Powers was first elected to represent Georgia on the American Legion's national executive committee in 1954, and he was appointed by successive national commanders to act as a liaison between the national executive committee and the rehabilitation commission of the Legion. He has served as vice-chairman and chairman of the national membership and post activities committee, and he has been active in several capacities on the national rehabilitation commission. Powers has also worked on the liaison committee of the national internal affairs commission, the advisory committee to the national

commander, the resolutions subcommittee, and the national reorganization committee.

On October 11, 1962, the last day of the American Legion's forty-fourth annual convention at Las Vegas, Nevada, both Powers and Joe L. Matthews, Jr., of Texas were nominated to succeed Charles L. Bacon of Kansas City, Missouri as national commander. Their respective supporters staged parades up and down the aisles of the convention hall. At the end of the roll-call vote Powers had about two-thirds of the votes. A subsequent motion by Matthews to make the election unanimous was adopted by the convention.

Among the prominent speakers who were heard by the 3,016 delegates to the convention were former President Harry S. Truman; Attorney General Robert F. Kennedy; J. Edgar Hoover, director of the FBI; and George Meany, president of the AFL-CIO. The convention adopted a resolution calling for vigorous action, including economic sanctions, against the Castro regime in Cuba and advocated a strong pension program for disabled, aging, and unemployable veterans. Other resolutions recommended full support of the House Committee on Un-American Activities and the passage of new laws to deter sabotage and acts of treason in time of peace, as well as an investigation of the American Civil Liberties Union. After some debate, a resolution was adopted, asking Congress to enact legislation permitting spoken prayer in public schools.

Shortly after his election Commander Powers visited the Caribbean area for a briefing by military commanders of the Antilles Defense Command. Following President Kennedy's naval blockade of Cuba on October 22, 1962 to counter the Soviet military buildup there Powers sent a message to the President, congratulating him on "the courageous and necessary stand" that he had taken to counter this threat and pledging "the full force and support of the Legion in this and any other actions" that the government might consider necessary to remove Communism from the hemisphere.

Speaking to a group of top-level American Legion officers and staff members at Washington, D.C. a few weeks later, Commander Powers said that an important objective in 1963 would be "to increase liaison between members of . . . Congress and Legionnaires in their home districts and states." He noted that Legion-supported reforms in veterans' programs did not fare very well in 1962 and cited as an example the defeat of a measure that would have re-opened National Service Life Insurance for one year. He pointed out that the measure might have passed, if more Legionnaires had been effectively organized to make their demands known to Congress.

In a foreign policy address to the Women's Forum on National Security at Washington, D.C. on January 15, 1963 Powers said: "We have played this deadly serious game of international cat and mouse just about as far as we can pursue it—for in this game of give and take we have learned that the Communists will take everything we are willing to give. . . . As viewed by the American Legion, the primary purpose of our foreign policy should be to protect and to advance America's interests in world affairs, and the primary purpose of our national security program is to provide the muscle to make that foreign policy effective." At the request of Senator Herman Talmadge of Georgia the speech was included in the *Congressional Record* (January 17, 1963).

Powers is a member of the Cherokee Heights Methodist Church in Macon, and he has served as president of its men's Bible class. He has continued to be active in the Boy Scout movement, as a scoutmaster and troop commissioner, and he has managed an American Legion junior baseball team, which won the Georgia state championship one year. Powers has been co-chairman of the Keep Georgia Green Committee and of the National Employ the Physically Handicapped Committee. His organizational and civic interests also include the Georgia Farm Bureau, the Georgia Master 4-H Club, the Macon Little Theater, and the Macon Community Concert Association. He is a member of the American Legion Department Service Officers Association.

On December 6, 1931 James E. Powers married Katherine McCamy of Rome, Georgia, a former librarian. They have one son, James Ellis Powers, Jr., an engineer with the National Aeronautics and Space Administration at Houston, Texas, and two grandchildren. A ruggedly built, broad-shouldered man, Jimmie Powers is six feet one inch tall, weighs 225 pounds, and has brown hair and blue eyes. He has been described as being "as dependable and sturdy as Stone Mountain." A fellow Georgia Legionnaire has said of Powers: "He is a man everyone turns to as a leader, as an advisor, as a friend. He never seems to think of himself. He is a gentleman in speech and deed. His ruling attitudes are good humor, friendship and sincerity. Hate, spite and meanness are alien to him. He has been a hard taskmaster for us, but a harder one for himself, for he has called on all of us to work mightily for the American Legion but none of us will ever catch up with what he has done himself."

Reference

American Legion Mag 73:13+ D '62 pors

PRASAD, RAJENDRA Dec. 3, 1884-Feb. 28, 1963 Indian statesman; lifelong associate of Mohandas Gandhi; first president of India (1950-62). See *Current Biography* (April) 1950.

Obituary

N Y Times p36 Ap 1 '63

PRINZ, JOACHIM May 10, 1902- Rabbi; author; organization official
Address: b. 621 Clinton Ave., Newark, N.J.; h. 306 Elmwynd Dr., Orange, N.J.

One of the outstanding American representatives of world Jewry and a leading exponent of the creative continuity of the Jewish heritage is Dr. Joachim Prinz. He has been rabbi of Temple B'nai Abraham in Newark, New Jersey since 1939 and national president of the American Jewish Congress since 1958. As a young rabbi of the Jewish community in Berlin from 1926 to 1937 Prinz was one of the first German-Jewish leaders

JOACHIM PRINZ

to recognize the danger of the rising Nazi movement, and his sermons and writings were an inspiration to the Jews of Germany, faced with persecution after Hitler's rise to power. Since his arrival in the United States in 1937 Dr. Prinz has stood in the forefront of the struggle against bigotry and for the preservation of Jewish life, and his frankness in speaking out for the principles he believes in has frequently involved him in controversy.

A native of Burckhardtsdorf in Upper Silesia, Joachim Prinz was born on May 10, 1902, one of four children of Joseph Prinz, a department store owner, and Nani (Berg) Prinz. Reared in a prosperous and enlightened German-Jewish atmosphere, Joachim Prinz learned English as a child. At fifteen he became an adherent of the Zionist movement of Theodor Herzl, which aimed at establishing a Jewish homeland in Palestine, an act looked upon as something akin to heresy by the assimilated middle-class Jews of Germany. After graduating from secondary school in Oppeln, Upper Silesia in 1921, Prinz studied philosophy and art history at the universities of Breslau and Berlin, and he received his doctor of philosophy degree at the University of Giessen in 1924. In the following year he was ordained a rabbi by the Jewish theological seminary in Breslau.

Invited to Berlin in January 1926, Prinz became the youngest ordained rabbi to serve the Jewish community of that city, and he soon attained an immense popularity, especially among the younger generation. He fostered Hebrew and Yiddish cultural aspirations, promoted a school of Jewish studies in Berlin, and wrote many articles. His continued adherence to Zionism was looked upon with disfavor by leaders of the Jewish community, who had high hopes for increasing German national acceptance and cultural assimilation during the era of the Weimar Republic.

(Continued next page)

PRINZ, JOACHIM—*Continued*

In the years before Hitler's rise to power Dr. Prinz warned of the consequences of Nazism and criticized those Jewish leaders who failed to recognize the impending danger. In his book *Jüdische Geschichte* (1931) he traced the history of the Jews and pointed out that the Jewish people were still living in the "twilight of the ghetto." In the midst of the despair that gripped the Jews of Germany after 1933, Dr. Prinz's sermons and books were a source of inspiration and hope, and attendance at his services mushroomed. His fearless attacks upon the government from his pulpit and from public platforms throughout Europe caused him to be arrested repeatedly by the Gestapo.

In his book *Wir Juden* (1934), a best seller, Prinz called upon his people to take pride in their cultural heritage and advocated the emigration of Jews from Germany. Other books by Prinz, dealing with Jewish history, culture, religion, and education, include *Illustrierte Jüdische Geschichte* (1933), *Die Geschichten der Bibel* (1934), *Die Reiche Israel und Juda* (1935), *Der Freitagabend* (1935), and *Das Leben im Ghetto* (1937). Some of these books have been translated into Spanish and Portuguese, and have attained considerable popularity among Jewish communities in Latin America.

In early 1937 Prinz visited the United States upon the invitation of Rabbi Stephen S. Wise, and as a result decided to immigrate to America with his family. His farewell meeting in Berlin, when he addressed some 2,000 members of his congregation, was attended by Adolf Eichmann, then a minor Gestapo official. (All Jewish meetings during this period were under strict surveillance of the Gestapo.) Eichmann subsequently issued a report to his superiors in which he stated that the fact that Prinz was immigrating to America instead of Palestine convinced him that the Jews were planning a worldwide conspiracy with headquarters in New York. The report is believed to have launched Eichmann's career.

Following a brief arrest by Nazi authorities in Berlin, Prinz was ordered to leave Germany. His expulsion order was signed by Eichmann. He arrived in New York on August 1, 1937 and for the next two years he toured the country, raising funds for the United Palestine Appeal and lecturing on European and Near Eastern affairs. On September 9, 1939 he was installed as rabbi of Temple B'nai Abraham in Newark, New Jersey upon recommendation of Rabbi Wise, who described Prinz as "one of the most gifted and brilliant young men . . . in the rabbinate."

In addition to his work on behalf of his congregation Dr. Prinz has taken an active part in national and world Jewish affairs. In 1946 he became a member of the executive board of the World Jewish Congress, which links Jewish organizations and communities of some sixty countries. He was chairman of the American delegation at its second plenary assembly at Montreux, Switzerland in June 1948 and has served as a member of its world executive.

In 1952 Prinz became vice-president of the American Jewish Congress. He has also served as chairman of its administration committee and of its commission on international affairs. In the latter position he initiated the publication of materials analyzing the Arab refugee problem and documenting anti-Jewish activities by Arab authorities. At its national convention at Miami Beach, Florida in May 1958 the American Jewish Congress elected Prinz as its president for a two-year term, succeeding Dr. Israel Goldstein. He was re-elected in 1960 and 1962. The American Jewish Congress, which represents some 300,000 Jews in the United States, was founded in 1918 with the purpose of defending American liberties and promoting the unity and creative survival of the Jewish people.

Dr. Prinz has consistently battled for civil liberties and human rights. In 1954 he instituted a libel suit against Conde McGinley, the editor of the rabidly anti-Semitic publication *Common Sense*, who had accused him of being a Communist. Prinz was awarded $30,000, which he never collected. His victory was viewed as a landmark in the fight against bigotry, indicating that racial and religious libels could be effectively challenged in the courts. In April 1960 he led a picket line in front of a Woolworth store in New York City protesting discrimination against Negroes at lunch counters in Southern states.

When a wave of anti-Semitic vandalism swept the United States in 1959 and 1960, Prinz warned against dismissing such action as a mere fad. He proposed in a letter to President Dwight D. Eisenhower that a White House conference be convened to deal with bigotry and lawlessness, and he called upon churches, schools, and government to take action against bigotry. On the other hand, under his guidance the American Jewish Congress rejected certain proposals for federal legislation against libel of groups as detrimental to civil liberties. Prinz has spoken out against federal aid to religious and private schools, and he has urged states to grant exemptions from Sunday closing laws to members of religions that do not recognize Sunday as the Sabbath. Other areas of particular concern to Dr. Prinz are the recent resurgence of anti-Semitism in the Soviet Union and continuing anti-Jewish activities in Arab countries.

In recent years Prinz has made several trips to his native Germany. In Berlin in the summer of 1956 he preached to the now decimated congregation on the site of his former pulpit, but rejected an invitation to return permanently to the Jewish community of Berlin. In talks with West German officials at Bonn in 1959 Prinz observed that the leaders of postwar Germany were men of good will, but he noted that strong anti-Semitic tendencies still prevailed among the German people. "Germany has failed to teach its youth about the crimes of Hitlerism," Prinz told Joseph Wershba of the New York *Post* (January 15, 1960). "There's been no 'moral rearmament' —instead there's been an emphasis on prosperity."

After Israeli agents captured Adolf Eichmann in Argentina in 1960, Prinz defended Israel's right to conduct the trial of the Nazi executioner on the grounds that Eichmann's crimes were directed specifically against the Jewish people. Prinz has also urged that the United States ratify the Genocide Convention, which is aimed at preventing similar crimes in the future.

Although Prinz had been a lifelong Zionist, he left the Zionist movement in 1948, when Israel became a nation, and he disagrees with Israeli Prime Minister David Ben-Gurion's view that Jews living outside Israel are not living a full Jewish life. Prinz believes that since Zionism had fulfilled its purpose with the creation of the state of Israel, the Zionist movement has become obsolete. In its place Prinz has proposed a new movement, based on the concept of Jewish "peoplehood," and dedicated to the unity of the Jewish people. Such a movement would forge new and vital links between the Jews of the United States and Israel. Although Prinz has been criticized for his position by Zionist leaders, his views have received considerable support among leaders of the American Jewish Congress.

On the American scene Dr. Prinz has been concerned with the creative survival of Jewish life. Although he no longer sees anti-Semitism as threatening the extinction of the Jews, he feels that Judaism is threatened from within by an increasing degree of assimilation and disintegration, a lack of identification with Jewish life, and widespread ignorance of Jewish culture and tradition. To counteract these tendencies Prinz has urged an expanded program of Jewish education for adults as well as children. In his book *The Dilemma of the Modern Jew* (Little, 1962), Prinz reviews the history of Jewish persecution and progress since the French Revolution and pleads for the preservation of the Jewish heritage and identity.

In his home community, Essex County, New Jersey, Prinz has served as chairman of the United Jewish Appeal and as president of the Jewish Educational Association. He is a member of the board of directors of the Jewish Community Council and of the Heart Association of Essex County. In 1956 he became a director of the Conference on Jewish Material Claims against Germany, and since 1958 he has served on the editorial boards of *Judaism* and of the *Reconstructionist*. He has contributed a chapter to *The Great Jewish Books* (Horizon Press, 1952), edited by Samuel Caplan and Harold U. Ribalow. Hebrew Union College conferred an honorary D.D. degree on Dr. Prinz in 1959.

Dr. Joachim Prinz has been an American citizen since 1944. He was first married on December 25, 1925 to Lucie Horowitz, who died on January 14, 1931, and he has one daughter, Lucie (Prinz) Berkowitz, from this marriage. On May 24, 1932 he married Hilde Goldschmidt, and they have three children, Michael, Jonathan, and Deborah. The Prinzes also have an adopted daughter, Jo, who had lost her family and had been at Auschwitz for four years. Dr. Prinz is five feet five inches tall, weighs 160 pounds, and has graying black hair and brown eyes. He is frank and direct in his manner of speaking. Often working as much as seventeen hours a day, Prinz is always available to members of his congregation for counseling . His favorite recreations are reading, art appreciation, and gardening. On June 5, 1962 Dr. Prinz was honored at a testimonial dinner at the Essex House in New York City, marking his sixtieth birthday and the twenty-fifth anniversary of his arrival in the United States.

References

Who's Who in America, 1962-63
Who's Who in World Jewry (1955)

QUAY, JAN EDUARD DE (kwī yän ä′dü-ärt dĕ) Aug. 26, 1901- Former Premier of the Netherlands; economist
Address: h. Waalsdorperweg 161, The Hague, the Netherlands

In May 1959 Jan Eduard de Quay, a former teacher, rose out of political obscurity to take over the difficult task of forming a new Netherlands government after the resignation of Premier Willem Drees, who had headed various Dutch cabinets for ten years. A compromise choice acceptable to all major parties, de Quay set up a conservative coalition government, which for the first time since the end of World War II did not include the socialist parties. De Quay himself belongs to the Catholic People's party, a strong group that supports free enterprise and Dutch unity with the West. Before becoming Premier he had been for thirteen years the Queen's Commissioner (Governor) of the Dutch province of North Brabant and for nearly twenty years a teacher at the Catholic School of Economics in Tilburg. After the general elections held in May 1963 the de Quay cabinet automatically went out of office. De Quay was one of four members of the Catholic People's party who tried, but failed, to form a new cabinet.

The son of a Dutch general, Jan Eduard de Quay was born on August 26, 1901 in 's Hertogenbosch (Bois-le-Duc), the capital of North Brabant, a southern province of the Netherlands. Upon completing his secondary education at St. Willibrordus College in Katwijk he entered the State University of Utrecht and majored in psychology. He obtained the doctor's degree in 1927 after submitting the thesis "Het aandeel der sensorische en motorische componenten in het verloop van leer- en arbeidsproces," about the role played by sensory and motor responses in the teaching and work processes. De Quay studied for several months at Yale and Harvard universities in 1927 and 1928.

As a lecturer from 1928 to 1934 and as professor from 1934 to 1946 de Quay taught business administration and applied psychology at the Catholic School of Economics in Tilburg, North Brabant. He also served as an assistant in the psychological laboratory of the State University of Utrecht in 1928-29, with the Advisory Bureau for Business Organizations in 1930, and as an adviser in applied psychology to C. and A. Brenninckmeijer from 1931 to 1933. From 1933 to 1946 he was director of the Technical Economic Institute and editor-secretary of the periodical *Economie*.

Until 1940 de Quay was chairman of the Society for National Security, and for a few days after the Nazis invaded the Netherlands in May 1940, until the Dutch ended their formal resistance, he fought with the Dutch army as an artillery major. In July 1940 he joined with the

JAN EDUARD DE QUAY

and a member of the advisory commission of the National Purchasing Bureau, which advised the government on its buying power. De Quay is the principal editor of the three-volume work *Het Nieuwe Brabant* (The New Brabant), published between 1952 and 1955.

The Catholic People's party, to which de Quay belongs, is the avenue of political expression for most of the Roman Catholics who make up about 38.5 percent of the Dutch population. It favors small property, corporative organizations, and limited state control of economic life and supports a foreign policy of co-operation with the United Nations and the West. It has been a major partner in all coalition cabinets since World War II. Of about equal strength in Parliament is the Labor party, a moderate socialist party that favors some production and distribution planning and socialization in production, banking, and transportation. Willem Drees of the Labor party served as Premier of various cabinets from 1948 to 1958.

Friction within the Parliament (Staten-Generaal) over tax policies brought about the resignation in December 1958 of the Drees cabinet. Queen Juliana named a caretaker government headed by Louis J. M. Beel, which dissolved the lower chamber of Parliament. General elections of March 1959 resulted in a reconstituted lower chamber in which the 150 seats were divided among the Catholic People's party (49), the Labor party (48), the Liberal party (19), the conservative Anti-Revolutionary (14) and Christian Historical Union (12) parties, and the Political Reform, Communist, and Pacifist Socialist parties.

The process of forming a new cabinet was lengthy and difficult. The responsibility for this had been assigned to de Quay, whose chief political asset, according to the New York *Times* (January 6, 1962,) "was that no one in any important party had anything against him, and the situation called for a compromise choice." In May 1959 de Quay succeeded in forming a conservative coalition cabinet, excluding the Labor party for the first time since the end of World War II.

A few months after he was sworn into office on May 19, 1959 de Quay made clear in a speech to Parliament his intention "to end a situation where the citizen relies on the state rather than on his own initiative and where the government continuously interferes with each and every aspect of social life in the Netherlands." He called for the reduction of social welfare benefits and farm subsidies, rejected a 4 percent general wage increase recommended by trade unions, and suggested that wage agreements be arrived at through collective bargaining of workers with private employers rather than by government rule. He further led government opposition to price-fixing policies in industry. In the budget planned for 1960 the public deficit was reduced from $500,000,000 to less than $250,000,000 by cutting back on agricultural and housing aid. However, more money was allocated to projects like an anti-flood plan, the development of Rotterdam's new harbor, Europoort, and a large road construction program. Every effort was made by the de Quay government to keep Dutch currency stable and to quash every inflationary trend in the economy.

Governor of the province of Groningen and with the chief commissioner of the Rotterdam police in publishing an appeal to the nation to support a Netherlands Union that was being formed to maintain contact between the Dutch and the German occupying authorities. De Quay and other leaders of the union worked to obtain an agreement that Dutch legal processes would be respected, and for about a year the Germans permitted this group to engage in a certain amount of political activity. This tolerance did not last, however, and in 1942 and 1943 de Quay was imprisoned as a hostage at Haaren and at St. Michielsgestel.

In October 1944, following the liberation of the southern Dutch provinces by Allied forces, Pieter S. Gerbrandy, Premier of the Dutch government-in-exile, appointed de Quay chairman of the board of commissioners in charge of economic affairs in the liberated areas. On April 4, 1945, when the Gerbrandy cabinet had been reorganized to include several ministers from the southern provinces, de Quay was named Minister of War. He held this post until June 23, 1945, when the first postwar cabinet was formed in the Netherlands with Willem Schermerhorn of the Labor party as Premier.

The Catholic People's party won the elections of May 17, 1946, with the Labor party coming in a close second, and a coalition cabinet headed by Louis J. M. Beel of the Catholic People's party was established on July 3, 1946. The following November de Quay was appointed Queen's Commissioner (Governor) of the province of North Brabant. His work over the next thirteen years enhanced his reputation as a good administrator and sound economist. In 1952 he was appointed chairman of the Council for Emigration Affairs. He also became board chairman of the North Brabant Electricity Society, commissioner and adviser of the Netherlands Bank, a member of the Institute for Cultural Relations,

Late in December 1960 the de Quay government resigned after the lower chamber of Parliament had overruled it and voted to raise the number of government-subsidized houses planned for 1960 from 80,000 to 85,000. On January 2, 1961 de Quay withdrew his resignation, however, and the cabinet continued as before. Industrial workers in the Netherlands did well in 1962, with wages increasing by an average of 6 percent and prices remaining stable. About 1,500,000 workers were covered in several agreements to limit to 2.7 percent eventual wage increases. Farmers, however, fared less well because of overproduction, and it was found necessary to set up an Agricultural Development and Reorganization Fund of about $7,000,000 to help them.

Surrender to the United Nations in August 1962 of Netherlands sovereignty over West New Guinea under pressure from Indonesia was a severe blow to Dutch pride, particularly as de Quay had already undertaken reforms in that colony. Early in 1961 he had initiated a ten-year development program to build roads, ports, and airfields, to raise production of coconut, copra, and nutmeg, and to prepare more Papuan natives for administrative and teaching posts. His government had installed a New Guinea Legislative Council in which twenty-three out of twenty-eight members were Papuans. De Quay answered Indonesian charges of insincerity quietly and reasonably, and in September 1961 he suggested that Dutch New Guinea be placed under United Nations jurisdiction and that the Papuans eventually be given the right to decide their own future.

This was not satisfactory to Indonesia, however, and on August 15, 1962 the Dutch Ambassador to the United Nations and the Indonesian Foreign Minister signed an agreement turning West New Guinea over to the United Nations until May 1, 1963, when sovereignty would be transferred to Indonesia. The final status of New Guinea was to be decided by local plebiscite in 1969. The agreement was sponsored by the United States. "There is no cause for joy in the Netherlands," commented the Dutch Foreign Minister Joseph M. A. H. Luns. He declared that the agreement had been accepted by the Dutch only because of United States pressure. "The Netherlands could not count on the support of its allies," de Quay said in a television address to the Dutch people, "and for that reason we had to sign."

The new Dutch Parliament elected in May 1963 was of much the same composition as its predecessor; the Catholic People's party remained the strongest. Four prominent members of this party—Carl Romme, Win de Kort, Louis J. M. Beel, and finally de Quay—were asked to form a new coalition cabinet, but it was not until July 23, 1963 that Victor Marijnen succeeded in forming a four-party coalition cabinet and became the new Premier.

Jan Eduard de Quay and Maria van der Lande were married in 1927, and they are the parents of five sons and four daughters. Designated a Commander of the Order of Orange-Nassau in 1959, de Quay is also a Knight of the Order of Netherlands Lion. He is a methodical, hardworking man and is soft-spoken and amiable.

He has a good sense of humor and often tells jokes on himself, frequently about his below-average height.

References

> N Y Times p2 Ja 6 '62 por
> Toronto Globe and Mail p8 Ap 7 '62 por
> International Who's Who, 1962-63
> International Year Book and Statesmen's Who's Who, 1963
> Who's Who in America, 1962-63
> Wie Is Dat? (1956)

RADCLIFFE, CYRIL JOHN, 1ST VISCOUNT RADCLIFFE Mar. 30, 1899- British jurist; public official
Address: h. "Hampton Lucy House," Hampton Lucy, Warwickshire, England; 5 Campden Hill Gate, Duchess of Bedford Walk, London, W.8, England

Lord Radcliffe's membership in the peerage of Great Britain is the result of achievement and service rather than of circumstance of birth. A brilliant career as a barrister, as wartime director general of the Ministry of Information, and as a King's Counsel led in 1944 to a knighthood. Five years later he was appointed a Lord of Appeal in Ordinary, becoming one of the few men to hold this high office without previous service as a judge. In 1962 he became Viscount Radcliffe, adding this title to the life peerage as a baron that accompanied his appointment as a Lord of Appeal. Lord Radcliffe has been chairman of a number of influential commissions and committees; he is one of Britain's most widely respected public servants. He is a Knight Grand Cross of the Order of the British Empire and a Privy Councillor and holds honorary degrees from several universities.

Cyril John Radcliffe was born on March 30, 1899, in Llanychan, North Wales, one of the four sons of Captain Alfred Ernest Radcliffe, a regular army officer, and the former Sybil Harriet Cunliffe. He obtained his secondary education at Haileybury College, a noted public school in Hertfordshire, and then in 1917 went into the British army. Barred by poor sight from service with a fighting regiment, Radcliffe enlisted in the Labour Corps, a unit engaged in construction work. He served in the Labour Corps for nearly two years, mostly in France, and was released a year after the end of World War I with the rank of second lieutenant.

Continuing his interrupted education, Radcliffe in 1919 went up to New College, Oxford, from which he graduated in 1921 with first class honors in "Greats"—classics and philosophy. He then sought a fellowship at another Oxford college, All Souls. Discovering that fellowships there were granted in only two courses of study, one of which was law, he read law furiously for a year and in 1922 was accepted as a Fellow of All Souls. There he prepared himself for a career as a barrister, a lawyer in England who has the exclusive right to argue cases in court. A brilliant student, he was named an Eldon Law Scholar in 1924. The same year he was called to the bar from the Inner Temple, one of the four Inns of Court. Fellowship in All Souls carried no resi-

Wide World

VISCOUNT RADCLIFFE

dential obligation, and, though Radcliffe was a Fellow there until 1937, he began to practise law in London as soon as he had been admitted to the bar. In 1935 he "took silk," that is, he became a King's Counsel and an acknowledged leader in his profession.

In 1939, at the outbreak of World War II, Radcliffe joined the Ministry of Information as chief press censor. Two years later, after a period as controller of the press and censorship division, he was appointed director general of the ministry, a position he held until the end of the war in 1945. A writer in the London *Times* (May 16, 1961) commented on this period in these terms: "To work with him is a joy. No one who had dealings in the highest reaches of the Ministry of Information during the war will forget the sanity and calm always to be found in his office."

Meanwhile, in 1943, Radcliffe had become a bencher—a member of the governing body—of the Inner Temple. In 1944 he was made a K.B.E. Now Sir Cyril Radcliffe, he returned in 1945 to legal practice as a distinguished barrister whose services were widely sought. In 1946 he was retained by the Labour government of the day in its nationalization of the Bank of England, previously owned by private stockholders. Subsequently he advised mine owners on the valuation of their property when the coal industry was taken over by the government.

Thereafter, important public appointments came in rapid succession from the Labour government and from the Conservative government that followed it in 1951. In 1947 Radcliffe served as chairman of the Punjab and Bengal boundary commissions, arbitrating the tangled boundaries between India and Pakistan. In 1948 he was made a G.B.E., and in May 1949 he was appointed a Lord of Appeal in Ordinary, one of that small group of eminent jurists that, in effect, exercises the rights and responsibilities vested in the House of Lords as Britain's highest

court of appeal. It was the first time in fifty years that such an appointment had gone to a man who had not previously served as a judge. The Lords of Appeal automatically receive life peerages and the right to sit and vote as barons in the House of Lords. Sir Cyril chose to be styled the First Baron Radcliffe of Werneth, a suburb of Oldham, Lancashire, which was at one time the home of his father's family. At fifty, he was the youngest of the "law lords." In 1949 Lord Radcliffe also received two additional honors, becoming a Privy Councillor and a Fellow of his alma mater, New College, Oxford.

His next public appointment followed in 1951, when he became chairman of the Royal Commission on Taxation of Profits and Income, an exacting assignment that continued until the commission made its final report in 1955. A year later, as constitutional commissioner for Cyprus, he headed the mission that toured that troubled island and formulated the first proposals for a new constitution. His proposals, which envisaged a limited form of self-government instead of the immediate self-determination demanded by the Cypriots, were angrily rejected.

In May 1957 Lord Radcliffe was named chairman of a nine-man committee of inquiry set up by the Chancellor of the Exchequer to investigate the country's monetary and credit system. The committee made the first full study of Britain's financial status and structure in nearly thirty years. Its report, published in 1959, was very widely reviewed and discussed. Finding that officials in the Bank of England and related institutions knew far too little about what they were doing, it called for the collection and publication of new statistics in many areas. No fundamental changes in Britain's monetary system were sought, but certain shifts of emphasis in existing policy were recommended. The *Economist* (August 22, 1959), in a generally favorable review, regretted that the report was a unanimous one, believing that this implied some compromises, but described it as "the best textbook that exists on the British financial mechanism, and probably the only one comprehensible to the layman."

Two assignments of a quite different nature followed. In May 1961 Prime Minister Harold Macmillan named Radcliffe chairman of a five-man committee of inquiry to investigate Britain's security procedures and practices, which was established in response to growing public anxiety over violations of the Official Secrets Act by civil servants. In its report in April 1962 the committee said it was disturbed by the number of Communists and Communist sympathizers in the civil service and its professional associations and trade unions and emphasized that "the biggest single risk" was "general lack of conviction that any substantial threat exists." The report led to an intensification and expansion of counterespionage measures within the civil service.

Later in 1962 Radcliffe was picked by Macmillan as head of a tribunal that was to conduct a "trial of truth" to determine whether rumors of widespread immorality and treason in the Admiralty had any foundation. These rumors had arisen out of the case of William J. C. Vassall, a former Admiralty clerk. Vassall, a homosexual, had been blackmailed into spying for the Soviet Union and was jailed for eighteen years in October 1962. Shouts of approval followed the announcement in the House of Commons of Lord Radcliffe's appointment.

The tribunal was given wide powers of subpoena and cross-examination. The full extent of those powers was demonstrated early in 1963, when two newspapermen who refused to disclose the sources of stories they had written about Vassall were turned over to the High Court. Both men, Reginald Foster and Desmond Clough, received prison sentences. A violent controversy followed this action, which was regarded in many quarters as a threat to the freedom of the press. However, it was in most cases not the Radcliffe tribunal but the law itself that was attacked.

From 1952 to 1955 Lord Radcliffe was chairman of the general advisory council of the British Broadcasting Corporation. In February 1957 he became chairman of the British Commonwealth International Newsfilm Agency Trust, and in November 1957 he was appointed a trustee of the British Museum. He is a life trustee of the Shakespeare Birthplace Trust and of Sir John Soane's Museum. Lord Radcliffe is also deputy chairman of the Court of London University and has been since 1960 chairman of the governors of that university's School of African and Oriental Studies. From 1946 to 1949 he was vice-chairman of the General Council of the Bar.

In 1951 Lord Radcliffe gave the annual series of Reith Lectures on the BBC, speaking on "Power and the State." In 1953 he was Montagu Burton Lecturer at the University of Glasgow and two years later delivered the Lloyd Roberts Lecture to the Royal Society of Medicine. He was Rosenthal Lecturer at Northwestern University, Illinois, in 1960 and gave the 1961 Rede Lecture at Cambridge and the 1962 Romanes Lecture at Oxford. His Reith Lectures were subsequently published as *The Problem of Power* (Macmillan; Secker & Warburg, 1952); his Rosenthal Foundation lectures as *The Law and its Compass* (Northwestern Univ. Press, 1960; Faber, 1961); and his Rede Lecture as *Censors* (Cambridge Univ. Press, 1961). All three publications, like his speeches and reports, reveal what a London *Times* writer (May 16, 1961) called "a brilliant mind" and "a lucid pen," as well as a profound concern for the freedom and dignity of the individual.

On July 11, 1962 Lord Radcliffe was created a viscount in Queen Elizabeth's Birthday Honours. He took the title Viscount Radcliffe, of Hampton Lucy, the Warwickshire village near Stratford-on-Avon where he has one of his two houses. Lord Radcliffe received an honorary LL.D. degree from the University of Wales in 1957, from the University of St. Andrews in 1959, and from Northwestern University in 1960. He has an honorary D.C.L. degree from Oxford University (1961), and he is an honorary member of the Institute of Civil Engineers and an honorary Fellow of the Institute of Bankers. He is a member of Brooks's Club.

On December 11, 1939 Lord Radcliffe married Antonia Mary Roby Benson, daughter of the first Baron Charnwood. They have no children. He is a member of the Church of England; as is traditional with the "law lords," he admits no political affiliation. He has blue-gray eyes and what he describes as "gray-white" hair, is five feet nine inches tall, and weighs about 168 pounds. He is a connoisseur of art and of books, and his collection of impressionist and postimpressionist paintings was valued in 1957 at $140,000. Lord Radcliffe confesses to an interest in comic strips and films and is a faithful theatergoer and a friend and supporter of actors, directors, writers, and designers. "Culture," he once said, "is a word that makes some people reach for a gun, like Marshal Goering. But I do not see how a country that is worth living in can get on without a reverence for it."

"Few careers are better known to the public than that of Lord Radcliffe," a London *Times* writer (May 16, 1961) has commented. "Yet the man himself remains elusive. . . . He commands great devotion [but] as often as not it is the outcome of admiration for his gifts and the selfless way he uses them rather than because there has been some personal intimacy." But, the article continued, far from being a "disembodied intellect," he is "a man who feels deeply." In addition, the *Times* writer said: "He is slowly coming to fill the role in our society . . . akin to that of an American Judge such as Holmes, Brandeis, Frankfurter, or Learned Hand. The British Constitution does not readily offer outstanding legal minds the chance to play such a role. When it does come about the effect can be lasting."

References

London Times p6 My 16 '61
N Y Times p6 Ap 7 '62 por
Burke's Peerage, Baronetage, and Knightage, 1963
Kelly's Handbook of the Titled, Landed and Official Classes, 1961-62
Who's Who, 1963

RAMSEY, NORMAN F(OSTER) Aug. 27, 1915- Physicist; university professor
Address: b. Lyman Laboratory, Harvard University, Cambridge 38, Mass. h. 55 Scott Rd., Belmont, Mass.

As an experimental physicist, Norman F. Ramsey owes his international reputation largely to his work on the properties of the atomic nucleus, but he is also noted for his wide-ranging interests and accomplishments. During World War II he led a group at Massachusetts Institute of Technology that developed the first three-centimeter radar systems. Later he directed a project at Los Alamos that turned a nuclear device into a practical weapon. He was chief scientist at the Tinian Island base in the Marianas, from which the first A-bomb missions were flown. Since 1950 he has been a professor of physics at Harvard.

The son of General Norman Foster Ramsey and his wife, the former Minna Bauer, Norman Foster Ramsey was born in Washington, D.C. on August 27, 1915. At that time his father, a graduate of the United States Military Academy, was serving as assistant to the Chief of Ordnance in Washington. A brother, John George Ramsey, is no longer living. Just before Norman's high school days began, his father had been assigned to the Command and General Staff School at

NORMAN F. RAMSEY

Fort Leavenworth, Kansas. Norman attended the Leavenworth High School, was president of his class, and graduated in 1931.

Deciding on a career in science, Norman Ramsey majored in physics at Columbia University, where he was also a teaching assistant in mathematics. He won the Van Aminge and Van Buren prizes in mathematics, was elected to Phi Beta Kappa, and obtained his B.A. degree in 1935. As a graduate student he held a Kellett Fellowship of Columbia from 1935 to 1937, a Tyndall Fellowship of Columbia in 1938-39, and a Carnegie Fellowship of the Carnegie Institution in Washington in 1939-40. He studied both at Cambridge University in England, which awarded him the B.A. degree in 1937 and the M.A. degree in 1941, and at Columbia, where he earned his Ph.D. degree in 1940. His thesis, on rotational magnetic moments of hydrogen molecules, was published in the *Physical Review*, August 1, 1940. Many years later, in 1954, he returned to Cambridge to take his Sc.D. degree, and in 1954-55 he was a Guggenheim Fellow at Oxford University.

United States entry into World War II was impending as Ramsey completed his graduate studies at Columbia. He went immediately to the Massachusetts Institute of Technology Radiation Laboratory, where as a research associate from 1940 to 1943 he had a major part in the development of the magnetron transmitter for radar. The resulting three-centimeter radar systems are now widely used. From 1940 to 1942 he was also an associate at the University of Illinois. In 1942 he was appointed expert consultant to the Secretary of War, a position in which he served until the war's end. He was also a consultant to the National Defense Research Committee from 1940 to 1945.

In one of his important wartime assignments Ramsey headed a group of young scientists whose mission was to convert a nuclear device into an operating weapon. The first work was done in New Mexico, where Ramsey was group leader and associate division chief from 1943 to 1945 at the Los Alamos Laboratory of the Atomic Energy Project. In 1945 Ramsey's group went to the Marianas to man the Atomic Energy Laboratory at the Tinian Island bomber base, from which the first atom bombing missions were flown. The scientists lived at the base and were briefed with bomber crews.

Also during the war Norman Ramsey was associated with Columbia University as assistant professor of physics from 1942 to 1945. He was promoted to associate professor in 1945. While still at Columbia, soon after the war, he helped set up the Brookhaven National Laboratory for Nuclear Research at Camp Upton on Long Island, and in 1946-47 he headed the physics department there. He left Columbia in 1947 to join the faculty at Harvard University as associate professor. Since 1950 he has been professor of physics.

At Columbia, Ramsey had worked with the Nobel prizewinner I. I. Rabi on studies of the electrical and magnetic properties of the atomic nucleus and at Harvard continued his investigations, studying the effect of magnetic fields on a stream of relatively slowly moving molecules. His range of interests is illustrated by the list given in *American Men of Science* (1960-62): nuclear moments, molecular beams, high energy particles, nuclear interactions in molecules, deuteron quadrupole moment, diamagnetism, molecular structure, thermodynamics, proton-proton scattering, billion volt accelerators, atomic masers, and electron scattering. He has written more than 125 papers on these subjects in scientific journals and is the author of several books, including *Nuclear Moments* (Wiley, 1953) and *Molecular Beams* (Oxford, 1956).

As chairman of the Harvard Nuclear Physics Committee (since 1948) and director of the Harvard Nuclear Laboratory (from 1948 to 1950 and in 1952), Professor Ramsey worked on the development and operation of Harvard's first postwar cyclotron, which was built in 1949. The purpose of the 125,000,000-electron-volt atom smasher was to study what particles make up atomic nuclei and what forces keep these particles together. Ramsey was appointed in 1956 to the executive committee for the 6,000,000-electron-volt Cambridge Electron Accelerator, a joint project of Harvard and the Massachusetts Institute of Technology.

In 1955 Professor Ramsey announced a startling result of a series of abstruse mathematical calculations which, under the particular conditions involved, contradicted the second law of thermodynamics. Because on the Kelvin temperature scale zero is the absolute zero, and all other temperatures are positive, it had until now always been thought that no temperatures of matter could be below absolute zero. Ramsey's calculations showed that some atoms among many near absolute zero could actually have negative absolute temperatures, and in this situation, a machine could take heat from a higher negative temperature, perform work, and return it to a lower negative temperature. Following this the heat would flow back to the higher negative temperature without extracting energy from the system.

Along with two Harvard associates Professor Ramsey announced in 1960 an atomic clock expected to be a hundred thousand times more accurate than the best atomic clocks then known. Called masers (Microwave Amplification by Stimulated Emission of Radiation), such clocks originally used gaseous ammonia molecules or synthetic ruby crystals. Ramsey's clock depends on high-energy atomic hydrogen. Since his hydrogen clock is far more accurate than any known standard to which it could be compared, the only way to check it was to build an identical one and synchronize the two.

President Dwight D. Eisenhower named Ramsey in November 1960 to the general advisory committee of the Atomic Energy Commission. In 1963 he headed a panel of scientists convened by the Presidential Scientific Advisory Committee and the AEC advisory committee to consider the future needs of the nation in high-energy accelerator physics. The panel made three major recommendations: first, for the construction at the University of California Lawrence Radiation Laboratory of a 200 bev (billion electron volt) machine, which would have six times the energy of the one at Brookhaven; second, for studies leading to a 600-1000 bev machine to be installed at Brookhaven in the 1970's; and third, for the construction at Brookhaven of "storage rings," to allow collisions of protons moving at high speeds in opposite directions.

The upper limit on accelerators does not now lie in today's technology, but rather on the availability of funds. Professor Ramsey told a conference in Palo Alto in June 1963 that the "most exciting" machine that could now be conceived would be a nuclear particle accelerator of 100,000 bev. To wrest basic cosmic secrets from nature, such a machine would be estimated to cost $100 billion. Nuclear physicists dream about the discoveries that could be made with such equipment. In his New York Times column (June 30, 1963) William L. Laurence pointed out that "the world of the atom is so fantastic that it requires a complete readjustment in our concepts of space and time. In the world of the atomic nucleus, a billionth of a second is a very long time, a trillionth of an inch is a measure of great length, and a quadrillionth of a gram is a mass of great weight." One might say that as the size of the cosmos to be investigated goes down to billionths, the cost of research goes up by billions.

Professor Ramsey has filled other important governmental advisory positions. One of the most challenging was as science adviser in 1958-59 to Paul-Henri Spaak, Secretary General of the North Atlantic Treaty Organization. On leave from Harvard, Ramsey headed a fifteen-member committee of scientists who advised on all NATO activity in research and applied science and the production of scientific manpower. In other government appointments he has served on the board of trustees of the Brookhaven National Laboratory (from 1952 to 1955), the Air Force scientific advisory board (from 1948 to 1954), and the Department of Defense panel on atomic energy (since 1953).

Among the honors that Ramsey has received are the Presidential Certificate of Merit (1947) for his wartime radar work and the E. O. Lawrence Award (1960). He is a Fellow of the American Academy of Science and of the American Physical Society, of which he has been a council member since 1956. He also belongs to Sigma Xi, the honorary society for scientific research, and the National Academy of Sciences and was on the board of editors of the *Review of Modern Physics* from 1953 to 1956.

Norman Foster Ramsey and the former Elinor Jameson, who were married on June 3, 1940, have four daughters: Margaret Foster, Patricia Gail, Winifred Bauer, and Janet Carter. Professor Ramsey is tall and slender, six feet one inch in height and 160 pounds in weight; he has graying hair and hazel eyes. His hobbies are active ones: swimming, skiing, playing tennis, sailing, and walking. A biographical sketch in the New York *Times* (February 6, 1958) noted that "unlike the storied professor who can solve all manner of professional problems but is helpless around the house, Dr. Ramsey can fix a leaky faucet and do other chores."

The *Times* profile quoted Dr. M. Stanley Livingston of Harvard, who described Professor Ramsey as being admired for complete candor "with everyone and everything" and called him an extremely likable extrovert. Ramsey has decided opinions on a variety of matters and, according to Livingston, is almost always right "or close to it."

References

N Y Times p8 F 6 '58 por
American Men of Science 10th ed (1960-62)
International Who's Who, 1962-63
Who's Who in America, 1962-63

RAPHAEL, CHAIM (rā'-f'l ᴋīm) July 14, 1908- British government employee; author; scholar

Address: b. Her Majesty's Treasury, Great George St., London, S.W.1, England; h. 21 Greycoat Gardens, London, S.W.1, England

An unexpected assignment during World War II, to work in British internment camps for European refugees, initiated Chaim Raphael's career in government service. He subsequently served for fifteen years with the British Information Services in New York and is currently head of the British Treasury's information division. He is also, according to Joseph Wershba in the New York *Post* (October 23, 1962) "a former Oxford don, a prodigious Hebrew classical scholar, a popularizer of economics, an author of ingenious detective novels, a wit, raconteur, pixie, sensualist and romanticist. He is the perfect mirror image of his latest book, *Memoirs of a Special Case*. It is the autobiography of an Englishman who enjoys being a Jew." Raphael writes his novels under the pseudonym Jocelyn Davey.

Chaim Raphael was born on July 14, 1908 in the North of England industrial town of Middlesborough, Yorkshire, the fifth in a family of seven children. He spent his early years in South

CHAIM RAPHAEL

Shields, Durham, where his father, a Russian *émigré*, was cantor in the local synagogue. At the age of fourteen, Raphael won a scholarship to a rabbinical school in Portsmouth, Hampshire. There he boarded, studying the Bible, the Talmud, and Jewish history in the evenings and over weekends and attending the Portsmouth Grammar School by day for his secular education.

The English grammar school typically offers a secondary education of an academic, rather than vocational, nature. The headmaster of Portsmouth Grammar School during Raphael's years there was the Reverend Dr. Walter John Barton, a remarkable teacher who later became canon of Salisbury Cathedral. Barton and his wife saw in Raphael a potential scholar. They encouraged him, coached him, and took him with them on a Christmas visit to Florence that Raphael still remembers with deep pleasure and satisfaction. Thus, at a formative period in his youth, Raphael experienced very intensely the impact of two great traditions, the Jewish and the Christian. "These two influences," he wrote recently, "have remained with me in my life."

With Barton's encouragement and help, Raphael worked hard. In 1927 he was awarded an open scholarship in modern history to University College, Oxford. There he read philosophy, politics, and economics, earning his baccalaureate in 1930. For his postgraduate work, Raphael turned back to Hebrew studies. He won the James Mew Scholarship in Post-Biblical Hebrew in 1931 and the following year received both his M.A. degree and his appointment as Oxford's Cowley Lecturer in Hebrew. From 1933 to 1936 he also held the Kennicott Fellowship in Biblical Hebrew.

Raphael taught at Oxford for seven years. He began a book on the Midrash, the Biblical commentaries of the early rabbis, and the Kennicott Fellowship made it financially possible for him to travel in Spain and the Middle East. In 1936

he spent six months in Palestine, a moving and formative experience for him, both as a scholar and a Jew. During his stay he cast around hopefully but unsuccessfully in the Dead Sea area for ancient Hebrew documents that might help him with his book. Rumors that such documents existed were confirmed years later by the discovery of the Dead Sea scrolls.

In his fictionalized autobiography, *Memoirs of a Special Case,* Raphael wrote of his years at Oxford: "In my youth I had been pulled in opposite directions by my intensely orthodox Jewish upbringing and the non-Jewish world around me; but now I had stumbled into a way of living that seemed to bring everything together, and with a sense of constant discovery. There was infinite room in my Hebrew studies for all that I felt about my Jewish past. Everything I read fitted in and added colour and variety—rabbinical legends, classical history, Freud, archeology—it was like peeling an endless onion, with sharp recognition bringing tears of excitement to one's eyes. And on the other side was Oxford. . . . To be reading my father's copy of the Talmud in that ancient, pinnacled background, followed by dinner at High Table and port in the Senior Common Room was some sort of special benediction."

Raphael's book on the Midrash was finished in 1939 and accepted for publication by Oxford University Press, but World War II intervened in September of the same year, and the book never appeared. Not long after, Raphael was spending a last weekend at Oxford before joining the Royal Air Force when he was abruptly called upon to do an entirely different kind of war work. All over Britain, German refugees, many of them Jewish, had been placed in internment camps. Several hundred of them, transmigrants with visas pending for the United States, had been accommodated in a camp near London. By an administrative error, their documents had been taken from them and lost. Raphael's assignment as liaison officer for internment camps was to make good the error—to secure visas for the alarmed and confused refugees and get them out of England.

The assignment was one of great complexity. Documents to replace the missing ones had to be secured from relatives, refugee organizations and consulates all over the world, and visas had to be secured from the American consulate in London. As the German submarines tightened their grip on the Atlantic, the supply of ships to the refugees to the United States dwindled. Raphael worked against time, acquiring a motorbike from the army to take him with maximum speed from the camp to the United States consulate, cutting red tape wherever he could. When at last the supply of ships dried up, hundreds of the refugees had been safely dispatched to New York.

Raphael's successful handling of this assignment brought him another—similar and no less burdensome. Early in the war, Britain had shipped several thousand European refugees to Canada. Most of them wanted to immigrate to the United States, where they had family and friends. The Canadian authorities were willing to release them if the United States would first provide visas; the United States authorities were willing to provide visas if Canada would first release the internees. Neither side would make the first move. Raphael's task was to find some way of breaking the deadlock. After some months of unsuccessful effort, Raphael met the *diseuse* Ruth Draper. She was concerned about an Italian boy, the child of friends, who was interned in one of the camps. With Raphael's encouragement, Miss Draper appealed to the Canadian Prime Minister, Mackenzie King, and secured the boy's release into her care. That was a beginning. Within three months all the refugees had found guarantors in the United States, and the problem was solved.

In 1942 Raphael was transferred to New York as an economist with the British Information Services. He remained in that post until the end of the war, when he accepted an invitation to stay on with BIS as director in charge of economic information. Raphael remained in New York until 1957, when he returned to England as deputy head of the information division of Her Majesty's Treasury. In 1959 he became head of the division, a post he has held ever since. He was named an Officer of the Order of the British Empire in 1951.

Chaim Raphael had started to write during the 1930's while he was at Oxford, contributing articles on current affairs to newspapers and magazines. In 1948 he began to write stories for the American magazine *Commentary.* His first full-length work of fiction followed in 1956. It was *A Capitol Offense* (Knopf, 1956; Doubleday paperback edition 1961), published in England as *The Undoubted Deed* (Chatto, 1956) and written under the pseudonym of Jocelyn Davey.

A Capitol Offense introduced the Oxford philosophy don and British secret agent Ambrose Usher, who is sent to Washington to investigate security leakages in the British Embassy and soon finds himself embroiled in a freakish murder. "Short, apple-round and learnedly garrulous," wrote the reviewer for *Time* magazine (July 28, 1958), "Ambrose ambles through his adventures preceded by a pillar of chaos. While bodies are felled and dark deeds are done all about him, the philosophy don lets Bach's Magnificat sing through his mind, ruminates about Hegel, and numbs his listeners with a flow of quotes from the Bible, Shakespeare, major poets and minor lyricists."

Reviewers praised the book's wit and erudition (though some thought it too learned for the average thriller reader), and it was a Book Society choice in England. Similar enthusiasm greeted two subsequent installments in the adventures of Ambrose Usher, also written under the Jocelyn Davey pseudonym: *The Naked Villany* (Knopf; Chatto, 1958; Doubleday paperback, 1961) and *A Touch of Stagefright* (Chatto; Clarke, Irwin, 1960; Penguin, 1963). All three of the Ambrose Usher stories drew on Raphael's own background and interests—*The Naked Villany,* for example, taking all its clues from the Bible. Raphael, whom Julian Symons has called "the Aldous Huxley of detection," made himself known as

the author when readers began to suppose that Sir Isaiah Berlin had written the books.

Raphael's latest book, written under his own name, is *Memoirs of a Special Case* (Little; Chatto, 1962), a collection of sketches, several of them first published in *Atlantic Monthly* and *Commentary,* that are partly autobiographical and partly fictional. Raphael began to write the memoirs in 1957, when he returned from New York, in an attempt to "catch up with" himself. "But," he wrote in his introduction to the book, "the self is an elusive creature. At first, memories came back simply and factually, and I found it easy to put them down that way. But once I had unlocked the door much more came through than I had bargained for . . . Memories and dreams of many people and many things shook themselves free of time and place. I let it all flow, for if something impelled me to write this way in fact and fantasy, this too was part of the self I had been looking for."

Memoirs of a Special Case deals with Raphael's boyhood and education, his visits to Spain and to Palestine, and his work in the wartime internment camps. It is essentially an examination of his twofold background, as an Englishman and a Jew, and is pervaded by a sense of the Jewish tradition. "If I say that the Jew is a 'special case,'" Raphael has written, "it is not in self-pity but in the recognition of a sense of fullness and colour that comes from being aware of and enjoying one's roots." Some reviewers felt that the mixture of fact and fiction had created an awkward hybrid, but most received the book with warm enthusiasm, praising its humor, vitality, and intelligence. Alfred Kazin saw in it "the enormous joy in being Jewish—the joy it brings of all the perspectives on history and the immediate world."

Chaim Raphael was married in 1934 to Diana Rose, a painter. They have two grown children, Adam and Jacqueline. Raphael is five feet eight and a half inches tall, weighs 175 pounds, and has brown eyes. His receding black hair is now graying. His recreations include swimming, travel, Biblical studies and, according to *Who's Who,* America—a country he revisits regularly. Raphael, who knows the Bible intimately in both English and Hebrew, is said to find in the Old Testament admirable solutions for his day-to-day professional problems. He is also, like Ambrose Usher, a lover of music. Raphael's clubs are the Reform and Jack's.

References

Raphael, Chaim. Memoirs of a Special Case (1962)
Who's Who, 1963

RAY, (JACKSON HARVELLE) RANDOLPH June 11, 1886-May 31, 1963 Former Rector of the Protestant Episcopal Church of the Transfiguration, popularly known as the Little Church Around the Corner (1923-58). See *Current Biography* (April) 1945.

Obituary

N Y Times p84 Je 2 '63

RAYE, MARTHA Aug. 27, 1916- Comedienne; actress; singer
Address: b. c/o William Morris Agency, 151 El Camino, Beverly Hills, Calif.

After fifteen years of absence from Hollywood, Martha Raye returned to the screen in 1962 in the Metro-Goldwyn-Mayer production of *Jumbo*. In it she played the kind of role for which she had been hailed a decade earlier as America's leading television comedienne—that of a homely knockabout whose singing voice can produce some of the most memorable "pop" singing of her generation. This rare combination of talents has made Martha Raye a star for more than a quarter of a century. In her durability she somewhat resembles her older friend Jimmy Durante, with whom she has often clowned on radio and television and who shared co-star billing with her in *Jumbo*.

Martha Raye, whose original name was Margie Yvonne Reed, was born into show business on August 27, 1916, in the charity ward of a hospital in Butte, Montana. Her parents, Pete and Peggy (Hooper) Reed, were Irish immigrants whose song-and-dance act, billed as "Reed and Hooper," took them to carnivals and vaudeville houses throughout the United States. Margie was only three years old when she joined her parents' act. "I must have been hypnotized by the spotlight," she told Hollywood columnist Sidney Skolsky (New York *Post,* July 8, 1962). "I can't imagine being anything but an entertainer." Originally taught to read and write by her mother, she picked up her education wherever she could, and she attended public schools in Montana, Roman Catholic schools in Chicago, and the Professional Children's School in New York City.

At the age of fifteen she sang, danced, and performed the comedy lead in a children's act whose members included Jackie Heller, Hal LeRoy, Sonny O'Day, and Buddy and Vilma Ebsen,

all of whom later became prominent in show business. After taking the stage name Martha Raye from a telephone book, she went on her own, as a member of the Benny Davis Revue, and later with the Ben Blue Company. She also toured the Loew's circuit, performed with Will Morrisey's act for three years, and was featured in *Earl Carroll's Sketchbook* and in Lew Brown's Broadway musical comedy *Calling All Stars*. In 1936 she met the motion picture director Norman Taurog, who was so impressed with her flair for comedy that he signed her for the lead opposite Bing Crosby in the film *Rhythm on the Range* (Paramount, 1936). Her swinging delivery of "Mr. Paganini" in this film catapulted her to stardom.

Miss Raye soon became one of the busiest and most popular comediennes in Hollywood. She appeared in the Paramount films *College Holiday* in 1936; *Artists and Models, Double or Nothing, Waikiki Wedding,* and *Hideaway Girls* in 1937; *College Swing, Give Me a Sailor,* and *Big Broadcast of 1938* in 1938; *Never Say Die* and *$1,000 a Touchdown* in 1939; and *The Farmer's Daughter* in 1940. She also had roles in the Republic production *Navy Blues* (1937) and in the Universal films *The Boys From Syracuse* (1940), *Keep 'Em Flying* (1941), and *Hellzapoppin* (1941).

In 1940 Miss Raye co-starred on Broadway with Al Jolson in *Hold On to Your Hats,* a musical revue that ran for 158 performances. She appeared on Jolson's radio show for two years and made guest appearances with Eddie Cantor, Bob Hope, and other leading stars of radio. Returning to Hollywood in 1944, Miss Raye played in *Four Jills in a Jeep* (Twentieth Century-Fox), based on a USO tour of Army bases in England and North Africa, which she had made with Kay Francis, Carole Landis, and Mitzi Mayfair. Although the film was generally panned by the critics, Miss Raye's performance was widely praised. Archer Winsten wrote in the New York *Post* (April 6, 1944) that the star's comedy had "never been more raucous, rough and pleasing."

In 1947 Miss Raye was selected by Charles Chaplin for a major supporting role in *Monsieur Verdoux* (United Artists), Chaplin's mordant "comedy of murders" and his first production since *The Great Dictator*. Again the comedienne won critical acclaim. Howard Barnes wrote in the New York *Herald Tribune* (April 14, 1947): "Miss Raye makes altogether the best foil for the actor's miming. . . . In her rough and tumble scenes with the star something of the gaiety of the early Chaplin masterpieces is recaptured." Archer Winsten of the New York *Post* wrote that despite the full-size cast in the film, "only raucous Martha Raye holds her own with the . . . comedian. Her bull-in-a-china-shop personality is the perfect contrast for Chaplin's airy precision."

Miss Raye's rowdy comedy and slapstick style seemed like natural assets for the new medium of television. She did a number of guest appearances with Milton Berle on the *Texaco Show,* then became one of the alternating stars of *The All-Star Revue,* and later was star and mistress of ceremonies on her own NBC-TV *Martha*

MARTHA RAYE

Raye Show. Television critic Marie Torre, referring to Miss Raye's "unique status in television" during this period, noted that during the 1953-54 season she was "hailed as the country's No. 1 comedienne," and as "the unqualified queen of buffoons" (New York *Herald Tribune,* December 4, 1957).

Returning to the cabaret circuit, Miss Raye performed in a number of the leading night clubs in the United States, including the Copacabana in New York, the Sahara in Las Vegas, the Chez Paree in Chicago, and the Cal-Neva at Lake Tahoe. For several years she starred in her own night club, the Five O'Clock Club in Miami. She also continued to make occasional appearances on television. In January 1958, as a guest on the *Steve Allen Show,* she performed a sketch that a critic for the New York *Times* (January 27, 1958) found "extremely funny." In February 1959 she did a nineteen-hour telethon as a benefit for the Association for the Help of Retarded Children over WNEW-TV in New York, and helped to raise $352,000 in pledges. Her "herculean job," according to a reporter for *Variety* (February 11, 1959), was "topnotch . . . a combination of heart and talent."

In early 1958 Miss Raye briefly starred in a revival of *Annie Get Your Gun* at the City Center in New York, but was forced to leave the show because of illness. She also appeared in the plays *The Solid Gold Cadillac, Separate Rooms,* and *Calamity Jane* in summer stock, her favorite form of theater. When she appeared in the leading role in *Wildcat* at the Westbury, Long Island, Music Fair in August 1962, Hank McCann of the Long Island *Press* (August 15, 1962) noted that Miss Raye "achieved a rare Long Island distinction . . . a standing ovation at her curtain call. It was a rare occurrence and a stirring tribute to a real pro."

In 1962 Martha Raye starred, with Jimmy Durante, Doris Day, and Stephen Boyd in *Jumbo,* the Metro-Goldwyn-Mayer film version of the 1935 circus musical produced by Billy Rose. In the role of Madame Lulu, which producer Joe Pasternak and director Charles Walters created for her, Miss Raye demonstrated her versatility as a fortune teller, aerialist, clown, tattooed lady, snake charmer, imitation lioness, and human cannonball. Although critics could work up little enthusiasm for the film, they singled out Miss Raye's performance in it for praise. A reviewer for *Variety* (December 5, 1962) wrote: "Martha Raye, too long absent from the screen, only has room to swing a couple of times, but she makes them big," and Paul V. Beckley observed in a review for the New York *Herald Tribune* (December 7, 1962) that Miss Raye "can breathe life into [her lines] as only fine clowns can, making the grimace add golden weight to the words."

Martha Raye has been married six times. Her first husband was Hamilton (Buddy) Westmore, a Hollywood makeup expert, whom she wed in May 1937 and divorced in September 1938. She then married and divorced David Rose, orchestra leader and composer; Neal Lang, a hotel manager; Nick Condos, a dancer, who now serves as Miss Raye's personal manager; and Ed Begley, another dancer. In November 1958 Miss Raye married Robert O'Shea, her former bodyguard, from whom she is now separated. She has a daughter, Melodye Raye Condos, who is seeking her own career as a singer.

Miss Raye stands five feet three inches tall and weighs 122 pounds. She has brown hair, blue eyes, and a cavernous mouth that has become her trademark. She once bet a director at Paramount that her legs were as shapely as those of Marlene Dietrich—and won. She enjoys deep-sea fishing (she keeps a forty-four-foot boat in Florida) and interior decorating. Despite her haphazard education she speaks some Italian, French, Yiddish, Greek, and Spanish and reads omnivorously. She maintains a cottage in Nassau, a penthouse in Miami Beach, and a house in Kings Point, Long Island. In 1962 she moved back to California and purchased a home in the exclusive Bel-Air section of Los Angeles.

Perhaps as a by-product of the wholehearted way she throws herself into the pratfalls, splits, and other features of her slapstick performances, Miss Raye's health has occasionally faltered. During the USO tour of American bases in England and North Africa she made during World War II, she suffered an attack of anemia. In March 1962 she was found unconscious on a deserted stretch of beach near Malibu, California, near a home she had rented. She was treated for exhaustion and released from a hospital after two days.

According to Sidney Skolsky, Martha Raye's real personality affords a sharp contrast to the public image she has created as a "brash, slapstick, not-too-bright lady clown." The comedienne, Skolsky wrote in the New York *Post* (July 8, 1962), "loves every minute when she's performing" but is often lonely and "singing the blues" when she is off the stage. She told Skolsky: "Few people actually know me, or take me seriously. It's great for my career though, I guess." In a more pensive mood, she added: "I thought success in show business was the answer to everything. It isn't. I don't know what is."

Skolsky's description of Martha Raye was confirmed by another Hollywood columnist, Louella O. Parsons, early in 1963: "Like many great entertainers who thrive on audience reaction, Martha is 'on' at the drop of a cue. At a party she will sing and clown her heart out for hours. She's boisterous, hilarious, loud. But get her alone and you'll find a soft-spoken, serious, thoughtful woman who talks with honesty and simplicity." Martha Raye summed up her personal and professional history in an interview with Marie Torre of the New York *Herald Tribune* (December 4, 1957). She put it simply: "My career is my whole life. I'll always work."

References

N Y Post Mag p3 Jl 8 '62 por

International Motion Picture Almanac, 1963

Who's Who in America, 1950-51

RENNE, ROLAND R(OGER) (rĕn'ē) Dec. 12, 1905- Agricultural economist; university president; United States government official

Address: b. Department of Agriculture, Washington 25, D.C.; Montana State College, Bozeman, Mont.; h. 1815 Sourdough Rd., Bozeman, Mont.

Because agriculture has come to play an important role in international affairs President John F. Kennedy created a new post—Assistant Secretary of Agriculture for international affairs—and appointed to it early in 1963 Roland R. Renne, a man of wide experience in agriculture, economics, public service, and education. Renne has been president of Montana State College in Bozeman, Montana since 1944. He is a nationally known agricultural economist who has also been a farmer, and he has served on a number of government agricultural missions in foreign countries. He is on leave from his college for the year 1963.

The third of five children of Fred Christian and Caroline A. (Young) Renne, Roland Roger Renne was born on December 12, 1905 in Greenwich, New Jersey. He has a sister, Mrs. Sarah (Renne) Riggins, and three brothers, Fred W., a farmer; Henry E., superintendent of the Vineland Training School Farm; and Evan W., a Presbyterian minister. Roland Renne grew up on his father's large dairy and diversified farm in southern New Jersey. He attended the Bridgeton (New Jersey) High School and then the Hopewell Township High School in Shiloh, New Jersey, from which he graduated in 1923. In the spare time left to him after his school work and the farm chores were completed he managed and played on the baseball team.

Renne's desire to be an agricultural economist dates back to his early high school years. "My father used to take me to town on Saturdays," he recently recalled, "when he would deliver eggs to the stores and buy groceries for the next week's needs. I early became intrigued by the fact that my father asked the grocer what he was paying for eggs and then after he had sold his eggs . . . asked the grocer what he was charging for sugar or flour. . . . This seemed to me to be highly inconsistent in the process of fair bargaining between buyer and seller, and when I asked my father why this was this way, he said he did not know except it had always been this way. I decided I would try to find out why, because it seemed to me that if the grocer determined the price of things he sold, then the farmer should determine the price of the things he had for sale. This, of course, got me into economics, and particularly agricultural economics, and . . . I determined that I wanted to be an agricultural economist."

To prepare for his chosen career Renne enrolled in 1923 at Rutgers University in New Brunswick, New Jersey, where he majored in agriculture and took part in several extracurricular activities. He was captain of the cross-country track team; manager of the rifle team; business manager of *Targum*, the school newspaper; chairman of the Interscholastic Debate League; and captain of the debate team. An excellent student, he was elected to Phi Beta Kappa and awarded the Grant Prize in Agriculture as the most outstanding member of his senior class. He graduated from the university in 1927 with the B.S. degree.

Renne took graduate work in agricultural economics, with minors in public law, American history, and land economics, at the University of Wisconsin and obtained the M.Sc. degree in 1928. His thesis was called "The Federal Reserve Board and the Agricultural Depression Beginning in 1920." Two years later, in 1930, Renne was awarded the Ph.D. degree, after he had submitted a dissertation entitled "The Tariff on Dairy Products." While studying at Wisconsin, Renne served as a graduate Fellow and as a graduate assistant in agricultural economics. Later, he was a Raleigh Foundation Fellow.

From July 1, 1930 to July 1, 1934 Renne was an assistant professor of agricultural economics at Montana State College in Bozeman, Montana, and he divided his time between teaching and research. In 1935 he was promoted to the rank of associate professor, and one year later he was made a full professor. Renne became head of the department of economics in 1938 and head of the department of agricultural economics and economics in 1939. He was named acting president of Montana State College in 1943, and since July 1944 he has been the president of the college, responsible for administration and general supervision of all the teaching, research, and co-operative extension service programs.

Roland R. Renne was not one to retire into the ivory towers of Academe. For a number of years he combined his teaching and administrative duties with practical work on an eighty-acre farm that he operated two miles from the Montana State campus. He regularly rose early to complete the milking, haying, and other farm chores before going to his office. The story is told that on the night of his inauguration as president he returned late to his farm to discover one of his prize ewes having lambing trouble. Hurriedly discarding his academic robes for overalls, he rushed to the barn and successfully delivered the lamb.

The modern farmer, Renne believes, should take advantage of the new technological, chemical, biological, and agricultural resources that are becoming available to him in this "atomic age of agriculture." Moreover, he must think not only in terms of his own farm, region, or nation but in international terms. Renne has tried to adapt the curriculum to the complexity of contemporary national and international realities. The need for understanding other peoples will require less specialization at the undergraduate level, he feels, and more synthesis of materials that cut across traditional course lines. He has envisioned an accelerated program that would establish divisions or centers for the study of international problems and policies.

Montana State College has grown under Dr. Renne. Half of the total number of students who have ever enrolled at the college did so since Renne took office, and the number of graduate students doubled within a period of eight years. In an interview in the *Christian Science Monitor* (August 14, 1948) Renne outlined his hopes for the agricultural students who are to be America's future farmers: "I want them to appreciate the distinguished character of farming; to realize what agriculture means to the world; to understand the fundamentals of economics in a business that touches everything; I want them to lead richer lives and, once in a while, to play."

Renne served as state price officer for Montana with the Office of Price Administration during World War II, and he helped to plan the Point Four program of aid to foreign countries. From July 1951 to August 1953 he was on leave of absence from Montana State College to serve in the Philippines as chief of an Economic Cooperation Administration technical and economic mission. For several months in the summer and fall of 1958 Renne headed an agricultural survey mission in Peru, which was sponsored by the International Bank for Reconstruction and Development and the Food and Agriculture Organization of the United Nations. A year and a half later, in January and February 1960, he acted as a special consultant to the United States technical mission to Ethiopia on a multimillion-acre land settlement and development project.

President John F. Kennedy nominated Renne to be Assistant Secretary of Agriculture for international affairs on January 24, 1963; the nomination was confirmed by the Senate on March 1. This was a new post, Renne has explained, "created because of the increasing importance and involvement of agriculture in international trade and economic and technical assistance." All activities in these areas in the Department of Agriculture fall under his jurisdiction. He is also the director of the Commodity Credit Corporation.

One of the most important problems facing the Assistant Secretary is the need to lower the trade barriers erected by the European Economic Community (Common Market) countries against American agricultural exports, particularly poultry, feedgrains, fruits, and vegetables. He is also concerned with improving United States technical assistance programs throughout the world, particularly in Latin America. "The U.S. Department of Agriculture," he recently said, "with its technical know-how and extensive resources in agricultural sciences, agricultural production, and marketing will work cooperatively with the Agency for International Development in helping to provide, along with the Land Grant Colleges and Universities of the nation, the necessary agriculturally trained manpower resources needed for effective economic and technical assistance programs in the less developed and newly developing countries of the world."

In order to take the post Renne was given a one-year leave of absence from the presidency of his college by the Board of Regents of Montana. In April 1963, when the acting president, P. C. Gaines, became ill, the board demanded that Renne return to Bozeman or resign the presidency. Renne refused, saying that he had accepted the Washington assignment in good faith and would serve out his year. The board later appointed another acting president, but a New York *Times* article (April 13, 1963) reported, "It is predicted that when [Renne's] contract as president of the college expires next April, it will not be renewed." The article placed

ROLAND R. RENNE

this controversy against the background of a political struggle between liberals and conservatives for control of the Montana higher education system. It suggested that the conservative faction, led by Governor Tim M. Babcock, had hoped for the resignation of Renne, who is a liberal Democrat.

Renne brought to his present government post a long and distinguished record of public service on the local, state, and national levels. He has been a member of the advisory council of the Montana State Planning Board from 1934 to 1941 and from 1957 to the present, and he served in a similar capacity with the Pacific Northwest Council of the National Resources Planning Board from 1935 to 1938. After the end of World War II he served on the postwar planning commission, Bozeman Chamber of Commerce, and on the Land-Grant Colleges Postwar Agricultural Policy Committee. From 1948 to 1954 Renne was on the United States Forest Advisory Board, and from 1949 to 1952, on the United States Advisory Council on Indian Affairs. In 1950-51 he was also a member of the President's Water Resources Policy Commission. More recently, from 1960 to 1962 he served on the health research facilities council of the National Institutes of Health.

In addition to many journal articles and experiment station bulletins on public administration and agricultural economics, Renne has written several textbooks. These include *Land Economics* (Harper, 1947; 1958); *The Government and Administration of Montana* (Crowell, 1958), and *The Montana Citizen* (State Publishing Co., Helena, Montana, 1937; 1960), a textbook on government for Montana schools that he wrote with J. W. Huffman. He was visiting professor of economics at the University of Chicago in 1940 and visiting professor of local government at Cornell University in 1941-42. He holds an honorary Litt.D. degree from Rutgers University

RENNE, ROLAND R.—*Continued*

(1947); an honorary LL.D. from the University of the Philippines (1953); and an honorary doctorate from the National University of Asunción, Paraguay (1962). He was also the recipient of the National 4-H Alumni Recognition Award in 1962.

Renne belongs to the Society for International Development, the American Economic Association, the American Academy of Political and Social Science, and the American Association for the Advancement of Science. He has served on the editorial committee and is a past vice-president of the American Farm Economics Association. He has also been president of the Western Farm Economics Association, and he holds membership in the American Rural Sociological Society, the National Municipal League, the International Conference of Agricultural Economists, and national and regional educational associations. He is a member of Phi Kappa Phi and Alpha Zeta.

Roland R. Renne and Mary Kneeland Wisner of Bozeman, Montana were married on August 9, 1932. They have four children, Mrs. Karen Schaefer (Renne) Many, Roger Lewis, Joan Eleanor, and Paul Wisner. Renne stands five feet four inches tall, weighs 151 pounds, and has hazel eyes and gray hair. He is a past president of the Bozeman Rotary Club and a Presbyterian. His favorite recreations are handball, squash, tennis, swimming, hiking, and travel.

References

Christian Sci Mon p6 Ag 14 '48 pors
American Men of Science 10th ed (1960-62)
Who's Who in America, 1962-63
Who's Who in American Education, 1961-62

REYNOLDS, ROBERT RICE June 18, 1884-Feb. 13, 1963 Former United States Democratic Senator from North Carolina; founder of the Vindicators and American Nationalist party, dedicated to "100 percent Americanism"; identified with isolationist and extreme right-wing groups. See *Current Biography* (October) 1940.

Obituary

N Y Times p36 Ap 1 '63

RICHARDSON, TONY June 5, 1928- British director; producer

Address: b. Woodfall Film Productions Ltd., 11a Curzon St., London, W.1, England

In the eleven years that have gone by since he left Oxford University, Tony Richardson, the director and producer, has caused one of the greatest stirs in the British theater since the departure of George Bernard Shaw and has become one of the most important newer influences in the British film industry. Richardson began his career in 1953, as a television director for the British Broadcasting Corporation. In 1955 he joined the English Stage Company as associate artistic director, and he became its

joint artistic director a few years ago. When he launched John Osborne's *Look Back in Anger* as his first production for the English Stage Company, he introduced a powerful new talent and ushered in a renaissance in the British theater.

Among the plays Richardson has directed on Broadway—most of them first staged by the English Stage Company—have been *Look Back in Anger*, Osborne's *The Entertainer*, and Shelagh Delaney's *A Taste of Honey*. All have been adapted for motion pictures by Richardson for Woodfall Film Productions, the company he owns in partnership with Osborne. Other films that he has directed or produced for Woodfall and has stamped with his own brand of uncompromising poetic realism, include *Saturday Night and Sunday Morning, The Loneliness of the Long Distance Runner,* and *Tom Jones.* Richardson has also staged plays for the Shakespeare Memorial Theatre and in London's West End.

Tony Richardson was born on June 5, 1928 in Shipley, Yorkshire to Clarence Albert Richardson, a druggist, and his wife, the former Elsie Evans Campion. For secondary school Richardson attended Ashville College, Harrogate, which during World War II was evacuated to the Lake District. There academic discipline collapsed, and Richardson spent much of his time hiking alone about the countryside. "I hated all authority," he once told a *Time* interviewer (January 18, 1963). According to the *Time* article, he hopes that this "essential attitude" has never left him.

After the war, Richardson entered Wadham College, Oxford University. Fascinated by the theater for as long as he could remember, he joined Oxford's famous dramatic society. He was its president from 1949 to 1951 and directed a number of its productions, including *The Duchess of Malfi, Peer Gynt, Romeo and Juliet,* and *King John.* He left Oxford in 1952 with a B.A. degree in English.

Richardson's professional career began in 1953, when he joined the British Broadcasting Corporation's television service and learned his craft as a director in that demanding medium. He directed a number of productions for the BBC, among them *Othello* and Dostoievsky's *The Gambler.* At this time Richardson made his first film, one of the earliest in a series sponsored by the British Film Institute's Experimental Film Fund. *Momma Don't Allow,* with Karel Reisz as joint director, followed a number of young Londoners to the Wood Green Jazz Club for an evening of dancing and listening to the traditional jazz music of Chris Barber. At a time when Britain's Teddy-boys were being condemned as delinquents, Richardson's documentary was startling in its uncondescending sympathy and its identification with the mood of its subjects.

At the BBC Richardson had met the director George Devine, in whom he found a fellow enthusiast for the idea of a truly contemporary theater. In 1955, when Devine joined the newly formed English Stage Company, Richardson followed him as associate artistic director. The English Stage Company, with modest subsidies from the Arts Council and from private patrons, set out, in Richardson's words, "to make the creative writer and the theatre mutually aware of each other." It took as its headquarters the 600-seat Royal Court Theatre in London's Knightsbridge area, where fifty years earlier Granville Barker had introduced the plays of Ibsen and Shaw to startled British audiences.

The English Stage Company presented its first two productions in April 1956, and the first play directed for the company by Tony Richardson opened on May 8. It was a work that had, until then, been rejected by every management and agent who had seen it—John Osborne's lunging attack on contemporary British society, *Look Back in Anger*. The play aroused a sensation, leaving most critics in a state of shocked indignation. The few who liked it, however, liked it very much indeed, greeting it with an enthusiasm that, as the play was televised and repeatedly revived, at the Royal Court and elsewhere, was soon seen to be justified. In retrospect it is clear that *Look Back in Anger* marked the beginning of a new era in the British theater, restoring vigor, realism, and social protest to a stage that had, in Arthur Miller's words, been "hermetically sealed from life." The play established the twenty-eight-year-old Richardson as a director to be reckoned with.

After that spectacular beginning, Devine and Richardson made the Royal Court a major outlet for the explosion of theatrical vitality that they had released with *Look Back in Anger*. This vitality has expressed itself in two quite different genres—the impassioned realism of Osborne and his successors, and the so-called "theatre of the absurd" of Ionesco, Beckett, and Simpson.

The plays that Richardson has staged at the Royal Court include examples of both schools and a number of classical revivals and unclassifiable experiments. His second production for the English Stage Company, in June 1956, was Nigel Dennis's social satire *Cards of Identity*. In 1957 he directed another Osborne play, *The Entertainer;* a double bill comprising Ionesco's *The Chairs* and Giradoux's *The Apollo de Bellac; The Making of Moo*, a satire on religion written by Nigel Dennis in collaboration with Richardson; Carson McCuller's *The Member of the Wedding;* and William Faulkner's *Requiem for a Nun.* By the end of 1957 Murray Schumach could report in the New York *Times* (December 29, 1957): "Mr. Richardson and his troupe have stirred up the London stage as have few things since Shaw."

Richardson, who now shares with George Devine the title of artistic director of the English Stage Company, has in recent years been able to direct fewer productions at the Royal Court. In spite of his heavy commitments elsewhere, however, he has since 1958 staged the following plays there: *Flesh to a Tiger*, by the Jamaican writer Barry Reckord; Tennessee Williams' *Orpheus Descending; Look After Lulu*, a farce by Noel Coward based on Feydeau's *Occupe toi d'Amélie;* Middleton and Rowley's *The Changeling; A Midsummer Night's Dream;*

Julie Hamilton

TONY RICHARDSON

and Osborne's *Luther.* Chekhov's *The Seagull* and Brecht's *St. Joan of the Stockyards* have been scheduled for the Royal Court's 1963-64 season, to be directed by Richardson and to star his wife, Vanessa Redgrave.

Richardson's work for the theater in England has not been confined to the Royal Court. In 1958 he staged *Pericles* at the Shakespeare Memorial Theatre, Stratford-upon-Avon, winning praise for an "unforgettably beautiful presentation," and the following year directed Paul Robeson in *Othello* there. The production was an extraordinary success, although some critics felt that Richardson had stressed speed and liveliness at the expense of poetry. In December 1962 he directed Sir Laurence Olivier in David Turner's *Semi-Detached* at the Saville Theatre in London's West End, but the play was not well received.

A number of English Stage Company productions have found their way to Broadway, many of them directed by Richardson. The first was *Look Back in Anger*, which opened at the Lyceum Theatre in October 1957. It ran for over 400 performances at the Lyceum and won the Drama Critics Circle award as the best foreign play of the season. In January 1958 Richardson directed Ionesco's *The Chairs* and *The Lesson* at the Phoenix Theatre, and in February brought Osborne's *The Entertainer* to the Royale Theatre as his third American production. The play was welcomed, with some reservations, and Richardson's handling of a brilliant cast headed by Sir Laurence Olivier again drew praise from the New York critics.

Richardson's next New York offering, *Requiem for a Nun*, lasted for only a few performances at the John Golden Theatre in 1959, but was triumphantly followed in October 1960 by Shelagh Delaney's *A Taste of Honey*, which Richardson co-directed with George Devine. The

RICHARDSON, TONY—*Continued*

play earned both critical and popular acclaim and enjoyed a long run at the Lyceum Theatre. Less successful was William Inge's *Natural Affection,* which opened at the Booth Theatre in January 1963, although both Richardson's direction and Kim Stanley's acting won enthusiastic notices.

John Osborne's most recent play, *Luther,* directed by Richardson in Paris and London, was hailed in both cities as a major work, but an uneven one, whose success owed much to Richardson's staging and Albert Finney's acting. It opened in New York on September 25, 1963. That autumn Richardson directed three productions for David Merrick in New York, with scarcely a break between them. The first was *Luther;* the second was Brecht's *Arturo Ui,* which ran briefly at the Lunt-Fontanne Theatre in November; and the third was the extensively rewritten version of Tennessee Williams' *The Milk Train Doesn't Stop Here Any More,* which opened at the Brooks Atkinson Theatre on January 1, 1964. These and his projected productions for the English Stage Company were scheduled to occupy him until February 1964, to be followed by a year and a half of film making. His film schedule included a motion-picture version of Evelyn Waugh's *The Loved One,* to be shot on location in California in the summer of 1964 for the Filmways Company.

Rather than sell the screen rights of *Look Back in Anger* to an established company, Richardson and Osborne decided in 1958 to form their own film company, Woodfall Film Productions Ltd. The Osborne play, their first production, made its debut in 1959 with Richardson as director and a cast that included Richard Burton, Mary Ure, and Claire Bloom. Many critics preferred the screen to the stage version, praising Richardson's "sensitive, beautifully modulated direction," and his avoidance of cinematic clichés.

Woodfall's second film was *The Entertainer.* Sir Laurence Olivier contributed a virtuoso performance as the seedy music hall comedian of the title, as he had in the play, and Richardson again directed. *Saturday Night and Sunday Morning,* Woodfall's next film, was directed by Karel Reisz, jointly produced by Richardson and Harry Saltzman, and launched a brilliant new star in Albert Finney. The film, based on Alan Sillitoe's novel, reached the United States in 1961, where it repeated the success it had already enjoyed in Britain.

During 1960 Richardson made his first Hollywood film, the Twentieth Century-Fox production *Sanctuary,* based both on Faulkner's novel of the same title and his *Requiem for a Nun.* The result, according to Richardson himself, was "very bad." The experience convinced him that the gigantic Hollywood production companies, cautiously protecting their huge investments, were an anachronism. At a press conference in October 1960 he said: "It's impossible to make films that appeal to everyone, and the only solution is to make them at a nonprohibitive cost, and try to adhere to a strong, independent point of view that will appeal to at least one body of customers—the ones who want to be stimulated by provocative ideas."

Richardson followed his own prescription closely in his next film for Woodfall. This was the screen version of *A Taste of Honey,* which he produced, directed, and wrote in collaboration with Shelagh Delaney. Working with a budget of $350,000 (much of it, ironically enough, derived from his *Sanctuary* fee), he selected an almost unknown cast and filmed on location in an attempt to escape the artificiality of the studio. It was released in 1961.

The film with which Richardson has identified most clearly is *The Loneliness of the Long Distance Runner,* which he directed and produced from a short story by Alan Sillitoe. The solitary running of the reform school boy whose story the film tells reminded Richardson painfully of his own lonely hikes at "the horrible off-white sort of public school" that he had attended during World War II. Denied permission to visit British reform schools for background, Richardson went anyway, masquerading as a social worker. The film created another new star, Tom Courtenay, and added another triumph to Woodfall's lengthening list of successes.

From the gritty, industrial present Richardson turned back to eighteenth-century England for his next film, *Tom Jones,* adapted by John Osborne from Henry Fielding's novel. "I wanted to get away from the rainy, industrial cities of the North," Richardson has explained. "I wanted something full of color and fun and it suddenly hit me that *Tom Jones,* which I'd loved since childhood, was it." He wanted to prove that his generation has not only a flair for social realism, but also a healthy sense of humor. By far Woodfall's most expensive production to date, with a budget of some $1,500,000, *Tom Jones* has enjoyed both an artistic and commercial success since its release in 1963. Richardson set out to make an authentic period piece, and by and large both British and American critics have felt that, with this bawdy and bucolic romp, he succeeded.

In 1962 Tony Richardson married the actress Vanessa Redgrave, daughter of Sir Michael Redgrave. They have one daughter. Richardson is a lanky man with black hair and the long, thin face of a classical actor. A casual dresser, he often wears windbreakers and shirts without ties. *Who's Who* lists his recreations as "directing plays and films."

References

Who's Who, 1963
Who's Who in the Theatre (1961)

ROOSEVELT, (ANNA) ELEANOR

Oct. 11, 1884-Nov. 7, 1962 Humanitarian; writer; wife of Franklin D. Roosevelt; First Lady (1933-45); United States representative to the United Nations (1945, 1947-52, and 1961); chairman of the U.N. Commission on Human Rights (1946-51); was influential in the Democratic party; was often selected in international polls as "the world's most admired woman." See *Current Biography* (January) 1949.

Obituary

N Y Times p1+ N 8 '62

ROUTLEY, T(HOMAS) CLARENCE Mar. 11, 1889-Mar. 31, 1963 Former secretary and president of the Canadian Medical Association. See *Current Biography* (January) 1956.

Obituary

Toronto Globe and Mail p41 Ap 2 '63

ROWLEY, JAMES J(OSEPH) Oct. 14, 1908- Chief of the United States Secret Service

Address: b. Treasury Bldg., Washington 25, D.C.; h. 3225 Oliver St., Chevy Chase, Md.

To James J. Rowley, chief of the United States Secret Service, belongs the dual task of protecting the President of the United States from possible harm and of apprehending counterfeiters of United States currency. Rowley, who worked his way through evening high school and earned two law degrees at night, began his career as an investigator for banks and entered government service in 1937 as a special agent for the Federal Bureau of Investigation. Assigned to the White House detail of the United States Secret Service in 1939, he became chief of that detail in 1946. Since then he has guarded the lives of four Presidents and their families. On September 1, 1962 Rowley succeeded Urbanus E. Baughman as chief of the Secret Service.

James Joseph Rowley was born on October 14, 1908 in the Bronx, New York to James Joseph and Bridgett (McTeague) Rowley. Both of his parents were natives of Ireland who settled in the Fordham area of the Bronx, where Rowley attended the local Roman Catholic parochial schools. He has a brother, the Reverend Frank P. Rowley, S. J., a chaplain in the Hudson State Hospital in Poughkeepsie, New York, and a sister, Mrs. Marjorie Borise, an executive secretary with the Blue Cross in New York. An outstanding athlete in high school, Rowley excelled in baseball, football, basketball, and track, and was offered three college scholarships. Before he could complete high school, his father, a painter for the city of New York, was killed in an accident on the job, and Rowley had to help support his family. He continued his schooling at night while working as a credit investigator for the Bank of the United States in New York City from 1926 until 1930. He graduated from Fordham Evening High School in 1929.

From 1930 to 1936, while studying law at St. John's University in Brooklyn, New York, Rowley worked as an investigator on liquidation work for the New York State Banking Department, serving as liaison between its banking division and its legal department. While at the university he was a member of Taft Inn and treasurer of Phi Delta Phi legal fraternity. He received his LL.B. degree from St. John's in 1935 and his LL.M. in 1936.

In 1937 Rowley joined the Federal Bureau of Investigation as a special investigator in the Charlotte, North Carolina area. He left the FBI to join a private law firm in the following year, but returned to government service when the partnership did not materialize. In November 1939 Rowley was assigned to the White House detail of the United States Secret Service and

JAMES J. ROWLEY

has remained with it since that time, except for the period from April 1943 to August 1945, when he served as a private in the United States Army.

During his Secret Service career Rowley's main concern has been the protection of four presidents: Franklin D. Roosevelt, Harry S. Truman, Dwight D. Eisenhower, and John F. Kennedy. At first he acted as an advance man in protective planning on Presidential trips. In 1946 he was appointed supervising agent of the White House detail, traveling right at the President's side, and keeping constantly on the alert for possible trouble. On photographs of the President of the United States Rowley is often seen as an anonymous figure, always scanning the crowd for a suspicious move or gesture that might mean a possible assassination attempt. President John F. Kennedy likes to recall that once, during the 1948 election campaign, when he was a freshman Congressman, Rowley pushed him aside to make way for President Truman. On September 1, 1961 Rowley was sworn in as chief of the Secret Service in a ceremony attended by President Kennedy. He succeeded retiring chief Urbanus E. Baughman, who had served in this office for thirteen years.

As Chief of the Secret Service, Rowley heads an agency created in 1865 by Secretary of the Treasury Hugh McColloch primarily for the purpose of suppressing counterfeiting. It was only after the assassination of President William McKinley in 1901 that Secret Service men were regularly assigned to guard the President and members of his immediate family. In 1951 Congress authorized the Secret Service also to protect the President-elect, and the Vice-President at his request. (A bill is pending in Congress making it mandatory to protect the Vice-President or whoever is next in the succession to the Presidency. The bill would also permit the service to guard a President for six months after he leaves office.)

(Continued next page)

ROWLEY, JAMES J.—*Continued*

Under the act of 1951 the Secret Service is authorized, among other things, to "detect and arrest any person committing any offense against the laws of the United States relating to coins, obligations, and securities of the United States and of foreign governments." The service also administers the execution of warrants issued under authority of the United States, offers and pays rewards for services or information leading to the apprehension of criminals, and investigates tort claim cases involving the Treasury Department personnel and property, and violations of the Gold Reserve Act of 1934 and the Silver Purchase Act of 1934. The Secret Service has a staff of some 706 employees, including the uniformed White House police and the Treasury guard responsible for protecting the main Treasury building and the cash and bonds in its vaults, and about 325 agents operating in sixty-three cities throughout the United States. The salary of the Secret Service chief is $18,500 per year, and his appointment is not subject to Senate confirmation.

According to Rowley, the task of guarding Presidents has become more difficult with the advent of the jet age; it requires three times as many men as it once did. In former years it was enough to send a few men ahead to prepare for the President's arrival by train, but now agents must be sent well in advance to set up security procedures at airports. Security problems are especially troublesome when Presidents visit foreign countries. One of Rowley's most difficult assignments was President Eisenhower's visit to Asia in 1960, when Secret Service agents guarding the President were mobbed by crowds of well-wishers in Korea, Manila, and New Delhi. In stressing the need for an enlarged Secret Service staff Rowley cites the riots that greeted former Vice-President Richard M. Nixon during his visit to South America in 1958 and the unrest faced by former Presidential press secretary James C. Hagerty in Japan in 1960 (which led to the cancellation of President Eisenhower's trip to that country).

The tensest moment in Rowley's career came in 1950, when Puerto Rican nationalists made an attempt on President Truman's life, resulting in the killing of one White House guard and the wounding of two others. "The biggest threat to a President's life is from the self-deluded who become the dupes of terroristic or subversive organizations," Rowley once said. "They think that if you knock off the head man, you throw the country into confusion and inertia. They think they become heroes in their own groups." To function effectively the Secret Service must keep in step with the latest technological developments in such fields as communications, explosives, electronics, radiation-detection, photographic processing, and high-speed printing.

Although the White House detail gets more publicity, the detection of counterfeit money and the apprehension of counterfeiters is a major function of the Secret Service. During the twelve months preceding September 1962 counterfeiting operations in the United States almost doubled, and some $4,000,000 in counterfeit currency was manufactured. The Secret Service confiscated about $3,500,000 of this before it got into circulation and arrested almost 700 counterfeiters. In addition, more than 3,100 forgers of government checks were arrested by Secret Service agents.

Testifying before a House Appropriations subcommittee in February 1962, Rowley warned Congress of the sharp rise in counterfeiting operations. "Counterfeiting on any scale represents a danger," he said, "and the government must act speedily to see that the integrity of its money is protected." He asked for fifty-eight new agents and for increased funds, so that the Secret Service could step up all phases of its operations. (The House Appropriations Committee subsequently cut the number of additional agents allowed to the Secret Service to less than thirty, and reduced the overall budget request by more than $500,000.)

Rowley takes his worries about his responsibility for guarding the President home with him. "If we get a report of some new method of assassination I'll think about it at night, trying to devise a way to counter it," he says. He wants to elevate the dignity of the Secret Service and is trying to make the public more aware of its role. According to Rowley, the ideal Secret Service agent should be alert, intelligent, and able to make quick decisions. He must be a team man, self-assured, but not overly aggressive.

James J. Rowley was married on April 15, 1940 to Mabel Rita Cluen, whom he met on a blind date in New York and courted by long distance from Washington. They have three daughters, Claudia, Linda, and Donna. The oldest daughter is a student at St. Joseph College in Emmitsburg, Maryland, and the two younger girls attend Immaculata Seminary in Washington. Organizations to which Rowley belongs include the Society of Former Special Agents of the Federal Bureau of Investigation and the International Association of Chiefs of Police.

A handsome, square-jawed man with graying brown hair and blue eyes, Rowley is five feet eleven inches tall and weighs 184 pounds. Belying the stereotype of a Secret Service man as a humorless, uncommunicative sort of person, Rowley is an easygoing man with a friendly smile and a gentle manner. He dresses impeccably and has a modest and courteous demeanor. His position as chief of the Secret Service requires less traveling than his previous position as chief of the White House detail, which kept him on the road for the greater part of the year. His favorite leisure-time activities include swimming, golf, and reading.

References

N Y Herald Tribune II p3 S 17 '61 por
N Y Post p32 S 7 '61 por
N Y Times p15 Ag 2 '61 por
Washington (D.C.) Post A p2 Ag 2 '61 por
Who's Who in America, 1962-63

RYAN, JOSEPH P(ATRICK) May 11, 1884-
June 26, 1963 President of the International
Longshoremen's Association (1927-53). See *Current Biography* (January) 1949.

Obituary

N Y Times p32 Je 27 '63

RYAN, ROBERT (BUSHNELL) Nov. 11,
1909- Actor
Address: b. 259 S. Beverly Dr., Beverly Hills,
Calif.; h. 88 Central Park West, New York 23

Originally chosen by movie producers because
his rugged frame and handsome features seemed
to typify the red-blooded, two-fisted American,
Robert Ryan has for more than twenty years
portrayed saints and sinners in some seventy film
roles. Ryan, who has never balked at playing
unsympathetic characters, won special praise for
his portrayals of a vicious racist in *Crossfire*
(1947), of an aging and battered fighter in
The Set-Up (1948), and of the evil shipmaster
in the 1962 film *Billy Budd*. Ryan began his
career on the legitimate stage, and he returned
to it for appearances in the 1954 production of
Shakespeare's *Coriolanus* and the American
Shakespeare Festival's *Antony and Cleopatra*
with Katherine Hepburn in 1960. Ryan's "American" look and previously untapped singing voice
won him the title role of *Mr. President*, the
Irving Berlin musical which opened on Broadway in October 1962. He has always found
time for participation in politics and education
and for the promotion of better race relations
and of peace in the nuclear age.

Robert Bushnell Ryan was born on November
11, 1909 (some sources give 1913) in Chicago,
the only child of Timothy and Mabel (Bushnell)
Ryan. His father, the son of an Irish immigrant,
was a prosperous building contractor. His mother
was of English background. At the age of eight,
Ryan recalls in *Parents' Magazine* (September
1954), "my father arranged for me to take boxing lessons. My mother countered by fixing me
up with instruction on the violin. I never became a violin virtuoso, but I did turn out to be
an expert boxer."

Ryan attended Loyola Academy, a Jesuit school
in Chicago, where he excelled in scholarship as
well as athletics. His admiration for Shakespeare
dates from this period, when one of his teachers
spent an entire semester on *Hamlet*. After his
graduation from the academy in 1927, Ryan
entered Dartmouth College. Although his father
hoped he would join him in the construction
business, Robert Ryan wanted to become a
writer. While at Dartmouth, he played football,
took part in track and field events, and edited
the college newspaper. He was the first freshman to win the college's heavyweight boxing
championship, remaining undefeated in four
years of intercollegiate competition. He became
a member of Psi Upsilon, where one of his fraternity brothers was Nelson Rockefeller, and he
won a first prize in a playwriting contest in
1931. He graduated in 1932 with a B.A. degree
in English.

Barrett—Howard

ROBERT RYAN

There was a surplus of college graduates during the first years of the Depression and—as
Ryan soon discovered—not enough literary jobs
to go around. He dug sewer tunnels under Chicago, stoked coal on a freighter bound for Africa,
worked as a miner, and herded horses in Montana. He also collected bills for a loan shark in
Chicago, but his compassion for the poor families he was collecting from prompted him to quit
after two weeks. Later he worked as supervisor
of supplies for the Chicago Board of Education
and as a paving supervisor for the WPA. With
more free time, Ryan was able to renew his interest in drama. He joined a little theater group
in Chicago in 1937, and after a few months
decided he preferred acting to writing plays. He
was offered an opportunity, without pay, to stage
and direct a play at a private school for girls.
The production was a success and Ryan began
to study drama seriously under the tutelage of
veteran actor-director Edward Boyle.

In 1938 a modest windfall of $2,000—the
result of investing $400 in a single oil well stock
during his high school days—enabled Ryan to
continue to support his widowed mother and at
the same time finance a trip to Hollywood.
There he enrolled at the Max Reinhardt Workshop and continued individual study, this time
with dramatic coach Vladimir Sokoloff. In the
following year he met and married another
drama student, Jessica Cadwalader. He made his
stage debut at the Belasco Theater in Los Angeles in 1940, but when given a try-out at Paramount Studios he was told that he was "not the
type" for motion pictures.

The Ryans then left Hollywood for the Eastern
strawhat circuit, where they were hired by a
stock company in Roslyn, Long Island "for room,
board, and $2 a week apiece." They eked out
their income with the last of the oil well money
and with Jessica Ryan's earnings as a model. A
supporting role in the play *A Kiss for Cinderella,*

RYAN, ROBERT—*Continued*

starring Luise Rainer, brought Ryan his first favorable critical notices. In December 1941 he was cast with Tallulah Bankhead, Joseph Schildkraut, and Lee J. Cobb in the Broadway production of Clifford Odets' play, *Clash By Night*. Although the play closed after forty-nine performances, it brought Ryan to the attention of Hollywood scouts, who felt that his granitic appearance would be ideal for a role in Pare Lorentz's projected film, *Name, Age, and Occupation*.

Although the Lorentz film was shelved, Ryan returned to Hollywood under contract to RKO Radio Pictures and made his film debut in *Bombardier*, released in 1943. Concentrating mainly on portrayals of war heroes and other heroic types, he also appeared during this period in the RKO productions *The Sky's the Limit, The Iron Major, Behind the Rising Sun, Gangway for Tomorrow, Tender Comrade,* and *Marine Raiders*. In January 1944 he entered the Marine Corps, serving as an infantry training instructor at Camp Pendleton and San Diego, California, and he was discharged as a private first class in November 1945.

While at the Camp Pendleton discharge center, Ryan met writer Richard Brooks, who had just completed a novel about the Marine Corps called *The Brick Foxhole* (Harper, 1945). After reading the book Ryan told Brooks he would like to play the role of Montgomery if the novel were ever filmed. Back at RKO Studios in 1947 the director Edward Dmytryk offered Ryan the desired role in *Crossfire*, the screen version of Brooks' novel. In the film Ryan portrayed a bigoted psychopath who kills a Jewish war veteran while in a drunken rage. *Crossfire* won the award for the best social film at the 1947 Cannes Film Festival. Bosley Crowther, in the New York *Times* (July 23, 1947), called Ryan's portrayal "frighteningly real," and Alton Cook, writing in the New York *World-Telegram* (July 22, 1947), described it as "an unusually intelligent performance." Ryan's prestige in Hollywood was enhanced by another challenging role, in *The Set-Up*, in 1949. As the aging but determined fighter, Stoker Thompson, Ryan did a "first-rate acting job," according to Otis L. Guernsey, Jr., of the New York *Herald Tribune* (March 30, 1949).

Crossfire and *The Set-Up* established Ryan in the top echelon of film stars, but the roles that followed in war films, Westerns, and crime exposés provided him with more revenue than acting scope. His postwar films for RKO have included *Woman on the Beach* and *Trail Street* (1947); *Return of the Bad Men, Berlin Express,* and *The Boy with Green Hair* (1948); *The Woman on Pier 13, Born to be Bad,* and *The Secret Fury* (1950); *The Best of the Badmen* and *On Dangerous Ground* (1951); *Clash By Night* (1952); *Escape to Burma* (1955); and *Back From Eternity* (1956). He also appeared in the Metro-Goldwyn-Mayer productions *Act of Violence* (1948), *Caught* (1949), *The Naked Spur* (1953), and *Her Twelve Men* (1954); the Twentieth Century-Fox films *Inferno* (1953), *The Tall Men* (1955), *House of Bamboo* (1956),

and *The Canadians* (1961); Warner Brothers' *About Mrs. Leslie* (1954); and the United Artists releases *Men in War* (1957), *Lonelyhearts* (1958), and *Day of the Outlaw* (1959).

Ryan was singled out for praise by reviewers for his performance as a bullying rancher in *Bad Day at Black Rock* (MGM, 1955); for his portrayal of the Georgia farmer Ty Ty Walden in the film version of Erskine Caldwell's earthy novel *God's Little Acre* (United Artists, 1958); for his role as a Negro-hating ex-convict in *Odds Against Tomorrow* (United Artists, 1959); for his appearance as the Alaska pioneer Thor Storm in the film version of Edna Ferber's novel *Ice Palace* (Warner Brothers, 1960); and for his performance as the sadistic Master Claggart in Peter Ustinov's production of Melville's *Billy Budd* (Allied Artists, 1962). Ryan also appears in a "cameo" role as John the Baptist in the religious epic *King of Kings* (MGM, 1961), and he is one of many stars in the epic war film *The Longest Day* (Twentieth Century-Fox, 1962). In 1963 he was chosen for the role of General Santander in the forthcoming *Simon Bolivar*, a film based on the life of the South American liberator.

Ryan has been identified with a group of film stars—referred to by columnist Joe Hyams as "Hollywood standbys"—who work constantly, turn in superior performances, and enjoy substantial incomes. As a free-lance actor Ryan receives a percentage of the profits of each film, in addition to, or in lieu of, a flat salary. In recent years he has selected those roles that are most satisfying to him and are not likely to type him. To do so, he reads about 200 scripts a year.

In 1954 Ryan temporarily interrupted his film career to accept the title role in the Phoenix Theatre's production of Shakespeare's *Coriolanus* in New York City. Although Ryan's performance was praised by Brooks Atkinson, it received unfavorable notices from a number of critics. The experience whetted his interest in Shakespeare, however, and he established a class for aspiring Shakespearean actors in Hollywood. In the summer of 1960 Ryan played Mark Antony opposite Katherine Hepburn's Cleopatra in the American Shakespeare Festival's production of *Antony and Cleopatra* at Stratford, Connecticut.

The leading role that Ryan accepted in the Irving Berlin musical *Mr. President* was a marked departure from his usual assignments. He was suggested for it by Katherine Hepburn and hired after an audition assured composer Berlin that Ryan could carry a tune. Written by Howard Lindsay and Russel Crouse and directed by Joshua Logan, the show centers about an American President and his wife who go on an international goodwill tour shortly before retiring from the White House. The Washington opening night at the National Theatre on September 26, 1962 was distinguished by an audience that included President and Mrs. John F. Kennedy and an entourage of political and diplomatic personalities.

Like a number of other Hollywood actors Ryan has worked in television. He joined a team of rotating stars—Dick Powell, David Niven,

Jack Lemmon, and Charles Boyer—in a series of half-hour dramas on NBC-TV during the 1957-58 season. Each actor owned a portion of the production, which was filmed at Dayton Studios. Despite the variety of offerings and the competence of the stars, however, the series, *A Turn of Fate*, did not succeed with television critics, who disliked the material. Ryan has starred in two television spectaculars: he had the title role in a *Playhouse 90* production of F. Scott Fitzgerald's *The Great Gatsby* on June 29, 1958; and he played the dying writer of Ernest Hemingway's *The Snows of Kilimanjaro* on the *Buick-Electra Playhouse* on March 25, 1960. He has also appeared on the *Zane Grey Theatre* and on other television programs.

When he is not busy with acting commitments Ryan devotes his energies to his family and to civic responsibilities. He is a founder, and has served as the president of, a theater group at the University of California at Los Angeles, which has presented, among other productions, Berthold Brecht's *Mother Courage*, Dylan Thomas' *Under Milkwood*, and T. S. Eliot's *Murder in the Cathedral*, in which Ryan played the role of Saint Thomas à Becket in 1959.

The Oakwood Elementary School in the San Fernando Valley owes its existence to the Ryans, who had become concerned about North Hollywood's overcrowded school conditions. Although private, it is open to anyone, and scholarships aid children whose parents cannot afford the tuition. Ryan was the school's first president and Mrs. Ryan was the second; both are still members of the board of trustees. The school has cost the Ryans over $40,000.

Like the late Humphrey Bogart, Robert Ryan has become one of the most active Democrats in Hollywood. He donated several thousands of dollars to the party's 1958 gubernatorial campaign, and in February 1962 he joined a group of actors in a radio program challenging the right-wing John Birch Society. (The program touched off anonymous threats to bomb Ryan's home.) Ryan says that he is interested in "just about all organizations working for better race relations and disarmament." In September 1959 he and Steve Allen acted as co-chairmen to organize the Hollywood chapter of the National Committee for a Sane Nuclear Policy. He is a board member of its national committee and served as chairman of a "Stars for Sane" show presented at Town Hall in New York City in March 1963.

Since 1950 Ryan has served on the board of directors of the Westwood International Center. He is a member and past vice-president of the Academy of Motion Picture Arts and Sciences. Ryan is also a past president of the Southern California Chapter of the United World Federalists, and he belongs to the American Civil Liberties Union and similar organizations. Although he was reared as a Roman Catholic, Ryan takes an active interest in the Society of Friends, of which his wife is a member.

Robert Ryan and Jessica Calwalader were married on March 11, 1939. They have three children, Timothy, Cheyney, and Lisa. Mrs. Ryan is the author of four books for young people. The Ryans make their home in Bronxville, New York, and they own a rambling country house in North Hollywood, with an acre of land and a menagerie for pets. Ryan also owns a small office building in Beverly Hills. Described by Frank Quinn in the New York *Sunday Mirror* (May 25, 1958) as a "quiet, soft-spoken but friendly person," who is "serious but with a ready smile that warms," Ryan is six feet four inches tall, weighs 190 pounds, and has brown eyes and brown hair touched with gray at the temples. He enjoys walking, cares little for night life, and prefers to spend his free time with his family.

References

Cue 29:8+ Jl 30 '60 pors
N Y Post p43 Mr 7 '63 por
Pageant 14:24+Mr '59 por
International Motion Picture Almanac, 1963
Who's Who in America, 1962-63

SADDLER, DONALD (EDWARD) Jan. 24, 1920- Choreographer; dancer
Address: b. c/o Deborah Coleman Agency, 200 W. 57th St., New York 19; h. 320 W. 56th St., New York 19

A choreographer of considerable versatility and imagination, Donald Saddler has created dances for the ballet, the musical comedy stage, television, and films. His theater credits include *Wonderful Town* (1953), for which he won an Antoinette Perry Award, and *Milk and Honey* (1961). His original ballets *Winesburg, Ohio* and *This Property is Condemned* were presented at the Jacob's Pillow Dance Festival in 1958. Saddler, who began his career as a dancer with the Ballet Theatre company in 1940, has also directed a number of summer theater musical productions.

Born in Van Nuys, California on January 24, 1920, Donald Edward Saddler was reared in Los Angeles, California. He was the youngest of twelve children—six boys and six girls—of Elmer Edward Saddler, a rancher, and Mary Elizabeth (Roberts) Saddler. He attended Lynwood Junior High School in Lynwood, California and the David Starr Jordan High School in Los Angeles, from which he graduated in 1936. He took part in track and football and won a speech contest for Southern California, sponsored by the Junior Red Cross. Saddler studied journalism at Los Angeles City College for two years.

Saddler's admiration for dancer-choreographers like Angna Enters, Harald Kreutzberg, and Fred Astaire led him to study dance with Carmalita Maracci. He financed his lessons by working as a dancer in films, including *Rosalie* and *Girl of the Golden West*. He made his debut in California in 1938 and at the International Casino Show in New York in 1939. Joining the company of the Ballet Theatre (now the American Ballet Theatre) at its inception late in 1939, he came under the tutelage of Anthony Tudor, Anton Dolin, and Michel Fokine. He also

DONALD SADDLER

studied ballet with Elisabeth Anderson Ivantzova and dramatics with Beno Schneider.

Appearing with the Ballet Theatre from 1940 to 1943 and again for several years after World War II, Saddler danced, among others, the parts of Alias in Eugene Loring's *Billy the Kid,* the Rose Cavalier in Dolin's *Princess Aurora,* the Bartender in Jerome Robbins' *Fancy Free,* the Friend in *Swan Lake,* and Eusebius in *Carnaval.* He was one of the Queen's Lovers in a Ballet Theatre world première of Fokine's *Bluebeard,* presented in Mexico City and New York City in the fall of 1941. He also danced the adagio in Frederick Ashton's *Les Patineurs* (The Skaters) and had roles in David Lichine's *Helen of Troy,* and in Tudor's *Lilac Garden, Gala Performance,* and *Undertow.* He has been the partner of Maria Tallchief, Nora Kaye, Alicia Markova, Alicia Alonso, and Maria Karnilova.

From May 1943 to February 1946 Saddler served with the United States Army, rising from the rank of private to that of corporal. He choreographed and took part in six presentations of the soldier revue *Merrily We Roll Along,* the USO productions *As You Were* and *Bonanza Days,* and the Air Corps' *Speak Low.* Stationed in Alaska, he gave dance concerts at Seward, Anchorage, and Fort Richardson, where he was also staff announcer and assistant production manager of the post's radio station.

Having completed his military service Saddler returned to the Ballet Theatre in 1946. The company appeared during the summer of 1946 in England at Covent Garden and then toured the United States during the 1946-47 season. It performed at the New York City Center in the spring and fall of 1947 and played a season at the Metropolitan Opera House. Meanwhile, Saddler had also been engaged to appear in *High Button Shoes,* which opened on Broadway in October 1947, and in which he danced a tango with Helen Gallagher. During the 1949-50

Broadway season he appeared in *Dance Me a Song,* in which he was the partner of Joan McCracken, and during the 1950-51 season he was a principal player in *Bless You All,* in which he partnered Valerie Bettis. Saddler has danced with Esther Junger and in the Mexican films *Yolanda* and *Los Tres Mosqueteros.*

More active today as a choreographer than a dancer, Saddler has staged dances for musical comedies, the ballet, television, and motion pictures. He was the choreographer for the films *April in Paris* (1952), *By the Light of the Silvery Moon* (1953), *Young at Heart* (1955), and *The Main Attraction* (1962).

His first choreographic assignment for Broadway was the arrangement of the dances and musical numbers for Leonard Bernstein's *Wonderful Town,* a musical comedy based on the play *My Sister Eileen,* which opened on February 25, 1953 and ran for 559 performances. The dance numbers included an exuberant "Conga!", led by the show's star, Rosalind Russell; a mock game, "Pass the Football"; a depiction of a job hunt, "Conquering New York"; and a night club scene in slow motion in which couples are shown futilely trying to dance on a tiny crowded elevated dance platform.

"For his movement vocabulary Mr. Saddler has, for the most part, utilized actions derived from popular or social dance forms," Walter Terry wrote of *Wonderful Town* (New York *Herald Tribune,* March 8, 1953). "He has called upon the techniques of ballet and modern dance and upon freshly devised theatrical movement to support, invigorate, and extend the elemental figures of ballroom dancing. . . . With 'Wonderful Town' he has won the right to recognition as an artist-craftsman equipped to function on the most demanding of theatrical thoroughfares, Broadway." Saddler won an Antoinette Perry (Tony) Award for his work in *Wonderful Town.* He was the director for a production of *Wonderful Town,* starring Carol Channing, at the Greek Theatre in Hollywood.

Saddler's next contribution to Broadway was the choreography for the revue *John Murray Anderson's Almanac,* which opened on December 10, 1953 with Hermione Gingold, Billy De Wolfe, Harry Belafonte, Orson Bean, and Nanci Crompton. In addition to arranging some ballet episodes, he planned movements for the singers and actors. "When it came to planning action for the song-pluggers and the skit-players, he did as masterful a job of dance creation as I have ever seen accomplished in this very special movement area," Walter Terry wrote in the New York *Herald Tribune* (December 20, 1953). "Gestures, steps and patterns were never incidental. Indeed they were definitive in giving physical form to the rhythms of song, in delineating character, in evoking mood." In 1956 Saddler contributed the choreography to *Shangri-La,* the musical version of James Hilton's book *Lost Horizons,* which had a short run on Broadway.

Between 1954 and 1960 Saddler choreographed a number of productions for the Italian musical stage. Working on almost one show a year, he arranged dances and musical numbers for *Tobia la Candida Spia* in 1954; for *La Patrona di*

Raggio di Luna in 1955; for *Buona Notte, Bettina* in 1956; for *L'Adorabile Giulio* in 1957, for *Un Trapezio per Lisistrata* in 1958; and for *Un Manderino per Teo* in 1960. For his work with *Tobia la Candida Spia* and *Buona Notte, Bettina* he received the Maschera d'Argento, the Italian equivalent of an Antoinette Perry Award. In 1960 he also arranged the dances and musical numbers for the London musical *When in Rome.*

Saddler directed musical productions at the Dallas State Fair in the summers of 1957 and 1959 and at the Carousel Theatre, a theater-in-the-round, in Framingham, Massachusetts in the summer of 1958. While staging *New Girl in Town* at the Carousel in July 1958 he daily traveled the 100 miles from Framingham to Lee, Massachusetts, where he was presenting two original ballets at the Jacob's Pillow Dance Festival.

At Jacob's Pillow, Saddler and four other dancers, including Maria Karnilova, performed the world première of Saddler's ballet, *Winesburg, Ohio,* based on Sherwood Anderson's book. By welding movement and music with spoken dialogue, the ballet tried to depict the private tragedies of five people in a small town. Saddler danced the part of a guilt-ridden Peeping-Tom minister; the others portrayed a mother and son, a prostitute, and a spinster. The second ballet presented at Jacob's Pillow in July 1958 was Saddler's adaptation of Tennessee Williams' play *This Property is Condemned,* which he first created for the Ballet Theatre Workshop in 1957. It sketched the story of a young girl destined to follow her sister into prostitution. Walter Terry, reviewing the ballets in the New York *Herald Tribune* (July 13, 1958), wrote, "These two theater-dance pieces not only represent Mr. Saddler's versatility but also his increasing mastery of a difficult area of dance creation, his taste and tenderness in communicating the secrets of the heart while telling clearly the surface drama which holds them captive."

At the Jacob's Pillow Dance Festival two seasons later, in 1960, Saddler appeared as a guest artist with Valerie Bettis' Dance Theater, dancing the role of Macbeth opposite Miss Bettis in *The Golden Round,* sequences drawn from Shakespeare's tragedy. He also appeared in Miss Bettis' *Early Voyagers,* based on themes and characters from Truman Capote's *Other Voices, Other Rooms.* In June 1961 he and Maria Karnilova portrayed Vernon and Irene Castle doing dances of the 1920's as part of a program, *America Dances,* at the tenth season of the Boston Art Festival. For the same program Saddler choreographed and danced, with Miss Karnilova, some satires of the current choreographic styles of Jerome Robbins and Agnes de Mille.

Saddler's creation of a ballet based on *Romeo and Juliet* and a short dance sequence based on *A Midsummer Night's Dream* for the *Bell Telephone Hour* (NBC-TV) in March 1961 prompted Walter Terry of the New York *Herald Tribune* once again to praise Saddler for his imaginative and exciting choreography. Saddler had previously staged incidental dances for the *Bell Telephone Hour* in the 1960 season, and he did so

again in 1962. Later in the 1961 season Saddler added to his Broadway credits by doing the choreography for *Milk and Honey,* a musical about Israel, which he visited to gather material for the show. The dances he provided included a hora; a work dance, showing the clearing of the land; and a Yemenite wedding.

In the summer of 1962 Saddler participated in a unique project, sponsored by the Rebekah Harkness Foundation. At Watch Hill, Rhode Island, near the estate of Mrs. Rebekah Harkness Kean, six choreographers were provided with time and space and the services of a full dance company and pianists. For twelve weeks they were encouraged to create ballets as they pleased, without thought of commercial commitment or success. Six "ballets-in-progress" that were evolved during the summer were given a private showing at New York's Fashion Institute of Technology in October 1962. Saddler has also been commissioned by the Rebekah Harkness Foundation to create a children's ballet for the Robert Joffrey Ballet.

A bachelor, Donald Saddler is five feet eleven inches tall, weighs 155 pounds, and has blue eyes and brown hair. During his free time he pursues his interest in Italian Renaissance art and in photography, reads, and does theatrical research in museums. He also likes to travel. But his vocation is his most compelling concern, for he has said, "To me, when one is not dancing, one is not alive. I must dance in order to live."

References

Christian Sci Mon p12 Je 22 '45 por

N Y Herald Tribune IV p4 Jl 13 '58

Chujoy, Anatole, ed. Dance Encyclopedia (1949)

SAMUEL, HERBERT (LOUIS) 1ST VISCOUNT Nov. 6, 1870-Feb. 5, 1963 British statesman; member of the House of Commons (1902-18, 1929-35); member of the House of Lords (since 1937); served in several cabinets; a leader of the Liberal party in Parliament. See *Current Biography* (April) 1955.

Obituary

N Y Times p36 Ap 1 '63

SANDBURG, CARL (AUGUST) Jan. 6, 1878-
Author; folk singer
Address: h. Connemara Farm, Flat Rock, N.C.

NOTE: This biography supersedes the article that appeared in *Current Biography* in 1940.

As poet, novelist, historian, biographer, folklorist, and storyteller, Carl Sandburg has for some sixty years proclaimed his faith in the collective wisdom of the American people and through his writings has built a bridge between frontier America and twentieth-century industrial society. Early in life Sandburg came into immediate contact with the common man while he was a manual laborer, hobo, soldier, Socialist organizer, and newspaperman. Since then he has

Wide World

CARL SANDBURG

written more than 1,000 free verse poems, produced a monumental biography of Abraham Lincoln, and established himself as an authority on folk music. Sandburg has won two Pulitzer Prizes, in addition to many other honors, and is probably more widely read by American high school students than any other living writer. To Rebecca West he is, like Burns, "a national poet."

Carl Sandburg, who was christened Carl August Sandberg, is a native of Galesburg in the prairie country of Illinois, an area associated with the early career of Abraham Lincoln. He was born on January 6, 1878, the second of seven children of August and Clara Mathilda (Anderson) Sandburg, who had come to the United States from Sweden. Sandburg recalls his father as a frugal, semiliterate, and devout man, who earned "forty dollars in good months and nineteen dollars in bad" as a helper at the Chicago, Burlington & Quincy Railroad blacksmith shop.

Carl Sandburg wanted to become a writer by the time he was six. An avid reader, he enjoyed history and biography and devoured the daily newspapers. He obtained his education in Galesburg elementary schools and attended the Swedish Lutheran Church and Sunday school. Although he grew up in a conservative Republican atmosphere, his interest in social justice was aroused by such events as a local railway engineers' strike and the Chicago Haymarket riots of 1886.

From the age of eleven Sandburg helped to earn his keep, sweeping floors and cleaning cuspidors in a law office, delivering newspapers, and performing other odd jobs. After completing the eighth grade he left school to take a full-time job delivering milk. Later he was a handyman in a drugstore, carried water for a road crew, sold refreshments and rented out boats at a resort, harvested ice at a frozen lake, shifted scenery in a theater, and worked at a racetrack, a bottling

plant, a brickyard, and a pottery. He also shined shoes at a barber shop, hoping to learn the barbering trade, and he made an unsuccessful attempt at running a mail-order business.

Dissatisfied with his "dead-end" jobs, Sandburg decided in June 1897 to head westward by freight train to work in the Kansas wheat harvest. After a few months on the road he returned to Galesburg, where he became apprenticed to a housepainter. When the United States declared war on Spain, Sandburg decided to join the army, and on April 26, 1898 he enlisted in Company C, Sixth Infantry Regiment of the Illinois Volunteers. He served for eight months in Puerto Rico but did not see combat duty.

After his discharge Sandburg enrolled at Lombard College in Galesburg, working in his spare time with the Galesburg fire department. At the end of his freshman year he was selected as a candidate for the United States Military Academy at West Point, but he returned after two weeks, having failed tests in arithmetic and grammar. Back in Lombard College Sandburg captained the college basketball team, sang in the glee club, edited college publications, and delivered a prize-winning oration. His literary aspirations were encouraged by Professor Philip Green Wright, who organized the Poor Writers Club at Lombard and who helped to arouse Sandburg's interest in Lincoln.

Sandburg left Lombard College in 1902 without graduating and worked for a time as an advertising manager for a department store and as a stereoscope salesman. He remained in contact with Professor Wright, who privately published his first two volumes of poems, In Reckless Ecstasy (1904) and The Plaint of a Rose (1905), and a volume of his essays, Incidentals (1905), through his Asgard Press. These early works of Carl Sandburg were formal and classical in style, optimistic and romantic in vein.

In 1907 Sandburg moved to Milwaukee to become district organizer for the Social Democratic party of Wisconsin. He contributed articles and poems to the International Socialist Review, the Leader, LaFollette's Weekly, and other publications, and wrote for the Milwaukee Daily News, which in 1909 published his first article on Abraham Lincoln in observance of the Lincoln centennial. From 1910 to 1912 he served as secretary to Milwaukee's Socialist Mayor, Emil Seidel.

Late in 1912 Sandburg went to Chicago to work as a feature writer for the Daily Socialist. In 1913 he became associate editor of System, and he wrote articles dealing with industrial reform. For a time he also worked as a reporter for Day Book, a tabloid newspaper founded by E. W. Scripps, which operated without advertising and presented the viewpoint of the wage earner. After Day Book suspended publication in 1917 Sandburg worked briefly as a reporter for the American Federation of Labor press.

Sandburg first received wide recognition when some of his poems were published in Poetry: A Magazine of Verse, founded by Harriet Monroe in 1912. In March 1914 Poetry published "Chicago," which won Sandburg the $200 Helen Haire Levinson prize that year. "Chicago" was the leading poem in Sandburg's Chicago Poems

(Holt, 1916), which, by emphasizing the seaminess of city life, shocked those whose ears had been attuned to the poetry of the genteel tradition. A reviewer for the Boston *Transcript* (May 13, 1916) dismissed it as "a book of ill-regulated speech that has neither verse nor rhythm" and predicted, "This phase of our poetic art will pass, it is too positive to last," but a critic for *Review of Reviews* (June 1916) noted that Sandburg "has shaped poetry that is like a statue by Rodin."

Although a number of his poems and essays were pacifist, Sandburg refused to join his fellow socialists in their antiwar stand after the United States entered World War I. He worked briefly in 1917 as an editorial writer for William Randolph Hearst's Chicago *American* but quit in distaste after three weeks and became a reporter for the Chicago *Daily News*, with which he remained for twelve years. There he became associated with a number of noted writers, including Ben Hecht, Charles MacArthur, Floyd Dell, and Harry Hansen in a literary movement known as the Chicago Renaissance. A new volume of Sandburg's poems, *Cornhuskers* (Holt, 1918), dealing mainly with rural life, was recognized by Phillips Russell in the New York *Call* (November 10, 1918) as representing "that vigorous, urging spirit that is revising our art and poetry as well as our economics."

In 1918 Sandburg went to Norway and Sweden to report on the Finnish revolution for the Newspaper Enterprise Association. Returning home, he covered the Chicago race riots of 1919 in a series of articles for the *Daily News* that stressed the need for better opportunities for Negroes and called for a federal investigation of race relations. The articles were published in a book, *Chicago Race Riots* (Harcourt, 1919), with an introduction by Walter Lippmann. Sandburg's assignment as motion-picture editor with the *Daily News* later in 1919 left him with more leisure to devote to his own writings. His next two volumes of poetry were *Smoke and Steel* (Harcourt, 1920) and *Slabs of the Sunburnt West* (Harcourt, 1922). For his own daughters he wrote a series of children's fairy tales, *Rootabaga Stories* (Harcourt, 1922) and *Rootabaga Pigeons* (Harcourt, 1923).

Sandburg's massive study of Abraham Lincoln, conceived during his boyhood in Galesburg, was undertaken with the purpose of counteracting sentimental Lincoln biographies by presenting an unvarnished portrait. While living in Elmhurst, a Chicago suburb, in the early 1920's, Sandburg traveled widely in search of Lincoln materials. Along the way he made many public appearances before university and literary groups, giving lectures, reciting his poetry, and singing folk songs.

The first two volumes of Sandburg's Lincoln biography, *Abraham Lincoln: The Prairie Years* (Harcourt, 1926), covering Lincoln's youth and early career, were almost universally acclaimed, although some critics categorized them as creative writing rather than objective history. A shortened version for children was published with the title *Abe Lincoln Grows Up* (Harcourt, 1928).

Sandburg's *American Songbag* (Harcourt, 1927) is an annotated compilation of some 280 songs and ballads—some of them reaching print for the first time—that he had collected over the years. In preparing the book Sandburg enlisted the aid of composers, arrangers, singers, musicians, and musicologists. The work was later supplemented by the *New American Songbag* (Associated Music Publishers, Inc., 1951). Sandburg has also recorded folk songs, poems, and narratives for Lyrichord Discs, Caedmon Records, and other companies.

In 1928 Sandburg moved with his family to the sand dune country of Harbert, Michigan. The title poem of his next book of poems, *Good Morning, America* (Harcourt, 1928), was selected as the Phi Beta Kappa poem at Harvard University in 1928. Other works by Sandburg published during his early years at Harbert include *Steichen the Photographer* (Harcourt, 1929), a biography of his noted brother-in-law, Edward Steichen; *Potato Face* (Harcourt, 1930), a book of "Rootabaga stories" for adults; *Early Moon* (Harcourt, 1930), a book of poems for children; and *Mary Lincoln, Wife and Widow* (Harcourt, 1932).

Sandburg paid tribute to the common man of America—his folk speech, his creeds, and his humor—in the long and affirmative poem *The People, Yes* (Harcourt, 1936). In *Literary History of the United States* (Macmillan, 1946) Willard Thorp referred to it as "one of the great American books" and added: "A foreigner will find more of America in *The People, Yes* than in any other book we can give him. But he will have to spell it out slowly." After its publication Sandburg continued his research and writing on Lincoln, touring the United States during the winter months in folk song recitals.

His long and arduous years of research culminated in the publication in 1939 by Harcourt, Brace and Company of *Abraham Lincoln: The War Years*, for which he won the Pulitzer Prize in history in 1940. More than a biography, this four-volume work of over 1,000,000 words is also a history of the Civil War era, ending with the death of Lincoln. The historian Allan Nevins, writing in the *Saturday Review of Literature* (December 2, 1939), called it "one of the greatest of American biographies . . . a magnificent piece of history." Other contributions by Sandburg to the study of Lincoln and the Civil War era include *Storm Over the Land* (Harcourt, 1942), a photographic record of the Civil War; *The Photographs of Abraham Lincoln* (Harcourt, 1944), on which he collaborated with Frederick Hill Meserve; and *The Lincoln Collector: The Story of Oliver R. Barrett's Great Private Collection* (Harcourt, 1949). Sandburg's six-volume biography of Lincoln has been condensed into one volume with the title *Abraham Lincoln: The Prairie Years and the War Years* (Harcourt, 1954).

From 1941 to 1945 Sandburg wrote a weekly political column for the Chicago *Times* syndicate, supporting the Allied war effort. Some of his wartime writings were published in *Homefront Memo* (Harcourt, 1943). He appeared on radio broadcasts for the Office of War Information and wrote the commentary for the government film *Bomber* and the captions for Edward Steichen's mural photography show *Road to Victory*, presented in 1942.

(*Continued next page*)

SANDBURG, CARL—*Continued*

Sandburg's epic novel, *Remembrance Rock* (Harcourt, 1948), covers a period of American history extending from the days of the Pilgrims to the end of the Civil War period. The book received mixed reviews. In 1951 Sandburg was awarded his second Pulitzer Prize, for his *Complete Poems* (Harcourt, 1950). His autobiographical *Always the Young Strangers* (Harcourt, 1952), an account of the first twenty years of his life, was acclaimed by Robert E. Sherwood in the New York *Times* (January 4, 1954) as "the best biography ever written by an American."

Well beyond retirement age, Sandburg continued to be tirelessly active. He wrote the prologue to Edward Steichen's photographic exhibit *The Family of Man,* which opened at the Museum of Modern Art in New York City in January 1955 and was later shown in many countries of the world. On February 12, 1959, the 150th anniversary of Lincoln's birth, Sandburg became the first private citizen to address a joint session of both houses of Congress.

His most recent volumes of poetry are *Wind Song* (Harcourt, 1960), *Harvest Poems: 1960* (Harcourt, 1960), and *Honey and Salt* (Harcourt, 1963). *The Sandburg Range* (Harcourt, 1957) is an anthology of his works. *The World of Carl Sandburg,* a dramatization adapted and directed by Norman Corwin, was presented on Broadway in 1960, starring Bette Davis. In recent years Sandburg has appeared on a number of television programs. He has written forewords for some twenty books of other authors, and his poems continue to appear in magazines.

Sandburg has often been accused of writing without form. "Well, I'm not some sort of *addict* for form," he told Mark Harris in an interview for *Life* (December 1, 1961). "But if I lack *form* all the proverbs of Solomon, all the psalms of David, the book of Ecclesiastes, and the Old Testament—they are all lacking form." Self-described as a radical and a political independent, Sandburg has taken part in Democratic political campaigns in recent years, but he has turned down requests that he run for Congress. When Harry Golden once asked him about his religious beliefs, Sandburg replied: "I am a Christian, a Quaker, a Moslem, a Buddhist, a Shintoist, a Confucian, and maybe a Catholic pantheist or a Joan of Arc who hears voices—I am all of these and more."

In 1919 and 1921 Sandburg shared the Poetry Society of America prize. The Swedish government conferred on him the Royal Order of the North Star in 1938 and made him a Commander of the order in 1953. The King of Sweden presented him with a special gold medal in 1959 for his accomplishments in the fine arts. In 1940 Sandburg was elected to membership in the American Academy of Arts and Letters, which conferred on him its gold medal for historical and biographical writing in 1952. Sandburg has also received the Poetry Society of America medal (1953), the silver medal of the Civil War Round Table (1954), and the Albert Einstein Award of Yeshiva College (1956), among other awards. Some thirty-four colleges, including the University of Uppsala in Sweden, have conferred honorary doctorates on him, and schools throughout the United States have been named in honor of Sandburg.

Since 1945 Carl Sandburg has lived on Connemara Farm near Flat Rock, North Carolina with his wife, the former Lillian Paula Steichen, whom he married on June 15, 1908, and their two oldest daughters, Margaret and Janet. Sandburg's younger daughter, Helga, is a poet and a novelist and is the mother of his two grown grandchildren. At Connemara the Sandburgs breed and raise goats. Harry Golden has noted that although Sandburg is not quite six feet tall, he conveys the impression of "incredible height," and that his physical stature and facial features resemble those of an American Indian chief. Although Sandburg is generous with his friends he has simple tastes and spends little on himself. For relaxation he takes walks, and he spends about a half hour daily singing in his mellow, untrained baritone voice to the accompaniment of his bell-shaped guitar.

References

Golden, Harry. Carl Sandburg (1961)
Sandburg, Carl. Always the Young Strangers (1952)
Twentieth Century Authors (1942; First Supplement, 1955)
Who's Who in America, 1962-63
Zehnpfennig, Gladys. Carl Sandburg: Poet and Patriot (1963)

SAXON, JAMES J(OSEPH) Apr. 13, 1914-
United States government official

Address: b. Treasury Department, Washington 25, D.C.; h. 6024 Western Ave., Chevy Chase, Md.

The appointment of James J. Saxon as Comptroller of the Currency in November 1961 brought into the Kennedy administration a man who advocated sweeping alterations in the banking industry and who felt that his office should take the lead in this change. In the relatively short time that he has held office, Saxon has boldly set forth to reform the banking industry by presenting to the President the first major overhaul of the system since 1933 and has moved vigorously to modernize all aspects of the comptroller's operations. His fifteen years of experience as a Treasury Department expert and five years as special counsel for the First National Bank of Chicago have given him undisputed qualifications for the top post in currency affairs.

James Joseph Saxon was born to Samuel Joseph and Catherine Ann (Mulhanney) Saxon on April 13, 1914 in Toledo, Ohio, where his father worked as a railroad traffic agent. His first school was Good Shepherd School in Toledo. From 1928 to 1931 he attended St. Charles Preparatory School in Catonsville, Maryland, but returned to Toledo to complete his secondary education at St. Johns High School. After he had graduated from St. Johns College, also in Toledo, he went to Washington, D.C. for postgraduate work in economics and finance at Catholic University. He then entered Georgetown University Law School in Washington and obtained his LL.B. degree in 1937.

A career in government was a natural choice for Saxon. He remained in Washington and in 1937 entered the United States Treasury Department as a securities statistician in the Office of the Comptroller of Currency, the agency he would be appointed to head twenty-four years later. After four years there, he was transferred to the Stabilization and Foreign Funds Control. In 1941 he became United States Treasury attaché to the Governor of Hawaii, but before the end of the year he was appointed Treasury attaché to the United States High Commissioner to the Philippine Islands, Francis B. Sayre.

At the outbreak of fighting between the United States and Japan, Saxon was responsible for the disposition and control of enemy and alien property in the Philippines, where he handled the takeover of Japanese banks. In December 1941 he left the Philippines with Sayre for Corregidor. There he served as Treasury adviser to both Sayre and General Douglas MacArthur. In this post he removed by submarine some $80,000,000 worth of gold bullion from the island before it fell to the Japanese.

Shortly after his return to the United States in April 1942, Saxon was again sent abroad to handle difficult currency problems. As Treasury representative he went to Hawaii, Puerto Rico, Algiers, Dakar, French West Africa, Casablanca, and Tangier. He represented the North African Economic Board in 1943 in co-ordinating reciprocal lend-lease policy and procedures with the United States Army and French authorities. The Treasury assigned him to duty in London and Paris in 1944, and the following year he served as financial attaché to the American Legation in Stockholm.

Late in 1945 Saxon was recalled to Washington to become special assistant to the director of the Treasury's division of monetary research, a position in which he worked with the National Advisory Council, the International Monetary Fund, and the International Bank. Beginning in 1947 he was assistant to the Secretary of the Treasury, John W. Snyder, with responsibilities that included press and public relations. In one of his many trips abroad in behalf of the department, Saxon accompanied Snyder on a twelve-country financial crisis mission in Europe in July 1949, and in Rome in November 1951 he advised Snyder on matters relating to the NATO meeting. In 1950 he had been named special assistant to the Treasury's general counsel. His task was to help survey the legal and operating procedures of the chief counsel of the Bureau of Internal Revenue, and ultimately he assisted in the 1952 Internal Revenue Service reorganization.

In 1952, after fifteen years in the Treasury Department, Saxon resigned. An avowed Democrat, he went to work in the Presidential campaign of 1952 on the Democratic National Committee, as assistant to the chairman, Stephen A. Mitchell. After Dwight D. Eisenhower's election, Saxon joined the staff of the American Bankers Association as assistant general counsel in the Washington office. He specialized in the fields of taxation and legislation and formed close relationships with key members of Congress in the banking field, with whom he would later deal as Comptroller of the Currency.

JAMES J. SAXON

Saxon acquired further firsthand knowledge of banking as attorney to the First National Bank of Chicago, a position that he accepted in August 1956 and held for five years. He was also director, secretary, and counsel of First Capital Corporation of Chicago, an affiliate of the First National Bank of Chicago. On behalf of the bank he testified before Congressional committees in support of the reserve requirements bill in 1959 and later in support of United States membership in the Inter-American Development Bank and in the International Development Association. He made other visits to Capitol Hill as secretary and associate counsel to the advisory committee to the Senate Banking and Currency Committee for the study of federal statutes governing financial institutions and credit.

Chosen by President John F. Kennedy to succeed Ray M. Gidney, a holdover of the Eisenhower administration, Saxon took his oath of office as Comptroller of the Currency on November 16, 1961. A recess appointment, it had to wait until early 1962 for Congressional confirmation. The post of comptroller pays $20,500 annually. His duties, as defined by the National Bank Act of 1863 involve general supervision of national banks; his approval is required for bank mergers and organization of new banks; and he names receivers when a national bank is insolvent. The dual banking system that has evolved from the statutes has created a situation in which states have the right to control banks that prefer to remain apart from the national system. These banks now outnumber national banks by roughly nine to five, but total assets in the two are about equal—$150 billion. The total number of United States banks is about 13,500.

From the start, Saxon has seen his role of comptroller as that of a leader of the banking industry. He arrived in Washington with twenty four single-spaced typewritten pages outlining

SAXON, JAMES J.—*Continued*
what he thought was wrong with the banking
system and offering suggestions for revision. He
also came with the understanding that there
would be fuller co-operation than his predecessor
had enjoyed between the Justice Department and
comptroller on possible antitrust suits, but this
agreement, as reported in *Business Week* (August
4, 1962), soon dissolved into somewhat strained
relations between the two departments.

Saxon's first step in office indicated that he
intended to revamp, broaden, and modernize the
banking system: he instituted an industry-wide
survey of banking problems and appointed committees to make recommendations on important
issues. Within a few months a 189-page report
projecting a new framework for the national
banking system was handed to the President, the
first major plan for revision of the system since
1933. Recommendations included stripping the
Federal Reserve Board of its regulatory, non-
monetary functions; permitting statewide branching by national banks despite state laws to the
contrary; reorganizing federal control of banking
by giving the comptroller responsibility for holding companies and national banks while bringing
the Federal Deposit Insurance Corporation under
the Treasury Department and having it supervise
state banks.

Saxon moved rapidly to carry out some of the
proposals. He improved such operations as bank
examinations, stock options, and office procedures,
which he already had authority to change. However, implementation of the broader concepts of
the report, the so-called "substantive issues,"
would require Congressional action. In revitaliz-
ing the banking industry Saxon liberally chartered
new national banks and approved branches for
existing ones, an action called controversial by
many bankers. His report urged that federal
chartered banks be allowed to branch within
twenty-five miles of their home office and within
the same state, regardless of any curbs on state
bank branching, and this issue caused a bitter
battle over states-versus-national control of banking expansion. Many national banks have rallied
around Saxon, but state banks have maintained
that he is challenging the existing dual-banking
system. They are aware of increased competition
that might bring pressure on state authorities to
follow Saxon's lead and are united in their dislike
of his "expansionist policies."

In testimony before the House Banking and
Currency Committee in May 1963, Saxon defended his regulating policies. He said that private initiative alone determines whether to seek
approval to set up a new national bank or
branch. "Enclaves of monopoly, and stagnant,
unprogressive banks," he told the committee,
"should not be safeguarded against the insistent
pressures for expansion in a growing economy."

A dispute in another area of banking arose
between Comptroller Saxon and the Securities
and Exchange Commission, over the regulation
of common trust funds of banks and the question
of whether banks must comply with the full-
disclosure provisions of the Securities Act of 1933.
Saxon opposed the SEC view that it has the responsibility of protecting those who participate
in a common trust fund just as it protects investors in mutual funds. He has also disagreed
with the Federal Reserve Board on the right of
banks to underwrite state and municipal revenue
bonds.

James J. Saxon is a member of the District of
Columbia and Illinois bar associations, Amer-
ican Bar Association, Federal Bar Association,
Delta Theta Phi law fraternity, National Tax
Association (bank tax committee), Tax Execu-
tives Institute, Council of Profit Sharing Indus-
tries, National Capital Democratic Club, Chi-
cago Association of Commerce and Industry,
Illinois State Chamber of Commerce, Navy
League of the United States, and American
Judicature Society. He attends the Roman Catho-
lic Church. He and his wife, the former Dorothy
Stewart Bell, whom he married on December 30,
1944, have six children: James Joseph, Jr.,
Stephen Mulhanney, Dorea Webb, Kevin Bell,
Catherine Frances, and Lucy Ives.

As comptroller, according to the *National Observer* (May 6, 1963), "Saxon has applied a
veneer of glamor to one of Washington's most
prosaic posts." He is a graying, dapper man,
forthright and vigorous in manner and notably
articulate. During the first five months of 1963
his schedule called for some forty speeches. *Time*
(October 18, 1963) reported that the conservatives
"frown on the fact that he has all his speeches
bound between fancy colored covers, has launched
a grandiose quarterly, *National Banking Review*,
to propagate his views."

References

Bsns W p96+ Ag 4 '62 por
N Y Herald Tribune p3 N 15 '61 por
N Y Times p49 S 22 '61 por
Nat Observer p10 My 6 '63 por
Time 80:90 O 5 '62 por
Washington (D.C.) Post E p3 Jl 7 '63

SCHERMAN, HARRY Feb. 1, 1887- Business
executive; organization official; writer
Address: b. Book-of-the-Month Club, Inc., 345
Hudson St., New York 14; h. 322 E. 57th St.,
New York 22

> NOTE: This biography supersedes
> the article that appeared in
> *Current Biography* in 1943

Once described as "probably the greatest bookseller in the history of the country," Harry Scherman, the founder and prime mover of the Book-
of-the-Month Club, has played a major role in
meeting the demand of the American public for
high-quality reading. Scherman began his career
as a journalist and free-lance writer and worked
for several years as a copywriter for advertising
firms. In 1916 he helped to found the Little
Leather Library, which distributed large numbers
of low-cost editions of literary classics, and which
was a direct forerunner of the Book-of-the-Month
Club. Scherman, who became president of the
Book-of-the-Month Club in 1931 and chairman
of the board in 1950, is also known for his efforts
to make the general public understand the problems of economics and finance. His writings in
this field, including the book *The Promises Men
Live By* (1937), have received wide acclaim.

Since its establishment in 1926 the Book-of-the-Month Club has placed some 186,000,000 books into American homes through mail subscription. In making the best books available to the public, the club uses the services of a board of five noted literary figures who choose from among the books of all American publishers, and whose decisions are independent of the management of the organization. A pioneer in its field, the Book-of-the-Month Club served as a model for the approximately 120 book clubs that now exist in the United States.

Harry Scherman was born in Montreal, Canada on February 1, 1887, the fourth in a family of five children, two of whom died at an early age. His father, Jacob Scherman, a native of Cardiff, Wales, owned a general store in Montreal. His mother, Katharine (Harris) Scherman, was born in Manchester, England. Both of his parents were of the Jewish faith. At the age of two, Harry Scherman moved with his family to the United States. His parents later became separated, and Harry Scherman was brought up with his brother and sister in a Philadelphia boarding house by his mother.

Scherman, who recalls his childhood as a happy one, attended Philadelphia public schools, where he was a good student. His love for reading, which he developed at an early age, was inspired by his family. Although he was too small to make the school teams, he played baseball and football with a neighborhood athletic club in North Philadelphia. At the Central High School, Scherman was at the head of his class, and he excelled in Latin and Greek. He contributed articles and stories to student publications and wrote a prize-winning essay. His graduating class of 1905 included Alexander Woollcott and Ed Wynn.

Having won a scholarship awarded by the city of Philadelphia, Scherman entered the Wharton School of Economics and Finance at the University of Pennsylvania and added to his income by writing free-lance articles for local newspapers. Uncertain as to whether he should follow a career in engineering, medicine, literature, or journalism, Scherman temporarily dropped out of school. He returned to the University of Pennsylvania in 1906, enrolling in its School of Law, but left again in April 1907, after less than a year, to join his family in New York City. There he accepted an offer from Louis Lipsky for a job as a reporter with the *American Hebrew*, a weekly newspaper owned by Cyrus Sulzberger.

Working for a salary of $12 a week, Scherman reported on books, plays, political events, and social life for the *American Hebrew*. At the same time he tried unsuccessfully to establish himself as a creative writer. During this period he also wrote free-lance articles for New York and Philadelphia newspapers and collaborated with his brother William on free-lance advertising assignments. On one occasion he served as press agent for a Russian theatrical company that was visiting New York.

Scherman left the *American Hebrew* in 1912 to concentrate on free-lance advertising, hoping to save enough money to enable him to return to creative writing. For a time he wrote advertising copy for the Osborne Calendar Company. Hav-

HARRY SCHERMAN

ing saved a substantial sum, Scherman set out to see the United States, but he lost his money as a result of bad investments and eventually returned to New York. Although he had abandoned plans for creative writing, he wanted to remain close to the literary field, and he decided to apply his talents to the marketing of books.

In 1913 Scherman joined the mail order advertising firm of Ruthrauff and Ryan as a copywriter and succeeded in promoting books that had been difficult to sell. A year later he took a job with the J. Walter Thompson Company, then a mail order advertising firm specializing in books and correspondence courses. During this period Scherman became associated with a circle in Pleasantville, New York that included Walter Lippmann and other aspiring intellectuals. Among them were Charles and Albert Boni, who conceived the idea of marketing low-cost, miniature leather-bound editions of literary classics.

Greatly interested in this venture, in 1916 Scherman joined with the Boni brothers and with Maxwell Sackheim, a colleague at the J. Walter Thompson Company, in establishing the Little Leather Library Corporation. Scherman then left his job at the J. Walter Thompson Company, much against the advice of his employer, and became president and manager of the Little Leather Library Corporation. The books offered by the Little Leather Library included the Bible, Shakespeare, Tennyson, Plato, Dante, and Whitman, and eventually sold for as little as ten cents a copy. While it lasted, the Little Leather Library distributed some 48,000,000 volumes.

In 1920 Scherman and Sackheim established their own advertising firm, specializing in selling books by mail. Meanwhile, the Little Leather Library had reached its saturation point, and business had begun to decline. The Boni brothers left the corporation to launch the Modern Library, and in 1924 Scherman and Sackheim sold the controlling interest in the Little Leather Library to Robert K. Haas. For a time Scherman

SCHERMAN, HARRY—*Continued*

experimented with a book-of-the-week club, which offered fifty-two classics a year to subscribers, and with a scheme for selling albums of records by mail, which did not succeed, owing to the advent of radio.

The Book-of-the-Month Club, which was founded in 1926 by Scherman, Sackheim, and Haas, grew out of Scherman's assumption that the public's demand for good books was far greater than the supply available through bookstores. The main problem was making the books conveniently available to the public. Although literary classics could be sold by mail, this could not be profitably done with single new books, since the cost of promotion and selling was too high. Scherman and his associates conceived of an organization that would distribute groups of newly published books to individual subscribers by mail over a period of time. The books would be chosen for their quality by an independent panel of experts, and the club would thus establish its reputation as a competent selector of good books.

The $40,000 that constituted the original capital of the Book-of-the-Month Club, Inc., was the only money invested in it until the club began to offer shares to the public in 1947. Haas contributed half of the original sum; Scherman and Sackheim each put up one fourth. Haas became the first president of the corporation. Scherman succeeded Haas as president in 1931, serving until 1950, when he was named chairman of the board. He was succeeded as president by Meredith Wood, who was later succeeded by Axel G. Rosin. Although he is now nominally retired, Scherman continues to take an active part in the affairs of the club, and he and members of his family own a majority of the shares of stock in the corporation.

The original editorial board of the Book-of-the-Month Club consisted of Henry Seidel Canby, Dorothy Canfield, Heywood Broun, Christopher Morley, and William Allen White. These judges were later succeeded by Amy Loveman, Clifton Fadiman, John Marquand, Gilbert Highet, Basil Davenport, and John Mason Brown. The judges agree upon the club selections at a monthly luncheon held in Scherman's office. Scherman, who warns against underestimating the average reader, rejects the notion that the selections of the judges might be over the heads of the general public.

The Book-of-the-Month Club buys its selections from publishers at a special discount and pays a royalty to the publisher on each sale. The subscriber has a wide range of alternate books to choose from if the current selections are not to his liking. Although the club does not reduce prices it offers special free dividends to subscribers, including classics, anthologies, and reference works. Until January 1951 Scherman edited the club's magazine, the Book-of-the-Month Club *News.*

When the Book-of-the-Month Club began its operations in April 1926 it had 4,750 subscribers who received the club's first selection, Sylvia Townsend Warner's *Lolly Willowes.* The figure increased almost tenfold—to 46,539—by the end of the year and rose to 110,588 in 1929. During the years of the Depression the club managed to hold its own, and during World War II it witnessed a rapid increase in its membership, which reached a peak of 889,305 in 1946. In recent years the membership has become stabilized at about 500,000, a level which, Scherman believes, is about the optimum for the efficient operation of the club.

Over the years the Book-of-the-Month Club has sometimes been criticized for allegedly offering unfair competition to booksellers, but Scherman has pointed out that the club has been largely responsible for the boom in book publishing, of which the book stores have been the prime beneficiaries. Although its editorial board has occasionally been criticized for its selections, the club has generally succeeded in bringing the best of current literature to subscribers. Nobel Prize winners whose works have been among the club's selections include Sinclair Lewis, John Galsworthy, Thomas Mann, George Bernard Shaw, Pearl Buck, Ernest Hemingway, and Eugene O'Neill. A number of its selections later received Pulitzer Prizes, including works by Stephen Vincent Benet, Margaret Mitchell, Marjorie Kinnan Rawlings, Carl Van Doren, Carl Sandburg, Samuel Eliot Morison, Arthur Miller, and MacKinlay Kantor. Writers introduced by the club include Frederick Lewis Allen, Clyde Brion Davis, Pierre van Paassen, William L. Shirer, and J. D. Salinger. The club has also introduced to American readers a number of foreign authors in English translation, such as Erich Maria Remarque, Mika Waltari, and Sigrid Undset.

Since 1959 the Book-of-the-Month Club has been giving Dorothy Canfield Fisher Library Awards to small libraries for the purchase of books. At first there was a single award of $5,000 and in 1960, 1961, and 1962 nine additional awards of $1,000 were given. Beginning in 1963 fifty awards were made, to one library in each state: one of $5,000, nine of $1,500, and forty of $1,000. Later the number was increased to fifty-two to include the Virgin Islands and Puerto Rico.

Scherman is much interested in economics, especially monetary theory, and he has conveyed his views on this topic to the American public in many articles. His best-selling book, *The Promises Men Live By: A New Approach to Economics* (Random House, 1937), has been widely praised, although some reviewers have criticized its conservative economic views. (Scherman is a staunch advocate of the profit system.) Other books by Scherman are *The Real Danger in Our Gold* (Simon & Schuster, 1940); *Will We Have Inflation?* (Simon & Schuster, 1941); and *The Last Best Hope on Earth: A Philosophy for the War* (Random House, 1941). His essay "Invisible Greenbacks," written during World War II at the request of the United States Treasury Department and first published in the *Saturday Evening Post,* is one of the most frequently reprinted articles in the history of American journalism.

In 1937 Scherman became director-at-large of the National Bureau of Economic Research. He was its president in 1950, 1951, and 1954 and chairman of the board in 1952-53 and 1955-56, and he continues to serve as director-at-large and member of the executive committee. Since 1942 he has been a trustee and member of the research and policy committee of the Committee for Economic Development, an organization of business economists. The organization's policy statement, "Economic Growth in the United States: Its Past, Present and Future," was drafted by a special committee headed by Scherman in 1957-58, and it has been widely circulated.

On June 3, 1914 Harry Scherman married Bernadine Kielty, a former teacher, editor, and writer, and an early staff member of the Book-of-the-Month Club. They have two children: Katharine Whitney Scherman (Mrs. Axel G. Rosin), who has written several books; and Thomas Kielty Scherman, a well-known orchestra conductor. Scherman is noted for his integrity, his modesty, and his ability to inspire confidence. His clubs are the Players, the Lotos, and the Century. When in early 1963 the Scherman Foundation, which had been founded in his honor, donated some 22,000 books to the libraries of the New York City schools, Scherman requested that in the selection of titles the main emphasis be placed on the "joy and fun of reading."

References

> Lee, Charles. The Hidden Public: The Story of the Book-of-the-Month Club (1958)
> Who's Who in America, 1962-63
> Who's Who in World Jewry (1955)

SCHUCK, ARTHUR A(LOYS) June 20, 1895-Feb. 25, 1963 Former chief executive of the Boy Scouts of America (1948-60). See *Current Biography* (April) 1950.

Obituary

> N Y Times p36 Ap 1 '63

SCHUMAN, ROBERT June 29, 1886-Sept. 4, 1963 French statesman and political economist; Premier of the French Republic (1947-48) and Cabinet Minister (1946-52); closely associated with development of the European Coal and Steel Community and the Common Market; president of the European Parliament (1958-60); recipient of Charlemagne Prize (1958). See *Current Biography* (January) 1948.

Obituary

> N Y Times p1+ S 5 '63

SCHWEITZER, PIERRE-PAUL (shvī'tsĕr) May 29, 1912- International Monetary Fund official

Address: b. International Monetary Fund, 19th and H Sts., N.W., Washington 25, D.C.

France owes its remarkable postwar economic recovery to a great extent to the banker Pierre-Paul Schweitzer, a former director of the French Treasury and deputy governor of the Bank of France. One of the international organizations with which he had worked in helping to rebuild

his country's economy is the International Monetary Fund, which is both a specialized agency of the United Nations and an independent organization. In September 1963 Schweitzer gave up his brilliant career in the French civil service to become the fourth managing director and chairman of the board of the IMF, succeeding Per Jacobsson in a post of considerable international authority.

Pierre-Paul Schweitzer was born on May 29, 1912 in Strasbourg, Alsace-Lorraine, a territory that was in German hands at the time of his birth, but reverted to France after World War I. One of two sons of Paul and Emma (Munch) Schweitzer, he belongs to a small French Protestant elite that has played an important role in banking and in many other fields. He is a nephew of the philosopher and missionary surgeon Dr. Albert Schweitzer and, on the maternal side, of the conductor Charles Munch. Jean-Paul Sartre is his second cousin.

Until he was seventeen, Schweitzer was educated at private and state schools in the Strasbourg area—the Collège de Bouxwiller, the Lycée de Haguenau, and the Gymnase Protestant de Strasbourg. Leaving the latter secondary school in 1929, Schweitzer enrolled at the University of Strasbourg. He graduated in 1932, *summa cum laude* and as laureate of the university, with degrees in both law and economics. Schweitzer's postgraduate work took him to Paris, where further academic distinction awaited him. In 1933 he obtained postgraduate degrees in civil law and economics at the University of Paris, again graduating *summa cum laude*. There followed two more years of study at the École Libre des Sciences Politiques, (Free School of Political Sciences), which Schweitzer left in 1935 with yet another *summa cum laude* degree.

In 1936 Schweitzer joined the French civil service as an assistant inspector of finances. The *inspecteurs des finances* are a select corps to which the present French Foreign Minister, Finance Minister, and Ambassador to the United States have all belonged. World War II began in 1939, the year that Schweitzer achieved the rank of full inspector of finances, and he joined the French Army as a second lieutenant in the infantry. In the months before the fall of France in 1940, Schweitzer was promoted to the rank of captain, wounded in action, and captured. For Schweitzer, that was by no means the end of the war. He escaped, went underground in Paris, and soon became a leader in the Resistance. In 1944 the Nazis caught him again. Schweitzer, who made an unsuccessful attempt at suicide, was tortured and deported to the notorious Buchenwald concentration camp in Germany. There he survived until Buchenwald was taken by American forces in 1945.

After this "temporary interruption," as he has called it, Schweitzer resumed his career, becoming in 1946 deputy director of the department of international finance at the French Treasury. A year later he was sent to Washington as alternate executive director for France of the International Monetary Fund. Thus, at a fairly early stage in his career, he entered the field of international economics and gained firsthand

PIERRE-PAUL SCHWEITZER

knowledge of the IMF and the Washington scene. Schweitzer spent a year in Washington and in 1948 returned to Paris as secretary general of France's interministerial committee on questions of European economic co-operation— as his country's representative, that is, to the newly formed Organization for European Economic Cooperation. The OEEC was set up in 1948 to co-ordinate the economic activities of European countries receiving aid under the Marshall Plan.

By 1949 Schweitzer was back in Washington, where he served until 1953 as financial counselor to the French Embassy. It was during those years that the United States poured billions of dollars in Marshall Plan aid into France, and that "American officials," according to Joseph R. Slevin in the New York *Herald Tribune* (June 2, 1963) "were bluntly and insistently telling the French how they ought to be running their country. Mr. Schweitzer relayed many of the exchanges and his quiet diplomacy did much to prevent an angry blow-up."

Schweitzer was recalled to Paris in 1953 to take up a major appointment. He became the director—the chief professional officer—of the French Treasury. In that post he was responsible for taxation, money, budgeting, and economic and commercial policies, which in the United States are distributed among five officials. Nor was this all. Schweitzer became at the same time a director of the French National Railroads, of Air France, and of the Bank of Algeria, and an auditor of the Bank of France and of the Crédit National.

As director of the Treasury, Schweitzer inherited an economic structure that he himself has described as "pretty much a museum piece," and set about converting it into a modern system. In 1957 France embarked upon discussions with the International Monetary Fund. Schweitzer, his country's chief spokesman in the discus-

sions, became a close friend of Per Jacobsson, then recently appointed as the fund's managing director. The IMF offered loans and advice that contributed greatly to France's extraordinary economic recovery. Schweitzer played a major part both in shaping the recovery program that finally emerged and in implementing it. Measures taken during his administration included the effective use of IMF and American aid; the drawing up of targets for industry under Le Plan, France's blueprint for economic growth; and the revaluation and stabilization of the franc.

In 1960 Schweitzer left the top office of the Treasury to continue his work from a new vantage point, as deputy governor of the Bank of France. Serving also in a host of subsidiary roles, he relinquished his connection with the National Railroads, the Crédit National, and the Bank of Algeria, but took on two new responsibilities as Treasury representative on the boards of the French Petroleum Company and the French Refinery Company. He also continued to serve as a director of Air France and, in two posts that he had accepted in 1958, as a director of the European Investment Bank and as an alternate governor for France of the International Bank for Reconstruction and Development, better known as the World Bank. According to the New York *Herald Tribune* (July 8, 1963), Schweitzer is today "the man most credited with converting France from a mock capitalism to one of the strongest economic powers in the world."

Per Jacobsson died in May 1963 and Schweitzer, Jacobsson's own choice, at once came under consideration as his successor. Schweitzer did not at first welcome the idea of his being appointed, saying that it would involve "great personal sacrifice." There were moreover some doubts about the wisdom of appointing a French national to the post, which had traditionally gone to natives of less powerful countries. These objections were overcome, and on June 21, 1963 Schweitzer was named managing director of the IMF and chairman of its board of directors for a five-year term. His post, which he took up on September 1, 1963, pays an annual tax-free salary of $40,000.

The IMF was established in 1944 by the United Nations Monetary and Financial Conference of forty-four nations at Bretton Woods, New Hampshire. Its aims are to expand international trade and to stabilize exchange rates. The fund makes loans to countries with short-term currency problems, arranges a pattern of exchange rates based on the value of gold and the United States dollar, and gives advice to members on fiscal, monetary, and credit policy. It now has 102 members and resources of about $21 billion.

During Jacobsson's tenure the IMF had grown into a powerful force in international finance. Jacobsson himself, although he was a conservative in his economic philosophy, was an ebullient and articulate individual who expressed his strong views freely. Schweitzer shares Jacobsson's monetary orthodoxy, his faith in stable prices and sound currency, and his belief in economic planning and the co-ordination of aid to underdeveloped countries. As managing director of the IMF, Schweitzer is, however, expected to be less vocal than his predecessor. "The difference between myself and Jacobsson," Schweitzer told a *Newsweek* interviewer (July 1, 1963), "is that he was an economist and I am a banker. Above all, I hesitate to give myself to theorizing."

Schweitzer faces a crucial period in international economics. World liquidity is threatened by the rapid growth of international trade, and the stability of the dollar is threatened by America's huge balance of payments deficit. The Kennedy administration has initiated drastic action to overcome the latter problem. If it should succeed in ending the American payments deficit, however, the problem of maintaining liquidity would be exacerbated, since it is the United States deficit that now feeds liquidity.

These problems have important implications for the future of the IMF. Schweitzer has so far resisted suggestions that any fundamental change in the IMF's role, or any new international credit agency, is necessary to maintain international liquidity. But Britain called for some such mechanism at the 1962 annual meeting of the IMF, and President John F. Kennedy is thought to be leaning to the British view. At its annual meeting in the fall of 1963 the IMF decided to make a full-dress study of the international payments system. Simultaneously, the Paris Club, made up of the ten nations controlling 80 percent of the free world's supply of gold and foreign exchange, undertook a similar study that may also influence the future of the IMF.

For his services to France during World War II, Schweitzer was named a Commander of the Legion of Honor and awarded the Croix de Guerre (1939-1945) and the Medal of the Resistance with rosette. He is also a Commander of the Order of the National Economy, a Commandeur du Mérite Postal and an Officier du Mérite Agricole. On August 7, 1941 Schweitzer married Catherine Hatt; they have two children, Louis and Juliette. Schweitzer is brown-haired and brown-eyed, stands six feet tall, and weighs 160 pounds. He has been described as somewhat reserved in manner, elegant, urbane, and decisive. His hobbies are playing bridge and gardening. He is a Lutheran.

Comparing Schweitzer with Per Jacobsson, a writer for the Manchester *Guardian* (June 24, 1963) commented, "Let it be said first of all that Pierre-Paul Schweitzer is a highly trained and cultured French finance official whose intellectual capacity is probably equal to that of the formidable Dr. Jacobsson. He is a man of courage and character. . . . If he lacks the expansive personality of his late predecessor and has still to gain the personal influence that European and American authorities that Dr. Jacobsson had built up over the years, M. Schweitzer has probably a more disciplined mind and a greater capacity for administration."

References

N Y Herald Tribune V p3 Je 2 '63
Newsweek 62:55 Jl 1 '63 por
Toronto Globe and Mail Globe Mag p7 S 28 '63 por
Washington (D.C.) Post E p3 S 15 '63 por
International Who's Who, 1963-64
Who's Who in France, 1963-64

SCHWIDETZKY, OSCAR (OTTO RUDOLPH) Dec. 31, 1874-Oct. 10, 1963 Medical and surgical instruments maker and inventor; developer of the Ace bandage and the Asepto syringe; inventor of specialized hypodermic needles. See *Current Biography* (December) 1943.

Obituary

N Y Times p37 O 11 '63

SEEGER, PETE(R) May 3, 1919- Folk singer; folklorist; musician

Address: b. c/o Harold Leventhal, Suite 602, 200 W. 57th St., New York 19; h. Dutchess Junction, Beacon, N.Y.

A "reincarnated troubadour," "America's tuning fork," and the "Thomas Jefferson" of folk music, Pete Seeger is perhaps more responsible than anyone else for the vogue of folk music in the United States. Since taking to the road in the late 1930's he has presented a cross-section of American life in song to audiences throughout the world, and he is considered one of the best-informed scholars in folk music. A master of the five-string banjo, Seeger is also an authority on the guitar, the recorder, and the Trinidad steel drums. Over the years he has recorded some fifty albums for Folkways, Columbia, and other companies, and his activities also include song writing, film production, and research, editing, and writing in the folk music field. Although Seeger's acute sense of social justice and his insistence on freedom of speech and association have brought him into conflict with the House Un-American Activities Committee and caused him to be blacklisted by television networks, he has acquired a huge following, especially among young people, and his audiences have included some Rockefellers as well as hoboes and migratory workers.

Descended from Colonial settlers who came to New England some 300 years ago, Pete Seeger counts among his ancestors religious dissenters, Revolutionary War soldiers, and abolitionists. His family, mostly New Englanders and Pennsylvanians, is "shot through with pedagogues, doctors, occasional businessmen, and occasional artists." (The World War I poet Alan Seeger, author of the famous poem "I Have a Rendezvous with Death," was an uncle of his.) A native of New York City, Peter Seeger was born on May 3, 1919 to Dr. Charles Louis Seeger, a musicologist, conductor, author, and educator who is on the faculty of the University of California at Los Angeles, and to Constance de Clyver (Edson) Seeger, a violinist and teacher. He has two older brothers, Charles L. and John P.; through his father's second marriage, to the late Ruth Crawford Seeger (also a noted musicologist), he has a half-brother, Michael, and three half-sisters, Margaret (Peggy), Barbara Mona, and Penelope.

After completing his primary education at public schools in Nyack, New York and at the Spring Hill School in Litchfield, Connecticut, Seeger attended secondary school at Avon Old Farms, a private boarding school in Avon, Connecticut, where he took part in dramatics, edited the

PETE SEEGER

ords. He also accompanied the Lomaxes on field trips, recording songs in remote areas of the country, and he appeared on Lomax's CBS radio program, along with Woody Guthrie and Leadbelly.

In 1940 Seeger joined with Lee Hays, Woody Guthrie, Millard Lampell, and others in the Almanac Singers, a group that toured the United States and recorded albums of sea shanties, "sodbuster ballads," work songs, and union and topical songs. Later, Seeger teamed up with Guthrie, singing at migrant camps and union halls in the South and Southwest, touring Mexico, collaborating on the writing of labor and anti-Fascist songs, and singing on overseas broadcasts for the Office of War Information. Inducted into the Army in 1942, Seeger spent three and a half years with Special Services, entertaining troops in the United States and the South Pacific and adding soldier songs to his repertoire.

After his discharge, with the rank of corporal, in December 1945, Seeger, along with others, founded People's Songs, Inc., and he became its national director. People's Songs, a union of songwriters, as well as a research center and clearing house for folk songs, grew out of Seeger's conviction that the United States was ripe for a folk music revival, which, he felt, would be given its main impetus by organized labor. The organization, which began rather modestly, had a membership of about 3,000 at its peak and counted among its leading members such singers, musicians, and scholars as Alan Lomax, Lee Hays, Woody Guthrie, Sonny Terry, Betty Sanders, Tom Glazer, and Waldemar Hille. It published a monthly bulletin and a *People's Song Book*, popularized current topical songs and traditional folk songs from all over the world, furnished songs to unions and other organizations on request, and conducted weekly "hootenannies," or informal folk song sessions. During the early postwar years Seeger also made a short folk music film, *And Hear My Banjo Play*, produced in 1946, and he appeared in a revival of the folk play *Dark of the Moon* when it was performed by the Los Angeles Repertory Theatre. In 1948 he toured the United States in behalf of the Progressive party's Presidential candidate, Henry A. Wallace.

The folk music revival was given momentum by the appearance of the Weavers, a four-member singing group established in 1948 by Seeger, Lee Hays, Ronnie Gilbert, and Fred Hellerman. After making their professional debut at the Village Vanguard in New York City in late 1949 the Weavers appeared on national radio and television programs, sang in leading night clubs and in theaters throughout the United States, and turned such folk songs as "On Top of Old Smoky," "Goodnight, Irene," and "So Long, It's Been Good to Know You" into national hits. By 1952 sales of their recordings for Folkways and Decca exceeded 4,000,000 copies. The Weavers disbanded temporarily in 1952 and were reconstituted in 1955. Seeger left the group in 1957 because of other commitments.

On his own, Seeger continued his folk singing tours in the 1950's, performing before capacity crowds in New York's Carnegie Hall and Town

school paper, and had ambitions of becoming an artist or a journalist. Having been exposed mainly to classical music during his childhood, Pete Seeger had little contact with any music at the grass roots. His interest in folk music, and particularly in the five-string banjo, was first aroused when in 1935 he accompanied his father to a folk festival in Asheville, North Carolina. The experience was a revelation and opened a new world to him.

In 1936 Seeger entered Harvard University, where he majored in sociology and served as secretary of the Harvard Student Union. He decided to cut short his formal education, however, and left Harvard in 1938 during his sophomore year, to seek his fortune on the open road. Roaming through the New England countryside, he painted rural landscapes in watercolors and bartered them for his basic needs. In the next few years he covered thousands of miles, often by riding the rods or hitchhiking, traveling through the Depression-ridden United States as a folk singer. He performed on street corners and in hobo jungles, migrant camps, saloons, and churches. Along the way he learned "a little something from everybody," picking up songs and banjo techniques from farmers, workers, and mountaineers, and building a vast repertoire of ballads and blues, spirituals, lullabies, work songs, and country dance tunes.

Among the major influences upon Seeger's life and career during this period were the Oklahoma balladeer and folk composer, Woody Guthrie; the "king of the twelve-string guitar," Huddie Ledbetter (Leadbelly); and the curator of the Archive of American Folk Song at the Library of Congress, Dr. John A. Lomax, and his son, Alan. As part of his self-education as a folk musician, Seeger spent considerable time in Washington, listening to the recordings in the Archive of American Folk Song and working as an assistant in the archive, classifying rec-

Hall and throughout the United States, Canada, and the British Isles. In the winter of 1954-55 he gave a series of six concerts entitled "American Folk Music and its Origins" at Columbia University's Institute of Arts and Sciences. He also was featured at the National Folk Festival in St. Louis, and in the late 1950's and early 1960's he helped to organize the Newport (Rhode Island) Folk Festivals, in which he has been a participant.

In 1955 Seeger was called before a subcommittee of the House Committee on Un-American Activities investigating alleged subversive influences in the entertainment field. Refusing to answer questions put to him by the committee regarding his political beliefs and associations, Seeger chose to cite the First Amendment to the Constitution, guaranteeing freedom of speech and association, rather than the Fifth, allowing the individual to avoid self-incrimination, which would have safeguarded him from prosecution. "In my whole life I have never done anything of any conspiratorial nature," he declared at the time of the hearing. "I resent very much and very deeply the implication of being called before this committee."

Indicted on ten counts of contempt of Congress, Seeger went on trial before the United States District Court in New York City in March 1961, and was found guilty on all counts by a jury that had deliberated for one hour and twenty minutes. Upon being sentenced to one year in prison by Judge Thomas F. Murphy on April 4, 1961, Seeger declared: "I have never in my life supported or done anything subversive to my country. I am proud that I have never refused to sing for any organization because I disagreed with its beliefs." To illustrate his position he then offered to sing a song, but he was refused permission by the court to do so. Later he told an interviewer for *Variety* (March 21, 1962): "I'd sing for the John Birch Society or the American Legion, if asked. So far they haven't."

On May 18, 1962 the United States Court of Appeal by unanimous decision, reversed Seeger's conviction on the ground that the indictment had failed to define with sufficient clarity the authority of the subcommittee to hold the hearings. Although the indictment against Seeger has been dismissed he is still banned by some television networks and his concerts continue to be picketed by the American Legion and other organizations. When the American Broadcasting Company banned Seeger and the Weavers from its weekly folk music program *Hootenanny*, which made its television debut on April 6, 1963, several folk singers, including Joan Baez, declined invitations to appear on the program. The ABC network later issued a statement that it would consider using Seeger if he signed an affidavit regarding his political affiliations, but he refused to do so on constitutional grounds.

Pete Seeger's popularity stems largely from his informal style and his mesmeric ability to get his audiences to take an active part in his concerts. He sings in a light, pleasing baritone, trying to recreate the atmosphere in which the songs were originally sung. His long-necked five-string banjo, which has become his trademark, was made to his own design, and he plays it in several styles. His instruction manual, *How to Play the Five-String Banjo*, was published privately in 1948 and revised in 1954. His other publications include *The Twelve-String Guitar as Played by Leadbelly*, *The Steel Drums of Kim Loy Wong*, and several songbooks. Seeger serves on the editorial staff of the folk music magazine *Sing Out!* and as an adviser to the new topical song periodical *Broadside*, and he has written for these and other publications.

During his thirteen years with Folkways Records and Service Corporation, Seeger made forty albums, including four volumes of *American Favorite Ballads* and three volumes of *Frontier Ballads*, and children's songs, Civil War songs, industrial ballads, African freedom songs, and instructional records for banjo and guitar. In 1961 he signed a contract with Columbia Records, but he still records occasionally for Folkways. As a writer of songs Seeger has also met with success. His "Where Have All the Flowers Gone?" became a hit in 1961. Another hit, which he wrote with Lee Hays, is "If I Had a Hammer," and he collaborated with the Weavers in writing "Kisses Sweeter Than Wine." In another, related activity Seeger produces educational short subjects through Folklore Research Films, which he and his wife had founded. In the summer of 1963 Seeger embarked with his family on a global singing tour covering some twenty-one countries, including Australia.

On July 20, 1943 Peter Seeger married Toshi-Aline Ohta, who is of Japanese and Virginian parentage. They have a son, Daniel Adams, and two daughters, Mika Salter and Virginia S. (Tinya). The Seegers live near Beacon, New York, some sixty miles north of New York City in a two-room log cabin overlooking the Hudson River, which they have built with the help of friends. Tall and lanky, Pete Seeger stands at six feet one and a half inches, weighs 165 pounds, and has thinning brown hair and blue eyes. On his concert tours he drives around the country in an old station wagon and wears work shoes and vivid shirts, socks, and ties. His favorite recreations are skiing, sailing along the Hudson in a small boat, and rambling through the woods near his home.

Indifferent to material gain, Seeger often turns down bids for concert engagements to tour Negro colleges in the South or to give benefit performances for the Freedom Riders and for other causes. He is not particularly disturbed by the commercialism that has generally accompanied the recent folk music boom. "Folk music is a living, vibrant thing again," he told an interviewer for *Look* (August 27, 1963). "To me, this is the musical reflection of a new national maturity; we are trying to identify with our country again." Of his own role as a folk singer Seeger said in an interview with J. C. Barden for *High Fidelity* (January 1963): "I feel I'm building a healthy musical life for people who seem to have lost it somewhere in the machine age."

References

Hi Fi 13:51+ Ja '63 pors
Sing Out! 4:4+ My '54 por
Lawless, Ray M. Folksingers and Folksongs in America (1960)

SENSENICH, ROSCOE L(LOYD) Nov. 20, 1882-Jan. 19, 1963 Physician; specialist in internal medicine; president of the American Medical Association (1948-49). See *Current Biography* (June) 1949.

Obituary

N Y Times p36 Ap 1 '63

SEYMOUR, CHARLES Jan. 1, 1885-Aug. 11, 1963 Fifteenth president of Yale University (1937-50); professor of history at Yale (1918-37). See *Current Biography* (May) 1941.

Obituary

N Y Times p21 Ag 12 '63

SHEPARD, E(RNEST) H(OWARD) Dec. 10, 1879- British book illustrator; painter

Address: Woodmancote, Lodsworth, Sussex, England

One of the more endearing figures in contemporary children's literature is A. A. Milne's Winnie-the-Pooh. It is impossible to visualize that portly bear and his entourage except as they were first portrayed nearly a half century ago by the English illustrator and artist E. H. Shepard. A precociously talented draftsman, Shepard learned his craft at the Royal Academy Schools, where he won the Landseer scholarship and a British Institution prize. Shepard began his career as an illustrator of books, magazines, and newspapers in 1902. Before World War I he began to sell his cartoons to *Punch* and in 1921 became its senior staff editor. A few years later, in 1924, he began his long and felicitous association as illustrator for A. A. Milne. Through his delicate and gently humorous drawings Shepard has interpreted nearly fifty books, and in his long career he has probably given more pleasure to young readers than any other British

Gwen Morgan

E. H. SHEPARD

illustrator. In his autobiography, of which two volumes—*Drawn from Memory* (1957) and *Drawn from Life* (1962)—have been published, he has revealed a literary style as inimitable as his drawings.

Ernest Howard Shepard was born on December 10, 1879 at 55 Springfield Road, St. John's Wood, London. His father was Henry Dunkin Shepard, an architect and adviser to University College Hospital, London University. His mother, the former Harriet Jessie Lee, was the daughter of a watercolor painter, William Lee. Shepard was the youngest of three children. His brother Cyril was killed in action on the Somme in World War I. His sister Ethel, a pianist and organist, died in 1941 after many years as deaconess of St. Hilda's Church, Lahore, India.

When Shepard was four, the family moved to 10 Kent Terrace, on the edge of Regent's Park not far from Baker Street. It was very much the world that he was to capture in his illustrations for the books of A. A. Milne—the secure, privileged, but now vanished world of Christopher Robin. Shepard lived in a large house, with balconies and stucco columns, and stained-glass door panels designed by his father. There were a close and warm family relationship, a comfortable cook and a beloved nursemaid, toy horses and lead soldiers, kind uncles and formidable aunts.

The Shepards were a cultured family, with many friends in the arts. One party given when Shepard was seven or eight included songs by the noted singer and actor Hayden Coffin and recitations by Sir Herbert Beerbohm Tree. The children were given violin lessons and taken to concerts, private viewings, theaters, and museums. As some children might describe such excursions in their diaries, Shepard recorded his in sketches. Some of these have been preserved, showing that Shepard at seven already possessed an astonishingly mature talent. His draftsmanship was a source of pride to his parents, who early decided that he should become an artist.

Shepard attended an elementary school near his home until he was nine. The following year he sustained a profound and lasting blow with the early death of his mother. In *Drawn from Life* he has described the closeness of their relationship and her encouragement of his drawing. "She, almost more than Father," he wrote, "inspired me to persevere. After her death I missed her companionship terribly and determined to justify her faith in my talent."

For a year after Mrs. Shepard's death, the children stayed with aunts in Gordon Square, London. Ernest Shepard had private lessons for a time at his father's studio, where he made many sketches of a cast of the *Venus de Milo,* and later spent an unhappy period at the St. John's Wood Preparatory School. However, his student and family life improved in 1892, when the family was reunited at an attractive new house in Hammersmith, London, and Shepard and his brother entered Colet Court, the lower-form school of St. Paul's Preparatory School. Two years later, when he was fourteen, he went to St. Paul's School itself, a noted British public school that at that time enjoyed an unequaled academic reputation.

At St. Paul's, where Shepard played Rugby football and cricket, his artistic talent was recognized. Faculty members decided that he should try for a scholarship to the Royal Academy Schools—the schools of painting, sculpture, and architecture maintained since 1768 for the free tuition of "all students who shall be qualified to receive advantage from such studies." In his last year at St. Paul's Shepard was placed in a special drawing class as its only member. He also began to take additional classes on Saturday mornings at Heatherley's, a long-established art school in London, and in September 1896, having left St. Paul's, he became a full-time student at Heatherley's.

Although Shepard greatly enjoyed student life at Heatherley's, the teaching, according to *Drawn from Life,* "was not good." Most of his time was devoted to drawing "from the antique." He was not encouraged to do any painting, and he learned nothing of construction or design. Nevertheless, because his heart was set on a scholarship to the Royal Academy Schools, he doggedly endured the formal curriculum. The drawings on which his scholarship application was to be judged were completed late in 1896, and in the spring of the following year he was accepted. Shepard studied at the Royal Academy Schools from 1897 to 1902.

Although tuition was free at the schools, Shepard's father was by this time in some financial distress, and there was little money. In his second year, however, Shepard won the Landseer scholarship, and the following year a British Institution prize. These two awards together brought him for a time an income of £100 a year —not inconsiderable in those days—augmented by his first commissions as a book and magazine illustrator. In 1901 he secured his first studio, a small one in Chelsea, which he shared with a fellow student called George Swaish. The same year he had two pictures hung at the Royal Academy's summer exhibition—"A Devonshire Valley" and a portrait of his sister Ethel.

Shepard left the Royal Academy Schools in 1902, and two years later he married a fellow student, Florence ("Pie") Chaplin. With their small capital and a nominal weekly rental, they set up house in a tiny cottage at Shamley Green in Surrey. Just before his marriage Shepard had sold his first oil painting, but in the years that followed he relied for his income primarily on black and white drawings for the illustrated papers, and on illustrations for books. He also bombarded *Punch* with a stream of cartoons and began to sell regularly to that magazine in 1907.

During the second year of World War I Shepard joined the Royal Artillery as a lieutenant. He served in France with the 105th Siege Battery from May 1916 to November 1917, seeing action on the Somme, at Arras, and in the series of engagements known as the Third Battle of Ypres. He won the Military Cross and was promoted to the rank of captain before his trans-

fer to Italy, late in 1917. He served in Italy, at Montello and Asiago, until April 1919, when he was discharged from the army with the rank of major.

Returning to civilian life, Shepard resumed his association with *Punch*. In 1921 he joined the staff of the magazine, and the same year was elected to that venerable institution, the "Punch Table." This is the group of senior staff members who meet regularly to discuss the theme and treatment of each week's major political cartoon. They confer around a table, once the property of a local tavern where the meetings began, which bears the carved initials of many illustrious members, past and present—among them Shepard's own.

Although Shepard has over the years contributed many cartoons to *Punch* and other illustrated magazines, it is as a book illustrator, and above all as an illustrator of children's books, that he is best known. He earned a prominent place in the history of children's literature with his illustrations in the 1920's for the Christopher Robin poems and stories of A. A. Milne: *When We Were Very Young* (Methuen, 1924; Dutton, 1925); *Winnie-the-Pooh* (Methuen; Dutton, 1927); and *The House at Pooh Corner* (Methuen; Dutton, 1928). It is generally recognized that the phenomenal success of these books owed much to what has been called the "exquisite aptness" of Shepard's drawings. According to *A Critical History of Children's Literature* (Macmillan, 1953), by Cornelia Meigs and others, Shepard "has come to be considered as the only possible artistic interpreter of A. A. Milne's poems and stories . . . , so surely does he catch in his illustrations every nuance of humor and ingenuousness."

Shepard's delicate and economical line, supplanting the colorplate work of the previous decade, was very much of the 1920's, and Shepard has been called the most characteristic illustrator of that period. But if, as Marcus Crouch wrote in *Treasure Seekers and Borrowers* (Library Association, 1962), Shepard's style "matched the humorous homely fantasy of the 'twenties admirably," his success has by no means been confined to those years. Indeed, many authorities, including Crouch, believe that his finest work was done in the 1930's, when he illustrated Richard Jefferies' *Bevis* (J. Cape, 1931; P. Smith, 1932) and a number of books by Kenneth Grahame, including *Dream Days* (Methuen; Lane, 1928); *The Golden Age* (Lane; Dodd, 1931); *The Wind in the Willows* (Methuen; Saunders, 1931); and *The Reluctant Dragon* (Methuen, 1938; Saunders, 1939). *Bevis*, first published in 1882, had little success until the story was matched with Shepard's illustrations, and Shepard's "pleasantly homely" interpretation of *The Wind in the Willows* is widely regarded as his best work.

Shepard's output was small during the 1940's, but he has since then produced a spate of work that includes Anna B. Stewart's *Enter David Garrick* (Methuen, 1950; Lippincott, 1951); Mrs. Molesworth's *Cuckoo Clock* (Dent; Dutton,

SHEPARD, E. H.—Continued

1954); Roland Pertwee's *Operation Wild Goose* (Oxford Univ. Press, 1955); and *The Islanders* (Bobbs, 1955); B. D. Rugh's *Crystal Mountain* (Muller; Houghton, 1955); Malcolm Saville's *Susan Bills* (Houghton, 1954); *Susan Colling's Frogmarten* (Collins, 1954; Knopf, 1955); Mrs. Ewing's *The Brown-Isles* (Dent; Dutton, 1955); and versions of *Tom Brown's Schooldays,* Hans Christian Andersen and Greek fairy tales. In the 1950's he also illustrated two books by Eleanor Farjeon that were particularly admired—*The Silver Curlew* (Oxford; Viking, 1953) and *The Glass Slipper* (Oxford; Viking, 1955). According to Marcus Crouch, they signaled a "return to his best style," being "full of the humorous detail and invention that had made him the definitive illustrator of Milne."

As an illustrator of adult books, Shepard was until recently best known for a series of anthologies that included *Everybody's Boswell* (Harcourt, 1930); *Everybody's Lamb* (Harcourt, 1933); and *Everybody's Pepys* (Harcourt, 1941); and for his illustrations of Lawrence Housman's plays about Queen Victoria: *Victoria Regina* (J. Cape; Scribner, 1940); *Gracious Majesty* (J. Cape; Scribner, 1940); and *Golden Sovereign* (J. Cape; Scribner, 1940). In the past few years, however, Shepard has delighted a wide new audience with his illustrated autobiography, of which two volumes have so far appeared. *Drawn From Memory* (Methuen, 1956; Lippincott, 1957) describes his childhood at 10 Kent Terrace; *Drawn From Life* (Methuen, 1962; Dutton, 1963) carries the story on from about 1890 until the time of his first marriage, in 1904. Both volumes have been praised by the critics and warmly received by their many readers for their gentle humor and the detailed picture that they present of English middle-class life in the late-Victorian period.

Shepard was married to the artist Florence Eleanor Chaplin on September 28, 1904. She died in 1927, leaving two children, Graham Howard, now deceased, and Mary Eleanor Jessie, who is the wife of E. G. V. Knox, a former editor of *Punch*. On November 12, 1944 Shepard was married again, to Norah Radcliffe Mary Carroll, a hospital nurse. He now lives with his wife in Sussex. Shepard, who is five feet three inches tall and weighs 129 pounds, has gray eyes and light-brown hair, only now turning gray. He is a member of the Church of England, and his clubs include the Savage and the Lansdowne. His recreations are motoring, gardening, and sailing. Among children's book illustrators of this century, wrote Frank Eyre in *Twentieth Century Children's Books* (British Council, 1952), "the illustrator who has given most pleasure is undoubtedly Ernest H. Shepard, whose delightful line drawings for *The Wind in the Willows* and A. A. Milne's books are as inimitable as the work of Tenniel."

References

Shepard, Ernest H. Drawn from Life (1962)
Who's Who, 1963

SHOEMAKER, SAMUEL M(OOR) Dec. 27, 1893-Oct. 31, 1963 Clergyman; honorary canon to the Ordinary of the Protestant Episcopal Diocese of Pittsburgh; former rector of Calvary Episcopal Church in New York City (1925-51); author and lecturer. See *Current Biography* (April) 1955.

Obituary

N Y Times p25 N 2 '63

SHOPE, RICHARD E(DWIN) Dec. 25, 1901- Physician; animal pathologist

Address: b. Rockefeller Institute, 66th St. and York Ave., New York 21; h. Ridge Rd., Kingston, N.J.

A physician turned researcher in animal pathology, Richard E. Shope has gained international recognition in the field of virology. He was the first to isolate an influenza virus, the first to establish the feasibility of animal immunization against influenza, and the first to offer an explanation of the pandemic of Spanish influenza of 1918-19. In studying viruses in animals in the laboratory and under natural conditions, Shope has contributed important techniques to the combating of viruses in man. Through his many experiments with animals he has added considerably to the understanding of malignant tumors, and he has furnished veterinarians with valuable information on the treatment of virus diseases in animals. In studying mosquitoes as carriers of the dreaded sleeping sickness, he succumbed to this often fatal disease. He is the first human being from whom the virus responsible for sleeping sickness has been isolated and is one of the few to recover without permanent brain damage. Nobel Laureate Wendell M. Stanley has called Shope "the best example of a virus hunter I know."

Richard Edwin Shope was born to Charles Cornelius Shope, a physician, and Mary (Hast) Shope, a former schoolteacher, on Christmas Day, 1901 in Des Moines, Iowa. He has a brother, Raymond Shope, and a sister, Mrs. Ellen LeBourdais. In his youth Shope developed an interest in animals on the family farm near Des Moines, where he raised pigs, ran a milk route, and acquired an elementary knowledge of poultry anatomy by dressing chickens. He attended public schools in Des Moines and graduated from East High School in 1918.

Shope originally intended to study forestry at Iowa State College in Ames (now Iowa State University of Science and Technology), but when he presented himself for registration he found the office closed. He then decided to hop a freight train for Iowa City, where he enrolled in a premedical course at the State University of Iowa. While a medical student he began to feel that he would prefer medical research to the practice of medicine. Interested in the relationship of blood cholesterol to tuberculosis, he obtained laboratory space from Dr. Oscar H. Plant, professor of pharmacology, and began to carry out studies on dogs because of their high cholesterol level. He received his M.D. degree in 1924 and the next year continued his experiments with dogs while serving as an instructor in pharmacology in the School of Medicine.

In 1925 Shope received a call that determined the direction of his life's work. Dr. Paul A. Lewis at the animal pathology laboratory of the Rockefeller Institute in Princeton, New Jersey, was looking for an assistant, and Dr. Plant recommended Shope for the job. Shope was assistant at the animal pathology laboratory (1925-30), associate (1930-34), associate member (1934-40), and member (1940-49). In 1949 he went to the Merck Institute in Rahway, New Jersey, where he remained for three years, and in 1952 he became associated with the Rockefeller Institute in New York City, as member and professor.

During his first three years at the Rockefeller Institute in Princeton, Shope continued to do research on the relationship of tuberculosis and cholesterol. Then, in 1928, when an epidemic of hog cholera struck Iowa, Dr. Paul Lewis suggested that Shope return to the Middle West to study the causative virus. His Iowa assignment turned out to be short-lived, however, for he soon switched his attention to research on swine influenza, on the suggestion of Dr. Charles Murray, professor of veterinary bacteriology at Iowa State College. Before 1930 there was little known about swine influenza, and Shope soon became fascinated with the subject.

Hog influenza had first appeared in 1918, the same year in which the Spanish influenza pandemic had occurred. It became apparent to physicians, virologists, and veterinarians that the disease that afflicted millions of hogs resembled the virulent human variety. Although the human influenza had disappeared, there was no assurance that it would not return, especially since hog influenza recurred every autumn. Shope succeeded in solving the mystery of hog influenza, and it makes for a prime detective story.

From previous medical literature Shope learned that Dr. Richard Pfeiffer had associated a particular bacillus with the influenza pandemic of 1889-92. Now in 1928 Dr. Shope and Dr. Paul A. Lewis wanted to know if Pfeiffer's bacillus could be detected in Iowa hogs stricken with the disease. Shope made autopsies on hogs in Iowa, and lung specimens were mailed by air to Lewis for him to study in Princeton.

Encouragement came early. Lewis identified P. bacillus from the first two samples sent to him, and the scientists were able to transmit the flu from a sick pig to a healthy one through cultures. Hoping that they had identified the causative agent, they performed a series of experiments to prove their hypothesis. Suddenly they could not repeat their results. P. bacillus was present in the infected hogs as before, but from pure cultures the contagion no longer made healthy ones sick. At this vexing point in the experiments, Shope found an important clue: crude lung suspensions of bronchial mucus from diseased pigs did establish the infection in normal swine. Shope now believed that swine influenza could be attributed to a virus.

He filtered the bacteria out of the crude lung suspensions and innoculated pigs with the clear filtrate. A virus was present, clearly enough, but

H. Boudakian
DR. RICHARD E. SHOPE

it produced an illness far milder than epidemic hog flu. Then, in 1932, came a striking observation: pigs who had recovered from the mild virus illness proved to be immune to severe flu, and the basis for the first influenza vaccine had been discovered. However, this discovery did not yet provide a comprehensive understanding of the flu cycle. Shope began to suspect that both P. bacillus and virus were required to induce severe flu. Either one alone was not very dangerous, but in concert they might be lethal agents. How could the annual reappearance of the combination be accounted for? Perhaps by the possibility that one of them went "underground" for part of the year, in which case the virus seemed to be the most likely candidate.

Shope then suspected the common hog parasite, the lungworm. He traced the course of the virus, therefore, through the life cycle of the lungworm, which as it moves along from pig lung to stomach to ground to earthworm and back to pig's mouth in rooting can, in effect, disappear for long periods of time. Once he had established this mechanism, Shope had also established the cause of severe influenza in swine: the combined action of a virus and a bacterium. Dr. Shope also holds the P. bacillus and the flu virus in combination responsible for the human influenza pandemic of 1918-19, but that would have to be established experimentally with human beings.

Although Dr. Shope's work with influenza is perhaps his best-known achievement, he has made many other notable contributions in animal pathology. He has shown, for example, that Pseudorabies (or Mad Itch) is caused by a pseudorabies virus for which pigs act as intermediate hosts. Appropriately named, Mad Itch causes cattle and swine to bite and tear themselves until they die. His work on rabbit tumors is an impressive contribution to research on

SHOPE, RICHARD E.—*Continued*

cancer. While studying tumors of Midwestern cottontails, he found a virus causing similar growths in domestic rabbits that can eventually become malignant. This was the first time that a potentially cancerous tumor was shown to be caused by a virus.

From 1942 to 1944, during World War II, Shope served as director of the War Disease Control Station in Grosse Isle, Quebec. The United States and Canadian governments feared that rinderpest, a fatal cattle disease, might be used by the enemy as an agent of biological warfare. Dr. Shope was assigned to developing a method of immunization, and he succeeded with a "live virus" vaccine that has been used to combat rinderpest throughout the world.

Recently Shope has been doing research on Eastern equine encephalitis, a virus inflammation transmitted by mosquitoes, that is often called "sleeping sickness." The virus was first found in the blood of a horse, and human beings are highly susceptible. There is no known cure. About 50 percent of its victims die, and most of the survivors suffer from paralysis of the brain or mental defectiveness. Facing these dangers, Dr. Shope went to southern New Jersey in 1960 to collect virus-bearing mosquitoes. Bitten, he soon displayed sleeping sickness symptoms, and a co-worker, Dr. Delphine Clark, recovered "live virus" in his blood, the first to be taken from a living person. Extremely fortunate in regaining his health in a few weeks, Dr. Shope promptly returned to his work on the disease.

Dr. Shope sits on many scientific advisory committees, including those of the United States Public Health Service, the National Academy of Sciences, and the National Cancer Institute. He holds honorary degrees from Yale University, Rutgers University, the University of Chicago, and the University of Pennsylvania in the United States, and from the University of Utrecht in Holland and Justus-Liebig University in Giessen, Germany. His many awards include the Semi-Centennial Research Award of Sigma Xi, the John Phillips Memorial Medal of the American College of Physicians, the Kober Medal of the Association of American Physicians, the Albert Lasker Award, and the Bertner Foundation Award. He holds memberships in the National Academy of Sciences, the American Philosophical Society, and the Harvey Society, among many other groups.

On July 28, 1925 Richard Edwin Shope married Helen Madden Ellis, a former schoolteacher. They have four children: Richard Edwin, Jr.; Robert Ellis; Nancy Helen (Mrs. Richard Fitz-Gerrell); and Thomas Charles. Dr. Shope is slender, nearly six feet two inches tall, blue-eyed, brown-haired, and weighs 180 pounds. He is a Republican, a Presbyterian, and a member of the Century Association. He enjoys fishing and gardening.

When Dr. Peyton Rous presented the Kober Medal to Dr. Shope in 1957, he noted that this was only the second time the Association of American Physicians had so honored contributions to the health of domesticated animals. In his remarks he said: "Dr. Shope is beyond all else a naturalist . . . his feeling for animals is not sentimental but compassionate . . . to watch how he handles them is a delight."

References

> Time 75:68 Ja 18 '60 por
> American Men of Science 10th ed (1960-62)
> Who's Who in America, 1962-63
> Williams, Greer. Virus Hunters (1959)

SILVER, ABBA HILLEL Jan. 28, 1893- Rabbi; author; organization official

Address: b. The Temple, E. 105th St. and Silver Park, Cleveland, Ohio; h. 19810 Shaker Blvd., Cleveland, Ohio

> BULLETIN: Abba Hillel Silver died on November 28, 1963. *Obituary*: N Y Times p1+ N 29 '63
>
> NOTE: This biography supersedes the article that appeared in *Current Biography* in 1941.

A chief architect of the Jewish homeland in Israel and one of America's most prominent representatives of Reform Judaism is Rabbi Abba Hillel Silver, who since 1917 has been the spiritual leader of The Temple in Cleveland, Ohio. A militant Zionist since his early youth, Dr. Silver stood in the vanguard of the Zionist movement during the crucial years that preceded the establishment of the independent state of Israel in May 1948. On the American scene Silver has been a consistent champion of civil liberties and social justice. His writings, which include the books *Religion in a Changing World* (1930), *The World Crisis and Jewish Survival* (1941), *Where Judaism Differed* (1956), and *Moses and the Original Torah* (1961), are regarded as major contributions to Biblical scholarship and to the understanding of the Jewish religion.

A native of Neinstadt, Schirwindt, Lithuania, Abba Hillel Silver was born on January 28, 1893 to Rabbi Moses and Dinah (Seamon) Silver. The family included an elder brother, Maxwell, and three sisters: Bessie (Mrs. Samuel E. Liebow); Pearl (Mrs. Jacob Michelson), who is deceased; and Rose (Mrs. Jacob Matlow). Rabbi Moses Silver, who represented the third successive generation of ordained rabbis in his family, earned his living as a soap manufacturer. He was the author of two volumes of Biblical commentary, published under the title *Hishukei Kessef* (Filigree of Silver).

In June 1902 the Silvers settled on the Lower East Side of New York City, and Moses Silver became a teacher in a Hebrew school. The political Zionist movement of Dr. Theodor Herzl profoundly impressed Abba Silver, and in 1904 he and his brother Maxwell established the Dr. Herzl Zion Club, the first Hebrew-speaking Zionist organization in America, which conducted debates and performed plays in Hebrew. Abba Silver was elected president of the club in 1906. Although the club met with criticism by opponents of the Zionist ideal, it received the encouragement and guidance of Rabbi Moses Silver.

Following in the family tradition of scholarship, Abba Hillel Silver was an excellent student at Townsend Harris High School, from which he graduated in 1911. With the approval of his father he entered Hebrew Union College in Cincinnati, Ohio, the leading center of Reform Judaism in the United States, which Maxwell Silver also attended. At the same time he enrolled in the University of Cincinnati to obtain a general college education. Completing a nine-year program at Hebrew Union College in four years, Silver was ordained a rabbi in 1915, the same year he took his B.A. degree from the University of Cincinnati.

From 1915 to 1917 Silver served as rabbi at the Eoff Street Temple (Congregation L'Shem Shamayim) in Wheeling, West Virginia. In the latter year he served in France, where his ministry to Allied troops won him the French decoration, Officier de l'Instruction Publique in 1919. Installed as rabbi of The Temple (Tifereth Israel) in Cleveland, Ohio in 1917, Silver succeeded the venerable Rabbi Moses Gries. Although some of the more conservative members of his congregation criticized Silver's Zionist and liberal cosmopolitan views, The Temple grew into one of the foremost synagogues in the United States under his leadership.

In 1925 Silver received his D.D. degree from Hebrew Union College, after submitting a dissertation that was later expanded and published as *A History of Messianic Speculation in Israel From the First Through the Seventeenth Centuries* (Macmillan, 1927; Beacon, 1959). The book is a documented collection of ancient and medieval prophetic writings and is considered a classic contribution to the study of Messianic ideas. In *The Democratic Impulse in Jewish History* (Bloch, 1928) Silver traces Jewish social thought to ancient times and notes the contributions of Judaism to democracy. His book *Religion in a Changing World* (R. R. Smith, 1930), is a collection of sermons stressing the relationship between political liberalism and modern religion, the absence of any real conflict between science and religion, and the need for better communication between Jew and non-Jew. Reviewing the book in *Outlook and Independent* (May 27, 1931), E. B. Chaffee wrote: "Dr. Silver writes with rare beauty and a depth of insight which places him easily in the front rank of our religious leaders." H. Y. Williams noted in *World Tomorrow* (March 1931) that "these sermons are splendid as far as they go," but that "one does not need to be told that they were preached to a wealthy congregation."

A strong advocate of civil liberties and social justice, Silver opposed the post-World War I anti-Red hysteria that was manifested in the Palmer raids of 1921. He supported organized labor in its demand for the closed shop, and he resigned from the Cleveland Chamber of Commerce because of its antiunion stand. Silver was instrumental in effecting the adoption of state and federal unemployment insurance legislation. In 1928 he persuaded the Consumers League of Ohio to undertake a study of this problem, and as a member of a state commission appointed by the Governor he helped draft Ohio's first unemployment insurance law. President Herbert Hoover appointed Silver a member of a committee to help alleviate unemployment. Silver also

Karsh, Ottawa

RABBI ABBA HILLEL SILVER

helped bring about the arbitration of industrial disputes, and he helped introduce the city manager system in Cleveland.

As a leader of the American Zionist movement Silver addressed the international Zionist conference in London in 1920, sharing the platform with such noted statesmen as Lord Balfour and Dr. Chaim Weizmann. During the 1920's Silver was identified with the Zionist group led by Louis D. Brandeis. When a controversy arose between Brandeis and Weizmann over the administration of philanthropic funds, Silver, who supported Brandeis on this issue, left the leadership of the American Zionist movement. He was, however, among the first of the dissenters to return to active Zionist service, and he supported Weizmann's proposal for an extended Jewish Agency for Palestine, which was ratified in Zurich in 1929.

During the early years of Nazism in Germany, Silver, together with Samuel Untermeyer, organized an anti-Nazi boycott at a time when such a move was still opposed by some Jewish leaders as unduly provocative. Organizations to which Silver belonged in the 1930's included the National World Court Committee and the American League for India's Freedom. He served as president of the Cleveland Bureau of Jewish Education from 1924 to 1932 and of the Cleveland Jewish Welfare Federation from 1935 to 1941. As president of the United Palestine Appeal from 1938 to 1943 and as co-chairman of the United Jewish Appeal from 1938 to 1944 Silver helped raise many millions of dollars for Jewish settlement in Palestine and for Jewish relief. In his book *The World Crisis and Jewish Survival* (R. R. Smith, 1941) Silver expressed confidence in the ability of the Jewish people to survive in the face of war and persecution.

During the 1940's Silver worked closely with the Zionist leader Dr. Emanuel Neumann to gain support for the creation of an independent

SILVER, ABBA HILLEL—Continued

state of Israel. He played an active role at the extraordinary conference of American Jewry held at New York in 1942, at which the Biltmore program was adopted, defining clearly for the first time the establishment of a Jewish commonwealth as the goal of Zionism. He also took part in the work of the American Jewish Conference, founded in 1943 to help World Jewry meet postwar problems and to support Zionist aims. An American Zionist Emergency Council, established in 1943, was administered at first by Silver and Rabbi Stephen S. Wise and later by Silver alone.

In 1944 the American Zionist Emergency Council brought the cause of statehood for Palestine before the United States Congress. Addressing a Congressional committee in February 1944, Silver declared: "Just as there is an England, a France, and a Germany, there must be a land of Israel in order that the status of the Jewish people might be normalized throughout the world." Although bipartisan Congressional resolutions favoring a Jewish state failed to pass in 1944, both major parties included pro-Zionist planks in their respective platforms for the 1944 election campaign.

As a result of a controversy between the "Silver activists" and the "Wise moderates" Silver was forced to resign his co-chairmanship in the Emergency Council in December 1944. However, in July 1945 he was recalled to the chairmanship, and in 1945-46 he served as president of the Zionist Organization of America. In December 1945, following a vigorous campaign of the Emergency Council among the American people, a concurrent resolution was adopted by both houses of Congress, favoring a "Jewish national home" and a "democratic commonwealth" in Palestine.

In the following months Silver put pressure upon the Truman administration in the United States and upon the British Labour government to bring about a solution of the Palestine problem. He criticized as a delaying device the British proposal, agreed to by President Truman, for an Anglo-American Commission of Inquiry, and he also opposed a subsequent British proposal for the federalization of Palestine. At the twenty-second Zionist Congress at Basel in December 1946 Silver led the militant faction against the moderate position represented by Weizmann, who still favored negotiations with Great Britain. The congress overwhelmingly reaffirmed the Biltmore program, which called for the reconstitution of all of Palestine as a Jewish commonwealth. The action of the congress is believed to have influenced the British decision in February 1947 to bring the issue before the United Nations.

During 1947 Silver, as chairman of the American section of the Jewish Agency for Palestine, skillfully presented the case for a Jewish homeland to the U.N. The General Assembly gave final sanction to the creation of a Jewish state in a resolution passed on November 29, 1947 by a vote of 33 to 13 with eleven abstentions, and the state of Israel was officially proclaimed on May 14, 1948. Silver subsequently resigned his leadership of the Zionist movement because of a controversy with Israeli leaders, but he continued to work independently on behalf of Israel. Silver's philosophy of Zionism, which views Jewish history and the Jewish people in their entirety, differs from the Israeli Prime Minister David Ben-Gurion's rejection of all Zionist activity that is not based upon the state of Israel.

A collection of Silver's addresses on the Zionist question, delivered between 1942 and 1948, was compiled in his book *Vision and Victory* (Zionist Organization of America, 1949). Speaking on the German question in a sermon delivered in March 1951, Silver said: "The re-arming of Germany means putting militarism in the saddle again in Germany, and aggressive nationalism. It means weakening still further whatever democratic forces and sentiment there still remain in the country. It means the blossoming anew of a neo-Nazism. It means the prelude to a third World War."

In January 1953 Silver gave the official prayer at the inauguration of President Dwight D. Eisenhower. In the following month, at a banquet at the Waldorf Astoria Hotel in New York City honoring his sixtieth birthday, Silver delivered a major policy address in which he expressed concern about the problems confronting Israel and about evidences of growing anti-Semitism and anti-Zionism in the Soviet Union. At another banquet, in Cleveland, a charitable and educational foundation was set up in Silver's name, to promote his religious, civic, and social projects in Cleveland.

Silver's book *Where Judaism Differed; An Inquiry Into the Distinctiveness of Judaism* (Macmillan, 1956) emphasizes the individuality of the Jewish religion. His most recent work is *Moses and the Original Torah* (Macmillan, 1961). On the occasion of his seventieth birthday he was honored by the publication of a volume of essays *In the Time of Harvest* (Macmillan, 1962), edited by his son Daniel Jeremy Silver.

Dr. Silver is now Rabbi Emeritus of The Temple in Cleveland. He serves as chairman of the Israel Bond Organization, and he is honorary president of the Zionist Organization of America. Honorary doctorates were conferred upon him by Western Reserve University (1928), Hebrew Union College (1941), the University of Tampa (1951), and Dropsie College (1957). He has received the National Service Award of Phi Epsilon Pi (1948); the B'rith Sholom Award (1948); the Cardozo Memorial Award of Tau Epsilon Rho (1949); the Award of Merit of the Jewish World Veterans (1951); the Award of Merit of Zeta Beta Tau (1953); the Eisenmann Award of the Cleveland Welfare Federation (1957); the Human Relations Award of the National Council of Christians and Jews (1958); and the Louis D. Brandeis Award of the American Zionist Council (1963). The Israeli communities of Nathanya, Ramat Gan, and Tel Aviv have conferred honorary citizenship upon him.

In 1940 Silver was Dudleian Lecturer at Harvard University. He has served as university preacher at Harvard, Cornell, Syracuse, Purdue, New York University, and the University of Chicago; as national chaplain of the Jewish War Veterans; and as a board member of the Hebrew University in Jerusalem and the Institute of

Technology in Haifa. He was president of the Central Conference of American Rabbis from 1945 to 1947 and has served as vice-president of the Jewish Academy of Arts and Sciences and as a trustee of the American Civil Liberties Union. Other organizations in which Silver has been active include the National Child Labor Committee, the American Birth Control League, the Jewish Publication Society of America, the Ohio Race Betterment Association, the Ohio Commission on Unemployment Problems of the Negro, the Council of Democracy, the Council of Jewish Federations and Welfare Funds, the Cleveland chapter of the American Red Cross, the Cleveland Associated Charities, and the Cleveland Jewish Welfare Federation. His clubs are the Alathians, the Oakwood, and the City Club of Cleveland.

On January 2, 1923 Abba Hillel Silver married Virginia Horkheimer, the daughter of a leader of the Jewish community in Wheeling, West Virginia. They have two sons, Daniel Jeremy (who was ordained a rabbi in 1952) and Raphael David. According to a sketch in *Life* (April 6, 1953), Dr. Silver "has the imposing look of an ancient Jewish leader. Tall and dark, he has a massive head and a shock of graying black hair. When he preaches, his words come out in organ tones."

References

International Who's Who, 1962-63
Silver, Daniel Jeremy, ed. In the Time of Harvest (1962)
Who's Who in America, 1962-63
Who's Who in World Jewry (1955)

National Institutes of Health—
Vernon E. Taylor

DR. JOSEPH E. SMADEL

SMADEL, JOSEPH E(DWIN) (smä-děl') Jan. 10, 1907- Medical scientist; United States government official
Address: b. Laboratory of Virology and Rickettsiology, Division of Biologics Standards, National Institutes of Health, Bethesda 14, Md.; h. 1440 Hemlock St., N.W., Washington, D.C.

BULLETIN: Joseph E. Smadel died on July 21, 1963. *Obituary:* N Y Times p29 Jl 23 '63

The 1962 winner of the $10,000 Albert Lasker Award for Clinical Medical Research is Dr. Joseph E. Smadel, who has been chief of the laboratory of virology and rickettsiology in the division of biologics standards of the National Institutes of Health since 1960. The highly coveted honor was bestowed on Dr. Smadel in November 1962 in recognition of his pioneering work between 1947 and 1952 in showing that the antibiotic chloromycetin (chloramphenicol) could be used to cure diseases like typhoid fever, scrub typhus, epidemic typhus, and Rocky Mountain spotted fever. This discovery reduced fatality rates significantly and affected millions of people throughout the world. Smadel was also cited for his contributions toward the control of cholera, plague, and psittacosis. In addition, he has done research on smallpox, vaccinia (cowpox), influenza, encephalitis, poliomyelitis, and leptospirosis.

An authority on viral and rickettsial diseases, Dr. Smadel was an associate director of the National Institutes of Health from 1956 to 1960. Before he became associated with the institutes he had worked for the Walter Reed Army Institute of Research (1946-56), the United States Army (1942-46), and the Rockefeller Institute for Medical Research (1934-42). The Lasker Award jury called Dr. Smadel's contributions to the control of cholera, typhus, and typhoid "especially timely and important to the health of [South-East Asia], so critical to our allies, and to our military and civilians who serve our nation in the Far East."

Born in Vincennes, Indiana on January 10, 1907, Joseph Edwin Smadel is the son of Joseph William Smadel and his wife, the former Clara Green. He obtained his early education in the local schools and graduated from the high school in Vincennes in 1924. After taking his B.A. degree at the University of Pennsylvania in 1928 Smadel attended the university's Graduate School of Medicine for one year. He then transferred to the Washington University School of Medicine in St. Louis, where he took his M.D. degree in 1931. Retaining his connection with Washington University, Smadel completed a one-year internship and a one-year residency in pathology at the Barnes Hospital in St. Louis. In 1933-34 he served as an assistant in medicine at the Washington University School of Medicine, teaching courses and doing research on viral diseases.

In 1934 Smadel was invited to join the staff of the Rockefeller Institute for Medical Research in New York City, where he had the opportunity to work and study with some of the most distinguished virologists in the United States. He began his association with the institute as an assistant resident; in 1936 he was appointed an associate and in 1939 an associate member. He also served as physician to Rockefeller Hospital and as acting pathologist of the institute.

(Continued next page)

SMADEL, JOSEPH E.—Continued

Smadel's publications between 1934 and 1937 were principally concerned with his study of experimentally induced nephritis in rats. During his eight years with the institute, from 1934 to 1942, he also conducted laboratory and clinical research on virus diseases, including encephalitis and lymphocytic choriomeningitis. One of his papers on the latter disease, "Identification of the Virus of Lymphocytic Choriomeningitis" (with M. J. Wall), appeared in the *Journal of Bacteriology* in 1941. In addition, Smadel worked with a team of researchers headed by Dr. Thomas M. Rivers, isolating constituents of elementary bodies of vaccinia (cowpox), and he collaborated with Rivers on experiments that led to the identification of the virus that causes infectious myxomatosis, a fatal disease of rabbits.

When World War II began, Smadel took a leave of absence from the Rockefeller Institute to enter the Medical Corps of the United States Army as a captain. In 1942-43 he was stationed at the Army Medical School of the Walter Reed Army Medical Center in Washington, D.C., where he did research on virus and rickettsial diseases. The latter are caused by Rickettsia, a group of micro-organisms, and include scrub typhus, epidemic typhus, Rocky Mountain spotted fever, psittacosis (parrot fever), rickettsialpox, and Q fever. Smadel spent two years, from 1943 to 1945, in the European Theater of Operations as chief of the virus department and commanding officer of a detachment at the 1st Medical General Laboratory. When he returned to the United States in 1945 he was assigned for a year to the department of virus and rickettsial diseases at the Walter Reed Army Institute of Research.

Following his discharge in the rank of lieutenant colonel in 1946 Smadel was invited to remain at the Walter Reed Army Institute of Research as a civilian scientist and was appointed chief of the department of virus and rickettsial diseases. In 1950 he also became technical director of research of the communicable diseases division of the Walter Reed Army Institute of Research, holding the two posts simultaneously until 1956.

During the 1940's Smadel discussed in professional papers various kinds of encephalitis, including the West Nile variety; Japanese encephalitis vaccine; the morphological structure of Rickettsiae; psittacosis; Q fever and vaccination for Q fever; influenza; and some types of typhus, including scrub typhus. In 1946 the first two papers in a series of studies on scrub typhus by Smadel and others were published in the *Journal of Experimental Medicine* and the *Proceedings of the Society for Experimental Biology and Medicine*.

In 1947 Smadel's and E. B. Jackson's paper, "Chloromycetin, an Antibiotic with Chemotherapeutic Activity in Experimental Rickettsial and Viral Infections," was published in *Science*. This was among the earliest of many publications between 1947 and 1952 that testify to Smadel's pioneering work in showing that certain infectious diseases could be treated successfully with chloromycetin (chloramphenicol). Working with British scientists in Malaya, Smadel found that the new antibiotic could cure scrub typhus, and

he was the first to demonstrate its effectiveness against epidemic typhus, typhoid, and Rocky Mountain spotted fever. Later studies, in which Smadel served as a volunteer subject, showed that chloromycetin made patients immune to further attacks. Fatalities from these diseases were reduced from 12 percent to less than 3 percent.

Smadel explained in a press interview in November 1962 that a few thousand cases of typhoid are still reported in the United States each year, although a full-scale epidemic is unlikely. He believes that in these remaining isolated instances the typhoid is transmitted to young people by an elderly person who has had the illness at one time and has carried the bacilli in a quiescent form. With injections of chloromycetin, cortisone, or other antibiotics the illness can be completely cured. When the disease is eradicated in this way, few of the young victims become carriers, and thus typhoid will present a negligible problem in the United States in the future.

The appointment of Dr. Joseph E. Smadel to the post of associate director of intramural research at the National Institutes of Health was confirmed in 1956. Four years later he was designated chief of the laboratory of virology and rickettsiology in the division of biologics standards. The division is responsible for maintaining standards of quality and safety of biological products such as vaccines, antitoxins, therapeutic serums, and blood derivatives. Since these products are all derived from living organisms such as bacteria and viruses, they are all potentially dangerous to the user. Close surveillance of production and constant improvement in quality are essential.

In another interview (New York *World-Telegram and Sun*, November 24, 1962) Smadel cautioned that those "diseases which our antiseptic society has come to regard as exotic or even medieval actually are merely dormant, ready to break out right in our own back yard any time that there's a letdown in public health measures." He gave as an instance, cholera, which for years had been confined to the Ganges delta region in India in an endemic form but which suddenly spread in 1958 and 1959 to Thailand, in 1961 to Hong Kong, and later to the Philippines, Formosa, Indonesia, and West New Guinea. As another example of the delicate balance between disease control and epidemics, Smadel mentioned rickettsialpox, first detected in New York in the late 1940's and subsequently found elsewhere along the Atlantic seaboard, in Korea, and in the Soviet Union. Smadel explained that rickettsialpox occurred more frequently among human beings in areas where more efficient garbage disposal (as incineration) has eliminated a rodent population on which the blood-sucking mite that transmits the infecting organism relies for sustenance.

Since he began his research activities in 1934 Smadel has written, often with others, about 200 articles for scientific publications. He has been invited by authors of medical texts to provide chapters on epidemic, murine, and scrub typhus; smallpox and vaccinia; Q fever; Rocky Mountain spotted fever; rickettsialpox; psittacosis; hemorrhagic fever; lymphocytic choriomeningitis;

and general aspects of viral and rickettsial diseases. These have appeared in such definitive volumes as *Principles of Internal Medicine,* edited by T. R. Harrison (McGraw, 1958); *Viral and Rickettsial Infections of Man,* edited by T. M. Rivers and F. L. Horsfall, Jr. (Lippincott, 1959); and *Textbook of Medicine,* edited by R. L. Cecil and R. F. Loeb (W. B. Saunders, 1951; 1955; 1959). Smadel was a visiting lecturer in virology at the University of Maryland from 1950 to 1954 and a visiting professor of rickettsial diseases at the University of Pennsylvania School of Medicine from 1950 to 1956.

Professional organizations to which Smadel belongs are the American Epidemiological Society, the American Association of Immunologists, (of which he was president in 1958), the American Society for Experimental Pathology, the Society of American Bacteriologists, the American Society of Tropical Medicine and Hygiene, and the Harvey Society. He is a Fellow of the New York Academy of Sciences, the American Public Health Association, and the American Association for the Advancement of Science. He is also a member of the National Academy of Sciences, the American Association of Pathologists and Bacteriologists, the Society for Experimental Biology and Medicine, the American Society for Clinical Investigation, the Washington Academy of Medicine, the Association of Military Surgeons, and the Association of American Physicians.

Smadel has served on a number of advisory boards and committees: the advisory panel on medical sciences of the Department of Defense (1958-60); the advisory medical board of the Leonard Wood Memorial (1956-60); the advisory scientific board of the Gorgas Memorial Institute of Tropical and Preventive Medicine, Inc. (since 1957); and the research and standards committee of the American Public Health Association (1950-57). From 1948 to 1958 Smadel took part in the work of the committee on virus research and epidemiology of the National Foundation for Infantile Paralysis (now the National Foundation). Since 1955 he has been a member of the technical committee on poliomyelitis vaccine of the United States Public Health Service, and since 1959, of the research committee of the National Foundation. He was the director of the commission on immunization (1946-52), the commission on hemorrhagic fever (1952-54), and the commission on rickettsial diseases (since 1954) of the Armed Forces Epidemiological Board.

In addition to the Albert Lasker Award for Clinical Medical Research, which consisted of $10,000 and a gold statuette of the Winged Victory of Samothrace (representing in this case victory over death and disease), Smadel has received the United States of America Typhus Commission Medal (1946), the Gordon Wilson Medal (1949), and the Howard Taylor Ricketts Medal (1953). The Exceptional Civilian Service Award was bestowed on Smadel in 1950, and the alumni of Washington University cited him for his unique contributions in 1956. In 1959 he was honored with the James D. Bruce Memorial Award and the Stitt Award. An honorary M.Sc. degree was conferred on Smadel by Yale University in 1950. Jefferson Medical College gave him

an honorary D.Sc. degree in 1955, and the University of Maryland School of Medicine gave him an honorary D.Sc. degree in 1962. Dr. Joseph E. Smadel was married to Elisabeth Moore on July 1, 1936.

References

American Men of Science 10th ed (1960-62)
Directory of Medical Specialists (1961)
Who's Who in America, 1962-63

SMALL, JOHN D(AVIS) Oct. 11, 1893—Jan. 23, 1963 Rear Admiral of the United States Navy (retired); business executive; head of the Civilian Production Administration (1945-46); chairman of the munitions board of the Defense Department (1950-53). See *Current Biography* (February) 1946.

Obituary

Washington (D.C.) Post B p6 Ja 25 '63

SMITH, SYLVESTER C(OMSTOCK), JR.
Aug. 27, 1894- Lawyer; organization official
Address: b. Prudential Insurance Co. of America, Prudential Plaza, Newark, N.J.; h. 1 Merrywood Dr., West Orange, N.J.

Although he calls himself a "country lawyer," Sylvester C. Smith, Jr., the eighty-sixth president of the American Bar Association, could more aptly be described as a "lawyer's lawyer." He is a man who "loves and lives for the law" and is dedicated to the idea that the independence of the lawyer must be preserved. For twenty years, from 1918 to 1938, Smith practised law privately in Phillipsburg, New Jersey; since 1938 he has worked for the Prudential Insurance Company of America, of which he is now general counsel. He has served his community and state in many capacities, including those of county prosecutor and member of the New Jersey highway authority. Before he became its president on August 10, 1962 for a one-year term, Smith had long been active in the American Bar Association.

Sylvester Comstock Smith, Jr., was born on August 27, 1894 in Phillipsburg, New Jersey to Sylvester Comstock and Mary Elizabeth (Davis) Smith. One of five children—the others are Harold D., Sydney, Marian H., and Ellen S. Whitesell—he grew up in Phillipsburg, where his father, a lawyer, had a trial practice. Smith credits his father with instilling in him his deep regard for the law. After his graduation from Phillipsburg High School in 1911 he attended Lafayette College in Easton, Pennsylvania, where he majored in civil engineering at the insistence of his father. According to a profile in the New York *Times* (February 22, 1961), the senior Smith once had a case involving complicated blueprints and became convinced that a good lawyer in a mechanical age must have a thorough knowledge of civil engineering. Sylvester Smith, Jr., received his civil engineering degree in 1915.

Continuing his studies at New York Law School, Smith received his LL.B. degree in 1918 (he had been admitted to the New Jersey bar the previous year). Upon graduation, he en-

SYLVESTER C. SMITH, JR.

listed in the United States Navy as a seaman for World War I service. After his discharge he returned to Phillipsburg, where he practised law with his father in the firm of Smith & Smith until 1928 and with associates until 1938. In 1921 Sylvester Smith, Jr., was named prosecutor of the pleas for Warren County, a post his father had held before him. He served in this position from 1921 to 1926 and from 1928 to 1938. From 1921 to 1941 he was town attorney for Phillipsburg; between 1921 and 1938 he also served as attorney for other townships and municipalities in Warren and Hunterdon counties and was several times appointed special assistant attorney general of New Jersey to try important criminal and civil cases.

Smith gave up private practice in 1938 to become associate general solicitor for the Prudential Insurance Company of America in Newark, New Jersey. In 1944 he became the company's general attorney and the following year was named its general solicitor. In 1948, ten years after he had joined Prudential, Smith was named to his present post of general counsel. He now heads a staff of more than 150 lawyers as the chief legal officer for. the gigantic insurance company. He feels that lawyers must retain their independence and has put this concept in force at Prudential, where the law department occupies three floors of the modern Newark headquarters. According to the New York *Times* profile, Smith's department retains the atmosphere and characteristics of a law office, including the traditional leather chairs and used and comfortable furniture.

Smith was nominated president-elect of the American Bar Association on February 21, 1961 and formally elected in August 1961 at the association's annual convention in St. Louis, Missouri. On August 10, 1962 he automatically became president of the ABA for a one-year term, succeeding John C. Satterfield. The American Bar Association, the national organization of the legal profession, is the principal spokesman on national issues for its more than 100,000 members, who include lawyers, judges, and law teachers. When Smith was nominated as ABA president-elect, the New York *Times* profile writer noted: Smith "is a man who loves and lives for the law. But he has so mastered it that, his associates say, he is relaxed and serene in the most trying legal circumstances."

Before his election to the presidency Smith had held key positions in the American Bar Association. In 1936 he helped to bring about the reorganization by means of which the House of Delegates was established as the ABA's policy-making body. The following year he chaired a special committee that directed the ABA's successful campaign against President Franklin D. Roosevelt's plan to enlarge the United States Supreme Court. After serving almost twenty years in the House of Delegates—most of them as the elected state delegate from New Jersey—he was elected in 1958 chairman of the House of Delegates for a two-year term. At that time he criticized the decisions that had been handed down by the Supreme Court in 1957 as having produced "a black year in law enforcement, dominated by decisions in which the guilty criminal was often the fond object of the court's doting tenderness."

Other positions he held in the ABA include membership in the association's board of governors from 1940 to 1943 and chairmanship of the ABA committee that successfully supported creation by Congress of the administrative office of the United States Courts. As chairman of the association's administrative law committee in 1943, he played an important role in the group's advocacy, before Congress, of the Administrative Procedure Act, which later was enacted to regulate activities of the federal administrative agencies.

During Smith's tenure, the ABA has taken action on many significant measures. These include the retention of the controversial canon 35 in its code of judicial ethics, which provides that cameras and broadcasting equipment be barred from the courtroom during a trial. The ABA's support of the canon was reaffirmed after a special committee, formed to review canon 35, had submitted its opinion that distractions made by cameras and equipment would make it more difficult for judges to see that trials were fair. Revision of the canon had been urged by newspapers and radio and TV broadcasters on the ground that it interfered with freedom of the press.

As president of the ABA, Smith also took part in setting up a world conference on peace through law. The purpose of the conference, which was held in Athens, Greece, in July 1963, was to determine how lawyers could better resolve international legal disputes and bolster international law and legal institutions. Also during Smith's term in office, the ABA sponsored a book, *Democracy and Communism in World Affairs*. For years the association had urged that high school students be taught the facts about Communism, and the book was prepared especially for high school teachers. The group also backed a proposal by President John F. Kennedy to establish a public defender system in federal courts so that "the right to competent counsel may be assured to every man accused of crime, regardless of his means." In June 1963 Smith was one of forty-six eminent lawyers who issued a statement calling upon the Governor of Alabama to comply with a court order forbidding him to block Negro enrollment at the state university, and in August 1963 Smith invited the National Bar Association, many of whose members are Negroes, to affiliate with the ABA.

In 1955 Smith was appointed by Governor Robert B. Meyner of New Jersey, a former associate of his in Phillipsburg, to a nine-year term as member of the New Jersey highway authority; Smith is now treasurer of the authority. He is also the president of the Bureau of Municipal Research of the City of Newark, of which he was a founder. Smith has written *The Supreme Court Fight, Modern Trends in Pleading and Trial Practice*, and *Improving Administration of Justice in Administrative Process*, and he is also a contributor to *The Life Insurance Contract*.

Smith holds honorary LL.D. degrees from Lafayette College (1951), Marietta College (1962), and the New York Law School (1962). He belongs to the Essex County, Warren County, New Jersey State, American, Inter-American, and International bar associations and to the American Judicature Society, the Association of the Bar of the City of New York, and the Association of Life Insurance Counsel. He is a Democrat and an Episcopalian.

Sylvester Comstock Smith, Jr., married Thalia E. Graff on May 17, 1922. She died on March 1, 1958. Their two daughters are Mrs. Page E. (Smith) Bigelow and Thalia Barbara. Smith has blue eyes and gray hair, stands five feet nine inches tall, and weighs 165 pounds. His favorite recreations are sailing his forty-three-foot sloop, the *Teal*, and following the games of the Lafayette College football team. He belongs to the Essex Club, the Harkers Hollow Golf Club, the Northampton County Country Club, the Bay Head Yacht Club, the New York Yacht Club, and the Cruising Club of America.

References

N Y Times p17 F 22 '61 por
Martindale-Hubbell Law Directory, 1962
Who's Who in America, 1962-63

SOKOLSKY, GEORGE E(PHRAIM) Sept. 5, 1893-Dec. 12, 1962 Journalist; industrial consultant; conservative columnist for the New York *Herald Tribune* (1935-40) and the Hearst syndicate, King Features (since 1944). See *Current Biography* (May) 1941.

Obituary

N Y Times p36 Ap 1 '63

SORDONI, ANDREW J(OHN) Feb. 11, 1887-Feb. 27, 1963 Industrialist; Republican member of the Pennsylvania Senate (1927-38); president of the American Automobile Association (1954-56). See *Current Biography* (July) 1956.

Obituary

Philadelphia Inquirer p34 F 28 '63

STANDLEY, W(ILLIAM) H(ARRISON) Dec. 18, 1872-Oct. 25, 1963 United States Navy Fleet Admiral (ret.); Chief of Naval Operations (1933-36); United States Ambassador to the U.S.S.R. (1942-43). See *Current Biography* (May) 1942.

Obituary

N Y Times p27 O 26 '63

STARCH, DANIEL Mar. 8, 1883- Psychologist; market research consultant
Address: b. Boston Post Rd. and Beach Ave., Mamaroneck, N.Y.; h. 14 Burgess Rd., Scarsdale, N.Y.

With his recent development of a method of measuring the sales effectiveness of advertising, Daniel Starch climaxed some forty years of pioneering work in advertising research. He is the chairman of Daniel Starch and Staff, which he founded in 1923, a market research organization perhaps best known for its readership surveys of advertisements in magazines, newspapers, and business publications. The Starch reports on ad readership, on the effectiveness of specific kinds of advertising, and on the selling power of advertising have had a major influence on the development of the advertising business.

The son of a Midwest farmer, Daniel Starch was born to Frank and Theresa (Starch) Starch on March 8, 1883 in La Crosse, Wisconsin. His father, a native of Sudetenland in Bohemia, had moved to the United States with his own parents in 1855. Daniel and his three brothers (Emil, Benjamin, and John) and two sisters (Lydia and Anna) grew up on their father's 420-acre farm— the largest in La Crosse—which produced wheat, corn, and dairy products.

Even before he began attending the one-room schoolhouse located on the farm, Daniel Starch knew how to read, having learned from an older brother. He read voraciously, although he had meager time for diversion between farm chores, and later when he attended Charles City Preparatory School in Iowa, he was active in the debating and literary society. After graduating in 1899, he entered Morningside College, Sioux City, Iowa, where he worked at various jobs to help meet his educational expenses. One of his jobs for many years, tending a coal furnace, required him to get up at five o'clock in the morning.

At Morningside, Starch majored in psychology and mathematics. When he received his B.A. degree in 1903, he was nineteen years old, the youngest in his graduating class. Fascinated by the new field of experimental psychology, he enrolled at the State University of Iowa in Iowa City on a fellowship to study for his M.A. degree in psychology and education, which was granted in 1904. It was twenty years before the university again awarded the master's degree to a student as young as Starch. He continued his work in psychology at the State University of Iowa, writing his doctoral thesis on the localization of sound. He received his Ph.D. degree in 1906 and remained at the university for another year as an instructor in psychology. The next year he went to Wellesley College in Massachusetts as an instructor in experimental psychology. While

Kaiden-Kazanjian

DANIEL STARCH

teaching at Wellesley, he also studied experimental psychology at Harvard University.

In 1908 Starch joined the staff of the University of Wisconsin as an instructor in psychology. He advanced to assistant professor in 1912 and from 1917 to 1919 held the title of associate professor. During his twelve years in Madison he wrote several books in which he applied the findings of psychology to advertising and to education: *Principles of Advertising—A Systematic Syllabus* (University Cooperative Co., 1910); *Advertising, Its Principles, Practice and Technique* (Scott, 1914); *Educational Measurements* (Macmillan, 1916); and *Experiments in Educational Psychology* (Macmillan, 1917). His growing reputation in the psychology of advertising won him an appointment in 1919 as lecturer at the Harvard Graduate School of Business Administration, where he remained until 1927, becoming assistant professor in 1921 and associate professor in 1923. He had received a commission as a captain in the Army Signal Corps in November 1918, too late to serve in World War I.

Shortly before leaving Wisconsin for Massachusetts in 1919, Starch had begun research in marketing when the Gorton-Pew Fisheries Company asked him to make observations and reports on housewives' reactions to new canned codfish cakes. He distributed samples to housewives and recorded their responses a week later. While teaching at Harvard, he did research for the Liberty Mutual Insurance Company to find an appeal for automobile liability insurance advertisements. He found that an ad showing a picture of an automobile wreck was most effective in attracting attention. Later studies have supported Starch's conclusion, and Liberty Mutual continues to use the same theme.

One of Starch's most important contributions in the field of market research, according to his own evaluation, is the use of the recognition method for measuring readership of advertise-

ments. In 1921, undaunted by the skepticism of marketing executives in regard to his chances for success, he attacked the problem of readership measurement through the application of a concept that had previously been tried only under laboratory conditions. Instead of using the recognition method in interviewing people who had been exposed to dummy ads that were read within a given time limit, Starch applied it in measuring response to published material that the interviewees had read outside the laboratory, in the natural course of their lives.

Starch included a report on the readership-scoring method in his *The Principles of Advertising* (Shaw, 1923), a successful book that remained a standard text in the field for some years. In 1923 he founded his own research company, Daniel Starch and Staff, and the following year when the American Association of Advertising Agencies asked him to direct its newly established research department, he agreed to take the assignment only on a part-time basis. One of his projects for the advertising association was a qualitative study of newspaper and magazine circulation.

Radio was a new medium in the mid-1920's when Starch decided to give up teaching and spend more time on research. He made the first comprehensive study of the size of the nation's radio audience, for the National Broadcasting Company, which had been in existence for only two years and wanted to know how many families had radios. To make an accurate survey, in 1928 Starch formulated a probability-sample procedure to determine to what extent a random sample of a particular area would be universally representative. When the Bureau of Census took the first governmental survey two years later, Starch's projected estimate for 1930 was within 4 percent of the number established by the census that year.

Using his recognition method for measuring readership, Starch began in 1932 a massive program of studying magazine advertising. This time, he was not greeted with skepticism and discouragement. The country was deep in the Depression, and advertisers were very careful as to how they spent their money. Both Starch's research capabilities and the field of advertising were on trial. Still going on today, the program has expanded to include some eighty magazines and many important newspapers. Over the years, Starch's reports have been a major influence in the development of advertising copy techniques and in the growth of advertising as a powerful force in the American economy.

A few years ago Daniel Starch and Staff made a study of its own findings on high-rated advertisements and reported that three factors contribute to the success of an ad. The first, simplicity, means that the ad should not be cluttered and confusing but should function as a unit. In the second place, the advertisement should be realistic; it should be a blend of elements which make sense to and concern the reader. Finally, the ad should establish a personal relationship with the reader, perhaps by directly addressing him, by offering him benefits or novelty, or by answering his questions or problems. "Factors such as these," the report stated (*Editor and Publisher*, April 11, 1959), "do not produce a simple and slick formula, but they do provide fruitful direction for writing an ad."

One outstanding question about advertising had long remained unsolved: How much does advertising increase sales? This question, too, has been answered by Daniel Starch, after fourteen years of work formulating his Netapps (net-ad-produced-purchases) method. In 1958, when he reported his progress in an article for the *Harvard Business Review* (May-June, 1958), he said, "Results have been promising, and considerable progress has been made. . . . I was trained as an experimental psychologist and have always felt that a true scientist never gives up trying to solve problems, no matter how intricate they are, provided any light on their solution is valuable to society."

Data accumulated since 1944 by Daniel Starch and Staff had established methods for measuring the purchases of a product by perceivers of advertising messages within the week after they saw the ad and methods for measuring the purchases made by non-perceivers within the same week. Starch has explained in *Printer's Ink* (February 16, 1962), "The thought suddenly flashed into my mind in November 1959 that if ten per cent of non-ad readers buy a product without ad stimulation, then ten per cent of ad readers, too, would buy the product without ad stimulation, even though they read the ad." Combining this concept with the measurements made of purchases during the control period and using his readership method, Starch was able accurately to formulate a way to measure the sales due to ad stimulation. The Netapps method is applicable to all advertising media.

Aside from his contributions in the field of advertising research, Starch's writings have included articles in professional journals in education and psychology and in the *Encyclopaedia Britannica*. He collaborated with Roger Barton on a book about economic booms and depressions, *Faith, Fear and Fortunes* (R. R. Smith, 1934), and he wrote *How To Develop Your Executive Ability* (Harper, 1943). He belongs to the American Psychological Association, American Association for the Advancement of Science, American Marketing Association, Market Research Council, the Harvard Club in New York City, and the Scarsdale Golf Club. His Greek-letter societies are Sigma Xi, Alpha Delta Sigma, and Phi Delta Kappa, among others. He has received many awards, including a certificate of achievement from the University of Iowa in 1947, the Converse Award in Marketing Research at the University of Illinois in 1951, and election to the Marketing Hall of Fame of the American Marketing Association also in 1951.

On August 26, 1913 Daniel Starch married Amy Jane Hopson, a public school teacher whom he had met in Madison, Wisconsin. He has blue eyes and is five feet seven inches tall and weighs 152 pounds. His colleagues are often impressed by the thoroughness and determination in his approach to his work. A *Printer's Ink* biographical sketch, which mentions his "old-world dignity and charm," quotes his observations on his role in advertising, "No one will ever be able to make the perfect ad. And I don't think this is bad. The making of an advertisement is a creative process—and it always will be. All that research can do is to help the creator do a better and more precise job."

References

J of Marketing 21:265+ Ja '57
Ptr Ink 278:54+ F 16 '62 por
National Cyclopaedia of American Biography current vol F (1939-42)
Who's Who in America, 1962-63

STARKER, JANOS (shtärk'ĕr yä'nōsh) July 5, 1924- Cellist

Address: b. Indiana University, Bloomington, Ind.

The cello virtuoso Janos Starker has been making headlines in the world of music since he started his professional career at the age of ten. A child prodigy, he began to play the cello when he was seven and performed as cellist in a string quartet at the Budapest Conservatory of Music at eleven. Starker established his international reputation as a first cellist with the Dallas Symphony Orchestra, the Metropolitan Opera orchestra, and the Chicago Symphony Orchestra. Since then he has gone on to distinguish himself as a soloist with leading orchestras both in the United States and abroad. He is especially known for his performances of the relatively limited chamber repertoire for cello, in which he has impressed the critics with his finished phrasing, controlled and refined tone color, masterly double stopping, musicianship, and style.

Janos Starker was born in Budapest, Hungary on July 5, 1924; one of three sons born to Sandor Starker, a tailor, and Margit (Chajkin) Starker. He lost both his brothers, Tibor and Ede, in World War II. Growing up in music-loving Budapest, the boy was introduced to music at an early age by his mother and father, and he decided to be a solo cellist at the age of seven. He obtained his academic training at the Zrinyi Gymnasium and his musical training at the Franz Liszt Academy of Music, both in Budapest. The teacher who most influenced him at the Franz Liszt Academy was Adolf Cziffer, who in turn had been a pupil of the famous cello virtuoso and professor at the Conservatory of Budapest, David Popper. While studying at the Franz Liszt Academy, Starker became acquainted with Geza de Kresz, a violinist and teacher, and during the summers Starker joined de Kresz and two of his most promising students in the performance of string quartets. "We used to measure how well we did," Starker has said, "by the number of girls who sobbed during the Debussy slow movement."

After graduating from the Franz Liszt Academy of Music, Starker held the chair of first cellist with the Budapest Opera orchestra and the Budapest Philharmonic Orchestra. During World War II, in 1944 and 1945, he served in the Hungarian civil defense. In 1946 he left Hungary because he "did not like the atmosphere" and gave a series of concerts throughout Europe that laid the groundwork for his rapidly growing reputation as a virtuoso cellist. In 1948, the year in which Starker first came to the United States,

JANOS STARKER

he won the Grand Prix du Disque for his recording of Zoltán Kodály's Sonata for Cello Unaccompanied, Opus 8 (1915), which in 1963 was still available on the Angel Records label.

Once established in the United States, Starker took a post as first cellist with the Dallas Symphony Orchestra for its 1948-49 season. He then moved back East to occupy the chair of first cellist with the Metropolitan Opera orchestra from the season of 1949-50 through the season of 1952-53, continuing in the meanwhile his conquest of the critics in the United States that he had begun in Europe. When, in 1953, Fritz Reiner left the podium as conductor of the Metropolitan Opera orchestra to become conductor of the Chicago Symphony Orchestra, Janos Starker was the only musician whom he took along with him to the Midwest.

For his appearances as a soloist with the Chicago Symphony Orchestra from the season of 1953-54 through the season of 1957-58 Starker received acclaim from the local music critics. After Roger Dettmer of the Chicago *American* heard Starker perform Robert Schumann's Concerto in A for Cello and Orchestra, Opus 129, in 1956, he wrote, "Starker has grown from an important cellist to an incomparable one," an opinion echoed in other segments of the local press. His interpretation of Prokofiev's Concerto in E for Cello, Opus 58 (1935-38), perhaps the most fiendishly difficult concerto in the entire cello repertoire, was praised by a music critic of the Chicago *Tribune* as "a performance of extraordinary beauty, of virtuosity, elegance, and a moving reticence of style."

Starker's first return visit to Europe, in 1956, was a triumphant success. In addition to appearing as a soloist with leading orchestras, he gained an international reputation as an interpreter of chamber music. Starker had originally intended to start his career as a soloist without orchestral support in 1957, but when his parents were forced to escape from Hungary in the aftermath

of the 1956 revolution, he postponed it for another year.

After Starker appeared at the Hollywood Bowl in 1957 a music critic for the Los Angeles *Herald and Express* called him "one of the few ranking cellists of the day." At the Edinburgh Festival in the same year his performances evoked such critical comment as "prodigious artistry," "stunning technical prowess," and "a beautiful exhibition of playing, sensitive, elegant, and intuitive." One member of the Edinburgh audience when Starker played Johann Sebastian Bach's Suites for Cello Unaccompanied was Desmond Shawe-Taylor of the *New Statesman and Nation*. He later wrote: "His masterly phrasing, pure tone, varied dynamics, and subtle rubato confirmed an impression that he is the most notable interpreter of such music since Casals."

Since 1958 Starker has been a professor of music at Indiana University, where a large number of students have the benefit of long-term study under his guidance. He is teaching young cellists to surmount the technical difficulties of their instrument and to develop their approaches to the cello in their own way. Starker believes that the cello is an unfamiliar solo instrument to the concert-going public in the United States because the great composers wrote comparatively little music for the cello virtuoso. He feels that few cellists command a basic understanding of their instrument and settle for lower standards than those accepted for the violin. By serving as string consultant to community orchestras scattered throughout the United States, Starker further helps to develop the potential of the cello, which lags far behind the violin in repertoire and in performance technique.

Slow in making his concert debut in New York City, Starker waited until April 14, 1960 when he gave a sonata recital with Mieczyslaw Horszowski, pianist at the Grace Rainey Rogers auditorium of the Metropolitan Museum of Art. The event was eagerly awaited by New York music lovers who knew Starker's artistry only through his recordings. Reviewing the debut in the New York *Times* (April 15, 1960), Harold C. Schonberg wrote: "It took no time at all for Mr. Starker to prove what his many recordings suggested—that he is certainly the equal of any living cellist." Paul Henry Lang of the New York *Herald Tribune* (April 15, 1960) acclaimed Starker as "a superlative cellist, equipped with an abundance of technique and a magnificent tone," and called the recital "an artistic event of the first magnitude."

When Starker gave his second New York recital, in 1961, and his third, in 1962, the critics did not revoke their earlier enthusiasm. Martin Bernheimer informed the readers of the New York *Herald Tribune* on January 20, 1961 that "the Hungarian cellist not only tackled three of Bach's difficult unaccompanied suites, he also gave each one individuality, produced enough sonority and color to make an orchestra jealous, and—in general—amply repaid a large audience for being undaunted by snow and storm." The following winter Francis D. Perkins reported in the New York *Herald Tribune* (January 5, 1962): "Janos Starker who made a remarkable impression in his first two recitals . . . again gave a performance that marked him as one of today's foremost cellists when he appeared here last night."

An enduring record of Starker's virtuosity is available on the many discs that he has made for the Period, Angel, and Deutsche Grammophon labels. Starker began to make records for the old Period label when he was still first cellist with the Metropolitan Opera orchestra, and his recorded performances range over the entire cello literature from Antonio Vivaldi to Béla Bartók. His recordings of the Bach Suites for Cello Unaccompanied have threatened the long established supremacy of Pablo Casals' historic interpretations of the suites; his recordings of the works of fellow Hungarian Zoltán Kodály have been highly esteemed by collectors and critics.

Janos Starker married Eva Uranyi on November 11, 1944. By this marriage, which ended in divorce, he has a daughter, Gabrielle Edith. On June 22, 1960 he married Donna Rae Busch. Starker is five feet nine inches tall and weighs about 150 pounds. He is bald except for a border of black hair and has an assertive jaw and thick eyebrows. In his leisure hours he likes to write short stories and articles, to swim, to play ping-pong, and to discuss current events. He is a Lutheran and a member of the American Federation of Musicians. The Chicago Conservatory of Music awarded him an honorary doctorate in music in March 1961.

Reference

Who's Who in America, 1962-63

STEINBECK, JOHN (ERNST) Feb. 27, 1902-
Author
Address: b. c/o McIntosh & Otis, 18 E. 41st St., New York 17

> NOTE: This biography supersedes the article that appeared in *Current Biography* in 1940.

In honoring the California novelist John Steinbeck as the 1962 recipient of its Nobel Prize in Literature, the Swedish Academy affirmed its determination that the award reflect international esteem for a writer's total statement, the sum of his experience. Steinbeck's critical reputation has been in gentle, and sometimes savage, eclipse since *The Grapes of Wrath*—the last of the prewar triad of novels (*In Dubious Battle* and *Of Mice and Men* are its companions) that documented American social extremity and human sorrow with abrasive passion. Yet against a sense of decline that not even the ambitious realistic allegories of the last decade, *East of Eden* and *The Winter of Our Discontent*, could entirely dispel, the jurors of the academy set his "simple joy of life . . . great feeling for nature— the tilled soil, the wasteland, the mountains and the ocean coasts." The citation read, "To John Steinbeck, United States, for his at one and the same time realistic and imaginative writings, distinguished as they are by a sympathetic humour and a social perception."

Much of his art is the history of a place: of the fertile California valley and town of Salinas, Monterey County. John Ernst Steinbeck was born there on February 27, 1902, of German, Irish, and Yankee extraction, the only son of John

Paul Farber

JOHN STEINBECK

Ernst Steinbeck, Sr., for many years the treasurer of Monterey County. The sheltering mountains, the tide pools and littoral of Monterey Bay fed the intimacy with nature that markedly shapes his imagination. From his mother, Olive (Hamilton) Steinbeck, who was a teacher in the public schools of the Salinas Valley area (an authentic portrait of her exists in *East of Eden*), he derived a sense of the intensity of literary power, which was to make certain books more real than experience. His early favorites included *Crime and Punishment, Madame Bovary, Paradise Lost,* and *The Return of the Native.* His childhood reading was dominated by Malory's *Le Morte d'Arthur,* which he confessed in 1957 to having been "more affected by . . . than by anything else except possibly the King James version," as Peter Lisca quotes him in *The Wide World of John Steinbeck* (Rutgers Univ. Press, 1958). "Later it caused a fairly intensive study of Anglo-Saxon, Old and Middle English all of which I suspect have had a profound effect on my prose." To this day, the image of the "primitive" Steinbeck is the mask of a well-read, sophisticated, and even scholarly personality.

After his high school years, when he excelled at track and basketball and spent summers as a hired hand on nearby ranches, Steinbeck entered Stanford University in 1920. During this casual academic adventure he sporadically contributed poems and comic satires to the school's periodicals, took courses in science and writing, but was not a candidate for a degree. In 1925 he went to New York, where during the next two years he worked intermittently as a reporter and ultimately as a bricklayer on the rising Madison Square Garden.

When he returned to California, he took a job as caretaker to a private estate in the High Sierras. In two mountain winters Steinbeck com-

STEINBECK, JOHN—*Continued*

pleted his first novel, *Cup of Gold,* six times re-worked from a story he had originally written at Stanford. Published in 1929 by Robert Mc-Bride & Company, it drew little attention, but at least made financially possible the novelist's marriage in 1930 to Carol Henning, of San José. Steinbeck later allowed *Cup of Gold* only a "certain lyric quality," yet Lisca sees in this "Life of Sir Henry Morgan, Buccaneer, with Occasional Reference to History," a rawly ambitious variation on the Faust theme, inexperienced and rife with extravagance, but prophetic perhaps, notably of the writer's later sexual attitudes. Negatively, Lisca thinks, its effect was to turn Steinbeck to "a simple but balanced prose, to the kind of people he had known since his childhood, and to that particular area of California where he had been born and had lived all his life—the Salinas Valley."

To a God Unknown (Ballou, 1933) and *The Pastures of Heaven* (Ballou, 1932) explore this familiar experience with experimental audacity. Neither significantly enhanced Steinbeck's fortunes, though a happy accident involving them was to mark a fortuitous change in his career. While the manuscript of *Tortilla Flat,* his next book, was making the rounds of publishers suspicious of its episodic structure, the New York editor Pascal Covici happened to visit a Chicago bookshop, where *The Pastures of Heaven* and *To a God Unknown* were pressed on him as achievements of notable promise. Covici was sufficiently interested to seek out *Tortilla Flat,* which he published in 1935, eighteen months after Steinbeck had submitted the book to his agents. The firm of Covici-Friede, both then and when it was later absorbed by the Viking Press, has published all of the novelist's subsequent work, and the relationship, personal and professional—particularly with Pascal Covici—has remained one of the most rewarding in Steinbeck's career.

Tortilla Flat far exceeded its publisher's mild expectations: it appeared on the best-seller lists for months and was denounced by the Monterey Chamber of Commerce, who feared its discouraging effect on the tourist trade. It received the California Commonwealth Club's annual gold medal for the best novel by a California writer, was adapted for the stage, and sold to Hollywood. *Tortilla Flat* has been called a sketchbook of the California *paisanos,* lightened by Steinbeck's relish of their highly colored individuality and given ironic depth by his contemplation of their ambiguously eccentric moralities. Steinbeck's burlesque of epic form stands as one of his most distinctive creations, replete with themes and moral attitudes he would take up again and freshly examine in *Cannery Row, Sweet Thursday,* and *The Wayward Bus.*

In announcing the Nobel award, Dr. Anders Osterling, secretary of the Swedish Academy, hailed as "incomparable" the stories gathered in Steinbeck's collection *The Long Valley* (1938). The most celebrated stories—those dealing with the education of the boy Jody into the realities of nature, responsibility, and human suffering—had been separately issued in 1937 and were reprinted in a 1945 illustrated edition, on both occasions as *The Red Pony.* His themes of lead-

ership in *The Long Valley* were a prelude to *In Dubious Battle* (1936), that coldly dramatic novel of a California strike in the thirties, which in its working-class realism, its moral neutrality, and potent sense of what Steinbeck calls "a terrible kind of order" is unique among the proletarian writings of the Depression. The French writer André Gide thought *In Dubious Battle* the best psychological portrayal that he knew of Communism.

Steinbeck's growing reputation had prepared an audience for his famous parable of free will and necessity, *Of Mice and Men* (1937), with its lumbering, inarticulate Lennie, meant—as Steinbeck himself wrote—"to represent . . . the powerful yearning of all men." *Of Mice and Men* had begun as a play (a form Steinbeck was later to explore in his adaptations of *The Moon is Down* and *Burning Bright*), and after its success as a novel, he translated it for the theater. Its 1937 opening on Broadway brought Steinbeck the Drama Critics Circle Award for that season, honoring his "direct force and perception in handling a theme genuinely rooted in American life . . . his refusal to make this study of tragical loneliness and frustration either cheap or sensational." But Steinbeck was already living and working with a group of migrants heading for California, and in April 1939 *The Grapes of Wrath* was published by the Viking Press.

The Grapes of Wrath, as Peter Lisca notes, "did not have a chance of being accepted and evaluated as a piece of fiction. From the very beginning it was taken as substantial fact and its merits debated as a document rather than as a novel." To an America still convalescent from the Depression, its tragic rendering of the forced migration of the "Okie" Joad family became a dramatization of the flight of the dispossessed everywhere. Not since *Uncle Tom's Cabin* had an imaginative work provoked such a national explosion of protest, indignation, and defense. "No novel of our day has been written out of a more genuine humanity," Louis Kronenberger wrote in the *Nation,* "and none, I think, is better calculated to awaken the humanity of others." *The Grapes of Wrath* won for its author the 1940 Pulitzer Prize and was later filmed by Darryl F. Zanuck.

Notoriety was not congenial to Steinbeck, and at the height of the clamor over *The Grapes of Wrath,* he went with his friend the marine biologist Ed Ricketts, who figures as Doc in *Sweet Thursday* and *Cannery Row,* on a scientific expedition to the Gulf of California. They emerged with *Sea of Cortez* (1941), a journal of travel, with observations on marine animals of the Panamic faunal province. On America's entry into the war, and at the suggestion of General "Hap" Arnold, Steinbeck toured Army Air Force bases and wrote a straightforward account of their life and training, *Bombs Away* (1942).

In 1943 Steinbeck went as foreign correspondent for the New York *Herald Tribune* to North Africa and the Italian front; his dispatches were later collected as *Once There Was A War* (1958). In 1942 *The Moon is Down,* Steinbeck's abstract chronicle of the enemy occupation of a vaguely "Scandinavian" country, appeared and precipitated a bitter controversy in which the genuine critical issues were obscured by wartime psychology. It enjoyed favor among the European re-sistance movements, however, and the novelist was decorated by the King of Norway.

To a postwar world whose interests often lay elsewhere, John Steinbeck offered familiar images in *Cannery Row* (1945), *The Pearl* (1947), and *The Wayward Bus* (1947). While the latter two (like *East of Eden* and *Of Mice and Men*) have each sold over a million copies in paperback editions, they did little to extend the novelist's range or reputation. In 1947 Steinbeck was in-vited to Russia as "a leading proletarian writer," and on his return he published *A Russian Jour-nal* (1948), with photographs by Robert Capa. His motion picture scripts of his own stories *The Pearl* and *The Red Pony* were notably distin-guished, as was his study of Emiliano Zapata in his biographical film of the Mexican revolution-ary leader, *Viva Zapata!* (1952). About this time, Steinbeck lost his great mentor and friend, Ed Ricketts, to whose memory he pays tribute in the sketch "About Ed Ricketts," which pref-aces *The Log from the Sea of Cortez* (1951).

Another experiment in play-novelette form, *Burning Bright*—on vaguely mystical themes of sexual sterility—was not well regarded during its brief 1952 Broadway engagement, but *Pipe Dream*, a musical adaptation by Rodgers and Hammerstein of *Sweet Thursday* (1954), the se-quel to *Cannery Row*, opened in 1955 to popular success. In 1957 Steinbeck published a fantasy of contemporary France, *The Short Reign of Pippin IV; A Fabrication.*

East of Eden (1952) and *The Winter of Our Discontent* (1961) were serious bids for a critical reconstitution of the novelist's earlier reputation, yet what some commentators regarded as their overt moralizing, looseness of structure, and "af-fected" prose became sources of dispute. Begin-ning as a family chronicle, *East of Eden* devel-oped into a vast and intricate gloss on the Cain-Abel theme set in the Salinas Valley. Joseph Wood Krutch (New York *Herald Tribune Week-ly Book Review*, September 21, 1952) felt that "not even in *The Grapes of Wrath*" had Stein-beck "exhibited such a grasp upon himself and upon his materials," but Arthur Mizener spoke for more stringent critical opinion in observing that "so long as [Steinbeck] sticks to animals and children and to situations he can see to some purpose from the point of view of his al-most biological feeling for the continuity of life he can release the considerable talent and sen-sitivity which are naturally his. As soon as he tries to see adult experience in the usual way and to find the familiar kind of moral in it, the in-sight and talent cease to work and he writes like the author of any third-rate best-seller" (*New Republic*, October 6, 1952). The last part of the novel was filmed by Elia Kazan.

In *The Winter of Our Discontent*, Steinbeck deserted his customary scenes for New England, with his portrait of a scion of an old and dis-tinguished family who betrays his heritage of idealism through fear of insecurity. Although Granville Hicks in the *Saturday Review* (June 24, 1961) found it "neither convincing as a piece of fiction nor persuasive as a sermon," William Hogan (San Francisco *Chronicle*, June 22, 1961) praised it as "a tense, moving drama and an articulate comment on American manners and

morals today." Dr. Osterling of the Swedish Academy emphasized that *The Winter of Our Discontent* had favorably influenced the Nobel jury. With it, he said, Steinbeck "resumed his position as an independent expounder of the truth, with an unbiased instinct for what is genuinely American, be it good or bad."

Once blond, still blue-eyed, rugged and six-foot, John Steinbeck wears a Mephistophelean beard that gives him a Renaissance, piratical as-pect. He and Carol Henning were divorced in 1943. By his second wife, Gwyn Conger, whom he married on March 29, 1943, he has two sons, Tom and John. Since December 26, 1950 he has been married to Elaine Scott Steinbeck. He maintains an apartment in New York (of which he observes: "If you have lived in New York no place else is good enough") and owns a shingled cottage on a wooded two acres off Long Island's Sag Harbor. There, in a workshop se-cluded from the main house and designed by Steinbeck with Spartan simplicity, he works six hours a day, roughing out new stories in pencil. His work has been translated into thirty-three foreign languages.

His recent book, *Travels With Charley* (1962), a whimsical itinerary of a continent-spanning tour he shared with his French-born poodle Charley, was published only a few months before he received the Nobel prize and is subtitled *In Search of America*. Its intention might serve as epigraph to the journey of John Steinbeck's ca-reer, through which he has remained faithful to the certain testimony of his senses, his distrust of abstract ideas. "I began to feel that Amer-icans exist, that they really do have generalized characteristics regardless of their states, their so-cial and financial status, their education, their religious and their political convictions," he would write in *Travels With Charley*. "But the more I inspected this American image, the less sure I became of what it is."

References

N Y Herald Tribune p41 O 26 '62
N Y Times p1+ O 26 '62 pors
Newsweek 60:65 N 5 '62 por
Lisca, Peter. The Wide World of John Steinbeck (1958)
Twentieth Century Authors (1942; First Supplement, 1955)
Who's Who in America, 1962-63

STORKE, THOMAS M(ORE) Nov. 23, 1876- Newspaper editor and publisher
Address: b. Santa Barbara *News-Press*, News-Press Bldg., Santa Barbara, Calif.; h. 1716 Santa Barbara St., Santa Barbara, Calif.

In 1951, on the occasion of his fiftieth anni-versary as a newspaper publisher and editor, Thomas M. Storke explained to a gathering of California editors his personal creed. "I believe," he said, "that the first obligation of a newspaper editor is to his community . . . that [he], better than any other single force, can form and develop character for his community . . . that with few exceptions, this is a lifetime job." The commu-nity that Storke has striven all his life to im-prove is his native Santa Barbara, California,

THOMAS M. STORKE

which he has seen develop from a Spanish-American pueblo of 3,000 into a city of 60,000.

Early in 1961, when the John Birch Society created fear and unrest in his area, Storke's newspaper carried an exposé of the society and an editorial that condemned it as totalitarian in its organization and methods and challenged its leaders to "come up from underground." For this crusade in behalf of his community and the nation, Storke won the 1961 Lauterbach Award of the Nieman Foundation of Harvard University for "outstanding work in defense of civil liberties," a 1962 Pulitzer Prize for editorial writing, and the 1962 Elijah Lovejoy Award from Colby College for courageous journalism. In 1958 Storke imparted his reminiscences in *California Editor* (Westernlore Press), a condensed and updated version of which was published as *I Write for Freedom* (McNally and Loftin) in 1962.

Thomas More Storke was born in Santa Barbara, California on November 21, 1876, but since his birth was recorded as having occurred on November 23, he considers the latter date as his official birthday. His ties to Santa Barbara and its Hispanic past derive from his maternal ancestry. His mother, Martha (More) Storke, was the great-great granddaughter of José Francisco de Ortega, a soldier who in 1782 dedicated the presidio of Santa Barbara for Spain. In Tom Storke's boyhood the Spanish influence still prevailed both in the town and in his home; as a child he spoke Spanish as fluently as English. His father, Charles Albert Storke, was an Easterner who had fought in the Union Army. Settling in California after the Civil War, he chose law as his profession, became active in Democratic politics, and eventually became a mayor and state legislator. Thomas More Storke had two sisters, Mrs. Minita (Storke) Banks and Mrs. Alice Carey (Storke) Maynard, who are no longer living; he also has a half-sister, Mrs. Jane

(Law) Latimer, and a half-brother, S. Westbrook Law.

One of Tom Storke's favorite pastimes in his youth was horseback riding. In his spare time he earned pocket money by tending a cow and selling milk to neighbors and by doing odd jobs. When he was nearly thirteen his father took him to a session of the state legislature—an experience that Storke feels began his lifelong interest in politics. In 1894, although he had only completed his junior year in high school, his father decided that he was ready for college and enrolled him at Stanford University. As a freshman Tom Storke lived at Encina Hall, where he met a fellow student, Herbert Hoover. The following year he moved to the Alpha Pi Chapter House of the Kappa Alpha (Southern) fraternity, where he earned his room and board as house manager. Majoring in economics, Storke graduated with the B.A. degree in 1898.

Not having decided upon a career on graduating from Stanford, Storke tried his hand for one afternoon at reporting for the Santa Barbara *Daily News.* Since he proved unsuccessful as a reporter, he consented to his father's proposal that he manage a family sheep ranch on Santa Rosa Island. The brief encounter with the world of journalism, however, remained on his mind, and a few months later he returned to the mainland, where he obtained a six-dollar-a-week reporting job on the Santa Barbara *Morning Press.* He stayed on its staff for about six months and then agreed to tutor the two teen-age sons of Dr. Seward Webb, vice-president of the New York Central Railroad. Later, on his first trip East, he accompanied the Webb party on a transcontinental tour.

Returning to Santa Barbara, Storke resumed his job with the *Morning Press,* and he soon became its night editor. The *Press,* however, was being used by its owners to further their own private interests rather than the public welfare, which so dissatisfied Storke that he dreamed of having his own newspaper. With A. S. Petterson, a top reporter who had unsuccessfully tried to found a newspaper in Santa Barbara, Storke on December 29, 1900 bought the *Daily Independent,* then the weakest of the town's three papers. He had intended to handle only the publishing side, while Petterson was to be the editor, but a few weeks later, when Petterson begged out of the struggling venture, Storke bought him out and took over all responsibilities.

The first issue of Storke's *Independent* was published on January 2, 1901, with an editorial extolling Santa Barbara's climate and natural beauty and exhorting the citizenry to improve the area even more. Later that year Storke persuaded the hotel magnate Milo Potter to erect a luxury hotel in Santa Barbara. The city was launched on its new industry of playing host to tourists and wealthy people in retirement. Although his early financial situation was precarious, Storke characteristically refused to publish advertisements of patent medicine quacks. At first he met costs by job printing and through loans, and gradually he was able to build up advertising, circulation, and prestige.

In 1909 a man unknown to Storke asked him to sell the *Independent,* and since Storke did not want to sell, he priced it at a then "ridiculous figure" of $40,000. The offer was accepted, however, and he was obligated to sell the paper, only to discover that the buyer had acted for public utility interests against whose projected increase in utility rates Storke had been fighting. Burdened by free time after selling the newspaper, Storke went into the oil business in Bakersfield.

Unable to buy back the *Independent,* Storke in March 1913 acquired the Santa Barbara *Daily News* and once more assumed the task of rehabilitating a paper that had seen better days. His new publication soon outflanked the *Independent* in advertising and circulation, and it was not long before he was able also to retrieve his former paper. For the next twenty years he published under the merged masthead of the *Daily News & Independent.* In 1914 Storke was appointed United States postmaster of Santa Barbara, a job he held through 1920. During World War I, owing to lack of time, he was obliged to give up editorial work for his newspaper, and he delegated it to his father, who wrote vigorous editorials under the name of "The Old Man."

During his early adulthood Storke took part in politics only on the local level; he made his debut in state politics in 1902 as a delegate to the state Democratic convention. Storke considers himself a true independent: although he has always been a registered Democrat and his paper is considered pro-Democratic, his publications for nearly fifty years have supported more Republicans than Democrats. His first serious interest in national politics was aroused in 1918 when he met William Gibbs McAdoo, then Secretary of the Treasury, who became his intimate friend. McAdoo asked him to go with the California delegation to the 1920 national Democratic convention, and during the 1920 campaign Storke first met Franklin Delano Roosevelt, who was running with the Presidential candidate James Cox.

Six months before the 1920 Republican convention Storke had had a conversation with the lawyer Samuel Untermeyer, in which Untermeyer predicted that a comparatively unknown Senator from Ohio, Warren G. Harding, would be nominated as the Republican contender and elected President of the United States. His story —that Harding had been preselected by a small group of powerful men in New York—sounded incredible to Storke. History proved Untermeyer right, and when Storke attended the Democratic convention of 1924 as a delegate, he witnessed a similar phenomenon in his own party: the convention became deadlocked, and what Storke calls the "Wall Street interests" or the "invisible forces" enlisted their "compromise" choice on the 103d ballot—a weak candidate, John W. Davis, who would have no chance of beating Calvin Coolidge for the Presidency. Storke had joined the 1924 California delegation because McAdoo was seeking the Presidential nomination, and he had helped McAdoo make political contacts in California. After the convention debacle, he returned home, disgusted and disillusioned.

After resigning the postmastership of Santa Barbara in 1920, Storke moved his newspaper to new quarters that conformed to the Spanish architectural style that Storke has advocated for all of Santa Barbara's buildings. After the 1924 convention he threw himself into a program of civic improvement then going on in his native city, which received impetus from the demolition of the poorer sections of the city following the 1925 earthquake. The recovery of Santa Barbara after the earthquake, Storke has said, was the most inspiring event of his eighty-odd years.

Storke paid scant attention to national politics until the 1932 Democratic National Convention in Chicago. As a member of the California delegation, Storke played an important role in obtaining support for Franklin D. Roosevelt from the California group. Eventually, at a crucial point in voting, William McAdoo, who led the California delegation, cast California's forty-four votes in favor of Franklin Roosevelt. Following California's decision, state after state joined the Roosevelt camp; the deadlock that had developed around the other two leading contestants, Alfred E. Smith and John N. Garner, was broken.

When Storke returned home he bought the *Morning Press,* his only competitor, on September 30, 1932 to prevent it from going out of existence. It was a Republican paper, and Storke, feeling that the prevailing Republican opinion of Santa Barbara was entitled to an organ of expression, published it for six years independently of his own paper and under the editorship of the leading Republican news writer Paul Cowles. In 1938 he merged the two papers into the Santa Barbara *News-Press.* In 1937 he added to his possessions a radio station, KTMS. Today his annual payroll is about $1,000,000, and his circulation is around 35,000.

In the meantime McAdoo had been elected the junior Senator from California, and since most of the state patronage fell to him and he was not familiar with the California political scene outside of Los Angeles, Storke helped him dispense appointments. Finding himself "mixed up" in the New Deal era by reason of his acquaintance with important party figures, Storke turned this to account for Santa Barbara: in the New Deal years, when funds were freely available, he played an influential role in getting some $22,000,000 in federal aid for public improvements in Santa Barbara city and county. From November 8, 1938 to January 3, 1939 he served out the senatorial term of McAdoo, who had resigned.

Projects in which Storke was involved were the building of a federally financed post office and a new Santa Barbara airport; a successful campaign to get the Santa Barbara State College into the University of California system (1954), and an eighteen-year struggle to construct the Cachuma Dam, which ensures the area an adequate water supply. In 1951 he was appointed to the second California crime commission, and in 1955 he was named a regent of the University of California.

Thomas M. Storke's latest crusade for the welfare of Santa Barbara was his exposure of the John Birch Society, which had selected Santa Barbara as one of its earliest targets. A semisecret, ultraconservative group founded by Robert Welch in 1958, the society sowed distrust and fear by branding many people as Communists,

STORKE, THOMAS M.—*Continued*

from teachers and ministers to members of the Supreme Court and the President. In January 1961 the *News-Press* carried two stories about the society, and in February Storke wrote a front-page editorial condemning its "destructive campaign of hate and vilification" and urging it to "tell their fellow citizens exactly what they are up to." Later that year, when the society tried to sabotage UNICEF's Halloween children's collections, Storke himself contributed a check for "1,000 dimes." Often congratulated on his "courageous stand," Storke replied: "It was not a courageous gesture. . . . If I had *not* taken this stand I would have considered it cowardly."

In addition to the Lauterbach Award, the Pulitzer Prize for editorial writing, and the Elijah Lovejoy Award for his crusade against the John Birch Society, Thomas M. Storke has received many other honors. He holds honorary LL.D. degrees from the University of California (1960) and Colby College (1961). He belongs to the Santa Barbara Club, the University Club (Santa Barbara), the California Club (Los Angeles), and the Santa Maria Club, and he is a charter member of every country club in the area. He is also a charter member of Los Rancheros Visitadores, a group of horsemen that assembles every spring to re-enact old roundup treks of the rancheros. At his TMS Ranch in the Santa Ynez Valley, Storke raises white-faced Hereford cattle.

Thomas M. Storke is five feet ten inches tall, weighs 195 pounds, and has gray eyes and gray hair. By his marriage on March 9, 1904 to Elsie Smith, who died on July 4, 1918, he has three children: Jean Isabel (Mrs. Ernest Menzies), Elsie Margaret (Mrs. E. Morris Cox), and Charles Albert Storke 2d. On February 16, 1920 he married Marion Day, who had nursed his first wife through her final illness, and they have one son, Thomas More Storke, Jr. Storke's family is Episcopalian.

"It has been my good fortune," Storke said in *I Write for Freedom*, "to be given more than the normal share of active years. They have been exciting years. . . . Because I have a keen sense of history I have always, from the very beginning, had an awareness of who and what I was. I've been blessed more than most, perhaps, with the knowledge of what sort of an American I am—and I've never doubted my instincts. I have nothing but pity for the man who doesn't know where he should stand in any fight concerning the welfare of his nation."

References

N Y Times p9+ D 10 '61

Storke, Thomas M. California Editor (1958); I Write for Freedom (1962)

Who's Who in America, 1962-63

STORMS, HARRISON A(LLEN), JR. July 15, 1915- Business executive; aeronautical engineer

Address: b. 12214 Lakewood Blvd., Downey, Calif.; h. 1 Pine Tree Lane, Rolling Hills, Calif.

If a team of American astronauts lands on the moon by 1970, the approximate target date,

much of the credit for their journey will go to Harrison A. Storms, Jr., a vice-president of North American Aviation, Inc., and since December 1960 the president of its Space and Information Systems division. In November 1961 this division became the prime contractor for the National Aeronautics and Space Administration's Project Apollo, charged with constructing a spacecraft to carry three men on a round trip to the moon.

Space engineering is an infant science, which must evolve radically new designs to enable man and his vehicles to travel safely through a largely unexplored environment. But Storms is confident that human ingenuity will respond to this new challenge as it has to earlier ones. In his twenty years with North American Aviation, Inc., he has helped to develop a number of aviation prototypes—bombers, fighters, supersonic jets, and a rocket plane.

Harrison Allen Storms, Jr., was born on July 15, 1915 in Chicago, Illinois and grew up in Wilmette, a residential suburb of Chicago. He is the only child of Peggy Lucille (Ware) Storms and Harrison Allen Storms, associate manager for the North Shore Association, a motor vehicle club. As a boy, Harrison A. Storms, Jr., built model airplanes and tinkered with a Model-T Ford, and he was a member of the Boy Scouts. He has said that his father's interest in science encouraged him to attend college and to take advanced degrees.

After graduating from New Trier High School in Wilmette in 1934 he enrolled at Northwestern University in Chicago, where he studied mechanical engineering. An average student, he received the B.S. degree in 1938 and the M.Sc. degree in 1939, after he submitted a thesis entitled "Factors Influencing the Design of the Precombustion Chamber of a Diesel Engine." At college he organized an undergraduate chapter of the aviation society Alpha Eta Rho and became the first president of the Northwestern University student chapter of the American Society of Mechanical Engineers.

Storms next studied at the California Institute of Technology, receiving his B.S. degree in aeronautical engineering in 1940 and the degree of Aeronautical Engineer in 1941, after he had written the thesis "Some Aspects of the Effects of Propeller Operation on the Static Longitudinal Stability of an Airplane." At Cal Tech he worked as a research assistant in wind tunnel testing.

Color blindness kept Storms out of military service during World War II, but he made notable contributions to the war effort as an aircraft designer of planes like the B-25 bomber and the P-51 Mustang, one of the best American fighter planes of its time. Joining the aerodynamics group of North American Aviation, Inc., in 1941, he was advanced to the post of assistant group leader three years later and shortly thereafter to that of group leader. In 1951 he became assistant chief technical engineer, and in 1953 he was made chief technical engineer. Promoted to the position of research and development manager in 1956, he was named chief engineer of North American's Los Angeles division in 1957. He also became the engineering vice-president of the division.

As engineering vice-president, Storms had over-all responsibility for the design of the T-39 Sabreliner, a twin-engine utility Air Force trainer; the X-15, the first manned vehicle to rocket out of the atmosphere, for which he de-signed a cruciform-shaped tail to provide flight stability; and the six-engine jet B-70 (RS-70), a bomber and potential passenger plane, designed to fly at three times the speed of sound. Storms also helped to engineer the F-86 Sabrejet, which was used in Korea; the F-100, the first supersonic fighter plane; and the T-6, the T-28, the B-45, and the F-107.

North American Aviation, Inc., one of the largest corporations in the aerospace field, has five divisions in addition to the one at Los An-geles: the Autonetics division, an electronics com-pany; the Rocketdyne division, which produces liquid rocket engines; Atomics International, which does research and development of nuclear power programs; the Columbus (Ohio) division, which works on Army and Navy projects; and the Space and Information Systems division.

The Space and Information Systems division, which has been in operation since 1946, acquired its present name shortly after Storms became its president on December 5, 1960. At that time it was given a new charter, which assigned to it all responsibility for development of both manned and unmanned space exploration vehicles, anti-ICBM projects, and information processing sys-tems. Two major projects occupying the division are the production of the air-to-surface Hound Dog missile for the Air Force and the production for NASA of a paraglider that can be used to guide space boosters and capsules to "dry-earth" landings.

In November 1961 the division won out over four other bidders in one of the most important competitions ever held in the missile-space indus-try. It was awarded the $400,000,000 prime con-tract for the building of the Apollo spacecraft that will carry three men to the moon. This involves designing a "command module," a conical capsule in which the men will ride; a "service module," which is a fuel-power component; and the launch escape system, which will be mounted on top of the command module. The Space and Informa-tion Systems division also received from NASA a $140,000,000 contract to build the S-II stage of the Advanced Saturn booster that will send off the Apollo. The manufacture of the liquid fuel for the Saturn was assigned to the Rocketyne division. In the first quarter of North American Aviation's fiscal year 1962 the Space and Information Sys-tems division brought in $599,000,000 in con-tracts, compared to its $108,100,000 in sales dur-ing fiscal year 1961.

To Storms belongs much of the credit for the rapid growth of the Space and Information Sys-tems division and for its winning of the Apollo contract. Believing that "with a good team you can do anything," he began to assemble a high-caliber staff of scientists and engineers. From the Los Angeles division he brought many of the engi-neers who had worked on the X-15 project and who had been co-workers for many years. By July 1961, when NASA invited sixteen major aerospace companies to submit bids for the Apollo project, the Space and Information Systems division was ready to meet the challenge. "We took a calcu-

HARRISON A. STORMS, JR.

lated gamble," Storms recalls, "went out, and hired the best technical force available. We paid people salaries for jobs we didn't even have yet. By the time we were working on our Apollo pro-posal, we had the finest engineering-managment team I've ever seen." Of the 10,500 people em-ployed by the division about 1,000 work exclu-sively on the Apollo project.

In addition to its excellent staff North American Aviation, Inc., commands a $10,000,000 aerospace laboratory that contains the world's largest acoustical test facility, an environmental test chamber, and a privately owned wind tunnel. Another selling point that may have won North American the Apollo contract is the fact that, unlike other companies who co-operated in sub-mitting combined Apollo bids, North American submitted a single plan that streamlined manage-ment organization and concentrated decision-making and responsibility in a small group of executives. The complex project is co-ordinated by means of daily intra-project conferences and weekly discussions between NASA officials and project heads.

Storms's alma mater, Northwestern University, awarded him an alumni merit award in 1959 and an honorary D.Sc. degree in 1960, citing him as one of the nation's top aeronautical engineers. In 1961 the American Rocket Society, to which he belongs, presented him with its James H. Wyld Award for his "outstanding application of rocket power" in connection with the X-15 program. That year he also received the Richards Memorial Award from the American Society for Mechanical Engineers. A consultant on the aerospace panel of the United States Air Force Scientific Advisory Board, he is a former member of a Department of Defense research and steering group and of a number of NASA committees. He is a Fellow of the Institute of Aerospace Sciences.

Harrison A. Storms, Jr., married Phyllis Kathryn Wermuth on September 14, 1940. They have three children, Patricia Anne, Harrison Allen III, whose nickname is Skip, and Richard, who is

STORMS, HARRISON A.—*Continued*

called Ricky. Storms himself is nicknamed Stormy. At work he pushes insistently for results and demands the best from himself and his subordinates. He is informal in manner and impartial in his judgments. A slim man with brown hair and brown eyes, Storms weighs 150 pounds and stands five feet ten inches tall. He is a Roman Catholic. His hobbies are photography and working with electronic equipment. He once tried raising cattle on his nine-acre property in California.

Storms has called the building of the Apollo spacecraft and the S-II Saturn booster the greatest challenge of his career. "We have one of the finest technical design teams in the world," he has said. "In the final analysis we must rely on man's ingenuity. There are always barriers—the sound barrier, the heat barrier. . . . It is the inventive scientists who have found answers through gathering information, testing, proving."

References

Los Angeles Times p1 S 25 '60
N Y Times p15 O 16 '58 por
Sat Eve Post 235:85+ My 5 '62 pors
Thomas, Shirley. Men of Space vol 4 (1962)
Who's Who in America, 1962-63

STRACHEY, (EVELYN) JOHN (ST. LOE) Oct. 21, 1901-July 15, 1963 Prominent member of the British Labour party; economist; Minister of Food (1946-50); Secretary of State for War (1950-51). See *Current Biography* (June) 1946.

Obituary

N Y Times p31 Jl 16 '63

STRATTON, JULIUS A(DAMS) May 18, 1901- University president; scientist; engineer
Address: b. Massachusetts Institute of Technology, Cambridge 39, Mass.; h. 111 Memorial Dr., Cambridge 39, Mass.

If the United States is to retain its scientific and technological leadership in a rapidly changing world, President Julius A. Stratton of Massachusetts Institute of Technology believes, American schools must meet the challenge of the present revolution in science through "education for excellence." Stratton, who deplores the American tendency to fear an intellectual elite, has devoted most of his career as an engineer, scientist, teacher, and administrator to M.I.T., probably the world's foremost institution of science and engineering. In November 1957, during the post-Sputnik crisis of that year, he took over as acting president after President James R. Killian, Jr., became special assistant for science and technology to President Eisenhower. Stratton was formally installed as M.I.T.'s eleventh president on June 15, 1959.

Julius Adams Stratton was born in Seattle, Washington on May 18, 1901, the son of Julius A. and Laura (Adams) Stratton. Both the Adams and the Stratton families had left New England to join at an early date in the westward movement. Stratton's grandfather, Curtis P. Stratton, went to Oregon by way of Cape Horn in 1852; his family (including Stratton's father) followed

two years later via covered wagon on the Oregon Trail.

As a child Stratton lived for a while in Germany with his family. He attended Broadway High School in Seattle and at the age of fourteen became an avid crystal set radio ham. During World War I he went to night school to qualify as a wireless operator, but the Armistice was signed before he was ready, and at seventeen he became instead a seagoing operator. He sailed first on coastal ships and later on runs to the Orient. In 1919 he enrolled at the University of Washington, but after a year he decided to attend Massachusetts Institute of Technology and shipped on a boat for Boston.

Stratton received his B.S. degree in electrical engineering in 1923. He studied French literature at the universities of Grenoble and Toulouse for a year and then returned to M.I.T. for graduate work in electrical engineering, obtaining his M.Sc. degree in 1925. From 1924 to 1926 he was an M.I.T. research associate in communications. Becoming more interested in the science underlying electrical engineering, Stratton went abroad again, this time to the Eidgenössische Technische Hochschule of Zurich, where he earned a D.Sc. degree in mathematical physics in 1927. He remained in Europe for another year on a traveling fellowship from M.I.T., studying principally at the universities of Munich and Leipzig.

Returning to M.I.T. in 1928, Stratton was appointed assistant professor of theory of electricity and magnetism in the department of electrical engineering. He moved to the department of physics in 1931 and advanced to associate professor of physics in 1935 and professor in 1941. He held the rank of professor until 1951, when he was made vice-president of M.I.T. In 1940 Dr. Stratton became one of the first members of M.I.T.'s newly established Radiation Laboratory. It was here that the major United States research for the development of radar was carried out. Detached from the laboratory in 1942 (although he remained a member until 1945), Stratton became expert consultant on radar in the office of the Secretary of War, where he organized a series of technical advisory committees to the Air Force on ground radar, radar fire control, and radar bombing. He also helped to establish a development program for aids to all-weather flying and made trips to Labrador, Greenland, North Africa, and Europe. For his wartime services he received the Medal for Merit from the Secretary of War.

Stratton's first major postwar task was to organize a successor to the wartime Radiation Laboratory. In 1946 the famed Research Laboratory of Electronics was established at M.I.T. with Stratton as its first director. There, co-operative effort among physicists, electrical engineers, and others provided a fruitful pattern for collaborative research that was later widely adopted and was instrumental in making M.I.T. what is perhaps the leading center of electronics and computor development in the United States. Stratton also served as chairman of the committee on electronics of the Research and Development Board from 1946 to 1948 and as both a member and chairman of the Naval Research and Advisory Committee.

In recognition of his work at M.I.T., in 1949 Stratton was appointed to the new office of provost. His responsibilities included the co-ordination of the programs of interdepartmental laboratories. While he was serving as vice-president and provost, in 1955, he headed a special seven-man committee of the National Academy of Sciences appointed at the request of President Eisenhower to consider reports that the government had withheld or cancelled research grants to scientists whose loyalty was in question. A year later, in April 1956, the committee recommended that questions about a scientist's loyalty should not exclude him from working on unclassified research grants. Scientists working on unclassified federal research should be judged on their "scientific integrity" alone, Stratton's committee found. In August of that year the White House announced that it would comply with the committee's report.

With his appointment in 1956 to the position of M.I.T. chancellor, Stratton became right-hand man to President Killian and administrator of the institute's entire academic program. He was named acting president in 1957 and president in 1959. Few academic institutions have undergone such dramatic changes as M.I.T. during the past two decades. Since Stratton's undergraduate days, it has evolved from a strictly technological school dedicated to turning out first-rate engineers to a leading research center for basic science as well. In 1923 M.I.T. spent some $2,000,000 on the education of its engineers; in 1958, while Stratton was acting president, it spent some $22,000,000 for operating costs and $56,000,000 on sponsored research projects. Central to the institute's present educational philosophy is the recognition of the importance of the humanities as well as science, and its courses range from politics to psychology, literature to interstellar space. No small part of the credit for this goes to Dr. Stratton, who raised the department of humanities and social science to the same standing as the institute's other professional schools.

Although Stratton believes in the need for a broad cultural knowledge on the part of a modern scientist or engineer, he is quick to stress the need a modern engineer has for more basic science, and he advocates "a higher level of achievement in mathematics, physics and chemistry." Education in science and engineering has now "gone critical," he says, but warns that although the fields of science and engineering are growing closer, "we could make no more disastrous error than to attempt to recreate the engineer in the image of a scientist," as Fred M. Hechinger quotes him in the New York *Times* (February 19, 1961).

To meet the challenge of providing technological leadership for the United States, under Stratton's guidance M.I.T. coupled the start of its 1961 centennial celebration with a "Second Century Fund" drive to raise $66,000,000 to be used on its curriculum, laboratory facilities, professorships, student scholarships, and buildings. (When the drive ended in May 1963 it was announced that $98,000,000 had been raised.) At the same time the institute is basically changing its internal structure by building five graduate centers where scientists and engineers in related fields will pool their skills in co-operative research. A $6,000,000 Center for Earth Sciences, for example, will bring together professors and graduate students in geology, geophysics,

JULIUS A. STRATTON

meterology, geochemistry and oceanography to study the problems of the earth. During Stratton's terms of provost, chancellor, and president, other outstanding changes have taken place at M.I.T. The School of Industrial Management, the School of Humanities and Social Science, and the Center for International Studies were founded, and the famed Lincoln Laboratory and Instrumental Laboratory were established in response to government needs for crucial research effort in special fields.

Stratton is the author of *Electromagnetic Theory* (McGraw-Hill, 1941), a widely used book in its field, and co-author of *Spheroidal Functions* (Wiley, 1956). As vice-president of the National Academy of Sciences, Stratton became in 1962 the chairman of a committee to study the relationship of engineers to the academy. He is a trustee and member of the executive committee of the Ford Foundation, the Committee for Economic Development, the Rand Corporation, and the Boston Museum of Fine Arts and a trustee of Vassar College and Pine Manor Junior College. He is also a trustee for the Carnegie Foundation for the Advancement of Teaching, the Pacific Science Center Foundation, and the WGBH Educational Foundation; a Fellow of the National Academy of Sciences, the American Philosophical Society, the American Physics Society, and the American Institute of Radio Engineers; and a member of the National Science Board, the Corporation of Educational Services, Inc., and the Woods Hole Oceanographic Institute.

Many colleges and universities have conferred honorary doctorates on Stratton, including Harvard, Brandeis, Notre Dame, and Johns Hopkins. He was made an officer of the French Legion of Honor in 1961 and received the Certificate of Award from the United States Navy in 1957, the Medal of Honor of the Institute of Radio Engineers, and the Faraday Medal of the British Institute of Electrical Engineers in 1961 for his contribution to technological education and re-

STRATTON, JULIUS A.—*Continued*

search in radio communication. His clubs include St. Botolph Club (Boston), the Century Association (New York), and the University clubs of New York and Boston. He is a member of Tau Beta Pi, Sigma Xi, and Zeta Psi.

Julius A. Stratton married Catherine N. Coffman of Ivy, Virginia on June 14, 1935. They have three daughters, Catherine Nelson, Ann Cary, and Laura Adams. The Strattons own a farm in Newfane, Vermont where they spend their holidays. A humanist as well as a scientist, Dr. Stratton enjoys reading French and German history in the original. He has traveled widely; as a young teacher he made a vacation trip by boat down the Yukon River and went on an expedition among the headhunting Jivaros in the jungle at the headwaters of the Amazon River. During January and February of 1963 he and his wife made a five-week trip to Africa and India on behalf of the Ford Foundation to observe some of the foundation's activities abroad. A somewhat reserved man, Stratton dresses conservatively and, according to *Time* (December 15, 1958), "has become known for a quiet manner" and his "earnest efforts to resolve clashing points of view, and for a broad understanding of how to bridge the shifting boundaries between scientific disciplines."

References

Time 72:49 D 15 '58 por; 73:66 Je 29 '59 por; 77:58 Ap 7 '61
Who's Who in America, 1962-63
American Men of Science 10th ed (1960-62)

STRUVE, OTTO Aug. 12, 1897-Apr. 6, 1963
Astronomer who specialized in stellar spectroscopy and the study of double stars; university professor; directed a number of observatories since 1932, including the Leuschner Observatory of the University of California (1950-59) and the National Radio Astronomy Observatory (1959-63). See *Current Biography* (October) 1949.

Obituary

N Y Times p31 Ap 9 '63

SUBANDRIO (sū'băn-drē"ō) Sept. 15, 1914-
Foreign Minister of the Republic of Indonesia

Address: b. Ministry of Foreign Affairs, Djakarta, Indonesia

When the Netherlands and Indonesia signed a United Nations agreement in August 1962 transferring West New Guinea to Indonesian sovereignty, Dr. Subandrio, the Indonesian Foreign Minister, declared that his nation's "struggle for independence" was finally completed. The pact capped a long, hard battle by the energetic former surgeon, who was one of the principal architects of the campaign that gained for his country the last part of the former Dutch East Indies retained by the Netherlands after Indonesia won unconditional independence in 1949.

Dr. Subandrio, who was appointed Foreign Minister by President Sukarno in April 1957, has always given the impression that while he is a firm believer in his country's independent foreign policy, he has not overlooked the value of neutralism in the cold war. And he has accepted military and economic aid both from the East and West. Regarded by admirers and critics alike as Indonesia's most able Foreign Minister since the island country proclaimed its independence in August 1945, Dr. Subandrio has been called a "smooth spokesman" for President Sukarno's policy of "guided democracy." In November 1963 Sukarno appointed himself to the additional position of Premier and named Subandrio the first of three Deputy Premiers.

Like many other Indonesians, Subandrio has only a single name. He was born on September 15, 1914 in Kepandjen, East Java and was a "Raden" by birth, a title denoting a Javanese aristocrat. As a student, Subandrio was active in the nationalist youth movement. He attended the Medical College in Jakarta and in 1941 graduated as a surgeon. He joined the staff of the Jakarta Central Hospital, but because of his activity in the anti-Japanese underground, Dr. Subandrio was forced to leave the hospital when the Japanese occupied the island during World War II, in 1942. From 1942 to 1945 he ran a private clinic in the city of Semarang.

On August 17, 1945, after the surrender of the Japanese, Indonesian nationalists under the leadership of Sukarno proclaimed the country's independence from Dutch rule. Dr. Subandrio immediately gave up his private practice and organized an information unit in Central Java. He served as head of the Central Java division of the Ministry of Information until the following year when he was appointed secretary general of the Indonesian Ministry of Information.

On his first diplomatic assignment Dr. Subandrio went to Europe in 1947 as a special envoy of the Indonesian government to try to rally world opinion in support of his country's fight for freedom against Dutch rule. He set up an information office in London, where he was the Indonesian representative to Great Britain. On December 27, 1949, while Dr. Subandrio was still serving as chargé d'affaires in London, Indonesia won its full sovereignty. He was named his country's first Ambassador to the Court of St. James the following March.

After four more years in London, as Ambassador to Great Britain, in 1954 Subandrio was named Indonesia's first Ambassador to the Soviet Union. He remained in Moscow until 1956 when he was summoned back to Jakarta and named secretary general of the Indonesian Ministry of Foreign Affairs. In April 1957 he was appointed Minister of Foreign Affairs in the cabinet of Premier Djuanda.

As Foreign Minister, Dr. Subandrio was a leading figure in Indonesia's bitter struggle for West New Guinea. The Indonesians claimed that West New Guinea (West Irian) was part of the old Netherlands East Indies and should have been turned over to them by the Dutch. The Dutch, however, contended that the natives of West New Guinea, the Papuans, were of a different race from the Indonesians and had no desire to become part of Indonesia.

In October 1957 Foreign Minister Subandrio asked the United Nations General Assembly to open new Dutch-Indonesian negotiations to settle the West New Guinea dispute. He warned that Indonesia would use force to take the territory from the Netherlands if the appeal to the General Assembly proved unsuccessful. In November the U.N. defeated a resolution calling for renewed negotiations, and less than a week later the Indonesian government adopted sweeping new measures against Dutch nationals. The measures included the seizure of Dutch-owned warehouses, shipping lines, shuttle railways, and other Dutch enterprises. The government also announced that it planned to deport the majority of the 46,000 Dutch nationals.

While the anti-Dutch campaign continued, Dr. Subandrio denied press reports that the Communists were playing a major part in the seizure of Dutch properties. (The Communist party in Indonesia is the largest in Asia outside of China.) "I want to stress that I do not want Indonesia to become Communist," he said in December 1957, and he warned, "If no indication is forthcoming from the Netherlands showing willingness to come to terms in the way of negotiations, the Indonesian government will be forced to implement its policy without reservations."

Early in 1958 dissident groups on Sumatra and outlying islands openly rebelled against the central government, protesting "Javanese domination." Sumatra, for example, provided the government with more than half its revenues, but the Sumatran rebels charged that most of the money was used for development of Java. The insurgents also hit at President Sukarno's "guided democracy" government, maintaining that under it the Communists were seizing more and more power. Relations between the governments of the United States and Indonesia became strained during the revolt when Indonesia accused the United States of having connived at providing material aid to the rebels while professing a policy of nonintervention.

Relations between the two countries took a decided turn for the better after the United States agreed in mid-August 1958 to sell light arms and other equipment to Sukarno's government. In a speech before the American Association of Indonesia in Jakarta, Dr. Subandrio said: "We hope this will mark the beginning of better appreciation and more confidence in each other. Delivery of arms to Indonesia is an important fact in itself, but on the other hand, the political evaluation which led to the new transaction is of more importance for future relationship between our two countries." The Indonesian Foreign Minister had earlier praised Secretary of State John Foster Dulles for saying that the Indonesian revolution should be dealt with "without intrusion from without." On December 7, after talks with Dulles in Washington, Dr. Subandrio announced that he had been able to eliminate all misunderstandings between the United States and Indonesia.

Further evidence that the United States was altering its position toward Sukarno came in February 1959 with the announcement of another and larger arms deal with Indonesia. United States officials explained that the government had found leading members of the Indonesian regime increasingly wary of Communism and of Soviet influence. On July 8, 1959 President Sukarno

Wide World

DR. SUBANDRIO

announced the formation of a new ten-man "inner" cabinet, led by himself as Premier and including Dr. Subandrio as Minister of Foreign Affairs. Communists were excluded from the new cabinet.

Later in the year Indonesia took a tougher stand against Communist China by curbing the travel of Chinese Communist diplomats because of their "meddling" in Indonesia's internal affairs. Red Chinese diplomats, according to official charges, had been roaming the West Java countryside and inciting alien Chinese against Indonesian regulations that had been enforced to break the Chinese control of the rural economy. Dr. Subandrio accused the Chinese of "capturing power in the Indonesian people's economic life" by practices that included disregard of justice and humanitarian principles.

Indonesia stepped up its drive to weaken the Chinese stranglehold on its rural economy on January 1, 1960, when it banned all aliens from engaging in retail trade in rural areas—a move that affected about 300,000 Chinese. After a meeting with the Chinese Communist Ambassador to Indonesia, Huang Chen, Dr. Subandrio told newsmen that he had warned the Chinese envoy that Indonesia had some "concern" about Communist China's "inclinations" toward Indonesia and that his country wanted to be friends with all countries, but not at the expense of its national interests and self-respect.

That Indonesia was still very much a neutralist nation, however, was manifested in early 1960. The United States Export-Import Bank announced loans totaling $47,500,000 to the southeast Asia country on January 28. On February 28 Soviet Premier Nikita S. Khrushchev signed an agreement for Soviet credit of $250,000,000 to Indonesia.

In its struggle with the Netherlands, meanwhile, for possession of West New Guinea, Indonesia had gained little headway, and in August 1960 the two countries severed diplomatic rela-

SUBANDRIO—*Continued*

tions. Foreign Minister Subandrio told a meeting of Jakarta university students in January 1962, "If the Dutch want war over West Irian, we will accommodate them." Negotiations over West New Guinea continued, however, and with the help of the United States diplomat Ellsworth Bunker, an agreement was reached early in July 1962 between Dr. Subandrio and Jan Herman van Roijen, the Ambassador of the Netherlands. On August 15, 1962 the thirteen-year dispute was settled in the United Nations Security Council when Dr. Subandrio and Ambassador Roijen signed an accord on the future transfer of West New Guinea to Indonesia. The agreement called for the temporary administration of the territory by the United Nations beginning October 1, 1962. Indonesia took over full administration of West New Guinea (West Irian) on May 1, 1963.

According to a biographical sketch in the New York *Times* (December 30, 1961), Dr. Subandrio is regarded as a voluble statesman who would much prefer to make a 500-word speech than reply "no comment" to a ticklish question. His diplomatic achievements—which included signing an amity pact with Red China a year after the two countries had almost broken off diplomatic relations—caused one diplomat to describe him as "one of the greatest flying trapeze artists of his time."

Dr. Subandrio's wife, Hurustiati, whom he married in 1940, is also a medical doctor. They have one son, Budoyo. Dr. Subandrio is a Moslem and speaks several languages, including English, Dutch, and Russian. The bespectacled, black-haired statesman is of slight build. He has a quick sense of humor and is widely read. For relaxation he enjoys tennis and dancing.

References

N Y Times p5 D 30 '61 por
Asia Who's Who (1960)
International Who's Who, 1962-63
International Year Book and Statesmen's Who's Who, 1963

SUMMERSKILL, EDITH (CLARA), BARONESS SUMMERSKILL Apr. 19, 1901- British politician; physician

Address: b. House of Lords, London, S.W.1, England; h. Pond House, Millfield Lane, Highgate, London, N.6, England

NOTE: This biography supersedes the article that appeared in *Current Biography* in 1943.

An ardent feminist, Edith Summerskill "has a record that might deliberately have been conceived to answer any male advocate of the notion that women are the weaker sex." She became a physician at twenty-three and a Member of Parliament at thirty-seven, and she served as a Minister of the Crown in the two postwar Labour governments and then as chief spokesman for the Opposition on matters of health. Her uncompromising campaigns for equality for women, for the abolition of professional boxing, and for a host of frequently unpopular social reforms have made her public

life one of ceaseless controversy. In 1961 she received a life peerage, enabling her to carry her crusading zeal into the House of Lords as Baroness Summerskill of Ken Wood.

Edith Clara Summerskill was born in London on April 19, 1901, to William and Edith Summerskill. Her father was a physician and a radical who had once stood for Parliament as an Independent. As a girl, Edith Summerskill often accompanied her father when he visited his patients, inheriting from him her choice of a career and the belief, as a Manchester *Guardian* writer put it (January 17, 1961), that "the diagnostic approach is not enough. The good physician must go on, with compassion and practicality, to assault the causes of disease on whatever battleground they were to be found."

Edith Summerskill attended King's College, London, and in 1918—at a time when only 4 percent of British physicians were women—went as a medical student to Charing Cross Hospital, also in London. In 1924 she emerged as a qualified physician—a member of the Royal College of Surgeons and a licentiate of the Royal College of Physicians. A year later she married Dr. E. Jeffrey Samuel, who had been a student with her at the Charing Cross Hospital, and for some years they practised medicine together.

Confronted on her daily rounds by the afflictions of London's poor—rickets caused by malnutrition, tuberculosis by dirty milk, high maternal mortality by a general disregard for hygiene—Dr. Summerskill became more and more frustrated. She and her husband joined the small group of doctors who, in the early days of the Socialist Medical Association, were already planning a free and comprehensive national health service.

The association, which she served for many years as vice-president, was at that time small and without influence. The power to reform rested, she realized, not with doctors but with politicians. In 1931 she took her first step into public life, entering local politics by the back door as a co-opted (non-elective) member of the maternity and child welfare committee in Wood Green, London. Three years later she ran for elective office in the Middlesex County Council election, standing as Labour candidate for the Green Lanes division of Tottenham. Although the ward was regarded as a safe Conservative seat, Dr. Summerskill won and remained a member of the Middlesex County Council until the pressure of other work forced her to resign in 1941.

Also in 1934 Dr. Summerskill made her first attempt to enter national politics, standing as Parliamentary candidate for the London constituency of Putney, another Conservative stronghold. She lost the election, but reduced the Conservative majority from 22,000 to 2,500. A second attempt, at Bury, Lancashire in the 1935 general elections, was also unsuccessful. Undaunted, Dr. Summerskill ran again in the 1938 by-election for West Fulham, London, and won the seat from the Conservatives. She was Member of Parliament for West Fulham from 1938 to 1955, when the constituency was swallowed up in the redrawing of Parliamentary boundaries. In that year she was returned to Parliament from the Lancashire borough of Warrington, whose representative she remained until her elevation to the House of Lords in 1961.

When she took her seat in the House of Commons in 1938, Dr. Summerskill became, as she put it, "the personification of what were once outrageous ideas—a woman doctor and a woman M.P." She continued to practise medicine, although she was by then the mother of two 'children and a world traveler. In 1931 she had visited Russia to examine public health conditions there. She went to Spain during the civil war at the invitation of the Spanish Government to study the condition of refugees, and in 1938 she lectured on the subject in the United States. Shortly before World War II she inspected maternity and child welfare services in Italy, again by governmental invitation.

When World War II began in 1939, Dr. Summerskill found new responsibilities and a new cause for which to fight. She served on the women's consultative committee set up to advise the government on the wartime employment of women, on the select committee that inquired into the conditions of women in the services, and on the select committee on equal compensation for civilian war injuries. Believing that women should share male responsibilities as well as mole rights, she campaigned indefatigably for their admission to the country's Home Guard. She founded the Women's Home Defence Movement, which taught women to use weapons against a potential invader, and demonstrated her own proficiency by scoring seven bull's-eyes out of ten on the House of Commons rifle range. The Home Guard began to enroll women in April 1943.

When the Labour government came to power in July 1945, Dr. Summerskill was immediately given junior ministerial rank as Parliamentary Secretary to the Ministry of Food. It was only then that she relinquished her regular medical practice. In 1948 she saw the introduction of Britain's National Health Service, for which she had fought long and hard. Another high point of her five years at the Ministry of Food was the passing of the 1949 Milk (Special Designations) Act—the so-called Clean Milk Bill, which she had helped to frame and which she introduced in the House of Commons. In 1949 Dr. Summerskill was made a member of the Privy Council.

She broke new ground again, and even more spectacularly, in 1950, when she became Minister of National Insurance, the third woman and the first married one to become a member of the British cabinet. Typically, she expressed her approach to the appointment by saying: "I want to be a Minister of Human Relations." Her tenure lasted only until 1951, when the Labour government fell, and was especially notable for the pioneering work she did on legislation entitling workers to compensation for industrial injury and diseases. With the Labour party out of office, Dr. Summerskill became Opposition spokesman on matters of health, applying herself, in the words of a New York Times profile (January 17, 1961), "against anyone, either Labor friend or Tory foe, who stood in the way of what she believed was in the

Wide World
DR. EDITH SUMMERSKILL

best interests of Britain, the Labor party and women."

During her years in Parliament, Dr. Summerskill has fought many battles on diverse issues. In the public mind, however, she is probably most closely associated with the struggle for equal rights and a secure financial status for women. "I like men very much," she has said, "but . . . I want women to get a square deal." She has served as president of the Married Women's Association, a kind of trade union for wives, and has sought legislation which would give married women a legal right to a fair share of the family income.

Her first book was Babies Without Tears (Hutchinson, 1941), dealing with another issue on which she has campaigned tirelessly—the right of women to painless childbirth. It is largely owing to her efforts that anesthesia for childbirth is now available to all British women. So far Dr. Summerskill has had less success with her crusade to abolish professional boxing. This she has made the subject of bills in both Houses of Parliament and of a book, her second, called The Ignoble Art (Heinemann; British Book Service, 1956). It emphasized the brutalizing effects of the sport on participants and audiences and the physical damage sustained by professional boxers. Her bill would impose a penalty of up to 200 pounds or three months' imprisonment for organizing a boxing match for profit. It failed hopelessly in the House of Commons but came within six votes of negotiating its second reading in the House of Lords on May 10, 1962, following the deaths of several professional fighters from brain injuries received in the ring.

A third book, Letters To My Daughter (Heinemann; British Book Service) followed in 1957. These affectionate and revealing letters, spanning the years from 1944 to 1956, were written to Dr. Summerskill's daughter, Shirley, when she was a schoolgirl, an Oxford undergraduate,

SUMMERSKILL, EDITH—*Continued*

and a medical student. The author's sincerity and simplicity come through very clearly, as do her views on many subjects. Some readers were troubled by the book's unusually frank discussion of sexual problems. Dr. Summerskill has frequently spoken on radio and television and has written many magazine articles, pamphlets, and reports.

On January 16, 1961 Edith Summerskill became Baroness Summerskill of Ken Wood, one of six life peers named at that time in a move to strengthen Labour representation in the House of Lords. She became the sixth woman to sit in the British Parliament's upper house since women were first admitted there in 1959. "Of course I shall continue to be an active parliamentarian," Lady Summerskill promised. "The House of Lords . . . is just another part of Parliament. I am the same person as I was yesterday, with the same convictions, the same ideals, and I shall fight just as actively for them."

She has been as good as her word. Although new peers traditionally speak on noncontroversial topics for the first time, her maiden speech attacked increased National Health Service charges and the American drug companies, which she said were making huge profits out of the Service. She has since demonstrated all her old fire on such varied topics as boxing, oral contraceptives, the thalidomide tragedy, and the attendance records of other members of the House of Lords.

Lady Summerskill is a former member of the Labour party's National Executive Committee, and was its chairman in 1954-55. She is much interested in foreign affairs, and not even World War II could keep her at home. In 1944 she toured the United States, Australia, New Zealand, Ceylon, India, and Egypt, traveling under conditions of extreme discomfort and some danger. She has made a special study of the Middle East, visiting that region many times. Among her more important journeys abroad were her 1946 trip to Washington as leader of Britain's delegation to the U.N. Food and Agriculture Organization conference; her 1953 journey to Strasbourg as a British representative to the Council of Europe's consultative assembly; and her trip to China in 1954 as a member of a Labour party delegation that included Clement Attlee and Aneurin Bevan.

Lady Summerskill was married to Dr. E. Jeffrey Samuel on August 7, 1925. They have two children, Michael, a barrister, and Shirley, a physician, who have inherited their mother's fierce individualism and who have elected to use her maiden name, as she has continued to do. "People who think of [Edith Summerskill] only as a relentless public figure are far wide of the truth," a Manchester *Guardian* profile writer (January 17, 1961) noted. She and her husband "have established a deeply happy, relaxed and successful relationship." She has said that if she had to choose between her career and her home life she would unhesitatingly sacrifice the former.

Lady Summerskill has gray eyes and auburn hair, now touched with gray. She is slender, straight-backed, and nearly five feet ten inches tall. The *Guardian* profile describes her as "a woman of the greatest possible personal kindness" but one who "will pursue, with understanding, but without pity, those who oppose her on every issue she believes important." There are many such issues, and her sometimes humorless determination to set the world right whether it likes it or not is irritating to many. But Lady Summerskill continues to follow what the *Guardian* profile calls "her straight, dedicated path, contemptuous of compromise, apparently, but not always in reality, invulnerable to criticism." In *Letters To My Daughter*, Edith Summerskill wrote: "To be happy in politics, you must possess your own soul." Norman Shrapnel commented in the *Guardian* of March 21, 1960, "She does, so perhaps she is."

References

> Manchester Guardian p6 Mr 21 '60 por; p7 Ja 17 '61
> N Y Times p2 Ja 17 '61 por
> Washington (D.C.) Post p18 Ap 27 '61
> Burke's Peerage, Baronetage, and Knightage, 1963
> International Who's Who, 1962-63
> International Year Book and Statesmen's Who's Who, 1963
> Summerskill, Edith. Letters To My Daughter (1957)
> Who's Who, 1963

SWALLOW, ALAN Feb. 11, 1915- Publisher; teacher; editor; author

Address: 2679 S. York St., Denver 10, Colo.

The founder, owner, and sole employee since 1940 of the small publishing firm that bears his name, Alan Swallow is dedicated to issuing "works of quality which do not have a chance to make their way in commercial publishing." Under the imprint of Alan Swallow, Publisher, he brings out poetry, fiction, and literary criticism and bibliography; under the imprint of Sage Books he publishes books about the American West. A teacher of English at Western universities from 1940 to 1954, he left the academic world in 1954 to continue his publishing activities full time. He has written several books of poetry, and he has edited a number of little magazines, which, he feels, perform the same function in the magazine field as the "little publisher" does in book publishing.

Alan Swallow was born on February 11, 1915 in Powell, Wyoming to Edgar Austin Swallow, a farmer, and Alta Helen (Myers) Swallow. His sister Vera Helen (Swallow) Cowel lives in Fort Collins, Colorado. His other sister, Virginia Grace (Swallow) Robinson, died in 1945. At the Powell High School, from which he graduated in 1932, Swallow played football, belonged to the debating team, and worked for the student newspaper. When he had completed his secondary schooling he enrolled at the University of Wyoming at Laramie, where he majored in English and won the president's book for outstanding work in English, philosophy, and sociology. He was a member of the debating team for three years and won several contests. After his graduation with the B.A. degree in 1937, when a

Phi Beta Kappa chapter had been established at the university, he was elected to the honorary society as an alumnus.

Swallow began writing poetry and prose in his teens. In college he was news editor and columnist for the student newspaper, the editor of a student literary magazine, and the editor of the Wyoming *Quill*, the writing society publication. He also founded his own little literary magazine, *Sage,* after which he later named one of his publishing enterprises, Sage Books. "As graduation approached," Swallow has recalled, "I was still not clear how to make a go of things with my interest in writing, and so I applied for scholarships. Eventually I landed at Louisiana State University with Robert Penn Warren and Cleanth Brooks."

Holding a reading fellowship for one year and a teaching fellowship for two years, Swallow studied English at Louisiana State University from 1937 to 1940. He received his M.A. degree in 1939, after writing the thesis "Method of Composition in the Poems of Sir Thomas Wyatt" and his Ph.D. degree in 1941, after submitting the dissertation "Method of Poetic Composition in Early English Renaissance, Skelton to Sidney." At Louisiana State Swallow was elected to the honorary society Phi Kappa Phi. He began his publishing activities on a part-time basis during his last year of graduate study at Louisiana State, in 1939-40. He felt that much of the work of the young writers studying under Warren and Brooks merited publication, and he began to print it on a hand press with handset type. The first book was called *Signets: An Anthology of Beginnings.*

The only fiction by Swallow that was published in his post-college years was *Two Stories* (Swallow Pamphlets, 1953), but he has written several books of poetry: *XI Poems* (Prairie Press, 1943); *The Remembered Land* (Decker Press, 1946); *The War Poems of Allan Swallow* (Fine Editions Press, 1948); and *The Nameless Sight: Poems 1937-56* (Prairie Press, 1956). Swallow could not earn a living as a poet, however, and he began to teach in 1940. For two years he was an instructor of English at the University of New Mexico, teaching composition, literature, debate, and journalism. He was an associate professor of English at Western State College in Gunnison, Colorado from 1942 to 1943 and then entered the United States Army as a private. After two years of administrative and educational work in the medical corps he was released in 1945 with the rank of technical sergeant.

From 1946 to 1948 Swallow was an assistant professor of English at the University of Denver and from 1948 to 1954 he was an associate professor of English there. In addition to teaching literature and composition courses, he directed the writing program, one of the few in the United States that grants M.A. and Ph.D. degrees in creative writing. From 1947 to 1954 he also directed the University of Denver Press. In 1947 Swallow received a postwar creative writing fellowship from the Rockefeller Foundation. During the 1940's he somehow found enough free time to edit ten anthologies of verse and modern fiction.

From 1941 to 1942 Swallow published and edited the magazine *Modern Verse.* He was

ALAN SWALLOW

poetry editor of the *New Mexico Quarterly* from 1942 to 1948 and editor of *Author & Journalist* from 1951 to 1953. Since 1954 he has edited and published *PS* (poems and stories), and since 1955 he has been managing editor of *Twentieth Century Literature.* His handbook for writers, *The Beginning Writer,* was published by Johnson Publishing Company in 1954.

Swallow has long been connected with literary quarterlies and little magazines, both as associate editor and as a member of editorial boards. Since 1949 he has published the *Index to Little Magazines.* Little magazines, in his opinion, perform an important corrective and supplementary function, since they serve as forums for poetry and new and experimental writing seldom published in mass magazines.

The function of the "little publisher," according to Swallow, is analogous to that of the little magazine. He has been a "little publisher" for more than twenty years, whose firm has become one of the best known of its kind. From 1940 to 1954 he published on a part-time basis, and in 1954, the first year in which his business yielded enough profit, he left teaching and engaged in publishing on a full-time basis.

Swallow has published continuously under his major imprint, Alan Swallow, Publisher, since 1940, except for a brief period of six months in 1942 when the firm was known as Swallow and Critchlow. (Swallow and Critchlow published his book *The Practice of Poetry.*) In an essay, "The Problems of Publishing Poetry," written in 1957 and reprinted in Swallow's *An Editor's Essays of Two Decades* (Experiment Press, 1962), Swallow reveals the method by which he has been able to reduce the financial burden of publishing poetry (and other new work) for which there is a limited demand: "To substitute work for money. This has been the method by which I have continued to publish poetry. . . . My original premise was that if I could reduce the out-of-pocket expenses to payment for materials and work which

SWALLOW, ALAN—*Continued*

I could not perform, I could sell enough copies to pay that out-of-pocket expense and a royalty to the author. This has worked fairly consistently. I taught myself to print . . . thus reducing costs to paper, postage, and, usually, binding. As I have continued in the work and my "list" has become more and more established as a serious and significant list of verse, the sales have increased enough so that now I purchase composition."

The Alan Swallow list contains titles in poetry, literary criticism and bibliography, and fiction. On it are several books by the poet and critic Yvor Winters, whose merits Swallow was early to appreciate, and poetry collections by J. V. Cunningham, Thomas McGrath, Edgar Bowers, and Alan Stephens, all of whom Swallow considers among the best modern poets. Many more poets are published in Swallow's Key Poets and New Poetry series. In the category of fiction Swallow has published, along with others, novels by several Western writers at odds with current intellectual fashions. In an essay, "The Mavericks," written in 1959 and published in *An Editor's Essays of Two Decades*, Swallow voices his confidence in the talent of these novelists, who are generally ignored by publishers and reviewers. He mentions Janet Lewis, Vardis Fisher, Frank Waters, Frederick Manfred, and Edward Loomis. He has also published *The Fathers*, a novel, *Poems*, and *Collected Essays* by Allen Tate, several books by Anaïs Nin, and inexpensive offset editions of English Renaissance poets.

A subsidiary imprint of Alan Swallow is Sage Books, which offers nonfiction, fiction, and poetry about the American West. Some representative Sage Books titles are *Red Wind of Wyoming* (poems); *Manual of the Plants of Colorado; Calamity Was the Name for Jane; Ghost Trails to Ghost Towns; The Law Goes West; Silver, Gold and Black Iron; Chuck Wagon Cookbook;* and *The Buffalo Harvest.* From 1947 to 1953 Swallow owned Sage Books with a partner, Horace Critchlow, but in 1953 the corporation was dissolved, and Sage Books became a subsidiary imprint of Alan Swallow. Sage Books is planning a new venture, the Rio Grande Press, Inc., which will reissue out-of-print and scarce nonfiction classics of the Southwest. In the fall of 1959 Swallow entered the quality paperback field with Swallow Paperbooks. He also publishes Western Sage Paperbooks. From 1947 to 1951 about twenty-one titles were published under the joint imprint of Swallow Press and William Morrow and Company, including *Anchor in the Sea: An Anthology of Psychological Fiction* (1947) and *Some Poems of Sir Thomas Wyatt* (1949), both edited by Swallow. (The Swallow-Morrow titles were later incorporated into the Swallow list.)

Swallow, who publishes about thirty titles a year (including some eight volumes of new verse), edits, designs, packages, addresses, and ships the books himself from his house and garage in Denver. He has approximately 300 titles in print, and he ships out some 70,000 books a year, divided about equally between the Sage and Swallow imprints. He is also the distributor for Bancroft Pamphlets and for Experiment Press

books. The Experiment Press is the book publishing outlet for a poets' co-operative, Experiment Group, which was formed in the 1940's as the result of a letter of invitation sent to a number of experimental poets by Swallow and Meade Harwell.

Writing in *An Editor's Essays of Two Decades* of the contributions made to publishing by the "small, dedicated publisher," Swallow said, "There is one great virtue in it: in the estimation of new work, the matter of critical judgment becomes paramount. The difficulty with commercial publishing is that the judgment can be blunted by many factors, including notions of the possible economic picture for the book. . . . The 'little publisher' . . . can assert his taste and judgment. He need not compromise so much. And although no one taste can do the whole job . . . if his taste is strong, he will bring to light some excellent work. Some excellent work missed by him may be brought to light by another 'little publisher' of different taste and judgment. Hence the correctives to an inadequate 'commerce' of publishing lie in the supplements to commercial publishing methods."

Swallow belongs to the Colorado Authors League, of which he was president in 1958-59, the Denver Westerners, the American Civil Liberties Union, and the Western Writers of America. He is a Democrat. Since June 20, 1936 he has been married to the former Mae Elder. They have one daughter, Ida Karen. Five feet ten inches tall and weighing 180 pounds, Swallow has gray eyes and gray hair. A sports car fan, he also likes to watch baseball games and horse races. When Swallow left his teaching post at the University of Denver in 1954 the future of his full-time publishing venture looked uncertain. "Frankly, even in those days I figured I would be begging for a teaching job in a couple of years," he has recalled (*Saturday Review,* July 22, 1961). "So now I feel I'm one of the world's luckiest guys, to be concentrating so single-mindedly, working so many hours, on something I want so much to see done—and have a modest living out of it! I tell you the whole business continues to look promising as my interest in really good books continues to grow."

References

N Y Times Bk R p8 Jl 16 '61
Sat R 44:33+ Jl 22 '61 por
Who's Who in the West (1962)

TAMM, IGOR (EVGENYEVICH) July 8, 1895- Physicist

Address: b. Academy of Sciences of the U.S.S.R., Lenin Prospekt, Moscow, U.S.S.R.

A leading Soviet scientist, Dr. Igor Tamm has been in the vanguard of his country's nuclear physics program as a researcher and teacher for more than thirty years. In 1958 he shared a Nobel Prize in Physics with his colleagues Pavel A. Cherenkov and Ilya M. Frank. His international reputation is based mainly on the theory of the radiation of an electron moving in a medium with a velocity higher than that of light in that same medium, known technically as the "Cherenkov effect." Essentially his work has been directed at uniting the Einstein theory of relativity, sometimes regarded in Soviet Russia as anti-Marxist idealism, with quantum mechanics. He has made significant contributions to problems dealing with the quantum theory of solids, the beta theory of nuclear forces, the theory of elementary particles, and controlled thermonuclear fusion. Tamm's position as a leading scientist within the Soviet Union and his international prestige have won for him a greater amount of freedom to criticize the government than is generally accorded most Soviet scientists. As a teacher he has urged such reforms in scientific training as the elimination of work programs.

Igor Evgenyevich Tamm, the son of Eugen Tamm, a civil engineer, and his wife, the former Olga Davydova, was born on July 8, 1895 in Vladivostok. When he was four years old his family moved to the Ukraine and settled in Kirovograd (then called Elisavetgrad). He attended Russian schools through the Gymnasium before he matriculated in 1913 at the University of Edinburgh in Scotland. (The practice of enrolling in foreign universities was not uncommon in pre-Revolutionary Russia.) In the summer of 1914 Tamm's studies were interrupted by the outbreak of war in Europe, and he returned to Russia.

In spite of Russian military defeats in Eastern Europe and the subsequent political crises in Russia, Tamm managed to complete his university education. In 1918 he received his Ph.D. degree in physics and obtained a faculty position at Crimean University in Simferopol. From 1920 to 1922 he taught at the Odessa Polytechnic Institute and then went to Moscow to work as a senior engineer at Glav-electro. At this time Tamm was also associated with several universities simultaneously. He taught at the Sverdlov Communist University from 1922 to 1925 and was in the theoretical physics department of the Second Moscow University as an assistant professor (1923-27) and professor (1927-29). In 1924 he joined the faculty of the University of Moscow, where he received a full professorship, and in 1930 he was appointed head of the physics department. In late 1941, because units of the German Army were approaching the environs of Moscow, the university was relocated, and Tamm temporarily relinquished his duties with the institution.

As a teacher Dr. Tamm helped to expand the simple laboratory facilities at the University of Moscow into a large-scale research center and to improve the quality of physics instruction throughout Russia. He revised course materials to make room for the teaching of quantum mechanics and Einstein's theory of relativity. As a research scientist he concentrated on experiments involving the basic problems of theoretical physics, such as the theory of elementary particles and the quantized field theory and its applications.

In 1930 Dr. Tamm formulated a quantum theory that explained acoustical vibrations and the scattering of light in solid bodies. For the next two years he worked on a theory of light diffusion by free electrons based on the Dirac electron formula. During 1932 and 1933 Tamm

Novosti Press Agency

IGOR TAMM

examined some of the problems and discrepancies in the quantum theory of solids and became aware of the existence of surface electronic states in semiconductor metals. His scientific explanation indicating the possibility of electrons tightly bound into states on the surface of a laboratory sample became known as "Tamm's levels." It had a direct bearing on the development of transistor electronics in the Soviet Union.

In 1934, while Igor Tamm was serving as chairman of the theoretical department of the Lebedev Physics Institute of the Soviet Academy of Sciences, he became involved in a project conducted by Pavel A. Cherenkov, who was working closely with Tamm's former teacher, the Academician Sergei I. Vavilov. In the laboratory Cherenkov had observed that an extremely faint but constant blue light was emitted by water and other transparent substances when exposed to gamma radiation from radioactive substances. Further experiments by Cherenkov proved that the light was not simply conventional luminescence. The blue glow was strongly polarized, had a rainbow-like spectrum, and was generally given off in the direction of gamma ray beams. Cherenkov, however, was unable to find a satisfactory explanation of the eerie illumination.

In spite of Cherenkov's unsuccessful attempts to resolve the mystery of the blue glow, Tamm and his laboratory assistant, Ilya M. Frank, had by 1937 theoretically substantiated the radiation effect as observed by Cherenkov. They based their explanation on a classical electromagnetic interpretation that a charged particle traveling through a medium with a velocity greater than the phase velocity of light in the medium gives out an electromagnetic shock-wave effect. The emission of the Cherenkov radiation is the electronic analogue of the sonar boom made by airplanes moving faster than the speed of sound in air. A functional application for the Cherenkov radiation phenomenon was a device devel-

TAMM, IGOR—*Continued*

oped by scientists in the United States and Great Britain. Known as the Cherenkov counter, the device is made of a dielectric such as glass, water, or clear plastic, which permits charged particles to enter it at a speed greater than the speed of light within the material. The counter has proved useful in detecting individual charged particles of very high energy that exist for only a split second. This device facilitated the discovery of antiprotons at the University of California and has been employed in *Sputnik III* in studying cosmic rays within space for such antimatter.

In the late 1940's Tamm concentrated on the fundamental problems inherent in the theory of elementary particles and, as a result, established the Tamm-Dancoff method. This is a technique for approximating the wave function of a system of interacting particles, especially nucleons and mesons, by describing it as a superposition of a certain number of possible states. In 1950 Tamm conducted experiments with A. D. Sakharov that suggested the use of electrical charges in ionized gases as a means of acquiring controlled thermonuclear power.

With the publication in 1934 of two scientific treatises entitled *Neutron Magnetic Moment* and *Exchange Forces Between Neutrons and Protons,* Dr. Tamm gained a reputation as one of the foremost physicists in the Soviet Union. In the same year he announced the formulation of the beta theory of nuclear forces that held that each force field must have its own field quanta, just as every electromagnetic field has its photons, or quanta of light energy. Tamm reasoned that nuclear forces should have their own field quanta, though he was unable to explain the actual nuclear forces with the then known elementary particles. However, a year later a Japanese physicist, Hideki Yukawa, used Tamm's calculations to predict the existence of other elementary particles called mesons. The project earned Yukawa the Nobel Prize in 1949 and established Tamm's hypothesis as scientifically valid.

In addition to the two volumes listed, Dr. Tamm has published a long bibliography on theoretical physics, covering studies on the photoelectric effect in metals, cosmic rays, elementary particles with higher spins, and the energy-time indeterminate relationship in non-relativistic quantum electrodynamics. He is the author of *Principles of Electricity Theory* (published in 1929 and reprinted in 1956), the chief Soviet text on the theory of the electromagnetic field. He also wrote *The Relativistic Theory of Nucleon Interaction* (1953) and *Theory of Magnetic Thermonuclear Reactions* (1958). His major scientific papers are well-known to the Western world since they have been published in German and English scientific journals.

The 1958 Nobel Prize in Physics, worth $41,420, was bestowed on Igor Tamm, Pavel A. Cherenkov, and Ilya M. Frank for their distinguished work on the Cherenkov radiation effect. They were the first Russians ever named to receive the Nobel Prize in Physics. According to

Harry Schwartz, a specialist in Soviet affairs, the honor gave "definitive international recognition to the high quality of experimental and theoretical research in physics being done in the Soviet Union" (New York *Times,* October 29, 1958).

The government of the Soviet Union has awarded Tamm the Stalin Prize, the Order of Lenin (twice), and the Order of the Red Banner of Labor. He also received the title of Hero of Socialist Labor. Dr. Tamm has represented his government at scientific conferences in the Soviet Union and Europe. In 1958 he was a delegate to the East-West conference on policing a nuclear test ban and the International Conference on High-energy Physics held concurrently in Geneva.

In 1953 Igor Tamm was given the title of Academician and elected to full membership in the Soviet Academy of Sciences. Composed of some 400 outstanding scientists, the Academy functions as a ministry that distributes funds and directs research activities in accordance with government plans. On occasion Professor Tamm has been a vigorous and outspoken critic of governmental bureaucratic oppression in the Academy. Late in 1956 he served as spokesman for dissident elements among the members of the Academy at a meeting convened to elect a new president. He pointed out that past general meetings had not abided by the charter provisions that the direction of basic scientific work be governed by majority vote. He also contended that bureaucratic control of the Academy's research had brought about a waste of time, manpower, and resources. Tamm also holds membership in the Polish Academy of Sciences and the American Academy of Arts and Sciences.

A distinguished-looking, white-haired man who speaks English with a Scottish burr, Igor Tamm has the reputation of being an able, candid, and courageous scientist. He has been praised for his warmth and humanity. When he appeared on a CBS television interview in May 1963, the Washington *Post* (May 24, 1963) described him as "no word-wielding propagandist, no defensive diplomat, no smug philistine, but a cultured scientist whose stature allows him a breadth of outlook and a candor of expression denied to many of his countrymen." During the interview Tamm called the obsessive distrust between the East and the West the major barrier to progress in disarmament. He recommended a "drastic change in our political thinking which starts from the point of view that no war at all is possible." Dr. Tamm is a not a member of the Communist party. He married Natalie Shuiskaia on September 16, 1917. The couple has two children, Irene and Eugen.

References

N Y Times p2 N 23 '59 por
Collier's Encyclopedia Yearbook, 1959
International Who's Who, 1963-64
Levitan, Tina N. Laureates: Jewish Winners of the Nobel Prize (1960)
Who's Who, 1963
Who's Who in America, 1962-63
Who's Who in the USSR, 1961-62

TEMPLETON, ALEC July 4, 1910-Mar. 28, 1963 Blind pianist and composer; gave many performances in concert halls and on radio and television as both a musical satirist and classical pianist. See *Current Biography* (March) 1940.

Obituary

N Y Times p36 Ap 1 '63

TENNANT, SIR WILLIAM GEORGE Jan. 2, 1890-July 26, 1963 British naval officer; knighted and made an admiral in 1948; directed evacuation of British troops at Dunkirk in 1940; served as commander in chief, America and the West Indies station, from 1946 until his retirement in 1949. See *Current Biography* (February) 1945.

Obituary

N Y Times p17 Jl 27 '63

TER-ARUTUNIAN, ROUBEN (tĕr ä-rōō-tōō' nē-ăn rōō-bĕn') July 24, 1920- Theatrical designer

Address: 360 E. 55th St., New York 22

The imaginative scenic and costume designs of Rouben Ter-Arutunian, which range from the realistic to the symbolic, have within the past decade made him prominent in the worlds of theater, dance, television, and opera. They have brought him critical acclaim as well as an Emmy award (1957), an Outer Circle Critics Award (1958), and an Antoinette Perry (Tony) award (1959). Ter-Arutunian is a naturalized American of Russian-Armenian descent who immigrated to the United States in 1951. He has created designs for the American Shakespeare Festival Theatre and Academy, including its permanent dramatic set, and for Broadway hits like *New Girl in Town* (1957), *Who Was That Lady I Saw You With?* (1958), *Redhead* (1959), and *Advise and Consent* (1960). He has also worked for the New York City Opera Company, the Los Angeles Civic Light Opera Company, the San Francisco Opera, and the Opéra-Comique in Paris.

Of Armenian descent, Rouben Ter-Arutunian was born in Tiflis, Russia on July 24, 1920 to Guegam Ter-Arutunian, a lawyer, and Anaida (Seylanian) Ter-Arutunian. He was reared in Berlin and Paris and educated in European schools. From 1927 to 1930 he attended elementary school in Berlin, and from 1930 to 1938 he studied at the Hohenzollern Schule in that city. Following his graduation from the Hohenzollern Schule he took a year of training for a projected career as a concert pianist.

Ter-Arutunian's vocational interests changed at about this time, however. Influenced by performances of the Ballets de Colonel de Basil that he had seen in 1936 and 1938, he decided to make his career in painting and design. From 1939 to 1941 he attended the Reimann Art School, and in 1943 he studied film music at Berlin's Hochschule für Musik. At the Friedrich-Wilhelm University in Berlin from 1941 to 1943 and at the University of Vienna in 1943-44 he took courses in the history of art, theater, literature, and philosophy.

Friedman—Abeles

ROUBEN TER-ARUTUNIAN

Ter-Arutunian's first professional costume designs were made in 1940 for the dancers of the Berlin Staatsoper. In 1943 he designed the costumes for a Dresden Opera production of Bedrich Smetana's *The Bartered Bride* and in 1944, for a Vienna Opera presentation of Richard Strauss's *Salome*, given in honor of Strauss's eightieth birthday. After World War II, in 1946, Ter-Arutunian planned club interiors and the scenery and costumes for military shows for the Special Services of the United States Third Army in Bavaria and Heidelberg. He went to Paris in 1947 for three years of study at L'École Nationale Supérieure des Beaux-Arts, where he was an *élève definitif* in the studio of the painter Jean Souverbie. In 1950 he created costumes and scenery for the Opéra-Comique production of the ballet *Concerto*.

On January 2, 1951 Rouben Ter-Arutunian immigrated to the United States, where he first joined the CBS television network as a staff designer. During the three years that he worked for CBS-TV he designed for a variety of shows, including *Studio One*. From 1954 to 1956, as a staff designer at NBC-TV, Ter-Arutunian created designs for *Producer's Showcase, Hall of Fame, Wide, Wide World, Opera Theatre*, and the Kaiser Aluminum show. Among the television shows to which he contributed designs between 1955 and 1959 were the *Bell Telephone Hour, Swing Into Spring*, with Benny Goodman; and productions of Jean Anouilh's *Antigone;* Shakespeare's *The Tempest, The Taming of the Shrew*, and *Twelfth Night* (for which he received an Emmy award in 1957); Mozart's *The Magic Flute* and *Abduction from the Seraglio;* and Lukas Foss's *Griffelkin*. Ter-Arutunian was also the designer for the original television production of Igor Stravinsky's and George Balanchine's *Noah and the Flood*, given in June 1962. Harriet Van Horne in the New York *World-Telegram and Sun* (June 15, 1962) praised the retelling of the

TER-ARUTUNIAN, ROUBEN—Continued

Genesis story and said, "The most arresting contribution was made by Rouben Ter-Arutunian, who designed the highly stylized sets and the primitive, grotesque masks worn by the principals."

Meanwhile, in 1953 Ter-Arutunian had begun to plan costumes and settings for the New York City Opera Company. Productions he worked on between 1953 and 1959 were Béla Bartók's *Bluebeard's Castle,* Maurice Ravel's *L'Heure Espagnole,* Rossini's *La Cenerentola,* a musical version of Franz Kafka's *The Trial,* Humperdinck's *Hansel and Gretel,* Douglas Moore's *The Devil and Daniel Webster* and Lee Hoiby's *The Scarf,* which Ter-Arutunian originally designed for the Spoleto Festival in 1958. He also designed a San Francisco Opera production of Norman dello Joio's *Blood Moon* in 1961 and contributed to the New York City Ballet's *Souvenir* (1955) and *The Seven Deadly Sins* (1958) and to productions of Martha Graham and Paul Taylor.

The theater provided yet another showcase for Ter-Arutunian's creations beginning in 1956, when he was asked by the American Shakespeare Festival Theatre to design the stage and a permanent dramatic set for its summer productions at Stratford, Connecticut. He devised a platform stage projecting over the pit, with numerous possibilities for exits and entrances. For three sides of the inner stage he created tall, narrow strips of lattice, sections of which could be shifted to suit the needs of different plays. He also designed the scenery and costumes for two of the plays presented by the festival theater in the summer of 1956—*King John* and *Measure for Measure.* Brooks Atkinson in the New York *Times* (July 8, 1956) said that Ter-Arutunian's scenery was "excellent—daring in design, exhilarating in effect. . . . It mirrors the vitality of the plays. It creates moods; it has life."

When the American Shakespeare Festival Theatre company moved to New York City for the winter, it took his set along. The set served as the background for three plays presented at the Phoenix Theatre in January, February, and March of 1957—*Measure for Measure, The Taming of the Shrew,* and John Webster's *The Duchess of Malfi.* Ter-Arutunian's festival stage and set continued to be used by the American Shakespeare Festival Theatre in subsequent seasons. In 1960 he was asked to make some alterations in the stage design, principally the elimination of two proscenium posts for greater freedom of movement on the sides of the stage and the removal of the lattice work, which it was felt diverted the attention of the audience from the actors. The lattice pieces were replaced by a semi-dome encompassing the playing area. In 1957 Ter-Arutunian did the scenery and costumes for the festival theater's productions of *Othello* and *Much Ado About Nothing* and the scenery for *The Merchant of Venice.* He also designed for the same company the productions of *Twelfth Night,* given in June 1960, and *Antony and Cleopatra,* given in August 1960.

In 1957 Ter-Arutunian outlined his first designs for a Broadway play—the musical *New Girl in Town,* based on Eugene O'Neill's *Anna Christie,* which opened in May of that year. His saloon and waterfront settings were called festive and colorful by critics. The next musical for which he planned the settings, in 1958, required a great deal of ingenuity on his part. *Who Was That Lady I Saw You With?,* a comedy by Norman Krasna, had some thirteen different scenes, including a teacher's office, a livingroom, FBI headquarters, a Chinese restaurant, and an elevator in the Empire State Building. Ter-Arutunian provided for quick scene changes with rolling and split-level devices. Praising the settings in the *New Yorker* (March 15, 1958), John Lardner wrote, "The scenery, which is the work of a man, or possibly a group, named Rouben Ter-Arutunian, is controlled by a number of miracles of modern engineering among which I identified a ski lift, a trolley turntable, a vertical waffle iron, a hydromatic gearshift, several coal chutes, and a set of those small windows you find in the Automat." Ter-Arutunian received an Outer Circle Critics Award for his settings.

An assignment of quite a different nature was undertaken by Ter-Arutunian later in 1958 on commission from the NBC *Opera Theatre.* This was to design the décor for Gian-Carlo Menotti's musical drama *Maria Golovin,* which dealt with the jealous love of a young blind man for a married woman. Ter-Arutunian's settings included a cage-like "spidery villa surrounded by tangled-wire trees" and a barred prison; they were called "stunning" and extremely adroit by Winthrop Sargeant in the *New Yorker* (November 15, 1958). *Maria Golovin* had its world première at the American Theatre at the Brussels World Fair in August 1958. In November it played at the Martin Beck Theatre in New York, in December at the La Scala in Milan, and in March 1959 at the New York City Center.

For the musical *Redhead,* starring Gwen Verdon, which opened in New York in February 1959, Ter-Arutunian designed settings that included a waxworks, a music hall, and a pub, and lavish costumes that won him a Tony award. In 1960 he did the décor for the dramatization of Allen Drury's novel *Advise and Consent,* providing movable panels of white, gray, and black that, according to Howard Taubman (New York *Times,* November 18, 1960), "helped to give visual variety to the action."

In 1961 Ter-Arutunian devised costumes and settings for the musical *Donnybrook!,* and in 1962 for *A Passage to India,* Santha Rama Rau's adaptation of the E. M. Forster novel. Early in 1962 he also did the settings for *The Umbrella,* a play by Bertrand Castelli that had only nine performances in Philadelphia before it closed down. His costumes and settings were seen in the spring of 1963 in *Hot Spot,* a musical about the Peace Corps that starred Judy Holliday, and in two Off Broadway one-acters by Lorees Yerby, *Save Me a Place at Forest Lawn* and *The Last Minstrel,* as well as in *Arturo Ubi,* which ran briefly on Broadway in November 1963.

Rouben Ter-Arutunian is five feet nine inches tall, weighs 145 pounds, and has black hair and gray eyes. He is unmarried. Listening to music, taking walks, and sunning at the beach are his favorite recreations. He has been a naturalized American citizen since 1957. His religious affiliation is with the Armenian Christian Church.

References
Who's Who in America, 1962-63
Who's Who in the Theatre (1961)

TERESHKOVA, VALENTINA (VLADIMIR-OVNA) (tĕ-rĕsh-kŏ′và và-lĕn-tē′nà vlà-dē-mēr-ŭv′nà) Mar. 6, 1937- Soviet woman cosmonaut

Address: b. Scientific Research Institute of Aviation Medicine, Petrovsky Park, Moscow, U.S.S.R.

The Soviet cosmonaut Valentina Tereshkova became the world's first spacewoman on June 16, 1963, when her spaceship *Vostok VI* blasted off for a flight that lasted three days and encompassed forty-eight orbits of the earth. Lieutenant Tereshkova, a former cotton mill worker, was twenty-six years old at the time of her flight. She had been selected in 1962 as a potential cosmonaut primarily on the basis of her experience as an amateur parachutist. Valentina Tereshkova was the sixth Soviet cosmonaut and the tenth person to go into orbit. The four American astronauts who preceded her made a combined total of thirty-four orbits—fewer than she achieved in a single flight. Lieutenant Tereshkova's record has itself been exceeded by only two of her countrymen, one of whom—Lieutenant Colonel Valery F. Bykovsky—had gone into space two days before she did and returned to earth a few hours after her on June 19. In the autumn of 1963 she was promoted to the rank of captain.

Valentina Vladimirovna Tereshkova was born on March 6, 1937 in the village of Maslennikovo, near the 900-year-old city of Yaroslavl on the Volga River. Her father was Vladimir Tereshkov, a tractor driver who fought with the Red Army and was killed in action early in World War II. Her mother is Elena Fyodorovna Tereshkova, a former worker at the Krasny Perekop cotton mill in Yaroslavl, now retired. Miss Tereshkova has a brother, Vladimir, who is a driver, and a sister, Ludmilla, who works at the Krasny Perekop mill.

Vladimir Tereshkov's death at the front left his wife, Elena, in straitened circumstances, with three small children to raise, and Valentina experienced deprivation as a child. It was not until 1947, when she was ten, that she started to school, and seven years later, in 1954, she went to work as an apprentice at the Yaroslavl Tire Factory. She continued her education while working at the tire factory by attending classes at an evening school. Late in 1954 she joined her mother and sister at the Krasny Perekop mill, where she learned to operate a coarse linen loom. She also joined Komsomol (Young Communist League) and enrolled in a correspondence course for training in cotton technology.

An ardent Communist, Valentina Tereshkova was soon taking an active part in the mill's branch of Komsomol. She also adopted a hobby that was soon to be of great significance in her life—parachute jumping. In 1959 she joined the Yaroslavl Air Sports Club, and before long she was directing a group of amateur enthusiasts at the mill. Meanwhile, Miss Tereshkova continued her Komsomol work, serving on committees and becoming involved in such projects as the building of homes for fellow employees and the beautification of the mill's grounds. In 1960, at the age of twenty-three, she was elected secretary of her branch of Komsomol. In the same crowded year she completed her correspondence course in cotton-spinning technology and received a first-

Wide World

VALENTINA TERESHKOVA

class certificate of proficiency as a parachutist. Election followed to the Yaroslavl regional committee of Komsomol, and in February 1961 she became a candidate member of Komsomol's parent organization, the Communist party itself.

In April 1961 Yuri Gagarin became the first man to orbit the earth, and the achievement fired Miss Tereshkova's imagination. Writing to the authorities, she cited her proficiency as a parachutist and volunteered her services as a cosmonaut. She was accepted. In March 1962, just before joining the cosmonaut training unit, she became a full member of the Communist party, one of the youngest in the Soviet Union. By American standards of selection it seems remarkable that Valentina Tereshkova was accepted into the training program for cosmonauts, since she lacked any experience as a test pilot. However, it has been suggested that the relatively great size of the Soviet spaceships, made possible by larger rockets, allows room on board for automatic back-up equipment, and enables the Russians to be far less demanding in selecting pilots than the Americans can afford to be.

Before women were admitted to cosmonaut training, Soviet scientists made extensive tests with animals to determine the effects of space flight on the female organism. According to Soviet sources, the tests showed that women could stand the physical and emotional stresses involved as well as men, and that they might indeed be better equipped to orientate themselves in space and to tolerate high G-forces. Miss Tereshkova, at any rate, is said to have astounded her male colleagues in the cosmonaut training unit by her physical endurance and stamina. If, as is reported, she followed much the same training program as the men, she must have spent a long period in a "chamber of silence," been exposed to forces up to fifteen times the force of gravity, been placed in a thermal chamber producing alternately high and

TERESHKOVA, VALENTINA—*Continued*

low temperatures, and must have spent brief periods in a state of weightlessness.

Valentina Tereshkova's technical training was no less rigorous and apparently imposed greater demands on her than the physical aspects of the course. Fellow cosmonaut Yuri Gagarin has said of her: "I watched her at practice and in class a great deal. It was hard for her to master rocket techniques, study spaceship designs and equipment, but she tackled the job stubbornly and devoted much of her own time to study, poring over books and notes in the evening." Reportedly Miss Tereshkova received some training in the piloting of conventional aircraft as an introduction to the technique of space flight. At the end of 1962, about nine months after the beginning of her cosmonaut training, she received the military rank of junior lieutenant.

At 3 P.M. (Moscow time) on June 14, 1963 Lieutenant Colonel Valery F. Bykovsky was launched into orbit in the spaceship *Vostok V* from the Soviet space center at Baikonur, Kazakhstan. He was still aloft two days later when at 12:30 P.M. on June 16, Valentina Tereshkova was rocketed into a similar orbit in the spaceship *Vostok VI*. Soon afterward, Lieutenant Tereshkova made her first radio report from space. Using her radio call name, she said: "This is Seagull. I see the horizon. A light blue, a blue band. This is the earth. How beautiful it is! Everything goes fine." Later she was seen on television screens in the Soviet Union and Eastern Europe, smiling broadly, a pencil and a log book floating in front of her face in a state of weightlessness. Instruments in the cabin showed ground control that Lieutenant Tereshkova was reacting well to space conditions from the first. She ate lunch during her first orbit and dinner on her third. Premier Nikita S. Khrushchev spoke to her by radio telephone and warmly congratulated her. By 10:00 P.M. on the first day she had completed seven orbits, had finished her supper, and was preparing to sleep.

Awakening at 6:10 A.M. on June 17, Lieutenant Tereshkova began the day with exercises and then proceeded with other assigned tasks. *Vostok VI* had entered an orbit whose altitudes ranged from 113.7 to 144.8 miles above the earth. The spaceship traveled at a speed of approximately 18,000 miles an hour, circling the earth every 88.3 minutes. The size and power of *Vostok VI* were not disclosed, but American NASA officials estimated that the rockets that propelled it must have had a thrust of about 1,200,000 pounds, as against the 362,000 pounds of the Atlas rockets that have so far propelled American spaceships.

From time to time the two orbiting Vostoks were not far apart. Early on June 17 the two cosmonauts announced by radio that they were only 3.1 miles from each other. The relatively short distance separating the two spaceships and the fact that each previous Soviet cosmonaut flight had represented a great technical advance led space experts in the West to believe that a rendezvous in space would be attempted. Later on June 17, however, *Vostok V* sank to a dangerously low apogee of only 102 miles from earth and *Vostok VI* lost radio contact with ground control. Tass reported that Lieutenant Tereshkova had fallen asleep off schedule and had to be awakened by Bykovsky. The "group flight" continued uneventfully on June 18 without the two Vostoks again reaching a point close to rendezvous.

At 11:20 A.M. (Moscow time) on June 19, Valentina Tereshkova returned safely to earth, having completed forty-eight orbits and having traveled about 1.2 million miles in seventy hours, fifty minutes. At some undisclosed point while re-entering the atmosphere, she was ejected from the spacecraft, completed the landing by parachute, and came down in a glade near a village about 380 miles northeast of Karaganda, Kazakhstan. Soon afterward, in a telephone conversation with Premier Khrushchev, she reported that she was well and that the only injury she had sustained in landing was a bruised nose. She also informed him that the villagers had welcomed her "very cordially in the Russian manner, with bread and salt." At 2:06 P.M. on the same day, approximately 330 miles northwest of Karaganda, Bykovsky landed safely, having completed eighty-two orbits—a new space flight record.

A joyous reunion followed between Bykovsky and Lieutenant Tereshkova on June 20, and two days later the pair were hailed in a massive ceremony in Moscow's Red Square. They received an emotional and affectionate welcome from Premier Khrushchev, who called for peace and international co-operation in space and chided the West for its "bourgeois" notion that woman is the weaker sex. He pointed out that Valentina Tereshkova's flight was longer than those of all four American astronauts put together and announced that a bust would be erected in Moscow in her honor. Lieutenant Tereshkova said that she was "boundlessly happy" to be the first woman in space and continued: "In space, too, our men will not feel lonely now. Let them feel there, too, friendly womanly support." She was, she said, ready for further space flights.

The group flight of Bykovsky and Valentina Tereshkova caused much speculation in the West. Since a similar if shorter flight had already been made by Soviet cosmonauts Nikolayev and Popovich in 1962, it had been widely supposed that the Bykovsky-Tereshkova flight would introduce some startling space maneuver. Western experts had forecast that *Vostok V* and *Vostok VI* would be joined in space, that a third spaceship would be orbited at the same time, or that Bykovsky would stay aloft for eight days—the calculated time required to make a round-trip journey to the moon. When none of these predictions was fulfilled, it was suggested that some unannounced error or technical malfunction had intervened—perhaps Bykovsky's unexplained loss of altitude on June 17.

Soviet sources did not comment directly on these conjectures. The communiqué announcing Lieutenant Tereshkova's launching merely said: "The flight is being made to continue the study of the effect of various space-flight factors on the human organism, including a comparative analysis of the impact of these factors on the organisms of a man and a woman; to carry out new medical-biological research, and to further improve and perfect the system of piloted spaceships in conditions of simultaneous flight." It has also been pointed out that women will need to go into space if an "island of life" is ever established on a long-term basis in outer space. At a news conference on June 25, Lieutenant Tereshkova said that her mission had been "for one day, with a possible extension to three." She had chosen to stay aloft for three days, she said, because she felt well and her ship was functioning perfectly.

Valentina Tereshkova—"Valya," as she is now affectionately known to millions of Soviet citizens —is a blue-eyed blonde. She has an oval face with a cleft chin and is said to resemble Ingrid Bergman. Her figure is trim and athletic, and she wears her hair in the short "kitten" style popular with Moscow's young women. She wears little make-up, but has an acknowledged weakness for smart clothes and high heels. On June 22, at a reception in the Kremlin, she was named a Hero of the Soviet Union, her country's highest honor, and received from the Chairman of the Presidium, Leonid I. Brezhnev, the Order of Lenin and the Gold Star Medal. She also holds many honors and citations from the Soviet Union, Cuba, and Mexico. Valentina Tereshkova's favorite composers are Tchaikovsky, Verdi, and Beethoven; her favorite writers are Leo Tolstoy and Mikhail A. Sholokhov.

During October 1963 Valentina Tereshkova, accompanied by her fellow cosmonaut Yuri Gagarin, traveled to Cuba, where she was a guest of the Cuban Women's Federation, and to Mexico, where she attended a general conference of the International Aeronautical Federation. In New York City that same month she received a standing ovation at the General Assembly of the United Nations. On November 3, 1963, in a civil ceremony at one of Moscow's two wedding palaces, Valentina Tereshkova married the cosmonaut Andrian Nikolayev.

References

N Y Herald Tribune p13 Je 17 '63 por
N Y Times p8 Je 17 '63 por

TISSERANT, EUGÈNE, CARDINAL (tēs-rän′) Mar. 24, 1884- Roman Catholic prelate

Address: b. Curia Vescovile di Ostia, Porto e Santa Rufina, Via della Dataria 94, Rome, Italy; h. Via Giovanni Prati 4, Rome, Italy

The librarian and archivist of the Roman Catholic Church is the dean of the College of Cardinals, French-born Eugène Cardinal Tisserant. A "Curia cardinal," Tisserant is a member of several of the Vatican congregations that assist the Pope in the central administration of the Roman Catholic Church, including the Congregation of Ceremonies, of which he is prefect. He is also bishop of the Italian dioceses of Ostia, Porto, and Santa Rufina. An expert in manuscripts and Semitic paleography, Cardinal Tisserant became pro-prefect of the Vatican Library in 1930. From 1936, when he was elevated to the cardinalate, until 1959 he was secretary of Congregation for the Eastern Church. On June 15, 1962 he was elected to the French Academy.

Wide World

EUGÈNE CARDINAL TISSERANT

Eugène Gabriel Gervais Laurent Tisserant was born in Nancy, France on March 24, 1884. He was the fourth of six children of Marie Auguste Hippolyte Tisserant and Octavie Léonie Héloise (Connard) Tisserant. His three sisters —Marie, Claire, and Louise—were older than Eugène; his two brothers—Charles and Henri —were younger. Eugène learned to read when he was three. Among the books he read as a boy were the scientific textbooks owned by his father, a veterinarian. When he was ten there came into the Tisserant household an inheritance that was to strengthen his love of books: the 2,000-volume library of a bibliophile uncle. Other books, including classics of French and world literature, were lent him by his schoolteachers.

Latin and German were the subjects in which Tisserant began his formal primary education in 1891 at a school conducted by the Sisters of Christian Doctrine of Nancy. From 1892 to 1896 he studied under diocesan priests at the school of St. Léopold in Nancy, where during his last year he decided against a naval career and in favor of the priesthood. In 1896 he entered the College of St. Sigisbert, Nancy, which awarded him his baccalaureate degree in 1900. From 1898 to 1900 he also took courses in the school of science of the University of Nancy.

In October 1900, at the age of sixteen, Tisserant entered the Major Seminary of Nancy. In becoming a student for the priesthood, he did not abandon his love for the exact sciences. For recreation he read manuals of differential and integral calculus, and he envisioned his life as a priest coupled with that of a professor of science. Two new areas of interest opened to him at the seminary, however. He was introduced to library science as a student-assistant in the institution's library, and he became aware of the importance of Syrian and Arabic literature for the study of

TISSERANT, EUGÉNE, CARDINAL—*Cont.*

early and medieval Christian thought. While studying theology he also learned Hebrew, Syriac, and Assyrian and decided to specialize in the study of the Old Testament.

During his last year, 1903-04, at the Nancy seminary Tisserant taught physics to first-year students. In 1904-05 he studied under Father Lagrange at the Biblical School of St. Stephen in Jerusalem. After completing a year of military service in Toul, France, Tisserant went to Paris, where between 1906 and 1908 he worked for a diploma in Hebrew, Syriac, Arabic, Ethiopic, and Assyrian at the Catholic Institute. At the same time he studied Arabic at the École des Langues Orientales Vivantes; oriental archeology and Greek, Assyrian, and Arabic paleography at the Sorbonne's École des Hautes Études; and Greek sculpture as well as the Egyptian language at the École du Louvre.

Ordained at Nancy on August 4, 1907, Tisserant went to Rome in 1908 to become professor of Assyrian at the University of St. Apollinare and curator of oriental manuscripts at the Vatican Library. It was to the library that he gave most of his time, devoting himself first of all to cataloging the Arabic manuscripts in the Borgia collection. Between 1910 and 1914 one of his other major projects was the compilation for the Gesellschaft der Wissenschaften zu Göttingen a union list of oriental translations, dispersed through several Italian libraries, of the Greek version of the Old Testament known as the Septuagint.

Beginning in 1908 Tisserant contributed to *Revue Biblique, Revue de l'Orient Chrétien,* and other scholarly journals. His *Ascension d'Isaie,* a translation from the Ethiopic version, was published in Paris by Letouzey and Ané in 1909. From Greek manuscripts in the Vatican and British museums he edited *Codex Zuquinensis rescriptus Veteris Testamenti* (Tipografia Poliglotta Vaticana, 1911). From the Arabic he translated *Le Calendrier d'Abû'l-Barakât* (Firmin-Didot, 1913). He examined countless manuscripts in the course of compiling *Specimina codicum orientalium* (Pustet, 1914), which has been called "the indispensable companion and guide of all students of oriental paleography." A collection of cuneiform texts that he made during a trip to the Near East in 1911-12 was cataloged in the *Revue d'Assyriologie* in 1921.

When World War I broke out Tisserant joined the French infantry as a corporal, and he was wounded in September 1914. He spent the next two years as an interpreter in the office for the Near East in the general staff headquarters in Paris. In 1917 and 1918 he served on the staff of the French Expeditionary Forces in Palestine and Syria. Discharged with the rank of first lieutenant, he was decorated with the Croix de Guerre.

Returning to the Vatican Library in May 1919, Father Tisserant became assistant to the prefect, Monsignor Giovanni Mercati, later that same year. Among his duties were supervision of personnel and direction of the manuscript-restoration laboratory. In 1921 he was honored with the title of monsignor. Pius XI, after becoming Pope in 1922, started a program of increasing the collections, the shelf space, and

the efficiency of the Vatican Library. Monsignor Tisserant took part in negotiations for the acquisition of several important collections. In 1923 he toured the Balkans and the Near East, examining and purchasing manuscripts and books.

The modernization of the Vatican Library began in the late 1920's with the collaboration and subsidy of the Carnegie Endowment for International Peace. In 1927 Monsignor Tisserant spent two and one-half months in the United States, visiting forty-two libraries. After his return to Rome he persuaded Pius XI that American steel catalog cabinets and stacks should be purchased for the new wing to the Vatican Library, a former horse stable then being renovated. Tisserant supervised the erection of a three-tier, 260-foot stack in the new wing, which was opened on December 20, 1927.

Tisserant helped prepare a code of rules for organizing a central catalog of the library's printed books and organized the printing of cards similar to those of the Library of Congress. After becoming pro-prefect of the library in 1930, he assumed full direction of the indexing of the library's 60,000 manuscripts. Many physical improvements were made during his pro-prefecture. These included additional tiers of stacks, suitable quarters for the catalog department, new quarters and equipment for photographic services, a new repair shop for manuscripts, and a new prints room. Through his efforts a library school was established at the Vatican in 1934.

While serving in the Vatican Library, Tisserant attended many library conferences. In 1933, when he was a member of the International Library Committee, he addressed the American Library Association in Chicago. "Our task as librarians is similar to that of the priestesses of Vesta, to whom was committed the care of the sacred fire," he said. "And this is the reason why nothing is unworthy in our life if we consider our duty toward humanity." All the tasks of librarianship are noble, he concluded, "if we feel that we are helping humanity in its trend toward that spiritual unity which would be the result of unity of culture."

On June 15, 1936 Pope Pius XI named Tisserant a Cardinal and appointed him to succeed Luigi Cardinal Sincero, who had died, as secretary of the Sacred Congregation for the Eastern Church. The newest of the ministries which make up the Roman Curia, or central administration of the Roman Catholic Church, this congregation was created in 1917. Its jurisdiction covers 8,000,000 Catholics who do not use the Latin rite in worship but who are in union with Rome: Ruthenians (including Ukrainians), Rumanians, Italo-Greeks, Italo-Albanians, Uniate Russians, Bulgarians, Greeks, Maronites, Syrians, Egyptian and Ethiopian Copts, Chaldeans, Syro-Malabars in India, and Armenians.

As dean of the Sacred College of Cardinals, Tisserant was the most prominent Roman Catholic Church prelate during the interregnum between the death of Pope Piux XII and the election of Pope John XXIII in October 1958. He next gained notice in the international press a year later in reports regarding efforts at Church unity. Two Roman Catholic priests attending meetings of the central committee of the World Council of Churches in August 1959 suggested that a meeting between Roman Catholic and Eastern Orthodox churchmen be held the following year with a view to reunion. Cardinal Tisserant denied that he had anything to do with the suggestion and said that he doubted that the priests had received instructions from the Vatican. In September, however, the Vatican radio announced that Eastern Orthodox and Roman Catholic churchmen would hold unofficial theological discussions in Venice in 1960 with a view to reunion.

In November 1959 Cardinal Tisserant resigned his position as secretary of the Sacred Congregation for the Eastern Church. He explained to newsmen that Pope John preferred that he devote himself to scientific work. He was also reported as saying that he left the Eastern congregation post to devote himself more fully to his work as church librarian and archivist. He retained his position as prefect of the Sacred Congregation of Ceremonies. Tisserant was a member of the Central Preparatory Commission for Vatican II, the ecumenical council called by Pope John XXIII. The commission held its last session in June 1962. On September 5, 1962 Pope John named him to a ten-man presidency council that would help preside over Vatican II. The ecumenical council opened with Mass in St. Peter's Basilica on October 11, 1962. The celebrant was Cardinal Tisserant.

In addition to being prefect of the Sacred Congregation of Ceremonies, Tisserant is a member of the Consistorial Congregation, the Congregation for Extraordinary Ecclesiastical Affairs, and the congregations of rites, of seminaries and universities, of the sacraments, and of the affairs of religious. He remains a member of the Congregation for the Eastern Church.

The pressure of administrative work has kept Tisserant's scholarly publications to a minimum since 1920. His "L'Inventaire sommaire des manuscrits arabes du fonds Borgia à la Bibliothèque Vaticane" appeared in *Miscellanea Francesco Ehrle* (Tipografia del Senato, 1924). He published *Codices Armeni Bibliothecae Vaticanae* (Typis Polyglottis Vaticanis, 1927) and collaborated on *Codices Aethiopici Vaticani et Borgiani* (Bybliotheca Vaticana, 1935-36). His historical study *Luigi Maria Grignion de Montfort, le scuole di carità e le origini dei Fratelli di San Gabriele* was published in Rome by Tipografia del Senato in 1943. Some of his speeches were collected under the title *L'Église militante* (Bloud & Gay, 1950). He contributed the article on pontifical libraries to the *Dictionnaire de sociologie* (Letouzey, 1936) and that on the Syro-Malabare Church to *Dictionnaire de théologie catholique* (Letouzey, 1941).

Eugène Cardinal Tisserant is five feet eight inches tall and weighs about 180 pounds. His eyes are hazel and his hair and beard white. He is sturdy and vigorous for his age and often has a twinkle in his eye. His hobby is stamp collecting. He holds honorary doctorates from Manhattan College and the universities of Louvain, Princeton, Nijmegen, Coimbra, and Vienna, among others. He is a life member of the American Library Association and the American Association for the Advancement of Science, a Grand Master of the Knights of the Holy Sepulchre, and honorary president of the Pontifical Academy of Science. A Grand-Officier of the Légion d'Honneur, he received its Cordon and Grand Croix in 1957. He was elected by the French Academy in 1962 to fill the seat that the death of Duke Maurice de Broglie had left vacant among "the forty immortals."

References

Lib Q 22:214+ Jl '52
N Y Herald Tribune p3 O 9 '58 por
Semaine Religieuse p1+ Jl 1 '62 por
Dictionnaire Biographique Français Contemporain (1954)
International Who's Who, 1962-63
Tisserant, Eugène. Recueil (1946)
Who's Who, 1963

TOLLEFSON, THOR C(ARL) May 2, 1901- United States Representative from Washington; lawyer

Address: b. House Office Bldg., Washington 25, D.C.; h. 4704 29th Place, N.W., Washington 8, D.C.; 3839 East G St., Tacoma, Washington

Convinced that sea power is essential to world leadership, Thor C. Tollefson has repeatedly fought for expansion of the United States merchant marine and has become identified with forward-looking shipping legislation. Since 1947 he has represented the Sixth Washington Congressional District and since 1955 has been the ranking Republican on the House of Representatives Merchant Marine and Fisheries Committee. He was successful in 1954 in amending the Mutual Security Act with a provision that 50 percent of all foreign aid cargo must be carried by American ships, and more recently he helped to obtain government assurance that the United States would receive at least 50 percent of the traffic resulting from its grant to the United Nations Congo Fund.

Thor Carl Tollefson was born to Christian and Bertha (Jacobson) Tollefson on May 2, 1901 in Parley in northwestern Minnesota, the small Norman County community where he attended public grade school. In 1912, when he was ten years old, the family moved to Tacoma, Washington, where Christian Tollefson, a merchant, died three years later. To support his brothers and sisters while they obtained a high school education, Thor Tollefson left high school at the age of fifteen and went to work in local mills and in shipyards as a mechanic.

Then in 1922, at the age of twenty-one, Tollefson was able by working nights to return to the Lincoln High School in Tacoma. He served as president of the student body, participated in three sports, and was valedictorian of his class at graduation two years later. To put himself through college and law school at the University of Washington, he worked for one year at various jobs and for five years as manager and president of his social fraternity, Alpha Sigma Phi. During the summer months he worked in the mills of Tacoma.

The University of Washington Law School, where Tollefson was elected to the Phi Delta Phi

THOR C. TOLLEFSON

honor society, awarded him the LL.B. degree in 1930. After being admitted to the Washington bar in the same year, he entered private practice in Tacoma. Early active in local Republican party organizations, he began in 1930 an eight-year membership on his precinct committee and also joined the Tacoma Men's Republican Club, of which he was later elected president. He was appointed deputy prosecuting attorney for Pierce County (in which Tacoma is located) in late 1932 and served in that office through the following year. In 1934 he returned to private practice, but four years later he was elected prosecuting attorney for Pierce County. He was a delegate to the Republican State Convention in 1936, 1938, 1940, and 1942.

Since 1932 the Democrats had dominated the Washington political scene, controlling the state legislature and filling both seats in the United States Senate and most of the six seats in the House of Representatives. In the November 1946 nationwide Republican landslide, however, the Republicans in Washington elected one Senator, Harry B. Cain, and captured five of the seats in the House of Representatives. In the Sixth Congressional District, Thor Tollefson defeated John Main Coffee, the Tacoma attorney and New Deal Democrat who had represented the area since 1937. Tollefson was re-elected in all subsequent biennial elections.

At the time of his first election, the Sixth District included Pierce County and the greater part of King County, to the north. Later, on the basis of the 1950 census, the state received a seventh seat. The King County areas were detached from Tollefson's district, and much of Kitsap County, across Puget Sound from Tacoma, was substituted.

Soon after he was seated in the Republican-controlled Eightieth Congress, in January 1947, Representative Tollefson was assigned to the House Merchant Marine and Fisheries Commit-

tee, on which he had the distinction of being named chairman of the fisheries subcommittee in his freshman term. In June 1947 Tollefson's subcommittee heard protests by Southern California fishing interests that the presence of the floating cannery *Pacific Explorer* in tuna fishing waters off Costa Rica constituted unfair competition. The subcommittee recommended that the Reconstruction Finance Corporation take steps to see that this government-owned vessel contracted by the Pacific Exploration Company be operated "for the benefit of the entire fishing industry." At a hearing on reciprocity early in the following year Tollefson argued against cutting tariffs on fish industry products, and in April 1950 he championed the cause of five Texas trawlers seized by Mexico for allegedly fishing for shrimp in territorial waters. He characterized the seizure of the trawlers, which eventually paid fines, as "an act of piracy."

In his general voting record in his early, as well as later, years in Congress Tollefson was far from being a down-the-line Republican partisan. In his freshman term he favored banning of portal-to-portal pay suits and voted for the 1948 tidelands oil bill and the Mundt-Nixon subversive activities control bill. During the same period, however, he voted against the Taft-Hartley bill and favored extending rent controls. Sympathetic toward much of the Truman foreign policy, he voted for Greek-Turkish aid and the Voice of America bill and opposed placing a rigid limit on foreign aid grants. He was one of the "top ten" liberal Republicans (headed by Jacob K. Javits of New York) whom Ralph Bendiner of the New York *Times* characterized in September 1951 as "well disposed to internationalism and some New Deal measures."

During the second session (1954) of the Republican-dominated Eighty-third Congress, Tollefson served as acting chairman of the Merchant Marine and Fisheries Committee. He suggested in February 1954 that the Navy Department could save $11,400,000 by adopting Maritime Administration methods in laying up fifty-seven T-2 type tankers on loan from the Maritime Administration. In an address to the Propeller Club in New York on May 21 of that year Tollefson accused the government of "foggy thinking" with respect to merchant ship operation. Three days later he introduced in the House of Representatives legislation calling for construction of sixty cargo and cargo-passenger ships a year. "An immediate ship construction program," he said, "is vital to the national defense of our country. . . . Because of lack of cargo and troop carrying vessels prior to World War II we almost lost the war."

On June 30, 1954 Tollefson moved to restore to the Mutual Security Act an amendment, deleted by the Foreign Affairs Committee, requiring that 50 percent of all foreign aid cargoes go in American vessels. His motion was adopted by voice vote, and in August the House unanimously approved a Senate version of a measure containing the 50-50 clause. Tollefson also favored legislation assuring that 20 percent of all government shipbuilding would be allocated to the Pacific Coast. Suggesting in November 1954 to the Foreign Operations Administration and the Army Engineers that increased use of Puget Sound ports would result in saving of time and money, Tollefson noted that Washington state ports were "nearer the Philippines than, for instance, is San Francisco." As the ranking Republican on the Merchant Marine Committee in the Democratic-controlled Eighty-fourth Congress (1955 and 1956) Tollefson co-sponsored with the new chairman, Herbert C. Bonner of North Carolina, a bill authorizing construction of an experimental atomic merchant vessel.

Among Washington state Republicans, Tollefson was considered a probable choice in 1956 for nomination as Governor, but in May 1956 he withdrew from the gubernatorial race and announced that he would seek re-election to Congress instead. Again the ranking Republican on the Merchant Marine Committee, Tollefson proposed in early 1957 that existing laws be broadened to permit Pacific Coast shipyards a greater share in government construction. When urging haste in planning and building the nuclear-powered ship that had been authorized the previous year, he suggested that it be built on the West Coast. In December 1957 a Tollefson bill calling for the United States to stake a claim in part of Antarctica was endorsed by the National Security Council. He was one of a nine-member delegation from the Merchant Marine Committee that traveled to both Europe and the Far East in 1959 to gather data for a study on steamship conferences and rate-making practices.

In key voting during the Eighty-sixth Congress Tollefson opposed the Tennessee Valley Authority self-financing bill (May 1959), recorded a "yea" for the Landrum-Griffin labor reporting bill (August 1959), and voted against the Powell anti-segregation amendment to the school construction bill of 1960 (May). After the Democrats took over control of the government in 1961, he supported such Kennedy administration bills as the $394,000,000 authorization for redevelopment of economically depressed areas (March) and the creation of the Peace Corps (September). He opposed extension for two years of the law permitting Mexicans to enter the United States for farm work (May). During the 1962 session of the Eighty-seventh Congress he voted against the setting up of an urban affairs and housing department (February) and against new fiscal 1963 authorization for foreign economic aid (July and September), but favored granting the President authority to cut tariffs through the Trade Expansion Act (February). In November 1962 Tollefson won his ninth election to Congress, defeating his Democratic opponent, Dawn Olson, by 72,241 to 31,603 votes.

Of medium stature, Representative Thor C. Tollefson is five feet seven inches tall and weighs about 175 pounds. He has brown hair and blue eyes. He belongs to several benevolent and fraternal organizations, including the Elks and the Eagles, and is a thirty-second degree Mason (Shriner and Scottish Rite). He is also a member of the Kiwanis Club in Tacoma and of the Sons of Norway. His religious affiliation is with the Central Lutheran Church. Mrs. Tollefson, whose maiden name was Eva M. Keuss, was a stenographer and secretary before her marriage on November 24, 1934. The Tollefsons have three daughters, Rosemary, Karley, and Janie.

References

Biographical Directory of the American Congress, 1774-1949 (1950)
Congressional Directory (1963)
Who's Who in America, 1962-63
Who's Who in the West (1960)
Who's Who in United States Politics (1952)

TOWNES, CHARLES H(ARD) July 28, 1915- Physicist; university professor and administrator

Address: b. Massachusetts Institute of Technology, Cambridge, Mass.

The technological revolution in the United States has received tremendous impetus during the past decade from the work of Charles H. Townes in the field of electronic physics. Since 1961 the provost of Massachusetts Institute of Technology, Townes is a former professor of physics at Columbia University and a former vice-president and director of research at the Institute for Defense Analyses in Washington, D.C. His experiments since World War II in radio astronomy, microwave spectroscopy, and atomic clocks and relativity have been outstanding scientific accomplishments. He has been especially honored for his work on the theory and application of the maser, an amplifying device for which he holds the basic patent. The maser has produced results of far-reaching importance in communications, in astronomical research on the nature of planets and galaxies, and in testing cosmological theories.

Charles Hard Townes, who is of English and Scottish ancestry, was born on July 28, 1915 in Greenville, South Carolina, one of the six children of Henry Keith Townes, an attorney, and the former Ellen Sumter Hard. He has three sisters, Aurelia Schawlow, Ellen Taylor, and Mary Nyland, and two brothers, Henry K. Townes, an entomologist at the University of Michigan, and George F. Townes, a lawyer. Charles Townes was reared in Greenville and graduated from the local high school in 1931. His home was on the outskirts of the city, surrounded by fields and woods that stimulated his boyhood interest in birds and insects.

At Furman University in Greenville, where he held a fellowship to pay his tuition, Charles Townes majored in modern languages and physics. He earned a high academic rating and served as a student assistant in the sciences during his sophomore, junior, and senior years. He was also the curator of the college museum and a member of the band, glee club, swimming team, and newspaper staff. When he graduated in 1935 with the B.A. and M.A. degrees, he won the prize for being the best scholar in the senior class and the medal for outstanding work in the sciences.

Assigning second place to his interest in languages and natural history, Townes decided to undertake graduate work in physics because of its "beautiful logic." He studied for a master's degree at Duke University, where he held a

CHARLES H. TOWNES

teaching assistantship while writing his thesis on Van der Graaf generators. He also took courses in French, Russian, and Italian. After receiving the M.A. degree in 1937, Townes entered the California Institute of Technology to continue his research for the doctorate. His dissertation, on which he worked with Professor W. R. Smythe, "The Spin of Carbon Thirteen," was published in 1939 in *Physical Review*.

After receiving the Ph.D. degree in physics in 1939, Townes was employed as a member of the technical staff of the Bell Telephone Laboratories in New York City and Murray Hill, New Jersey. During World War II he was principally occupied with the design of radar bombing systems and navigation devices at both the Bell Laboratories and at various Air Force test centers. Townes continued his theoretical work also, studying the structure of nuclei, measurement of nuclear moments, hyperfine structure of molecules, and radio astronomy. In his studies of microwave spectroscopy he was one of three scientists who independently discovered high-resolution microwave spectroscopy of gases.

In 1948, soon after he had resigned from Bell Telephone Laboratories, Townes accepted an academic post as associate professor of physics at Columbia University. He was appointed executive director of the university's Radiation Laboratory and promoted to a full professorship in 1950. Two years later he was named head of the physics department for a three-year period and executive officer of the laboratory, supervising research involving the use of microwave radar in the analysis of molecules. The Radiation Laboratory is jointly sponsored by the Army Signal Corps, Office of Naval Research, Air Research and Development Command, and Columbia University.

Dr. Townes, his colleagues, and graduate students used short-wave radar, which had become a useless military tool, to investigate the electromagnetic spectrum in the region between the shorter infrared or "heat" radiations and the longer radio waves. Radio frequencies in this area were similar to the end-over-end rotation of molecules. Modifications in frequencies demonstrated the effects of electrical and magnetic interaction between the rotating motion of the molecules and spinning nuclei within the constituent atoms.

As Dr. Townes expanded his molecular wave experiments, he conceived the idea of developing an instrument to measure time more absolutely and irrespective of the motions of sun and stars. He called this device a "maser," from the initials of its description, microwave amplification by stimulated emission of radiation. Scientists had long recognized disturbances in the motions of celestial bodies caused by changes in the earth's rotations and changes in the rate at which the earth moves around the sun. The upsets were entirely unpredictable and caused the loss or gain of a second or more every year. The device developed by Townes aimed to put the world on an exact schedule without consideration of the seasonal variations in the speed of rotation, the shifting of the internal structure of the earth, and the normal slowing down and speeding up of the yearly revolution.

Since its development in 1954, the atomic clock that uses the maser has proved more accurate than any previous timing device, varying no more than one second every three hundred years. To test its validity, Townes and his associates built a second model to work in conjunction with the first. Both masers vibrated at the same frequency, thus establishing the soundness of the principle. The extreme degree of accuracy was attributed to the absence of electric circuits that were found in all other instruments. Instead, the maser used a stream of ammonia molecules flowing through an electrostatic field. While the low-energy molecules were disposed of, the high-energy molecules were concentrated in a small resonant cavity. The latter vibrated at twenty-four billion cycles a second with a frequency variation of only a small fraction of one cycle a second over a short period of time such as a few seconds.

Once the immediate practical benefits of Dr. Townes's invention were established, scientists used the maser to make more accurate measurements of the earth's rate of rotation, to amplify radio signals too weak for ordinary vacuum tubes, to check the frequency of oscillation of a wide variety of molecules and atoms, and to maintain radio and television on precise frequencies, especially in short-wave long-distance telephone and TV fields.

The maser was used to conduct laboratory tests of Einstein's theory of relativity. Scientists made measurements of the frequency of an electromagnetic wave as it traveled in the same direction and in an opposite direction to that of the motion of the earth in its orbit around the sun. The maser measured extremely high frequencies, yielding results with an accuracy of one part in a million million. After conducting "the most precise physical experiment in history" for one year of the earth's orbit (November 1958-59), scientists confirmed the validity of relativity. It was established that the velocity of light (186,000 miles per second) remained constant regardless of the motion of the observer.

One variation of Dr. Townes's invention, the three-level solid state maser, was introduced late in 1957 by Harvard University astronomers who used a crystal instead of gas as the operating medium of the device. The following year Dr. Townes and Naval scientists conducted an examination of the planet Venus, including a temperature check, with a fifty-foot radio telescope equipped with a maser in which the operating medium was a synthetic ruby. An outgrowth of Professor Townes's maser has been the laser (light amplification by stimulated emission of radiation). This continuous "talking" beam of light has been used to improve methods of radio and television transmission, to maintain telephone conversations without wires, and to perform knifeless surgery. In May 1962 scientists used the laser to flash a beam on the moon, the first time man illuminated another celestial body.

Although interested in administrative work, Townes hesitated for some time in 1959 when he was offered the position of vice-president and director of research of the Institute for Defense Analyses in Washington. He accepted on the condition that while on leave from Columbia, he could give one day a week to directing the work of his graduate students. Established in 1956 at the request of the Joint Chiefs of Staff and Department of Defense, the I.D.A. is a nonprofit organization designed to bring together scientists and government defense planners. Columbia and Massachusetts Institute of Technology are among I.D.A.'s eight member institutions.

In September 1961 Townes left I.D.A. to become provost of Massachusetts Institute of Technology, where he had the opportunity to teach and experiment as well as responsibility in directing the institute's enormous research and teaching program. "I found myself finally making a choice, a more or less overt choice, to undertake administrative work at M.I.T. rather earlier in life than I would have expected," Townes has explained, as Theodore Berland quotes him in *The Scientific Life* (Coward, 1962). "I did it out of a desire to see what could be done. I like to experiment in different directions and this was something of an experiment—one which I went into very seriously, however, with the expectation that I'd really enjoy it."

A prolific author, Dr. Townes has written more than 125 articles that have appeared in American and foreign journals. He collaborated with his brother-in-law Arthur L. Schawlow to write *Microwave Spectroscopy* (McGraw, 1955), which reviewers called a well-written book on a new and important branch of experimental physics. Townes edited *Quantum Electronics* (Columbia Press, 1960), the proceedings of a conference sponsored by the Office of Naval Research in 1959. He has served on the editorial boards of several scientific periodicals, including *Physical Review* and *Journal of Chemical Physics*. Townes was the national lecturer for Sigma Xi in 1950 and Richtmyer lecturer of the American Physical Society in 1959.

For his accomplishments in science, Dr. Townes has been honored by the Franklin Institute, National Academy of Sciences and American Academy of Arts and Sciences. He received a Guggenheim Fellowship in 1955 and two Fulbright Fellowships to teach in France and Japan. The New York City Science Writers gave him the Page-One Award in 1958 and the Air Force cited him for exceptional service the following year. An honorary Litt. D. degree was conferred on him by his alma mater, Furman University, in 1960.

The many professional organizations to which Townes belongs include the American Philosophical Society, American Astronomical Society, and the Institute of Radio Engineers. He is a Fellow of the American Physical Society, of which he served as a council member in 1959. Townes has been elected to the National Academy of Sciences, American Academy of Arts and Sciences, and the physical societies of France and Japan. He is a member of the Scientific Advisory Board and a consultant to the President's Science Advisory Board, National Bureau of Standards, and the Brookhaven National Laboratory.

Charles H. Townes has brown hair and blue eyes, is six feet one inch tall, and weighs 175 pounds; he speaks with a slight Southern accent. On May 4, 1941 he married Frances Hildreth Brown, an employee of International House in New York whom he had met on a ski trip. With their four daughters—Linda Lewis, Ellen Screven, Carla Keith, and Holly Robinson—the Towneses spend their leisure time skin diving, traveling, and mountain climbing (in 1955 Townes climbed the Matterhorn). Townes is a political independent and an active Presbyterian layman. In relating science and religious feeling, he sees science as a part of religion. "There is a tremendous emotional experience [in scientific discovery] which I think is similar to what some people would normally describe as religious experience, a revelation," he has said (*The Scientific Life*). "In fact, it seems to me, a revelation can be viewed as a sudden discovery of understanding of man and man's relation to his universe, to God, and his relation to other men."

References

American Men of Science 10th ed (1960-62)
Berland, Theodore. The Scientific Life (1962)
International Who's Who, 1962-63
Who's Who in America, 1962-63
World Biography (1954)

TRAPHAGEN, ETHEL Oct. 10, 1882-Apr. 29, 1963 Fashion designer; founder and director of Traphagen School of Fashion. See *Current Biography* (December) 1948.

Obituary

N Y Times p35 Ap 30 '63

TRAUTMAN, GEORGE M(cNEAL) Jan. 11, 1890-June 24, 1963 President and treasurer of the National Association of Professional Baseball Leagues (the minor leagues) (1947-63). See *Current Biography* (October) 1951.

Obituary

N Y Times p33 Je 25 '63

TUCHMAN, BARBARA W(ERTHEIM)
(tŭk'măn) Jan. 30, 1912- Author; historian

Address: h. 875 Park Ave., New York 21; Cos Cob, Conn.

The 1963 Pulitzer Prize for general nonfiction went to Barbara W. Tuchman for her best-selling *The Guns of August,* a history of the beginning phases of World War I. Mrs. Tuchman is a historian whose idea of heaven, according to Max Lerner, is the National Archives and the manuscript division of the Library of Congress. She received her training as a chronicler of world events in the 1930's, working as a researcher for the Institute of Pacific Relations in New York and Tokyo and as an editor, writer, and European correspondent for the *Nation.* In addition to her prize-winning history of the war, which, she says, "is the chasm between our world and a world that died forever," she has written three other historical books and a number of articles. Of her role as a historian, Mrs. Tuchman has remarked: "I belong to the 'How' school rather than the 'Why.' I am a seeker of the small facts, not the big Explanation; a narrator, not a philosopher."

Mrs. Tuchman was born Barbara Wertheim in New York City on January 30, 1912. Her father, Maurice Wertheim, an international banker, publisher, philanthropist, and sportsman, was a founder of the Theatre Guild and a president of the American Jewish Committee. Through her mother, Mrs. Alma (Morgenthau) Wertheim, she is a granddaughter of the noted businessman and diplomat Henry Morgenthau, Sr., a niece of Henry Morgenthau, Jr., who served as Secretary of the Treasury under President Franklin D. Roosevelt, and a cousin of the United States Attorney for New York, Robert M. Morgenthau, who was the Democratic candidate for Governor in 1962. She has two sisters, Josephine (Mrs. Ralph Pomerance), who is active in peace movements, and Mrs. Robert E. Simon, Jr.

Barbara Tuchman experienced her first encounter with World War I in early August 1914, while accompanying her parents on a visit to her maternal grandfather, then the American Ambassador to Turkey. On board an Italian ship on the Mediterranean, headed for Constantinople, the family witnessed an exchange of shots between the British warship *Gloucester* and two German naval vessels, the *Breslau* and the *Goeben.* Many years later she devoted a chapter in *The Guns of August* to this first naval engagement of World War I.

Although she was too young at the time to remember the Anglo-German naval battle, Mrs. Tuchman recalls that she became fascinated with history and world affairs early in life. Contributing to her interest in the historical was the Twins series of children's books by Lucy Fitch Perkins. Later literary influences were works by G. A. Henty, Sir Arthur Conan Doyle, Jane Porter and, in particular, the historical novels of Alexander Dumas. She obtained her secondary education at the Walden School in New York City and spent summers in Europe with her parents. In 1929, after her graduation from the Walden School, she entered Radcliffe College, where she studied under Irving Babbitt and C. H.

McIlwain, and wrote a honors thesis entitled "The Moral Justification for the British Empire."

Imbued with social consciousness and a desire to get out into the world, Barbara Wertheim accompanied her grandfather to the World Economic Conference in London in 1933, the same year that she graduated from Radcliffe with a B.A. degree. In 1934 she began work as a research assistant for the Institute of Pacific Relations in New York City and a year later was sent to the organization's branch office in Tokyo. Upon her return to New York in 1935 she took a position as an editorial assistant and writer with the *Nation,* then owned by her father. (Wertheim sold the *Nation* in 1937 because of a disagreement with its editors.) Max Lerner, one of the editors of the *Nation* at the time, recalls Barbara Wertheim as "a petite, dark, intense girl," who wrote a number of editorial columns and occasional signed feature articles for the magazine.

In 1937 Barbara Wertheim went to Spain as correspondent for the *Nation,* reporting from Madrid during the Spanish Civil War. She then worked for a while in London as a staff writer for the magazine *The War in Spain.* Her first book, *The Lost British Policy: Britain and Spain Since 1700,* was published in 1938 by United Editorial Ltd. in London. Upon her return home in September 1938, during the week of the Munich agreement, she worked as a free-lance writer for the *Nation,* and in the following year she became the United States correspondent for the British journal of opinion *New Statesman and Nation.* On June 18, 1940 she married Dr. Lester Reginald Tuchman, who is president of the medical board of City Hospital in Queens and attending physician at Mount Sinai Hospital in New York City. From 1943 to 1945 Mrs. Tuchman took time out from her duties as housewife and mother to serve as an editor at the news desk of the Office of War Information, dealing with Far Eastern affairs.

In her second book, *Bible and Sword; England and Palestine from the Bronze Age to Balfour* (New York Univ. Press, 1956), Mrs. Tuchman expresses sympathy for the Zionist cause and emphasizes the impact of Palestine's political geography upon its rulers through the ages. She maintains that the Balfour declaration of 1917, favoring a Jewish homeland in Palestine, was a logical product of British conscience and ambition. Mrs. Tuchman's next book was the monographic study *The Zimmerman Telegram* (Viking, 1958), which she based on primary source materials. It describes the suspenseful political and diplomatic developments brought about by the cable sent in January 1917 by the German Foreign Minister, Arthur Zimmerman, to the German Ambassador in Washington, Count von Bernstorff, for forwarding to von Eckhardt, the Imperial German Minister in Mexico. The telegram proposed a German-Mexican alliance in return for territorial concessions in the Southwestern United States. A condensed version of the book was published in *Reader's Digest* in January 1959.

The Guns of August, published by the Macmillan Company in January 1962, sketches in the diplomatic prelude to World War I and the military history of its first thirty days, from the invasion of Belgium on August 4 to the eve of the Battle of the Marne on September 4, 1914. The subject had been suggested to Mrs. Tuchman by Cecil Scott, an editor with the Macmillan Company. To prepare herself for her project Mrs. Tuchman in August 1959 undertook an on-the-spot survey of the areas where the early land battles of World War I had taken place. She closely followed the routes that the German armies had taken through Luxemburg, Belgium, and northern France in their attempt to reach Paris. During the two and a half years required to complete the book, Mrs. Tuchman worked mainly at the New York Public Library and the New York Society Library, delving through books, letters, state documents, diaries, and other materials, published and unpublished. As a journalistic historian rather than as an expert on military strategy, Mrs. Tuchman emphasized the human factor, stressing the weaknesses of national leaders in a time of crisis, whose actions during the first thirty days of the war largely determined the course of events in the years to come. Her treatment of the conflict as it developed in Europe contrasts with many economic and Marxian interpretations of World War I.

The Guns of August was praised by William L. Shirer as "one of the finest books in years." Clifton Fadiman, writing in the *Book-of-the-Month Club News* (February 1962), speculated that it "may turn out to be a historical classic" and added: "Its virtues are almost Thucydidean: intelligence, concision, weight, detachment." Although the military historian Gordon A. Craig predicted in the New York *Herald Tribune* (January 28, 1962) that "few readers who take up her account will be able to put it down without finishing it," he criticized its failure to give an account of the Austro-Hungarian armies. (Mrs. Tuchman explains her reasons for omitting the Austrian and Balkan combat areas in the introductory note to her book.) According to Bruce Bliven in the *New Yorker* (April 14, 1962), "Mrs. Tuchman leans toward seeing issues as black and white but her control of her material is so certain and her opinions are so passionate that it would be risky to argue with her."

A Book-of-the-Month Club selection for February 1962, *The Guns of August* became a best seller, both in its hard-cover edition and as a paperback, issued by the Dell Publishing Company. *The Guns of August* appeared in England with the title *August 1914*, and it has been published in many European countries and in Japan. It is being made into a motion picture to be released by Universal-International in August 1964 to commemorate the fiftieth anniversary of the outbreak of World War I. According to Max Lerner, the book has stimulated an interest in World War I that may rival the current mania for the American Civil War, and President John F. Kennedy was so fascinated by *The Guns of August* that he presented a copy to Prime Minister Harold Macmillan during his visit to the United States in June 1962. Barbara Tuchman is now working on a new book that deals with "La Belle Époque"—the twenty-year period preceding the beginning of World War I.

Frank Pemberton

BARBARA W. TUCHMAN

Over the years she has contributed articles to the *Nation,* the *New Republic,* the *Atlantic Monthly, Esquire, American Heritage, Foreign Affairs, Pacific Affairs* and other publications.

Mrs. Tuchman tries to adhere to the school of the noted nineteenth-century German historian Leopold von Ranke, who insisted that the historian must make every effort to write history as it actually occurred, although she concedes that his goal is one that will forever remain beyond reach. "We can never be certain that we have recaptured it as it really was, but the least we can do is stay within the evidence," she said in a dinner address to the Radcliffe chapter of Phi Beta Kappa in April 1963. Finding history far more interesting than fiction, she maintains that it presents a greater challenge and responsibility to the writer. Of the systematizers and philosophers of history, like Arnold J. Toynbee, who try to fit the past into prefabricated patterns, Mrs. Tuchman is somewhat skeptical. "If the historian will submit himself *to* his material instead of trying to impose himself *on* his material, then the material will ultimately speak to him and supply the answers," she has said.

Mrs. Barbara W. Tuchman, who is now divorced, has three daughters: Lucy (Mrs. David Eisenberg), a 1961 graduate of Radcliffe; Jessica, now a student at Radcliffe; and Alma, who attends the Brearly School in New York City. Mrs. Tuchman is five feet five inches tall, weighs 119 pounds, and has gray hair and gray eyes. A skier and poker player, she also indulges in gardening at her home at Cos Cob, Connecticut. She is a member of the Cosmopolitan Club in New York City and since 1960 has served as a trustee of Radcliffe College. Mrs. Tuchman fears that the lessons of history are sometimes lost on the statesmen of the present day. "I'm not for sitting back in 1962 and saying, Look what fools they

TUCHMAN, BARBARA W.—*Continued*

were," she told Joseph Wershba in an interview for the New York *Post* (February 18, 1962). "Anyone who wants to talk of the stupidity of 1914 has only to remember the Bay of Pigs in 1961."

References

Christian Sci Mon p7 My 17 '62 por; p2 N 3 '62 por
N Y Post Mag p2 F 18 '62 por
N Y Times p35 My 7 '63 por
New Yorker 38:42+ O 6 '62
Radcliffe Quarterly 47:29+ My '63 por
Washington (D.C.) Post B p2 F 5 '63 por; F p12 F 17 '63 por
Who's Who of American Women, 1964-65

TUGWELL, REXFORD G(UY) July 10, 1891-

Political scientist; educator; economist; author

Address: b. University of Puerto Rico, Rio Piedras, Puerto Rico; h. MD3 Finca Universitaria, University of Puerto Rico, Rio Piedras, Puerto Rico

> NOTE: This biography supersedes the article that appeared in *Current Biography* in 1941.

Rexford G. Tugwell, former Governor of Puerto Rico and leading proponent of the New Deal programs of Franklin D. Roosevelt, believes that government is "an expression of man's effort to control his environment and shape it as a means to his ends," and that it should reasonably secure every man against the risks and hardships of life. He put some of his liberal ideas into practice in the Department of Agriculture during the 1930's —as Assistant Secretary, then Under Secretary, of Agriculture and as administrator of the Rural Resettlement Administration. He also effected a number of reforms in Puerto Rico while he was Governor of the island from 1941 to 1946.

Since his retirement in 1957 Tugwell has been a consultant to the chancellor of the University of Puerto Rico. A teacher of economics at Columbia University from 1920 to 1937, he was a professor of political science at the University of Chicago from 1946 to 1957 and the director of its Institute of Planning from 1946 to 1952. Tugwell has written many books and articles on government and economics.

Rexford Guy Tugwell, the oldest of four children of Charles Henry and Edessa (Rexford) Tugwell, was born on July 10, 1891 in Sinclairville, a village in Chautauqua County in western New York State. His two brothers died in infancy, and his sister, eight years younger than he, is no longer living. His mother, a former teacher in a one-room school, was active in the intellectual activities of Chautauqua. A devotee of romantic literature, she often read the poetry of Thomas Moore, Longfellow, and Tennyson aloud to Tugwell. From his father, a hard-working entrepreneur, he acquired a knowledge of practical affairs. In his autobiographical *The Light of Other Days* (Doubleday, 1962) Tugwell recalls that he had a happy and affectionate home life, in which the tenets of Congregationalism were followed, but not too strictly.

Tugwell learned to read early, and during his frequent respiratory illnesses (including asthma attacks), he turned to books as a solace. Although he read widely, he was a poor student in the small schools he attended, where, he recalls, he was rarely challenged or required to make more than minimal efforts. Outside of school Tugwell fished and swam, skated and skied, played basketball and volleyball, hunted "coons," and went to sugaring offs.

In relating his own boyhood in *The Light of Other Days* Tugwell evokes an idyllic picture of village life at the turn of the century. "Yet it has to be said that the boys and girls who were growing up in rural America at the beginning of the century," Tugwell wrote in *The Light of Other Days,* "would not turn out to be the kinds of citizens needed for their times. Even the civic virtues and the more general ideals, so faithfully held, would be dangerously anachronistic." *The Light of Other Days* tries to trace the influences that brought about genuine liberty, but also much moral selfishness, in America, and that eventually led its people to sanction the "final sin" of dropping the atomic bomb on Hiroshima and Nagasaki in 1945.

Tugwell first emerged from the parochial world of Sinclairville when he took a six-month trip to Colorado with his parents in 1902. Two years later the Tugwells left Sinclairville permanently, moving to Wilson, New York. Charles Tugwell, who had been a cattle dealer and then the manager of a canning plant in Sinclairville, became the manager and part owner of a canning plant in Wilson and eventually the president of a bank. Rexford Tugwell worked each summer during his college years as a hand in the canning factory and as a traveling field man who judged the correct time to harvest each farmer's crop for canning. He made the acquaintance of the impoverished Sicilians who were seasonal workers in the factory, and he came to question the fairness of a system in which workers were given the lowest possible wages.

From his youth Tugwell felt the desire to write, and he first saw his words in print in the Niagara Falls *Gazette,* to which he contributed news of the Wilson community for one year. He attended Wilson High School, but found its courses inadequate for college preparation. After passing some preliminary regents examinations with the help of his principal, he transferred to Masten Park High School in Buffalo. There he thought of becoming a biologist, but was discouraged by his limited grasp of mathematics. A member of the high school literary society, he wrote for the *Masten Park Chronicle.* He also played football until his asthma attacks forced him to stop. During his last year at Masten Park, he worked for the Buffalo *Courier,* checking the courts and city departments for routine news.

Like his move to Wilson from Sinclairville, Tugwell's move to Buffalo broadened his horizons. Developing a social awareness, he began to question the morality of profit-seeking and unrestrained competition. No political party seemed to offer any satisfactory program for alleviating the hardships suffered by many. He was aware that he had somehow become a part of "the fraternity of those who dissented from orthodoxy."

In 1911 Tugwell enrolled at the Wharton School of Finance and Commerce of the University of Pennsylvania, from which he received the B.S. degree in economics in 1915, the M.A. degree in 1916, and the Ph.D. degree in 1922. There he was introduced to the scientific management principles of the American efficiency engineer Frederick Winslow Taylor. He became managing editor of the *Daily Pennsylvanian* and a member of Delta Upsilon. After serving from 1915 to 1917 as an instructor in economics at the University of Pennsylvania, Tugwell became an assistant professor of economics at the University of Washington for one year. He then went to Paris to manage the American University Union, and on his return in 1920 became an instructor in economics at Columbia University. He remained at Columbia until 1937, where he was promoted to assistant professor in 1922, associate professor in 1926, and professor in 1931. With L. H. Keyserling he co-edited a book, *Redirecting Education* (Columbia Univ. Press, 1935), which contained essays on the teaching of social science.

Beginning with his Ph.D. thesis, *The Economic Basis of Public Interest* (George Banta, 1922), Tugwell wrote and edited (sometimes with others) several books that criticized the existing laissez-faire economy and that called for economic planning and for the governmental regulation of industry to serve social, rather than individual, ends. Some of these are *The Trend of Economics* (Knopf, 1924), *American Economic Life and the Means of its Improvement* (Harcourt, 1925), *Industry's Coming of Age* (Harcourt, 1927), and *The Industrial Discipline and the Governmental Arts* (Columbia Univ. Press, 1933), the last two directly derived from Taylor's principles.

In the summer of 1927 Tugwell visited the Soviet Union with a delegation of trade unionists, and on his return he co-edited and contributed a chapter on Russian agriculture to the book *Soviet Russia in the Second Decade* (Day, 1928). In 1928 he made a survey of American agricultural problems for the New York Governor, Al Smith, whom he supported for the Presidency that year. During the 1932 Presidential campaign he was one of Franklin D. Roosevelt's close advisors, and he served in Roosevelt's administration under Henry A. Wallace as Assistant Secretary of Agriculture, from 1933 to 1934, and Under Secretary of Agriculture, from 1934 to 1936.

One of Roosevelt's "brain-trusters," Tugwell became a leading spokesman for New Deal programs, and he advanced many original ideas for economic, social, and agricultural reform. In a newspaper interview in January 1933 he advocated the spending of $5 billion for relief and redistribution of purchasing power; the rapid spending of public works money; and higher income and inheritance taxes, and he urged that consumer protection be part of the National Recovery Act.

Tugwell supported soil conservation and crop reduction, rather than the dumping of farm surpluses. From 1935 through 1936 he was administrator of the Rural Resettlement Administration,

REXFORD G. TUGWELL

which relocated farmers from unproductive to fertile land and provided advice on scientific methods of farming. His green-belt "Tugwell-towns" have served as models for private and government low-income suburban housing projects. He administered the land-use program for soil erosion control and rural rehabilitation and electrification. He is credited with originating currency legislation and the processing tax, and he was instrumental in the formation of the Civilian Conservation Corps. He also worked on the government housing board, the surplus relief administration, the commercial policy committee, and the public works board. His book *The Battle for Democracy* (Columbia Univ. Press, 1935) is a collection of his Washington speeches favoring a democratic economy and the New Deal.

Tugwell's bold views on the government's role in regulating industry and establishing social welfare programs brought him savage criticism from right-wing politicians, who accused him of being a Communist. But Tugwell once called himself a conservative bent on saving capitalism from itself, and his superior in the Department of Agriculture, Henry A. Wallace, said of him at that time, "Men of Tugwell's courage and insight are rare." Tugwell resigned his federal posts late in 1936 and became executive vice-president of the American Molasses Company.

In April 1938 Mayor Fiorello H. LaGuardia appointed Tugwell chairman of the New York City Planning Commission to succeed A. A. Berle. That year Tugwell prepared the first annual capital budget for New York City; he wrote the budget again in November 1940. In December 1940 Harold Ickes, United States Secretary of the Interior, asked Tugwell to go to Puerto Rico to investigate methods of enforcing a law there, forbidding corporations from owning more than 500 acres of land. Tugwell thus made the acquaintance of Luis Muñoz Marín, then president of the Puerto Rican senate, who had campaigned for enforcement of the law, and with Muñoz's

TUGWELL, REXFORD G.—*Continued*

support he became chancellor of the University of Puerto Rico in July 1941. Shortly thereafter President Roosevelt asked Tugwell to take the post of Governor of Puerto Rico, succeeding Guy J. Swope. The United States Senate confirmed his appointment in August 1941 and Tugwell resigned as chancellor of the university in September 1941 to take up the Governorship.

In *The Stricken Land* (Doubleday, 1946) Tugwell describes his five years as Governor of Puerto Rico during wartime. His administration did much to improve the economic and political situation despite problems resulting from the extreme poverty of the people, the bitter opposition of political parties no longer in power, the shortages caused by the submarine blockade, and the need for military preparedness. Tugwell believes that the achievements of his 1942 legislative program represent the second genuinely creative period of his public life. They included the Planning Act and the establishment of a budget bureau, a central statistical office, and the Development Bank. His proposals for reorganization of the civil service and modernization of the police force were defeated by the legislature. *Puerto Rican Public Papers of R. G. Tugwell* was published in 1945, and Tugwell's *The Place of Planning in Society*, with special reference to Puerto Rico, was published in 1954.

In 1946, after Roosevelt's death, Tugwell was invited to return to the academic world as a professor of political science and director of the Institute of Planning at the University of Chicago. Realizing that any beneficial influence he might have in Washington on behalf of Puerto Rico was now gone, and challenged by the opportunity to direct research on more effective government planning, Tugwell resigned as Governor of Puerto Rico in June 1946 and went to the University of Chicago, where he was professor of political science until his retirement in 1957 and director of the Institute of Planning until 1952. For a while he was a member of the Progressive party, and in 1948 he worked for the national Wallace for President committee.

Concerned with the potential danger to civilization in the atomic age, Tugwell worked for two years with an eleven-man committee at the University of Chicago to draft a constitution for a world government, which was made public in March 1948. His book *The Chronicle of Jeopardy* (Chicago Univ. Press, 1955) gives his reactions to the atomic threat during 1945-55. Tugwell has given his personal impressions of three eminent political leaders, Muñoz, La Guardia, and Roosevelt, in *The Art of Politics* (Doubleday, 1958). He has also written *The Enlargement of the Presidency* (Doubleday, 1960), *Early American Policy: Six Columbia Contributors* (with others, Columbia Univ. Press, 1960), and *The Democratic Roosevelt* (Doubleday, 1957).

Tugwell was visiting professor of political science at the London School of Economics from 1949 to 1950, and Hillman lecturer at Howard University in 1959. He taught a summer course at Columbia University on the American Presidency in 1962. At present he is a consultant to the chancellor of the University of Puerto Rico.

Recipient of a Woodrow Wilson Foundation award in 1958, he had also received an honorary Litt.D. degree from the University of New Mexico in 1933 and an honorary LL.D. degree from the University of Puerto Rico in 1953. He is a member of the International Institute of Planners, the American Political Science Association, the Cosmos Club in Washington, D.C., and the Hamilton Street Club in Baltimore.

On June 7, 1914 Rexford G. Tugwell married Florence E. Arnold, from whom he was divorced in August 1938. They have two daughters, Tanis and Marcia. He and his second wife, the former Grace Falke, whom he married in November 1938, have two sons, Tyler and Franklin. Tugwell has blue eyes and white hair and is five feet ten inches in height. He is a Unitarian. Tugwell wrote, in *The Light of Other Days*, "I had had a good life—work I believed in, repeatedly enlivened with controversy, set among pleasant scenes, and rich with the affection of family and friends."

References

Tugwell, Rexford G. The Light of Other Days (1962); The Stricken Land (1946)
Who's Who in America, 1962-63

TYNAN, KENNETH (PEACOCK) Apr. 2, 1927- British drama critic; author; theater literary manager

Address: b. British National Theatre, 22 Duchy St., London, S.E.1, England; h. 120 Mount St., London, W.1., England

The most influential drama critic in Great Britain, Kenneth Tynan joined the weekly *Observer* in 1954 and has since earned comparison with Hazlitt, Shaw, and Beerbohm as a critic of the first rank. Tynan has become identified with a new vitality in the British theater, and it has been said that he "not only espoused the new English realism . . . but in a way summoned it." Only twenty-seven when he joined the staff of the *Observer*, he already enjoyed a national reputation as an *enfant terrible* that he had gained as an undergraduate at Oxford and as the precocious drama critic of the *Spectator* (1951-52), the *Evening Standard* (1952-53), and the *Daily Sketch* (1953-54). In 1958 he went to the United States for two seasons as drama critic of the *New Yorker*. Tynan has worked as an actor and as a director and has written several books. In 1963 he served as chairman of the International Drama Conference and became the first literary manager of the British National Theatre, which opened in October.

Kenneth Peacock Tynan was born on April 2, 1927 in the industrial city of Birmingham, England. Godfrey Smith, in a profile for the *Sunday Times* magazine (August 25, 1963) has reported that Tynan's father, Sir Peter Peacock, began his career as a dollar-a-week clerk, amassed a considerable fortune as a store owner, and was at one time mayor of Warrington, Lancashire. According to Tynan, before his death in 1948, Peacock legally adopted the family name of Tynan's mother, a Lancashire girl of Irish extraction and equally humble origins called Letitia Rose Tynan. Peacock, a Liberal and a Methodist, had no interest in the arts and wanted his son to become a lawyer. It was Tynan's mother who introduced him to the theater, taking him on occasional jaunts to London to see plays by Noel Coward and musicals by Ivor Novello.

Tynan attended public elementary schools in Birmingham and then went on to the King Edward VI School in the same city. There he played cricket for the school team, and there the Tynan legend began to take shape. At fifteen he took part in a mock parliamentary election, and as independent candidate advocated repeal of laws governing homosexuality and abortion. When the headmaster demanded the withdrawal of this platform, Tynan called a protest meeting that ended in something like a riot. Asked to withdraw from the election, Tynan handed the headmaster his resignation and that of the three other candidates.

At the age of ten Tynan had discovered Birmingham's repertory company and had become addicted to the theater. Soon he was traveling further afield. In 1943, when he was sixteen, he saw a performance of *Hamlet* at Stratford that so excited him that he felt an urge to capture the experience in words. An actor friend challenged him to produce a review in an hour, as professional critics must. The result won praise from the late James Agate, then the authoritative critic of the *Sunday Times* magazine. In this and subsequent precocities of Tynan, Agate saw "a great dramatic critic in the making."

Two years later, in October 1945, Tynan went up to Magdalen College, Oxford. Godfrey Smith, a contemporary of Tynan's at the university, wrote in the London *Sunday Times* magazine (August 25, 1963): "I don't think even the substantial faction who loathed him would deny that this will go down in the history books as Tynan's Oxford." Tynan at Oxford habitually wore a purple doeskin suit and a gold satin shirt; he so outraged his enemies that he was burned in straw effigy by Rugger thugs in Broad Street. Tynan reacted by driving a borrowed car through the flaming bonfire. He became editor of the *Cherwell*, the undergraduate newspaper; drama critic of the university magazine, the *Isis;* editor of a broadsheet called *Avant Garde;* and secretary of the famous Oxford Union debating society, where his speeches invariably packed the house.

Before he left Oxford, Tynan also served as president of the university's Experimental Theatre Club, where he directed five plays (including *A Toy in Blood*, his own adaptation of *Hamlet*) and acted in nine productions. He wrote for and appeared in three Experimental Theatre Club revues, and still found time to throw parties for the Old Vic Company, the cast of *Anna Lucasta*, and for Gertrude Lawrence. He came down from Oxford in 1948 with second-class honors in English, already committed to a career in the theater.

Tynan went to work in 1949 as the director of a repertory company at Lichfield, Staffordshire and the following year directed his first London production, *A Man of the World*, which opened at the Lyric, Hammersmith, and later moved to the Phoenix Theatre. Later in 1950 he took a production of *Othello* on a tour financed by the British Arts Council. As an

Wide World

KENNETH TYNAN

undergraduate, Tynan had sold a review to the *Spectator,* a weekly magazine which at that time invited contributions from students. Early in 1951 he began to write regularly for the magazine as its dramatic critic.

In May 1951 occurred Tynan's first and so far his only professional appearance as an actor. Alec Guinness was directing *Hamlet* at London's New Theatre for the Festival of Britain and asked Tynan to take the part of the Player King. Tynan objected that he lacked the experience, but finally accepted. The production was a failure, and Tynan was singled out for harsh criticism by Beverley Baxter in the London *Evening Standard.* Tynan replied in a coruscating letter. Soon afterward he was hired by the *Evening Standard,* and in 1952 he succeeded Baxter as the newspaper's theater critic.

Tynan stayed with the *Evening Standard* until the end of 1953, worked briefly for the *Daily Sketch,* and, in the spring of 1954, joined the *Observer* as its theater critic. He thus, at the age of twenty-seven, achieved a commanding position in British dramatic criticism roughly comparable with that occupied in the United States by Walter Kerr. He brought to his work a supple and epigrammatic literary style, extraordinary erudition, and a talent for the provocative assertion that has delighted, irritated, and unfailingly stimulated his nationwide audience.

At first, as Tynan has himself confessed, he had small use for realism in the theater. "I revered poetic plays about the death of kings," he wrote in *Curtains,* "especially if they had not been performed since the seventeenth century." For him, "drama was apart from life, instead of a part of it." Gradually, under the influence of writers like Bertolt Brecht and Arthur Miller, he "became aware that art, ethics, politics and economics were inseparable from each other . . . that no theatre could sanely flourish until there was an umbilical connec-

TYNAN, KENNETH—Continued

tion between what was happening on the stage and what was happening in the world." His influence grew until, as Godfrey Smith observed in the *Sunday Times* magazine (August 25, 1963), "he crystallized the aspirations of the New Wave that re-invigorated the British theatre in the 1950's."

In 1958 Tynan left the *Observer* for two seasons as theater critic of the *New Yorker*. His impact on the American theatrical scene was immediate. He is said to have been almost entirely responsible for the selection by the New York Drama Critics Circle of Lorraine Hansberry's *Raisin in the Sun* as prize play of 1958-59. The success of Jack Gelber's *The Connection* has also been attributed largely to his influence. On the other hand, his murderously witty attacks on what he considered second-rate drama made him many enemies, and David Merrick threatened to ban him from his theaters. Richard Watts has said that, within months of his arrival, the mere dropping of his name at theatrical parties was enough to provoke violent argument.

Nor was Tynan's impact in the United States confined to the theater. In January 1960 British television audiences saw a program prepared by Tynan called *We Dissent*, in which twenty-five United States citizens aired nonconformist views on certain aspects of the American scene. Participants in the program, presented to "combat the false idea . . . that America was a land of intellectual conformity," included Alger Hiss, Norman Thomas, Robert M. Hutchins, Norman Mailer, Mort Sahl, Allen Ginzberg, and Jules Feiffer. On May 5, 1960 Tynan was summoned before a closed session of the Senate internal security subcommittee. He was questioned about *We Dissent* and also about his signing of a newspaper advertisement expressing sympathy for the Castro regime in Cuba. "I submit," Tynan wrote in *Harper's Magazine* (October 1960), "that governmental grilling of foreign newspapermen is not a practice that one instinctively associates with the workings of Western Democracy."

In 1960 Tynan returned to the *Observer*, where he remained until he took up his present post as literary manager of the British National Theatre. As yet it has no home of its own, though one was authorized by Parliament as long ago as January 1949. It will stand on the South Bank of the Thames, near the Royal Festival Hall, where in 1951 Tynan protested against building delays by standing in full mourning on the deserted site. The new building is now scheduled for completion in 1965 or 1966. Meanwhile, the National Theatre will be housed in what was the famous Old Vic Theatre, where it opened on October 22, 1963, with a production of *Hamlet*.

Long a propagandist for a national theater, Tynan has accepted his new assignment for an initial period of a year. As literary manager, he will guide Sir Laurence Olivier, artistic director of the National Theatre, in the choice of plays and texts, commission new plays, arrange for translations, and write program notes. Eventually, it is hoped, a different play will be presented every night, about two-thirds of them established classics, the rest revivals and new plays. Tynan will continue to write for the *Observer*, but not as resident theater critic. In his valedictory column in that newspaper (August 25, 1963) he wrote: "I have prayed . . . for a national theatre; and the challenge of helping that enormous dream to take shape was something out of which I could not decently chicken. . . . It is the commercial theatre that sets up barriers between critic and artist. . . . In a non-commercial theatre, where profit and loss are not the first considerations . . . critic and artist can work together in the common pursuit of perfection."

Tynan's first book was *He That Plays the King* (Longmans, 1950), an intensely personal view of the theater, which was published when its author was twenty-three. His friend Orson Welles contributed a foreword, and the book's audacious judgements irritated some reviewers but delighted most with their intellectual exuberance *Alec Guinness* (Rockliff, 1953; Macmillan, 1955) was a study of the actor's work that has been reprinted repeatedly. It was followed by *Persona Grata* (Wingate, 1953; Putnam, 1954), a collection of 100 impressionistic profiles of personalities in the arts, illustrated with Cecil Beaton's photographs. Tynan's fourth book was *Bull Fever* (Harper; Longmans, 1955), an "evocative and well-informed" critique of a highly theatrical art that had captured Tynan's imagination when he saw his first bullfight in 1950. *Curtains* (Atheneum; Longmans, 1961) was a highly praised collection of Tynan's reviews and other writings.

In 1956 Tynan was co-author with Harold Lang of a radio feature called *The Quest for Corbett*, published in 1960 by Gaberbocchus. From 1956 to 1958 he served as a script editor for Ealing Films. Tynan makes much of his income by writing for leading magazines in the United States and England. He plans to write a book about his generation at Oxford, to be called *Now, Alas, Demolished,* but does not believe that he will ever write a play, "the hardest of all things you can do with a pen." Tynan has achieved his reputation as a brilliant public speaker, earned on platforms and television screens in many parts of the world, in spite of a persistent and sometimes acute stammer. He scored a triumph in September 1963, when he served as chairman of the International Drama Conference, held as part of the Edinburgh Festival. According to John O'Callaghan in the *Guardian* (September 9, 1963): "Any assessment of the conference must remark Mr. Tynan's courage and self-control as general supervisor. Never can there have been such a volatile assembly of artists, showmen, and charlatans. To have kept them from assaulting one another was achievement enough. To have stirred them to a series of sensible debates bordered the miraculous." Tynan is a Fellow of the Royal Society of Literature.

Kenneth Tynan was married in 1951 to Elaine Dundy, the American actress who wrote the best-selling novel *The Dud Avocado* and, more recently, a play called *My Place* that ran for a month in London in 1962. They have a daughter, Tracy, named after a character once played by Katherine Hepburn, who is her god-mother. Tynan is a little over six feet tall and cadaverously thin, with hair that has been described as "butter-colored." His favorite re-creations include eating and watching bullfights. According to a fellow critic, Tynan "has already earned a footnote in any history of the stage. Whether he will have a chapter to himself we shall now see."

References

London Sunday Times p16 Ag 25 '63 pors
International Who's Who, 1963-64
Who's Who in the Theatre (1961)

VALLEE, RUDY (văl'ē) July 28, 1901- Entertainer

Address: 7430 Pyramid Place, Hollywood, Calif.

NOTE: This biography supersedes the article that appeared in *Current Biography* in 1947.

Rudy Vallee's widely acclaimed performance in the Broadway musical hit *How to Succeed in Business Without Really Trying* has proved that he is one of the most durable and versatile entertainers in the United States. Beginning his career as a saxophonist and bandleader in the 1920's, Vallee was one of the first crooners and a popular radio and vaudeville personality over the next two decades. The megaphone through which he crooned his theme song, "My Time is Your Time," and his nickname, "The Vagabond Lover," (derived from one of his songs and from his first movie) became inseparably associated with him. From 1929 to 1939 he and his band, the Connecticut Yankees, appeared on the *Fleischmann Hour* over NBC radio.

As television largely replaced radio, and public taste changed, Vallee lost some of his luster as an entertainer. In the 1950's he toured nightclubs in the United States and Canada with a solo comedy-singing act. Foreshadowed by some of Vallee's movie roles in the 1940's and 1950's, his portrayal of a pompous corporation executive in *How to Succeed in Business Without Really Trying* returned him to the limelight in 1961 and won him new recognition for his acting ability. Vallee has written two autobiographies, *Vagabond Dreams Come True* (Dutton, 1930) and, with Gil McKean, *My Time is Your Time* (Obolensky, 1962).

Rudy Vallee was born Hubert Prior Vallée in Island Pond, Vermont, near the French-Canadian border, on July 28, 1901. (He adopted the name "Rudy" in the 1920's from Rudy Wiedoeft, a saxophonist he admired.) Of French-Irish descent, he was one of three children of Charles Alphonse and Katherine (Lynch) Vallée. His older sister, Kathleen Vallée Lenneville became a music teacher, and his younger brother, William Lynch Vallée, became a magazine writer. Early in his childhood the family moved to Westbrook, Maine, where his father opened a drugstore. Rudy Vallee's first musical instrument, which he received when he was four, was an enameled metal drum upon which he banged to allay the pain of the earaches that often plagued him. He

RUDY VALLEE

later learned to play a complete set of drums, the piano, and the clarinet.

Rudy Vallee was only nine when he began to help out in his father's drugstore. At Westbrook High School he chose the industrial training course, but both work and school bored him, and he therefore joined the United States Navy in 1917, only to be discharged a few weeks later when it was discovered that he was only fifteen. Returning to Westbrook High and the drugstore, Vallee took some comfort from the records and demonstration phonograph that his father had added to the stock. Within a few weeks, however, he again left the drugstore and became janitor, usher, and operator of the hand-cranked projection machine at the local movie house, the Star Theater.

In 1918 Vallee began commuting between Westbrook and nearby Portland to a job as head usher at the DeLuxe Strand Theater. It was here that he got his first C melody saxophone from a fellow employee. At that time the saxophone was still a rarity; there were perhaps 100 saxophonists in the United States, and there was no adequate teacher in Portland. Applying his clarinet techniques and inspired by phonograph recordings of Rudy Wiedoeft, Vallee taught himself to play. In trying to reproduce Wiedoeft's "wave-like" sounds on the instrument, Vallee hit upon a vibrato or "singing saxophone" effect that later became associated with him. By 1920 he was playing with the Strand Theater orchestra as a local celebrity.

In 1921 Vallee entered the University of Maine, but the following year he transferred to Yale University, where he majored in Spanish and joined the Sigma Alpha Epsilon fraternity. To pay for his tuition and board he played with a college group in the dining hall, and two or three times a week with bands under the Jack Cipriano-Bill Bolton management at dances and parties between New York and Boston. He began to carry a truncated megaphone in the bell of

VALLEE, RUDY—Continued

his baritone sax and to sing through it occasionally with the band. In the summer of 1923 he played an engagement at the Rendez-vous nightclub in New York City.

Taking a leave of absence from Yale, Vallee spent nine months in London from September 1924 to June 1925. He played with a band at the Hotel Savoy, made recordings, and gave private saxophone lessons. Among the songs that he picked up in London and popularized in the United States was "My Time is Your Time," which later became his theme song on the *Fleischmann Hour.* In the summer of 1925 he played at Old Orchard Beach, Maine, and in the fall he resumed his studies at Yale and his band engagements several times a week. The following summer, with a band called the Yale Collegians, he went on a vaudeville tour that took him as far as Chicago. As a senior, Vallee led the eighty-piece Yale football band.

After receiving his Ph.B. degree in 1927, Vallee played in the Boston and New York City areas at hotels, country clubs, society functions, and dances with the Yale Collegians, a Vincent Lopez band, and Ben Bernie ensembles. In January 1928 he formed his own eight-piece band, which played its opening engagement at the new, exclusive Heigh-Ho Club in New York City. The following month WABC began to broadcast the music of Vallee and his band live from the club. First called the Yale Collegians, the band was later renamed the Connecticut Yankees.

The program was an immediate success, and for one year the Connecticut Yankees broadcast from the club about twenty times a week over WABC and other radio stations. Vallee's salutation, "Heigh-ho, everybody!" became his byword over radio. He sang, announced and talked about the songs himself, and had his band change keys from one number to another to avoid monotony. Describing these early programs to a *Show Business Illustrated* interviewer (January 23, 1962), Vallee said: "We couldn't afford a big band in those days. Nor could we afford an announcer. There wasn't even room for a brass section in our format. So partly by design and partly by accident, the jaded New York listener . . . suddenly heard music with no brass, two strings, two saxes and a lot of piano. They also heard an announcer named Rudy Vallee, a guy who spoke through his nose like Coolidge . . . and made a song interesting."

While appearing at the club, Vallee also conducted a band for tea dances at the Lombardy Hotel. After leaving the Heigh-Ho in January 1929 the Connecticut Yankees appeared on the Keith circuit, at the Palace Theater, and for ten weeks at the Paramount Theaters in New York and Brooklyn. (They returned to the Paramount in October 1929 for a twenty-one month run.) Meanwhile, Vallee's band acquired new headquarters at the Versailles nightclub on East 60th Street, which was renamed the Villa Vallee, and Vallee invested in a new Greenwich Village nightspot, the Daffydill Club.

In October 1929 Standard Brands signed Vallee and his augmented band for an hour-long weekly radio show over WNBC to advertise Fleischmann's Yeast. Over the next decade the *Fleischmann Hour* achieved top popularity. At first featuring band music and singing by Vallee, it was changed in 1932 into radio's first variety show on which Vallee, as master of ceremonies, introduced established or new talent. Key scenes from Broadway hits and first-person accounts of unusual experiences were also presented.

In the summer of 1930 the Connecticut Yankees toured the East and the Middle West, and in 1931 they again appeared throughout the United States. After leaving the Villa Vallee in 1931 the Connecticut Yankees played at the Hotel Pennsylvania for two years. Vallee appeared in *George White's Scandals of 1931* and in *George White's Scandals of 1936.* He also formed a talent agency in the 1930's and, later, two music companies. During the week of George VI's coronation in May 1937 Vallee played an engagement in London.

In his regular club appearances and on the radio Vallee introduced many new songs that later became hits. Some of the hundreds of songs with which he became associated are "I'm Just a Vagabond Lover" (words and music by Vallee), "Deep Night" (lyrics by Vallee), the University of Maine "Stein Song," "Good Night Sweetheart," "I Kiss Your Hand, Madame," "Lover Come Back To Me," "Springtime in the Rockies," "Honey," "Marie," and the "Whiffenpoof Song" of Yale University.

The popularity of Vallee and his song "I'm Just a Vagabond Lover" led RKO to film *The Vagabond Lover* (1929). Characterizing his performance as "almost laughable," Vallee added: "When I saw the première, I thought I was ruined for life." Hollywood, however, continued to cast him as a crooner in other films, among them *Sweet Music* (1935), *Gold Diggers in Paris* (1938), *Second Fiddle* (1939), *Time Out for Rhythm* (1941), and *Too Many Blondes* (1941). Playing opposite Claudette Colbert in *The Palm Beach Story* (1942), Vallee was a resounding success as John D. Hackensacker III, a stuffy millionaire.

In October 1939 Vallee ended his ten-year association with Fleischmann's Yeast. He returned to the air in March 1940 with a weekly show, *The Sealtest Hour,* sponsored by National Dairies, which used historical events as background material and featured guest stars and Vallee in humorous sketches. It ran through 1941, after which Vallee switched from sponsor to sponsor for relatively short periods of time. In the fall of 1940 Vallee invested in a Hollywood nightclub, the Pirate's Den.

Following America's entry into World War II, Vallee enlisted in the United States Coast Guard, where he rose in rank from chief petty officer to lieutenant, senior grade. He continued to broadcast during 1942 (with his salary going to the Coast Guard Welfare Fund) but left radio entirely in 1943 to assume full-time duties as bandmaster of the Eleventh Naval District Coast Guard Band, based in Wilmington, California. A twenty-piece group when he took over, it was later augmented to forty-seven pieces and earned a reputation as one of the finest service bands in the country. The band entertained groups in all the services and played at war bond rallies.

Vallee returned to radio in 1944 and for the first time produced and directed his own program, *Villa Vallee*. The show was first built around apparent radio rehearsal sessions and then around a night club, owned by Billie Burke, where anything could happen. *Villa Vallee* was sponsored by Procter and Gamble for Drene Shampoo through August 1946. Philip Morris cigarettes sponsored Vallee in another show from 1946 to 1947.

Upon his return to civilian life Vallee also resumed his movie career. His last film role before he entered the Coast Guard had been that of a yacht-owning millionaire in *Happy-Go-Lucky* (1943). In 1945 he was seen in *Man Alive* and, as himself, in *It's in the Bag*. *People Are Funny* and *The Fabulous Suzanne* followed in 1946, and the *The Bachelor and the Bobby-Soxer* in 1947. Of his performance in the last film, Alton Cook of the New York *World-Telegram* (July 25, 1947) wrote, "You will discover once again that Rudy Vallee, playing a pompous, jealous suitor, is developing into one of our better light comedians." Also in 1947 Vallee appeared in *I Remember Mama*. In 1949 Vallee had parts in *Father Was a Fullback*, *The Beautiful Blonde From Bashful Bend*, and *Mother is a Freshman*, and in 1950 he portrayed a prissy jukebox tycoon in *The Admiral Was a Lady*. He appeared in *Ricochet Romance* in 1954, in *Gentlemen Marry Brunettes* in 1955 and in *The Helen Morgan Story*, as himself, in 1957.

With the advent of television Vallee auditioned for a number of programs in the new medium. "I got some good offers," he explained in a *Saturday Evening Post* interview (June 23, 1962), "but I didn't like the way I looked on the screen." He has, however, appeared as a guest star on the *Ed Sullivan Show* and other programs and has acted in *Kraft Theater* productions. Embarking on a new career as a nightclub comedian in 1949, over the next twelve years Vallee developed a solo act that was about three-quarters comedy and one-quarter crooning and that contained, in his opinion, "the best collection of minister, priest, and rabbi stories ever told." In 1954 he played the part of a priest in a summer stock production of Jean Kerr's *Jenny Kissed Me*, and he repeated the role at the Pasadena Playhouse in 1956.

In October 1961 Vallee returned to Broadway for the first time since 1936 in the Abe Burrows-Frank Loesser musical *How to Succeed in Business Without Really Trying*. A New York *Herald Tribune* reviewer (October 16, 1961) observed, "Rudy Vallee is very funny . . . in a tough-minded, high-handed, majestically incompetent way. As a corporation president who steadies his nerves by knitting covers for his golfclubs . . . Mr. Vallee is reflective, sober, and preposterous." Most critics experienced a moment of nostalgia when Vallee cupped his hands to his mouth like a megaphone and sang "Grand Old Ivy," a satire on college songs, in a way reminiscent of his own style of the 1930's. In June 1962 for his performance Vallee received a citation from the Outer Circle, a group of drama critics for out-of-town newspapers and other publications.

Vallee was president of the American Federation of Actors in 1937. He belongs to ASCAP, to the American Federation of Musicians, the Screen Actors' Guild, the Academy of Motion Picture Arts and Sciences, the Amateur Cinema League, the National Association of Performing Artists, the American Arbitration Association, and the American Legion (including its Société des 40 Hommes et 8 Chevaux). His clubs are the New York Athletic, the Lambs, the Friars, and the Yale Club of New York. In 1936 he received an honorary M.A. degree from Suffolk Law School.

Vallee is a tall, slender man with gray eyes and gray hair. He has been married to the former Eleanor Kathleen Norris, his fourth wife, since September 3, 1949. His first marriage, to Leonie Cauchois in 1928, was annulled the same year. His marriage to Fay Webb in July 1931 ended in divorce in May 1936; his marriage to Bette-Jane Greer in December 1943 ended in divorce in 1944. Vallee has five miniature poodles and a German shepherd dog. He lives in a large house just north of Hollywood that he has named "Silvertip." Born a Roman Catholic, Vallee has characterized himself as a "questioning free-lance believer." He protests when journalists call his appearance in *How to Succeed in Business Without Really Trying* a comeback. Speaking to a *Show Business Illustrated* interviewer (January 23, 1962), he insisted that he had never been out of the show business spotlight, and added, "I'll be front page news until the day I die."

References

Sat Eve Post 235:24+ Je 23 '62 pors
Show Bsns Illus 2:32+ Ja 23 '62 pors
Washington (D.C.) Post p12 D 3 '61 pors
Vallee, Rudy. My Time is Your Time (1962); Vagabond Dreams Come True (1930)
Who's Who in America, 1962-63

VANDERCOOK, JOHN W(OMACK) Apr. 22, 1902-Jan. 6, 1963 Radio news commentator for National Broadcasting Company (1940-46) and American Broadcasting Company (1953-60); explored and wrote about South America, Africa, the West Indies, and Pacific islands. See *Current Biography* (April) 1942.

Obituary

N Y Times p36 Ap 1 '63

VANDIVERT, WILLIAM (WILSON) (văn'-dĭ-vûrt) Aug. 16, 1912- Photographer
Address: b. 5 Union Sq., New York 3; h. 21 E. 10th St., New York 3

A topflight professional photographer for almost thirty years, William Vandivert has ranged his camera's eye over such diverse subjects as the Battle of Britain, the American paper industry, and the family life of the mink. His techniques are as varied as his subject matter, embracing everything from aerial photography to microphotography and from 35mm "available light" photography to the most elaborate studio work. One of the original *Life* staff photographers and a founding member of Magnum Photos, Inc.,

WILLIAM VANDIVERT

Vandivert now works as a free lance. His work has appeared in leading news, science, art, fashion, and photography magazines, both here and in England. With his wife, Rita Vandivert, writing the text for his photographs, he has produced two books on animals and one about children in the Soviet Union.

William Wilson Vandivert was born in Evanston, Illinois on August 16, 1912, the oldest of three sons of Virginia (Wilson) Vandivert and Roderick McClean Vandivert, an advertising executive. His younger brothers are Samuel Waldo and Roderick McClean, Jr. William Vandivert spent his early years in New Jersey and Illinois and attended Wheaton (Illinois) High School. After graduating from high school in 1928 he enrolled at Beloit College in Wisconsin, where he studied chemistry and played football and basketball, but lack of funds forced him to leave after two years. He later studied at the Art Institute in Chicago and spent a year learning lithography as a management trainee with the United States Printing and Lithograph Company.

This threefold background in chemistry, art, and lithography led to Vandivert's interest in photography, and in March 1935 he borrowed a 35mm camera from a friend to experiment with some pictures. The following month he showed them to the managing editor of the Chicago *Herald-Examiner,* who hired him as a candid camera reporter. Shortly thereafter Vandivert got his first scoop: assigned to cover an electrocution at Joliet prison, he hid a 35mm camera in his trousers and, in violation of prison rules, snapped the first photographs ever taken of a condemned man being executed in the electric chair.

In 1936 Vandivert did some work for *Time* and obtained his first important assignment in industrial photography from *Fortune.* Later that year he was invited to join the staff of *Life,* then a new experimental picture magazine. For the next two years he worked for *Life* in the Midwest, covering strikes and other local news, and in December 1938 *Life* sent him to its London office. During World War II Vandivert served in Europe, as a Canadian war correspondent in 1940-41 and as an American war correspondent from 1941 to 1946. He flew with the RAF, went on maneuvers with the British army, and, perched on the cliffs of Dover with a 40 cm. Leica with telephoto lens, he recorded Luftwaffe-RAF encounters 15,000 feet in the air during the Battle of Britain in 1940. He roamed the streets taking pictures during the heaviest raids and, sharing the experience of many Londoners, was bombed out of his home four times.

Effectively reporting the war news, however, involved more than just having courage or being on the spot. As Vandivert wrote in 1941: "Since the war photographer is going to be where things are happening that he has never dreamed of, he must know the cameras he uses so well that they become part of him. Automatically, while taking in a scene, he must stop down his lens, focus his camera, shoot calmly and purposefully no matter what kind of hell is breaking loose." In 1942 the Museum of Modern Art held a one-man show of Vandivert's war photography. Entitled "Two Years of War in England," it included a picture of a blitzed British baby lying silent and bandaged in its sunlit hospital bed.

At the end of his assignment in England, *Life* sent Vandivert all over Europe and to Latin America, India, Burma, and China. From these places he sent pictures of every kind, including human interest, political, and industrial photos and pictures of celebrities, children, and animals. In 1946 Vandivert left the *Life* staff to become a founding member of Magnum Photos, Inc., a photographic agency, with four other photographers, Robert Capa, Henri Cartier-Bresson, George Rodgers, and David Seymour. In 1947 Vandivert also served as consultant to the Curtis Publishing Company.

As a free-lance photographer, Vandivert has placed work in *Life, Time, Fortune, Scientific American, Look,* the *Saturday Evening Post Collier's, McCall's, Pageant, Harper's Bazaar, Art News, Argosy, Holiday, U.S. Camera, Popular Photography,* and *Modern Photography.* He has also done advertising illustration and industrial photography. In 1961, with Stewart Holbrook and George Loh, he prepared the International Paper Company's *Yankee Loggers,* a memoir of "woodsmen, cooks, and river drivers" in the New England woods. He also provided the photographs for *The World of Mead,* published by the Mead Corporation, a large paper company.

Vandivert's wife, the former Rita Andre, whom he married on June 7, 1940, has collaborated with him on four books: she did the research and wrote the text, and he supplied the photographs. Their first collaboration was *Common Wild Animals and Their Young,* a Dell paperback original published in 1957 (with line drawings by Carl Burger). The text gives details on the habits, life cycle, and mating of the coyote, bobcat, red fox, mink, black bear, and eleven other American mammals and is illustrated by 127 photographs.

"Successful animal photography," the Vandiverts wrote in the introduction, "requires a camera, an animal, limitless patience and—most important of all—an idea for the picture or series." The photographs were taken in the open woods, in outdoor enclosures, and in the studio. Using Rolleiflex and Leica cameras with several lenses, and high-speed strobe lighting equipment to capture the action of the fast-moving animals, Vandivert was able to photograph the flight of a deer, bear cubs at play, and a mother racoon nursing her young. Many of these studies were shown at a photographic exhibition of wild animal young at the American Museum of Natural History in 1958. The Vandiverts did a second book about animals, for children, *The Porcupine Known as J.R.* (Dodd, 1959), based on the antics of a porcupine pup that spent a summer with them.

In the summer of 1959 Vandivert approached *Look* magazine with some ideas for a photographic story about the Soviet Union. *Look* gave him the assignment, and he spent a month in Russia taking pictures of adults and children. His wife had done such thorough research before the trip that he knew exactly what to look for. "It was a matter of looking, waiting, watching the people," he explains, "until I found the seconds, the moments, that brought my ideas into focus." Vandivert's picture story on Russia —showing workers in factories, families at home, vacationers, children at school and camp—appeared in the June 21, 1960 issue of *Look*.

Besides completing his assignment for *Look* Vandivert amassed enough photographs for another children's book. Published by Dodd, Mead in 1960 with a text by Mrs. Vandivert, *Young Russia: Children of the USSR at Work and at Play* shows American children how their Russian counterparts live. The photographs, taken in schools in Moscow, Stalingrad, and Kiev, provide glimpses of typical Russian city children from infancy (when they are cared for in co-operative nurseries) up to about fifteen years of age. The Vandiverts have also collaborated on *Gregory*, published by Hamish Hamilton in London in 1961.

Vandivert is six feet five inches tall, weighs 240 pounds, and has gray eyes and gray hair. He and his wife have one daughter, Susan. Vandivert is a Christian Scientist and a Democrat. His hobbies are swimming, walking, woodworking, and nature study (both observation and photography). He is a member of the Overseas Press Club of America, the New York Zoological Society, the Museum of Modern Art, and the Coffee House Club.

Vandivert believes that to succeed on the imaginative level, a photographer must possess a solid, competent technique and follow his own bent, rather than the current fashion. He is never casual in his approach to an assignment, no matter how routine. "Take pains to produce always at your own highest level," he advises. "Try to translate into pictorial ideas some particular concept which has not been especially well stated previously. Don't stand still and don't try to get by on past achievements."

References

Fortune 25:12+ F '42 por
U.S. Camera 23:60+ Ap '60 por

VAN DYKE, DICK Dec. 13, 1925- Comedian; actor

Address: b. c/o CBS Television Network, 485 Madison Ave., New York 22; h. 4849 Encino Ave., Los Angeles, Calif.

A master of the art of pantomime, the tall, gangling, rubber-faced comedian and song-and-dance man Dick Van Dyke has emerged as one of television's most popular personalities. Van Dyke, who started in show business as a night-club entertainer, has appeared on a variety of television programs since he arrived in New York City in 1955. In 1960 and 1961 he scored a hit with his performance in the starring role of the Broadway musical *Bye Bye Birdie,* and he also stars in its motion picture version. Since October 1961 he has had his own weekly comedy program, the *Dick Van Dyke Show* (CBS-TV), which has won an Emmy award from the National Academy of Television Arts and Sciences. John Crosby of the New York *Herald Tribune* (August 31, 1960) describes Van Dyke as "a very likeable comedian with a lot of talent of the left-footed, foot-in-mouth, double-take variety."

Dick Van Dyke was born on December 13, 1925 in West Plains, Missouri, the son of a trucking agent. His younger brother, Jerry, is a nightclub comedian. During his childhood he moved with his family to Danville, Illinois, where he made his friends laugh with his clowning antics while attending high school. He also appeared in school plays and civic theater productions, but at the time he did not seriously consider a career in show business. During World War II Van Dyke served in the Air Force for two years. His performance in a service show greatly impressed a fellow airman, Byron Paul, who began to guide him, and who later became Van Dyke's personal manager.

Van Dyke's debut in the entertainment world had to wait, however, for upon his discharge from the Air Force he and a friend, Wayne Williams, decided to open an advertising agency in Danville. The agency went bankrupt a year later, and in 1947 Van Dyke teamed up with an old friend, Philip Erickson, for a comedy-pantomime act. Calling themselves "The Merry Mutes," the two comedians toured nightclubs from coast to coast, and they later became known as "Eric and Van." The act was not always a financial success, and on one occasion Van Dyke was evicted from an apartment because he was unable to pay the rent.

Eric and Van broke up as a team in 1953, and after a brief period of single appearances in nightclubs Van Dyke accepted an offer from a television station in Atlanta, Georgia, where he became master of ceremonies of the daytime programs *The Merry Mutes Show* and *The Music Shop.* Two years later he moved to New Orleans, where he performed on his own television variety program, *The Dick Van Dyke Show,* which became highly successful.

Van Dyke moved into major network television in June 1955, when he came to New York City to accept an offer from the CBS television network for a seven-year contract. His first assignment for CBS was to act as master of ceremonies of *The Morning Show,* a task that

DICK VAN DYKE

had previously also been performed by Walter Cronkite, Jack Paar, and John Henry Faulk. On this program, which catered to early morning risers, Van Dyke specialized in telling children's stories and performing comedy monologues. In 1956 he was master of ceremonies of *Cartoon Theater*, an evening show. CBS later kept Van Dyke occupied with guest appearances on various programs, but he failed to receive the kind of assignments that he would have liked.

When in the summer of 1958 CBS refused his request for a daytime show, Van Dyke requested and obtained a release from his contract. "I want to stay with the housewives," he told Marie Torre of the New York *Herald Tribune* (June 3, 1958). "I can't think of a more delightful way to make a living." Recalling his encounter with CBS he added: "I kept asking for a daytime show and they kept saying I ought to have a nighttime comedy show and when I said 'okay,' they told me it was a bad time for comedy. I just got tired of waiting for comedy to come back. It's not that I'm ambitious. I just want to work."

After the termination of his contract Van Dyke became a free-lance performer on television. In the summer of 1958 he substituted for Garry Moore, who was on vacation, and he also appeared with singer Andy Williams over ABC-TV. He later received some good spots on television specials, and he often made guest appearances on such programs as the *Phil Silvers Show*, the *Ed Sullivan Show*, and *To Tell the Truth*. In October 1958 Van Dyke became host of the *Mother's Day* series (ABC-TV), a daily panel show for housewives, and in 1959 he served as master of ceremonies of *Laugh Line* (NBC-TV), a completely ad-libbed weekly comedy show that featured such performers as Elaine May, Mike Nichols, and Orson Bean. He also made a pilot film for a situation comedy titled *Poor Richard*, in 1959, but the show failed to find a sponsor.

In February 1959 Van Dyke displayed his acting talents in a straight dramatic role in "Trap for a Stranger," presented on the *United States Steel Hour* (CBS-TV). On Thanksgiving Day, 1960 he delighted audiences in a comedy revue entitled *No Place Like Home* (NBC-TV), in which he appeared with Rosemary Clooney, José Ferrer, and Carol Burnett. As host of *Flair*, a weekday afternoon ABC radio program, which began in October 1960, Van Dyke was described by a reviewer for *Variety* (October 5, 1960) as having "a style and projection that makes most of the local deejay jabbernicks sound out of the stone age."

Van Dyke made his debut on Broadway in the fall of 1959 in the musical revue *The Girls Against the Boys*, in which he was able to perform some of his own material. Although the show, which also featured Bert Lahr, Nancy Walker, and Shelley Berman, was not well received by the critics and closed after sixteen performances, Van Dyke was praised for his contribution. A critic for *Variety* (September 30, 1959) reviewing the show's pre-Broadway tryout in Philadelphia, wrote that Van Dyke "shines when his material permits," and Kenneth Tynan commented in the *New Yorker* (November 14, 1959) that "a versatile comic named Dick Van Dyke adds color to a lot of drab spots" in the revue.

A few months later Van Dyke was given the chance to exhibit his talents in a more successful vehicle when he was chosen for the role of Albert Peterson, the manager of a rock 'n' roll singer in the musical comedy hit *Bye Bye Birdie*, starring opposite Chita Rivera. Choreographed by Gower Champion, with book by Michael Stewart, music by Charles Strouse, and lyrics by Lee Adams, *Bye Bye Birdie* played on Broadway from April 14, 1960 to September 9, 1961. Van Dyke was described as "one of the best of the younger singing and dancing comedians" by John Beaufort, who reviewed the show for the *Christian Science Monitor* (April 23, 1960). A critic for *Newsday* (April 20, 1960) wrote that "the droll, loose-limbed Dick Van Dyke . . . more than fulfills the promise he made in that shortlived revue, *The Girls Against the Boys*." John Chapman commented in the New York *Sunday News* (April 24, 1960) that "Dick Van Dyke, whose affable mugging and gentle joking has entertained daytime television watchers, is a most attractive and sincere agent—and he has nimble feet."

On October 3, 1961 Van Dyke began to star in his own weekly comedy program, the *Dick Van Dyke Show* (CBS-TV), which writer-producer Carl Reiner created especially for him. Reiner reportedly had originally planned a show with himself in the leading part, but was so impressed by Van Dyke's Broadway performance that he gave the role to him. The program, which also stars Mary Tyler Moore, Rosé Marie, and Morey Amsterdam, was described by Muriel Fischer in the New York *World-Telegram and Sun* (October 4, 1961) as a show with "a potpourri plot involving a TV comedy writer, his colleagues, his wife, their precocious son, a teen-aged baby sitter, neighbors and doctor." Although the show was not universally received with enthusiasm Van Dyke told Marie Torre of the New York *Herald Tribune* (September 29, 1961): "I feel optimistic about our chances for success. We have a believable premise and situations that are alternately warm and funny."

A reviewer for *Variety* (October 11, 1961) noted that the *Dick Van Dyke Show* was "about par" as situation comedies go, but that it "could be carried beyond its potential by the bright and talented cast." The show was described as the "most insistently comic" of the new situation comedies in *Newsweek* (January 1, 1962), while a reviewer for *Show* (February 1962) noted that it had "that rare commodity in a family situation series—honest comedy." Bob Williams wrote in the New York *Post* (April 5, 1962) that while the series was somewhat "flimsy" in its content, it persists as the best cast situation comedy on the air."

Although the sponsors of the *Dick Van Dyke Show* were reported for a time to have considered dropping the program because it had not lived up to rating expectations, its continuance for the 1962-63 season under renewed sponsorship has been assured. On May 23, 1962 the *Dick Van Dyke Show* received an Emmy award from the National Academy of Television Arts and Sciences as the best comedy program of the 1961-62 season, and in October 1962 it was ranked among the ten most popular television programs. Van Dyke owns a small share in the show.

Although Van Dyke prefers the theater, he decided to enter the more lucrative medium of motion pictures when Columbia Pictures Corporation offered him the leading role in the filmed version of *Bye Bye Birdie*. The picture, which also stars Janet Leigh, went into production in 1962. Van Dyke's role in the film has been considerably expanded from the original Broadway version. Since Hollywood rarely uses the original cast in filming a Broadway hit, Van Dyke maintains that he got the role by default. "I understand Laurence Harvey didn't have time to play the role and some other guys weren't interested, or something like that," he told Vernon Scott of the New York *World-Telegram and Sun* (April 27, 1962).

Van Dyke has been cast opposite Julie Andrews in the Walt Disney production *Mary Poppins*, based on a popular children's book, and he has negotiated for the film rights to the book *Zoomar* by the late comedian Ernie Kovacs. He has also discussed with Stan Laurel of the former comedy team of Laurel and Hardy the possibility of making a film based on the life of Laurel, whom he resembles facially. In the future Van Dyke hopes to be able to act in some straight dramatic roles of the lighter variety, such as have been performed by Jack Lemmon and Cary Grant.

In addition to his other activities Van Dyke has continued to make occasional appearances on special television programs. In February 1962 he appeared on a special comedy revue titled *Henry Fonda and the Family*, and in May 1962 he drew mixed reviews for his pantomime of a country boy visiting the city, on the *Andy Williams Show* (NBC-TV). For his performances on Broadway, Van Dyke received a Theater World Award in May 1960, as the most promising young actor of the current season. In October 1960 he was cited at a March of Dimes luncheon for "accomplishments in his chosen field and for his contributions of time and energy on behalf of the country's less fortunate citizens."

On February 12, 1948 Dick Van Dyke married his childhood sweetheart, Marjorie Willett, on the *Bride and Groom* radio show. They have four children: Christian, Barry, Stacey, and Carrie Beth. Van Dyke, who is six feet one inch tall and weighs 147 pounds, is constantly trying to put on weight, but with little success. Unassuming and untheatrical in his manner, he regards himself as "lazy and irresponsible," although he has never been known to miss an appointment on the movie set or before television cameras. With his family he lives in the exclusive Mandeville Canyon area of Los Angeles in a large house which he is redecorating himself. His hobbies include painting, sculpture, making home movies, racing miniature sports cars, and attending track meets and road races. His favorite composers are Johann Sebastian Bach, Cole Porter, and Henry Mancini. He spends much time with his children and he teaches Sunday school.

Discussing the nature of comedy in an interview with Jack Leahy for the New York *Sunday News Magazine* (November 18, 1962) Van Dyke concludes: "I think it's a mistake even to try to figure out a definition of comedy. You could lose your sense of humor in the attempt. A guy who feels good and then tries to find out why he feels good may soon find he has no reason for it and wind up feeling miserable."

References

N Y Post Mag p3 S 16 '62 por
N Y Sunday News Mag p4 N 18 '62 pors
Sat Eve Post 235:25 Jl 28-Ag 4 '62 por

VANOCUR, SANDER (văn-ō'-kĕr) Jan. 8, 1928- News commentator
Address: b. 4001 Nebraska Ave., Washington 16, D.C.; h. 3122 Ordway St., Washington, D.C.

Since January 1961 Sander Vanocur has held one of the choicest journalistic assignments in the free world—that of White House correspondent, along with Ray Scherer, for the National Broadcasting Company. A former reporter for the Manchester *Guardian*, Vanocur is one of only three Americans who have been staff journalists for British daily newspapers. He came to the National Broadcasting Company from the New York *Times*.

Vanocur has covered Presidential press conferences, accompanied Mrs. Jacqueline Kennedy to India and Pakistan, and once received a curtsy from Caroline Kennedy when he presented her with a book called "Nancy Nurse." He remains unaffected, however, by the glamor of frequent contact with the Kennedys. "I hope never to become a news 'specialist,'" he has said. "The world is full of real-life drama, and it's everywhere, not just in one area or field. If I had become a doctor, I'd be a general practitioner. And, as a newsman, I love the tag, 'general assignment.'"

Sander Vanocur was born in Cleveland, Ohio on January 8, 1928, the son of Louis and Rose

NBC-TV Photo

SANDER VANOCUR

(Millman) Vinocur. (He spells his name differently from his father, a lawyer who is now County Administrator of Lake County, Illinois.) Vanocur has one sister, now Mrs. Roberta Friedkin. Reared in both Cleveland and in Peoria, Illinois, Vanocur graduated from Western Military Academy in Alton, Illinois in 1946. He then attended Northwestern University, where one of his classmates and a fellow member of the debating team was Newton N. Minow, now chairman of the Federal Communications Commission. After his graduation from Northwestern in 1950, Vanocur went to England to study at the London School of Economics. In 1952 he entered the United States Army and, after serving two years in Austria and Germany, he was discharged with the rank of first lieutenant.

Returning to England, Vanocur joined the staff of the Manchester *Guardian* as a reporter. Not too long afterwards he began his career as a news broadcaster when, as a sideline to his job with the Manchester *Guardian*, he did a weekly news analysis for the North American Service of the British Broadcasting Company. He also wrote for the *Observer* (London) and for a short time served as a "stringer" (a reporter who serves another publication or news agency part-time in addition to his regular assignment) for the Columbia Broadcasting System in London. As a reporter in England he covered a wide variety of assignments including the retirement of Winston Churchill and the romance of Princess Margaret and Group Captain Peter Townsend.

In 1955 Vanocur joined the city staff of the New York *Times*. For a time he covered a police beat in the borough of Queens, an assignment he does not look back upon with any particular nostalgia, and "dabbled in everything from sports to obits." In September 1957 he became a Washington correspondent for NBC News, and in 1958 he was transferred to Chicago as its roving Midwestern correspondent. He covered the

Chicago parochial school fire that late in 1958 took the lives of scores of children, toured the United States with Soviet Premier Nikita S. Khrushchev, and reported the dramatic school desegregation in Little Rock, Arkansas.

While he was roving correspondent in the Midwest for NBC News, Vanocur once described his current mode of life. "I spend most of my time in hotels and airplanes," he said. "When I do return to Chicago, I usually see most of it from the air, hurrying from airport to airport in a helicopter. So when my wife is on the beach with our son, she can point up to airplanes passing overhead and say, 'There goes Daddy.' She has an 8-to-5 chance of being correct."

In 1960 Vanocur was assigned to cover John F. Kennedy's bid for the Democratic Presidential nomination, and he followed the campaign trail for months, through the primary elections, the national Democratic convention in Los Angeles, and the election. When John F. Kennedy was installed in the White House in January 1961, Vanocur was transferred from Chicago to the White House beat, which he shares for NBC News with Ray Scherer.

Vanocur also covered the 1960 Republican national convention in Chicago and followed Vice-President Richard M. Nixon for part of his election campaign. For the first of the televised Nixon-Kennedy debates, in September 1960, Vanocur was selected as one of the newsmen to question the two Presidential candidates on the aid. One query that he put to Vice-President Nixon, some observers have suggested, may have seriously hurt the Republican nominee's chances. Vanocur asked Nixon to comment on President Dwight D. Eisenhower's remark, made some days earlier, that if given a week, he might think of a major idea suggested by Nixon that had been adopted by the Administration. Nixon's reply that Eisenhower probably made the remark facetiously and that it would have been "improper" for the President to go into detail about the recommendations made to him by members of his official family was not considered by many political observers to have removed the sting from Eisenhower's remark.

Far from showing partisanship when he asked his questions, Vanocur looked upon the debate "as an opportunity to pin both men down." He told John P. Shanley of the New York *Times* (December 17, 1961), "I spent an entire morning working on the questions that I would ask during that program. I thought it was most important to ask searching questions of both of the candidates." He pointed out that during the same telecast he had asked Senator Kennedy an equally difficult question: how, if elected, he expected to push his program through Congress when he had failed to do so in the Congressional session of August 1960 following his nomination for the Presidency.

As NBC's White House correspondent, Vanocur contributed a chapter called "No Reason For Despair" to *Memo to JFK from NBC News* (Putnam, 1961), in which National Broadcasting Company newsmen around the world assessed some of the problems faced by the new administration. Vanocur submitted his view that the country was "ably governed," and noted that "after six months of rather close observation of the President and the people around him, I see no reason for despair."

One of the people around the President with whom Vanocur has had considerable professional contact is the First Lady. He has conducted two exclusive television interviews with Mrs. Kennedy and is enthusiastic about her. After covering the trip of the Kennedy family to Paris in 1961, Vanocur wrote in *Memo to JFK:* "Mr. Kennedy went to Paris armed with the most important and popular export since Coca-Cola replaced Pernod in Parisian sidewalk cafes—his wife, Jacqueline. . . . At one luncheon, the French President almost completely ignored the woman on his left and talked in animated fashion throughout the luncheon with Mrs. Kennedy. Since General de Gaulle usually speaks to no one below the rank of President and God, Mrs. Kennedy's achievement was a formidable one."

Vanocur is a student and critic of the ways in which radio and television, his own media, and newspapers handle the news. When he received the annual Broadcast Leadership Award from the Yale Broadcasting Company in May 1962, Vanocur expressed the view that radio and television should provide more coverage in depth of the President and his administration, with more interpretive comment on the meaning of White House actions and less emphasis on the superficial. In December 1961 he told a convention of NBC affiliated broadcasters that newspapers are becoming more and more filled with trivia. He said: "Totaling what we put out in a week and comparing it to what many information-starved citizens read in their daily newspapers in many of our cities, I think there is no question but that at the end of the week the person who has faithfully tuned in . . . has a much better picture of what is going on in this world than the person who has to depend on many of our newspapers."

Sander Vanocur has brown eyes, dark hair, and stands six feet tall. He lists tennis, golf, and loafing as his favorite recreations. On March 3, 1956 he married the former Edith Pick, a native of Vienna, whom he met when she was a fashion designer in London. They have two sons, Nicholas and Christopher. Despite the long hours that he puts in on his White House assignment, Vanocur sees more of his family now than he did when he was stationed in Chicago; then he was away from home about 80 percent of the time.

Much as he enjoys his present assignment, Vanocur is tantalized by visions of the job opportunities afforded by future technological developments in mass communications. In a guest column for Marie Torre of the New York *Herald Tribune* (August 17, 1961) he wrote: "The possibility of television transmissions from Western Europe to the United States within a short time interests me. There will be an exciting story unfolding in Western Europe during the next ten to fifteen years and I feel that after I have spent a reasonable period of time at the White House, I would like to return to the Continent, perhaps with a roving assignment."

Reference

N Y Times II p2 D 17 '61 por

VAN VOLKENBURG, J(OHN) ("JACK") L(AMONT) Dec. 6, 1903-June 11, 1963 First president of the Columbia Broadcasting System television network (1951-56); president of M-E Productions. See *Current Biography* (January) 1955.

Obituary

N Y Times p33 Je 13 '63

VAN WATERS, MIRIAM Oct. 4, 1887- Penologist

Address: h. 14 Clark St., Framingham, Mass.

For more than forty years as a penologist and social worker Miriam Van Waters dedicated herself to transforming institutions for women offenders from places of confinement and punishment to centers of rehabilitation. Harry Elmer Barnes, writing in *Saturday Review* (July 14, 1962), called her "the outstanding woman in American correctional history, distinguished as much for her dynamic personality as for her vision, courage, and determination."

Superintendent of the Massachusetts State Reformatory for Women at Framingham from 1931 to 1957, Dr. Van Waters had previously introduced modern penological methods as an administrator of institutions for delinquent girls in Oregon and California, and as the referee at the Los Angeles Juvenile Court. She has written two books and done major research in her field. Dr. Van Waters has always been guided by concern for the individual inmate and by the knowledge that 95 percent of all prisoners must eventually be released. Prison, she believes, must prepare the inmate for a return to normal life, not with less respect for the law than he had before, but with more.

Miriam Van Waters, the second of six children of George Browne and Maude Ophelia (Vosburg) Van Waters, was born in Greensburg, Pennsylvania on October 4, 1887. The ties between parents and children—Miriam, Ruth, Rebekah, George, and Ralph—were close. (The oldest child, Rachel, had died in infancy.) When Miriam was a child the family moved to Portland, Oregon, where George Van Waters, a liberal Episcopal rector, founded some seventeen parishes, a school for boys, and a girls' school, St. Helen's Hall. Miriam Van Waters acquired her elementary education at home, learning Latin, Greek, history, mathematics, music, art, and literature from her father and from young divinity students who visited the Van Waters home. She also read a good deal on her own and tried her hand at writing verse and novels. At the age of fourteen she took complete charge of the large Van Waters household for several months while her mother was absent, and the discipline and understanding she gave to her young sisters foreshadowed her work with girls in later years. Completing her secondary education, she graduated from St. Helen's Hall with honors in 1904.

At the University of Oregon Miss Van Waters was editor in chief of the *Oregon Monthly,* a campus correspondent for the Portland *Oregonian,* a member of the debating team and dra-

MIRIAM VAN WATERS

matic club, and winner of a $100 Beekman Prize for oratory. She was elected to Phi Beta Kappa and graduated with a B.A. degree in philosophy in 1908 and an M.A. degree in psychology in 1910. Awarded a fellowship at Clark University, Miss Van Waters began studying social psychology under the noted American psychologist G. Stanley Hall, and during her first year there she undertook, at Hall's request, a study of three hundred delinquent girls. After her first year Miss Van Waters switched her field of study to anthropology and prepared a much praised library-based dissertation on the adolescent girl in primitive society. She received her Ph.D. degree in 1913. While at Clark she worked as an assistant at the Child Welfare Institute in Worcester.

After leaving Clark, Dr. Van Waters became a probate officer of the Boston Children's Aid Society at Boston Juvenile Court. In the spring of 1914 she returned to Portland, Oregon to take up a post as superintendent of the Frazer Detention Home. In the course of reforming the home, she hired medical, recreational, dietary, and psychological staff, did away with physical punishment, and tested each child to weed out mental defectives. It was at this time that she made a decision not to keep juvenile court records, because she believed that, passed as these were from administration to administration, they were not safe repositories of "crudely written adult interpretations of children's misdeeds."

Ill with tuberculosis and attendant heart trouble, Dr. Van Waters moved to California in 1915 and spent some time in a sanatorium. Without hope at first of returning to active institutional work, she began to write articles on correctional and social work problems, one of which, "Four Kinds of Social Workers," was widely published. In 1916 she spent six months at Cannon Beach, Oregon, where she tutored her brother George for university enrollment.

Dr. Van Waters returned to California in the spring of 1917 and took over the superintendency of Juvenile Hall, a detention home in Los Angeles. "It is difficult for anyone who does not live in an institution to realize the proposition I'm up against," she wrote to her father at this time. "I am happy in it—thoroughly. But constant vigilance, eternal conferences, infinite series of emergencies are one's weekly job." Overcoming innumerable obstacles, she brought reforms to Juvenile Hall as she had to the Frazer Detention Home and as she was to do to the women's reformatory at Framingham. In 1919, in addition to her responsibilities at Juvenile Hall, she assumed administration of El Retiro, an experimental home and school devoted to re-educating young Juvenile Court wards. Also, to help alumni of El Retiro, Dr. Van Waters founded the Los Angeles Business Girls' Club.

After studying law to prepare herself for the position Miriam Van Waters in 1920 became the referee of the Los Angeles Juvenile Court, where she investigated cases and made recommendations for their disposition. The following year a philanthropist, Mrs. Ethel Sturges Dummer, made it possible for Dr. Van Waters to take a six-months' leave of absence from the court to visit industrial training and reform schools for girls in twenty-six states and recommend federal grants to those with constructive policies. Her findings were published as a federal survey, and these, together with her first book, *Youth in Conflict* (New Republic, 1925), established Dr. Van Waters' national reputation in the fields of social work and penology.

Dr. Van Waters planned, in writing *Youth in Conflict,* "to show the meaning of delinquency in modern life—how it is not just drift or 'badness' but a genuine struggle, a conflict misunderstood . . . how youth is in conflict with home, school, church, courts, and community." The book is based on twelve Los Angeles Juvenile Court cases. J. C. Lathrop, writing in *Survey* (March 15, 1925), saw in it the "brilliancy and sheer charm characteristic of Miriam Van Waters' mind and works." "Never in my knowledge," he wrote, "has the delinquency disclosed in the Juvenile Court and its treatment been discussed with a more scientific approach, a nicer human understanding, a more uncompromising sense of reality."

Reactions to her book were gratifying. The Los Angeles police captain in charge of juvenile affairs asked her to co-operate with him in reorganizing police work with children. The Laura Spelman Rockefeller Foundation invited her to head a major research project on adolescent problems in home and school. She directed some of the foundation-sponsored Fellows who gathered facts, formulated teaching methods for parents, and worked with groups of parents. The methods that were evolved in California were to be carried to other states. Shortly after her book appeared, also, Dr. Felix Frankfurter of the Harvard Law School asked her to supervise the juvenile aspects of the Harvard Law School Crime Survey. She was to survey eight courts, parks, playgrounds, social agencies, churches and industries, as these related to children under seventeen, and three industrial schools for delinquents.

Shuttling between her offices in Massachusetts and California, Dr. Van Waters returned to Los Angeles in June 1927 to find that her house and most of the manuscript for her second book had been destroyed by fire. She also encountered, not for the first or last time, that despair of reform penologists—interference in their work by politicians, officials, and the public who demanded "tough prisons." Her gains at El Retiro had been practically wiped out. Dr. Van Waters rewrote the manuscript of her book, which was published as *Parents on Probation* by New Republic, Inc., in 1927. Margery Mansfield wrote of this book in the New York *Herald Tribune* (May 13, 1928): "She places the family in historical perspective, and child and parent in the great human drama. She is not afraid of literary and scientific references and her mind plays over her subject like a ray of light."

Meanwhile, Dr. Van Waters had represented California at a White House-sponsored committee established to draw up federal standards for juvenile courts. She had served as president of the Los Angeles mental hygiene clinic, taught a course on social diagnosis at the University of California, and lectured frequently in the Los Angeles area on such topics as the juvenile court, the mental hygiene movement, adolescence, parent-child relations, and children's personality problems. In 1928 she wrote the first of twenty annual articles on juvenile delinquency for the *Encyclopædia Brittanica*. In 1929-30 she was president of the National Conference of Social Workers, and during 1930 and 1931 she was chief consultant on juvenile offenders for the National Commission on Law Observance and Enforcement (Wickersham Commission), set up by President Herbert Hoover to investigate federal prisons.

In November 1930 Miriam Van Waters formally resigned from her refereeship of Juvenile Court, and in the summer of 1931 she moved to Cambridge, Massachusetts. In December 1931 she was appointed superintendent of the Massachusetts State Reformatory for Women at Framingham, and she took over her new job in March 1932. She succeeded Jessie Hodder, who had made the reformatory one of the most progressive houses of detention for women and girls in the United States, but there was still room at Framingham for the introduction of additional reforms on the lines that Dr. Van Waters had been advocating for years.

At Framingham as at her previous institutions, juvenile court records were not kept, because Dr. Van Waters considered them an unfair obstacle to growth and change by young offenders. She also refused to accept political patronage appointees for responsible posts on her staff. Full psychological and medical inspection of each inmate was made upon admission. More freedom and privileges were granted to "students"—as Dr. Van Waters called the inmates—than is usual in prisons. There were no fences around the institution, and inmates were free to stroll around most of the 300 acres. Visiting hours were liberalized and outsiders were encouraged to form friendships with inmates. Jewish, Protestant, and Roman Catholic chaplains were encouraged to work with the prisoners.

The women and girls under Dr. Van Waters at Framingham were among the first prisoners in the country to receive spending money in return for work like gardening and sewing, and they were allowed to keep pets. Special educational facilities were set up for those who needed them, and inmates were given time off from work to attend classes. Dr. Van Waters led the formation of clubs to fill special needs of the inmates. Separate facilities and instruction were provided for mothers with children. The parole club prepared members for release, the rangers' club emphasized nature and the outdoors, a birthday club celebrated inmates' birthdays each month. There were a branch of Alcoholics Anonymous and literary, drama, glee, social, and sports clubs, among others. Many of the reforms were supported by private funds. "By 1947 the Framingham Reformatory for Women was better than any place Dorothea Dix could have prayed for in her revolt against the charnel houses of her time," Burton J. Rowles wrote in *The Lady at Box 99; The Story of Miriam Van Waters* (Seabury Press, 1962). "It was a model worthy of the national praise it received, and it was the institutional image of Miriam Van Waters."

Successive Massachusetts commissioners of correction approved of her reforms at Framingham, some of them giving enthusiastic support, until 1948. In that year there was a legislative investigation into "lax conditions" at the reformatory, during which Dr. Van Waters defended vigorously her use of modern penological methods. She was supported by many prominent persons, including Eleanor Roosevelt. In June 1948, however, she was ordered by Commissioner Elliott E. McDowell to return to the rules of 1923. All outside privileges were removed, outside work was prohibited, mothers were separated from their children, and many other reforms were nullified. "At a stroke of a pen," Dr. Van Waters wrote at this time, "we were thrown back into the conditions of a quarter century ago. . . . It is a complete end to rehabilitation." Commissioner McDowell, acting on a report by his assistant, Frank A. Dwyer, Jr., ordered her removal, and on December 27, 1948 Governor Robert F. Bradford announced that she would be fired, but that her discharge would be deferred until Governor-Elect Paul A. Dever took office on January 6 of the following year.

After her removal in January 1949 Governor Dever appointed a commission of three distinguished persons to re-examine the case. The commission vindicated Dr. Van Waters of all blame on March 4, 1949. Reinstated, she served as head of the Framingham reformatory for eight more years (although she was not able fully to restore the reforms), and she finally resigned for reason of age on October 31, 1957.

A small, slender woman, Miriam Van Waters is five feet two inches tall. She is still lively and busy at the age of seventy-five. Her adopted daughter, Sarah Ann (Mrs. Richard Hildebrandt), is no longer living. Dr. Van Waters is a member of the Episcopal Church. She holds honorary doctorates from the University of Ore-

VAN WATERS, MIRIAM—*Continued*

gon, Smith College, Coolidge Law School, Bates College, and Western College for Women. She has served as president of the American League to Abolish Capital Punishment.

References

Harper 198:81+ Je 9 '49
Newsweek 33:22 Ja 31 '49 por
Rowles, Burton J. The Lady at Box 99 (1962)
Who's Who in America, 1950-51
Who's Who of American Women (1958-59)

VILA, GEORGE R(AYMOND) (vĭl′à) Mar. 12, 1909- Rubber company executive
Address: b. United States Rubber Co., 1230 Avenue of the Americas, New York 20; h. "Windy Hill Farm," Far Hills, N.J.

During the thirty years that George R. Vila, president and chief executive officer of the United States Rubber Company, has spent in the rubber industry he has seen its manufacturing scope expand from tires as its almost only important product to many thousands of items, including chemicals, plastics, and synthetic rubber goods. A chemical engineer, Vila himself contributed directly to the industry's growth and diversification through his role in the development of synthetic rubber during World War II. He became president of the United States Rubber Company in November 1960 and its chief executive officer in January 1962. With annual sales reaching nearly $1 billion, the United States Rubber Company ranks below only Goodyear Tire & Rubber Company and Firestone Tire & Rubber Company among the nation's largest rubber concerns.

A native of Philadelphia, Pennsylvania, George Raymond Vila was born there on March 12, 1909 to Joseph S. and Rachel P. (McCulley) Vila. He completed secondary school in Philadelphia and then studied at Wesleyan University in Middletown, Connecticut, where he received his B.A. degree in 1932. For graduate work in chemistry he attended Massachusetts Institute of Technology in Cambridge, which granted him the M.Sc. degree in chemical engineering in 1933.

Graduating in a Depression year, Vila readily accepted a position with the Boston Woven Hose & Rubber Company as a production and development engineer. "I didn't choose the rubber industry," Vila told John M. Lee in a interview for the New York *Times* (February 4, 1962). "There was no choice in those days. Jobs were scarce, and you were fortunate to get one at all." He would, he explained, have preferred the chemical business since at that time the rubber industry meant natural rubber and cotton tire cord and "didn't have the scope it has today."

The Boston Woven Hose & Rubber Company, now merged in American Biltrite, was regarded as a leading producer of industrial rubber goods, and in three years at its Cambridge plant Vila obtained an excellent grasp of many phases of the rubber business. When he left in 1936 to join Naugatuck Chemical, a division of the United States Rubber Company, his purpose was to get into sales work. The Naugatuck chemical plant in Connecticut, a division of United States Rubber since 1911, had been the first chemical acquisition in the rubber industry. The division produced sulphuric acid for use in reclaiming rubber and eventually began developing antioxidants and other rubber chemicals. Then, after it had succeeded in compounding latex, the milky fluid found in rubber plants, it carried out research on polystyrene, agricultural chemicals, synthetic rubber, and plastics.

For somewhat over five years beginning in 1936 Vila was occupied as a technical salesman for the rubber chemicals department at Naugatuck. Then in 1942, after the United States had entered World War II, he was transferred to the division's research and development department, where he worked on GR-S (Government Rubber-Styrene) synthetic rubber. He was promoted to research and development manager for synthetic rubber in the following year. Besides pioneering in the development of GR-S rubbers, he adapted statistical control methods to the manufacture of synthetic rubber, in one of the earliest applications of statistical quality control concepts to a chemical manufacturing process. Vila reported to the American Chemical Society in a paper "Use of Organic Chemicals in Compounding Synthetic Rubber" in September 1942. Other papers by Vila, entitled "Action of Organic Acceleration in Buna S," "Plastication and Processing of GR-S," and "Approach by Statistical Methods to Manufacture of Synthetic Rubber," appeared in technical periodicals in 1942, 1943, and 1944 respectively.

A member of the technical industrial intelligence committee of the Joint Chiefs of Staff during World War II, Vila was sent to Germany in 1945 to study the progress of that country's synthetic rubber industry. The information that the mission obtained on cold polymerization helped him after his return to Naugatuck in initiating the research work that led to the development of cold GS-S. He was awarded a Certificate of Appreciation by the United States government for this achievement. Later in 1945 he became assistant general development manager for the Naugatuck chemical and synthetic rubber divisions of United States Rubber.

When the company wanted someone to boost division sales after the war, Vila, as he says modestly, "happened to be in position." He was appointed sales manager for Naugatuck Chemical's latex and plastic products in 1946 and three years later was promoted to general sales manager for Naugatuck Chemical. In 1953, after he had attended during the preceding year the advanced management program of Harvard's Graduate School of Business Administration, he advanced to assistant general manager of the Naugatuck division. On March 1, 1957, upon becoming general manager of Naugatuck, he was elected a vice-president of United States Rubber.

Chartered as a corporation in 1892, the United States Rubber Company had operated since 1929 under a committee management plan introduced by du Pont chemical executives called in to strengthen the company's financial position at the onset of the Depression. "The essential feature of the system," it is explained in *Business Week* (October 22, 1960), "is to place most top operating responsibilities in the hands of the executive committee. In U.S. Rubber, this body was usually made up of the board chairman, president and four vice-presidents who had no individual operating responsibilities." Through absorption of the Gillette Rubber Company, the Firestone Footwear Company, the Fisk Rubber Corporation, and other concerns, United States Rubber had rapidly grown in the 1930's and by the middle 1950's had expanded elevenfold.

As the company became larger and more diversified, its executive committee was unable to cope with some of its new and complex problems. In October 1957 Harry E. Humphreys, Jr., president of United States Rubber since 1949, discarded the old system. Under a new setup he became chairman of the board and chief executive officer and was succeeded as president by John W. McGovern. The executive committee's functions were divided among individual executives including two group executive vice-presidents responsible to the president. Vila was named group executive vice-president responsible for the Naugatuck Chemical, international, textile and plantation divisions, Latex Fiber Industries, and Dominion Rubber Company, Ltd., of Canada. Another group vice-president was appointed for tires, footwear, and mechanical goods. Two years later the tire division, which accounted for about half of United States Rubber sales, was made a separate group with its own vice-president, and in January 1962 it was reorganized as the United States Rubber Tire Company, with P. C. Rowe as president.

With President McGovern reaching United States Rubber's retirement age of sixty-five, George R. Vila was elected on October 17, 1960 to take office as his successor at the beginning of the following month. The company had enjoyed its peak sales of $977,000,000 and its top stock rating in 1959, but slumped slightly in 1960. At the end of that year, accordingly, the new president announced plans to spend more than $53,000,000 in 1961 on a research, modernization, and development program with emphasis on what was described as "quality control through automation of tire production systems and improving nation-wide distribution of tires." Another plan called for the construction by 1965 of more than 200 United States Rubber tire shopping centers, and, in addition, in September 1961 the company acquired 40,000 shares of the Pan-American Tire Company of Florida, which operated retail stores.

Meanwhile, Vila himself had played a leading part in negotiating with the Borden Company the foundation of Monochem, Inc., to produce raw materials for their respective chemical products at a $50,000,0000 complex of plants to be erected in Louisiana. In September 1961 Vila announced that United States Rubber scientists had developed three new types of synthetics superior to many materials used for conveyor

Pach Bros., N.Y.

GEORGE R. VILA

belts, golf balls, and tires. "We have shaken ourselves free," he declared, "from the molecular designs of mother nature. . . . We can now build molecules exactly to the specifications we wish."

On January 9, 1962 Vila was elected chief executive officer of United States Rubber, succeeding Humphreys, who continued to serve as chairman of the board. Toward the end of the following month United States Rubber acquired over 100,000 of the shares of the Masland Duraleather Company, producers of vinyl film and sheets; and in April United States Rubber announced the development of a new chemical binding agent called CVC for preventing separations in tires and tubes. In the autumn of 1962 ground was broken for the erection at Opelika, Alabama, of a new $20,000,000 plant for the manufacturing of United States Rubber's line of passenger car tires.

Since March 1961 Villa has been a director of the Aero Service Corporation and since July 1962, of the ACF Industries, Inc., which manufactures railroad freight cars, missile and aircraft components, and other heavy equipment. Vila is also a director of the National Agricultural Chemical Association and the Rubber Manufacturers Association, a past director of the Manufacturing Chemists' Association, and a member of the American Chemical Society, the Chemists' Club, and the Society of the Plastics Industry. His social club is the Lotus in New York City and his fraternity, the Psi Upsilon. He attends the Episcopal Church. George R. Vila and Katherine Elizabeth Miller were married on October 4, 1941 and have two sons, John D. and Richard L.

Both Vila and his wife are ardent collectors of antiques. Another of Vila's hobbies is skiing. As John M. Lee pictures him in the New York *Times* (February 4, 1962), "Vila . . . is a hard-driving man of average height, solid build and dark complexion. His attitude is pleasant, yet con-

VILA, GEORGE R.—Continued

fident, candid and direct. He appears to operate effortlessly, yet gives the impression there is power to spare."

References

Bsns W p100+ O 22 '60 pors
Investors' Reader 10:18+ N 9 '60 por
N Y Herald Tribune p32 O 20 '60 por
N Y Times p51 O 20 '60 por; p90 Ja 10 '62 por
N Y World-Telegram p49 O 17 '60 por
Rubber World 143:10 N '60 por
International Who's Who, 1962-63
Poor's Register of Directors and Executives, 1962
Who's Who in America, 1962-63
World Who's Who in Commerce and Industry (1961)

VILLON, JACQUES July 31, 1875-June 9, 1963 French painter; helped usher in the Cubist movement; exhibited in early Cubist shows in Paris (1911, 1912) and in the New York Armory Show (1913); won Carnegie Prize (1950) and Grand Prix, Venice Biennale (1956). See Current Biography (January) 1956.

Obituary

N Y Times p31 Je 10 '63

VON HASSEL, KAI-UWE See Hassel, Kai-Uwe von

VON KÁRMÁN, THEODORE May 11, 1881-May 6, 1963 Aerodynamicist; often called "father of the supersonic age"; his analyses of the action of fluids led, among other things, to the development of efficient aircraft structures, of wind and shock tunnels for testing aircraft, and of supersonic jets, guided missiles, and rockets; director of aeronautics center at California Institute of Technology, 1930-49; founder and chairman of advisory council for air research and development of the North Atlantic Treaty Organization (1951-63). See Current Biography (May) 1955.

Obituary

N Y Times p39 My 8 '63

VON WICHT, JOHN Feb. 3, 1888- Painter
Address: 55 Middagh St., Brooklyn 1, N.Y.

The abstract paintings of John Von Wicht, which are included in the permanent collections of several American and European museums, range from severe geometric designs to brilliantly colored, lyrical compositions. They demonstrate the versatility of the German-American artist, who has developed over the past forty years independently of artistic fashions. During the 1940's Von Wicht was a scow captain, and his many harbor abstractions reflect this experience. He has also worked in color lithography and, during the 1930's, in stained glass and mosaic.

John Von Wicht, one of a minister's large family of children, was born on February 3, 1888

in Malente, Schleswig-Holstein, Germany. He spent the early years of his life among the lakes, fields, and forests of northern Germany, and his earliest drawings, dated 1905 and 1906, depict this scenery with the precision and meticulousness of a Dutch landscape painter. John Von Wicht attended elementary school in Malente and high school in Lübeck. Around the turn of the century his family moved to Oldenburg, where he continued his academic studies.

Between 1905 and 1908 Von Wicht was apprenticed to a local painter and decorator, Bakenhus. In the paint shop he watched painters create beautiful patterns fortuitously as they sampled colors by streaking them on a wall, and he began to gain a sense of color and texture. "I saw the beauty of paint itself," he has said, "but I could not use this understanding then . . . without knowing why it was beautiful. We North Germans always have to know—and it has taken me a lifetime to find out why that wall could affect me with such wonder."

When an early painting by Von Wicht, Peasant Interior, was sold at the opening of a Bremen museum exhibition, the Von Wichts foresaw a career in the arts for their son. But practical considerations dictated that he learn applied arts, and in 1909 he enrolled in the private art school of the Grand Duke of Hesse at Darmstadt. Under the painter Friedrich Wilhelm Kleukens, Von Wicht learned to master such arts as poster and book cover design and lettering. One of his assignments was to do a series of drawings of plants: to learn precision and a sense of proportion he was required to observe the growth of a plant and to convey in his drawings not only an impression of its appearance but a sense of its structure.

This experience and others like it greatly influenced Von Wicht's concept of painting, for, according to Dorothy Seckler in Arts (November 1957), "Von Wicht was able to identify nature, its organic and efficient functioning of parts to a whole, with structure in the picture itself. Thus the picture is most like nature when its parts are also in the most perfect and dynamic correspondence, when it offers a parallel contrast of strong and delicate, and, above all, when the white space between shapes are in sizes and proportions of the greatest strength."

In 1911 Von Wicht went to Berlin and for the next three years studied in the School of Fine Arts at the Academy of Berlin. Under Professor E. Doepler, Jr., he studied applied arts, including lithography and the techniques and history of mosaics and stained glass. During 1912 and 1913 Von Wicht traveled through Scotland, England, and the Orkney Islands, executing paintings and lithographs. He had his first one-man show of prints and drawings in Scotland, followed by exhibits in Berlin and Stockholm. Although many of his fellow artists were painting in blazing colors during this period, Von Wicht did not immediately follow their lead. The work done on his trip to Great Britain is notable for its starkness and sweeping, simplified curves.

Von Wicht served in the German army in World War I, and battle wounds left him in a state of near-paralysis for several years. During his recuperative period he returned to painting and drawing, but in 1923 he decided that the chaos of postwar Berlin held little for him, and, with his wife, he immigrated to the United States. The Von Wichts settled in Brooklyn Heights (where they still live), which was then host to a flourishing art colony inhabited by Kuniyoshi, Robert Laurent, Maurice Sterne, Stephen Hirsch, and other artists. Von Wicht became an American citizen in 1936.

Although he never stopped working in the fine arts, Von Wicht busied himself for more than twenty years in the applied arts. Between 1923 and 1925 he worked for the United States Printing and Lithographing Company in Brooklyn, and from 1925 to 1928 he designed mosaics and stained glass windows for Ravenna Mosaics, Inc. From 1932 to 1934 he was a sketch artist with the Rambusch Decorating Company of New York City, designing and executing decorative work in paint, mosaic, and stained glass for churches and public buildings.

Between the mid-1920's and the early 1940's Von Wicht received numerous commissions from architects and builders for murals, mosaics, and stained glass work. He designed and painted ceiling decorations for the Fulton Savings Bank in Brooklyn, the Pan American Airways Terminal in Miami, and the Neurological Institute at McGill University in Montreal, Canada. He completed two murals for the Pennsylvania Railroad station at Trenton, New Jersey, a mural for the United States Post Office building in Brewerton, Alabama, and ceiling decorations and a mural for the Federal Court House in Knoxville, Tennessee. He prepared the designs and cartoons for mosaics for a Roman Catholic church in Atlantic City, for the St. Louis (Missouri) Cathedral, for Christ Church in New York City, for a Department of Health building in New York City, and for the Williamsburg Savings Bank in Brooklyn. In 1936 he held a one-man show at the Architects' Building in New York City.

In 1939 Von Wicht designed and executed six murals and a mosaic panel for the United States building at the New York World's Fair (1939-40). He was commissioned by the Libbey-Owens-Ford Glass Company in 1940 to design and render in color a large vitrolit mural for the Toledo Public Library. In 1941 the R. H. Macy Company hired him to design and render color schemes as a color specialist in their architectural department. In 1943 Von Wicht executed an architectural mural for the children's toy room of the Museum of the City of New York and designed and painted a globe for an exhibition at the Museum of Modern Art.

In executing his commerical designs, for which he frequently consulted Byzantine and medieval mosaic and stained glass work, Von Wicht gained a color sense that benefited his serious painting. He came to perceive color in terms of the shape, size, and position of color areas and to regard it as "symbolic, affecting the senses and emotions through direct impact rather than through descriptive correspondence" (*Arts*, November 1957). In other ways, however, his commercial work deflected Von Wicht from his major artistic concerns.

Consequently around 1942 Von Wicht decided to find an occupation entirely different from painting. He heard that the United States Army

JOHN VON WICHT

was looking for scow captains and, since he had always been interested in the sea, he became captain (and crew) of a scow that transferred food to Army transports lying in New York harbor. In 1947 he took command of the scow *Dorothy*, in which he hauled tires and automobiles from Tarrytown, New York to New York City to be reloaded for export. At times Von Wicht found the job almost too agreeable. "Really, it would be better for a representationalist than for an abstractionist," he once said. "The scenery was so beautiful that from the beginning I realized I must be careful to save it for relaxation. For my painting, I've learned to hide myself inside the cabin and not peek out."

A capacity for self-discipline has been a prominent trait of Von Wicht since his early days at Darmstadt, and his development as an artist has always been independent of the trends of his time. In the middle 1930's, when other painters were concerned with social realism or the American scene, Von Wicht voluntarily limited himself to painting severe geometrical forms on flat surfaces: "I wanted to put down a single line of a certain length, a certain thickness and at a certain angle. It was important that it divide the canvas into two unequal parts and that these remain in equilibrium—a matter of feeling, not measurement." One of his best known abstractions of this period is *Force* (1937), a dynamic arrangement of opposing curves and angles that achieved a two-dimensional momentum rarely obtained by American painters. *Force* was displayed in 1939 at Von Wicht's first one-man show of paintings in America, held at the jewelry store of Theodore A. Kohn in New York City.

In January 1944 Von Wicht exhibited oils and gouaches at the Artists Gallery, and in December 1945 he had a show of gouaches at the Kleemann Gallery. By 1947 he was selling from six to twelve paintings a year, deriving an income

VON WICHT, JOHN—Continued

that about equaled his salary as a scow captain. Harbor themes often appeared in his abstractions. Reviewing his exhibition at the Kleemann Gallery, held in April 1947, a New York Times critic (April 11, 1947) remarked: "Jutting planes and angles of massive water-front structures were ready-made semi-abstractions that simply required the deft hand of Von Wicht to transfer them to the two-dimensional canvas." Another art reviewer praised the oils for their rich and resonant colors, sensuous textures, and "free, swinging, lyrical rhythms." Concurrently with the Kleemann show Von Wicht displayed paintings at the Riverside Museum. In 1947 he also exhibited at the Mercer Art Gallery at Mercer University in Georgia and at the Art Gallery Education Building at the University of California in Los Angeles.

After passing through a period of Cubism during which the forms in his painting took on a limited solidity, Von Wicht began, in the 1950's, to concentrate on a new development of color. Brilliant, luminous, free-floating, exuberant designs filled his oils, gouaches, drawings, and prints. He joined the Passedoit Gallery in 1950, and his work was exhibited there in 1950, 1951, 1952, 1954, 1956, and 1957.

In 1954 Von Wicht visited the MacDowell Colony for creative artists (primarily musicians) in Peterboro, New Hampshire. Stirred to emotional response by the music he heard, Von Wicht decided to create a series of paintings that would depict the mood and movements he perceived in several modern musical compositions. The oils were shown at the Passedoit in 1954. A piano quintet was interpreted in terms of light feathery color forms, while larger, blockier forms represented a symphony. Rhapsodic Variations showed cloudy, fragmented grey and white shapes, and, according to a New York Times reviewer (November 4, 1954), "one large canvas in heavier shapes and hues effectively suggests the harsh character of orchestration in much contemporary work."

At Von Wicht's show at the Passedoit in 1956 compositions incorporating a new nature theme appeared among the harbor paintings that he had long been creating. Perhaps this resulted from his frequent visits to the country—to Vermont, to the MacDowell Colony, and to Yaddo, a former estate near Saratoga Springs, New York where artists can live and work. Connected with the nature theme were calligraphic symbols, which Von Wicht used in oils, oils on rice paper, and prints. He had one-man shows at the Bertha Schaefer Gallery in New York in 1960 and 1962.

Since the early 1940's Von Wicht has been promoting the art of color lithography in America. In 1953 he showed some of his prints at the John Herron Art Institute in Indianapolis, and he taught the techniques of color lithography at the John Herron Art School in May 1953. He taught painting at the Art Students League of New York in 1951 and 1952. In 1954 he had an exhibition of prints at the Carl Schurz Memorial Foundation in Philadelphia.

Von Wicht received prizes for his lithographs at the Brooklyn Museum Print Show in 1951, from the Brooklyn Society of Artists in 1953, from the Print Club, Philadelphia, in 1953, and from the Society of American Graphic Artists in 1954. The Brooklyn Society of Artists awarded him a prize for watercolor in 1945, a prize for oil in 1948, and honorable mentions for oil in 1950, 1951, and 1954. He received honorable mentions for oil in 1952, 1953, and 1954 and a gold medal in 1957 from the Audubon Artists, Academy of Design. He also holds a prize for gouache from the North Shore Long Island Society Festival. Von Wicht is a member of the Federation of Modern Painters and Sculptors, Artists Equity Association, Audubon Artists, American Abstract Artists, Scenic Artists, Brooklyn Society of Artists, and the International Institute of Arts and Letters.

His work is represented in the Whitney Museum of Art, the Brooklyn Museum, the Museum of Modern Art, the Philadelphia Museum, the Library of Congress, and in university and private collections. It has also been exhibited in New York City, Philadelphia, Detroit, Des Moines, Cincinnati, St. Louis, and cities in Virginia, and in France, Germany, and Italy. Von Wicht is vigorous in appearance, ruddy in complexion, and has a direct, piercing gaze. Since 1914 he has been married to the former Kunigunde Petz. When one of his paintings is to be a large one, he places the canvas on the floor to work on it.

References

Arts 32:32+ N '57 pors
New Yorker 23:21 S 20 '47
Who's Who in American Art (1962)

WACHUKU, JAJA (ANUCHA) (wä-chū′kô zhä′zhä) 1918- Nigerian Minister of Foreign Affairs and Commonwealth Relations; lawyer

Address: b. Ministry of Foreign Affairs and Commonwealth Relations, Lagos, Nigeria

One of the most outspoken and fiery of the diplomats from the new African states at the United Nations is Jaja Wachuku, who has represented the Federation of Nigeria at the U.N. since it became an independent state within the British Commonwealth of Nations on October 1, 1960. A native of Eastern Nigeria and a lawyer who was trained at the University of Dublin, Wachuku was the Nigerian Minister of Economic Development from October 1960 to July 1961, when he became the Nigerian Minister of Foreign Affairs and Commonwealth Relations.

The most populous country in Africa with over 35,000,000 inhabitants, Nigeria was under British administration for about 100 years. After World War II increasing pressures for autonomy led to the formation of the Federation of Nigeria in 1954, to the granting of internal self-government in 1957, and to complete independence in 1960. In West Africa not far from Ghana, Nigeria is divided into Northern, Western, and Eastern Regions, each with its own premier and legislative bodies.

Descended from twenty generations of Ngwa Ibo chieftains, Jaja Anucha Wachuku was born to Ndubisi and Nganchiwa Wachuku at Nbawsi in Eastern Nigeria in 1918. "It's a good thing to be well-born," Wachuku was once quoted as saying in the New York *Post* (April 4, 1961). "A chief, like a king, is not only a political and social institution, but the personification of the best in the community. He must be humble. And he must serve."

After attending St. George's primary school at Umuomainta, Nbawsi, and the Aba Division and Government School at Afikpo, Wachuku entered Government College, a secondary school, at Umuahia in 1931. He then studied at the Higher College at Yaba in 1935-36 and at the Gold Coast People's College at Adidome and the New Africa University College at Angloga. Having chosen law as his profession, Wachuku matriculated at Trinity College, Dublin, in 1939 and obtained his B.A. degree in legal science in 1943. At Trinity he belonged to the University of Dublin branch of the Students Christian Movement and to the College Historical Society, which awarded him a medal for oratory in 1944. A founder of the Dublin International Club, he was its secretary from 1943 to 1945. In 1945 he represented the Association of Students of African Descent, Ireland, at a Pan-African congress held in Manchester, England. Wachuku was an LL.B. Law Prizeman and a member of the Honourable Society of King's Inns, Dublin.

From 1944 to 1947 Wachuku practised law at the Irish bar. While holding a research scholarship in the department of international law at the University of Dublin, he made a study of the juristic status of protectorates in international law and received his M.A. degree in 1947. He returned to Nigeria in 1947 after spending six weeks in London as the legal and constitutional adviser to the National Council of Nigeria and the Cameroons (N.C.N.C.) Pan-Nigerian London delegation on constitutional reform.

On his return to Eastern Nigeria Wachuku set up a law practice near his birthplace and joined the N.C.N.C., the independence-minded political party founded in 1944. In 1949 Wachuku formed the New Africa party, a radical youth wing, which became affiliated with the N.C.N.C. a year later. From 1949 to 1952 he was a member of the Ngwa Native Authority Council.

In 1951 Wachuku was elected to the Eastern House of Assembly as second member for the Aba division, and the following year he was seated in the federal House of Representatives at Lagos as first member for the Aba division and Owerri province. He has since served continuously in the federal legislature. In 1952 and 1953 he was chairman of the N.C.N.C. parliamentary party and deputy leader of the N.C.N.C. government formed by Azikiwe. Early in 1953, however, he found himself disagreeing with some of Azikiwe's policies, and he resigned from the N.C.N.C. to help form the new National Independence party (later the United National Independence party—U.N.I.P.), which allied itself with the N.C.N.C.'s rival in advocating nationalism, the Action Group. It was as adviser and alternate delegate of U.N.I.P. that Wachuku attended Nigerian constitutional conferences in London in 1953 and Lagos in 1954 that evolved a new constitution, effective on October 1, 1954, which established the Federation of Nigeria.

United Nations

JAJA WACHUKU

In the federal elections of November 1954 the N.C.N.C. under Azikiwe won majorities in both Eastern and Western Nigeria, and Wachuku, who had been elected as first member for Aba on the U.N.I.P. ticket, was deputy leader of the Opposition in the federal House from 1955 to 1957. He also served on the House Finance Committee for two years beginning in 1956. Wachuku rejoined the N.C.N.C. in 1957. In 1958 and 1959 he was chairman of the Business Committee of the federal House, a member of a parliamentary committee on Nigerianization of the federal public service, and secretary of the N.C.N.C. federal parliamentary party.

At the constitutional conference in London in October 1958 the Nigerians were promised independence in two years, provided that a new legislature, to be elected in December 1959, could agree on the solution of certain basic problems relating to Nigerian unity. Wachuku served as secretary of the N.C.N.C. delegation at this meeting, and before the elections of December 1959 he was responsible for adjudicating the numerous appeals presented by N.C.N.C. candidates against the party nominations. In the elections the Northern People's Congress captured most of the seats, with the N.C.N.C. taking second place. The N.P.C. and N.C.N.C. formed a coalition government, and on May 2, 1960 Wachuku was elected to succeed Sir Frederic Metcalf as Speaker of the House of Representatives, becoming the first Nigerian in that post.

On October 1, 1960 the Federation of Nigeria became an independent state within the British Commonwealth of Nations. Azikiwe was named Governor-General, and Wachuku became Minister of Economic Development in the coalition government headed by Sir Abubakar Tafawa Balewa, the N.P.C. leader. On July 17, 1961 Wachuku gave up his portfolio of Economic

WACHUKU, JAJA—Continued

Affairs to become Minister of Foreign Affairs and Commonwealth Relations.

Jaja Wachuku first visited the United States as a member of an economic mission in July 1960, and in October 1960, when Nigeria became the ninety-ninth member of the United Nations, he accompanied the Nigerian Premier, Sir Abubakar, to New York as Nigeria's Acting Permanent Representative to the U.N. and chairman of the Nigerian delegation to the fifteenth session of the General Assembly. Wachuku lost no time in making the presence of his nation felt at the U.N. On November 1, 1960 he delivered the first of several speeches on the subject of better representation for African nations on important agencies and committees of the U.N. Wearing embroidered robes and speaking with a British accent, he addressed the General Assembly's Special Political Committee and demanded African representation on the Economic and Social Council, UNESCO, and on the Security Council. (In October 1962 Morocco and Nigeria contended for a Security Council seat vacated by the United Arab Republic, and Morocco won, 73 to 35, in a secret General Assembly vote.) On November 17, 1960 Wachuku was appointed chairman of the newly created Conciliation Commission for the Congo, and in December he was one of a three-man advance group that traveled to Leopoldville to open a commission office.

In answer to the proposal of Adlai E. Stevenson, United States Representative to the U.N., in March 1961 that African nations take the initiative in developing an aid program "by, of, and for Africa," Wachuku immediately demanded propositions "that are not intended to hoodwink anybody, that are not intended to mesmerize us." He expressed disappointment that Stevenson had not indicated how much money the United States would contribute. Several days later Wachuku declared that Africa was becoming a third force between East and West, and that Nigeria needed investment capital and technical advice. "We want co-operation," Wachuku said, "but we are not willing to trade our hard-won independence."

On October 10, 1961 in the General Assembly, Wachuku criticized the big powers for failing to provide world leadership. "I am losing confidence in the great powers," he said. "They are climbing from the pedestal of greatness to the pedestal of insanity. We expect leadership from them; they give us destruction. We expect wisdom from them; they give us lack of knowledge. We expect objectivity from them; they present us with blurred vision." In December 1961 he proposed that both the Chinese Nationalists and the Chinese Communists be seated in the United Nations.

In the United Nations in November 1961 Wachuku presented a draft resolution that called for complete independence of the entire African continent by 1970. In October 1961 he had attended a five-day conference on Africa, sponsored by the United States National Commission for UNESCO, and in January and May 1962, at Lagos, he attended conferences of foreign ministers on African unity.

Wachuku was a member of the Central and Eastern Regional Board of Education of Nigeria from 1952 to 1954 and chairman of the Eastern Regional Board of Education from 1952 to 1954 and from 1957 to 1960. He also served as chairman of the Eastern Region scholarship board during 1952 and 1953. From 1956 to 1959 he was a member of the Electricity Corporation of Nigeria.

Jaja Wachuku and his wife, the former Rhoda Idu Onumonu, have five children: Chinedum, Onyeuwalu, Ndubisi, Emeruwa, and Akubiara. He is short and stocky and prefers to wear the embroidered cap and "uwe," or native robe, of Eastern Nigeria. He has a reputation as a brilliant, shrewd, and witty speaker with an instinctive gift for the dramatic and was described in the New York Times (February 17, 1961) as "not unaware that native dress makes him a striking figure in the halls of the United Nations and before the television cameras." Cricket, football, tennis, and gardening are among his recreations, and in 1961 he was elected a director of the International Recreation Association for three years. Wachuku believes that sound relations between the United States and Nigeria would go far to stabilize the world situation.

References

N Y Post p40 Ap 4 '61 por
N Y Times p2 F 17 '61 por
Directory of the Federation of Nigeria, 1962
International Who's Who, 1962-63
Segal, Ronald. Political Africa (1961)
Who's Who in America, 1962-63
Who's Who in Nigeria (1956)

WAGMAN, FREDERICK H(ERBERT) Oct. 12, 1912- Librarian; organization official

Address: b. 210 General Library Bldg., University of Michigan, Ann Arbor, Mich., h. 1407 Lincoln Ave., Ann Arbor, Mich.

At its eighty-first annual conference, held at Miami Beach, Florida in June 1962, the American Library Association announced the election of Frederick H. Wagman as first vice-president and president-elect, to succeed James E. Bryan as president in 1963. Wagman began his career as a college instructor of German and taught at Columbia University, Amherst College, and the University of Minnesota. After serving as an official with the United States Bureau of Censorship during World War II he spent eight years in administrative positions with the Library of Congress. Since 1953 he has been director of the University of Michigan Library, one of the great research libraries in the United States. Wagman took office as president for 1963-64 at the ALA's eighty-second annual conference, in Chicago in July 1963.

Frederick Herbert Wagman was born in Springfield, Massachusetts on October 12, 1912, the only child of Robert and Rebecca (Gaberman) Wagman. He grew up in Amherst, Massachusetts and attended Amherst High School, where he took part in debating and declamation, played baseball, contributed to the school magazine, and was a member of the school orchestra. After graduating in 1929 he went to Amherst College on a four-year tuition scholarship, studying German and English literature. To help meet expenses he worked in the college library and also took jobs as a bookkeeper, salesclerk, and general factotum in a men's clothing store. In 1932 Wagman won first prize in a local Shakespeare essay contest, and in the same year he wrote the top prize-winning essay in a national essay contest on Goethe that was sponsored by the Carl Schurz Memorial Foundation to commemorate the 100th anniversary of Goethe's death. His essay, "Goethe's Conception of Personality," was published by the foundation in 1933.

After graduating *magna cum laude* from Amherst in 1933 with the B.A. degree Wagman attended Columbia University on a William Addison Hervey Memorial Scholarship. He obtained his M.A. degree in German literature in 1934. In the following year Wagman was awarded an Ottendorfer Memorial Fellowship with a travel grant by New York University, and he went to the University of Göttingen in Germany to spend a year at postgraduate work. However, because of the tensions developing in Nazi Germany, he moved to Zurich before he had completed a year there. His research culminated in the book *Magic and Natural Science in German Baroque Literature* (Columbia Univ. Press, 1941), which was issued simultaneously in three series and was sold out. He obtained the Ph.D. degree from Columbia University in 1942.

Beginning his career as a teacher of German, from 1933 to 1935 Wagman was an instructor in extension at Columbia University, and in 1936-37 he was a teaching fellow at Amherst College. He was an instructor in German at the University of Minnesota from 1937 to 1942. Volunteering his knowledge of German to help the United States war effort, Wagman became a reader with the United States Office of Censorship at Miami, Florida in 1942. Within a few weeks he advanced to a position of greater responsibility in that office, and in less than a year he moved to Washington, D.C., where he headed the planning unit in the postal division of the United States Office of Censorship. A few months later he was placed in charge of training programs and became head of the regulations section. As regulations officer he supervised the drafting and approval of regulations that governed the work of the 13,000 employees in field positions at the Office of Censorship.

Although Wagman had no degree in library science, his interest in literature and the influence of two instructors at Amherst College during his undergraduate days motivated him to enter librarianship. When the Office of Censorship closed at the end of the war Wagman applied for a position with the Library of Congress. One of his references at the time of his application wrote that "Wagman is precisely the type of person who is in a position to make a real contribution to such an activity as that which a great reference library offers." Originally hired as director of the library's division of the adult blind, Wagman was assigned to the position of acting director of personnel when he reported for duty in September 1945.

University of Michigan
News Service

FREDERICK H. WAGMAN

During his eight years with the Library of Congress, under the direction of Dr. Luther H. Evans, Wagman served in a number of administrative positions. These included acting director of administrative services, assistant director for public reference, director of the processing department, deputy chief assistant librarian, and director of administration. Perhaps the most notable achievement of the library during this period was the publication of the Library of Congress Catalog in a series of volumes, which first appeared while Wagman was in charge of the processing department.

In August 1953 Wagman left the Library of Congress to succeed Warner Rice as director of the library of the University of Michigan at Ann Arbor. The University of Michigan Library consists of a general library, dedicated in 1920, and an undergraduate library, a number of divisional libraries, and several special libraries and collections. Under Wagman's administration the library expanded rapidly and by 1962 its holdings consisted of about 3,000,000 volumes, some 17,600 periodicals, and over 135 newspapers. The opening of the new undergraduate library in January 1958 was one of the most important achievements of Wagman's administration. It provides seating for 2,300 persons, and it has such special features as study rooms for the blind, an audio room for listening to recordings that may be used by 151 students at a time, an exhibit area, and a print study gallery. Other recent additions to the University of Michigan Library include a storage library and a new medical school library. A physics and astronomy library is under construction, and a new music library and an annex for the general library are being planned.

(Continued next page)

WAGMAN, FREDERICK H.—*Continued*

In addition to effecting improvements in the material structure of the University of Michigan Library, Wagman has undertaken changes in its administration, with the aim of improving services to faculty and students. He has started extensive decentralization of administration, creating a level of what Dan Lacy in the *ALA Bulletin* (September 1962) refers to as "middle management." With the opening of the undergraduate library new facilities were established to make the collections of the main library more accessible to faculty and graduate students for research and advanced study. The cataloging used in the library was simplified and the divisional and special libraries were integrated more closely with the curricula and research programs of the schools that they serve. The reorganization of the library has been so successful that Wagman receives many calls to serve as a consultant in the planning and building of university libraries.

Long active in the American Library Association, Wagman has served on many of its committees. From 1950 to 1959 he was chairman of its National Union Catalog subcommittee, and in 1952-53 he was on its nominating committee. He was a member of the board on catalog policy and research of the division of cataloging and classification in 1952-53 and of its catalog code revision committee from 1954 to 1962. From 1953 to 1957 he was on its resources board, serving as its chairman in 1956. In 1958 he was chairman of the special committee of five, which drafted the ALA Goals for Action, and he has served on the greater ALA committee that planned the growth and development of the association. Wagman has also served on the committee on resources since 1958; the American Library Association-American Book Publishers Council joint committee on reading development (1955); the advisory committee to the membership committee (1960-1963); the New York World's Fair library exhibit exploratory committee (1962-63); and the Library of Congress-ALA liaison committee (1962-63). He was a member of the ALA council from 1957 to 1961 and chairman of the committee on appointments in 1962 and 1963.

At the ALA's eighty-first annual conference at Miami Beach, Florida, June 17-23, 1962, it was announced that Wagman had been chosen first vice-president and president-elect by mail ballot among the ALA's approximately 26,500 members. On July 19, 1963 he was installed as president at the inaugural banquet of the eighty-second annual conference, at Chicago, succeeding James E. Bryan of Newark, New Jersey. Dan Lacy, writing in the *ALA Bulletin* (September 1962) commented that Wagman would "bring to ALA the same capacity for clear organization and easy and lucid administration" that he had shown in his other positions.

In addition to his activities for the ALA Wagman also served, in 1959-60, as president of the Michigan Library Association. During his administration a drive was undertaken to increase state support for public libraries. He has been librarian of the Michigan Academy of Arts, Science and Letters since 1953 and a director of the Council on Library Resources, Inc., since

1958. Wagman is on the executive board of the Association of Research Libraries and has served on several of its committees, including the committee on Near Eastern materials, of which he was a member from 1957 to 1962. He has served on the national board of the National Book Committee since 1961 and on the steering committee for National Library Week since 1962.

Over the years Wagman has written many articles for professional journals, such as *Publishers' Weekly, Library Quarterly, College and Research Libraries, Library of Congress Information Bulletin, Michigan Librarian,* and *Texas Library Journal.* He has served as co-sponsor of two conferences that were held in Ann Arbor under the auspices of the University of Michigan. The first dealt with the development of lifetime reading habits and college studies. Its proceedings were published under the title *Reading for Life* (Univ. of Michigan Press, 1959). The second conference, held in 1962, concerned itself with the use of paperbound books in education.

Frederick H. Wagman is five feet eleven inches tall, weighs 190 pounds, and has brown hair and brown eyes. He married Ruth Jeanette Wagman, a teacher, on November 21, 1941. They have two children, Elizabeth Laura and William George. Wagman is a member of Phi Beta Kappa and Phi Kappa Phi honorary fraternities, and he belongs to the University Club of Ann Arbor and the Rotary Club. He is a Democrat. His favorite recreations are reading and swimming. In 1958 Amherst College conferred an honorary L. H. D. degree on him. When Wagman left the Library of Congress in 1953, Verner W. Clapp, writing in *College and Research Libraries* (October 1953), described him as "a winner of confidence, wise in council, and fun to work with."

References

ALA Bul 56:732+ S '62 por
Facts and Faces: The ALA Council in 1963 (1963)
Who's Who in America, 1962-63
Who's Who in Library Service (1955)

WAGNER, AUBREY J(OSEPH) Jan. 12, 1912-
United States government official; engineer
Address: b. 403 New Sprankle Bldg., Knoxville, Tenn.; h. 1600 Cedar Lane, Knoxville 18, Tenn.

As chairman of the board of the Tennessee Valley Authority, Aubrey J. Wagner heads a United States government agency that since its creation in 1933 has been the focus of much controversy on the issue of public vs. private power. Through its system of dams and steam plants, TVA provides navigation of the Tennessee River and its tributaries, flood control in the areas around the Tennessee and Mississippi rivers, and large amounts of electric power that it wholesales to communities and to the federal government. Wagner is a TVA career man. He joined TVA in 1934 as an engineering aide and advanced through successive promotions to the posts of general manager (1954-61), director (1961-62), and finally board chairman. President John F. Kennedy named him to the latter post on June 23, 1962 to succeed Herbert D. Vogel.

Aubrey Joseph Wagner, the son of Joseph M. and Wilhelmina (Filter) Wagner, was born in Hillsboro, Wisconsin on January 12, 1912 and grew up on his father's dairy farm. He has two brothers, Richard K. Wagner, of Forsyth, Kentucky, and Eldon C. Wagner, of Madison, Wisconsin, and a sister, Mrs. Mark Maun, of Grosse Pointe, Michigan. After graduating in 1927 from Hillsboro High School, where he took part in 4-H Club work, forensics, and dramatics, Wagner enrolled at the University of Wisconsin in Madison.

Majoring in civil engineering, Wagner was elected to the general honor fraternities Phi Kappa Phi and Phi Eta Sigma, and he became secretary of the engineering honorary Tau Beta Pi and president and secretary of Chi Epsilon, the honor society in civil engineering. He also served as chairman of the Engineers' St. Patrick's Day parade and belonged to Lambda Chi Alpha, to Scabbard and Blade, and to the drill and rifle teams. A *magna cum laude* graduate, he received the Theodore Herfurth Efficiency Award and took the B.S. degree in 1933.

Wagner held various jobs in highway engineering, surveying, and soil erosion control before he joined the Tennessee Valley Authority in 1934 as an engineering aide in the general engineering and geology division. Assigned to the navigation program, he took part in the planning and construction of Tennessee River navigation facilities. After successive promotions to junior hydraulic engineer, assistant hydraulic engineer, associate navigation engineer, and navigation engineer, he attained the position of assistant chief of the river transportation division. His studies of transportation economics were made to develop low-cost water transportation as part of TVA's program of integrated resource development.

In 1948 Wagner was named chief of the navigation and transportation branch in Knoxville, Tennessee. He assumed responsibility for the general planning of TVA's navigation program, including engineering and economic aspects connected with the increasing commercial use of the improved Tennessee waterway. Wagner served in 1950 on the committee on domestic water navigation projects and national policy of the President's Water Resources Policy Commission. In 1951 he was appointed assistant general manager and in 1954 general manager of TVA. The general manager is the chief administrative officer for TVA. He co-ordinates and directs the execution of the decisions, programs, and policies of the board of directors and approves management methods, organization changes, and major personnel appointments.

Succeeding Brooks Hays in 1961, Wagner became one of the three directors of the Tennessee Valley Authority. The three-man board, composed of a chairman, vice-chairman, and director, is appointed by the President and approved by the Senate. The establishment of general programs and policies, the evaluation of results, and the approval of major items are the responsibility of the board of directors.

The Tennessee Valley Authority, a corporation created by Congress on May 18, 1933, was established to develop navigation of the Tennessee River and its tributaries and to institute flood

AUBREY J. WAGNER

control in the areas surrounding the Tennessee and Mississippi rivers. The dams that were built or acquired for these purposes also made possible the large-scale production of electric power. TVA is also charged with encouraging conservation of natural resources and with developing improved chemical fertilizers to aid agriculture.

Seven states—Tennessee, Kentucky, Alabama, North Carolina, Georgia, Virginia, and Mississippi—have benefited from TVA's program of power distribution, flood control, and river navigation. Controlling forty-eight dams and ten steam plants, TVA has the largest power system in the United States. All the plants and twenty-eight of the dams are owned by the agency. Primarily a wholesaler of electricity, TVA sold 21.2 billion kilowatt-hours in 1961 to about 150 rural and municipal co-operative distribution systems, which retailed the power to 1,450,000 customers. Forty-six percent of the electric power produced by TVA was used by federal defense agencies in 1961.

On June 23, 1962 Wagner was named by President John F. Kennedy to succeed Herbert D. Vogel as chairman of the board of TVA. He was the second TVA career man to be appointed to this post. An Associated Press release from Knoxville, Tennessee stated that "Wagner is the kind of man folks here like to see become chairman," and quoted a member of the TVA staff as saying, "I doubt if anyone has walked and boated up and down the (Tennessee) River's navigation system as much as Red [Wagner]."

In July 1962 Wagner reported that nineteen retail distributors of TVA electricity had reduced power rates in 1961-62, creating savings of more than $1,000,000 for 160,000 consumers. Three months later, in October, Wagner released a report for fiscal 1962, which revealed that TVA had grossed a record $252,098,000 in power revenues and had taken in a record $109,236,000 in net power proceeds. He said that these unprece-

WAGNER, AUBREY J.—*Continued*

dented results "emphasize the contributions of electricity in the regional development program, with further increases in the usefulness of TVA power and further reductions in the cost to consumers."

Under the leadership of Wagner, TVA hopes to expand, and one of the projects being considered for the future is the building of a nuclear-fueled power plant. As Wagner has pointed out, however, nuclear fueling would have to be "really economical" before it could replace TVA's present methods of generating power. Abundant supplies of low-cost coal are available in the Tennessee Valley region, and coal-burning steam plants are now used by TVA to supplement water power for generating electricity.

Aubrey J. Wagner married Dorothea J. Huber on September 9, 1933. They have three sons, Joseph Michael, Karl Edward, and James Richard, and a daughter, Audrey Grace (Mrs. J. Donald Elam). Wagner is five feet ten inches tall, weighs 175 pounds, and has sandy hair and blue eyes. He is a director of the East Tennessee Heart Association and belongs to the American Society for Public Administration and the Tennessee Archeological Society. He is a member and past director of the Fort Loudoun Association, which is devoted to restoring the pre-Revolutionary frontier fort for which one of the TVA lakes is named. Politically Wagner is an independent.

A Lutheran, Wagner is a past president of St. John's Lutheran Church Council in Knoxville, Tennessee. He has taken part in the Boy Scout program since 1935, and he was awarded the Scoutmaster's Key in 1951 and the Silver Beaver award in 1956. On May 4, 1962 he received the Distinguished Service Citation from the University of Wisconsin at its fourteenth annual Engineers' Day Program. His favorite recreation is fishing.

References

Christian Sci Mon p10 Je 25 '62 por
Who's Who in America, 1962-63

WALKER, STANLEY Oct. 21, 1898-Nov. 25, 1962 Journalist; author; was city editor of New York *Herald Tribune* (1928-35) and wrote a book about this job, *City Editor* (1934); wrote several other books and many articles. See *Current Biography* (November) 1944.

Obituary

N Y Times p25 N 26 '62

WALLACE, GEORGE C(ORLEY) Aug. 25, 1919- Governor of Alabama; lawyer

Address: b. State Capitol, Montgomery, Ala.; h. Governor's Mansion, 1142 S. Perry St., Montgomery, Ala.

On January 14, 1963, at inaugural ceremonies in Montgomery, Alabama, on the same spot where President Jefferson Davis once took the oath of office to the Confederacy, George C. Wallace was installed as forty-seventh Governor of Alabama, and the South acquired a new leader in its battle against racial integration. Within the first year of his term of office Wallace stood "in the schoolhouse door" in an attempt to block enrollment of Negro students at the University of Alabama, and he later postponed the opening of integrated public schools.

A leading spokesman for states' rights and an avowed segregationist, Wallace was formerly a member of the Alabama legislature and a circuit judge. After his election as Governor with the greatest popular vote ever received in Alabama, he defiantly proclaimed: "I say segregation now, segregation tomorrow, segregation forever!"

George Corley Wallace was born to George C. and Mozell (Smith) Wallace at Clio, Alabama on August 25, 1919. A farmer's son, George Wallace and his brothers, Jack and Gerald, and his sister, Marianne, attended local schools and helped out on the farm. In 1936, while attending Barbour County High School, Wallace won the state Golden Gloves bantamweight boxing championship and held the title for the following year. He also made the high school football team and was a quarterback when he graduated in 1937. Wallace enrolled in the University of Alabama Law School in 1937, the same year that his father died, leaving the family with limited financial resources. He worked his way through law school by boxing professionally, waiting on tables, serving as a kitchen helper, and driving a taxi. Finding time to take part in school activities, he was president of his freshman class, captain of the university boxing team and freshman baseball team, president of the Spirit Committee, and a member of the highly regarded Law School honor court. He received his law degree in 1942.

In October of the same year Wallace volunteered for pilot training in the United States Army Air Force, but in 1943 he was hospitalized with spinal meningitis and was forced to give up pilot training. Upon his release from the hospital he became a flight engineer on a B-29 assigned to the 20th Air Force in the Pacific. After performing many aerial combat missions over Japan, Wallace was honorably discharged in December 1945 with the rank of flight sergeant.

Wallace returned home and in 1946 served as an assistant attorney general for Alabama. The following year, running as a candidate from Barbour County, he was elected to the Alabama Legislature. He served two terms in the legislature, where he distinguished himself as one of its most eloquent orators. Wallace was twice voted one of the legislature's most outstanding members, and during his two terms in the legislature he was responsible for introducing many measures. Among these was the Wallace Act, which to date has provided for the construction of five state trade schools to increase skilled labor potential in Alabama. The Wallace Industrial Act has attracted more than 100 new industries to the state. Wallace also sponsored the Alabama GI and Dependents Scholarships Act, which provides college and trade school tuition to children and widows of war casualties. His antilottery bill is credited with thwarting racketeers in Alabama, and his Highway Responsibility Law and his Natural Gas District Act have helped city governments in supplying services. Other highlights of Wallace's legislative career include his fight for more mental hospitals and tuberculosis hospitals and old-age pensions. He also led filibuster battles against a sales tax increase bill.

George Wallace was elected judge of the Third Judicial Circuit in 1953—a position that he held until January 1959. While in the judiciary chair he became known as the "Fighting Judge" because of his defiance of the United States Civil Rights Commission. In 1959 he was cleared of contempt of court charges after he refused to turn over voter registration records to the commission looking into charges of discrimination against prospective Negro voters. When he was cleared of the contempt charge, Wallace declared: "These characters from the Civil Rights Commission and Justice Departments were backed to the wall—they were defied and backed down. This 1959 attempt to have a second Sherman's March to the Sea has been stopped in the Cradle of the Confederacy."

While serving as a legislator and judge, Wallace also was active in the Democratic party. In 1948 he gained national attention, when as a delegate to the Democratic National Convention, he was a leader in the floor fight against a strong civil rights plank. Although a strong advocate of states' rights and segregation, he refused to join other members of the Alabama delegation who walked out of the convention in protest against the civil rights plank. Wallace also placed the name of Senator Richard Russell of Georgia in nomination for the Vice-Presidency during the 1948 Democratic National Convention. His showing at the 1948 convention led to his being chosen to represent Alabama on the platform committee at the Democratic National Convention in 1956, where his committee work produced a civil rights plank "as weak as a wet splinter," according to one critic.

In 1958 Wallace entered the Democratic primary for Governor of Alabama and was defeated by John Patterson by a vote of 314,000 to 250,000. According to Robert E. Baker in the Washington Post (May 31, 1962), Wallace told friends that Patterson had "out-segged" him (meaning that Patterson had posed as a more determined segregationist than he) and promised that it would not happen again. In 1962 Wallace again entered the Democratic gubernatorial primary, in which a victory is tantamount to being elected Governor in Alabama.

"Wallace campaigned up and down the state like "a one-man army at war with the Federal Government," according to the Saturday Evening Post (March 2, 1963). He vowed that if elected he would ask the legislature to give him the "right to assign pupils to schools that are threatened with integration." He assured cheering crowds, "When the court order comes, I am going to place myself in the position so that it must be directed against me and not some lesser official. I shall refuse to abide by any illegal federal court order, even to the point of standing in the schoolhouse door." On May 30, 1962 Wallace defeated State Senator Ryan de Graffenried in the Democratic gubernatorial runoff by 70,000 votes, and in November of that year, running on a segregation and economy platform, he was elected Governor of Alabama.

Paul Robertson

GEORGE C. WALLACE

In his inaugural speech in January 1963, Wallace repeated his campaign pledges and shouted his defiance of federal intervention in Alabama affairs. "I draw the line in the dust and toss the gauntlet before the feet of tyranny. . ." Wallace declaimed. As Governor, he lived up to his campaign promise to reduce the cost of government. "I never had money to waste and I'm certainly not going to waste someone else's money," he told taxpayers. He put more than one-quarter of the state's 4,000 automobiles up for sale, asked the legislature to slash his own office budget by more than $100,000, and sold one of the state's two yachts.

On June 11, 1963 Governor Wallace kept his campaign pledge to prevent desegregation of Alabama schools when he barred the path to two Negro students trying to register at the University of Alabama. Backed by state troopers and armed highway patrolmen, Wallace made his stand in front of Foster Auditorium, the university's registration center, where he blocked entrance to James A. Hood and Vivian J. Malone, who were accompanied by federal officers. After Deputy United States Attorney General Nicholas Katzenbach demanded that Wallace comply with federal court orders and allow the students to enter, the Alabama Governor issued a proclamation saying that the central government had no right to usurp state authority in the operation of the public schools, colleges, and universities. He pointed out that he was not barring the doorway "for defiance's sake, but for the purpose of raising basic and fundamental constitutional questions. My action is a call for strict adherence to the Constitution of the United States as it was written—for a cessation of usurpation and abuses." However, four hours later, after President John F. Kennedy signed an executive order federalizing the Alabama National Guard and ordered units of the 31st Division to the campus, Governor

WALLACE, GEORGE C.—*Continued*

Wallace stood aside and the Negro students registered without further incidents.

In September 1963, after several cities in Alabama had been ordered by a federal court to integrate their schools, Wallace sent state troopers to a consolidated school in Tuskegee to delay opening the fall term. Though the school board of Tuskegee had agreed to obey the federal court integration order, armed state patrolmen and troopers surrounded the school on September 2 and turned away students and teachers. Wallace explained that he had postponed the school opening for a week because there was reasonable cause to fear "breaches of the peace." Then on September 4 Wallace ordered more than 600 state troopers and special state police into Birmingham, where three schools were about to be desegregated. However, acceding to the request of local authorities, he and the troopers stayed away from the schools and two Negro pupils enrolled at one of them.

The next day, however, after a night of rioting in which the home of a Negro lawyer was bombed and another Negro was shot to death, the schools that had been ordered to integrate were closed. Wallace announced that the school board had acceded to his request and that the schools were closed temporarily. The next day Wallace sent state troopers to Huntsville and Mobile. At Huntsville helmeted troopers kept the students away from four schools. On September 10, after a ten-day period of confusion that involved the reopening and closing of schools within Alabama, President Kennedy once again federalized the Alabama National Guard. The Department of Defense in Washington, D.C., ordered the National Guard to their respective armories, away from all public schools. The federal directives then left the local police in control, who agreed to follow and to enforce federal orders relating to school integration.

After the school integration crisis Governor Wallace embarked on a series of speaking engagements, at college campuses and with panel groups. He says he plans in 1964 to enter Presidential primaries in the North; in the South his political strategy involves the naming of Democratic Presidential electors who are free to withhold support for the nominee. In a close election the required majority of the Electoral College would then be difficult to attain.

In May 1943 George C. Wallace married Lurleen Burns, whom he had met as a student at the University of Alabama. They have four children, Bobbie Jo, Peggy Sue, George, Jr., and Janie Lee, who, Wallace says, was named after Robert E. Lee. Wallace holds memberships in the American Legion, Veterans of Foreign Wars, Eastern Star, Disabled American Veterans, Shriners, Woodmen of the World, Masons, Moose, Elks, and Civitan. He is also a member of the Alabama Council for Better Schools and Alabama Parent Teachers Association and is on the board of directors of the Alabama Tuberculosis Association and the Alabama Pension Institute.

Known as "Little George" to his friends, George C. Wallace stands five feet seven inches tall, weighs 155 pounds, and has black hair and brown eyes. He lists fishing as his favorite recre-

ation. For more than twenty years he taught Sunday school at the First Methodist Church in Clayton. In August 1963 he challenged the federal government when, at his urging, the Alabama Board of Education adopted a resolution requiring every public school in the state to open its daily program with readings from the Bible. In June 1963 the United States Supreme Court had ruled that Bible reading in public schools was unconstitutional. "I want the Supreme Court to know we are not going to conform to any such decision," Wallace said. "If this is ever challenged while I am governor . . . I'm going to that school and read it myself."

References

N Y Times p21 Ja 27 '59 por; p26 My 14 '63 por
N Y World-Telegram p3 My 31 '63 por
Newsday p47 Ap 27 '63 por
Sat Eve Post 236:12 Mr 2 '63
New York Times. Men in the News (1962)

WALTER, FRANCIS E(UGENE) May 26, 1894-May 31, 1963 Democratic United States Representative from Pennsylvania (1933-63); chairman of the House Un-American Activities Committee; chairman of the immigration and naturalization subcommittee; co-author of the McCarran-Walter Act restricting immigration. See *Current Biography* (June) 1952.

Obituary

N Y Times p21 Je 1 '63

WARD, ROBERT (EUGENE) Sept. 13, 1917- Composer; business executive
Address: b. Galaxy Music Corp., 2121 Broadway, New York 23; h. 34 Hart Place, Nyack, N.Y.

Robert Ward, whose opera *The Crucible* won the 1962 Pulitzer Prize in Music, is convinced that opera "belongs on the stage and not in the orchestra pit." He feels that operas are mainly vocal vehicles and that dramatic color and effect should not be transferred from the singers to the orchestra as is done in many contemporary operas. In addition to *The Crucible*, for which he also won a New York Critics Circle citation in 1962, Ward has composed another opera, *Pantaloon;* four symphonies; and music for orchestra, chamber groups, and piano as well as for voice and chorus. From 1946 to 1956 he taught at the Juilliard School of Music; since 1956 he has been the executive vice-president and managing editor of the Galaxy Music Corporation.

Robert Eugene Ward was born in Cleveland, Ohio on September 13, 1917 to Albert E. Ward and Carrie (Mollenkopf) Ward. He has two brothers, David, an architect, and Albert, who until his recent retirement was active in radio and television work, and two sisters, Rhea and Margaret, who are teachers. Ward grew up in Cleveland, where his father had a moving and storage business. He attended local elementary schools and the John Adams High School, from which he graduated in 1934. While in high school, he was active in choral work and sang in several Gilbert and Sullivan operettas. He studied piano for two years with Ben Burtt and made his first attempts at composition at that time.

In 1935 Ward enrolled as a scholarship student at the Eastman School of Music of the University of Rochester. A composition major, he studied under Bernard Rogers, Howard Hanson, and Edward Royce. At the Eastman School he wrote *Fatal Interview* for soprano and orchestra, which was first conducted by Howard Hanson at Rochester in 1937, and several other vocal compositions. Hanson also conducted performances of Ward's *Slow Music for Orchestra* in 1938 and *Ode for Orchestra* in 1939. While an undergraduate at the Eastman School, Ward held the post of music librarian. He received a MacDowell Colony Fellowship in 1938, and he graduated with a bachelor of music degree in 1939.

In New York City, where he moved after graduation, Ward entered the Juilliard Graduate School on a fellowship. He studied composition under Frederick Jacobi for a year and conducting with Albert Stoessel and Edgar Schenkman from September 1940 to December 1941. During the summer of 1941 he also studied with Aaron Copland at the Berkshire Music Center in Massachusetts. From January 1940 to 1941, while still attending Juilliard, Ward was a music instructor at Queens College and wrote for the magazine *Modern Music*. During this period he also wrote *First Harvest* (1940), *Yankee Overture* (1940), three songs for soprano or tenor and piano, and Symphony No. 1 (1941), for which he won a Juilliard publications award.

Ward was inducted into the United States Army as a private in January 1942 and sent to Fort Riley, Kansas, where he composed most of the musical score for the Army show *The Life of Riley*. He attended the United States Army music school at Fort Myer, Virginia and wrote an orchestral piece, *Adagio and Allegro*, in 1943. His next assignment was in the Pacific, as leader of the 7th Infantry Division band. He was awarded the Bronze Star for meritorious service during a Japanese attack on the island of Attu in the Aleutians, and he and the band were cited for outstanding service during their tour of United States outposts in the Pacific. Ward composed most of the "jazzy," energetic *Jubilation, an Overture* (1946) during the campaigns of Leyte and Okinawa in 1944 and 1945. In December 1945 Ward was discharged with the rank of warrant officer, junior grade.

Returning to Juilliard, Ward completed his his study of conducting with Schenkman and obtained his postgraduate study certificate in May 1946. Shortly thereafter he joined the Juilliard faculty, where he remained for the next ten years, and he also became an associate in music at Columbia University, where he taught until 1948. From 1952 to 1955 Ward was music director at the Third Street Music School Settlement, and from 1954 to 1956 he served as assistant to the president of the Juilliard School. In 1944, while still in military service, he had received an Alice M. Ditson Fellowship from Columbia University, and in 1946 he was given a $1,000 grant by the American Academy of Arts and Letters.

ROBERT WARD

Ward's Symphony No. 2 (1947) was first performed in New York in May 1948, by the CBS Symphony Orchestra at the annual Festival of Contemporary American Music, sponsored by the Alice M. Ditson Fund of Columbia University. The concert, which also contained works by other contemporary composers, was reviewed by Noel Straus in the New York *Times* (May 17, 1948). According to Straus, Ward's symphony was suave and rich in texture. "The first movement was forceful, with well contrasted themes," he wrote, "but the crown of the work was the slow movement, with its romantic, intense content, and graceful melodic outlines." On January 31, 1950 the symphony was included in a Carnegie Hall concert program of the Philadelphia Orchestra, under Eugene Ormandy. "Robert Ward's Second Symphony . . . is a young man's work," Virgil Thomson wrote in the New York *Times* (February 1, 1950). "It is exuberant and warm, also boisterous and more than a little noisy. The life in it comes from the rhythm, which is never plodding, and from a certain naturalness in the melodic content. This tuneful material is mostly not first-class, but nowhere is it self-conscious or affected."

Over the next decade Ward composed several additional orchestral works: *Concert Music* (1948); *Night Music* (1949), based on blues; *Jonathon and the Gingery Snare* (1950), a piece for young people that makes heavy use of percussion instruments; Symphony No. 3 (1950); *Fantasia* for brass choir and timpani (1953); and *Euphony for Orchestra* (1954). He also wrote for piano *Lamentation* (1948); *Bagatelle* (1949); *Angels* (1949); and *Scherzo* (1950) as well as *Sonata for Violin and Piano* (1950) and *Arioso and Tarantelle* (1954) for cello and piano. Ward also composed *Sacred Songs for Pantheists* (1951) and several choral pieces during this period. The composer held Guggenheim Fellowships for composition in 1949-50 and 1951-52.

WARD, ROBERT—Continued

In June 1956 Ward resigned from his Juilliard posts to become executive vice-president and managing editor of the Galaxy Music Corporation.

Ward's first opera, *Pantaloon*, was given its première on May 17, 1956 by the Columbia University Opera Workshop at the Juilliard School of Music. Ward and his librettist, Bernard Stambler, based their opera on Leonid Andreyev's play *He Who Gets Slapped*. *Pantaloon* "is dramatic and lyrical; it holds the attention and engages one's sympathies," Howard Taubman wrote in the New York *Times* (May 18, 1956). Nine days later, in the *Times*, Taubman noted: "Mr. Ward's abundance of ideas is disarming. His music pours out with a generosity that is in strong contrast to the barren scores of some other contemporary operas. It is a pleasure to encounter a composer who is prodigal of invention. . . . It is enough for the present to greet him as a man with a future in the opera house." The three-act opera was again performed in April of 1959, under the title *He Who Gets Slapped*, by the New York City Opera Company.

On October 26, 1961 Ward's second opera, *The Crucible*, was performed by the New York City Opera Company. Written under a Ford Foundation grant, it was an adaptation of Arthur Miller's play, *The Crucible*, which dealt with the Salem witch trials of 1692. Ward and Bernard Stambler worked closely with Miller in transforming the play into an opera. Ward said that he first became interested in the play when he paid a chance visit to an Off Broadway production of it fifteen months earlier. He told Alan Rich of the New York *Times* (October 22, 1961) that two things in particular had attracted him to *The Crucible*. One was the "rich orchestration of its language, the stylized rhetoric that Miller had put into the mouths of his harried townspeople," and the other was the "line of the plot, which was projected so strongly that it would come through even when compressed into a singable libretto."

Ward adheres to the Italian operatic tradition as exemplified by Verdi and Puccini in that he makes the voice and not the orchestra the center of action. "Fascinating things go on in the pit in operas like 'Wozzeck,' but not much seems to go on the stage," he noted (New York *Herald Tribune*, October 22, 1961). "I may be old fashioned, but my feeling about opera is that everything must happen in the voice," he told Alan Rich. In 1962 Ward won the Pulitzer Prize in Music and the New York Critics Circle citation for *The Crucible*.

In addition to those compositions already listed, Ward's works include Symphony No. 4, created for the La Jolla Festival and Nikolai Sokoloff in 1958, *Divertimento for Orchestra* (1961), and *Hymn and Celebration*, first performed by the Phoenix Symphony Orchestra under Guy Taylor in March 1962. He has also composed band music. At present Ward is working on another opera—a comic one—tentatively entitled "Lady From Colorado."

The president of the American Composers Alliance in 1955-56, Ward is now chairman of its board of governors. He is also vice-chairman and a director of the American Music Center and a member of the music committee of the Henry Street Settlement. He has contributed articles and reviews to *Modern Music, Juilliard Review* and the National Federation of Music Clubs magazine. He has no religious or political affiliation.

Robert Ward is five feet nine and a half inches tall, weighs 192 pounds, and has graying hair and brown eyes. On June 19, 1944 he married Mary Raymond Benedict, a teacher. They have five children, Melinda, Jonathon, Mark, Johanna, and Timothy. The composer and his family live in Nyack, New York, a suburb of New York City, where he is a member of the Nyack Field Club and the Nyack Boat Club. An avid reader, Ward is always on the lookout for some written work that may be adaptable for opera. He also is an accomplished conductor and has appeared as guest conductor of his own music on several occasions. For five years he conducted the Doctors' Orchestral Society. Among the instruments he plays are the piano, clarinet, and viola. "All just enough to get by," he says.

References

Music Mag 164:6+ Jl ' 62 por
N Y Times II p11 O22 '61

Ewen, David. American Composers Today (1949)
Grove's Dictionary of Music and Musicians (1960)
Slonimsky, Nicolas. Baker's Biographical Dictionary of Musicians (1958)
Who's Who in America, 1962-63

WATSON, JAMES DEWEY Apr. 6, 1928- Biologist; university professor

Address: b. Department of Biology, Harvard University, Cambridge, Mass.; h. 10 Appian Way, Cambridge, Mass.

Since 1953 scientists have been guided by the Nobel Prize-winning discoveries of James Dewey Watson, a Harvard University biology professor, toward amazing new insights into the mysteries of life and reproduction. The classic one-page paper that Watson and Francis H. C. Crick contributed to the British journal *Nature* on April 25 of that year has been called a twentieth-century Rosetta stone that provides the code for translating puzzling biological observations into the precise language of molecules.

In this paper and a second one that followed on May 30, 1953, Watson and his British colleague presented a model for the molecular structure of deoxyribonucleic acid (DNA) and showed that this model could explain how living cells reproduce themselves in their own likeness, why some men are white and others red, and how evolutionary changes and mutations can occur. In its fruitfulness for further discovery, the Watson-Crick model has been compared to Newton's laws of motion, Darwin's theory of evolution, and Einstein's relativity theories. In recognition of their work, Watson and his collaborators, Crick and Maurice H. F. Wilkins, were accorded many honors, including the Nobel Prize for Medicine in 1962. Watson's further contributions include studies on the molecular structure of viruses and on the mechanism of protein biosynthesis.

Born to James Dewey and Jean (Mitchell) Watson in Chicago, Illinois on April 6, 1928, James Dewey Watson attended the University of Chicago Nursery School, Horace Mann Elementary School, and South Shore High School. As a boy, he was a bird watcher, Watson once told a *Fortune* reporter (June 1960), "a pleasant way to get some science when you're young, but not as an adult." After two years of high school, at the age of fifteen, Watson was an early entrant in the College of the University of Chicago, where in the next four years he earned both the Ph.B. and B.S. degrees, conferred in 1947. Recalling Watson's undergraduate work, Professor Charles E. Olmstead, chairman of the department of botany, said at the time of the announcement of the Nobel award, "He took two courses under me, and received an *A* in both courses. He must have been very keen, because I don't give very many *A*'s."

Still interested in bird study, Watson wrote to Indiana University about the opportunities for graduate study in ornithology. Although Indiana had no specialty in this field, he decided to go to Bloomington, where he was strongly influenced by the scientists Tracy M. Sonneborn, Ralph Cleland, S. E. Luria, and Hermann J. Muller, who is a Nobel laureate in genetics. In this climate Watson's interest in ornithology faded, and he wrote his doctoral thesis on bacterial viruses, a form that lies on the borderline between the giant molecules of the organic chemist and living matter. Watson's Ph.D. degree from Indiana was granted in 1950.

Plunging into postdoctoral research the same year, Watson went to the University of Copenhagen under a National Research Council fellowship. In 1951 he joined Francis H. C. Crick at the Cavendish Laboratory of Cambridge University. Here, under a fellowship of the National Foundation for Infantile Paralysis, he began one of his most productive periods. Perhaps the name Cavendish Laboratories brought visions of stately academic buildings to Watson's mind, but it bothered him not at all to learn that he and Crick were to do their work in a shabby shack known locally as The Hut. According to *Time* (October 26, 1962), "Watson, tieless, rumpled . . . fitted the picture perfectly."

A casual visitor, glancing inside The Hut, would hardly have recognized it as a scientific laboratory, much less the birthplace of one of biology's most fruitful concepts. Here, among a welter of old books, Watson and Crick began putting together an elaborate three-dimensional jigsaw puzzle, out of pieces of wire and colored beads and steel rods and oblongs of sheet metal. They sought a model of the deoxyribonucleic acid molecule that would fit all the known facts and that might yield a molecular explanation of how living matter reproduces itself.

These were the facts. Biologists had long since known that the genes in reproductive cells determine the form that their offspring will take. Later, the biochemists had found out that the basis of gene function, and of heredity, lay in the large and very complex molecule known as deoxyribonucleic acid. Chemists knew that this

Wide World

JAMES DEWEY WATSON

DNA molecule was made up of just six kinds of pieces (in an almost infinite variety of arrangements): a sugar, a phosphate group, and four basic units containing nitrogen. As other clues, Watson and Crick had the predictions of Linus Carl Pauling, Nobel laureate at California Institute of Technology, that the DNA molecule would be shaped like a long coil or spiral. Also at hand were reports of the X-ray diffraction studies of Maurice H. F. Wilkins, of King's College, University of London, clearly revealing that the DNA molecule was indeed some kind of spiral.

With these facts plus their background of knowledge about the affinities of chemical substances and the possible geometries of molecules, Watson and Crick finally evolved a model of the DNA molecule that—however different from earlier ideas—met all the requirements of the observed data. The model may be visualized as a very long ladder whose sides are made of link chain and whose rungs or steps are attached to every second link in each of the two chains. Each chain has alternating links in the sequence: sugar, phosphate, sugar, phosphate, the rungs being supported by, and attached to, the sugar links only.

Each rung, moreover, consists of two pieces, which fit together at the middle of the rung like round pegs in round holes, and square pegs in square holes; and there are only four kinds of pieces from which the rungs can be assembled. These pieces correspond to the four nitrogen-containing bases: adenine and thymine, and guanine and cytosine. The pieces can be attached to the chain in any order, but when one half of a rung is decided, the other half is automatically fixed. Adenine always pairs with thymine, and guanine always mates with cytosine. To complete the picture, it was found that the internal forces are such that the ladder must twist itself into a long spiral.

(Continued next page)

WATSON, JAMES DEWEY—*Continued*

This is a much simplified picture of the DNA model that Watson and Crick described in their April 25, 1953 paper in *Nature* in these modest words: "We wish to suggest a structure for the salt of deoxyribose nucleic acid (DNA). This structure has novel features that are of considerable biological interest." Nevertheless, the two scientists were well aware of the significance of their discovery. They added: "It has not escaped our notice that the specific pairing we have postulated immediately suggests a possible copying mechanism for the genetic material."

Just a month later, in *Nature* (May 30, 1953), Watson and Crick developed further implications of their model for genetics, pointing out the probability that the precise sequence of bases down the ladder probably carries the genetic information necessary for building identical new cells. They proposed the concept that the DNA ladder entwists, splits down the middle dividing each rung in two, and then the resulting halves gather up sugar, phosphate, and each of the four bases, until two new spiral ladders identical with the original have put themselves together. Thus each half of the ladder serves as a mold or template for assembling new ladders. Laboratory proof that precisely this process does occur earned Professor Arthur Kornberg of Stanford University a Nobel Prize in 1959.

While making the further point that their model could explain a number of phenomena besides genetic replication—for example, spontaneous mutation—Watson and Crick were not without humor in wondering how their DNA molecules could coil and uncoil as theory demanded "without everything getting tangled"; however, they "thought this objection [would] not be insuperable." That it is not insuperable has been shown by other scientists who have added proof after proof of the correctness of the Watson-Crick model.

After completing his work at Cambridge, Watson became in 1953 a senior research fellow in biology at California Institute of Technology. Then, in 1955, he moved to Harvard University as assistant professor of biology; he advanced to associate professor in 1958 and professor in 1961. In 1957 he again collaborated with Crick in proposing a structure of viruses, which was confirmed in 1962 by the electron microscope studies of Dr. Robert Horne of the Institute of Animal Physiology, Babraham, Cambridge, England. More recently, Professor Watson has been concerned with the mechanism of protein biosynthesis, while teaching Harvard and Radcliffe biology classes.

Professor Watson was the recipient (with Crick) of the John Collins Warren Prize of the Massachusetts General Hospital, 1959; the Eli Lilly Award in biochemistry of the American Chemical Society, 1960; (with Crick and Wilkins) the Albert Lasker Award of the American Public Health Association, 1960; and (with Crick and Wilkins) the 1962 Nobel Prize for Medicine, for "discoveries concerning the structure of nuclear acids and its significance for information transfer in living material." The University of Chicago awarded him the honorary D.Sc. degree in 1960. He is a member of the American Academy of Arts and Sciences and the Society of Biological Chemists.

James Dewey Watson was described in the New York *Times* (October 19, 1962) as impatient with the traditional approach to biological problems. He delivers his Harvard lectures from carefully organized notes, but is said sometimes to give his students the impression that he is "muttering into his shirt pocket." He is slender, brown-haired, and informal in manner. Reporters pressing Watson for speculation about race improvements that might ultimately emerge from his Nobel Prize-winning discoveries got this laconic reply: "I'd say if you want to have an intelligent child, you should have an intelligent wife."

References

Fortune 61:57 Je '60 por
N Y Times p27 O 19 '62 por
Time 80:46 O 26 '62 por
American Men of Science 10th ed (1960-62)
Who's Who in America, 1962-63

WAUGH, SIDNEY (BIEHLER) Jan. 17, 1904-June 30, 1963 Sculptor whose works adorn several governmental buildings in Washington, D.C. and many museums; known also for the glassware he had designed for the Steuben Glass Company since 1934. See *Current Biography* (July) 1948.

Obituary

N Y Times p29 Jl 1 '63

WEIS, MRS. CHARLES W(ILLIAM), JR. July 8, 1901-May 1, 1963 Former United States Representative from New York (1959-63); member of executive committee of the Republican National Committee (1954-63). See *Current Biography* (December) 1959.

Obituary

N Y Times p35 My 2 '63

WEIS, JESSICA McCULLOUGH *See* Weis, Mrs. Charles W(illiam), Jr.

WELCH, LEO D(EWEY) Apr. 22, 1898- Corporation chairman; industrialist; banker
Address: b. 3029 Klingle Rd., N.W., Washington, D.C.

The industrialist and banker Leo D. Welch set aside plans for retirement in February 1963 when President John F. Kennedy asked him to serve as chairman of the board and chief executive officer of the new and controversial Communications Satellite Corporation. He was confirmed by the Senate in April 1963. Welch is well qualified to direct the activities of this government-sponsored and government-regulated private corporation, which was set up after one of the bitterest Congressional battles in recent years. Beginning his career as a trainee with the First National City Bank of New York, Welch spent some twenty-five years in its service, as managing supervisor of its South American branches and later as vice-president of its Caribbean operations. He joined the Standard Oil Company of New Jersey as treasurer in 1944 and rose through the ranks to become, in 1960, the chairman of its board of directors.

Leo Dewey Welch, the son of William F. and Mary E. (Compton) Welch, was born in Rochester, New York on April 22, 1898. He grew up in Rochester and attended the Charlotte (New York) High School, from which he graduated in 1915. He then went on to the University of Rochester, where he majored in languages and received his B.A. degree in 1919. From August to November 1918 he served in the United States Naval Reserve. Although his father, a contractor, wanted him to enter the family business after his college graduation, Leo Welch entertained other ambitions. Capitalizing on his training in languages, he embarked on a career with the First National City Bank of New York, joining the bank's branch in Buenos Aires, Argentina as a trainee.

Welch remained in South America until 1943, serving as managing supervisor of the bank's branches in Argentina, Chile, and Uruguay. From 1936 to 1940 he was also director of the Central Bank of Argentina, and in 1936-37 he was president of the United States Chamber of Commerce in Argentina. He served as president of the Argentine Trade Promotion Corporation from 1941 to 1943. Welch was recalled from South America in 1943 to be promoted to vice-president in charge of the First National City Bank's Caribbean operations.

Highly regarded in the banking community for his business acumen and especially for his skill in international trade and finance, Welch is also noted for diplomatic finesse, which he acquired during his sojourn in Latin America. He had dealt with foreign governments so long that, as he has noted, he had in effect "become a part of the foreign environment" (New York *World-Telegram and Sun*, May 4, 1960). In recognition of his services to Argentina and Chile both governments awarded Welch the Order of Merit with the title of Commander.

In 1944 Welch made what he called "the unique switch" to America's largest oil company, the Standard Oil Company of New Jersey. Oil companies traditionally develop executive talent from within their own organizations. But as World War II neared its end, Standard Oil of New Jersey found itself faced with new and complex foreign currency problems. When company officials overheard Welch briefing bank customers on economic problems abroad, they were sufficiently impressed to take a close look at his qualifications and offer him the job of treasurer of their company.

As treasurer of Standard Oil of New Jersey, Welch traveled extensively to find foreign capital to finance the major portion of the expanding company's overseas ventures. His domestic responsibilities included supervising the company's investment portfolio and dealing with problems in marketing, public relations, and executive development. His job also took him into politics and diplomacy. As he has observed, "Oil is such

Wide World

LEO D. WELCH

a tremendous factor in the economy of every country that the government is looking over your shoulder all the time." At Standard Oil of New Jersey, Welch continued his climb to one of the top corporate jobs in the United States. He was elected a director of the company in 1953 and a vice-president in 1956. In 1958 he became an executive vice-president and a member of the executive committee, and in 1960 he was elected chairman of the board.

As a leading spokesman for the highly regulated oil industry, Welch has been concerned with what he sees as a problem of over-regulation by government. Speaking at the company's eightieth annual stockholders' meeting on May 23, 1962 Welch maintained that the nation's economic growth was menaced by "the shadow cast by big government over the freedom of decision by management." He noted that industrial confidence was being weakened by increasing efforts to control prices, the frequency of charges and investigations by the government, restrictions on mergers, punitive taxes on foreign investments, discrimination against large firms, and other factors. At the same time Welch recognized the need for government and business to straighten out their differences. The growing economic competition from abroad, he pointed out, "will not permit the luxury of feuding between government and business."

Welch had originally planned to retire in the spring of 1963, but the challenge of heading the Communications Satellite Corporation was too exciting to turn down. The choice of Welch as chairman of the board and chief executive officer of the corporation was announced by the White House on February 27, 1963 and confirmed by the United States Senate on April 25, 1963 over the opposition of a small group of Senators who maintained that the Senate did not have the constitutional authority to confirm officials of a privately owned concern.

(Continued next page)

WELCH, LEO D.—*Continued*

In his present position Welch has the opportunity to draw on every facet of his past experience in management, finance, politics, and diplomacy. The nature of the organization he heads and the kind of work it was set up to handle make for complexities that the ordinary corporate executive never meets. The Communications Satellite Corporation was established by Congress under the communications satellite bill, which was enacted in August 1962 over the opposition of a liberal bloc of Senators who favored public ownership. It was set up as a private corporation with the responsibility of developing and operating in conjunction with other countries a global communications system using satellites as relay stations. Although privately owned, the Communications Satellite Corporation is much more closely supervised and regulated by the government than other private corporations.

As its chairman, Welch faces many domestic and foreign problems. He is responsible for co-operating with four government agencies: the National Aeronautics and Space Administration, the Federal Communications Commission, the Department of State, and the Department of Defense. All have some statutory supervision over corporation operations. Welch also has to deal with such private communications carriers as the American Telephone and Telegraph Company and the Radio Corporation of America. On the foreign front, he is charged with negotiating arrangements with other countries for the placing and use of the satellites.

Equally imposing are the technical and financial hurdles that must be overcome. Welch and his colleagues in Tregaron, the former estate in Washington, D.C. of the late Ambassador Joseph E. Davies where the corporation is housed, are being asked to start from scratch the first commercial venture into space, an enterprise that may cost $200,000,000 or more, on the basis of a technology that is still unproved and with little hope for profits for at least a decade. Comsat, as the corporation is often called, plans to offer its stock for sale by early 1964. By law half of its shares will be offered to communications carriers, the other half to the general public. In the meantime the corporation has negotiated with ten banks to borrow up to $5,000,000. Before Comsat can operate a profitable satellite system, its scientists must develop satellites that will operate in space for several years. Satellites launched to date have gone off the air in a matter of weeks or months. To Welch these problems represent challenges that he fully intends to overcome. Although he had planned to slow down his activities in the coming years he finds himself on an accelerated pace, working days, nights, and weekends. On those rare occasions when he can get away from his job he relaxes at Hill and Dale Farms near Berryville, Virginia, a cattle farm that he bought in August 1963.

Welch still maintains his connection with the First National City Bank of New York, having served on its board of directors since 1956. He is a director of the Commonwealth Fund in New York City, and in 1962-63 he was a director of the International Telephone and Telegraph Company. He is vice-chairman of the United States Council of the International Chamber of Commerce; a trustee of the University of Rochester and of the Committee for Economic Development; and a member of the Council on Foreign Relations.

On January 27, 1926 Leo D. Welch married Veronica Purviance, whose father represented Armour & Company in South America. They have a daughter, Gloria, a former Vogue model, who is married to Emmet Whitlock, a New York broker, and one grandchild. Welch is six feet two inches tall, weighs 175 pounds, and has blue eyes and thinning gray hair. He dresses conservatively, and he has a reputation for remaining calm in the most provocative situations. Welch belongs to the University Club (New York City), Maidstone Club (East Hampton, New York), National Golf Links of America (Southhampton, New York), Links Golf Club (Roslyn, New York), Jockey Club (Buenos Aires), Twenty-Nine (New York City), Clove Valley (New York) Rod and Gun Club, Augusta National Golf Club, Lyford Cay (Nassau), and the Links (New York City). He is fond of shooting game and fishing, and keeps in shape by taking regular, strenuous walks. During his younger days in Argentina he was an excellent polo player. He does some oil painting, mostly of landscapes. His favorite preoccupation, however, is with the daily international scene, and he says: "To me there's nothing as absorbing as the history we're living in this rapidly changing world" (New York *World-Telegram and Sun*, May 4, 1960).

References

N Y Post Mag p2 Ap 28 '63 por
N Y World-Telegram p51 My 4 '60 por
Newsday p51 F 28 '63 por
Who's Who in America, 1962-63
World Who's Who in Commerce and Industry (1961)

WIDMARK, RICHARD Dec. 26, 1914- Actor; producer
Address: b. 139 S. Beverly Dr., Beverly Hills, Calif.

An actor who has starred in nearly every picture in which he has played, Richard Widmark reached film prominence fifteen years ago with his chilling portrayal of a laughing killer in *Kiss of Death* (1947). Since then he has had a diversity of parts, mostly ruggedly masculine, including that of the American prosecutor in *Judgment at Nuremberg* (1961). Before beginning his screen career, Widmark was a successful actor in radio and the theater in New York. A few years ago he formed his own film producing company, Heath Productions, which has made *Time Limit* (1957) and *The Secret Ways* (1961).

Richard Widmark was born in Sunrise, Minnesota on December 26, 1914 to Mae Ethel (Barr) Widmark and Carl H. Widmark, a salesman. His younger brother, Donald, is no longer living. When Richard Widmark was a child his family traveled around a good deal, living at Sioux Falls, South Dakota; Henry, Illinois;

Chillicothe, Missouri; and Princeton, Illinois. He attended high school in Princeton, where he played football, acted with the dramatic club, wrote for the student newspaper, and was senior class president. When his class graduated in 1932 he gave the commencement address. In Princeton he took a job as doorman at the local motion picture theater so that he could see all the films; he had loved going to the movies ever since his grandmother first took him when he was three years old.

At Lake Forest (Illinois) College, where he held a full four-year scholarship, Widmark majored in speech and political science. He won a first prize in the McPherson oratory contest and third prize in a state oratory contest, belonged to the honorary society Iron Key, played football and baseball, and was senior class president. To help support himself he held a part-time job as a waiter in the college dining hall. After graduating in 1936 with the B.A. degree he made a summer tour of France and Germany and then taught as an instructor in the Lake Forest College drama department from 1936 to 1938. During his years at the college, both as an undergraduate and as an instructor, he acted in some thirty modern plays, and he has said that his work in drama under Professor R. C. Tomlinson at Lake Forest influenced his choice of acting as a career. He explained further, in a *New Yorker* interview (November 4, 1961), "I suppose I wanted to act in order to have a place in the sun. I'd always lived in small towns, and acting meant having some kind of identity."

In 1938 he went to New York, where a former classmate who was producing radio programs gave him a part in a radio series called *Aunt Jenny's Real Life Stories*. Widmark's excellent diction was an asset, and over the next ten years he appeared—often as a neurotic young man—on many other radio shows. These included *Big Sister; Joyce Jordan, M.D.; David Harum; Stella Dallas; Pepper Young's Family; Front Page Farrell; Grand Central; Kate Smith's Program; Columbia Workshop; March of Time; Cavalcade;* and *Inner Sanctum.*

Rejected for Army service during World War II because of a perforated eardrum, Widmark entertained servicemen under the auspices of the American Theatre Wing and served as an air-raid warden. He made his Broadway debut on March 17, 1943 as a young Army Air Corps lieutenant in the comedy *Kiss and Tell*. Late in 1943 he played Harry Bird, a writer, in a short-lived production of William Saroyan's *Get Away Old Man.*

Another production in which he appeared was *Trio*, a controversial play touching on lesbianism that opened on December 29, 1944 and ran for sixty-seven performances before it was closed by the License Commissioner. Widmark's part was that of a young college student who fights to free the girl he loves from domination by an older woman. "Widmark does a remarkable job," a New York *Herald Tribune* reviewer (December 30, 1944) wrote. "His tense underplaying sustains the most faltering moments of the play." Widmark left the cast on February 17, 1945 to begin rehearsals for *Kiss Them For Me.*

On Broadway for three months beginning March 20, 1945, *Kiss Them for Me* dealt with

Horst Fanke, Hamburg

RICHARD WIDMARK

three naval aviators, fresh from combat in the Pacific, who want to devote an unauthorized four-day Stateside leave to wine, women, and song. Widmark was generally commended by drama critics for his portrayal of the most perceptive member of the trio. In December 1945 and January 1946 he played Jim Baird, an idealistic State Department official, in S. N. Behrman's *Dunnigan's Daughter*. During the 1946-47 season he co-starred in the Chicago production of Elmer Rice's *Dream Girl.*

Although Widmark prospered in radio and the theater, he had always wanted to act in movies more than in plays. "I learned the fundamentals of acting on the stage," he explained in the 1961 *New Yorker* interview. "Movie acting, however, is the most difficult kind of all to do." Early in 1947, despite the director's objections that he seemed too well-bred and intellectual, Widmark was cast in his first movie role as the sadistic killer Tom Udo in *Kiss of Death,* which was filmed on location in New York City. In one of his big scenes Widmark, laughing like a hyena, pushed an old woman in a wheel chair down a flight of steps. Critics acclaimed Widmark's performance as first-rate, and *Kiss of Death* made him a prominent film actor. To act in *Kiss of Death,* Widmark had had to sign a seven-year contract with Twentieth Century-Fox, and between 1947 and 1954 he made more than twenty pictures for the company. Often assigned "bad man" or military roles, he usually elicited approval from the film critics.

In *The Street With No Name* (1948) Widmark played a gang leader, in *Road House* (1948) a double-crossing proprietor, and in *Yellow Sky* (1949) one of a group of malcontent Civil War veterans who become outlaws. *Down To the Sea in Ships* (1949), in which Lionel Barrymore played a crusty old sea captain who wants his young grandson to learn about the sea, afforded Widmark a sympathetic role as the grandson's friend and teacher. A New York

WIDMARK, RICHARD—Continued

Herald Tribune reviewer (February 23, 1949) said, "Widmark is excellent as the young mate who knows about marine biology as well as trade winds."

Widmark portrayed a daredevil pilot in *Slattery's Hurricane* (1949), and in *Night and the City* (1950) he was a cabaret hustler who dreams of big-time money. In *No Way Out* (1950) he took the role of a psychotic Negro-hater. His performance in *Panic in the Streets* (1950) as a young United States Public Health doctor who tracks down the carriers of a lethal plague germ was called memorable by a *New Yorker* reviewer.

Widmark was cast as a Marine lieutenant in *Halls of Montezuma* (1951), as commander of an underwater demolition team in *The Frogmen* (1951), and as a parachuting forest fire fighter in *Red Skies of Montana* (1952). He next appeared in *Don't Bother to Knock* (1952) and in *O. Henry's Full House* (1952). He departed from his more usual characterizations in the comedy *My Pal Gus* (1952), in which he played a bonbon manufacturer too busy to devote time to his small son. A *Variety* reviewer (November 12, 1952) commented: "Widmark is very good as the tough, rags-to-riches father, showing both good comedy feeling as well as the more touchingly dramatic flavor required in the final scene."

The military theme cropped up again in Widmark's next few films: he portrayed the leader of a meteorological team in Mongolia during World War II in *Destination Gobi* (1953), a hard-as-nails drill sergeant in a basic-training camp in *Take the High Ground* (MGM, 1953), and a submarine commander in *Hell and High Water* (1954). In *Pickup on South Street* (1953) he was cast as a gangster who works with Communist spies. In 1954 Widmark appeared in *Garden of Evil* and *Broken Lance,* both Westerns. When his contract with Twentieth Century-Fox expired Widmark became an independent. "I knew I had to get away from Fox," he explained in the 1961 *New Yorker* interview. "I was being switched around from movie to movie without getting a chance to do much that I liked."

In 1955 Widmark appeared in *A Prize of Gold* as an Air Force sergeant who steals gold from the government for a noble purpose and in *Cobweb* as a chief psychiatrist in a mental clinic. He acted in two Westerns, *Backlash* and *The Last Wagon,* in 1956 and in the same year portrayed a best-selling author lost in the jungles of Mexico in the thriller *Run for the Sun.*

Widmark made his debut as a producer in 1957 with the well-received picture *Time Limit,* produced by his company, Heath Productions, and released through United Artists. The film dealt with an Army major facing trial for treason because, as a brainwashed prisoner in North Korea, he supposedly defected to and aided the enemy. Widmark portrayed a dedicated judge advocate who is dissatisfied with the surface evidence and probes deeper for motives. Heath Productions was also associated in the creation of *The Trap* (1959), in which Widmark played a courageous lawyer, and in 1961 Heath produced *The Secret Ways,* released by Universal-International, which was less of a critical success than *Time Limit.* Filmed mostly on location in

Vienna, *The Secret Ways* concerns an American adventurer (Widmark) who is paid to spirit an anti-Communist leader from behind the Iron Curtain.

Reviewers gave only a lukewarm reception to the film version of Shaw's *Saint Joan* (1957), in which Widmark played the Dauphin, and to the comedy *Tunnel of Love* (1958), in which he was the philandering husband of a childless wife, a role created by Tom Ewell on Broadway. Widmark then appeared in the Westerns *Warlock* (1959), *The Alamo* (1960), and *Two Rode Together* (1961).

Learning the lines for his role as the American prosecutor, Colonel Tad Lawson, in Stanley Kramer's production of *Judgment at Nuremberg* (1961) took Widmark about six weeks. A fictional version of the trial of four Nazi judges accused of giving legal sanction to German war crimes, the picture raises the question of to what degree the individual is responsible for crimes he has committed or condoned at the behest of the state. Widmark, with the rest of the star-studded cast—including Burt Lancaster, Spencer Tracy, Maximilian Schell, Montgomery Clift, Marlene Dietrich, and Judy Garland—received excellent critical notices.

In 1962 Widmark appeared in the Cinerama production *How the West Was Won,* which received good notices in *Variety* on its release in Europe late in the year. "Widmark makes a vital impression as the head man of the construction team building the railroad," the *Variety* reviewer (November 7, 1962) wrote. Also in 1962 Widmark starred in *Flight From Ashiya,* made in Japan, about American airmen who rescued some Japanese sailors during World War II.

Although he intends to keep on acting Widmark has in recent years become increasingly interested in production, and he hopes to make about two pictures a year—one for himself and one for a big releasing company. He feels it is important to shoot on location (because travel and television have made audiences familiar with actual locales) and to spend more time on rehearsals before the shooting of scenes. In 1962 Widmark, with the director Fred Zinnemann and the actor Whit Bissell, helped a group of students from the University of Southern California make a fifteen-minute noncommercial film, *Off the Highway.*

Richard Widmark and his wife, the former Jean Hazlewood, were married on April 5, 1942 and have one child, Anne Heath Widmark. The actor is five feet eleven inches tall, weighs 165 pounds, and has blue eyes and blond hair. He objects to the prying approach of fan magazines to actors, and he firmly keeps business separate from his home. The Widmarks own a house in Brentwood, California and a farm-ranch between Santa Barbara and Los Angeles, where they grow barley and raise cattle. Widmark is a Democrat and belongs to the Riviera Country Club in California and the Coffee House in New York City.

Riding, swimming, playing golf and tennis, reading, painting, and listening to music are among Widmark's hobbies. Blessed with a good memory, he first learns the lines of his parts by rote with the help of his wife or daughter and then concentrates on polishing the interpretation.

"Getting launched was easy for me," he recalls of his early career (*New Yorker*, November 4, 1961). "Too easy, perhaps. That's probably why I never got that dedicated feeling. I never considered myself a dedicated artist, and don't now. I've never had the feeling I'd die if I didn't get a certain part. Just the same, I love to work, and I work hard. Acting has always been my work, and it's part of my life."

References

Colliers 123:23+ Ap 16 '49 por
Life 26:81+ Mr 28 '49 por
New Yorker 37:60+ N 4 '61

International Celebrity Register (1959)
International Motion Picture Almanac, 1963
Ross, Lillian and Ross, Helen. The Player (1962)

WILHELMINA (HELENA PAULINE MARIA) Aug. 31, 1880-Nov. 28, 1962 Princess and former Queen of the Netherlands; succeeded to the throne in 1890 and abdicated in favor of her daughter, Juliana, in 1948. See *Current Biography* (January-June) 1940.

Obituary

N Y Times p1+ N 28 '62

WILKINS, MAURICE H(UGH) F(REDERICK) Dec. 15, 1916- Biophysicist
Address: b. King's College, University of London, Strand, London, W.C.2, England; h. 30 St. John's Park, Blackheath, London, S.E. 3, England

For more than a decade Maurice H. F. Wilkins, a British biophysicist, has been using X-rays to shed new light on the fundamentals of biology. Together with Francis H. C. Crick, a fellow Englishman, and James Dewey Watson, an American, he won the 1962 Nobel Prize for Medicine for determining the structure of the deoxyribonucleic acid (DNA) molecule, which is believed to carry the genetic code that makes possible the transfer of hereditary characteristics from parent to child in all living things.

When the first reports by Wilkins and others on the double spiral structure of the DNA molecule appeared in the spring of 1953 in the British journal *Nature,* a ripple of excitement stirred the world of biology. Molecular biologists believe that this discovery may well lead in to man's control of cell-forming processes and to the elimination of birth defects, hereditary diseases, and cancer. Wilkins, who is currently working at the Sloan-Kettering Institute for Cancer Research in New York, is deputy director of the biophysics unit of the Medical Research Council in London. He is also an honorary lecturer of biophysics at King's College, University of London, where the unit is based. Before joining the Medical Research Council unit in 1946 he worked during World War II on the Manhattan Project, which created the atomic bomb, at the University of California in Berkeley.

Maurice Hugh Frederick Wilkins was born in Pongaroa, New Zealand on December 15, 1916 to Edgar Henry and Eveline Constance Jane

MAURICE H. F. WILKINS

(Whittaker) Wilkins, both of Dublin, Ireland. His father had a strong bent for research, but his duties as a school doctor in New Zealand left him little opportunity to pursue it. At the age of six Maurice Wilkins was taken from New Zealand to England to attend King Edward's School in Birmingham. Later he studied at St. John's College, Cambridge University, where he obtained his B.A. degree in 1938, the year before England's entry into World War II. At the direction of the Ministry of Home Security and Aircraft Production, he went to Birmingham University to do graduate research under Sir John Randall on the improvement of radar screens. His fundamental studies on the luminescence of solids and the electron trap theory of phosphorescence earned him the Ph.D. degree in 1940.

Moving from radar to weapons as England's war crisis deepened, Wilkins joined the physicists working under Sir Marcus Oliphant on the separation of uranium isotopes for atomic bombs. When Britain's military nuclear research was transferred to the United States, Wilkins went with it, as a member of the Manhattan Project at the University of California in Berkeley. There he pursued mass spectrograph studies of the separation of uranium isotopes.

As the war neared its end Wilkins began to think of changing his field of specialization from pure physics to biophysics. He is quoted in the *Saturday Review* (March 2, 1963) as saying, "Partly on account of the [atomic] bomb, I lost some interest in physics." He read Erwin Schrödinger's book *What is Life?* (1944) and discussed the question of changing fields with the physicists Sir John Randall, Harrie S. Massey, and Sir Marcus Oliphant, who all felt that physics could contribute to biological understanding. When his receipt of the Nobel Prize for contributions to biology was announced, Wilkins said in an interview (New York *Herald Tribune,* October 19, 1962): "During the war, I got interested in going into the biology field. After the war, I did it with considerable trepidation, but

WILKINS, MAURICE H. F.—Continued

I thought I'd have a bash at it." In 1945 Wilkins became a lecturer in physics at St. Andrews University in Scotland, and in 1946 he went to King's College, University of London, where he joined the biophysics unit of the Medical Research Council. (The council is responsible for promoting medical research in Britain.) He has been with the unit ever since, becoming its deputy director in 1955.

In 1946, the same year that Wilkins went to King's College, scientists at the Rockefeller Institute announced that the genes, which had long been known as the units inside living cells that transmit hereditary characteristics, were made up of deoxyribonucleic acid (DNA), an extremely complicated chemical substance. Fascinated by this discovery, Wilkins began to wonder whether it would be possible to learn the exact structure of this giant molecule.

With his collaborators, he began to study DNA molecules under the microscope by illuminating them with one color of transmitted light and another color of reflected light. He applied this dichroism pattern analysis to DNA samples that he had assembled from several different sources. And, as often happens in science, progress came from an unexpected direction.

It was his customary procedure to have his DNA samples in a gel and to orient his materials under the microscope with a glass rod. He noticed that whenever he removed the glass rod from the gel, a thin fiber like the strand of a spider web spun itself between the surface of the gel and the tip of the glass rod. Recalling the literature on structure studies of crystalline proteins, he soon realized that these fibers would be ideal for analysis by X-ray diffraction techniques.

Pressing the department's only X-ray equipment into immediate service, he was quickly rewarded for his flash of insight. His X-ray diffraction patterns clearly indicated that the structure of the DNA molecule was a double spiral, like a rope ladder that is fixed at the top and twisted a number of times about its own length. He also found that DNA samples from widely varying sources all showed the same double spiral pattern.

Wilkins passed on his findings to James Watson, an American biologist, and Francis Crick, a British biochemist, who in the early 1950's was collaborating on theoretical studies of DNA structure at the Cavendish Laboratory of Cambridge University. Watson and Crick seized on the concept of the double spiral structure and, co-ordinating it with the known chemical constitution of DNA and the theoretical constraints on the assembly of its various parts into a stable molecule, soon developed the now famous Watson-Crick model of DNA.

Shortly afterward Watson and Crick also showed how the DNA molecule could carry the genetic information required for building new living cells identical with their parents and how mutations or cell abnormalities can occur. For their contributions to an understanding of DNA, they shared the 1962 Nobel Prize for Medicine with Wilkins. Wilkins later refined his X-ray techniques and added experimental confirmation of the Watson-Crick model. The Nobel Prize, which in 1962 amounted to nearly $50,000, was awarded to the three men by the Royal Caroline Institute of Sweden on October 18, 1962.

It has been said that science is like a great cathedral—the work of a few architects and many artisans. The grand design having been laid out by Wilkins, Watson, and Crick, the artisans now went to work with a will. Thousands of experiments were performed, all bearing witness to the soundness of the architecture. No fundamental revision of the DNA model has been needed, although refinements have followed. Wilkins has contributed to this refinement in studies reported in 1960 and since.

One of the more recent concepts of molecular biologists is that of a substance termed "messenger RNA," which is closely related to DNA and which is believed to transmit the code specified by the DNA "tape." In 1962 Wilkins obtained the first clear X-ray diffraction patterns of RNA and showed it to have a helical structure very similar to that of DNA.

In view of the progress that has been made in the past decade it seems likely that some day control over the processes by which cells reproduce themselves will be achieved. This is particularly desirable because mistakes sometimes occur in nature that human. beings would like very much to correct—like those in which healthy cells produce cancerous ones. Wilkins continues to work on the problem of the ribonucleic acids at the Sloan-Kettering Institute for Cancer Research in New York, where he has been a visiting scientist since 1962.

In 1958 Maurice H. F. Wilkins was made an honorary lecturer in the department of biophysics at King's College, and in 1959 he became a Fellow of the Royal Society. He shared the $5,000 Albert Lasker Award of the American Public Health Association with Watson and Crick in 1960. In the fall of 1962 he lectured in the United States. By his marriage in 1959 to Patricia Ann Chidgey, Wilkins has a daughter, Sarah Fenella, and a son, George. He has been described as being tall, slender, and blond and as having a courtly manner. Wilkins is a man of precision who has a strong dislike for overstatement. In the first draft of his Nobel Prize lecture he wrote: "Nucleic acids are very remarkable." On second thought, he crossed out the word "very."

References

N Y Herald Tribune p3 O 19 '62
N Y Times p27 O 19 '62
Sat R 46:57 Mr 2 '63 por
Who's Who, 1963
Who's Who in America, 1962-63

WILLIAMS, G(ERHARD) MENNEN Feb. 23, 1911- United States government official; lawyer

Address: b. Department of State, Washington 25, D.C.; h. 1401 31st St., N.W., Washington 7, D.C.

NOTE: This biography supersedes the article that appeared in *Current Biography* in 1949.

As the leading representative of the United States Department of State to a continent where most of the nations have achieved independence within the last few years, G. Mennen Williams has a job that President John F. Kennedy has termed "a position of responsibility second to none in the new administration." Beginning his career as a young lawyer with the Social Security board, Williams has served in various state and federal positions. As Governor of Michigan from 1948 to 1960 he was responsible for many important reforms, and he holds the distinction of having served the greatest number of consecutive terms of any state Governor in American history. Since taking office as Assistant Secretary of State for African affairs on February 1, 1961 he has been an articulate, if at times controversial, spokesman on the various problems involving the continent of Africa.

Of English, Welsh, French, and German lineage, Gerhard Mennen Williams was born in Detroit on February 23, 1911 to Henry Phillips and Elma (Mennen) Williams. His father's family, one branch of which was well-known at the time of the Revolutionary War, owned a prosperous pickle factory in Detroit and was active in Michigan real estate. His maternal grandfather, who had immigrated to the United States from Germany, founded a well-known soap and pharmaceutical firm, the Mennen Company. This connection accounts for Mennen Williams' nickname, "Soapy." G. Mennen Williams and his two younger brothers, Henry Phillips and Richard, were given a careful upbringing by their parents. The family was devoutly Episcopalian, and Mennen sang in the church choir and acted as crucifer during Sunday services at St. Paul's Cathedral in Detroit. He took piano and dancing lessons, but his main interests as a boy were reading and physical culture. By the time he was eight years old he had accompanied his parents on trips to Cuba, Alaska, and Panama.

Williams obtained his early education at the Liggett School in Detroit and at the Detroit University School. In 1925 he entered the Salisbury School, an exclusive Episcopalian preparatory school in Connecticut. During his five years there he served as chapel prefect, took part in athletics, wrote poetry for a student magazine, and received the highest grades in the school's history. His study of the history of English serfdom and of the Industrial Revolution influenced him in his determination to champion the cause of the underdog.

At Princeton University, where he attended the School of Public and International Affairs, Williams obtained high honors in history and was recommended for a Rhodes Scholarship. He won two varsity letters in athletics and was a member of the rowing team. Williams also served as secretary of the local chapter of Phi Beta Kappa; regional president of the National Student Federation; and president of the student senate, the Quadrangle Club, and the Young Republican Club. When he graduated with the B.A. degree in 1933 he ranked in thirty-seventh place in a class of 476 students.

Dissuaded from pursuing a diplomatic career by a family friend who was with the diplomatic service, Williams enrolled in the University of Michigan Law School. He served on the editorial staff of the *Michigan Law Review* and was a member of the student senate, the Order of the Coif, and the Liberal Club. It was during

G. MENNEN WILLIAMS

this period that he changed his political affiliation to the Democratic party, although his family remained staunchly Republican. Williams graduated in 1936 in the upper 10 percent of his class. Because of his scholarly achievements he received the degree of J.D. instead of the customary LL.B. degree.

In June 1936 Williams went to Washington, D.C. as an attorney for the Social Security board, and he helped prepare briefs for the Supreme Court case that resulted in the upholding of the constitutionality of the Social Security act. The following year he was recalled to Michigan to serve as assistant attorney general in the administration of the liberal Governor Frank Murphy, whom he had met earlier and who became a major influence on his career. Williams prepared a milk marketing bill, did special work on the Governor's housing study commission, and served as liaison officer to the antitrust section of the United States Department of Justice.

Following the defeat of Governor Murphy in his bid for re-election in 1938, Williams resigned from government service to travel in the Middle East and Europe. While he was still on his tour, Murphy was named United States Attorney General and recalled Williams to serve as his administrative assistant and personal aide, a position that entailed considerable challenge and responsibility. When Murphy was appointed to the Supreme Court in 1940 Williams transferred to the criminal division of the Justice Department, where he conducted investigations involving fraud and gained some trial experience. He resigned in 1941 to become executive assistant to Brunson McChesney, assistant to the general counsel in the Office of Price Administration.

In 1942 Williams enlisted in the United States Naval Reserve and was commissioned a lieutenant (j.g.). He was an air combat intelligence officer for two and a half years in the Pacific, serving on the aircraft carriers *Essex, Bunker Hill, Hornet,* and *Yorktown* and taking part in ten campaigns.

(Continued next page)

WILLIAMS, G. MENNEN—Continued

In addition to receiving the Legion of Merit with Combat "V" he was named in three Presidential unit citations. In February 1946 he was discharged with the rank of lieutenant commander and in April of that year he returned to the OPA as deputy director of the Michigan office in Detroit, where he worked with local price control boards throughout the state.

When the OPA was dissolved Williams headed a special office set up to find new jobs for its employees. In 1947 he joined with Hicks and Martha Griffiths as a partner in the Detroit law firm of Griffiths, Williams, and Griffiths, and in the same year he was appointed by the Republican Governor Kim Sigler as a Democratic member of the state liquor control commission. Although the position was not a particularly significant one, it enabled Williams to advance himself in Michigan state politics.

In the spring of 1948 a newly organized group of young liberals formed the Michigan Democratic Club and supported G. Mennen Williams for the Governorship. Although at first he was not considered to be an important candidate, his chances were greatly increased with the backing of the AFL and the CIO. The labor leaders were seeking a man independent of ties to James R. Hoffa, who had thrown the support of the International Teamsters' Union to his own hand-picked candidate. Because of labor's support, Williams narrowly won the Democratic nomination with a plurality of about 8,000 out of 285,113 votes.

In the general election of November 1948 Williams ran against Governor Kim Sigler on a liberal nine-point platform that included demands for improved housing, education, civil rights, farm programs, veterans' benefits, and roads. The program also called for an increase in state unemployment compensation and for repeal of the state's controversial Bonne-Trippe labor relations act. Although the Republicans carried Michigan in the Presidential election and in the voting for the state legislature, Williams was elected Governor over Sigler by a plurality of some 163,000 votes. Michigan law calls for gubernatorial elections to be held every two years. In 1950 Williams ran against former Governor Harry F. Kelly and won by a majority of 8,618 votes after a recount. In 1952 he again won after a recount. He was re-elected in 1954, 1956, and 1958. His record of six terms has never been equaled by any other American Governor.

As Governor of Michigan, Williams enforced a strong program of civil rights. He led the state to enact a fair employment practices law as well as "Rule Nine," which prohibits discrimination against minority groups in the buying and selling of real estate. He appointed the first Negro in the United States to hold a cabinet post since Reconstruction days, and he named several Negroes to judgeships in the Michigan courts. To enlist public support for his programs, he made effective use of study commissions consisting of prominent men from both parties. Such commissions were responsible for planning the Mackinac Bridge project, recommending legislation to aid the physically handicapped, proposing general reforms in election methods, improving the youth correction system, and approving many other important measures.

Williams' greatest test as Governor was his tax battle with the Republican-controlled legislature in 1959. He had consistently advocated taxes on personal income and corporation profits to ensure adequate revenue, but the legislature refused to enact his proposals and the battle was fought to a stalemate. A temporary tax measure was finally passed to provide necessary funds pending the adoption of a new state constitution in the spring of 1963. The difficult tax battle was apparently one of the factors that influenced Williams in his decision not to run for re-election in 1960.

During his years as Governor of Michigan Williams took an active part in national Democratic politics. He served as vice-chairman of the Democratic National Committee, as chairman of its nationalities division, and as a member of its advisory council. When John F. Kennedy was elected to the Presidency in 1960 one of his first appointments was that of Williams to the post of Assistant Secretary of State for African affairs to head one of several regional bureaus within the Department of State. In this post, which had been handled by the Assistant Secretary for the Middle East until one year previously, Williams heads the Bureau of African Affairs and is responsible for the general conduct of foreign relations with African nations. He supervises the political, economic, security, public affairs, social, consular, and administrative policies for Africa. His department is also concerned with maintaining and supervising relations with African missions in the United States and with the operation of American foreign service establishments on the African continent. Williams' appointment evoked misgivings on the part of some observers, who questioned his qualifications for the post.

Since taking office on February 1, 1961 Williams has made several trips to Africa, visiting virtually every part of the continent to study conditions at first hand and to explain United States policy to the Africans. On his first fact-finding trip, in February 1961, he was strongly criticized by white settlers in Kenya for having said in effect that Africa belongs to the Africans. The criticism subsided somewhat when Williams later explained that he had intended the phrase to include all those who regard Africa as their permanent home, regardless of the color of their skins. While he rejects the concept of colonialism, Williams feels that the white man does have a place in Africa provided he does not expect special privileges but seeks only what he is entitled to on the basis of his contributions. He has stressed the need for greater investment in Africa but has warned: "American capital must help with nation-building along with profit-taking or it will not be welcome" (New York Times, September 26, 1962).

In an interview in the U.S. News and World Report (June 4, 1962) Williams said: "Our policy toward Africa is motivated by two things. One is that Americans really do have a humanitarian interest to help people. But we also have a self-interest, because, in the long run, our security is dependent upon a stable world. We want to help those people to build up their economic and political stability to the point where they're useful, contributing members in the world." Noting that Americans tend to be too preoccupied with the threat of Communism, Williams believes that aid should not be given solely for the purpose of stopping African countries from dealing with the Communists. "No African leader is going to become a Communist," he declared. "The Africans are so imbued with their own sense of independence that they are going to be independent of Russia, independent of the United States."

Williams belongs to the Detroit, Michigan, and American bar associations. He is a Grand Officer of the Order of Orange-Nassau (Netherlands) and a Grand Commander of the Royal Order of Phoenix (Greece) and has been decorated with the Humane Band of African Redemption (Liberia) and the Polonia Restituta (Polish government-in-exile). He has been awarded honorary degrees by Lawrence Institute of Technology, Wilberforce University, Ferris Institute, Michigan State University, University of Michigan, Aquinas College, St. Augustine's College, and the University of Liberia.

On June 26, 1937 G. Mennen Williams married Nancy Lace Quirk, a member of a prominent family of Ypsilanti, Michigan. They have three children: G. Mennen, Jr., Nancy Quirk, and Wendy Stock. Williams is six feet three inches tall, weighs 235 pounds, and has crew-cut graying hair. His trademark is a green polka-dot bow tie, which he wears even in the conservative atmosphere of the State Department. His hobbies include tennis, golf, riding, square dancing, and the study of American history. He enjoys leading a quiet home life with his family.

Although he was born to wealth, Williams is little concerned with social status. His administration as Governor of Michigan was noted for its atmosphere of honest folksiness and lack of pomp and formality. Of his appointment to the State Department position, a career diplomat has remarked that he welcomed the idea of a "gregarious, rough-and-tumble politician, without frozen ideas and uninhibited by protocol and bureaucratic timidity, coming in to handle a rough-and-tumble area like Africa" (Democratic Digest, January-February 1961).

References

Fortune 49:87 Ja '54 por
Newsday p46 D 2 '60 por
N Y Herald Tribune p4 D 2 '60
N Y Times p26 Ap 30 '59 por
Sat Eve Post 229:32+ O 27 '56 por
McNaughton, Frank. Mennen Williams of Michigan (1960)
New Frontiersmen (1961)
Who's Who in America, 1962-63

WILLISTON, SAMUEL Sept. 24, 1861-Feb. 18, 1963 Dean of the American legal profession, whose drafts on laws of contracts and sales form the basis of commercial laws in many states; professor of law at Harvard University Law School, 1895-1938. See Current Biography (December) 1954.

Obituary

N Y Times p36 Ap 1 '63

WILSON, COLIN (HENRY) June 26, 1931-
Writer
Address: h. Tetherdown, Trewallock Lane, Gorran Haven, Cornwall, England

Colin Wilson, the self-educated son of a British factory worker, achieved dazzling literary success at the age of twenty-four with the publication of his first book, The Outsider (1956). A few months later the mass media and the literary establishment that had created his reputation as a prophet of his generation destroyed it in an about-face without parallel in publishing history. Wilson is now climbing patiently back to a stable position as one of England's most versatile and provocative young writers. Most of Wilson's books, including his first novel, Ritual in the Dark (1960), have been published by Victor Gollancz Ltd. in England and the Houghton Mifflin Company in America.

Colin Henry Wilson was born in England on June 26, 1931, the first child of Arthur and Anetta (Jones) Wilson. He is a native of Leicester, the county seat of Leicestershire and a center of boot and shoe manufacturing. His father is employed in that industry as a factory worker. Anetta Wilson, an omnivorous reader, is apparently the only source of her eldest son's intellectualism, which, however, is not shared by her other children, Barry, Rodney, and Susan.

Whatever the reason, Colin Wilson "could no more help writing than a dog with fleas can help scratching," as he said in his introduction to Sidney Campion's The World of Colin Wilson (Muller, 1962). His early ambitions were scientific rather than literary, however. At the age of eleven he discovered science fiction and was soon ransacking his public library for books on psychiatry, philosophy, and all the sciences.

When he was thirteen he wrote a paper defending Albert Einstein against the English mathematician and astronomer Edward A. Milne, and his first full-length book, begun the following year, was an attempt to summarize the world's entire scientific knowledge. "Until I was fourteen I intended to be a scientist—had a great admiration for Einstein," Wilson said recently. "My ambition was to develop the atomic bomb, and when this was done in 1945, I lost interest in science. However, I had also been writing since I was nine . . . and admiration for [George Bernard] Shaw decided me to be a writer." Although he was known to his contemporaries as "the Professor," and in spite of his extraordinary breadth of reading, Colin Wilson left Leicester's Gateway Secondary Technical School in July 1947 with an unremarkable scholastic record. Thus, at sixteen (as is still common in England) his formal education ended and he went to work.

Colin Wilson's first employer was a Leicester wool company, Cranbourne Products Ltd., where he was required to weigh and distribute hanks of wool. This hard and tedious work drove him to seek an antidote to boredom and he threw himself more than ever into writing, beginning among other things a long play

Oswald Jones

COLIN WILSON

based on Shaw's *Man and Superman*, which he had heard performed on the radio several months earlier. As his creative instinct quickened, his interest in science diminished even further.

It was, ironically, at this time that he was offered a position as laboratory assistant at the Gateway School, which with some misgivings he accepted. Instead of studying for a science degree, however, he spent his ample leisure and intense nervous energy writing plays and a long story called "The Mirror." In July 1948, after a year during which his lack of interest in science had become obvious, the headmaster "regretfully sacked him."

There followed two similar years of writing, reading, and uninteresting employment: one (1948-49) as a civil servant in a tax collection office at Leicester and nearby Rugby, and the second (1949-50) as an aircraftman, second grade, in the Royal Air Force. Discharged from his duties as an RAF clerk in the spring of 1950, Wilson left the Royal Air Force "determined never again to surrender to self-contempt and boredom in an office" (*The World of Colin Wilson*). Between 1950 and 1956, when *The Outsider* was published, he worked at a variety of "meal-ticket" jobs—as a carnival ticket salesman, as a ditchdigger, as a builder's laborer, on farms, in laundries and coffee shops, and for eighteen months in a plastic factory—but his drive to literary success never faltered.

During these years Wilson's intellectual interests broadened and deepened. He spent the winter of 1950-51 in Paris and Strasbourg and settled in London in 1951. Reading voraciously in public libraries, he discussed what he learned and thought with other young writers and transformed it into a stream of unperformed plays, unpublished stories, essays, journals, and letters. In 1953 he flirted briefly with politics: he joined the London Anarchist

Group and the Syndicalist Workers Federation of North London. Although he enjoyed the opportunity to speak in public and to write and produce a political review, he soon tired of the Anarchist party line.

In 1954 Wilson began writing a novel that was published in 1960 as *Ritual in the Dark*. Throughout the summer he spent his days writing at the British Museum and his nights in a sleeping bag on Hampstead Heath or any other convenient open space to eke out his small savings. Early in 1955 he completed the first part of *Ritual in the Dark* and began work on another book, which was published in 1956 as *The Outsider*.

Wilson's "Outsider" is the man, often an artist, who "sees too deep and too much." He cannot escape the consciousness that life is futile, doomed, and chaotic. The entire structure of society is, in his view, designed to insulate man from this unbearable truth. The Outsider, unable to accept the comfortable illusions that make life tolerable, is thus alienated from the rest of humanity. As Wilson describes the Outsider's predicament by giving examples from the lives and works of Albert Camus, T. E. Lawrence, Ernest Hemingway, Franz Kafka, T. S. Eliot, Shaw, Nietzsche, and others, it becomes apparent that he advocates a kind of existentialist acceptance by the Outsider of his vision of life, however terrible. It also appears that Wilson's existentialism comes closer to the religious mysticism of Kierkegaard than to the intellectualism of Jean-Paul Sartre.

The initial critical response in Britain to *The Outsider* was favorable. Philip Toynbee, for instance, writing in the *Observer* (May 27, 1956), called it "an exhaustive and luminously intelligent study of a representative theme of our time . . . a real contribution to an understanding of our present predicament." In the United States the book came in for some strong criticism, however. Newton Arvin, writing in the New York *Times* (September 9, 1956), for example, said that the book is "a well-intentioned effort on the part of a very youthful but quite untrained and uncritical intelligence to deal with some difficult and painful contemporary problems, and quite failing to hit the mark," and H. J. Muller, writing in the New York *Herald Tribune Book Review* (September 2, 1956), called it "full of fashionable literary allusion" and "half-baked." In any case, *The Outsider* became an immediate best seller and was translated into twelve languages. Wilson, at twenty-four, was suddenly a celebrity: press and television interviews sought him out; *Life* magazine photographed him; and the sculptor Laurence Bradshaw made a bust of him.

What happened then has been discussed as a unique literary phenomenon by a number of critics, and at some length by Kenneth Allsop in *The Angry Decade* (Owen, 1958). The newspapers had exploited Wilson's "rags to riches" story, his extreme youth, his unconcealed faith in his own genius, his Shavian talent for outrageous self-advertisement. Now they tired of the game and turned on him, subjecting his private life to merciless publicity. This reached a climax in February 1957, when his future father-in-law, mistaking Wilson's blood-curdling notes for *Ritual in the Dark* for a private diary, threatened to horsewhip him.

Later in 1957, with the publication of *Religion and the Rebel,* it became apparent that the literary establishment had experienced a similar change of heart. Wilson's second book extended the argument of the first, discussed some additional Outsiders, and included an autobiographical introduction. The reviewers dismissed it as egocentric, inaccurate, unoriginal, or merely embarrassing and accused its author of megalomania, neo-Fascism, and "pugnacious ignorance." Philip Toynbee condemned it and went on to temper his earlier praise for *The Outsider.* In fact, as Kenneth Allsop commented, *Religion and the Rebel* and *The Outsider* "are the halves of one book. . . . To pretend that virtues belong to one half and vices to the other is dishonest."

Colin Wilson received these attacks stoically. Unshaken in his determination "to finish as the greatest writer European civilization has produced," he worked harder than ever. His next book was *The Stature of Man* (1959), published in England and Canada the same year as *The Age of Defeat.* It mourned "the vanishing hero" in modern literature, arguing that humanity needs its heroes if all individuality is not to be crushed by bureaucratic institutions. Bad reviews outweighed the good, and Wilson was accused of sloppy thinking and a careless use of his sources.

The first real break in the chorus of disdain came with the publication of *Riutal in the Dark.* The novel is about a writer, Gerard Sorme, who befriends a mass murderer and is briefly won over by the man's argument that any action, however horrible, is justified if it offers an escape from the limits of personality. Sorme eventually rejects the fallacy and grows a little in self-knowledge. Reviews of this and of Wilson's subsequent books were more evenly balanced. Although some critics were savage, others thought it the work of a born storyteller. And many who condemned it for poor technique and an excess of philosophical talk were won over by the author's sincerity, vitality, and "inquisitive ardour."

Another novel followed. *Adrift in Soho* (1961) was a picaresque story about an inexperienced youth learning from an expert how to live by his wits in London's Greenwich Village and subsequently rejecting this irresponsibility. The London *Times Literary Supplement* (September 8, 1961) called it "a small book" but "surely a signpost to a distinguished career as a novelist."

Wilson's interest in crimes of violence as an expression of the individual's alienation from society was reflected in *The Encyclopedia of Murder* (Barker, 1961; Putnam, 1962). Written jointly with Patricia Pitman, it provided brief accounts of some 300 murders, of all places and times, and was generally well received. A somewhat harsher press greeted *The Strength to Dream* (1962), in which Wilson used his familiar technique of summarizing and discussing a large number of books, this time for the purpose of illuminating the nature and workings of the imagination. Early in

1963 Dial Press published Wilson's novel *The Sex Diary of Gerard Sorme,* and later that year the Houghton Mifflin Company published his novel *The Violent World of Hugh Greene.*

Among his recreations Wilson lists "writing plays, which are seldom produced." Two, however, had noncommercial performances in 1960: *The Metal Flower Blossom,* a "highbrow farce" about Bohemian London; and *Viennese Interlude,* a curtain-raiser originally written as a prologue to a play about Strindberg. Works in progress include "Towards a New Existentialism" and "The Origins of the Sexual Impulse"; a novel, "The World of Violence"; and an autobiography, "Voyage to a Beginning." Wilson has been an editor of and a contributor to *Encounter, London Magazine, Time and Tide,* and the *Chicago Review.* He also contributed to a symposium by so-called "angry young men," edited by Tom Maschler and published under the title *Declaration* (MacGibbon, 1957; Dutton, 1958). "Although I would not consider myself an 'engaged' writer," Wilson has written, "I am passionately opposed to capital punishment. Am also for total disarmament, but not for Britain alone abandoning the Bomb."

In 1960 Colin Wilson married Pamela Joy Stewart, a librarian. They and their daughter, Sally Elizabeth, live in Cornwall. Wilson also has a son, Roderick Gerard, by his marriage in 1951 to Dorothy Betty Troop. The writer is a Socialist and, although he has no church affiliation, is "deeply sympathetic to Roman Catholicism." He is six feet tall, weighs 156 pounds, and says he has "blue-ish" eyes and "muddy brown" hair. Wilson's main hobby is music, and he has a collection of over 3,000 long-playing records. His clubs are the Dionysus, the Savage, and the Wig and Pen. He is a member of the Society of Authors. For two months in 1961 he was enabled by a Ford Foundation grant to visit the United States and go on a lecture tour arranged by the Institute of Contemporary Arts, Washington, D.C.

"[I] am not and never have been an 'Angry Young Man,'" Wilson said recently. "I consider my life work that of a philosopher, and my purpose, to create a new and *optimistic* existentialism, a deliberate break-away from Sartre and Heidegger, in the tradition of British empiricism and Husserl's phenomenology." Whether or not he will succeed remains to be seen, but he is equipped for the attempt with an intellect that Kenneth Allsop calls "formidable in his own chosen routes," with an absolute faith in his own genius and with prodigious energy.

References

Life 41:73+ O 1 '56 pors
N Y Times Bk R p8 Jl 1 '56; p8 S 20 '59; p8 O 22 '61
Sat R 39:37 S 8 '56 pors

Allsop, Kenneth. The Angry Decade; A Survey of the Cultural Revolt of the Nineteen-Fifties (1958)
Author's and Writer's Who's Who (1960)
Campion, Sidney R. The World of Colin Wilson (1962)
Who's Who, 1963

WILSON, (JAMES) HAROLD Mar. 11, 1916-
British political leader
Address: b. House of Commons, London, S.W.1,
England; h. 12 Southway, Hampstead Garden
Suburb, London, N.W.11, England

NOTE: This biography supersedes
the article that appeared in
Current Biography in 1948.

On February 14, 1963, a month after the death
of Hugh Gaitskell, the British Labour party
elected a new leader. He was the Right Honourable Harold Wilson, O.B.E., Member of Parliament for Huyton, Lancashire, and his party's
spokesman on foreign affairs. There is wide
agreement that, as Maurice Green wrote in the
London *Daily Telegraph* (February 15, 1963),
"in sheer intellectual power and in capacity for
debate and administration, he is the best leader
that the Labour Party could have chosen."

An Oxford don at twenty-one, a member of
the British cabinet at thirty-one, and Leader of
the Opposition at forty-six, Harold Wilson has
not necessarily reached the apex of his career.
The Conservative government must call a general
election not later than October 1964. If, as many
pollsters predict, Labour wins that election,
Harold Wilson will be Prime Minister of England—the youngest since William Pitt.

James Harold Wilson was born on March 11,
1916 in Huddersfield, Yorkshire, England, to
James Herbert Wilson, an industrial chemist,
and Ethel Wilson. He attended the Milnsbridge
Council School and then the Royds Hall Secondary School in Huddersfield until he was fourteen, when his family moved to Cheshire. Wilson completed his secondary education at the
Wirral Grammar School in Bebington, where he
played good cricket, captained the Rugby football team, and won a scholarship that took him
to Oxford University.

As an undergraduate at Jesus College, Wilson
read "Modern Greats"—philosophy, politics, and
economics—and won two university essay prizes,
the Gladstone Memorial Prize and the Webb
Medley Economics Scholarship. He did some
long-distance running and served on the committee of the university's Liberal Club (preferring
this to the Labour Club because, he has said, the
latter was then dominated by Communists).

In 1937, when he graduated with first class
honors, Wilson stayed on at Oxford to become,
at twenty-one, lecturer in economics at New
College and one of the university's youngest dons.
Lord Beveridge, architect of England's "welfare
state," was then master of Oxford's University
College. Wilson became his research assistant
while still at New College and in 1938 joined
him as a Fellow of University College. Beveridge
subsequently described him as the ablest research
student he had ever had.

With the outbreak of World War II in 1939
Wilson volunteered for the army but, thanks to
his growing reputation as an economist, was
drafted instead into the civil service. He served
as an economic assistant in the War Cabinet
Secretariat in 1940-41 and then in various capacities at the Ministry of Fuel and Power. In 1943
he became the ministry's director of economics
and statistics.

A year later Wilson was adopted as prospective Labour candidate for Ormskirk in Lancashire and resigned from the civil service. Just
before the 1945 election, out of his wide knowledge of every branch of the mining industry, he
published *New Deal for Coal* (Contact Publications, 1945), prefiguring Labour's policy for nationalization of that industry. The same year he
was appointed praelector in economics at University College, Oxford, but he gave up the appointment when, in July 1945, he found that he
had won election to Parliament in Labour's landslide victory.

Wilson was at once given a junior ministerial
position as Parliamentary secretary to the Ministry of Works; he was one of the three new
Labour M.P.s to go straight to the "front bench."
In March 1947 he moved to the Board of Trade
as secretary for overseas trade and in September
of the same year succeeded Sir Stafford Cripps
as President of the Board of Trade (a position
roughly equivalent to Secretary of Commerce).
He became at the same time a member of the
Privy Council. A senior minister at thirty-one,
Wilson was the youngest British cabinet member
of this century.

According to Maurice Green, writing in the
London *Daily Telegraph* (February 15, 1963),
Wilson was "one of the best departmental Ministers that Labour ever produced." His most
notable achievement during his four years at the
Board of Trade was to scrap many of the controls that restricted British industry and that were
favored by Stafford Cripps and most doctrinaire
Socialists. Wilson worked hard to increase exports and demonstrated toughness and tenacity
during the prolonged Moscow trade talks of 1947,
when he bargained night after night—often until
six in the morning—with Soviet Deputy Premier
Anastas I. Mikoyan. He carried on talks with
trade delegations from all over the world and
made a highly successful coast-to-coast tour of
Canada. In 1946, 1947, and 1949 he led the
British delegations to the Food and Agriculture
Organization conferences in Washington, D.C.
and traveled throughout the United States.

In the general elections of February 1950 Wilson stood as M.P. for the new Lancashire division of Huyton. He was successful and has represented that constituency ever since. The Labour
party retained power, though with a greatly reduced majority, and Wilson resumed his post at
the Board of Trade. In April 1951 Aneurin
Bevan, leader of the party's rebellious left wing,
resigned as Minister of Labour in protest over
the introduction of nominal charges in the
formerly free National Health Scheme, and over
what he regarded as the excessive scale of the
cabinet's rearmament program. Wilson resigned
with him. Soon after, the Labour government
was swept from office.

Harold Wilson thus became associated with
the left wing of his party, and to some extent he
still is. But it soon became apparent that he
could not be labeled an unequivocal Bevanite.
In April 1954 Bevan resigned from the Parliamentary Committee of the Labour party—the
so-called "shadow cabinet." This time Wilson
did not emulate him. He was next in line for
membership of the Parliamentary Committee,
and he agreed in the name of party unity to take
Bevan's place there.

"Wilson emerged from the Bevanite conflict," said a *New Statesman* profile writer (April 11, 1959), "as a militant who was willing to risk his career for principles, but also as a pragmatist who, once the fire had gone out of Bevanism, could . . . make himself essential to the official leadership." Thereafter, his "sense of the political game has enabled him to consolidate a position of power." In 1956 Wilson became the principal Opposition spokesman on economic affairs —the "shadow" Chancellor of the Exchequer.

At the party's 1960 conference, however, Wilson was once more in rebellion, failing to support Hugh Gaitskell on two crucial issues. One was the move to amend Clause 4 of the party's constitution, which pledges Labour to widespread nationalization. Wilson agreed that Clause 4 needed modernization, but felt that other policy matters should be decided first. He also allied himself with advocates of unilateral disarmament, not because he was a unilateralist, but because he was opposed to what was then the alternative, Labour support for an independent nuclear deterrent. The party subsequently adopted the views he expressed then, but at the time he was much criticized for what many regarded as his disloyalty. In the fall of 1960, when he ran against Gaitskell for leadership of the party, he was soundly defeated, 166 votes to 81.

Wilson nevertheless retained his place in the "shadow cabinet" and in November 1961 became the Opposition's spokesman on foreign affairs. He had by then developed a flair for hitting upon issues calculated to embarrass his Conservative opponents. This, combined with an extraordinary and infallible memory and a savage wit, made him a formidable adversary when he challenged the government on such matters as Britain's attempts to enter the European Common Market and to maintain her own nuclear arsenal.

In November 1962 Wilson ran against George Brown for deputy leadership of the party and was defeated by 133 votes to 103. Two months later Hugh Gaitskell died, and Wilson was again in competition with Brown, this time for the leadership. The first ballot was inconclusive, but eliminated a third candidate, James Callaghan. At the second ballot, on February 14, 1963, Wilson beat Brown by 144 votes to 103 and became Leader of the Opposition.

At a press conference the next day, Harold Wilson pledged himself to maintain the party unity achieved by Hugh Gaitskell and to lead his party to victory in the next elections. Many political commentators believe that both pledges can be fulfilled. A Gallup Poll made in mid-February 1963 gave Labour a 15.5 percent edge over the Conservative government in public esteem. Under these circumstances rebellion within the Labour party is considered unlikely. Wilson has moreover demonstrated his willingness to forget past enmities by declaring that he would represent "no special group, no special policy, but the whole party."

In a televised statement on February 27, 1963 the new Leader of the Opposition said that the Labour party, if it came to power, would end restrictive practices in industry, eradicate inequalities in taxation and education, and put more money into scientific research. The steel industry would be renationalized. On foreign

British Inf. Services

HAROLD WILSON

affairs, Wilson has committed his party to firm support of the North Atlantic Treaty Organization. He favors NATO control of nuclear arms, is opposed to such bilateral or small-scale agreements as that under which Britain is to have Polaris-armed submarines, and believes it is "nonsense" for Britain to try to maintain an independent nuclear deterrent. On this and other issues he is, according to *Newsweek* (February 25, 1963), "much more in tune with President Kennedy's Administration than is the present Tory government."

For his wartime work in the civil service Harold Wilson was made an O.B.E. in 1945. He has been a member of his party's national executive committee since 1952 and of its Parliamentary committee since 1954. He was chairman of the party in 1961-62 and of the Fabian Society in 1954-55. Wilson is also chairman of the Public Accounts Committee of the House of Commons. One of the most traveled Members of Parliament, he has been a frequent visitor to the United States, Canada, and Russia, as well as to places nearer home. In 1958 he visited China for talks with Chou En-lai. According to the *New Statesman* (February 15, 1963), Wilson "is one of the handful of politicians capable of expressing himself on paper with the skill, economy and regard for time of the professional journalist." Wilson's *The War on World Poverty*, published in 1953 by Gollancz in England and by Bond Street Publications in the United States, proposed ways in which the plight of the underdeveloped nations could be alleviated. He has also written pamphlets for the Labour party and for the National Peace Council and contributed widely to periodicals.

In 1940 Harold Wilson married Gladys Mary Baldwin, an amateur poet and daughter of a Congregational minister. With their two sons, Giles and Robin, they live in a modest house in a London suburb. Wilson's sole relaxation is an occasional round of golf at the Hampstead Golf Club. Maurice Green in the *Daily Telegraph*

WILSON, HAROLD—*Continued*

(February 15, 1963) describes him as being "of medium height and medium build, with a rather average sort of face from which an average pipe usually protrudes. . . . Never at a loss for a phrase or an idea, he shines and impresses in any company. . . . His personality and humor . . . have a certain youthful, bubbly quality which the years have so far failed to suppress. Cool-headed and unemotional, perhaps, but not austere." The cultured accent acquired at Oxford has not been allowed entirely to eradicate the homelier delivery of Yorkshire, and Wilson's classlessness is a distinct political asset in class-conscious England.

The consensus is that Harold Wilson is formidably equipped as Leader of the Opposition, but harder to measure as a potential Prime Minister. He has few intimates and remains something of an enigma even to his associates in the Labour party. His critics see him as a self-seeking opportunist, lacking in political convictions, "searching for the point of balance in his party and perching on it." They accuse him of disloyalty to both Bevan and Gaitskell. His supporters deny this, contending that the decisions he made in 1954 and 1960 were honestly and painstakingly arrived at and pointing out that party policy now coincides with Wilson's then controversial views. They see him, says an *Observer* reporter (February 17, 1963), "as a sort of homespun Kennedy, complete with brains trust."

Maurice Green, writing in the *Daily Telegraph* (February 15, 1963), remarked: "Often he gives the impression of a man having to seek compromises between strong socialist and egalitarian instincts, and a most businesslike brain. . . . From him one would expect a policy distinctly Socialist in intention, but conditioned in execution by respect for good economics and good administration."

References

London Daily Express p7 F 15 '63 pors
London Daily Telegraph p12 F 15 '63
N Y Times (Western Edition) p2 F 15 '63 por
Newsday p38 Ap 2 '63
Newsweek 61:42+ Ap 15 '63 por
Time 82:34+ O 11 '63 pors
Toronto Globe and Mail p4 F 18 '63 por
Washington (D.C.) Post p4 F 24 '63 por
Chambers's Biographical Dictionary (1961)
International Year Book and Statesmen's Who's Who, 1963
Who's Who, 1963

WIRTZ, W(ILLIAM) WILLARD Mar. 14, 1912- United States Secretary of Labor; university professor

Address: b. Department of Labor, Washington 25, D.C.; h. 5009 39th St., N.W., Washington, D.C.

NOTE: This biography supersedes the article that appeared in *Current Biography* in 1946.

Technological changes, unemployment, and foreign competition cause most of the problems that threaten increased prosperity in the United States and beset its Secretary of Labor, W. Willard Wirtz. For ten years a professor of labor law at Northwestern University, he also has an impressive background in government administration during World War II and in mediating labor disputes. President John F. Kennedy appointed him to the cabinet post in August 1962 to succeed Arthur J. Goldberg, who became an Associate Justice of the Supreme Court.

William Willard Wirtz, the oldest of five children of William Wilbur and Alpha Belle (White) Wirtz, was born on March 14, 1912 in DeKalb, Illinois, where his father was a teacher at the Northern Illinois State Normal School. Willard Wirtz himself attended Northern Illinois State Teachers College (as it was renamed in 1921) for two years after his graduation from the local high school in 1928. He enrolled in 1930 in the University of California at Berkeley and the following year transferred to Beloit College in Wisconsin. In college, as in high school, he played on the football team and was a member of the debating society and the dramatics society. He also served as president of the student body and was elected to Phi Beta Kappa. In 1933 he received his B.A. degree with honors in sociology.

Wirtz's first job was as a high school teacher of English and American history in Kewanee, Illinois. Before the end of his first year, in 1934, he made up his mind to study law. He entered Harvard Law School, became editor of the *Law Review,* and graduated with an LL.B. degree in 1937. That year he began his career as a university teacher with an instructorship in law at the University of Iowa. He remained there until 1939 when he became an assistant professor in the School of Law of Northwestern University.

In 1942 Wirtz accepted his first assignment in Washington. He served as assistant general counsel to the Board of Economic Warfare, which distributed supplies in the war effort for the United States and its allies. Later in the year he was transferred to the National War Labor Board to serve on its appeals committee as chairman. In this position from 1943 to 1945 and then as counsel and as public member of the War Labor Board in 1945, he worked for the settlement of crippling labor disputes and the stabilization of wages until the termination of the wartime agency in October 1945.

When the National Wage Stabilization Board was set up in the Department of Labor in 1946 to replace the War Labor Board, Wirtz became its chairman and a public member. The new board was responsible for approving wage reductions and increases and for determining whether increases in wages might be used by employers as a basis for price increases. Wirtz headed a staff of from 700 to 900 employees charged with settling several thousand cases involving wage stabilization. In directing the changeover of wage scales from a wartime to a peacetime basis, Wirtz helped to work out a formula for an equitable wage-price policy. Matching an estimated 33 percent increase in the cost of living from January 1941 to September 1945, the Wage Stabilization Board established a general pattern of wage increases. The Price Control Board reviewed these increases before granting requests for price increases in industry.

By November 1946 government wage and price controls had been lifted. The few remaining functions of the Wage Stabilization Board were transferred to other government agencies, and Wirtz supervised the board's liquidation in early 1947. At this time he returned to teaching law, and as a full professor of law at Northwestern University, he specialized in labor law from 1946 until 1954.

After Adlai E. Stevenson became Governor of Illinois, he scoured the state for able men to serve in his administration. In 1950 he met W. Willard Wirtz, whom he appointed to the part-time post of Liquor Control Commissioner. At the same time, from 1950 to 1956, Wirtz served on the Winnetka (Illinois) Library Board. Of the simultaneous positions, he says with typical humor, "I felt that every time I read a book, I had to take a drink, and vice versa." Stevenson and Wirtz became good friends and in 1955 formed a law partnership in Chicago. When Stevenson ran for President in 1956 on the Democratic ticket, Wirtz was a top strategist in his campaign. After Stevenson's defeat, they helped to establish the law firm of Stevenson, Rifkind & Wirtz, which they maintained until 1960. Wirtz dealt with hundreds of labor-management disputes and served on many Taft-Hartley Law boards of inquiry.

In January 1961 Arthur J. Goldberg was appointed Secretary of Labor by President Kennedy. Wirtz, with two decades of experience as an arbitrator in the adjustment of labor disputes and as a specialist in labor law, was an ideal choice for his assistant. Goldberg persuaded Wirtz to give up his lucrative Chicago law practice to join the New Frontier as Under Secretary of Labor. His appointment was confirmed by Congress on January 20.

At the Labor Department, Wirtz worked quietly, often behind the scenes, in settling labor disputes and traveled widely as Goldberg's representative in labor mediation. He was most active in crises in the transportation industry, handling the bitter dispute between the airlines and Flight Engineers Union skillfully and mediating in the West Coast shipping strike. At the same time he earned the respect of labor and industry for his work on the President's Advisory Committee on Labor-Management Policy.

A successful labor mediator and arbitrator like Wirtz, a *Christian Science Monitor* editorial (September 1, 1962) pointed out, must possess "complete integrity, which earns the trust, confidence and respect of both sides. With this must go an industriousness that searches to the bottom of the problems involved, a patience with personal emotional committments, and a determination to find areas of agreement." After a short time in office Wirtz acquired the reputation around Washington as "Goldberg's solid backstop who, besides being an excellent mediator, had a fine hand for administration and a fertile mind," Milton Viorst reported in the *New York Post* (August 31, 1962).

Wide World

W. WILLARD WIRTZ

In August 1962, while Wirtz was hard at work in round-the-clock meetings trying to end the dispute between the telegraphers union and the Chicago & North Western Railway he received the news that Secretary Goldberg had been elevated to the Supreme Court. At the same time he was notified that President Kennedy had chosen him to be the new Secretary of Labor. Wirtz took the oath of office on September 25, 1962. His appointment was commended within the ranks of both industry and labor. George Meany, president of the AFL-CIO, called it "a fine appointment." Wirtz, he said, "has the experience, background and understanding that are necessary in this difficult role."

As Secretary of Labor, W. Willard Wirtz administers a department originally created by Congress in 1884 and lodged in the Interior Department. In 1903 it was relocated in the Department of Commerce and Labor, and it was not until 1913 that labor leaders won their battle for "equal rights" with business by having a department of their own. The purpose of the Department of Labor is to improve working conditions and advance opportunities for profitable employment of workers. In 1947 Congress established an independent Federal Mediation and Conciliation Service reporting directly to the President to deal with labor disputes. Despite this separate organization, the Secretary of Labor has retained the role of personal mediator in disputes.

In his new position Wirtz has sought to limit his work as mediator, preferring to devote his energy and thought to developing solutions for the national problems of full employment and manpower retraining to cope with increased industrialization and technological change. He cites the "fact of change" as the common denominator of the issues facing the United States. In a Labor Day speech in 1961 he said that the adversaries of labor are

WIRTZ, W. WILLARD—*Continued*

the "forces of technology, of foreign competition, of stagnation, of complacency."

Wirtz has gone on record against shortening the work week and against compulsory arbitration, and he strongly backs the administration's trade expansion bill. Such concepts as "featherbedding" and "right-to-work," Wirtz believes, tend to corrupt debate and prejudice the real issues. He has advocated a $40,000,000 bill to strengthen and expand college-level technical training, and in his first few weeks in office he approved programs sending many workers back to school for retraining under the new Manpower Development and Training Act. He has consistently attacked public apathy toward unemployment, has opposed the theory that high rates of joblessness are normal, and has described as "utterly reprehensible" the idea current in some economic circles that a 4 percent unemployment rate is desirable to maintain economic stability. One solution for full employment that Wirtz endorses is a large and significant tax cut as soon as possible. But he has urged government economists to look at employment in terms of the human needs for education, health, transportation, recreational facilities, and a higher standard of living.

When he took office, Wirtz inherited several labor disputes. The Chicago & North Western Railway strike ended soon after his appointment. In November 1962, when the New York *Daily News* was closed down in a Newspaper Guild strike, Wirtz himself swung into action. After eight almost sleepless days of intense mediation, he personally concluded successful negotiations to avert a possible city-wide news blackout.

Later in November he also announced a complete accord between the pilots and flight engineers unions and Trans World Airlines, which had been in prolonged dispute. TWA is the first major carrier to reach agreement with the unions on all aspects of the crew-complement issue and other working conditions, and Wirtz called the settlement a milestone. Before the end of 1962 he was personally involved in efforts to settle the New York newspaper strike and the East Coast and Gulf ports dock strike —two difficult disputes that continued into the following year.

Standing six feet one inch tall and weighing 190 pounds, Wirtz has the build of a football player. He wears horn-rimmed glasses, has graying crew-cut hair, and is seldom without a pipe. On September 8, 1936 he married Mary Jane Quisenberry, of St. Louis, whom he had met at Beloit College. Their sons are Richard, a graduate student at Princeton University, and Philip, a high school student. The whole family shares Wirtz's enthusiasm for bowling, tennis, golf, and fishing.

W. Willard Wirtz is a member of the National Academy of Arbitrators and the American Bar Association. His Greek-letter societies, besides Phi Beta Kappa, are Beta Theta Pi and Delta Sigma Rho. He is known for his sense of humor, and he often calls upon his sharp wit during tense bargaining sessions. As A. H. Raskin remarked, however, in the New York *Times Magazine* (November 11, 1962), "There

is nothing frivolous in Wirtz's approach to his job." Raskin described him as a reflective man who "brings an abhorrence of cant and a clinical precision in the use of words" to labor-management affairs.

References

Nat Observer p2 S 3 '62 por
N Y Post p35 Ag 31 '62 por
N Y Times p8 Ag 31 '62 por
U S News 53:25 S 10 '62
International Who's Who, 1962-63
Who's Who in America, 1962-63

WOODSMALL, RUTH F(RANCES) Sept. 20, 1883-May 25, 1963 International women's welfare worker; general secretary, Young Women's Christian Association (1935-48). See *Current Biography* (July) 1949.

Obituary
N Y Times p29 My 27 '63

WOOLLEY, MONTY Aug. 17, 1888-May 6, 1963 Stage and screen actor; best known for his portrayal of Sheridan Whiteside in the Broadway and film versions of the Kaufman-Hart comedy *The Man Who Came to Dinner*. See *Current Biography* (July) 1940.

Obituary
N Y Times p41 My 7 '63

WRIGHT, JOHN J(OSEPH) July 18, 1909- Roman Catholic prelate

Address: b. Catholic Diocese of Pittsburgh, 111 Blvd. of Allies, Pittsburgh, Pa.; h. 5078 Warwick Terrace, Pittsburgh, Pa.

The bishop of the Roman Catholic diocese of Pittsburgh, the Most Reverend John J. Wright, is no sectarian shepherd. To the care of his own religious flock he has brought a vision that embraces national Catholic problems, Catholic-Protestant ecumenical relations, and the state of the international human community. Formerly for nine years the bishop of the diocese of Worcester, Massachusetts, Wright was installed as bishop of Pittsburgh in 1959.

Bishop Wright's first American ancestors came from England and Ireland over a century ago. The oldest of six children, John Joseph Wright was born in the Dorchester section of Boston, Massachusetts on July 18, 1909 to John J. Wright, a paper-factory clerk, and Harriet L. (Cokely) Wright. At Boston Latin School, which he attended until 1927, he distinguished himself in scholarship and debate. Nights and summers he worked at the Hyde Park branch of the Boston Public Library as stack boy for twenty-five cents an hour.

The library job, and another in the city room of the Boston *Post*, helped pay his way through Boston College, where he continued to amass academic and debating honors. He was voted by the class of 1931 as the member who did the most for the college. Taking his B.A. degree in 1931, Wright entered St. John's Seminary, Brighton,

Massachusetts. At the end of a year at the seminary he was one of the top two in his class and was sent to Rome to finish his studies. He lived at the North American College in the Italian capital while studying theology at the Pontifical Gregorian University. He was ordained a priest in the chapel of the North American College by Cardinal Marchetti-Solvaggiani on December 8, 1935.

After his ordination Wright remained in Rome for further study at the Pontifical Gregorian University. During vacations and while he was writing his thesis he did voluntary parish work in Edinburgh, Scotland; Southwark, England; and Périgueux, France. He developed a love for those countries and their heroes, particularly for France and Joan of Arc. (His bishop's crosier, closer to the prototype of the simple shepherd's crook than most, was designed in France, and his bishop's miter bears the *fleurs-de-lis*.) He received the Licentiate in Sacred Theology degree in 1936 and the Doctor of Sacred Theology degree in 1939. His doctoral thesis was later published as *National Patriotism in Papal Teachings* (Stratford, 1942).

Returning to Massachusetts, Father Wright became, at thirty, professor of philosophy at St. John's Seminary, Brighton. In 1943 he was appointed secretary to the archbishop of Boston, William Cardinal O'Connell. He retained the position under Archbishop (now Cardinal) Richard J. Cushing, who succeeded O'Connell in September 1944. Named a monsignor with the rank of papal chamberlain in December 1944, Wright rose in monsignoral rank to domestic prelate in June 1946. He was consecrated titular bishop of Aegea and auxiliary bishop of Boston on June 30, 1947.

In January 1950 Worcester became the see city of a new diocese, the boundaries of which formerly fell within the diocese of Springfield. Wright was appointed bishop of the new diocese on January 28, 1950. Archbishop Cushing of Boston presided at Wright's installation as first bishop of Worcester on the morning of March 7, 1950. The diocese of Worcester measures fifty miles north and south and forty miles east and west. Catholics within this area comprise about half the general population. The number, some 250,000 during Wright's tenure and now over 300,000, divides about equally into the faithful of Irish, French-Canadian, and Italian descent. One of the tasks to which Wright set himself as bishop of Worcester was to give these people of different national backgrounds a sense of solidarity as Roman Catholics while encouraging, particularly among the French-speaking, a conservation of tradition. He also tried to make the parishes of the diocese more integrated in the local Yankee communities.

The solution of the religious-sociological problems was facilitated rather than hindered by another problem, an ecological one. The unsettling city-to-suburb shift that Wright found on his arrival in Worcester gave him an opportunity to work on fresh ground. Old parish boundaries had to be changed and new parishes had to be erected because some city churches had lost most of their parishioners to suburban and rural areas where existing facilities were in-

BISHOP JOHN J. WRIGHT

adequate to cope with the new flood of population.

Thirty new parishes were established in the diocese of Worcester during Wright's years there. The churches in the new parishes were built with the population spread and the Yankee environment in mind. They were, on the average, small. Many were built in colonial style, with local wood or stone, and named after saints, like Richard of Chichester, native to the country from which the original settlers came. Wright sees the parish as becoming "perhaps . . . less and less the administrative unit and more and more the educative and . . . the liturgical center." St. Vincent's Hospital in Worcester was also built under Bishop Wright's direction.

When Bishop John F. Dearden of Pittsburgh was appointed archbishop of Detroit in December 1958, Wright was named as his successor in Pittsburgh. Wright was installed as eighth bishop of Pittsburgh on March 18, 1959. Among his distinguishing acts as bishop of Pittsburgh was the foundation, in 1961, of a Pittsburgh branch of the Oratory. The Oratory, a congregation of priests without special vows, was founded by Philip Neri in 1564. Each house is autonomous, so that the name Oratory is specific as well as generic. The Pittsburgh Oratory is patterned after that planned by John Henry Cardinal Newman for Oxford University. It is an intellectual apostolate to Roman Catholic students on general college and university campuses.

A minor but significant action of Wright in Pittsburgh involved the annual pledge of Roman Catholics to accept and follow the judgments of the Legion of Decency on the morality of movies. The pledge is optional, but the communal manner in which it is handled in many dioceses sometimes obscures this fact. In Pittsburgh, Wright has minimized the extraneous communal aspect. It was he who suggested the changing of the name of the Pittsburgh Morals Court to that which it now bears, the Magistrates Court. He

WRIGHT, JOHN J.—Continued

initiated the formal religious celebration of Labor Day in the Pittsburgh diocese and was one of those who helped bring into being the Pittsburgh fair-housing ordinance. When Wright became bishop there were 853,347 Roman Catholics in the diocese of Pittsburgh out of a total population of 2,250,000.

Unhappy with the factionalism within Christendom, Bishop Wright has often engaged in interdenominational dialogue on the subject. Because the barriers to unity are sociological as well as religious, he places greater hope in individuals than in groups. Unlike some other Roman Catholic ecumenicists, he sees more common ground in the practice of charity than the acceptance of natural law. He has engaged in interfaith dialogue as well.

Wright's combined interests in ecumenicism and in the Roman Catholic lay retreat movement led to his planning an unusual project in 1961. The retreat, traditionally practised by Roman Catholic priests, monks, and nuns, is an annual withdrawal into seclusion and silence for meditation abetted by the homilies of a retreat master. In recent years the practice has become more common among Roman Catholic laymen, a development looked upon with favor by Bishop Wright, who is episcopal moderator of the lay retreat movement. To spread understanding of the movement among Christian clergyman Wright conducted a retreat at Marydale Retreat House, Erlanger, Kentucky, from September 12 to September 14, 1961. The retreatants were Protestant ministers.

In many contexts Bishop Wright has revealed his wariness of blind enclosure in the walls of time and place. Active in the Catholic Association for International Peace, he has lamented the apathy of American Catholics toward peace and international problems generally. Playing upon the international connotations in both names, he commented in an interview with Donald McDonald in the Catholic Messenger (July 9, 1959) regarding meetings about the whole, worldwide human community: "We know why the Universalists are there. We don't know why the Catholics aren't." In a talk at North Catholic High School, Pittsburgh, on April 23, 1960, he said: "In order to enter the service of peace, history . . . must be made the deliverer not only from the influence of other times, but from the undue influence of our own, from the tyranny of environment and the pressure of the air we breathe. . . . He is a blind jingoist, indeed, who fails to recognize to what a great extent our American children have become the victims of a . . . histoire dirigée. . . . We must develop their sense of the broad highway of history."

Although Wright sometimes eschews the term, the Roman Catholic intellectual receives his sustained and sympathetic attention. He distinguishes intellectuals from scientists. The scarcity of Roman Catholic scientists deplored by some Roman Catholic educators leaves him cold: "I'm not sure that a lack of dominant interest in science is a lack that I personally would passionately regret," he told Donald McDonald in the Catholic Messenger interview. "I might as well admit that I would much prefer that Catholics wrote the poetry and philosophy . . . than that a Catholic had played any great part in producing the thing [the nuclear bomb]."

Bishop Wright was a member of the theological commission that prepared the agenda on dogma and morality for the Ecumenical Council of the Roman Catholic Church, which opened at the Vatican on October 10, 1962, and he attended the council along with some 2,500 other prelates. He was president general of the National Catholic Educational Association in 1960-61, national honorary chairman of Catholic Book Week in 1962, and honorary chairman of the thirty-eighth annual Catholic Library Association Conference in 1962. He received the Italian Order of Merit in 1957 and became an officer in the French Legion of Honor in 1958. He is a Fellow of the American Academy of Arts and Sciences. Several universities, including Notre Dame, Georgetown, and Fordham, have granted him honorary degrees. Since his installation as bishop of Pittsburgh he has delivered a weekly broadcast over radio station KDKA in that city.

Robert L. Reynolds wrote in Jubilee (February 1956) of Wright after observing him in Worcester in the mid-1950's: "A strenuous routine . . . is neither exhausting nor boring for Bishop Wright, an energetic and gregarious man who genuinely enjoys meeting people, who likes them, and who is liked in return. Private conversation with him reveals a quick, probing, retentive mind and a fund of humorous stories, told with a fine sense of timing and a gift of mimicry. Some of his anecdotes gently satirize the provincialism of the Boston Irish. . . . He epitomizes a new generation of New England Catholics—more urbane, open-minded and tolerant."

References

Jubilee 3:6+ F '56 pors
Pittsburgh Catholic Supplement p3+ Mr 19 '59 pors
American Catholic Who's Who, 1962 and 1963
Who's Who in America, 1962-63

YEVTUSHENKO, YEVGENY (ALEXANDROVICH) (yĕf-tōō-shĕn'kō yĕf-gān'ē) July 18, 1933- Poet
Address: b. c/o E. P. Dutton & Co., 201 Park Ave S., New York 3

The most popular of contemporary Russian poets, Yevgeny Yevtushenko, might be considered the Soviet counterpart of what in parliamentary democracies is termed the "loyal opposition." Following in the tradition of earlier Russian poets who have spoken out against injustices —men like Alexander Pushkin, Vladimir Mayakovsky, and Boris Pasternak—Yevtushenko is regarded as the leading spokesman for the bewildered generation of young Russians who grew to maturity since the death of Joseph Stalin in 1953.

Although Yevtushenko bears full allegiance to Russia and to the Communist cause, he is undaunted in his criticism of bureaucracy, chauvinism, dogmatism, and other abuses existing in Soviet society. One of his most famous poems, "Babiy Yar," is a condemnation of anti-Semitism. The fact that his criticisms, and those of other young Russian poets, are tolerated by the authorities, is seen by some Western observers as a hopeful sign, indicating a greater degree of intellectual freedom in the Soviet Union. Since the publication of a volume of his *Selected Poems* in English translation in 1962, Yevtushenko has attained considerable recognition in Great Britain and in the United States.

Of Ukrainian, Latvian, Tartar, and Russian peasant stock, Yevgeny Alexandrovich Yevtushenko was born on July 18, 1933 in Zima, a small lumber station on the trans-Siberian railway, about 150 miles west of Irkutsk. His great-grandfather, Joseph Yevtushenko, a suspected subversive, was exiled from the Ukraine during the repressions that followed the assassination of Czar Alexander II in 1881, and died on the way to Siberia, where his children subsequently settled. During his early childhood "Zhenya" Yevtushenko lived in the old quarter of Moscow with his mother, Zinaida Yevtushenko, a geologist and singer, whose surname he adopted. His maternal grandfather, a lieutenant general in the artillery, disappeared during Stalin's Red Army purges of 1938, and his paternal grandfather, Rudolph Gangnus, also vanished about that time, arrested on charges of spying. Yevtushenko's parents were divorced in the early 1940's. He has a younger sister, Yelena.

During World War II Yevtushenko was evacuated to his home town, Zima. When he was only ten years old he wrote his first novel, and at the age of twelve he wrote lyrics to Russian folk tunes, which attained some popularity. He returned to Moscow in 1944. At fifteen he was falsely accused of stealing some records and expelled from school, and he ran away to Kazakhstan to join his father. After taking part in geological expeditions in Kazakhstan and in Altai, he returned to his mother in Moscow. As a boy Yevtushenko was fond of sports, especially soccer, ping-pong, and cycling, and he knew jujitsu.

In 1949, while preparing to become a professional soccer player, Yevtushenko had his first poem published in *Sovietsky Sport*, a sports journal. He subsequently began to turn out large numbers of poems, which appeared regularly in the newspapers *Komsomolskaya Pravda* and *Literaturnaya Gazeta*, in popular journals such as *Ogonyok* and *Smena*, and in the literary monthlies *Novy Mir*, *Oktyabr*, and *Molodaya Gvardia*. Written largely in a Stalinist vein, these early poems did not provoke any great controversy. Yevtushenko's first book of poetry, *The Prospectors of the Future*, which was published in 1952 by the Soviet Writer publishers, was praised by the official party critics. As a result of its publication, he was invited to join the Gorky Literary Institute and the Writers' Union. Yevtushenko studied for several years in the department of poetry at the institute, but he did not distinguish himself as a scholar and left without graduating.

After Joseph Stalin's death in 1953 Yevtushenko temporarily abandoned political themes and wrote love poems. His second book, *Trety*

Sovphoto

YEVGENY YEVTUSHENKO

sneg (Third Snow), published in 1955, was attacked by the official critics, but also made him nationally popular almost overnight. In his lengthy poem "Zima Junction," published in *Oktyabr* in 1956, Yevtushenko describes a visit to his home town in 1953, after several years of absence. The poem reflects the confusion and search for values of a young man in post-Stalin Russia, in contrast to his relatively carefree childhood. A critic reviewing the poem in *Znayama* in 1957 called Yevtushenko a "frivolous, captious idler," and berated him for failing to portray the "heroism of labor."

In 1956 and 1957 Yevtushenko published additional volumes of poems, including some of his best work. In these poems, marked by nonconformity, he treats both personal and social themes, and conveys strong feelings of human sympathy. ("I won't forgive anyone coldness of heart," he declares in a poem published in 1956.) In another poem, published in the following year, he reveals his cosmopolitanism with the declaration, "I feel everything in the world/And everything in the world is all in me!" His poem "The Nihilist," also published in 1957, deals with a young nonconformist who sacrifices his life to save a friend. Although Yevtushenko's popularity continued to grow, he drew the hostility of orthodox Stalinist critics, who conferred on him such labels as "pessimist," "revisionist," "formalist," and "escapist." In 1957 he was expelled from Komsomol, the Communist youth organization, as a "nihilist." (He was reinstated in 1959.)

Yevtushenko's book *Luk i Lira (Longbow and Lyre)*, published in 1959, contains poems about Georgia, including translation from the Georgian language. In the same year he published *Stikhi Raznykh Let (Poems of Several Years)*,

YEVTUSHENKO, YEVGENY—Continued

an anthology containing some of his best short poems. The book was printed in 20,000 copies and was sold out almost immediately. Another book, *Yabloko (The Apple),* published in 1960, was somewhat less favorably received. His latest book, *Vzmakh Ruki (A Sweep of an Arm),* containing some of his most powerful poems, was printed in 1962 in 100,000 copies. Yevtushenko has observed that under present conditions the number of copies printed of a book by a Soviet poet is determined more and more by his public popularity rather than by his official position, as had been the case during the Stalin era. Some of Yevtushenko's poems were included in an anthology of Soviet Russian poetry, published in Moscow in 1957.

Yevtushenko's poems have been translated into some sixteen languages, including Polish, Bulgarian, Romanian, Czech, Italian, and French. A representative collection of twenty-two of his poems, including the autobiographical "Zima Junction," has been translated into English by Robin Milner-Gulland and Peter Levi, S.J., and was published in 1962 by E. P. Dutton & Company and Penguin Books, under the title *Selected Poems.* Well received in England and the United States, the collection includes poems recalling the terrors of the Stalin regime and criticizing the bureaucracy. It also includes love lyrics and pastoral poems and deals with such themes as the conflict between appearance and reality, the joy of freedom, and the inevitability of death. One of his best-known poems, "Babiy Yar," which he wrote in 1961 and recently revised, recalls the massacre of some 96,000 Russian Jews by the Nazis in 1944, and contains an indictment of continuing anti-Semitism in the Soviet Union. The poem ends with the lines: "No Jewish blood runs among my blood, /but I am as bitterly and hardly hated /by every anti-Semite/as if I were a Jew. By this/I am a Russian." The poem was one of the sources that inspired Dmitri Shostakovich to compose his Thirteenth Symphony.

In recent years Yevtushenko has given readings before enthusiastic audiences at universities, theaters, clubs, and factories. In 1961 he made an estimated 250 of such presentations. His appearance on Poetry Day in October 1961 before a crowd of some 5,000 in Moscow's Mayakovsky Square led to such a tumult that a policeman remarked: "Better a revolution than a poet." Some of Yevtushenko's poems have been set to music and have become quite popular in this form. He has also translated a number of foreign poems into Russian. Currently Yevtushenko is working on a novel about Russia's new generation of intellectuals.

Since 1960 Yevtushenko has been permitted to travel abroad, and he has visited Bulgaria, France, Ghana, Cuba, the United States, and Great Britain. During visits to Cuba he has had several meetings with Premier Fidel Castro, whom he greatly admires, and he has written a script for a Soviet motion picture about the Cuban revolution, which was filmed in Cuba in 1962. He visited the United States in 1961. In the spring of 1962 Yevtushenko visited England, where he met such noted literary figures as T. S. Eliot, C. P. Snow, Kingsley Amis, and Alan Silli-

toe. He made many public appearances, which evoked much comment in the British press. A filmed interview of Yevtushenko made during his visit to England has been presented in the United States by Chet Huntley over NBC-TV. When the American poet Robert Frost visited the Soviet Union in 1962 Yevtushenko served as his host.

Described as a "middlebrow" poet, Yevtushenko is considered by some critics as less talented than some other contemporary Russian poets (notably Vladimir Berestov and Andrei Vosnesensky). Nevertheless, he seems to have captured the imagination of Russia's youth, and he is generally regarded as "the unchallenged spokesman of the new Russian literary generation." Although Yevtushenko feels some kinship to the Beat Generation of the United States and the Angry Young Men of Great Britain, he distinguishes between these movements and his position. "Like the beatniks we hate falsehood and cant, but while the beatniks do not believe in any social system, we do believe in ours," he has said. "The purpose of our criticism is to improve the society in which we live."

Although he is not a member of the Communist party, Yevtushenko considers himself a staunch Communist. In an article in the London *Observer* following his visit to England, he wrote: "The very fact that in my poems I attack bureaucracy, dogmatism, chauvinism, means precisely that I am a Communist in my convictions. For me communism and bureaucracy by no means go together but are simply incompatible." He said in a poem published in July 1962: "I am a Communist by nature./ And communism orders me/ To be angrier and angrier/ Toward all that stands in its way." Despite his attacks upon certain aspects of Soviet society, Yevtushenko is gaining more and more acceptance in official Soviet circles. His supporters in high places include the novelist Ilya Ehrenburg and the editor of *Izvestia,* Alexis Adzhubei, the son-in-law of Premier Nikita S. Khrushchev.

Yevgeny Yevtushenko's first marriage in 1954, to Bella Akhmadulina, a noted poet, ended in divorce. His second wife, Galina Semyonovna, is a translator of literary works, including the writings of Somerset Maugham and J. D. Salinger. Tall and slender, Yevtushenko stands at six feet three inches, and has blond hair and a thin-featured face marked by a "spare but ardent asceticism." With his wife he lives in the outskirts of Moscow, in a new two-room apartment equipped with Scandinavian furniture and decorated with abstract paintings by his friends. Yevtushenko reads Western literature in Russian translation, including the works of J. D. Salinger, William Faulkner, and John Osborne. He especially admires the writing of Ernest Hemingway, about whom he has written a poem ("Encounter"). He is interested in music "in an amateur sort of way."

Chet Huntley of NBC-TV is quoted by Marya Mannes of the *Reporter* (June 7, 1962) as saying at the time of Yevtushenko's visit to England: "Yevtushenko represents possibly a new and bolder breed of the Soviet Union. He believes in Communism although he is not a member of the Communist party; he is certainly a loyal and highly patriotic Russian. However, he believes in a better Communism, a humane Communism, and a Communism based, in some degree at least, upon popular consent. . . . One of our best hopes is that more Yevtushenkos will be produced in the U.S.S.R."

References

N Y Times p34 S 27 '62 por
N Y Times Mag p12+ D 31 '61 por
Soviet Survey 25:75+ Jl-S '58
Time 79:28+ Ap 13 '62 pors
Everyman's Concise Encyclopaedia of Russia (1961)
Yevtushenko, Yevgeny. Selected Poems (1962); A Precocious Autobiography (1963

ZAHEDI, FAZLOLLAH 1897-Sept. 2, 1963 Iranian army officer and statesman; Minister of the Interior (1951); Premier of Iran (1953-55); later Iranian Ambassador to United Nations European headquarters; worked to improve Iran's relations with the West. See *Current Biography* (February) 1954.

Obituary

N Y Times p39 S 4 '63

ZELLERBACH, J(AMES) D(AVID) Jan. 17, 1892-Aug. 3, 1963 Industrialist; diplomat; board chairman of Crown Zellerbach Corporation; United States Ambassador to Italy (1956-60). See *Current Biography* (December) 1948.

Obituary

N Y Times p81 Ag 4 '63

ZORACH, WILLIAM (zŏr'äk) Feb. 28, 1887- Sculptor; painter

Address: 276 Hicks St., Brooklyn 1, N.Y.; Robinhood, Me.

NOTE: This biography supersedes the article that appeared in *Current Biography* in 1943.

During an era of American art that has favored nonobjectivism William Zorach has maintained his fame as a more or less representative sculptor whose monumental works reflect his magnanimity of spirit and whose smaller, intimate figures radiate a warmth of feeling that is alien to abstract art. He is a former lithographer who broke free of commercial art in the teens of the twentieth century to become an avant-garde oil painter and who gradually later found aesthetic fulfillment as an interpretative watercolorist and sculptor. In the 1920's when he introduced the ancient practice of direct carving in wood and stone, he was considered a pioneer. Now, the preference of many young artists in the United States for open, or transparent, molded sculpture, of which Jacques Lipchitz is a leading exponent, has put Zorach in the conservative camp. It has not, however, diminished his eagerness to explore the limits of direct carving with fresh concepts.

Wide World

WILLIAM ZORACH

Like Lipchitz, William Zorach is a native Lithuanian of Jewish background. He was born in Eurburg, then a part of Czarist Russia, on February 28, 1887 to Aaron and Toba (Bloch) Zorach. He was the seventh of ten children, of whom only two others are still living, a brother, Eddy Fink, and a sister, Ida C. Shoener. His mother was of peasant stock, and his father sailed a small freight barge on the Niemen River, until hostility toward the Jews drove him to try to make a living in America as a peddler of notions in rural areas.

William Zorach was four years old when his father sent for the family to join him in Port Clinton, Ohio. There they lived in a poverty that afforded the boy little contrast with his mud-floored log cabin home in Europe. In 1894 they moved to Cleveland, where Aaron Zorach set himself up in business as a junk dealer while his son worked at odd jobs in after-school hours. Since early childhood William had shown considerable skill in drawing and carving, and when he was in the seventh grade at Brownell School his teacher, a Miss Sterling, brought his talent to the attention of the supervisor of art in Cleveland's public schools, who gave him a letter of recommendation to the Morgan Lithograph Company of Cleveland.

Leaving school in the eighth grade, Zorach worked first as an errand boy with the Morgan company, then as an apprentice, and finally as a lithographer. From 1903 to 1906 he also studied drawing and painting in the evenings at the Cleveland School of Art. For several more years he had to rely on lithography for his livelihood, but by saving his earnings he was able to study for two winters at the National Academy of Design in New York City, where he won a medal for drawing and honorable mention for painting. In his spare time in New York he copied old masters at the Metropolitan Museum of Art.

In 1910 Zorach went to Paris, and since he did not know French, he enrolled at La Palette,

ZORACH, WILLIAM—*Continued*

where he could receive criticism in English. One of his teachers there, John Duncan Fergusson, had a marked influence on his early development. At La Palette he met Marguerite Thompson, an American student from California whom he later married. Her enthusiasm for cubism and Fauvism, as well as his own interest in Gauguin and Cézanne, greatly affected the direction of his work. Four of the five Fauve, or "wild," pictures that he sent to the Salon d'Automne in 1911 were accepted for exhibition.

Penniless by late 1911, Zorach returned to his lithographer's job in Cleveland, but a year later, in December, he moved to New York City and married Marguerite Thompson. He and his wife set up a studio in Greenwich Village, and both had paintings in the famed Armory Show of 1913. Zorach has said that he was "drunk with the possibilities of color and form," and when some critics objected to his red sea and green-skinned women, he explained that he used combinations of color and form not to copy nature but to express an inner feeling arising from his experiences in nature or life.

After a period of several years in which his paintings, such as *Spring, Number I* (1913), were predominantly Fauve, Zorach turned toward cubism, as in *Leo Ornstein—Piano Concert* (1918). John I. H. Baur has pointed out in *William Zorach* (Praeger, 1959) that although Zorach appreciated the creation of abstract design as the "essential contribution" of modern art to aesthetics, his own cubist paintings "are filled with a warmth of sentiment totally alien to pure abstraction." More personal for Zorach, Baur believes, is the fluid, semiabstract style of a series of drawings, water colors, and oil paintings that he worked on in the Yosemite Valley during the summer of 1920.

During an earlier summer, in 1917, spent at a New Hampshire farm, Zorach had become involved in sculpture when somewhat by chance he found an interesting butternut panel from which he made a carved relief, *Waterfall*. With no formal training in sculpture, but with a mature grasp of plastic design, he began to find greater satisfaction in carving than in painting. Between 1917 and 1922 he produced some dozen pieces in wood, as well as several terracottas, and in 1922 he abandoned oil painting altogether for sculpture. He has, however, continued to paint in watercolor and in 1932 won the Logan Medal and Prize at the Art Institute of Chicago International Watercolor Exhibition.

Some characteristics or mannerisms of Zorach's cubist paintings, such as angularity of line, were carried over into his early carved pieces. But in his sculpture the credos of modern art mattered less to him than primitive carvings of the past— of the Africans, the Persians, the archaic Greeks, and the Egyptians. In his affinity for direct carving in wood and massive blocks of stone, he led the way in the United States toward a revival of the practices and skills of ancient sculptors.

In teaching sculpturing, Zorach has explained that the material that a sculptor selects often determines his basic design. The foreword to the catalogue of his retrospective exhibition at the Art Students League Gallery in November 1950 quotes him, "A piece of sculpture is made up of silhouettes which move in a spiral, which must function at every angle of the sphere. I like to be able to roll a stone piece around on the ground so that I can look at it from every position. You cannot do this with a model of clay." Among his sculptures that seem to derive their shape from the material itself are *Floating Figure* (1922), *Pigeon* (1930), and *Reclining Cat* (1935).

In many other notable carvings, including *The Artist's Wife* (1924) and *Child with Cat* (1926), both in Tennessee marble, Zorach took less direction from his stone. He carved his *Mother and Child* (1927-30) entirely in the round from a three-ton block of Spanish Florida Rosa marble. One of his masterpieces, this sculpture, which is now owned by the Metropolitan Museum of Art, was exhibited in January 1931 at the Downtown Gallery in New York in a one-man show. Edward Alden Jewell of the New York *Times* hailed the exhibition as an event that marked a "prodigious advance" in the realm of sculpture. *Mother and Child* brought Zorach the Logan Medal and $1,500 prize for sculpture of the Chicago Art Institute in 1931.

Turning for the moment from stone to clay, in the early 1930's Zorach molded two important statues that were cast in metal: the aluminum *Spirit of the Dance* (1932) and the bronze *The Embrace* (1933). *Spirit of the Dance*, commissioned for Radio City Music Hall in New York, became a center of controversy when S. L. Rothafel ("Roxy"), the Music Hall manager, refused to exhibit it because he thought it too nude. Nelson A. Rockefeller joined other art lovers in protesting Rothafel's rejection of the statue, and it was eventually exhibited at Radio City.

Zorach's significant work in connection with public commissions includes the over-life-size marble figure of Benjamin Franklin (1936-37) for the Benjamin Franklin Post Office in Washington, D.C.; a monument, *Builders of the Future* (1939), for the New York World's Fair; a relief, *Man and Work* (1953), for the facade of the Mayo Clinic building in Rochester, Minnesota; and a monumental high relief for the new Municipal Court Building in New York City (1961).

According to Baur, over the past two decades Zorach has developed principally along classical lines, as is evident in his *Devotion* (1946), and *The Family* (1957). At the same time he often departs from classicism in the direction of both the romantic and the primitive. Almost all of his work, however, expresses much the same spirit of nobility, serenity, tenderness, joyousness—the meditative outlook on life of an artist who does not hire professional models and who finds his inspiration in his family and friends, the places where he has lived, and the animals that he has known.

Since 1923 Zorach has spent part of each year at his farm near the sea at Robinhood, Maine, where the color and motion of the landscape perhaps encouraged him to continue his painting in watercolor. His watercolors *Windy Day— Lowe's Point* (1950) and *Robinhood Marina*

(1958), for example, testify to his delight in his summer home. Away from his farm, he has always given considerable time to teaching. Interested in progressive education, he taught from 1920 to 1935 in a number of progressive schools in and around New York, including Rosemary Hall in Greenwich, Connecticut. During three summers, from 1932 to 1935, he lectured on the history of sculpture at Columbia University, and for more than thirty years, from 1929 to 1960, he was an instructor of sculpture at the Art Students League. He is the author of many articles in art periodicals and of the book *Zorach Explains Sculpture* (American Artists Group, 1947).

During the Roosevelt administration Zorach served as a juror on the section of fine arts for the Treasury Department in Washington. He is a member of the board of the Sculptors' Guild and a past vice-president of the Society of American Painters, Sculptors, and Gravers. Among his recent awards is the Gold Medal of the National Institute of Arts and Letters (1961), and he has honorary degrees from Bowdoin College (1958) and Colby College (1961). Since 1931 he has had exhibitions periodically at the Downtown Gallery in New York, and major retrospective exhibitions of his work were held at the Art Students League Gallery in November 1950 and the Whitney Museum of American Art in New York in the fall of 1959.

Stocky and sturdy in build, Zorach stands five feet ten inches tall and weighs 190 pounds; he has gray eyes and gray hair. He and his wife, the former Marguerite Thompson, whom he married in 1912, have a son, Tessim, and a daughter, Dahlev (Mrs. Adolph Ipcar), also an artist. Zorach, who once described himself as "a simple person, close to the earth," finds his recreation chiefly in farming and swimming.

In an overall characterization of Zorach's work for the foreword of the catalogue of the sculptor's exhibit at the Art Students League, Larry Campbell wrote: "There is always a conviction that life is exalted and filled with dignity. His sculptures are never esoteric, although they may be mysterious. But it is the mystery of life that is breathed into them, rather than a mystery of confusion, or a mystery of statement."

References

Baur, John I. H. William Zorach (1959)
Ritchie, Andrew Carnduff. Sculpture of the Twentieth Century (1952)
Who's Who in America, 1962-63
Who's Who in American Art, 1959

BIOGRAPHICAL REFERENCES

American Architects Directory, 1962

American Bar, 1963

American Catholic Who's Who, 1962 and 1963

American Medical Directory, 1961

American Men in Government (1949)

American Men of Science 10th ed (1960-62)

ASCAP Biographical Dictionary of Composers, Authors, and Publishers (1952)

Asia Who's Who (1960)

Author's & Writer's Who's Who (1960)

Baseball Register, 1963

Bénézit, E., ed. Dictionnaire des Peintres, Sculpteurs, Dessinateurs et Graveurs (1948-55)

Biographical Directory of the American Congress, 1774-1961 (1962)

Biographical Encyclopedia of Pakistan, 1955-56

Biographic Directory of the USSR (1958)

Burke's Landed Gentry (1952)

Burke's Peerage, Baronetage, and Knightage, 1963

Business Executives of America (1950)

Canadian Who's Who, 1958-60

Catholic Who's Who, 1952

Chemical Who's Who, 1956

Chi è? (1961)

China Yearbook, 1960-61

Chujoy, A., ed. Dance Encyclopedia (1949)

Congressional Directory (1963)

Congressional Quarterly Almanac, 1963

Contemporary Authors (1963)

Davidson, G. Opera Biographies (1955)

Department of State Biographic Register, 1963

Dictionnaire Biographique Français Contemporain (1954)

Directory of American Judges (1955)

Directory of American Scholars (1957)

Directory of British Scientists, 1963

Directory of Medical Specialists (1963)

Directory of Medical Women, 1949

Directory of the American Political Science Association, 1953

Ewen, D., ed. Composers of Today (1936); Living Musicians (1940; First Supplement, 1957); Men and Women Who Make Music (1949); American Composers Today (1949); European Composers Today (1954); The New Book of Modern Composers (1961); Popular American Composers (1962)

Feather, Leonard. Encyclopedia of Jazz (1960)

Grove's Dictionary of Music and Musicians (1955)

Hindustan Year Book and Who's Who, 1962

Hoehn, M. A., ed. Catholic Authors (1957)

Hvem er Hvem? 1959

International Motion Picture Almanac, 1963

International Television Almanac, 1963

International Who's Who, 1963-64

International Who's Who in Poetry (1958)

International Who's Who in World Medicine, 1947

International World Who's Who (1949)

International Year Book and Statesmen's Who's Who, 1963

Italian-American Who's Who (1946)

Japan Biographical Encyclopedia & Who's Who, 1961

Japan Who's Who, 1950-51

Jews in the World of Science (1956)

Junior Book of Authors (1956)

Kelly's Handbook to the Titled, Landed and Official Classes, 1963

Kleine Slavische Biographie (1958)

Kraks Blå Bog, 1961

Kürschners Biographisches Theater-Handbuch (1956)

Kürschners Deutscher Gelehrten-Kalender, 1961

Leaders in Education (1948)

Martindale-Hubbell Law Directory, 1963

Menke, Frank G. The Encyclopedia of Sports (1959)

Middle East, 1963

More Junior Authors (1963)

Nalanda Year-Book and Who's Who in India and Pakistan, 1958

National Cyclopaedia of American Biography current vols. A-I (1926-59)

New Century Cyclopedia of Names (1954)

Österreicher der Gegenwart (1951)

Panorama Biografico degli Italiani d'Oggi (1956)

Poor's Register of Directors and Executives, 1963

Quem é Alquém (1947)

Quien es Quien en la Argentina, 1958-59

Quien es Quien en Venezuela, Panama, Ecuador, Colombia, 1956

Radio and Television Who's Who (1956)

Religious Leaders of America, 1941-42

Slavonic Encyclopedia (1949)

Slonimsky, Nicholas. Baker's Biographical Dictionary of Musicians (1958)

Thompson, O., ed. International Cyclopedia of Music and Musicians, 1956

Turkin, H., and Thompson, S. C.
Official Encyclopedia of Baseball (1959)
Twentieth Century Authors
(1942; First Supplement, 1955)

Vem är Det, 1963
Vem och Vad, 1948

Warfel, H. R. American Novel-
ists of Today (1951)
Webster's Biographical Diction-
ary (1959)
Wer ist Wer? (1962)
Who is Who in Music (1951)
Who Knows—and What (1954)
Who's Who, 1963
Who's Who in Advertising, 1963
Who's Who in America, 1962-63
Who's Who in American Art
(1962)
Who's Who in American Edu-
cation, 1961-62
Who's Who in Art, 1962
Who's Who in Australia, 1962
Who's Who in Austria, 1959-60
Who's Who in Belgium (1962)
Who's Who in British Science,
1953
Who's Who in California, 1961
Who's Who in Canada, 1962-63
Who's Who in Chicago and
Illinois (1950)

Who's Who in Colored America,
1950
Who's Who in Engineering, 1959
Who's Who in France, 1963-64
Who's Who in France (Paris),
1953-54
Who's Who in Germany (1960)
Who's Who in Insurance, 1962
Who's Who in Israel, 1962
Who's Who in Italy, 1957-58
Who's Who in Labor (1946)
Who's Who in Latin America
Pts 1-7 (1946-51)
Who's Who in Library Service
(1955)
Who's Who in Modern China
(1954)
Who's Who in Music and Musi-
cians, 1962
Who's Who in New England
(1949)
Who's Who in New York, 1960
Who's Who in New Zealand
(1962)
Who's Who in Philosophy
(1952)
Who's Who in Railroading in
North America (1959)
Who's Who in Switzerland:
1960-61
Who's Who in the East, 1964-65
Who's Who in the Midwest
(1963)
Who's Who in the Netherlands,
1962-63
Who's Who in the South and
Southwest (1961)

Who's Who in the Theatre
(1961)
Who's Who in the United Na-
tions (1951)
Who's Who in the USSR, 1961-
62
Who's Who in the West (1963-
64)
Who's Who in U.A.R. and the
Near East, 1959
Who's Who in United States
Politics (1952)
Who's Who in World Aviation
and Astronautics (1958)
Who's Who in World Jewry
(1955)
Who's Who of American
Women, 1964-65
Who's Who of Southern Africa,
(1962)
Who's Who of the Federation of
Rhodesia and Nyasaland, Cen-
tral and East Africa, 1962
Wie is Dat? (1956)
Winchester's Screen Encyclo-
pedia (1948)
Women Lawyers in the United
States (1957)
Women of Achievement (1940)
Wood, C. TV Personalities vols.
1-3 (1955-57)
World Biography (1954)
World Diplomatic Directory,
1951
World Who's Who in Com-
merce and Industry (1964-65)

PERIODICALS AND NEWSPAPERS CONSULTED

NOTE: Most of the publications below are listed in Wilson Company periodical indexes found in most libraries. For addresses, subscription price, etc., consult your librarian.

ALA Bul—American Library Association Bulletin
Am Artist—American Artist
Am Assn Univ Women J—Journal of the American Association of University Women
Am Bar Assn J—American Bar Association Journal
Am Hist R—American Historical Review
Am Mercury—American Mercury
Am Pol Sci R—American Political Science Review
Am Scholar—American Scholar
Am Sociol R—American Sociological Review
Am W—American Weekly (discontinued)
America—America
Américas—Américas (incorporating Bul Pan Am Union)
Ann Am Acad—Annals of the American Academy of Political and Social Science
Arch Forum—Architectural Forum, the Magazine of Building
Arch Rec—Architectural Record
Archaeology—Archaeology: A Magazine Dealing with the Antiquity of the World
Art N—Art News
Arts—Arts
Arts & Arch—Arts & Architecture
Atlan—Atlantic Monthly
Aviation W—Aviation Week and Space Technology

Barrons—Barron's
Bet Hom & Gard—Better Homes and Gardens
Book-of-the-Month Club N—Book-of-the-Month Club News
Books Abroad—Books Abroad
Bsns W—Business Week
Bul Atomic Sci—Bulletin of the Atomic Scientists

Can Hist R—Canadian Historical Review
Cath World—Catholic World
Chem & Eng N—Chemical and Engineering News
Christian Cent—Christian Century
Christian Sci Mon—Christian Science Monitor
Colliers—Collier's (discontinued)
Commonweal—Commonweal
Cong Digest—Congressional Digest
Cong Q—Congressional Quarterly Weekly Report
Coronet—Coronet (discontinued)
Cosmop—Cosmopolitan
Cue—Cue
Cur Hist—Current History

Dance Mag—Dance Magazine

Ed—Education
Ed & Pub—Editor & Publisher
Ed Res Reports—Editorial Research Reports
Esquire—Esquire
Etude—Etude (discontinued)

Facts on File—Facts on File
For Affairs—Foreign Affairs
For Policy Bul—Foreign Policy Bulletin
Forbes—Forbes
Fortune—Fortune

Gen Army—Generals of the Army and the Air Force and Admirals of the Navy (discontinued)
Good H—Good Housekeeping

Harper—Harper's Magazine
Hi Fi—High Fidelity; The Magazine for Music Listeners
Hi-Fi/Stereo R—Hi-Fi/Stereo Review
Holiday—Holiday
House & Gard—House & Garden

Illus Lond N—Illustrated London News
Ind Woman—Independent Woman (continued as Nat Bsns Woman)

J Am Med Assn—Journal of the American Medical Association

Ladies Home J—Ladies' Home Journal
Lib J—Library Journal
Life—Life
Look—Look

McCalls—McCall's
Macleans Mag—Maclean's Magazine
Mag Wall St—Magazine of Wall Street and Business Analyst
Manchester Guardian—Manchester Guardian
Mlle—Mademoiselle
Mus Am—Musical America
Mus Courier—Musical Courier
Mus Mod Art—Museum of Modern Art Bulletin

NEA J—Journal of the National Education Association
N Y Herald Tribune—New York Herald Tribune
N Y Herald Tribune Bk R—New York Herald Tribune Book Review
N Y Post—New York Post
N Y Times—New York Times
N Y Times Bk R—New York Times Book Review
N Y Times Index—New York Times Index
N Y Times Mag—New York Times Magazine
N Y World-Telegram—New York World-Telegram and Sun
Nat Bsns Woman—National Business Woman
Nat Geog Mag—National Geographic Magazine
Nat Observer—National Observer
Nation—The Nation
Nations Bsns—Nation's Business
Nature—Nature
New Engl Q—New England Quarterly
New Repub—New Republic
New Statesm—New Statesman
New Yorker—New Yorker
Newsday—Newsday
Newsweek—Newsweek

Opera N—Opera News

Pol Sci Q—Political Science Quarterly
Pop Mech—Popular Mechanics Magazine
Pop Phot—Popular Photography
Pop Sci—Popular Science Monthly
Ptr Ink—Printers' Ink
Pub W—Publishers' Weekly

Read Digest—Reader's Digest
Reporter—The Reporter
Rotarian—Rotarian

Sat Eve Post—Saturday Evening Post
Sat Night—Saturday Night
Sat R—Saturday Review
Sch & Soc—School and Society
Sci Am—Scientific American
Sci Mo—Scientific Monthly (combined with Science)
Sci N L—Science News Letter
Science—Science (incorporating Sci Mo)
Show—Show
Show Bsns Illus—Show Business Illustrated (discontinued)
Spec—Spectator
Sports Illus—Sports Illustrated
Sr Schol—Senior Scholastic

Theatre Arts—Theatre Arts
This Week—This Week Magazine
Time—Time
Times Lit Sup—London Times Literary Supplement
Toronto Globe and Mail—Toronto Globe and Mail
Toronto Globe and Mail Globe Mag—Toronto Globe and Mail Globe Magazine
Travel—Travel

U N R—United Nations Review
U S Dept State Bul—United States Department of State Bulletin
U S News—U. S. News & World Report

Variety—Variety
Vital Speeches—Vital Speeches of the Day
Vogue—Vogue

Washington (D.C.) Post—Washington Post
Wilson Lib Bul—Wilson Library Bulletin

Yale R—Yale Review

NECROLOGY

This is a list of biographees' obituaries that are in the yearbook, including those of late 1962. Deaths that occurred in late 1963 are recorded in the early 1964 issues of CURRENT BIOGRAPHY.

Ali, Mohammed
Anderson, Samuel W.
Armstrong, David W.
Austin, Warren R.

Barber, Mary I.
Ben-Zvi, Isaac
Beveridge, Sir William
Bohr, Niels
Braque, Georges
Brigham, Clarence S.
Brooke, Alan, 1st Viscount Alan-brooke
Brooks, Van Wyck

Campbell, Grace
Carton de Wiart, Adrian
Casey, Robert J.
Chavez, Dennis
Clapp, Gordon R.
Coty, René
Cresap, Mark W., Jr.
Cunningham, Andrew Browne, 1st Viscount Cunningham
Curtice, Harlow H.

Dale, Chester
Davis, Tobé Coller
Dryfoos, Orvil E.
Du Bois, W. E. B.

Eisenschiml, Otto

Ferguson, Garland S.
Flagstad, Kirsten
Foyle, William Alfred
Freyberg, Bernard Cyril, 1st Baron Freyberg
Frost, Robert

Gaitskell, Hugh
Galloway, Irene O.
Gardner, Ed
Gasser, Herbert S.
Graham, Philip L.
Griswold, A. Whitney

Hamilton, Edith
Harbach, Otto A.
Hart, Merwin K.
Hatch, Carl A.
Herskovits, Melville J.

Holenstein, Thomas
Hornsby, Roger
Humphrey, Helen F.
Hurley, Patrick J.

Irene

Jacobssen, Per
Janney, Russell
John XXIII, Pope
Johnston, Eric A.
Jones, Joe

Kalmus, Herbert T.
Kassem, Abdul Karim
Kauffmann, Henrik
Kefauver, Estes
Kennedy, Thomas
Kerr, Robert S.
Kessing, O. O.
Kirk, Alan Goodrich

La Farge, Oliver
Langner, Lawrence
Laughton, Charles
Lemonnier, André
Lequerica y Erquiza, José Félix de
Loutfi, Omar
Low, Sir David

McDevitt, James L.
McGranery, James P.
MacLean, Basil C.
Mattei, Enrico
Mattingly, Garrett
Mead, George H.
Mehaffey, Joseph C.
Melcher, Frederic G.
Milam, Carl H.
Morgenstierne, Wilhelm Munthe de
Morris, William Richard, 1st Viscount Nuffield
Murphree, Eger V.

Odets, Clifford
Olds, Irving S.
Olsen, John
O'Mahoney, Joseph C.
Oxnam, G. Bromley

Patterson, Alicia
Pease, Lute

Perkins, C. H.
Pew, Joseph N., Jr.
Phillips, Morgan
Piaf, Edith
Picard, Frank A.
Piccard, Jean Felix
Powell, Dick
Prasad, Rajendra

Ray, Randolph
Reynolds, Robert Rice
Roosevelt, Eleanor
Routley, T. Clarence
Ryan, Joseph P.

Samuel, Herbert, 1st Viscount Samuel
Schuck, Arthur A.
Schuman, Robert
Schwidetzky, Oscar
Sensenich, Roscoe L.
Seymour, Charles
Shoemaker, Samuel M.
Silver, Abba Hillel
Smadel, Joseph E.
Small, John D.
Sokolsky, George E.
Sordoni, Andrew J.
Standley, W. H.
Strachey, John
Struve, Otto

Templeton, Alec
Tennant, Sir William George
Traphagen, Ethel
Trautman, George M.

Vandercook, John W.
Van Volkenburg, J. L.
Villon, Jacques
Von Kármán, Theodore

Walker, Stanley
Walter, Francis E.
Waugh, Sidney
Weis, Mrs. Charles W., Jr.
Wilhelmina, Princess of the Netherlands
Williston, Samuel
Woodsmall, Ruth F.
Woolley, Monty

Zahedi, Fazlollah
Zellerbach, J. D.

CLASSIFICATION BY PROFESSION—1963

Advertising
Starch, Daniel

Agriculture
Bellmon, Henry
Carvel, Elbert N.
Holyoake, Keith J.
Renne, Roland R.

Archaeology
Gordon, Cyrus H.

Architecture
Mumford, Lewis

Art
Clark, Sir Kenneth
Dickinson, Edwin
Mostel, Zero
Shepard, E. H.
Ter-Arutunian, Rouben
Von Wicht, John
Zorach, William

Aviation
Cochran, Jacqueline
Dougherty, Dora
Gilruth, Robert R.
Storms, Harrison A., Jr.

Business
Beeching, Richard
Carvel, Elbert N.
Cary, William L.
Clay, Lucius D.
Cochran, Jacqueline
Copeland, Lammot du Pont
Darin, Bobby
Egbert, Sherwood H.
Eisenschiml, Otto
Greene, Hugh Carleton
Gullander, W. P.
Hughes, Harold E.
Lee, Peggy
Mosbacher, Emil, Jr.
Muir, Percy
Onassis, Aristotle Socrates
Plumley, H. Ladd
Scherman, Harry
Starch, Daniel
Swallow, Alan
Vila, George R.
Ward, Robert
Welch, Leo D.

Dance
Nureyev, Rudolf
Plisetskaya, Maya
Saddler, Donald
Ter-Arutunian, Rouben

Diplomacy
Dowling, Walter C.
Jones, Howard P.
Moscoso, Teodoro
Nehru, B. K.
Pearson, Lester Bowles
Subandrio
Williams, G. Mennen

Education
Beranek, Leo L.
Blanchard, Hazel A.
Calder, Ritchie
Cary, William L.
Coggeshall, L. T.
Collins, James
Debye, Peter J. W.
Dickinson, Edwin
Dougherty, Dora
Edel, Leon
Franklin, John Hope
Gordon, Cyrus H.
Gordon, Kermit
Green, Constance McLaughlin
Greenstein, Jesse L.
Gross, Paul Magnus
Hamilton, Edith
Hess, Victor Francis
Hoggart, Richard
Infeld, Leopold
Kellogg, Winthrop N.
Keppel, Francis
Küng, Hans
Langer, Susanne K.
Morgenthau, Hans J.
Mumford, Lewis
Nabrit, S. M.
Ohlin, Lloyd E.
Park, Thomas
Popper, Karl R.
Quay, Jan Eduard de
Ramsey, Norman F.
Renne, Roland R.
Starker, Janos
Stratton, Julius A.
Swallow, Alan
Townes, Charles H.
Tugwell, Rexford G.
Wagman, Frederick H.
Ward, Robert
Watson, James Dewey
Wirtz, W. Willard

Engineering
Ammann, O. H.
Gilruth, Robert R.
Holmes, D. Brainerd
O'Neill, Eugene F.
Storms, Harrison A., Jr.
Stratton, Julius A.
Vila, George R.
Wagner, Aubrey J.

Finance
Cary, William L.
Gordon, Kermit
Kimbrel, M. Monroe
Saxon, James J.
Schweitzer, Pierre-Paul
Welch, Leo D.

Government— Foreign
Banda, Hastings
Beeching, Richard
Ben Bella, Ahmed
Bosch, Juan
Brezhnev, Leonid I.
Brown, George
Chavan, Y. B.
Clark, Sir Kenneth
Crosland, Anthony
Dorticós, Osvaldo
Eshkol, Levi
Grimond, Jo
Guevara, Ernesto
Hassel, Kai-Uwe von
Holyoake, Keith J.
Jagan, Cheddi
Kawakami, Jotaro
Messmer, Pierre
Nabarro, Sir Gerald
Nehru, B. K.
Nyerere, Julius K.
Pearson, Lester Bowles
Quay, Jan Eduard de
Radcliffe, Cyril John, 1st Viscount Radcliffe
Raphael, Chaim
Schweitzer, Pierre-Paul
Subandrio
Summerskill, Edith, Baroness Summerskill
Wachuku, Jaja
Wilson, Harold

Government— United States
Bellmon, Henry
Burdick, Quentin N.
Carvel, Elbert N.

Cary, William L.
Celebrezze, Anthony J.
Clay, Lucius D.
Coggeshall, L. T.
Dowling, Walter C.
Friedman, Herbert
Gilruth, Robert R.
Gordon, Kermit
Hoff, Philip H.
Holmes, D. Brainerd
Hughes, Harold E.
Jones, Howard P.
Kennedy, Edward M.
Keppel, Francis
Love, John A.
McIntyre, Thomas J.
Moscoso, Teodoro
Pittman, Steuart L.
Powers, James E.
Renne, Roland R.
Rowley, James J.
Saxon, James J.
Tollefson, Thor C.
Tugwell, Rexford G.
Wagner, Aubrey J.
Wallace, George C.
Welch, Leo D.
Williams, G. Mennen
Wirtz, W. Willard

Industry

Beeching, Richard
Copeland, Lammot du Pont
Dykstra, John
Egbert, Sherwood H.
Gullander, W. P.
Nabarro, Sir Gerald
Storms, Harrison A., Jr.
Vila, George R.
Welch, Leo D.

International Relations

Clay, Lucius D.
Dowling, Walter C.
Holyoake, Keith J.
Jones, Howard P.
Moscoso, Teodoro
Nehru, B. K.
Pearson, Lester Bowles
Schweitzer, Pierre-Paul
Subandrio
Wachuku, Jaja
Williams, G. Mennen

Journalism

Calder, Ritchie
Storke, Thomas M.
Tuchman, Barbara W.
Vanocur, Sander

Labor

Davidson, Roy E.
Wirtz, W. Willard

Law

Allen, Florence E.
Burdick, Quentin N.
Cary, William L.
Celebrezze, Anthony J.
Chavan, Y. B.
Dorticós, Osvaldo
Hoff, Philip H.
Kennedy, Edward M.
Love, John A.
McIntyre, Thomas J.
Morgenthau, Hans J.
Pittman, Steuart L.
Radcliffe, Cyril John, 1st Viscount Radcliffe
Rowley, James J.
Smith, Sylvester C., Jr.
Tollefson, Thor C.
Wachuku, Jaja
Wallace, George C.
Williams, G. Mennen
Wirtz, W. Willard

Library Service

Brode, Mildred H.
Colwell, Eileen
Tisserant, Eugène, Cardinal
Wagman, Frederick H.

Literature

Albee, Edward
Bosch, Juan
Creasey, John
Durrell, Lawrence
Hamilton, Edith
Hoggart, Richard
Maugham, Somerset
Muir, Percy
O'Connor, Edwin
Porter, Katherine Anne
Pound, Ezra
Raphael, Chaim
Sandburg, Carl
Steinbeck, John
Swallow, Alan
Wilson, Colin
Yevtushenko, Yevgeny

Medicine

Banda, Hastings
Churchill, Edward D.
Coggeshall, L. T.
De Kruif, Paul
Fister, George M.
Guevara, Ernesto
Jagan, Cheddi
Li, C. H.
Shope, Richard E.
Smadel, Joseph E.
Subandrio
Summerskill, Edith, Baroness Summerskill
Watson. James Dewey

Military

Chavan, Y. B.
Clay, Lucius D.
Cooper, Leroy Gordon, Jr
Hassel, Kai-Uwe von
McDonald, David L.
Messmer, Pierre
Tereshkova, Valentina

Motion Pictures

Ashcroft, Dame Peggy
Benny, Jack
Berlin, Irving
Bolt, Robert
Chamberlain, Richard
Darin, Bobby
Duke, Patty
Finney, Albert
Holloway, Stanley
Kubrick, Stanley
Lamorisse, Albert
Lee, Peggy
Mastroianni, Marcello
Mills, Hayley
Mills, John
Morley, Robert
Mostel, Zero
Pinter, Harold
Raye, Martha
Richardson, Tony
Ryan, Robert
Saddler, Donald
Vallee, Rudy
Van Dyck, Dick
Widmark, Richard

Music

Baez, Joan
Barber, Samuel
Benny, Jack
Berlin, Irving
Chamberlain, Richard
Cook, Barbara
Darin, Bobby
Guthrie, Woody
Hines, Jerome
Lee, Peggy
Leinsdorf, Erich
McCracken, James
Madeira, Jean
Morath, Max
Raye, Martha
Sandburg, Carl
Seeger, Pete
Starker, Janos
Ter-Arutunian, Rouben
Vallee, Rudy
Ward, Robert

Nonfiction

Allen, Florence E.
Beranek, Leo L.
Calder, Ritchie
Clark, Sir Kenneth

Clay, Lucius D.
Cochran, Jacqueline
Collins, James
Colwell, Eileen
Creasey, John
Crosland, Anthony
Debye, Peter J. W.
De Kruif, Paul
Durrell, Lawrence
Edel, Leon
Eisenschiml, Otto
Franklin, John Hope
Gollancz, Victor
Gordon, Cyrus H.
Green, Constance McLaughlin
Guthrie, Woody
Hamilton, Edith
Hess, Victor Francis
Hoggart, Richard
Huddleston, Trevor
Huxley, Sir Julian
Infeld, Leopold
Küng, Hans
Landau, Lev
Langer, Susanne K.
Maugham, Somerset
Morgenthau, Hans J.
Mosconi, Willie
Muir, Percy
Mumford, Lewis
Partridge, Eric
Popper, Karl R.
Porter, Katherine Anne
Pound, Ezra
Renne, Roland R.
Sandburg, Carl
Scherman, Harry
Shepard, E. H.
Silver, Abba Hillel
Smith, Sylvester C., Jr.
Starch, Daniel
Storke, Thomas M.
Summerskill, Edith, Baroness Summerskill
Swallow, Alan
Tuchman, Barbara W.
Tugwell, Rexford G.
Tynan, Kenneth
Van Waters, Miriam
Wilson, Colin

Organizations

Alcock, Norman Z.
Blanchard, Hazel A.
Brode, Mildred H.
Davidson, Roy E.
Fister, George M.
Gross, Paul Magnus
Gullander, W. P.
Kimbrel, M. Monroe
Park, Thomas
Plumley, H. Ladd
Powers, James E.
Prinz, Joachim
Scherman, Harry
Smith, Sylvester C., Jr.
Wagman, Frederick H.

Philosophy

Collins, James
Langer, Susanne K.
Mumford, Lewis
Popper, Karl R.

Photography

Vandivert, William

Politics— Foreign

Banda, Hastings
Ben Bella, Ahmed
Bosch, Juan
Brezhnev, Leonid I.
Brown, George
Chavan, Y. B.
Crosland, Anthony
Dorticós, Osvaldo
Eshkol, Levi
Grimond, Jo
Guevara, Ernesto
Hassel, Kai-Uwe von
Holyoake, Keith J.
Jagan, Cheddi
Kawakami, Jotaro
Messmer, Pierre
Nabarro, Sir Gerald
Nehru, B. K.
Nyerere, Julius K.
Pearson, Lester Bowles
Quay, Jan Eduard de
Summerskill, Edith, Baroness Summerskill
Wachuku, Jaja
Wilson, Harold

Politics— United States

Bellmon, Henry
Burdick, Quentin N.
Carvel, Elbert N.
Celebrezze, Anthony J.
Hoff, Philip H.
Hughes, Harold E.
Kennedy, Edward M.
Love, John A.
McIntyre, Thomas J.
Saxon, James J.
Tollefson, Thor C.
Wallace, George C.
Williams, G. Mennen

Psychology

Dougherty, Dora
Kellogg, Winthrop N.
Starch, Daniel

Publishing

Gollancz, Victor
McCabe, Gibson
Scherman, Harry
Storke, Thomas M.
Swallow, Alan

Radio

Ashcroft, Dame Peggy
Benny, Jack
Bolt, Robert
Greene, Hugh Carleton
Holloway, Stanley
Morath, Max
Pinter, Harold
Raye, Martha
Vallee, Rudy
Vanocur, Sander
Widmark, Richard

Religion

Huddleston, Trevor
Küng, Hans
Paul VI, Pope
Prinz, Joachim
Silver, Abba Hillel
Tisserant, Eugène, Cardinal
Wright, John J.

Science

Alcock, Norman Z.
Beeching, Richard
Beranek, Leo L.
Brode, Mildred H.
Calder, Ritchie
Coggeshall, L. T.
Cooper, Leroy Gordon, Jr.
Debye, Peter J. W.
De Kruif, Paul
Drake, Frank D.
Eisenschiml, Otto
Friedman, Herbert
Gilruth, Robert R.
Greenstein, Jesse L.
Gross, Paul Magnus
Hess, Victor Francis
Huxley, Sir Julian
Infeld, Leopold
Kendrew, John C.
Landau, Lev
Li, C. H.
Nabrit, S. M.
O'Neill, Eugene F.
Park, Thomas
Perutz, M. F.
Popper, Karl R.
Ramsey, Norman F.
Shope, Richard E.
Smadel, Joseph E.
Storms, Harrison A., Jr.
Stratton, Julius A.
Tamm, Igor

Tereshkova, Valentina
Townes, Charles H.
Watson, James Dewey
Wilkins, Maurice H. F.

Social Science

Crosland, Anthony
Gordon, Kermit
Guevara, Ernesto
Morgenthau, Hans J.
Mumford, Lewis
Nehru, B. K.
Ohlin, Lloyd E.
Quay, Jan Eduard de
Renne, Roland R.
Starch, Daniel
Tuchman, Barbara W.
Tugwell, Rexford G.
Van Waters, Miriam

Social Service

Gmeiner, Hermann
Huddleston, Trevor
Ohlin, Lloyd E.
Van Waters, Miriam

Sports

Beatty, Jim
Brumel, Valeri
Carter, Don
Clay, Cassius
Fischer, Bobby
Hornung, Paul
Laver, Rod
Lombardi, Vince
McKinley, Chuck
Mosbacher, Emil, Jr.

Mosconi, Willie
Pennel, John

Technology

Ammann, O. H.
Beranek, Leo L.
Brezhnev, Leonid I.
Brode, Mildred H.
Cooper, Leroy Gordon, Jr.
Dougherty, Dora
Drake, Frank D.
Dykstra, John
Eisenschiml, Otto
Friedman, Herbert
Gilruth, Robert R.
Greenstein, Jesse L.
Gross, Paul Magnus
Holmes, D. Brainerd
Mumford, Lewis
O'Neill, Eugene F.
Ramsey, Norman F.
Storms, Harrison A., Jr.
Stratton, Julius A.
Tereshkova, Valentina
Townes, Charles H.
Vila, George R.

Television

Ashcroft, Dame Peggy
Benny, Jack
Bolt, Robert
Chamberlain, Richard
Clark, Sir Kenneth
Cook, Barbara
Darin, Bobby
Duke, Patty
Greene, Hugh Carleton
Hagen, Uta

Holloway, Stanley
Lee, Peggy
Mills, John
Morath, Max
Morley, Robert
Mostel, Zero
Pinter, Harold
Raye, Martha
Ryan, Robert
Saddler, Donald
Ter-Arutunian, Rouben
Vallee, Rudy
Van Dyck, Dick
Vanocur, Sander

Theater

Albee, Edward
Ashcroft, Dame Peggy
Benny, Jack
Berlin, Irving
Bolt, Robert
Cook, Barbara
Duke, Patty
Finney, Albert
Hagen, Uta
Holloway, Stanley
Mastroianni, Marcello
Maugham, Somerset
Mills, John
Morley, Robert
Mostel, Zero
Pinter, Harold
Raye, Martha
Richardson, Tony
Ryan, Robert
Saddler, Donald
Ter-Arutunian, Rouben
Tynan, Kenneth
Vallee, Rudy
Van Dyck, Dick
Widmark, Richard

CUMULATED INDEX—1961-1963

For the index to 1940-1950 biographies, see CURRENT BIOGRAPHY 1950 Yearbook. For the index to 1951-1960 biographies, see CURRENT BIOGRAPHY 1960 Yearbook. The dates after names indicate monthly issues and/or yearbooks in which biographies and obituaries are contained.

Abbas, Ferhat Mar 61
Adams, Eva B(ertrand) Sep 62
Adderley, Cannonball See Adderley, J. E. Jul 61
Adderley, Julian E(dwin) Jul 61
Adoula, Cyrille Mar 62
Ahmad, Imam of Yemen obit Nov 62
Alanbrooke, 1st Viscount See Brooke, A. obit Sep 63
Albee, Edward (Franklin) Feb 63
Albers, Josef Jun 62
Alcock, Norman Z(inkan) Mar 63
Ali, Mohammed obit Mar 63
Allan, John J(ames) obit Jan 61
Allen, Arthur A(ugustus) Jan 61
Allen, Florence E(llinwood) Jul 63
Alpert, George Sep 61
Amies, (Edwin) Hardy Mar 62
Amini, Ali Jan 62
Ammann, O(thmar) H(ermann) Jan 63
Anderson, George W(helan), Jr. Nov 62
Anderson, Dame Judith Feb 61
Anderson, Samuel W(agner) obit Jan 63
Anderson, Victor E(manuel) obit Oct 62
Andrić, Ivo Feb 62
Appel, Karel Mar 61
Armstrong, David W(illiam) obit Mar 63
Arnold, Edwin G(ustaf) obit Jan 61
Arquette, Cliff(ord) Jun 61
Ashcroft, Dame Peggy Sep 63
Askey, E(dwin) Vincent Feb 61
Astor, Mary Nov 61
Atkinson, (Justin) Brooks Feb 61
Austin, Warren R(obinson) obit Feb 63
Avery, Sewell (Lee) obit Jan 61

Babbitt, Milton (Byron) Sep 62
Bacon, Charles L(angston) May 62
Baez, Joan Nov 63
Bailey, John M(oran) Jun 62
Bainton, Roland H. Jun 62
Balch, Emily Greene obit Mar 61
Balewa, Sir Abubakar Tafawa Sep 61
Ball, George W(ildman) Feb 62
Banda, Hastings (Kamuzu) Jan 63
Bandaranaike, Sirimavo May 61
Bannow, Rudolph F(rederick) obit Sep 62
Barber, Carl Jerome See Barber, J. Apr 62

Barber, Jerry Apr 62
Barber, Mary I(sabel) obit Apr 63
Barber, Samuel Sep 63
Barnard, Chester I(rving) obit Sep 61
Barnett, Ross R(obert) Sep 61
Barnsley, Alan (Gabriel) See Fielding, G. Feb 62
Barr, Alfred H(amilton), Jr. Jan 61
Barr, John A(ndrew) Jan 61
Barrett, Frank A. obit Jul 62
Barringer, Emily Dunning obit Jun 61
Barth, Karl Nov 62
Barton, Bruce Feb 61
Batcheller, Hiland G(arfield) obit Jul 61
Bates, Sanford Jan 61
Batt, William L(oren), Jr. Sep 62
Beaton, Cecil (Walter Hardy) Jul 62
Beatty, Jim Jan 63
Beatty, Warren May 62
Beck, Bertram M(aurice) May 61
Beebe, (Charles) William obit Sep 62
Beecham, Sir Thomas obit May 61
Beeching, Richard Sep 63
Behan, Brendan (Francis) Mar 61
Békésy, Georg von Dec 62
Bell, David E(lliott) Jun 61
Bellmon, Henry (Louis) Jul 63
Bemelmans, Ludwig obit Dec 62
Ben Bella, Ahmed Feb 63
Ben-Zvi, Isaac obit Jun 63
Bender, George H(arrison) obit Sep 61
Bennett, Henry Gordon obit Oct 62
Bennett, John C(oleman) Jan 61
Bennett, Robert Russell May 62
Benny, Jack Nov 63
Benson, John obit Nov 62
Beranek, Leo L(eroy) Mar 63
Berelson, Bernard (Reuben) Jul 61
Bergen, John J(oseph) Jun 61
Bergquist, Kenneth P(aul) Mar 61
Berle, Adolf A(ugustus), Jr. Jun 61
Berlin, Irving May 63
Bess, Demaree (Caughey) obit Sep 62
Bettelheim, Bruno Jul 61
Bettmann, Otto L(udwig) Nov 61
Beveridge, Sir William (Henry) obit May 63

Biddle, Anthony J(oseph) Drexel obit Jan 62
Bimson, Carl A(lfred) Mar 61
Bingham, Millicent Todd Jun 61
Bishop, Joey Apr 62
Blair, David Jan 61
Blair, James T(homas), Jr. obit Sep 62
Blanchard, Hazel A(nn) Jun 63
Block, Joseph L(eopold) Jun 61
Boeschenstein, Harold Feb 61
Bohr, Niels (Henrik David) obit Jan 63
Bok, William Curtis obit Jul 62
Boland, Frederick H(enry) Feb 61
Bolt, Robert (Oxton) Jul 63
Booth, Arch N(ewell) Dec 61
Boring, Edwin G(arrigues) Mar 62
Borzage, Frank obit Sep 62
Bosch, Juan Jun 63
Boucher, Anthony Jun 62
Boulanger, Nadia May 62
Bowater, Sir Eric (Vansittart) obit Nov 62
Boyd, Stephen Dec 61
Boyle, William M(arshall), Jr. obit Nov 61
Brady, William T(homas) Jan 61
Bramuglia, Juan A(tilio) obit Nov 62
Brand, Oscar Jun 62
Braque, Georges obit Oct 63
Brazzi, Rossano May 61
Breckinridge, Aida de Acosta obit Jul 62
Brewster, (Ralph) Owen obit Feb 62
Brezhnev, Leonid I(lyich) Jan 63
Bridges, (Henry) Styles obit Jan 62
Bridgman, P(ercy) W(illiams) obit Nov 61
Brigham, Clarence S(aunders) obit Oct 63
Bristol, Lee H(astings) biog Sep 62 obit Nov 62
Britten, (Edward) Benjamin Apr 61
Britton, Edgar C(lay) obit Oct 62
Brode, Mildred H(ooker) Sep 63
Brook, Peter (Stephen Paul) May 61
Brooke, Alan (Francis), 1st Viscount Alanbrooke obit Sep 63
Brooks, Overton obit Dec 61
Brooks, Van Wyck obit Jun 63
Brown, George (Alfred) Dec 63
Brown, Harold Sep 61
Bruce, David K(irkpatrick) E(ste) Sep 61

495

Bruce, Howard obit Sep 61
Brumel, Valeri Apr 63
Bryan, James E(dmund) Jun 62
Bryant, C(ecil) Farris Sep 61
Buchanan, Scott (Milross) Sep 62
Buchman, Frank N(athan) D(aniel) obit Nov 61
Buck, Solon J(ustus) obit Jul 62
Buckley, William F(rank), Jr. Jun 62
Budd, Ralph obit Mar 62
Buechner, Thomas S(charman) Feb 61
Buitoni, Giovanni Jun 62
Bundy, McGeorge Mar 62
Burchfield, Charles (Ephraim) May 61
Burdick, Quentin N(orthrop) May 63
Burke, William R(ichard) Jul 61
Burnett, Carol Jun 62
Burns, James MacGregor Dec 62
Burr, Raymond (William Stacy) Sep 61
Butler, Paul M(ulholland) obit Feb 62

Caffrey, James J(oseph) obit May 61
Cage, John (Milton, Jr.) Sep 61
Calder, (Peter) Ritchie Apr 63
Calvin, Melvin Apr 62
Campbell, Grace (MacLennan Grant) obit Jul 63
Canaday, John (Edwin) May 62
Canby, Henry Seidel obit Jun 61
Cannon, Cavendish W(elles) obit Dec 62
Caplin, Mortimer M(axwell) Sep 61
Cardona, José Miró See Miró Cardona, José Nov 61
Carpenter, Malcolm Scott Sep 62
Carr, Robert K(enneth) Apr 61
Carroll, Diahann Sep 62
Carroll, Joseph F(rancis) Apr 62
Carroll, Thomas H(enry 2d) Jul 62
Carter, Don(ald James) Mar 63
Carton de Wiart, Adrian obit Jul 63
Case, Francis (Higbee) obit Sep 62
Cassini, Oleg (Loiewski-) Jul 61
Castillo (del Rey), Antonio (Cánovas del) Sep 62
Carvel, Elbert N(ostrand) Jun 63
Cary, William L(ucius) Jan 63
Casey, Robert J(oseph) obit Jan 63
Celebrezze, Anthony J(oseph) Jan 63
Chamberlain, (George) Richard Jul 63
Champion, George Apr 61
Chancellor, John (William) Jan 62

Chaplin, Charles (Spencer) Mar 61
Charles-Roux, François (-Jules) obit Sep 61
Chavan, Y(eshwantrao) B(alwantrao) Apr 63
Chavchavadze, George obit Apr 62
Chavez, Dennis obit Jan 63
Cheshire, (Geoffrey) Leonard Jan 62
Chiari, Roberto F(rancisco) Feb 61
Churchill, Edward D(elos) Feb 63
Clapp, Gordon R(ufus) obit Jun 63
Clark, Sir Kenneth (Mackenzie) Sep 63
Clay, Cassius (Marcellus, Jr.) Sep 63
Clay, Lucius D(uBignon) Jun 63
Cleveland, (James) Harlan Sep 61
Close, Upton obit Jan 61
Cobb, Geraldyn M. See Cobb, J. Feb 61
Cobb, Jerrie Feb 61
Cobb, Ty(rus Raymond) obit Oct 61
Cobham, Charles John Lyttelton, 10th Viscount Apr 62
Coblentz, W(illiam) W(eber) obit Nov 62
Coburn, Charles obit Nov 61
Cochran, Jacqueline Jun 63
Cockrell, Ewing obit Apr 62
Coggeshall, L(owell) T(helwell) Sep 63
Coleman, Ornette Jun 61
Compton, Arthur H(olly) obit May 62
Collins, James (Daniel) Dec 63
Colwell, Eileen (Hilda) Jul 63
Connally, John B(owden, Jr.) Jul 61
Connor, John T(homas) Apr 61
Cook, Barbara Feb 63
Cook, Donald obit Dec 61
Cooke, Leslie E(dward) Jun 62
Cooper, Gary obit Jul 61
Cooper, Leroy Gordon, Jr. Sep 63
Copeland, Lammot du Pont May 63
Corea, Sir (George) Claude (Stanley) biog Mar 61 obit Nov 62
Corson, Fred Pierce, Bishop May 61
Coty, René (Jules Gustave) obit Jan 63
Coward, Noel (Pierce) Mar 62
Cox, Archibald Jul 61
Cox, Herald R(ea) Apr 61
Creasey, John Sep 63
Cresap, Mark W(infield), Jr. obit Sep 63
Crosland, (Charles) Anthony (Raven) Sep 63
Crosley, Powel, Jr. obit Jun 61

Cunningham, Andrew Browne, 1st Viscount Cunningham obit Sep 63
Curtice, Harlow H(erbert) obit Jan 63

Dale, Chester obit Jan 63
Dalton, (Edward) Hugh (John Neale) Dalton, Baron obit Apr 62
Darin, Bobby Mar 63
Darling, Jay Norwood obit Mar 62
Davey, Jocelyn See Raphael, Chaim Dec 63
Davidson, Roy E(lton) Sep 63
Davies, Clement (Edward) obit May 62
Davis, Joan obit Sep 61
Davis, Meyer Jun 61
Davis, Miles (Dewey, Jr.) Jun 62
Davis, Tobé Coller obit Feb 63
Day, Dorothy May 62
Day, J(ames) Edward May 62
Dayal, Rajeshwar Feb 61
Dean, H(enry) Trendley obit Jul 62
Dean, Sir Patrick (Henry) May 61
Dearborn, Ned H(arland) obit Oct 62
Debye, Peter J(oseph) W(illiam) Sep 63
Decker, George H(enry) Jan 61
De Forest, Lee obit Oct 61
De Kruif, Paul (Henry) Jul 63
Delaney, Shelagh Apr 62
Del Castillo (del Rey), Antonio (Cánovas) See Castillo (del Rey), A. Sep 62
Dempsey, John (Noel) Jun 61
Dennis, Eugene obit Mar 61
De Quay, Jan Eduard See Quay, J. de May 63
De Toledano, Ralph See Toledano, R. de Dec 62
De Wohl, Louis obit Oct 61
Dichter, Ernest Jan 61
Dickerson, Nancy Hanschman See Hanschman, N. Sep 62
Dickinson, Edwin Sep 63
Dickson, (Horatio Henry) Lovat Sep 62
Djanira Jan 61
Dobrynin, Anatoly F(edorovich) Sep 62
Dobzhansky, Theodosius (Grigorievich) Sep 62
Dolci, Danilo (Bruno Pietro) Sep 61
Donald, David (Herbert) Sep 61
Donnelly, Phil M. obit Nov 61
Donovan, James B(ritt) Jun 61
Dooley, Thomas A(nthony) obit Mar 61
Dorticós (Torrado), Osvaldo Feb 63
Dougherty, Dora (Jean) Mar 63
Dowling, Walter C(ecil) Mar 63
Downey, Sheridan obit Jan 62
Drake, Frank D(onald) Jan 63

Drozniak, Edward Jul 62
Dryfoos, Orvil E(ugene) biog Jan 62 obit Jul 63
Du Bois, W(illiam) E(dward) B(urghardt) obit Oct 63
Dubuffet, Jean Jul 62
Duffy, Edmund obit Nov 62
Duke, Angier Biddle Feb 62
Duke, Patty Sep 63
Dulles, Eleanor Lansing Sep 62
Dunham, Franklin obit Jan 62
Dunrossil, William Shepherd Morrison, 1st Viscount obit Apr 61
Durrell, Lawrence (George) Jul 63
Dworshak, Henry C(larence) obit Oct 62
Dykstra, John Apr 63

Eady, Sir (Crawfurd) Wilfrid (Griffin) obit Feb 62
Eberhart, Richard (Ghormley) Jan 61
Eddy, Manton S(prague) obit Jun 62
Edel, (Joseph) Leon Jul 63
Edwards, Vincent Oct 62
Egbert, Sherwood H(arry) Jun 63
Eichelberger, Robert L(awrence) obit Dec 61
Einaudi, Luigi obit Jan 62
Eisenschiml, Otto Oct 63
Eisler, Hanns obit Nov 62
Eklund, (Arne) Sigvard Jul 62
Eliot, T(homas) S(tearns) Oct 62
Ellis, Elmer Jul 62
Elvehjem, C(onrad) A(rnold) obit Oct 62
Emanuel, Victor obit Jan 61
Ernst, Max Oct 61
Ernst, Morris L(eopold) Feb 61
Eshkol, Levi Oct 63
Evans, Maurice Jun 61
Ewell, Tom May 61
Eyring, Henry Oct 61

Fairless, Benjamin F(ranklin) obit Feb 62
Farrell, Eileen Feb 61
Faulkner, William obit Sep 62
Fay, Frank obit Dec 61
Feiffer, Jules Oct 61
Feis, Herbert Oct 61
Ferguson, Elsie obit Jan 62
Ferguson, Garland S(evier) obit Jun 63
Ferguson, Harry (George) obit Jan 61
Ferriss, Hugh obit Mar 62
Fielding, Gabriel Feb 62
Fine, Benjamin Mar 61
Finney, Albert Oct 63
Fischer, Bobby Oct 63
Fister, George M(organ) Jun 63
Fitch, Robert Elliot Apr 62
Fitzgerald, Barry obit Feb 61
Flagstad, Kirsten obit Jan 63
Fleming, Sam(uel) M. Jun 62

Florence, Fred F(arrel) obit Feb 61
Flynn, Elizabeth Gurley Oct 61
Foerster, Friedrich Wilhelm Jul 62
Folkers, Karl (August) Oct 62
Ford, Edward Charles See Ford, W. Apr 62
Ford, Gerald R(udolph), Jr. Mar 61
Ford, Whitey Apr 62
Forrester, Maureen (Kathleen Stewart) Jul 62
Foster, Sir Harry (Braustyn Hylton) Hylton- See Hylton-Foster, Sir H. (B. H.) Jan 61
Foster, William Z(ebulon) obit Nov 61
Foyle, William Alfred obit Jul 63
Franciosa, Anthony Jul 61
Francis, Connie Jul 62
Franklin, John Hope Oct 63
Freyberg, Bernard Cyril, 1st Baron Freyberg obit Sep 63
Friedman, Herbert Sep 63
Frische, Carl A(lfred) Oct 62
Frost, Robert (Lee) obit Mar 63
Fuchs, Joseph (Philip) Oct 62

Gable, Clark obit Jan 61
Gagarin, Yuri (Alekseyevich) Oct 61
Gaither, H(orace) Brown, Jr. obit Jun 61
Gaitskell, Hugh (Todd Naylor) obit Feb 63
Galloway, Irene O(tillia) obit Feb 63
Gardiner, James Garfield obit Mar 62
Gardner, Ed(ward Francis) obit Oct 63
Gasser, Herbert S(pencer) obit Jul 63
Gavin, James M(aurice) Sep 61
Gavin, John Sep 62
George, Zelma W(atson) Oct 61
Gerstacker, Carl A(llan) Oct 61
Gesell, Arnold L(ucius) obit Sep 61
Gilmore, Voit Feb 62
Gilruth, Robert R(owe) Oct 63
Gingrich, Arnold Feb 61
Giordani, Francesco obit Mar 61
Glaser, Donald A(rthur) Mar 61
Glenn, John H(erschel), Jr. Jun 62
Gmeiner, Hermann May 63
Goldberg, Arthur J(oseph) Jul 61
Golden, Clinton S(trong) obit Sep 61
Gollancz, Victor Oct 63
Goodman, Benny Oct 62
Goodspeed, Edgar J(ohnson) obit Mar 62
Googe, George L(ogan) obit Dec 61
Goossens, Sir Eugene obit Sep 62
Gorbach, Alfons Oct 61

Gordon, Cyrus H(erzl) May 63
Gordon, Kermit Jul 63
Gordon, Lincoln Feb 62
Gore, Sir (William) David Ormsby- See Ormsby-Gore, Sir (W.) D. Mar 61
Goulart, João (Belchior Marques) Sep 62
Goulet, Robert (Gerard) Sep 62
Gove, Philip B(abcock) Oct 62
Graham, John Oct 62
Graham, Martha Jun 61
Graham, Philip L(eslie) obit Oct 63
Grant, Gordon (Hope) obit Jul 62
Green, Constance (Winsor) McLaughlin Oct 63
Greene, Hugh Carleton Sep 63
Greenebaum, Leon C(harles) Jan 62
Greenstein, Jesse L(eonard) Sep 63
Gregory, Dick Jun 62
Gregory, Edmund B(ristol) obit Mar 61
Grimes, Tammy (Lee) Jul 62
Grimond, Jo(seph) Oct 63
Griswold, A(lfred) Whitney obit Jun 63
Groat, Dick May 61
Groat, Richard M(orrow) See Groat, D. May 61
Gross, Paul Magnus May 63
Gross, Robert E(llsworth) obit Nov 61
Guevara (Serna), Ernesto Jun 63
Guggenheim, Peggy Oct 62
Guggenheimer, Mrs. Charles S. See Guggenheimer, M. Oct 62
Guggenheimer, Minnie Oct 62
Guinzburg, Harold K(leinert) obit Jan 62
Guion, Connie M(yers) Feb 62
Gullander, W(erner) P(aul) Oct 63
Gunther, John Feb 61
Guthrie, Woody May 63

Hagen, Uta Oct 63
Halaby, Najeeb E(lias) Oct 61
Hall, Peter (Reginald Frederick) Feb 62
Hall, William Edwin obit Mar 61
Hamilton, Edith biog Apr 63 obit Jul 63
Hammarskjöld, Dag (Hjalmar Agne Carl) obit Nov 61
Hammond, John Hays, Jr. Jul 62
Hand, (Billings) Learned obit Nov 61
Hanschman, Nancy (Conners) Sep 62
Hansen, Carl F(rancis) Oct 62
Harbach, Otto A(bels) obit Mar 63
Hardenbrook, Donald J(ohnson) Jul 62
Hargrave, Thomas J(ean) obit Apr 62

Harkness, Douglas S(cott) Oct 61
Harper, Marion, Jr. Mar 61
Harris, Harwell Hamilton Jan 62
Harrison, James L(erlie) Oct 62
Hart, Edward J(oseph) obit Jun 61
Hart, Merwin K(imball) obit Jan 63
Hart, Moss obit Feb 62
Hartigan, Grace Sep 62
Hartle, Russell P(eter) obit Jan 62
Harvey, Laurence May 61
Hassel, Kai-Uwe von May 63
Hatch, Carl A(twood) obit Nov 63
Hayakawa, Sessue Sep 62
Head, Matthew See Canaday, J. May 62
Heath, Edward (Richard George) Oct 62
Heineman, Ben W(alter) Jan 62
Heller, Walter W(olfgang) Sep 61
Herbster, Ben M(ohr) Jul 62
Herlihy, James Leo Sep 61
Herskovits, Melville J(ean) obit Apr 63
Hess, Elmer obit Jun 61
Hess, Max (Jr.) Oct 61
Hess, Victor Francis Oct 63
Hesse, Hermann biog Oct 62 obit Oct 62
Hesselgren, Kerstin obit Oct 62
Hester, James M(cNaughton) Jun 62
Heyrovský, Jaroslav Jul 61
Hillyer, Robert Silliman obit Feb 62
Hilsberg, Alexander obit Nov 61
Hines, Jerome Feb 63
Hocking, William Ernest Mar 62
Hodes, Henry I(rving) obit Apr 62
Hodges, Gil(bert Ray) Oct 62
Hoff, Philip H(enderson) Sep 63
Hofmann, Klaus H(einrich) Apr 61
Hofstadter, Robert Oct 62
Hoggart, (Herbert) Richard Oct 63
Holbrook, Hal May 61
Holenstein, Thomas (Emil Leo) obit Jan 62
Holland, Sir Sidney (George) obit Nov 61
Holloway, Stanley Feb 63
Holman, Eugene obit Oct 62
Holmes, D(yer) Brainerd Mar 63
Holt, Isabella obit May 62
Holyoake, Keith J(acka) Feb 63
Hornsby, Rogers obit Feb 63
Hornung, Paul (Vernon) Feb 63
Horsfall, Frank L(appin), Jr. Jan 61
Houk, Ralph (George) Jul 62
Houle, Cyril O(rvin) May 62
Hours, Madeleine See Hours-Miédan, M. Apr 61
Hours-Miédan, Magdeleine Apr 61

Howe, C(larence) D(ecatur) obit Feb 61
Howe, Gordie Mar 62
Howe, Gordon See Howe, Gordie Mar 62
Hu Shih obit Apr 62
Hubbard, Bernard (Rosencrans) obit Jul 62
Huddleston, (Ernest Urban) Trevor Oct 63
Hudson, Rock Oct 61
Hughes, Harold E(verett) Jun 63
Hughes, Richard J(oseph) Jul 62
Humphrey, Helen F. obit Oct 63
Hurley, Patrick J(ay) obit Sep 63
Husing, Ted obit Oct 62
Huxley, Sir Julian Oct 63
Hylton-Foster, Sir Harry (Braustyn Hylton) Jan 61

Ikeda, Hayato May 61
Infeld, Leopold Jul 63
Irene obit Jan 63
Ives, Irving M(cNeil) obit Apr 62

Jack, Homer A(lexander) Jul 61
Jackson, Eugene B(ernard) Jun 61
Jacobson, Leon Orris Oct 62
Jacobsson, Per obit Jun 63
Jagan, Cheddi (Berret) Apr 63
Janney, Russell obit Sep 63
Johannesen, Grant Jun 61
John XXIII, Pope obit Jul 63
John, Augustus (Edwin) obit Jan 62
Johnson, Harold Ogden obit Apr 62
Johnson (Justin) Leroy obit Jun 61
Johnson, Rafer (Lewis) Jun 61
Johnston, Eric A(llen) obit Oct 63
Jones, Candy Oct 61
Jones, Sir Harold Spencer obit Jan 61
Jones, Howard P(alfrey) Jul 63
Jones, Joe obit Jun 63
Jones, Shirley Oct 61
Jonsson, John Erik Jan 61
Jordan, Marian (Driscoll) obit Jun 61
Joxe, Louis Apr 61
Jung, Carl Gustav obit Sep 61

Kahn, Herman Oct 62
Kaiser, Henry J(ohn) Mar 61
Kaiser, Jakob obit Jul 61
Kalmus, Herbert T(homas) obit Sep 63
Kampmann, (Olfert) Viggo (Fischer) Jan 61
Kasavubu, Joseph Mar 61
Kassem, Abdul Karim (El-) obit Mar 63
Katsh, Abraham I(saac) Mar 62
Kauffmann, Henrik (Louis Hans) obit Jul 63

Kaufman, George S(imon) obit Sep 61
Kawakami, Jotaro Mar 63
Kay, Hershy Mar 62
Kefauver, (Carey) Estes obit Oct 63
Keldysh, Mstislav (Vsevolodovich) Feb 62
Kellogg, Winthrop N(iles) Apr 63
Kendrew, John C(owdery) Oct 63
Kennedy, Edward M(oore) Sep 63
Kennedy, Jacqueline (Lee Bouvier) Oct 61
Kennedy, (John) Arthur Nov 61
Kennedy, John B(right) obit Oct 61
Kennedy, John F(itzgerald) Jul 61
Kennedy, Thomas obit Feb 63
Kennelly, Martin H(enry) obit Jan 62
Keppel, Francis May 63
Kerner, Otto Oct 61
Kerr, Clark Apr 61
Kerr, Robert S(amuel) obit Feb 63
Kessing, O(liver) O(wen) obit Mar 63
Kestnbaum, Meyer obit Feb 61
Khouri, Faris el- obit Feb 62
Kimbrel, M(arvin) Monroe Jun 63
Kindelberger, J(ames) H(oward) obit Oct 62
Kingman, Dong (Moy Shu) Oct 62
Kiplinger, W(illard) M(onroe) Jan 62
Kirk, Alan Goodrich obit Dec 63
Kirk, Russell (Amos) Sep 62
Klahre, Ethel S(usan) May 62
Kline, Clarice (Lenore) May 61
Kobak, Edgar obit Jul 62
Koestler, Arthur Jan 62
Korth, Fred (H.) Jul 62
Kosaka, Zentaro Sep 61
Kovacs, Ernie obit Mar 62
Krag, Jens Otto Oct 62
Kreisler, Fritz obit Mar 62
Kruif, Paul (Henry) De See De Kruif, P. Jul 63
Kubrick, Stanley Feb 63
Küng, Hans Jul 63
Kutchuk, (Mustafa) Fazil Feb 61

Labouisse, Henry R(ichardson) Oct 61
La Farge, Oliver (Hazard Perry) obit Oct 63
Lamorisse, Albert (Emmanuel) Jun 63
Landau, Lev (Davidovich) Jul 63
Langer, Susanne K(atherina Knauth) Nov 63
Langner, Lawrence obit Feb 63
Larson, Leonard W(infield) May 62
Laughton, Charles obit Jan 63
Laver, Rod(ney George) Feb 63
Law, Vernon S(anders) Apr 61
Lawrence, Carol Nov 61

Lawrence, (Frederick William Pethick-Lawrence), 1st Baron Pethick- See Pethick-Lawrence, (F.W.P.-L.) obit Nov 61

Lederle, John W(illiam) Feb 61

Lee, Laurence F(rederick) obit Oct 61

Lee, (Nelle) Harper Nov 61

Lee, Peggy Mar 63

Lefèvre, Théo(dore Joseph Albéric Marie) Jun 62

Léger, Alexis Saint-Léger Apr 61

Lehmann, Inge Nov 62

Lehmann-Haupt, Hellmut E(mil) Mar 61

Leigh, Robert D(evore) obit Mar 61

Leinsdorf, Erich Oct 63

Lemmon, Jack Feb 61

Lemonnier, André (Georges) obit Jul 63

Lequerica y Erquiza, José Félix de obit Jul 63

Lesage, Jean Nov 61

Lewis, Jerry Nov 62

Lewis, John (Aaron) Jan 62

Lhevinne, Rosina Nov 61

Li, C(hoh) H(ao) Apr 63

Lichtenberger, Arthur (Carl), Bishop Apr 61

Lilly, John C(unningham) Nov 62

Lindsay, John V(liet) Nov 62

Lipchitz, Jacques Apr 62

Lippmann, Walter Nov 62

Lober, Georg (John) obit Feb 62

Loeb, James (Isaac), Jr. Jan 62

Lombardi, Vince May 63

Lorge, Irving (Daniel) obit Apr 61

Loutfi, Omar obit Jul 63

Louw, Eric H(endrik) Mar 62

Love, J(ames) Spencer obit Mar 62

Love, John A(rthur) Nov 63

Low, Sir David (Alexander Cecil) obit Nov 63

Luccock, Halford E(dward) obit Jan 61

Luce, Henry R(obinson) Jan 61

Luhan, Mabel Dodge obit Oct 62

Lumumba, Patrice (Emergy) obit Apr 61

Luthuli, Albert John Feb 62

Macapagal, Diosdado Nov 62

McCabe, Gibson Feb 63

McCarthy, Clem obit Jul 62

McClintic, Guthrie obit Jan 62

McCloy, John J(ay) Nov 61

McConnell, F(owler) B(eery) obit Feb 62

McCormack, John W(illiam) Apr 62

McCormick, Myron obit Oct 62

McCracken, James (Eugene) Nov 63

McCracken, Joan obit Jan 62

McCune, Francis K(imber) Mar 61

McDevitt, James L(awrence) obit May 63

McDonald, David L(amar) Nov 63

McDowall, Roddy Apr 61

McGee, Gale (William) Nov 61

McGinley, Phyllis Nov 61

McGovern, John W. Nov 61

McGranery, James P(atrick) obit Feb 63

McIntyre, Thomas J(ames) Nov 63

McKeen, John E(lmer) Jun 61

McKinley, Chuck Nov 63

MacLean, Basil C(larendon) obit Apr 63

McMurrin, Sterling M(oss) Jun 61

McNamara, Robert S(trange) Sep 61

McNeely, Eugene J(ohnson) Nov 62

McSwigan, Marie obit Sep 62

Macy, John W(illiams), Jr. Jan 62

Madeira, Jean (Browning) Oct 63

Malone, George W(ilson) obit Jul 61

Manzu, Giacomo Mar 61

Mao Tse-tung May 62

Marais, Jean Apr 62

Margai, Sir Milton (Augustus Strieby) Feb 62

Maris, Roger (Eugene) Nov 61

Mark, Herman F(rancis) May 61

Marks, Simon, 1st Baron Nov 62

Martin, Edmund F(ible) Jan 62

Marvel, Mrs. Archie D. Apr 62

Marvel, Elizabeth Newell See Marvel, Mrs. A. D. Apr 62

Marx, Chico obit Dec 6!

Mastroianni, Marcello Jun 63

Mattei, Enrico obit Jan 63

Mattingly, Garrett obit Feb 63

Maugham, (William) Somerset Jan 63

May, Elaine Mar 61

Mead, George H(ouk) obit Feb 63

Mearns, David C(hambers) Jul 61

Medawar, Peter Brian Apr 61

Meerloo, Joost A(braham) M(aurits) Jan 62

Mehaffey, Joseph C(owles) obit Apr 63

Melcher, Frederic G(ershom) obit Apr 63

Mellers, Wilfrid (Howard) Feb 62

Melton, James obit Jun 61

Menderes, Adnan obit Nov 61

Meng, John J(oseph) Nov 61

Merrick, David Jan 61

Messer, Thomas M. Nov 61

Messick, Dale Jul 61

Messmer, Pierre (August Joseph) Nov 63

Meštrović, Ivan obit Mar 62

Milam, Carl H(astings) obit Oct 63

Milhaud, Darius May 61

Miller, Harry W(illis) Mar 62

Miller, J(oseph) Irwin Nov 61

Miller, Watson B(ahan) obit Apr 61

Miller, William E(dward) Feb 62

Mills, Hayley Apr 63

Mills, John May 63

Minow, Newton N(orman) Oct 61

Miró Cardona, José Nov 61

Mitropoulos, Dmitri obit Jan 61

Moffo, Anna May 61

Mohammed V, King of Morocco obit Apr 61

Monroe, Marilyn obit Oct 62

Montini, Cardinal Giovanni Battista See Paul VI, Pope

Moore, Charlotte Emma See Sitterly, C. M. Jan 62

Morath, Max (Edward) Nov 63

Morgenstierne, Wilhelm (Thorleif) Munthe de obit Sep 63

Morgenthau, Hans J(oachim) Mar 63

Morison, Samuel Eliot Sep 62

Morley, Robert Nov 63

Morris, William Richard, 1st Viscount Nuffield obit Oct 63

Morrison, William Shepherd See Dunrossil, W. S. M., 1st Viscount obit Apr 61

Morse, Robert (Alan) Nov 62

Morton, Elizabeth Homer Jul 61

Morton, Florrinell F(rancis) Jul 61

Mosbacher, Emil, Jr. Mar 63

Mosconi, Willie Jun 63

Moscoso (Mora Rodríguez), (José) Teodoro Oct 63

Mosel, Tad Nov 61

Moses, Anna Mary Robertson obit Feb 62

Mössbauer, Rudolf L(udwig) May 62

Mostel, Zero Nov 63

Motherwell, Robert (Burns, 3d) Nov 62

Motley, Arthur H(arrison) Jan 61

Mowrer, Edgar Ansel Jul 62

Muench, Aloisius (Joseph), Cardinal obit Apr 62

Muir, P(ercival) H(orace) See Muir, P. Apr 63

Muir, Percy Apr 63

Mumford, Lewis Mar 63

Murphree, Eger V(aughan) obit Jan 63

Murphy, (Eleanor) Patricia Apr 62

Murray, James E(dward) obit May 61

Murray, John Courtney May 61

Murray, Thomas E(dward) obit Sep 61

Murtaugh, Daniel (Edward) Feb 61

Nabarro, Sir Gerald (David Nunes) Nov 63

Nabrit, James M(adison), Jr. Jan 61

Nabrit, S(amuel) M(ilton) Jan 63

Nash, Philleo Nov 62

Nehru, B(raj) K(umar) Feb 63

Neill, A(lexander) S(utherland) Apr 61
Nestingen, Ivan A(rnold) Mar 62
Neuberger, Maurine B(rown) Oct 61
Neutra, Richard J(osef) Jul 61
Newhart, Bob Mar 62
Newhouse, Samuel I(rving) Mar 61
Nichols, Mike Mar 61
Nicklaus, Jack (William) Nov 62
Nikolayevna-Tereshkova, Valentina (Vladimirovna) See Tereshkova, V. Dec 63
Nitze, Paul H(enry) Feb 62
Nuffield, 1st Viscount See Morris, W. obit Oct 63
Nureyev, Rudolf (Hametovich) Jul 63
Nyerere, Julius K(ambarage) Apr 63

O'Brien, Lawrence F(rancis) Nov 61
O'Casey, Sean Nov 62
Ochoa, Severo Jun 62
O'Connor, Edwin (Greene) Nov 63
Odets, Clifford obit Nov 63
Odlum, Mrs. Floyd B(ostwick) See Cochran, J. Jun 63
Ogburn, Charlton obit Apr 62
Ogilvy, David M(ackenzie) Jul 61
Ohlin, Lloyd E(dgar) Apr 63
Olav V, King of Norway Jan 62
Olds, Irving S(ands) obit Apr 63
Olsen, John (Sigvard) obit Mar 63
O'Mahoney, Joseph C(hristopher) obit Jan 63
Onassis, Aristotle Socrates Mar 63
O'Neill, Eugene F(rancis) Apr 63
Oppenheimer, Harry Frederick Feb 61
Ormsby-Gore, Sir (William) David Mar 61
Orr, Louis M(cDonald) obit Jul 61
Osgood, Charles E(gerton) Apr 62
Osmeña, Sergio obit Dec 61
Oxnam, G(arfield) Bromley obit Apr 63
Ozbirn, Catharine (Freeman) See Ozbirn, Mrs. E. L. Jan 62
Ozbirn, Mrs. E. Lee Jan 62

Page, Ruth Jun 62
Pant, Govind Ballabh obit May 61
Pape, William Jamieson obit Mar 61
Park, Thomas Jan 63
Parker, Cola G(odden) obit Sep 62
Parry, Albert Apr 61
Parsons, Talcott Jan 61
Partridge, Deborah (Cannon) See Wolfe, D. Dec 62

Partridge, Eric (Honeywood) Jan 63
Pate, Randolph McC(all) obit Oct 61
Patterson, Alicia obit Sep 63
Paul VI, Pope Nov 63
Pearson, Lester Bowles Nov 63
Pease, Lute obit Nov 63
Peden, Katherine (Graham) May 62
Pennel, John (Thomas) Nov 63
Perkins, C(harles) H(arvie) obit Apr 63
Perse, St.-John See Léger, A.S.-L. Apr 61
Perutz, M(ax) F(erdinand) Nov 63
Peterson, Esther (Eggertsen) Dec 61
Pethick-Lawrence, (Frederick William Pethick-Lawrence), 1st Baron obit Nov 61
Petri, Egon obit Jul 62
Pettit, Robert (E. Lee) Oct 61
Pevsner, Antoine obit Jun 62
Pew, Joseph N(ewton), Jr. obit Jun 63
Phillips, Morgan (Walter) obit Feb 63
Piaf, Edith obit Nov 63
Picard, Frank A(lbert) obit Apr 63
Picasso, Pablo Nov 62
Piccard, Auguste obit May 62
Piccard, Jean Felix obit Mar 63
Pierce, Bob Dec 61
Pierce, J(ohn) R(obinson) Feb 61
Pinter, Harold Nov 63
Piston, Walter (Hamor, Jr.) Dec 61
Pittman, Steuart L(ansing) Jan 63
Player, Gary Nov 61
Plisetskaya, Maya (Mikhailovna) Jun 63
Plumley, H(arold) Ladd Apr 63
Pompidou, Georges (Jean Raymond) Nov 62
Popper, Karl R(aimund) Jan 63
Porter, Katherine Anne Mar 63
Portinari, Candido obit Mar 62
Poston, Tom Apr 61
Pound, Ezra (Loomis) May 63
Powdermaker, Hortense Feb 61
Powell, Dick obit Feb 63
Powers, James E(llis) Jun 63
Prasad, Rajendra obit Apr 63
Price, (Mary) Leontyne May 61
Prinz, Joachim Feb 63
Pucci, Emilio Feb 61

Quadros, Jânio da Silva Jun 61
Quay, Jan Eduard de May 63

Rabaut, Louis Charles obit Jan 62
Radcliffe, Cyril John, 1st Viscount Radcliffe Jun 63
Raeder, Erich obit Jan 61
Ramadier, Paul obit Dec 61

Ramírez, Pedro P(ablo) obit Sep 62
Ramsey, DeWitt C(linton) obit Nov 61
Ramsey, Norman F(oster) Dec 63
Randall, Tony Jan 61
Randolph, Jennings Jan 62
Rankin, John E(lliott) obit Jan 61
Raphael, Chaim Dec 63
Rasminsky, Louis Dec 61
Ratoff, Gregory obit Feb 61
Rawlings, Sir (Henry) Bernard (Hughes) obit Dec 62
Ray, (Jackson Harvelle) Randolph obit Jul 63
Ray, Satyajit Mar 61
Rayburn, Sam(uel Taliaferro) obit Jan 62
Raye, Martha Jul 63
Read, Sir Herbert (Edward) Mar 62
Reece, B(razilla) Carroll obit May 61
Reiner, Carl Apr 61
Reischauer, Edwin O(ldfather) May 62
Renne, Roland R(oger) Jun 63
Resor, Stanley B(urnet) obit Dec 62
Reybold, Eugene obit Jan 62
Reynolds, Robert Rice obit Mar 63
Richardson, Tony Dec 63
Richberg, Donald R(andall) obit Jan 61
Richter, Sviatoslav (Teofilovich) Feb 61
Riecken, Henry W(illiam) Dec 61
Rigg, Edgar T(aylor) Jun 61
Rivers, Thomas M(ilton) obit Jul 62
Robarts, John P(armenter) Dec 62
Robertson, D(avid) B(rown) obit Dec 61
Robinson, Henry Morton obit Mar 61
Robinson, Spottswood W(illiam), 3d Mar 62
Robus, Hugo Dec 62
Rogers, Carl R(ansom) Dec 62
Rogers, Frank B(radway) Jun 62
Rogers, Rutherford David Jun 62
Rollins, Carl Purington obit Jan 61
Rombauer, Irma (von) S(tarkloff) obit Dec 62
Roosa, Robert V(incent) Dec 62
Roosevelt, (Anna) Eleanor obit Jan 63
Rose, (Iain) Murray Jun 62
Rostow, Eugene V(ictor) Apr 61
Rostow, Walt W(hitman) May 61
Rothko, Mark May 61
Routley, T(homas) Clarence obit Jun 63
Rowley, James J(oseph) Jan 63
Rubattel, Rodolphe obit Dec 61
Rudolph, Wilma (Glodean) Sep 61

Rusk, (David) Dean Jul 61

Russell, Donald J(oseph) May 62

Russell, James S(argent) Jan 62

Ryan, Joseph P(atrick) obit Sep 63

Ryan, Robert (Bushnell) Dec 63

Saarinen, Eero obit Nov 61

Saddler, Donald (Edward) Jan 63

Salant, Richard S. Nov 61

Salinger, Pierre (Emil George) Jul 61

Samuel, Herbert (Louis), 1st Viscount Samuel obit Mar 63

Sandburg, Carl (August) Dec 63

Sandström, (Alfred) Emil (Fredrik) obit Sep 62

Sanford, (James) Terry Nov 61

Satterfield, John C(reighton) Jul 62

Savage, Augusta (Christine) obit May 62

Sawyer, John E(dward) Jul 61

Saxon, James J(oseph) Dec 63

Schell, Maria (Margarethe Anna) Jun 61

Schell, Maximilian Dec 62

Scherman, Harry Jul 63

Schoeppel, Andrew F. obit Mar 62

Schröder, Gerhard Dec 62

Schuck, Arthur A(loys) obit Apr 63

Schuman, Robert obit Nov 63

Schuman, William (Howard) Dec 62

Schweitzer, Pierre-Paul Dec 63

Schwidetzky, Oscar (Otto Rudolph) obit Nov 63

Scofield, Paul Mar 62

Seaborg, Glenn T(heodore) Dec 61

Seeger, Pete(r) Dec 63

Senghor, Léopold Sédar Mar 62

Senior, Clarence (Ollson) Dec 61

Sensenich, Roscoe L(loyd) obit Feb 63

Seymour, Charles obit Nov 63

Seymour, Whitney North May 61

Shepard, Alan B(artlett), Jr. Dec 61

Shepard, E(rnest) H(oward) Dec 63

Sherrod, Robert (Lee) Dec 62

Shirer, William L(awrence) May 62

Shoemaker, Samuel M(oor) obit Dec 63

Shope, Richard E(dwin) Dec 63

Shotton, Burt(on Edwin) obit Oct 62

Shriver, R(obert) Sargent (Jr.) Dec 61

Shurlock, Geoffrey M. Jan 62

Sides, John H(arold) Jan 61

Sidi Mohammed, Sultan of Morocco See Mohammed V, King of Morocco obit Apr 61

Silver, Abba Hillel May 63

Sinclair, Upton (Beall, Jr.) Dec 62

Sitterly, Mrs. Bancroft Walker See Sitterly, C. M. Jan 62

Sitterly, Charlotte Moore Jan 62

Skidmore, Louis obit Dec 62

Slocum, (Manly) Harvey obit Jan 62

Smadel, Joseph E(dwin) biog May 63 obit Sep 63

Small, John D(avis) obit Mar 63

Smith, Carleton Apr 61

Smith, Elizabeth Rudel Dec 61

Smith, Margaret (Madeline) Chase Mar 62

Smith, Oliver Sep 61

Smith, Sylvester C(omstock), Jr. Jul 63

Smith, Walter Bedell obit Nov 61

Snell, Peter (George) Dec 62

Snow, C(harles) P(ercy) Dec 61

Snow, Sir Charles Percy See Snow, C. P. Dec 61

Sokolsky, George E(phraim) obit Jan 63

Sordoni, Andrew J(ohn) obit Apr 63

Sorensen, Theodore (Chaikin) Dec 61

Souvanna Phouma, Prince of Laos Nov 62

Spahn, Warren (Edward) May 62

Speicher, Eugene (Edward) obit Jul 62

Sporborg, Mrs. William Dick obit Feb 61

Spottswood, Stephen Gill Apr 62

Stace, W(alter) T(erence) Apr 61

Stahr, Elvis J(acob), Jr. Sep 61

Stainback, Ingram Macklin obit Jun 61

Standley, W(illiam) H(arrison) obit Dec 63

Starch, Daniel Jan 63

Starker, Janos May 63

Steacie, E(dgar) W(illiam) R(ichard) obit Nov 62

Stefansson, Vilhjalmur obit Nov 62

Steinbeck, John (Ernst) May 63

Stelle, John obit Sep 62

Stevenson, Adlai E(wing) Sep 61

Stikker, Dirk U(ipko) Feb 62

Stokes, Anson Phelps, Jr. Jul 62

Storke, Thomas M(ore) Dec 63

Storms, Harrison A(llen), Jr. Jan 63

Strachey, (Evelyn) John (St. Loe) obit Sep 63

Stratton, Julius A(dams) May 63

Straus, Nathan obit Nov 61

Struve, Otto obit Jun 63

Stuart, J(ohn) Leighton obit Nov 62

Subandrio Mar 63

Suggs, Louise Jan 62

Summerskill, Edith (Clara), Baroness Summerskill Jul 63

Sunderland, Thomas E(lbert) Apr 62

Swallow, Alan Feb 63

Swann, W(illiam) F(rancis) G(ray) obit Mar 62

Swift, Harold H(iggins) obit Sep 62

Switzer, Mary E(lizabeth) Jan 62

Tafawa Balewa, Sir Abubakar See Balewa, Sir Abukakar Tafawa Sep 61

Tamm, Igor Dec 63

Tati, Jacques Feb 61

Taylor, A(lbert) Hoyt obit Jan 62

Taylor, Maxwell D(avenport) Dec 61

Teagle, Walter C(lark) obit Feb 62

Teague, Walter Dorwin obit Jan 61

Teale, Edwin Way Dec 61

Templeton, Alec obit May 63

Tennant, Sir William George obit Sep 63

Ter-Arutunian, Rouben Jun 63

Tereshkova, Valentina (Vladimirovna) Dec 63

Terry, Luther L(eonidas) Oct 61

Terry-Thomas Mar 61

Tisserant, Eugène, Cardinal Apr 63

Thant, U Feb 62

Thomas, John Charles obit Feb 61

Thomas, Norman (Mattoon) Jul 62

Thomas, Terry- See Terry-Thomas Mar 61

Thompson, Dorothy obit Mar 61

Thurber, James Jan 62

Tillinghast, Charles C(arpenter), Jr. Feb 62

Timberlake, Clare H(ayes) Jan 61

Titov, Gherman (Stepanovich) Dec 62

Tobias, Channing H(eggie) obit Jan 62

Toledano, Ralph de Dec 62

Tollefson, Thor C(arl) Feb 63

Tower, John G(oodwin) Dec 62

Townes, Charles H(ard) Mar 63

Tozzi, Giorgio Oct 61

Traphagen, Ethel obit Jun 63

Trautman, George M(cNeal) obit Sep 63

Travell, Janet G(raeme) Dec 61

Tree, Marietta Dec 61

Tree, Mrs. Ronald See Tree, Marietta Dec 61

Trujillo Molina, Rafael Leónidas obit Oct 61

Tshombe, Moise (-Kapenda) Dec 61

Tuchman, Barbara W(ertheim) Dec 63

Tugwell, Rexford G(uy) Jan 63

Turner, Ewald (Walter) May 62

Turner, R(ichmond) Kelly obit Apr 61

Tydings, Millard E(velyn) obit Apr 61

Tynan, Kenneth (Peacock) Dec 63

Udall, Stewart L(ee) May 61
Unitas, John Feb 62

Vallee, Rudy Apr 63
Vance, Cyrus R(oberts) Dec 62
Vandercook, John W(omack) obit Feb 63
Vandiver, S(amuel) Ernest Jul 62
Vandivert, William (Wilson) Mar 63
Van Dyke, Dick Mar 63
Van Loen, Alfred Feb 61
Vanocur, Sander Jan 63
Van Pelt, John V(redenburgh) obit Sep 62
Van Volkenburg, J(ohn) ("Jack") L(amont) obit Jul 63
Van Waters, Miriam Mar 63
Vertès, Marcel biog Apr 61 obit Jan 62
Vickers, Jon Mar 61
Viereck, George Sylvester obit May 62
Vila, George R(aymond) Mar 63
Vilar, Jean (Louis Côme) Apr 62
Villon, Jacques obit Jul 63
Volpe, John A(nthony) Feb 62
Von Békésy, Georg See Békésy, Georg von Dec 62
Von Hassel, Kai-Uwe See Hassel, K. von May 63
Von Kármán, Theodore obit Jun 63
Von Wicht, John Jan 63

Wachuku, Jaja (Anucha) Apr 63
Waddington, C(onrad) H(al) Apr 62
Wagman, Frederick H(erbert) Jul 63
Wagner, Aubrey J(oseph) Jun 63
Wagner, Richard Apr 62
Wahlen, Friedrich T(raugott) Jun 61
Wald, Jerry obit Sep 62
Walker, Stanley obit Jan 63

Wallace, George C(orley) Dec 63
Wallgren, Mon(rad) C(harles) obit Nov 61
Walter, Francis E(ugene) obit Jul 63
Ward, Robert (Eugene) Jul 63
Walsh, Chad Feb 62
Walsh, William B(ertalan) May 62
Walter, Bruno obit Apr 62
Ward, Paul L(angdon) Mar 62
Watson, James Dewey Apr 63
Watson, Lucile obit Sep 62
Watts, Alan (Wilson) Mar 62
Waugh, Sidney (Biehler) obit Sep 63
Waymack, W(illiam) W(esley) obit Jan 61
Weaver, Robert C(lifton) Apr 61
Webb, James E(dwin) May 62
Weber, Max obit Dec 61
Weis, Mrs. Charles W(illiam), Jr. obit Jun 63
Weis, Jessica McCullough See Weis, Mrs. C. W., Jr. obit Jun 63
Welch, Leo D(ewey) Dec 63
Welles, Sumner obit Nov 61
Welsh, Matthew E(mpson) Jun 62
Wenner-Gren, Axel (Leonard) obit Jan 62
Wesker, Arnold Feb 62
Westmoreland, W(illiam) C(hilds) Jun 61
Whalen, Grover A(loysius) obit Jun 62
Wheelwright, Jere (Hungerford, Jr.) obit Mar 61
White, Byron R(aymond) Dec 62
Whitton, Rex M(arion) May 62
Wickens, Aryness Joy Sep 62
Widmark, Richard Apr 63
Wiesner, Jerome B(ert) Dec 61
Wilcox, Francis O(rlando) Apr 62
Wilhelmina, Princess of the Netherlands obit Jan 63
Wilkins, Maurice H(ugh) F(rederick) Jun 63

Wilkinson, Bud See Wilkinson, C. Apr 62
Wilkinson, Charles (Burnham) Apr 62
Williams, G(erhard) Mennen Jun 63
Williston, Samuel obit Apr 63
Wills, Royal Barry obit Feb 62
Wilson, Charles E(rwin) obit Dec 61
Wilson, Colin Apr 63
Wilson, (James) Harold May 63
Winiarski, Bohdan (Stefan) Feb 62
Wirtz, W(illiam) Willard Feb 63
Wolfe, Deborah (Cannon) Partridge Dec 62
Wolman, Leo obit Dec 61
Wood, Louise A(letha) Jul 61
Wood, Natalie Apr 62
Woodsmall, Ruth F(rances) obit Jul 63
Woodward, Robert F(orbes) Dec 62
Woolley, Monty obit Jun 63
Wright, John J(oseph) Feb 63
Wright, Sir Michael (Robert) Jul 61
Wright, Richard obit Jan 61

Yamasaki, Minoru Mar 62
Yevtushenko, Yevgeny (Alexandrovich) Feb 63
Youlou, Fulbert Dec 62
Young, Owen D. obit Sep 62

Zacharias, Ellis M(ark) obit Oct 61
Zahedi, Fazlollah obit Nov 63
Zellerbach, J(ames) D(avid) obit Nov 63
Zog I obit Jun 61
Zorach, William Feb 63
Zorlu, Fatin Rustu obit Nov 61